BUSINESS POLICY

MANAGING STRATEGIC PROCESSES

MGMT 690

BUSINESS POLICY

MANAGING STRATEGIC PROCESSES

JOSEPH L. BOWER
Donald Kirk David Professor of
Business Administration

CHRISTOPHER A. BARTLETT
Professor of Business Administration

HUGO E.R. UYTERHOEVEN
Timken Professor of Business Administration

RICHARD E. WALTON
Wallace Brett Donham Professor of
Business Administration

All of the Graduate School of
Business Administration
Harvard University

Eighth Edition

Boston, Massachusetts   Burr Ridge, Illinois   Dubuque, Iowa
Madison, Wisconsin   New York, New York   San Francisco, California   St. Louis, Missouri

Irwin/McGraw-Hill

*A Division of The **McGraw·Hill** Companies*

Senior sponsoring editor:	Kurt L. Strand
Editorial coordinator:	Michele Dooley
Senior marketing manager:	Kurt Messersmith
Project editor:	Mary Conzachi
Production supervisor:	Dina L. Treadaway
Designer:	Heidi J. Baughman
Cover designer:	Margaret Armour
Art studio:	Jay Bensen Studios
Graphics supervisor:	Charlene Breeden
Compositor:	Alexander Graphics, Inc.
Typeface:	10/12 Melior
Printer:	R.R. Donnelley & Sons Company

Library of Congress Cataloging-in-Publication Data

Business policy : managing strategic processes / Joseph L. Bower . . .
  [et al.]. —8th ed.
      p.   cm.
   Includes bibliographical references.
   ISBN 0-256-11591-5
   1. Corporations—United States—Case studies.   2. Industrial
management—United States—Case studies.   I. Bower, Joseph L.
   HD2785.B78 1995   95–2575
   658.4′012—dc20

Printed in the United States of America
  4 5 6 7 8 9 0 DO 2 1 0 9

To
Kenneth R. Andrews and
C. Roland Christensen
For reasons they know well

PREFACE

The eighth edition of *Business Policy* text and casebook marks a watershed in the life of what has turned out to be a 30-year teaching and research project. For the first time since its 1965 publication, the text has been completely rewritten rather than modified.

We have retained in this edition those cases that our users have found most helpful in accomplishing the objectives of their courses. Nonetheless, we have sometimes changed the way in which they are used to reflect a new approach to the subject matter of the book. Ten of the holdover cases are on the list of all-time best sellers of the Harvard Business School Publishing Division. But we have added a number of new cases that have proven powerful vehicles for learning about the challenges of general management in the turbulent and competitive global markets of the 1990s.

In the eighth edition, we have emphasized five basic educational themes. First, the material focuses on the roles, tasks, and skills of the general manager in leading the overall enterprise or business unit, in contrast to the tasks of a manager whose responsibilities are limited to a functional specialty. Second, our text and cases highlight strategic management as a key function and responsibility of the line general manager, not as a staff planning activity. Third, we emphasize the extent to which an organization's strategy is built by administrative processes over time as opposed to being designed in an analytic process at a moment in time. Fourth, the extent to which building strategy and building an organization are interdependent tasks is reflected in the structure of the book, its text, and the cases. This represents a major departure from the "formulation followed by implementation" structure of preceding editions and reflects major improvements in the development of general management cases. Finally, a study of this material emphasizes the importance of general management practice as a professional activity. General managers are responsible to multiple constituencies with conflicting needs and goals.

They must manage those organizations so as to achieve economic, social, and ethical goals.

The fourth of these themes is worth further attention. The development of the concept of corporate strategy has exploited the power of the basic idea that structure should follow strategy. Great insight into the appropriate nature of organizational purpose and design has been achieved by examining these topics in sequence with an analytic perspective. Considerable progress in the field of strategy has been possible precisely because of this separation and sequencing. But as the cases in previous editions revealed and the text asserted, and as research in our field has proven for two decades, the two topics are not independent from a general manager's perspective, nor can they be managed in an orderly sequence.

As the pace of competition has accelerated, an accurate reflection of the challenges of general management requires a framework that views these problems as occurring simultaneously. Our focus in this text on the general manager as strategist, organization builder, and doer reflects this objective.

Attention to the role of the general manager in managing these strategic processes has changed as business leaders have come to better understand the value of a positive work environment and constantly improving capability. Both require the involvement of a committed workforce at all levels.

The evolution of this book has been encouraged by many individuals— business managers, academic instructors, and students—who have taken the time and effort to send us suggestions for improvements. We are in their debt. Their continuing interest has helped us to develop a course in general management that can be taught effectively at undergraduate, graduate, and executive seminar levels.

Whatever the course name, all students of general management participate in a long-term, evolving intellectual adventure. The basic administrative processes and problems with which we are concerned have been part of organizational life for centuries, and date as an academic field to the first business policy course at Harvard Business School in 1908.

This edition builds on substantial contributions made by former and present colleagues; it carries their efforts further along the way to better understanding and greater applicability. In particular, this book abandons the pedagogical approach of separating sharply the formulation and implementation of strategy. It continues the trend toward more international material and more cases concerned with the process of transforming organizations so that they can engage more effectively in the competitive battles that characterize most industries around the globe.

The specific core ideas, the concepts of corporate strategy and managing strategic processes, were developed at Harvard Business School in the 1960s and early 1970s under the leadership of three now emeriti professors: Kenneth R. Andrews, C. Roland Christensen, and Edmund P.

Learned. Two of this book's authors, Joseph L. Bower and Hugo E. R. Uyterhoeven, worked closely with them in the development of the early course. Christopher A. Bartlett has worked to apply these ideas to international strategic management, and Richard E. Walton has brought to bear his extensive research on the transformation of human behavior in organizations. Over the years, other colleagues have made important contributions through the writing of cases, doing research in general management, and teaching in the MBA and executive programs.

The concept of *corporate strategy* articulated in this textbook has been derived from the careful study in hundreds of company situations of the uniformities that constitute the way decisions about corporate purpose are made and carried out. Distinguishing more from less successful experience has led to a theory about how the tasks involved in giving direction to an organization in competitive conditions can be made more effective. We call it corporate strategy to distinguish it from popular presentations of economic strategy.

The idea that perceived strategy at a point in time is the outcome of *managed organizational processes* over time rather than the result of detached analysis has been built up from research and case studies on the making of business unit and corporate strategy. It has been particularly important in helping students and managers to understand why it is so extraordinarily difficult to "turn around" a large previously successful corporation.

We develop at length that the primary function of the general manager is to lead a continuous process of determining the nature of the enterprise, setting and revising goals, building layer upon layer of corporate capability relevant to those goals, and driving day-to-day activity so that over time the organization prospers as its environment changes. By emphasizing the leadership of process in addition to the generation of strategic vision, we have recognized that a general manager is as much the builder of the organization and a leverager of ongoing organizational performance, as he or she is a strategist, and that depending on the circumstances any one of these three roles may be most important.

While our conceptual scheme is not elegant in the conventional sense that the disciplines seek simple formulaic power, we believe that it has great power in application in each unique corporate setting. Although it has not been derived from theoretical modeling or management science, it is based on long experience. The authors, besides being familiar with and having contributed to the literature of strategic management and organizational behavior, have been teaching and doing research in general management for a combined total of more than a century. They have written and supervised more than 400 case studies of domestic, foreign, and multinational companies. They have served as consultants to about 200 companies on general management problems, and serve or have served on the many different corporate boards of directors. Apart from case collections, they have authored ten research monographs.

We have concluded from this varied experience that no comprehensive positive theory of general management is currently possible. The combination of objective and subjective elements, of economic, social and personal purposes, and of complex ethical and social responsibilities makes automatic outcomes impossible. Close competitive analysis may point to a desired generic economic strategy for a busines unit. A unique corporate strategy, however, will reflect the judgment, aspiration, desire, and determination of many fallible human beings in ways that no theoretical model can prescribe. All-purpose management formulas are transparent fantasies. We cannot tell you from our conceptual scheme what the corporate strategy should be for any one company that we do not know, nor what the plan of action should be for that company's general manager. This book will help you find out, in a company you do know, how to approach your own conclusion.

How is this thinking about general management work related to the task of learning in the classroom? We summarize our answer as follows:

> The uniqueness of a good general manager lies in one's ability to lead effectively organizations whose complexities he or she can never fully understand, where a capacity to control directly the human and physical forces comprising that organization is severely limited, and where he or she must make or review and assume ultimate responsibility for present decisions which commit concretely major resources for a fluid and unknown future.
>
> These circumstances—lack of knowledge, lack of an ability to control directly, and a mixture of past, present, and future time dimensions in every decision—make the concept of strategy so important for the generalist, senior manager. For strategy gives a manager reasonably clear indications of what one should try to know and understand in order to direct an organization's efforts. It counsels on what to decide, what to review, and what to ignore. It gives guidelines as to which critical, central activities and processes one should attempt to influence or, on rare occasions, attempt to control. It encourages a general manager to view every event and question from multiple time dimensions.
>
> Chester Barnard said that the highest managerial traits are essentially intuitive, "being so complex and so rapid, often approaching the instantaneous, that they could not be analyzed by the person within whose brain they take place." If Barnard is correct, and we think that he is, how do those of us interested in management education strive to contribute to the development of future general managers? We do this first by disciplined classroom drill with the concept of strategy. Drill in the formal and analytic sense—what is the current strategy of the firm? What are its strengths and weaknesses? Where, in the firm's perceived industry, are profit and service opportunities? And how can those corporate capacities and industry opportunities be effectively related? We then ask, What new capabilities must be created? How can the work environment be transformed so that organization

members will perceive the need to acquire them? Which individuals must be engaged in the process so that it succeeds? And what sequencing of strategic, organizational, and interpersonal action will effect intended change? This framework of questions helps to give order to the familiar chaos of complex organizations. It provides the manager with a map relating past, present, and future, industry and company–specific decisions to wider objectives.

Moreover, this analytic classroom process focuses attention on a key administrative skill—the process of selecting and ordering data so that management asks the critical questions appropriate to a particular situation. Here the choice of abstraction level is key, for the question has to be stated in a way that avoids the specific that has no meaning and the general that has no content.

We seek also, via the classroom case discussion process, to educate in the nonlogical—that mixture of feeling and sentiment, comment and commitment, certainty and uncertainty—that goes into every decision and judgment. Such directed group discussions force attention to the human dimensions through which the analytic framework is filtered in real life. It serves further to emphasize the ongoing or process nature of the general manager's world.

It is a combination of these two forces—the analytic framework of strategic planning and the process framework emphasizing human interaction, the complexities of persons, and the difficulty of communication and persuasion—that make up our educational fare.

The need is great for professionally trained generalists—those men and women who make our organized society's critical decisions. We continue to believe that this challenge will be met, at least in part, by all of us who work in the general management area, both in academic and practical pursuits, throughout this country and the world. And we hope this book will be of some help in meeting that challenge.

Joseph L. Bower

—

Acknowledgments

The history of the Business Policy course at Harvard Business School began in 1911, when a small group of instructors first developed a course outline and materials for a pioneering venture in education for general management. Those of us who currently teach and do research in the business policy arena are in debt to those pioneers who provided the academic platform on which current efforts rest. We wish to especially recognize and thank efforts of A. W. Shaw, the first policy professor at Harvard Business School, M. T. Copeland, George Albert Smith, Jr., and Edmund P. Learned, who provided almost 60 years of dedicated leadership to course ideals and development, and Kenneth R. Andrews and C. Roland Christensen who built and sustained the modern policy course both by introducing the concept of corporate strategy and by preserving the course's central focus on the leadership function of the general manager. We are in their debt, as we are to those colleagues who worked under their leadership and who assisted in past course development.

Many members of the Harvard Business School faculty have contributed to the constant development of our field. We appreciate the help of present members of the group teaching related courses, Joseph L. Badaracco, Norman A. Berg, James L. Heskett, Cynthia A. Montgomery, Michael E. Porter, Malcolm S. Salter, Howard H. Stevenson, David B. Yoffie, and Michael Y. Yoshino.

Our sincere appreciation goes to the supervisors and authors of the cases included in this edition. To the following our thanks: Myra M. Hart for work on the Bright Horizons Children's Centers, Inc.-1987 case prepared originally by Johanna M. Hurstak and Professor Ralph Z. Sorensen; Howard H. Stevenson and Professor C. Roland Christensen for Head Ski Company, Inc.; for the original case material used in Phil Knight: CEO at NIKE (1983), Professor C. Roland Christensen and David C. Rikert; for Serengeti Eyewear, Professor David A. Garvin and Jonathan West; for Crown Cork and Seal in 1989, Professor Stephen P. Bradley and Sheila M.Cavanaugh; for

Asahi Breweries, Ltd., Professor Malcolm S. Salter and Jiro Kokuryo; for Wal-Mart Stores, Inc., Professor Stephen P. Bradley and Sharon Foley; for Apple Computer-1992, Professor David B. Yoffie; for Bill Gates and the Management of Microsoft, Philip M. Rosenzweig; for Salvatore Ferragamo, SpA, Andrall E. Pearson; for Schlumberger Ltd., E. Tatum Christiansen; for BayBank Boston, Associate Professor J. Gregory Dees; for RU 486 (A), Professor Joseph L. Badaracco and Christopher Sturr; for The Adams Corporation (A), Professor C. Roland Christensen; for Colgate Palmolive: Company in Transition (A), Professor James L. Heskett; for Johnsonville Sausage Co. (A), Assistant Professor Michael J. Roberts; for Lincoln Electric Company, Professor Norman A. Berg and Norman Fast; for Cleveland Twist Drill (A), Associate Professor Richard G. Hamermesh and Nasswan Dossabhoy; for Richardson Hindustan Ltd. (Abridged), Professor Francis J. Aguilar; and for Ben & Jerry's Homemade Ice Cream, John Theroux.

Although the text for this book is new, it reflects its roots in the concepts and principles articulated so well in the earlier text material authored by Kenneth R. Andrews. It also has been influenced greatly by the teaching faculty of the MPP and GMP courses at Harvard Business School during the 1990–94 period and numerous unnamed doctoral candidates in Business Policy who have discussed the course with us. Ken Andrews and Chris Christensen are both enjoying busy and productive lives in retirement. But the thousands of students and faculty with whom they worked know how much they have contributed to thinking about all aspects of general management in business schools everywhere but especially in practice. They remained focused on the human and ethical aspects of leadership at a time when analytic nostrums were epidemic. They were our teachers and friends, and we have dedicated this book to them.

Dean John H. McArthur and Warren F. McFarlan, Director of the Division of Research, provided us with intellectual support and practical administrative assistance. We are in their debt. A special thanks to the reviewers for this book: T. K. Das, Baruch College; Professor Andrew Deile, Mercer University; Professor Joseph Monroe, Rensselaer Polytechnic Institute; Dr. Ben B. Sutton, Our Lady of the Lake University; Professor Frank L. Winfrey, Kent State University.

Marguerite Dole took on the management task of producing this book and carried out the assignment with her usual blend of efficiency and good humor.

We hope this book, within which the efforts of so many good people are compressed, will contribute to constructive concern for corporate purpose and accomplishments and to the continuing and effective study and practice of general management in private, nonprofit, and public organizations.

JLB
CAB
HU
REW

CONTENTS

BUSINESS POLICY

MANAGING STRATEGIC PROCESSES

Introentilen

■

The General
Management Perspective
and Business Policy

This book is about the work of general managers, those executives with responsibilities for running an entire business as opposed to a function like finance or a process like human resource management. There are general managers in all kinds of organizations, nonprofit as well as profit-making, but the cases in this book describe the problems of business managers.

Some general managers run companies and others run subsidiaries or profit centers. Much is similar in the general management work of these different kinds of managers, and this book is concerned with both of them. But it is also true that some general managers are responsible for their entire company, and we are particularly concerned in this book with this critical work of corporate leadership. We will usually speak of this top role as "chief executive officer" or, less formally, as "the president."

There is something special about this role. Harry Truman captured a great deal of it when he said, "The buck stops here." The chief executive is responsible for the results of the corporation's behavior, the earnings, the balance sheet, the quality of the products and services, the safety of plant facilities, the citizenship of the company in the towns and countries where it operates—everything. In large companies, chief executives go to sleep each night knowing that the next day's headlines may include some terrible gaffe or even crime committed by an employee. And when something goes wrong, the chief executive is supposed to be able to explain the problem knowledgeably whether it is surprisingly low earnings, the result of a change in some government's policy, or an environmental disaster.

At the same time, customers look to the chief executive as the ultimate salesperson for the company. Where customers are large relative to total sales, selling is actually something the president does. But in all companies, the president is the person to whom the markets look as the chief spokesperson. The smiling face of Sam Walton represented Wal-Mart, and his presence in his stores reflected his conclusion that the customers were right. Especially in the United States with its strong populist tradition, anonymous is a negative description when applied to a chief executive.

Equally important to the work of the president, the people of the organization look to him or her for personal leadership. The chief executive operates on a stage with bright lights on most of the time. All actions and words are interpreted for meaning, and inconsistencies are duly noted. What is the president saying, and does he "walk the way he talks"? The values of the organization, its standards of performance, and generally the way people are treated inevitably reflect the way the president behaves.

Sometimes, the comprehensiveness of these responsibilities is experienced as a real burden by company leaders. Especially if they were entrepreneur founders of their organizations, they sometimes yearn for the "freedom" they experienced in their companies' formative years. (Usually this means they have forgotten their dismay with the behavior of their financiers!) How well they deal with these almost unlimited responsibilities depends on their personality and their physical condition. An important characteristic of chief executives is simply their stamina. John Harvey-Jones, famous as the chief executive who turned around the U.K. chemical giant ICI, has remarked that physical and intellectual toughness are key attributes of business leaders.[1]

BUSINESS POLICY AS A FIELD OF STUDY

Many business management students aspire to the role described above. Many others see top management as their ultimate client for consulting or banking services, or their employer. For all, understanding the role of the general manager and the skills required in the job is central to understanding the nature of a business and how it is managed. As a field of business administration, *business policy* "is the study of the functions and responsibilities of senior management, the crucial problems that affect the success of the total enterprise, and the decisions that

---

[1] John Harvey-Jones, *Making It Happen: Reflections on Leadership* (London: Collins, 1988).

determine the direction of the organization, shape its future, and, when well implemented, secure its achievement."[2]

Today, the subject of business policy is taught under a wide range of names. At many schools the title "Strategic Management" is used to reflect the body of research that has been carried out in the last 15 years in that field. Elsewhere, the problems of economic strategy are separated from those of leadership. The research and literature that provide the foundation for this book, as well as its previous editions, find the core problems of general management in the indivisibility of the twin tasks of shaping the purpose of the organization and managing the processes by which the organization operates. Except for narrow pedagogical purposes, it is not even right to separate from the study of the work of general management the vital contribution the president can make by leveraging the day-to-day performance of the organization.

It is precisely to emphasize the importance of process and action in the functions and responsibilities of senior management that we have shifted emphasis in this edition from the more analytic "business policy," with its emphasis on the core concept of corporate strategy, to the more dynamic "general management," with its balanced view of purpose and process interacting.

A CONCEPT OF "GENERAL MANAGEMENT"

Even the brief review that we have made of general management responsibilities reveals the comprehensiveness and complexity of the job of chief executive. In order to make sense of the job and to study its functions, it is useful to consider it in terms of three roles, *strategist, organization builder,* and *doer*. These three roles encompass the tasks of

- crafting the strategy of the organization and communicating it to the organization.
- managing the resource allocation process so that it reflects the strategy.
- managing the selection, training, and progress of the people organization and building a positive work environment, designing the structure and systems that provide context for the operations—both so that capabilities increase in areas that permit moving toward strategic objectives.
- intervening personally where necessary to drive forward and raise the quality of day-to-day performance.

---

[2] Joseph L Bower et al., *Business Policy: Text and Cases, 7th edition* (Homewood, IL: Irwin, 1991), p.2.

We shall see as well that the job involves learning from the reactions of suppliers, customers, competitors, and other constituencies interested in the corporation so as to give order to the process by which strategy evolves. This necessity to reflect while in action is one of the most demanding aspects of the president's job.[3]

The General Manager as Strategist

Anyone who has taken part in any organized activity, from helping to push a car out of a snowbank to working for a large corporation, knows that there is a need to coordinate activity around a common goal and that the goal had better be realistic. This is a key component of the work of leadership, and it involves thinking about what needs to be done, communicating what has been decided, and motivating others to contribute their efforts. When we consider these activities from the perspective of shaping the purpose of the organization, we speak of the general manager as strategist. While great intellect is often required to lead the problem solving involved in crafting an effective corporate strategy, the work of strategist is not merely analytic. An effective strategy cannot be discovered in a library and delivered to an organization on paper or in a speech to be implemented. Much as for Moses after he acquired the Ten Commandments from the Lord, time and effort are required to convert a wise vision into an informed organization. In today's jargon we would say it is a "continuous process."

The role is daunting. To begin, many take part in the process. Their ideas and knowledge need to be tapped. At the same time, careful thought about the future reveals just how uncertain is our understanding of what may happen. Even if we know with near certainty that particular conditions will develop, where and when are highly unpredictable. Leaders soon discover that the strategic questions that keep them awake at night are sufficiently frightening to be disabling to most of their colleagues. While management theorists may value planning that is "outside the box," leaders know or soon discover that most of their employees are more than content with the comfortable arrangements inside the box. Indeed, most of their colleagues' careers are premised on the notion that the knowledge they have accumulated will continue to be useful in an organization that will only be incrementally different in the future.

---

[3] Donald A Schon has called attention to this critical skill of professionals in action. His book *The Reflective Practioner: How Professionals Think in Action* (New York: Basic Books, 1983) makes an important contribution to our understanding of what professionals do when they use knowledge to guide action.

The difference between great strategists and unemployed prophets is that the former is able to get others to see the wisdom of their vision and build a coalition that will act on it. It is this aspect of strategic work rather than formulating the intellectual content of the economic strategy that falls almost uniquely on the chief executive's shoulders. It relates to the work of marshaling and allocating resources so that the capabilities of the organization are directed in line with strategy. And it involves to a critical degree shaping the character of the people of the organization and the environment in which they work. The strategic aspects of these tasks mean that they are not just the province of the finance and human resource management organizations.

The General Manager as Organization Builder

Whether an organization is successful over time depends as much on its capabilities as on what it is trying to do. Achieving more means that those capabilities must be improved. We will see in the cases that sometimes the means to achieve objectives can be acquired in the market as equipment or licensed technology. But the capabilities that are critical to strategic progress reside in the processes and practices of the organization: what the organization knows how to do and is able to do.

Giving shape to processes and practices involves designing the organization and its systems for measure and information, for planning, for budgeting and control, and for reward and punishment. These architectural activities are complemented by choosing ventures and projects that build the strength of the organization. Two adages (both framed before gender neutral language became prevalent) guide this highly idiosyncratic process: "A man must walk before he can run," and, "A man's reach must exceed his grasp, or what's a heaven for." The leader's responsibility for building the organization requires not only driving it to take on ever more difficult tasks at a pace that is at least the equal of competitors, but also assessing the consequences of failure so that the inevitable unforeseeable setbacks will not destroy the company. When to develop a new product line, when to enter a foreign market, and when to improve value added by building a scarce skill center in-house are decisions that turn on judgments about the ability of people to grow and the consequences of failure. These vital decisions, in turn, depend on judgments about the motivation and skill of people, and their ability to work together.

The General Manager as Doer

Though least glamorous and hardest to conceptualize, the way a general manager uses time in the day has an enormous impact on the organization. His or her ethical and intellectual standards, working hours, approach to people, attention to customers, and consideration of family are the models for the senior management. Their example is education for the subordinate executives. In this way, the individual shapes the behavior of the company and its reputation in the community.

The general manager also has a critical influence in his or her choices of where or when to intervene. In the cases of this book we see general managers stepping out of their managerial role in order to work as inventors, salespeople, team leaders at critical moments in the innovation process, risk takers, catalysts for change, and simple cheerleaders driving people to feats that they did not know they were capable of achieving.

THE SKILLS OF THE GENERAL MANAGER

In performing these three roles, general managers draw on many skills. The list of useful abilities is long, and few have all. General managers must have sufficient *analytic* skill to be capable of diagnosing both the economic and administrative components of a situation. In doing so they must be able to deal with vital detail as well as the big picture. Research on the intellectual skills of effective managers reveals that their particular strength is the ability to see patterns in detail and link these to useful concepts.[4]

General managers also need to develop good *judgment*. In effect, they need to be able to apply their experience and analysis quickly and decisively so that problems get resolved early. The cases include many examples of managers who have the courage to see that something is not working well, and act on their intuition. C. Roland Christensen, an author of earlier editions of this book, defined *intuition* as "knowledge and experience processed so as to be instantly available wisdom." General managers learn quickly that they must develop and rely on this resource.

Closely related to judgment but possibly different is the ability to apply special kinds of intuition that Americans call *street smarts* because they are not taught in schools. Some people are remarkably good at understanding the motives of individuals and are able to anticipate on that basis how they are likely to behave. Reasoning in this fashion, they are also able to deal with individuals and situations with remarkable effectiveness. This particular set of skills is thought of as being acquired at birth or while growing up, but is extremely valuable.

General managers also need *creativity, the ability to take risks,* and *the ability to integrate.* Repeatedly, the skill that distinguishes an effective leader is the ability to invent a solution that turns a problem into an

---

[4] While academics and professionals such as lawyers are usually superior to managers at dealing with abstraction or rigorous detail, neither are as good at bridging between the two.

opportunity. By making a necessity of their vision and objectives, great general managers are able to drive thinking into new channels producing original solutions. In the same spirit, they see when taking a risk is worth the potential cost and move forward boldly. While avoiding foolhardy acts, they have the stomach for confrontation or investments that might fail. (The difference between foolhardy and acceptable risk often turns on self-confidence that if things begin to turn out badly in the future, one can develop a creative solution not readily apparent in the present.) Both creativity and risk taking in management are aided by an integrative perspective. The ability to link vision and exhaustive detail in a comprehensive view enhances the chance for success and reduces the likelihood of surprise outcomes.

An absolutely vital skill is the ability to *communicate* clearly one's vision and logic. General managers are constantly engaged in sharing their view of a question, a problem, an objective, or a program of action. Unless they can effectively engage the attention of subordinates, peers, superiors, and other relevant constituencies such as investors, they cannot succeed. The more varied the constituencies with which a manager must communicate, the more demanding the task. The nature of the message is also important. One of the hardest tasks we will study is the dismantling of unsuccessful organization. General managers that can engage their organization in the enthusiastic and effective exit from a business have unusual skill. Like surgeons, they can cut deeply into an organization in order to produce a healthier company.

Finally, and perhaps most valuable of all, general managers rely on their skills with people. Depending upon their personality, style, and experience they are able to enlist the commitment and trust of those with whom they work. The cases in this book display some who are charming, some who are mysterious, and some who inspire fear. But all effective general managers develop a way of communicating to those with whom they work that they are reliable sources of help—good ideas, good information, and good spirits, all grounded in good intentions.

If this list of skills appears long and demanding, we would ask you to remember that it is intended to evoke the results of a career rather than a course. We return to the list in the last chapter when we consider the challenge of building a career in general management. Before that, however, we focus on the three basic roles of a general manager just described, noting those skills that are especially important to particular tasks.

We begin with the role of strategist, considering first what corporate strategy really means. In subsequent chapters we work with the economic, organizational, and societal elements of building a strategy. This leads us directly into the interrelated work of building and transforming organizations.

Bright Horizons Children's Centers, Inc.—1987

THE OPPORTUNITY

In 1985, Jack Reynolds and his wife, Anne Whitman, celebrated the arrival of their first child, an event that eventually triggered the birth of Bright Horizons Children's Centers. After an initial period of at-home care, the couple anticipated placing their daughter in a quality day care facility. They had planned ahead for that day by placing her name on the waiting list at 12 different centers near their home and work. Confident that at least one appropriate space would become available, they inspected each of the centers. They found that most were only marginally satisfactory, and among all of them, no place materialized. The couple soon discovered that most of their friends were experiencing the same problems in finding quality care for their children.

Reynolds discussed the problem with a personal friend in the business, Lois Baker. Baker was an expenenced child care specialist, working at Kinder Care Learning Centers, who was able to provide valuable industry and operating insights. Convinced of both the need and the opportunity it represented, Reynolds prepared a preliminary business plan for a network of quality child care centers in his "spare time" while working as a management consultant at Bain and Company. With a working plan for a child care network he had dubbed *Edukids*, he began contacting venture capitalist firms. He found little interest in the concept, except at Bain Capital. There, the investors felt the plan had merit, but they could not consider any commitment without seeing a top-quality management team in place and at least one site negotiated.

While the plan was still in process, Jack Reynolds discussed the idea with his former Bain associate, Roger Brown, and Linda Mason, both of whom had just returned to the Boston area. Both Brown and Mason were graduates of the Yale School of Organization and Management who had a longstanding interest in child welfare. In 1980, as part of their graduate internship program, they each managed Cambodian refugee programs in Thailand. Upon their return, the two coauthored a book, *Rice, Rivalry, and Politics*, based on their experience in the management of relief efforts. They chose consulting work after graduation in 1982, he with Bain and she with Booz, Allen, and Hamilton, but, when they were offered the opportunity to initiate and manage a Save the Children Federation relief effort in the Sudan, they departed for Africa in 1985. While in Africa, the two directed a $14 million program and managed a staff of 600 professionals scattered across a country roughly the size of the Eastern seaboard of the United States served by a road system with fewer paved miles than existed in the state of Rhode Island. Though they often worked independently in different parts of the country, the two divided management responsibilities when possible. Brown concentrated on fund raising, agency relationships, and general administration while Mason concentrated on recruiting and coordinating personnel, setting up worksites, and overseeing operations.

When they returned from the Sudan in 1986, the couple's combination of business management skills, start-up experience (albeit nonprofit), and their strong commitment to children's programs made them potentially attractive partners for Reynolds' child care idea. Mason and Brown were attracted to the venture because it enabled them to "put down roots," to continue working together, and to extend their ongoing commitment to children's well-being, though in "less distressing conditions" than they had encountered abroad. Compared with battling hunger in regions devastated by drought and war, providing child care for prosperous parents seemed simple and straightforward. Yet, from the beginning, Mason and Brown intended to do much more than

create successful centers. They wanted to "transform the way people think about child care." Brown noted that he was extremely ambitious in his personal goal to reach beyond Reynolds' venture . . . to have a significant influence on the child care industry.

> I'm just an ambitious person, but ambitious not so much in the traditional sense that I'm eager to make a lot of money. In fact, I'm so ambitious that money is not even that important to me. I think the idea of this bigger challenge of trying to build an enterprise that somehow does something good for the world at the same time that it is a good place for people to work and can function in the mainstream of business . . . that's a real ambitious goal.

Speaking of Mason and himself as a team, he went on:

> [We have] ambition to put ourselves in a position where we will be able to be spokespeople and can be recognized as leaders, and to achieve the fairly complex and challenging goal of building an institution that is successful.

THE DECISION

Before making a final decision to join the project that Reynolds, Whitman, and Baker were already planning, Mason and Brown undertook extensive market research. They worked with Reynolds to refine and complete a 60-page business plan, renaming the business Bright Horizons Children's Centers, Inc. They agreed to assume leadership for the venture and next turned their total energies to the financing. The couple wanted to demonstrate that the idealism associated with nonprofit endeavors could survive and flourish in a disciplined, for-profit venture. They saw Bright Horizons as an opportunity to provide high-quality child care through a financially stable organization. Though they had explored the possibility of starting such a business as a parent-funded cooperative, they found insufficient interest among the parent group they surveyed. The venture-funded, for-profit alternative that Bright Horizons represented would give them the platform to start a large number of centers, to grow rapidly, and to begin influencing the way America thought about child care while experiencing the excitement of building and managing a successful new business. Brown felt that there was little difference in the management of an enterprise whether it was for-profit or nonprofit. "It's just a question of who your boss is and who you have to ask for money."

Potential investors were nervous about Mason's and Brown's "nonprofit mentality" and worried about the advisability of having the couple function as coequal heads of the proposed company. The venture capitalists were convinced of the viability of the plan but needed assurance on the suitability of the management team. At the insistence of one venture capitalist, the couple were evaluated by a West Coast psychologist. Though the idea initially infuriated Mason and amused Brown, the evaluation turned out to be an unexpected boon and the report, a strong selling tool. "It testified," said Brown, "that we have a vigorous marriage and are great at working together, that we're pitbulls and once we sink our teeth into something we don't let go." Two of the other founders also took active management roles, Baker as director of operations and Whitman as marketing manager. Reynolds, who was by then working with North American Management, an investment management firm, chose to invest and to serve on the board of directors, but not to be involved in day-to-day management.

A commitment by the developer of One Kendall Square, a new office complex in Cambridge, to provide space for the first center provided the final impetus for the venture capital agreement. After months of research and multiple investor presentations, Bright Horizons became one of the first child care companies to secure venture funding: a $2 million commitment from Bessemer Venture Partners and Bain Capital with a minority investment from North American Management Corporation. Under the terms of the deal that closed in March 1987, the venture capital firms received common shares and convertible, redeemable preferred shares carrying a 13 percent noncash dividend rate. The dividends were to be accrued annually but not paid out. Only if the preferred shares were redeemed, rather than converted, would the dividend actually be tendered. On a postconversion basis, the venture capitalists' collective holdings totaled approximately 55 percent of the equity. The remaining 45 percent was retained by the company to be used to reward management, including Mason, Brown, and other managers. The lead investors, Bain Capital and Bessemer Ventures, would provide management oversight as members of the Bright Horizons board of directors, which would also include Brown (as chairman), Mason, and Reynolds. The founders had a vision of quality child care that motivated them, but they were aware that their investors were primarily interested in the return on their investment. They would most likely want to do an initial public offering around the fifth year of operation and would target a 30–40 percent annualized return on their investment.

The initial $2 million capitalization was intended to finance growth through the first two years and result in the opening of nine New England centers by the end of 1988. A second round of financing was planned at that stage, with initial investors expected to participate if Bright Horizons was meeting or exceeding its plan (see Exhibit 1).

THE MARKET

Center-based child care was a $6 billion industry in 1985 and had an annual growth rate of 15 percent (see Exhibit 2). In 1960, 20 percent of American women who had children under six worked outside the home. By 1985, more than 50 percent did so. While the need for child care was rapidly increasing, the availability of the extended family network, once the mainstay of child care, was declining. Whereas 59 percent of children with working mothers were cared for by a relative in 1965, the percentage had dropped to 41 percent in 1982 (see Exhibit 3). In contrast with many European countries, there were few public facilities in the United States to fill the gap.

Three general categories of child care services were available: in-home ("nanny") care, family day care, and center-based care. In-home care, while offering parents the greatest flexibility, was typically the most expensive option and accounted for less than 10 percent of the child care market. Family day care, in which one or more children were supervised in a caretaker's typically unlicensed home, was the most likely alternative to relative-provided care and accounted for approximately 30 percent of child care in 1982. Center-based care accounted for 21 percent of the child care market in 1982 and was the fastest growing segment. By 1990, the centers were expected to account for 32 percent of total child care. Most were neighborhood-based, but several for-profit chains had already started up and had proven themselves financially successful by the mid-1980s. Revenues for center-based care were projected to reach $12 billion by 1990. Though research indicated that 50 percent of the demand was for worksite-based child care, only 5 percent of the centers were located at or near work by 1987.

Large national chains claimed 10 percent of the total center-based child care revenues in 1987. The remaining 90 percent was shared by single center operations and small organizations of two to four centers, most of which were nonprofit. The growth rate for the chains was significantly outpacing the single center openings, with a projected annual growth rate of 30 percent from 1985 to 1990. Most of the growth was expected to come from newer entries.

The Bright Horizons business plan provided information about four of the largest national day care chains: Kinder Care Learning Centers, La Petite Academy, Children's World, and Children's Discovery Centers (see Exhibit 4). Their explosive growth resulted in financial success, but in some cases it also brought a reputation for inferior quality. The largest chain, Kinder Care, considered itself the McDonald's of child care, expanding from its humble beginnings in Montgomery, Alabama, in 1969 to more than 1,000 centers nationwide by 1986. Revenues had an average annual growth rate of 28 percent in the decade from 1975 to 1985 with an average net return on sales of 8 percent. In spite of its financial success, it was asserted that some of its corporate clients, including The Campbell Soup Company, canceled contracts after employees complained to management about the quality of care. Kinder Care had a record of paying its employees close to the minimum wage and experienced turnover rates reported to be among the highest in the industry. The National Child Care Staffing Study considered staff wage level the single most accurate predictor of quality in child care.

Though Kinder Care had purchased a network of 30 Massachusetts centers in 1982, it had found the state's regulatory environment very tough and had chosen not to expand further. The company had, in fact, closed two of the centers since the acquisition. La Petite Academy was founded in 1970. Headquartered in Kansas City, Missouri, it had concentrated its growth in the Midwest and South. Children's World had 248 centers in 1986. The company operated primarily in the Southwest and the Washington, DC, area, but had announced an aggressive growth plan after its acquisition by Grand Metropolitan in 1983 and was rumored to be planning an entry into the Boston market. Children's Discovery Centers was a venture-funded operation, founded in Connecticut in 1984. Though it had 13 centers in Connecticut, it had not established a presence elsewhere in New England. The venture group that had funded the start-up was in the process of selling its shares in 1987, and the future direction of the company was unclear. None of the major chains served the professional market that Bright Horizons had targeted, and all had chosen a residential location strategy. Kinder Care was beginning to establish some workplace centers by the mid-1980s but had not made that a major strategic thrust.

New England was thought to be an especially attractive market for Bright Horizons. Low unemployment in the mid-1980s inspired vigorous competition among corporations to recruit and retain valuable employees. With a high percentage of professional working women in the market, on-site day care was seen as a valuable and still unusual amenity that could make the difference in choosing among employment options. The Northeast was not well served by the major child care industry players. According to the Bright Horizons business plan, there were 10.7 such centers per million people in the South, 8.8 in the West, 5.8 in the Midwest, with only 2.2 per million in the Northeast. Expensive real estate and stringent licensing requirements were formidable barriers to entry. Bright Horizons felt it had significant advantages because of the New England connections already established through investors and advisors and Lois Baker's expertise in the licensing area.

THE STRATEGY

Reynolds, Mason, and Brown developed the Bright Horizons business plan according to a different vision of child care. The defining components of the Bright Horizons strategy included:

- quality positioning
- parent/child orientation
- worksite location
- corporate- or developer-subsidized rents
- regional dominance

Quality

Bright Horizons defined quality along several dimensions. One dimension was the continuity of care for a child at one center from birth to 6 years of age. Most child care centers offered limited or no infant/toddler spaces because such care required a higher staff/child ratio, was costly to operate and difficult to staff, and usually operated at lower profit margins. By establishing different tuitions for each age group based on the teacher/child ratio, Bright Horizons planned to offer continuous child care in a single location for all of a child's preschool years.

Though Bright Horizons expected the typical center to accommodate 100 children, the plan for the opening of facilities in Massachusetts, where Bright Horizons would have to work with tight space in existing buildings, was based on centers with a capacity of 80 children. In the model, spaces were allocated approximately 17 percent infants, 23 percent toddlers, and 60 percent preschoolers (see Exhibit 5). Brown projected that each center would ramp up to 80 percent capacity within the first seven months and that enrollment would stabilize at that level (see Exhibit 6). The ramp-up rate was largely dependent upon when the center opened. Many child care programs followed an academic year schedule, so parents often made their commitments in the late summer, making it more difficult to fill the older preschool categories in the winter and spring. Mason and Brown believed the ramp-up time could be smoothed, however, since infants and toddlers arrived at any time during the year.

Perhaps the most important element of quality care was the relationship between teacher and child, requiring faculty with a natural affinity for children and sufficient training to design stimulating activities for them. Thus, teachers with Early Childhood Education degrees would be recruited. To preserve the teacher/child relationships, staff turnover was to be minimized. The attention to staffing reflected Mason's and Brown's belief that the faculty was 99 percent of the quality. In addition to the human care provided by the trained staff,

Bright Horizons was planning to emphasize the importance of the physical space as essential in supporting the quality program. Centers would be open, light-filled, and well-furnished with educational toys. To encourage parents to visit with the children at the center or to linger and talk with teachers, each center would include a comfortable living room area.

Parent/Child Orientation

Bright Horizons developed a sliding-scale tuition schedule with rates for preschool children comparable to those at competitor centers and higher rates for toddlers and infants (see Exhibit 5). The target market consisted of working families with one to two children aged 0–6 years with a combined annual income of $40,000 or more. Through participation in local tuition support programs, Mason and Brown were planning to extend the affordability of Bright Horizons' programs to families from a wide spectrum of incomes and ethnicity. They were also establishing a nonprofit foundation, the Horizons Fund, for charitable contributions to provide care to children of battered women and homeless children.

Worksite Location

Bright Horizons' founders chose the channel of day care delivery that had the largest unmet need, the worksite. By placing the child care centers near the parents' workplace, Bright Horizons expected to create a family-oriented program that fostered daytime parent/child interaction. The plan also enabled Bright Horizons to receive financial support from corporate sponsors to defray the costs of operating, thus keeping the tuition costs of the high-quality care in a more affordable range.

Corporate- or Developer-Subsidized Rents

Bright Horizons sought reduced or free rent at each of its locations. Rent, including utilities, real estate taxes, and insurance, typically averaged 22–25 percent of a center's revenues. Bright Horizons' plan called for these occupancy costs to be no more than 10–11 percent of revenue. Brown was the primary advocate for this strategy and, in his negotiations with potential sponsors, used what he described as an "ice water approach" by immediately announcing that Bright Horizons could not pay market rates (typically $12–$15 psf rent + other occupancy costs) but could consider rent in the $5–$7 range. He then explained the rationale of substituting increased salaries for a portion of the rent savings to offer the high-quality care at a competitive price.

Brown was adamant about minimizing the fixed costs in a business with traditionally low profit margins (6–8 percent after taxes). In addition to his negotiating strategy, he began educating himself about real estate by attending industry association meetings and reading trade literature. He stressed that "if we don't do the real estate right, we won't survive."

Regional Dominance

In order to manage the company's expansion, Mason and Brown planned to build strong local recruiting networks, establish regional identity with quality child care, and develop systems for close monitoring of center operations. The strategy dictated the development of clusters of child care centers, each one comprising 8 to 12 centers within two to three hours' driving distance of one another.

THE IMPLEMENTATION

With the other founders, Mason and Brown established a clear set of corporate values that they planned to operationalize in the business. The values were intended to be the guiding principles for decision making at all levels. Dubbed *RNTOBS* for short, they included:

- Respect (for child, parent, faculty)
- Nurturing
- Trust
- Openness to change
- Balance (between program, faculty, parents, environment)
- Sustainability

These values were represented in the Bright Horizons logo by the six rays around the sun, symbol of the child at the center of all activities. Mason and Brown assembled an advisory board of individuals who would support and enhance the basic values and the quality mission of Bright Horizons while providing important industry contacts (see Exhibit 7).

Jim Rouse, a real estate developer, commented when he joined Bright Horizons' advisory board, "Profit is the discipline that hauls dreams into focus." Mason and Brown believed that their most important task was to create successful, highly reputable child care centers as models to attract new corporations and developers as sponsors. Once that was done, they anticipated a period of sharply accelerated growth with a second geographic region being opened in year three. In the longer term, acquisition of existing centers would also become a part of the company's growth strategy. With money in the bank and one center on the drawing board, Mason and Brown were ready to start making the dream come true.

EXHIBIT 1
FINANCIAL MODEL FROM ORIGINAL BRIGHT HORIZONS BUSINESS PLAN, 1986

Financial model: Based on 52-week year, center with 80-children capacity. Figures have been simplified and rounded.

Fixed costs (annual)

Rent	$33,000
Depreciation of leasehold improvements (4-year depreciation schedule)	17,000
Other expenses including liability insur.	10,000
	$60,000

Year one start-up fees

(legal, architectural, etc.)	6,000

Contribution per student per week

Revenue per student ($/week)		$135.00	
Staff compensation ($/student/week)	$93.00		
Food cost ($/student/week)	4.85		
Supplies ($/student/week)	3.33		
Total variable costs ($/student/week)		$101.18	
Contribution ($/student/week)		33.82	
Annual contribution per center, based on 80% occupancy: $33.82 × 52 × 64 =			$112,550
Contribution per center during first six "ramp-up" months: averaging 29% occupancy			$ 20,600

Growth Scenario

Year*	Centers	Cumulative Cash Needs
1	3	$ 896,000
2	6	1,900,000
3	12	2,900,000
4	24	3,800,000
5	48	4,400,000

Cumulative 93 centers†

Average projected corporate overhead expense for year 1: $53,000/month

*Bright Horizons' first fiscal year (FY 1988) dated from July 1, 1987, to June 30, 1988.
†This figure was reduced to 87 In the final plan.

EXHIBIT 2
GROWTH IN CENTER-BASED CARE MARKET, 1975–1990E

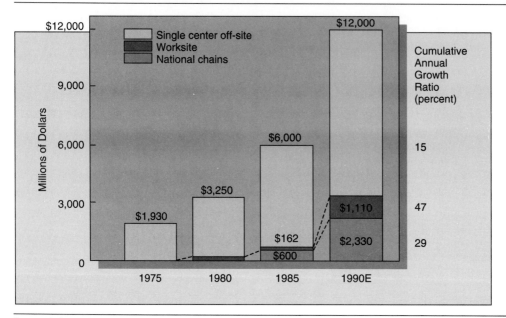

Source: Industry Analysis Reports: Drexel, Burnham, Lambert.

EXHIBIT 3
CHILD CARE INDUSTRY SEGMENTS, 1958–1990E

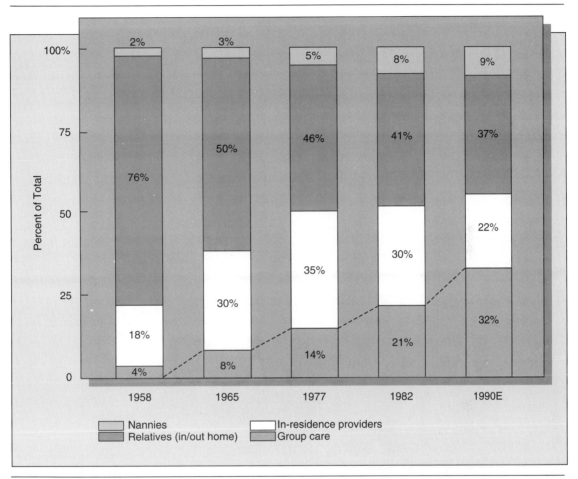

Source: U.S. Bureau of the Census.

EXHIBIT 4
SELECTED COMPETITORS' PERFORMANCE

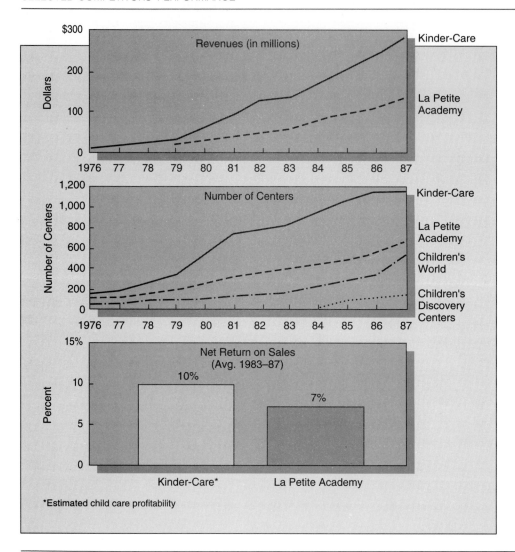

Source: Bright Horizons Business Plan, 1986.

EXHIBIT 5
BRIGHT HORIZONS CENTER CONFIGURATION

	Children	Teachers*	Child:Teacher Ratio	Monthly Tuition
Infant (up to 15 months)	14	4	3.5:1	$780
Toddler (up to 2 yrs, 9 months)	18	4	4.5:1	640
Preschooler (up to 6 years)	48	5	9.6:1	460
Total	80	13	6.15:1	

*This did not include a limited number of part-time teachers typically hired to handle the early morning and late afternoon hours at each center.

EXHIBIT 6
BRIGHT HORIZONS CENTER PROJECTED RAMP-UP RATES

Month	1	2	3	4	5	6	7
Students	5	11	18	26	35	45	64

EXHIBIT 7
MEMBERS OF BRIGHT HORIZONS ADVISORY BOARD

Member	Title	Background
Dr. T. Berry Brazelton	Nationally renowned pediatrician and child advocate.	Pioneering scientific research used by physicians nationally. Authored/produced books and videotapes on child-rearing.
Phyllis Dobyns	Vice President of Operations, Save the Children Federation	Over 20 years of international development and relief work.
Robert Avinger	EVP Sterling Capital Management Company	Ph.D. Economics, Duke University. Professor of economics, Davidson College, 12 years. Visiting economist to Federal Trade Commission in 1970s.
Bart Harvey	Deputy Chairman of the Enterprise Foundation	Formerly Managing Director of Corporate Finance, Dean Witter Reynolds. Lobbied Congress to maintain incentives for the creation of low-income housing. Leading spokesperson for the housing needs of poor people in the United States.
Jim Rouse	Founder and former Chairman and CEO, Rouse Company (a major U.S. real estate development firm) Founder and current Chairman, Enterprise Foundation (an organization addressing housing needs of the urban poor)	Designed and developed Columbia, Maryland, a fully self-sufficient city filled with open land, residents of socioeconomic and racial diversity, and with child care in every neighborhood.
Patrica T. Rouse	Cofounder, Secretary–Treasurer, and Trustee of The Enterprise Foundation	Board member of WorldTimes, Mediators Productions, and Columbia Bancorp. Appointed by President Bush as Director of the Commission on National and Community Service. Board member to several foundations in Maryland.
Dr. Edward F. Zigler	Sterling Professor of Psychology, Yale University, and head of the Psychology Section of the Yale Child Study Center Director of Yale's Bush Center in Child Development and Social Policy	The first Director of the Office of Child Development and Chief of the Children's Bureau from 1970 to 1972. Architect of U.S. Head Start program. Board member/consultant to over 20 organizations; author or editor of 20 books and over 500 chapters and journal/media articles.
Greg Winter	Manager of Real Estate Development and Project Manager for the Prudential Center Redevelopment Project, Prudential Center Property Company, Inc.	Engineering a $500 million redevelopment of the Prudential Center in downtown Boston. Worked for the Economic Development and Industrial Corporation of Boston, 4 years.

Head Ski Company, Inc.

In 1967 the Head Ski Company, Inc., seemed to be at a turning point. In its 17 years of existence, the company had enjoyed great success as a specialized manufacturer of high-quality skis under the entrepreneurial leadership of its founder, Howard Head. Recently, however, the company had moved to a more structured management organization and had embarked on several diversification ventures.

Head Ski had been formed in 1950 to sell metal skis designed by its founder. In the company's first year, six employees turned out 300 pairs of skis. By the 1954–1955 skiing season, output reached 8,000 pairs, and by 1965 it passed 133,000. Growth in dollar sales and profits was equally spectacular. When Head went public in 1960, sales were just over $2 million and profits just under $59,000. By 1965 sales were up to $8.6 million and profits had reached $393,713. In the next two years, volume continued to rise, although less dramatically. In the 53-week period ended April 30, 1966, sales were $9.1 million and profits $264,389. In the year ended April 29, 1967, sales were $11.0 million and profits $401,482. (For financial data, see Exhibit 1.)

THE INDUSTRY

Skiing was one of the most dynamic segments of the growing market generated by leisure-time activities. The industry association, Ski Industries America (SIA), estimated that skiing expenditures—including clothing, equipment, footwear, accessories, lift tickets, travel, entertainment, food, and lodging—had risen from $280 million in 1960 to $750 million in 1967, and were projected to reach $1.14 billion by 1970, reflecting both an increasing number of skiers and greater per capita expenditures. In 1947, the number of active skiers in the United States was estimated at less than 10,000. SIA believed there were 1.6 million in 1960 and 3.5 million in the 1966–1967 ski season, and predicted 5 million for 1970. Another industry source estimated that the number of skiers was increasing by 20 percent a year.

Of the $750 million total skiing expenditures in the 1966–1967 season, an estimated $200 million was spent at retail for ski equipment and skiwear. A wide variety of skis was available in several price ranges, as shown in Table A. Although many manufacturers made all three types of skis and some had multiple brands, the industry was highly fragmented. Ninety-eight manufacturers belonged to the SIA.

Observers noted that the ski industry was changing rapidly. *Ski Business* summed up an analysis of recent trends as follows:

- Imports of low-priced adult wood skis into the United States are skidding sharply.
- U.S. metal skis are gaining faster than any other category.
- The ski equipment and apparel market is experiencing an unusually broad and pronounced price and quality uptrend.
- Ski specialty shop business appears to be gaining faster than that of the much publicized department stores and general sporting goods outlets.
- The growth in the national skier population is probably decelerating and may already have reached a plateau.[1]

As the *Ski Business* article emphasized, the market was growing even faster in dollar value than in physical volume:

> Foreign skis clearly lost in 1966 at the gain of domestic manufacturers. (The total of imported and domestic skis sold in the United States is believed to be running at over 900,000 pairs annually.) By conservative estimate, U.S. metal-ski production in 1966 (for shipment to re-

TABLE A
NUMBER OF SKI BRANDS (AND MODELS)
BY PRICE RANGE

Price Range	Wood	Metal	Fiberglass
<$50	69	0	0
$50–100	27	22	24
		(28 models)	(35 models)
>$100	3	28	39
		(73 models)	(81 models)
All price ranges	85	49	53

Source: *Skiing International Yearbook*, 1967.

tail shops for the 1966–1967 selling season) was up by at least 40,000 pairs from 1965 . . .

But far more important than the domestic American ski gain (which will continue now that American fiberglass ski makers are entering the market) is the remarkable upward price shift. Thus while 10 percent fewer foreign skis entered the United States in 1966, the dollar value of all the skis imported actually rose by more than 10 percent or $700,000 . . . Here was the real measure of growth of the ski market; it was not in numbers, but in dollars.

The principal beneficiary of this remarkable upward shift in consumer preference for higher product quality is, of course, the ski specialty shop. The skier bent on purchasing $140 skis and $80 boots will tend to put his confidence in the experienced specialist retailer. The ski specialist shops, themselves, are almost overwhelmed by what is happening. Here's one retailer's comment: "Just two or three years ago, we were selling a complete binding for $15. Now skiers come into our shop and think nothing of spending $40 for a binding."

Most of the department store chains and sporting goods shops contacted by *Ski Business* were also able to report increased business in 1966–1967, but somehow the exuberant, expansionist talk seems to have evaporated among

---

[1]John Fry, *Ski Business*, May–June 1967, p. 25.

nonspecialty ski dealers. Montgomery Ward, for instance, says that ski equipment sales have not come up to company expectations. Ward's has specialized in low-end merchandise for beginning and intermediate skiers . . . Significantly, department stores or sporting goods shops which reported the largest sales increases tended to be those which strive hardest to cast their image in the ski specialist mold.[2]

Ski imports served both the low-priced and the high-priced market, as shown in Exhibit 2. Most of the decline in import volume is due to a sharp reduction in the number of Japanese skis; most other countries actually increased their ski exports to the United States. More than half the 530,000 pairs of skis imported from Japan were thought to be children's skis, which helped explain the low average valuation of the Japanese product ($6.84 a pair f.o.b.).[3]

The market for skis retailing at $100 or more was estimated at approximately 250,000 pairs a year. Sales of the leading competitors in this high-priced segment are shown in Table B. Fischer was believed to have worldwide sales of $15–18 million. Kniessl was thought to be about the same size as Head worldwide, but only about one-tenth Head's size in the United States. Another large company, AMF Inc., was entering the market with a fiberglass ski offered by its Voit recreational products division. Voit also manufactured water skis, a wide variety of aquatic equipment, and rubber products. AMF's 1966 sales were $357 million, with bowling equipment representing 22 percent of the total and other recreational equipment approximately 20 percent.

---

[2]Ibid.
[3]Ibid.

TABLE B
HIGH-PRICED SKIS

Brand	Type	Estimated Sales (000 pairs)	Price Range
Head (U.S.)	metal	125	$115–175
Hart (U.S.)	metal	44	100–175
Kniessl (Austria)	epoxy	20	150–200
Yamaha (Japan)	epoxy	13	79–169
Fischer (Austria)	wood, metal, epoxy	13	112–189

Source: *Skiing International Yearbook*, 1967.

A skier's choice of equipment was determined in part by his skill level. (Appendix A outlines the differences in construction and performance among skis of various types.) Of the 3.5 million skiers active in 1966–1967, 17,000 were regarded as racers; 75,000 were considered experts; and another 100,000 were sufficiently skillful to be classed as strong recreational skiers.

THE MARKET

Skiing was considered to be a sport that attracted the moderately well-to-do and those on the way up. A 1965 *New York Times* article outlined the costs of participation:

> A statistical study released early this year by the Department of Commerce disclosed that the American skier has a median age of 26.2 and a median annual income of $11,115. Moreover, it showed that about two-thirds of all skiers are college graduates.
>
> How do these young, affluent, and intelligent men and women spend their skiing dollars? At a typical resort, a person might spend each day $10 for accommodations, $10 for food, $5 for a lift ticket, and $10 for renting everything needed to attack the slopes from pants and parka to skis, boots, poles, and bindings . . .

The initial purchases of a person determined to have his or her own good equipment and to look well while skiing could easily be about $200. For this amount, a skier could buy everything from winter underwear to goggles and perhaps even have a bit left over for a rum toddy in the ski lodge the first night of his trip.

For instance, ski boots cost from $20 to $150 and average $50 a pair. Skis range from $30 to $200 and poles from $5 to $35.

When it comes to apparel, costs vary considerably. Snow jackets or parkas might cost as little as $20 or as much as $1,000 for those made with fur. Many jackets are available, though, at about $30.

Stretch pants have an average price of about $20. Other apparel requirements for skiing include sweaters, which retail from $10 to $50; winter underwear, which costs about $5; and ski hats and caps, which sell for $3 and up.[4]

Fashion consciousness was apparent in the design of ski equipment and skiwear and in the advent of a new type of skier. *The Wall Street Journal* reported on this phenomenon under the headline, "The Nonskiers: They Flock to Ski Resorts for the Indoor Sports."

Want to take up a rugged, outdoor sport? Cross skiing off your list.

The sport has gone soft. Ski resorts now have all the comforts of home—if your home happens to have a plush bar, a heated swimming pool, a padded chairlift, boutiques, and a built-in baby sitter . . . Skiing, in fact, has become almost an incidental activity at some ski resorts; indeed, some of the most enthusiastic patrons here at Squaw Valley and other resorts don't even know how to ski. They rarely venture outdoors.

So why do they come here? "Men, M-E-N. They're here in bunches, and so am I, baby," answers slinky, sloe-eyed Betty Reames as she selects a couch strategically placed midway between the fireplace and the bar . . .

Squaw Valley houses half a dozen bars and restaurants and often has three different bands and a folksinger entertaining at the same time. Aspen, in Colorado, throws a midwinter Mardi Gras. Sun Valley, in Idaho, has a shopping village that includes a two-floor bookstore and boutique selling miniskirts.

Life has also been made softer for those skiers who ski . . . Also some resorts are making their chairlifts more comfortable by adding foam padding. But even that isn't enough for some softies. "What? Me ride the chairlift? Are you crazy? I'd freeze to death out in the open like that," says blonde Wanda Peterson as she waits to ride up the mountain in an enclosed gondola car. She doesn't stand alone. The line of the gondola is 200 strong; the nearby chairlift, meanwhile, is all but empty . . .

For beginning skiers most resorts offer gentle, meticulously groomed inclines that make it almost impossible to fall. "We try to make it so that the person who has no muscle tone and little experience can't be fooled, can't make a mistake," says one resort operator. "Then we've got him. He's a new customer as well as a happy man."

Once he gets the hang of it—whether he's any good or not—the happy man starts spending lots of money, and that's what the resorts love.[5]

Capitalizing on the concern for style, some manufacturers of skiwear and ski equipment developed new colors and annual

---

[4]*New York Times*, December 12, 1965.

[5]*Wall Street Journal*, February 1967.

model changes to inspire a sense of product obsolescence and fad purchases.

HEAD COMPANY HISTORY

The first successful metal ski was developed by Howard Head, chairman and founder of the company bearing his name. Combining the experience of an aircraft designer with dedication to a sport he enjoyed, he spent more than three years developing a ski that did not break, turned easily, and tracked correctly without shimmying and chattering. Others had tried to produce metal skis, but Head succeeded almost five years before the introduction of the next competitive product, the Hart metal ski. *Ski Magazine* described the factors underlying Howard Head's success:

> He was obsessed, to be sure, and being relatively unencumbered by stockholders, high overhead, and strong yearnings for luxurious living, he was well braced for the long haul . . .
>
> "I made changes only where I had to make them," he has said of the days when his skis were undergoing trial by fire. "When they broke, I made them stronger only where they broke."[6]

In 1960 Howard Head described the early years of his enterprise and the trials that surrounded it:

> Twelve years ago I took six pairs of handmade metal skis to Stowe, Vermont, and asked the pros there to try them out. It had taken about a year to make those six pairs of skis. The design, based on engineering principles of aircraft construction, was radically different from any ever tried before. I thought it was

sound but the pros weren't a bit surprised when all six pairs promptly broke to pieces. After all, others before me had tried to make metal skis and all they had proved was what everyone knew anyway—a ski had to be made of wood.

> That was in January 1948. Today about 60 percent of all high-grade skis sold in the United States are metal skis. The reasons for this revolution in the ski manufacturing industry are simple. People like the way metal skis ski, they like their durability, and they like their easy maintenance . . .
>
> Many small refinements and changes in design have been introduced through the years because of our continued testing and development program and to meet the advances in technique and changes in skiing conditions. But the basic structural design hasn't changed, which speaks well for the original concept.[7]

Howard Head traced his involvement in the ski business to his personal interest in technical problems:

> When I started out, I was a mechanical design engineer—the whole origin of the business was the feeling that it should be possible to build a better ski. What started as an engineering puzzle ended as a business.
>
> I distinctly remember wondering at that time whether we would ever grow to the point where we would be making 5,000 pairs of skis a year.

Price–volume considerations had little influence on Head's initial marketing policy. Although most skiers were then using war surplus skis that cost $20, including bindings, the first Head metal skis were priced at $75. As Howard Head

---

[6]*Ski Magazine*, January 1964.

[7]"On Metal Skis," manuscript by Howard Head, 1960.

described it, quality was the overriding consideration:

> The great disadvantage of all metal skis is simply their high price. This became apparent to us when we were pioneering the original metal ski and found it was going to cost a good bit more than a wood ski. We didn't let that stop us because we believed the striking advantages of a metal ski more than compensated for its high price. As it turned out, even with a higher initial price, Head Skis proved to cost less in the long run because they are so durable . . .
>
> In the early days people had no way of knowing the skis would last so long that they actually ended up costing less than cheaper skis. They simply liked them enough to go ahead and buy them in spite of the price.[8]

The Head skis found a market that was quite unexpected. Despite their high price, they appealed more to relatively inexperienced skiers than to racers. Among skiers, Heads became known as "cheaters" because they could make almost anyone look good. "They practically turn themselves," it was said. Soon the black plastic top of the Head ski became a ubiquitous status symbol on the slopes.

PRODUCT POLICY

The keynote of Howard Head's product policy was quality. His fundamental belief was that the consumer should get all he pays for and pay for all he gets. Over the years, the product line was considerably upgraded. Several times the company recalled particular models or produc-

tion runs of skis that had been found defective. One executive commented that recalls had been made without hesitation, even when the company was in a precarious financial condition.

Asked what distinguished his company from its competition, Howard Head replied:

> I believe it is a tradition of attention to detail which grew out of its entrepreneurial history. In every aspect we attempt to follow through. Service, dealer relations, product quality, style, advertising, are all important and must be done in the best way we know how.
>
> We stress continued emphasis on quality of product and quality of operating philosophy. We pay meticulous attention to the individual relationships with dealers and the public.
>
> I have attempted to make creativity, imagination, and standards of perfection apply across the board. This was always our desire, and we only failed to live up to it when the business got too big for the existing staff. The philosophy remained constant, and now we have the people to live up to it.
>
> We get a return on this attention to detail. The feedback from success allows us to maintain the necessary staff to insure continuation of this philosophy. We allow no sloppiness.

Head skis came in one color—black. Different models were indicated only by the color (blue, red, yellow, or black) of the base and of the name "Head" embossed on the top of the ski. The use of a chrome top was once considered but rejected because it would be difficult to see against the snow and would create glare. Moreover, black was preferred as a conservative color that would go with anything. Howard Head explained that he

---

[8]Ibid.

CRITICAL FEATURES OF A SKI'S DESIGN

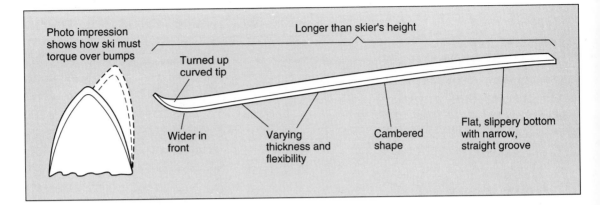

"did not want to complicate the consumer's choice."

> I deeply believe in sticking to function and letting style take care of itself. We have stuck so rigorously to our black color because it is honest and functional that it has become almost a trademark. While we constantly make minor improvements, we never make an important model change unless there is a performance reason for it. In other words, we skipped the principle of forced obsolescence, and we will continue to skip it.

This consciously chosen policy was staunchly maintained, while competitors introduced six or eight different colors and yearly color changes to keep up with fashion.

Apart from color and style, skis had to be designed to perform well on the slopes. Specifically, the three critical functions were tracking, traversing, and turning.[9]

Producing a ski that would perform well in all three respects required a delicate balancing of design considerations.

Ski distributors and retailers interviewed described some critical features of a ski's design. As shown above, the ski had to be flexible, designed with a cambered or arched shape to distribute the skier's weight over the entire ski, and manufactured so as to be straight, without warp or twist. The tip of the ski had to be pointed and turned up to permit the skier to navigate difficult terrain and soft snow without changing direction. The bottom of the ski was also critical: it had to provide a slippery surface for ease of travel and had to be perfectly flat except for a center groove which helped the skier

---

[9]*Tracking*: A ski pointed down a slope and allowed to run freely should hold a straight course—over bumps and through hollows and on every type of snow surface. *Traversing*: A ski should be able to hold a straight line while moving diagonally across a slope over obstacles and various snow conditions. *Turning*: When a skier releases the edges of his skis, the skis must be capable of slipping sideways, and when edged, they must bite into the snow evenly. (A skiing turn is nothing more than a sideslip carved into an arc by the controlled bite of the edges.)

to achieve tracking stability. The edges of the ski had to be sharp for holding and turning purposes. All of those interviewed stressed that for maximum performance, the skier had to select skis of the proper length.

Howard Head found a proper combination of these elements for the recreational skier in his earliest metal ski. This Standard model underwent substantial improvement in the following years. Until 1960, however, the goal of providing the best ski for experts eluded Head and other metal ski makers. As Head put it, "During the early years at Head Ski, we were too busy making the best ski we could for the general public to spend much time developing a competition ski."

Experts complained that metal skis were too "soft" and tended to vibrate badly at racing speeds. This problem was substantially solved in 1960, when Head introduced its Vector model. The Competition followed in 1962 and later entirely replaced the Vector. In these skis, an imbedded layer of neoprene dampened vibrations and considerably improved performance. Whereas most competitors in the 1960 Squaw Valley Olympics had stuck to their wooden skis, by the end of 1962 Head skis were in wide use. Of 141 racers who finished among the top six in races conducted by the international Professional Ski Race Association in Canada and the United States, 77 had used Head skis. About half the skis used in the U.S. National Junior and Senior Championships that year were also Heads.

By 1966 Head had established itself as an important factor in the ski racing world. An American had set the world speed record—106.527 mph—on Head skis. In major international competitions in 1966, one-third of all finishers in the top 10 places at all events were on Head skis, and

HEAD'S COMPETITION SKI

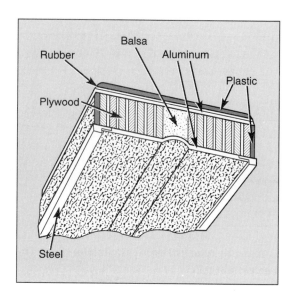

Head was the outstanding single manufacturer on the circuit, with 18 gold medals, 15 silver medals, and 15 bronze medals.

The 1968 Head line included a ski for every type of skier, from the unskilled beginner to the top professional racer, as described in Appendix B.

Head experimented constantly with new designs and frequently introduced minor modifications to improve the performance and durability of its product. A major change in product construction, such as a move to the fiber-reinforced plastic ski, was thought unlikely, however. Howard Head commented:

> We think that the metal sandwich construction is the best material. We do not see this situation changing in the foreseeable future. Certainly now, the other exotic materials are not gaining ground. They lack the versatility of application of the metal sandwich ski. The epoxy or fiber-reinforced plastic skis have low durability and don't have the wide performance range of our skis.

We believe that the advantage of the metal ski is that you can build in any performance characteristic you desire. Naturally, we have a research department investigating other materials, but until a major improvement is found we should stick to our basic material. We can always build the best ski for beginners, and we can adapt that ski to get the performance required by experts.

MARKETING POLICIES

Head's emphasis on quality extended beyond the product to the dealer and service network. The company sold only through a limited number of franchised dealers who had satisfied management that they knew something about skis and skiing. Ten district sales managers were employed; they sold to about 900 dealers throughout the United States. Of these, about 85 percent were ski specialty shops, 12 percent were large full-line sporting goods stores, and the remainder were full-

A FIBER-REINFORCED PLASTIC SKI

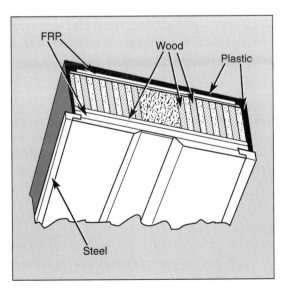

line department stores (see Exhibit 3). Head skis were distributed in Europe through an exclusive distributor, Walter Haensli of KIosters, Switzerland, who had sold 19 percent of Head's 1964 output. His share of sales appeared to be declining gradually.

The company believed that a Head franchise was valuable to a dealer. Many large stores that wanted to sell Heads were turned down, and Saks Fifth Avenue waited eight years before it was given a franchise. As Howard Head described it, the dealer played a critical role in Head sales:

> Getting Saks Fifth Avenue as a dealer is consistent with our operating philosophy of expecting the same quality from our dealers as from ourselves.
>
> Once they become a dealer, however, we get to know the people involved and work closely with them. Increasingly, we are recognizing the business value of providing more assistance and leadership to our dealers in helping them to do a better job for their customers.
>
> Even a large, well-managed department store or sporting goods store may need help in the specialized area of skis. They may need help in display stock selection, or even personnel selection. We are increasingly concerned about the type of personnel who sell skis. There is a high degree of dependence on the salesman. He must be a good skier himself.
>
> We have seen instances of two department stores of essentially identical quality in the same area, where one store could sell 8 pairs of skis a year and the other 300, simply because of a different degree of commitment to getting the right man to sell. Skis can only be sold by a floor salesman who can ski and who can sell from personal experience.

The company was convinced that selling skis was an exacting business. The ski size had to be matched to the individual's height and body weight; flexibility had to be chosen correctly depending on use, and bindings had to be mounted properly.

Head offered extensive after-sale service. Dealers were expected to maintain service facilities for minor repairs, and skis were sent back to the factory for sharpening edges, rebuilding the plastic portion of the ski, or matching a single ski if the mate had been broken beyond repair. Even in the busiest part of the season, service time was kept under three weeks.

In March 1967, Harold Seigle, the newly appointed president and chief operating officer of Head, issued a "management news bulletin" outlining the company's marketing philosophy:

1. Our current selective dealer organization is one of Head Ski Company's most valuable assets, next to the product itself.
2. Our continued sales growth will be based on a market-by-market approach aimed at increasing the effectiveness of our present dealers and by the very selective addition of new dealers wherever present dealers prove to be inadequate rather than by mass distribution and merchandising techniques.
3. Our future marketing efforts, particularly personal selling, advertising, merchandising, and sales promotion, will be geared to the specific needs of our dealers to sell all Head Ski products.
4. We want and will have the finest sales forces in the industry . . . who rely upon personal integrity, service, and hard work to do a professional selling job rather than inside deals and short cuts.
5. We feel that, next to quality products, strong personal selling at the

manufacturer's level and the retail level is paramount to our continued success and tends to transcend other facets of marketing that contribute to the sale of merchandise.

Advertising was done on a selective basis. A marketing journal reported:

> The company invests about 2 percent of gross sales in advertising, split between the skiing magazines (50 percent) and *Sports Illustrated, The New Yorker,* and *Yachting*—"the same kind of people like to sail."
>
> The most effective promotion, however, is probably the ski itself. Head is delighted at the growing demand for his skis in the rental market. "We sold 10,000 pairs—almost 10 percent of our business—for rental last year," he points out, "and everyone who rents those skis becomes a prospect."[10]

Ski rental was seen as the best way to introduce a customer to the ease of skiing on Heads. Accordingly, Head gave dealers an additional 12–15 percent discount on skis purchased for rental.

In general, the Head Ski Company took a soft-sell approach. Unlike many sporting goods companies, Head did not rely on personal endorsements of famous skiers. According to one executive, it was impossible under American amateur rules even to feature an amateur skier on a poster. Professional endorsements were probably ineffective anyway, since so many other sporting goods companies used them, and most people knew that such testimony could be bought. In an effort to get actual news pictures of famous skiers or racers using Head skis, the company did lend skis to racers for one

---

[10]*Sales Management/The Magazine of Marketing,* February 5, 1965.

year. Even this practice was expensive and had to be tightly controlled. A good skier might need upwards of nine pairs of skis a year, which would represent an expenditure of nearly $1,000. On the other hand, Head felt this type of promotion yielded a significant secondary benefit of product development information.

Head also collaborated with United Airlines in making a promotional film showing famous ski slopes. Head was mentioned in the title, at the end, and occasionally in the body of the show. The film was popular with ski clubs and other organizations that wished to promote interest in the sport.

Head skis received additional publicity through skiwear and resort advertisements. As *Sales Management* put it:

> So great is the worldwide prestige of Head skis that although Howard Head claims he makes no promotional tie-in deals, the ski buff can hardly miss seeing the familiar black skis in ads for anything from parkas to ski resorts. They're status symbols.[11]

PRODUCTION

Head skis were produced in three steps. The Detail Department made up the various components parts, including the core, the nose piece, the tail piece, the top plastic, the top and bottom skins, the running surface, and the edges. The separate pieces were then assembled in the Cavity Department. Here, too, the various layers were laid into a mold and heated and bonded under controlled temperature and pressure. The skis were then roughed out on a band saw. From this point on, all work was done on the skis as a pair. In the

Finishing Department, the skis were ground to final form, buffed, polished, and engraved.

Manufacture involved a great deal of handwork, of which 70 percent required a high degree of skill. Because of the basic nature of the assembly process, operations did not lend themselves to mass production techniques.

Howard Head commented on the difficulty of the manufacturing process and on the relationship between costs and price:

> [There are] approximately 250 different operations, involving a great number of specially developed machines, tools, and processes. None of the processes is standard. It all had to be developed more or less from scratch.
>
> Some of the special-purpose machines involved are those for routing the groove in the bottom aluminum, for attaching the steel edges, and for profiling the ski after it comes out of the presses. Also there are the bonding procedures that require an unusual degree of control of heat and pressure cycles.
>
> Supplementing all the special-purpose machines, we have learned to make rather unusual use of band saws. A good example of a demanding band-saw operation is the profiling of the plywood and plastic core elements. Since the stiffness of a ski at any point goes up as the square of the spacing between the top and bottom sheets, i.e., the core thickness, a normal band-saw tolerance of about .010 inch would grossly affect our flexibility pattern and would be out of the question. However, by special adapters and guides, we are actually able to band saw these parts in high production at about 10 seconds apiece to a tolerance of plus or minus .002 inch over the entire contour.
>
> An example of effective but low cost equipment in our factory is the press used to laminate 3 feet × 10 feet sheets

[11]Ibid.

of plywood core material to their corresponding sheets of sidewall plastic. This operation requires a total load of some 90,000 pounds. By using a roof beam as the reaction point, the floor for a base, and three screw jacks for pressure, we are able to produce enough material for 600 pairs of skis at one shot with equipment costing a total of about $250.

It's been our policy from the start to put absolute emphasis on quality of product. We never compromise on old material, nor reject a new one on the basis of cost. In principle, if better skis could be made out of sheet platinum, I suspect we would wind up with it. In other words, it is our policy to make the best product we can regardless of cost and then price it accordingly to the trade.

At the beginning of 1967, Head's 105,668-square-foot plant in Timonium, Maryland, was divided between manufacturing and warehouse facilities (93,040 square feet) and office space (12,628 square feet). The plant included a cafeteria, locker rooms, and shower areas for the workers. In May, Head completed the fifth addition to the plant since its construction in 1959.

Production at Head was on a three-shift basis throughout the year, with skis being made for inventory during the slow months. There were over 600 employees.

Six attempts had been made to unionize the plant, but all had been rejected, several times by three-to-one majorities. One warehouse employee with 12 years' seniority said, "It's a nice place to work. We don't need a union. If you have a problem, Mr. Head will listen to you."

All employees received automatic step raises based on seniority, as well as merit reviews and raises. In addition a profit-sharing trust plan had generally added 6–7 percent to the employees' salary.

These funds became fully vested after three years.

Another important benefit for exempt salaried employees was the year-end bonus plan. The amount of the bonus depended on the employee's salary class and the company's profitability. For the lowest-paid group, the bonus was 3 percent if pretax profits on sales were under 2 percent, but 10–11 percent if profits were 8–12 percent. For the middle group, no bonus was paid if profits were 2 percent or below, but the rate was 20–22 percent if profits ranged between 8 and 12 percent. Rates for the top group were not disclosed, but it was indicated that their bonus plan was even more steeply skewed. For most of the past several years, the payoffs had been at or near the upper range.

FINANCE

The initial financing of Head Ski Company was $6,000 from Howard Head's personal funds. In 1953, Howard Head sold 40 percent of the stock in the company for $60,000. This, together with retained earnings and normal bank debt, financed expansion until 1960, when common stock was issued. Additional financing was required to continue the rapid expansion, and in January 1965 a $3,527,500 package was sold, made up of 5½ percent convertible subordinated debentures in the face amount of $2,125,000, and 42,500 shares of common stock. Until the stock issue of 1965, Howard Head had owned 42.4 percent of the common stock, and the other directors and officers had owned 46.1 percent. Full conversion of the new issue would represent 17.1 percent ownership. At no time had there been any question about Howard Head's commanding role in any important decisions.

Expansion was viewed by many in the company as a defensive tactic. They reasoned, "If you do not grow as fast as the market will allow you to, you are taking a substantial risk that someone else will come in and take that market away from you." In addition, the new funds provided capital for two diversifications started in 1966: the Head Ski and Sportswear Co., and the Head plastics division.

Although Head's earnings growth had slowed (see Exhibit 1), the stock market continued to evaluate its prospects at 29 to 60 times previous years' earnings. During the period January 1966 to July 1967, the company's stock price ranged from 9⅜ to 17¾. As recently as January 1965, the stock had sold at 22¾.

ORGANIZATION

Before the appointment of Harold Seigle as chief operating officer in January 1967, Howard Head presided directly over the various departments and marketing functions. There was no overall marketing director. Even in the 1960–1966 period, when the company had an executive vice president, Mr. Head indicated that he had concerned himself with the operating details of the business.

Harold Seigle reorganized the company along functional lines. Reporting to the president were the vice president for operations, the treasurer, and the directors of marketing, quality control, and personnel. Of the 26 managers appearing on the organization chart (Exhibit 4), 12 had been with Head one year or less. Asked about the potential difficulties of that situation, Head responded, "I would only say that if you are to have a lot of new people, you must have one man in command who is an experienced and gifted professional at utilizing people. My job is to support and use that man."

Howard Head reviewed the steps through which the organization had reached its current structure:

I think that this is typical of the kind of business that starts solely from an entrepreneurial product basis, with no interest or skills in management or business in the original package. Such a business never stops to plan. The consuming interest is to build something new and to get acceptance. The entrepreneur has to pick up the rudiments of finance and organizational practices as he goes along. Any thought of planning comes later. Initially he is solely concerned with the problems of surviving and building. Also, if the business is at all successful, it is so successful that there is no real motivation to stop and obtain the sophisticated planning and people-management techniques. Such a business is fantastically efficient as long as it can survive. One man can make all of the important decisions. There is no pyramidal team structure.

In our case this approach worked quite successfully until about 1955, when we sold 10,000 pairs of skis and reached the $500,000 sales level. The next five years from 1955 to 1960 saw a number of disorganized attempts to acquire and use a more conventional pyramidal organizational system. To put it succinctly, what was efficient at the $500,000 level was increasingly inefficient as we reached $1 million, then $2 million in sales. One man just couldn't handle it. I made too many mistakes. It was like trying to run an army with only a general and some sergeants. There were just no officers, to say nothing of an orderly chain of command.

In 1960 came the first successful breakthrough, where I finally developed the ability to take on a general manager who later became an executive vice president. It was hard for me to learn to operate under this framework. The most striking thing missing from this period was a concept of people management. I spent five years gradually learning not to either over- or under-delegate.

Let me interject that the final motivation necessary to make a complete transition to an orderly company came because the company got into trouble in 1965–1966. Even five years after the beginning of a team system, the company got into trouble, and this was the final prod which pushed me to go all the way. It is interesting that it took 12 years. Up until 1960 the company was totally under my direction. From 1960 to 1965 we stuttered between too much of my direction and not enough.

The chief difficulty for me was to learn to lay down a statement of the results required and then stay out of details. The weakness was in finding a formula of specifying objectives, then giving freedom as long as the objectives were met.

The appointment of Hal Seigle as president brought us a thoroughly sophisticated individual who can bring us the beginning of big business methods. On my part, this change has involved two things: first, my finally recognizing that I wanted this kind of organization; second, the selection of a man with proven professional management skills.

Unfortunately, with an entrepreneur there are only two courses which can be taken if the company is to grow beyond a certain size. He can get the hell out, or he can really change his method of operation. I am pleased that this company has made the transition.

Now more than ever the company is using my special skills and abilities, but I am no longer interfering with an orderly and sophisticated management and planning system. We have given the company new tools to operate with, and I have not pulled the rug out from under them.

I am reserving my energies for two things. First, there is a continuation of my creative input—almost like a consultant to the company. Second, I have taken the more conventional role of chairman and chief executive officer. In this role I devote my efforts to planning and longer-range strategy.

I feel that I can serve in both capacities. I can only be successful in the role of creative input if I can be solely a consultant without authority. It has to be made clear in this role that anything said is for consideration only. It has been demonstrated that this role is consultative, since some of my suggestions have been rejected. I like this role because I like the freedom. I can think freer, knowing that my suggestions will be carefully reviewed.

Of course, in areas of real importance like new product lines such as binding or boots, adding new models to the ski line, or acquisitions, etc., I must exert authority, channeled through the president.

Before joining Head, Harold Seigle had been vice president and general manager of a $50 million consumer electronics division of a $150 million dollar company. His appointment was viewed as "contributing to a more professional company-operating philosophy." He hoped to introduce more formalized methods of budget control and to "preside over the transition from a 'one man' organization to a traditionally conceived functional pattern."

Seigle introduced a budgeting system broken down into 13 periods each year. Reports were to be prepared every four weeks comparing target with actual for each of the revenue or expense centers, such as marketing, operations, the staff functions, and the subsidiaries. The hope was eventually to tie the bonus to performance against budget. Previously statements had been prepared every four weeks, but only to compare actual results against the previous year's results.

Being new to the company, Seigle found he was spending much of his time on operating problems. He believed, however, that as the budget system became completely accepted and operational, he would be able to devote more of his time to looking ahead and worrying about longer-term projects. He said: "Ideally, I like to be working 6 to 18 months ahead of the organization. As a project gets within 6 months of actual operation, I will turn it over to the operating managers." He had hired a manager for corporate planning with whom he worked closely.

A VIEW TOWARD THE FUTURE

Head's first diversification was to ski poles, which were relatively simple to manufacture and could be sold through existing channels. As with the skis, Head maintained the highest standards of quality and style. The poles were distinguished from the competition by their black color and their tapered shape and extra-light weight, which were then unavailable on other high-priced, quality ski poles. At $24.50, Head's prices were well toward the upper end of a spectrum that ranged as low as $5 for some brands. Success in selling poles encouraged the company to look at other products it might add.

Two further steps were taken toward diversification in late 1966, when Head formed a plastics division and established a subsidiary, Head Ski and Sportswear, Inc.

The plastics division's activity centered on high molecular weight plastics. A March 1967 press release described this activity:

Head Ski Co., Inc. has signed a license agreement with Phillips Petroleum Company . . . to use a new method developed by Phillips for extrudIng ultra-high molecular weight high-density polyethylene into finished products . . .

Developmental equipment has been installed at the Head plant here and limited quantities of sheet have been extruded and tested in the running surface of Head skis with excellent results . . Production of ski base material is scheduled for this spring . . .

In addition to its own running surface material, the Head plastics division has been developing special ultra-high molecular weight high-density polyethylene compounds to serve a variety of industrial applications . . .

Ultra-high molecular weight high-density polyethylene is an extremely tough abrasion-resistant thermoplastic capable of replacing metal and metal alloys in many industrial areas. Compared with regular high-density resins, the ultra-high molecular weight material has better stress-cracking resistance, better long-term stress life, and less notch sensitivity.

Company executives considered the diversification into skiwear the more important move. Howard Head described the logic of this new venture:

Skiwear is "equipment" first and fashion second. We are satisfied that our line of skiwear is better than anything done before. It represents the same degree of attention to detail which has characterized our hardware line.

The president of the new subsidiary, Alex Schuster, said:

Many people thought that Head should stay in hardware such as poles, bindings, and wax. As I see it, however, by going into skiwear we are taking advantage of ready-made distribution and reputation.

There is no reason why the goodwill developed through the years can't be related to our endeavor.

This new market offers a greater potential and reward than the more hardware-oriented areas. Any entry into a new market has difficulties. These can only be solved by doing things right and by measuring up to the Head standards. Having a Head label commits us to a standard of excellence.

Assuming that we live up to those standards, we shall be able to develop into a supplier in a small market, but with formidable potential. We are creating a skill base for further diversification.

Our products are engineered, not designed. We are concerned with the engineered relationship among fabric, function, and fit. The engineering details are not always obvious, but they are related to functional demands. Emphasis is placed on function over fashion, yet there is definite beauty created out of concern for function. We are definitely in tune with fashion trends.

We will provide a complete skiing outfit—pants, parkas, sweaters, accessories, socks, and gloves. We will offer a total coordinated look.

Along with the design innovations, we shall offer innovations in packaging, display, and promotion. We have to go beyond simply preparing the proper apparel.

Head Ski and Sportswear did both manufacuring and subcontracting. The products that had the highest engineering content were made in the Head plant. Sweaters were contract-made to Head specifications by one of Europe's leading sweater manufacturers.

The collection was first shown to dealers in April 1967 and was scheduled for public release for the 1967–1968 skiing season. The initial reponse of dealers and the fashion press was extremely encouraging. *Ski Business* reported:

> *Head's Up.*
> . . . way up, in fact 194 percent ahead of planned volume on its premier line of skiwear.
>
> Anyone who expected Howard Head's entry into the world of fashion to be presented in basic black was in for a surprise. Ironically the skiwear collection that blasted off with the hottest colors in the market is offered by a man who is totally color blind . . .
>
> *On pants:* The $55 pant was the big surprise. It was our top seller—way beyond expectations—and the basic $45 pant came in second in sales. Another surprise was the $70 foam waisted pant for which we only projected limited sales—it's a winner . . .
>
> *On orders:* "Way beyond expectations. Ninety percent of the orders are with ski shops and 10 percent with the department stores. Naturally we are committed to selling to Head Ski dealers but it definitely is not obligatory."[12]

The sportswear subsidiary had been set up in a separate plant five miles from Head's Timonium headquarters. It was an autonomous operation with a separate sales force and profit responsibility. The initial premise was that the sportswear would be distributed through current Head dealers, but Harold Seigle indicated the marketing decisions of the sportswear division would be made independently of decisions in the ski division. Although Head dealers were offered the Head sportswear line, it was not sold on an exclusive basis. Distribution would be directly from factory salesmen to the dealer. Within the company, the need for a separate and

---

[12]John Fry, *Ski Business*, May–June 1967, p. 46.

Samples of the new Head Skiwear

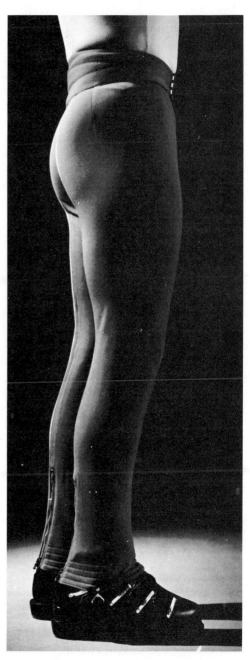

different type of sales force was acknowledged. As one executive phrased it, "I can't imagine our ski salesmen trying to push soft goods. Our salesmen got into the business first and foremost because they were excellent skiers." As with skis and poles, the product line was to be maintained at the high end of the spectrum in both quality and price.

Harold Seigle believed Head would continue to grow rapidly in the future. He saw the potential of doubling the ski business in the next five years. Although he characterized the sportswear business as a "good calculated risk," he thought it offered the potential of expanding to annual sales of $5–8 million. Beyond that, he felt that Head might go in three possible directions. First, he believed that Head should once again explore the opportunities and risks of moving into the other price segments of the ski market, either under another brand or with a nonmetallic ski. Although he estimated Head could sell 50,000 or more pairs of skis in a lower price range, the risks were high. Seigle also felt Head should explore the opportunity in other related ski products, such as boots or bindings. Finally, he believed Head should eventually expand into other specialty sporting goods, preferably of a counterseasonal nature.

In looking to these new areas, Harold Seigle believed Head should adhere to a two-part product philosophy:

> Any new product which Head will consider should (1) be consistent with the quality and prestige image of Head Ski; (2) entail one or more of the following characteristics:
> a. high innovative content
> b. high engineering content
> c. high style appeal
> d. be patentable.

We will consider getting into new products through any of the normal methods such as internal product development, product acquisition, or corporate acquisition. If we are to move into a new area we definitely want to have a product edge. For example, if we were to manufacture a boot, we would want to be different. We would only seriously consider it if we had a definite product advantage, such as if we were to develop a high-quality plastic boot.

Howard Head, in speaking of the future, voiced the following hopes:

> I would like to see Head grow in an orderly fashion sufficient to maintain its present youth and resiliency. That would mean at least 20–25 percent per year. This statement does not preclude the possibility that we might grow faster. We believe the ski business alone will grow 20–25 percent per year. As our staff capabilities grow, we will probably branch out into other areas.
>
> As to our objectives for the next five years, I would say that the first corporate objective is to maintain healthy growth in the basic ski business. It is the taproot of all that is good in Head. Second, we must be certain that any new activity is carefully selected for a reasonable probability of developing a good profit and an image platform consistent with the past activity of Head.

APPENDIX A

TYPES OF SKIS

Wood Skis

If you are on a tight budget, well-designed wood skis at low prices are available from domestic and foreign manufac-

CROSS SECTION OF A WOOD SKI

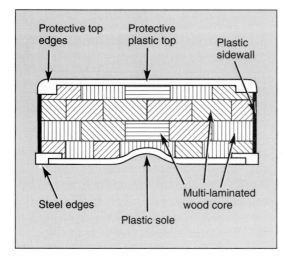

turers. Wood is a bundle of tubular cellulose cells bound together in an elastic medium called lignin. The internal slippage of wood skis not only lets them torque over the bumps in traverse, but damps any tendency to vibrate or chatter on hard, rough surfaces. There are wood skis for any snow, and any speed, and they are fun to ski on. Their only problem is a lack of durability. Wood skis are fragile. Besides, as wood skis are used, the internal slippage of the fibers increases, and they lose their life.

In choosing a wood ski, it is probably wise to pay more than the minimum price. Multiple laminations of hickory or ash, a soft flex pattern, interlocking edges, polyethylene base, plastic top and sidewalls, and tip and tail protectors are some of the features a beginner or intermediate should look for in a better wood ski. When you get past the $40 to $70 range, your own dealer's recommendations will be your best guarantee of value.

FRP Skis

A few years ago there were only a handful of "epoxy" skis on the market, and skiers were eyeing them with mixed interest and distrust. Now the available models have multiplied almost unbelievably. New companies have been formed, and many of the established manufacturers have now brought out versions of their own. The plastic skis are still new enough for most skiers to be confused about their true nature—and with good reason, since there are so many types.

The word *epoxy* is part of the confusion. The true family resemblance of all the skis that are currently being lumped under that designation is the use of glass fibers locked into a plastic medium to create layers of great strength. The plastics engineers use the term *fiber-reinforced plastic* (FRP) to designate this type of structural solution. It is very strong.

The reinforcing layers used in these new designs derive their strength from the combined strength of millions of fine glass fibers or threads locked in the plastic layer. The potential strengths of materials in this family of structural plastics can exceed those of aluminum or steel. Unfortunately, there is no simple way to evaluate them or describe the materials actually in use. The wide variety of glass fibers, resins, and systems of molding and curing the fiber-reinforced layer produces a wide range of results. These can be evaluated only by laboratory tests or, finally, by actual in-service results.

FRP materials are being used for all sorts of sporting goods, industrial, and space-age applications. The strength-to-weight ratio is attractively high, and the possibility of creating new reinforced shapes by means of molding operations has proved to be attractive enough to encourage a great deal of experimentation. Skis seem to adapt to this structural technique.

Metal Skis

In the search for more durable skis, the metal skis took over the quality market about a decade ago, and are widely accepted as ideal for both recreational skier and expert. Except for specialized racing uses, the wooden skis have been largely outmoded in the better ski market. Today, the fiber-reinforced plastic designs are the only challengers to the primacy of the metals.

Metal skis obtain their strength from aluminum sheets that are light in weight but very strong. The structure of a metal ski is somewhat like an "I" beam; when the ski is bent, the bottom sheet is stretched and the top sheet is compressed. The core material serves as the web—the vertical portion of the "I"—and must be attached to the top and bottom metal sheets securely enough to resist the shearing stress that occurs when the ski is bent.

Service Potential of Metal Skis

The possibility of rebuilding and refinishing metal skis has been one of the key sales attractions of the metal ski in this country. So long as bonding remains intact, only the effects of wear and tear—rocks, skis banging together, rough treatment in transportation, etc.—limit the life of the skis. The possibility of having the plastic surfaces and edges, or even the structural members themselves, replaced has strong appeal for the skier investing well over $100 in his skis. The rebuilding potential also tends to keep the trade-in and used resale value of the skis higher,

making it less expensive for the skier to move to higher-performance or more recent models as his skiing ability—or his desire for something new—dictates. The American companies were the first to develop rebuilding techniques, but more recently European factories have been establishing service centers in the United States.

There are three basic elements of FRP construction: the plastic material or resin; the glass fibers themselves; and the method of combining, curing, and shaping the composite reinforcing layer. Variation of any of these three elements affects the characteristics of the end product.

Service Potential of FRP Skis

One of the problems facing the manufacturers of fiber-reinforced plastic skis has been how to service and rebuild them—once the normal wear and tear of skiing has taken its toll. Only the metal skis, it has seemed, could be refinished and rebuilt.

Though it is true that you cannot heat up an FRP ski, melt the glue, resand, recoat, and reconstruct it quite as easily as you can a metal ski, progress has been made in this direction during the past season. Several manufacturers have set up regional service centers.

What these various service centers can accomplish is considerable. They are replacing bases and edges. They are renewing and refinishing top surfaces. In some cases, the structural fiberglass members can be separated from the wood core and replaced, producing in effect a brand new ski. The sum of all this is real benefit to the average skier, who is unwilling to discard a pair of skis every season or so. The gap between metal and FRP skis, as far as service potential is concerned, is being narrowed. You will find that the costs range over approximately the same spread as metal skis and that guarantee provisions are similar.

<hr>

APPENDIX B

THE HEAD PRODUCT LINE, 1968

The most important design consideration is you—the type of skier you are and where you ski. That's why your dealer was able to offer you nine different models of Head Skis to choose from. You can be sure the model he helped you select was the optimum—for you.

Standard—The Most Forgiving Ski: For beginners of average size and athletic ability up to intermediates learning stem christies. Also for the better, occasional skier who prefers an easygoing, lively, light-weight ski that practically turns for him.

The *Standard* is medium soft in flex overall for easy turning and responsiveness. Engineered side camber and relative overall width contribute to ease and slow-speed stability. Its light weight and torsional rigidity make traversing and other basic maneuvers simple. Thin taper in the tip allows the *Standard* to cut easily through the heaviest snow, instead of ploughing.

> Standard. $115.00 Thirteen sizes from 140 to 215 cm. Black top, sidewalls, and bottom; white engraving.

Master—More of a Challenge: For the skier who has mastered the basic techniques and wants to begin driving the skis

and attacking the slope. As lively as the *Standard*, this is also the ski for the heavier, more athletic beginner who wants more "beef" underfoot.

The *Master* is like the *Standard* in basic shape but thicker and heavier. The tip radius is longer for extra shock absorption. Slightly stiffer flex overall acts as a heavy-duty shock absorber over bumps.

> Master. $135.00 Nine sizes from 175 to 215 cm. Black top and sidewalls; blue base and engraving.

The Fabulous 360—The Most Versatile Ski: Finest all-around ski ever made—for the skier beginning stem christies on through the expert class. Remarkable for its ease of turning as well as its steadiness and precision, the *360* is the serious skier's ski for attack or enjoyment on the slope, under any condition of snow or terrain.

With its smooth-arcing flex pattern, the *360* has the supple forebody of the other recreational skis, but is slightly stiffer at the tail. Its side camber is similar to that of the *Giant Slalom*. Narrower overall than the *Standard* or *Master*. Rubber damping in the lightweight top-skin unit makes the *360* a very responsive ski, allowing the expert to control his turns beautifully and set his edges precisely. Tip splay is designed to give easiest entrance through snow and to provide excellent shock absorption, particularly in heavily moguled areas.

> The Fabulous 360. $115.00 Eleven sizes from 170 to 220 cm. Black top and sidewalls; yellow base and engraving.

Slalom—The Hot Dog: For the expert skier who likes to stay in the fall-line, slashing through quick short-radius turns on the steepest, iciest slopes. The *Slalom* has been totally redesigned this year to fit

Appendix A Source: *Skiing International Yearbook*, 1967, pp. 63–68. Copyright by Ziff-Davis Publishing Co. Reprinted with permission.

the special needs of the expert recreational skier, who wants the lightest, fastest-reacting, and best ice-holding ski possible.

Slalom is Head's narrowest ski overall. And, thanks to the lightweight topskin unit and core, it is also one of Head's lightest skis. Lightness and narrowness allow for carved or pivoted turns, reflex-fast changes in direction. Special engineered side camber and relative softness at the thin waist give the ultimate in "feel" and control on ice. Neoprene rubber gives the damping and torque necessary for a top-performance ice ski.

> Slalom. $160.00 Five sizes from 190 to 210 cm. Black top and sidewalls. Racing red base and engraving.

Downhill—Bomb!: Widest and heaviest Head ski, the *Downhill* is for the advanced skier—recreational or competitor—who wants to blast straight down the slope. It offers the ultimate in high-speed performance, tracking ability, and stability over bumps and moguls.

The long tip splay and supple forebody are the secret of the *Downhill's* exceptional speed advantage. It virtually planes over the surface of the slope. With its firm midsection and tail acting like the rudder of a hydroplane, the *Downhill* affords the skier utmost control coupled with great turning ability at slower speeds. Heavy-duty topskin unit and added rubber damping contribute to the stability and high-speed "quietness" of the *Downhill*. This is the elite international-class racing ski, and experts have found it an excellent powder ski as well.

> Downhill. $175.00 Seven sizes from 195 to 225 cm. Black top and sidewalls. Yellow base and engraving.

Giant Slalom—Grace Plus Speed: The "GS" incorporates the best features of the *Downhill* and *Slalom* models. It offers the expert skier—recreational and/or competitor—the optimum in stable all-out speed skiing, combined with precise carving and holding ability in high-speed turns. It is another favorite on the international racing circuit.

The *Giant Slalom's* ability and precision come from a unique combination of sidecut and relatively stiff flex. The "GS" is similar to the *360* in overall dimensions, but has a stiffer flex pattern than the *360*, particularly underfoot. This gives the "GS" the versatility of the *360* but with greater control at high speeds. Tip splay is designed for maximum shock absorption and easy riding.

> Giant Slalom. $165.00 Nine sizes from 175 to 215 cm. Black top and sidewalls. Yellow base and engraving.

Youngster's Competition—Junior Hot Dog: Carrying the *Giant Slalom* engraving, this ski is designed for expert youngsters who want, and can handle, a faster, more demanding ski than the small size *Standard*. Similar in cut and performance characteristics to the *Giant Slalom*, but without the "GS's" neoprene damping, to provide the junior racer with easier turning ability.

> Youngster's Competition. $120.00 Two sizes, 160 and 170 cm. Black top and sidewalls; yellow bottom and engraving.

Shortski—Fun Without Effort: Not just a sawed-off *Standard*, but a totally different ski with totally different proportions. Very wide for its length, quite stiff overall, the *Shortski* is the only ski of its kind with an engineered side camber. Ideal for quick learning of the fundamentals of skiing. Also for the older or more casual skier who enjoys being on the slopes and wants the easiest-possible tracking and turning ski ever built.

Shortski. $115.00 Four sizes from 150 to 190 cm. Black top, sidewalls, and bottom. White engraving.

Deep Powder—Sheer Buoyancy on the Slopes: Super soft flexibility and buggy-whip suppleness allow this specialized ski to float in powder, while maintaining easy turning plus full control and tracking ability on packed slopes.

The *Deep Powder* is very wide and soft overall, with a "hinge-like" effect in the forebody that enables it to glide through the deepest powder.

Deep Powder. $115.00 Five sizes from 195 to 215 cm. Black top, sidewalls, and bottom. White engraving.

———————

Source: Head's Ski *Handbook*, 1968.

EXHIBIT 1

A. Consolidated Balance Sheet	As of April 29, 1967	As of April 30, 1966	As of April 24, 1965
Assets			
Current assets			
Cash	$ 263,896	$ 233,330	$ 162,646
Short-term commercial paper receivable	1,200,000	800,000	1,200,000
Notes and accounts receivable—less reserve	242,632	174,127	334,503
Inventories—valued at lower of cost or market	3,102,069	3,522,235	2,815,042
Prepayment and miscellaneous receivables	402,879	223,864	207,279
Total current assets	$ 5,211,476	$ 4,953,556	$ 4,719,470
Fixed assets, at cost			
Buildings—pledged under mortgage	$ 1,010,149	$ 1,012,085	$ 1,014,738
Machinery and equipment	1,540,707	1,059,274	847,974
Other	715,809	213,692	147,336
	$ 3,265,945	$ 2,285,051	$ 2,010,048
Less accumulated depreciation	1,123,203	892,153	822,255
Total fixed assets	$ 2,142,742	$ 1,392,898	$ 1,187,793
Other assets			
Unamortized bond discount and expenses	$ 252,004	$ 263,564	$ 277,636
Cash surrender value of life insurance	133,568	120,589	103,117
Other	70,194	22,364	28,583
Total other assets	$ 455,766	$ 406,517	$ 409,336
Total assets	$ 7,809,984	$ 6,752,971	$ 6,316,599
Liabilities and stockholders' equity			
Current liabilities			
Accounts payable	$ 829,826	$ 299,040	$ 521,031
Current portion of long-term debt	23,100	21,000	20,600
Accrued expenses	549,720	413,865	451,062
Income taxes payable	333,514	299,452	39,102
Other	51,120	91,271	94,899
Total current liabilities	$ 1,787,280	$ 1,124,628	$ 1,126,694
Long-term debt			
Mortgage on building (5¾) payable to 1978	$ 331,115	$ 376,036	$ 396,646
Convertible subordinated debentures	2,125,000	2,125,000	2,125,000
		2,501,036	2,521,646
Less current portion		21,000	20,600
Total long-term debt	$ 2,456,115	$ 2,480,036	$ 2,501,046
Commitments and contingent liabilities/ stockholders' equity			
Common stock—par value 50¢ per share (authorized 2,000,000 shares; outstanding 1966, 915,202 shares; 1965, 882,840 shares adjusted for 2-for-1 stock split-up effective September 15, 1965)	459,401	457,601	220,710
Paid-in capital	1,679,700	1,679,700	1,820,323
Retained earnings	1,412,488	1,011,006	647,826
Total stockholders' equity	$ 3,566,589	$ 3,148,307	$ 2,688,859
Total liabilities and stockholders' equity	$ 7,809,984	$ 6,752,971	$ 6,316,599

EXHIBIT 1 (continued)

B. Consolidated Statement of Earnings

	52 Weeks Ended April 29, 1967	53 Weeks Ended* April 30, 1966	52 Weeks Ended* April 24, 1965	52 Weeks Ended* April 25, 1964
Net sales	$11,048,072	$9,080,223	$8,600,392	$6,018,779
Cost of sales	7,213,188	6,357,169	5,799,868	4,033,576
Gross profit	$ 3,834,884	$2,723,054	$2,800,524	$1,985,203
Expenses:				
Selling, administrative, and general	$ 2,756,939	$2,029,531	$1,697,659	$1,169,392
Research and engineering	327,857	239,851	303,884	102,358
Total expenses	$ 3,084,796	$2,269,382	$2,001,543	$1,271,750
Income before income taxes and nonrecurring charges	$ 750,088	$ 453,672	$ 798,981	$ 713,453
Federal and state income taxes	348,606	221,034	392,515	367,542
Income before nonrecurring charges	$ 401,482	$ 232,638	$ 406,466	$ 345,911
Nonrecurring debt expense—after giving effect to income taxes			63,678	
Net earnings	$ 401,482	$ 232,638	$ 342,788	$ 345,911
Net earnings as restated	401,482	264,389	393,713	376,788
Earnings per share before nonrecurring charges	.44	.26	.51	.40
Earnings per share after nonrecurring charges	.44	.26	.43	.40
Earnings per share as restated		.29	.49	.48

Note: Earnings per share are based on average shares outstanding of 904,237 in 1966 and 801,196 in 1965 after giving effect to the 2-for-1 stock split-up effective September 15, 1965, and the 3-for-1 stock split on July 7, 1964.

*Earnings restated April 29, 1967, to give effect to an adjustment in the lives of depreciable assets for federal income tax purposes.

C. Summary of Financial Data

	52 Weeks Ended April 29, 1967	53 Weeks Ended April 30, 1966	52 Weeks Ended April 24, 1965	52 Weeks Ended April 25, 1964	52 Weeks Ended April 27, 1963
Net sales	$11,048,072	$9,080,223	$8,600,392	$6,018,779	$4,124,445
Net earnings	401,482	264,389	393,713	376,788	191,511
Expenditures for plant and equipment	1,027,854	304,102	558,865	513,130	272,154
Depreciation	249,961	238,161	211,683	132,497	79,719
Working capital	3,424,196	3,828,928	3,542,857	1,525,015	654,676
Plant and equipment and other assets, net	2,598,508	1,799,415	1,745,839	1,187,246	701,875
Long-term debt	2,456,115	2,480,036	2,501,046	1,176,647	287,245
Shareholders' equity	3,566,589	3,148,307	2,787,650	1,535,614	1,069,306
Earnings per share	.44	.29	.49	.48	.25
Average shares outstanding	916,542	904,237	801,196	777,600	777,600

Source: Company records.

Note: Average shares outstanding reflect the 2-for-1 stock split-up effective September 15, 1965, and 3-for-1 stock split on July 7, 1964. Statistical data for the years 1963 to 1966, inclusive, have been adjusted to reflect retroactive adjustments.

EXHIBIT 2
1966 SKI IMPORTS BY COUNTRY OF ORIGIN

| | Number of Pairs | Increase (Decrease) from 1965 | Value ($000s) | Average Value per Pair ($)* | |
				1966	1965
Japan†	529,732	(89,632)	$3,626	7	6
Austria	72,536	(20,872)	1,512	21	21
West Germany	44,736	9,959	1,010	23	18
Yugoslavia	22,540	5,122	255	11	11
Finland	10,184	5,411	98	10	9
Italy	7,494	351	196	26	14
Canada	7,091	6,350	150	21	23
France	5,257	2,828	265	50	49
Switzerland	2,835	1,155	124	44	39
Sweden	2,767	1,131	22	8	9
Australia	2,307	2,307	114	49	
Norway	1,125	(698)	18	16	6
Belgium	129	129	6	49	

Source: *Ski Business*, May–June 1967, p. 31.

*F.o.b. plant price: does not include charges for shipping, handling, tariff (16⅔%), excise tax, or profit for trading company or wholesaler.

†More than half the Japanese imports were thought to be children's skis, which helps explain the low average pair value.

EXHIBIT 3
NUMBER OF HEAD DEALERS

	On January 1	Newly Franchised	Terminated or Not Renewed	At Year-End
1967	900*	30	na	—
1966	727*	na	na	900
1965	670	96	39	727
1964	560	167	57	670
1963	454	136	30	560
1962	390	105	41	454

Source: Company records.

Note: In addition the franchised dealers had approximately 300 branches that are not included in the above figures.

*Estimated.

EXHIBIT 4
HEAD ORGANIZATION CHART, JUNE 1967

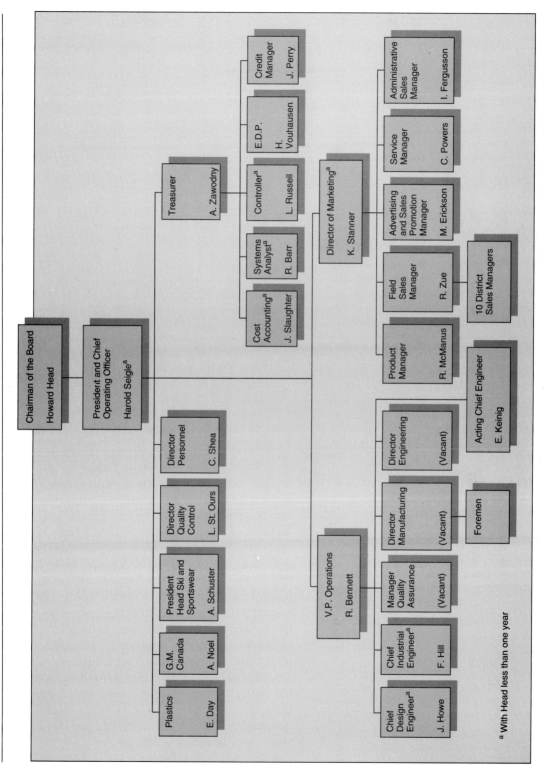

Phil Knight: CEO at NIKE (1983)

I have always felt that if we had the right product at the most economical cost, we'll figure out a way to sell it. Everybody talks about our marketing, and it has been good. But it's been good because we've had a good product with enough margin for the right marketing expense. And it's all worked because of the people we've had.

Phil Knight, Spring 1983

NIKE STRATEGY

History

In 1962, during his final semester at Stanford Business School, Phil Knight wrote a term paper about a business opportunity to create a better track shoe. Knight had been a track star himself as an undergraduate at the University of Oregon in Eugene, where he had run a 4:13 mile on coach Bill Bowerman's track team.

In spring 1983, he reflected on the term paper and the origins of his business idea:

Adidas shoes were beginning to dominate the U.S. market, and it didn't make any sense, because West Germany was not the place to put shoe machinery. I thought it might be possible to take over the market with low-priced, but high-quality and smartly merchandised imports from Japan, as had already happened with cameras and other optical equipment.

Following graduation in 1962, Knight visited Japan and presented himself as a shoe importer, using the name "Blue Ribbon Sports" (BRS), to Onitsuka, the manufacturer of Tiger brand shoes. He received exclusive rights for BRS to distribute Tiger shoes in the western United States. When the first 50 pairs arrived in 1964, Knight and coach Bowerman each invested $500 and officially launched BRS. In its early years, BRS was primarily a company of athletes selling to other athletes. Phil Knight worked as a CPA, later as a business school professor, not turning his full attention to BRS until 1969. By then, the product was improved, thanks to Bowerman's design changes, and the company was building a strong brand name among serious athletes. According to

Knight, BRS's growing popularity resulted in "reverse leverage": order-rich and cash-poor!

By 1972, sales were $2 million, and Onitsuka decided it wanted to do its own U.S. distribution. Onitsuka offered to buy 51 percent of BRS and threatened to end all supplies if the company refused.

Knight and his colleagues scrambled for alternatives. Armed with their own design, they persuaded Japan's sixth largest trading company, Nissho Iwai, to find the manufacturing sources *and* to provide financing and export/import services to BRS. The new shoes were called NIKE (a name Jeff Johnson, NIKE's first full-time employee, said appeared to him in a dream) and bore the "swoosh" logo (created by a now-famous graduate design student for $35). Knight recalled:

> There have been some real triumphs along the way. I can remember in 1976 . . . we'd never had a guy make the Olympic team in NIKE shoes, and thought we had a good chance in the Olympic trials down in Eugene. In the first event, we were 1, 2, 3, and I just went berserk!! While you can feel good about the financial performance and things like that, moments of elation like the race in Eugene are real treasures.

Knight felt that NIKE morale was aided by the product. "There's a feeling of 'We did it!' when you see the product on the feet of someone crossing the finish line on TV." That tie to the values and ideals of sports was fundamental at NIKE.

Despite the focus on product excellence, the company remained aware it was a business. Knight remarked:

> Profit is like the score in a dual track meet. It's the way you decide if you've won or lost. But how you get there—that is through your values, the training, the

trying to take every step better than anybody else. We'd like to be the biggest and best in our business in the world. And we're a growth company, not 15 percent, but 30 percent or more. Sure, we could slow down our growth, tighten up, and pay some dividends—but that's not who we are, not who we intend to become.

Bob Woodell, who had joined Knight in 1967, added:

> It's easy to get caught up in getting shoes on eight zillion athletes in the next Olympics or whatever. But profit is how this game is scored. We play this game in good part for the competition of it, not just to have more money or so the stock will be worth more. We'd really like to believe that the young whippersnappers from Oregon, who everybody thinks are country bumpkins, can be best in the world.

NIKE went public in late 1980. By 1982, every world record in men's track from the 800 meter to the marathon had been set by athletes wearing NIKE shoes. The product line now included shoes for the not-so-serious athlete and athletic clothes. Sales had risen to $694 million by year-end 1982, from $2 million 10 years before, and net earnings had grown from $60,000 to $49 million over the same period. (See Exhibit 1 for financial details.) NIKE had displaced Adidas as the dominant force in the United States.

The Athletic Footwear and Apparel Industry

Until the late 1960s, the U.S. athletic footwear market was divided between the ubiquitous canvas sneaker and a small market (approximately 10 percent) of specialized performance shoes for sports such as football, soccer, and track. These latter shoes were primarily imported. Athletic clothes were dominated by generic gray "sweats" used by all except more serious sportspeople.

In the 1970s came the revolution: America discovered jogging, and health and fitness in general became national obsessions, particularly for the younger and more affluent. By 1982, according to industry experts, nearly 35 million people ran frequently, and half the population was doing some form of exercise—most wearing a new generation of sports shoes and clothing designed to aid performance and prevent injury. A lighter running shoe or a sleeker speed skating suit could cut important tenths of a second from the time of a world-class competitive athlete. For the average runner, a shoe's proper cushioning and support were important to reducing injury to feet, shins, and knees. Two other factors fueled the dramatic change in this industry—comfort and style. One industry observer commented:

> Running was never the lifeblood of running shoe sales. Comfort was. And anyone who tried on a running shoe was reluctant to step back into a less comfortable conventional shoe. No wonder women want to walk to work with high heels under their arms and running shoes on their feet.

The overall branded athletic footwear market in the United States grew from about $800 million in 1978 to about $1.9 billion in 1982. This represented about half of the total athletic shoe dollar volume (the other half consisted of cheap, unbranded shoes from dozens of sources) and 15 percent of all footwear sales. Similarly, the active-wear apparel market grew from around $3 billion in 1977 to $6 billion in 1982, which represented less than 10 percent of the total apparel market.

As the market took off in the mid-1970s, performance shoe companies, rather than the sneaker makers, met demand. Rapid innovation flourished as the companies sought to develop shoes that the top athletes would wear and that influential trade sources, such as *Runners' World*, would rate highly. As one observer explained, "In the emerging market for an unfamiliar product, consumers relied on a brand name, established by the implicit or explicit endorsement of an athlete or by the ratings. And later, as the shoes became fashionable, that brand name again sold the shoes." Athletes and sporting event organizers discovered that the shoe companies were willing to pay for visibility, and "promotion" (as it was called) became a lucrative—or expensive, depending upon your side of the fence—proposition.

In 1982, NIKE dominated the branded athletic shoe market with an estimated 30 percent market share; Adidas followed with 19 percent, then Converse (9 percent), Puma (7 percent), and Keds (7 percent). Adidas and Puma were West German companies focusing on technically more sophisticated shoes for specialty sports and performance-conscious athletes. Adidas was the worldwide leader in athletic footwear and apparel with $2 billion in sales in 1982—40 percent came from apparel. (For more detail, see Exhibit 2.)

A growing number of specialty companies also were targeting speciflc market segments. New Balance, originally aimed at runners, grew from $1.6 million in 1976 to $50 million in 1982 as it broadened its line to include basketball, tennis, and leisure shoes, as well as athletic apparel. The company manufactured in the United States and initially sold to specialty running stores, later expanding to top department stores. Other specialty names were Brooks ($16 million) for running shoes and Etonic ($37 million) for golf and tennis shoes (acquired by Colgate-Palmolive in 1976).

Finally, several older sneaker companies moved to participate in the running/ exercise boom. Converse was acquired by Allied Chemical in 1976 and was again sold to managers and investors in 1982 (1982 sales reached $200 million). Another was Keds (1979 sales of $83 million), which Stride Rite acquired from Uniroyal in 1979.

The Activewear Apparel Business

In the late 1960s, Adidas became the first athletic footwear company to exploit its brand name by introducing sports clothing for athletes. By 1982, almost every major competitor had followed suit. Observers agreed that a strong brand awareness was a necessity for a footwear company as it took the plunge into apparel. "Fundamentally," one explained, "the brand name conjured up an authentic, athletic image that appeals to the athlete, for on- and off-track wear, and to the consumer who doesn't actively participate, but who identifies with athletes and the active lifestyle." Apparel, however, was clearly different from shoes: "The apparel world is driven by fashion, not technical performance. It is fast-paced, products die quickly, and there is an army of copiers waiting in the wings to knock off whatever design is hot."

Several footwear companies, New Balance and Etonic among them, supplied only "authentic performance" clothing. Others, including NIKE and Adidas, sold both performance and ath-leisure items. At the authentic end of the active-wear spectrum, the footwear companies competed with a number of small specialty outfits that focused on high-performance clothing for athletes. At the ath-leisure end of the active-wear spectrum, they competed with the major sportswear houses, including Levi Strauss, Izod La Coste, and Merona, as well as the hundreds of smaller sportswear firms that were aggressively developing active-wear lines.

NIKE's Evolving Strategy

Although NIKE continued to compete primarily in the branded athletic footwear business, by 1982, sales of other items had risen to 16 percent, from 3 percent in 1978. The footwear product line strategy accommodated expanding athletic sports and ath-leisure sales. Based on the original racing shoe, NIKE exploited its design capabilities, marketing channels, and its name recognition to other sports (soccer, football, tennis, etc.), to other users (joggers, nonathletes, children), to other features (greater specialization of sole, lacing, and external materials for different individuals' comfort), and to other products (leisure shoes, apparel).

From 1972 to 1982, NIKE's footwear line grew from 13 to 156 basic models, or, with color and material variations, to 270 separate products. NIKE shoes were offered in a standard array of sizes (each in one width) at suggested retail prices from $15 to $90. NIKE managers viewed the footwear market as a pyramid (Table 1), with a small peak (serious athletes) and a broad base (the millions of Americans who wore athletic footwear in a casual, or "street," way). During the 1970s, the company maintained its strong position at the top of this pyramid. In addition, its presence extended downward to much larger segments—although it continued through-

TABLE 1
THE MARKET PYRAMID

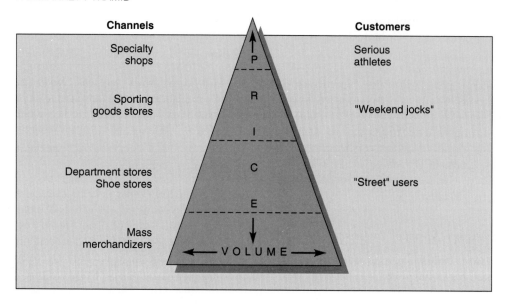

out most of the decade to avoid the low-end mass merchandiser base. Achieving this expansion, managers believed, was due to the strength of the NIKE brand name. And this, they insisted, was based on the company's reputation at the top.

NIKE's marketing activities, therefore, consistently focused on the top of this pyramid. Most, falling under the rubric of "promotion," involved getting NIKE shoes on the feet of visible athletes and NIKE's name associated with sports—Knight's "word-of-foot" policy. NIKE spent about $20 million in 1982 on promotion. At the same time, NIKE remained active at the grassroots level, sponsoring local races, presenting clinics for area high school coaches and trainers, and donating shoes to promising local athletes. NIKE employees themselves, typically athletes or former athletes, added credibility to these business efforts. The company's advertising budget (about $6 million in 1982, with 60 percent earmarked for co-op programs with dealers) targeted serious participants through specific sports media such as *The Runner* magazine. Ad messages ranged from quite technical to more mood-oriented.

Bill Bowerman instilled a development ethic from the outset. In 1978, the company outgrew Bowerman's kitchen and opened its R&D center in Exeter, New Hampshire. An early innovation was the patented "Air Sole" (gas under pressure encapsulated within the midsole material to provide superior cushioning). In 1982, NIKE spent $5.7 million (approximately 1 percent of sales) on R&D, which placed it ahead of almost all competitors. One industry observer commented, "While all the companies are doing some research, NIKE will tend to produce the more revolutionary advances and the others the more evolutionary ones."

Although NIKE established its own manufacturing facilities in Exeter, New Hampshire, in 1974, and in Saco, Maine, in 1978, accounting for 7 percent of output, sourcing shoes in the low-cost Far East, with 70 percent of output from Korea alone, was a cornerstone of Knight's original concept. (See Exhibit 3 for a typical cost buildup.) It remained the dominant practice as the company grew through the 1970s, although handling the intricacies of growing trade protectionism and import quotas required ingenuity. What made the approach work, executives believed, was the company's ability to find and develop contract factories, closely monitor them for quality, and forecast production needs effectively. Once a source was developed, NIKE expatriate technicians continued to work closely with it. "This has been the real key," production executive Ron Nelson explained. "Our people are living there and working with the factories as the product is going down the lines. This is a lot different from accepting or rejecting the product at the end of the line—especially at the end of a three-month pipeline to the Unites States!"

The heart of NIKE's production scheduling system was the Futures sales program. Started in the early 1970s, it eventually accounted for about 65 percent of footwear sales. Under the program, a retailer ordered five or six months in advance of delivery. In return, the retailer received a 5 to 7 percent discount and guaranteed delivery during a two-week window around the target date. This was valuable to retailers who competed in a rapidly growing business notorious for unreliable suppliers. As one said, "You can count on three things in this world—death, taxes, and Futures." And it was valuable for NIKE: retailer shelf space was committed to NIKE, the company received reliable, early information on trends, and most important, 65 percent of production was presold goods.

The basic pattern for NIKE's sales and distribution was also set in the early years. The company used independent sales representatives, paid entirely on commission, to reach an expanding base of accounts. The representatives were largely order takers, and NIKE itself performed all order processing, credit, and physical distribution work from three increasingly automated regional warehouses/offices in Oregon, New Hampshire, and Tennessee. The Futures program was the key sales program. By year-end 1982, the account base had expanded to 9,500 accounts (operating 13,000 outlets) in the four retail channels. (See Exhibit 4.)

Cash and credit were always problems in the early years of NIKE, when it operated on a nine-month business cycle with only six months' financing. To raise the necessary cash, NIKE depended on the goodwill of local bankers. Later, NIKE negotiated interest-bearing payables with its new Japanese "partner" Nissho Iwai. In 1980, NIKE went public. (See Exhibit 5.)

NIKE T-shirts were introduced at the 1972 Olympic trials, but the company did not seriously enter the business until 1978. Its first steps were faltering. As *Fortune* reported, "The company made an almost fatal first step when it aimed the introductory line at lower-middle class consumers instead of its usual, richer buyers." Bob Woodell was assigned to the division in early 1980. With a strong brand name, NIKE's apparel line grew quickly. Sales rose from $2 million in 1979 to an estimated $100 million for 1983, while the number of styles increased from 45 to 270. Observing this growth, one specialty store owner commented, "NIKE apparel is nothing special in and of itself. But it has the

NIKE name on it." NIKE used the same independent representative agencies to sell the line, although the agencies usually hired salespeople who handled only apparel. Sales were concentrated in department and specialty stores, and limited advertising appeared in magazines such as *Seventeen* and *Rolling Stone*.

NIKE entered the international market in the late 1970s and rapidly lined up local distribution channels in Europe, Latin America, and the Asia/Pacific region. These were supported by marketing assistance from regional NIKE offices and sourced from NIKE contract factories in the Far East. International sales grew quickly from 1 percent of total sales in 1978 to 6 percent in 1982, but the company found the reality of building a business in these international markets to be more expensive, complex, and time-consuming than expected. Executives noted several issues:

- Market strategy. In the U.S. market, NIKE established its consumer acceptance in running and then expanded its product line into other sport shoes. In most other countries, however, running was significantly less popular than in the United States. Should NIKE attempt to develop credibility for its brand name through running shoes or by directly tackling the most popular sport in each region (e.g., soccer in Europe)?

- Operations. Many executives believed that some distributors (typically private companies that marketed, sold, and warehoused the NIKE products) were undercapitalized and/or unwilling to tackle the market as aggressively as NIKE wanted. One option under consideration was the purchase of several distributors. This would provide greater control, but would also, of course, require significant capital expenditures and pose the challenge of managing foreign operating units.

- Product strategy. There was disagreement about the appropriate level of country-specific products for major markets such as Europe and Japan. On-site managers typically argued for more market-tailored products, while the domestic managers argued for less.

- General business conditions. These differed widely from area to area and often presented significant business challenges to NIKE. In Europe, for example, the Common Market tariff barrier forced the company to source many shoes from European factories, including two it had purchased in 1981–1982.

Because of the complexity of its international business, NIKE executives were considering a plan to focus the company's efforts on three major markets—Japan, Europe, and Canada—rather than continuing to push aggressively on a broad scale. In 1982, 63 percent of NIKE's $43 million international sales were in Europe, 28 percent in Japan, and 3 percent in Latin America. Nearly all international sales were in footwear.

In 1980, NIKE made an unsuccessful foray into leisure shoes with the "Air Casual." Even further away from the "real athlete" or "ath-leisure" markets, this strictly casual shoe made no pretense at any possible athletic use and was purely fashion-oriented. This first failure slowed the initial development of this segment, which reached $14 million in sales by 1982.

NIKE MANAGEMENT

Phil Knight's Leadership

The source of NIKE's leadership and spirit was Phil Knight, considered a man with strong passions and an overriding commitment to excellent products. A person unafraid of making decisions when necessary, he also strongly believed in teamwork and maintaining an informal, open atmosphere across the organization. A major strength was his ability to gain commitment at the highest practical level. While NIKE managers often found it hard to articulate the experience of working with Knight, three common observations emerged: He tended to provide *general direction*, rather than specific orders; he expected people to *keep in touch* with him on relevant issues; and he was, like Bowerman, often referred to as a *teacher*. Remarked a senior manager:

> His style is to give some general directions, not a lot of specifics. You get a general feeling, and that's what you go out and try to do. For example, I've been working on a contract with an athlete. Knight told me, "Don't spend much money, but don't let anybody else sign her." What the hell does he mean by that? It may be impossible, but I'll try to do something of that nature.

Another added:

> One thing Knight has taught us is that you can always do something better. He's not a stroker, doesn't let you gloat on a success. "Not bad!" is a supreme accolade. Perhaps that's where we avoid some of the phoniness found in so many places.

While Knight routinely saw several formal reports, his "control system" was largely informal, based upon keeping in touch. For this approach to work, of course, both Knight and his subordinates had to be sensitive to which issues were sufficiently important to keep in touch about, and able and willing to be reasonably open about them. Clearly, these characteristics took time to develop. Knight typically talked with his closest associates every couple of days. "With those who really understand this place," he said, "I can count on being told about what's

going right *and* what's going wrong in their area." One senior manager explained, "On major things, you touch base with him, just keep him generally informed. He doesn't need a lot of details. If he has confidence in you, on many things you just do it."

Of his role in the organization, Knight said:

> When I'm at what I consider my best, I am thinking in conceptual terms—where we want to be, how we are going to get there. Then I'll go out and spend some time in the area I've been thinking about and really probe in depth. Actually, this is what I ought to be doing. It's a constant fight to avoid getting overwhelmed by daily operating issues and ceremonial duties.

The values of competition, excellence, individual effort, team commitment, and a never-ending pursuit of improvement could be traced to Knight and his core management's participation in Bill Bowerman's track team at the University of Oregon. They learned much more than technical skills from him. "It wasn't anything magic," Knight recalled, "just his ideas of competitive response, of working hard, of having character, of all those corny things that your parents teach you. But he put them on you like a tattoo so that you'd never forget them." Said Knight, "You can't make a silk purse out of a sow's ear. But take an athlete with some talent, and with motivation and desire, he can do much more than a super talent who sits on his ass."

Organizational Evolution

In the early years at NIKE, Knight hired "simply good people," who were expected to do everything and moved rapidly from one position to another to bring their individual skills to a particular problem. This eventually became basic management philosophy. According to Knight:

> The idea that the brains are all at the top of an organization is really kind of silly. And nobody at the top ever does anything—it's the folks down the line that make it work. I learned that early. I had a great concept about bringing in shoes from Japan to compete with the German shoes, but I wouldn't have gotten far with it if I hadn't bumped into Jeff Johnson. He really made it work. And Jeff in turn had to rely on other people. I have a lot of respect for how we did that, and I guess that's the way this company has always worked.

Knight kept NIKE's formal structure relatively flat, functional, and flexible. He believed that this "simpler setup" had been a help to the growing company, yet he was aware that increasing size was driving managers to divide jobs into small components, which inevitably made the organization more complex (e.g., the product line reorganization in 1982 broke down one "unmanageable" job into four). Knight was clear, however, in his belief that structural actions could not be divorced from a consideration of the people involved.

Said Phil Knight:

> We've always tried to look for ability more than specialties. In the beginning, we didn't have an industry to draw on and never had enough money to hire guys that were expert in an area. We just sort of all banded together, recognizing that maybe we weren't good enough individually to do this, but somehow, collectively, we could make this thing go okay. I think that's a lot of the message of NIKE's success.

NIKE's senior group consisted, in the words of one inside observer, "of entrepreneurs—with a capital E." While many were athletes, or at least read the sports pages first, the strong bonds among them seemed to reflect camaraderies based on deeper, shared values: a desire to accomplish something of value, a healthy cynicism, self-confidence, a willingness to be a part of a team. They were proud of their achievements, but most could step back and poke a little fun at themselves, too.

Managers who joined NIKE in later years often had to prove themselves before becoming accepted as team members. David Chang, a former architect who joined in 1982 to develop sourcing in China, commented on his settling-in experiences:

> Despite all the seemingly jocular, fraternity house sort of things, there is a great deal of pressure on new people. It's not the pressure of an IBM or ITT, but the pressure of lack of direction, of not having the familiar accoutrements of job descriptions, performance goals, and organization charts to tell you what you're supposed to do. After being at NIKE a couple of weeks, for example, I went into Del's office and said, "Could you give me a little direction as to what I'm supposed to do?" Strasser was there, and he broke into peals of laughter. For months, he would poke his head into my office and ask, "Have you gotten any direction yet?" as if that was the most absurd thing in the world to ask for.
>
> A new person needs to have a strong sense of self, yet not be defensive. You can't be afraid to say "I don't know" or to ask for help. There's a feeling here that nobody knows it all; this is a business where we're writing the book from scratch.

In the early 1980s, the company modified its functional organization with a product-line unit. Apparel and International were assigned to separate units (see Exhibit 6), and the U.S. domestic footwear marketing operation was split into four product lines. The organization remained fluid enough, however, to respond to significant market changes or special events; for example, a "marketing group" was set up to prepare for the 1984 Los Angeles Olympics.

A shortage of talented managers led to further periodic organizational changes. The promotions function, for example, was decentralized to product lines in early 1982, only to be recentralized nine months later. Knight explained, "In an organization our size, the structure we choose clearly depends on the people we have to work with ... But after a while, we began to see certain benefits in the very fact of moving. People developed a broader understanding, and that's helpful." "It is unusual," one observer commented, "to find an organization in which so many people perceive problems and issues broadly, as company issues, rather than narrowly, as functional or territorial ones." Or, in Knight's words, "We tend to have specialists in the company not the job."

Meetings

Meetings, NIKE's principal communication and problem-solving mechanism, occurred at all organizational levels and ranged from informal conversations to formal product-line reviews. Most meetings were scheduled in response to needs rather than according to preset cycles; these sessions were open and sprinkled with humor, yet reflected an underlying seriousness of purpose. Managers ap-peared able to discuss issues along multiple dimensions, and several often took the lead in moving a session forward. "We don't invite the organization chart to a meeting," Bob Woodell said, "we invite people who can contribute to the issue."

For executive decision making, three "concentric" circles radiated from Knight. Knight had worked a long time and formed very close relationships with several of his managers—Woodell, Strasser, and Hayes, in particular (the group was known as the "Gang of Four"). Said Del Hayes:

> Generally speaking, the top group tries to have some knowledge of and feeling for what is going on in areas that may not be their direct responsibility. We try to do this through a series of meetings and through a continual interplay and exchange of ideas. You get a better grasp of what is happening on the whole and more of an appreciation for a problem in one area that may have a ripple effect in your area. In addition, you tend not to develop an overly protective sense of your empire, because you're more concerned with what's happening in the team and what can be the best bottom-line result. That has worked fairly well.

As Woodell described it:

> We go back a ways, and he is comfortable with us. We're real different, but have worked together long enough that we understand each other's strengths, can communicate reasonably quickly, have all done a lot of the jobs in the company. Knight's a difficult person to get to know, and few are close to him. With most people he avoids conflict and confrontation. But with Strasser, Hayes, and me, he'll absolutely seek it out.

Knight relied on the 11-person executive group (see Exhibits 6 and 7), known as "The Friday Club" (due to their regular biweekly Friday meetings), to provide companywide coordination. Twice a year the group went off-site for a week. "This is about the most enjoyable part of the business for me," Knight reported. Discussions were frank, and executives considered them critical opportunities to get back in touch with what everyone was doing and where the company was headed. Representative issues discussed during one meeting included:

- Production and R&D: ways to improve the new product transition from design to production; R&D priorities; factory capacities and capabilities.
- Control: the excess inventory situation; the growing space requirements in the Beaverton area.
- Marketing: the appropriate advertising/promotion balance (currently 1 to 3 in dollars); the Los Angeles Olympics; the overall marketing focus; the defective product return policy; broadening the sales pyramid (should retailers such as Sears be added?).
- People: Are the right people in the right slots?

A third "circle" included a larger group of managers involved in more impromptu meetings to respond to issues of the day. Kirk Richardson, who was in charge of the product lines at the time, described a meeting of this group:

> Several of us got real concerned that we were sapping our brand strength with some bonehead decisions and poor control in the sales area. We'd hammer away at this in staff meetings, and finally Woodell and Strasser said, "S___, let's get together and hash this thing out." So we got the relevant people from across the country together off-site for several days. Bob and Rob gave us a little direction, and we helped fill them in on what the problem seemed to be from our perspective. We then worked on it for a

couple of days and identified a series of concrete steps we thought we should take. We got back together with Woodell and Strasser, and they poked at us pretty hard and then said, "Let's do it."

Although various individuals, particularly the senior managers, served informally in coordinating roles over the years, the company recently began to define this job formally. For example, a major responsibility of a product-line manager was to coordinate all activities relating to that line—R&D, advertising, promotion, selling, and so forth. "We were tired," one noted, "of screw-ups like the sales reps pushing a shoe that we were phasing out."

Reports and Rewards

Traditionally, NIKE had used formal management reports and systems relatively little, although top management did consider two reports of particular importance. A daily summary of orders and shipments (in effect, Futures and sales) indicated whether things were going as expected; a comprehensive monthly accounting report detailed the whole operation, enabling trouble spots to be identified.

As the company grew, more and varied management systems were established, typically in response to specific needs. For example, middle managers in production scheduling, product line management, product development, and sales designed a formal planning tool to help coordinate their increasingly interdependent work. It was easier to install these systems than to gain full acceptance of, and adherence to, the discipline they imposed. Treasurer Gary Kurtz commented on the introduction of an annual budgeting process in 1978:

Budgets are part of the evolution of any company, and we're moving toward more bottom-line accountability by product area. There's been a reluctance to get involved initially, but we find it's a matter of education, of trying to get people to the point at which they understand the process and don't just treat it as a bureaucratic procedure. As I try to explain, running a business without good numbers would be like trying to manage a baseball team without the statistics.

While Knight approved the department budgets, formal reviews with the department managers were seldom conducted. Woodell saw the budget as a "scorecard" rather than a planning tool:

It's a kind of a financial plan with checkpoints so we can look at our results during the year and ask, how are we coming, are we ahead or behind, what's happening? It's not an authorization in advance to go spend money. As each decision comes along, you have to rethink it. We'll either decide to do it or we won't, and that process doesn't have a whole lot to do with budgets.

On the other hand, R&D Director Ned Frederick felt the budget system had brought a greater emphasis in product-line accountability:

We are more oriented toward managing profits today. We see this mostly from the product-line folks, in a decision not to go with a particular product or to change a product in some way so as to improve the gross profit margin. We've always had a lively dialogue with those folks, but the dialogue didn't used to be about gross profit margins.

Most people considered NIKE an exciting place to work, for the company, in effect, asked them to join a team. As Woodell expressed it, "What we like is for

people to come in and say, 'I want to contribute.' " In return, management "took care of" people, in part with pay, but more with opportunities for growth, responsibility, and contribution. As Knight explained, "It's really not so much salary as it is job responsibility, or the perception of it."

Wages and salaries were considered roughly comparable to those of other local companies. Each employee (including all managers) was reviewed once a year; annual raises were awarded at this time, with managers asked to tie the increase to individual performance. There was no organized incentive compensation program. Inevitably, how such procedures were administered varied, yet there was a general sense within NIKE that the company was "fair."

Challenges

Although executives identified many external threats to NIKE's continued success (ranging from the skills of particular competitors to political instability in the Far East), they consistently singled out the internal, organizational dimension as the most critical challenge. Most believed that NIKE's success to date was due in large part to the unconventional, freewheeling, entrepreneurial people it had attracted and the collegial style of working together it encouraged. And yet, as the company grew larger and its operations became more complex (employment had risen from 720 in 1978 to 3,600 in 1982, and there were nine NIKE locations in the Beaverton area alone), NIKE senior managers accepted—sometimes grudgingly, sometimes readily—the need for more "formal" management thinking, organization, and practices; and they took steps to move in this direction. Many of these changes were personally difficult. "We all see the need," one executive admitted, "but none of us wants to give up any freedom." These changes also touched a more fundamental nerve. "It's fine to develop structures and plans and policies," one senior executive explained, "if they are viewed, and used, as tools. But it is so easy for them to become substitutes for good thinking, alibis for not taking responsibility, reasons to not become involved. And then we'd no longer be NIKE."

Said Woodell in March 1983:

> The greatest threats to our continued success may well be internal. You see, NIKE, more than anything, is a group of people who have learned how to work well together, how to bring the best out of each other. NIKE is a spirit that means being smart about what you do, and busting your butt to do it well. It means talking to your friends and sharing ideas and not trying to go off and be a hero by yourself. It means trying things and having the freedom to recognize your mistakes and not be fired for them.
>
> And there's the danger. As we get used to being Number One, I worry that we'll become arrogant and start to believe we deserve the success, that we'll get lazy and stop reading the market. But more, as we continue to get larger and more spread out, I worry that we'll start to create our own little fiefdoms and stop talking to each other; that we'll substitute a two-inch thin policy manual for some broad principles and a lot of deep *thinking*; that we'll become just another big company.

A middle manager elaborated:

> There was a real dilemma here. Growth had led us to compartmentalize, to define jobs more narrowly. And this had created a kind of tunnel vision. For instance, about this time, orders come in from our sales force for the summer/fall

season. Typically, we try to ship these out by June 1. Well, it turns out one particular shoe was still in Korea and wasn't going to be in the States until June 10, which means it wouldn't have gotten to the stores until the third week in June. This shoe is a basketball shoe, which dealers usually don't place on the shelves until July 1, anyway. But because it said "ship June 1" on the order, a clerk decided to have the shoes air-freighted from Korea, which cost us an additional $50,000. The clerk did check with a supervisor, who was busy and who didn't really know what was going on either. This is what happens when people don't see the big picture. Yet, it is this very sense of freedom and autonomy that has made this company what it is. How do we preserve *it* while instituting the structure and systems we need?

As NIKE managers discussed their company and the internal challenges it faced, three primary areas of concern emerged: the continuing need to "emphasize the basics"; the necessity of continuing to "talk to each other"; and the challenge of "remaining a team."

Early in 1983, challenges in the marketplace also emerged. In March, the *New York Times* reported:

> In recent months, the cooling of NIKE's domestic shoe sales has pinched profits. On February 24, 1983, NIKE announced that earnings for the third quarter ended February 28 would show the first quarterly decline in the company's history—largely because of "lower than anticipated shoe sales," Gary Kurtz, NIKE's treasurer, said. The surprise statement, which prompted NIKE's over-the-counter per-share bid to drop to $16 from $23 a share in one week, followed a second quarter in which earnings were flat despite a 30 percent increase in revenue.

The sales shortfall sparked debate within NIKE. Some felt that it was a short-term response to the current recession. Others believed it reflected more fundamental issues. Overall, three factors were apparent, however: (1) Growth in the core domestic athletic footwear market was slowing; (2) NIKE's rapid growth during the previous decade had stretched systems and people; and (3) NIKE, as a publicly traded company, presented the original tightly knit entrepreneurial group with new challenges. Phil Knight commented:

In January (1983), it became clear that shipments and bookings weren't tracking the way we expected. As we dug into that situation, we realized that we weren't going to get the growth we had expected, and it became clear that over the next few years, the company is going to be a little different animal to manage. For example, as demand slows, we're going to have to manage the operating expenses more tightly.

I met with Woodell, Strasser, and Hayes in February and we realized that the process we had to go through—taking a good, hard look at the whole company and sort of confirming or realigning the directions in which we were headed as a company—would just be more efficient with four than with eleven. With those three guys, we had the major areas of the business pretty much covered. Woodell was sort of the administrator, Hayes the factory guy, and Strasser the creative guy.

Starting in March, we went around the company on a series of department audits, which is something we don't do in a normal year. We wanted to review what was going on, trying to check that people were working on the right things, to ask if we were getting the most benefit from major costs such as promo and advertising, to help people focus on some of the immediate problems. For example, in the production area, we realized we had too

much capacity and that we had to decide which factories to cut. There were some heated arguments about this, because the issues went beyond dollars and cents.

Woodell had the following to say:

We dug back into operations. The third-quarter earnings figure was really the first sign that everything we touched didn't turn to gold. Futures were down, and the product line seemed to be getting a bit stale. At the same time, there was a subtle shift in our marketplace. The athletic look wasn't the number one "in" thing anymore; people were starting to dress up a bit more.

We also started to see some cracks in the organization: It seemed to take forever to get a shoe to market, with so much coordination required between product management in Beaverton and development in Exeter. And when a product did come through, it sometimes wasn't the right one. Yet it would be unfair to say that these things caught us completely by surprise. We knew that growth was covering up a multitude of sins. We made a conscious decision not to try to clean most of them up while we were still riding the rocket straight up, but to wait until things started to slow down a bit. And now that's happening.

A middle manager responded to some of the ongoing changes:

Management hired individuals who had potential and gave them room to run. But now the senior managers are into too many decisions. For instance, we recently had a pricing meeting for a product line. We had done a lot of work and a lot of research. They reviewed it, didn't like it, and five minutes later we had a new pricing scheme. I question whether they are really close enough to the market to make decisions like that. And I know that it really affects the motivation of a lot of people when they see that their efforts haven't amounted to much.

Another comment was:

This recentralization, however, has really slowed things down. You get the feeling that senior management wants to be involved in lots of decisions. So you go to them and say, "Here's my problem; what do you want me to do?" And they say, "Let me think about it." Then, four or five days later when you haven't heard anything, you go back again.

In a surprise announcement in June 1983, Phil Knight appointed Bob Woodell as NIKE's president and COO. In classic NIKE fashion, Woodell had no job description beyond a general agreement with Knight. "We never talked," smiled Woodell. "Phil said, 'You do short-term, and I'll do long-term.' " Both men realized that for Woodell to be more than a ceremonial president, he would need "some of the trappings of power." To enable Woodell to establish a day-to-day working relationship with the management team, Knight "stayed in the background." He moved to a new office building two miles away and stopped going to operating meetings with Woodell.

EXHIBIT 1
FINANCIAL INFORMATION

Year	Sales ($Million)	Gross Margin	SG&A	Net Income	Inventory Turnover	Return on Equity
1976	14.1	28.8%	17.9%	4.3%		
1977	28.1	30.3	17.3	5.3		
1978	71.0	28.8	15.5	5.4		59%
1979	149.8	30.9	14.9	6.5		60
1980	269.8	27.1	14.8	4.6	4.81	45
1981	457.7	28.3	13.3	5.7	3.82	31
1982	693.6	36.9	13.7	7.1	3.41	37
1983	867.2	32.0	15.3	6.6	3.06	

Recent NIKE Financial Statements
(Balance Sheet as of May 31)
($Million)

	1983	1982	1981	1980
Assets:				
Cash	$ 13	$ 5	$ 2	$ 2
Accounts receivable	151	130	87	64
Inventory	283	203	120	56
Other	20	7	4	2
Current assets	$466	$345	$213	$124
Property, plant, and equipment	$ 61	$ 41	$ 24	$ 14
Less accumulated depreciation	(21)	(12)	(8)	(4)
Other	3	1	1	1
Total assets	$508	$375	$230	$135
Liabilities and stockholders' equity:				
Current portion of long-term debt	$ 2	$ 4	$ 7	$ 4
Notes payable to banks	132	113	61	37
Accounts payable*	91	74	42	37
Other	30	42	28	17
Current liabilities	$255	$233	$138	$ 95
Long-term debt	$ 11	$ 9	$ 9	$ 11
Other	1	1	0	0
Total liabilities	$267	$243	$147	$106
Common stock at stated value	$ 3	$ 2	$ 2	$ 0
Capital in excess of stated value	77	27	27	0
Retained earnings	161	103	54	29
Stockholders' equity	$241	$132	$ 83	$ 29
Liabilities and stockholders' equity	$508	$375	$230	$135

Source: Company annual reports and 10-Ks.

*Includes NIAC—Nissho Iwai American Corporation.

EXHIBIT 2
BRANDED ATHLETIC FOOTWEAR SUBMARKETS, 1982

Submarket	Racquet		Running		Basketball		Field		Other
% of total	35%		30%		15%		15%		5%
Leading competitors (market share)	NIKE Adidas Tretorn	40% 20% 6%	NIKE New Balance Adidas	50% 15% 10%	Converse Puma Nike	36% 30% 20%	Puma Adidas Hyde	30% 20% 10%	Hiking and walking: small but growing as older people discover walking.
Comments	Common for street use; tennis has not been growing but may in coming years.		Growth of 6% to 8% expected, depending on how long people continue to run, and how many are diverted to home exercise.		Beginning to decline: fewer teens; Title IX* bulge over.		Team sports, so depends on increase in industrial leagues; soccer will grow but at expense of football.		Leisure: moderate growth, unless a model captures imagination of young people.

Note: Data based on sales in athletic specialty and sporting goods channels only.

*Title IX, a federal statute, required that educational institutions provide athletic programs and facilities for women similar to those traditionally provided for men.

EXHIBIT 3
TYPICAL COST BUILDUP MODERATE-PRICED NIKE SHOE

Labor	$ 1.10	10%
Materials	5.20	48
Overhead and profit	2.70	25
Factory cost	$ 9.00	83
Shipping & duty	1.50	14
NIAC commission*	.36	3
NIKE cost	$10.86	100
NIKE margin	5.87	56%
Retailer cost	$16.73	
Retailer margin	12.22	58%
Retail price	$28.95	

Source: Company records.

*NIAC = Nissho Iwai American Corporation.

EXHIBIT 4
SUMMARY OF ACCOUNTS

Type	% of Accounts	% of Sales
National accounts*	—	15
Specialty shops	15	14
Department stores	27	19
Sporting goods stores	29	26
Shoe stores	29	26
	100	100

Source: Company records.

*Major customers such as J.C. Penney and Footlocker.

EXHIBIT 5
NIKE PUBLIC EQUITY OFFERINGS AND MARKET PERFORMANCE

NIKE went public on December 2, 1980, at $11 per share.* In anticipation of a public offering, the company had created two classes of stock: A—voting and B—nonvoting. Management maintained control of the voting shares, while the Class B shares were sold to the public. The Class B shareholders did, however, retain the imited right to elect one of the seven members of the board. The company offered its B shares to the public for a second time on October 14, 1982, at a price of $24.31 per share.

NIKE Public Offering Summary
(000s of shares)

Number of shares outstanding prior to offering: 32,352

	1st Offering	2nd Offering
Shares outstanding after offering	35,072	37,272
Class A	30,318	22,532
Class B	4,754	14,740
Share price at offering	$11.00	$24.31
Shares sold (all Class B)	4,754	3,000
Primary	2,720	2,200
Secondary	2,034	800[†]
Funds raised ($ millions)	52.3	72.9
Primary	29.9	53.5
Secondary	22.4	19.4
Company valuation ($ millions)	385.7	906.1
Directors' and officers' % of shares		
Total	57%	50%
Class A	65%	83%[‡]
P. H. Knight % of shares		
Total	46%	42%
Class A	53%	69%[‡]

NIKE Stock Performance

Quarter Ending	Price/Share* High	Low	P/E High	Low
5/31/81	11.50	8.50	14.0	10.4
11/30/81	13.88	8.88	10.8	6.9
5/31/82	15.25	12.36	11.2	9.1
11/30/82	27.12	20.00	20.5	15.1
5/31/83	21.37	15.12	13.7	9.7

Source: NIKE prospectus and annual report.

*All data adjusted for 2:1 split January 1983.

[†]Existing A shares are converted to B shares and then sold by these shareholders to the public.

[‡]Both the directors/officers and Knight's percentage is increasing as nondirector and nonofficer Class A shareholders sell their shares.

EXHIBIT 6
SKETCH OF THE NIKE ORGANIZATION

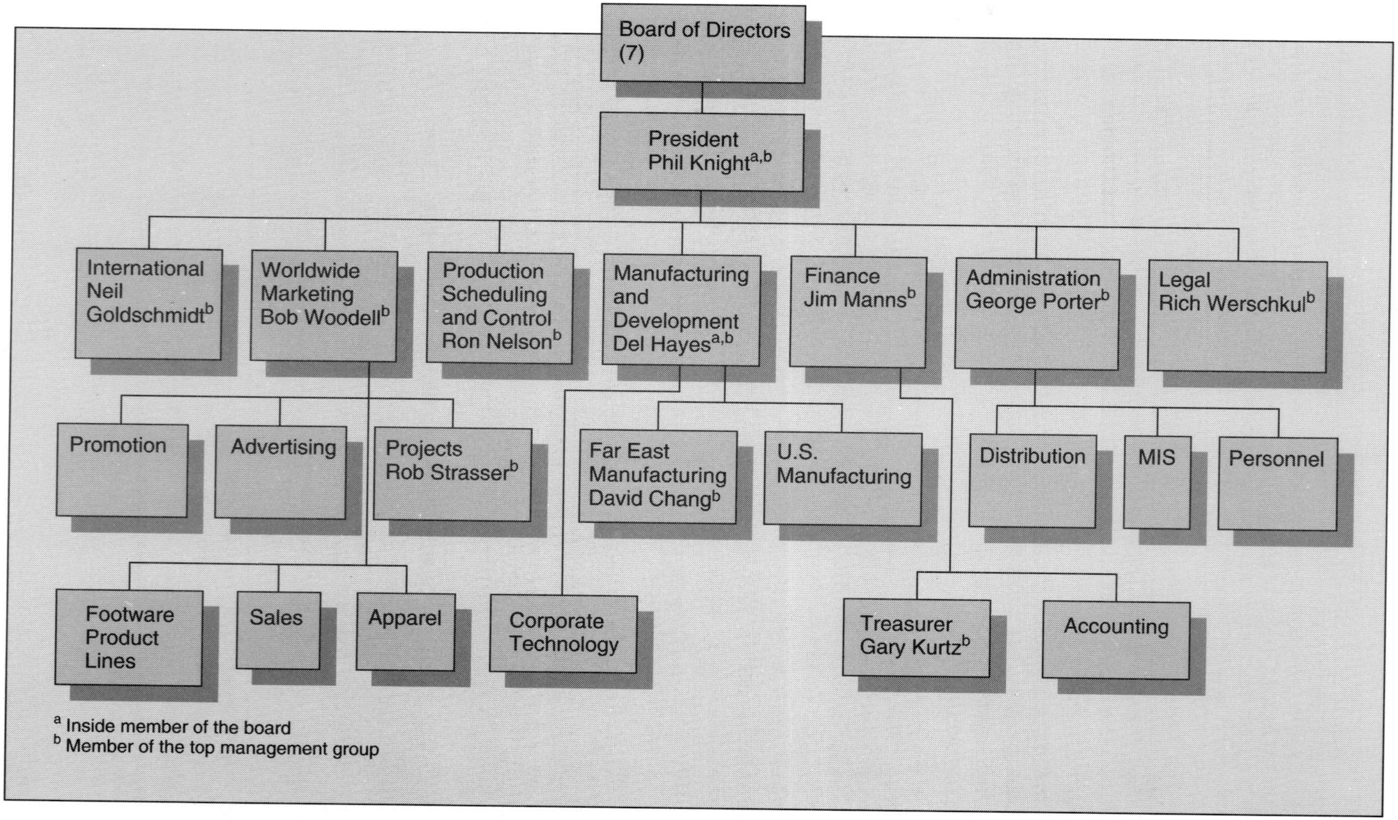

Board of Directors (7)

President Phil Knight[a,b]

International Neil Goldschmidt[b]

Worldwide Marketing Bob Woodell[b]

Production Scheduling and Control Ron Nelson[b]

Manufacturing and Development Del Hayes[a,b]

Finance Jim Manns[b]

Administration George Porter[b]

Legal Rich Werschkul[b]

Promotion

Advertising

Projects Rob Strasser[b]

Far East Manufacturing David Chang[b]

U.S. Manufacturing

Distribution

MIS

Personnel

Footware Product Lines

Sales

Apparel

Corporate Technology

Treasurer Gary Kurtz[b]

Accounting

[a] Inside member of the board
[b] Member of the top management group

Source: Researchers' interpretation.

EXHIBIT 7
PROFILES ON SOME OF THE FRIDAY CLUB EXECUTIVES

Phil Knight, 44, was a native of Portland. He believed his greatest strength was as a long-term thinker and planner. He was very competitive. Reflecting on the company's success, he said, "Hell, there is no secret. There is just the basic attention to details and doing all the parts of the business right."

Bob Woodell, 38, also a native of Portland, attended the Eugene campus of the University of Oregon, where he was a champion long jumper. He broke his back (in a sports accident) and his legs were permanently paralyzed. He held every post at NIKE, except legal and accounting. He was both fiercely independent and supercompetitive. Many saw him as an effective administrator. "Woodell has a lot of organizational strengths," one peer noted, "and does more creative, practical thinking than anyone I know."

Del Hayes, 47, a Minnesota native, was a CPA at Price Waterhouse, where he was previously Knight's boss. He provided the "numbers power" and a detailed appreciation of the manufacturing process. Hayes was described by one peer as "brilliant, with a totally quantitative mind, maybe the best in the world in things having to do with shoe factories and production."

Rob Strasser, 38, a Portland native, had been a new member of a local law firm in 1972 when he was placed on the Blue Ribbon Sports account in their dispute with Tiger Shoes. He joined NIKE in 1976, moved into marketing, and had worked in this general area ever since, including a stint as managing director of NIKE Europe (1980–82). Peers described him as incredibly creative—and equally "off-the-wall." "Seven of ten Strasser ideas may be crazy," one colleague explained, "but the other three will be just incredible." Others referred to him as "a cheerleader in the organization" and "the vice president in charge of stirring the pot." One remarked, "Every company needs one Strasser . . . and probably can't handle more than that."

David Chang smiled, "Why did I become a shoemaker? Well, as Knight says, 'None of us studied shoemaking in college, either.' " Born in the People's Republic of China, Chang, 52, studied architecture in the United States and had a successful practice in New York for 22 years. As relations with China thawed in the seventies, he reestablished ties there. This led to several consulting projects, including one with NIKE in 1981 to help the company establish production sources there. A year later, he joined the company full-time.

George Porter, 51, joined NIKE in late 1982 to head up a collection of administrative areas (including distribution, transportation, management information systems, and personnel) that, some managers noted, "the top four just aren't interested in." Porter came to NIKE with a significant business background (at Boise Cascade and Evans Corporation). Prior to that, he spent 12 years as a CPA at Price Waterhouse, where he had been Hayes's and, briefly, Knight's boss. "I was," he chuckled, "a known quantity to these guys."

Serengeti Eyewear: Entrepreneurship within Corning Inc.

Finally alone in his office, Zaki Mustafa, vice president and general manager of Serengeti Eyewear, relaxed and collected his thoughts. He had spent all of May 12, 1993, gathering opinions from members of Serengeti's management team. On the face of it, the choice before them was simple enough: whether to launch a new line of sunglasses called Eclipse. But it seemed that everyone in the firm had a slightly different opinion of what should be done.

Mustafa and his team were determined to maintain the momentum that had made Serengeti one of the fastest-growing and most profitable businesses within Corning. The Eclipse decision, however, involved considerable risk. Because the new product line was aimed directly at the medium-priced market, it would put

Copyright © 1993 by the President and Fellows of Harvard College. Harvard Business School Case 394-033 (revised May 13, 1994).

Serengeti on a collision course with Ray-Ban, the industry giant.

COMPANY AND INDUSTRY BACKGROUND

Serengeti Eyewear specialized in premium, technology-oriented sunglasses aimed at the high end of the sunglasses market. It was a division of Corning Incorporated, a 120-year-old worldwide organization with 1992 sales of $3.7 billion, 40 plants, 44 offices, and 33 clinical-testing or life-science laboratories. Corning's core business was specialty glass and materials, but it also produced consumer housewares, laboratory services, and opto-electronics. Company brochures described technology as "the glue that binds the firm together."

Corning possessed a substantial research capability, with centers in the United States, Japan, and France employing some 1,500 scientists, engineers, and support staff. Over time, they had developed such breakthroughs as fiber-optic cables and laminated glass, as well as products sold under the firm's consumer brands of Corelle, Corning Ware, Pyrex, Revere Ware, Steuben, Visions, and Vycor. Like Corning's other divisions, Serengeti drew heavily on the research laboratories for new product ideas.

Serengeti sunglasses, for example, featured "spectral control," a technology that reduced the distracting effect of blue light on vision. Many also featured another Corning innovation, photochromic lenses, that darkened in bright sunlight and lightened in lower light. Products were aimed at diverse audiences and uses. Serengeti's main product, Drivers, which accounted for 60 percent of the division's sales, was directed at automobile drivers. Other products targeted skiers, shooters, and sailors.

Analysts normally divided the $1.8 billion U.S. market for nonprescription sunglasses into four segments: low end, moderate, mid-range, and high end. Low-end sunglasses were priced at less than $25 and accounted for 6 percent of industry dollar sales. They normally contained plastic or polycarbonate lenses and simple plastic frames, and appealed to buyers who valued appearance over performance. Moderate-priced products sold for $25–$49.99 and accounted for 18 percent of industry sales. In this category, lenses were still primarily plastic, but came with additional features, such as polarization and diverse frame styles. The mid-range segment was the largest, accounting for 48 percent of industry sales. Mid-range sunglasses were priced at $50–$74.99, allowed a choice between polycarbonate and ground-and-polished lenses, and were

normally sold by department stores or specialists, such as sunglasses shops, optical stores, or sporting goods outlets. High-end sunglasses sold for $75 or more and accounted for 28 percent of industry sales. They came primarily with ground-and-polished lenses and often had optical quality frames, and were sold mainly by sunglasses shops and optical specialists, with smaller numbers offered by department stores and sporting goods outlets.

Within this market Serengeti faced several major competitors. (See Exhibit 1 for market shares in the $25 and up segments.) Ray-Ban, a division of optical glasses-maker Bausch and Lomb, was by far the most important. It was the goliath of the sunglasses industry with worldwide sales of over $500 million in 1992, and the only competitor to have built a strong and enduring brand image. Ray-Ban had long been identified with pilots and was featured in the popular movie *Top Gun*. It was slightly preferred by male buyers and competed strongly in all but the low end of the market. Oakley was a distant second to Ray-Ban, having recently emerged as the second-strongest brand in both the mid-range and high-end segments. It had developed a strong sports and athletic image and was preferred by men. Vuarnet, manufactured in France, enjoyed a European image. It sold better to women and had its roots in the ski industry. Designer and other brands accounted for the balance of the market and competed primarily on fashion and style.

THE EARLY YEARS

Serengeti evolved from Corning Sunglass Products, a division launched in 1982. For many years Corning had sold eyeglass blanks to eyeglasses manufacturers. Then, in 1964, after the company's scientists invented photochromic glass, it became a major supplier of sunglass blanks as well. Corning Sunglass Products was created to capture a larger share of the profits from the downstream consumer business. Its strategy was to price slightly above the market, winning a premium for superior quality while offering both low- and high-end sunglasses positioned as fashion accessories.

At the time, Corning had little experience in such businesses. It was more at home in scale-intensive markets, where it sold to original equipment manufacturers. Early signs for the new division were good, but after a year it began to sour. Manufacturing, quality, and distribution problems undermined Corning's reputation with consumers and retailers, while poor product positioning eroded sales. Substantial losses were incurred, and in June 1984 Corning's senior management discontinued one of the major product lines. A month later, they began to consider closing the entire venture, and in August 1984 decided to exit.

THE TURNAROUND YEARS

Zaki Mustafa assumed control of Serengeti after he and a small group at Corning Sunglass Products disagreed with senior management's decision to close the division. They believed that the early stumbling reflected poor positioning and Corning's inexperience in consumer markets, not inherent flaws in the product or business. In fact, Mustafa, who was at the time the Sunglass Products operations manager, believed that the primary problem was an unwillingness to listen to customers. He later summed up the situation:

Somewhat typical of an arrogant organization, we thought we could dictate to the market what we'd make and sell. It turned out that the market was controlling us, not the other way around.

In September 1984, in a private meeting with group president William Hudson, Mustafa argued that closure would be a mistake and asked for a second chance to make the business a success. Because he wanted to fundamentally reposition the division's products and approach, he requested full control, including independence from the rest of Corning's management structure. When Hudson asked why Corning should indulge his scheme, Mustafa responded that he could offer nothing more than his commitment—and that he was willing to bet his career on it. Three weeks later, he and his group were told that they had been given the chance to revive the sunglasses business.

They immediately developed both short- and long-term plans. Short-term, they focused on cutting costs and stabilizing the business. All low-end product lines were eliminated and their production contracts ended. Any remaining inventory was sold, and physical facilities were consolidated under one roof. Serengeti thus became the first unit of Corning to move into its own building, apart from other divisions but in a neighboring town. And because Mustafa wanted to build a new organization that would meet the needs of customers by offering quality products, he decided to focus for the long term on the division's high-end product line, called Serengeti, and to rename the business Serengeti Eyewear.

Operationally, Mustafa put development of a core team of people, unswervingly committed to the business, as his top priority. To get them, he assembled the entire sunglasses staff and made an offer: "Anyone who wants to leave today can do so, and the company will find you another job at Corning. But if you stay for a year and then we have to shut down, we cannot guarantee that the company will relocate you."

The initial impact was predictable. Mustafa recalled:

> The best and brightest left straight away, and the company's staff fell from 135 people to 35. But those who stayed showed commitment to the cause. Most of them were novices, especially in marketing, but today they run the business.

Mustafa's second fundamental decision was to return to Corning's traditional strength in technology. He and his team felt that Serengeti sunglasses should be repositioned as high-tech, high-end, functional products, rather than fashion accessories. Whereas the old products had hidden the Corning name so as not to detract from their fashion image (and not to offend other sunglasses manufacturers, who continued to purchase sunglass blanks from Corning), all future products would prominently display the name to take advantage of the company's technology reputation. Products were also repositioned as male-oriented. In the past, Serengeti had sold mainly to women because of its fashion focus. At the same time, the product line was reduced from 230 to 53 items to allow for more targeted marketing. Using this approach, the Serengeti line was relaunched in January 1985.

Word-of-mouth advertising was used aggressively in the early lean years. Mustafa and his staff donated hundreds of pairs of free sunglasses to opinion leaders in various high-profile sports and occupations: ski patrolmen, members of the U.S. Sailing Association, pilots, even state troopers. Their objective was to have the company's products seen in places where performance was paramount. At one time, booths were even established on ski slopes to allow skiers to take Serengetis for a "test run."

As the new team struggled to rebuild the business, Mustafa continued to wrestle with Corning to maintain independence. To insulate his managers from what he regarded as Corning's time-consuming corporate style, he personally attended required corporate meetings in their place. Earlier, in 1985, when group management had attempted to install an "oversight committee" to guide Serengeti, Mustafa had walked out of the first meeting in frustration, declaring that he was too busy to waste his time at such gatherings. Fortunately, his dramatic gesture persuaded corporate management to give Serengeti the leeway he sought. The alternative, he recalled later, was probably an abrupt end to his career at Corning.

Eventually success came, but only after several difficult years. During this period, every substantial new order was viewed as a milestone, and each day ended with the entire staff gathered together in the packing and shipping department. Sales manager Hugh Ogle remembered the time:

> We began in a very negative position with retailers following the product withdrawals of a few years before, so we had to bend over backwards to provide customer service. In the new building we were all together and could go into customer service to see orders coming in. That was good news and it kept us going. In fact, all the senior people would come in and pack orders themselves to ensure that every order was sent the next day.

As Sharon Stone, Serengeti's marketing manager, put it, "That was when we learned to serve customers and lost our arrogant attitude." But there was excitement, too, as Mustafa recalled:

> It was harrowing at the time. But somehow we never felt that much pressure. I used to go home so exhausted that I'd fall asleep in front of the TV still in my work clothes. I'd wake up, find that my wife had thrown a blanket over me, change clothes, and head back to work ... But everybody who was in the business was there by choice. It was a story about how people can pull together and fight a war.

THE GROWTH YEARS

Over a period of several years Serengeti's management team succeeded in resuscitating sales and then in scoring strong growth. Between 1985 and 1987 sales increased fourfold; at the same time gross margin grew nearly sixfold. Between 1987 and 1992 both sales and gross margin more than tripled. (See Exhibit 2 for additional financial information on sales, contribution, and ROE.) During this period Serengeti won a number of prestigious awards for technical and design excellence and was included on several "best products" lists. Growth was steady, except for a brief downturn in 1990. In order to meet aggressive sales goals the previous year, Serengeti sold into customers' warehouses ahead of final demand. When the expected demand failed to materialize, distributors and retailers were left with large inventories, depressing the next year's sales.

Growth was sustained by three main initiatives. First, Serengeti sales staff worked to restore and broaden their relationships with U.S. distributors and retailers. Because of the abrupt reversals of the early 1980s, many buyers remained suspicious that Serengeti would again switch its policy or product line without notice.

A satisfied and complete U.S. distribution network therefore demanded considerable time and investment. International expansion soon followed. Between 1987 and 1993 Serengeti moved to increase its reach, first into Canada and then into Europe and Asia. During this period, Mustafa established a goal of eventually drawing a third of company sales from each of the three regions of North America, Europe, and Asia. Finally, Serengeti expanded its product line by relying on further advances in technology. Between 1987 and 1993 several new products were added. Each drew on innovations developed in Corning's laboratories. Strata, a new high-end product in the $300 price bracket, was the most distinctive. Along with photochromic glass, blue-shift correction, and full ultraviolet (UV) protection, it featured a new system for polarizing light and reducing glare. All competitive glass polarizing systems required plastic laminates; Strata, by contrast, used a proprietary surfacing process, for which Serengeti held exclusive rights, that integrated a layer of polarizing glass directly onto the lens.

The idea and technology for Strata came from Corning's research laboratory in France. It was originally invented for another purpose, but its properties made it a natural for sunglasses. After hearing of the innovation through their research contacts, Mustafa and Ogle, then in operations, traveled to Geneva to meet Serge Renault, the scientist responsible, and learn more about the technology. They decided on the spot to go ahead with the product. The only problem was the high price Serengeti would have to charge because of Strata's complex manufacturing process.

Because few companies had ever tried to sell $300 sunglasses, Serengeti began cautiously with a "test launch." To limit exposure, one hundred retail outlets were selected for a trial run. In one week seven Serengeti employees set up all necessary product displays and trained all store personnel in the special features of the product. After collecting feedback from customers, the test was quickly judged a success, and Strata began to sell steadily.

The concept of a test launch took hold at Serengeti and was used again to enter the European market. There, Serengeti chose to launch its products by selling for the first year only in Finland, a country somewhat outside the European mainstream but regarded as representative enough to provide cultural and institutional learnings. After a successful test launch, distribution was broadened to other parts of Europe.

ORGANIZATION AND FUNCTIONS

Mustafa described the firm's organizational structure as "buckets to put people's tasks in, not watertight buckets, but buckets nonetheless." (See Exhibit 3 for an organization chart.) He added:

> The organization chart is for people who need to see the world through those filters. We don't actually operate that way. People here often share and swap assignments, for example, when someone is out of town . . . In fact, if there's been any influence from me, it's to keep things informal and fluid. There's a formal and an informal organization, and if there's one thing I've tried to cultivate, it's to let the informal organization dominate.

Marketing

Serengeti's marketing revolved around technology. According to Stone, the strat-

egy was straightforward: "We want to be on the leading edge of technology and in the mainstream of fashion." To that end, marketing was responsible for the coordination of design projects, pricing, development and planning of new point-of-sale displays, advertising campaigns, and public relations. In each area, marketing focused on the special features of the company's technology: photochromic lenses, spectral control, ultraviolet protection, and polarization. Many advertisements, for example, included detailed descriptions of Serengeti's features, which other sunglass manufacturers normally avoided. (See Exhibit 4 for a sample advertisement.)

Marketing was also responsible for new product development, including incremental changes to the existing line (new frames, styles, colors, and lens shapes) and major additions such as Strata. But the actual design work was outsourced to Smart Design, a small design specialist in New York City that worked closely with Serengeti's marketing staff to draw up new fashion ideas. In fact, in its early years Serengeti had also leaned heavily on outside consultants for marketing and positioning advice. But unlike design, most of these functions had been gradually brought in-house. Stone believed that a rapidly shifting consumer market required managers who knew their customers intimately and built that understanding into every decision they made. Marketing staff therefore stayed in touch with trends by spending at least some time every few months selling sunglasses from behind the counters of different retail outlets.

In recent years Stone had been able to shift her own attention away from crisis management and toward the long term. She observed:

In the beginning I didn't even know how to write a marketing plan. I was always absorbed by day-to-day tasks. Now I spend about 25 percent of my time with domestic customers, 25 percent with international customers, 25 percent training and developing my staff, and the rest on matters that simply come to the office. I'm in the field about half the time.

Sales

Because of Serengeti's distinctive positioning, sales staff approached their task somewhat differently than their counterparts at other companies. A technology message, they believed, required knowledgeable and informed retailers. Consequently, Serengeti sold primarily through optical shops and sunglass retail chains. Typically, Serengeti accounted for 25–30 percent of their total sunglass sales. Most sales were direct. However, distributors were used for selling to optical shops and retail chains with fewer than 15 stores; they accounted for less than 10 percent of sales. Fifteen national accounts were responsible for 80 percent of Serengeti's volume, and the total number of accounts was approximately 750. The leading accounts, like Sunglass Hut, Lenscrafters, and Pearle Vision, had hundreds of stores. Close relationships with these stores was considered a must, and Serengeti placed great emphasis on training retail assistants. According to Ogle, "We take every opportunity to stand up in front of our customers' people."

Serengeti's customer training program, for example, was longer and more detailed than those offered by competitors. Complete training of a client's staff might take up to 10 sessions, spread over two days. Sessions included slides, overheads, videos, technical manuals, and hands-on demonstrations of the technical performance of Serengeti products. The object was not only to acquaint customers with the company's products and encourage them to carry the line, but also to make the retailer's own staff as confident and skilled as possible in presenting the underlying technology story.

For similar reasons, sales staff invited different retailers to visit Serengeti headquarters every four to six weeks. Visitors came from diverse accounts and usually included the account's top executive, as well as members of his or her next layer of management. The aim was to help them learn as much as possible about the company's products, organization, and people, while at the same time allowing Serengeti management and employees to better understand their clients. New customers normally spent between one-half and a full day touring the facilities, visiting a special room set up permanently with point-of-sale displays, and meeting with the entire Serengeti staff.

During these visits, both sides made substantial presentations about their objectives and ideas. One of the goals of the meetings, according to Ogle, was to "expose customers to our values." Discussions covered a broad range of topics and questions: What is your business? What does your company do? How do you do it? What does Serengeti do well? In what areas is Serengeti a benchmark for the industry? What does Serengeti need to improve upon? Ogle observed:

> We tell them not to be shy, that we really want to get better at meeting their needs. And they're not. The presentations can

take as long as one and a half hours. And everybody in Serengeti who's here at the time attends, including the packers.

Partnership Programs, which helped customers set and then meet higher sales goals for the Serengeti products they sold, were another priority of the sales group. They began in 1989 when Serengeti was striving to double its own sales. To create a partnership, Ogle and Stone sat down with clients to establish joint sales goals, usually involving a substantial increase over previous years' performance. The two then worked with clients to determine how the targets would be met and how Serengeti could help through activities such as joint promotions.

Mustafa encouraged the sales staff to focus on long-term customer satisfaction, rather than quick sales. In one instance he liked to cite, an airline pilot wanted to purchase top-of-the-line Stratas but had been dissuaded by Mustafa, who was himself a pilot. He knew that Strata's polarizing feature would make it difficult to read the instrument panel and that the pilot would be better off with less expensive Drivers.

Operations

Serengeti's manufacturing was unusual for a sunglasses company in that it was almost entirely outsourced. Timothy Yu, operations manager, explained that outsourcing allowed the company to go anywhere to obtain the highest quality frames and parts while still maintaining maximum flexibility. Only lens blanks were manufactured internally, and that was done by Corning Incorporated, not Serengeti. Yu observed, "Our expertise is in

the glass itself, so we said to ourselves early on, 'Let's play to our strength and not tie up capital in things we're not good at.'"

Manufacturing was conducted at sites around the world. Lens blanks were melted and shaped at a Corning plant in Harrodsburg, Kentucky; most grinding and polishing was done by subcontractors in Japan; frames and assembly were assigned to partners in Japan, Hong Kong, France, Italy, and the United States. Because of their technical complexity, Strata lenses were manufactured in France, close to the research facility where the concept originated. Serengeti purchased all of the sunglass blanks made by Corning.

Serengeti preferred to rely on existing suppliers bound by long-term contracts rather than competitive bidding. Contracts were terminated only in extreme circumstances. Typically, one or two sources were used for each item. Of Serengeti's fourteen original suppliers, all but two were still with the company. Cost improvements were gained by careful negotiation, and the goal, according to Yu, was to ensure "a fair margin to both parties." If suppliers were not able to meet cost-reduction targets, Serengeti engineers provided manufacturing and technical assistance.

Serengeti's suppliers enjoyed a number of advantages. The usual practice in the optical business was for suppliers to be paid only after goods were received by the buyer; Serengeti, by contrast, paid when orders left the company. Information on forecasts and predicted demand was shared routinely. And if a supplier had to invest in new capacity to meet Serengeti's requirements, it was guaranteed orders for a certain period. Yu summarized the company's approach by saying, "We are very responsible buyers."

Serengeti did not have a separate quality assurance group, nor was there a single individual with responsibility for quality. In fact, there had been no formal quality improvement programs since 1985. Instead, much of the responsibility for quality rested with a network of country manufacturing managers (also called in-country process engineers) who reported directly to Connie Lapp, the manufacturing manager. These engineers were stationed in different regions of the world and worked on-site with suppliers on a daily basis. Their task was to advise suppliers of Serengeti's needs, assist with production problems, and ensure that standards were met. Manufacturers were not paid until inspection was completed and standards were verified. Inspection was carried out by in-country process engineers at the source plant and again by packers in the company's single warehouse, located adjacent to the offices, where every pair of sunglasses was checked before shipment. While there were variations across the product line, total manufacturing costs for Serengeti sunglasses followed the trade average of one-seventh the product's suggested retail price.

Because Yu felt that formal manufacturing systems were more of a burden than a help, he preferred to use direct feedback from customers and country manufacturing managers (whom he regarded as "the best advance warning system for quality problems") to guide his department. Problems were fixed as they arose. In mid-1993 Yu was resisting pressure from Corning's corporate staff to institute new quality control programs as well as a just-in-time system. He commented:

Our goal is zero defects. We were practicing customer satisfaction before they [Corning] were even tracking it. We know what's right for the customer; we know what's right for the business; we just do it . . . Now the battle is around inventory. Because Corning is an original equipment maker, it doesn't need inventory. But Serengeti does because we must have product on hand to meet the needs of a cyclical fashion industry. Forecasts are always going to be unreliable. Yet we promise to ship within 24 hours.

Operations staff spent much of their time getting to know suppliers personally. As Yu put it, "At Serengeti we believe in face-to-face meetings. Over the phone doesn't cut it. I want to see the person's expression and body language." This philosophy resulted in considerable overseas travel. For example, in 1992 Yu made six trips to Asia and three to Europe, each lasting about a week. The Japan country manufacturing manager came to Corning twice for similar periods, while his European counterpart came three times. Comparable, and occasionally more intensive, travel schedules were followed by Yu's predecessors as operations manager, Mustafa and Ogle. Mustafa had headed operations before taking the helm in the 1985 turnaround; at the time he had developed the concept of a supplier network. Ogle had followed Mustafa as operations manager before becoming sales manager; he estimated that in the mid-1980s he spent almost 90 percent of his time on the road.

Operations also included distribution and the customer service department, which handled orders, inquiries, and complaints from retailers and consumers. Mustafa gave the service staff clear guidelines for dealing with unhappy customers:

"Make the decision as if you were the one with a broken pair of sunglasses." To ensure rapid response, all customer service representatives were able to make on-the-spot decisions. Judgment calls were inevitable, and customers occasionally appealed decisions to higher levels of management. In such cases, Mustafa told the customer service staff, he would always back them up, even if he disagreed with the decision.

Systems

Two people were responsible for maintaining and developing Serengeti's information technology, including systems for customer service, ordering, inventory management, and distribution control. Despite their small number, they had succeeded in radically transforming the company's information systems.

Between 1982 and 1992 Serengeti used a system that was supplied by Corning to all divisions. It had been developed in the late 1970s and was based on an IBM mainframe and centralized data processing services. Unfortunately, the system allowed records to be accessed in only a limited number of ways. Because most of them were designed for Corning's commodity businesses, Mustafa felt that the approach was too rigid and slow to meet Serengeti's increasingly flexible requirements. In 1991 he called Gary Wheeler, then a systems manager at Corning's central information systems division, and invited him to rejoin Serengeti to upgrade its information technology. Wheeler had previously been with the Sunglasses division between 1982 and 1985. Mustafa gave him a clear mandate: to select hardware and software that was appropriate for Serengeti's special needs. Wheeler recalled:

> Zaki told me, "Put in a customer service system that is best for the business. Don't do what other people say; do what's best for *this* business. You can't be successful if you conform all the time." That created a real problem, because corporate information services had already made a substantial investment in a new replacement system that they wanted us to use. But it was still centralized, and we weren't sure that it would be best for our needs.

In fact, when Wheeler drew up a list of requirements for Serengeti's new system, he realized that it would have to meet the needs of four main groups: staff, customers, country manufacturing managers, and suppliers. At the bottom of the list were the requirements of Corning corporate, who wanted Serengeti connected to the company's electronic mail network but really needed only an occasional information update, not constant interaction.

After nine months of research, conversations with several other companies that had downsized their computer systems, and consideration of 15 alternative packages, Wheeler recommended that Serengeti move to a system of linked personal computers. The new system offered several features not found on the IBM: online help for all data fields, paperless entry, frequent updates, flexibility, and the ability to be used outside of Corning's usual hours, which was important for Serengeti's European and Asian suppliers. Moreover, the new system cost between $80,000 and $90,000 for both hardware and software, whereas the alternative proposed by the corporate information group would have cost $780,000.

MANAGEMENT STYLE

Mustafa believed that business should be based on shared values and that rigid rules and procedures obstructed customer service and flexibility. He therefore cultivated an informal management style.

Philosophy and Values

Mustafa was fond of quoting snippets of homespun philosophy to his colleagues. These were fondly called "Zaki-isms" because they neatly summarized his beliefs about life and business (see Exhibit 5). For example, Mustafa argued that values should be the starting point in business:

> Motivation to service and quality are not conscious acts at all. They have to be a reflection of what you are, and what you yourself believe. The issue of compatibility of style and belief is very important, and I think that belief comes first. If it's not in you, I don't know how to cultivate it. You can't create the capacity to be quality-oriented in people; you can only destroy it.

Mustafa worked hard to build an atmosphere of teamwork and mutual support at Serengeti. From the time he became general manager, he viewed team building as one of his major responsibilities. He always asked employees to put the team first and carefully selected personnel who would be at home in such an environment. Trust, Mustafa believed, was critical to creating an effective business team. He observed:

> We may not have the best and the brightest, but we all pull together. Don't worry about having the brightest people; worry about the team.
>
> Trust comes from interdependence, not independence. We've made a clear statement: "The individual is secondary to the organization."

Management at Serengeti did not merely espouse these values; they tried to live them. (See Exhibit 6 for excerpts from an employee climate survey.) A vital factor in Mustafa's assessment of a prospective employee's potential was the likelihood that he or she would become part of the team. He observed:

> There are some people who take great pride in excellent output of their own. Others take great pride in excellent output of the group. I'm always looking for people in the second category.

Prospective employees were therefore screened extremely carefully for fit with these values. As Ogle put it, "We check chemistry as well as resumes." The hiring-in process involved extensive interviews with managers throughout the company. One recent hire summarized the process by saying, "I didn't feel like I was being hired; I felt like I was being adopted."

Mustafa also believed that it was important to involve everyone in the business fully, from top management to warehouse personnel. He shared virtually all information, including financial and performance data, with the entire staff. Yu commented on the company's norms of equality:

> Typical firms are like an army, with a caste system. We don't have that here. There is no reserved parking (except for visitors), no separate dining areas, no separate bathrooms. And everybody, including the packers, attends the annual sales meeting.

Mustafa believed that this approach should extend beyond working relationships. In 1985, at the end of his first year as general manager, he sent all hourly workers an invitation to the annual Christmas party. He recalled:

> None of them showed up. I was very disappointed and later asked them why they hadn't attended. It turned out that they thought my invitation wasn't serious, that it was merely a casual note. So the next year I visited each one personally to invite them. By the third year, we had full attendance.

Mustafa emphasized that building teamwork and trust was a two-way street: He had to trust employees if they were to trust him. He gave an example of what that approach meant for management: "When we moved into our own building, I was told that we needed a security system in the warehouse and packing area to prevent theft. I wouldn't do it." At the same time, he set demanding goals and expected high performance. Mustafa stressed self-reliance, and several Serengeti employees noted that he asked more of them than their previous bosses. Lapp observed:

> Working for Zaki is probably the most challenging thing you could do. Why? Because if you have a normal ego and ambition you often think to yourself, "So much achievement would be fine." But he thinks you could do so much more. He doesn't care about where you went to school, or anything like that; he goes right to your soul. And because of that, I've been able to achieve more.

To illustrate her point, Lapp described an occasion when she had expressed doubts to Mustafa about her ability to perform a new and more demanding job. He responded by asking her to write down 10 good things about herself and put the list on his desk by the next morning. She found the task almost impossible and hoped he would forget. But Mustafa kept asking. Finally, several weeks later she forced herself to write down everything she could think of and gave him the list. She remembered what happened next:

> He threw it in the trash. I asked, "What are you doing? Aren't you going to look at the list?" He replied, "It doesn't matter what I think, it's what you put on the list that's important." That's what I got for all my agonizing and worrying about what he would think. But I could do a lot better list now.

Mustafa believed that an important part of his job was caring for his staff. He commented:

> I regard myself not just as a business manager, but as a surrogate father for our people. I say to our employees, "You worry about your work, I'll worry about you." I am a friend, and I do it because I get a lot of pleasure out of it.

Decision Making

Most decisions at Serengeti, even very important ones, were reached with a minimum of memos, reports, and formal meetings. Indeed, Serengeti had no scheduled meetings of any kind, other than with customers and suppliers. According to Mustafa, "If an individual thinks a meeting is needed, it happens. But seldom. I spend a good part of my day visiting people, chatting with them over coffee. That's how we usually make decisions."

Mustafa stressed that informality did not mean shooting from the hip or working without the facts. At Serengeti large amounts of information were collected before reaching a conclusion. In this sense,

Mustafa felt that Serengeti's decision-making style was different from that of many other entrepreneurial companies:

> We're actually very cautious and conservative in what we do. We think things through, and that requires a lot of information. Some businesses describe themselves as entrepreneurial, but they're really irresponsible. They operate by the seat of their pants, just a brief conversation or two, then move to a decision. We don't. A true entrepreneur takes a long-term view.

Not all information, however, was treated equally. Mustafa believed that quantitative information often took the place of managers developing "a sense about what's right." For this reason, he strove for numbers that were "directionally correct" while avoiding artificial precision and extensive documentation. He explained:

> In this business we emphasize the ability to become comfortable with qualitative information. We have two principles: Always deal with the broad picture before getting into the details, and always get the rationale right before running the numbers. If there's one legacy I want to leave here, it's that people look at the broad picture first and do a logic check.
>
> Unfortunately, the bureaucrats want documentation. You can give them perfect information, or, at the risk of accuracy, you can give them directionally correct information and save several days of work. But at no point in time, for any reason, have I ever misled people directionally.

James Stokes, Serengeti's controller, who had worked elsewhere in Corning, believed that Mustafa had a reputation within the company for being cavalier with numbers. But Stokes thought that he simply used them in a different way:

> I don't accept the traditional view that Zaki is not interested in numbers, that he's not numbers oriented. What he's really interested in is directional analysis, rather than precise predictions. When numbers are relevant, he studies them exhaustively.

Mustafa recognized that the combination of informality, a team orientation, and his approach to numbers could weaken individual responsibility. He therefore insisted on strict accountability:

> I always tell people, "Don't say to me, 'To the best of my knowledge,' 'As advised by,' 'To the best of my ability,' 'As I'm told,' or whatever. Either it is or it isn't. Check it out. Don't rely on a third party." Our presumption is that if you're going to make a decision, you need to have firsthand information, because we want firsthand ownership and results. Anything that smacks of covering your tracks, like approvals or memos, is frowned on.

Or as Stone jokingly summed up the culture, "If you don't meet results, we take out a gun and shoot you—but we're unhappy about it."

Running the Business

To achieve these ends, Mustafa estimated that he spent about a third of his time on the road. Of that, 40 percent was spent visiting customers, 40 percent visiting suppliers, and the balance visiting Serengeti employees in the field. His customer visits were primarily with small accounts, he observed, "because they need more reinforcement that we care about them." When not traveling, Mustafa usually arrived at the office between 7:00 and 7:15 and left between 6:30 and 7:00; he tried to be the first one in and the last out so that "things were never a rush." About

10–15 percent of his time was spent on matters that he handled himself, such as budgets, reviews of financial performance, and attendance at corporate meetings. Several hours each week were devoted to meeting with customers at Serengeti. The remaining time either was spent wandering around visiting with employees or was unscheduled free time.

Mustafa's employee visits were unstructured and seemingly random. Often, he simply arrived at the company cafeteria and sat down with whoever was there. At other times, he wandered the hallways, dropping in on people in their offices. Free time was even less programmed. Some was spent mulling over what he had heard on his visits—in his words, "letting the mind wander." As much as two hours a day was spent reading, usually newspapers and business journals from around the world. And some time was spent indulging his interests in flying, tennis, and other recreations. Mustafa strove for a balanced life and drew a sharp distinction between a hard worker and a workaholic. He commented, "Make sure you have some free time, and be comfortable with it. There's a busyness problem for many managers. A balanced life is possible, providing you don't take pride in a full calendar, lots of phone calls, and back-to-back meetings."

THE NEW PRODUCT LINE DECISION

For several years Serengeti had been exploring the idea of a higher-volume product. Young people aged 18–24 were a special target because the company currently had no products aimed specifically at them. Yet as a group they represented 24 percent of all purchases in the $25–$49.99 price segment and 27 percent of purchases in the $50–$74.99 segment.

Moreover, at the $75 price point there were few competitive offerings, and a leading sunglass chain had observed, "The first one who does something branded with this market wins." The proposed product line fit this niche. It had emerged in late 1992 from casual discussions between Lapp and a friend at Corning laboratories.

Lapp had raised the idea of developing a cheaper, fixed-tint lens; the scientist had responded by saying that he was working on "something better." He and his group had already created a test lens that blocked 100 percent of ultraviolet (UV) rays. (Most existing glass lenses met the national standard of 95 percent UVA protection; 100 percent UVA blockage, however, was technologically difficult for glass.) The new manufacturing process was likely to result in sunglasses with a suggested retail price of approximately $80. And while the lens was neither photochromic nor polarized, it was distinctive in an important respect. By operating at a point on the spectrum that scientists call "neutral C," it offered completely undistorted color.

The proposed new product, tentatively called Eclipse, would be positioned as "Earth-friendly." The technology, on which Serengeti would hold exclusive rights, would also be marketed slightly differently. Research suggested that young people were less interested in the traditional Serengeti technologies of photochromic lenses and spectral control but were far more concerned that their sunglasses block 100 percent of UV rays. In addition, they seemed to like the idea of "natural color." Stone observed:

> The biggest challenge now is coming up with a technology story. We don't offer "me-too" products. So we need to find a scientist with imagination, just like we

did with Drivers and Vermilion [another Serengeti product], to help us tell the story that explains why the lens is great. Our sales force needs one, and I feel comfortable that we can sell young people on performance. After all, they buy high-tech sneakers and high-tech stereo equipment, and they're better at computers than we are. As long as you meet their primary needs of style and price, it'll be fine.

Bausch and Lomb, of course, was certain to react to Eclipse. At the moment, there was limited direct competition between the two companies, mostly between high-end Ray-Bans and discounted Drivers. Yet Bausch and Lomb had already decided, in response to competition, to raise its advertising budget from a reported $2.7 million in 1992 to $7 million in 1993. Stone predicted, "They will try to use price as a blocking tool, offering retailers heavy promotions and price specials on basic Ray-Bans like Wayfarers." But she added:

> If we test Eclipse at the largest retail chains, and they have had a hand in designing the product, they'll be much harder to move. Nobody wants to see their baby killed. That's why our retail chains, which have a one-third share of the high-end business, will play such a big role in the development of the new line.

Mustafa, however, remained concerned about the product's risks. He feared that "neutral C" might not provide a compelling sales advantage and that the company's technology reputation might be undermined as a result. Cannibalization was a worry as well. Drivers, Serengeti's leading seller, carried a list price of $130, but could be found discounted for substantially less. Mustafa feared that Eclipse might hurt its sales. Perhaps most troubling were the organizational implications. Would Serengeti's approach to business succeed in the medium-priced market? Or was it appropriate only for competition as a high-end specialist?

There was an even deeper concern. What would happen if the new line failed? Since 1985 Serengeti had earned considerable latitude from corporate management because of its continued growth and profitability. Mustafa knew he had the authority to make the Eclipse decision without seeking approval from Corning management. But would Serengeti be able to maintain its independence if it suffered a major financial reversal? The opportunity, Mustafa knew, was enormous, but was Eclipse worth the risk?

EXHIBIT 1
1993 U.S. SUNGLASSES MARKET SHARES (UNITS)

	Total Sunglasses Bought At:			
	$25–$49.99 %	$50–$74.99 %	$75+ %	All Categories, $25 and above
Ray-Ban	39	48	28	38
Oakley	8	16	16	13
Vuarnet	5	9	10	7
Serengeti	3*	5*	14	7
Designer	14	8	12	11
Other/don't know	31	14	20	24

Source: Merltat research.

*Serengeti's sales at these price points reflect heavy discounting by retailers, usually for special promotions.

EXHIBIT 2
FINANCIAL SUMMARY ($ IN MILLIONS)

	1985	1986	1987	1988	1989	1990	1991	1992
Sales	$5.0	$11.0	$19.0	$32.5	$45.0	$38.7	$52.3	$62.0
Contribution	−3.0	−0.9	2.5	4.7	7.9	3.4	9.6	10.1
ROE%*	−104%	−56%	−7%	10%	23%	−6%	39%	37%

Source: Company records.

*To compute the equity of its divisions, Corning used the following calculations:

Operating assets = inventory + net fixed assets @ book value (including precious
        metals) + accounts receivable − accounts payable
        (12% of sales) ± goodwill

Corning assets = operating assets − minority assets

Total equity = operating equity (60% of Corning assets) + investment in equity
        companies − minority interest in equity

EXHIBIT 3
ORGANIZATION CHART

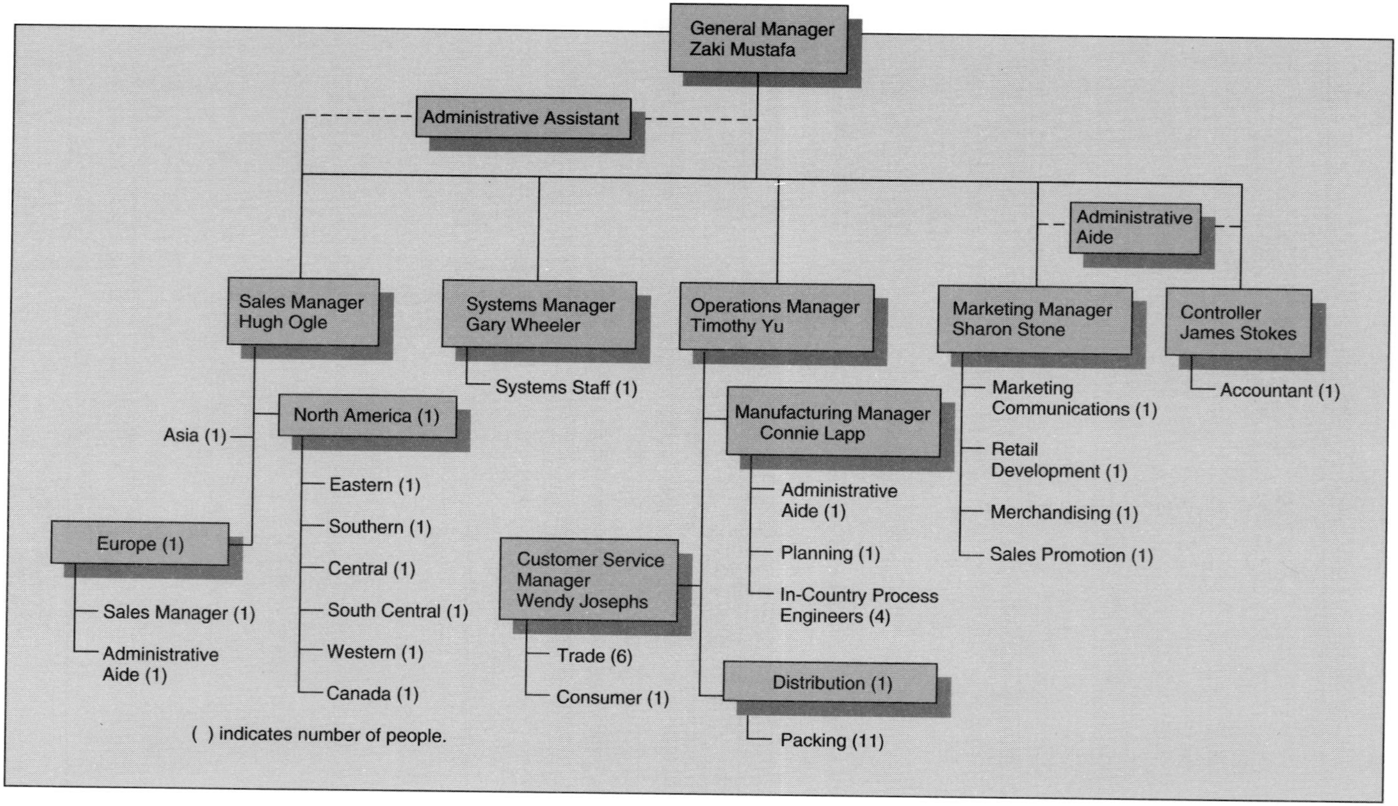

General Manager
Zaki Mustafa

Administrative Assistant

Administrative Aide

Sales Manager
Hugh Ogle

Systems Manager
Gary Wheeler

Systems Staff (1)

Operations Manager
Timothy Yu

Marketing Manager
Sharon Stone

Controller
James Stokes

Accountant (1)

Marketing Communications (1)

Retail Development (1)

Merchandising (1)

Sales Promotion (1)

Manufacturing Manager
Connie Lapp

Administrative Aide (1)

Planning (1)

In-Country Process Engineers (4)

Distribution (1)

Packing (11)

Customer Service Manager
Wendy Josephs

Trade (6)

Consumer (1)

North America (1)

Eastern (1)

Southern (1)

Central (1)

South Central (1)

Western (1)

Canada (1)

Asia (1)

Europe (1)

Sales Manager (1)

Administrative Aide (1)

( ) indicates number of people.

Source: Company records.

EXHIBIT 4
SERENGETI ADVERTISING

Exhibit 4   Serengeti Advertising

EXHIBIT 5
"WHAT I TAUGHT THE HARVARD BUSINESS SCHOOL"

In 1992 Zaki Mustafa attended the Harvard Business School's Advanced Management Program. On his return, Technical Products Division staff organized a dinner and presented him with a book, "What I Taught the Harvard Business School," which contained a collection of "Zaki-isms." The following are excerpts:

On Boston:	There is no place like home. Home is where the heart is. Boston does not qualify.
Harvard Business School:	. . . is where you go when you have a 50 percent ROE budget and you don't have any idea how to get there.
	or . . . when the five-year plan needs to be done.
Cases:	. . . should have executive summaries so you don't have to read the stupid things.
Customers:	. . . is where you go when there's a:

      • staff meeting
      • staff trip
      • quality trip
      • KRI discussion
      • strategy setting meeting
      • period review
      • quarterly review
or . . .
      • TO GET SALES

On winning:	Winning isn't everything but it sure beats losing.
	Without victory there is no survival.
	Win without risk, triumph without glory.
On American business:	American business thrives on organizational change:

      • Restructuring
      • Centralization
      • Decentralization
But as long as American business rewards style over substance, its erosion is likely to continue.

On people:	I'd rather have terrifically talented people with no product than a terrific product with no people, because people can improvise.
On caring:	Caring about issues means we see ourselves as forces for change and improvement.
The radical heart:	The *radical heart* keeps us focused on a vision of the future . . . on the opportunity, not the risk, of finding out what is possible.
	The *radical heart* wishes to be practical but is willing to live on the frontier with its danger and is of the belief that human beings have only begun to reach their potential.

EXHIBIT 6
CORNING EMPLOYEE SATISFACTION SURVEYS

In January 1990 Corning conducted a wide-ranging Climate Survey to assess employees' views of the workenvironment. The following is a selection of the results for all divisions in the Technical Products group, including Serengeti:

	Total Tech Products	Advanced	Materials	Optical	LA/AP	Serengeti
Organizational outcomes						
Overall effectiveness	84*	81	87	88	75	86
General satisfaction	67	55	75	79	50	76
Work satisfaction	79	77	88	82	68	79
Pay satisfaction	48	41	52	69	21	49
Working conditions	63	70	48	49	67	90
Training satisfaction	66	59	70	65	63	62
Benefits satisfaction	51	74	50	73	40	24†
Intent to stay	61	59	65	69	38	73
Job security	61	59	65	68	42	74
Organizational culture						
Market sensitivity	66	51	61	74	64	78
Innovativeness	72	54	84	74	62	71
Capacity to act	57	41	56	68	46	65
Total quality‡	65	62	69	74	68	46
Openness	65	55	66	58	61	65
Intergroup cooperation	54	43	53	60	45	65
Valuing diversity	67	51	81	69	63	60
Corning values						
Total quality	72	61	67	73	67	89
Integrity	77	78	81	73	63	83
Performance	78	78	74	70	72	94
Leadership	65	52	45	73	58	92
Technology	74	65	64	80	63	94
Independence	79	64	79	87	66	94
The individual	61	48	57	63	39	78

Source: Company records.

*Percent of employees expressing favorable view.

†Serengeti was the only business to include the corporate union group in its survey. Union benefits were negotiated at the corporate level, not the business level.

‡Refers to the use and application of Corning's quality system, policies, and tools.

Chapter 1

■

What Is Strategy?

INTRODUCTION

Perhaps no abstract business concept has been so widely accepted as the concept of *strategy*—the idea that a company ought to have goals and a plan for how and why they will be achieved. The concept of corporate strategy was first defined in the early 1960s by Kenneth Andrews as "the goals of the firm and the pattern of policies and programs designed to achieve those goals."[1] It is hard to imagine that in the early 1960s corporate strategy was a new idea. Military strategy had been discussed for many years, and strategy for games of various sorts was understood. But the idea that the management of a company would have a strategy or ought to have a strategy was novel.

The late development of the idea is easier to understand if we remember that companies themselves are relatively recent inventions. Craftsmen belonged to guilds that more or less regulated how their functions ought to be performed. Others in commerce, like trappers, fishermen, or traders, were adventurers of sorts. Bankers were often agents of one crown or another. Those that were not at least government sponsored were suspect and often at risk unless they had one form or another of protection. In the United States the first joint stock companies were set up in the early 19th century as government-chartered monopolies to accomplish a purpose, such as building and operating a turnpike or a canal. Almost everywhere, family was the key economic unit.

---

[1] Kenneth R Andrews, *A Concept of Corporate Strategy* (Homewood, IL: Irwin, 1967). The text was first published in the first edition of this casebook in 1964. The Andrews definition follows from the business historian Alfred D Chandler, Jr., who introduced this notion of strategy in order to explain the need of major corporations to change their structure dramatically.

Economists wrote about companies as if they had no discretion. Steel companies made steel and that was all there was to it. The idea that there were choices to be made in markets, products, and processes received little attention. Indeed, any room that management had to choose how to configure, price, or distribute products was conceived as imperfection in the markets that gave company management the opportunity to develop and exploit monopoly power.

To most people, the economists' view is exactly how business appeared. A pharmacy might be more conveniently located than another; the cooking at one restaurant might be better than another; and one shoemaker might be more skilled than another; but within a geographic region, businesses were local proprietorships with little variation in range of goods carried, menu, or product features.

With the advent of large markets, now-legendary entrepreneurs built the great industrial and commercial enterprises that shaped modern industrial economies. In *The Visible Hand*, Alfred D. Chandler, Jr., chronicled the development of companies with the resources to invest in differentiated approaches to serving customers. In Ohio, Rockefeller used new refinery technology to build a vast petroleum-based empire. Independent refiners in Pennsylvania fought back, building a pipeline across the Alleghenies to exploit the economies of a tidewater location. Henry Ford exploited the economies of mass production, turning the Model T into an icon symbolizing the start of the automobile age. In turn Alfred Sloan, Jr., and Pierre DuPont used product innovation to provide consumers with a steadily improving automobile. Woolworth built a national chain of local general stores. The Rosenwalds used the catalog to build Sears.

The records of these companies show management working systematically to think through what their purposes ought to be and how to achieve them. It is not that company executives spent all or even most of their time devoted to such seminal issues. But many leaders devoted important attention to such questions, and the consequences of getting strategy right were dramatic. On the other hand, some 30 years of the first half of the 20th century were spent in economic boom or depression or at war. We can imagine that getting goods out the door or survival were the two main modes of operation during most of that time.

There is an important point here to which we return in later chapters. Beginning with Henry Mintzberg, management scholars have noted that when one watches chief executives, they do not spend a lot of their time making strategy, or even planning.[2] They are constantly engaged in

---

[2] Henry Mintzberg, "The Manager's Job: Folklore and Fact," *Harvard Business Review*, July–August 1975, pp. 49–61. See also Wrapp, "Good Managers Don't Make Policy Decisions," *Harvard Business Review*, September–October 1967, pp. 91–99.

talking with people, usually about day-to-day matters of the business. Other scholars led by Jeffrey Pfeffer and William Salancik have built a school of thought called *resource dependence* that describes management as substantially unable to affect change in the fortunes of their companies because they are completely dependent on whether rapidly changing markets will reward them with success.[3]

Both Mintzberg and the resource dependence theorists would suggest that the pattern of logical relationships that we are calling corporate strategy is something that is found after the fact. They see the orderly explanation of policies and programs in the service of goals as retrospective rationalization—something that is at best learned over time. In fact, managements do build strategy step by step. We examine the process in Chapter 5. But the concept of strategy plays many roles in general management, and we need to know what it is before we think about building it.

Let's return to the story of how the concept of strategy was developed. It was apparent from hundreds of case studies that when management in most companies did consider the future, the normal mode of thinking was what one might call long-range planning. Attempts were made to forecast the demand for products, and on that basis investments were made in productive capacity. Among larger companies, it was common to have an economics department that sought to tie estimates of national or global economic growth to developments of importance to a particular industry. For example, Armstrong Tile used macroeconomic analysis to estimate how swings in the housing cycle would affect the demand for roofing and flooring materials, while General Motors attempted to manage inventories of cars and trucks using the same kind of data.

The problem was that planning of this sort seemed to have limited use in steering the long-term fortunes of individual companies. The Linde division of Union Carbide had a dominant position in industrial gases (oxygen and nitrogen for chemical and steel makers), but the Air Products company made steady inroads in their business.[4] The makers of manual typewriters all recognized that their competitor IBM had a wonderful growing business in computers. With the advice of the best bankers and management consultants, they all entered the computer industry and destroyed their companies. In the farm equipment industry, John Deere was successful while Massey-Ferguson and J. I. Case failed. There had to

[3] Jeffrey Pfeffer and William Salancik, *The External Control of Organizations: A Resource Dependence Perspective* (New York: Harper & Row Publishers, 1978). See also I Dierx and K Cool, "Asset Stock Accumulation and Sustainability of Competitive Advantage," *Management Science* 35, pp. 1504–1511, 1989; and W Wernerfelt, "A Resource-Based View of the Firm," *Strategic Management Journal* 5, pp. 171–180, 1984.

[4] "Air Products and Chemicals," Harvard Business School Case #9-375-370.

be something other than economic forecasts and long-range plans to explain such dramatic contrasts in company experiences.

In fact, when one stopped to ask why one company in an industry performed better than another, one thing was clear: In addition to the capabilities of the people and factories, some companies had positioned themselves in relation to suppliers, customers, and competitors far better than others. In the first industry study made from this perspective, Kenneth Andrews noted that some Swiss watch companies were doing very well while others faltered.[5] The U.S. typewriter, tire, and farm equipment industries yielded similar findings.[6] The specific mix of goals, policies, and programs and the allocation of resources to serve those programs gave one company an advantage over competitors that was significant and long-lasting and in that sense was strategic.

The source of that advantage could be broad or narrow. The Air Products company, for example, had turned a weakness into a strength. As a small, technology-based entrant in a large industry, they lacked the financial strength to build facilities based on their own balance sheet. Instead, they built oxygen plants to serve the then-new basic oxygen-process steel producers on the sites of the steel plants and leased them to the steel companies. The leases in turn provided top-rated collateral against which Air Products could borrow. In a final twist, Air Products oversized these facilities and used the marginal-cost product that was beyond the needs of the steel manufacturer to penetrate the rich merchant gas market. With a conventional balance sheet of two-thirds equity and conventional costs, it took Union Carbide many years to work through how Air Products was competing and then to devise a response based on its own strengths.

A good strategy is often hard for competitors to recognize. In the late 1950s TIMEX introduced an inexpensive pin-lever watch to compete with fine jeweled watches made in the United States and Switzerland.[7] Because the watch was cheap and welded shut and because there was very little margin and no service income, it was of no interest to jewelers, the main channel of distribution for watches. In order to get distribution, TIMEX found and used drugstore chains that were happy to have higher-priced goods to sell. And in order to create awareness of their product and its sturdy qualities, TIMEX turned to TV advertisement in ways no watch had ever been displayed. Divers in Acapulco and race-horses were used to show that "TIMEX took a lickin' and kept on tickin'."

---

[5] Kenneth R Andrews, *Problems of General Management* (Homewood, IL: Irwin, 1961).

[6] Norm Berg, William Guth, and Seymour Tilles developed these series. Later Tilles would use his research as one of the founders and principal researchers at the Boston Consulting Group.

[7] "Timex, Inc.," Harvard Business School Case #9-373-080.

For the manufacturers of a jeweled watch, the pin-lever product with its mass merchandiser distribution and TV ads was a joke. The entire Swiss industry as well as American standards such as Hamilton were in very serious trouble before they even recognized that they faced formidable competition.

We see the same phenomenon again and again. The American Big Three car producers seemed unable to understand the significance of the Volkswagen Beetle and later the Japanese at the small-car end of the market. By the time they recognized the importance of the changes in the profile of demand and in manufacturing process, they had lost a third of the U.S. market.

IBM commanded as much as three-quarters of the world's markets for mainframe computers. IBM management responded late but effectively to Digital's development of the minicomputer and Apple's introduction of the desktop computer. But IBM failed to see how the steadily increasing power and decreasing cost of the microprocessor would transform the information systems market in ways that would permit Intel and Microsoft to emerge as dominant players despite the fact that IBM possessed in its own labs the technical strength to lead.

What can it mean that managers of outstanding companies miss major competitive moves just because the source of the thrust is an entrant with a new concept? How can it be that small cars were misunderstood? Did they forget Henry Ford?

STRATEGY DEFINED

The concept of corporate strategy was developed to help managers think about questions of this magnitude. Strategy has to do with the life and death of firms. Whatever is precedent setting, has a major impact, or affects the values and goals of a firm is strategic.

Let us reexamine Andrews's definition of corporate strategy as "the goals of the firm and the pattern of policies and programs designed to achieve those goals." In this sense every firm has a strategy to the extent that its behavior is guided by some purpose. Whether the strategy is explicit and sound are entirely different but very important questions.

In order to identify the strategy of a firm we need to answer a series of questions about products and processes.

> Over the long term, what is the firm trying to accomplish?
>
> What are the products and services that the firm sells?
>
> To which markets does it sell them?
>
> What is the operational model of the firm?
>
> What is the economic model?

What are its principal functional policies?

- R&D
- Production
- Marketing
- Sales
- Finance

What are its principal management policies?

- Organization
- Information
- Personnel
- Planning
- Resource allocation

From a competitive perspective, which capabilities of the firm are of distinctive importance in the sense that they are important to customers and distinct relative to competitors?

While it may be difficult to answer these questions, most of them are clear. Two need some development.

By the *operational model of the firm* we mean the activities in which it has chosen to engage. In effect, where the firm begins, where it ends, and how it adds value are choices that management must make. For example, Nike designs athletic footware, even performing R&D, but does not own factories. It adds value through skillful design, sourcing, marketing, distribution, and coordination of these functions. In contrast, Honda adds value through great design and manufacturing skill. They are master manufacturers.

By the *economic model of the firm* we mean the relationship among price, variable costs, fixed costs, and the balance sheet. Firms differ widely in their gross margins, their operating profits, their asset turnover, and their financing. Some combinations are much more problematic than others. For example, a firm in the fashion business that does not enjoy high gross margins but invests heavily in fixed assets is at substantial risk. In the late 1970s Burlington Mills invested heavily in a vast automated factory to make denim for the fashion jeans that everyone was wearing. As world capacity expanded and price competition increased, gross margins shrank. Then when fashion turned, Burlington found itself with far too large a plant to run.

On the basis of the answers to these questions it is possible to identify the strategy of a company. As we discuss in Chapter 2, this type of industry and competitor analysis is an extremely useful management exercise. But it is also a good exercise for students learning how to use the concept of strategy. Indeed, the appropriate first step in preparing the cases in this section is to answer the questions and try to summarize the strategy in one paragraph.

By way of example, it is interesting to consider the Heublein company, a manufacturer of food and beverages whose principal product in 1975 was Smirnoff vodka. A business policy case study of the company was prepared prior to its acquisition by R. J. Reynolds at a time when Heublein was considering the purchase of the Hamm's brewery. A student prepared the following summary of Heublein strategy:

> Heublein aims to market in the United States and via franchise overseas a wide variety of high-margin, high-quality consumer products concentrated in the liquor and food business, especially bottled cocktails, vodka, and other special-use and distinctive beverages and specialty convenience foods, addressed to a relatively prosperous, young-adult market and returning over 15 percent of equity after taxes. With emphasis on the techniques of consumer goods marketing [brand promotion, wide distribution, product representation in more than one price segment, and very substantial offbeat advertising directed closely to its growing audience], Heublein intends to make Smirnoff the number one liquor brand worldwide via internal growth [and franchise] or acquisitions or both. Its manufacturing policy rather than full integration is in liquor to redistill only to bring purchased spirits up to high-quality standards. It aims to finance its internal growth through the use of debt and its considerable cash flow and to use its favorable price–earnings ratio for acquisitions. Both its liquor and food distribution are intended to secure distributor support through advertising and concern for the distributor's profit.

It is highly unlikely that such a statement existed within Heublein. But in this rather dense, infelicitous paragraph (that still tells us nothing about the human side of Heublein or its values) we learn a great deal about how Heublein intends to grow, how it operates, and the shape of its economics—enough to make us wonder whether a low-margin, down-market product like Hamm's beer could possibly fit. It might have helped Heublein management to prepare such a document.

Explicit Strategy   Managers and researchers often find that when they ask the executives of a particular company for a statement of their strategy, there is "no there there." As we guessed with Heublein, it is not common for companies to try to compress their objectives in a short comprehensive summary. (Oddly enough, since the concept of corporate strategy became popular, it is the security analysts who have adopted the practice. Many find it a useful way of communcating their understanding of a company's strategy to their readers.) Beyond some vague generalization that might apply to many other companies, there is no sharp ends–means identifying statement of objectives and policy.

A company in many businesses may find it difficult to explain how it is trying to succeed except by "maximizing value for the shareholder serving customers using the technical and managerial skills of our outstanding teams of women and men." What corporate strategy is for a business in a single industry and what it might be versus strategy for a diversified firm is a profound issue addressed later in the chapter.

On the other hand, some firms take strategy very seriously and confine their thinking to a limited circle of top executives. For firms such as these, an explicit strategy is a contradiction in terms. They keep their strategic intentions in the narrowest circle, even preferring to be thought of by outsiders as not possessing a strategy.

Even where there is an explicit statement of strategy, some like Mintzberg would suggest that it is not a careful, forward-thinking statement of intent. Rather, such a strategy statement rationalizes past actions in a way that clarifies and makes sense of corporate history so that members of the company can act in the future in a manner that is consistent with the past formula for success. Mintzberg calls this *emergent strategy*, reflecting its origins in the unfolding history of the firm, in contrast to *intended strategy*, which is the product of more or less rational analysis of appropriate purpose.[8]

Based on his studies of the role of systems in 20 large companies, Robert Simons argues that strategy does function as emergent doctrine. He describes its function as a *boundary system* in the sense that rather than making clear to managers where they should be headed, strategy defines boundaries excluding activities that are inappropriate because they lie outside broad arenas defined as within the corporation's mission.[9]

For the management of still other firms, a statement of strategy is not so much an articulation of the logic of corporate purpose as it is a rallying cry designed to point the dispersed efforts of a large group in a particular direction. It is the vision. Several Japanese companies have used strategic objectives in this way. Kawai of Komatsu (the Japanese earth-moving equipment company) urged his organization to "Maru C!"—surround Caterpillar. And Canon chose "beat Leica" as its early objective.

C. K. Prahalad and Gary Hamel use the phrase "strategic intent" to capture the use of strategy in this role. Prahalad and Hamel argue that for

[8] Henry Mintzberg, "Of Strategies, Deliberate and Emergent," *Strategic Management Journal*, pp. 257–272 (1985).

[9] Robert Simons, "Strategic Orientation and Top Management Attention to Control Systems," *Strategic Management Journal* 12, no. 1 (January 1991) pp. 49–62.

a general manager, strategy has to be seen in this light. In turbulent environments, it is impossible to develop strategic plans in any detailed sense that is useful to the members of a large corporation. Indeed, a detailed top-down prescription would be more likely to interfere with the ability of corporate subunits to devise imaginative responses to competitive moves and environmental shifts.

Hiro Itami has provided a compelling analysis of strategic action in a company to explain this result. Itami argues that in an age where technology and capital are highly mobile, a company's most valuable assets are invisible. They are knowledge the company has of its markets and how to apply technology, the knowledge markets have of the company and how it performs (reputation), and the knowledge embedded in the organization of how to link technological capability and market knowledge. Itami argues that the central task of management is to build these knowledge-based capabilities of the organization. This building is accomplished by undertaking tasks that stretch the organization—that go beyond "fit." This dynamic strategic process is constrained by any framework for planning and analysis that boxes activities inside some logical explicit framework. (In this line of thought, Hamm's might have been right for Heublein *if* its management wanted to develop the new set of capabilities required to succeed in the lower end of the beer market.)

A final source of confusion in the use of the language of strategy is that a very popular use of *strategy* is based on still another perspective. Michael Porter has introduced the idea of *competitive strategy*, which he defines as the "*ends* (goals) for which a firm is striving and the *means* (policies) by which it is seeking to get there." As he notes, this definition actually rephrases Andrews. What has made Porter's analysis so popular is that having adopted a broad definition of strategy it then narrows focus on the economic dimensions of strategy, providing for the reader a powerful framework for analyzing industry and competitive forces. We examine this framework in the next chapter.

At this stage, you may be wondering, "What on earth am I supposed to learn if all these distinguished academics cannot agree on how to use the same words?" If you take the perspective of a general manager you need not worry. As long as you know what you are doing, you can use the concept of strategy to identify the approach of a competitor based on its past moves, to clarify the strengths and weaknesses of your own company by identifying emergent strategy, to test the detailed logic of your own intentions working closely with a few key colleagues, to work out in further detail the economic game plan for a particular business, or to provide a rallying cry that gives a sense of meaning and direction to the entire organization.

Strategy is a logic of ends and means. It can be applied retrospectively and prospectively, in detail or in general. Its use can inspire or demoralize an organization. These ideas are developed in Chapters 2, 3, and 5. But we can begin to understand how and why this is true if we turn to the question "Is the strategy sound?"

Sound Strategy

Strategic thinking reveals core propositions about a company in a way that makes it obvious how they should be tested. At its essence, a sound strategy must be internally consistent and congruent with its environment.

Internal Consistency. Imagine a runner who planned to prepare for a world-class marathon with months of heavy drinking and smoking. We would be deeply suspicious as to his or her true intent or degree of sanity. The same kind of test is appropriate when we are assessing the soundness of corporate strategy, and the same kinds of conclusions can be drawn. For years, auto manufacturers thought it normal to pursue demanding quality objectives at the same time that antagonistic relations were pursued with the UAW union and that significant portions of factory floor space were set aside to repair the predictable defects from the line. Similarly, teleretailers that sought to achieve the image of friendly service rewarded their sales representatives on the number of calls processed in an hour. In both cases, personnel policies were not consistent with product policy.

Another important element, beyond the test of whether extant policies are internally consistent, involves the basic matter of whether the company has the full complement of resources to undertake its objective, and if it does not, whether it sees the building of the requisite capability as an element of the strategy. While it may be surprising, companies often embark on ventures while lacking critical capabilities. The quixotic efforts of the mechanical typewriter companies to follow their mastery of keyboards into electronic computers is a transparently silly example. But there are more subtle examples. In the same industry, RCA and GE both developed successful lines of computers and entered the industry, but failed to recognize that the market that IBM had shaped leased their machines rather than bought them. As a consequence, the proceeds of a sale were only realized over several years. For cash-rich IBM, this was no problem, but the financial demands of success were more than RCA or GE wanted to deal with given the need for cash of their other businesses.

As the computer example suggests, it is not always easy to see which capabilities will be key. In the 1970s, the consumer products group of Union Carbide was a powerhouse with important brands such as Prestone antifreeze, Glad plastic products, and Eveready batteries. As the leading producer of many of the ingredients used in disposable diapers, Union

Carbide thought it natural to turn this production and marketing capability to the rich market that Procter & Gamble had developed with Pampers. Market tests of the product and powerful advertisements gave early indications that the venture would be successful. What Carbide had not understood was that making a disposable diaper was a demanding mechanical process requiring capabilities far different from those they had developed in the manufacture of chemicals and plastics. P&G was a master of such processes and as a consequence incurred far lower costs than Carbide. Despite their success in the market, Carbide had to withdraw.

Environmental Consistency.   Equally important to the soundness of a strategy is the validity of the environmental analysis on which it is based. In a sense, Union Carbide's mistake was to misunderstand the strength of a competitor. But companies also stumble strategically because they misunderstand their market. The capabilities that they apply to the business are not appropriate to meet customer needs.

An intriguing example of this problem is provided by the entry of the petrochemical divisions of oil companies into the fertilizer business during the 1970s. From a production and cost side, analysis revealed that giant integrated oil companies had a clear advantage in the production of ammonia fertilizer over traditional agricultural chemical companies. And the post-1973 oil crisis revenues gave them plenty of financial resources to invest. Several, such as Gulf Oil, built large state-of-the-art facilities to manufacture ammonia fertilizer. What they did not understand was the behavior of their customers. Farmers want to put fertilizer on their fields at a particular moment, perhaps within a one-week period when the season and the weather are precisely right. That means that in a particular region of the country, one years' sales have to be delivered ready for application in a very short period. During that period, the distribution system has little time for sleep. Companies such as Gulf found that the distribution problem—so unlike gasoline or even polyethylene—was far beyond what their managers could cope with. They exited the business with substantial losses.

These stories of capable giants failing illustrate how vital to a successful strategy is the understanding of the particular set of capabilities required by a particular market opportunity. They complement the stories demonstrating the importance of congruent internal policies and programs. Together they make the point that strategy is about fit among the many elements of a firm's activities and between the firm and its environment. Despite differences in language and beliefs concerning the ability to influence environmental circumstances, managers and scholars all agree that long-term success is always associated with this kind of strategic fit. This book is concerned with the role general managers play and the skills they apply in making that fit happen.

In making it happen the concept of strategy plays three roles. To begin, it defines the idea of *market opportunity*. In a similar way it permits sorting out which of a *corporation's capabilities* are critical to success. And perhaps most importantly, a well-conceived and articulated strategy gives members of the organization a clear understanding of the *mission and values* that guide their diverse activities. In large companies with businesses all over the geographic and product map, this clarity of purpose permits the kind of delegation necessary for people to be involved in and enthusiastic about their jobs.

A STRATEGIC VIEW OF MARKET OPPORTUNITY

An absolutely essential idea underlying the concept of corporate strategy is that the same markets pose different opportunities for individual companies. As we have already seen in the introduction, in the market for athletic footwear, Nike and Reebok were offering different product concepts. Similarly, while Apple and IBM may both have been active in the market for personal computers, they were selling very different products. The nature of the opportunity depended upon what each company and its management brought to the endeavor.

Another example makes the point clearer. To understand why tiny Canon could successfully attack giant Xerox's hold on the copier market in Japan, it is not enough to know that the demand for small copiers was great because the inability of computer keyboards to deal with kanji meant most documents were still handwritten. Equally important was establishing why Canon might fulfill that demand better than Xerox using capabilities available to Canon. Xerox had built its position serving the high-volume needs of corporations for multiple copies of substantial documents. Their marketing, sales, and distribution staff focused on the needs of corporate document centers. Canon conceived that there would be a big demand for small copiers that could be located near each group of desks in an office if, independent of Xerox patents, they could develop a plain paper technology copier with a small footprint based on Canon skills in optics and miniaturization and new skills with chemical processing. This line of thinking might have been wrong, but it was specific to Canon and could be tested by measuring size, cost, and quality objectives against Canon capabilities.

The cases presented here contain many unusual definitions of opportunities. Linda Mason and Roger Brown saw theirs in the arena of child care. In the United States in the 1980s the prevalence of working mothers meant there was obviously a need for child care. But they defined opportunity quite narrowly in terms of high-quality teachers and facilities that, in turn, required a particular kind of financing for their centers. At

Microsoft, Bill Gates saw opportunity in the ability of outstanding operating system software to capture the value added in the information processing industry. And at The Body Shop, Anita Roddick saw opportunity in her ability to develop or imitate traditional cosmetic products based on natural ingredients.

A strategic definition of opportunity is not merely a recognition of the existence of a lot of potential customers. It goes further by defining a group of customers that can be served well relative to competitors using core skills of the company. Strategy is a hypothesis about how the company can serve customers, given its ability to perform in a specified way. And like all good science, strategies are revised and improved as experience provides direction.

A STRATEGIC VIEW OF CAPABILITIES

The second role of strategy is to define the competencies of a company in terms of market need. As opposed to inward-looking inventories of skills that an organization might possess, a strategic view measures the resources of a company against the needs of customers and the strengths of competitors. The idea of defining opportunity in terms of competence, then, is mirrored in the definition of competence in terms of opportunity. Whether a company possesses "competence" is determined by competitors and customers, not internal assessments.

This specificity and action orientation is reflected in the way managerial discussions about strategy have moved from the somewhat passive language of "corporate resources" to the currently popular phrase "core competences." Whereas the latter refers to those capabilities of the firm that are critical to its strategic success, resources evokes more of an inventory. This distinction may seem like just words, but for a general manager, it is all-important. Knowing what skills are key helps greatly in knowing where to invest. The shift of focus from assets and resources to competence or capability also tends to shift focus outward to the ability of the organization to use tangible or intangible resources in satisfying customer needs. This shift is important because capabilities tend to reside in the organization, its practices, and its people, rather than in balance sheet assets that are easily acquired in the market.[10]

This change in the way words have been used to discuss the "inside the company" part of strategic analysis reflects important research and thinking during the last decade. Although the formulations of strategic

---

[10] A powerful analysis of the strategic dynamics of capability is provided in Hiroyuki Itami, *Managing Invisible Assets*, Harvard University Press, Chapter 1 and passim.

analysis were usually correct in the sense that they allowed for the possible importance of almost any factor of production, a review of writing from the 1960s suggests that the ability to manufacture and deliver products and services was given far less emphasis than it would be today. It is a clear exaggeration to say that "operations weren't strategic," but they did not get a lot of attention. Discussions of strategy emphasized the difficulty of figuring out *what* to do, not *how* to do it.

In fact, careful studies of manufacturing during the early 1980s revealed huge differences in cost and yield across facilities within the *same* companies.[11] The spread of "best practice" campaigns reflects the appreciation for this finding among management. In the same period, consultants at the Boston Consulting Group were among the first to focus on the time companies took for operating activities and new product development.[12] They found that as much as 95 percent of the time it took between a customer order and delivery was waiting. Activities that took months could be reduced to days. In terms of better customer service and lower inventories these changes were strategic—not merely good operations. The differences in new product introductions were even more dramatic. Fast-cycle innovators such as Toyota and Honda took as much as two years less than their U.S. and European counterparts to develop new car models. A decade of such differences meant that the cars offered by competitors were no longer comparable products, independent of price.

This greater understanding of the strategic significance of organizational capabilities has transformed the way we manage companies. The problems general managers face in developing specific capabilities are addressed directly in Chapters 6 and 7 of this book. For the present, we need to focus on how to understand what we mean by competence or resource or capability when we try to identify the strategy of a firm.

In the 1950s, the sociologist Philip Selznick developed the idea of "distinctive competence."[13] Based on his in-depth studies of organizations as varied as the Soviet Commintern and the TVA, he noted that in the life of any organization particular events shaped its fundamental character in a manner analogous to the development of personality in an individual. It was not merely that skills were developed. Values that

---

[11] Robert H Hayes, Steven C Wheelwright, and Kim B Clark, *Dynamic Manufacturing* (New York: Free Press, 1988).

[12] George Stalk and Thomas Hout, *Competing Against Time: How Time-Based Competition Is Reshaping Global Markets* (New York: Free Press, 1990). See also Joseph L Bower and Thomas Hout, "Fast Cycle Capability for Competitive Power," *Harvard Business Review*, November 1988.

[13] Philip Selznick, *Leadership in Administration: A Sociological Interpretation* (Berkeley: University of California Press, 1984).

influenced how these skills would be applied also emerged. The success of leaders depended on undertaking activity that exploited the historically shaped distinctive competence.

One could use this idea to explain many intriguing business developments. For example, in the decade before Tom Watson, Jr., took over IBM and led the development of its formidable technical capabilities, IBM was able to hold share in the information system markets of the early 1950s on the basis of its sales force's strength—its scale, commitment, and understanding of the needs of its customers. Long before marketers had coined the phrase, IBM's sales force was "selling solutions" to the information problems of corporate customers using dated electronic accounting machines while competitors such as Sperry Rand were selling computers (that most customers could not use). Understanding the commercial data processing needs of their customers was a distinctive competence of IBM.

At Harvard Business School, where the authors work, our predecessors saw the importance of teaching about management by simulating the process of management problem solving in the classroom using cases. How we teach is what we teach. Cases have evolved from executives in the classroom, to printed documents that were no more than short descriptions of a difficulty at a company, to carefully constructed exercises that use video, computers, and role playing by competing teams to portray the challenges facing particular managers. Using "the case method" is a distinctive competence of our school, and we build on it to serve aspiring managers everywhere.

What Selznick saw was that leaders had to understand the distinctive competence of their organization so that the missions they undertook were congruent with the tasks that could be performed well. The TVA, for example, had been established to bring hydroelectric power and income support for farmers in the Tennessee Valley. In order to move forward, important alliances were made with the local Farm Bureaus dominated by the large farmers. These in turn provided powerful supporters in the Department of Agriculture and among the farm bloc in Congress. But because income redistribution was low on the agenda of these supporters, the TVA was successful only in the development of electric power.

Later, IBM would find that it had to develop new competences in microprocessors and software in order to deal with developments of the 1980s. It appears that IBM had no problem building wonderful new skill centers but had great difficulty in incorporating those capabilities into the body of understanding that shaped the strategic perspective of the company. Its distinctive competence changed more slowly than its skills. There are those who assert that the inability of its top management to loosen the grip of the descendants of that great commercial sales organization on the strategic decisions of the company was at the heart of its loss in profitability at the end of that decade.[14]

We can see this same lesson played out in the unsuccessful efforts of other companies to respond to change in their environment. The profitability of Sears, Roebuck operations in the 1960s and 1970s, for example, was built in large measure on the ability of their well-trained sales force to "trade customers up" from the "good" products advertised in the newspapers to the "better" and "best" products shown on the floor. But this represented a high-cost format that was very difficult to modify when K-Mart and Walmart—the super discounters—brought leading brands at low prices to the new malls. With Sears apparently unclear on what to sell, the distinctive capability of their sales force was strategically of less value.

STRATEGY AS A SUMMARY OF CORPORATE VALUES

The consequences of the obsolescence of Sears strategy are recounted in *The Big Store*.[15] What is so striking is the loss of focus in the organization. As Sears's leadership explored the challenge of managing a financial services conglomerate, the company somehow lost its soul. The merchants of Sears were unclear of their mission and how they fit just at the time that new competitive formats were provoking changes in customer behavior.

> "We are facing up to the new realities of the American market," (Sears CEO) Telling said. . . . In considering the way Telling had "stunned the financial community" by snapping up (stockbroker) Dean Witter and (real estate broker) Coldwell Banker, *The New York Times* wondered if the move meant that Sears had "run up against a growth ceiling in its retail business."
>
> After a year of busting themselves up and trying to do better, many a Headquarters and Field merchant had to admit that he knew what Ed Telling meant by the new realities. The Sears American . . . was headed for extinction. Maybe what the experts had to say was true. Maybe the day of the big general store was over.[16]

What this change in spirit illustrates is the role of strategy as a summary of corporate values. In a fundamental way, the strategy of an organization tells its members who they are and how they relate to the world around

---

[14] The discussion of Charles Ferguson and Charles Morris in *Computer Wars: How the West Can Win in a Post-IBM World* (New York: Times Books, 1993) provides a colorful description of the powerful role played by marketers in the mainframe computer group in blocking key software products.

[15] Donald R Katz, *The Big Store* (New York: Viking, 1987), chapter 16, pp. 324–326.

[16] *Ibid.*

them. The concept of corporate strategy, by linking how an organization functions with what it is trying to accomplish, provides a statement of identity that has far more than economic, analytic, or intellectual content.

- The ground staff and crew of Southwest Airlines know that they are part of an organization dedicated to speedy, friendly, spartan air travel at low cost. They know that they are uniquely profitable among airlines because of what they do as individuals, and it gives pleasure and meaning to their work.[17]

- The sales and assistants and "till operators" at Britain's great retailer, Marks & Spencer, know that they are the front line of the leading provider of retail value in the country. Their job includes identifying shoddy merchandise and taking it off the floor as well as making credit judgments about customers.

- The workers on the factory floor of Lincoln Electric put their personal stamp on the welding machinery they produce. They express pride at being part of a very hardworking, high-quality organization.

- When Johnson & Johnson was faced with the Tylenol crisis (some mad individual had found a way to put poison in some of the bottles), their strategy, as reflected in their corporate credo, provided the organizing principles that guided action around the world as their far-flung organization implemented the decision to take the affected product off the market.

Strategy is critical as a summary of values because the scale and scope of the modern corporation makes it extremely difficult for the leadership to communicate regularly with employees concerning how business should be done. Under such circumstances, it is easy for a company to become a consortium or even a galleria in which the only unifying theme is money, and colleagues become rivals. General managers know that they must rely on the judgment of thousands who are dealing daily with suppliers, customers, regulators, and competitors. The standards of performance that influence the behavior of these members determine the reputation of the company in the markets and in the community, and thereby how the members feel about themselves. Those standards can be made clear and important through the strategy of the company.

The centrality of values in business is not a new phenomenon. Certainly there were always owners and managers who recognized the power of a good reputation and a committed workforce. The founders of

---

[17] "Southwest Airlines," Harvard Business School case #9-694-023. See also James L Heskett, W Earl Sasser, and Leonard Schlesinger, *Service Breakthroughs: Changing the Rules of the Game* (New York: Free Press, 1990).

Procter & Gamble, the Singer Company, and International Harvester built their empires on a reputation for quality. Jobs at IBM and Kodak meant lifetime employment with good benefits, training, and a supportive work environment. But business also encompassed unrestrained economic warfare with National Cash Register salesmen taking axes to the products of the competition, Colorado Fuel & Iron using dynamite on rivals' camps, and U.S. Steel using private militia to break the steelworkers' union. And recent times reveal no end to the steady drumbeat of fraud in banking, copyright theft, software piracy, and day-to-day "sharp dealing."

General managers have recognized that the values of the organization, as embodied in the strategy and reflected in the work environment, function as the "software" of the organization, providing purposive influence as powerful as the traditional "hardware" such as the economic portfolio, the organization chart, measurement and information systems, and compensation. This recognition is a somewhat mixed blessing, for it is miserably difficult to manage the values of an organization and virtually impossible to recover once the internal or external constituencies of the organization believe that the expression or use of values is hypocritical. It is also difficult to deal with the many contradictory imperatives to which a modern company must respond. The responsibilities to owners, employees, customers, and community are seldom congruent, especially for a multinational corporation. We address these issues in chapters 3 and 4.

For now we turn to the somewhat easier task of reconciling economic demands in the formulation of strategy. To do that we have to look very carefully at the structure of industry and the behavior of competitors.

■

Crown Cork & Seal in 1989

John J. Connelly, Crown Cork & Seal's ailing octogenarian chairman, stepped down and appointed his longtime disciple, William J. Avery, chief executive officer of the Philadelphia can manufacturer in May 1989. Avery had been president of Crown Cork & Seal since 1981 but had spent the duration of his career in Connelly's shadow. As Crown's new CEO, Avery planned to review Connelly's long-followed strategy in light of the changing industry outlook.

The metal container industry had changed considerably since Connelly took over Crown's reins in 1957. American National had just been acquired by France's state-owned Pechiney International, making it the world's largest beverage can producer. Continental Can, another long-standing rival, was now owned by Peter Kiewit Sons, a privately held construction firm. In 1989 all or part of Continental's can-making operations appeared to be for sale. Reynolds Metals, a traditional supplier of aluminum to can makers, was now also a formidable competitor in cans. The moves by both suppliers and customers of can makers to integrate into can manufacturing themselves had profoundly redefined the metal can industry since John Connelly's arrival.

Reflecting on these dramatic changes, Avery wondered whether Crown, with $1.8 billion in sales, should consider bidding for all or part of Continental Can. Avery also wondered whether Crown should break with tradition and expand its product line beyond the manufacture of metal cans and closures. For 30 years Crown had stuck to its core business, metal can making, but analysts saw little growth potential for metal cans in the l990s. Industry observers forecast plastics as the growth segment for containers. As Avery mulled over his options, he asked, Was it finally time for a change?

THE METAL CONTAINER INDUSTRY

The metal container industry, representing 61 percent of all packaged products in the United States in 1989, produced metal cans, crowns (bottle caps), and closures (screw caps, bottle lids) to hold or seal an almost endless variety of consumer and industrial goods. Glass and plastic containers split the balance of the container market with shares of 21 percent and 18 percent, respectively. Metal cans served the beverage, food, and general packaging industries.

Metal cans were made of aluminum, steel, or a combination of both. Three-piece cans were formed by rolling a sheet of metal, soldering it, cutting it to size, and attaching two ends, thereby creating a three-piece, seamed can. Steel was the primary raw material of three-piece cans, which were most popular in the food and general packaging industries. Two-piece cans, developed in the 1960s, were formed by pushing a flat blank of metal into a deep cup, eliminating a separate bottom, a molding process termed "drawn and ironed." While aluminum companies developed the original technology for the two-piece can, steel companies ultimately followed suit with a thin-walled steel version. By 1983, two-piece cans dominated the beverage industry, where they were the can of choice for beer and soft drink makers. Of the 120 billion cans produced in 1989, 80 percent were two-piece cans.

Throughout the decade of the 1980s, the number of metal cans shipped grew by an annual average of 3.7 percent. Aluminum can growth averaged 8 percent annually, while steel can growth fell to an average of 2.6 percent per year. The number of aluminum cans produced increased by almost 200 percent during the period 1980–1989, reaching a high of 85 billion, while steel can production dropped by 22 percent to 35 billion for the same period (see Exhibit 1).

Industry Structure

Five firms dominated the $12.2 billion U.S. metal can industry in 1989, with an aggregate 61 percent market share. The country's largest manufacturer—American National Can—held a 25 percent market share. The four firms trailing American National in sales were Continental Can (18 percent market share), Reynolds Metals (7 percent), Crown Cork & Seal (7 percent), and Ball Corporation (4 percent). Approximately 100 firms served the balance of the market

Pricing Pricing in the can industry was very competitive. To lower costs, managers sought long runs of standard items, which increased capacity utilization and reduced the need for costly changeovers. As a result, most companies offered volume discounts to encourage large orders. Despite persistent metal can demand, industry operating margins fell approximately 7 percent to roughly 4 percent between 1986 and 1989. Industry analysts attributed the drop in operating margins to (1) a 15 percent increase in aluminum can sheet prices at a time when most can makers had guaranteed volume prices that did not incorporate substantial cost increases; (2) a 7 percent increase in beverage can production capacity between 1987 and 1989; (3) an increasing number of the nation's major brewers producing containers in-house; and (4) the consolidation of soft drink bottlers throughout the decade. Forced to economize following costly battles for market share, soft drink bottlers used their leverage to obtain packaging price discounts.[1] Overcapacity and a shrinking customer base contributed to an unprecedented squeeze on manufacturers' margins, and the can manufacturers themselves contributed to the margin deterioration by aggressively discounting to protect market share. As one

---

[1]Salomon Brothers, *Beverage Cans Industry Report*, March I, 1990.

manufacturer confessed, "When you look at the beverage can industry, it's no secret that we are selling at a lower price today than we were 10 years ago."

Customers Among the industry's largest users were the Coca-Cola Company, Anheuser-Busch Companies, Inc., Pepsico Inc., and Coca-Cola Enterprises Inc. (see Exhibit 2). Consolidation within the soft drink segment of the bottling industry reduced the number of bottlers from approximately 8,000 in 1980 to about 800 in 1989 and placed a significant amount of beverage volume in the hands of a few large companies.[2] Since the can constituted about 45 percent of the total cost of a packaged beverage, soft drink bottlers and brewers usually maintained relationships with more than one can supplier. Poor service and uncompetitive prices could be punished by cuts in order size.

Distribution Due to the bulky nature of cans, manufacturers located their plants close to customers to minimize transportation costs. The primary cost components of the metal can included (1) raw materials at 65 percent; (2) direct labor at 12 percent; and (3) transportation at roughly 7.5 percent. Various estimates placed the radius of economical distribution for a plant at between 150 and 300 miles. Beverage can producers preferred aluminum to steel because of aluminum's lighter weight and lower shipping costs. In 1988, steel cans weighed more than twice as much as aluminum.[3] The costs incurred in transportmg cans to overseas markets made international trade uneconomical. Foreign markets were served by joint ventures, foreign subsidiaries, affiliates of U.S. can manufacturers, and local overseas firms.

Manufacturing Two-piece can lines cost approximately $16 million, and the investment in peripheral equipment raised the per-line cost to $20–25 million. The minimum efficient plant size was one line, and installations ranged from one to five lines. While two-piece can lines achieved quick and persistent popularity, they did not completely replace their antecedents—the three-piece can lines. The food and general packaging segment—representing 28 percent of the metal container industry in 1989—continued using three-piece cans throughout the 1980s. The beverage segment, however, had made a complete switch from three-piece to two-piece cans by 1983.

A typical three-piece can production line cost between $1.5 and $2 million and required expensive seaming, end-making, and finishing equipment. Since each finishing line could handle the output of three or four can-forming lines, the minimum efficient plant required at least $7 million in basic equipment. Most plants had 12 to 15 lines for the increased flexibility of handling more than one type of can at once. However, any more than 15 lines became unwieldy because of the need for duplication of set-up crews, maintenance, and supervision. The beverage industry's switch from three- to two-piece lines prompted many manufacturers to sell complete, fully operational three-piece lines "as is" for $175,000 to $200,000. Some firms shipped their old lines overseas to their foreign operations where growth potential was great, there were few entrenched firms, and canning technology was not well understood.

Suppliers Since invention of the aluminum can in 1958, steel had fought a losing battle against aluminum. In 1970,

---

[2]T. Davis, "Can Do: A Metal Container Update," *Beverage World* (June 1990): 34.

[3]J. J. Sheehan, "Nothing Succeeds Like Success," *Beverage World* (November 1988): 82.

steel accounted for 88 percent of metal cans, but by 1989 had dropped to 29 percent. In addition to being lighter, of higher, more consistent quality, and more economical to recycle, aluminum was also friendlier to the taste and offered superior lithography qualities. By 1989, aluminum accounted for 99 percent of the beer and 94 percent of the soft drink metal container businesses, respectively.

The country's three largest aluminum producers supplied the metal can industry. Alcoa, the world's largest aluminum producer with 1988 sales of $9.8 billion, and Alcan, the world's largest marketer of primary aluminum, with 1988 sales of $8.5 billion, supplied over 65 precent of the domestic can sheet requirements. Reynolds Metals, the second largest aluminum producer in the United States, with 1988 sales of $5.6 billion, supplied aluminum sheet to the industry and also produced about 11 billion cans itself.[4] Reynolds Metals was the only aluminum company in the United States that produced cans (see Exhibit 3).

Steel's consistent advantage over aluminum was price. According to The American Iron and Steel Institute in 1988, steel represented a savings of from $5 to $7 for every thousand cans produced, or an estimated savings of $500 million a year for can manufacturers. In 1988 aluminum prices increased an estimated 15 percent, while the lower steel prices increased by only 5 percent to 7 percent.

According to a representative of Alcoa, the decision on behalf of the firm to limit aluminum price increases was attributed to the threat of possible inroads by steel.[5]

Industry Trends

The major trends characterizing the metal container industry during the 1980s included (1) the continuing threat of in-house manufacture; (2) the emergence of plastics as a viable packaging material; (3) steady competition from glass as a substitute for aluminum in the beer market; (4) the emergence of the soft drink industry as the largest end user of packaging, with aluminum as the primary beneficiary; and (5) the diversification of, and consolidation among, packaging producers.

In-house Manufacture Production of cans at "captive" plants—those producing cans for their own company use—accounted for approximately 25 percent of the total can output in 1989. Much of the expansion in in-house manufactured cans, which persisted throughout the 1980s, occurred at plants owned by the nation's major food producers and brewers. Many large brewers moved to hold can costs down by developing their own manufacturing capabllity. Brewers found it advantageous to invest in captive manufacture because of high-volume, single-label production runs. Adolph Coors took this to the extreme by producing all their cans in-house and supplying almost all of their own aluminum requirements from their 130 million pound sheet rolling mill in San Antonio, Texas.[6] By the end of the

---

[4]Until 1985, aluminum cans were restricted to carbonated beverages because it was the carbonation that prevented the can from collapsing. Reynolds discovered that by adding liquid nitrogen to the can's contents, aluminum containers could hold noncarbonated beverages and still retain their shape. The liquid nitrogen made it possible for Reynolds to make cans for liquor, chocolate drinks, and fruit juices.

[5]L. Sly, "A 'Can-Do Crusade' by Steel Industry," *The Chicago Tribune* (July 3, 1988): 1.

[6]Merrill Lynch Capital Markets, *Containers and Packaging Industry Report*, March 21, 1991.

1980s, the beer industry had the capacity to supply about 55 percent of its beverage can needs.[7]

Captive manufacturing was not widespread in the soft drink industry, where many small bottlers and franchise operations were generally more dispersed geographically compared with the brewing industry. Soft drink bottlers were also geared to low-volume, multilabel output, which was not as economically suitable for the in-house can manufacturing process.

Plastics   Throughout the 1980s, plastics were the growth leader in the container industry with their share growing from 9 percent in 1980 to 18 percent in 1989. Plastic bottle sales in the United States were estimated to reach $3.5 billion in 1989, with food and beverage, buoyed by soft drinks sales, accounting for 50 percent of the total. Plastic bottles accounted for 11 percent of domestic soft drink sales, with most of their penetration coming at the expense of glass. Plastic's light weight and convenient handling contributed to widespread consumer acceptance. The greatest challenge facing plastics, however, was the need to produce a material that simultaneously retained carbonation and prevented infiltration of oxygen. The plastic bottle often allowed carbonation to escape in less than four months, while aluminum cans held carbonation for more than 16 months. Anheuser-Busch claimed that U.S. brewers expected beer containers to have at least a 90-day shelf life, a requirement that had not been met by any plastic can or bottle.[8] Additionally, standard produc-

tion lines that filled 2,400 beer cans per minute required containers with perfectly flat bottoms, a feature difficult to achieve using plastic.[9] Since 1987, the growth of plastics slowed somewhat apparently due to the impact on the environment of plastic packaging. Unlike glass and aluminum, plastics recycling was not a "closed loop" system.[10]

There were many small players producing plastic containers in 1988, often specializing by end use or geographic region. However, only seven companies had sales of over $100 million. Owens-Illinois, the largest producer of plastic containers, specialized in custom-made bottles and closures for food, health and beauty, and pharmaceutical products. It was the leading supplier of prescription containers, sold primarily to drug wholesalers, major drug chains, and the government. Constar, the second largest domestic producer of plastic containers, acquired its plastic bottle operation from Owens-Illinois, and relied on plastic soft drink bottles for about two-thirds of its sales. Johnson Controls produced bottles for the soft drink industry from 17 U.S. plants and six non-U.S. plants, and was the largest producer of plastic bottles for water and liquor. American National and Continental Can both produced plastic bottles for food, beverages, and other products such as

---

[7]Salomon Brothers Inc, *Containers/Packaging Beverage Cans Industry Report*, April 3, 1991.

[8]A. Agoos, "Aluminum Girds for the Plastic Can Bid," *Chemical Week* (January 16, 1985): 18.

[9]B. Oman, "A Clear Choice?" *Beverage World* (June 1990): 78.

[10]In response to public concern, the container industry developed highly efficient "closed loop" recycling systems. Containers flowed from the manufacturer, through the wholesaler/distributor, to the retailer, to the consumer, and back to the manufacturer or material supplier for recycling. Aluminum's high recycling value permitted can manufacturers to sell cans at a lower cost to beverage producers. The reclamation of steel cans lagged that of aluminum because collection and recycling did not result in significant energy or material cost advantages.

tennis balls (see Exhibit 4 for information on competitors).

Glass Glass bottles accounted for only 14 percent of domestic soft drink sales, trailing metal cans at 75 percent . The cost advantage that glass once had relative to plastic in the popular 16-ounce bottle size disappeared by the mid-1980s because of consistently declining resin prices. Moreover, soft drink bottlers preferred the metal can to glass because of a variety of logistical and economic benefits: faster filling speeds, lighter weight, compactness for inventory, and transportation efficiency. In 1989, the delivered cost (including closure and label) of a 12-ounce can (the most popular size) was about 15 percent less than that of glass or plastic 16-ounce bottles (the most popular size).[11] The area in which glass continued to outperform metal, however, was the beer category, where consumers seemed to have a love affair with the "long neck" bottle that would work to its advantage in the coming years.[12]

Soft Drinks and Aluminum Cans Throughout the 1980s, the soft drink industry emerged as the largest end user of packaging. In 1989, soft drinks captured more than 50 percent of the total beverage market. The soft drink industry accounted for 42 percent of metal cans shipped in 1989, up from 29 percent in 1980. The major beneficiary of this trend was the aluminum can. In addition to the industry's continued commitment to advanced technology and innovation, aluminum's penetration could be traced to several factors: (1) aluminum's weight advantage over glass and steel; (2) aluminum's ease of handling; (3) a wider variety of graphics options provided by multipack can containers; and (4) consumer preference.[13] Aluminum's growth was also supported by the vending machine market, which was built around cans and dispensed approximately 20 percent of all soft drinks in 1989. An estimated 60 percent of Coca-Cola's and 50 percent of Pepsi's beverages were packaged in metal cans. Coca-Cola Enterprises and Pepsi Cola Bottling Group together accounted for 22 percent of all soft drink cans shipped in 1989.[14] In 1980, the industry shipped 15.9 billion aluminum soft drink cans. By 1989, that figure had increased to 49.2 billion cans. This increase, representing a 12 percent average annual growth rate, was achieved during a decade that exprienced a 3.6 percent average annual increase in total gallons of soft drinks consumed and a 3.4 percent average annual increase in per capita soft drink consumption.

Diversification and Consolidation Low profit margins, excess capacity, and rising material and labor costs prompted a number of corporate diversifications and subsequent consolidations throughout the 1970s and 1980s. While many can manufacturers diversified across the spectrum of rigid containers to supply all major end use markets (food, beverages, and general packaging), others diversified into non-packaging businesses such as energy (oil and gas) and financial services.

Over a 20-year period, for example, American Can reduced its dependence on domestic can manufacturing, moving into totally unrelated fields such as insurance.

---

[11]N. Lang, "A Touch of Glass," *Beverage World* (June 1990): 36.
[12]Lang, "A Touch of Glass."

[13]U.S. Industrial Outlook, 1984–1990.
[14]The First Boston Corporation, *Packaging Industry Report*, April 4, 1990.

Between 1981 and 1986 the company invested $940 million to acquire all or part of six insurance companies. Ultimately, the packaging businesses of American Can were acquired by Triangle Industries in 1986, with the financial services businesses reemerging as Primerica. Similarly, Continental Can broadly diversified its holdings, changing its name to Continental Group in 1976 when can sales dropped to 38 percent of total sales. In the 1980s, Continental Group invested heavily in energy exploration, research, and transportation, but profits were weak and they were ultimately taken over by Peter Kiewit Sons in 1984.

While National Can stuck broadly to containers, it diversified through acquisition into glass containers, food canning, pet foods, bottle closures, and plastic containers. However, instead of generating future growth opportunities, the expansion into food products proved a drag on company earnings.

Under the leadership of John W. Fisher, Ball Corporation, a leading glass bottle and can maker, expanded into the high-technology market and by 1987 had procured $180 million in defense contracts. Fisher directed Ball into such fields as petroleum engineering equipment, photoengraving, and plastics, and established the company as a leading manufacturer of computer components.

Major Competitors in 1989

For over 30 years, three of the current five top competitors in can manufacturing dominated the metal can industry. Since the early 1950s, American Can, Continental Can, Crown Cork & Seal, and National Can held the top four rankings in can manufacturing. A series of dramatic mergers and acquisitions among several of the country's leading manufacturers throughout the 1980s served to shift as well as consolidate power at the top. Management at fourth-ranked Crown Cork & Seal viewed the following four firms as constituting its primary competition in 1989: American National Can, Continental Can, Reynolds Metals, and Ball Corporation. Two smaller companies—Van Dorn Company and Heekin Can—were strong competitors regionally (see Exhibit 5).

American National Can   Representing the merger of two former, long-established competitors, American National—a wholly owned subsidiary of the Pechiney International Group—generated sales revenues of $4.4 billion in 1988. In 1985, Triangle Industries, a New Jersey–based maker of video games, vending machines, and jukeboxes, bought National Can for $421 million. In 1986, Triangle bought the U.S. packaging businesses of American Can for $550 million. In 1988, Triangle sold American National Can (ANC) to Pechiney, S.A., the French state-owned industrial concern, for $3.5 billion. Pechiney was the world's third largest producer of aluminum and, through its Cebal Group, a major European manufacturer of packaging. A member of the Pechiney International Group, ANC was the largest beverage can maker in the world—producing more than 30 billion cans annually. With more than 100 facilities in 12 countries, ANC's product lines of aluminum and steel cans, glass containers, and caps and closures served the major beverage, food, pharmaceuticals, and cosmetics markets.

Continental Can   Continental Can had long been a financially stable container company; its revenues increased every year without interruption from 1923 through the mid-1980s. By the 1970s, Continental had surpassed American Can as the largest container company in the United States. The year 1984, however, represented a turning point in Continental's history when the company became an attractive takeover target. Peter Kiewit Sons Inc., a private construction firm in Omaha, Nebraska, purchased Continental Group for $2.75 billion in 1984. Under the diection of Vice Chairman Donald Strum, Kiewit dismantled Continental Group in an effort to make the operation more profitable. Within a year, Strum had sold $1.6 billion worth of insurance, gas pipelines, and oil and gas reserves. Staff at Continental's Connecticut headquarters was reduced from 500 to 40. Continental Can generated sales revenues of $3.3 billion in 1988, ranking it second behind American National. By the late 1980s, management at Kiewit considered divesting—in whole or in part—Continental Can's packaging operations, which included Continental Can USA, Europe, and Canada, as well as metal packaging operations in Latin America, Asia, and the Middle East.

Reynolds Metals   Based in Richmond, Virginia, Reynolds Metals was the only domestic company integrated from aluminum ingot through aluminum cans. With 1988 sales revenues of $5.6 billion and net income of $482 million, Reynolds served the following principal markets: packaging and containers; distributors and fabricators; building and construction; aircraft and automotive; and electrical. Reynolds's packaging and container revenue amounted to $2.4 billion in 1988. As one of the industry's leading can makers, Reynolds was instrumental in establishing new uses for the aluminum can and was a world leader in can-making technology. Reynolds's developments included high-speed can-forming machinery with capabilities in excess of 400 cans per minute, faster inspection equipment (operating at speeds of up to 2,000 cans per minute), and spun aluminum tops which contained less material. The company's next generation of can end-making technology was scheduled for installation in the early 1990s.

Ball Corporation   Founded in 1880 in Muncie, Indiana, Ball Corporation generated operating income of $113 million on sales revenues of $1 billion in 1988. Considered one of the industry's low-cost producers, Ball was the fifth largest manufacturer of metal containers as well as the third largest glass container manufacturer in the United States. Ball's packaging businesses accounted for 82.5 percent of total sales and 77.6 percent of consolidated operating earnings in 1988. Ball's can-making technology and manufacturing flexibility allowed the company to make shorter runs in the production of customized, higher-margin products designed to meet customers' specifications and needs. In 1988, beverage can sales accounted for 62 percent of total sales. Anheuser-Busch, Ball's largest customer, accounted for 14 percent of sales that year. In 1989, Ball was rumored to be planning to purchase the balance of its 50-percent-owned joint venture, Ball Packaging Products Canada, Inc. The acquisition would make Ball the number two producer of metal beverage and food containers in the Canadian market

Van Dorn Company   The industry's next two largest competitors, with a combined market share of 3 percent, were Van Dorn Company and Heekin Can, Inc. Founded in 1872 in Cleveland, Ohio, Van Dorn manufactured two product lines: containers and plastic injection molding equipment. Van Dorn was one of the world's largest producers of drawn aluminum containers for processed foods and a major manufacturer of metal, plastic, and composite containers for the paint, petroleum, chemical, automotive, food, and pharmaceutical industries. Van Dorn was also a leading manufacturer of injection molding equipment for the plastics industry. The company's Davies Can Division, founded in 1922, was a regional manufacturer of metal and plastic containers. In 1988, Davies planned to build two new can manufacturing plants at a cost of about $20 million each. These facilities would each produce about 40 million cans annually. Van Dorn's consolidated can sales of $334 million in 1988 ranked it sixth overall among the country's leading can manufacturers.

Heekin Can James Heekin, a Cincinnati coffee merchant, founded Heekin Can in 1901 as a way to package his own products. The company experienced rapid growth and soon contained one of the country's largest metal lithography plants under one roof. Three generations of the Heekin family built Heekin into a strong regional force in the packaging industry. The family sold the business to Diamond International Corporation, a large, diversified, publicly held company, in 1965. Diamond operated Heekin as a subsidiary until 1982, when it was sold to its operating management and a group of private investors. Heekin went public in 1985. With 1988 sales revenues of $275.8 million, seventh-ranked Heekin primarily manufactured steel cans for processors, packagers, and distributors of food and pet food. Heekin represented the country's largest regional can maker.

CROWN CORK & SEAL COMPANY

Company History

In August of 1891, a foreman in a Baltimore machine shop hit upon an idea for a better bottle cap—a piece of tin-coated steel with a flanged edge and an insert of natural cork. Soon this crown-cork cap became the hit product of a new venture, Crown Cork & Seal Company. When the patents ran out, however, competition became severe and nearly bankrupted the company in the 1920s. The faltering Crown was bought in 1927 by a competitor, Charles McManus.[15]

Under the paternalistic leadership of McManus, Crown prospered in the 1930s, selling more than half of the United States and world supply of bottle caps. He then correctly anticipated the success of the beer can and diversified into can making, building one of the world's largest plants in Philadelphia. However, at one million square feet and containing as many as 52 lines, it was a nightmare of inefficiency and experienced substantial losses. Although McManus was an energetic leader, he engaged in nepotism and never developed an organization that could run without him. Following his death in 1946, the company ran on momentum, maintaining dividends at the expense of investment in new plants. Following a disastrous attempt to expand into plastics and a ludicrous diversification in metal bird cages, Crown reorganized along the lines of the much larger Continental Can, incurring additional personnel and expense that again brought the company near to bankruptcy.

At the time, John Connelly was just a fellow on the outside, looking to Crown as a prospective customer and getting nowhere. The son of a Philadelphia blacksmith, Connelly had begun in a paperbox factory at 15, and worked his way up to become eastern sales manager of the Container Corporation of America. When he

---

[15]R. J. Whalen, "The Unoriginal Ideas That Rebuilt Crown Cork," *Fortune*, October 1962.

founded his own company, Connelly Containers, Inc., in 1946, Crown promised him some business. That promise was forgotten by the post-McManus regime, which loftily refused to "take a chance" on a small supplier like Connelly. By 1955, when Crown's distress became evident, Connelly began buying stock and in November 1956 was asked to be an outside director—a desperate move by the ailing company.[16]

In April 1957, Crown Cork & Seal teetered on the verge of bankruptcy. Bankers Trust Company withdrew Crown's line of credit; it seemed that all that was left was to write the company's obituary when John Connelly took over the presidency. His rescue plan was simple—as he called it, "just common sense." Connelly's first move was to pare down the organization. Paternalism ended in a blizzard of pink slips. Connelly moved quickly to cut headquarters staff by half to reach a lean force of 80. The company returned to a simple functional organization. In 20 months Crown had eliminated 1,647 jobs or 24 percent of the payroll. As part of the company's reorganization, Connelly discarded divisional accounting practices; at the same time he eliminated the divisional line and staff concept. Except for one accountant maintained at each plant location, all accounting and cost control were performed at the corporate level; the corporate accounting staff occupied one-half the space used by the headquarters group. In addition, Connelly disbanded Crown's central research and development facility.

The second step was to institute the concept of accountability. Connelly aimed to instill a deep-rooted pride of workmanship throughout the company by establishing Crown managers as "owner-operators" of their individual businesses. Connelly gave each plant manager responsibility for plant profitability, including any allocated costs. (All company overhead, estimated at 5 percent of sales, was allocated to the plant level.) Previously, plant managers had been responsible only for controllable expenses at the plant level. Although the plant managers' compensation was not tied to profit performance, one senior executive pointed out that the managers were "certainly rewarded on the basis of that figure." Connelly also held plant managers responsible for quality and customer service.

The next step was to slow production to a halt and liquidate $7 million in inventory. By mid-July Crown paid off the banks. Connelly introduced sales forecasting dovetailed with new production and inventory controls. This move put pressure on the plant managers, who were no longer able to avoid layoffs by dumping excess products into inventory.

By the end of 1957, Crown had, in one observer's words, "climbed out of the coffin and was sprinting." Between 1956 and 1961, sales increased from $115 million to $176 million and profits soared. Throughout the 1960s, the company averaged an annual 15.5 percent increase in sales and 14 percent in profits. Connelly, not satisfied simply with short-term reorganizations of the existing company, developed a strategy that would become its hallmark for the next three decades.

CONNELLY'S STRATEGY

According to William Avery, "From his first day on the job, Mr. Connelly structured the company to be successful. He took control of costs and did a wonderful job taking us in the direction of becoming

---

[16]R. J. Whalen, "The Unoriginal Ideas That Rebuilt Crown Cork," *Fortune* (October 1962): 156.

owner-operators." But what truly separated Connelly from his counterparts, Avery explained, was that while he was continually looking for new ways of controlling costs, he was equally hell-bent on improving quality. Connelly, described by *Forbes* as an individual with a "scrooge-like aversion to fanfare and overhead," emphasized cost efficiency, quality, and customer service as the essential ingredients for Crown's strategy in the decades ahead.

Products and Markets Recognizing Crown's position as a small producer in an industry dominated by American Can and Continental Can, Connelly sought to develop a product line built around Crown's traditional strengths in metal forming and fabrication. He chose to emphasize the areas Crown knew best—tin-plated cans and crowns—and to concentrate on specialized uses and international markets.

A dramatic illlustration of Connelly's commitment to this strategy occurred in the early 1960s. In 1960, Crown held over 50 percent of the market for motor oil cans. In 1962, R. C. Can and Anaconda Aluminum jointly developed fiber-foil cans for motor oil, which were approximately 20 percent lighter and 15 percent cheaper than the metal cans then in use. Despite the loss of sales, management decided that it had other more profitable opportunities and that new materials, such as fiber-foil, provided too great a threat in the motor oil can business. Crown's management decided to exit from the oil can market.

In the early 1960s Connelly singled out two specific applications in the domestic market: beverage cans and the growing aerosol market. These applications were called "hard to hold" because cans required special characteristics either to contain the product under pressure or to avoid affecting taste. Connelly led Crown directly from a soldered can into the manufacture of two-piece steel cans in the 1960s. Recognizing the enormous potential of the soft drink business, Crown began designing its equipment specifically to meet the needs of soft drink producers, with innovations such as two printers in one line and conversion printers that allowed for rapid design change-over to accommodate just-in-time delivery.[17] After producing exclusively steel cans through the late 1970s, Connelly spearheaded Crown's conversion from steel to aluminum cans in the early 1980s.

In addition to the specialized product line, Connelly's strategy was based on two geographic thrusts: expand to national distribution in the United States and invest heavily abroad. Connelly linked domestic expansion to Crown's manufacturing reorganization; plants were spread out across the country to reduce transportation costs and to be nearer customers. Crown was unusual in that it did not set up plants to service a single customer. Instead, Crown concentrated on providing products for a number of customers near their plants. In international markets, Crown invested heavily in developing nations, first with crowns and then with cans as packaged foods became more widely accepted. Metal containers generated 65 percent of Crown's $1.8 billion 1988 sales, while closures generated 30 percent and packaging equipment 5 percent.

Manufacturing When Connelly took over in 1957, Crown had perhaps the most outmoded and inefficient production fa-

---

[17]In the mid-1960s, growth in demand for soft drink and beer cans was more than triple that for traditional food cans.

cilities in the industry. Dividends had taken precedence over new investment, and old machinery combined with the cumbersome Philadelphia plant had generated very high production and transportation costs. Soon after he gained control, Connelly took drastic action, closing down the Philadelphia facility and investing heavily in new and geographically dispersed plants. From 1958 to 1963, the company spent almost $82 million on relocation and new facilities. From 1976 through 1989, Crown had 26 domestic plant locations versus nine in 1955. The plants were small (usually two to three lines for two-piece cans) and were located close to the customer rather than the raw material source. Crown operated their plants 24 hours a day with unique 12-hour shifts. Employees had two days on followed by two days off and then three days on followed by three days off.

Crown emphasized quality, flexibility, and quick response to customer needs. One officer claimed that the key to the can industry was "the fact that nobody stores cans" and when customers need them "they want them in a hurry and on time . . . Fast answers get customers." To accommodate rush orders, some of Crown's plants kept more than a month's inventory on hand. Crown also instituted a total quality improvement process to refine its manufacturing processes and gain greater control. According to a Crown spokesperson, "The objective of this quality improvement process is to make the best possible can at the lowest possible cost. You lower the cost of doing business not by the wholesale elimination of people, but by reducing mistakes in order to improve efficiency. And you do that by making everybody in the company accountable."

Recycling In 1970, Crown formed Nationwide Recyclers, Inc., as a wholly owned subsidiary. By 1989, Crown believed Nationwide was one of the top four or five aluminum can recyclers in the country. Whlle Nationwide was only marginally profitable, Crown had invested in the neighborhood of $10 million in its recycling arm.

Research and Development (R&D) Crown's technology strategy focused on enhancing the existing product line. As one executive noted, "We are not truly pioneers. Our philosophy is not to spend a great deal of money for basic research. However, we do have tremendous skills in die forming and metal fabrication, and we can move to adapt to the customer's needs faster than anyone else in the industry."[18] For instance, Crown worked closely with large breweries in the development of the two-piece drawn-and-ironed cans for the beverage industry. Crown also made an explicit decision to stay away from basic research. According to one executive, Crown was not interested in "all the frills of an R&D section of high-class, ivory-towered scientists . . . There is a tremendous asset inherent in being second, especially in the face of the ever-changing state of flux you find in this industry. You try to let others take the risks and make the mistakes . . ."

This phllosophy did not mean that Crown never innovated. For instance, Crown was able to beat its competitors into two-piece can production. Approximately $120 million in new equipment was installed from 1972 through 1975, and by 1976 Crown had 22 two-piece

---

[18]R. G. Hamermesh, M. J. Anderson, Jr., and J. E. Harris, "Strategies for Low Market Share Business," *Harvard Business Review* (May–June 1978): 99.

lines in production—more than any other competitor.[19] Crown's research teams also worked closely with customers on specific customer requests. For example studies of the most efficient plant layout for a food packer or the redesign of a dust cap for the aerosol packager were not unusual projects.

Marketing and Customer Service   The cornerstone of Crown's marketing strategy was, in John Connelly's words, the philosophy that "you can't just increase efficiency to succeed; you must at the same time improve quality." In conjunction with its R&D strategy, the company's sales force maintained close ties with customers and emphasized Crown's ability to provide technical assistance and specific problem solving at the customer's plant. Crown's manufacturing emphasis on flexibility and quick response to customer's needs supported its marketing emphasis on putting the customer first. Michael J. McKenna, president of Crown's North American Division, insisted, "We have always been and always will be extremely customer driven."[20]

In can manufacturing, service sells. Competing cans were made of identical materials to identical specifications on practically identical machinery, and sold at almost identical prices in a given market. At Crown, all customers' gripes went to John Connelly, who was the company's best salesman. A visitor recalled being in his office when a complaint came through from the manager of a Florida citrus-packing plant. Connelly assured him the problem would be taken care of immediately, then casually remarked that he would be in Florida the next day. Would the plant manager join him for dinner? He would indeed. As Crown's president put the telephone down, his visitor said that he hadn't realized Connelly was planning to go to Florida. "Neither did I," confessed Connelly, "until I began talking."[21]

Financing   After he took over in 1957, Connelly applied the first receipts from the sale of inventory to get out from under Crown's short-term bank obligations. He then steadily reduced the debt/equity ratio from 42 percent in 1956 to 18.2 percent in 1976 and 5 percent in 1986. By the end of 1988, Crown's debt represented less than 2 percent of total capital. Connelly discontinued cash dividends in 1956, and in 1970 repurchased the last of the preferred stock, eliminating preferred dividends as a cash drain. From 1970 forward, management applied excess cash to the repurchase of stock. Connelly set ambitious earnings goals, and most years he achieved them. In the 1976 annual report he wrote, "A long time ago we made a prediction that someday our sales would exceed $1 billion and profits of $60.00 per share. Since then, the stock has been split 20-for-1, so this means $3.00 per share." Crown Cork & Seal's revenues reached $1 billion in 1977, and earnings per share reached $3.46. Earnings per share reached $10.11 in 1988 adjusted for a 3-for-1 stock split in September 1988.

International   A significant dimension of Connelly's strategy focused on international growth, particularly in developing countries. Between 1955 and 1960, Crown received what were called "pioneer

---

[19]In 1976, there were 47 two-piece tinplate and 130 two-piece aluminum lines in the United States.

[20]*One Hundred Years,* Crown Cork & Seal Company, Inc.

[21]Whalen, "The Unoriginal Ideas That Rebuilt Crown Cork."

rights'' from many foreign governments aiming to build up the industrial sectors of their countries. These ''rights'' gave Crown first chance at any new can or closure business introduced into these developing countries. Mark W. Hartman, president of Crown's International Division, described Connelly ''as a Johnny Appleseed with respect to the international marketplace. When the new countries of Africa were emerging, for example, John was there offering crown-making capabilities to help them in their industrialization, while at the same time getting a foothold for Crown. John's true love was international business.''[22] By 1988, Crown's 62 foreign plants generated 44 percent of sales and 54 percent of operating profits. John Connelly visited each of Crown's overseas plants. (See Exhibit 6 for a map of plant locations.)

Crown emphasized national management wherever possible. Local people, Crown asserted, understood the local marketplace: the suppliers, the customers, and the unique conditions that drove supply and demand. Crown's overseas investment also offered opportunities to recycle equipment that was, by U.S. standards, less sophisticated. Because can manufacturing was new to many regions of the world, Crown's older equipment met the needs of what was still a developing industry overseas.

Performance Connelly's strategy met with substantial success throughout his tenure at Crown. With stock splits and price appreciation, $100 invested in Crown stock in 1957 would be worth approximately $30,000 in 1989. After restructuring the company in his first three years, revenues grew at 12.2 percent per year while income grew at 14.0 percent over the next two decades (see Exhibit 7). Return on equity averaged 15.8 percent for much of the 1970s while Continental Can and American Can lagged far behind at 10.3 percent and 7.1 percent, respectively. Over the period 1968–1978 Crown's total return to shareholders ranked 114 out of the *Fortune* 500, well ahead of IBM (183) and Xerox (374).

In the early 1980s, flat industry sales, combined with an increasingly strong dollar overseas, unrelenting penetration by plastics, and overcapacity in can manufacturing at home, led to declining sales revenues at Crown. Crown's sales dropped from $1.46 billion in 1980 to $1.37 billion by 1984. However, by 1985 Crown had rebounded and annual sales growth averaged 7.6 percent from 1984 through 1988 while profit growth averaged 12 percent (see Exhibits 8 and 9). Over the period 1978–1988 Crown's total return to shareholders was 18.6 percent per year, ranking 146 out of the *Fortune* 500. In 1988, *Business Week* noted that Connelly—earning a total of only $663,000 in the three years ending in 1987—garnered shareholders the best returns for the least executive pay in the United States. As an industry analyst observed, ''Crown's strategy is a no-nonsense, back-to-basics strategy—except they never left the basics.''[23]

John Connelly's Contribution to Success

Customers, employees, competitors, and Wall Street analysts attributed Crown's sustained success to the unique leadership of John Connelly. He arrived at

---

[22]*One Hundred Years,* Crown Cork & Seal Company, Inc.

[23]''These Penny-Pinchers Deliver a Big Bang for Their Bucks,'' *Business Week,* May 4, 1987.

Crown as it headed into bankruptcy in 1957, achieved a 1,646 percent increase in profits on a relatively insignificant sales increase by 1961, and proceeded to outperform the industry's giants throughout the next three decades. A young employee expressed the loyalty created by Connelly: "If John told me to jump out the window, I'd jump—and be sure he'd catch me at the bottom with a stock option in his hand."

Yet Connelly was not an easy man to please. Crown's employees had to get used to Connelly's tough, straight-line management. *Fortune* credited Crown's success to Connelly, "whose genial Irish grin masks a sober salesman executive who believes in the 80-hour week and in traveling while competitors sleep." He went to meetings uninvited and expected the same devotion to Crown of his employees as he demanded of himself. As one observer remembered:

> The Saturday morning meeting is standard operating procedure. Crown's executives travel and confer only at night and on weekends. William D. Wallace, vice president for operations, travels 100,000 miles a year, often in the company plane. But Connelly sets the pace. An associate recalls driving to his home in the predawn blackness to pick him up for a flight to a distant plant. The Connelly house was dark, but he spotted a figure sitting on the curb under a street light, engrossed in a loose-leaf book. Connelly's greeting as he jumped into the car: "I want to talk to you about last month's variances."[24]

Avery's Challenge in 1989

Avery thought long and hard about the options available to him in 1989. He considered the growing opportunities in plastic closures and containers, as well as glass containers. With growth slowing in metal containers, plastics were the only container segment that held much promise. However, the possibility of diversifying beyond the manufacture of containers altogether had some appeal, although the appropriate opportunity was not at hand. While Crown's competitors had aggressively expanded in a variety of directions, Connelly had been cautious and had prospered. Avery wondered if now was the time for a change at Crown.

Within the traditional metal can business, Avery had to decide whether or not to get involved in the bidding for Continental Can. The acquisition of Continental Can Canada (CCC)—with sales of roughly $400 million—would make Canada Crown's largest single presence outside of the United States. Continental's U.S. business—with estimated revenues of $1.3 billion in 1989—would double the size of Crown's domestic operations. Continental's Latin American, Asian, and Middle Eastern operations were rumored to be priced in the range of $100 million to $150 million. Continental's European operations generated estimated sales of $1.5 billion in 1989 and included a workforce of 10,000 at 30 production sites. Potential bidders for all or part of Continental's operations included many of Crown's U.S. rivals in addition to European competition: Pechiney International of France, Metal Box of Great Britain (which had recently acquired Carnaud SA), and VIAG AG, a German trading group, among others.

Avery knew that most mergers in this industry had not worked out well. He also thought about the challenge of taking two companies that come from completely different cultures and bringing them together. There would be inevitable emotional and attitudinal changes, particularly

---

[24]R. J. Whalen, "The Unoriginal Ideas That Rebuilt Crown Cork," *Fortune*, October 1962.

for Continental's salaried managers and Crown's "owner-operators." Avery also knew that the merger of American Can and National Can had its difficulties. That consolidation was taking longer than expected and, according to one observer, "American Can would be literally wiped out in the end."

Avery found himself challenging Crown's traditional strategies and thought seriously of drafting a new blueprint for the future.

EXHIBIT 1
METAL CAN SHIPMENTS BY MARKET AND PRODUCT, 1981–1989 (MILLIONS OF CANS)

	1981	%	1983	%	1985	%	1987	%	(Estab.) 1989	%
Total Metal Cans Shipped	88,810		92,394		101,899		109,214		120,795	
By market										
For sale:	59,433	67	61,907	67	69,810	69	81,204	74	91,305	76
Beverage	42,192		45,167		52,017		62,002		69,218	
Food	13,094		12,914		13,974		15,214		18,162	
General packaging	4,141		3,826		3,819		3,988		3,925	
For own use:	29,377	33	30,487	33	32,089	31	28,010	26	29,490	24
Beverage	14,134		16,289		18,160		14,711		17,477	
Food	15,054		14,579		13,870		13,167		11,944	
General packaging	189		171		59		72		69	
By product										
Beverage:	56,326	63	61,456	67	70,177	69	76,773	70	86,695	72
Beer	30,901		33,135		35,614		36,480		37,276	
Soft drinks	25,425		28,321		34,563		40,293		49,419	
Food:	28,148	32	26,941	29	27,844	27	28,381	26	30,106	25
Dairy products	854		927		1,246		1,188		1,304	
Juices	13,494		11,954		11,385		11,565		12,557	
Meat, poultry, seafood	2,804		3,019		3,373		3,530		3,456	
Pet food	3,663		3,571		4,069		4,543		5,130	
Other	7,333		7,470		7,771		7,555		7,659	
General packaging:	4,336	5	3,997	4	3,878	4	4,060	4	3,994	3
Aerosol	2,059		2,144		2,277		2,508		2,716	
Paint: varnish	813		817		830		842		710	
Automotive products	601		229		168		128		65	
Other nonfoods	863		807		603		582		503	
By materials used										
Steel	45,386	52	40,116	45	34,316	37	34,559	34	35,318	29
Aluminum	42,561	48	48,694	55	58,078	63	67,340	66	85,477	71

Source: *Can Shipment Report*, Can Manufacturers' Institute, 1981–1989.

EXHIBIT 2
TOP U.S. USERS OF CONTAINERS, 1989

Rank	Company	Soft Drink/ Beverage Sales ($000)	Principal Product Categories
1	The Coca-Cola Company* (Atlanta, GA)	$8,965,800	Soft drinks, citrus juices, fruit drinks
2	Anheuser-Busch Companies, Inc.[†] (St. Louis, MO)	7,550,000	Beer, beer imports
3	Pepsico Inc. (Purchase, NY)	5,777,000	Soft drinks, bottled water
4	The Seagram Company, Ltd. (Montreal, Quebec, Canada)	5,581,779	Distilled spirits, wine coolers, mixers, juices
5	Coca-Cola Enterprises, Inc.* (Atlanta, GA)	3,881,947	Soft drinks
6	Philip Morris Companies, Inc. (New York, NY)	3,435,000	Beer
7	The Molson Companies, Ltd. (Toronto, Ontario, Canada)	1,871,394	Beer, coolers, beer imports
8	John Labatt, Ltd. (London, Ontario, Canada)	1,818,100	Beer, wine
9	The Stroh Brewery Company[‡] (Detroit, MI)	1,500,000	Beer, coolers, soft drinks
10	Adolph Coors Company[§] (Golden, CO)	1,366,108	Beer, bottled water

Source: *Beverage World*, 1990–1991 Databank.

*The Coca-Cola Company and Coca-Cola Enterprises purchased (vs. in-house manufacture) all of its cans in 1989. Coca-Cola owned 49% of Coca-Cola Enterprises, the largest Coca-Cola bottler in the United States.

[†]In addition to in-house manufacturing at its wholly owned subsidiary (Metal Container Corporation). Anheuser-Busch Companies purchased its cans from four manufacturers. The percentage of cans manufactured by Anheuser-Busch was not publicly disclosed.

[‡]Of the 4.5 billion cans used by The Stroh Brewery in 1989, 39% were purchased and 61% were manufactured in-house.

[§]Adolph Coors Company manufactured all of its cans, producing approximately 10–12 million cans per day, five days per week.

EXHIBIT 3
COMPARATIVE PERFORMANCE OF MAJOR ALUMINUM SUPPLIERS (DOLLARS IN MILLIONS)

	Sales	Net Income	Net Profit Margin %	Long-Term Debt	Net Worth	Earnings Per Share
Alcan Aluminum						
1988	$8,529.0	$931.0	10.9%	$1,199.0	$4,320.0	$3.85
1987	6,797.0	445.0	6.5	1,336.0	3,970.0	1.73
1986	5,956.0	177.0	3.0	1,366.0	3,116.0	.79
1985	5,718.0	25.8	.5	1,600.0	2,746.0	.12
1984	5,467.0	221.0	4.0	1,350.0	2,916.0	1.00
ALCOA						
1988	9,795.3	861.4	8.8	1,524.7	4,635.5	9.74
1987	7,767.0	365.8	4.7	2,457.6	3,910.7	4.14
1986	4,667.2	125.0	2.7	1,325.6	3,721.6	1.45
1985	5,162.7	107.4	2.1	1,553.5	3,307.9	1.32
1984	5,750.8	278.7	4.8	1,586.5	3,343.6	3.41
Reynolds Metals*						
1988	5,567.1	482.0	8.7	1,280.0	2,040.1	9.01
1987	4,283.8	200.7	4.7	1,567.7	1,599.6	3.95
1986	3,638.9	50.3	1.4	1,190.8	1,342.0	.86
1985	3,415.6	24.5	.7	1,215.0	1,151.7	.46
1984	3,728.3	133.3	3.6	1,146.1	1,341.1	3.09

Source: *Value Line*

*Reynolds Metals Company is the second largest aluminum producer in the United States. The company is also the third largest manufacturer of metal cans with a 7 percent market share.

EXHIBIT 4
MAJOR U.S. PRODUCERS OF BLOW-MOLDED PLASTIC BOTTLES, 1989 (DOLLARS IN MILLIONS)

Company	Total Sales	Net Income	Plastic Sales	Product Code	Major Market
Owens-Illinois	$3,280	$(57)	$754	1,3,4,5	Food, health and beauty, pharmaceutical
American National	4,336	52	566	1,2,3,6	Beverage, household, personal care, pharmaceutical
Constar	544	12	544	1,2,3,4,6	Soft drink, milk, food
Johnson Controls	3,100	104	465	2	Soft drink, beverages
Continental Can	3,332	18	353	1,2,3,4,5,6	Food, beverage, household, industrial
Silgan Plastics	415	96	100	1,2,3,4,6	Food, beverage, household, pharmaceutical, personal care
Sonoco Products Co.	1,600	96	N/A	1,3,4,6	Motor oil, industrial

Source: *The Rauch Guide to the U.S. Plastics Industry, 1991*: company annual reports.
Product code: (1) HDPE; (2) PET; (3) PP; (4) PVC; (5) PC; (6) multilayer.

EXHIBIT 5
COMPARATIVE PERFORMANCE OF MAJOR METAL CAN MANUFACTURERS (DOLLARS IN MILLION)

Company*	Net Sales	SG&A as a % of Sales	Gross Margin	Operating Income	Net Profit	Return on Sales	Average Assets	Average Equity
Ball Corporation								
1988	$1,073.0	8.1%	$161.7	$113.0	$47.7	4.4%	5.7%	11.6%
1987	1,054.1	8.5	195.4	147.6	59.8	5.7	7.8	15.7
1986	1,060.1	8.2	168.0	150.5	52.8	5.0	7.6	15.2
1985	1,106.2	7.5	140.7	140.5	51.2	4.6	8.1	16.4
1984	1,050.7	7.9	174.1	123.9	46.3	4.4	7.8	16.6
1983	909.5	8.2	158.2	114.6	39.0	4.3	7.3	15.6
1982	889.1	8.4	147.4	100.5	34.5	3.9	6.9	15.8
Crown Cork & Seal								
1988	1,834.1	2.8	264.6	212.7	93.4	5.1	8.6	14.5
1987	1,717.9	2.9	261.3	223.3	88.3	5.1	8.7	14.5
1986	1,618.9	2.9	235.3	202.4	79.4	4.9	8.8	14.3
1985	1,487.1	2.9	216.4	184.4	71.7	4.8	8.6	13.9
1984	1,370.0	3.1	186.6	154.8	59.5	4.4	7.3	11.4
1983	1,298.0	3.3	182.0	138.9	51.5	4.0	6.2	9.3
1982	1,351.8	3.3	176.2	132.5	44.7	3.3	5.2	7.9
Heekin Can, Inc.								
1988	275.8	3.7	38.9	36.4	9.6	3.5	4.8	22.6
1987	230.4	4.0	33.6	30.2	8.8	3.8	5.8	26.3
1986	207.6	4.1	31.1	28.0	7.0	3.4	5.4	27.5
1985	221.8	3.2	31.8	29.0	6.8	3.1	5.2	42.5
1984	215.4	2.7	28.4	26.5	5.5	2.6	4.3	79.7
1983	181.6	3.2	24.4	22.8	3.8	2.1	3.3	102.7
1982†	—							
Van Dorn Company								
1988	333.5	16.5	75.3	26.7	11.7	3.5	6.6	12.2
1987	330.0	15.7	73.6	28.4	12.3	3.7	7.7	12.7
1986	305.1	16.3	70.4	26.5	11.7	3.8	7.7	12.9
1985	314.3	15.1	75.6	33.6	15.4	4.9	10.6	19.0
1984	296.4	14.7	74.9	36.5	16.8	5.7	12.9	24.9
1983	225.9	14.8	48.5	20.1	7.4	3.3	6.8	12.8
1982	184.3	16.1	37.7	12.7	3.6	2.0	3.5	6.6
American Can Company‡								
1985	2,854.9	22.6	813.4	1,670.0	149.1	5.2	5.2	10.9
1984	3,177.9	18.0	740.8	168.3	132.4	4.2	4.9	11.2
1983	3,346.4	15.0	625.4	123.6	94.9	2.8	3.5	9.7
1982	4,063.4	16.1	766.3	113.4	23.0	0.6	0.8	2.4
1981	4,836.4	15.0	949.6	223.0	76.7	1.2	2.7	7.2
1980	4,812.2	15.8	919.5	128.1	85.7	1.8	3.1	8.0
National Can Company§								
1983	1,647.5	5.1	215.3	93.5	22.1	1.3	2.7	6.3
1982	1,541.5	4.6	206.3	100.7	34.1	2.2	4.4	10.0
1981	1,533.9	4.6	191.7	86.3	24.7	1.6	3.1	7.5
1980	1,550.9	5.4	233.7	55.0	50.6	3.3	6.4	16.7
The Continental Group, Inc.‖								
1983	4,942.0	6.3	568.0	157.0	173.5	3.5	4.4	9.4
1982	5,089.0	6.4	662.0	217.0	180.2	3.5	4.3	9.6
1981	5,291.0	7.2	747.0	261.0	242.2	4.6	5.9	13.6
1980	5,171.0	7.2	700.0	201.0	224.8	4.3	5.5	13.7
1979	4,544.0	6.5	573.0	171.0	189.2	4.2	5.3	13.1

Source: *Value Line* and company annual reports (for SGA, COGS, and asset figures).

*Refer to Exhibit 3 for Reynolds Metals Company.

†Figures not disclosed for 1982.

‡In 1985, packaging made up 60% of total sales at American Can, with the remainder in specialty retailing. In 1986 Triangle Industries purchased the U.S. packaging business of American Can. In 1987, American National Can was formed through the merger of American Can Packaging and National Can Corporation. In 1989, Triangle sold American National Can to Pechiney, S.A.

§In 1985, Triangle Industries bought National Can.

‖In 1984, Peter Kiewit Sons purchased The Continental Group.

EXHIBIT 6
CROWN CORK & SEAL FACILITIES, 1989

EXHIBIT 7
CROWN CORK & SEAL COMPANY CONSOLIDATED STATEMENT OF INCOME
(DOLLARS IN MILLIONS, YEAR-END DECEMBER 31)

	1956	1961	1966	1971	1973	1975	1977	1979
Net Sales	$115.1	$177.0	$279.8	$448.4	$571.8	$825.0	$1,049.1	$1,402.4
Costs, expenses, and other income:								
Cost of products sold	95.8	139.1	217.2	350.9	459.2	683.7	874.1	1,179.3
Sales and administration	13.5	15.8	18.4	21.1	23.4	30.1	34.8	43.9
Depreciation	2.6	4.6	9.4	17.0	20.9	25.4	5.6	16.4
Net interest expense	1.2	1.3	4.6	5.1	4.4	7.4	31.7	40.1
Provision for taxes on income	.1	7.6	12.7	24.6	26.7	34.9	48.7	51.8
Net income	.3	6.7	16.7	28.5	34.3	41.6	53.8	70.2
Earnings per common share (actual)	(6.01)	.28	.80	1.41	1.81	2.24	3.46	4.65
Selected financial statistics								
Return on average equity	0.55%	9.66%	16.44%	14.05%	14.46%	15.20%	15.88%	15.57%
Return on sales	0.24	3.76	5.99	6.35	6.00	5.04	5.13	5.00
Return on average assets	0.32	6.00	6.76	7.25	8.00	7.69	9.13	8.93
Gross profit margin	16.76	21.43	22.37	21.76	19.69	17.13	16.68	15.90
Cost of goods sold/sales	83.24	78.57	77.63	78.24	80.31	82.87	83.32	84.29
SGA/sales	11.73	8.65	6.56	4.70	4.09	3.65	3.32	3.13

CROWN CORK & SEAL COMPANY CONSOLIDATED STATEMENT OF FINANCIAL POSITION
(DOLLARS IN MILLIONS, YEAR-END DECEMBER 31)

	1956	1961	1966	1971	1973	1975	1977	1979
Total current assets	$50.2	$66.3	$109.4	$172.3	$223.4	$265.0	$340.7	$463.3
Total assets	86.5	129.2	269.5	398.1	457.5	539.0	631.1	828.2
Total current liabilities	15.8	24.8	75.3	110.2	139.6	170.0	210.8	287.1
Total long-term debt	20.2	17.7	57.9	41.7	37.9	29.7	12.8	12.2
Shareholders' equity	50.3	77.5	110.8	211.8	243.9	292.7	361.8	481.0
Selected financial statistics								
Debt/equity	0.40	0.23	0.52	0.20	0.16	0.10	0.04	0.03
Capital expenditures	1.9	11.8	32.7	33.1	40.4	49.0	58.9	55.9
Book value per share of common stock	1.57	2.74	5.19	10.62	13.13	16.64	23.54	31.84

Source: Adapted from annual reports.

EXHIBIT 8
CROWN CORK & SEAL COMPANY CONSOLIDATED STATEMENT OF INCOME
(DOLLARS IN MILLION EXCEPT EARNINGS PER SHARE, YEAR-END DECEMBER 31)

	1981	1982	1983	1984	1985	1986	1987	1988
Net sales	$1,373.9	$1,351.9	$1,298.0	$1,369.6	$1,487.1	$1,618.9	$1,717.9	$1,834.1
Costs, expenses, and other income:								
Cost of products sold	1,170.4	1,175.6	1,116.0	1,172.5	1,260.3	1,370.2	1,456.6	1,569.5
Sales and administrative	45.3	44.2	42.9	42.1	43.0	46.7	49.6	50.9
Depreciation	38.0	39.9	38.4	40.2	43.7	47.2	56.9	57.2
Interest expense	12.3	9.0	9.0	8.9	12.2	6.2	8.9	10.0
Interest income	—	—	—	—	—	—	(15.2)	(14.8)
Total expenses	1,266.1	1,268.6	1,206.2	1,263.6	1,359.2	1,470.3	1,556.8	1,672.9
Income before taxes	107.8	83.2	91.8	105.9	127.9	148.6	161.1	161.2
Provision for taxes on income	43.0	38.5	40.2	46.4	56.2	69.2	72.7	67.8
Net income	64.8	44.7	51.5	59.5	71.7	79.4	88.3	93.4
Earnings per common share	1.48	1.05	1.27	1.59	2.17	2.48	2.86	3.37

Note: Earnings per common share have been restated to reflect a 3-for-1 stock split on September 12, 1988.

SELECTED FINANCIAL STATISTICS

	1981	1982	1983	1984	1985	1986	1987	1988
Return on average equity (%):	11.72%	7.94%	9.34%	11.42%	13.94%	14.34%	14.46%	14.45%
Return on sales	4.72	3.31	3.97	4.35	4.82	4.91	5.14	5.09
Return on average assets	7.38	5.19	6.20	7.31	8.58	8.80	8.67	8.61
Gross profit margin	14.81	13.04	14.03	14.39	15.25	15.36	15.21	14.42
Cost of goods sold/sales	85.19	86.96	85.97	85.61	84.75	84.64	84.79	85.58
SGA/sales	3.30	3.27	3.30	3.07	2.89	2.88	2.89	2.78
Net sales ($):								
United States	775.0	781.0	749.9	844.5	945.3	1,010.3	985.5	1,062.5
Europe	324.0	304.4	298.7	283.0	282.8	365.6	415.6	444.2
All others	283.6	273.1	259.1	261.3	269.3	269.0	342.5	368.6
Operating profit ($):								
United States	62.8	58.9	55.0	67.1	88.9	92.8	95.4	70.6
Europe	20.6	19.0	24.0	17.2	17.0	21.9	22.4	33.4
All others	40.0	37.3	33.1	38.3	40.6	39.6	64.9	66.1
Operating ratio (%):								
United States	8.1	7.5	7.3	7.9	9.4	9.7	9.6	6.6
Europe	6.3	6.2	8.0	6.0	6.0	5.9	5.4	7.5
All others	14.1	13.6	12.7	14.6	15.0	14.7	18.9	17.9

Source: Adapted from annual reports.

Note: The above sales figures are before the deduction of intracompany sales.

EXHIBIT 9
CROWN CORK & SEAL COMPANY CONSOLIDATED STATEMENT OF FINANCIAL POSITION
(DOLLARS IN MILLIONS, YEAR-END DECEMBER 31)

	1981	1982	1983	1984	1985	1986	1987	1988
Current assets:								
Cash	$ 21.5	$ 15.8	$ 21.0	$ 7.0	$ 14.8	$ 16.5	$ 27.6	$ 18.0
Accounts receivables	262.8	257.1	240.6	237.6	279.0	270.4	280.7	248.1
Inventory	206.2	184.4	170.2	174.6	171.9	190.1	228.1	237.6
Total current assets	490.6	457.3	431.7	419.2	465.6	477.0	536.4	503.8
Investments	12.4	14.6	26.7	28.8	41.5	43,7	NA	NA
Goodwill	11.2	10.8	9.6	10.3	11.8	14.1	16.7	16.5
Property, plant, and equipment	368.4	357.8	353.7	348.0	346.9	404.0	465.7	495.9
Other noncurrent assets	NA	NA	NA	NA	NA	NA	79.1	57.0
Total assets	882.6	840.6	821.7	806.4	865.8	938.8	1,097.9	1,073.2
Current Liabilities:								
Short-term debt	22.7	21.6	24.4	42.0	16.3	17.2	44.0	20.2
Accounts payable	193.0	165.6	163.1	177.9	197.1	220.1	265.9	277.6
U.S. and foreign taxes	17.3	4.7	11.4	6.0	11.4	11.3	28.4	23.3
Total current liabilities	233.0	191.9	198.8	225.8	224.8	248.5	338.2	321.2
Long-term debt	5.8	5.6	2.8	2.7	2.2	1.4	19.7	9.4
Other	14.5	18.5	12.8	15.8	31.2	29.3	0.0	0.0
Total long-term debt	20.3	24.1	15.6	18.5	33.5	30.7	19.7	9.4
Deferred income taxes	55.5	57.7	57.8	60.7	71.3	79.2	89.4	93.7
Minority equity in subsidiaries	7.2	7.2	5.2	3.7	4.7	3.8	5.0	0.9
Shareholders' equity	566.7	559.8	544.3	497.8	531.5	576.6	645.6	648.0
Liability and owners' equity	882.6	840.6	821.7	806.4	865.8	938.8	1,097.9	1,073.2

SELECTED FINANCIAL STATISTICS

	1981	1982	1983	1984	1985	1985	1987	1985
Debt/equity	1.02%	0.99%	0.51%	0.54%	0.42%	0.24%	3.06%	1.45%
Debt/(debt + equity)	3.5%	4.1%	2.7%	3.5%	6.0%	5.0%	3.0%	1.4%
Shares outstanding at year end (M)	14.5	14.0	13.2	11.5	10.5	10.0	9.5	27.0
Capital expenditures ($M)	$63.8	$50.3	$55.5	$53.8	$50.9	$94.0	$99.5	$102.6
Shares repurchased ($'000)	75.4	528.3	863.1	1,694.5	1,006.0	677.1	638.7	2,242.9
Stock price: High*	$12.00	$10.00	$13.00	$15.75	$29.62	$38.25	$46.87	$46.72
Stock price: Low*	$8.00	$7.00	$10.00	$11.75	$15.12	$25.25	$28.00	$30.00

Source: Adapted from annual reports.

*Restated for 9/1988 stock split.

Asahi Breweries, Ltd.

In mid-January 1989, president Hirotaro Higuchi of Asahi Breweries was faced with a major investment proposal. Implementation of the proposed investment plan would expand brewing and packaging capacity of Asahi up to 2,100,000 kiloliters per year in 1990 from the existing level of 880,000 kiloliters. The expansion would require investments of 100 billion and 130 billion yen in 1989 and 1990, respectively, to expand production capacity. (The 1988 year-end exchange rate stood at $1 = ¥125.) This plan would push the Japanese beer industry's total capacity up by 30 percent between 1987 and 1990 (assuming competitors' capacities remained at present levels). Exhibits 1, 2, 3, and 4 show details of the investment and associated profit plans as well as related financial data for Asahi.

Asahi Breweries and its president were two of the brightest lights of the Japanese business community in 1988. The company recorded a 71.9 percent beer sales volume increase in 1988 while the industry as a whole grew only 7.6 percent. This had pushed the company's market share from 10.5 percent to 20.6 percent between 1986 and 1988. Prior to Asahi's challenge, Japanese beer drinkers were said to be so brand loyal that the maximum market share gain for a company could only be around 1 percent per year. The dramatic shift in Asahi's market share, however, appeared to negate this presumption.

Asahi seemed to have created a social phenomenon. The "dry" taste concept that the company introduced with its "Super Dry" beer had such appeal to consumers that the competing beer manufacturers rushed to sell their own "dry" beers. Dry beer was a kind of draft beer that was fermented to a higher degree than ordinary beer. This gave it a lower sugar level, higher alcohol content, and subsequently, a "sharper" taste.

Prior to Asahi's introduction of dry beer, there were two major kinds of beer sold in Japan: one was the more traditional, richer tasting lager beer; the other was the steadily growing and lighter tasting draft beer. The two were quite similar in their production processes, except that lager beer was heat pasteurized at the end whereas draft was not. By this traditional definition, dry beer was merely a kind of draft beer. However, its growth and differentiated image were seemingly making it into an independent market segment.

Since long industry experience had shown that beer drinkers in Japan did not change their taste preferences very quickly, Asahi's decision to change the taste of its core product was considered an extremely risky proposition by most observers both inside and outside the industry. Not surprisingly, Asahi's initial success, based on its break with established beliefs and expectations, attracted wide attention.

Until 1986, Asahi Breweries was regarded as a marginal player, barely surviving in the highly concentrated beer industry. In 1985, the Japanese beer industry was dominated by the giant Kirin, holding over a 60 percent share. By 1985 Asahi had a 9.9 percent share and was a distant number three in the industry. It was considered only a matter of time before the company would be taken over by Suntory, a whiskey giant that entered the industry as a latecomer. The story of Asahi's success was thus one of a miraculous comeback by an underdog challenging the invincible giant.

The History of the Japenese Beer Industry and the Kirin Legacy

The Japanese beer industry began in the late 19th century. The industry was fragmented at the beginning but concentrated over the years. By the 1940s the industry had only two companies, Dai Nippon, which held roughly 75 percent of the market, and Kirin. Dai Nippon was essentially a group of companies with localized brands bound by common ownership.

During the second world war, emphasis was placed on supplying the soldiers fighting at the front. In this period, masses of Japanese were exposed to the taste of beer for the first time. Prior to the 1940s, beer was still a novel and expensive item. The generation that fought in the war subsequently formed the core of the first mass consumer segment after the war. This generation defined what the "right" kind of beer was in Japan. They preferred a richer, heavier, and more bitter taste compared to the present younger generations.

After the war, occupation forces implemented their policy of splitting up dominant companies in excessively concentrated industries. As a result, Dai Nippon Breweries was split into Sapporo Breweries (originally named Nippon Breweries) and Asahi Breweries in 1949. At the time of the division, Sapporo was the market share leader with 38.6 percent, followed by Asahi with 36.1 percent and Kirin with 25.3 percent.

The history of the Japanese beer industry from the war to the 1980s was essentially that of Kirin building a formidable empire. From its 25.3 percent share in 1949, Kirin had expanded to hold 63.8 percent of the market by 1976. Many reasons were cited for Kirin's advance. First, when Dai Nippon was split, Kirin was left as the only national player. Dai Nippon was divided geographically, with Asahi mainly inheriting the factories, brand, and distribution channels in western Japan and Sapporo taking those in the east. Since Dai Nippon was a group of localized brands, Sapporo and Asahi had to start as regional players.

Second, Kirin was credited with identifying the market trends effectively. Immediately after the war, beer was still an expensive item, and the majority of consumption took place in restaurants and other commercial locations. Beer consumption at home was then only 25 percent of total industry sales. Sapporo and Asahi focused their efforts in expanding sales in their traditional strength, the commercial market. Kirin, on the other hand, focused its attention on the home consumption market by developing an extensive distribution network. With rising incomes and the spread of refrigerators in homes, beer consumption in the home grew rapidly, and so did Kirin.

Perhaps the most important achievement by Kirin in the period was developing its top-quality image as "the beer of beer lovers." The top 10 percent of beer drinkers were estimated to consume 50 percent of the total consumption, and when the next 10 percent was included, the number reached 75 percent. Kirin captured the heart of this heavy beer drinker market. In addition, according to market research conducted at the time, the top three reasons for choosing a brand were "quality," "what I have always drunk," and "reputation." Thus, Kirin could virtually lock up its commanding position, leveraging on its quality image and consumers' brand loyalty.

Instead, the trend in the late 1970s and early 1980s was toward product differentiation based upon packaging and product image. Numerous sizes of beer cans and bottles were sold to address the different market segments, for example, minibarrels for small group get-togethers. In addition, characters such as penguins or raccoons were used to attract consumer attention. Advertising focused on creating a product image rather than on explaining the product.

The perceived conservatism of consumers made beer manufacturers conservative about the taste of their products. Kirin's pasteurized lager beer became the indus-try standard, and competitors did not try to differentiate the taste of products very much. Kirin became the favorite target for the promoters of strict antitrust law implementation. Kirin at this point felt that any additional increase in market share would lead to a forced breakup of the corporation by the government. As a result, Kirin shifted its attention to diversifying into nonbeer businesses in order to maintain growth.

An important exception to this was nonpasteurized draft beer. Draft beer was recognized by the consumers as good-tasting beer. However, because quality control of draft was difficult, draft was originally only served fresh during the summer at beer halls. Bottled or canned products for home use did not exist until the 1960s. Even then the perception remained in consumers' minds that draft was a summer-and-beer-hall-only product, and bottled/canned draft was somehow not real draft beer. Sales of canned and bottled draft beer nevertheless grew steadily, and by 1985 the draft segment was 41 percent of the total beer market. Sapporo, Asahi, and Suntory were all pushing draft beer for home consumption as a weapon against Kirin.

Kirin, on the other hand, maintained that for bottles and cans their pasteurized lager beer was the "right" formula. The thought within Kirin was that, since they had secured their leadership position through sales of lager, it was unwise for them to commit to nonlager products. Kirin refused to market bottled draft beer for home consumption until 1985, when they decided that this segment was becoming too large to be ignored. In spite of draft's advance, however, Kirin's pasteurized lager beer still had a commanding 52.7 percent share in 1985, and Kirin as a whole had a 61.3 percent market share.

Exhibits 5, 6, 7, and 8 show the comparative production and performance data of Japan's beer manufacturers.

Industry Economics of the Modern Japanese Beer Industry

Production The process of producing beer was basically uniform among all the beer companies. Malt and hops were used as primary raw materials with other grains added according to necessity and taste. The production process used yeast to ferment sugar present in the primary raw materials. The development of large outdoor tanks in the late 1960s had added substantial economies of scale to the brewing process.

An important production-related issue was the dramatic seasonality of sales. Consumption of beer was heavily concentrated in the summer season. Since stale beer was extremely unpopular in Japan, this sales pattern created large fluctuations in capacity utilization. Exhibit 9 shows the seasonal demand patterns. The effect of the seasonality was not identical across all competitors. In the past, Kirin with its more popular product experienced relatively constant sales. Other competitors experienced larger fluctuations, absorbing the demand during the short-supply summer months while being overwhelmed by the clout of Kirin during the off-peak season and running with substantial excess capacity.

In the course of its growth, Kirin aggressively sought to cover the nation with a network of production facilities. Since beer was a bulky product relative to its price, this gave Kirin a logistics cost advantage where sufficient sales were achieved in the markets surrounding the individual plants.

Distribution Distribution was structured into a two-layered system of distributors and retailers. Both the distributors and retailers were licensed by the government; new licenses were strictly limited.

There were basically two kinds of distributors. One was the general distributor, found primarily around the Tokyo area, that dealt with all four brands of beer. The other was the exclusive distributor that dealt with only one or a limited number of brands. Exclusive distributors were strongly represented in the more traditional Osaka area.

The distribution system tended to work as a barrier against new entrants to the industry or major share increase by any player. With the widely held perception that beer was a commodity and that differentiation was not effective except in limited niche segments, the objective of the beer producers had been to create a close personalized relationship with distributors. Kirin, in particular, had strong bargaining power over the distributors because of its historical popularity and product shortage. Takara, a distillery, attempted to enter the beer market in 1957 but was forced to retreat after failure to secure distribution.

Retailers were typically liquor stores that sold to both consumers and commercial operations that served alcohol. Retailers independently selected which beers to sell.

One important element in the distribution of beer in Japan was the emphasis on "fresh rotation." Consumers preferred to drink beer as fresh as possible and could distinguish beers more than a few months old. Brewers had taken to labeling the brewing date on the bottle to address this concern.

Marketing The retail price of beer in Japan was virtually regulated at a uniform level by the Ministry of Finance. Government policy of securing a stable source of revenue from domestic beer sales resulted in heavy taxes on beer in Japan. Heavy dependence on beer tax revenue provided an incentive for the government to maintain healthy beer companies. Maintenance of a minimum price level was perceived as necessary, because Kirin had the power to drive the smaller players into financial difficulty and monopolize the industry.

Price competition did, however, exist at the distribution level in the form of producer rebates to distributors and distributor rebates to retailers. Producer rebates to distributors played a relatively smaller role since transactions in this part of the distribution chain carried lower margins than distributor/retailer transactions. Distributors traditionally were forced to give retailers higher rebates for Asahi's products than the more popular Kirin beer. This made Asahi's exclusive distributors financially weaker than Kirin's distributors. For general distributors, the rebate structure also made Asahi's beer less attractive to push.

On the advertising front, a minimum level of expense was necessary regardless of the size of the sales in order to maintain brand recognition. Thus, in 1985, for instance, Asahi's advertising budget was 62 percent of Kirin's while its sales were only 20 percent as large. (See Exhibit 5 for comparative financial data.)

Cost and Price Structure Variable costs as a percentage of sales could be estimated by adding logistics costs, promotion costs (rebates), and liquor tax to the raw materials cost. In Asahi's case this was around 76 percent in 1987. (See Exhibit 2.) All of the beer companies sold the standard large bottle (0.633 liter) to distributors at a uniform price of 4,756 yen per case (20 bottles). Distributors, in turn, sold a case of beer to retailers at 5,178 yen. The case price at retail to consumers was 6,200 yen. (Prices exclude rebates.)

Asahi Breweries, Ltd.

The breakup of Dai Nippon in 1949 was a severe blow for Asahi Breweries. "The destructive force of the breakup was enormous. Asahi had to start with a negative tone and fell into a vicious circle," recalled executive vice president Takanori Nakajo. Managing director Mitsuro Matsuwake added, "Immediately after the breakup, the Asahi brand was not sold in Tokyo. Sapporo was in the same position in Osaka. Kirin, on the other hand, had brand recognition and distribution capability in both places. Business people who traveled between the two major business centers thus tended to choose Kirin, since consumers preferred to stick to one brand if they could."

Asahi went into a long period of decline as Kirin gradually increased its share. One mistake was its agreement to allow Suntory, a whiskey giant and a newcomer to the industry, to use its distribution channels. Suntory, using its own financial power, gained from the whiskey business, gradually pushing Asahi aside. Another mistake, often pointed out by industry analysts, was Asahi's focus on the relatively stagnant commercial market instead of the growing home consumption segment. Advisor Yoshio Oka, former managing director, claimed that was all Asahi could do. "At the time of the breakup, the commercial market was both larger and more influential than the home consumption market. Asahi at the time was faced with the task of creating a marketing channel from scratch in eastern

Japan. It was thus only natural for us to aim at the bigger segment in those markets where we needed to create initial sales volume."

Although sales stagnated, Asahi was regarded as the innovator in the industry. Vice chairman Tooru Takenawa explained, "We have always been trying new things, but we were always pushed back by the clout of Kirin. Asahi, for instance, was the first to start differentiating its product through packaging innovations as with the introduction of the 'minibarrel' in 1977." This was a small-sized barrel that could be used at home to serve draft beer. It became a sensation in the marketplace. "But this idea was copied by our competitors quickly," Takenawa added. The success induced others to come in, and when they did, they snatched the market away from Asahi. In addition, it triggered a proliferation of packaging types and stock-keeping units which worked to the disadvantage of Asahi, whose total volume was smaller and who could only secure smaller shelf space than other competitors. With Kirin displaying a full line of beer products, little shelf space was kept for Asahi.

In addition to the beer business, Asahi provided soft drinks, pharmaceuticals, and specialty foods and also ran a real estate business. Together, these nonbeer businesses generated 21.4 percent of corporate sales in 1987. These diversified businesses either used the by-products of brewing or exploited other assets and skills employed in its beer business.

On the financial side, Asahi had close relations with Sumitomo Bank as their primary source of financing. Since 1971, the president of Asahi had always come from Sumitomo. Each president invested substantial effort in restructuring Asahi. Executive Auditor Shigeji Nakakoji sum-

marized their policy as follows: "In general, the focus was on cost cutting, trying to regain equilibrium by contraction. During this period, the whole company was managed by the accounting department."

Crisis Situation in the Early 1980s

By the late 1970s, Asahi was in a downward spiral. A mediocre image of both the company and its product led to slow sales. Slow sales in turn led to slow inventory turns, which caused a deterioration in taste and product image. Lower sales necessitated steeper rebates and higher advertising costs per bottle.

The problem at Asahi was not that its sales personnel were lazy. The general manager of the Sales Division, Kazuo Takahashi, said:

> On the contrary, we were trying much harder than our competitors' sales force. We might have depended too much, however, on personal relationships between the salespersons and the buyers. This was a time-consuming method, requiring our salespeople to make very frequent visits. Also, because our product was not perceived as attractive, and those distributors carrying multiple company products did not push our products aggressively, our sales people had also been visiting retail stores and drinking places. Kirin's people just visited distributors and sold more than Asahi salespeople. The morale of the sales force was naturally low because they saw little progress, no matter how hard they tried.

The management control system malfunctioned, too. Because strong emphasis was placed on increasing sales and market share, there was a tendency to try to push products into the distribution channel at the end of the fiscal year. This not only resulted in a reactionary dip in sales in the subsequent month, but much more seriously, it caused deterioration of taste due to longer stocking.

Another controversial element of the control system was the productivity index. In order to acquire productivity data, the company used an index that showed plant efficiency "assuming the plant was running at full capacity." This assumption had to be made because otherwise sluggish sales would eclipse improvements achieved on the production line. Using this index, Asahi managed to eliminate sufficient personnel at the plants to make the company a low-cost producer during the late 1970s and early 1980s. There was, however, a disadvantage as executive vice president Toshiomi Fukuchi explained: "Production originally started this system to help sales efforts. But in reality, the index created such a mentality among production people toward cost that they ended up focusing, so to speak, on producing unsalable products efficiently."

Distrust among employees was perhaps the most serious problem of all. Many felt that since they were working as hard as any of the competitors' counterparts, it must be somebody else in the organization who was doing a mediocre job and ruining the company. The production people felt that their products were as good as any in the market and that it was the mediocre sales force who let the product sit in the distribution channel and deteriorate. On the other hand, the sales force felt that the engineers were egocentric and insensitive to consumer tastes.

For Asahi employees, 1981 was a particularly depressing year, as the company was forced to implement an early retirement program that removed 550 people from an organization that only employed

3,200. Asahi also became the target of a "green mail" attempt by a health care institution. Asahi was eventually saved by the Sumitomo Bank and a friendly chemical company who took over the aggressor's shares, but the incident left a negative image of the company in many consumers' eyes.

The Murai Era

In 1982, Sumitomo Bank decided to send its executive vice president, Tsutomu Murai, to the troubled Asahi as president. Murai had a reputation as a turnaround manager, having been credited for going in as executive vice president and saving Mazda, an auto manufacturer, shortly after the 1973 oil crisis.

Murai explained his initial impression upon arriving at Asahi as follows:

> I found at Asahi, as at Mazda, a rigid, vertical organization. Everyone was looking upward—to the strong CEO. An organization cannot be effective on this basis because it will eventually become risk averse; distance will build up between top management and line management; divisions and departments within the organization will become self-chartered; and the central administrative function will begin to swallow up all the resources, both human and financial. These are all the signs of an organization in decline, and both Asahi and Mazda shared these characteristics. By the time I got to Asahi, I had seen it before.

One of Murai's first actions as president was to instruct his managers to formulate an explicit company credo. General managers of different functions were gathered to discuss the overall goals of the corporation. In this process, many of the conflicts that functional departments had with each other were discussed in light of overall corporate goals. See Exhibit 10 for the credo formulated at the time.

On a more personal basis, Murai frequently hosted small groups of managers to informal nights out where they were given an opportunity to talk directly with the president. To facilitate such communication, Murai often organized a study group of managers who were assigned reading materials that would be discussed over drinks. He also insisted that a facility be made to host such casual meetings at a nearby location.

Some of the most common words and phrases used by Asahi managers to describe Murai included "accessible, good communicator, dauntless, cheerful, prepares a positive environment and waits for subordinates to come up with the right idea, and ignites the middle management." Murai described his initial goals as follows: "As a new CEO, I knew I had to do two things successfully: first, I had to be perceived as arriving without prejudice; second, I had to feel the organization with my own hands and avoid the 'Naked King' syndrome. A Naked King is a CEO whose aides protect him from seeing the real picture."

During his effort to understand the company, Murai found a report prepared by McKinsey and Company in 1980 that analyzed Asahi's problems and gave four general recommendations: (1) improve the corporate image, (2) implement a market-needs-oriented product development program instead of a technology-driven one, (3) make efforts to convey the positive aspects of Asahi and its products, and (4) guarantee the fresh rotation of beer. This report had been disregarded by the previous president, but Murai found the analysis to be credible and decided to ask for

concrete action plans to implement these recommendations.

To facilitate the process, Murai created two cross-functional task forces: the Corporate Identity Introduction Team and the Total Quality Control Introduction Team. Reflecting Murai's philosophy that operating managers are the driving force behind a company, seven- to eight-member CI and TQC Introduction Teams were chosen from the deputy general manager and section chief level.

The TQC Introduction Team began by focusing on customer satisfaction and the scientific use of data. Subsequently, all 600 managers above the section chief level were brought in for training sessions designed to encourage managers from different functional areas of the company to discuss the common topic of quality.

TQC activities began on a corporate-wide basis in January 1984. Quality Control Circles were set up on the shop floor where employees were encouraged to make suggestions on how to guaranee the delivery of high-quality fresh beer to customers. At the corporate level, a Quality Assurance committee was organized by general managers of various functional departments to deal with suggestions from the field, complaints from the customers, and other related issues.

In the meantime, the Corporate Identity Team focused on improving the image of the company with the public, as well as raising the self-perception and expectations of the company's employees. Murai had experience in successfully implementing a CI program when he was with Mazda.

The CI Introduction Team started with a survey of how Asahi and its products were perceived by the consumers. The results were summarized in the following three points:

1. Asahi's presence in the marketplace was not felt by consumers.
2. Asahi's efforts were not recognized by consumers.
3. The company lacked the capability to communicate effectively with the public or to identify trends in the market.

Based on these findings, the CI team went ahead to discuss the future directions Asahi should take. To win the support from the rest of the organization, the process of formulating these points was purposefully designed to incorporate a wide range of employees.

Through the process of conceptualizing the present situation and the future direction, the need for a symbol to represent the efforts of Asahi was strongly felt. A proposal was made to completely change the corporate trademark and product labels. This became an extremely controversial proposition. The conventional trademark of the rising sun had close to 100 years of history, and many employees, as well as Asahi's distributors, felt proud of it. Strong opposition also came from branch managers, who claimed that there were many consumers who identified with the traditional trademark.

An important development in the CI process that took place in parallel with the corporate trademark debate was the proposal for changing the taste of Asahi beer. This proposal stemmed from a separate study conducted by the marketing division, which had run market trials in conjunction with the product development division. A blind test involving 5,000 beer drinkers revealed that consumer preference was changing away from the bitter and rich taste represented by Kirin to a more refreshing "sharper" taste.

This finding was turned into a new product proposal by the Corporate Identity team, which was beginning to question whether Asahi's products really matched the needs of the consumers. "We were very fortunate," Marketing Division general manager Yasuo Matsui said, "that CI was under way. People were willing to question taboos." The beer industry was so conservative, the fear for losing existing market by changing taste so strong, and the pride of the engineers in the existing product so strong that it had always been a taboo to suggest changing taste.

During the fall of 1985, the management committee finally decided to implement a full change in the corporate trademark in conjunction with a major revision in taste. Taste was changed to emphasize sharpness rather than richness and bitterness. Attention was paid, however, to the conservative attitudes toward richness. While "richness" and "sharpness" were technically contradictory, efforts by engineers brought about a product that seemed to meet both criteria. The all new "Asahi Draft" was born with completely new labels and a new taste that was designed to match that of contemporary beer lovers.

"The reason why the organization was able to make such a daring decision in violation of industry norms," a number of executives explained, "was probably because Asahi was at the edge. People knew Asahi beer could not continue anyway if we did nothing and kept on losing. We had little left to lose, so we could bet it all."

Through these corporate-sponsored programs, the atmosphere of the corporation became more open and lively. This new spirit, however, was not translating into results. The 0.2 percent share increase that followed Murai's installation as president in 1983 soon started to slide. By 1985, it was at 9.9 percent, only 0.7 percent above Suntory's. Sympathetic distributors and retailers were starting to give up on Asahi. The number of retailers carrying Asahi was starting to drop sharply. Many executives pointed out that this was a most dreaded trend for any consumer products manufacturer, one that could lead to a total collapse. There was a strong feeling of crisis within the company.

Higuchi Comes In

In the spring of 1986, Hirotaro Higuchi succeeded Murai as president. Higuchi was another Sumitomo banker who was following a fast track to become the youngest executive vice president in the bank's history. Murai and Higuchi knew each other well for a long time within the bank. In 1986, Murai was reaching the age of 68 and requested the bank to send Higuchi to succeed him for what was expected to be the demanding battle of implementing the dramatic changes that had been planned.

Higuchi was described by his subordinates as a "quick response person, always talking in concrete terms, hates abstract philosophy, high-spirited, a romantic person that pursues ideals, comes up with his own ideas, does not wait for subordinates' coordinated decisions." Everybody interviewed by the casewriters agreed that his management style was top-down. Higuchi described his own management posture as follows:

> Ensuring profit is the responsibility of the president, and the president only. The rest of the organization's members should be dreamers that suggest what-

ever they feel is worthwhile for themselves and the corporation. They shouldn't worry about numbers. It is then up to the president to decide which ideas should be implemented to align the efforts into a profitable format. These decisions are ultimately mine.

"Decision making at Asahi accelerated after Higuchi came," Corporate Planning General Manager Masui said. "Higuchi gets mad when he finds that he is not informed, particularly of bad news. He doesn't want delays either." Public Relations Section Manager Naoki Izumiya said:

> There is a big contrast between Murai's style and Higuchi's. Murai tried to set the environment and wait for things to develop. Murai was also philosophical, and his words were conceptual. Higuchi, on the other hand, is more action oriented. He comes up with his own ideas, and his instructions are concrete and specific. At a meeting, for instance, Murai would be the last to speak and Higuchi is the first to speak. Because Higuchi requires people to report anything substantial and to do so fast, he is quite busy. Murai was not so specific about reports.

Immediately after he joined Asahi, Higuchi became involved in the launching of the new Asahi Draft. He made several significant policy decisions at this point. The first was recalling all the beer in the distribution channel that carried the old label. "This cost us 1.5 billion yen," Higuchi looked back and said, "but we had to show our commitment to quality and the new image. I have learned through my experience at the bank that it generally pays to get rid of bad operation even if you have to throw in extra money just to do it." There were arguments against this action suggesting that if Asahi sold the old product in peripheral markets at steep discount, the product could be sold out. Higuchi's action ran the risk of wiping out the company's net profit, which was at the 1.4 billion yen level in 1985. Higuchi's decision, however, was firm.

The second policy was the choice of raw materials. Higuchi instructed the organization to use the best quality malt available even if it meant higher cost. As a result, Germany became their source of malt.

Third, Higuchi declared that the company would spend "as much money on advertising and promotion as necessary until operating profit dropped down to zero." This was a departure from the traditional policy of containing advertising budget within a framework that ensured a certain level of operating profit.

Looking back to this period, the Engineering Division General Manager Yukio Tsukamura commented, "Mr. Higuchi came in and started telling us to spend as much money as we need on facilities to improve quality. Before then, we were really cost focused and weren't used to spending that much. So in the end, we couldn't spend that much. I think Mr. Higuchi made his statements intentionally to change the way we think."

The advertising and promotion of the new Asahi Draft focused on its "better taste." A caravan distributed minisized cans to 1,000,000 people who would test drink and hopefully spread the word of the new product. Heavy advertising was also implemented using mass media, particularly newspapers. It was expected that newspapers would logically convey Asahi's message on why new Asahi Draft tasted better than other beers.

In 1986, the sales of Asahi Breweries grew 9.7 percent over the previous year. In the beginning everybody, including the company's employees themselves, was still skeptical about whether Asahi's revolutionary strategy would be successful, but soon signs of improvement began to appear. The former Public Relations director and a CI member, Hirofumi Tange, recalled, "After a while, the distribution people began to understand that Asahi's determination was for real. And we made a point in convincing all the 160,000 retailers to taste our beer. Then they started to push Asahi products seriously."

Super Dry

In the summer of 1986, while Asahi Draft was gaining ground, a new plan was proposed and rejected by Higuchi in an executive meeting. The plan was to introduce a new product called "Super Dry" in 1987. Super Dry was intended to further the trend that Asahi Draft started toward emphasizing "sharpness" over "richness" common to lager beers.

The basis for Higuchi's initial rejection of Super Dry was that it came too soon after launching the successful Asahi Draft. He thought introducing a new product would dilute the image and effort expended on Asahi Draft. Higuchi explained, "I hesitated because I knew Asahi had the reputation among its distributors for launching lots of new products and giving up soon when they didn't work." Similar in terms of product concept, Super Dry was also certain to cannibalize the Draft.

The Super Dry development team persisted, however. Higuchi later commented, "I originally rejected the idea. But the young guys kept on coming to me. Finally, they came to me and made me drink the product. I changed my mind. The new beer really tasted good." It was decided to market Super Dry from the beginning of the 1987 season.

In March 1987 Higuchi decided to invest 70 billion yen to expand Asahi's capacity by 50 percent by 1988. Corporate Planning General Manager Kenichiro Masui recalled:

> The difficult thing about capacity planning is that it requires over a one-year lead time from when you commit to an investment plan until the capacity comes on-line. Thus in the spring of 1987, we had to make up our mind about 1988 capacity before looking at the 1987 sales data. So we made the plan for 1988 capacity based on 1986 data and came up with what we thought was a very aggressive plan of 30 percent capacity increase. But Higuchi didn't like it. At the top management meeting where the plan was presented, he asked the engineering people what the maximum capacity expansion they could handle was, and when they answered 50 percent, that became the plan.

Government regulations complicated capacity expansion. It was necessary to acquire a license to open a plant at new locations. As Executive Vice President Takemasa Yoneyama explained, "The Ministry of Finance restricts the issuance of licenses when they see potential for industrywide excess capacity."

In 1987, Asahi increased its sales by 33 percent with the boost from Super Dry. Vice Chairman Tooru Takenawa analyzed the success of the Super Dry, saying that "the timing of several factors was right. Kirin's core supporters were getting older; people were bored with the packaging and the cute mascots; draft was good but was already too old an idea to create a major change. So, when Asahi presented consumers with Super Dry, a product that was developed through a careful analysis of their changing tastes, the consumers were ready to react."

The Dry Wars

In 1987, when dry was initially introduced, Kirin ignored it stating that it was a niche and fad item. Kirin maintained that its product was the best-tasting beer and that consumers would come back to it soon after trying a novel item. After a while, however, Asahi's competitors started to recognize that dry was becoming more than a niche product. Furthermore, statistics showed Super Dry eating into Kirin's core market. Other beer companies decided to sell dry beer of their own in early 1988. Following the tradition of the industry, these products were not differentiated in either concept, content, or packaging. Direct confrontation was at hand.

Sales General Manager Takahashi recalled:

> We didn't mind others launching a similar product using dry as the name. What upset us was the fact that their design of packaging was almost identical to ours. Our competitors probably thought they could take over the dry market by launching an indistinguishable product which would eliminate the psychological link between Asahi and dry in the minds of consumers. Kirin boasted that they would become the top seller of dry.

Asahi responded by demanding that packaging and concept statements be changed in the spirit of protecting Asahi's development efforts. Squabbling among the beer companies over packaging attracted the attention of the press as a fight over intellectual property rights. Intellectual property rights were, at the time, becoming a focal point of trade conflict between the United States and Japan and had become a favorite topic of discussion. The confrontation was given the name of "Dry Wars."

This dispute had an effect of emphasizing to the consumers that Asahi was the one who originally introduced dry beer. Once the consumers recognized that Asahi Super Dry was the "real" dry beer, the competitors' advertisements for dry beer benefited Asahi more than themselves.

During the summer of 1988, Asahi could supply only approximately 70 percent of the orders placed. This caused not only lost sales, but more importantly, failure to live up to distributors' expectations of the company. It became increasingly clear that Asahi had established itself as the dominant player when it came to dry beer. It also seemed that dry beer was becoming a stable independent segment within the market. These developments pushed Asahi's competitors into changing their strategy. In a dramatic about-face, their new strategy focused on trying to convince consumers that dry beer was a fad product and that the taste was really not as great as Asahi claimed.

Asahi's competitors implemented their strategy in two ways. First, they went back to pushing their strongest product lines. Thus, Kirin started to reemphasize that lager was the best-tasting beer, while Sapporo pushed their popular "Black Label Draft" and Suntory its 100 percent malt beer. Second, they rushed the development of new products that were to become the next generation after dry. In the fall of 1988, Sapporo launched a new draft beer product, "Fuyu Monogatari (Winter Tale)," which was beginning to pick up in popularity. Other developments were apparently in the planning stages at Asahi's competitors.

At the end of 1988, consumers, retailers, distributors, and industry watchers were all watching the development of the beer market with great curiosity. *The Wall Street Journal* reported on December 5 that "the losers in Japan's dry-beer war are striking back, hoping to create a 'post dry' era." Exhibit 8 shows the most recent market share figures of the competitors by product category.

At the same time, Asahi was experiencing growth problems. Personnel General Manager Yutaka Tamino said, "Besides engineers and technicians, there is a shortage of sales and administrative staffs. Our plan is to increase the number of permanent employees from 3,200 to 4,000 over the next three years." Rapid expansion of sales also put pressure on distribution channels. A general manager explained, "Exclusive distributors are experiencing a huge volume increase and are in need of funds and expertise to expand their physical capacity." There were problems with general distributors, too. "Those distributors that were sympathetic to Asahi in the past were the smaller distributors. To increase our volume we also need the larger distributors. We face a delicate balance between our volume goal and important ties with those distributors that have been loyal to us through the bad times."

The Future

Views were mixed about the future of "Super Dry." While the competitors and some of the industry watchers talked about the "post dry" era, Asahi maintained that dry beer would last. Marketing Director Matsui said, "Dry is not a fad because it was created to match the long-term trend in the consumers' preferences. We should not overreact to competitors' moves."

Managing Director Koichiro Iwaki, in charge of corporate planning, added, "The industry sales volume has prospects for growing at around 7 percent for the next few years. Asahi's goal is to capture most of the increment. I know there are people who point out difficulties in our plan. But we should be trying to figure out how to accomplish our goal, rather than analyzing why it cannot be done."

Asked about the financial risks involved in the proposed investment, Finance Division Hiroshi Okada answered:

> Asahi, being an old company, has a lot of securities and real estate that we purchased a long time ago at a low price. As a result, we have a large sum of undervalued assets. With the recent rise in stock and land prices, these undervalued assets grew to around 600 to 700 billion yen. So even if the expected sales do not materialize and we get stuck with excess capacity, there is no fear of bankruptcy. In addition, the number of shares outstanding for Asahi is relatively low because we have not been able to issue very much in the past. Consequently, dividend burden for us is low. So now that our stock price has risen to the 2,000 yen level, we can fund all of the investment with equity financing without the fear of seriously diluting our earnings. We have issued stock recently and secured 100 billion yen. All in all, we are pretty safe in terms of cash flow.

Higuchi personally managed the company's portfolio of investments.

As he considered the investment proposal, Higuchi reminded himself of what he had often expressed to others:

> My natural instinct as a manager tells me to grow, to become the biggest, the most powerful. I am, however, always telling my people that the goal of the corporation is not to become a big company but to become a good company. A good company is one which has good product and good culture as well as being recognized by the public to have good people who are courteous and humble. There is no value in our existence otherwise.

EXHIBIT 1
OPERATION AND INVESTMENT PLAN FOR ASAHI BREWERIES (AS OF JANUARY 1, 1989)*
(BILLIONS OF YEN EXCEPT AS OTHERWISE NOTED)

	1986	1987	1988 (Estimate)	1989 (Projection)	1990 (Projectioin)	1987 Kirin	1987 Sapporo	1987 Suntory
Sales	259.4	345.1	545.0	780.0	1,000.0	1,266.3	467.0	780.0
Of which beer	200.0	271.2	460.0	670.0	870.0	1,182.4	440.0	215.7
Operating profit[†]	2.6	3.5	14.0	16.0	20.0	69.6	14.5	25.7
Ordinary profit[‡]	5.3	9.4	14.0	16.0	20.0	80.8	13.1	47.4
Net profit[§]	1.5	2.5	4.8	6.0	7.0	34.1	5.3	16.4
Permanent employees (people)	2,747	2,944	3,160	3,340	3,700[‖]	7,557	3,791	4,772
Depreciation expense	4.0	5.0	8.0	15.0	30.0	22.9	10.3	15.6
Investment in production capacity	10.0	20.0	70.0	100.0	130.0	NA	NA	NA
Production capacity (thousand kl)	550.0	580.0	880.0	1,450.0	2,100.0	2,886.0	1,086.0	520.0
Advertising and promotional expense	27.0	38.0	50.0	—	—	54.0	24.0	81.0

Source: Company data.

*Effects of projectod tax changes are excluded.

[†]Calculated as sales, rninus cost of goods, and SG&A.

[‡]Calculated as operating profit, plus nonoperating income, minnus nonoperating expenses. Nonoperating income consisted mainly
of interest and capital gains from investments while nonoperating expenses consisted mainly of interests on corporate debt.
Asahi's profit plan assumed that for the years 1988 through 1990, nonoperating income and expenses would be equal.

[§]Profit after tax. Calculated as ordinary profit plus extraordinary income less extraordinary expense.

[‖]In addition to its permanent workforce, Asahi planned to hire 2,000 or so temporary employees to help increase sales.

EXHIBIT 2
DETAILED BREAKDOWN OF COSTS, 1987

		1987	% of Sales
Cost of goods sold		267,214	77.4
Of which:	Liquor tax	158,445	45.9
	Raw material	74,571	21.6
	Labor	8,103	2.3
	Depreciation	3,850	1.1
	Power and light	1,545	0.4
	Other overhead	9,193	2.7
	Real estate	1,815	0.5
	Inventory adjustments	9,689	2.8
SG&A		74,389	21.6
Of which:	Promotional expense	19,222	5.6
	Advertising expense	18,902	5.5
	Logistics expense	10,584	3.1
	Provision for bad debt	72	0.0
	Salary	7,433	2.2
	Bonus	2,598	0.8
	Depreciation	1,227	0.4
	Other	14,347	4.2
Nonoperating expense		8,497	2.5
Extraordinary expense		1,748	0.5
Of which:	Write-off	836	0.2

Source: Condensed from corporate financial reports.

EXHIBIT 3
INCOME STATEMENT, 1985–1987 (MILLIONS OF YEN)

Year Ending December 31	1985	1986	1987
Sales	236,383	259,357	345,112
Cost of goods	186,187	202,867	267,214
Gross profit	50,195	56,489	77,897
SG&A	45,796	53,842	74,389
Operating profit	4,398	2,646	3,507
Nonoperating income*	3,283	8,348	14,378
Nonoperating expense*	4,411	5,673	8,497
Ordinary profit	3,270	5,321	9,388
Extraordinary income[†]	2,776	15	19
Extraordinary expense[‡]	1,582	1,286	1,748
Profit before tax	4,464	4,050	7,659
Provision for tax	3,100	2,540	5,150
Net profit	1,364	1,510	2,509

Source: Condensed from corporate financial reports.

*Nonoperating income and expense consisted mainly of financial income and expense.

[†]Extraordinary income consisted mainly of profit from sales of assets.

[‡]Extraordinary expense consisted mainly of a special provision for retirement pensions and a write-off of undepreciated assets.

EXHIBIT 4
BALANCE SHEETS, 1985–1987 (MILLIONS OF YEN)

Year (Year-Ends)	1985	1986	1987
Cash and securities*	18,197	42,801	78,312
Notes receivable	15,542	15,991	17,870
Accounts receivable	15,225	19,591	39,967
Inventory	21,328	18,419	20,400
Other	14,771	16,641	18,478
Total current assets	85,063	113,443	175,027
Tangible fixed assets	39,979	46,177	64,962
Intangible fixed assets	580	1,236	1,883
Investments and other[†]	14,116	20,702	24,362
Total fixed assets	54,675	63,115	91,207
Total assets	139,738	181,558	266,234
Notes payable	5,529	7,753	4,408
Accounts payable	6,054	7,397	19,127
Short-term loan	17,699	5,921	24,481
Unpaid liquor tax	15,992	26,433	40,136
Deposit	31,368	33,623	40,322
Other	18,747	22,379	34,207
Total current liabilities	95,389	103,506	162,681
Bond	4,600	7,060	4,540
Convertible bond	0	20,000	5,333
Long-term loan	972	12,260	8,657
Total other[‡]	5,934	5,511	5,170
Long-term liability	11,506	44,831	23,700
Paid-in capital	15,918	15,918	61,284[§]
Retained earnings	16,923	17,302	18,566
Shareholder's equity	32,841	33,220	79,850
Total liabilities and shareholders' equity	139,736	181,557	266,231

Source: Condensed from corporate financial reports.

*Consisted of cash, deposits, and short-term investments in securities.

[†]Consisted of long-term Investments in securities, long-term loans, and other long-term investments.

[‡]Consisted mainly of provisions for retirement oompensation fund.

[§]As of December 31, 1987, the number of shares outstanding equaled 270,388,791.

EXHIBIT 5
COMPARATIVE PERFORMANCE OF JAPANESE BEER PRODUCERS, 1984–1987

	Asahi				Sapporo				Kirin				Suntory			
	1984	1985	1986	1987	1984	1985	1986	1987	1984	1985	1986	1987	1984	1985	1986	1987
Sales (billion yen)	224.4	236.4	259.4	345.1	379.9	402.6	436.0	467.0	1,151.8	1,210.9	1,221.8	1,266.3	761.5	767.5	749.5	780.0
Of which beer	175.0	178.6	200.0	271.2	357.1	378.7	411.9	440.0	1,079.2	1,138.4	1,151.6	1,182.4	177.8	190.0	196.3	215.7
Sales per employee (million yen)	83.3	88.5	94.4	117.2	99.5	106.3	116.3	123.2	153.2	161.0	162.8	167.6	161.6	160.4	156.5	163.4
Operating profit (billion yen)	4.3	4.4	2.6	3.5	12.2	12.2	15.1	14.5	60.7	65.5	72.1	69.6	30.2	32.8	25.1	25.7
Ordinary profit	2.8	3.3	5.3	9.4	9.8	10.7	12.4	13.1	66.6	73.3	79.3	80.8	17.3	22.9	14.7	47.4
Shareholders' equity (billion yen)	32.6	32.8	33.2	79.9	47.5	50.5	76.6	108.6	235.7	262.6	294.7	323.0	146.4	153.9	157.9	173.6
Total assets	145.2	139.7	181.6	266.2	206.6	206.6	256.6	365.8	604.4	647.1	690.2	813.5	600.0	605.9	591.8	693.5
Equity/total assets (%)	22.5%	23.5%	18.3%	30.0%	23.0%	24.5%	29.8%	29.7%	39.0%	40.6%	42.7%	39.7%	24.4%	25.4%	26.7%	25.0%
Operating profit/sales (%)	1.9%	1.9%	1.0%	1.0%	2.6%	2.7%	2.8%	2.8%	5.3%	5.4%	5.9%	5.5%	4.0%	4.3%	3.3%	3.3%
Personnel (persons)	2,695	2,672	2,747	2,944	3,819	3,787	3,749	3,791	7,519	7,521	7,507	7,557	4,713	4,785	4,789	4,772
Average age (years old)	41.0	41.4	41.3	40.8	40.4	41.0	41.6	41.1	37.7	38.2	38.7	39.0	35.0	35.4	35.9	36.4
Advertising expense (billion yen)	8.9	7.9	11.7	13.9	11.0	12.1	13.3	15.1	15.9	18.9	15.9	18.4	26.7	22.8	22.9	27.1
Promotional expense	10.8	11.7	14.9	19.2	6.6	7.2	9.3	8.7	23.1	23.0	29.8	35.2	40.8	40.8	47.8	53.6
Total marketing expenses	19.6	19.7	26.6	38.1	17.6	19.3	22.6	23.9	39.0	36.9	45.7	53.5	67.5	63.6	70.7	80.7
Marketing expenses/sales (%)	8.8%	8.3%	10.3%	11.0%	4.6%	4.8%	5.2%	5.1%	3.4%	3.0%	3.7%	4.2%	8.9%	8.3%	9.4%	10.4%
Fixed assets (billion yen)	48.9	40.0	46.2	65.0	79.6	80.4	104.0	142.0	193.7	206.2	205.2	208.7	132.0	130.0	129.1	136.0
Stock price (year high, yen/share)	393	450	1,110	2,010	535	706	1,460	2,300	633	796	1,780	3,170	NA	NA	NA	NA

Source; Asahi Breweries.

147

EXHIBIT 6
SALES VOLUME OF BEER SHIPPED IN JAPAN BY NATIONAL BRAND MANUFACTURERS,
1975–1988 (THOUSAND KL)

	Total (Growth)	Kirin (Share)	Sapporo (Share)	Asahi (Share)	Suntory (Share)
1975	3,928.1	2,380.8	795.1	529.4	222.8
	8.9%	60.6%	20.2%	13.5%	5.7%
1976	3,639.3	2,321.9	669.6	429.4	218.4
	(7.4)%	63.8%	18.4%	11.8%	6.0%
1977	4,124.2	2,554.1	806.7	496.1	267.2
	13.3%	61.9%	19.6%	12.0%	6.5%
1978	4,430.4	2,751.3	868.4	513.9	296.8
	7.4%	62.1%	19.6%	11.6%	6.7%
1979	4,475.8	2,815.3	859.4	496.8	304.4
	1.0%	62.9%	19.2%	11.1%	6.8%
1980	4,513.8	2,807.6	889.2	496.5	320.5
	0.8%	62.2%	19.7%	11.0%	7.1%
1981	4,617.1	2,894.0	927.9	473.2	322.0
	1.3%	62.7%	20.1%	10.2%	7.0%
1982	4,733.5	2,946.6	946.5	473.1	367.3
	2.5%	62.2%	20.0%	10.0%	7.8%
1983	4,908.7	3,006.6	981.4	502.2	418.5
	3.7%	61.3%	20.0%	10.2%	8.5%
1984	4,645.8	2,858.7	904.8	464.6	417.6
	(5.4%)	61.5%	19.5%	10.0%	9.0%
1985	4,746.9	2,910.2	931.0	467.8	437.8
	2.2%	61.3%	19.6%	9.9%	9.2%
1986	4,930.3	2,946.6	1,012.0	516.9	454.8
	3.9%	59.8%	20.5%	10.5%	9.2%
1987	5,302.7	3,023.6	1,090.2	684.4	504.6
	7.6%	57.0%	20.6%	12.9%	9.5%
1988	NA	NA	NA	NA	NA
	7.6%*	50.5%[†]	19.8%[†]	20.6%*	8.9%[†]

Sources: 1975–1967 data from Nikkan Keizai Tsushin. 1988 data from the following sources:
*Asahi Breweries
[†]Japan Economic Journal (minor inconsistency with *, due to survey method differences).
Note: Besides the national brands, there was one local brand, Orion Beer, sold only in Okinawa with a 0.7% share of the national market in 1987. Also, figures include foreign brands, produced under license and shipped by each company.

EXHIBIT 7
SHARE OF DRAFT BEER SALES FOR NATIONALLY MARKETED
BRANDS, 1980–1987

	All Beers	Kirin	Sapporo	Asahi	Suntory
1980	21%	3%	45%	46%	100%
1981	25	5	55	56	100
1982	30	5	65	64	100
1983	33	5	70	75	100
1984	37	9	73	80	97
1985	41	14	78	83	96
1986	44	15	81	85	95
1987	50	18	85	91	96

Source: Nikkan Keizai Tsushin.

EXHIBIT 8
1988 MONTHLY MARKET SHARE OF NATIONALLY MARKETED BRANDS CONSUMED AT HOME BY MAJOR PRODUCT
CATEGORY (ALL FIGURES REPRESENT PERCENT SHARE OF THE TOTAL BEER MARKET)

	January	February	March	April	May	June	July	August	September	October	November
Asahi	11.2	13.5	16.0	16.2	17.3	19.1	18.7	20.3	23.1	21.9	20.5
Sapporo	16.9	17.2	15.8	18.2	17.5	17.4	16.5	18.1	16.0	16.2	18.2
Kirin	66.0	64.1	61.8	59.7	59.1	57.8	58.5	56.4	56.3	55.9	56.2
Suntory	5.6	5.0	5.8	5.6	5.6	5.5	5.6	4.9	4.6	5.3	4.7
Dry beer subtotal	6.2	8.3	17.3	23.2	27.6	31.0	34.8	36.0	35.1	30.5	28.1
Asahi	6.2	7.8	10.3	11.3	12.8	15.3	15.4	17.0	19.3	17.7	17.3
Sapporo	NA	0.2	1.4	3.5	4.2	3.9	4.6	4.9	4.4	3.7	3.3
Kirin	NA	0.3	4.3	6.7	9.0	10.2	12.8	12.4	10.3	7.5	6.5
Suntory	NA	0.0	1.3	1.7	1.6	1.6	2.0	1.7	1.1	1.7	1.0
Draft beer subtotal	NA	33.4	30.0	29.6	27.3	26.8	25.8	25.5	23.5	24.7	24.6
Asahi	NA	5.0	5.3	4.4	4.4	3.6	3.2	3.1	3.5	4.0	2.9
Sapporo	NA	15.0	12.9	13.6	11.9	11.8	10.4	11.4	9.9	10.8	12.9
Kirin	NA	8.7	7.6	7.9	8.0	8.3	9.1	8.5	7.9	7.3	6.4
Suntory	NA	4.7	4.2	3.7	3.0	3.1	3.1	2.5	2.2	2.5	2.4
Lager beer subtotal	NA	57.9	52.2	46.9	42.9	40.6	37.5	36.6	38.8	41.7	44.0
Asahi	NA	0.6	0.5	0.4	0.1	0.1	0.2	0.3	0.2	0.2	0.2
Sapporo	NA	2.0	1.5	1.2	0.8	0.8	0.8	1.1	0.9	0.9	1.3
Kirin	NA	55.1	49.9	45.1	41.8	39.2	36.3	35.0	37.5	39.9	42.0
Suntory	NA	0.2	0.3	0.2	0.2	0.3	0.2	0.2	0.2	0.2	0.3
Malt 100% beer subtotal	NA	NA	NA	NA	1.6	1.6	1.6	1.6	1.9	3.0	3.3
Asahi	NA	NA	NA	NA	0.0	0.0	0.0	0.0	0.0	0.0	0.0
Sapporo	NA	NA	NA	NA	0.6	0.8	0.8	0.7	0.7	0.8	0.8
Kirin	NA	NA	NA	NA	0.3	0.2	0.4	0.4	0.6	1.3	1.4
Suntory	NA	NA	NA	NA	0.7	0.6	0.4	0.5	0.6	1.0	1.1

Source: Shakai Chosa Kenkyusho Ltd.

Note: Data are compiled through monthly survey since using sampling methods.

EXHIBIT 9
MONTHLY SHIPMENT OF BEER

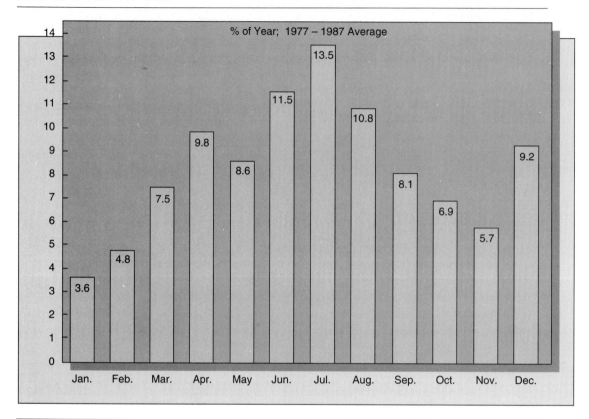

% of Year; 1977 – 1987 Average

Source: HBS estimates.

EXHIBIT 10
CORPORATE PHILOSOPHY OF ASAHI BREWERIES, LTD.

We at Asahi Breweries, Ltd., through our business activities including alcoholic and nonalcoholic beverages, food, and pharmaceuticals, wish to contribute to the health and well-being of people the world over. By thus contributing to society as a whole, the Company seeks to attain the trust and confidence of the consumer and develop still further.

1. Consumer Orientation

Identifying the best interests of consumers, we endeavor to meet their demands by creating products suited for contemporary tastes and lifestyles.

2. Quality First

Open to consumer opinion of our products, we consistently enhance quality level and extend technological capabilities in order to market the finest products in the industry.

3. Respect for Human Values

Our Company firmly believes that human beings are the core of the business, and follows the principle of human values through developing human resources and implementing fair personnel management. Each employee is encouraged to fully utilize his or her own potential, and work to realize an open, positive-thinking corporate culture.

4. True Partnership Between Labor and Management

Our Company aims to strengthen harmonious relations between labor and management based on mutual understanding and trust. Both parties work hand in hand for corporate development as well as the welfare of all employees.

5. Cooperation with Business Associates

We seek to build strong relations with all our business associates and affiliates in a spirit of coexistence and coprosperity based on mutual trust. At the same time, we are determined to accept and fulfill our responsibilities as the core of the Asahi group companies.

6. Social Responsibilities

We at Asahi, through securing and expanding the base of our operations, desire to fulfill our responsibilities to stockholders and the local communities in which we operate. Also, in carrying out business activities, we sincerely observe the moral principles of management based on social standards.

Wal-Mart Stores, Inc.

In *Forbes* magazine's annual ranking of the richest Americans, the heirs of Sam Walton held spots five through nine in 1993 with $4.5 billion each. Sam Walton, the founder of Wal-Mart Stores, Inc., died in April 1992 and left his fortune to his wife and four children. Wal-Mart was a phenomenal success with a 20-year average return on equity of 35 percent, compound average sales growth of 34 percent, and compound earnings per share growth of 23 percent. Sales per square foot of nearly $300 at Wal-Mart surpassed the industry average of $220, and at the end of 1993, Wal-Mart had a market value of $65 billion. Wal-Mart was one of the first retailers to invest heavily in information technology, and it was a widely held belief that Wal-Mart had revolutionized many aspects of retailing.

David Glass and Don Soderquist faced the challenge of following in Sam Walton's footsteps. Glass and Soderquist, CEO

Copyright © 1994 by the President and Fellows of Harvard College. Harvard Business School case 794-024 (revised April 26, 1994).

and COO, had been running the company since February 1988 when Sam, retaining the chairmanship, turned the job of CEO over to Glass. Their record spoke for itself—the company went from sales of $16 billion in 1987 to $67 billion in 1993, with earnings more than tripling from $628 million to $2.3 billion.

The main issue faced by Glass and Soderquist was how to sustain the company's phenomenal performance. Headlines in the press started to appear which expressed some doubt: "Growth King Running into Roadblocks," "Can Wal-Mart Keep Growing at Breakneck Speed?" and "Wal-Mart's Uneasy Throne." In April 1993, the company confirmed in a meeting with analysts that 1993 growth in comparable store sales would be in the 7–8 percent range, the first time the company had fallen under a 10 percent growth rate since 1985. Sellers lined up so quickly that the New York Stock Exchange temporarily halted trading in the stock. From early March through the end of April 1993, the stock price fell 22 percent to 26⅝. With sales forecast to reach $87 billion in 1994, and Supercenters targeted as the prime growth vehicle, Glass and Soderquist had their work cut out for them.

DISCOUNT RETAILING—GENERAL BACKGROUND

Discount stores emerged in the United States in the mid-1950s. They followed on the heels of supermarkets, which sold food at unprecedentedly low margins. Discount stores extended this approach to general merchandise by charging gross margins that were 10–15 percent lower than those of conventional department stores. To compensate, discount stores cut costs to the bone: fixtures were distinctly unluxurious, in-store selling was limited, and ancillary services, such as tailoring, delivery, and credit, were scarce.

The discounters' timing was just right. Consumers had become increasingly better informed since World War II. Supermarkets had educated them about self-service, many categories of general merchandise had matured, and TV had intensified advertising by manufacturers. Government standards also bolstered consumers' self-confidence. Many were ready to try cheaper, self-service retailers except for products that were big-ticket items, technologically complex, or "psychologically significant."

Discount retailing burgeoned as a result, with many players entering the industry at the local, regional, or national level. Sales grew at a compound annual rate of 25 percent from $2 billion in 1960 to $19 billion in 1970. During the 1970s, the industry continued to grow at an annual rate of 9 percent, with the number of new stores increasing by 64 percent; and in the 1980s at a rate of 7 percent, but with the number of stores increasing by only 11

percent. Sales reached $106 billion by 1992, up 10 percent from the previous year. However, the number of stores increased by less than 1 percent, and this trend toward fewer new store openings was attributed to a more cautious approach to expansion by discounters, who placed increasing emphasis on the refurbishment of existing stores. Industry analysts predicted that discount store sales would increase about 5 percent annually over the next five years. Exhibit 1 depicts the average economics of discounting in 1990.

Of the top 10 discounters operating in 1962, the year Wal-Mart opened for business, not one remained in 1993. Several large discount chains, such as King's, Korvette's, Mammoth Mart, W. T. Grant, Two Guys, and Woolco, failed over the years or were acquired by survivors. As a result, the industry became more concentrated: In 1986 the top five players accounted for 62 percent of industry sales; in 1992 they accounted for 74 percent of sales, and discount store companies that operated 50 or more stores accounted for 86 percent of sales. Exhibit 2 shows the top discounters in 1992. Ames, which acquired Zayre in 1989, filed for Chapter 11 protection in 1990 and emerged from bankruptcy after losing more than $200 million in 1991. Hills unveiled its Chapter 11 reorganization plan in June 1993, over two years after it filed for court protection from its creditors. Rose's Stores and Jamesway filed for Chapter 11 protection in 1993.

WAL-MART HISTORY

Providing value was a part of the Wal-Mart culture from the time Sam Walton opened his first Ben Franklin franchise store in 1945; during the 1950s, the number of Walton-owned Ben Franklin franchises increased to 15. After his idea for opening stores in small towns was turned down by the Ben Franklin franchise, Sam and his brother Bud opened the first "Wal-Mart Discount City" store in 1962. For years, while he was building Wal-Marts, Sam continued to run his various Ben Franklin stores, gradually phasing them out by 1976. The company expanded rapidly, initially in the South and then into the upper Midwest, the Southwest, and the Southeast.

There were two key aspects behind Sam's plan for growing Wal-Mart. It began with locating stores in isolated rural areas and small towns, usually with populations of 5,000 to 25,000. He put it this way: "Our key strategy was to put good-sized stores into little one-horse towns which everybody else was ignoring."[1] About one-third of Wal-Mart stores were located in areas that were not served by any of its competitors. Sam was convinced that discounting could work in small towns: "If we offered prices as good as or better than stores in cities that were four hours away by car, people would shop at home."[2] The second part of the plan involved the pattern of expansion. David Glass explained, "We are always pushing from the inside out. We never jump and then backfill."[3]

By 1970, Sam steadily expanded his chain to 30 discount stores in rural Arkansas, Missouri, and Oklahoma. But the cost of goods sold—almost three-quarters of discounting revenues—rankled. As Sam put it, "Here we were in the boondocks, so we didn't have distributors falling over themselves to serve us like competitors in larger towns. Our only alternative was to build our own warehouse so we could buy in volume at attractive prices and store the merchandise."[4] Since warehouses, at $5 million or more apiece, were rather capital-intensive, Walton took the company public and raised $3.3 million.

By 1993, 55 percent of Wal-Mart stores faced direct competition from Kmart stores, and 23 percent from Target. However, 82 percent of Kmart stores and 85 percent of Target stores faced competition from Wal-Mart.[5] Further geographic growth would undoubtedly increase the competition with other major retailers. Wal-Mart was penetrating the West Coast and the Northeastern states, and by 1993, it operated in 45 states, with stores planned for Rhode Island, Vermont, Washington, Hawaii, and Alaska. Exhibit 3 maps Wal-Mart's discounting network at the beginning of 1993, when Wal-Mart operated 1,880 Wal-Mart stores (including 30 Supercenters), 256 warehouse clubs (Sam's Clubs), 64 warehouse outlets (Bud's), and four hypermarkets. Sam's Club was a wholesale/retail cash-and-carry membership warehouse operation. Merchandise was displayed in pallet-size quantities and was sold at wholesale prices. A supercenter was a combination Wal-Mart discount store and supermarket under one roof. Bud's carried closeout, damaged, and overrun merchandise and utilized former Wal-Mart discount store locations. The plans for 1993 included 150 new Wal-Mart stores and 65 Sam's Clubs. It also planned to expand or relo-

---

[1]Sam Walton with John Huey, *Sam Walton, Made in America* (New York: Bantam Books, 1992).

[2]*Business Week*, November 5, 1979, p. 145.

[3]*Business Week*, November 5, 1979, p. 146.

[4]*Forbes*, August 16, 1982, p. 43.

[5]George C. Strachan, "The State of the Discount Store Industry," *Goldman Sachs*, April 6, 1994.

cate approximately 100 of the older Wal-Mart stores (about half would be made into Supercenters) and 25 Sam's Clubs. Exhibit 4 compares Wal-Mart's performance with that of its competitors; Exhibit 5 summarizes Wal-Mart's history over the past decade.

SAM'S LEGACY

Sam Walton died in April of 1992 at the age of 74 after a long fight with cancer. His memorial service was broadcast to every store over the company's satellite system. Sam Walton had a philosophy which drove everything in the business: He believed in the value of the dollar and was obsessed with keeping prices below everybody else's. On buying trips, Sam's rule of thumb was that trip expenses should never exceed 1 percent of the purchases, which meant sharing hotel rooms and walking instead of taking taxis.

Sam instilled in his employees, called associates, the idea that at Wal-Mart they have their own way of doing things. Sam tried to make life at Wal-Mart unpredictable, interesting, and fun. He even danced the hula on Wall Street when he lost a bet to David Glass. Glass bet that the company would produce a pretax profit of more than 8 percent in 1983. Sam said of the event, "Most folks probably thought we just had a wacky chairman who was pulling a pretty primitive publicity stunt. What they didn't realize is that this sort of stuff goes on all the time at Wal-Mart."[6]

Sam spent as much time as possible in his own stores and checking out the competition. He was known to count the number of cars in Kmart and Target parking lots, and tape-measure shelf space and note sale prices in Ames. Sam knew his competitors intimately and copied their best ideas. He got to know Sol Price, who created Price Club, and then redid the concept with Sam's Club.

Sam said that the most important ingredient in Wal-Mart's success was the way the company treated its associates. If you want the people in the stores to take care of the customers, you have to make sure you're taking care of the people in the stores. There was one aspect of the Wal-Mart culture that bothered Sam from the time Wal-Mart became really successful. "We've had lots and lots of millionaires in our ranks. And it just drives me crazy when they flaunt it. Every now and then somebody will do something particularly showy, and I don't hesitate to rant and rave about it at the Saturday morning meeting. I don't think that big mansions and flashy cars are what the Wal-Mart culture is supposed to be about—serving the customer."[7]

Sam described his management style as "management by walking and flying around." Others at Wal-Mart described it as "management by wearing you down" and "management by looking over your shoulder." On managing people, he said, "You've got to give folks responsibility, you've got to trust them, and then you've got to check up on them." Wal-Mart's partnership with its associates meant sharing the numbers—Sam ran the business as an open book and maintained an open-door policy. The corporate mission was to excel by empowering associates, maintaining technological superiority, and building loyalty among associates, customers, and suppliers.

---

[6]Sam Walton, *Made in America*.

[7]Sam Walton, *Made in America*.

MARKETING

Wal-Mart's promotional strategy of "everyday low-prices" meant customers were offered brand-name merchandise for less than in department and specialty stores. When a customer walked into a Wal-Mart store, he or she was met by a "People Greeter," an associate who greets customers and hands out shopping carts. Wal-Mart had few promotions—while other major competitors typically ran 50 to 100 advertised circulars annually to build traffic, Wal-Mart offered 13 major circulars per year. At Wal-Mart, advertising expense was typically 0.5 percent of sales, versus 1.8 percent at Kmart, 2.7 percent at Sears, and the 1.2 percent industry average. Wal-Mart's "satisfaction guaranteed" policy meant merchandise could be returned to any Wal-Mart store with no questions asked.

Competitive changes in discount retailing were reflected in Wal-Mart's decision to change its marketing slogan from "Always the low price—Always" to "Always low prices—Always." Wal-Mart used the first slogan when building its chain by offering better prices than small-town merchants. Wal-Mart increasingly competed against rivals such as Kmart, Target, and Toys 'R' Us, when no one always had the lowest price. See Exhibit 6 for a comparative pricing study between Wal-Mart, Kmart, and Bradlees.

Merchandise was tailored to individual markets and, in many cases, individual stores. Information systems made this possible through "traiting," a process which indexed product movements in the store to over a thousand store and market traits. The local store manager, supported by inventory and sales data, chose which products to display based on customer preferences and allocated shelf space for a product category according to the needs in his or her own store. Wal-Mart was very competitive in terms of prices, and its store managers had more latitude in setting prices than did their counterparts in "centrally priced" chains such as Caldor and Venture. A study in the mid-1980s found that when Wal-Mart and Kmart were located right next to each other, Wal-Mart's prices were roughly 1 percent lower; when Wal-Mart, Kmart, and Target were separated by 4–6 miles, Wal-Mart's average prices were 10.4 percent and 7.6 percent lower, respectively. In remote locations, where Wal-Mart had no direct competition from large discounters, its prices were 6 percent higher than when it was right next to Kmart.

Wal-Mart was known for its national brand strategy, and the majority of its sales consisted of nationally advertised branded products. However, private label apparel made up about 25 percent of apparel sales in Wal-Mart. Wal-Mart gradually introduced several other private label lines in its discount stores such as Equate in health and beauty care and Ol' Roy in dog food. "Sam's American Choice" private food label was introduced in 1991. A year later, there were about 40 items in the Sam's line, consisting of products such as cola, tortilla chips, chocolate chip cookies, and salsa. Sam's Choice offered an average 26 percent price advantage over comparable branded products, with the range of the advantage being 9–60 percent.[8] Sam's Choice, considered the company's premium-quaulty line, also sold in Sam's Clubs (in larger club packs) and Supercenters. Although private label appeared to be a departure from Wal-Mart's national brand strategy, it fit into the

---

[8]*Supermarket News*, May 4, 1992.

corporate mission of providing quality products at the lowest possible prices.

In an effort to replace foreign-sourced goods sold in Wal-Mart stores with American-made goods, Wal-Mart developed its "Buy American" program. A letter was mailed to U.S. manufacturers in 1985 inviting them to participate in the program. In its 1989 annual report, the company stated that it converted or retained over $1.7 billion in purchases, at retail, that would have been placed or produced offshore, and created or retained over 41,000 jobs for the American workforce.

Store Operations

The company leased about 70 percent of Wal-Mart stores and owned the rest. Rental expense accounted for 0.8 percent of sales in 1990, compared to the industry average of 1.8 percent. An average Wal-Mart store was 80,000 square feet, with the newer units about 100,000 square feet. Construction costs were about $20 per square foot. Starting in the 1980s, Wal-Mart did not build a discount store at a location where it could not be expanded at a later date. Wal-Mart sales per square foot were $300, compared to Target at $209 and Kmart at $147. During 1992, no single store location accounted for as much as 1 percent of sales or net income. A Wal-Mart store devoted 10 percent of its square footage to inventory, compared with an industry average of 25 percent, and kept operating expenses at 15.8 percent of sales, versus 21 percent for the industry average.

The majority of Wal-Mart stores were open from 9 AM to 9 PM six days a week and from 12:30 PM to 5:30 PM on Sundays. Some Wal-Mart stores and most of the Supercenters were open 24 hours. Store managers priced products to meet local market conditions. Sales were primarily on a self-service, cash-and-carry basis with the objective of maximizing sales volume and inventory turnover while minimizing expenses. Customers could use Visa, MasterCard, the Discover card, or a layaway plan available at each store location.

Wal-Mart stores were generally organized with 36 departments and offered a wide variety of merchandise, including apparel, shoes, housewares, automotive accessories, garden equipment, sporting goods, toys, cameras, health and beauty aids, pharmaceuticals, and jewelry. License fees, mainly from pharmaceuticals, made up 0.1 percent of Wal-Mart's sales, versus the industry average of 0.2 percent.

Category	Wal-Mart	Industry Averages
Softgoods (apparel, linen, fabrics)	27	31
Hardgoods (hardware, housewares, auto supplies)	27	26
Stationery and candy	11	9
Sporting goods and toys	9	9
Health and beauty aids	9	11
Pharmaceuticals	6	
Gifts, records, and electronics	6	9
Shoes	3	3
Jewelry	2	2
Total	100%	100%

Electronic scanning of the Uniform Product Code (UPC) at the point of sale began in Wal-Mart stores in 1983. By 1988, UPC scanning was installed in nearly all Wal-Mart stores. Kmart began installing UPC scanning in mid-1986 and finished in 1990, a two-year lag behind Wal-Mart. Store associates used hand-held barcode scanning units to price-mark merchandise. These scanners, which utilized radio frequency technology, communicated with the store's computerized inventory system to ensure accurate pricing and improve efficiency. Shelf labeling rather than product price tags was used in many stores. Wal-Mart initiated a system to track refunds and check authorizations, which helped reduce shrinkage, a euphemism for pilferage or shoplifting, by identifying an item stolen from one Wal-Mart store which was submitted for refund at another store.

Electronic scanning and the need for improved communication between stores, distribution centers, and the head office in Bentonville, Arkansas, led to the investment in a satellite system. When electronic scanning was first used, the scanned data was transmitted to Bentonville over telephone lines, which had limited capacity. A satellite was launched in 1983 to solve this problem and was later used for video transmissions, credit card authorizations, and inventory control. The satellite allowed sales data to be collected and analyzed daily, so managers could immediately learn what merchandise was moving slowly and thus avoid overstocking and deep discounting. In an individual Wal-Mart store, daily information such as sales by store and department, labor hours, and inventory losses could be compared to the results for any time period, for any district or region, or for the nation. From 1987 to 1993, Wal-Mart spent over $700 million on its satellite communications network, computers, and related equipment.

DISTRIBUTION

Wal-Mart's two-step hub-and-spoke distribution network started with a Wal-Mart truck-tractor bringing the merchandise into a distribution center, where it was sorted for delivery to a Wal-Mart store—usually within 48 hours of the original request. A technique known as "cross-docking" enabled goods to be continuously delivered to warehouses, repacked, and dispatched to stores often without ever sitting in inventory. Merchandise replenishment originated at the point of sale, where information was transmitted via satellite to Wal-Mart headquarters or to supplier distribution centers. About 80 percent of Wal-Mart stores' purchases were shipped from its own 22 distribution centers—as opposed to 50 percent for Kmart. In recent years, Wal-Mart's cost of inbound logistics, which was part of costs of goods sold, averaged about 2.8 percent of sales, compared to its competitors' at 4.5–5 percent of sales. The balance of purchases were delivered directly from suppliers, who stored merchandise for Wal-Mart stores and billed the company when the merchandise left the warehouse.

Each store received an average of five full or partial truckloads a week. Because Wal-Mart stores were grouped together, one truck could resupply several on a single trip. Any merchandise that had to be returned was carried back to the distribution center for consolidation. Since many vendors operated warehouses or factories within Wal-Mart's territory, trucks also picked up new shipments on the return trip. Wal-Mart's trucks were running 60 percent full on backhauls, and its truck fleet consisted of more than 2,000 trucks and 2,500 drivers. A store selected one of four options regarding the frequency and time of day it wanted to receive shipments—over half selected night deliveries. An accelerated delivery plan, designed for stores located within a certain distance of a distribution center, allowed merchandise to be delivered within 24 hours.

A typical distribution center was about one million square feet, staffed by 700 associates, operated 24 hours a day, designed to serve the distribution needs of approximately 150 stores, and highly automated. When orders were pulled from stock, a computerized "pick to light" system guided associates to the correct location. Wal-Mart was expanding its distribution network to service its growing number of stores by opening million-square-foot distribution centers in Wisconsin, Pennsylvania, Arizona, and Utah in 1993.

VENDOR RELATIONSHIPS

Wal-Mart was known in the business as being a tough negotiator. When vendors visited the company's headquarters in Bentonville, they were shown not into buyers' offices but to one of about 40 interviewing rooms equipped with a table and four chairs. Wal-Mart eliminated manufacturers' representatives from negotiations with suppliers at the beginning of 1992, and the reps tried unsuccessfully to take the matter to the Federal Trade Commission. Wal-Mart's sourcing standards were tough, and limited sourcing to vendors who limited workweeks to 60 hours, did not employ child labor, and provided safe working conditions. Wal-Mart centralized its buying at the head office, and in 1993 no single supplier accounted for more than 3.7 percent of the company's purchases.

Sam Walton said that when Wal-Mart opened for business, Proctor & Gamble would dictate how much they would sell to Wal-Mart and at what price. In 1993, Wal-Mart was P&G's largest customer, doing about $3 billion in business annually, or about 10 percent of P&G's total revenue. P&G was one of the first manufac-

turers to share information with Wal-Mart by computer and reportedly had a team permanently based in Bentonville.

By the late 1980s, a vendor-managed inventory system was utilied by companies such as Wrangler and GE to replenish stocks in Wal-Mart stores and warehouses. Every evening, Wal-Mart transmitted sales data to Wrangler, whose software interpreted the data to deliver orders for various quantities, sizes, and colors of jeans from specific warehouses to specific stores. Wal-Mart transmitted warehouse inventory data to GE Lighting every evening to enable GE to determine how much merchandise to deliver to Wal-Mart's warehouses. This "orderless order-entry system" meant that GE produced to order rather than inventory, thus improving their own and Wal-Mart's performance.

Introduced in 1990, the "retail link" program gave more than 2,000 suppliers computer access to Wal-Mart point-of-sale data. Manufacturers analyzed sales trends and inventory positions of their products on a store-by-store basis. The installation of electronic data interchange (EDI) enabled an estimated 3,600 vendors, representing about 90 percent of Wal-Mart's dollar volume, to receive orders and interact with Wal-Mart on an electronic basis. EDI started out as a means of sharing purchase order information with suppliers, and expanded to forecasting, planning, replenishing, and shipping applications. Wal-Mart used EDI-invoicing with over 65 percent of its vendors and used electronic funds transfer with many of them.

HUMAN RESOURCE MANAGEMENT

Wal-Mart's culture stressed the key role of associates, who were motivated by more responsibility and recognition than their counterparts in other retail chains. Information and ideas were shared—in individual stores, associates knew the store's sales, profits, purchases, and markdowns. Glass said, "There are no superstars at Wal-Mart. We're a company of ordinary people overachieving."[9] Associates were recognized by suppliers as being totally committed to the company: "Wal-Mart is a lean operation managed by extremely committed people," said an executive at a leading manufacturer. "It's very exciting being anywhere near these people. They live to work for the glory of Wal-Mart. This may sound like B.S., but it's incredible. Our production, distribution, and marketing people who visit Wal-Mart can't believe it."[10]

Wal-Mart introduced programs to involve the associates in the business. In the "Yes We Can Sam" suggestion program, associates suggested ways to simplify, improve, or eliminate work. Associates implemented over 400 suggestions in 1991 resulting in an estimated savings of over $38 million. The "store within a store" emphasis began in 1986 and supported, recognized, and rewarded associates in the management of their area of merchandise responsibility. Department managers became store managers of their own "store within a store" with sales in many instances exceeding $1 million. The "shrink incentive plan" provided associates with bonuses of up to $200 if their store held shrinkage below the company's goal. Shrinkage was approximately 1 percent of

sales in 1990 compared to the industry average of 1.6 percent.

Training at Wal-Mart was decentralized, with management seminars offered at the distribution centers rather than the home office, exposing the store managers to the distribution network. New associates received training before a store opened—from 10 to 12 assistant managers brought in from other Wal-Mart stores. Assistant managers were described this way: "They know better than to get comfortable, because the company's growth demands that assistants move on average every 24 months. Beth Brock, an Oklahoman who now runs a store in California, is an ultimate Wal-Mart warrior, having moved eight times in 10 years with the company. Her reward? Store managers can earn more than $100,000 a year, which goes a long way in most towns."[11]

Wal-Mart employed 520,000 full- and part-time staff and was the largest employer after the federal government and General Motors. The company was non-unionized, with 40 percent employed as part-time sales associates. Managers and supervisors were compensated on a salaried basis, with additional compensation based on store profits. Other store personnel were paid an hourly wage with incentive bonuses awarded on the basis of the company's productivity and profitability. Part-time associates who worked at least 28 hours per week received health benefits. Estimated payroll expense in 1990 was about 10 percent of sales compared to the industry average of 10.4 percent.

Profit sharing was available to associates after one year of employment. Based

[9]Wendy Zellner, "OK, So He's Not Sam Walton," *Business Week*, March 16, 1992.

[10]Emily DeNitto, "In Dry Grocery, Wal-Mart Sees Selective Success," *Supermaret News*, May 4, 1992.

[11]Bill Saporiot, "A Week Aboard the Wal-Mart Express," *Fortune*, August 24, 1992.

on profit growth, Wal-Mart contributed a percentage of every eligible associate's wages to his or her plan, which the associate took when leaving the company—in either cash or Wal-Mart stock. The company added $500 million to employee profit-sharing accounts since 1986, or 9 percent of net income. Eighty percent of the money was invested in Wal-Mart stock by a committee of associates. One general office associate had $8,000 in profit sharing in 1981; in 1991 she had $228,000. A retired hourly associate started off making minimum wage, $1.65 an hour, when he was hired in 1968. In 1989 when he was making $8.25 an hour, he retired and took $200,000 in profit sharing. A Wal-Mart truck driver in Bentonville joined the company in 1972; in 1992 he had $707,000 in profit sharing.[12] A stock ownership plan provided for the purchase of the company's common stock, with a 15 percent match by the company for up to $1,800 of annual stock purchases. About 50 percent of associates participated in the stock purchase plan.

MANAGEMENT

The Wal-Mart management team, with only a few exceptions, was made up of executives in their 40s and 50s who started working for the company after school and rose through the ranks as the company grew. David Glass, president and CEO, was one of the few who started his career outside of Wal-Mart. He worked for Consumers Markets in Missouri after graduating from college, joined Wal-Mart in 1976 as executive VP of finance, and later became chief financial officer. In 1984 Wal-ton engineered a job switch between Glass, then the CFO, and Jack Shewmaker, the president. Glass was known as an operationally oriented executive and was an important contributor to the sophisticated distribution system in place today. Don Soderquist, Wal-Mart's chief operating officer since 1987, left his job as president of Ben Franklin Variety Stores in Chicago to join Wal-Mart in 1980.

Glass's administrative style emphasized frugality. "He is one of the tightest men on the face of the earth," said an executive VP at Wal-Mart.[13] Glass rented subcompacts and shared hotel rooms with other Wal-Mart executives when he traveled. At headquarters, he paid a dime for his cup of coffee like everyone else. This didn't mean he wasn't a very rich man—his 1.5 million Wal-Mart shares were worth $82 million in 1992. Since suffering a heart attack in 1983, Glass tried to limit his long hours and late nights at the office.

Glass was on the road two or three days per week visiting stores. Since visiting every store was impossible, Glass used the company satellite to talk to employees by speaking into a foot-high microphone on his desk which was heard in every Wal-Mart across the country. Fifteen regional vice presidents operating from Bentonville spent about 200 days a year visiting stores. They managed a group of 11–15 district managers, who in turn were each in charge of 8–12 stores. Heading out to stores each week began early on Monday morning, when regional VPs, buyers, and 50–60 corporate officers boarded the company's fleet of 15 aircraft. They returned to Bentonville on Wednesday or Thursday "with at least one idea which would pay

---

[12]Sam Walton, *Made in America.*

[13]*Business Week*, March 16, 1992.

for the trip." The fact that Wal-Mart did not operate regional offices was thought to save the company about 2 percent of sales each year.

Friday morning was the weekly merchandise meeting. Glass said, "In the merchandise meetings, I force us to talk about how individual items are selling in individual stores."[14] According to Glass, "We all get in there and we shout at each other and argue, but the rule is that we resolve issues before we leave."[15] Guests were often invited to the meeting, including GE CEO Jack Welch, who commented, "Everybody there has a passion for an idea, and everyone's ideas count. Hierarchy doesn't matter. They get 80 people in a room and understand how to deal with each other without structure. I have been there three times now. Every time you go to that place in Arkansas, you can fly back to New York without a plane."[16]

The next day at 7 AM, Wal-Mart's entire management team and general office associates, along with friends and relatives, assembled in the auditorium for the Saturday morning meeting. The meeting combined entertainment with no-nonsense business, with the purpose of sharing information and rallying the troops. Don Soderquist ran through regional results, market share data, and weekly and quarterly numbers for the divisions, and regional VPs reported on the performance of new stores. No accomplishment was too small to go unrecognized. Cheers went up for a variety of reasons: stock ownership among associates was up, three associates

had 10-year anniversaries, the week's special item was selling well in selected Wal-Mart stores. Invited guests included former NFL quarterback Fran Tarkenton, country singer Garth Brooks, and comedian Jonathan Winters. On Monday, the process started over again with decisions implemented in the stores that morning.

EXPANSION AND DIVERSIFICATION

Wal-Mart started out as a discount store chain. In the early 1980s, the company began testing several new formats. Wal-Mart opened the first three Sam's Clubs in 1983, and soon after, the first Dot Deep Discount Drugstore in Iowa, and Helen's Arts and Crafts store in Missouri. Wal-Mart sold its three Helen's stores in 1988 and its 14 Dot stores in 1990.

In 1987, Wal-Mart opened its first two Hypermart U.S. stores and its first Supercenter. Wal-Mart borrowed the hypermarket concept, which originated in France in the 1960s, and built four. Each was a combination grocery and general merchandise store of over 220,000 square feet, carried 20,000–30,000 items, and had gross margins of 13–14 percent. Wal-Mart later dropped the Hypermart concept in favor of the smaller Supercenter format.

In 1990, Wal-Mart purchased McLane Company, a Texas retail grocery supplier, to service its Supercenters. McLane had 14 distribution centers which supplied convenience and grocery stores across the country. In 1992, McLane's sales increased 16 percent to nearly $3 billion. Wal-Mart also acquired Western Merchandisers, a wholesale distributor of music, videos, and books, and Phillips Companies, which operated 20 grocery stores in Arkansas.

Wal-Mart developed a chain of close-out stores called Bud's, named for Sam Walton's older brother, James "Bud" Wal-

[14]Wendy Zellner, "OK, So He's Not Sam Walton," *Business Week*, March 16, 1992.

[15]Bill Saporito, "A Week Aboard the Wal-Mart Express," *Fortune*, August 24, 1992.

[16]Bill Saporito, "What Sam Walton Taught America," *Fortue*, May 4, 1992.

ton, and there were 77 Bud's at the end of 1993. A Bud's store, which generated $6–$7 million annually in sales, was housed in a former Wal-Mart discount store location when the discount store outgrew the site. About 75 percent of Bud's merchandise was Wal-Mart surplus merchandise, and the rest was close-out goods shipped directly from vendors.

SAM'S CLUBS

A warehouse club used high-volume, low-cost merchandising, leveraged its buying power, minimized handling costs, and passed the savings on to its members. A club was able to derive above-average returns on investment despite gross margins of 9–10 percent. A high inventory turnover rate resulted from a limited number of stock-keeping units (SKUs), with inventory essentially financed through trade accounts payable (as much as 80–90 percent in some cases), resulting in minimal working capital needs. Membership fees comprised about two-thirds of operating profits. Warehouse clubs were pioneered by Price Club in the 1970s; Sam's Club opened in the early 1980s, and within four years, Sam's sales surpassed Price Club's to make it the largest wholesale club in the country. By 1992, Sam's was twice the size of Price Club with $12.3 billion in sales, compared to Price Club's $6.1 billion.

The operating philosophy at Sam's Club was to offer a limited number of SKUs (about 3,200 versus up to 30,000 for a full-size discount store) in pallet-size quantities in a no-frills, warehouse-type building. Name-brand merchandise at wholesale prices was offered to members for use in their own operations or for resale to their customers. Sam's was run by a separate team of managers from the discount stores, and would often co-locate with a Wal-Mart, with the two generating sales of $80–140 million a year. Although the Discover card was accepted, Sam's were mostly cash-and-carry operations. Both business and individual members paid an annual membership fee of $25. To join as a business member, a valid state/city tax permit or a current business license was required; individual members came from groups such as the federal government, schools and universities, utilities, hospitals, credit unions, and Wal-Mart shareholders. At the start of 1994, there were 325 Sam's Clubs, which operated seven days a week. Unlike Wal-Mart stores, Sam's received about 70 percent of its merchandise via direct shipments from suppliers rather than from the company's distribution centers.

Sales at Sam's Club rose 31 percent in 1992 (compared with 43 percent in 1991), the highest of any warehouse club chain (see Exhibit 7 for the top warehouse clubs by volume). Sam's sales accounted for 39 percent of the industry's volume in 1992, up from a 35 percent share in 1991. However, for the first time, comparable store sales in Sam's Clubs were down 3 percent in the first quarter of 1993, compared to first quarter 1992 results. Although sales in the warehouse club industry were projected to grow to $39 billion in 1993, up from $32 billion in 1992, most of the growth was expected to come from clubs "filling in" their existing market areas, rather than entering entirely new regions. Sam's chose to cannibalize its own sales by opening clubs close to one another in many markets, rather than giving competitors any openings. Overcapacity in the industry generated intense competition, and further consolidation in the industry was likely.

Wal-Mart acquired The Wholesale Club in 1991, which operated 28 wholesale clubs in the Midwest. The units were remodeled and incorporated into the Sam's Club network. In November 1993, Sam's Club agreed to acquire 91 of Kmart's 113 PACE clubs, giving Sam's entry to Alaska, Arizona, Rhode Island, Utah, and Washington, and expanding its presence in the massive California retail market. For Kmart, the sale marked a major step in its plan to shed specialty store businesses and focus on its core discount stores. In October 1993, Price Co. and Costco Wholesale Corp merged to form the 206-store PriceCostco Inc. chain.

SUPERCENTERS

A supercenter was a combination supermarket and discount store under one roof (see Exhibit 8 for a Supercenter layout). Wal-Mart's largest Supercenters combined a grocery section of 60,000 square feet with a discount section of 130,000 square feet. The grocery section offered about 17,000 SKUs of food, and the discount section about 60,000 SKUs of nonfood items. Limited package sizes and brands were offered to keep costs low, versus the supermarket's strategy of carrying a large assortment of products. Wal-Mart also introduced the "Great Value" private label grocery line consisting of 350 items. In addition, Supercenters often contained a bakery, deli, and convenience shops such as portrait studios, photo labs, dry cleaners, optical shops, and hair salons. About 450 associates staffed a Supercenter, 70 percent of which were full-time. There were about 30 cash registers at a central checkout area, with stores open 24 hours, seven days a week. Wal-Mart had 30 Supercenters in operation by the beginning of 1993 doing $1 billion in

sales. By the end of the year, there were 68 Supercenters with sales of $2.1 billion.

The grocery section of a Supercenter competed for food sales with supermarkets, independent food stores, discount retailers, and warehouse clubs. Food retailing was a $380 billion industry made up of local and regional operators rather than national chains (see Exhibit 9 for the financial position of the major supermarket chains). Independent stores accounted for 42 percent of supermarket sales two decades ago and only 29 percent in 1992. Operating margins within the industry were extremely low—a typical supermarket was lucky to squeeze out a 2 percent profit margin (see Exhibit 10 for supermarket versus Supercenter profitability). Specialty departments, such as bakeries, seafood shops, floral boutiques, and deli sections, increased customer traffic and offered higher margins of 35–40 percent. In 1992, discount retailers and warehouse clubs sold $16.3 billion worth of food, and about 20 percent of supermarkets sold general merchandise as well as food. These combination supermarkets, or "superstores," ranged in size from 45,000–65,000 square feet, with about 25 percent of the space devoted to nonfood merchandise. Supermarket companies were opening a higher percentage of combination stores over conventional units. Sales of general merchandise (including health and beauty aids) in combination supermarkets grew over 80 percent from $6.4 billion in 1985 to $11.6 billion in 1992, and the number of stores increased 37 percent from 2,670 to 3,650. Nonsupermarket sales of food, which accounted for 8 percent of food sales, was predicted to grow to over 20 percent by the year 2000.

The supercenter format had produced impressive growth, with sales in 1992 increasing 16 percent to $11.4 billion, up from $9.8 billion in 1991. Two super-center chains, Meijer and Fred Meyer, continued to lead the field in sales and store count, though analysts expected them to remain regional (see Exhibit 11 for a list of the top supercenter chains). Food, which typically accounted for 60 percent of sales, was the key ingredient in a successful discount/grocery operation because of its powerful traffic draw. Profits generally came from the higher-margin general merchandise side of the store. According to industry analysts, Wal-Mart Supercenters were "looking for a profit equal to or greater than $50 per square foot, which is not even approached by any other leading retailer except Toys 'R' Us."[17] Kmart had 22 combination outlets, known as Super Kmarts, at the end of 1993. Kmart planned to open 60–75 more Super Kmarts in 1994, and as many as 100 more in 1995. The company was shifting much of its investment in remodeling old Kmart discount stores into building new Super Kmarts, each of which usually replaced one or more traditional discount stores in a market.

Wal-Mart's first Supercenters were located in small towns in Arkansas, Missouri, and Oklahoma. Supercenters replaced the oldest Wal-Mart discount stores, drew customers from up to 60 miles around, and capitalized on Wal-Mart's familiarity and low-price image. Fleming Companies, the number two food wholesaler in the United States, was reportedly supplying half of the grocery items in the Supercenters. McLane division opened a 700,000-square-foot distribution center in Arkansas in early 1993, which serviced the Supercenters and 20

Phillips Companies supermarkets and would eventually service the grocery sections of 90 Supercenters. A second food distribution center opened in Texas in the fall of 1993.

MANAGEMENT CHALLENGES

Glass and Soderquist acknowledged that the current Wal-Mart was a different company from the one Sam Walton left. Its enormous size and the fact that the economy was stagnant presented them with challenges that Sam did not face. There was additional pressure on Glass because he followed a popular company founder. "You can't replace a Sam Walton," said Glass, "but he has prepared the company to run well whether he's there or not"[18] Glass's top priority was to maintain as much communication as possible with Wal-Mart associates.

The drop in the value of Wal-Mart stock was the highest-profile problem that faced Glass and Soderquist. They held a company-wide satellite broadcast to explain to associates, half of them shareholders, why Wal-Mart stock was down. Soderquist recalled, "Most associates were not planning to sell their stock the next day, we pointed out. We simply reassured them that the price of the stock would in time reflect the company's performance." He added, "There is a lot of pressure on management to perform. We have a lot of responsibility to our associates. Right now, we think the stock represents a great buying opportunity. All we have to do is work hard, and the stock will take care of itself."[19]

[17]Wendy Zellner, "When Wal-Mart Starts a Food Fight, It's a Doozy," *Business Week*, June 14, 1993.

[18]Wendy Zellner, "OK, So He's Not Sam Walton," *Business Week*, March 16, 1992.

[19]Jay L Johnson, "We're All Associates," *Discount*

It was uncertain whether gaining share in the supermarket industry would be as easy as it was with discount stores. The ability to undercut small-town supermarkets was reduced by the razor-thin margins on which the business already operated. Several supermarket chains began to feature larger package sizes in an effort to combat the warehouse clubs, and most had private label lines, which were attractively packaged, priced lower than name brands, and carried higher margins.

There were several additional challenges confronting Wal-Mart as it entered 1994:

- Wal-Mart was testing several of its retail formats in Mexico, the company's first foray into international markets, by entering into a joint venture with Mexico's largest retailer, Cifra S.A. Together, they planned to open warehouse clubs, supercenters, and discount stores in the metropolitan areas of Mexico City, Monterey, and Guadalajara. With Kmart planning to open in Singapore in 1994, analysts believed Wal-Mart was also looking closely at ventures in Thailand, China, and Indonesia. Management's concern was—would these formats be successful outside the United States?
- Wal-Mart purchased 122 Woolco stores across Canada from Woolworth Corp. in March 1994. As part of its acquisition proposal, Wal-Mart pledged to offer employment to almost all of Woolco's 16,000 employees, and give Canadian suppliers the opportunity to supply Wal-Mart's Canadian stores.

- Opposition was growing from many small towns groups, who accused Wal-Mart of forcing local merchants out of business. In Vermont, plans to build the state's first Wal-Mart were tied up in court for over two years.
- Wal-Mart was found guilty of pricing pharmaceutical items below cost in its Supercenter in Conway, Arkansas. Three independent pharmacies won the court case, and Wal-Mart was ordered to stop selling below cost. Wal-Mart's general counsel announced the company was appealing what he termed an "anticonsumer" decision. A separate suit was pending in another part of Arkansas. Wal-Mart lost a similar case in 1986 in Oklahoma—it settled out of court during its appeal and agreed to raise prices in the state.
- Target ran ads blasting Wal-Mart's price comparisons with Target, stating that prices were often wrong and noting that "this never would have happened if Sam Walton were alive." Wal-Mart responded that it still maintained and followed Sam Walton's policies, and Target was simply wrong.

Glass summed up the new challenges facing Wal-Mart: "For a lot of years, we avoided mistakes by studying those larger than we were—Sears, J.C. Penney, Kmart. Today we don't have anyone to study," and "When we were smaller, we were the underdog, the challenger. When you're number one, you are a target. You are no longer the hero."[20]

Merchandiser, August 1993.

---

[20]Ellen Neuborne, "Growth King Running into Roadblocks," *USA Today*, **April 27, 1993.**

EXHIBIT 1
THE INDUSTRYWIDE ECONOMICS OF DISCOUNTING
IN 1990 (% of sales)

Net sales	100.0%
License fees and other income	0.2
Cost of goods sold	73.7
Payroll expense	10.4
Advertising expense	1.2
Rental expense	1.8
Miscellaneous expense	7.8
Operating income	5.4
Net income	3.4

Source: *Operating Results of Mass Retail Stores* (International
Mass Retail Association), September 1990.

EXHIBIT 2
TOP DISCOUNT DEPARTMENT STORES ($ million)

Chain		Sales 1992	Sales 1993	% Change from 1992	Number of Stores			Average Store Size (000 Sq. Ft.)
					1/1992	1/1993	1/1994	
Wal-Mart*	Ark.	$39,414	$49,740	26.2%	1,720	1,880	2,030	81
Kmart†	Mich.	25,013	26,948	7.7	2,249	2,282	2,326	80
Target	Minn.	10,390	11,743	13.0	463	506	554	110
Ames‡	Conn.	2,284	2,123	−7.0	371	309	309	65
Caldor	Conn.	2,130	2,414	13.3	128	136	150	95
Bradlees	Mass.	1,831	1,881	2.7	127	126	126	80
Hills§	Mass.	1,750	1,800	2.9	154	154	154	67
Venture	Mo.	1,718	1,863	8.4	84	93	105	100
ShopKo	Wis.	1,683	1,737	3.2	109	111	117	90
Rose's‖	N.C.	1,404	1,383	−1.5	217	232	215	43
Family Dollar	N.C.	1,159	1,297	11.9	1,759	1,885	2,035	7
Dollar General	Tenn.	921	1,125	22.1	1,522	1,617	1,799	6
Jamesway#	N.J.	855	789	−7.7	122	108	94	60

Source: *Discount Store News*, July 5, 1993, and *Value Line*.
NA: Not available.
*Wal-Mart: Sales are for discount stores only.
†Kmart: Sales are U.S. Kmart discount stores only, excluding Super Kmarts and other specialty retailers.
‡Ames: Acquired Zayre in 1989. filed for Chapter 11 protection in April 1990, emerged from Chapter 11 in
December 1992.
§Hills: In Chapter 11. Filed its plan of reorganization in June 1993.
‖Rose's: Filed for Chapter 11 protection in 1993.
#Jamesway: Filed for Chapter 11 protection in 1993.

EXHIBIT 3
STORE AND DISTRIBUTION CENTER LOCATIONS, JANUARY 1993

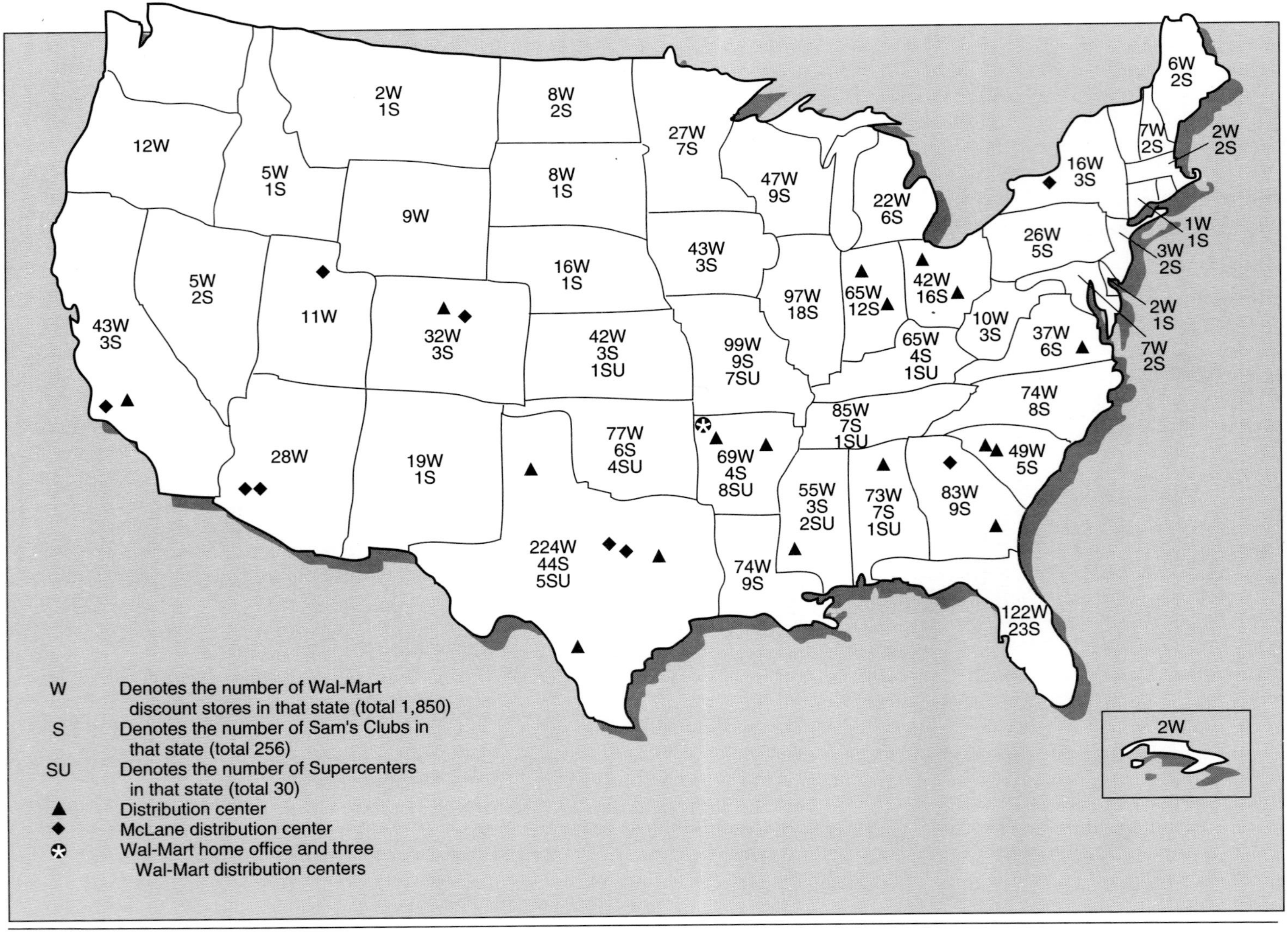

W   Denotes the number of Wal-Mart discount stores in that state (total 1,850)
S   Denotes the number of Sam's Clubs in that state (total 256)
SU   Denotes the number of Supercenters in that state (total 30)
◄   Distribution center
◆   McLane distribution center
✪   Wal-Mart home office and three Wal-Mart distribution centers

EXHIBIT 4
FINANCIAL PERFORMANCE OF SELECTED DISCOUNTERS (%)

	Five-Year Average*			1993 or Latest 12 Months		
	Return on Equity	Sales Growth	Earnings-per-Share Growth	Return on Sales	Return on Capital	Debt/Capital
Wal-Mart	31.2	28.2	25.0	3.5	17.3	40.3
Kmart	13.8	8.1	NM	1.9	8.5	39.5
Target	15.8	10.5	12.1	1.8	8.1	56.9
Venture Stores	28.7	6.8	15.4	2.5	16.7	31.1
Shopko Stores	18.7	9.7	12.1	2.5	9.5	45.2
Family Dollar	21.5	14.4	23.6	5.0	22.5	0.0
Dollar General	16.1	8.7	37.3	4.2	21.9	2.6

Source: "Forbes Annual Report on American Industry," *Forbes Magazine*, January 3. 1994.
NM: Not meaningful.
*Five-year growth rates are based on 1993 or the latest fiscal year-end results.

EXHIBIT 5
WAL-MART STORES, INC. ($ million)

	1983	1984	1985	1986	1987	1988	1989	1990	1991	1992	1993
Operating flows											
Net sales	$4,667	$6,401	$8,451	$11,909	$15,959	$20,649	$25,811	$32,602	$43,887	$55,484	$67,345
License fees and other income	36	52	55	85	105	137	175	262	403	501	NA
Cost of goods sold	3,418	4,722	6,361	9,053	12,282	16,057	20,070	25,500	37,786	44,175	53,444
Operating, selling, general, and administrative expenses	893	1,181	1,485	2,008	2,599	3,268	4,070	5,152	6,684	8,321	10,333
Interest cost	35	48	57	86	114	131	138	169	266	323	440
Taxes	161	231	276	396	441	488	632	752	945	1,172	1,358
Net income	196	271	327	450	628	837	1,076	1,291	1,608	1,995	2,333
Balances											
Current assets	1,006	1,303	1,784	2,353	2,905	3,631	4,713	6,415	8,575	10,198	NA
Property, plant, equipment, and capital leases	628	870	1,303	1,676	2,145	2,662	3,430	4,712	6,434	9,793	
Current liabilities	503	689	993	1,340	1,744	2,066	2,845	3,990	5,004	6,754	
Long-term debt	41	41	181	179	186	184	185	740	1,722	3,073	
Long-term obligations under capital leases	340	450	595	764	867	1,009	1,087	1,159	1,556	1,772	
Common shareholders' equity	735	985	1,278	1,690	2,257	3,008	3,966	5,366	6,990	8,759	
Share Informaton											
Net Income per share	.09	.12	.15	.20	.28	.37	.48	.57	.70	.87	1.02
Dividends per share	.01	.01	.02	.02	.03	.04	.06	.07	.09	.11	.13
Book value per share	.33	.44	.57	.75	1.00	1.33	1.75	2.35	3.04	3.81	4.75
End-of-year stock price ($)	2½	2⅜	4	5⅞	6½	7⅞	11¼	15⅛	29½	32	25
Financial ratios*											
Return on assets	16.5%	16.4%	14.8%	14.5%	15.5%	16.3%	16.9%	15.7%	14.1%	12.9%	NA
Return on shareholders' equity	40.2%	36.7%	33.3%	35.2%	37.1%	37.1%	35.8%	32.6%	30.0%	28.5%	NA
No. of stores at end of period											
Discount stores	642	745	859	980	1,114	1,257	1,399	1,570	1,714	1,850	1,953
Sam's Wholesale Clubs	3	11	23	49	84	105	123	148	208	256	419
Supercenters						2	3	3	6	30	68

Source: Wal-Mart annual report, January 31, 1993; Salomon Brothers; Bloomberg; *Value Line.*
*On beginning-of-year balances.
NA: Not available.

EXHIBIT 6
WAL-MART DISCOUNT STORES—COMPARATIVE PRICING STUDY, BERLIN, NEW JERSEY, JANUARY 1993

Item	Size	Unit Price			Average Price	Variance from Average Price		
		Wal-Mart	Kmart	Bradlees		Wal-Mart	Kmart	Bradlees
Black & Decker drill	½-inch drive	$43.97	$44.96	$44.99	$44.64	$(0.67)	$ 0.32	$ 0.35
Stanley Power Lock	16 feet; inch	11.97	9.94	9.99	10.63	1.34	(0.69)	0.64
Rustoleum	12-ounce can	2.94	2.94	3.09	2.99	(0.05)	(0.05)	0.10
Thompson's Water Seal	One-gallon can	9.47	9.98	9.99	9.81	(0.34)	0.17	0.18
Duracell batteries	Two AA size	1.44	1.45	2.71	1.87	(0.43)	(0.44)	0.84
Valvoline motor oil	10W-30 quart	0.84	0.91	1.49	1.08	(0.24)	(0.17)	0.41
Champion spark plugs	Regular set of four	3.92	5.12	5.99	5.01	(1.09)	0.11	0.98
WD-40	12-ounce can	1.74	1.97	2.99	2.23	(0.49)	(0.26)	0.76
Coleman lantern	—	17.94	19.97	29.99	22.63	(4.69)	(2.66)	7.36
Wilson tennis balls	Package of three	2.96	2.38	2.49	2.61	0.35	(0.23)	(0.12)
Kodak film	Gold 200; 24 exposure	2.88	3.27	4.29	3.48	(0.60)	(0.21)	0.81
Old Spice aftershave	4-ounce package	4.42	4.42	5.19	4.68	(0.26)	(0.26)	0.51
Tylenol Extra Strength	60 tablets	4.64	5.20	4.99	4.94	(0.30)	0.26	0.05
Oil of Olay facial cleanser	2½-ounce package	5.52	5.58	8.49	6.53	(1.01)	(0.95)	1.96
Tampax	24-count box	3.46	3.59	4.49	3.85	(0.39)	(0.26)	0.64
Noxzema	10-ounce jar	2.65	2.79	3.59	3.02	(0.34)	(0.23)	0.57
Pepto Bismol	8-ounce bottle	3.58	2.64	3.99	3.40	0.18	(0.76)	0.59
Vaseline	3½-ounce package	1.54	1.54	1.79	1.62	(0.08)	(0.08)	0.17
Preparation H	1-ounce package	3.59	3.68	3.99	3.75	(0.16)	(0.07)	0.24
J&J Baby Powder	24-ounce package	2.93	2.97	3.99	3.31	(0.38)	(0.34)	0.68
Crest toothpaste (regular)	6.4-ounce tube	1.24	1.24	2.29	1.59	(0.35)	(0.35)	0.70
Reynolds Wrap	75 square feet	3.79	3.89	4.59	4.09	(0.30)	(0.20)	0.50
Easy-Off oven cleaner	16-ounce can	2.73	2.69	3.29	2.90	(0.17)	(0.21)	0.39
Cascade dishwasher powder	50-ounce box	2.27	2.29	3.29	2.62	(0.35)	(0.33)	0.67
Fantastik spray cleaner	22-ounce bottle	1.97	1.87	2.29	2.04	(0.07)	(0.17)	0.25
Lysol disinfectant	38-ounce bottle	2.45	2.43	3.99	2.96	(0.51)	(0.53)	1.03
Woolite	18-ounce bottle	3.59	3.39	3.87	3.62	(0.03)	(0.23)	0.25
Scotch tape	22.2 yards	0.94	0.95	1.19	1.03	(0.09)	(0.08)	0.16
Crayola crayons	—	1.96	2.05	2.15	2.05	(0.09)	0.00	0.10
GE light bulbs	4 regular; 60 watt	1.34	1.67	2.29	1.77	(0.43)	(0.10)	0.52
Planters peanuts	16-ounce can	2.38	2.37	3.69	2.81	(0.43)	(0.44)	0.88
Oreo cookies	16-ounce package	1.84	1.79	1.99	1.87	(0.03)	(0.08)	0.12
Glad trash bags	50 count	5.35	5.58	6.99	5.98	(0.60)	(0.40)	1.01
Presto Salad Shooter	—	22.59	22.94	34.99	26.84	(4.25)	(3.90)	8.15

Source: Salomon Brothers Inc., January 1993.

171

EXHIBIT 7
TOP WAREHOUSE CLUBS ($ million)

Chain		Sales 1992	Sales 1993	% Change from 1993	Number of Stores		Average Store Size (000 Sq. Ft.)
					1/1993	1/1994	
Sam's Club	Ark.	$12,339	$14,746	19.5%	256	419	115
Price Club*	Calif.	6,100⎱	15,498	—	84⎱	206	117
Costco†	Wash.	5,700⎰			89⎰		115
Pace‡	Colo.	4,360	NA	NA	114	NA	107
BJ's Wholesale Club	Mass.	1,786	1,961	9.8	39	54	110
Smart & Final	Calif.	765	NA	NA	124	174	16
Mega Warehouse Foods	Ariz.	293	409	39.6	22	35	50
Warehouse Club	Ill.	241	255	5.8	10	10	100
Wholesale Depot	Mass.	200	225	12.5	8	9	100
Source Club§	Mich.	10	110	1,000	3	7	130

Source: *Discount Store News*, July 1993; *Discount Merchandiser*, November 1993; company annual reports.

*Price Club: Sales exclude Canadian clubs and membership fees. Price Club and Costco merged In October 1993. Sales for the combined PriceCostco are shown for 1993.

†Costco: Sales excludes Canadian clubs and membership fees.

‡Kmart sold 14 Pace Clubs to Wal-Mart in June 1993 and sold 91 additional Pace Clubs to Wal-Mart in January 1994.

§Meijer announced In December l993 that it planned to close its seven Source Clubs in order to free up resources for Its supercenters.

EXHIBIT 8
WAL-MART SUPERCENTER—STORE LAYOUT

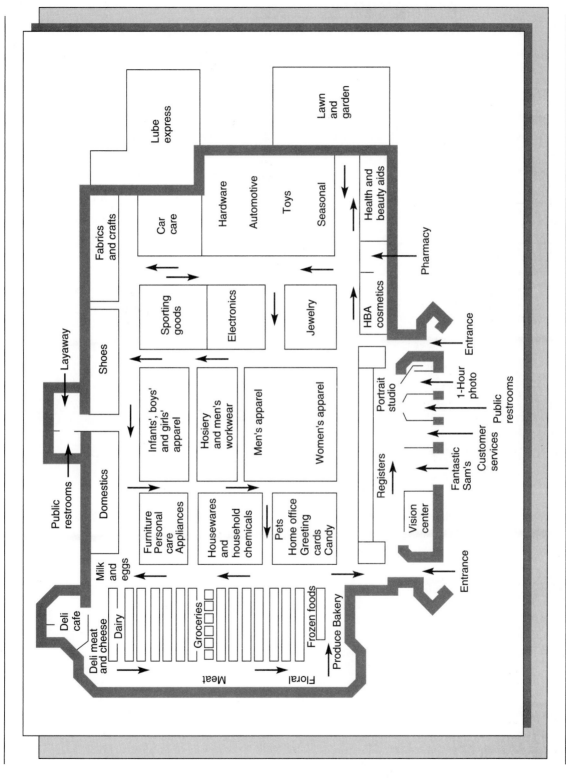

Source: Salomon Brothers, January 1993.

173

EXHIBIT 9
TOP 10 SUPERMARKETS ($ million)

| Chain | | Sales 1992 | Sales 1993 | % Change from 1992 | Five-Year Average (%)* | | ROS % 1993 | Gross Margin 1993 |
					Return on Equity	Sales Growth		
Kroger	Ohio	$22,144	$22,384	1.1%	1.4%	4.5%	0.8%	23.4%
Safeway Stores	Calif.	15,151	15,215	0.4	NE	NM	0.8	27.1%
American Stores	Utah	15,049	18,750	24.6	14.1	10.4	1.3	28.2%
A&P	N.J.	10,499	10,380	−1.1	4.7	2.7	0.13	28.6%
Winn-Dixie	Fla.	10,337	10,832	4.8	23.2	3.8	2.2	22.6%
Albertson's	Id.	10,173	11,385	11.9	24.0	10.8	3.0	26.5%
Food Lion	N.C.	7,195	7,610	5.8	28.5	19.3	1.5	19.5%
Publix†	Fla.	6,600	NA	—	NA	NA	NA	NA
Ahold USA	N.J.	6,300	NA	—	22.1	6.8	NA	NA
Vons	Calif.	5,595	5,145	−8.0	14.4	10.9	1.3	26.0%

Sources: *Stores*, July 1993; "Forbes Annual Report on American Industry," *Forbes Magazine*, January 3, 1994; *Value Line*; company annual reports.
NM: not meaningful.
ME: negligible.
MA: not available.
*1993 or latest five years.
†Privately held company.

EXHIBIT 10
SUPERCENTER PROFITABILITY

	Average Supermarket (40,000 sq. ft.)	Wal-Mart Supercenter (150,000 sq. ft.)
Investment		
Fixtures	$ 1,400,000	$ 2,100,000
Working capital	500,000	2,000,000
Pre-opening expenses	200,000	600,000
Total Investnent	$ 2,100,000	$ 4,700,000
Operating Statistics		
Sales	$20,000,000	$50,000,000
EBIT	700,000	3,100,000
EBIT margin	3.5%	6.2%
EBIT/investment	33.3%	66.0%

Source: *Supermarket News*, May 4, 1992.

EXHIBIT 11
TOP SUPERCENTER CHAINS ($ million)

Chain		Sales 1991	Sales 1992	Sales 1993	Number of Stores			Average Store Size (000 Sq. Ft.)
					1/1992	1/1993	1/1994	
Meijer	Mich.	$4,400	$5,043	$5,440	65	69	76	150
Fred Meyer	Ore.	2,702	2,854	2,979	94	94	127	147
Wal-Mart Supercenter*	Ark.	600	1,100	3,100	10	30	68	150
Smitty's[†]	Ariz.	580	650	NA	24	28	32	105
Bigg's	Ohio	350	450	NA	6	7	7	190
Super Kmart	Mich.	255	313	NA	6	9	22	160
Big Bear Plus	Ohio	190	280	NA	9	12	14	120
Holiday Mart	Hi.	100	117	NA	3	3	3	85
Twin Valu	Minn.	110	110	NA	2	2	3	180
Carrefour	Penn.	80	110	NA	1	2	2	160
Laneco	Penn.	100	110	NA	14	15	16	80

Source: *Discount Store News*, July 5. 1993; company annual reports.

*Wal-Mart Supercenter: Includes four Hypermart USAs.

[†]Smitty's Includes Smitty's and Xtra supermarket chain.

Komatsu Limited

In late January 1985 Chairman Ryoichi Kawai of Komatsu Limited, the world's second-largest earth-moving equipment (EME) company, saw the quarterly financial results of Caterpillar Tractor Co. (Cat), its archrival. With his understanding of the industry and of his competitor's problems, he was not surprised to see Cat's losses continuing but was not expecting the figure to be so high. The $251 million fourth-quarter loss brought the company's full-year loss to $428 million, closing out Cat's third straight unprofitable year. Although it meant that Komatsu appeared to be closing in on a competitor that had dominated the industry for so long, Kawai knew his competitor well enough to understand that Cat would fight hard to regain its preeminent position.

The realization that the industry structure was changing led Kawai to reflect on Komatsu's position. Since his company had become a major player in the indus-

try, it might be necessary to reappraise its competitive strategy. "After all," mused Kawai, "one important lesson to be drawn

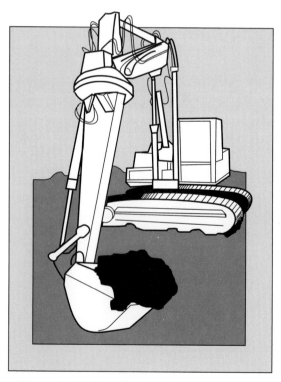

Illustration by Jane Simon

from Cat's decline is that success today does not necessarily imply success tomorrow.''

WORLD EME INDUSTRY

The demand for EME depended mainly on the general level of construction and mining activities, and both industries had undergone considerable change during the 1970s.[1] In the construction industry, for example, it became increasingly clear that in most developed countries the major nonrecurring construction expenditures such as highway programs, water management programs, land clearing, and housing had been largely completed. In the last quarter of the century, developing countries would probably provide most of the large remaining infrastructure projects.

Among developing countries, financing considerations played a significant part in buying decisions for all capital equipment. Further, the state sector was often a significant buyer, and for EME, the buying behavior typically stressed up-front bidding procedures that regularly included not only machines but also spare parts for a period of two years or more.

The mining industry had also undergone considerable change during the 1970s. In many less-developed countries (LDCs) mining belonged to the state sector. This contributed to the surplus production and widely gyrating prices of many minerals. The economic uncertainty and political instability in several of the traditional source countries caused min-

---

[1]A detailed industry review is contained in the companion case, "Caterpillar Tractor Co.," HBS Case No. 9-385-276, and only a brief summary of the key issues is presented here.

ing companies to explore mineral development in developed countries such as Australia. In the energy sector, the oil crises of 1973 and 1979 triggered a construction boom in the Middle East, and major developments elsewhere as other sources of energy were tapped.

The worldwide EME industry had traditionally been dominated by a handful of firms, almost all of them North American. The industry giant was Cat, based in Peoria, Illinois. Throughout the 1960s and the 1970s the company held a market share of over 50 percent. (Exhibit 1 shows the market share trend from 1971 to 1984.) The company built an unmatched reputation for quality and service in construction equipment. Its dealer network in North America and abroad, particularly in Europe and Latin America, had been an important source of its strength. The company's carefully planned competitive strategy emphasized the building of advanced, enduring machines using components made in specialized plants (mostly in the United States), selling them at premium prices, and offering fast, high-quality field service. Cat's high point came in 1981, when the sales and profits hit record levels of $9.2 billion and $580 million, respectively.

Industry Developments Since 1981

As the U.S. recession deepened in the early 1980s, the value of contracts signed by the top 400 U.S. construction companies fell by a third from $170 billion in 1981 to $115 billion in 1983. Much of Europe and Latin America was also in the throes of a recession, and the overseas portion of U.S. construction companies' contracts fell by 45 percent from 1981 to 1983.

During the same period many LDCs, particularly in Latin America and Africa, faced uncertain economic environments with low commodity prices, problems associated with debt servicing and new borrowing, and recession in their principal export markets such as the United States and Western Europe. Furthermore, the softening of oil prices meant that the Middle East no longer remained the center of activity for large construction contracts as it had been in the 1970s. The only economies with much economic resilience were in the Far East.

The competition in the EME industry had intensified during this period. The substantial capacity built during the more prosperous years of the late 1970s far exceeded industry demand. IBH, a German firm formed through the acquisition of many smaller European companies, registered extraordinary growth for several years. By 1983, however, this major European competitor faced bankruptcy proceedings. International Harvester (IH), an industry veteran, was forced to sell its EME business to Dresser in 1983. Almost all the companies had suffered losses since 1981, with U.S. exporters particularly hurt by a dollar that appreciated 40 percent between 1981 and 1984 in trade-weighted terms.

Cat's performance, however, held the attention of most industry observers. Although it had been known to pay generous hourly rates to its workers, Cat's labor relations had deteriorated. In the October 1982 wage negotiations, the company, citing the labor cost differential of more than 45 percent compared with its Japanese rival, sought to contain costs. Cat's treasurer was quoted as saying, "We can handle a 10 to 15 percent differential but not 45 percent."

The United Auto Workers union (UAW) would have none of it. Citing Cat's extraordinarily good performances in prior years, the UAW demanded a share in the prosperity. However, considering the company's worries about future prospects, the UAW made what in other days would have been a generous offer: to continue the old contract for three years with cost-of-living allowances (COLA) continued as before plus 3 percent raises annually, but no new add-ons. The company turned down the union proposal and stuck to its offer: no basic pay increases for three years; COLA for two of the three years but at a trimmed-down rate. Further, Cat wanted reductions in paid time off and more management flexibility in work scheduling between areas without having to consider workers' seniority.

A bitter 204-day strike (one of the largest on record against a major U.S. company) was finally broken in May 1983. Facing inventory shortages and the prospect of its dealer network not being able to meet customer demand, Cat conceded to almost all the union's demands except the additional 3 percent annual increase in COLA. Said one industry analyst, "The settlement will do little to ameliorate what has become a hostile relationship between Cat and the UAW."

With the strike behind it, the company was optimistic that it would post a profit in 1984. Indeed, a robust U.S. economic recovery lifted Cat's domestic sales 30 percent above 1983 levels. Foreign sales also increased 11 percent in 1984, with strong gains in Canada, Australia, Japan, and Europe offsetting overall declines in developing countries. Although total physical volume increased 26 percent over 1983 levels, sales revenue rose by only 21 percent due to "intense price competition." Cat managers blamed excess industry capacity and the strength of the U.S. dollar for this situation.

In response to continuing losses, Cat initiated a cost-reduction program in 1982, and management claimed that its 1984 costs were 14 percent below 1981 levels adjusted for inflation and volume. Furthermore, the company consolidated the operations of five U.S. plants and halted the construction of a national parts warehouse, resulting in 1984 write-offs of $226 million. In late 1984 management decided to close five other facilities. The full benefits of the consolidations and closings were not reflected in 1984's results, but management indicated that its efforts "could permit the company to be moderately profitable in 1985," acknowledging that this implied gaining sales at the expense of competitors. (Selected financial data for the period from 1979 to 1984 appear in Exhibit 2.)

KOMATSU LIMITED

In 1983 Komatsu Limited, the Osaka-based Japanese company with its headquarters in Tokyo, had consolidated net sales of $3.2 billion, with 81 percent of the sales emanating from the EME sector and the balance from a diversified base of manufactures, such as diesel engines, presses, machine tools, industrial robots, solar batteries, and steel castings. Yet, only two decades earlier, Komatsu had been just one of many small local equipment manufacturers living in the shadow of Cat.

Background

Komatsu was established in 1921 as a specialized producer of mining equipment. The company's basic philosophy since its earliest days emphasized the need to export. The founder of the company, Mr. Takeuchi, had stressed in his management goals statement as early as 1921 the requirement for management to have two important perspectives—an "overseas orientation" and a "user orientation." A year later Komatsu acquired an electric furnace and started producing steel castings. In 1931 the company successfully produced a two-ton crawler type of agricultural tractor, the first in Japan. During the Second World War Komatsu became an important producer of bulldozers, tanks, howitzers, and so forth.

In the postwar years the company reoriented itself toward industrial EME. The company's bulldozer was much in demand in the late 1950s as Japan's postwar reconstruction started in earnest. There was little competitive pressure on Komatsu either to augment its product line or to improve the quality of products. The company president acknowledged, "The quality of our products in terms of durability during that period was only half that of the international standards." Unable to persuade dealers to sell its equipment, the company set up its own branch sales offices and authorized small local repair shops to be Komatsu service agents. Given the poor quality of the machines, it is not surprising that customers complained of the company's poor service capability. Thus, despite the booming demand and the tariff-sheltered market, by 1963, Komatsu remained a puny, $168 million manufacturer of a limited line of EME, lacking technical know-how to produce sophisticated machines.

The turning point came in 1963, when the Japanese Ministry of International Trade and Investment (MITI) decided to open the EME industry to foreign capital investment. MITI felt it was necessary to continue to protect the emerging Japanese auto and electronics industries. As a quid pro quo, the EME industry was to be opened up since MITI officials believed that Japan did not possess a long-run competitive advantage in this industry. Cat decided to take advantage of the opportunity, and Komatsu was suddenly faced with a formidable competitor in its own backyard. Komatsu opposed the proposed Mitsubishi–Cat joint venture, but MITI was only willing to delay the project for two years. Yashinari Kawai, Komatsu's president, decided he must immediately take advantage of the Japanese government's policies, which demanded that foreign companies help the Japanese companies in return for access to Japan's markets. He planned to make his company a competitor of world standards.

The 1960s

In his single-minded drive for survival, Kawai set two goals: the acquisition of the necessary advanced technology from abroad and the improvement of product quality within the company. A manager who had been at Komatsu during this time recalled:

> Our mission was made very clear by the president. There was no question that the rapid upgrading of quality standards was the priority task that had to be promoted. It was the only way Komatsu could survive the crisis.

The company entered licensing arrangements with two major EME manufacturers in the United States—International Harvester and Bucyrus–Erie. The former was well known for its wheel-loader technology, and the latter was a world leader in excavator technology. Komatsu also concluded a licensing and technology collaboration agreement with Cummins Engine in the United States, which led the world in diesel engine development. Komatsu paid a substantial price for this technological access, not only in financial payments but also in restrictions on exports that it had to agree to as part of the arrangements. Recognizing that its dependence on these licensees left it vulnerable, the company established its first R&D laboratory in 1966 to focus on the application of electrical engineering developments.

Komatsu also launched a quality upgrading program in its factories. The program, one of the first to reflect the Total Quality Control (TQC) concept, was an adaptation and extension of the well-known Japanese quality-control-circles system in manufacturing operations. The objective of TQC was to ensure the highest quality in every aspect of Komatsu's operations. A company spokesperson explained, "The TQC umbrella spreads over all our activities. Virtually everything necessary to develop, to produce, and to service our products—and to keep customers around the world satisfied with those products' high performance, reliability, and durability—is incorporated into our scheme of Total Quality Control." All personnel—from top management to every worker on the assembly line—was expected to strive for TQC. Komatsu management was proud of receiving the highly coveted 1964 Deming Prize for quality control within three years of launching TQC.

In 1964 the company also began Project A. The project aimed to upgrade the quality of the small and medium-sized bulldozers, Komatsu's primary domestic market product. A top manager recalled, "The president commanded the staff to ignore the costs and produce world-standard products. He told us to disregard the Japanese Industrial Standards [JIS]." The first batch of upgraded products reached the market in 1966. The project produced spectacular results. The durability of the new products was twice that of the old ones, and despite the fact that Komatsu doubled the length of its warranty period, the number of warranty claims actually decreased by 67 percent from the previous level.

At this stage the company launched the second phase of Project A as cost reductions took precedence. Every aspect of design, production facilities, parts assembly, assembly-line systems, and the operation processes was subjected to thorough scrutiny, and costs were pared down. Between 1965 and 1970 the company increased its domestic market share from 50 percent to 65 percent despite the advent of the Mitsubishi–Caterpillar joint venture in Japan.

The company also benefited in other ways as reflected by the company president's comments:

> The product quality improvement activities greatly improved the quality of work within the company. A crisis atmosphere prevailed in the company when the project was being implemented, resulting in a spirit of unity between the management and staff. This was perhaps the most valuable achievement of the project.

The Early 1970s

By the early 1970s Komatsu's management sensed the need for aggressive expansion abroad. The company had achieved dominance within Japan. With domestic construction activity leveling off, however, it appeared as if the EME market was reaching maturity with little prospect of substantial growth. Meanwhile, management was aware of the rise of natural resources activities throughout the world, and particularly the construction boom in the Middle East in the post-1974 period.

Up until the 1960s the company's exports were largely based on inquiries received from abroad. The first large export order came from Argentina in 1955. During the early 1960s the company began opening a market in Eastern bloc countries. Yashinari Kawai was committed to promoting Japan's trade relations with the USSR and China. He and his son Ryoichi, a promising young Komatsu manager, conducted extensive negotiations in both countries and developed excellent relations with many high-level officials.

In the mid-1960s the company turned its attention to Western Europe. Large-scale shipments to Italy were followed by exports to other countries. In 1967 Komatsu Europe was established as a European marketing subsidiary to better coordinate the delivery of parts and the provision of field service. In the same year the first Komatsu machines were exported to the United States. In 1970 Komatsu America was established to develop business in the huge North American market. In most of these markets Komatsu concentrated on selling a limited product line, typically crawler-tractors and crawler-loaders, which were the most common equipment on construction sites. By pricing 30 to 40 percent below similar Cat equipment, the company soon established a foothold in most target markets.

Unlike Cat, whose servicing dealer network covered the globe, Komatsu had no such sales and service system. Even in Japan the company was trying to supplement its company-owned branches and small repair shops with an independent dealer structure. Overseas, Komatsu found it even more difficult to establish strong sales and service capabilities. Companies with the resources and skills to be strong dealers were already locked into one of the competitive EME distribution networks. To ensure good service by those dealers it had signed up, Komatsu maintained extensive parts inventories in each country—"a deliberate overkill," according to one dealer. When it could not get dealers, however, Komatsu handled the sales function directly, at least initially. Its links with Japanese trading companies helped to locate important projects, and the company's overseas subsidiaries would often follow these up to sell directly to government agencies or large companies.

In 1972 Komatsu launched a new project called Project B. This time the focus was on the exports. The large bulldozer, the company's man export item, was chosen for improvement. The aim was similar to Project A's: to upgrade the quality and reliability of its large bulldozer models and bring them up to world standards, then work on cost reductions. Once these aims were realized, the company planned to launch similar efforts for the other lines of export products such as power shovels. Although Project B's main objective was to develop the company's overseas markets, the new machines were also offered in Japan and further reinforced Komatsu's domestic position.

The mid-1970s also saw the beginnings of efforts to penetrate the markets of LDCs, and in particular the fast-growing industrializing countries in Asia and Latin America. In 1974 the company established a new presale service department that provided assistance from the earliest stage of planned development projects in LDCs. The services that the department made available to LDCs free of cost included advice on issues such as site investigation, feasibility studies, planning of projects, selection of machines, training

of operators, and so on. Komatsu also started developing its own exclusive dealer network in some of the large LDCs. In Southeast Asia and Africa, where payment terms for imported machines often involved some form of countertrade, the company also used the services of Japanese trading companies. With all these efforts, Komatsu's ratio of exports to total sales grew from 20 percent in 1973 to 41 percent in 1974 and to 55 percent in 1975.

During the early 1970s the company's R&D efforts continued apace with some attention to basic research as well as product development. Much of the effort, however, focused on the needs of the domestic market since the licensing arrangements constrained export efforts in some important new product areas. New excavator models were brought onto the market in this period, as were completely new products such as pipe layers, large dump trucks, and hydroshift vehicles.

The Late 1970s

By 1976 the Japanese market was highly concentrated, with Komatsu taking a 60 percent share and the Mitsubishi–Cat joint venture left with slightly over 30 percent. However, there was no indication of much market growth in the near future, since worldwide demand for construction equipment was slowing. Komatsu management decided to focus on improving the competitiveness of its products.

A four-part cost-reduction plan was initiated, the first part being dubbed the "V-10 campaign." The V-10 goal was to reduce the cost by 10 percent while maintaining or improving product quality. The second part of the overall plan called for reducing the number of parts by over 20 percent. The third part aimed at value engineering, specifically focusing on redesigning the products to gain economies in materials or manufacturing. The fourth part was a rationalization of the manufacturing system. By the end of the decade the company was well on its way to achieving all these goals.

As Komatsu planned this ambitious cost-reduction plan, an unexpected development occurred that required immediate management attention. In the fall of 1977 the Japanese yen began appreciating rapidly against most major currencies. For example, the yen/dollar exchange rate went from 293 at the end of 1976 to 240 a year later. Management responded by adopting a policy of using a pessimistic internal yen/dollar exchange rate of 180 for planning purposes. Manufacturing was responsible for achieving a cost structure that could be profitable even at this "worst-scenario" rate. After trading at a high of ¥179 to the dollar in mid-1978, the yen weakened considerably against the dollar and most other currencies in 1979 (see Figure A).

During the late 1970s Komatsu also accelerated its product development program. Between 1976 and 1981 the number of models offered in the five basic categories of EME (bulldozers, excavators, dump trucks, loaders, and graders) increased from 46 to 77. When Komatsu introduced its off-highway dump trucks and hydraulic excavators earlier than Cat, management proudly hailed the company's new leadership in technical development and innovation. "We are not content to produce the same type of equipment year after year," said one technical manager, "but are always looking at the latest technical developments and are trying to see how we can adapt them to our products." An example of this approach was the application of electronic technology to all types of machinery. Komatsu had the dis-

tinction of introducing the world's first radio-controlled bulldozers, amphibious bulldozer, and remote-controlled underwater bulldozer. These unique products were aimed at special uses such as toxic dump sites and underwater mining.

The 1980s

Until 1980 Komatsu was impeded by the narrow product line it offered abroad. According to a senior manager, the market for EME could be divided into the bidding market (dominant in most developing countries) and the commercial market (dominant in most developed countries). Although Komatsu's bulldozers and loaders were generally adequate to meet the needs of the former, demand in such markets was highly erratic. Any company that aspired to become a global competitor needed to gain a strong foothold in the commercial market, and to do so, it was almost a competitive necessity to be a full-line manufacturer with an extensive sales and service network.

The decision to become a full-line supplier, however, meant that Komatsu had to reevaluate its licensing relationships with technology suppliers. In exchange for help in obtaining essential know-how from Bucyrus–Erie and International Harvester for the manufacture of excavators and loaders, Komatsu signed agreements giving American licensers a tight grip over Komatsu's exports of its products and a veto over the introduction of competing products in Japan. In 1980 Komatsu objected to Bucyrus–Erie's terms restricting the export of two new products using the latter's technology. When Bucyrus demurred, Komatsu appealed to Japan's fair trade commission. After appropriate deliberations, the government agency agreed with Komatsu that it was a restrictive

FIGURE A
CURRENCY MOVEMENTS: EFFECTIVE EXCHANGE RATES (1975 AVERAGE = 100)

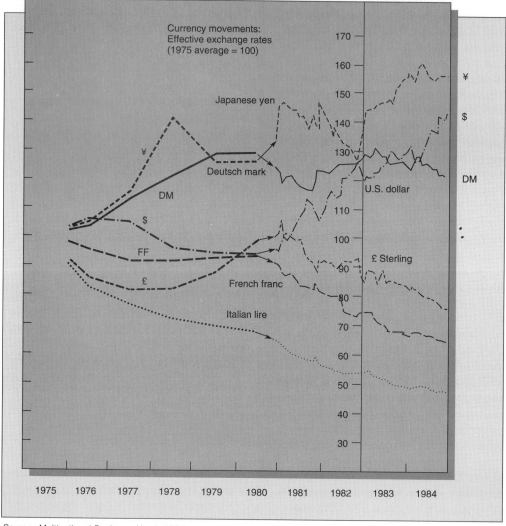

Source: *Multinational Business*, No. 4, 1984.

business practice that impaired competition. This finding allowed Komatsu to buy its way out of the contract, paying Bucyrus $13.6 million to get the data it wanted and another $6 million for royalties on the balance of the contract in May 1981. In early 1982 Komatsu had an opportunity to buy out of its obligations to International Harvester. When financially strapped Harvester was looking for cash, Komatsu bought back IH's half interest in its loader business for $52 million.

One senior manager of Komatsu summed up the approach very matter-offactly: "Komatsu had digested its licensed technology and had established its own technology. Therefore, we just got out of the various licensing agreements." Freed of the constraints of the licensing agreements, Komatsu could sell hydraulic excavators and wheel loaders to world markets. The company emerged as a full-line competitor.

In the early 1970s Komatsu started to reorganize its distributor network worldwide, aiming to supplement the direct sales offices with more servicing dealers similar to Cat's. In 1983 the company had eight marketing subsidiaries abroad, more than 20 overseas offices, and some 160 distributors in foreign countries. It maintained liaison offices in Havana, Warsaw, Moscow, and Peking (Beijing). In the United States, it established five regional centers for parts distribution and service. At each of these centers Japanese engineers were available to help dealers' repair departments with significant problems.

Komatsu management recognized that its 56 dealers in the United States were no match for the Cat distribution system. On average, only 30 percent of a Komatsu-America dealer's sales were of the company's products. Without exception, they all carried other lines as well, such as Clark and Fiat-Allis. Dealers were reluctant to become exclusive, often citing the small field population of Komatsu machines and its narrow product line. As the company broadened its product range, it began a heavy advertising campaign in specialist trade magazines, stressing its full-line capability and its product reliability.

Komatsu celebrated its sixtieth anniversary in 1981. That year it launched a new program called "EPOCHS," which stood for "Efficient Production-Oriented Choice Specifications." The project's theme was reconciliation of two contradictory demands. The aim was to "improve production efficiency without reducing the number of product specifications required by the market." The overseas expansion in the 1970s taught management that customer requirements varied widely by market and by application. For example, in Australia prospects were excellent in coal and iron-ore mining, but the tough operating requirements surpassed the capabilities of machines designed for Japanese construction applications. Komatsu responded by designing bulldozers, power shovels, and dump trucks adapted to mining conditions in Australia. To better its competition, it sent field engineers to survey Australian miners and elicited their comments and complaints about the equipment. The company then incorporated the needed improvements into its products.

As its export market increased, the company faced demands to adapt its products to suit the user requirements in different countries and diverse applications. These requirements varied with each country's environmental conditions and legal requirements. Such adaptations, however, were costly in terms of production efficiency, parts inventory, and field service management. The purpose of the EPOCHS project was to allow the company to respond to the diverse market needs without compromising its cost position.

The project focused attention on the linkages between production and marketing requirements, thereby reinforcing the spirit of TQC, which emphasized the connection between user needs and product development. The EPOCHS project led to the development of a standardized core module for major products and the required number of parts to create the market-determined variety of finished models. This approach was expected to reconcile the contradictory needs of the production and marketing departments.

By the end of 1983 the company's manufacturing had become fully integrated, producing almost all of its components and parts in-house (it was the largest producer of steel castings in Japan, for example). Komatsu prided itself on what it called the "integrated" and "concentrated" production system. From the selection of raw materials to the production and assembly of finished products, it was all part of a single, coordinated system. Further, main components of Komatsu products, regardless of size, were manufactured exclusively in individual plants.

Komatsu products were manufactured in 14 separate plants, 13 of them in Japan. The fully owned Brazilian subsidiary produced medium-sized bulldozers for Brazil and other countries in the region. In 1975 the company established a 49-percent-owned Mexican joint venture for the production of large-scale bulldozers for Mexico and neighboring countries.

Komatsu continued to emphasize its commitment to R&D. By 1982 four separate research labs specialized in production engineering, design engineering, electrical applications, and electronic applications. Product development centers were located in four major plants. A new research laboratory integrating the engineering and electrical labs was in the offing in 1982. The R&D expenditures as a percentage of sales increased from 4.3 percent in 1981 to 5.3 percent in 1982 and to 5.8 percent in 1983. In comparison, the average for the Japanese mechanical equipment industry was 1.7 percent in 1982.

The R&D staff was elated when the company decided in 1981 that it was ready to participate in the International

Construction Equipment Exposition (Conexpo) in Houston. Komatsu displayed some machines not previously seen— prototypes of products that would be marketed in 1982 or later. One of the main attractions at Conexpo was Komatsu's 1,000 hp bulldozer, bigger than Cat's top-of-the-line 700 hp machine. Officially, Cat's response was cool, saying that it had no plans to follow suit. But according to Komatsu managers, the most interested observers at their exhibit were Cat technicians. One Komatsu manager reportedly photographed four Cat managers examining and measuring the company's equipment at the exposition. "Ten years ago," he smiled, "we would have been the ones caught doing that."

Nonetheless, concern persisted about the depressed state of the construction industry worldwide, and Komatsu managers began talking increasingly about other business opportunities. In 1979 top management launched a companywide project called "F and F." The abbreviation stood for "Future and Frontiers," and its objective was to develop new products and new businesses. The project encouraged suggestions from all employees, asking them to consider both the needs of society and the technical know-how of the company. Management followed up on many of the 3,500 suggestions submitted, eventually leading to the development of such diverse new products as arc-welding robots, heat pumps, an excavating system for deep-sea sand, and amorphous silicon materials for efficient exploitation of solar energy.

Komatsu's R&D laboratories played an important role in this new diversification thrust, and the company planned to quadruple the number of research professionals within five years. Further, a joint research agreement with Cummins Engine provided for the sharing of information on diesel equipment improvements, including a heat pump Komatsu had developed that reportedly cut fuel costs by about 40 percent. The company also announced a breakthrough in developing a cast-iron alloy that was superior to the conventional aluminum alloy in heat resistance, noise generation, and fuel economy for use in high-speed diesel engines.

In the early 1980s Japanese-made industrial robots accounted for 80 percent of the world market, and Komatsu was already one of the top manufacturers focusing on arc-welding and material-handling robots, which it also put to use in its own factories.

Komatsu In 1984

By 1984 Komatsu managers had good reason to be proud of their company's record of the previous two decades. (See Exhibit 3 for a summary of the financial results of the company.) It still held a 60 percent market share in Japan, helped in part by sales to its fully owned construction and real estate subsidiaries. The company's domestic sales and service network was acknowledged to be the most extensive and efficient in Japan. Sales activities were conducted by 10 regional offices, 50 branch offices, and over 100 other sales offices. In addition, 100 independent dealers handled Komatsu products and were backed by the company's computerized parts supply system, which guaranteed a replacement part within 48 hours anywhere in the world.

Exports expanded so that they represented well over half of Komatsu's total sales in 1983. The company continued to strengthen its relationships with the Eastern bloc and had a backlog of orders for equipment for the Siberian natural re-source project. The Reagan administration's embargo in December 1981 on the sale of Cat pipe-laying equipment to Russia handed the total business to the Japanese company. Komatsu also signed a contract with the Soviets to develop a scraper based on a Russian design, using Japanese components, and was collaborating with the Russians on a big crawler-dozer and dump truck. Komatsu's sales to the Soviet Union were soon expected to overtake Cat's.

Worldwide, the company's marketing efforts gathered momentum. In Australia, its products were well received in mining circles. Referring to his company's decision to buy Komatsu's machines, the managing director of one of the largest mining companies in Australia said:

> Having come to consider the market its monopoly, Caterpillar became very off-hand with its customer relations. Our analysis suggested that the Komatsu machines offered significant dollar savings and outperformed the equivalent Caterpillar equipment. Komatsu's spares backup should be rated good. The operators also seemed to like the machines.

Despite competitors' suggestions to the contrary, Komatsu dealers generally denied that they were still competing mainly on price. A U.S. dealer commented:

> When you're selling against number one, you need some price advantage. But we tell contractors we can give then 10 percent more machine for 10 percent less money. That's not selling price in my book.

Although Komatsu had undoubtedly been highly successful over the previous two decades, the company's senior management felt that stagnant world demand would lead to fierce competition in the EME industry and could threaten Komatsu's growth. The internal consensus was that the existing distribution network represented a point of vulnerability. Almost inevitably, a senior Komatsu marketing executive compared his company with Cat:

> We have some gaps in our overseas sales network. Caterpillar's distribution network surpasses that of Komatsu in terms of capital, assets, number of employees, and experience. Caterpillar has greater strength in user financing and sales promotion. Indeed, some of our major dealers went bankrupt in the 1980 recession, and that taught us a major lesson about the need for financially strong dealers.

Managers hoped that Komatsu's continued efforts to produce new and differentiated products would help it to build a network of exclusive distributors overseas. Although the company could point to some progress on this objective in Europe, Asia, and Australia, it faced a much tougher task in the United States, where its market share was only 5 percent in 1983 (see Exhibit 4).

Responding to the demands of local governments, the company had commenced assembly operations in Brazil and Mexico. It was also working on a joint-venture proposal with its local dealer in Indonesia, where it held a 70 percent market share in the EME business. But Komatsu's preference had consistently been to design, manufacture, and export machines from Japan, despite the potential problems related to such a highly centralized production system. The rise of trade frictions between the European Community and the United States on the one hand and Japan on the other represented the most obvious risk in the early 1980s. A dumping complaint had been filed against

Komatsu in Europe, and the EEC Commission was considering the imposition of countervailing duties. Another risk for a centrally sourced company was the possible loss of competitive position due to adverse exchange rate movements. And finally, the logistical economics of shipping heavy equipment around the world could become a burden. According to the president of Komatsu-America Corporation, freight for bulldozers and loaders amounted to 6 to 7 percent of Komatsu's landed cost in the United States. For other machines it could be 10 percent or more.

Again, Komatsu managers compared their company with Cat:

> Caterpillar has production throughout the world. It is easier for them to shift production in response to protectionism, exchange rate fluctuations, and changes in other competitive factors. Komatsu has production plants only in a few developing countries, where it had to establish them [due to local government pressures]. Consequently, Komatsu has less flexibility in the face of changes in competitive factors.

Komatsu's market approach continued to emphasize the twin orientations toward overseas markets and consumer satisfaction laid down 60 years earlier by the founder. During the 1970s two additional themes had emerged. A senior manager described them succinctly: "The first is vertical integration based on the philosophy that you must start with good raw materials if you want to manufacture good machines. The second is the Total Quality Control [TQC] practices that pervade all our actions."

At Komatsu TQC went beyond just management practice. It epitomized management philosophy, representing the value system of the workers and managers alike. According to one top manager:

> It is the spirit of Komatsu. For every issue or problem, we are encouraged to go back to the root cause and make the necessary decisions. Not only does TQC help us resolve short-run management problems, but it also lays the foundation for future growth. Thus, it is a key to management innovation.

Komatsu extended its quality commitment to its dealers and suppliers. Working closely with suppliers, the company trained them in adopting its TQC system. The dealers were also encouraged to take advantage of its offer of free services to help implement such a system in their companies. In 1981 Komatsu achieved the distinction of being awarded the Japan Quality Control Prize, considered by many to be the world's supreme quality-control honor. Furthermore, its quality-control circle at the Osaka plant had twice won gold medals from the Union of Japanese Scientists and Engineers, topping the 178,000 quality-control circles of all companies in Japan.

The management practice of relying on the TQC system was supplemented by another system called the "PDCA" management cycle. The initials stood for Plan, Do, Check, and Act. The starting point for the PDCA cycle was the long-term plan announced by the top management team, and the company president's policy statement issued at the beginning of the year. Company president Ryoichi Kawai referred to this as "management by policy." He said:

> Personally, I believe that a company must always be innovative. To this end, the

basic policy and value of the target must be clarified so that all the staff members can fully understand what the company is aiming for in a specific time period. This is the purpose of the management by policy system.

The policy statements became the basis for management focus and follow-up action. As one of the managers described the PDCA system:

> A plan is made, it is executed, its results are checked, and then new actions are planned. Every activity is based on this cycle, including companywide management control systems, production, marketing, and R&D. Because of this, the corporate ability to achieve the targets set improves. These steps also improve the workers' morale and management's leadership.

The management team at Komatsu believed that the intertwined system of TQC, PDCA, and management by policy contributed to company performance and employee development. In the words of one senior manager:

> Tangible results from these systems have been twofold—increasing market share through quality improvement and productivity improvement leading to cost reduction. But equally important is the achievement of the intangibles such as improved communications among departments and setting up of clear common goals.

Ryoichi Kawai again:

> A human being donates his energy to work in order to enjoy and lead an enriched and satisfying life ... We think that it is necessary to satisfy the workers' monetary as well as other needs simultaneously. First of all, there is the satisfac-

tion of achievement in work. Second, there is the satisfaction of cooperating with a colleague and receiving the approval of others. Third, there is the satisfaction of witnessing an institution grow and achieve maturity. It is satisfaction, pride, and consciousness toward participation that make workers feel that they are contributing to a great objective and are doing important work in the company.

As a result, Komatsu had a long history of good labor relations, and the company believed this had been important in its ability to improve productivity and achieve cost competitiveness. Statistics compiled by Nomura Securities showed that between 1976 and 1981 labor productivity rose at an annual compound rate of 15.2 percent at Komatsu compared with the 10.6 percent annual rate at Cat. Both companies were investing heavily in plant capital expenditure during the period.

Despite the high productivity of its workers, the average Komatsu employee earned only 55 percent of the wages paid to Cat employees. Together with lower raw material costs (particularly steel), this low-cost, high-productivity labor force was clearly one of Komatsu's basic assets (see Tables A and B).

Pondering the Future

It was quite in character for Ryoichi Kawai, the chairman of Komatsu, to ponder the future direction for the company that he had headed since 1964, succeeding his father, Yashinari Kawai. Like his father, he had graduated from the elite Tokyo University and had served in the government bureaucracy. He became the youngest department head in MITI's his-

TABLE A
COST STRUCTURE OF A LARGE BULLDOZER
(equivalent to CAT D-6)

		Percent of Cost
Labor		35.0%
Components and subassemblies	12.4	
Overhead	18.0	
Assembly	4.6	
Purchased materials and components		49.6
Overhead		15.4
		100.0%

Source: Boston Consulting Group.

TABLE B
STEEL PRICE COMPARISON: UNITED STATES/JAPAN
($/ton)

	U.S.	Japan*	Japan/U.S.
Hot-rolled mill coil	494	359	73%
Hot-rolled steel plate	635	445	70%

Source: Boston Consulting Group.
Note: Assumed yen–dollar rate is $1 = ¥220.
*Contracted price. Actual prices are often lower due to negotiations between suppliers and the users.

tory before joining Komatsu in 1954. Like every other company executive, he had spent time with workers on the factory floor and was familiar with the company products and production processes.

Kawai had been described in the press as a "workaholic," who often spent his lunch time at his desk partaking of the $3 box lunch from the company cafeteria. He traveled abroad frequently to pursue business deals. Although considered a mild and gentle person, he reportedly had a tight grip on the company. In an interview with *Fortune* magazine, he hinted at his philosophy of life. "In the government you are only requested to do your best. In a company, it is one's duty to earn money and pay your workers. You can't get there by just doing your best."

Kawai greatly admired Cat and often spoke of modeling his company after it. Despite his generous praise of his American competitor, however, he seemed to cherish the idea of beating Cat some day. He likened the competition to a tennis match. "As you know, in a tennis tournament, you can be losing in the middle of the game but win at the late stage." This spirit of competition with Cat pervaded the entire company. Komatsu's in-house slogan was "Maru-C," which roughly translated meant "Encircle Caterpillar." Reportedly, the company continuously monitored events in Peoria, and one of the main jobs of Komatsu's executives in the United States was to keep tabs on any and all relevant press reports. Cat's monthly in-house letter to its employees, which featured new product introductions and other company-related news, was required reading for all Komatsu executives, and copies were sent by express mail to Tokyo for analysis at the corporate headquarters.

As Kawai continued to think about the possible changes in Komatsu's competitive strategy, he kept reminding himself that complacency is one vice his company had to guard against. "Eternal vigilance is not the price of liberty alone. It is also the price of prosperity."

EXHIBIT 1
MARKET SHARES OF MAJOR EME PRODUCERS

	1971	1972	1973	1974	1975	1976	1977	1978	1979	1980	1981	1982	1983	1984[‖]
Cat*	56.0%	55.0%	53.0%	53.0%	54.4%	56.1%	53.6%	51.9%	50.0%	53.3%	50.8%	45.7%	43.9%	43.0%
Komatsu	10.3	10.9	11.6	9.0	9.2	11.3	11.8	14.3	14.8	15.2	16.1	19.6	23.6	25.0
J.I. Case	6.7	6.9	8.9	8.3	7.2	7.4	8.5	9.4	10.5	10.3	9.7	9.9	9.6	10.0
Fiat–Allis†	4.3	4.0	3.8	7.3	7.7	6.3	6.5	6.1	5.8	5.7	5.3	5.8	4.8	4.3
Deere	5.8	6.2	6.3	6.1	4.7	5.2	6.6	6.7	7.1	6.6	5.0	4.8	5.9	6.5
International Harvester	11.0	10.0	10.1	9.7	10.0	7.6	7.2	6.6	7.1	5.1	4.7	3.5	3.3	3.0
Clark	5.9	6.0	6.3	6.6	6.8	6.1	5.8	5.0	4.7	3.8	3.2	2.9	3.1	3.5
Total	100%	100%	100%	100%	100%	100%	100%	100%	100%	100%				
IBH‡	—	—	—	—	0.5	0.5	0.6	0.7	1.4	4.2	5.3	7.8	5.8	4.7
Total industry sales (mil.)§	$4,063	$4,954	$6,190	$7,651	$8,840	$8,773	$10,130	$12,841	$14,027	$14,916	$14,788	$12,098	$10,956	$13,956
Year-to-year change	—	21.3%	24.9%	23.6%	15.5%	-0.8%	15.5%	26.8%	9.2%	6.3%	-0.9%	-23.3%	-9.4%	27.3%
Price increase‖	4%	5%	12%	10%	18%	6%	8%	9%	11%	12%	9%	5%	3%	0%
Real growth‖	—	16	13	13	(3)	(7)	7	18	(2)	(6)	(10)	(28)	(12)	27

Source: Wertheim & Co., Inc.

*Includes sales from Mitsubishi–Cat joint venture net of sales to and from Cat.

†Allis-Chalmers only before 1974.

‡IBH Holding AG—founded in 1975 with growth through acquisitions of 10 European equipment manufacturers through 1980. In 1980 IBH acquired Hymac (U.K.) and Hanomag (Germany). In 1981 IBH acquired Terex from General Motors.

§Excludes IBH up to 1980 but includes it thereafter.

‖Wertheim & Co., estimates.

EXHIBIT 2
SELECTED FINANCIAL DATA ON CATERPILLAR
($ in millions, except per-share amounts)

	1984	1983	1982	1981	1980	1979
Sales	$6,576	$5,424	$6,469	$9,154	$8,598	$7,613
Profit (loss) for year— consolidated	$(428)	$(345)	$(180)	$579	$565	$492
Profit (loss) per share of common stock	$(4.47)	$(3.74)	$(2.04)	$6.64	$6.53	$4.92
Return on average common stock equity	(13.8)%	(10.0)%	(4.9)%	15.9%	17.4%	16.9%
Dividends paid per share of common stock	$1.25	$1.50	$2.40	$2.40	$2.325	$2.10
Current ratio at year-end	1.5:1	2.5:1	2.87:1	1.50:1	1.71:1	1.88:1
Total assets at year-end	$6,223	$6,968	$7,201	$7,285	$6,098	$5,403
Long-term debt due after one year at year-end	$1,384	$1,894	$2,389	$961	$932	$952
Capital expenditures for land, buildings, machinery, and equipment	$234	$324	$534	$836	$749	$676
Depreciation and amortization	$492	$506	$505	$448	$370	$312
Research and engineering costs	$345	$340	$376	$363	$326	$283
Average number of employees	59,776	58,402	73,249	83,455	86,350	89,266
Average number of shares of common stock outstanding	95,919,938	92,378,405	87,999,086	87,178,522	86,458,748	86,406,162

Source: Annual reports.

EXHIBIT 3
SELECTED CONSOLIDATED FINANCIAL DATA ON KOMATSU LIMITED (millions of yen)

	1984	1983	1982	1981	1980	1979	1978
Net sales	¥713,472	¥750,530	¥810,379	¥703,705	¥647,773	¥558,229	¥479,732
Net income	22,642	26,265	32,639	33,257	27,766	23,746	19,617
Earnings per common share	27.2	32.6	41.9	44.0	37.8	32.8	27.6
Cash dividends per common share	8.0	8.0	8.0	8.0	8.0	8.0	8.5
Working capital at year-end	154,466	120,829	119,695	63,705	58,469	43,496	26,927
Property, plant, and equipment at year-end	157,617	143,182	134,223	120,225	110,579	107,767	110,459
Total assets at year-end	943,806	888,324	930,685	877,544	830,773	792,847	739,031
Long-term debt—less current maturities at year-end	80,722	57,442	67,731	48,443	62,755	76,925	70,871
Exchange rates	Yen per U.S. Dollar						
Rate at year-end	252	232	234	220	203	239	191
Average rate	239	238	248	222	225	220	204
Range of high and low rate	223–252	227–247	230–278	206–240	203–251	200–249	179–240

Source: Annual reports and Form 20F reports.

Note: Komatsu had a number of subsidiaries involved in construction, real estate development, overseas sales, and other activities in addition to the parent company, which was involved in earth-moving equipment manufacture.

EXHIBIT 4
KOMATSU'S SALES BY GEOGRAPHIC REGION

	1977	1978	1979	1980	1981	1982	1983
Japan	57.7%	62.4%	62.6%	56.7%	50.7%	41.8%	46.1%
Asia and Oceania	11.2	11.6	15.8	18.3	22.5	30.6	30.5
America (North and South)	18.7	15.7	12.3	11.8	11.8	7.8	7.5
Europe, Middle East, and Africa	12.4	10.3	9.3	13.2	15.0	19.8	15.9
Total	100.0	100.0	100.0	100.0	100.0	100.0	100.0

Source: Form 20F reports.

Corning Incorporated: A Network of Alliances

One Friday afternoon in late 1988, James Houghton, chairman and CEO of Corning, Inc., was preparing for a meeting of the Management Committee, the firm's senior decision-making body. Today, the group would consider the merits of three proposals, each originating from a different business sector.

During the five and a half years Houghton had headed Corning, he had brought major strategic and organizational change to the company. As a result, the business portfolio had been transformed, sales and earnings had reached a record level, and a new spirit had emerged in the organization. As he mentally reviewed the three proposals on the agenda for the meeting, Houghton recognized that the decisions reached today would greatly determine whether Corning would grow stronger in the coming years or whether the momentum built over the past five years would be reversed.

CORNING'S HISTORY

Since its founding more than a century earlier, Corning had enjoyed a strong reputation as a maker of specialty glass. In 1908, it became one of the first U.S. companies to establish a research laboratory, and from that point, technology-based research was at the core of operations, leading it into a growing diversity of businesses. As the company grew, it was credited with virtually creating and sustaining the town of Corning, New York. Corning's personal, informal, and caring style reflected its family-owned and controlled heritage. Its largest shareholders, the Houghton family, had also established a distinguished record of public service as ambassadors and members of Congress. (See Exhibit 1 for a company profile.)

Early on, Corning realized it could multiply gains by cooperating with other companies. In 1937, it combined its technology with PPG Industries' access to the construction industry to create Pittsburgh Corning. Owens Corning Fiberglas, formed as a joint venture with Corning and Owens-Illinois in 1938, was another highly successful partnership.[1] In 1943, Dow Corning was born of an oral agreement between Corning and Dow Chemical to jointly develop the silicone products invented by Corning. Over time, these ventures developed into separate companies, each with its own identity and culture.

When Amory Houghton, Jr., great-grandson of the founder, became the chairman in 1964, Corning's primary focus was on the U.S. market; most international markets were exploited opportunistically through export and licensing agreements. Where foreign operations existed, they were managed as satellites of the parent company, as Corning gradually acquired equity interests in local companies in several national markets.

Although such ventures typically provided Corning with local market access in exchange for technology transfer, they prevented the company from determining its own worldwide strategy. In order to transform Corning into a more international corporation, Amory Houghton acquired or took majority positions in most overseas joint ventures, while simultaneously increasing the company's control over wholly owned foreign subsidiaries. From 1965 to 1974, international sales increased from $35 million to $336 million. A separate international corporation was created and made responsible to James Houghton, vice chairman and younger brother of Amory.

The economic recession resulting from the 1973 oil shock caused a severe decline in Corning's profits. In response, management restructured operations drastically by disposing of several businesses, closing five plants, and reducing Corning's worldwide payroll by one-third in two years. A series of organizational changes culminated in the establishment of a product/area matrix structure.

But the integration of separately managed international and domestic operations proved time-consuming and distracting. When the recession of 1982 caused the company's profits to drop 30 percent, top management replaced the international matrix organization with product line operations in some businesses and geographical areas in others. The big lesson of the matrix experiment, according to one senior manager, was that management could not formalize the multiple informal relationships needed in Corning's complex operations and still hope to create a flexible, agile organization.

JAMES HOUGHTON AS CEO

Taking Charge

In April 1983, Amory Houghton retired as chairman, as he had planned. James Houghton succeeded him and brought his own hands-on leadership style to the office. He tried to visit 10 company locations each quarter to "talk, listen, and feel the atmosphere." An executive recalled:

> From the day Jamie took charge, he maintained an incredibly punishing schedule to remain highly visible even in the outposts. He was very open in his decisions, relentlessly firm, and clear in his purpose. But he was almost Japanese in his attempts to get people to agree and commit. Teams and committees abounded.

---

[1]An antitrust decree soon after World War II prevented Corning from taking an active management role in Owens Corning Fiberglas. Corning eventually sold its shareholding in the company in 1982.

People who were not team players did not fit Jamie's style, and most of them soon departed—including some capable senior people.

Houghton felt that the job of president and chief operating officer was too complicated for one person, so shortly after becoming CEO, he split the president's role into three group president positions reporting to him. He then set up a management committee composed of the three group presidents, the two vice chairmen, and himself as the chairman—a group soon dubbed the "six-pack" within Corning (see Exhibits 2 and 3). Houghton and the Management Committee focused especially on the work environment and company strategy.

Work Environment

As a first priority, the Management Committee moved to create more organizational discipline. Houghton explained:

> Our immediate challenge was that we had not been hitting our goals operationally. Morale was down and many in Corning were feeling like losers. So, we defined clear roles and responsibilities for all key managers. We began measuring their performance on both operating margins and return on equity, and we linked promotions and incentive programs very tightly to their performance.

Roger Ackerman, a Management Committee member, recalled the process of improving performance at Corning:

> There had been a phase when we did not make a corporate budget for six years. Jamie quickly made it clear that such performance would not be tolerated. When people would take their budgets to

the Management Committee and say they couldn't match corporate targets for the year, Jamie would tell them to come back when they had found ways to do it, then walk out of the presentation.

Houghton was increasingly feeling that Corning was falling behind its Japanese competitors in many areas. So, six months after becoming CEO, he decided to focus on establishing quality as Corning's competitive advantage. He recalled, "I didn't really know what we were getting into, but quality soon became a centerpiece of our strategy."

Despite the financial crunch facing Corning, Houghton allocated $5 million of corporate funds to the quality program and persuaded a respected senior executive to become the corporate director of quality. A Quality Institute with full-time instructors was opened in January 1984, with the Management Committee as its first batch of students. In his visits to company locations, Houghton hammered home his concern for quality as "the company's central long-term value." (See Exhibit 4 for details of the program.) Richard Dulude, a Management Committee member, remarked:

> Quality was Jamie's stamp on Corning. He had started a process that did more than just improve product quality—it put self-respect and confidence back in our people. It got people talking across internal boundaries and legitimized the idea that people across the organization could identify problems and solve them without approval from higher-ups.

In 1986, Houghton congratulated the organization on its achievements in meeting quality goals. He then immediately set even higher corporate quality goals for

1991 (Exhibit 4). Ackerman talked about the result:

> Over time, attitudes changed, and most people began to thrive on their new responsibilities. The scale of work increased dramatically, and the pace of life quickened. We began notching up a track record of reaching ambitious targets.

The Management Committee hoped to encourage flexibility and initiative in the workplace, and in 1988 took advantage of the opening of a new ceramics facility at Blacksburg, Virginia, to implement a new model. The experiment, which was dramatically successful, incorporated self-managed teams, coaches, coworkers, education, salaries, bonus payments based on overall plant performance, and a no-layoff policy. The Management Committee hoped to set up similar "partnership companies" across the board. The changes were very significant for middle management. Houghton reflected:

> Instead of bossing people around, managers are now being asked to be coaches and members of a team. It has been hard for many managers to see their authority shrinking. But we keep pounding away on the theme that in this changing workplace, middle managers need flexibility, a willingness to learn, and the ability to listen.

Houghton also moved to break the "glass ceiling" upon which the white male executives of U.S. operations stood, and above which women, minorities and non-U.S. executives seemed unable to rise. He initiated a time-bound program to achieve creative diversity in Corning.

The Corning Strategy Wheel

As a technology-driven company, Corning found itself being drawn into a wide diversity of businesses that were becoming increasingly difficult to fund as the technologies became more complex and faster-changing. Yet, despite its continued commitment to R&D, many of the innovations introduced in the late 1970s and the early 1980s had not translated into major marketplace successes. For over a year after it was formed, the Management Committee debated, What mix of businesses should Corning be in? Was the traditional technology-driven strategy right, or should Corning become market-driven instead? Finally, the committee formulated the operating principles of Corning (Exhibit 5). Houghton explained:

> In an attempt to give some focus to our diverse activities, we began to visualize our businesses as four segments of a wheel: consumer housewares, specialty materials, telecommunications, and laboratory sciences. At the center of the wheel are formal linkages that bind these segments and establish priorities. For Corning, these are technology, common values, and shared resources. The one big picture we share is a vision of Corning as the very best—as *world-class*.

Not only did the wheel give management a tool to communicate clearer objectives and priorities, but it was also used as a framework to help redefine Corning's business portfolio. In the mid-1980s, the Management Committee disposed of many mature and cyclical businesses such as light bulb glass and passive electronic components. (Exhibit 6 lists Corning's major businesses after this restructuring.) Houghton's objective was to replace the old-line businesses that had been sold with others that could "apply Corning's technical capabilities to young and expanding markets."

In 1986 Houghton reorganized operations to remove the last vestiges of a separate international organization and to make business managers responsible for their businesses worldwide. At the same time, each sector appointed a vice president of manufacturing and engineering to strengthen the function. Staff positions were cut by 20 to 30 percent and functions such as control and personnel were made a corporate responsibility (see Exhibit 2).

Achievements and Continuing Challenges

As a result of the restructuring, along with the improvements in the work environment, Corning's performance improved noticeably in the mid and late 1980s (see Exhibits 7, 8, and 9). No longer were journalists writing about Corning as a "country club," as a publication had once referred to it. Indeed, many investment analysts began to view it more as a high-tech company than as a mature industrial corporation.

Corning had historically been a technology-driven company, but it had often been unable to translate its innovations into profits. Among Corning's path-breaking achievements were the production of the first incandescent lamp bulb for Edison, the development of the all-glass television bulb, and the invention of commercially feasible optical fibers. However, Corning had often faltered in applying the innovations—it stayed on the sidelines while General Electric developed the electric bulb market; it failed to leverage its strong position in capacitors and resistors into a major presence in electronics components industry; in ophthalmics, it sat out the plastic lens surge and got mauled in the sunglasses market; and in tableware, it produced a total of four designs for nearly a decade, until its Japa-

nese competitors started taking the market away with innovative designs.

Houghton was determined to overcome this problem, but acknowledged the difficulty in identifying technologies the market would value:

> We continue to invest heavily in R&D, particularly keeping our basic research programs healthy. Amo supported the optical fiber business through thick and thin for 18 years before it became a big commercial product for us. I have to keep looking for the next optical fiber from among the numerous new technologies competing for R&D funds. I see tremendous opportunities in diverse businesses such as liquid crystal displays, memory disks, or ceramics, and we've committed to support R&D in all of them. Frankly, I just don't know which of the many business areas our next optical fiber will come from.
>
> But we've spent money on technology before and then screwed it up because we were late getting to the market. It is here that joint ventures have often proven useful in getting us to the market fast. We are also using them in new ways. As technologies have become more complex, specialized, and short-lived, even large, focused companies such as IBM have found it difficult to keep at the forefront of knowledge in all their relevant fields. Given our diversity of businesses, it's becoming increasingly difficult for us to find all the necessary financial and technical resources internally. Partnerships have become increasingly important not only for the diffusion of technology, but also for its development.

A NETWORK OF ALLIANCES

The 1980s brought new pressures and demands on U.S. companies to pursue joint ventures and acquisitions more aggressively for strategic purposes. *Fortune* magazine highlighted that from 1980 to 1988 over 2,000 major alliances had been formed between U.S. and European companies alone. The boom in strategic alliances, however, had its downside. A U.S.-based study reported that in the 10-year period ending in 1985, 57 percent of such alliances had not succeeded.[2]

Corning's Joint Ventures

Over a span of 60 years, Corning had formed more than 40 strategic alliances. Dulude reflected on Corning's reasoning behind the establishment of joint ventures:

> Our specific objective is to select a business structure that will provide the best chance of success in a particular market. Speed is often the key, and a partner may add expertise in manufacturing or marketing that will bring the product to market much faster. The question we have to ask ourselves is, Are we willing to spend the time needed to make a joint venture a success? It takes twice the management effort as compared to a wholly owned subsidiary, since we have to deal not only with the venture, but also with the partner.

Corning was widely recognized as one of the most successful companies in making joint ventures work. (Exhibit 10 details Corning's principal alliances.) Houghton suggested some reasons:

> Something in our culture helps. We have grown up in this company with the Dow Corning success, where a handshake sealed an agreement and led to a remarkable partnership. We know these things can be successful. Besides, there has been

a continuity in our relations with our partners at the chairman level. I make a point of getting together with the top person from each of our major partners once or twice a year just to have lunch and look the person in the eye to make sure our strategic visions match.

Corning also had a long tradition of letting a new venture operate independently without trying to "Corningize" it. Joint ventures typically reported to their independent boards. Ackerman explained:

> Rather than throwing Corning structure and practices on the alliances, we have relied on the entrepreneurial spirit. We have insisted on results, not procedures. We have first meshed their financial reporting with Corning, then established technology links. Often, we've stopped just there.

In their acquisitions, Corning management often simulated boards of directors internally and allowed them considerable freedom. Ackerman gave an example:

> Metpath [a wholly owned subsidiary] has very different management systems from the rest of Corning. Every joint venture and subsidiary relationship has its own spin, and they have all evolved in their own way.

The Network Organization

Corning was struggling with the increasing organizational complexity in its business sectors, when Houghton was struck by the concept of Corning as "an evolving network of wholly owned businesses and joint ventures." He recognized that operating in a network required a different perspective from operating in a hierarchy:

> A network is egalitarian. The parent company does not dominate its offspring units. All operations are part of a family,

---

[2]K. R. Harrigan, *Strategies for Joint Ventures* (Lexington, MA: Lexington Books, 1985).

some more distant cousins than the others, but all possessing some shared ethics and values. In fact, I now describe joint venture partnerships as part of our strategic wheel. We take technology from the hub and spread it across each sector of our network—to the inner wheel of our divisions and subsidiaries, and to the outer wheel of our alliances.

Historically, joint ventures had been loosely linked at the CEO level and more tightly integrated at the operating management level. Houghton felt, however, that the people responsible for sector strategies needed to be more directly involved. After an initial period on the board of a major new joint venture to give himself a feel for the business and the top managers, he would typically ask a group president to replace him in that position.

This arrangement linked the joint ventures much more directly to top management, and partnership issues were major agenda items at Management Committee meetings. But the greater integration of the joint ventures into the management process made new demands on the top executives, as Houghton explained:

> By forcing my senior managers to spend a lot more time worrying about our alliances, I have broadened and complicated the scope of their work. For example, I hold Roger Ackerman as responsible for Samsung Corning operations as for our U.S. television glass operations. The only difference between the two is that while one operation appears above the line in our annual report, the other appears below the line. My managers have become responsible for operations over which they do not have full authority. They are accountable for results over which they have only partial control. This means they have to use influence to shape priorities. They have to be comfortable negotiating rather than just deciding on important issues.

To make our network come alive, people at several levels have to move across invisible borders. This requires managers with a flexible style and a broad portfolio of skills, and such individuals are normally in very short supply. Both joint-venture partners have to recognize that moving bright, energetic people in and out of the alliances is not only acceptable—it is vital. We can't tolerate opportunistic practices like cherry-picking bright people from the alliances, or worse, filling them with parent company rejects.

One manager's views reflected the widely perceived impact that this had on management skill requirements:

> Operating successfully in a network requires a new mind-set. Our organization has come to be more team oriented. People rely less on formal power and share more information. Many middle levels have been eliminated, and we have a structurally more efficient, flatter organization. I have become more conscious of the highly interdependent nature of my work. Earlier, I used to deal with 6 to 8 people. Now I have direct line or dotted relations with about 15. We now live very well with apparent contradictions. For example, I am the worldwide manager for a business in which no operating manager directly reports to me.

In 1988 Corning recorded revenues on its consolidated statement of about $2.3 billion, which consisted of the sales of its divisions and subsidiaries. But the combined sales of its various joint ventures was about $3.0 billion (of which Corning's share approximated 50 percent, as recorded in Exhibit 9). As the network concept became better understood within the company, people began to look at joint ventures as something beyond peripheral investments. An executive described the changing perspective:

Although the concept of the Corning family has long been with us, it was only more recently that we realized what underexploited, hidden jewels our strategic alliances were. The network idea allowed us to hardwire these ventures more fully into our operations and break the linkage between size and importance. In a network, it became legitimate for small start-up operations, which previously could report only to middle management in a hierarchy, to get the high-level attention they needed.

Furthermore, we began to invite people from other companies in the network to participate in our management meetings. Their presence expanded our horizons, their entrepreneurial spirit enriched us, and I guess they learned from us as well. Although their greater involvement increased the variety of interests represented, we were all held together by a shared core of technology, expertise, and values. And we all had some controls in common—we were all linked to someone on the Management Committee, and we all required financial approvals at the board levels.

THE THREE PROPOSAIS

Corning had started as a specialty glass company. But as it had grown, the company had expanded beyond the core business into a variety of attractive new areas. Its range of partnerships had also increased. The three proposals to be considered by the Management Committee reflected Corning's emerging landscape.

The Centrifugal Forces in the Laboratory Sciences Sector

Gibson, president of the laboratory sciences sector, reflected on the increasing range of technologies and businesses that he was pursuing:

Corning's depressed earnings in the mid-1970s and the cyclicality of our traditional business allowed us to persuade top management of the need to diversify out of our existing laboratory sciences business base, which was dominated by laboratory glass, a mature business of selling test tubes and beakers to laboratories. With corporate support of our R&D efforts, we developed the technology for making porous glass, on which chemicals could be affixed for laboratory diagnosis, or on which enzymes could be immobilized. This breakthrough encouraged us to build on our limited position in the medical diagnostics field.

By 1985, Corning's medical diagnostics business had become significant, yet its operation was dwarfed by others in the industry (Exhibit 11). Gibson described the industry characteristics:

This business is an integrated operation with two parts—equipment and reagents. Like razors and razor blades, most companies were "giving away" the hardware—analytical instruments [that often incorporated Corning's porous glass] —and profiting on the software—the blood-testing reagents. The business was dominated by big, multiline players with huge R&D, or by biotechnology companies on the cutting edge of reagents research. We had entered from the hardware end, but the business really turned on the reagents.

In the meantime, Ciba-Geigy, the Swiss pharmaceuticals company, was looking for an opportunity to move into diagnostics. Gibson recalled:

We were a good strategic fit. We approached them to form a joint venture —mesh our proficiency at manufacturing and marketing with their biological research capabilities, and together crank up R&D expenditure in the operation.

But Ciba-Geigy people hated joint ventures—they had just seen one of their alliances go belly-up. I requested Jamie to fly over to Switzerland and meet the chairman of Ciba-Geigy's executive committee. They both liked each other, and the joint venture was established.

Ciba-Geigy paid $75 million to take a 50 percent share in Corning's medical diagnostics business, whose existing staff became employees of Ciba Corning. A series of "synergy teams" of scientists began transferring appropriate technology from the parent companies into Ciba Corning.

In 1986, soon after the venture was established, Houghton challenged Gibson to replace the sales Corning would lose in its consolidated statement. Gibson turned his attention to the laboratory testing industry. The industry consisted of three segments: clinical laboratory testing, pharmaceuticals testing, and environmental testing (Exhibit 11).

In 1982 Corning had acquired Metpath, one of the leading companies in the clinical laboratory testing field. Corning's experience with Metpath led Gibson to believe that a tremendous opportunity existed to consolidate the highly fragmented laboratory testing industry, which was fast growing out of its "mom-and-pop" store origins into professionalized facilities. Spurred by this vision, in 1987 he acquired Hazleton, an internationally recognized leader in pharmaceuticals testing, for about $115 miilion. By 1988, Corning had become a leader in the laboratory testing industry and had more than made up the revenue that had been lost on the consolidated statement by the transfer of the medical diagnostics business to Ciba Corning. Furthermore, the laboratory testing industry was expected to grow rapidly given the need for increased third-party,

professional testing for AIDS and chemical addiction.

Meanwhile, by 1988 annual R&D spending by Ciba Corning had been raised to $40 million, yet it was insufficient to close the gap with leaders in the medical diagnostics industry. For example, Abbott's R&D expenditure had risen to the $150 million range. Gibson noted:

> Medical diagnostics is a gigantic field, and we have an excellent, highly committed partner in Ciba-Geigy, which is willing to pour in even more funds to build the business. But I am not convinced we can, or should, match them. Ciba-Geigy would be very happy to buy our 50 percent share of Ciba Corning for about $150 million. We could pour these funds and the future R&D funding we would save into laboratory testing businesses.

Gibson had already made some initial overtures to companies in each of the three segments of the laboratory testing industry. He believed that Corning could acquire International Clinical Laboratories, a clinical laboratory testing firm, for about $300 million; G.H. Besselaar Associates, a pharmaceuticals testing company that evaluated new drugs, for about $50 million; and Enseco, an environmental testing firm, for about $125 million. Gibson figured that if these acquisitions came about, Corning would become the dominant firm in each of the three segments of the laboratory testing industry (Exhibit 11).

Thus, Gibson was proposing to the Management Committee that Corning sell its share of Ciba Corning (for about $150 million) and use the proceeds along with additional funding to purchase the three laboratory testing companies (for a total of about $475 million).

After Gibson had discussed his proposal with Houghton prior to the Management Committee meeting, Houghton expressed his concerns:

> I am in a quandary. On the one hand,
> Ciba-Geigy is a highly respectable com-
> pany with the same values as Corning, in
> the same league with the best of our
> partners. It is deeply committed to the
> medical diagnostics business and is will-
> ing to accept lower returns over the next
> several years as Ciba Corning builds the
> business. A long-run relationship with
> such a partner can only do good. But
> investment needs are high and profitabil-
> ity continues to be very poor [Exhibit 9].
> I am wondering whether the diagnostics
> business is central enough for us to sup-
> port it without a steady return for so
> long.
>
> But despite the fact that our laboratory
> testing business is one of our largest,
> most profitable, and fastest growing, it is
> a long way from our glass technology-
> based origins. Yet, Marty [Gibson] seems
> excited about its potential. It may come
> down to a debate about strategic fit and
> organizational commitment.

Charting Future Directions in the Communications Sector

Corning pioneered in the development
of optical fibers, which had much higher
message-carrying capacity than coaxial
cables. In 1970 Corning was able to trans-
mit telephone signals through optical fiber over long distances with minimal signal loss. The company spent the rest of
the decade investing in R&D and trying to
win market acceptance for the revolutionary new product in a conservative industry.

In the early 1970s, Corning moved to
exploit its optical fibers technology in
Europe. The government-owned telephone companies in France, the United
Kingdom, and Italy favored domestic suppliers. In response, Corning established
joint development agreements through fee
and licensing arrangements with the premier cable manufacturers of France and
the United Kingdom. In Germany, Corning entered into a joint venture with Siemens, the country's leading cable manufacturer, to form Siecor GmbH for the
purpose of making optical fibers.

As the European market began to blossom, in 1981 Corning entered into joint
ventures with its French and U.K. licensees along the lines of Siecor GmbH.[3] Corning set up manufacturing facilities through
its European joint ventures in order to
provide the optical fibers needed by the
European partners to manufacture fiber
optic cable for sale to their respective
national telephone companies.

Meanwhile, in the United States, AT&T,
which controlled about 75 percent of the
cabling business, had been developing its
own optical fiber. Despite years of effort,
Corning had been unable to convince the
independent copper cablers, who accounted for the rest of the market, to try its
fiber. Finally, Corning decided to integrate forward into cable making. In 1981
Corning and Siemens AG formed Siecor
Corporation for the purpose of making
fiber optic cable in the United States for
the U.S. market (using Corning optical
fiber). Each company contributed $50 mil-
lion, plus Corning brought its manage-

---

[3]In 1988 Corning was in the process of selling its
share in the French joint venture because Corning's
original partner had sold its share in the joint venture to one of Corning's competitors (as part of the
sale of the original partner's entire product line).
Furthermore, Corning believed that the evolving
rules of the European Economic Commission would
enable the French market to be served by one of the
other Corning European joint ventures.

ment and market knowledge to the alliance, and Siemens brought its cable-making know-how.

In 1983 MCI began buying fiber optic cable from Siecor Corporation. That same year, AT&T was broken up, and its captive cable market opened to outside suppliers. The fiber optic cable market in North America grew dramatically between 1982 and 1986. Industry capacity tripled by 1986, and fiber prices fell more than 70 percent by 1988. The result was a sharp drop in Corning's optical fiber revenues and profits (Exhibit 9). Siecor Corporation quickly became one of the largest makers of fiber optic cables in the world. While most of the U.S. market for fiber optic cables thus far had been in long-distance links, the market for local systems was expected to take off by the mid-1990s (Exhibit 12).

Dulude, the president of the communications sector, reflected on current challenges facing the optical fibers business:

> Before 1980, our entire fiber business was about $10 million with annual losses of $5 million. Today, the combined revenue of our divisions and alliances is over $1 billion, with good profitability. We are now planning for the next stage, when optical fiber enters homes, by developing tough new fibers more suited to local operations. We are proposing to the Management Committee to rapidly ramp up capacity to make optical fibers—by about 25 percent by 1990, and another 25 percent by 1991, at a cost of about $100 million.

Houghton commented on the opportunities and challenges facing Corning in optical fibers:

> In the 1980s, Corning held 150 patents on fiber and fiber-making processes, and we zealously protected our patents

against infringements. But our patents will expire in the early 1990s, and our business strategy in the United States has to adjust. Internationally, Eastern Europe and USSR offer outstanding opportunities, with decrepit phone systems and little copper to be replaced. We are contemplating entering several international joint ventures to access national markets quickly.

In order to make fiber optic cables more attractive to users, Corning began to consider offering sophisticated cable terminal peripherals, such as electronic receivers and transmitters, to large telecommunications and computer companies. Toward this goal, Corning formed PlessCor Optronics (PCO) in 1984—a joint venture with Plessey Corporation, U.K., and a management team led by an optoelectronic devices expert. In 1986, however, faced with an unfriendly takeover bid, Plessey Corporation sold its shares in PCO to Corning. By 1988, PCO sales had grown to about $10 million, although it was still incurring operating losses.

Dulude commented on this business:

> Just as we moved into cables in a big way with Siecor Corporation, we could push into peripherals in a big way. The principal potential users of the peripherals are developing their own production facilities. But we believe that IBM's in-house program is going slower than anticipated. We are proposing to the Management Committee that Corning offer IBM a partnership in PCO so that PCO becomes IBM's preferred second source, besides benefiting from IBM's knowledge of the technology and the market.

Therefore, Dulude's proposal to the Management Committee consisted of two parts: (1) invest $100 million in the three-year period 1989–91 in order to expand the U.S. optical fiber capacity to make the tough new fibers needed to service homes, and (2) offer IBM a partnership in PCO in order for PCO to become IBM's preferred second source for cable terminal peripherals.

While Houghton favored the U.S. capacity expansion in optical fibers, he had some qualms about the proposal to offer IBM a partnership in PCO:

> In PCO, we could have the seeds of another giant alliance. The question that I ask myself, however, is—how much should we remain focused on the huge, core potential, and how far should we allow interesting and potentially valuable expansion opportunities to lead us?

The Conundrum of the Television Glass Business

The color television glass business, a prized part of the specialty materials sector, also was offering new strategic and organizational challenges. The color television industry was increasingly dominated by the Japanese, who had developed superior technology and lower-cost manufacturability. Many industry analysts believed this dominance would increase as the industry approached a revolutionary new technology—High Definition Television (HDTV).

As the consumer electronics industry became more concentrated and fully integrated, competition among television glass suppliers also intensified (see Exhibit 13 for industry data).

In Asia, Corning was collaborating with Samsung to establish a substantial presence in the television glass business. But there were some differences between the partners on the eventual size and scope of the alliance.

In Europe, Corning and Schott were competing for business from two major customers, Philips and Thomson, both of whom were looking to integrate back into TV glass making. Feeling that too much investment would be needed to sustain a low-cost manufacturing position in Europe, Corning had offered to sell 80 percent of its business there to Thomson.

Meanwhile, Japanese TV set manufacturers began setting up facilities in the United States in the 1980s, and the U.S.-based TV set manufacturers began folding up one after the other in the face of the competitive onslaught. In the same period, Corning closed three television glass factories in the United States, and by 1988, it had only one remaining domestic plant in this once prized core business.

Following the Japanese TV set manufacturers, NEG, one of the two giant Japanese glass companies, entered the U.S. market by acquiring substantial shareholding in Owens Illinois, Corning's traditional domestic competitor in television glass. Asahi, the other Japanese glass company, had been a refractory materials licensee of Corning since the 1930s. During World War II, links between the two companies had been temporarily severed. But once the war ended, in a move emblematic of the close relations between them, Asahi unilaterally gave Corning the meticulously calculated license fee for refractory sales made in the war years. In 1965, the two companies formed Iwaki, a 50–50 joint venture to manufacture refractory materials in Japan, managed primarily by Asahi. Over time, while Corning wanted higher returns from Iwaki, Asahi was looking more for long-term growth. As a result, Corning was planning to dilute its holding in Iwaki.

As Corning tried to revitalize its U.S. television glass business, executives from the specialty materials sector were placing an intriguing proposal before the Management Committee—to sell Asahi 49 percent of Corning's U.S. television glass business for about $100 million and channel the proceeds into developing glass for liquid crystal displays.

A senior executive explained:

> Rather than fight on our own in an increasingly hostile environment in which capital and R&D costs are becoming prohibitive, we could convert our U.S. operations into a joint venture with Asahi. On their side, Asahi would gain access to the U.S. market and also to our melting, systems, and finishing technologies. We would gain access to Asahi's expertise in large-size television bulb and HDTV technology, especially the glass delivery systems and forming technology. And most importantly, we could benefit from their established relations with the Japanese TV manufacturers setting up facilities in the United States.
>
> When our salespeople began calling on the Japanese TV set manufacturers, we felt as if a veil came over them when they dealt with us. Their relationships with their Japanese suppliers ran very deep, while they were very distant with us. Last week, Asahi people escorted me to a meeting with the worldwide TV tube manager of a large Japanese company and introduced me properly to him. We had an extremely fruitful conversation. I wouldn't have even been able to meet him and discuss issues between us if it were not for the Asahi connection.

An alliance with Asahi would significantly alter the interweaving of relationships across companies in the tightly knit television glass and set assembly industries. As competition among European, Japanese, and Korean consumer electronics companies was intensifying, these companies developed an increasing concern about protecting proprietary knowledge. In many cases, this had put pressure on television glass suppliers to ensure the security of competitive information about downstream customers.

A decision on whether to create a U.S.-based television glass joint venture with Asahi would have important implications beyond the immediate situation. Houghton reflected:

> The proposed Asahi partnership would integrate alliances even deeper into our being. It's clear that such a venture would play a strategic role different from that of most other alliances. I want to be certain that such an alliance is appropriate for Corning and managed effectively. Besides, some of our senior employees would be transferred to this venture, and I would want to ensure that they knew that the company still looked on them as its own.

The Management Committee Meeting

As the members of the committee settled into their chairs, Houghton opened the meeting:

> I am sure that you all, like I, have formed some ideas about the three proposals we're going to discuss today. I suggest that we regard these as more than just incremental investment decisions. In my view, they present us with the opportunity to test our strategic vision for the company and to challenge our emerging concept of Corning as a network of alliances. We're confronting sensitive issues here, and our decisions today will, I believe, profoundly influence this company's future.

EXHIBIT 1
OWNERSHIP PATTERN AND COMPANY PROFILE IN 1988

Ownership Pattern	
Institutions	53%
Amory Houghton, Jr.	7.6
Arthur A. Houghton	8.2
Corning Investment Plans	5.5
Approximate number of shareholders	14,500

Company Profile		Of which:	
	Worldwide	In U.S.	Abroad
Employees	27,750	20,150	7,600
Plants	36	25	11
Sales/service offices	38	15	23
Laboratories	21	18	3

Corning owned 50% or less in 19 affiliated companies in 11
countries with combined sales of $3.0 billion. The numbers in this
table exclude these 19 affiliated companies.

Fortune 500 *Rank*				
	1988	1987	1986	1985
Sales	198	186	193	217
Assets	144	140	140	160
Income	136	111	101	119
Return on equity	158	271	221	282

Financial Performance, 1973–1989 ($ billion)																	
	89F	88	87	86	85	84	83	82	81	80	79	78	77	76	75	74	73
Assets	3.5	2.9	2.7	2.5	2.0	1.9	1.8	1.8	1.6	1.5	1.4	1.2	1.1	0.9	0.8	0.8	0.7
S/H equity	1.7	1.6	1.5	1.4	1.2	1.1	1.0	1.0	1.0	0.9	0.8	0.7	0.7	0.6	0.5	0.5	0.5
Sales	2.5	2.3	2.1	2.1	1.8	1.7	1.6	1.6	1.7	1.6	1.5	1.3	1.1	1.0	0.9	1.1	0.9
R&D	.10	.10	.10	.10	.09	.09	.09	.09	.08	.07	.07	.06	.06	.05	.04	.04	.04
Net income	.25	.21	.21	.18	.14	.10	.09	.07	.10	.12	.13	.10	.09	.08	.03	.05	.07

F = Forecast

EXHIBIT 2
THE ORGANIZATION STRUCTURE IN 1988

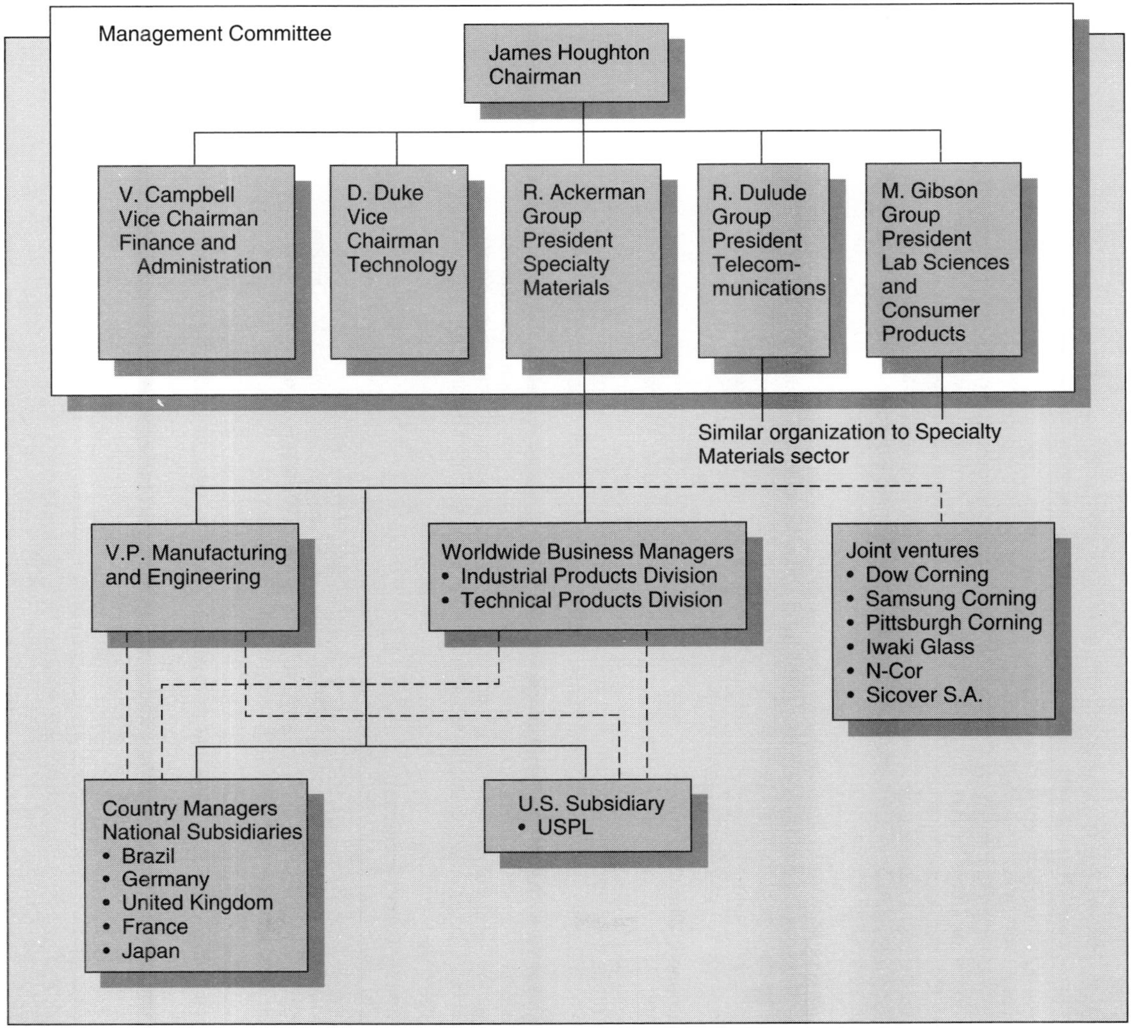

Management Committee

James Houghton
Chairman

V. Campbell
Vice Chairman
Finance and
Administration

D. Duke
Vice
Chairman
Technology

R. Ackerman
Group
President
Specialty
Materials

R. Dulude
Group
President
Telecom-
munications

M. Gibson
Group
President
Lab Sciences
and
Consumer
Products

Similar organization to Specialty Materials sector

Joint ventures
- Dow Corning
- Samsung Corning
- Pittsburgh Corning
- Iwaki Glass
- N-Cor
- Sicover S.A.

Worldwide Business Managers
- Industrial Products Division
- Technical Products Division

V.P. Manufacturing
and Engineering

U.S. Subsidiary
- USPL

Country Managers
National Subsidiaries
- Brazil
- Germany
- United Kingdom
- France
- Japan

EXHIBIT 3
BIOGRAPHICAL PROFILES OF MEMBERS OF THE MANAGEMENT COMMITTEE

James R. Houghton, Chairman and Chief Executive Officer

A graduate of Harvard College and Harvard Business School, Mr. Houghton joined Corning in 1962. He was named European area manager in 1965, vice president and general manager of the consumer products division in 1968, elected a director in 1969, and vice chairman responsible for international operations in 1971. He was elected chairman in 1983. Besides several subsidiary and joint-venture firms, Mr. Houghton was also a director of Metropolitan Life Insurance Company, CBS Inc., JP Morgan Co., and Owens-Corning Fiberglas Corporation. He also served as trustee of several institutions.

Roger G. Ackerman, Group President

Mr. Ackerman joined Corning in 1962 and served in various positions, including senior vice president and director of the manufacturing and engineering division, and president and chief executive officer of Metpath. He was named group president in 1985. Mr. Ackerman held a BS and an MS degree in engineering from Rutgers University.

Van C. Campbell, Vice Chairman

Mr. Campbell joined Corning in 1965 and progressed through a series of positions, including treasurer, vice president for finance, and senior vice president and general manager of the consumer products division. He was named vice chairman in 1983. Mr. Campbell received an AB degree from Cornell University in 1960 and an MBA from Harvard Business School in 1963.

David A. Duke, Vice Chairman—Technology

Dr. Duke joined Corning in 1962 and served in various positions, including vice president and general manager—telecommunications products, and director of research and development. In 1985, he was elected vice chairman—technology. Dr. Duke held BS, MS, and PhD degrees from the University of Utah.

Richard Duiude, Group President

Mr. Dulude joined Corning in 1957 and served in various positions, first in lighting glassware, and thereafter in international operations. He was named senior vice president and director of marketing and business development in 1980, and named group president in 1983. Mr. Dulude held a BME degree from Syracuse University and had completed the Senior Executive Program of the Sloan School of Management, MIT.

E. Martin Gibson, Group President

Mr. Gibson joined Corning in 1962 and held various positions, including vice president and general manager of the medical products division, vice president for personnel, and senior vice president and general manager of the medical and scientific division. He was named group president in 1983. Mr. Gibson received a BA degree from Yale University and an MBA from the University of Pennsylvania.

EXHIBIT 4
THE TOTAL QUALITY MANAGEMENT SYSTEM AT CORNING

The Policy

It is the policy of Corning to achieve total quality performance in meeting the requirements of external and internal customers. Total quality performance means understanding who the customers are, what the requirements are, and meeting those requirements, without error, on time, every time.

The Four Principles of the Total Quality Campaign

1. Meet the customer's requirements—Quality is meeting the customer's requirements. The customer is everyone an employee deals with. It's absolutely vital that we understand and agree on requirements before starting an assignment.
2. Error-free work—Errors are not acceptable.
3. Manage by prevention—Quality must be built into the work.
4. Measure by the cost of quality—The cost of quality is made up of three parts: error cost, detection cost, and prevention cost. Often, as prevention cost rises, overall cost of quality falls.

Organizing for Quality

- The Ouality Improvement Team
- Division Quality Executive
- The Management Committee
- The Corrective Action Team
- The Quality Council

Key Quality Events

1984   Quality institute opened, with the Management Committee as its first batch of students. Organization-wide climate survey.

1985   Corporate statement of Corning values.
James Houghton suggested, "Decide on your top three vital issues. Pick one. Remove it. Permanently."

1986   Goals set for 1991.

1987   National Quality Month chaired by James Houghton.
The year of delighting the customer.

1988   Focus on total quality skills: benchmarking, process management approach, service quality, customer/supplier partnerships, union–management quality reviews, workplace partnerships, and using criteria of the Baldrige award to judge quality.

Corporate Quality Goals Set in 1986 for 1991

1. To spend 5 percent of our time on education and training as a company.
2. To reduce by 90 percent the key errors in the company by using the "vital few" concept—picking the few most critical errors and solving them.
3. To introduce no new product that is not at least equal in quality to the product it's replacing or to the competition. You cannot ship your learning curve to the customer.

EXHIBIT 5
EXCERPTS FROM THE *CORNING VALUES* DOCUMENT

Our Purpose

Our purpose is to deliver superior, long-range economic benefits to our customers, our employees, our shareholders, and to the communities in which we operate. We accomplish this by living our corporate values.

Our Strategy

Corning is an evolving network of wholly owned businesses and joint ventures. We choose to compete in four global business sectors: *Specialty Materials, Consumer Housewares, Laboratory Sciences,* and *Communications.* Each segment is composed of divisions, subsidiaries, and alliances. Binding the four sectors together is the glue of common values, a commitment to technology, shared resources, dedication to total quality, and management links.

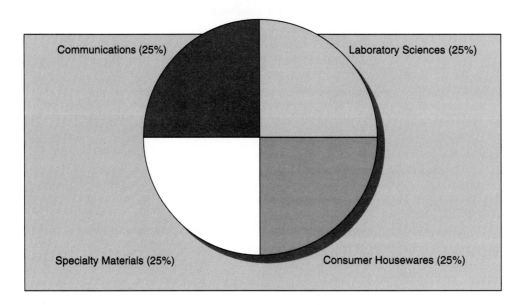

THE STRATEGY WHEEL OF CORNING

What We Value

- *Quality*
- *Independence*
- *Integrity*
- *Technology*
- *Performance*
- *The Individual*
- *Leadership*

Where We Want to Go—Our Financial Goals

- We will be consistently in the top 25 percent of the *Fortune 500* in financial performance as measured by return on equity.
- We will grow at an annual rate in excess of 5 percent in real terms.
- We will maintain a debt-to-capital ratio of approximately 25 percent and a long-term dividend payout of 33 percent.
- We will issue new shares of stock on a limited basis in connection with employee ownership programs and acquisitions with a clear strategic fit.

EXHIBIT 6
BUSINESS SECTOR PROFILE IN 1988

Sector	Major Businesses
Specialty Materials	Video displays, LCD displays, memory storage, automotive headlamps, emission-control products, and silicone-based products.
Communications	Optical fibers and fiber optic cables.
Laboratory sciences	Laboratory products and laboratory testing services.
Consumer housewares	Cookware, tableware, sunglasses, and crystal.

EXHIBIT 7
CONSOLIDATED FINANCIAL STATEMENTS, 1983–1988
($ MILLION, UNLESS OTHERWISE NOTED)

	1988	1987	1986	1985	1984	1983
Income statement						
Total revenue	$2,301.5	$2,130.0	$2,080.7	$1,786.6	$1,732.7	$1,589.4
Cost of sales	1,397.7	1,407.5	1,284.1	1,156.9	1,173.9	1,063.9
SG&A expenses	438.6	429.3	381.2	368.8	375.8	368.2
R&D expenses	95.2	99.8	103.5	87.5	94.3	89.3
Interest expense	41.0	39.9	34.2	39.1	38.2	44.5
Other expenses (gains)	58.4	8.0	132.2	88.9	(3.0)	(41.4)
Income before tax	**270.6**	**145.5**	**145.5**	**45.4**	**53.5**	**64.9**
Income tax	103.2	55.3	55.4	6.5	18.2	7.7
Income after tax	167.4	90.2	90.1	38.9	35.3	57.2
Equity share in affiliates' earning	125.0	98.9	76.8	71.8	53.4	35.0
Extraordinary credit*	(81.7)	18.4	14.9	25.7	11.6	
Net income	**210.7**	**207.5**	**181.8**	**136.4**	**100.3**	**92.2**
Balance sheet						
Cash	29.4	35.4	39.3	55.9	38.7	32.0
Short-term investment	127.1	220.0	163.7	55.8	70.9	109.1
Accounts receivable	397.5	364.8	342.6	275.0	244.4	251.4
Inventories	254.0	221.0	224.9	201.1	251.5	229.5
Deferred taxes	121.8	122.1	152.4	122.1	98.5	79.9
Total current assets	**929.8**	**963.3**	**922.9**	**709.9**	**704.9**	**701.9**
Investment in associated companies	805.9	683.3	569.1	519.9	389.6	340.6
Other investments	12.4	13.2	14.2	16.6	37.0	33.5
Net plant & equipment	991.5	909.7	859.4	708.6	641.8	610.9
Other assets	158.3	88.6	95.8	77.4	84.4	87.7
Total assets	**2,897.9**	**2,658.7**	**2,461.4**	**2,032.4**	**1,856.8**	**1,774.6**
Current liabilities	508.7	479.9	508.1	400.3	377.1	344.4
Other liabilities	223.2	117.3	132.7	81.4	61.2	50.8
Long-term loans	499.0	428.8	373.9	327.5	309.1	315.3
Deferred taxes	71.0	97.0	51.1	37.6	42.3	29.9
Minority S/H	35.3					1.5
Shareholders' equity	1,560.7	1,535.7	1,395.6	1,185.6	1,067.1	1,032.7
Total liabilities	**2,897.9**	**2,658.7**	**2,461.4**	**2,032.4**	**1,856.8**	**1,774.6**
Selected ratios (%)						
Return on equity						
Net income†	14	14	13	12	9	9
Divisions and subsidiaries‡	22	11	11	6	5	8
Joint ventures§	16	15	13	14	14	10
Shareholders' equity as % of total liabilities	54	58	57	58	57	58

*Generated by activities not connected with ongoing operations.
†Net income divided by shareholders' equity.
‡Income after tax divided by (shareholders' equity − investment in associated companies).
§Equity share in affiliates' earnings divided by investment in associated companies.

EXHIBIT 8
BUSINESS SECTOR PERFORMANCE, TOTAL OF DIVISIONS, SUBSIDIARIES, AND JOINT
VENTURES, 1983–1988 ($ MILLION, UNLESS OTHERWISE NOTED)

	%CAGR 1983–87	1988	1987	1986	1985	1984	1983
Revenues*							
Specialty materials	14%	$1,363	$1,227	$1,031	$ 895	$ 880	$ 711
Communications	8	732	824	857	733	578	488
Laboratory sciences	11	895	745	663	594	528	534
Consumer products	7	639	570	500	434	451	443
Miscellaneous (incl. R&D)	30	180	46	137	32	22	49
Total	11	3,809	3,412	3,188	2,688	2,459	2,225
Earnings[†] **(after tax)**							
Specialty materials	4%	119	122	90	109	103	99
Communications	12	75	71	96	126	68	42
Laboratory sciences	10	87	65	50	47	36	55
Consumer products	27	47	34	15	(22)	(6)	14
Miscellaneous (incl. R&D)	NM	(34)	(103)	(85)	(149)	(112)	(118)
Total	26	294	189	166	111	89	92
After-tax earnings **(as a % of revenues)**							
Specialty materials		9	10	9	12	12	14
Communications		10	9	11	17	12	9
Laboratory sciences		10	9	8	8	7	10
Consumer products		7	6	3	(5)	(1)	3
Miscellaneous (incl. R&D)		(18)	(224)	(62)	(466)	(509)	(241)
Total		8	6	5	4	4	4

Figures in parentheses indicate losses.

NM = not meaningful

*100% of revenues of divisions and subsidiaries plus 50% of revenues of joint ventures.

[†]100% of earnings (after tax) of divisions and subsidiaries plus Corning's share of joint venture companies' earnings (after tax).

EXHIBIT 9
BUSINESS SECTOR PERFORMANCE BY DIVISIONS AND SUBSIDIARIES AND BY JOINT VENTURES, 1983–1988 ($ MILLION, UNLESS OTHERWISE NOTED)

	% CAGR 1983–87	1988	1987	1986	1985	1984	1983
Revenues							
Divisions and subsidiaries							
Specialty materials	12%	$ 400	$ 386	$ 330	$ 324	$ 339	$ 227
Communications	(1)	363	522	581	488	435	374
Laboratory sciences	7	743	628	557	535	514	527
Consumer products	8	615	548	476	407	422	412
Miscellaneous (incl. R&D)	30	180	46	137	32	22	49
Total	8	2,301	2,130	2,081	1,786	1,732	1,589
Corning's share of joint venture companies*							
Specialty materials	15%	963	841	701	571	541	484
Communications	26	369	302	276	245	143	114
Laboratory sciences	85	152	117	106	59	14	7
Consumer products	(5)	24	22	24	27	29	31
Total	19	1,508	1,282	1,107	902	727	636
Earnings							
Divisions' and subsidiaries' earnings after tax							
Specialty materials	(9%)	37	46	30	58	53	60
Communications	(6)	33	47	76	100	58	45
Laboratory sciences	8	83	66	53	52	41	57
Consumer products	30	48	34	16	(22)	(5)	13
Miscellaneous (incl. R&D)	NM	(34)	(103)	(85)	(149)	(112)	(118)
Total	24†	167	90	90	39	35	57
Corning's share of joint venture companies' earnings after tax							
Specialty materials	16%	82	76	60	51	50	39
Communications	NM	42	24	20	26	10	(3)
Laboratory sciences	NM	4	(1)	(3)	(5)	(5)	(2)
Consumer products	NM	(1)	0	(1)	0	(1)	1
Total	29	127	99	76	72	54	35
After-tax earnings (as a % of revenues)							
Divisions and subsidiaries							
Specialty materials		9	12	9	18	16	26
Communications		9	9	13	20	13	12
Laboratory sciences		11	11	10	10	8	11
Consumer products		8	6	3	(5)	(1)	3
Miscellaneous (incl. R&D)		(18)	(224)	(62)	(466)	(509)	(241)
Total		7	4	4	2	2	4
Corning's share of joint venture companies							
Specialty materials		9	9	9	9	9	8
Communications		11	8	7	11	7	(3)
Laboratory sciences		3	(1)	(3)	(8)	(36)	(29)
Consumer products		(4)	0	(4)	0	(3)	3
Total		8	8	7	8	8	6

Figures in parentheses indicate losses.
NM = not meaningful.
*Calculated by casewriter from total revenue figures for joint venture companies with assumption that Corning's share is 50%.

†The compound annual growth rate (CAGR) of earnings of divisions and subsidiaries on a before-tax basis was 33%. Tax rate for divisions and subsidiaries was 12% in 1983, 34% in 1984, 14% in 1985, and 38% in 1986. 1987, and 1988.

EXHIBIT 10
MAJOR CORNING DIVISIONS, SUBSIDIARIES, AND JOINT VENTURES

Sector	Divisions	Subsidiaries	Joint Ventures
Specialty materials	Industrial products Technical products	Corning Brasil Corning France Corning GmbH (Germany) Corning Japan KK Corning Ltd., UK U.S. Precision Lens	Dow Corning, U.S. Iwaki Glass, Japan N-Cor, Japan Pittsburgh Corning, U.S. Samsung Corning, S. Korea Sicover SA, France
Consumer housewares	Consumer products Steuben	Corning Canada Corning Brasil Corning France Vitri Corning GmbH (Germany)	Iwaki-Corning, Malaysia Vitrocrisa Kristal, Mexico
Communications	Telecommunications products	Corning France	Fibres Optiques, France Metricor, U.S. Optical Fibres, Wales PCO Ltd., U.S. Siecor Corp., U.S. Siecor GmbH, Germany
Laboratory sciences	Science products	Metpath (U.S.) Hazleton Laboratories (U.S.) Corning Brasil	Ciba Corning, U.S. Genencor, U.S. MetWest, U.S. Unilab Corporation, U.S.

PRINCIPAL ALLIANCES

Company	Major Partners	Corning Shareholding	Date Established
Pittsburgh Corning, Pittsburgh	PPG Industries	50 %	1937
Dow Corning, Michigan	Dow Chemicals	50	1943
Iwaki Glass, Tokyo	Asahi Glass Company	49.4	1965
Siecor GmbH, Munich	Siemens AG	50	1973
Samsung-Corning, Seoul	Samsung Group	50	1974
N-Cor, Tokyo	NGK Insulators	50	1978
Optical Fibres, Clywood, Wales	BICC Plc	50	1981
Siecor, North Carolina	Siemens AG	50	1981
Fibres Optiques, France*	St. Gobain-Thomson	40	1981
Genencor, San Francisco	Genentech	25	1982
PCO, Los Angeles	M.K. Barnowski	80	1984
Ciba Corning, Massachusetts	Ciba-Geigy	50	1985

*In 1988, Corning was in the process of selling its share in the alliance.

EXHIBIT 11
U.S. MEDICAL DIAGNOSTICS INDUSTRY IN 1985 ($ MILLION)

	Estimated Revenue of Diagnostics	Estimated R&D Budget of Diagnostics
Abbott	800	100
Du Pont	300	50
Baxter	300	50
Hoffman-LaRoche	300	50
Behringer Mannheim	300	50
Ames (Beyer)	300	50
Coulter	300	50
Corning	150	25

Source: Company estimates.

U.S. LABORATORY TESTING INDUSTRY IN 1988

Industry Segment*	Clinical Laboratory Testing		Pharmaceuticals Testing		Environmental Testing	
Estimated market size ($ million)	6,000		1,500		600	
Annual market growth rate (%)	5%		15%		20%	
Principal companies (company revenue in parentheses)	SmithKline Beckman	(425)	Corning-Hazleton	(135)	Enseco[†]	(45)
	Hoffman LaRoche	(400)	Huntingdon	(55)	IT	(35)
	Corning-MetPath	(350)	Applied Bio-Sciences	(45)	NET	(25)
	National Health	(315)	G.H. Besselaar[†]	(20)		
	International Clinical Laboratories[†]	(190)				

Source: Company estimates.
*Market sizes are estimates for the merchant market only and do not include captive/in-house customers. The example of clinical laboratory testing market in 1988 is given below.

Estimate total annual demand	$25 billion
Catered by:	
Hospitals with in-house facilities	$13 billion
Physicians with own testing facilities	$ 6 billion
Commercial laboratories	$ 6 billion

[†]Acquisition by Corning under consideration.

EXHIBIT 12

| EVOLUTION OF U.S. OPTICAL FIBER MARKET (FIGURES ARE IN MILLION KILOMETERS) | | | | | GROWTH OF U.S. END-USE MARKETS FOR FIBER OPTIC CABLES | | | | | |

	Customer Segments					Year ($ millions)				
Year	Long Haul	Regional	Military and Others	Total	Segment	2000F	1995F	1988	1982	1977
1982	0.125	0.035		0.16	Telecommunications	2,500	900	415	70	5
1983	0.200	0.125	0.005	0.33	Data communications	950	400	100	1	1
1984	0.390	0.200	0.015	0.61	Military/government	450	225	70	10	1
1985	0.580	0.600	0.030	1.21	Video	75	35	11	1	—
1986	0.825	0.650	0.085	1.56	Others	175	65	14	3	—
1987	0.735	0.700	0.155	1.59						
1988	0.575	0.945	0.370	1.89						
1989F	0.460	1.300	0.640	2.40						
1990F	0.290	2.000	0.910	3.20	Total	4,150	1,625	610	85	7

Source: Company documents.

F = Forecast

Source: *Leading Edge Reports.*

GLOBAL FIBER OPTIC CABLE MARKET IN 1988

Region	North America		Europe		Japan and Korea	
Market size ($ million)	550		375		180	
Principal suppliers (% market shares in parentheses)	AT&T	(40)	BICC[†]	(30)	Sumitomo	(30)
	Siecor Corp.*	(30)	Alcatel	(20)	Furikawa	(30)
	Pirelli	(10)	Siemens[†]	(15)	Fujiora	(30)
	Northern Telecom	(7)	Pirelli	(10)	Others	(10)
	Alcatel	(5)	Others	(25)		
	Fitel	(3)				
	Others	(5)				

Sources: Merrill Lynch, company documents.

*Owned 50% by Corning and 50% by Siemens.

[†]Corning's European joint ventures were supplying optical fibers to these cable manufacturers.

PCO JOINT VENTURE

1984		Proposed	
Partner	% Shareholding	Partner	% Shareholding
Corning	40	Corning	65
Plessey Corp., U.K.	40	IBM	25
Management team	20	Management team	10

Source: Company documents.

EXHIBIT 13

MANUFACTURERS SERVING THE
U.S. COLOR TELEVISION MARKET

Company	Home Base	Market Share (%) 1989F	Market Share (%) 1988
Thomson-RCA	France	21	21
Zenith	U.S.A.	13	12
Philips	Holland	12	8
Sharp	Japan	6	6
Sony	Japan	6	6
Matsushita	Japan	5	6
Mitsubishi	Japan	5	4
Emerson	Holland	4	6
Toshiba	Japan	4	4
Goldstar	South Korea	2	3
Hitachi	Japan	2	2
Samsung	South Korea	2	2
Sanyo	Japan	2	1
Others		16	19
Total (million units)		19.4	20.2

TOP U.S. TELEVISION BRANDS

Brand	Market Share (%) 1990F	1988	1984	1980
RCA*	16.5	16.2	19.0	21.0
Zenith	11.0	12.8	17.5	20.5
Sony	6.9	6.5	6.5	6.5
GE*	5.0	6.0	7.6	7.5
Magnavox†	8.0	5.9	5.7	7.0
Sears	4.0	5.5	7.1	7.5
Sharp	5.2	4.4	2.5	1.5
Panasonic‡	3.2	3.8	4.0	2.0
Mitsubishi	3.5	3.5	2.0	1.0
Sylvania†	2.8	3.3	4.5	4.0
Emerson	3.6	3.3	1.0	0.0
Toshiba	4.6	3.0	1.4	1.0
Quasar‡	1.8	2.5	4.5	5.0
Montgomery Ward	2.0	2.5	2.5	2.3
Hitachi	2.4	2.5	2.5	1.7
Goldstar	2.0	2.0	1.0	0.0

Source: *TV Digest*, company documents.

F = Forecast   *Thompson brand   †Philips brand   ‡Matsushlta brand

PROJECTED SALES OF COLOR TV AND HDTV MARKETS IN UNITED STATES

Year	Total Units (million)	$ Billion Color TV	HDTV	Total
1990	20.8	6.6	0.0	6.6
1995	22.6	7.8	0.0	7.8
2000	25.0	5.3	12.6	17.9
2005	27.0	4.4	14.3	18.7

Source: *Electronic News*, company documents.

THE TELEVISION GLASS INDUSTRY

Principal TV Glass Manufacturers	Approximate Worldwide Sales of Color TV Bulbs ($ million) 1991F	1988	1985
Asahi	700	400	215
NEG	600	345	185
Samsung Corning	350	300	66
Owens Illinois	300	200	150
Schott	300	300	175
Corning	200	130	100

Source: Company documents.   F = Forecast

Chapter 2

■

Industry and Competitor Analysis

INTRODUCTION

Once a general manager adopts a strategic perspective, the problem of setting sensible objectives is always present. Company leaders are in the uncomfortable position of wondering how the myriad ups and downs of the economic, political, and social scene will affect their fortunes. What are the opportunities? What are the threats?

Because the answers to these questions can be measured only against the strengths and weaknesses of the company, probing to learn about the environment inevitably means reviewing internal affairs to assess the development of corporate capabilities. It is an endless process and a major source of stress for leaders. (This is especially true because general managers learn early that there are limits to the usefulness of sharing uncertainty with subordinates. It can be paralyzing for lower-level managers to understand how fragile their long-term prospects may be.) One reason corporate leaders are often found at industry forums and on the boards of various sorts of nonprofit organizations such as universities is that they find it useful to hear opinions from very different perspectives.

NONECONOMIC FACTORS

In thinking about the business environment it is common to find managers dividing issues along economic and noneconomic lines. This is especially true in the United States, where we tend to view the economy as the preserve of the private sector. This is more of an ideological belief than an observation based on evidence, but it is very apparent to U.S.

businessmen when they find themselves in foreign settings that they have a narrower view of government than do their overseas counterparts.[1] A typical reaction is that other countries should behave more like the United States, that active industrial policy is a form of cheating on "free trade."

Yet even Adam Smith thought that the British government could not leave shipbuilding to the forces of the market. It was too important to the British crown that its navy be strong and modern for it to rely merely on the market.[2] Much of what we protest in the industrial and trade policies of the French, Japanese, and Koreans is merely a sophisticated extension of Smith's line of thinking. (The line between mercantilism and national defense has become more muddled.) In turn, government support for agriculture (price supports), sugar beet producers (import quotas), steel (voluntary quotas and trigger prices), home owners (interest deduction), broadcasters (restraints on foreign ownership), and the 1986 Semiconductor Trade Agreement with Japan (market opening) are just a few of the ways in which the U.S. government intervenes to help its companies.

Similar points can be made with respect to the workforce. If managers believe that their "rights" as decision makers are independent of their behavior with respect to workers and that the government has no role in regulating employment, they may find it hard to implement some of the newer approaches to operating process and extremely difficult to function in foreign countries. From self-managed teams to worker participation in German supervisory boards, contemporary managers face circumstances in which very little can be taken for granted about how company leadership can move from intent to action. Even presuming that one knows what orders to give, a simple "top-down approach" is often substantially constrained by administrative infeasibility or law.

The simplest way of summarizing the issue is that almost nowhere else in the world does the government or the society take the view that the fate of the economy is best left in the hands of business managers. The point is very important for the role of general managers. The skills and experience that must be represented in the top management of a company differ if one assumes that relationships with the governments of the countries where one is operating are a central part of the task of leadership. The judgment that one brings to bear in considering strategic

---

[1] This point and its consequences have been beautifully developed in a series of books by George C Lodge, Jr., such as *The New American Ideology* (New York: Knopf, 1977). An excellent comparative analysis of U.S. and foreign views is in George C Lodge, Jr., and Ezra Vogel, eds., *Ideology and National Competitiveness* (Boston: Harvard Business School Press, 1987).

[2] Adam Smith, *The Wealth of Nations* (Chicago: University of Chicago Press, 1976), p. 144.

options needs to be far broader. And hence the way an aspiring business leader plans his or her management career is different.[3]

Having acknowledged the importance of noneconomic issues for general managers, or more precisely the important influence of political and social forces on economic matters, we can focus on the economic dimensions of strategy. Certainly the primary responsibility of a company's leadership is the long-term economic health of the enterprise. If it is true that society does not presume business to be at the center of the economic universe, it is also the case that businesspeople are expected to manage so as to keep their companies competitive and profitable. The Harvard Business School study of economic competition among nations (led by Michael Porter) has shown that, given the infrastructure and benign presence of an intelligent government, the most competitive industries, measured internationally, are those where company management focuses on succeeding in intense competition with local rivals.[4]

With new process technology, new materials, and new competition from vast industrializing countries like China and India keeping markets in turmoil over the next decade, management will have their hands full keeping track of and interpreting competitive conditions. For this purpose, companies have found it extremely useful to apply a framework for industry and competitor analysis.[5]

THE PRIMARY PROPOSITION: PROFIT POTENTIAL

As noted in Chapter 1, the concept of corporate strategy can be applied to any organization, no matter how complex. However, more focus is needed when a general manager considers the business environment. In order to examine the competitive possibilities of an industry, there needs to be some specification. What industry are we talking about? Precisely because strategy is an idiosyncratic notion, because it is unique to a

---

[3] Students interested in these untraditional aspects of business leadership may want to consult other work of the authors. Joseph Bower examined the political work of senior business managers in *Two Faces of Management* (Boston: Houghton Mifflin, 1983), chapter 6, pp. 114–165. Richard Walton's studies, *Strategic Negotiations: A Theory of Change in Labor–Management Relations* (Boston: Harvard Business School Press, 1994) focus on how the transformation of an organization's capabilities needs to be negotiated.

[4] Michael E Porter, ed., *The Competitive Advantage of Nations* (Boston: Harvard Business School Press, 1990).

[5] The text that follows relies very heavily on a framework for analysis developed by Michael E Porter and presented in his landmark book, *Competitive Strategy* (New York: The Free Press, 1980). While quotations are footnoted, no other acknowledgements will be made of what is often an adaption and modification of Porter's presentation.

company, the definition of industry may also be unique. Indeed, one dimension of competition is the way management chooses to define the industry in which it is competing. The company selling the solution to an information systems problem may well bill its customers for costs that include computers, but its definition of its industry and its competitors is likely to be very different from that of a company that sees itself in the computer industry. The stupendous growth of the firm founded by Ross Perot, EDS, can be understood in these terms.

Having recognized that we must return to consider how to define what industry we are in, the proposition that Michael Porter has argued most effectively is that "the state of competition in an industry depends on five basic forces . . . The collective strength of these forces determines the ultimate profit potential of an industry."[6] The five forces are the threat of entry, the threat of substitution, the bargaining power of suppliers and of customers, and the rivalry among existing firms. Together they establish the level of competition. And the level of competition sets a ceiling on how much profit can be earned on a sustainable basis.

The power of this proposition comes from this very strong conclusion. A firm may be lucky; its competitors may be badly managed; but over time it cannot earn more than the state of competition permits. In some tradable commodities such as petrochemicals or steel, where the power of suppliers is great and rivalry extremely intense, profit can be negative over long periods of time. Figure 2-1 shows the appalling performance of the leading U.S. petrochemical companies in the 1970s and the world steel industry in the 1980s. According to theory, companies should not experience losses over this length of time, but in capital-intensive industries of high interest to national governments, where there are numerous large firms competing, it is not unusual.

In contrast, other industries have had steady profits despite the turmoil. Figure 2-2 shows the profits of the leading U.S. investment banks over the last 10 tumultuous years. Despite changes in products, and despite stock market crashes, they have prospered because economies of scale and other advantages give them power over rivals and entrants in a market with low supplier and low customer power.

The importance of the profit potential proposition is that if structural conditions determine what the economic return from an industry might be over time, then structural analysis can tell a management a great deal about the attractiveness of their industry—or *different definitions of their industry*. If it is possible to make such judgments on the basis of objective analysis, it is certainly valuable to a general manager seeking to craft a powerful strategy.

---

[6] *Ibid.*, p. 3.

FIGURE 2–1
SPREAD FOR THE TOP 15 U.S. CHEMICAL COMPANIES, 1971–1980*

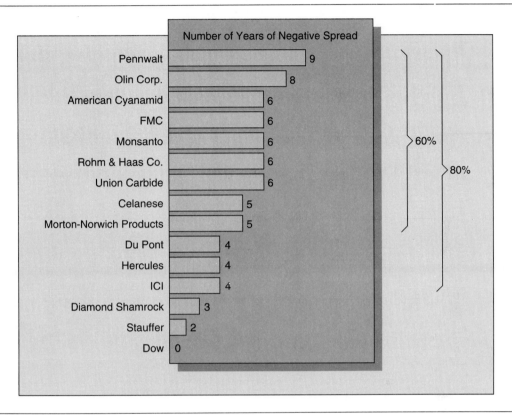

Reprinted from Dan Connell, "The Chemical Industry's $100 Billion Opportunity" (McKinsey & Company, 1982), pp. 1–12.
*Over 50 percent of total company's sales are chemicals; spread equals return on equity minus cost of equity.

STEEL
Worldwide Performance Is Horrible: 1979–89

	Number of Years ROE > 10%	Number of Years Operate at a Loss
United States	3	6
Japan	4	2
Germany	0	2
France	4	7
British Steel	3	6
Italsider	0	7
Hoogovens	5	6
Korea	0	0

FIGURE 2–2
LARGE INVESTMENT BANKS*
Pretax Profits

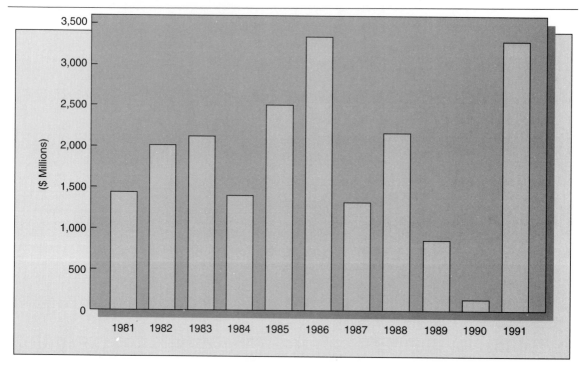

*Including Merrill and Shearson.
Source: Securities Industry Association.

STRATEGIC ANALYSIS OF INDUSTRY STRUCTURE

Strategic analysis of an industry begins with a careful exploration of the five forces listed.

The Threat of Entry

Newcomers to an industry are an important source of problems. At best, they are making a new investment similar to the existing rivals. As a consequence they are eager to earn a return. Sometimes, they misunderstand the economics of the industry and cause serious problems while they are learning. This was true in the market for ammonia fertilizer when oil companies entered, as discussed in Chapter 1. Other times they bring new product or process technology that seriously threatens existing participants. That is what happened to the U.S. car producers when the Japanese entered the U.S. market.

Whether the threat of entry is serious depends on whether there are barriers to entry. *Barriers* are structural forces that deter potential entrants. Some of the many factors that can deter entry are the following:

> *Economies of scale.* If the scale of efficient facilities is high, potential entrants may find it impossible to build a market position fast enough to pay back the required investment. As well as production, there may be economies in research (pharmaceuticals), advertising (mass market consumer goods), and after-sales service (home appliances).
>
> *Absolute cost advantages.* Incumbents may have positions that are simply not available to entrants. It may be, for example, that the good hydroelectric sites in a country or the places for a gas station at a major intersection are taken. The producers of wine in the region of Romanee Conti have had an unrivaled position since Roman times. There is no more land there for planting vines. But another commonly ignored source of advantage comes from constantly decreasing costs in process technology from learning or experience (many manufacturing processes). Still other advantages unavailable to entrants come from pioneer grants or subsidies from governments.
>
> *Capital requirements.* A related advantage to incumbents may come from the capital required to enter. Often firms may have a sound business idea based on new technology or a market concept but find it impossible to raise the capital needed to compete. This was the problem of Air Products until it saw how it could use the collateral of long-term leases to enter the industrial oxygen business.
>
> *Product differentiation.* Where an incumbent has invested heavily in unique product features (patented or otherwise) or a powerful brand image, potential entrants may find it difficult or impossible to enter. 3M has managed to use its knowledge of abrasives and coatings to create a stream of profitable niches for its "Scotch" brand products. It is reputed that Scotch tape earned more money for 3M than cellophane did for DuPont. The Walt Disney characters have proved so popular that they create insurmountable barriers in markets for all sorts of children's products.
>
> *Switching costs.* An almost natural form of differentiation arises through the phenomenon of switching costs. These are one-time costs incurred by a buyer when switching from one supplier to another. The costs may arise from small physical differences in formul-

ation of a product, from distribution set-up costs such as a pipeline, from the necessity of testing the quality of a new supplier, or from building a new relationship with the trust required to handle an oral contractual relationship with large stakes. Food packers and brewers, for example, are very reluctant to change the coatings used to protect the inside of their cans. Entrepreneurs often find it extremely difficult to change lawyers.

Access to distribution. It is often hard to bring a new product to market. We see this with new consumer products seeking shelf space in supermarkets, but there are other examples. Sony found that Matsushita could virtually shut it out of Japanese consumer markets and in response found it necessary to develop its transistor radio business first in the United States. More dramatically, the OPEC nations found that their power over world oil markets was somewhat limited by the control over the distribution of gasoline and heating oil by the major international oil producers.

Government policy. Governments often choose to control entry to their markets in favor of local producers, but often they also select specific participants. The nations of East Asia have restricted entry as part of their industrial and trade policy, but so have most OECD nations. The United States, for example, licenses radio and TV stations and confines the ownership of licenses to U.S. citizens. Until deregulated under Jimmy Carter, airlines were awarded routes by the government in a similar fashion. At a more mundane level, many states license those who sell liquor.

For a strategist, the threat of entry is a central consideration. For the incumbent, there is a constant question of whether to invest to create or raise barriers; while for an entrant, it is important to understand how expensive it may be to compete effectively. While economists and antitrust policy makers have tended to regard high barriers to entry as a serious cause for concern, it has been remarkable how many industries thought to be impenetrable have succumbed to clever, well-managed entrants. The U.S. markets for automobiles and steel were both highly concentrated and supplied by giant domestic producers, yet Japanese entrants were able to succeed using new process and product technology. It was difficult, but clearly not impossible.

Concerns about entry affect how fast incumbents will expand, whether they will license new technology to other firms, whether they will integrate vertically, and how they will treat international markets. Perhaps most centrally, the threat of entry is likely to affect pricing. Nothing deters an entrant more than an incumbent that produces products or services of increasing quality at low prices.

**The Threat of
Substitution**

Related to entry is the threat to an incumbent's market from products or services that substitute for what they are offering. The great economist Joseph Schumpeter pointed out that the real threat to existing producers was the "gale of competition" from innovation. Nylon stockings virtually eliminated silk; television news has reduced the market for newspapers; aluminum beverage cans took most of the market from steel; and powerful personal computers capped the market for mainframes.

For general managers, substitutes are a pervasive strategic consideration. There are almost always alternative ways for a customer to deal with a problem. Good public transit is a substitute for automobile travel if the cost is too high. Railroads fight truckers over the width and length of vehicles allowed on public roads.

Interestingly, shifts in prices change the feasibility of substitutes. In 1994, with the near demise of old growth forests, the price of lumber for home building had risen to the point where steel—which was always available—began to penetrate the home building market successfully. The awareness of earthquakes and hurricanes has also increased the demand for steel's strength and flexibility. Naturally, lumber companies will work to find ways of lowering costs and increasing strength. The use of laminate beams is one example. But also important will be the attitudes of builders and a distribution system capable of teaching those builders how to use the substitute product.

**The Power of
Suppliers and
Customers**

The idea of a series of links from steel manufacturer to builder highlights the extent to which the success of a company at one point in the chain from raw materials to final consumer depends upon others in that chain. The health of the entire chain is important to profitability. Thus when U.S. car manufacturers lost share to the Japanese, their component and raw material suppliers lost share as well even though the Japanese component suppliers were not present in the U.S. market. (They only entered later when the Japanese manufacturers who were their customers began to manufacture in the United States.)

Perhaps more fundamental, the value of the entire chain is determined by the price to the final consumer. The profitability of individual industries in the chain is determined by the relative power of that industry vis-à-vis its suppliers and customers. Powerful suppliers can extract value from an industry by raising prices, while powerful customers exercise their force by driving prices down. The relative power of the players depends upon structural forces.

Sources of supplier power are scale and concentration relative to the industry sold to, lack of direct competition due to product differentiation and lack of substitutes, high sensitivity of customer performance to supplier quality, high switching costs, and lack of dependence on the customer group. Relative profitability can also influence power since customers without profits have a very high incentive to cut input costs, while high profits can operate in the opposite fashion. U.S. discount retailers are famous, for example, as "brand killers." They use their tremendous volumes to drive down manufacturers' prices. But when in the process they destroy the image of the discounted products, they discover the importance of the temperate use of their power to preserve the profit in the total chain.

Sources of buyer power are the reverse of the coin: scale and concentration relative to suppliers, availability of direct competitors and substitutes, low sensitivity to supplier quality, low switching costs, and lack of dependence on the supplier group. The threat of backward integration is an important entry threat for customers. Historically the automobile industry has exercised awesome buyer power in most countries. High scale and concentration coupled with a very real threat of vertical integration have enabled car manufacturers to extract most of the profit from their transactions. Indeed, in the United States, the companies that manufacture tires for the Big Three seldom make any profit at all on their original equipment business. Nonetheless, they compete doggedly for every point of OEM market share because final customer loyalty means they have the chance to earn decent profits in the replacement tire market. The tire industry is particularly instructive on this point because, viewed by itself, its concentration and barriers to entry would lead one to expect high profits. As is clear in the Firestone case, however, the power of the buyers has made it a very difficult industry in which to make money.

Government

While Michael Porter does not include the government as an independent force in his framework for industry analysis, we believe that general managers should and that wise ones look at the government as a sixth force, especially those managers working outside the United States. For many managers, it is hard to think systematically about the government. As already noted, many have ideological blinders. But it is also difficult for managers that gather their experience in the context of a company and its markets to understand the way electoral and legislative politics play out, the way these intersect with the workings of administrative agencies, and the way both political and administrative forces are affected by the judicial system.[7] Almost always, companies that want to understand the

---

[7] See *Two Faces of Management*, Chapter 6 and passim.

strategic impact of government on their prospects find it useful to bring in outsiders who have spent their careers developing a grasp of the many aspects of government as it affects their industry.

All governments adopt policies and regulations that have a powerful force on the structure and hence profit potential of industry. By way of example, how the current health care debate in the United States is reflected in legislation will have a dramatic affect on the fortunes of enterprise in an arena representing one-sixth of the economy. In the meanwhile, pharmaceutical companies seeking to innovate find the behavior of the Food and Drug Administration to be a powerful drag on structural change. And in a much more mundane arena, how the courts treat the packaging used by Cott for its generic attack on Coca-Cola may have an important impact on the soft drink industry.

Rivalry among Competitors

The threat of entry and substitutes, buyer and supplier power, and governments provide the context for an industry. How profitable an industry turns out to be has a great deal to do with the nature of the battle among the incumbent companies. In some industries substantial cooperation creates conditions of profit that can then be fought for. In other cases, cutthroat competition leads to profitless growth.

The ultimate determinant of profitability is the nature of competition among an industry's incumbents. A good example of the range of possibilities is provided by the cement industry as described in a paper by French researchers.[8] They compared the performance of a regulated cartel among three U.K. producers with intense rivalry among four French gentlemanly oligopoists, a less concentrated group of German producers, and cutthroat competition among U.S. rivals. Prices were lowest, energy conservation the highest, and pollution the lowest in France. Germany was the next best performer, the legal cartel the next, and bloodthirsty competition the worst. By the 1990s conditions had become much more homogeneous across countries, but ownership of the U.S. industry was now largely in European hands. Profit was increasingly under pressure as coastal nations such as Greece subsidized the growth of industries built to export.

Even where structure and national context of industries is virtually identical, research has shown that profit can be very different. For example, Figure 2-3 compares prices and costs in ethylene oxide and propylene oxide, two chemical intermediates produced by large concen-

---

[8] Bernard Collomb and Jean-Pierre Ponssard, "Creative Management in Mature Capital Intensive Industries—The Case of Cement," *Journal of Enterprise Management*, November 1982.

FIGURE 2–3

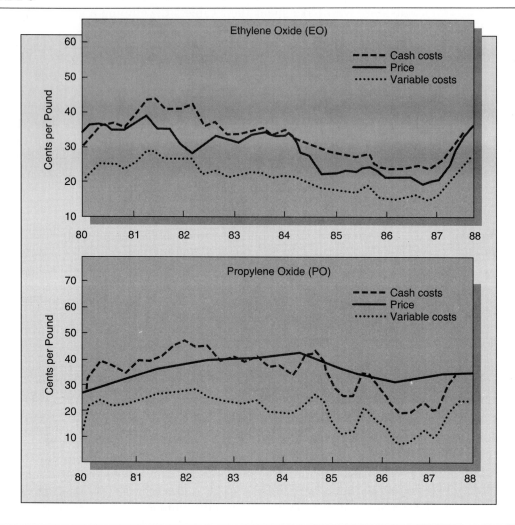

Source: Paine-Webber Commodity Chemical Chartbook

trated producers.[9] While there are slight differences in buyer power between the two industries, participants explain the difference by calling attention to the behavior of the leading companies.

---

[9] Joseph L Bower, "The Organization of Markets," Harvard Business School Working Paper #92-032, 1991.

The differences in question have to do with pricing and capital investment over time. In one case the leader tended to keep prices high until high capacity utilization made building new capacity attractive. The resulting overcapacity led to intense price competition making recovery of cash costs difficult. In the other case, the leader built capacity ahead of demand and priced so as to earn acceptable profits for itself but not so high as to encourage overbuilding. Its management was also careful to defend its market share fiercely when attacked but to avoid price wars with incumbents.

These differences reveal that the dimensions over which firms compete strategically are quite complex. They point to the role of industry and competitor analysis in the development of corporate strategy.

RELATING OPPORTUNITIES TO CAPABILITIES

Returning to our main theme, general managers face the problem of giving strategic direction and meaning to their corporation's activities. Industry and competitor analysis provides an orderly way to figure out the rules of the competitive game in a business: What do customers want and what will it take to win their business in a battle with the other firms out there? As such, this rather formal economic analysis is a way to sort out where opportunities lie and where viability is threatened, as well as to clarify what kinds of capabilities will be required to succeed in the battle.

Opportunities and Threats

Usually when one examines an industry in this fashion, there is a certain clear logic to the positions among the competing firms that represents their inheritance and their current capabilities. Sometimes a strategic weakness will be revealed that must be overcome if disaster is to be avoided. General Motors, for example, spent a good deal of the 1980s learning that it was a high cost producer of uninteresting cars. Fixing both problems was strategic but did not involve a change in strategy. Most incumbent participants can gain a lot by executing better. Costs can be lowered, working capital can be reduced, financing can be improved, and operating and innovating cycle times can be shortened. The differences can be staggering.

But the opportunity for unusually high sustained profits or the threat of quick destruction almost always develops because an industry is in transition. An industry thought to be mature may be exposed to new technology that will permit dramatically lower costs, which in turn will permit new uses in new markets. This is what happened to the shoe industry with the advent of innovative and stylish athletic footwear. An industry thought of as highly profitable may change as critical developments in components threaten to turn industry products into commodities. This is what happened to the computer industry with the explosion in memory and microprocessor capacity of exponentially decreasing cost and the standardization of operating software.

In order to identify opportunities and threats it helps to subject the results of industry and competitor analysis to an open-ended probing with the sort of questions listed next. In considering these questions, remember that the hard problem is to get imaginative answers. Because these questions inevitably involve the future, and because their answers have such powerful implications for the people of the company, finding good answers isn't easy. More often than not, the engineers and marketers responsible for a business think they have it well in hand.

1.   What apparent trends might change the underlying structure of the industry? Here three powerful drivers need to be examined: technology, customer behavior, and company strategies. By technology we do not mean just the physical processes by which things are made. We have in mind the broader definition that encompasses all the dimensions of how products and services are created and reach customers. According to this definition, the development of Wal-Mart's format of retail distribution was a technological change of threatening importance to Sears. By customer behavior we do not mean the decision of men to stop wearing ties at work. We also mean the growth in sophistication of buyers that leads them to conclude that a generic offering is as good as a brand. For example, customers were quickly ready to buy generic frozen orange juice but resisted generic colas until recently. (This may be because they believed that the generic colas did not taste good while the orange juice did.) The point of company strategy, of course, is that people often see the same thing but only some recognize that it is possible to implement dramatic change. Snapple turned a dull niche category—ice tea—into a soft drink sensation. TIMEX introduced the cheap reliable commodity watch. Nucor turned minimills into the coming edge of the steel industry.

2.   How might foreseeable changes in the social, political, and macroeconomic context affect the industry or the firm? It is now legend that after World War II, General Wood used his understanding of demographics, garnered from careful study of census data, to lead Sears Roebuck into a building program in the suburbs at the very moment that Sewell Avery had Montgomery Ward battening down the hatches to survive the great postwar depression that never came. There is nothing like fundamental change to open up opportunity for a company—or threaten its very existence. Who would have thought that tiny Church & Dwight could challenge the great Procter & Gamble and Colgate in toothpaste? And yet the environmental movement helped give the Arm & Hammer brand a

respectable 6 percent of the national market and has even enabled them to take a position in the market for laundry detergent!

3. What do analysis and observation of changes in management enable us to predict about changes in competitive behavior? It is often possible to make observations about the goals, assumptions, strategies, and capabilities of the management of competitors. The background in finance and domestic activities of GM's Roger Smith would have supported a reasonable prediction that he would not have a decent grasp of the changes that would be necessary in operations and management in order to make GM competitive in cost and product. In contrast, Jack Smith's background in turning around GM Europe would support the opposite view. In turn, a strong GM has very significant implications for all other auto competitors wondering what the rest of the 1990s might be like.

4. What critical capabilities will be required in order to compete in the future? Industry analysis can determine what skills will be critical to competitive success as the market and competition evolve. Manufacturers of consumer goods, for example, noting that retailers are moving to source many of their goods directly from the Far East, will need to have superior sources of product and, preferably, powerful brands desired by the consumer. Chemical companies will recognize the importance of biodegradability and build the relevant skill centers.

Determining what are critical capabilities is not always straightforward. Conventional analysis, for example, would say that newspapers are threatened by the telecommunication revolution. But a good deal of research suggests that most people buy newspapers as bulletin boards for local activities, including most importantly the advertisements of retail stores. Critical to thinking through the strategy for a local newspaper will be understanding how future shoppers will want to get their information.

5. Given the analysis of industry, competitors, and trends, what kinds of alternative direction might the company take? For general managers, this is where the rubber hits the road. It is all very well to acknowledge the staggering changes under way in economic, political, and social spheres, and even to see how these might threaten present success or offer an opening for radical improvement. But we shall see that developing sensible options that can be explored and tested against resources is a complex management task involving far more than intellectual analysis. It is at the heart of general management.

Assessing Capabilities and Weaknesses

To understand why developing and assessing concrete options is hard, it is useful to return to the idea set forth in Chapter 1 that opportunity and capability reflect each other. To understand how change in the environment can be exploited, it is critical to know what one's organization can do or can learn to do.

A most enjoyable example of this proposition is available in the popular series of novels about Captain Aubrey, who commands British men-of-war during the naval engagements of the Napoleonic wars.[10] The books are full of fascinating descriptions of encounters where Aubrey must judge the capability of his ship against an enemy, not just by counting the size and number of cannons, but by assessing the capability of the enemy's captain and the skill of the opposing crew relative to his own. When he misjudges the latter, he loses even though the opportunity he identified presents itself.

Each manager learns this reality of competition in his or her own way, but the lesson is vital. Undertaking tasks that require missing abilities can injure the firm. This is easiest to see when management adopts a course of action they cannot finance—often because the working capital requirements of rapid growth are not understood. That is often how companies go bankrupt. But it is also the case where a functional capability is missing. Especially interesting is how the Williams Company, which purchased an oil company fertilizer business, handled the problem. By changing the wholly owned distributors to franchisors, they totally changed the incentives—and hence the capabilities—of the distribution system. For owners, the prospect of a week or two of all-night work with farmers was not nearly as unattractive as it was for salaried employees.

In turn, understanding what is happening in the environment is key to knowing whether one's own organization is strong. Assessing the capabilities of one's organization involves precisely what Captain Aubrey had to do. It became especially critical when the United States began building a series of very large and heavily armed men-of-war such as the battleship *Constitution*. Assessment of capabilities involves watching one's organization in competition with another organization or knowing from past experience how good the team is. It also involves constant building of capabilities. (Since the Royal Navy was notoriously stingy, Aubrey often used his own resources in order to purchase powder for constant practice with his gun crews.) Recently, it has become common to take the leaders of an organization to visit competitors in another setting to get a sense for their capability relative to one's own. Visits to Japanese or outstanding U.S. plants are common. Benchmarking is another practice by which firms now measure themselves. Firms gather all kinds of intelligence,

---

[10] Patrick O'Brien has written 16 novels in this series. The first is *Master and Commander* (Philadelphia: Lippincott, 1969). Many dwell on Aubrey as a general manager—strategist, organization builder, and performer.

including value analysis of competitors' products and services, in order to establish how good they are by comparison. However it is accomplished, measuring one's skills against competitors is key to knowing whether a perceived opportunity can be exploited with any chance of success. Measuring oneself against the needs of future tasks is equally important but even harder. At the start, one can only guess the full range of challenges ahead.

In any event, for almost any company a usual experience is early failures. Microsoft knew that a software product that enabled a PC to behave like an Apple Macintosh would be a smashing success, but it was not until version 3.0 of Windows that their objective was achieved. In the meantime, they built up the capability needed to exploit the opportunity they had defined by learning from their failures.

It is on precisely this process of building up knowledge of technology and market and how to put them together that Itami focuses when he describes the idea of dynamic strategy. Getting to a strategy is an iterative process of learning how good one's organization may be and the exact nature of the opportunity. Building knowledge is the critical strategic process. It is why "the learning organization" has become a popular business buzz phrase.

Matching Opportunity and Capability

Traditionally, at this point in a discussion of strategy, there is a graphic such as Figure 2-4 that shows in principle how the intellectual constructs discussed in the chapter link up.

The problem with such a diagram, as is evident in the preceding paragraphs, is that strategy is almost never developed as the cascade of intellectual analysis portrayed. It is much more a process of building and learning. Before we can examine how that process is managed, we need to broaden our examination beyond the merely economic to take into account the values of those making strategy and the moral dimensions of corporate strategy.

FIGURE 2–4
SCHEMATIC DEVELOPMENT OF ECONOMIC STRATEGY

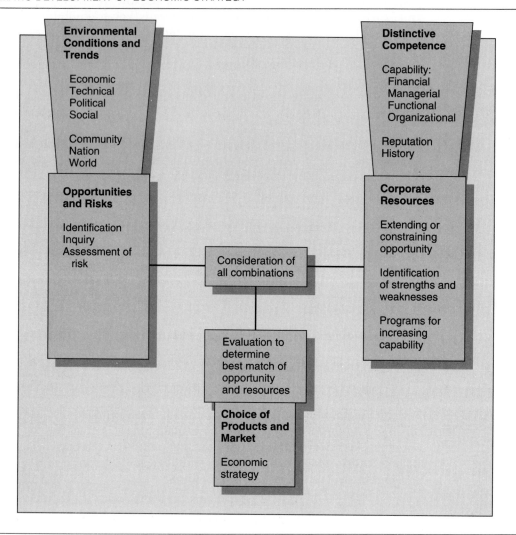

Harcourt Brace Jovanovich, Inc.

"Today we need your advice whether it makes strategic sense for us to become a major player in the publishing business," said Richard A. Smith, 66, chairman and CEO of General Cinema Corporation, to his board of directors at its regular meeting on December 14, 1990. He continued:

> Publishing is an industry we knew little about until recently, but we have been approached by Smith Barney about our possible interest to make a bid for Harcourt Brace Jovanovich. HBJ is on the ropes with close to a $2 billion debt load as a result of an earlier restructuring. Its junk bonds are way under water, its interest payments are hampering operations, and in two years its debt repayment schedule is certain to drive it into Chapter 11. Thus, HBJ's board has decided to look for a friendly acquirer. This seems our best chance to add another major operating business and use up most but not all of our $1.6 billion in cash. We are not asking for a vote today since we do not have a deal yet. However, I am anxious to get your opinions, assuming the price is right, whether the acquisition of HBJ is the right strategy for us. HBJ is also in the outplacement and insurance business, which impact the valuation but are not critical for our strategic discussion of whether publishing is a business we want to be in. We will have with us this morning our usual legal adviser and our investment banker. However, since First Boston was the architect of HBJ's restructuring, we have also asked Salomon Brothers to advise us. As consultants we have engaged McKinsey, which has extensive expertise in publishing, and Moseley Associates, which specializes in the field.

GENERAL CINEMA

Background

General Cinema had pioneered the drive-in movie theater in 1935 and the shopping center theater in Framingham in 1951, as well as the multiplex theater in 1963. Through expansion nationwide, it had become one of the country's major movie exhibition chains. Starting in 1968 with the cash flow from the movie theater business, combined with aggressive leverage, General Cinema had begun to acquire Pepsi franchised bottling operations to become the nation's largest independent Pepsi bottler. From 1968 through 1988, both bottling revenues and earnings grew at about 20 percent per year. In early 1989, General Cinema sold its soft drink bottling operations to PepsiCo for $1.77 billion, resulting in a $1.42 billion pretax gain. A fundamental change had occurred in the industry as Pepsi and Coke, according to the 1989 annual report, "pursued the strategic objective of controlling large parts of their distribution systems by acquiring more of their own bottling operations," limiting General Cinema's growth opportunities. This translated, in management's view, "into prospective annual earnings growth rates far below General Cinema's historical performance. The cash General Cinema received was by any measure the highest price ever paid for a multifranchise soft drink bottler and enabled the company to capture real value for its shareholders at a most propitious time."

Thus, General Cinema was left with a mountain of cash plus its original movie theater operations and its 59.8 percent equity interest in the Neiman-Marcus Group. General Cinema had obtained its Neiman-Marcus stake through the transformation of its original 1984 investment as a white knight in Carter Hawley Hale Stores. General Cinema's top management held the same positions at the Neiman-Marcus Group (NMG). NMG was in the middle of a significant capital investment program from which it had yet to reap the rewards. Even though General Cinema was satisfied with the scope of its retailing position, it had made a recent unsuccessful bid for Saks Fifth Avenue given its close fit with NMG. By 1990 the theater

operations had fallen on hard times, together with the rest of the industry, because of no-growth and high excess-capacity conditions. After its bottling sale, General Cinema had actively searched for a third operating business but without success. In spite of its intensive use of investment bankers and its close examination of a number of significant acquisition candidates, the all-time high in market values had so far precluded it from making a major acquisition.

General Cinema's primary objective was to "create value for its shareholders by providing a total return—appreciation in the market value of its shares plus dividends—well in excess of the rate of inflation." To achieve this objective the company was willing to make significant up-front investments, often of a marketing nature and which therefore had to be expensed immediately. While setting demanding targets, it was a patient investor, focusing on the long-term earnings potential of a business. This patience was facilitated by the one-third ownership of the Smith family, which caused a security analyst to comment in 1984 in a *Business Week* article entitled "Dick Smith's Midas Touch at General Cinema" that "it is a genius-like outfit of people playing with their own money." Over the years, General Cinema had made significant investments in Columbia Pictures, Heublein, and Cadbury Schweppes, all resulting in major capital gains. Except for Neiman-Marcus, finding another operating business had proven to be an elusive target. (See Exhibit 1 for financial data.)

The Board Presentation

The board discussion on the possible acquisition of HBJ began with the usual cautionary remarks by legal counsel:

You should feel free to take such notes as you require to assist in your deliberations, and to retain them for as long as you need to refer to them. But, as you are aware, virtually every transaction becomes the subject of litigation these days. From my experience, I can assure you that each page of your leftover notes—which must be produced in response to plaintiff's discovery requests—will consume hours of explanation during your deposition testimony, to say nothing of your preparation time with counsel. A helpful guide will be to write at the top of your note pad, "Ladies and Gentlemen of the Jury"!

The investment bankers then started the presentation with a background briefing on HBJ, for which the code name Eagle was used. HBJ, founded in 1919, had grown, frequently through acquisitions, during the previous three decades under the leadership of William Jovanovich. In May of 1987, Maxwell Communications informed HBJ of its desire to acquire the company. The $44 per share offer resulted in a big jump in HBJ's stock price, which was around $30 at the time. In response, HBJ announced and implemented a recapitalization plan during May–July of 1987. Each share was entitled to $40 in cash and one share of preferred stock (with a liquidation preference of $13.50). The cash portion aggregated about $1.6 billion, which required HBJ not only to resort to debt issues, with interest rates ranging between 13 percent and 14.75 percent, but also to sell a number of businesses. In November 1988 a refinancing plan was announced, including a 10.5 million share offering at $9.50 per share as well as additional high-yield debt securities. The stock price fluctuated around this level during some 12 months until it rose to $18 after HBJ's announcement that it would sell Sea World, which it had acquired in 1976. In late 1989, HBJ announced that operating performance would fall siguificantly short of the projections made at the time of recapitalization (see Exhibit 2), and the stock took a nosedive. Thereafter, everything went downhill, with several key executives resigning (including William Jovanovich in May 1990) and the stock dropping to around $1. In November 1990 Smith Barney was engaged to explore strategic options (see Exhibit 3 for selected financial data on HBJ).

The two investment bankers gave an overview of HBJ's operating segments (Exhibit 4). The investment bankers' preliminary discounted cash flow value for the publishing operations amounted to about $1.15 billion. HBJ's total value was estimated at a little over $1.4 billion. The investment bankers also covered a possible tender strategy for the junk bonds, a rate of return analysis, and the impact on General Cinema of a possible acquisition. The tender strategy for the junk bonds became a pivotal issue. Even though it would be a friendly transaction, the concurrence of management and shareholders would not suffice. The real power resided with the junk bond holders, who would have to be willing to tender at prices significantly below face value (see Exhibit 5). Only with at least 90 percent of the junk bonds tendered would the transaction make financial sense for General Cinema. Given this high uncertainty and the anticipated great length of time for the tender offer to proceed, how high would General Cinema's opportunity cost be by bidding for HBJ and not pursuing alternate opportunities? Thus, the strategic opportunity to enter the publishing industry and HBJ's position in it had to justify the risk, time, and opportunity cost.

"Well, Bob, is publishing a business you really want to run?" asked Dick Smith, referring to Robert J. Tarr, Jr., General Cinema's president and COO. Bob Tarr, to whom retailing and theaters reported, had been working with the two consulting firms. Tarr replied:

> This is what we have to figure out. Has the recapitalization permanently damaged some of HBJ's publishing properties or does this company, if properly capitalized, have a great future? Needless to say, we are concerned that we might be purchasing damaged goods. Reputation and image take years to build but can be destroyed overnight. Beyond this fundamental question, we will have io determine, with the help of our consultants, whether HBJ publishing meets our acquisition criteria. Specifically, does it have a significant inherent growth potential? How strong is their market position? Can some of HBJ's activities be profitably redefined or redirected? Do they have a distinctive competitive advantage through entry barriers?

General Cinema's acquisition criteria stressed the following three value creation opportunities:

1. Redefinition formats: Companies with a unique asset position (e.g., brands, market share, distribution strength, or manufacturing competence) which can be transferred or extended in new growth directions
2. Consolidation formats: Fragmented businesses or industries which, if consolidated, will provide economies of scale, entry barriers, and pricing leverage
3. Expansion formats: Companies with underexploited product or brand leadership whose potential can be expanded with increased marketing or distribution support; for example:

- line extensions
- channel extensions
- geographic extensions:
  - regional to national markets
  - foreign to domestic markets
  - domestic to foreign markets

Against this background, the consultants began their presentations. The remainder of this case is based entirely on the consulting reports prepared for management in November, for the board in December, and for a subsequent board meeting on January 4, 1991. For length and pedagogical reasons this case is not a complete portrayal of the consultants' presentations. Most of the recommendations have been omitted.

HARCOURT BRACE JOVANOVICH

The Book Publishing Industry

A $15 billion industry in 1989, book publishing had grown at a rate of 8.3 percent from 1982 to 1989, of which 1.6 percent was volume and 6.7 percent price (ahead of the 3.8 percent CPI increase). During the second half of the decade, increased concentration had been an important industry characteristic. Market share of the top 15 publishers had increased from 70 percent to 78 percent from 1986 until 1989, while the top six college textbook publishers went from 37 percent to 54 percent during the same time period. Most of this increase was achieved through acquisitions. In educational publishing alone, over $6 billion in transactions took place. McKinsey expected that "further industry consolidation is likely in the future since middle-sized publishers have the poorest operating performance [see Exhibit 6], leaving several large companies and niche players. After this consolidation, the industry structure may be more favorable for a return to higher profitability—for the survivors.''

In spite of this consolidation, operating margins had declined since 1987. Even though book publishing shareholders had seen a 17.3 percent return (share appreciation plus reinvested dividends) from 1980 through 1990 (compared with a 16.5 percent return for the S&P 500), stock prices nosedived toward the end of the decade, resulting in a 6.1 percent return for the 1985–1990 period (compared with 17.3 percent for the S&P 500). Fixed costs accounted for a large percentage of operating costs (see Exhibit 7) even though HBJ's corporate overhead amounted to less than 2 percent of sales. Investment levels were also substantial. Product development and plate, which was capitalized, averaged 28 percent of sales for the professional industry segment, 23 percent for the elementary-high school segment, and 15 percent for the college segment. For school publishers it often took several years before the investment could be recouped, if at all. Royalty advances were another investment, largely in the trade segment but also becoming more of a factor in the college segment. This cost and investment structure resulted in significant economies of scale in all phases of book publishing (see Exhibit 8). Book publishing also was a risky business, with only one of every five books being successful and with over 95 percent of all published books selling fewer than 20,000 copies. Libraries, which purchased 13 percent of all books sold, accounted for 55 percent of sales of low-volume books. Inventory writedowns and book returns were an important risk factor, with many titles having a short life.

In addition to industry concentration, McKinsey saw two major trends on the horizon: one coming from the market with its increasing customer fragmentation and the resulting desire for more custom products in educational markets, and the other, technological (i.e., "increased use of video/computer software in communicating information" [see Exhibit 9]). Moseley Associates, in its November 27, 1990, presentation to management had, however, stressed the "gap between the promise and implementation of technology":

- Publishing is a low-tech industry. Nonprint publishing has not, for the most part, been profitable:

    Database:
    - Lexis appears to be the only profitable service;
    - Incremental revenues for publishers already in data collection have not translated into significant profit.

    Software:
    - Abandoned by trade publishers, reflecting low home market penetration by personal computers;
    - Classrooms remain a limited market for publishers' software. Education remains a print business.
    - Pedagogical reinforcement programs are often provided gratis with important college texts.

    Audiovisual:
    - Never widely accepted as an integral part of the teaching process;
    - A few independent companies struggle for a dwindling share of the education market;
    - Audiocassettes get considerable fanfare but generate little revenue for trade publishers.

    Television:
    - Growing/grudging acceptance of educational TV in classroom;
    - Education's historic resistance to change will dampen growth of integrated modules

(TV/laser/computer) when they do become affordable.

Publishing on demand:

- The economics and technology of copying are making this concept more cost-effective. It will not go away, and ultimately will demand that publishers and copying interests find common and mutually profitable ground.

- The application of technology to the publishing process has not yet generated many schedule or cost benefits:

  - During 1988-1989 McGraw-Hill was forced to write off $172 million of premature investment in technology.

- Despite disappointing results thus far, publishers must anticipate future applications of technology in order to position themselves with respect to new publishing media and improvements in print publishing management.

A final trend stressed by both consultants was the growth potential in international markets. Exports of U.S. books in 1990 were estimated at $1.25 billion, up 70 percent over 1987. Trade books accounted for one-third, technical/scientific/medical for a quarter, and textbooks for almost 20 percent of exports, with the remainder going to other categories such as paperbacks.

College Publishing

The $3.5 billion college market had been characterized by above-average growth and operating margins (see Exhibit 10). Domestic college text publishers accounted for a 39.7 percent share of college market revenues, representing new books, to which an 8.1 percent share for ancillaries (audio/video/software/study guides) had to be added. New foreign texts took 3.5 percent of revenues, while noncollege books accounted for 28.9 percent. Among growing competitive threats were used texts (accounting for 15.8 percent of revenues) and photocopying services (with an estimated 4.3 percent market share). Used-book sales had increased by 23 percent per year since 1986 due to the emergence of used-book wholesalers and the relative pricing of new versus used books. The McKinsey study stated, "Bookstores can influence whether books are bought new from publisher or used from wholesaler; high profitability and better service from wholesaler makes them prefer used books." Said a sales representative, "Used books are killing us . . . you're better off as a wholesaler than a publisher to avoid development costs." As to photocopying, a college bookstore manager commented, "It's about 10 percent of our volume and is likely to increase after the copyright issues are settled . . . our university copy center wants to do a lot of it instead of Kinko's." According to Moseley, margins and return on assets, among the most attractive in publishing, were under increasing pressure for the following reasons:

- Higher manufacturing and selling costs;
- Shortened revision cycles;
- Increased royalty demands;
- Enrollment of traditional-age students will drop 23 percent in the period 1990–96:

  - More older, part-time, and minority students will require new kinds of materials.

- Faculty is aging; less experienced instructors will need additional (free) support materials.
- The percentage of returns has increased each year for the past three years.
- Prepublication costs continue to increase:

  - Plant cost must support lavish four-color formats;

- Heavy market research is required with respect to organization and subject coverage;
- More free materials are required (e.g., instruction manuals, test banks, integrated software).
- Marketing expense ratios are the highest in publishing:
  - Large field staffs are needed to visit campuses.
  - Complimentary copies can reach 10,000.

A new segment on the horizon was customized publishing (see Exhibit 11), involving a computerized publishing system that allowed customized material to be drawn from a database, thereby shortening the product life cycle and run length. It was expected that higher unit costs could be offset by the elimination of the used-book market and through lower plate, fulfillment, and inventory costs. The first custom textbooks were to be produced at USC in 1991 using technology developed jointly by McGraw-Hill/Kodak/R.R. Donnelley. A Prentice-Hall sales representative commented, "This could be really big . . . more popular with younger faculty . . . the technology is available . . . if it takes off, everyone will jump in." Firmly in the publishers' domain were the ancillary products, which had been growing at 20 percent per year. A publisher said, "We want to give students an educational package . . . which has continuity features to give students using our texts a logical progression through all levels of the discipline." A college sales representative added, "The toys are absolutely necessary to keep the business." Thus, according to McKinsey, "the product continuity concept is an attempt to create switching barriers on adoption decisions by creating an integrated series used throughout all levels of a discipline."

The McKinsey report indicated that "college market attractiveness varies by discipline, with the career-oriented 'hard-sciences' being most profitable, yet receiving the most attention by competitors." Computers ($150 million revenues) showed the highest growth, and together with math and engineering ($260 million), business economics ($390 million), and education ($155 million), were seen as the most attractive segments in terms of growth and profitability. Other sciences ($215 million), English literature/language ($145 million), and behavior/social sciences ($220 million) were rated as "average," while other humanities ($220 million) were at the bottom in terms of attractiveness. McKinsey stated that "competitors are seeking dominant positions within disciplines and complete representation across all disciplines to drive scale advantages, feed the product pipeline, and win orders." It concluded, "The most successful players in the college market derive superior profitability by achieving leadership in selected disciplines, building a strong editorial staff, and training their sales force to maximize adoption rates." (See Exhibit 12 for key success factors.) However, according to Moseley, "Market requirements are relatively predictable: Competitive activity is closely monitored, and a heavy peer review process influences publishing decisions and manuscript organization and coverage." Also, "Field sales staffs, the traditional source for editors, turn over 30–40 percent per year; salaries compare unfavorably with other industries, and the position, often the first out of college, proves unappealing to some." The sales force visited both bookstores and college professors. Since volume was driven by course adoptions, calling on professors was a key task for a sales representative.

By 1989, McGraw-Hill, which recently had acquired Random House, had 1989 college revenues of $216 million, behind Paramount-owned Simon and Schuster, which, after its Prentice-Hall acquisition, sold $246 million in the college market. In third place was the Wadsworth Group, belonging to Thomson, with $187 million in sales, having acquired South-Western. The combined revenues of $139 million of HBJ and HRW college books put it in fourth place, followed by Addison-Wesley (acquired by Pearson plc) with $113 million and Times Mirror, after the Richard D. Irwin acquisition, with $98 million in college revenues. Other college publishers with sales between $50 million and $75 million were J. Wiley & Sons, Houghton Mifflin, William C. Brown, and News Corp. through Harper & Row. These 10 publishers accounted for about $1.3 billion of the $1.8 billion new college text market.

HBJ's college activities covered all major disciplines, but market shares varied significantly:

1989 McKinsey Data	HBJ	HRW
Math and engineering	2.4%	2.5%
Computers	1.1	1.7
Science	0.8	9.2
Business	2.2	6.5
English literature	8.7	5.2
Humanities	4.3	7.3
Education	0.5	1.1
Social science	3.9	5.9
College share	2.6	4.9

HBJ's college market position was increased significantly through the 1986 acquisition of CBS publishing properties, which were still managed independently in 1990 and were separated into three business units. Holt, Rinehart and Winston, located in Fort Worth, Texas, published foreign language, humanities, and behavioral/social science textbooks. Dryden Press, headquartered in Chicago, published business textbooks. Saunders College from its Philadelphia location specialized in scientific titles. Through a sales force of 145, HRW College marketed some 2,200 titles, ringing up sales of $91 million in 1989 and supporting an editorial staff of 69 as well as a total 347-person headcount. HRW's president, 59, had joined HBJ in 1961 as a salesperson. HBJ College, headquartered in San Diego, California, sold $48 million of its 1,100 titles in 1989 through a sales force of 73 and supported an editorial staff of 72 as well as a 257-person total headcount. It had a strong presence in English, math, psychology, and accounting. Its president, 50, who was appointed in 1990, had joined HBJ College in 1966 as a salesperson. Moseley commented, "Antipathy between HBJ and HRW remains a problem."

McKinsey assessed HBJ's position in college publishing as follows: "HBJ is a major player in the college market, although its market share has fallen from 8.1 percent in 1987 to 7.0 percent in 1990. HBJ's position is strong but declining which appears to be due to lack of 'discipline' leadership, a deteriorating product development infrastructure, and a failure to achieve scale advantages from integrating its independent college businesses. HRW and HBJ appear to operate as independent companies (e.g., separate sales force)." McKinsey also presented the General Cinema directors with the assessment of HBJ's college position (see Exhibit 13). On November 26 it had also reported to management that "HBJ's percentage of sales from the top 20 titles continues to fall (27 percent in 1987 vs. 22 percent in 1990), while percentage of sales derived by newly published books has dropped from 38 percent in 1987 to 13 percent in 1990. Average sales per title has increased for new list between 1989 and 1990. HBJ's ability to attract top-name authors and design textbooks that are widely sought in the market may be decreasing." Also, HBJ "ranked number 10 in NACS's 1989 publishers rating based on responsiveness to bookstore needs, speed of fulfillment, return policy, and problem solving. Market interviews suggested no significant sales force problems." HBJ college operating margins remained in line with college publishing averages.

El-Hi Educational Publishing

The El-Hi (elementary and high school) market accounted for close to $2 billion of textbook sales and about $1.4 billion of other educational materials. Modest above-industry growth from 1982 to 1989 was achieved entirely through price increases. For the 1989–1996 period, McKinsey expected slightly lower unit-price increases and higher growth in the number of pupils, which, on balance, would result in slightly higher industry growth. Government funding for education stood at $161 billion in 1987, having grown at 7 percent per year since 1983. Six percent of educational funding came from the federal, 50 percent from state, and 44 percent from local governments. Only between 1 and 2 percent of these funds went to books and related ancillaries. In spite of high price increases, industry operating margins had declined since 1984, dropping from 15.6 percent in 1987 to 7.4 percent in 1989. Plate and editorial expenses had been rising as well as marketing expenses. Marketing expense ratios

increased from 23 percent in 1985 to 28 percent of sales in 1989 for the large publishers, primarily as a result of increased sampling and gratis copies, which cost 9 percent of sales in 1989.

The El-Hi market could be segmented in a number of ways. In terms of demographics, 31 percent of industry revenues went to states with a high Hispanic population requiring bilingual editions. Also, the market could be divided between open-territory states and adoption states, which developed master lists for school districts to choose from and which accounted for a little over half of industry revenues. The state selection process was critical because five adoption states accounted for 29 percent of El-Hi textbook sales in 1989: California, Florida, Georgia, North Carolina, and Texas. A final distinction was between the elementary and secondary markets, each of which consisted of a number of disciplines. The largest discipline for elementary schools, which accounted for 65 percent of El-Hi revenues, was reading/language ($758 million in revenues), followed by math ($209 million), science ($94 million), and social studies ($74 million). High schools purchased 35 percent of revenues, with reading/language the largest discipline ($185 million in revenues), followed by science ($115 million), social studies ($77 million), math ($70 million), and foreign languages ($64 million).

The differences between the elementary and secondary markets also had important implications for publishers. Moseley commented that "school sales representatives, no matter how competent, cannot sell effectively in both the K–8 and 7–12 areas; different (and incompatible) selling techniques are involved." According to McKinsey, "elementary school selling focuses on instructing teachers how to use materials." Also, single titles, common for secondary schools, were aimed at specialist teachers, requiring small investments. Elementary school series, aimed at generalist teachers, required large up-front investments. The development cycle and costs for both new and revised series were huge. A first phase of the development cycle, taking one and a half years, involved market research to analyze market/curriculum needs and competitor products, to define content outline, and to gain internal approval to develop a new series. The second phase consisted of content development and took one and a half to two years. Authors were selected, authors and editors worked on the new text, and internal reviews ensured curriculum compatibility. The final phase comprised the initial production, taking one year, and including the development of graphics, pictures, and layout, plate production, and initiation of the sales process with the finished materials. Elementary series for reading cost $35 million, while math/science series required $15 million and social studies $10 million. Secondary reading development costs came to $10 million, while math/science and social studies books cost $2 million each. Revised series took one and a half years of development time and required expenditures between one-third and one-half of new series.

McKinsey saw the El-Hi market changing and identified three trends: increasing local attention to education, a more diverse student population, and an increasing skill gap in the classroom. Curriculum decisions were reviewed by parents and local political leaders with local content (for example, urban versus rural or California versus Texas) being stressed more. Increased use of "pilot" programs occurred to determine text suitability. In terms of diversity, Texas and California

required Spanish language editions of K–8 series. With respect to skills, students were "relating less well to the print medium." Also, there was "pressure to make more use of computers and other 'high-tech' equipment in the classroom." Even though basic texts still accounted for 55 to 60 percent of sales, these trends had resulted in a 111 percent increase in ancillary products, a 638 percent increase in Spanish language titles, and a 37 percent annual growth in software sales. Also, Texas approved a video disk system as a text alternative. McKinsey concluded, "To compete effectively in this changing market and to adjust to declining margins, we believe publishers will need to develop new skills." (See Exhibit 14.)

McKinsey considered the El-Hi market as highly competitive. Except for HBJ, Scott-Foresman, and Houghton Mifflin, all the major players had used the acquisition route. According to Moseley, Paramount-owned Simon and Schuster, using the Silver Burdett and Ginn names for the elementary school market, was the leader with $300 million in El-Hi sales in 1989, followed by HBJ ($270 million), the Macmillan/McGraw-Hill joint venture ($250 million), Houghton Mifflin ($200 million), Murdoch-owned Scott-Foresman ($190 million), and two secondary school publishers, Raytheon-owned D.C. Heath ($140 million) and Pearson-acquired Addison-Wesley ($100 million). These top seven publishers had increased their combined market share from 1986 to 1989. Four other companies sold a total of $190 million, while the remaining $300 million in El-Hi sales were accounted for by smaller companies. McKinsey concluded that "competitors are pursuing aggressive product development, marketing, and sales strategies. Future winners will need more sophisticated management approaches to make trade-offs between investments in product development, marketing, and sales."

HBJ's acquisition of HRW from CBS, according to Moseley, "merged two powerful K–12 publishers." Moseley added, "HRW's strength in 7–12 science and mathematics were splendid complements to HBJ's strengths in secondary English and social studies. Although there was considerable product overlap, the problems were not insoluble. It was a different matter in K–8, however, with direct product overlap in elementary reading, mathematics, science, and social studies." After the acquisition, the kindergarten through grade 8 (K–8) activities were handled by HBJ School, located primarily in Orlando, with 1989 sales of $172 million and a head count of 350 (including 83 editorial and a salaried sales force of 85 plus 35 salaried consultants). The textbooks for grades 7–12 were published by HRW School, headquartered in Austin, Texas, with 1989 sales of $98 million and a head count of 260, which included 66 people in editorial and a salaried sales force of 70 supported by 14 staff technical consultants.

McKinsey and Moseley presented detailed assessments of HBJ's El-Hi activities. Market shares in 1989 for the various disciplines were as follows:

1989 McKinsey Data	HBJ School	HRW School
Reading, language, arts	10.5%	28.5%
Math	19.0	13.1
Science	11.7	22.9
Social studies	13.3	19.2
Foreign languages	—	14.8
Total market share	11.5%	14.6%

In the secondary market, HRW School had maintained its market share. It dominated the largest discipline, reading, where its leadership position had been reinforced by the successful introduction of a new literature series. It was also successfully selling college division texts for foreign language curricula. HRW School was also strong in science and social studies but traditionally weak in math. With respect to the latter, the consultants commented: "The curriculum is changing to 'an integrated approach,' and Eagle will not be ready until 1996. Management would invest more here if it had resources." In the elementary market, HBJ School's market share had dropped by almost 30 percent from 1987 to 1989. It had made "small revisions to several series in the same discipline instead of focusing resources on a single series." Its 1989 reading and math programs were poorly received and did not get adopted in several states.

McKinsey concluded: "It appears that HBJ has not been investing enough in the El-Hi business, resulting in the recent share losses." For example, from 1988 through 1990, editorial expense dropped from 3.3 percent to 2.2 percent and plant expense for plates used in the printing process from 23.9 percent to 10.6 percent of sales. The report quoted the following representative comments from interviews: "Over the past several years, they [HBJ] haven't been investing the resources required to be successful in El-Hi," "HBJ is submitting old programs with minimal revisions," and "Their debt problems have diverted their attention away from keeping up with curriculum changes." Major programs were under way for math (1992), reading (1993), and science (1994). In math, there was no clear leader, and the new program was expected to do well. In reading, according to the consultants, HBJ was "betting the farm" on its major revision.

McKinsey's assessment of HBJ's current position is shown in Exhibit 15. The consultants estimated that up to $450 million in textbook investment might be needed over the next six years to effectively compete in the El-Hi business. McKinsey stated:

> We expect that HBJ's market share will continue to erode over the next few years due to recent state adoption losses. Adoption losses preclude HBJ from competing in approximately 9 percent of the El-Hi market until these states readopt texts, typically six years later. In addition, although the data are sketchy, HBJ's position may continue to erode due to a possible lack of new programs in several upcoming adoption decisions.

In summary, McKinsey concluded, HBJ's "position is recoverable. Educators regard the quality of the program material as the most important aspect in making textbook selections. As long as HBJ invests in new programs, it will have an equal chance in the next round of buying decisions." It quoted a curriculum director: "We look at how the material matches our curriculum goals and teaching styles. It does not matter what they [the publisher] did last time. Each textbook decision is different." And a state adoption commissioner: "As long as they meet the state guidelines, they are on the list; last time does not count." Moseley concluded its commentary as follows: "But, with all the reservations, disclaimers, and doubts expressed above, we are nevertheless enormously and favorably impressed by the overall excellence of the combined HBJ/HRW School programs and products." It agreed with the comment of an HRW sales representative who stated, "We carry the best secondary school book bag in the business."

As to future opportunities in the El-Hi, McKinsey also commented that "further industry consolidation makes sense from an economic perspective, and publishers have begun searching for ways to consolidate (Exhibit 16). Once this consolidation has occurred, El-Hi profits are likely to improve (Exhibit 17). However, several factors may prevent El-Hi operating margins from returning to historic levels of 15 to 20 percent (Exhibit 18)."

Test Publishing

HBJ was also engaged in test publishing, largely for the K–12 market segment, through its wholly owned Psychological Corporation. The 1990 testing market was estimated at $950 million, largely consisting of four segments: industrial/employment/career (32 percent), K–12 (26 percent), college admissions (18 percent), and test preparation (18 percent). Recent annual growth for the K–12 segment had been in the double digits, as a result of an increasing testing trend in El-Hi education, and operating margins typically ranged between 20 percent and 25 percent. Historically, there had been little price competition. The K–12 testing market consisted of three distinct products: educational tests/materials, scoring services, and clinical tests. The first product, which accounted for the lion's share of the market, was sold to states and local school districts. There was an increasing trend toward state adoptions (32 states by 1990), in which event only one test was approved per state. Minimum competency testing was mandated by 42 states at selected grade levels. Many states, such as New York, Massachusetts, and California, had developed their own tests to save money and meet specific needs. Some states contracted with publishers to develop a test for their use. Local school districts had freedom to adopt additional achievement tests beyond state requirements.

Adoption decisions, which were heavily dependent on funding and budget constraints, were typically made every two years with little switching. In terms of key customer buying factors, McKinsey rated as high "compatibility between curriculum and test content" and "size and demographics of test norms" because of the "need to compare students to a similar population of large enough size to be accurate." Report formats, services, and support, as well as prices, were rated of medium importance. Rapport with the sales agent, however, could be the deciding factor. In total, some 40 million to 50 million tests were administered annually at $4 to $5 per test. The development costs for educational tests amounted to some $10 million, and the tests were revised every seven years. Five tests, offered by three companies, dominated the K–12 market: The Stanford and Metropolitan AT (Psychological Corporation), California AT and CTBS (McGraw-Hill/Macmillan), and the Iowa Basic Skills test (Houghton Mifflin's Riverside Press). Scoring services were performed either by test publishers or other vendors. Said an industry executive, "Scoring is where the high profits are in this industry." Clinical tests were not part of state adoptions, were administered one-to-one, and were sold by catalog. The 14-year revision cycle for clinical tests was twice that of educational tests.

McKinsey identified two key trends. One involved interactive testing through customized independent testing of students on PCs. One industry executive, however, observed, "This technology has a long way to go before it is used widely."

The other trend was a possible shift toward alternate format tests, fueled by the increased debate by test users and public interest groups over accuracy and fairness of standardized tests. Multiple-choice tests were heavily criticized, but it was unclear who would succeed in developing a superior product. The McKinsey report included the following representative quotes: "Eventually a superior format will be developed, but who is going to do it is uncertain . . . despite the vocal minority arguing tests are unfair, their use continues to increase;" "Alternate formats like open-ended math problems and essay questions will spell higher development, measurement, and labor costs for the industry;" and "How are you going to standardize the grading of essay questions?"

Psychological Corporation, with 1989 revenues of $69 million and operating margins at the high end of the testing industry, was the number one for-profit publisher in clinical and educational testing, with 13 state adoptions, holding a 40 percent market share of the for-profit K–12 educational market. The nonprofit Educational Testing Service had sales of $256 million but sold in different market segments and was not a direct competitor. Both Psychological Corporation's growth rate and operating margins exceeded industry averages even though, in 1990, it lagged behind other test publishers in number of sales representatives. These sales representatives were not interchangeable with those selling K–12 tests. Psychological Corporation also had a strong position in both emerging test formats and new growth opportunities, like report services and computerized testing. For example, it opened a writing assessment center in 1988 to respond to the movement away from multiple-choice tests, and it partnered with software companies to provide software-based tests. It made a significant recent investment in scoring facilities to move the bulk of scoring activities in-house (it previously contracted scoring). However, its scoring costs were slightly above scoring competitors. The McKinsey report included the following representative quotes:

> The publishers of the large tests like the SAT are entrenched and have developed their leadership position by historical precedent . . . Their large scale, mass use makes them impossible to displace . . . However, all publishers are basically the same.

> This is largely a fixed-cost business because test development is so expensive; after that, whoever can sell the most tests will make the most money.

> The purchase of standardized tests by school districts is highly dependent on educational funding levels. If funding is cut, test producers will suffer.

> Psychological Corporation is the only company I know of that has produced an open-ended question format test for K–12.

Professional Publishing

HBJ had strong positions in medical and scientific/technical publishing, with 25 percent of sales outside the United States. Both segments had grown at slightly below the rate of book publishing, although some disciplines like medicine or biological science grew much faster. Growth in the medical market was driven by the number of health care professionals, by increasing medical specialization, and by changing medical techniques and approaches. Operating margins averaged between 18 and 25 percent with low price

sensitivity, especially in journals and clinical books. Journals accounted for $650 million and books for $500 million of 1990 medical publishing revenues. The leader in 1990 in the combined book–journal market, with a 14 percent share, was Wolters Kluwer through its three affiliates, Lippincott, Aspen, and Raven. HBJ took 11 percent, followed by both Williams & Wilkins and Elsevier with 10 percent and Mosby-YearBook (Times Mirror) with 7 percent. The scientific/technical market in 1990 was $1.4 billion, of which $725 million was in books. Competitive conditions and operating margins were similar to the medical segment. Elsevier, particularly after its acquisition of Maxwell's Pergamon, held a 31 percent share in 1990, followed by Springer Verlag (11 percent), John Wiley (8 percent), HBJ and Kluwer Academic (5 percent each), as well as Plenum and McGraw-Hill (3 percent each).

HBJ competed in the medical market through Philadelphia-headquartered W.B. Saunders, with 1989 revenues of $97 million, acquired in 1986 from CBS. Saunders, with 1,200 titles in print, was a worldwide number one in the medical book segment and held strong market positions in veterinary, allied health, dental, and nursing. A sizable part of revenues came from subscription-based clinical series and journals, with 5 of its top 10 journals society owned. According to the Smith Barney offering memorandum:

> In the United States, clinical books are sold [directly to physicians] by a 65-person salaried plus commission sales force which is twice as large as the company's nearest competitor. [These] books are also sold through medical bookstores and by direct mail. Textbooks are sold by 28 salaried sales representatives who call on medical, dental, and veterinary school

professors, as well as the bookstores that service such institutions. Foreign sales are generated through HBJ's foreign operations. Journals are marketed through direct mail and society memberships as well as by the Saunders sales force and other HBJ affiliates.

The divisional president, according to Moseley, was considered "the best medical editor in the business."

In the scientific/technical market, serving professionals, researchers, and students at the graduate and postgraduate level, HBJ participated through its San Diego affiliate, Academic Press, with 1989 revenues of $68 million. Academic Press competed in all major science disciplines and was especially strong in life sciences. Its books consisted of 70 percent serials, 25 percent reference books, and 5 percent textbooks. It also published 107 journals plus another 80 through its London affiliate, edited by leading scholars and often sponsored by learned societies. Its major customers were libraries. Even though Academic Press employed five sales representatives to call on university bookstores, most of its sales were through direct mail, with space ads and conventions also being important.

McKinsey concluded that "both Saunders and Academic Press are favorably positioned against market requirements and key trends; as a result, their recent strong performance should continue." HBJ's position in terms of the key success factors, which were similar for the medical and scientific markets, are portrayed in Exhibit 19. McKinsey emphasized that for texts the "initial development was costly, but that established books had a long life. Author credibility was critical to success, and used-book sales were minimal." Subscription-based journals also had a long product life once established.

Exhibit 20 portrays the key trends as well as HBJ's position to meet their challenge. McKinsey concluded that "few are likely to significantly impact HBJ over the next several years."

Other Activities

HBJ Legal, located in Chicago, had 1989 sales of $35 million and an operating margin close to the HBJ average. It offered the nation's largest bar review program, holding a 60 percent market share and accounting for 65 percent of revenues. On-campus salaried plus incentive promoters solicited students through contacts with professors and administrators, posters, and newspaper advertisements. Moseley described these courses, which listed for $1,000–$1,300 with discounts for early sign-up and multiple courses, as follows:

> The keys to success in this business are sweating details and success rate of students passing the bar examinations. Successful competitors try to get down payments the first week students arrive on campus by offering discounts, price protection, and use of study materials. They fight over location of tables in student lounges and tear down each other's posters. This business cannot be run just from corporate; vigorous local organizations are needed for constant action.
>
> Being Number 1 carries with it the status of being the number one target for all competitors. Last year students were bombarded with leaflets suggesting that HBJ's "insolvency" could jeopardize BRI/BAR's ability to fulfill contracts.

HBJ Legal obtained 20 percent of its revenues as the leading publisher of law school study aids. It held the number two spot as publisher of graduate school entrance exam and CPA review programs, accounting for 10 percent of sales. Moseley commented, "The operations have for the most part been untouched by the parent. They require little if any services from corporate and management is quite capable of operating independently. The key executives are experienced and competent managers and are recognized authorities in the business. The firm is extremely market oriented and quite aggressive in protecting its territory. It has for the most part been unsuccessful in defining or penetrating new markets."

HBJ Trade, located in San Diego and New York, sold $25 million at a breakeven level in 1989, mostly in trade books (20 percent came from accounting and college guides). Its market share was below 1 percent, but it had the reputation as a specialist publisher of renowned literary figures and children's books. According to Moseley, "famous authors boost the reputation of the company in school and college marketing situations, especially English disciplines."

HBJ's international publishing activities were expected to ring up $131 million in revenues in 1989, 37 percent of which were sales in the United Kingdom, 38 percent in Canada, 7 percent in Australia, and 7 percent in Japan, with the remainder going to other countries. The U.K. operation, according to the Smith Barney offering memorandum,

> published scientific and medical books and journals, college textbooks, psychological tests, and school textbooks. The scientific, technical, and medical books, as well as imports from HBJ (U.S.), are sold by a sales force of six in the U.K. and six in Europe. The company also promotes books and journals through extensive mailing campaigns directly to consumers and through cooperative mailings with booksellers. School textbooks are sold by a commission sales force of 12. [In Canada] HBJ-Holt-Saunders Canada (Toronto) published primarily in the school and college markets, along with distribution of W.B. Saunders Company's and The Psychological Corporation's products. The school and college divisions account for over 75 percent of this unit's total revenue. Les Editions Etudes Vivantes (EEV) is HBJ's publisher of college textbooks in the French Canadian market. Les Editions HRW Ltee (HRW Ltee) is HBJ's elementary and secondary publisher in the French Canadian market. Agence D'Arc (ARC) publishes professional books for the use of the management of small and medium-size enterprises. All these Montreal companies operate in one location with centralized production, accounting, data processing, and warehousing services.

Mostly U.S. books, journals, and tests were sold by the Australian and Japanese subsidiaries and also by the Orlando-based HBJ International, which covered the rest of the world as well as American international schools and Department of Defense Dependents' schools. Most of the U.S. books sold in international markets, except for the United Kingdom and Canada, came from W.B. Saunders and the Academic Press.

Moseley pointed out that of the top six English-language publishing companies, only two were U.S. domiciled. Rupert Murdoch's News Corp. from Australia was the leader with $1.4 billion in sales, followed by Paramount (U.S.) with $1.2 billion, Hachette (France) with $1.1 billion, and Reed International (U.K.), Pearson (U.K.), and HBJ, each with $0.9 billion in sales.

EXHIBIT 1
GENERAL CINEMA CORPORATION—STATEMENT OF EARNINGS
(IN MILLIONS OF DOLLARS)

	1990	1989	1988	1987	1986
Revenues					
Specialty retail operations	$1,689	$1,468	$1,223	—	—
Theater operations	461	446	380	365	351
Beverage operations	—	261	721	675	639
Total	$2,150	$2,175	$2,324	$1,040	$ 990
Operating earnings					
Specialty retail operations	99	83	63	—	—
Theater operations	(11)	9	16	18	27
Theater restructuring	(34)	—	—	—	—
Beverage operations	—	11	62	92	90
Total	$ 54	$ 103	$ 141	$ 110	$ 117
Corporate activities					
Administrative expenses	(27)	(30)	(26)	(22)	(12)
Investment income less interest expense	20	35	(43)	7	17
Gain on sale of securities	129	83	33	26	4
Total	$ 122	$ 88	$ (36)	$ 11	$ 9
Earnings before taxes and minority interest	176	191	105	121	126
Gains (or loss) on discontinued operations (after tax)	—	855	—	(17)	—

Source: Annual reports.

EXHIBIT 2
COMPARISON OF OPERATING INCOME FORECASTS FOR THE PUBLISHING GROUP

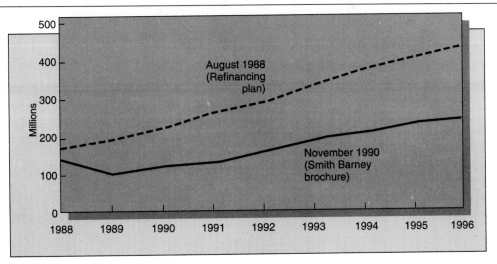

Source: First Boston and Salomon Brothers Inc.

EXHIBIT 3
SELECTED FINANCIAL DATA FOR HBJ (IN MILLIONS OF DOLLARS)

	Year Ended December 31				
	1989	*1988*	*1987*	*1986*	*1985*
Sales and revenues from continuing operations	$1,342	$1,271	$1,112	$ 807	$ 597
Recapitalization expenses	—	—	99	—	—
Interest expense (net)	351	314	164	22	18
Net (loss) income from continuing operations	(242)*	(94)	(107)	37	22
Publishing revenues†	886	868	791	526	451
Publishing operating income (before write-offs)	101	146	113	71	46
Total assets	2,644	3,235	2,911	2,413	1,364
Long-term debt	1,655	2,557	2,270	788	219

Source: HBJ 1989 annual report.

*Includes $126,801,000 of pretax write-offs.

†Includes outplacement affiliate.

EXHIBIT 4
HBJ PUBLISHING IN 1989 (IN MILLIONS OF DOLLARS)

*Revenues**		*Assets and Liabilities*	
College	$139	Accounts receivable	$ 139
HBJ School	172	Inventories	154
HRW School	98	Property and equipment (net)	96
Psychological Corporation	69	Plates and leasehold	
WB Saunders	97	improvements (net)	169
Academic Press	68	Publishing rights	150
Trade	25	Other intangibles	271
Legal	35	Other assets	55
United Kingdom	49		
Canada	50	Total publishing assets	$1,034
Japan	9		
Australia	9	Unearned subscription income	49
International	14	Accounts payable	152
	$834		
Depreciation and amortization	108	Capital expenditures	87

Source: Smith Barney and HBJ 1989 annual report.
*Before consolidation adjustments.

EXHIBIT 5
CAPITAL MARKETS OVERVIEW
Profile of the Outstanding Securities (dollars in millions)

Security	Book Value	Current Price	Market Value	Market Discount
Senior notes	$ 200	82.5%	$ 165	$ 35
Senior subordinateds	500	64.0	320	180
Subordinated debentures	200	36.0	72	128
Subordinated PIKs	398	25.0	100	298
Subordinated discount	398	21.0	107	291
Convertible subordinated	54	100.0	54	—
Other debt	109	100.0	109	—
Total debt	$ 1,860		$ 927	$933
Preferred	597	$0.563/share	34	563
Equity	(1,479)	$1.00/share	72	NM
Total	**$ 978**		**$1,033**	

Source: First Boston and Salomon Brothers Inc.

EXHIBIT 6
PUBLISHER PERFORMANCE—1988

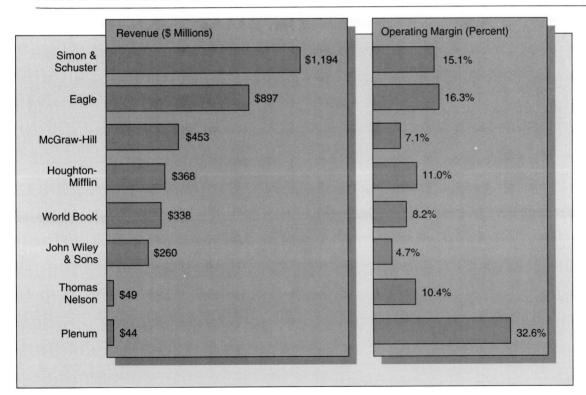

Source: BP reports presented during November 26, 1990, working session with management.

EXHIBIT 7
ESTIMATED FIXED COSTS FOR A TYPICAL BOOK PUBLISHER

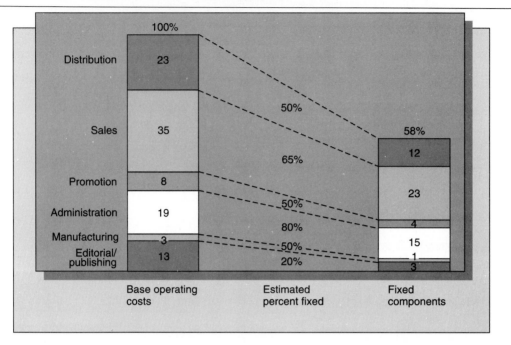

Source: McKinsey & Company, Inc., November 26, 1990, working session with management.

EXHIBIT 8
PUBLISHING ECONOMIES OF SCALE

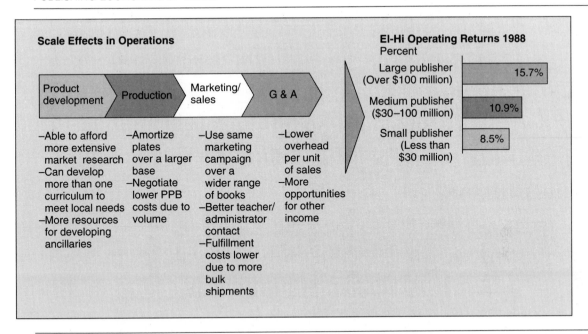

Source: McKinsey & Company, Inc., November 26, 1990, working session with management.
PPB = paper, printing, and binding

EXHIBIT 9
TECHNOLOGY IMPACT ON THE BOOK PUBLISHING INDUSTRY

Electronics: Changes in hardware and software technologies are beginning to impact the book publishing industry by offering electronic delivery of product and by reducing production costs and time. However, these changes provide Eagle with additional revenue enhancement and cost-reduction opportunities.

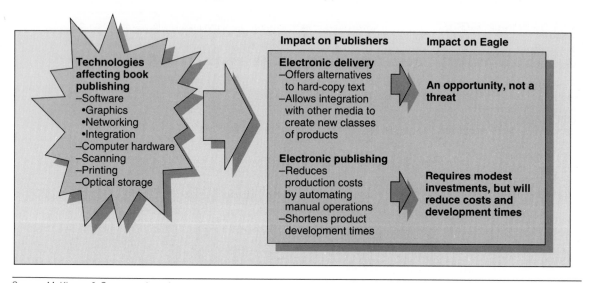

Source: McKinsey & Company, Inc., January 4, 1991, meeting with board of directors.

EXHIBIT 10
OPERATING MARGINS OF COLLEGE PUBLISHERS (PERCENT OF NET SALES)

Although segment profitability has been exceptional, margins slid from 1983 to 1986 as publishers increased marketing and sales expenses to win adoptions. In contrast, operating margins have improved from 1986 to 1988, largely as a result of industrywide price increases.

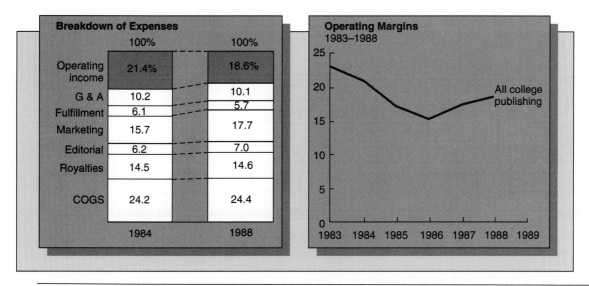

Source: McKinsey & Company, Inc., November 26, 1990, working session with management.

EXHIBIT 11
CUSTOM PUBLISHING OF COLLEGE TEXTS

Customized text publishing technology is still emerging but could drastically change the face of industry competition and cost structures.

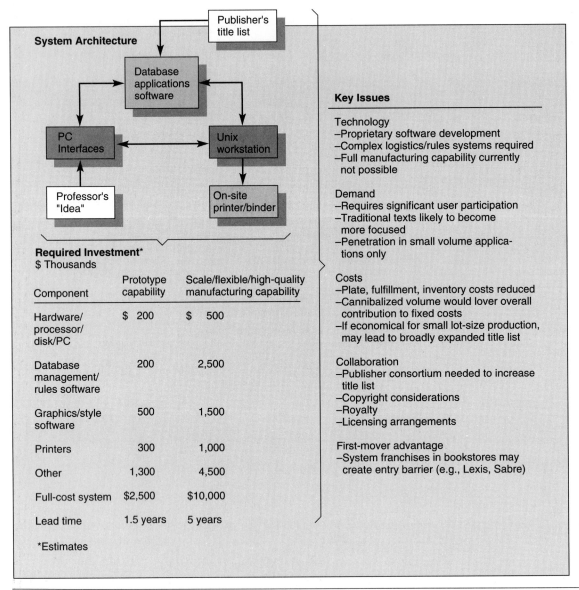

System Architecture

Publisher's title list

Database applications software

PC Interfaces

Unix workstation

Professor's "Idea"

On-site printer/binder

Required Investment*
$ Thousands

Component	Prototype capability	Scale/flexible/high-quality manufacturing capability
Hardware/ processor/ disk/PC	$ 200	$ 500
Database management/ rules software	200	2,500
Graphics/style software	500	1,500
Printers	300	1,000
Other	1,300	4,500
Full-cost system	$2,500	$10,000
Lead time	1.5 years	5 years

*Estimates

Key Issues

Technology
–Proprietary software development
–Complex logistics/rules systems required
–Full manufacturing capability currently not possible

Demand
–Requires significant user participation
–Traditional texts likely to become more focused
–Penetration in small volume applications only

Costs
–Plate, fulfillment, inventory costs reduced
–Cannibalized volume would lover overall contribution to fixed costs
–If economical for small lot-size production, may lead to broadly expanded title list

Collaboration
–Publisher consortium needed to increase title list
–Copyright considerations
–Royalty
–Licensing arrangements

First-mover advantage
–System franchises in bookstores may create entry barrier (e.g., Lexis, Sabre)

Source: McKinsey & Company, Inc., November 26, 1990, working session with management.

EXHIBIT 12
COLLEGE TEXTBOOK MARKET—KEY SUCCESS FACTORS

Factor	Description	Representative Quote
Attain dominant position within discipline.	• A dominant position works to attract top authors seeking maximum sales, which in turn leads to higher book adoption rates. • Creates editorial and sales efficiencies as employees can specialize, build competence, and develop reputations within specific disciplines.	• "I originally chose my publisher because he had the largest market share and coverage in the field . . . I've always stuck with the same publisher." —College professor and author of five popular textbooks
Play in many disciplines.	• Achieve scale advantages through sales force, fulfillment, and overhead leverage.	• "Our strategy is to become the largest college publisher." —McGraw-Hill

Build strong product-acquisition/development skills.	• Top-quality editors are instrumental in both winning noted authors and assuring that books appeal to target customer segment.
	• Increasing trend toward market-focused product development, for example:
	  • Market surveys and reviews
	  • Ancillary products
	  • Proactive author contracting
		• "Publishers need to devote a great deal of effort to making sure their products fulfill a large, real market need . . . that's where good editors are invaluable."
		—College sales rep

Build effective sales force.	• Recruiting, training, and managing of top sales force wins orders in an increasingly undifferentiated market and establishes relationships with key professors. • Achieves greater sales coverage and focus.	• "With so many textbooks of comparable content, adoption decisions are often made on the margin . . . and when that happens it's often the strength of the relationship or your superior knowledge that makes the sale." —College sales rep

Source: McKinsey & Company, Inc., November 26, 1990, working session with management.

EXHIBIT 13
EAGLE COLLEGE POSITION

	Discipline Strategy	Product Acquisition and Development	Production	Sales
Current Eagle position	• Participate in all major disciplines • Focus on large, introductory courses; little participation in intermediate and advanced-level courses • Dominant market share in several disciplines (e.g., chemistry, finance, art)	• Large number of new and revised titles expected 1991–93 • Reduced signings in HBJ college last several years due in part to deteriorating financial condition • Large number of new editors in both HBJ and HRW College (e.g., 10 editors in HBJ College with two years' experience or less) • Limited use of market research to shape product development	• Limited electronic publishing capabilities; currently systems installed in early '80s • No position in custom publishing	• HRW and HBJ compete directly in most disciplines • Recent reorganization of HRW sales force to develop discipline focus • Sales rep turnover rates exceed industry averages • Sampling expense ratio cut significantly in recent years; now lags competitors
Issues	• Current strategy not consistent with emerging market trends, e.g., competitors starting to follow more focused discipline strategies	• Recent signing/editorial staff inexperience likely to result in revenue fall-off in 1994–95 • Increasing marketing sophistication of competitors may require Eagle to develop additional marketing skills and increase spending	• Competitors have been investing in electronic publishing systems to reduce production costs—modest investments could reduce production costs by 25+% • Successful penetration of custom publishing could require sizable Eagle investments ($2–5 million +) to remain competitive	• Operating HRW and HBJ as separate companies forgoes scale economies

Source: McKinsey & Company, Inc., December 14, 1990, briefing package for board of directors.

EXHIBIT 14
EL-HI PUBLISHING—KEY SUCCESS FACTORS

	1970s	1980s	1990s	2000s
	Straightforward product/relationship business, stable market, predictable competition		Volatile/complex market, aggressive/unpredictable competitors	
	In the past		**In the future**	
Overall	• Focus on managing incremental change in the business		• Aggressively manage investment decisions across disciplines and markets	
Market research/ product development	• Review and comment on large state adoption criteria • Produce standard text in line with major market buying cycles		• Use sophisticated market research techniques to identify key local needs and teacher decision criteria • Incorporate specialized material geared to local curriculum needs • Reduce time needed to develop new material via integrated electronic publishing systems	
Marketing	• Do expensive "in-service" shows and "high-glitz" presentations • Stay in line with industry pricing		• Conduct local training sessions for teachers who use books in pilot programs • Develop and use teacher feedback • Develop creative pricing strategies	
Sales	• Maintain relationships with high-level administrators • High sampling • "Glad-handlers"		• Build presence with a broad range of decision makers • Sell "curriculum" expertise • "Professional sales force"	

Source: McKinsey & Company, Inc., December 14, 1990, briefing package for board of directors.

EXHIBIT 15
EAGLE RESPONSE TO INDUSTRY CHANGES

	Product Development	Production	Marketing/Sales	Financial/General Management
Current Eagle position	• Eagle does most work in-house, which is less expensive than commonly used practice of using vendors. • Editorial staff is very experienced for both K–8 and 7–12 (i.e., K–8 reading editorial staff all have 10 years' experience). • Eagle is increasing use of focus groups and customer interviews to determine market needs.	• Recently installed new inventory management systems. • Eagle has made minor investments in desktop publishing; however, position lags key competitors.	• Created marketing function in Austin for 7–12. • Eagle's sales force is experienced (average 15 years' experience). • Made sizable reductions in sampling expenses recently—to well below competitor averages.	• Starting to use DCF models to determine program investment levels.
Issues	• Eagle needs to get more marketing and sales manager input into product development process. • Eagle needs to cut development time cycle—currently at three years—to keep its editorial content competitive (some competitors at two years).	• Modest investments in electronic publishing could reduce production costs by over 25% and shorten development cycle.	• Eagle needs to rethink sampling policy before reduced sampling impacts revenues. • K–8 and 7–12 sales forces still have separate sales territories.	• Corporate management still wields considerable influence in day-to-day editorial decision making. • El-Hi business units are separated geographically.

Source: McKinsey & Co., Inc., December 14, 1990, briefing package for board of directors.

EXHIBIT 16
LIKELIHOOD OF FURTHER CONSOLIDATION

Economic pressures indicate further consolidation makes sense

Economic volume for basic programs is about 20–25 percent market share, making it impossible for six to seven large players to compete in all disciplines.

Large synergies exist for merging companies with complementary product lines.

Industry players with slow selling programs may eventually drop out because they face additional significant investment in programs that may not succeed against established leaders.

Recent activities indicate publishers are looking at how to consolidate

MacMillan/McGraw-Hill joint venture is doing very well and may be viewed as a good model going forward.

Some El-Hi publishing owners are trying to sell their business with limited success (no new entrants seem to be interested).

Eagle has had serious conversations with at least two other El-Hi publishers about potential joint ventures.

All seven companies are developing new 1993 reading programs; adoption decisions will determine the three to four winners; the three to four losers may not want to start over again in reading.

Source: McKinsey & Company, Inc., January 4, 1991, meeting with board of directors.

EXHIBIT 17
FUTURE EL-HI PROFITABLITY—FACTORS ENCOURAGING COOPERATION AND IMPROVED PROFITABILITY

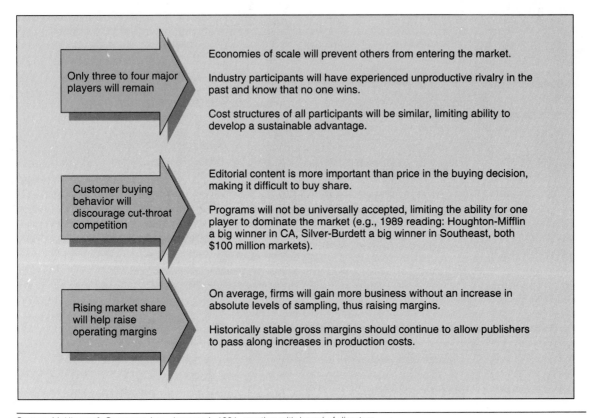

Only three to four major players will remain

Economies of scale will prevent others from entering the market.

Industry participants will have experienced unproductive rivalry in the past and know that no one wins.

Cost structures of all participants will be similar, limiting ability to develop a sustainable advantage.

Customer buying behavior will discourage cut-throat competition

Editorial content is more important than price in the buying decision, making it difficult to buy share.

Programs will not be universally accepted, limiting the ability for one player to dominate the market (e.g., 1989 reading: Houghton-Mifflin a big winner in CA, Silver-Burdett a big winner in Southeast, both $100 million markets).

Rising market share will help raise operating margins

On average, firms will gain more business without an increase in absolute levels of sampling, thus raising margins.

Historically stable gross margins should continue to allow publishers to pass along increases in production costs.

Source: McKinsey & Company, Inc., January 4, 1991, meeting with board of directors.

EXHIBIT 18
FUTURE EL-HI PROFITABILITY—FACTORS ENCOURAGING RIVALRY AND REDUCED PROFITABILITY

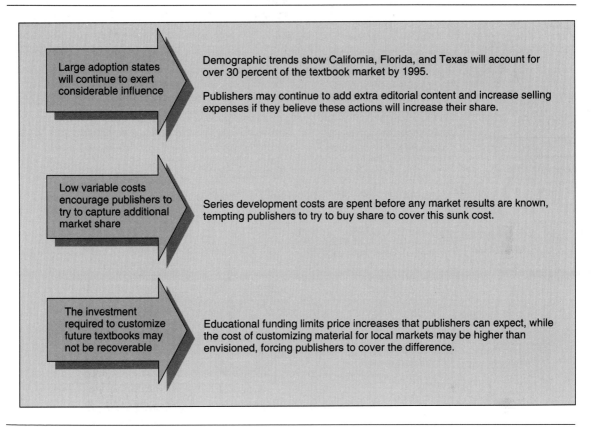

Large adoption states will continue to exert considerable influence

Demographic trends show California, Florida, and Texas will account for over 30 percent of the textbook market by 1995.

Publishers may continue to add extra editorial content and increase selling expenses if they believe these actions will increase their share.

Low variable costs encourage publishers to try to capture additional market share

Series development costs are spent before any market results are known, tempting publishers to try to buy share to cover this sunk cost.

The investment required to customize future textbooks may not be recoverable

Educational funding limits price increases that publishers can expect, while the cost of customizing material for local markets may be higher than envisioned, forcing publishers to cover the difference.

Source: McKinsey & Company, Inc., January 4, 1991, meeting with board of directors.

EXHIBIT 19
KEY SUCCESS FACTORS IN THE MEDICAL AND SCIENTIFIC/TECHNICAL MARKET (PRELIMINARY)

Key Success Factor	Publisher Requirements	Eagle's Position
Develop and maintain strong editorial department	• Requires editors that have 　• Technical knowledge of discipline 　• Intimate understanding of market requirements 　• Strong network of authors and key players in field • Expect low turnover in publisher's editorial department	• Eagle editorial investment increased to 6.4% in 1989 from 5.7% in 1988 • Eagle editorial department considered strong, but some concerns raised (e.g., "in general (Eagle's) material is good, but they may be getting comfortable with their position")
Attract quality authors	• Leading textbooks in specific subsegments achieve dominant share and are difficult to unseat	• Eagle has a number of leading titles (e.g., Nelson's *Textbook of Pediatrics*)
Support product release/maintain product position	• Support of new title introduction, e.g., advertising • Differential pricing for separate customer segments (e.g., medical students vs. attendings) • Strong channel management capabilities to address diverse distribution channels (e.g., retail, jobbers, direct mail, etc.)	• Sales force considered effective vs. competitors (e.g., "Eagle's sales rep is really on top of things") • Eagle's sales through alternate channels below industry averages (e.g., sales through wholesalers way below industry average)
Identify emerging segments	• Increasingly narrow specialization required, especially in journals • Strong editorial department with tight links to market needed to identify new trends	• Appears strong, for example 　• Number of new medical journal introductions increasing (from 4 in 1988 to 10 in 1989) 　• Strong growth in several high-growth subsegments (e.g., clinical reference)
Leverage strengths in college market	• Strength within a discipline across segments can 　• Improve overall reputation 　• Help attract authors • "McGraw-Hill had the editors, sales force, and in-house knowledge in the college market; it was easy to apply those strengths in the professional market."	• Some overlap in discipline focus between AP and Eagle college (e.g., physical sciences); coordination between groups unclear

Source: McKinsey & Company, Inc., November 26, 1990, working session with management.

EXHIBIT 20
KEY TRENDS IN THE MEDICAL AND SCIENTIFIC/TECHNICA1 MARKET (PRELIMINARY)

Key Trend	Description	Representative Quote	Eagle's Position
Rapid growth of electronic alternatives, e.g., CD-ROM, on-line databases	• Little market penetration to date (e.g., few title: on line) • More likely to impact materials that require frequent updating or where more sophisticated indexing/search routines increase the materials' usefulness • Currently, this technology is creating an incremental market with little cannibalization of core materials; longer term expect significant cannibalization • Significant up-front costs to write software interfaces/build database/acquire necessary hardware	• "I don't have the time to flip through three textbooks or a dozen journals—the computer can give me what I need in minutes." • "Our strategy is to price CD-ROM products so high that they can't cannibalize our core business."	• Eagle is investing in this area; future market positions are fluid and evolving

Constrained library budgets	• Libraries represent approximately 25% of market
	• Expect greater constraints on library budgets which may
	  • Make new journals more difficult to introduce
	  • Lead to fewer textbook purchases of updated new editions
		• "Every year we have to satisfy our members with less money."
		• "We have to make tough choices and cut the fringe journals."
			• Limited impact expected in core journal and textbook market (e.g., top 25 medical journals account for 91% of revenues)

Growth of nonprofit publishers in medical journal market	• Nonprofits now account for 25–30% of professional market • Nonprofits have lower cost structure; further reduces entry barriers		• Long-term industry trend; little near-term impact on Eagle
Strong growth of international markets	• International growth driven by journal sales • All publishers targeting international markets		• Eagle international journal growth 25% vs. 5% in United States

Source: McKinsey & Company, Inc., November 26, 1990, working session with management.

Firestone, Inc.: Globalization

Firestone, Inc., had long been the second largest North American tire manufacturer and one of the leaders in the world industry. Founded by Harvey Firestone in 1900, the company matured with the automobile industry, locating plants in more than a dozen countries and producing a full range of tires for cars, trucks, and off-road vehicles. In time this core business was augmented by plantations supplying natural latex, synthetic rubber facilities, and more than a thousand retail stores that complemented an extensive independent dealer network. For decades the company maintained a record of consistent, albeit lackluster, profitability.

In the late 1970s, however, Firestone was shaken by a series of crises, provoked by changing competitive conditions and inadequate management responses, which threatened the company's survival. With the situation deteriorating in the closing months of 1979, John Nevin was recruited as chief executive. During the next seven years, he restructured the corporation, reducing the scope of its operations and accumulating resources for diversification. Sales in 1987 were $3,867 million, down from $4,850 million in 1980; results from continuing operations recovered erratically from a $122 million loss to a $103 million profit; debt fell from $1,049 million to $429 million; and the company's stock price more than tripled.

The dynamics of the increasingly global tire industry were changing, however, and each of Firestone's domestic competitors had been either raided, acquired, or reorganized in the previous two years. In February 1988 Firestone had agreed to form a joint venture with Bridgestone Corp., the world's third largest tire producer, in what would be the largest investment to date by a Japanese company in a U.S. manufacturing firm.

The Tire Industry: Structure and Trends

Worldwide estimated tire demand in 1986 is shown in Exhibit 1. Sales were divided between original equipment (OE) and replacement markets. The former were strongly influenced by the location and growth of vehicle manufacturers, while the latter were related to the number of cars and trucks in service as well as to such factors as miles driven, replacement cycles, and tire durability (see Exhibit 2). The value of this global market, excluding the controlled economy countries, was thought to be approximately $34 billion. The 10 largest producers accounted for about 84 percent of the total in 1986, a proportion that had increased steadily in recent years as some companies expanded internally or through acquisition (see Exhibit 3).

Beginning in the mid-1970s the North American tire market was buffeted by rapidly changing competitive conditions. For years the field had been dominated by five domestic companies—Goodyear, Firestone, Uniroyal, General Tire, and B.F. Goodrich—together accounting for over 75 percent of industry sales, followed by a number of smaller firms which produced regional or private brand products for the replacement market. Then in the early 1970s Michelin, the largest European manufacturer and a private brand supplier to Sears Roebuck since 1966, initiated an aggressive sales campaign for its highly durable steel-belted radial tires, supporting these efforts with a U.S. factory in 1975.

The domestic producers had relied on bias ply tires and at first were reluctant to acknowledge that radials constituted a threat to the traditional construction. Radials, lasting about 40,000 miles, tripled the tire life compared with bias ply tires and also significantly improved fuel economy. Thus, the automobile companies were clamoring for radials, demand in the replacement market continued to grow, and soon a response became imperative. All of the domestic producers encountered difficulty digesting the massive

changes in product and process technology, generally centered around the problem of achieving adequate rubber-to-metal adhesion. The most conspicuous failure involved Firestone's "500" tire, which became the subject of a highly publicized 21 million unit recall, numerous lawsuits, and a $234 million writedown in 1978.

Other challenges to the U.S. tire industry's position emerged in these years. Difficult labor relations, marked by a long strike in 1976 and large wage settlements, drove costs upward. For a time margins were maintained by increasing tire prices, but then demand sagged sharply in 1979 and 1980 as the second oil shock restricted vehicle usage and the economy softened. More damaging still was the rapid growth in imported cars and tires, the latter jumping from 8 percent of the market in 1977 to more than 26 percent in 1987. Costs and excess capacity, especially for bias ply tires, became growing sources of concern. (See Exhibit 4 for trends relevant to the U.S. passenger car market.)

Changes were also occurring in tire distribution. The numbers of automobile dealers and full-service gasoline stations were declining, their places taken by independent tire stores and discount chains. The independents were more inclined to shop for low prices and private labels to broaden their product lines at the expense of the national brands. Often they were driven to this position by the discounters, for whom price was the determining factor in the purchase decision. Because the automobile manufacturers were reluctant to rely on a single supplier and tire technology was widely understood, product uniqueness was costly to achieve and difficult to sustain. The results were lower prices and a bruising struggle for market share in a business that by 1987 had just recovered to the volume levels of 1978. (See Exhibit 5 for U.S. market share data and Exhibit 6 for a capacity summary for 1979 and 1987.)

Globalization of the automobile industry in the 1980s presented yet another challenge for tire manufacturers. Joint ventures, technology sharing, component supply agreements, and sales and distribution arrangements among the major auto firms became commonplace as they sought to gain economies of scale in design and procurement and access to world markets (see Exhibit 7). Japanese and European companies also became more willing to locate facilities overseas to remain competitive, compensate for currency fluctuations, and lessen the danger of trade barriers. By the 1990s, some observers felt that their output in the United States would be two million or more vehicles. For the tire industry, these developments created new customers, potentially more complex supply relationships, and the need to think in global terms as well. Estimated market shares in 1987 for the OE and replacement markets in the United States, shown in Exhibit 8, reflect the opportunities for bonds to form between recent supplier and customer entrants.

Tire Industry Restructuring

The competitive conditions which prompted changes at Firestone were having an effect on the structure of the worldwide tire industry. The major producers chose or were forced to respond to market maturity, economic adversity, and globalization in a variety of ways, as the brief profiles below suggest.

Goodyear Tire and Rubber For many years the world's largest and most efficient tire manufacturer, Goodyear, was slow to react to Michelin's radial tire introduction in the United States. However, in 1972 it chose to meet the challenge head-on, spending over $3.2 billion in the following decade on plant and equipment, some $2 billion of it related to radials. By 1983, the company emerged with a strengthened competitive position, modern facilities, and an earnings record that remained substantially intact during the economic turbulence of the early 1980s (see Exhibit 9). Seeking growth, less dependence on the low-margin tire business, and an outlet for its steadily increasing uncommitted cash flow, Goodyear then turned to diversification by acquiring Celeron, an oil and gas company, for $820 million in stock and by expanding its aerospace business.

The equity markets responded poorly to Goodyear's diversification efforts: from a December 1982 high of $38 per share, its stock drifted down to $32 in September 1986 despite a rise in the New York Stock Exchange index during the same period. At that point Sir James Goldsmith, a prominent financier, acquired nearly 12 percent of the company's stock and offered to pay $49 per share ($4.7 billion) for the remainder. Alternatively he indicated that a takeover could be avoided if management adopted his reorganization plan, which called for significant cost cutting and the sale of the diversified business segments. The takeover bid was greeted with shock, indignation, and fear by Goodyear employees, government regulators, elected officials, and many prominent business leaders who felt that Goldsmith, for a quick gain, was attempting to dismember an outstanding company with a reputation for sound management and a long-term outlook. Nevertheless, during the next two months, Robert Mercer, Goodyear's chairman, announced his intention to sell the energy and aerospace units, slash overhead, and return Goodyear's focus to the tire industry. In November Goldsmith abruptly sold his interest to the company for $49.75 per share as part of an agreement which called for the repurchase from the public of an additional 36 percent of the outstanding stock at $50. (The stock subsequently rose to 76½ before settling in the high 50s.)

Following the recapitalization, Goodyear returned to its historic mission of being the world's largest tire producer. Industry observers generally rated its radial technology on a par with Michelin's and credited it with having highly automated and cost-efficient facilities. Moreover, with roughly 4,500 dealers and 2,000 company controlled-locations, Goodyear maintained a presence in every segment of the domestic replacement market. Overseas, it had the largest stake among U.S. companies in Europe[1] and Japan[2] and operated 22 plants elsewhere in the world. Major investments in capacity were planned in Korea to serve the Asian market.

Uniroyal–Goodrich Uniroyal had diversified into specialty chemicals, other auto parts, and rubber-based consumer goods in the 1970s such that by the end of the decade only 49 percent of sales were derived from tires and related products. Historically, the company's strength in tires had been in sales to General Motors and to a lesser degree Ford rather than to the replacement market. Faced with excess capacity, the conversion to radials, and a $120 million loss in 1979 on sales of $2,574 million, the company retrenched, closing two plants and cutting costs. When new car sales recovered after the 1982 recession, Uniroyal elected to service its OE customers rather than invest the capital to retain replacement tire volumes. Although sales declined to $2,122 million in 1984, profits had risen to $77.1 million, and the company's balance sheet was substantially improved.

In April 1985, Carl Icahn, a well-known corporate raider, acquired a 10 percent stake in Uniroyal and threatened a hostile tender offer for another 53 percent at $18 a share. (Six months earlier the stock had traded at $11 per share.) The company scrambled to locate a friendly suitor, ultimately striking a deal in May with Clayton & Dubilier, Inc., which organized a leveraged buyout for $22 a share financed with junk bonds. To recover its investment and retire the debt, the new owners immediately began to seek buyers for the company's various business segments and soon were left with the tire business only.

B.F. Goodrich had also sought to reduce its dependence on tires by investing heavily in specialty chemicals, polyvinyl chloride, and engineered plastic products. In 1981 the company abandoned the price-competitive OE market and concentrated its efforts on high-performance replacement tires. The Tire Group was viewed explicitly as a source of cash to finance additional diversification and by 1984 represented only 40 percent of total sales. Then in 1985, confronted by deteriorating PVC prices, overcapacity in the tire business, and persistent rumors of an impending takeover bid by Icahn, Goodrich took a $365 million charge to cover the costs of closing or selling several operations and

---

[1] Estimated European market shares in 1987 were Michelin, 40%; Continental, 13%; Pirelli, 12%; Goodyear, 12%; Firestone, 9%; Sumitomo/Dunlop, 6%; all others, 8%.

[2] Imports accounted for approximately 7% of the Japanese market in 1987 and were divided among Michelin, 53%; Continental, 21%; Pirelli, 12%; Goodyear, 6%; all others, 8%. Bridgestone had about 50% of the total market, followed by Sumitomo (17%), Yokohama (12%), and Toyo (7%).

announced its intention to restructure on its own.

In January 1986 Uniroyal and Goodrich agreed to place their tire operations in a joint venture which would have revenues exceeding Firestone's in the U.S. market. Neither partner had plants located outside of North America. At the time, the combination appeared ideal in that the businesses had complementary market positions and considerable opportunities for rationalization. However, the savings failed to materialize, and the task of combining Uniroyal's manufacturing capabilities with Goodrich's product development and marketing skills proved more difficult than expected. Finally, in December 1987, Goodrich agreed to sell its interest to Clayton & Dubilier for $225 million plus warrants to purchase 7 percent of the venture in the future.

General Tire Founded as a tire company in 1915, Genco diversified earlier than its competitors by acquiring broadcasting, soft drink bottling, and industrial products firms, so that by 1987 the General Tire subsidiary accounted for only 40 percent of corporate sales. General maintained a full line of passenger car and light truck tires and had successfully defended its position in both OE and replacement markets. On the other hand, it had neither overseas operations nor products to serve certain commercial segments, such as agricultural or off-road vehicles.

In March 1987 Genco received an unsolicited $2.2 billion tender offer ($100 a share) from a partnership affiliated with AFG Industries and Wagner & Brown, the former a closely held glass manufacturer and the latter an energy company. Three weeks later Genco countered with a proposal to repurchase 54 percent of its outstanding shares at $130, which caused the hostile bid to be withdrawn. Genco management indicated that the resulting debt would be retired by the divestiture of the tire, soft drink, and broadcast units, leaving the company in aerospace and plastics. In July an agreement was reached for the sale of General Tire to Continental Gummi Werke for $650 million.

Michelin The superior performance attributed to Michelin's radial tires enabled the company to dominate the European market and later to establish a coveted position in North America as a supplier to U.S. and Japanese automobile manufacturers (see Exhibits 5 and 8). The company attacked the replacement markets with forceful advertising, excellent quality, and aggressive pricing—and an attitude toward dealers that many termed arrogant. The burdens of rapid growth and depressed economic conditions contributed to $1.5 billion in losses from 1980 through 1984. The company recovered the following year, however, and in 1987, buttressed by record earnings, announced a plan to increase the capacity of its four U.S. plants by 30 percent at a cost of $275 million as part of a billion dollar worldwide investment program. Support for the expansion was provided by the award of a contract for the new GM-10 series cars, which some observers estimated could triple Michelin's share of the General Motors business.

Bridgestone With approximately 50 percent of its domestic market, Bridgestone had participated fully in the rapid growth of the Japanese automobile industry. However, until the purchase of Firestone's LaVergne truck tire plant in 1984, all manufacturing was located in Japan or in small facilities elsewhere in Southeast Asia. Regarded as conservatively managed, Bridgestone proceeded cautiously in the United States, initially emphasizing high-quality radial truck tires and replacement tires for Japanese cars, the latter exported from Japan. Then in 1987, the company announced its intention to invest $70 million to manufacture passenger car tires in the LaVergne facility, which happened to be in close proximity to Nissan's 240,000 unit assembly plant. Bridgestone's share of the automobile replacement market was approximately 2 percent in the United States and less than 1 percent in Europe. At then-current exchange rates ($1 = 125 yen) profits in 1987 were approximately $288 million on sales of $6.6 billion, of which exports from Japan accounted for 26 percent.

Continental Gummi Werke Strong ties to the German automobile industry provided Continental with both its core business and a reputation for well-engineered products which included power transmissions, air springs, rubberized fabrics, and the like. Although it had sales and technical agreements with General Tire and Uniroyal and maintained a small office in the United States to service its Volkswagen business, the company remained essentially a European producer until 1987, when the opportunity arose to acquire General Tire from Genco. Later in 1987, these companies entered into a joint venture with Yokohama Rubber Company and Toyo Tire and Rubber Company, the third and fourth largest Japanese tire producers, to purchase or build a facility in the United States, share research and manufacturing techniques, and produce radial truck tires to be molded and labeled for the partners' individual needs. Continental/General would own 51 percent, Yokohama 33.4 percent, and Toyo 15.6 percent. The agreement also called for the Japanese companies to produce passenger tires for Continental/General to sell to the Japanese car industry and for General to reciprocate for Yokohama and Toyo in the United States.

Pirelli From its strong Italian base, the Pirelli Group expanded into Germany and the United Kingdom, becoming the third largest European tire producer. Sales in 1987 were approximately $5.5 billion, divided among tires (44 percent), other rubber products (18 percent), and power and communication cable (38 percent). Operations overseas were limited, however, the most significant being in Brazil, where it rivaled Goodyear and Firestone for market leadership. In the United States, Pirelli had a small share of the Volkswagen business but was otherwise relegated to supplying high-performance replacement tires, which yielded a market share of about 1.5 percent. The company attempted to acquire 80 percent of Armstrong Tire Company, the fifth largest domestic tire manufacturer, from Armtek Corporation in 1987 but was unable to agree on the price.

Sumitomo Rubber Industries The second largest Japanese tire company was a member of the giant Sumitomo Group, one of the largest of that nation's *keiretsu*. Sales and pretax profits in 1987 were $2.15 billion and $9.2 million, respectively. In 1984 Sumitomo acquired Dunlop Holdings's six European tire plants, subsequently spending $130 million to increase their capacity by 25 percent. Two years later it purchased Dunlop's ailing operations in the United States, which were then modernized in preparation for a renewed effort to sell the growing number of foreign-based automobile manufacturers in North America and to expand Dunlop's 2.5 percent share of the replacement market.

Restructuring at Firestone: 1980–1981

On December 1, 1979, Nevin, then 53, became Firestone's first nonfamily chief executive following a six-year stint as CEO of Zenith Radio Corporation and a tour as president of Ford's Autolite Parts Division. Nevin described his initial impressions:

> The published information on Firestone didn't convey the severity of what was happening. It was hemorrhaging cash. Within a couple of weeks I realized we had a crisis and an organization that was not as demoralized as it should have been. Until the mid-1970s the company had always done well, even during the depression, and most of the management didn't understand that it didn't have the resources to compete in all segments of the tire business throughout the world. What I did would have been easier if they had.

During January and February, Nevin analyzed the situation and developed a short-term plan. He found that Firestone had negative cash flow of $392 million from 1977 through 1979 and the budget for 1980 anticipated an additional outflow of $236 million. Total debt had increased from 58 percent of equity to 72 percent during this period and was projected to grow to 85 percent by the end of the fiscal year. The North American Tire Division, its 17 plants operating at 59 percent of capacity, had lost $16 million after taxes in the first quarter with no relief in sight, while the remaining divisions earned just $2 million.

At the March directors' meeting, Nevin listed three objectives that were to guide his efforts over the next eight years:

- Strengthen Firestone's balance sheet by reducing debt.
- Improve profits from tire and related businesses in North America.

- Embark upon a diversification program to reduce Firestone's reliance on tire manufacturing for its future sales and profits.

Nevin also announced his intention to close seven plants in North America, most of them producing bias ply passenger car tires, withdraw from many of the company's private brand relationships, and institute an aggressive program to cut costs and liquidate receivables and inventory.

The results were dramatic. During the next year, the number of tire types produced by the North American Division was reduced from 7300 to 2600, inventory cut from 16.7 million to 9.7 million units, employment slashed by approximately 30 percent, debt reduced by $435 million, and cash increased by $232 million. Although the books showed a loss of $122 million for 1980, Firestone reported at its annual meeting that the liquidity crisis had passed and that the company was again profitable. (See Exhibits 10, 11, and 12 for income and cash flow and industry segment summaries for 1980–1987.)

In June 1981 Nevin presented the board with a more detailed and longer-range plan for achieving his objectives. He stated, "If Firestone's business strategy is based on the premise that assets should remain concentrated in the tire industry and that future success lies in the attainment of a dominant position in the tire industry worldwide, it is improbable that Firestone will earn returns on equity that exceed the 9 percent earned by other U.S. tire manufacturers in recent years . . . Firestone's strategic objectives should be based on attaining returns on equity equal to those earned by other major American corporations." Businesses which did not have the potential to meet this target (15 percent return on equity [ROE], which equated to an 18 percent operating profit on capital employed [ROCE]), would be liquidated or sold.

Using this guideline, Nevin outlined steps to prune Firestone's operations and amass funds and debt capacity to finance diversification. A bellwether example was his proposal to withdraw from the manufacture of radial truck tires in North America. Similar reasoning was applied to the cessation of radial off-road tire production. The 1981 plan for North American passenger car operations called for increased expenditures for modernization and conversion to radials, which were then yielding acceptable returns at the manufacturing level. Competing successfully for OE business was viewed as fundamental to the company's survival in the tire industry. The plan also wanted to expand the Firestone retail network to reduce the company's reliance on the large dealers and to take advantage of anticipated growth in the relatively stable automotive service market. Nevin's intent was to reduce overseas operations as a means of freeing resources for diversification even though they were projected to have an ROCE of 17.3 percent in 1981. "Firestone's future role in tire markets overseas should be that of a minority investor and a supplier of technology." By doing so, Nevin anticipated that assets invested in international tire operations could be reduced by $725 million by 1985. The four divisions comprising the Diversified Products Group in 1981 were concentrated in automotive parts which, in Nevin's view, did not provide Firestone with meaningful diversification. Those operations with high returns would be managed "to maximize profits" without substantial additional investment. The remaining units would be closed or divested.

Implementation of the strategic plan for the existing businesses was forecast to yield after-tax profits of $231 million or $4.00 per share in 1985, which was equivalent to an ROE of 12 percent. It would also result in unused debt capacity of $535 million and excess cash of $415 million. Were these resources invested so as to produce a 15 percent after-tax return, the corporation's ROE would increase to 16 percent. The plan also noted that:

> Firestone could substantially improve its return on equity by using excess cash to repurchase Firestone stock. That course of action would, however, leave Firestone tied to the tire industry and totally dependent upon that industry for its future. That course of action would involve very high risk.
>
> The businesses in which Firestone is today involved can be characterized as low-growth. They are also businesses in which Firestone's market share is significantly below that of the market leader. A corporation's strategic strength can be roughly measured by the extent to which it is engaged in businesses that offer high growth and in which it is the market leader.

Reappraisal: August 1985

In August 1985, Nevin again reviewed the company's progress and reassessed his program for the future. While asset sales had permitted further debt reductions and provided funds for the repurchase of stock, some from potential raiders (Icahn and Lawrence Tisch), operating cash flows had fallen to cover capital expenditures. Returns from the existing businesses were clearly below the levels anticipated in the 1981 plan, and little progress had been made on diversification.

Nevin acknowledged that some of the shortfall could be attributed to internal problems. However, the principal cause he attributed to unanticipated changes in

	1985 (millions)					
	1981 Plan			Actual		
	Operating Profit	Assets	ROCE	Operating Profit	Assets	ROCE
North American tire manufacturing	$215	$1,171	18%	$ (15) }	$1,421	—
Retail stores	147	1,016	14	18 }		
International Group	61	186	32	85	518	16%
Diversified products	117	333	35	57	228	25
	$540	$2,706	20%	$145	$2,167	7%

the competitive environment, specifically a flood of low-cost imported replacement tires, which led to a drop in dealer prices and an erosion in brand loyalty. Instead of increasing 3 percent in line with variable costs, Firestone's average price realizations actually declined 7 percent from 1981 to 1985, the difference in the last year amounting to about $200 million in lost operating profit.

With respect to diversification, Nevin indicated that he had been "reluctant to accept the risks associated with borrowing against tire and related assets in North America, which were producing totally inadequate levels of profit and cash flow, in order to fund a diversification effort."

Nevin's prescription for the immediate future was another contraction of Firestone's North American tire business. By closing up to four plants and further reducing the company's participation in the heavy truck, off-road, and low-end passenger car replacement markets, he estimated that $500 million in cash for diversification could be generated from working capital reductions. The company would then focus its attention on providing OE automobile and farm equipment manufacturers and the related replacement markets with "state of the art" premium-priced products, among them a new line of radials designed to challenge Good-

year's dominance in the high performance market segment. Conversely, the retail stores would be free to purchase low-end tires from any domestic or overseas producer in the event the company's manufacturing units could not supply them profitably at competitive prices.

Firestone: 1988

In North America the OE market accounted for approximately 46 percent of passenger and light truck tire sales in 1987 with the balance split between Firestone stores and independent dealers. Competition for OE business was based on technical assistance, especially in the design of tires to support the performance requirements of new cars, quality as determined by detailed customer audits, and cordial working relationships. Under normal conditions pricing was comparable among firms. By these criteria, Firestone considered itself to be in a leadership position at Ford and deadlocked for the top spot at General Motors. Moreover, the early attention given to overseas car manufacturers had resulted in a 27 percent share of their U.S. requirements, a close second to Goodyear.

There was general agreement that the North American tire industry was likely to exhibit little volume growth as increasing vehicle registrations were offset by improving tire longevity. The vice president of financial services for the tire unit noted:

> To stay technically proficient, it will be tough to limit capital expenditures to depreciation, but that's our objective. We may have to increase our IRR from a 20–25 percent hurdle rate to 35 percent. It's a heated internal debate: Why spend money when our overall returns are low, yet the industry demands that we stay competitive in pricing and meet OE specifications which are always getting tighter.

Internationally, Firestone sold approximately 26 million tires overseas divided among Europe (15 million), South America (10 million), and the rest of the world (1 million). Overseas, rather than across-the-board disinvestment, a pattern of geographical emphasis had evolved, centered around plants in Brazil, where Firestone enjoyed a 30 percent market share and healthy margins, France, and Spain, which Firestone operating managers argued were capable of competing in world markets.

By the end of 1987, Firestone had expanded its retail network to 1,506 locations. Sales of automotive parts and services had grown to $571 million representing approximately 60 percent of total store revenues. The vice chairman responsible for the retail and service operations commented on plans for the future:

> The market for automotive services, especially light maintenance, is vast, maybe $75 billion. No one has even 3 percent of it. The average American car is getting older, and the number of gas stations and repair shops has been declining. We see a big opportunity for growth and better margins if we have trained personnel and modern diagnostic and repair equipment, and can provide the customer sat-

isfaction to go along with the Firestone name. Our goal is to open 60, 90, and 120 stores in the next three years. We'll buy independent chains when they're available, but the big ones are about gone now, and there are only a few independents left with as many as 20 stores.

The company was able to expand store locations with essentially no investment by leasing the buildings and turning the inventory within the normal 90-day payment terms offered by the tire group and other suppliers. In the past, growth and profitability had been limited by management constraints. However, recently constructed training centers, which provided over 50,000 man-days of training in 1987 or about one week per retail store employee, were considered a major step in lifting this constraint.

The Diversified Products Group was composed of four divisions, all related in some fashion to Firestone's core rubber-based technology, with combined external sales in 1987 of $383 million and an operating profit of $84 million. The vice president responsible for the group reviewed his goals.

> Each of our existing divisions has a return on equity of 30 percent or more and together they have the potential for a 65 percent increase in sales by 1992. In addition, I'm looking for niche acquisitions that are compatible with our basic rubber technology and R&D capability; not huge ones, but singles and doubles that might add another $250 million in five years. Beyond that I'm targeting $100 million from new businesses so that by the end of the period the group will have sales of close to $1.0 billion.

With respect to diversification and Firestone's retail and service segment, Nevin commented:

We should make acquisitions when the combinations make sense. But in terms of my ego, I won't feel like a failure if I haven't done a $250 million deal before I retire. Our stockholders will be better off if we don't because we have to pay a premium to buy a company over what the shareholder can do for himself to diversify.

On the other hand, if I could find a way to put $250 million into our store system to grow it rapidly from 1,500 to 5,000 locations, I'd do it. We're the largest seller of automotive services in the country now except for Sears and still have less than 2 percent of the market. The growth potential is there, we have the infrastructure to manage it, and we could expand without having to push others out. I'd be disappointed if our retail sales haven't doubled in the next five years, but at that rate it can be done without much investment.

During Nevin's tenure Firestone's stock had risen from $9 to $31 per share. Contributing to this rise was the company's stock repurchase program, which had reduced the outstanding shares from 57.7 million in 1979 to 31.7 million in January 1988. With the exception of the most recent transactions, the purchases had been made at less than book value.

The Joint Venture Proposition

In Nevin's view the structural changes occurring in the automobile industry were altering the competitive characteristics of the tire business as well. As early as the summer of 1984, he had discussed with outside members of his board the benefits that might accrue to Firestone's shareholders from a joint venture which combined the tire units with those of an appropriate Japanese or European manufacturer. In the ensuing months exploratory discussions were held with seven potential partners,

but for a variety of reasons, including the magnitude of the transaction and Firestone's uneven financial record, each stagnated. In Bridgestone's case the issue was complicated by differing opinions in top management about the proper approach to the U.S. market, some contending that highly efficient greenfield capacity should be constructed once exports justified it, while others held that such volumes (8–9 million units) could not be achieved without significant OE business, which in turn necessitated domestic facilities and technical support. Nevertheless, Firestone continued intermittent discussions with several firms during the next three years.

On January 14, 1988, Akira Yeiri, president of Bridgestone, arranged a meeting with Nevin to review the possibility of a closer relationship, which he reported now had the unanimous support of his management. Yeiri suggested that Bridgestone acquire either all of Firestone's North American tire manufacturing operations or a majority interest in the company's global tire operations. He also expressed a strong desire to have an equity participation in the retail network. Nevin responded that Firestone was interested in a joint venture but preferred to retain ownership of the stores. He also explained that, because Bridgestone had declined his previous overtures, negotiations had proceeded with other tire companies (which were not identified) and that Bridgestone would have to proceed expeditiously.

On February 16, 1988, Firestone announced that it had agreed in principle with Bridgestone Corporation to form a joint venture to manage Firestone's worldwide tire business. Firestone would contribute all of its tire manufacturing assets having a book value of approximately $1.5 billion to a joint venture and in return receive $750 million from Bridgestone for a 75 percent interest and $500 million from the proceeds of a loan to be secured by the new entity. Firestone would retain the remaining 25 percent as well as the retail stores and the divisions in the Diversified Products Group. After tax payments and the funding of certain employee benefits, the company would have available net proceeds of approximately $1.0 billion.

Nevin at the time commented, "Of all the decisions I've made in my recent tire career, this is the first one I would call a 'win–win' situation—because it benefits shareholders, employees, customers, and all of the areas where we have operations." He indicated that Firestone would distribute a substantial portion of the after-tax proceeds to the shareholders. Firestone's stock soared from 9⅜ to 45⅛ on the news.

Subsequent Events

On March 6, Pirelli launched a tender offer for 100 percent of Firestone for $58 a share or about $1.86 billion. Concurrently, a letter was sent to Nevin which said in part, "We attempted to present in the clearest possible terms our continued interest in negotiating a purchase of, or joint venture with, Firestone's tire operations. Rather than choosing to negotiate with us, you announced your intention to pursue a joint venture with Bridgestone. Accordingly, we have no choice but to present a proposal directly to your shareholders." Pirelli management indicated that an initial round of discussions with Firestone had collapsed in March 1987. They were renewed later in the year but lapsed in February 1988.

Pirelli also revealed that, if its bid were successful, Michelin would buy Firestone's retail stores and the Brazilian tire operations for $650 million. In addition, Michelin would have an option to acquire 50 percent of Firestone's Diversified Products Group, including the synthetic and natural rubber divisions for $150 million. Pirelli also stated publicly that it was prepared to discuss the offer directly with Firestone management. Firestone's stock immediately jumped to 63⅛.

EXHIBIT 1
1986 WORLDWIDE TIRE DEMAND (MILLIONS OF UNITS)

	Passenger Car			Truck		
	Total	Replacement	OE	Total	Replacement	OE
United States	198	144	54	40	33	7
Japan	71	25	46	37	23	14
West Germany	39	20	19	4	2	2
France	28	17	11	3	2	1
United Kingdom	22	16	6	4	3	1
Canada	18	10	8	3	2	1
Italy	18	11	7	3	2	1
Australia	8	6	2	2	2	0
Eastern Europe and China	37	26	11	55	46	9
South, Central America	28	21	7	16	14	2
Others	50	34	16	20	16	4
Worldwide total*	517	330	187	187	145	42

Source: Goodyear, others.

*Plus an undetermined number of bicycle and motorcycle tires. In addition, it was estimated that 22 million tires were sold for industrial vehicles, 7 million for agricultural vehicles, and 1 million for aircraft.

EXHIBIT 2
1986 WORLDWIDE MOTOR VEHICLE PRODUCTION AND VEHICLES IN USE (MILLIONS OF UNITS)

	Production			Cars and Trucks in Use
	Cars	Trucks	Total	
Japan	7.81	4.45	12.26	28.9
United States	7.83	3.54	11.37	132.3
West Germany	4.31	.29	4.60	26.5
France	2.77	.42	3.19	21.6
Canada	1.07	.79	1.86	10.7
Italy	1.65	.18	1.83	22.9
Spain	1.28	.25	1.53	9.6
United Kingdom	1.02	.23	1.25	18.4
South Korea	.46	.14	0.60	n.a.
Others	2.36	.61	2.97	110.1
Total	30.56	10.90	41.46	381.0

Source: *Automotive News.*

EXHIBIT 3
TEN LARGEST TIRE MANUFACTURERS, 1986 (FIGURES IN $ MILLIONS)*

Ranking	Company/Headquarters	1986 Tire Sales	Percentage of Total Sales Generated from Tires	1985 Tire Sales	Percentage of Total Sales Generated from Tires	1984 Tire Sales	Percentage of Total Sales Generated from Tires
1	Goodyear/U.S.A.	$ 6,630	73	$ 6,190	74	$ 6,280	73
2	Michelin/France	6,155	92	4,494	92	4,232	92
3	Bridgestone/Japan	3,086	71	2,632	73	2,463	73
4	Continental-General/W. Germany†	2,741	71	1,292	70	844	68
5	Firestone/U.S.A.‡	2,265	65	2,523	66	2,641	66
6	Uniroyal–Goodrich/U.S.A.§	2,100‖	100	100	—	—	—
	B.F. Goodrich	—	—	1,184	37	1,387	40
	Uniroyal	—	—	953	45	976	46
7	Pirelli/Italy	2,068	44	1,694	46	1,584	45
8	Sumitomo/Japan	1,921	79	1,215	85	762	78
9	Yokohama/Japan	1,189	71	933	78	855	75
10	Toyo/Japan	632	60	620	65	589	68
	Total Top Ten	**$28,787**		**$23,730**		**$22,614**	
	% of Worldwide Sales	84%		79%		76%	

Source: *Rubber and Plastic News.*

*Figures for non-U.S. companies converted at August 1987 exchange rates.

†Continental purchased GenCorp's General Tire operations in 1987.

‡Firestone figures exclude all sales through Firestone retail stores. Including retail tire sales would Increase 1986 tire sales by $361 million and the percentage of sales from tires to approximately 75%.

§ Uniroyal and B.F. Goodrich combined tire operations in 1986.

‖ Estimate

EXHIBIT 4
UNITED STATES TIRE MARKET—PASSENGER CARS AND LIGHT TRUCKS

	1978	1979	1980	1981	1982	1983	1984	1985	1986	1987
(1) Units shipped (millions)										
Replacement	147	135	120	123	130	134	144	140	144	150
OE	57	51	37	37	33	44	52	55	54	53
Total	**204**	**186**	**157**	**160**	**163**	**178**	**192**	**195**	**198**	**203**
Replacement imported (%)	8.8%	11.2%	11.5%	14.0%	13.0%	17.2%	20.9%	23.9%	23.5%	25.2%
(2) Radial Construction (%)										
Replacement	42%	48%	54%	59%	64%	70%	75%	81%	85%	91%
OE	69	76	81	99.6	100	100	100	100	100	100
(3) Media price/tire ($)										
Radial	$63.88	$69.87	$72.71	$72.13	$65.00	$60.00	$55.50	$54.60	$53.80	$51.80
Bias	33.89	37.57	41.98	37.95	39.00	39.95	37.15	36.63	35.00	35.50
(4) Distribution channels (%)										
Independent dealers	60%	61%	63%	65%	67%	67%	68%	68%	68%	68%
Oil companies	6	5	5	5	4	4	4	3	3	2
Tire company stores	11	12	11	10	10	11	11	12	13	13
Chain, discount, and department stores	23	22	21	20	19	18	17	17	16	17
Total	**100**	**100**	**100**	**100**	**100**	**100**	**100**	**100**	**100**	**100**
(5) U.S. car sales										
Domestic	9,488	8,329	6,578	6,206	5,756	6,795	7,951	8,205	8,215	7,081
Imported	1,822	2,331	2,398	2,327	2,223	2,387	2,439	2,837	3,244	3,197

Sources: *Modern Tire Dealer, Ward's Automotive Reports*, and Salomon Brothers, Inc.

EXHIBIT 5
TREND IN SHARE OF U.S. PASSENGER TIRE MARKET (PERCENTS)

	Goodyear			Firestone			Uniroyal*			General			Goodrich*			Total Five U.S. Companies			Michelin		
	O.E.	Repl.	Total	O.E.	Repl.	Total	O.E.	Repl.	Total	O.E.	Repl.	Total	O.E.	Repl.	Total	O.E.	Repl.	Total	O.E.	Repl.	Total
1971	30.2	27.1	28.0	24.7	21.5	22.3	23.5	9.4	13.0	9.8	4.3	5.7	11.7	8.6	9.5	99.0	70.9	78.5	1.0	2.1	1.8
1975	34.4	25.0	27.3	20.7	24.2	23.4	23.1	8.7	12.3	11.0	5.5	6.9	9.4	8.8	8.9	98.6	72.2	78.8	1.3	5.0	4.0
1976	32.2	23.5	26.2	19.9	23.1	22.2	22.2	7.2	11.4	14.8	6.4	8.6	6.9	6.6	6.9	96.0	66.8	75.3	3.8	6.2	5.4
1977	32.4	25.1	27.5	19.9	23.7	22.5	20.3	7.0	10.9	15.2	6.4	8.9	8.3	6.2	7.0	96.1	68.4	76.8	3.6	7.0	5.9
1978	31.1	24.5	26.4	23.3	23.5	23.4	19.8	8.6	11.8	12.8	6.1	8.0	9.5	7.3	7.9	96.5	70.0	77.5	3.5	7.6	6.5
1979	26.9	25.0	25.5	23.5	21.8	22.2	23.8	8.5	12.6	12.6	6.2	7.9	9.2	7.3	7.8	96.0	68.8	76.0	4.0	8.8	7.5
1980	28.3	28.2	28.2	21.0	19.2	19.6	24.5	8.2	12.1	10.9	7.0	7.9	10.4	7.9	8.5	95.1	70.5	76.3	4.9	9.7	8.6
1981	30.3	28.5	28.9	21.6	14.1	15.8	23.3	8.0	11.5	12.6	8.4	9.3	5.6	8.0	7.5	93.4	67.0	73.0	6.6	10.2	9.4
1982	31.0	29.4	29.7	22.1	14.4	16.0	25.0	6.9	10.6	13.0	7.9	8.9	1.0	10.1	8.2	92.1	68.7	73.4	7.3	9.4	8.9
1983	32.4	27.7	28.9	25.0	14.0	16.7	22.2	6.0	10.1	13.1	7.0	8.5	1.0	10.4	8.1	93.7	65.1	72.3	6.3	9.1	8.4
1984	32.7	27.1	28.5	22.2	12.0	14.7	22.8	5.8	10.3	12.7	7.2	8.6	0.8	10.3	7.8	91.2	62.4	69.9	8.5	9.5	9.2
1985	33.3	25.8	27.9	22.2	11.0	14.1	21.6	6.4	10.7	13.0	7.3	8.9	0.7	10.3	7.6	90.8	60.8	69.2	8.8	10.7	10.2
1986	33.6	25.9	28.0	21.0	9.7	12.8	21.9	16.3	17.8	13.0	7.4	9.0	—	—	—	89.5	59.3	67.6	9.9	12.0	11.0

Note: Replacemant percentages include estimated sales of private brand tires.
*Uniroyal–Goodrich merged in 1986.

287

EXHIBIT 6
DOMESTIC PASSENGER CAR TIRE CAPACITY (UNITS IN THOUSANDS PER DAY)

Company	Plant	Constructed/ Rebuilt	1979 Capacity	1987 Capacity	% Radial
Armstrong	Des Moines, IA	1943	10	7	25
	Hanford, CA	1962	11	10	100
	Natchez, MS	—	8	Sold	0
	West Haven, CT	—	12	Closed	
	Nashville, TN	1973/76	8.5	13	100
	Total		**49.5**	**30 (−39%)**	**83**
Cooper	Findlay, OH	1919	8.4	13	70
	Texarkana, AR	1964/85	16.6	20	60
	Tupelo, MS	1959/84		10	100
	Total		**25**	**43 (+72%)**	**72**
Sumitomo/Dunlop	Buffalo, NY	1923/86	10	5	25
	Huntsville, AL	1969/86	18	23	70
	Total		**28**	**28 (+0%)**	**62**
Firestone	Albany, GA	—	25	Closed	
	Barberton, OH	—	6.5	Closed	
	Dayton, OH	—	12.5	Closed	
	Decatur, IL	1963	23.5	20	100
	Des Moines, IA	1945	17	0*	
	Los Angeles, CA	—	1	Closed	
	Memphis, TN	—	14.5	Closed	
	Oklahoma City, OK	1965	19.2	24	70
	Pottstown, PA	—	21	Closed	
	Salinas, CA	—	16.3	Closed	
	Wilson, NC	1973	15.8	20	100
	Total		**172.3**	**64 (−63%)**	**95**
Continental/GenCorp	Charlotte, NC	1967	19	19	100
	Mayfield, KY	1961	25	27	48
	Waco, TX	—	15.7	Closed	
	Mt. Vernon, IL	1973	12.5	13	100
	Total		**72.2**	**59 (−18%)**	**76**
Goodyear	Cumberland, MD	—	4.5	Closed	
	Fayetteville, NC	1969	29	45	100
	Freeport, IL	1964	14.5	2	0
	Gadsden, AL	1928/78	31.5	47	90
	Jackson, MI	—	21	Closed	
	Lawton, OK	1978	22	40	100
	Topeka, KS	1944	30	0*	
	Tyler, TX	1962/85	25	30	100
	Union City, TN	1968	46	44	100
	Total		**223.5**	**208 (−7%)**	**96**
Michelin	Greenville, SC	1975	25	25	100
	Lexington, SC	1981	0	15	100
	Total		**25**	**40 (+60%)**	**100**
Mohawk	Salem, VA	1968	13	13 (0%)	50
Uniroyal–Goodrich	Fort Wayne, IN	1961	18.4	20	100
	Miami, OK	—	5.8	Closed	
	Oaks, PA	—	18	Closed	
	Tuscaloosa, AL	1946	33.5	31	60
	Chicopee Falls, MA	—	17.2	Closed	
	Detroit, MI	—	14	Closed	
	Eau Claire, WI	1916/40	20.5	25	16
	Opelika, AL	1963	13.7	22	80
	Ardmore, OK	1969	32	33	100
	Total		**173.1**	**132 (−24%)**	**71**
	GRAND TOTAL		**781.6**	**617 (−21%)**	**84%**

Source: Donaldson, Lufkin, & Jenrette, *Rubber and Plastics News*.

*Converted to truck, agricultural, and off-road tires. In addition, Firestone closed or sold two Canadian and three nonpassenger car plants.

EXHIBIT 7
WORLDWIDE AUTOMOTIVE INTERRELATIONSHIPS—LARGEST TWELVE COMPANIES

	General Motors	Ford	Toyota	Nissan	Volkswagen	Renault	Peugeot	Fiat	Chrysler/AMC	Honda	Mazda	Mitsubishi
General Motors	XXX		1 (U.S.)	3,6 (Australia)				2,3 (U.S.)				
Ford		XXX		5,6 (U.S.) (Australia)	1,4,6 (Argentina) (Brazil)		3 (Europe)				2,3,4,5,6 (U.S.) (Asia)	
Toyota			XXX		4,6 (Germany)							
Nissan				XXX	3,4,6 (Japan)							
Volkswagen					XXX	6						
Renault						XXX	1,5,6 (France)		2,3,4,5,6 (U.S.)			
Peugeot							XXX	3,6 (Italy)				
Fiat								XXX				
Chrysler/AMC									XXX			2,3,4,5,6 (Japan)
Honda										XXX		
Mazda											XXX	3 (Japan)
Mitsubishi												XXX

Source: *Ward's Automotive International* and others.
Note: As of September 1987, ranked by annual volume starting from top left.
1 = Joint venture
2 = Equity arrangement
3 = Supplies or buys major components
4 = Marketing/distribution arrangements
5 = Technology agreement
6 = Manufacturing/assembly agreement

EXHIBIT 8
ESTIMATED 1987 BRAND SHARES—UNITED STATES
I. Original Equipment Passenger Tires

	General Motors	Ford	Chrysler	AMC	Volks-wagen*	Honda	Nissan	Nummi GM–Toyota	Mazda	Total
Goodyear	22.5%	23.5%	85%	55%	3.5%	32%	4%	50%	60%	33.4%
Firestone	21.5	40.5	1	—	—	—	33	50	40	21.9
Uniroyal–Goodrich	34.0	3.0	—	—	—	—	—	—	—	18.5
General Tire	17.5	11.5	—	—	—	—	63	—	—	12.9
Michelin	4.5	21.5	14	45	40.0	47	—	—	—	12.7
Continental	—	—	—	—	36.5	—	—	—	—	.4
Pirelli	—	—	—	—	20.0	—	—	—	—	.1
Dunlop/Sumitomo	—	—	—	—	—	21	—	—	—	.1
	100.0	100.0	100	100	100.0	100	100	100	100	100
1987 car production (thousands)	3,602	1,830	1,094	16	66	324	117	143	4	

*Volkswagen announced in 1987 that it would discontinue automobile production in the United States.

II. Replacement Passenger Tires*

Goodyear	16.0%	Dayton	2.0%
Firestone	9.0	Bridgestone	2.0
Michelin	8.5	Remington	2.0
Sears	7.5	Montgomery Ward	1.5
B.F. Goodrich	4.0	Jetzon-Laramie	1.5
General	3.0	Hercules	1.5
Multi-Mile	3.0	Atlas	1.5
Uniroyal	2.5	Stratton	1.5
Kelly Springfield	2.5	Western Auto	1.5
Cooper	2.5	Monarch	1.5
Dunlop	2.5	K Mart	1.5
Armstrong	2.5	Pirelli	1.5
Cordovan	2.0	Others	15.0

Source: *Modern Tire Dealer*.

*Includes private brand tires which may be imported or produced in the United States.

EXHIBIT 9
TIRE AND RELATED BUSINESS SEGMENT, 1980–1986 (AS REPORTED)

	1980	1981	1982	1983	1984	1985	1986
Goodyear*							
Sales	$7,016	$7,567	$7,103	$7,301	$7,648	$7,176	$7,844
Operating profit	502	633	586	538	608	452	487
Capital expenditures	201	230	261	342	430	571	532
Operating profit/sales	7.2%	8.4%	8.3%	7.2%	7.9%	6.3%	6.2%
Capital expenditures/sales	2.9	3.0	3.7	4.7	5.6	8.0	6.8
Firestone†							
Sales	$3,840	$3,746	$3,344	$3,356	$3,569	$3,404	$3,180
Operating profit	(43)	178	150	254	130	88	NA
Capital expenditures	135	173	177	196	245	197	215
Operating profit/sales	(1.1)%	4.8%	4.5%	7.6%	3.6%	2.6%	NA
Capital expenditures/sales	3.5	4.6	5.3	5.8	6.9	5.8	6.8
Uniroyal							
Sales	$1,117	$1,048	$939	$933	$1,018	NA	NA
Operating profit	4	69	67	78	85	NA	NA
Capital expenditures	20	24	27	28	43	NA	NA
Operating profit/sales	.4%	6.6%	6.1%	8.4%	8.3%	NA	NA
Capital expenditures/sales	1.8	2.3	2.9	3.0	4.2	NA	NA
Goodrich							
Sales	$1,294	$1,352	$1,275	$1,401	$1,500	$1,399	NA
Operating profit	65	79	75	79	93	68	NA
Capital expenditures	41	32	42	45	53	46	NA
Operating profit/sales	3.2%	5.8%	5.9%	5.6%	6.2%	.9%	NA
Capital expenditures/sales	3.2	2.4	3.3	3.2	3.5	3.3	NA
General							
Sales	$1,062	$981	$1,120	$999	$1,004	$1,179	$1,158
Operating profit	37	2	35	39	51	26	43
Capital expenditures	51	54	36	27	25	34	38
Operating profit/sales	3.5%	.2%	3.1%	3.9%	5.1%	2.2%	3.7%
Capital expenditures/sales	4.8	5.5	3.1	2.7	2.5	2.9	3.3

Note: Operating profits are shown before charges for discontinued operations.

*Goodyear sales include transportation-related products such as tubes, wheels, belts, and hoses.

†Firestone sales include all sales through Firestone retail stores including automotive parts and services.

EXHIBIT 10
FINANCIAL RESULTS, YEARS ENDING OCTOBER 31, 1980–1987 (AS REPORTED)

	1980	1981	1982	1983	1984	1985	1986	1987
Sales	4,850	4,361	3,869	3,866	4,001	3,836	3,501	3,867
Cost and expenses								
Cost of sales	4,063	3,448	3,000	2,852	3,187	3,080	2,711	2,979
SG&A	725	708	715	830	728	677	664	690
Provisions for restructuring	81	—	112	—	—	105	89	18
Other income and expense (net)	144	16	20	12	(18)	10	0	(23)
	5,013	4,172	3,847	3,694	3,897	3,872	3,464	3,664
Operating income	(163)	189	22	172	104	(36)	37	203
Income taxes	41	110	20	72	41	(30)	34	100
Income (loss) from continuing operations	(122)	79	2	100	63	(6)	3	103
Discontinued operations	—	50	—	—	26	—	16	20
Extraordinary credits	16	6	4	11	13	9	66*	22
Net Income	106	135	6	111	102	3	85	145
Income per share†								
Continuing operations	(2.11)	1.36	.04	2.03	1.36	(.14)	.08	2.81
Total	(1.84)	2.33	.11	2.26	2.21	.06	2.16	3.96
Shares outstanding at year-end	57,704	57,723	51,904	48,430	43,392	41,092	39,052	34,964
Employees	83,000‡	72,900	65,500	60,200	59,900	54,700	55,000	53,500
Stock Price								
Range	6⅛–9¾	9–13⅜	9⅛–14¼	13⅝–21⅞	15¾–23⅞	16⅛–22⅜	18½–29½	23–50
Year-end	9⅜	9⅞	14	21⅜	18⅜	18⅝	28⅛	30⅜

*Cumulative effect of change in pension recision accounting.

†Based on weighted average shares outstanding.

‡Employees at year-end 1979 were 107,500.

EXHIBIT 11
CASH FLOW 1980–1987, YEARS ENDING OCTOBER 31 (AS REPORTED)

	1980	1981	1982	1983	1984	1985	1986	1987	Total
Sources									
Income-continuing operations	(122)	79	2	100	63	(6)	3	103	222
Discontinued operations	—	50	—	—	14	—	25	—	89
Noncash Charges									
Depreciation	188	161	136	128	133	143	136	154	1,179
Provision for restructuring	81	—	94	—	—	104	89	18	386
	269	161	230	128	133	247	225	172	1,565
Asset sales									
Sale and leaseback-stores	—	—	—	20	—	35	123	27	205
Accounts receivable	—	—	100	251	171	—	72	—	594
Pension fund revision	—	—	—	—	—	240	—	—	240
Acquisitions and disposals (net)	11	204	28	78	50	20	(36)	149	504
	11	204	128	349	221	295	159	176	1,543
Noncash working capital	358	96	21	(167)	(155)	(124)	132	(31)	130
Total sources	**516**	**590**	**381**	**410**	**276**	**412**	**544**	**420**	**3,549**
Uses									
Capital expenditures	175	196	201	233	268	217	220	235	1,745
Dividends	17	35	32	29	37	34	31	35	250
Stock repurchase	—	—	75	63	93	49	57	147	484
Debt reduction (net)	131	179	125	31	117	15	124	(101)	621
Deferred taxes	80	(18)	(5)	12	12	94	22	22	219
Other (net)	13	12	15	(8)	(11)	11	33	74	139
Total uses	**416**	**404**	**443**	**360**	**516**	**420**	**487**	**412**	**3,458**
Net increase (decrease) in cash	100	186	(62)	50	(240)	(8)	57	8	91

EXHIBIT 12
FIRESTONE INDUSTRY SEGMENT AND GEOGRAPHICAL INFORMATION, 1987 (AS REPORTED)

	1981	1982	1983	1984	1985	1986	1987
Industry Segment							
Sales							
Tires and related products							
North America							
OE, wholesale	$2,180	$1,984	$2,042	$1,766	$1,666	1,382	1,335
Retail stores	343[†]	386[†]	498[†]	972	972	915	916
International	1,223	974	816	831	783	931	1233
Diversified products	615	525	510	432	432	321	383
	$4,361	$3,869	$3,866	$4,001	$3,836	$3,501	$3,867
Operating income							
Tires and related products							
North America							
OE, wholesale	85	73	144	19	(15)	*	*
Retail stores			(11)	18	*	*	*
International	93	77	110	122	85	*	*
Diversified products	56	23	30	40	57	*	*
	$234	$173	$284	$170	$145	$192	$262
Operating assets							
Tires and related products							
North America	1,574	1,563	1,450	1,489	1,421	*	*
International	754	558	537	555	518	*	
Diversified products	271	230	243	212	228	*	*
	$2,599	$2,351	$2,230	$2,256	$2,167	$2,002	$2,389
Capital expenditures							
Tires and related products							
North America	111	147	175	213	135	147	120
International	62	30	21	32	62	68	95
Diversified products	23	24	37	23	20	16	20
	$196	$201	$233	$268	$217	$231	$235
Geographical area							
Sales							
United States	2,860	2,660	2,788	2,869	2,773	3,453	2,493
Latin America	577	538	433	425	403	359	439
Europe	255	228	228	237	232	429[‡]	699[‡]
Other	689	443	417	470	428	260	236
	$4,361	$3,869	$3,866	$4,001	$3,836	$3,501	$3,867
Operating income							
United States	92	63	152	29	54	117	151
Latin America	32	55	68	70	59	37	69
Europe	23	15	17	15	10	32	52
Other	86	39	47	56	22	6	(10)
	$234	$173	$284	$170	$145	$192	$262

*Not available.

[†]Nontire parts and service only.

[‡]Sales increase due in part to the acquisition of a controlling interest in the Spanish affiliate.

Ingvar Kamprad and IKEA

With a 1988 turnover of 14½ billion Swedish Kronors (US $1 = SKr 6 in 1988) and 75 outlets in 19 countries, IKEA had become the world's largest home furnishings retailer. As the company approached the 1990s, however, its managers faced a number of major challenges. Changes in demographics were causing some to question IKEA's historical product line policy. Others wondered if the company had not bitten off too much by attempting major new market entries simultaneously in two European countries (U.K. and Italy), the United States, and several Eastern Bloc countries. Finally, there was widespread concern about the future of the company without its founder, strategic architect, and cultural guru, Ingvar Kamprad.

IKEA BACKGROUND AND HISTORY

In 1989, furniture retailing worldwide was still largely a fragmented national industry in which small manufacturers and distributors catered to the demands of

Copyright © 1990 by the President and Fellows of Harvard College. Harvard Business School case 390-132 (revised July 2, 1992).

their local markets. Consumer preferences varied by region, and there were few retailers whose operations extended beyond a single country. IKEA, however, had repeatedly bucked market trends and industry norms. Over three and a half decades it had built a highly profitable worldwide network of furniture stores (see Exhibit 1).

Company Origins

IKEA is an acronym for the initials of the founder, Ingvar Kamprad, his farm Elmtaryd, and his county, Agunnaryd, in Småland, South Sweden. In 1943, at the age of 17, Kamprad began his entrepreneurial career by selling fish, Christmas magazines, and seeds. Within a few years he had established a mail-order business featuring products as diverse as the new ballpoint pens and furniture. It was in furniture, however, that he saw the greatest opportunity.

Even as the pent-up wartime demand found expression in the post-war boom, the traditional Swedish practice of handing down custom-made furniture through generations was giving way to young householders looking for new, but inexpensive, furniture. But while demand was growing, interassociation supply contracts and agreements between Swedish manufacturers and retailers kept prices high while foreclosing entry. As a result, between 1935 and 1946 furniture prices rose 41 percent faster than prices of other household goods. Kamprad felt that this situation represented both a social problem and a business opportunity. He commented:

> A disproportionately large part of all resources is used to satisfy a small part of the population . . . Too many new and beautifully designed products can be afforded by only a small group of better-off people. IKEA's aim is to change this situation. We shall offer a wide range of home furnishing items of good design and function at prices so low that the majority of people can afford to buy them. . . . We have great ambitions.

When Kamprad's upstart company started participating in the annual furniture trade fair in Stockholm, traditional retailers complained that IKEA was selling imitations. In 1951, when the company was explicitly forbidden from selling directly to customers at the fairs, it responded by only taking orders. In 1952, such order-taking was banned at the fair, so Kamprad told employees to take down the names of potential customers and contact them after the fair. Subsequently, IKEA was forbidden from showing prices on its furniture. Finally, the retail cartel members pressured the manufacturers' cartel not to sell to IKEA. Kamprad responded by buying from a few independent Swedish furniture makers and by establishing new sources in Poland. To his delight, he found that his costs actually fell and he could charge even lower prices. "It resembles the monsters of old

times," fumed one retailer in a letter to the cartel. "If we cut one of its heads, it soon grows another."

In 1953, Kamprad converted a disused factory in Älmhult into a warehouse–showroom. Company sales grew from SKr 3 million in 1953 to SKr 6 million in 1955. By 1961, IKEA's turnover was over SKr 40 million—80 times larger than the turnover of an average furniture store (see Exhibit 2). Of a total SKr 16.8 million furniture mail-order business in Sweden, IKEA had SKr 16 million.

In 1965, Kamprad opened a second outlet in Stockholm. Sensitive to the impact of the automobile on shopping habits, he gave priority to creating ample parking space rather than the traditional focus on downtown location. His new store, built on the outskirts of the city, was the largest in Europe at the time.

Several of IKEA's basic practices were developed in this period: the self-service concept facilitated by the wide distribution of informative catalogs and the use of explanatory tickets on display merchandise, the knockdown kit that allowed stocks of all displayed items to be kept in store warehouses in flat pack boxes, and the development of suburban stores with large parking lots that brought the cash-and-carry concept to furniture retailing. Each of these practices resulted in economies that reinforced IKEA's position as the industry's low-price leader.

Between 1965 and 1973, IKEA opened seven new stores in Scandinavia, capturing a 15 percent share of the Swedish market. Rather than appealing to the older, more affluent consumers who had been the prime target of those offering the traditional, more expensive lines of furniture, Kamprad focused on younger buyers, who were often looking to furnish their first apartments. (See Exhibit 3 for customer data.) As the company grew, it strove to retain the relaxed, informal, fun atmosphere that characterized its stores in their early start-up years.

By 1973, IKEA sales were SKr 480 million. Although the Swedish furniture market doubled between 1963 and 1970, growth stagnated thereafter due to the low population growth rate and the saturated market. Kamprad felt IKEA had to expand internationally in order to continue growing.

Entry into Continental Europe

"It is our duty to expand," Kamprad said, dismissing those who insisted that furniture retailing was a strictly local business. "He ignored the economic downturn caused by the 1973 oil shock," remarked an executive, "and oddly, it worked in our favor. Our overhead costs were low, and the customers really appreciated our value-for-money approach." Because the German-speaking countries constituted the largest market for furniture in Europe, they became his priority, with Switzerland being the first target.

As in other European countries, Swiss furniture retailing was highly fragmented, with 67 percent of all firms employing three or fewer people. Most were in expensive downtown locations. IKEA opened a large store in the suburbs of Zurich in a canton which had about 20 percent of the country's consumer purchasing power. Ignoring the fact that furniture in Switzerland was of traditional design, had very sturdy construction, and was made from dark woods, the new store offered IKEA's line of simple contemporary designs in knockdown kits. Besides, rather than conform to the local service-intensive sales norms, the IKEA stores introduced self-service and cash-and-carry

concepts. By distributing half a million catalogs and backing them with humorous, off-beat advertising (see Exhibit 4), the new store attracted 650,000 visitors in its first year.

In 1974, IKEA opened near Munich. Not only was West Germany the largest and best-organized furniture market in Europe (estimated at DM 12 billion in 1973), but it was also its largest furniture producer and exporter. German retailers were set up as elaborate furniture showrooms, and they had adopted the role of order takers for manufacturers, holding little inventory of their own. As a result, consumers typically had to wait weeks for delivery, and manufacturers often faced sharp swings in demand as styles changed or the economy slowed.

Again IKEA promoted itself as "those impossible Swedes with strange ideas" (see Exhibit 4). Promising inexpensive prices, immediate delivery, and the quality image of the Swedish Furniture Institute's Möbelfakta seal, the company attracted 37,000 people to the store during its first three days.

German retailers responded vigorously. Their trade association complained that the Möbelfakta requirements of the Swedish Furniture Institute were "considerably below the minimum requirements for quality furniture in West Germany and neighboring countries." Following legal proceedings against IKEA for deceiving customers with the Möbelfakta seals, the German court put constraints on how IKEA could use the seals. Other retailers initiated legal action challenging the truthfulness of IKEA's aggressive advertising. Again, the courts supported the German retailers and curtailed IKEA's activities.

Nonetheless, business boomed, with IKEA opening 10 new stores in West Germany over the next five years. By the late

1970s, it had built a 50 percent share in the cash-and-carry segment of the West German market. Retailers who had earlier fought IKEA's entry began to acknowledge the potential of this new retailing concept, and imitators began to mushroom. IKEA continued opening stores in Europe and franchising others outside Europe into the 1980s. (Exhibit 5 details IKEA's worldwide expansion.)

IKEA'S CULTURE, STRATEGY, AND ORGANIZATION

As IKEA's spectacular growth and expansion continued, its unique management philosophy and organizational approach developed and changed. But at the core was the founder, Ingvar Kamprad.

Ingvar Kamprad

Ingvar Kamprad seemed driven by a vision larger than IKEA. "To create a better everyday life for the majority of people," he said, "once and for all, we have decided to side with the many. We know that in the future we may make a valuable contribution to the democratization process at home and abroad." One of his executives said of him, "He focuses on the human aspect. What motivates Ingvar is not profit alone but improving the quality of life of the people."

Throughout IKEA, Kamprad was revered as a visionary: someone who had foreseen—and helped accelerate—a major change in consumer needs and a structural shift in the furniture retailing industry. "He consistently turned problems into opportunities and showed us how it is not dangerous to be different," said one executive.

But Kamprad also paid extraordinary attention to the details of his business and could operate simultaneously on multiple levels. "Once, he was animatedly discussing a new strategy with us in a restaurant and we were at a critical point in the discussion," recalled one executive, "when he suddenly broke off, peered under the table, and knelt down to carefully study its construction. He commented on the design, then resumed the discussion as if there had been no break."

Another executive lamented his eye for detail. "In a group of 600 items, he will ask about a particular product, know its price, its cost, and its source, and he will expect you to know it, too. He checks everything and wants to do everything he can. He does not seem to believe in delegation. He is constantly bypassing formal structures to talk directly with front-line managers, particularly the designers and the purchasing group."

Kamprad's interest in front-line operations also extended to IKEA's staff. Whenever he visited a store he tried to meet and shake hands with every employee, offering a few words of praise, encouragement, or advice as he did so. The simple—some said spartan—values of his native Småland had stayed with Kamprad, and he still rose early, worked hard, lived simply, and took a commonsense approach to management.

One executive's account of his recent visit to a newly opened store in Hamburg captured much of Kamprad's management style:

> During his rounds of the new store, he made points that covered 19 pages of notes. They ranged from comments about the basic design—he felt the building had far too many angles, which added to construction costs—to the size of the price tags and the placement of posters in the store.

He invited the employees to stay after work—and almost all did—so he could thank them for their efforts, since most had transferred from a distant store site. The dinner was typical IKEA style—the employees went first to the buffet, the managers went next, and Ingvar Kamprad was among the last when only the remnants were left. After dinner, Ingvar shook hands and talked with all 150 present, finally leaving the store well past midnight. That experience will keep the motivation high for weeks. Each employee will go back home and tell his family and his friends that Ingvar shook hands with him.

When the store manager arrived at 6:30 the next morning, he found that Ingvar had been in the store for over an hour. Although he was staying in a modest hotel, he remarked that it was probably priced 5 DM too high. That story will probably circulate through the company as many others do—like the one about Ingvar driving around town late at night checking hotel prices, till he found one economical enough. It's all part of the aura and the legend that surrounds him.

IKEA's Management Philosophy and Practices

In many ways, IKEA developed as an extension of Kamprad and his view of life. "The true IKEA spirit," he remarked, "is founded on our enthusiasm, on our constant will to renew, on our cost consciousness, on our willingness to assume responsibility and to help, on our humbleness before the task, and on the simplicity in our behavior." Over the years a very distinct organization culture and management style had emerged.

The company operated very informally. It was reflected in the neat but casual dress of the employees (jeans and sweaters were the norm), in the relaxed office atmosphere with practically everyone sitting in an open-plan office landscape, and in the familiar and personal way the employees addressed each other—with the personal "du" rather than the more formal "sie" in Germany, and in France, with "tu" rather than "vous." Kamprad noted, "A better everyday life means getting away from status and conventions—being freer and more at ease as human beings." But a senior executive had another view: "This environment actually puts pressure on management to perform. There is no security available behind status or closed doors."

The IKEA management process also stressed simplicity and attention to detail. "Complicated rules paralyze!" said Ingvar Kamprad. An oft-repeated IKEA saying was "Retail is detail." Store managers and corporate staff alike were expected to fully understand the operations of IKEA's stores. The company organized "antibureaucrat weeks" that required all managers to work in store showrooms and warehouses for at least a week every year. The work pace was such that executives joked that IKEA believed in "management by running around."

Cost consciousness was another strong part of the management culture. "Waste of resources," said Kamprad, "is a mortal sin at IKEA. Expensive solutions are often signs of mediocrity, and an idea without a price tag is never acceptable." Although cost consciousness extended into all aspects of the operation, travel and entertainment expenses were particularly sensitive. The head-office travel department had circulated a pamphlet titled "Traveling for IKEA," which contained tips on qualifying for the most inexpensive air fares and listed economical, simple "IKEA hotels." "We do not set any price on time," remarked an executive, recalling that he had once phoned Kamprad to get approval to fly first class. He explained that economy class was full, and that he had an urgent appointment to keep. "There is no first class in IKEA," Kamprad had replied, refusing his request, "perhaps you should go by car." The executive completed the 350-mile trip by taxi.

The search for creative solutions was highly prized within IKEA. Kamprad had written, "Only while sleeping one makes no mistakes. The fear of making mistakes is the root of bureaucracy and the enemy of all evolution." Though planning for the future was encouraged, overanalysis was not. "Exaggerated planning can be fatal!" Kamprad advised his executives. "Let simplicity and common sense characterize your planning."

Kamprad had created company legends out of stories where creative common-sense experiments had changed the way the company did business. On opening day of the original Stockholm store, for example, the warehouse could not cope with the rush of customers. The store manager suggested that they be allowed to go into the warehouse to pick up their purchases. The result was so successful that future warehouses were designed to allow self-selection by customers, resulting in cost savings and faster service.

Because it had such a strong and unique culture, IKEA preferred not to recruit those who had already been immersed in another cultural stream. Nor was higher education necessary or even advantageous in IKEA. "The Stockholm-raised, highly educated, status-oriented individuals often find it difficult to adjust to the culture of the company," remarked one executive. "Besides, younger, more open recruits not only keep costs low, but they also absorb and amplify the enthusiasm of the company. We can develop them quickly by delegating responsibilities early, rotating them frequently, and offering rapid promotions to the high performers. The average age of a store manager is only 34."

An executive listed the characteristics of the successful new applicants to IKEA:

> They are people who accept our values and are willing to act on our ideas. They tend to be straightforward rather than flashy, and not too status-conscious. They must be hardworking and comfortable dealing with everyone from the customer to the owner to the cashier. But perhaps the most important quality for an Ikean is ödmjukhet—a Swedish word that implies humility, modesty, and respect for one's fellow man. It may be hard to translate, but we know it when we see it. It's reflected in things like personal simplicity and self-criticism.

The people and the values resulted in a unique work environment of which Kamprad was genuinely proud. "We take care of each other and inspire each other. One cannot help feeling sorry for those who cannot or will not join us," he said.

In 1976, Kamprad felt the need to commit to paper the values that had developed in IKEA during the previous decade. His thesis, *Testament of a Furniture Dealer*, became an important means for spreading the IKEA philosophy during a period of rapid international expansion. (Extracts are given in Exhibit 6.) With the help of this document, the organization strived to retain much of its unique culture, even as it spread into different countries. The big ideas contained in Kamprad's thesis were spread through training and "mouth to ear" transfer. Specially trained "IKEA ambassadors" were assigned to key positions in all units to spread the company's philosophy and values by educating their subordinates and by acting as role models. By 1989, about 300 such cultural agents had been trained in a special week-long seminar which covered not only the company's history and culture (presented personally by Kamprad), but also detailed training on how to spread the message.

The Adapting IKEA Strategy

At the heart of the IKEA strategy was its product range. Ingvar Kamprad called it "our identity" and set up clear and detailed guidelines on range, profile, quality, and price. While leaving considerable flexibility for fringe products, he decreed that IKEA should stand for essential products for the home—simple, durable, and well designed—priced to be accessible to the majority of the people.

In the 1980s, the product range had been expanded into a wide variety of household goods including carpets, wallpaper, pillows, table lamps, kitchen utensils and potted plants. In 1983, IKEA started a business group to develop a line of office furniture and supplies. In 1985, a workshop section began offering tools and other items useful for the home handyman.

In terms of overall range, IKEA had over 20,000 product offerings, of which 12,000 formed the core of simple, functional items common across IKEA stores worldwide. Of these, the 2,000–3,000 items displayed in the catalog received special attention since this was the centerpiece of the company's product promotion policy. Indeed, management saw the catalog as the principal means of educating consumers to the IKEA product line and concept. By 1988, the annual distribution of 44 million catalogs in 12 languages and 27 editions accounted for half the company's marketing budget.

In order to maintain its low-price reputation and allow catalog prices to be guaranteed for a year, management promoted an organizationwide obsession with cost control. The importance of production flexibility and responsiveness led to the following activities:

■ Finding low-priced materials: IKEA designers and buyers were always looking for less expensive, quality alternative materials and, in the early 1960s, led the trend to replace traditional teak with less costly oak materials. In the 1970s, IKEA helped win a broader acceptance of inexpensive pinewood furniture.

■ Matching products to capabilities: "We don't buy products, we buy production capacities," remarked a purchase executive. In an effort to maximize production from available capacity, IKEA constantly searched for unconventional means of supply. For example, it had offered contracts for table manufacture to a ski supplier and cushion covers to a shirt manufacturer with excess capacity. "If the suppliers have capacity, we ask them to produce first, and then we worry about selling the output. It is by ensuring our suppliers' delivery schedule security and by filling their available manufacturing capacity that we can maintain our unique price levels."

■ Developing long-term relations with suppliers: IKEA was willing to manage "difficult" low-priced sources and did so by supporting its suppliers both technically and financially even to the point of designing their factories, buying their machines, and setting up their operations. In order to meet cost objectives and maintain long-term supplier relationships, designers worked two to three years ahead of current products. By ensuring a high, steady volume of orders, IKEA encouraged the suppliers to invest and drive down manufacturing costs. In furniture alone, IKEA purchased from about 1,500 suppliers in more than 40 countries. Purchases were consolidated in 12 central warehouses, which maintained high inventories not only because of commitments to suppliers, but also to meet the company's 90 to 95 percent service level objective on catalog items.

But the most visible aspect of IKEA's strategy was its highly successful retail operations. The distinctive stores with their constant innovations had changed the face of furniture retailing in Europe. As IKEA expanded, tremendous internal competitiveness developed among the stores. "The newly set-up stores would look at the previously developed stores and try their hardest to improve on them," recalled an executive. "One would set up a green plant department, so the next would create a clock section." It was by this process that some of the unique distinguishing characteristics of the typical IKEA store emerged: supervised play areas for children featuring a large "pool" fiiled with red styrofoam balls, in-store cafes serving inexpensive exotic meals such as Swedish meatballs, and fully equipped nursery and baby-changing facilities.

Although this interstore competition resulted in numerous innovative new ideas, it also led to a certain amount of unnecessary differentiation and wheel reinvention. So much so that by the mid-1980s, some senior managers began proposing greater coordination and standardization of the diverse operations and multiple approaches. They argued that such standardization not only would project a clearer IKEA image, but could also result in considerable savings. An executive recalled:

> Hans Ax was the major champion of the "IKEA concept." He felt that we were spending too much on diverse development projects instead of taking the best ideas, standardizing our approach, and applying it to all the stores. As a result of this effort, a uniform concept has emerged. Guidelines have developed ranging from the basic color of the IKEA signs to the size of plants sold in our garden shops.

An important part of the IKEA concept was the development of standard in-store display areas. In every store there were five or six areas called studios which displayed some of the best-selling products. Under the IKEA concept, the locations of the studios within the retail store and their display settings were standardized, down to the last centimeter of layout design.

The concept also specified store architecture more precisely, defining the classic IKEA traffic flow that took customers through the store in a four-leafed clover pattern to maximize their exposure to the product line. It prescribed standard in-store facilities including baby-changing rooms, a supervised play area for children, information centers, and cafes. "We have become a little like McDonald's in our insistence that all the stores conform on these points," said one headquarters executive. "But we want to create a unique ambience that makes IKEA not just a furniture store, but a family outing destination that can compete with the entertainment park and the zoo for family time."

The Evolving Organization

When IKEA started internationalizing, Kamprad organized its non-Scandinavian business into an Expansion Group and an Operations Group. (See Exhibit 7.) The former was responsible for initial planning for a new market entry. First they sent in a construction team to set up the new facility. Then, two months before the opening, a "build-up" team from the first-year group would take charge, training the staff, establishing operations, and managing the opening. After about a year, they would hand over to the Operations Group.

This organization allowed rapid growth and also propelled many of IKEA's top managers to positions of responsibility. Recalled an IKEA executive:

> The pioneering spirit of a core group allowed our international expansion to succeed. With no guidelines except Ingvar's thesis and a general objective, young entrepreneurs would buy land, build and set up a store, and quickly move on to the next store. The pace was breathtaking. You could be hired on Monday and sent out on Thursday on a key mission. The company had unbelievable confidence in its people, and this experience created today's leaders in IKEA—Anders Moberg, Thomas Blomquist, and many others.

Responsibilities shifted frequently and careers progressed rapidly. Most senior executives were in their thirties. Jan Kjellman, IKEA's Product Range manager, had been administrative director of a German store, member of build-up groups for two stores, store manager in Holland, country manager for Holland and Belgium, Marketing manager, and then Product Range manager, all within the space of 12 years with IKEA. Anders Moberg, now IKEA's CEO, had started his career in store administration, moving to work in build-up groups before being appointed store manager in Austria and in Switzerland. He then led the IKEA entry into France as country manager while in his early thirties.

In the early 1980s, with a well-established international organization, IKEA retail was reorganized into four geographical regions, headed by regional managers. However, the purchasing, distrtbution, and design functions continued to be cen-

trally controlled and were staffed by specialists who rarely migrated to other functions. Most purchasers, for example, came from Småland, Kamprad's home region, whose inhabitants were renowned for their thriftiness. They rarely had a college education, and their job rotation and career growth were slower and more specialized than those of the retailers.

IKEA's senior management remained predominantly Scandinavian. "There is an efficiency in having such a homogeneous group," reasoned a Swedish manager of a foreign operation. "They instinctively follow the Scandinavian management philosophy of simple, people-oriented, non-hierarchic operations. But it can create problems when non-Scandinavians feel that their career prospects are limited."

Although there was no overt discrimination, some non-Swedes felt it was important to speak Swedish and understand the Smålandish psyche to be a member of the inner management circle since the dominant company ethic was viewed internally as systematized Smålandish common sense. Indeed, IKEA's president, Anders Moberg, had been publicly quoted as saying, "I would advise any foreign employee who really wants to advance in this company to learn Swedish. They will then get a completely different feeling for our culture, our mood, our values. All in all, we encourage all our foreign personnel to have as much contact with Sweden as possible, for instance, by going to Sweden for their holidays."

Over the years, the legal ownership structure of the IKEA group had been shaped by several influences. Above all, Kamprad wanted to ensure that the business would live on after him and would not be broken up in some kind of inheritance dispute. He and his family controlled a company whose income derived from franchise fees and royalties paid by IKEA stores. Operating profits were transferred to a charitable foundation Kamprad had set up in the Netherlands to escape stringent Swedish taxes and foreign exchange regulations. (See Exhibit 8.) Kamprad himself had moved to Lausanne, Switzerland, partly to escape the high Swedish taxes.

NEW DIRECTIONS AND FUTURE ISSUES

By the late 1980s, Kamprad and his management team were working on some bold new strategies to take IKEA into the next decade. Along with the new directions, however, came some questions about how long the company could maintain its remarkable record of growth and expansion.

New Horizons

In 1979, Kamprad had bought a faltering IKEA franchise in Canada, and turned it into a lucrative business within three years. Thereafter, management had been eyeing the United States, the largest furniture market in the world (estimated at $15 billion in 1985). The decision process leading to entry into the United States was in classic IKEA style, as Björn Bayley, head of the Canadian operations at the time, recalled:

> The U.S. market had enormous potential. There are 18 million people in New York alone—more than the population of Scandinavia. Add on the 24 million citizens of California, and prospects look very exciting.
>
> Once it became known within IKEA that we were planning to open stores in the United States, everyone wanted to come here. Three or four managers staked

out a claim to head the U.S. operations. But Ingvar was not ready to decide and, for several months, confusion reigned. Finally, Ingvar called me from a railway station in Stuttgart. He had decided to run the new U.S. stores as part of the Canadian operation. He wanted us to open two stores on the East Coast with as little hoopla as possible and, once these were successful, to follow with further expansion.

> In 1985, we opened a store in Plymouth Meeting near Philadelphia, and the following year another in Woodbridge, Virginia, near Washington, D.C. We supported each with an extensive media campaign and about one million catalogs. Despite the severe inventory shortages that resulted from unexpectedly heavy demand, the two stores had a turnover of over $77 million in 1986.

As usual, it didn't take long for imitators to appear. Indeed, a California-based retailer calling itself Stör began emulating IKEA's concepts so exactly—from product designs to ball-filled children's play areas—that the company launched legal proceedings against them. To preserve its image and to preempt imitators, management decided to accelerate its national expansion plans. By 1989, stores had been opened in Baltimore and Pittsburgh, and six more openings were scheduled by 1992.

In 1987, IKEA entered the U.K, a market estimated at £5 billion, and home of the only other large multinational furniture retailer—the more upscale Habitat. A successful entry in Warrington (in the northwest) was followed by the opening of the country's largest home furnishing store close to London at Brent Park. Plans for another 10 stores in the U.K were announced.

In 1989, IKEA opened its first store in Italy, one of Europe's largest furniture markets. Again its initial reception was excellent. For the first three days of operation, there were one-hour-long queues outside the store. As soon as it could obtain the necessary permits, the company hoped to expand south from its base in Milan.

IKEA had also taken the first steps in its plans to build a major presence in the Soviet Union and East Europe. Not surprisingly, the unconventional idea was hatched by Ingvar Kamprad in the mid-1980s. Recalled an IKEA executive, "Our entire East European strategy was mapped out by Ingvar on a small paper napkin. Just about every aspect of the entry strategy was laid out on this small piece of paper—we call it his Picasso—and for the past few years we have just built on and expanded that original vision."

The plans called for new skills and involved different risks. To source from 15 factories in the U.S.S.R. and many others in East Europe would require an investment in excess of SKr 500 million. The limited ability to transfer hard currency from East Europe forced the company to plan for extensive countertrade deals so that dividends and capital repayment could be replaced by furniture exports.

The idea initially aroused concern within the company. Some felt that it was too early to risk heavy resource dependence on the East Bloc countries, given their low reliability of service and poor quality image. Others were concerned that recent economic and political reforms in many of these countries could easily suffer major reversals. However, in face of Kamprad's persistence, IKEA was proceeding with this major thrust.

The site of its first East Europe outlet was in Budapest, where the company took a 50 percent share in a joint venture with a Hungarian retail chain. Soon after, it entered an agreement to open a store in Leningrad. In 1988, IKEA Poland decided to build a $25 million warehouse and retail center near Warsaw. As part of that plan, IKEA would buy furniture and establish a joint-venture woodworking factory in Poland. Outlets were also planned in Yugoslavia. An office in Vienna coordinated the administration of these various East European activities.

New Organization and Leadership

In 1986, Ingvar Kamprad appointed 35-year-old Anders Moberg as president. At the same time, IKEA operations were reorganized on functional lines (see Exhibit 9). At the top of the group was the four-person supervisory board, which reviewed the group's general direction. Under the supervisory board was the executive board, which was responsible for the day-to-day operations of the group. Except for Björn Bayley, all executive board members were based in IKEA's 50-person headquarters in Humlebaek, Denmark.

Of the group's four basic functions, product range, purchasing, and distribution service reported directly to Moberg in his operating capacity as head of wholesale. Ingvar Kamprad also continued his deep involvement with the purchase and product range functions, and often spent time discussing the intricacies of purchasing or design with managers five or more levels below him.

The leadership shift had an impact on the company's management style. Remarked one executive, "With over 13,000 employees worldwide, some began to push for a more formalized approach. Anders is more committed to systematization, and he delegates much more than Ingvar." In 1988 Moberg introduced a formal budgeting and planning process.

Business plans from the various country operations and product groups were integrated and modified at the executive board level. A corporate plan with three years' horizon was developed and sent back to the country units and the product groups to ensure their actions were in conformity with corporate plans.

Blanket cost consciousness at all levels was giving way to cost–benefit studies. Instead of seeking out the least expensive sites, the company was now more willing to locate new stores at A-class sites, where justified. Furthermore, while earlier stores had been built for the midweek crowds, newer store capacity was being matched with weekend crowds. Although many applauded the changes as overdue, some felt they were not coming fast enough:

> There is a time bomb ticking inside IKEA's growing profitability that makes employees less willing to sacrifice and more anxious to share the rewards. There is often a conflict between cost consciousness and efficiency. It's hard to keep the old spirit of frugality when the business is doing so well. But changes are coming—I noticed even Ingvar's new car has a premium metallic paint finish now!

Future Directions and Concerns

Overall, IKEA hoped to reach a turnover of SKr 19 billion by 1990 and perhaps three times that amount by the year 2000, principally through rapid geographical expansion. But there was some cause for concern. Said one executive, "We are currently making annual risk capital investment of about SKr 500 million, which translates to opening four to six new stores every year. But our expansion plans are much more ambitious today. In the United States alone, our rollout plan calls for two to three new stores every year, accelerating to five or six a year by the mid-1990s. I just hope we are not overextending ourselves."

Over the next few years, the median age and income level in most developed countries was expected to rise, while IKEA's target market segment of young low-to-middle income families would be shrinking. A senior executive reflected:

> We have to expand into other segments like office furniture and more traditional designs for the older, richer people. But we cannot risk making our profile too diffuse or distorting the IKEA image. Through extensive promotion, we are trying to decouple the consumers' linkage between ease of assembly and low price on the one hand and low product quality on the other. In our advertising also, we have started playing down the image of the "crazy Swedes," replacing it with a superior quality image. In entering the United States, for example, we did not resort to its traditional two-phase tactic of grabbing attention and then building a strong reputation. Instead, we have tried to project a sober image right from the beginning.

But perhaps the biggest concern was whether the rapid growth and increasing geographic spread of IKEA would make it difficult to retain the company's cultural values. With over 13,000 employees worldwide and 1,000 new recruits being added annually, many newcomers had only a vague sense of the IKEA way. Björn Bayley, head of North American operations, commented:

> The only constraint to our growth is people. At the top levels, our commitment to Ingvar's thesis still exists. But these days the pioneers are having to learn how to fill in forms. Yet we must keep the old pioneer spirit alive, even though in a company of this size it is

increasingly difficult to spread our core values and beliefs to the lowest levels. IKEA is adding about 10 percent to its workforce every year, in addition to normal personnel turnover, which can be as high as 20 percent in some departments. Inculcating the IKEA way into such a rapidly growing community is itself a tremendous challenge.

Another barrier we now face is the differences in attitudes between America and Scandinavia. U.S. retailing establishments have an annual personnel turnover in the 40 to 60 percent range. Although we are well below these figures, turnover is still undesirably high. Because of the low job security here, American employees are always looking for guidance—despite their higher education and need to achieve. The IKEA way requires openness and a willingness to take responsibility. We want people to stand up and disagree with authority if they have confidence in their beliefs. But despite intensive training programs it has been hard making the IKEA way their way of life here in the United States.

Even Kamprad conceded:

> The IKEA spirit was easier to keep alive in former days when we weren't so many, when we all reached each other and could talk with each other. Before, it was more concrete, the will to help each other, the art of managing with small means—being cost conscious almost to the point of stinginess, the humbleness, the irresistible enthusiasm, and the wonderful community through thick and thin. Certainly it is more difficult now when the individual is gradually being wiped out in the gray gloominess of collective agreements.

The importance of a homogeneous management group in maintaining this common cultural bond was also being debated within the company. "When we open in a new country, we need the top management to be culture bearers for IKEA," remarked an executive, "so they are Scandinavian. Once the local employees have learned how to live the IKEA way, they can rise within their national operations."

Of the 65 senior executives in IKEA, however, 60 were Swedish or Danish, and almost all the non-Scandinavians were concentrated in distribution services. Furthermore, most of the senior executives came from the retail side of business. Some in the company felt such similarity of background was no longer in IKEA's best interest, as reflected by the comments of one company executive:

> A lot about the IKEA culture is appealing. But sometimes I think there is too much ideology bordering on religion. You sell your soul to IKEA when you start internalizing the culture. Ingvar is obsessed with his own ideas, and there is an element of fanaticism and intolerance toward people who think differently. I, for one, react negatively to the stingy mentality that sometimes shows through our cost consciousness, or when Ingvar says that we can reach self-fulfillment only through our jobs—we work hard, but there is no reason that our jobs should necessarily so dominate our lives.

Concerns were also being raised about how far IKEA could or should push its common concept across all stores even as it rapidly expanded internationally. As one executive put it:

> Our common concept should leave sufficient room for creativity and freedom at the individual store level. Very often, market orientation and IKEA concept orientation clash. The U.S. market wants shelves with space for TV sets while European shelves are designed only for books. Should we adapt our line or continue to sell bookshelves in the United

States? The Scandinavian-designed bed and mattress is fundamentally different from the standard approach that is the norm in continental Europe. Should we continue to push the Scandinavian sleeping preferences on the rest of Europe?

But it's more than an issue of product design—it extends to how much we should adapt our organization and culture to different national environments. Humility may be a virtue in Europe, for example, but should we impose it on our U.S. organization? Or is the attitude of "success breeds success" more appropriate there? Should our business drive our culture, or should our culture drive our business?

But perhaps the deepest concern was one that was often unspoken. How well would IKEA survive Ingvar Kamprad's eventual departure from the company? To this concern, Ingvar Kamprad responded, "The IKEA ideology is not the work of one man but the sum of many impulses from all the IKEA leadership. Its supporting framework is massive." But others were less sanguine. One manager summed up the concerns of many: "Ingvar is a patriarch. His dominating personallty has been the life breath of the company, and you have to question how we will survive when he is gone."

EXHIBIT 1
IKEA CROWTH AND PERFORMANCE INDICATORS

Year	Turnover (m SKr)	Outlets	Countries	Coworkers	Catalogs (000s)
1954	3	1	1	15	285
1964	79	2	2	250	1,200
1974	616	10	5	1,500	13,000
1984	6,770	66	17	8,300	40,000
1988	14,500	75–83	19–20	13,400	44,000

Year	1979–1980	1980–1981	1981–1982	1982–1983	1983–1984	1984–1985	1985–1986	1986–1987	1987–1988
Turnover (billion SKr)	3.6	4.1	4.8	6.0	6.8	8.2	10.7	12.6	14.5
Estimated PAT (million SKr)	250	280	300	420	500	500	630	930	1,100
Total surface area (000 sq. m.)	425	458	483	533	606	825	907	953	973
Number of visitors (millions)	25	30	34	36	38	44	53	60	65

IKEA was a closely held private company. Accounting data were not made public. The company's capitalized market value was estimated conservatively at SKr 10 billion in 1987. Profits are best estimates from available information.

Region	% of Sales (1988)	Region	% of Purchases (1988)
West Germany	29.7%	Scandinavia	50%
Scandinavia	27.5	East Europe	20
Rest of Europe	28.5	Rest of Europe	22
Rest of the world	14.3	Rest of the world	8

Sources: 1. Company documents.
           2. *Affársvárlden*, December 8, 1987.

EXHIBIT 2
IKEA AND THE SWEDISH FURNITURE INDUSTRY: 1961

Personnel Functions in Swedish Furniture Stores in 1961

Personnel Occupied with:	IKEA	Furniture Stores	Furniture Sections of Department Stores
Selling	29%	42%	65%
Clerical	44	13	6
Warehouse	17	11	16
Transportation	5	13	5
Workshop	5	21	8

Productivity of Swedish Furniture Retailers in 1961

Measure	IKEA	Large Store*	Average Store
Annual turnover in 1,000 SKr/employee	202	114	93
Annual turnover in SKr/sq. m.	1,453	1,076	704
Rent as percent of annual turnover	0.6%	3.0%	3.4%
Annual stockturn	3.2	2.9	2.3

Source: R. Marteson, *Innovations in Multinational Retailing: IKEA in Swedish, Swiss, German and Austrian Markets*, doctoral dissertation (University of Gothenburg: Gothenburg, Sweden, 1981).
*Annual turnover SKr 1 million or more.

EXHIBIT 3
IKEA CUSTOMER PROFILE AND BUYER BEHAVIOR

				Profile of IKEA Customers (Stockholm, 1975)							
Age		*Children*		*Status*		*Income (000SKr)*		*Education (yrs)*		*Home*	
0–25	47%	0	55%	Married	65%	0–2	6%	0–6	24%	House	25%
25–35	32	1	22	Single	35	2–4	31	7–11	63	Apartment	63
35–45	14	2	16			4–6	25	12+	38	Condominium	12
45+	7	3	7			6+	38				

Buyer Behavior at IKEA (1975)			
Primary determinents of purchase	%		
Design	14%		
Price	44		
Quality	3		
Large assortment	16		
Catalog	11		
Recommendations	1		
Guarantees	0		
Others	11		
Total	100%		
Importance of criteria for store choice:	High	Low	No response
Design	69%	5%	26%
Price	54	11	35
Quality	90	0	10
Distance	19	66	15
Consumer atttitude to IKEA	Positive	Negative	Neither
Design	51%	10%	39%
Price	73	4	23
Quality	27	29	44
Distance	56	29	15
Purchase decisions were based on			
Prior visits to the store	37%		
Visits to other stores	72		
Information from catalog	78		

Source: R. Marteson (op.cit.).

EXHIBIT 4
INTRODUCTORY PROMOTION CAMPAIGNS OF IKEA IN CONTINENTAL EUROPE

Advertising Themes for IKEA Store Opening: Switzerland, 1973
(Six letters from Herr Bunzli)

No.	Theme	Abstract from the Advertisement
1.	The new sales concept	Jokes about Swiss unwillingness to transport and assemble furniture, even for lower prices.
2.	No delivery by IKEA	"That is a stupid thing."
3.	Assembly of knocked-down furniture	"You can't do that to us Swiss."
4.	The wood used for furniture	"No teak . . .we are not Swedes."
5.	The Swiss needing furniture as status symbol	"Swedes go home."
6.	Swiss quality	"Quality can come only from Switzerland."

Advertising Themes for IKEA Store Opening: Munich, 1974

No.	Theme
1.	Young people have more taste than money.
2.	We achieve the impossible.
3.	On October 17, we'll open Munich's furniture highway.
4.	At long last, the impossible furniture store will open on October 17.
5.	Trees off the ground we take, and furniture for you we make.

Promotion Campaigns: West Germany 1974–1979

No.	Campaign	Theme
1.	The day of the singles	Single visitors could get their socks washed at IKEA.
2.	The day of the baker	Crispy bread straight from the oven to all store visitors.
3.	The day of the barber	Free manicure and haircut to store visitors.
4.	The day of the breakfast	All visitors were offered free breakfasts.
5.	IKEA birthday	Free gifts to visitors.
6.	Rent a Christmas tree	Customers could rent a Christmas tree for 10 D Marks, refundable after Christmas if the tree was returned.
7.	Day of the sleeper	Offered 300 people the opportunity to test the new IKEA matttresses overnight in its store and buy them the next morning for 10 D Marks.

EXHIBIT 5
IKEA RETAIL OUTLETS WORLDWIDE

		Area in sq.m.*
Austria		
1977(81)	Vienna	23,500
1981	Wels	11,700
1989	*Graz†*	*14,900*
Belgium		
1984	Ternat (Brussels)	15,100
	Nossegem (Brussels)	11,100
1985	Wilrijk (Antwerp)	14,200
	Hognoul (Liège)	12,900
Canada		
1976(83)	Vancouver	14,700
1977(87)	Toronto	20,000
1978(85)	Edmonton	10,400
1979	Calgary	5,700
	Ottawa	6,600
1982	Quebec	9,600
1982(86)	Montreal	15,400
Denmark		
1969(75)	Tåstrup (Copenhagen)	39,500
1980	Århus	9,700
1982	Aalborg	6,700
1985	Odense	1,400
France		
1981	First establishment no longer in use	
1982(87)	Lyon	18,900
1983	Evry (south of Paris)	24,000
1985	Vitrolles (Marseilles)	15,700
1986	Paris-Nord	24,800
1988	*Lomme† (Lille)*	*15,100*
Italy		
1989	*Fulvio Testi† (Milano)*	*11,900*

		Area in sq.m.*
The Netherlands		
1979	Sliedrecht (Rotterdam)	16,600
1982(85)	Amsterdam	19,600
1983	Duiven	10,800
Norway		
1963(75)	Slependen (Oslo)	19,600
1984	Bergen	10,500
1988	*Forus† (Stavanger)*	*14,000*
Sweden		
1958	Älmhult	18,400
1965	Stockholm	44,000
1966	Sundsvall	11,800
1967(77)	Malmö	19,900
1972	Gothenburg	24,700
1977	Linköping	16,000
1981(87)	Jönköping	3,500
	Gävle	6,700
1982(88)	Helsingborg	11,600
1982	Örebro	2,300
1982(86)	Uppsala	13,000
1984	Västerås	10,900

		Area in sq.m.*
Switzerland		
1973(79)	Spreitenbach (Zürich)	25,500
1979	Aubonne (Lausanne)	17,500
1986	Emmen (Lucerne)	3,000
United Kingdom		
1987	Warrington	17,100
1988	*Brent Park† (London)*	23,300
United States		
1985	Philadelphia	15,000
1986	Woodbridge (Washington)	14,500
1988	*Baltimore†*	*19,700*
1989	*Pittsburgh†*	*19,900*
West Germany		
1974(86)	Eching	24,800
1975(78)	Godorf (Cologne)	16,100
1975	Dorsten	17,600
1976	Grossburgwedel (Hanover)	14,300
	Stuhr (Bremen)	12,900
1977	Kaltenkirchen (Hamburg)	8,000
1977(85)	Wallau (Frankfurt)	23,800
1978	Kamen (Dortmund)	14,200
	Stuttgart	4,300
1979	Berlin	17,700
	Kaarst (Düsseldorf)	14,200
1980	Kassel	4,200
1981	Poppenreuth (Fürth/Nuremberg)	19,100
	Schwalbach-Bous (Saarbrücken)	6,200
	Freiburg	6,100
	Walldorf	18,300
1983	Löhne-Gohfeld	6,200
1989	*Schnelsen† (Hamburg)*	*22,800*

Figures in brackets refer to the date of rebuilding.

*Incl. adjacent warehouses.

†Will be inaugurated after 88.08.31. Not included in total figures.

EXHIBIT 6
EXTRACTS FROM THE 11-PAGE DOCUMENT, *TESTAMENT OF A FURNITURE DEALER*

What is good for our customers is also good for us in the long run . . . We know we can have an important effect on practically all markets. We know that we may make a valuable contribution to the democratization process at home and abroad . . . That is why it is our duty to expand.

The following section describes our product range and price philosophy, which is the backbone of our work. Furthermore, we describe rules and methods which will continue to make IKEA a unique company.

1. The Product Range—Our Identity

Range: To cover the total home area, indoors as well as outdoors, with loose as well as fixed home furnishings. This range shall always be limited.

Profile: Our basic range shall be . . . simple and straightforward . . . durable and easy to live with . . . (and) shall express design, color, and joy. In Scandinavia [it] should be regarded as typically IKEA and outside Scandinavia as typically Swedish.

Quality: Throwaway products are not IKEA. But quality should never be an end in itself. It should always be adapted to the consumer's interests in the long run.

Changes: Our basic policy to serve the majority of people can never be changed.

2. The IKEA Spirit—A Strong and Living Reality

The true IKEA spirit is still founded on our enthusiasm, on our constant will to renew, on our cost consciousness, on our willingness to assume responsibility and help, on our humbleness before the task, and on the simplicity in our behavior . . . The IKEA spirit is still here, but it has to be taken care of and developed with time. Development, however, is not always equal to progress. It depends upon you, as a leader and a responsible person, to make development progressive.

3. Profit Gives Us Resources

Profit is a wonderful word! Let us rely on ourselves when it comes to creating resources. The aim for accumulating our resources is to obtain the best results in the long run.

4. To Reach Good Results with Small Means

Expensive solutions . . . are often a sign of mediocrity. We have no interest in a solution until we know what it costs.

5. Simplicity Is a Virtue

Bureaucracy complicates and paralyzes! Exaggerated planning can be fatal . . . Simplicity in our behavior gives us strength.

6. The Different Way

By daring to be different, we find new ways . . . I hope we never have two stores completely alike (because) a healthy appetite for experimenting will lead us forward.

7. Concentration of Energy—Important to our Success

The general who splits up his forces inevitably fails . . . We too have to concentrate. We cannot do everything everywhere, at the same time.

8. To Assume Responsibility—a Privilege

To assume responsibility has nothing to do with education, economy, or position. In our IKEA family we want to keep the human being in the center and to support each other . . . To make mistakes is the privilege of the active person.

9. Most Things Still Remain to Be Done—A Glorious Future

Happiness is not to reach one's goal but to be on the way. Experience is the drag on all evolution . . . Humbleness, will, and strengths are your secret weapons . . . Time is your most important asset. What we want, we can and will do. Together. A glorious future!

EXHIBIT 7
ORGANIZATION OF THE IKEA GROUP DURING THE 1970s

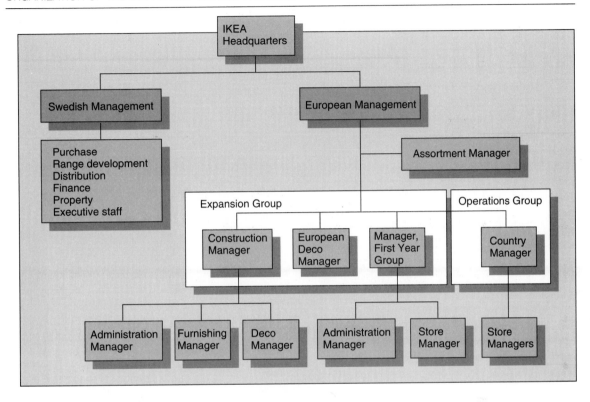

ORGANIZATION OF THE IKEA GROUP DURING THE EARLY 1980s

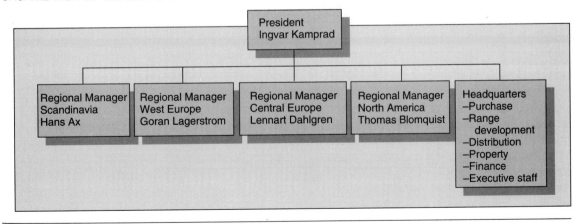

EXHIBIT 8
OWNERSHIP STRUCTURE OF THE IKEA GROUP

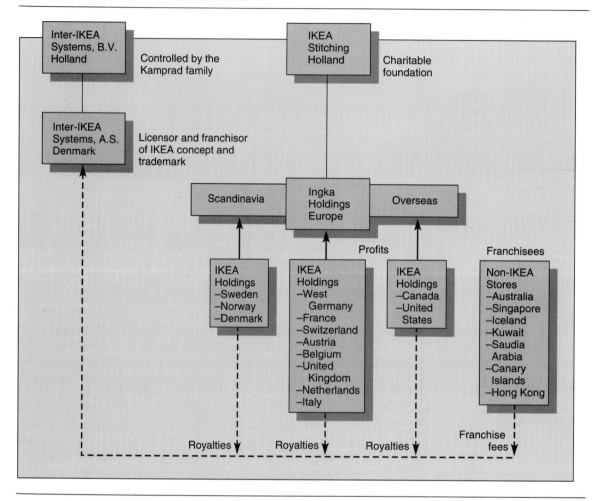

EXHIBIT 9
ORGANIZATION STRUCTURE OF IKEA AFTER 1986

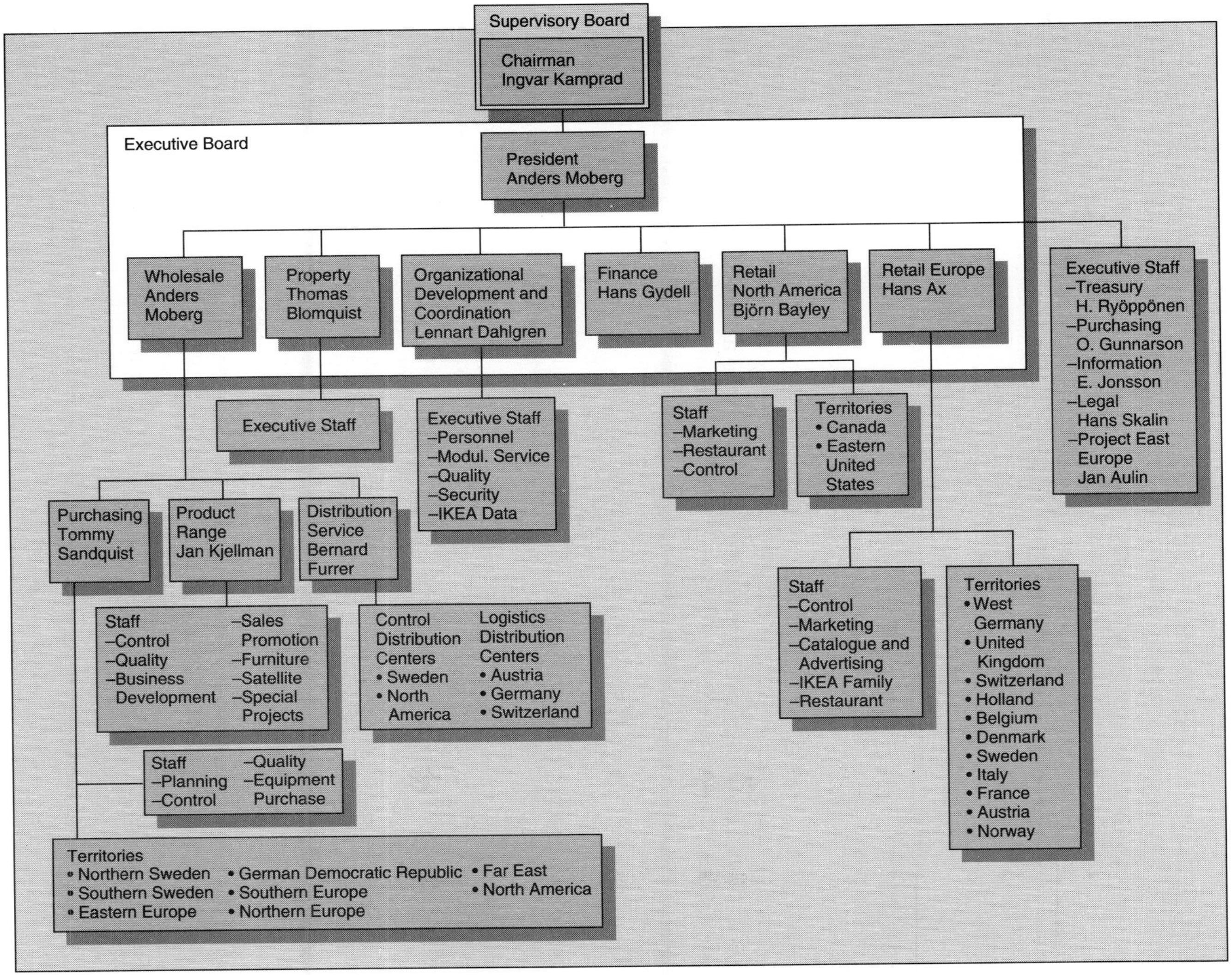

Supervisory Board
Chairman Ingvar Kamprad

President Anders Moberg

Executive Board

Executive Staff
- Treasury H. Ryöppönen
- Purchasing O. Gunnarson
- Information E. Jonsson
- Legal Hans Skalin
- Project East Europe Jan Aulin

Wholesale Anders Moberg

Property Thomas Blomquist

Organizational Development and Coordination Lennart Dahlgren

Finance Hans Gydell

Retail North America Björn Bayley

Retail Europe Hans Ax

Executive Staff
- Personnel
- Modul. Service
- Quality
- Security
- IKEA Data

Retail North America — Björn Bayley
Staff
- Marketing
- Restaurant
- Control

Territories
- Canada
- Eastern United States

Retail Europe — Hans Ax
Staff
- Control
- Marketing
- Catalogue and Advertising
- IKEA Family
- Restaurant

Territories
- West Germany
- United Kingdom
- Switzerland
- Holland
- Belgium
- Denmark
- Sweden
- Italy
- France
- Austria
- Norway

Executive Staff

Distribution Service Bernard Furrer
Control Distribution Centers
- Sweden
- North America
Logistics Distribution Centers
- Austria
- Germany
- Switzerland

Product Range Jan Kjellman
Staff
- Sales Promotion
- Furniture
- Satellite
- Special Projects

Purchasing Tommy Sandquist
Staff
- Control
- Quality
- Business Development

- Quality
- Equipment Purchase

Staff
- Planning
- Control

Territories
- Northern Sweden
- Southern Sweden
- Eastern Europe
- German Democratic Republic
- Southern Europe
- Northern Europe
- Far East
- North America

317

Apple Computer 1992

John Sculley, Apple Computer's charismatic CEO, sat in his small, interior glass office in Cupertino, California, reading the year-end results for 1991. The computer industry had just experienced its worst year in history. Average return on sales plummeted to under 4 percent and the ROE was under 11 percent. For the first time, worldwide PC revenues actually dropped by almost 10 percent, despite rising unit volume. Although Apple continued to outperform the industry, the intensity of competition was putting acute pressure on Apple's margins. "Our challenge," noted Sculley, "is not only to stay ahead of our competition, but we have to find some way to change the rules of the game. If computer manufacturers continue to make and sell commodities, everyone in our business will suffer." Changing a $50 billion global industry, however, was no easy task. Yet Sculley believed that Apple was one of the only companies that could do it. For Apple's next strategy session, he asked his staff to address two key questions: (1) could Apple change the structure of the industry, and if so how? and (2) what other alternatives were available?

A BRIEF HISTORY OF APPLE

Apple's legendary story began when Steve Wozniak (Woz) and Steve Jobs joined forces to produce the Apple I computer in the Jobs family garage in Cupertino. College dropouts in their early 20s, they formed Apple Computer Inc. on April Fool's Day, 1976. After selling 200 Apple I computers, mainly to hobbyists, they managed to obtain venture capital. Jobs sold his vision of making the personal computer easy to use for nontechnical people. His stated mission, which permeated the firm through 1992, was "to change the world through technology." The concept was one computer for every man, woman, and child. When Jobs and Woz announced the Apple II in March 1977, they began a revolution in computing, which changed the company *and* the world. Apple sold over 100,000 Apple IIs by the end of 1980, generating revenues over $100 million. Primarily selling into homes and schools, Apple was recognized as the industry leader. The company went public in December 1980, making the founders multimillionaires.

Apple's competitive position changed fundamentally when IBM entered the personal computer market in 1981. While Apple's revenues continued to grow rapidly, market share and margins fell precipitously. Apple responded to IBM with two new products, the Lisa and Macintosh (Mac). These innovative computers featured a graphical interface and a windowing operating system that allowed the user to view and switch between several applications at once. They also used a mouse to move and point to positions on the screen, making applications easier to use. However, both computers were incompatible with the IBM standard and even with the Apple II. The technologically sophisticated but expensive ($10,000) Lisa Computer was soon dropped. The Macintosh fared better but suffered because of limited software and low performance. By 1984, the company was in crisis.

A year before the introduction of the Lisa and Macintosh, Apple hired John Sculley to be its president and CEO. Sculley, 44, an MBA from Wharton and previously president of Pepsi's beverage operations, had spent most of his career in marketing and advertising. Sculley was to provide the operational expertise, and Steve Jobs the technical direction and vision. But Jobs resigned from Apple in September 1985 after a well-publicized dispute with Sculley and Apple's board of directors.

After its slow start, Apple's new Mac computer picked up steam. Between 1986 and 1990, Apple's sales exploded (see Exhibit 1). It introduced new, more powerful Macs that roughly matched the newest IBM personal computers in speed. Even more important, the Mac offered superior software and a variety of peripherals (e.g., laser printers) that gave Apple a unique market niche—the easiest computer to use in the industry with unmatched capabilities at desktop publishing. Apple's strategy of being the only manufacturer of its hardware and software made Apple's profitability the envy of the industry. By 1990, Apple had $1 billion in cash and more than $5.5 billion in sales. Return on equity, at 32 percent, was one of the best in the industry. Market share had stabilized at around 10 percent.

But the industry environment was changing rapidly. Rather than basking in success, Apple's management became convinced in the spring of 1990 that their position was unsustainable. According to Dan Eilers, V.P. of Strategic Planning at the time, "the company was on a glide path to history."

THE EVOLVING PERSONAL COMPUTER INDUSTRY[1]

The personal computer was a revolution in information technology that spawned a $50 billion hardware business, with another $30 billion in software and peripherals by 1991. During its short 15 years, the industry evolved through three successive periods. During its first five to six years, it was characterized by explosive growth and multiple, small competi-

---

[1] The description of the industry will focus primarily on the U.S. market, which was the trendsetter in PCs in the 1980s. PC penetration was much deeper in the United States than Europe and Japan, and trends in areas such as software and distribution generally started in the United States and filtered to Europe, then Japan within 1–3 years.

tors vying for a piece of the market. IBM's introduction of the IBM PC in 1981 launched a second stage in desktop computing. Over the next five years, the industry became a battle for standards and retail shelf space. Three firms emerged as the clear leaders during this period: IBM, Compaq, and Apple. The third era was one of increasing fragmentation. From 1986 through 1991–2, new manufacturers of IBM clones from around the world grabbed share from the industry leaders as new channels of distribution emerged and product innovation as well as revenue growth slowed.

In some ways, the personal computer was a very simple device. Most PCs were composed of five widely available components: memory storage, a microprocessor (the brains of the PC), a main circuit board called a motherboard, a disk drive, and peripherals (e.g., display, keyboard, mouse, printer, and so on). Most manufacturers also bundled their PC hardware with critical software packages, especially an operating system (the software required to run applications). But from the beginning, PCs have been available in almost infinite variety. They could vary in speed, amounts of memory and storage, physical size, weight, functionality, and so on.

During the early years of the industry, venture capital in the United States encouraged the entry of new firrns, which offered products in every conceivable shape and size. By 1980, new entrants flooded the market, promoting distinct standards and unique technical features. Almost every firm had a different configuration of hardware and software, making communication or sharing applications between machines virtually impossible. The first PCs introduced by Commodore and Apple had relatively little speed or memory. However, even these early computers allowed managers to perform tasks

that were either very time-consuming or reserved for expensive ($50,000 to >$1 million), multiuser mini and mainframe computers. For under $5,000, anyone could now do spreadsheet analysis and word processing.

Before IBM entered the market in 1981, most products were considered "closed" or proprietary systems. A closed system, like mainframes, minicomputers, and Apple's PCs, could not be copied or cloned because it was protected by patents or copyrights. However, closed systems typically rendered the computer incompatible with competitor's products. IBM's entry in 1981 changed the playing field by offering an "open" system. The specifications of IBM's PC were easily obtainable, allowing independent hardware companies to make compatible machines and independent software vendors (ISVs) to write applications that would run on different brands. Open systems had a big advantage for customers because they were no longer locked into a particular vendor's product, and they could mix and match hardware and software from different competitors to get the lowest system price. And as long as manufacturers could buy the key components, particularly Microsoft's DOS (disk operating system) and Intel's X86 family of microprocessors, they could manufacture a product that could piggyback on IBM's coattails. Between 1982 and 1986, the majority of the industry consolidated around IBM's MS-DOS/Intel X86 microprocessor standard. Among the various proprietary PC systems, which had included names like DEC, Xerox, and Wang, only Apple thrived.

Although IBM had created an open system that fostered imitators, few firms were capable of competing head-to-head with IBM. On the strength of its brand name and product quality, IBM captured almost 70 percent of the *Fortune* 1000 business market during its first four years. In addition, the personal computer was still a relatively new machine through the mid-1980s, and users were uncertain about quality, compatibility, service, and reliability. Concerns over the bankruptcies of companies, like Osborne and Leading Edge, as well as the occasional incompatible machine, led the majority of corporate buyers to buy brand-name computers through respected, high-service retail channels such as ComputerLand. Most retailers, however, only had space on their shelves for four or five major brands. In the mid-1980s, the typical retailer carried three core, premium brands: Apple, which was the leader in user friendliness and applications like desktop publishing; IBM, which was the premium-priced, industry standard; and Compaq, which built IBM-compatible machines with a strong reputation for quality and high performance. The multitude of smaller clone companies had to compete for the remaining one or two spaces on the retailer's shelf.

The early growth in PCs was built partly on rapidly changing innovative hardware and partly on exciting software applications. In its first five years, IBM and compatibles went through four major hardware product generations—the PC (based on Intel 8088), PC XT (based on 8086 and a hard drive), PC AT (based on Intel 80286), and 80386 PCs; in the meantime, Apple went from the Apple II to Macintosh—a major breakthrough in user-friendliness and functionality. The PC explosion was also fueled by software applications. Programs like Lotus 1-2-3 and WordPerfect were nicknamed "killer apps" because they were so powerful compared to their predecessors, everyone wanted them. Most of the best programs for business applications were written for

the IBM standard, while Apple dominated educational applications and graphics.

The late 1980s saw revolution turn into evolution in both hardware and software. On one front, the IBM PC standard became the MS-DOS/Intel-compatible standard. IBM tried to make PCs more proprietary in 1987 with the introduction of its PS/2 line of computers. Old IBM PC boards could not be plugged into the PS/2. Many customers, however, did not want to give up any compatibility with their prior purchases. As a result IBM faltered, losing almost half its market share. Since Intel and Microsoft provided all manufacturers with identical parts, it was IBM's clones that offered compatibility with the installed base. A new generation of PC clone manufacturers such as Dell and Gateway also found that most customers could no longer distinguish between low-priced and premium brands. Finally, the greatest differentiation in the industry had been between standards—IBM versus Apple. However, when Microsoft introduced its "Windows" 3.0 graphical user interface in 1990, the differences in user-friendliness between MS-DOS/Intel machines and Macs narrowed significantly.

By 1992, the PC business had changed from a high-growth industry to an industry with a few high-growth segments. The installed base of PCs approached 100 million units. New products, like notebook computers, and traditional products sold through new channels, like direct mail, continued to sell at double-digit growth rates. But the economics of PC manufacturing, sales, R&D, and software were fundamentally different compared to the early and mid-1980s.

MANUFACTURING AND R&D

A company could manufacture a personal computer box (with the most current, state-of-the-art microprocessor, but without a keyboard and screen) for as little as $540 in 1992. That box would typically carrry a wholesale price of $600. PC boxes with a last-generation microprocessor (i.e., an 80386) wholesaled for about $500. Firms, however, had different cost structures, which varied with their manufacturing strategy. Some firms were pure assembly operations, buying all of their components from independent vendors, while others designed and made their own computer boards. For under $1 million, an assembler could buy the equipment and lease enough space to make 200,000–300,000 PCs per year. It would cost that assembler about $480 for the boards, chassis, disk drives, and power supplies and another $60 in direct labor. If a firm designed and manufactured its own boards, the entry costs were somewhat higher. While you only needed one manufacturing line to be efficient, the initial capital costs for assembling computer boards was $5 million. One line would produce about 1000 boards per day. If the PC manufacturer produced its own boards, it could reduce the cost of the computer box by as much as $50. The price of the keyboard and monitor could add from $100 to more than $500 to the system's total costs, depending on the options. The costs of specialty PCs, like notebooks, were considerably higher. There were fewer standard components, the products required more special engineering, and there were only two major suppliers of LCD screens in the world, Japan's Sharp and Toshiba.

Location was another important variable in the manufacturing equation. Freight and duty costs for a complete system could be as much as 10–15 percent of total cost. As a result, many companies manufactured their boards in low-labor-cost locations (like Southeast Asia), then did final assembly near their market. The lowest-cost producers in the world in the early 1990s were probably the Taiwanese. Their advantages went beyond having low-cost labor. For instance, they designed their products for the lowest possible costs. Companies like Compaq, IBM, and Apple typically designed a PC to last up to 50 years, while Taiwanese engineers used a 10–15 year horizon. In addition, their overhead was usually minimal: manufacturing was often set up in warehouses rather than fancy air-conditioned factories.

R&D expenditures closely tracked a firm's manufacturing strategy. While the average R&D spending in computers was about 5 percent, PC manufacturers spent from 1 percent for a pure assembler to 8–10 percent for companies like Apple, which designed their boards, chips, and even the ergonomics of the keyboards and boxes. Since R&D costs on many key technologies were rising, there was a growing trend in the industry in the early 1990s to license technology from third parties, work collectively in consortiums, and whenever possible, buy off-the-shelf components and software rather than develop from scratch.

DISTRIBUTION AND BUYERS

Buyers of PCs could be roughly divided into three broad categories: business/government; education; and individual/home. Each customer had somewhat different criteria and different means for purchasing computers. The largest segment was business, with roughly 60 percent of the units and 70 percent of the total revenue. During the 1980s, personal computers were most often bought by individuals or small departments in corporations without much input from a corporation's MIS staff. Individual business PC buyers were usually unsophisticated about the technology and worried most about service, support, and compatibility. Brand name was especially important, and full-service computer dealers, such as Businessland and ComputerLand, built billion-dollar businesses servicing these customers.

By the early 1990s, individual business consumers had become more knowledgeable about the PC; in addition, more computers were purchased by technically trained MIS staff, who were operating under tight budgets. (See Exhibit 2.) Full-service dealers suddenly became an expensive channel. Demand exploded at "superstores" like CompuAdd and Staples as well as at mail order outlets, which offered computers and peripherals at 30–50 percent off list price. Even K Mart, Costco, and other mass merchandisers started to sell large volumes of PCs. (See Exhibit 3.) Since business organizations were increasingly demanding that their PCs be networked, another channel evolved, called value-added resellers or VARs. Most VARs were low-overhead operations that could buy computers in volume, package them with software or peripherals, and then configure the PCs into networks. Finally, some computer manufacturers bypassed third-party distribution entirely, selling directly through the mail with phone support for customer service.

The education and individual/home markets were driven by different channels and somewhat different criteria. In the early 1990s, education accounted for roughly 9 percent of units and 7 percent of revenues. While most schools had limited budgets for computers, the primary concern for most educators was the availability of appropriate software. The individual/home market comprised about 31 percent of units and 23 percent of revenues; however, the market was a complicated mixture of people who bought computers for business work at home and those who bought the computer for home uses. Most of these consumers bought PCs through mail order or other high-volume, low-priced channels.

PC MANUFACTURERS

In 1991, the four largest PC manufacturers were IBM, Apple, NEC, and Compaq, collectively accounting for roughly 37 percent of the world market. (See Exhibit 4.) But PCs were a truly global business, with more than 200 players from a dozen countries.[2] While U.S. firms had more than 60 percent of global revenues, small Taiwanese companies, like Acer, were gaining share in the very low end, and Japanese firms were the biggest players in portable computers, the fastest-growing PC segment. Toshiba, a huge Japanese conglomerate, dominated laptops (26 percent share in 1990), followed by NEC (15 percent). The United States was also the largest market for computers (39 percent), followed by Europe (36 percent) and Asia (25 percent).

In general, the majority of buyers could not easily distinguish between IBM and no-name PC brands in 1992. As a conse-

---

[2]Different geographic areas had different configurations of competitors: In North America, IBM, Apple, Compaq, and Dell had approximately 70 percent market share. In Japan, NEC had a proprietary standard, with almost 50 percent of the market. NEC had a relatively low share outside of Japan. The European market was dominated by U.S. competitors, with national champions such as Bull, Siemens, and Olivetti commanding large shares of their domestic markets.

quence, price competition had become the rule. For instance, on the same day in February of 1992, Apple and Dell Computer both slashed prices by almost 40 percent. Within a week, other competitors were cutting prices. "386" clones retailed for as little as $999.00, and "486" clones were selling for $1,600.00. Analysts repeatedly talked about a shake-out in the computer industry, yet there were no indications when and if a shakeout would occur. A few large mergers had taken place in the early 1990s, such as Groupe Bull's purchase of Zenith and AT&T's purchase of NCR. But the worldwide PC business was more fragmented in 1992 than in 1985. Despite the variety of competition, Apple's rivalry in the PC industry could be typified by three players: IBM—the worldwide leader; Compaq—the premium-priced leader in the MS-DOS/Intel segment; and Dell, a low-priced clone.

IBM　IBM's position in PCs was characteristic of many broad-line computer companies in the world, ranging from Digital Equipment to Siemens. Like its competitors in mainframes and minicomputers, IBM had a large installed base of customers that were tied to the company's highly profitable, proprietary technology. However, like most mini and mainframe companies, IBM was also a relatively high-cost producer of PCs that was struggling to create a unique position for itself in the 1990s. Despite suffering its first loss in history in 1991, IBM was still the world leader in computers, with $64 billion in revenue and the number one market share in PCs, minicomputers and mainframes (see Exhibit 5). IBM's trademark was its sweeping horizontal and vertical integration. One of the largest manufacturers of semiconductors, IBM had the largest direct sales forces in the computer industry

and sold more types of computers, software, and peripherals than any other company in the world. IBM's R&D budget of $6.6 billion exceeded the revenues of all but a few competitors. Nonetheless, IBM's market share had steadily declined in the PC business since 1984. IBM's products lost much of their differentiation as clones successfully attacked IBM with cheaper (and, in a few cases, technically superior) products; and after a dispute with Microsoft, IBM appeared to lose control over the operating system software (discussed below). To regain the initiative, IBM launched a blizzard of alliances in the 1990s, ranging from jointly developing the next generation of memory chips with Siemens and flat panel displays with Toshiba, to working with Apple on a next-generation operating system and with Motorola on microprocessors.

Compaq　Compaq got its start by selling the first successful IBM clone portable. In its very first year, Compaq generated $100 million in sales, making it the fastest-growing company in history. Compaq's subsequent growth and profitability were based on offering more power or features than comparable IBMs, usually at slightly higher prices. When Compaq launched the first PC with an Intel 80386 microprocessor, it became a trend-setter rather than just another clone. Compaq generally engineered its products from scratch, developing and manufacturing many custom components. However, Compaq did not make semiconductors, like IBM, nor did it develop software or manufacture peripherals, like Apple. Compaq was a pure PC hardware company that sold its products through full service dealers. In 1991, however, Compaq's position weakened considerably. Clones were quickly copying Compaq's PCs and even beating Compaq to market with some new products. The most damage was done by Dell Computer, which ran full-page ads in newspapers around the world suggesting that Dell offered comparable value at 50 percent off Compaq's list price. Although Compaq rarely sold its computers at list, the campaigns had a devastating impact. Compaq was put on the defensive with its customers, causing it to cut prices and streamline costs. Compaq's board fired the CEO and embarked on a new strategy of reducing costs and offering low-priced products through lower-cost channels.

Dell Computer   Michael Dell, a dropout from the University of Texas, started Dell Computer in Austin in 1984. The company's first product was an IBM PC/XT clone that it sold through computer magazines at one-half IBM's prices. From 1985 to 1990, Dell became the fastest-growing computer company in the world. By 1991, it was a half-billion-dollar company, offering a full line of PCs through direct mail. What made Dell distinctive was its unconditional money-back guarantee within 30 days, its toll-free customer service number, and a one-year contract with Xerox to provide next-day, on-site service within 100 miles of nearly 200 locations. Dell could bypass dealers because utilizing computer technology (i.e., running PCs with software tools that could tell the customer quickly how to fix a PC) could offer customers comparable or better service at much lower prices than a local dealer. Moreover, Dell generally copied Compaq or IBM's basic design while assembling the products with standard components. Yet even Dell was feeling pressure from lower-priced clones in 1992. Companies such as ALR, Packard Bell, and Gateway were doing to Dell what Dell had done to Compaq: copying the strategy with an even lower expense structure and

lower prices. Packard Bell, for instance, grew larger than Dell in 1990 by selling cheap clones exclusively through mass merchandisers; in the meantime, ALR started offering Dell clones with similar service at lower prices. Since ALR's overhead was only 14 percent of sales, with R&D of only 1.5 percent, Dell was forced to look for new ways to differentiate its products. By 1992, Dell was introducing new PCs every three weeks; its oldest product was 11 months old. Dell also planned to offer on-site service within four hours.

Suppliers

There were two categories of suppliers to the personal computer industry in the early 1990s: those supplying products that had multiple sources, like disk drives, CRT screens, keyboards, computer boards, and memory chips; and those supplying products that came from only one or two sources, particularly microprocessors and operating system software. The first category of suppliers were all producing products that had become commodities by 1992. Anyone in the world could buy memory chips or disk drives at highly competitive prices from a large number of companies, often from a wide variety of countries. Microprocessors and operating system software, on the other hand, were dominated by a small number of companies.

Every PC needed a microprocessor, which served as the brains of the computer. While several companies offered microprocessors, two companies dominated the industry: Intel, which was a sole source for the latest generation (386, 486, Pentiums) of chips for the MS-DOS standard; and Motorola, which supplied 100 percent of Apple's needs.[3] (See Exhibits 5 and 6.) Microprocessors were critical to the personal computer because in 1992, the leading software operating systems (OSs) could run only on specific chips. Most new OSs conceived since the late 1980s were developed for multiple microprocessors. But Apple's OS was originally written in the early 1980s and would run only on the Motorola chip, and Microsoft's MS-DOS would work only on Intel's X86.

Similarly, there were only two major suppliers of OSs for the PC market—Apple and Microsoft (see Exhibit 5). Since application programs like word processing or spreadsheets would have to be rewritten to run on a different operating system, even the huge PC market could not support multitude OS standards. In the early 1990s, analysts estimated that more than $40 billion in software was installed on the Intel/Microsoft standard and $4.5–$5.0 billion on the Motorola/Apple standard. For computer users to switch standards, they had to buy new hardware and software as well as incur substantial retraining costs. The economics of operating systems also made it difficult for multiple players to survive. While the marginal costs of producing software were negligible, it cost an estimated $500 million to develop a new-generation operating system, plus substantial ongoing development cost. Microsoft's dominance in this arena was based on its ability to sell to the huge installed base of Intel's X86 microprocessors, even though MS-DOS (and Windows) were widely acknowledged to be inferior to Apple's System 7. Microsoft

typically received about $15 from a manufacturer for every PC sold with MS-DOS, and approximately another $15 if the PC was sold with Windows. Finally, OSs were of little value without application programs written by independent software vendors (ISVs). The market share of an OS was critical in influencing an ISV's decision. A program written for MS-DOS, for instance, had a potential market of more than 80 million PCs; a program written for Apple's OS had roughly one-tenth the potential; and programs written for some of the other OSs, discussed below, had only one-tenth of Apple's possible market.

Events in the early 1990s suggested that the configuration of players in both microprocessors and operating systems might be changing. First, several new players entered the microprocessor arena, including imitators of Intel's chips as well as new competitors, such as IBM (with its RS6000 chip), Sun Microsystems, MIPS, and DEC. Most of these chips were designed in special ways, called RISC, which gave them some initial performance advantages over Intel and Motorola's existing products.[4] These RISC chips, however, could not run software directly compatible with Intel or Motorola in 1992. Second, there was an emerging battle over new operating systems. Microsoft's graphical user interface (GUI), Windows 3.0, worked on top of MS-DOS. Windows sold 10 million copies from its introduction in June of 1990 through March 1992, and was selling one million copies per month.

---

[3] Apple worked closely with Motorola to design their microprocessor. In addition, since Apple did not allow other vendors to make compatible products, Motorola was essentially a captive supplier to Apple.

[4] RISC stood for reduced instruction set computing. RISC chips were designed for greater speed than the traditional chips made by Intel and Motorola, known as CISC or complex instruction set computing. Intel was investing aggressively to narrow the gap.

Since Windows mimicked Apple's operating system, the differences between the Apple environment and the Microsoft/Intel world were less obvious.[5] Windows was also attracting the greatest ISV attention in the early 1990s. In the meantime, several companies were trying to compete directly with Microsoft by rewriting their operating systems to work on Intel's X86 chips. These firms included Sun and Steve Job's new company, NeXT. In addition, after IBM broke with Microsoft, it spent $1 billion to offer its own OS in 1992, called OS/2 2.0. While other vendors were not offering OSs compatible with the installed base, IBM hoped to stall Microsoft's momentum with a superior OS that would maintain compatibility with MS-DOS and Windows. Finally, both Microsoft and Apple were developing new OSs. Microsoft promised that its next product, Windows NT, would be available in late 1992. Microsoft claimed that Windows NT would match or exceed competitive products, be backward compatible with MS-DOS and Windows, and run on Intel, MIPS, and DEC microprocessors.[6] Apple's new OS, discussed below, was scheduled for release in 1994.

ALTERNATIVE TECHNOLOGIES

Like many high-technology businesses, there were a variety of substitutes either available or on the horizon. The most direct substitutes for PCs were technical workstations, powerful stand-alone computers that were used primarily by engineers for scientific applications, graphic-intensive applications, like designing airplane wings, and number-intensive applications, like financial transactions on Wall Street. Workstations comprised a highly competitive business dominated by four companies: Sun, DEC, Hewlett-Packard, and IBM. Each of these companies used their own RISC chip and incompatible OS. Historically, workstations were not only more powerful than PCs, but they were also much more expensive. By the early 1990s, all of the major workstation vendors had proclaimed that they, too, wanted to sell cheap versions of their computers for the mass market. In 1992, prices of low-end workstations dropped to less than $5000, making them competitive with high-end PCs and Macs.

Many analysts thought that much faster growth would come from other alternative technologies, like pen-based computers, palm-top computers, and mobile computing. All of these technologies were in their nascent stages in 1992. Pen-based computers allowed the user to point a stylus on a screen rather than use a keyboard. Both hardware and software innovations were required to make pen-based systems cost-effective. Microsoft had already announced a version of Windows for pen-based machines that was expected to compete with alternative OSs from a variety of start-up companies and Apple.

Hewlett-Packard and Japan's Sharp were the early entrants in the palm-top market. Their products were relatively primitive computers that could do very simple operations, like spreadsheets and word processing, as well as keep calendars and address books. Their advantage was size and price: These computers sold

---

[5] Apple had sued Microsoft over infringing its copyrights. Analysts did not expect Apple to win the lawsuit.

[6] Microsoft helped form the "ACE"—advanced computing environment—consortium in 1991 to help generate a coalition around the Windows NT OS. More than 80 computer companies originally committed to the standard; 12 months later, however, several of the leading firms broke ranks, including DEC and Dell.

for a few hundred dollars and could be carried in a shirt pocket. Sony also announced that it would offer for under $1000 portable "computer players" in 1992: book-size devices with CD audio capability that displayed text and video and ran Microsoft's MS-DOS software. Finally, several observers expected that all forms of computers would be networked in the 1990s, many with cellular phone connections. While analysts had talked about the merging of computer, telecommunications, and consumer electronics technologies for more than a decade, many industry executives believed that the integration of computers, phones, and videos would be a reality by the mid-to-late 1990s. Many consumer electronic products, like televisions, were beginning to use digital technologies, while computers were becoming sufficiently powerful to encode and manipulate video, sound, and data.

APPLE'S POSITION IN OCTOBER 1990

Apple held a peculiar position in the computer industry as it entered the 1990s. It was the only existing alternative hardware and software standard for PCs other than the MS-DOS/Intel standard. It was also unique because it was more vertically and horizontally integrated than any other PC company, with the exception of IBM. Historically, Apple designed its products, usually from scratch, specifying unique chips, disk drives, monitors, and even unusual shapes for its chassis. While it never backward integrated into semiconductors, it manufactured and assembled most of its own products in state-of-the-art factories in California, considered among the most automated and modern in the industry. In addition, Apple developed its own operating systems software

for the Mac, some of its applications software, and many of its peripherals, such as printers. About half of Apple's revenues came from overseas, and roughly half the U.S. sales were to education, where Apple had more than a 50 percent market share.

Analysts generally considered Apple's products to be easier to use, easier to network, and more versatile than comparable IBM machines. In many core software technologies like multimedia (integrating video, sound, and data), Apple had a two-year lead on vendors such as Microsoft. Since Apple controlled all aspects of the computer, from board design to software, it could offer a better computer "system" where all the parts—software, hardware, and peripherals—interacted in a coherent way. If someone bought an IBM and a clone, they could never be sure if one computer could be easily connected to another or whether two software programs from different vendors would lead the system to crash. Apple, on the other hand, gave customers a complete desktop solution. Hardware and operating system software were sold as a package, bundled together. This made Apple's customers the most loyal in the industry. As one analyst commented, "the majority of IBM and compatible users 'put up' with their machines, but Apple's customers 'love' their Macs."

Trouble started brewing, however, in the late 1980s. Apple had not aggressively lowered prices during the price war among competitors in the Microsoft/Intel standard. In addition, Apple's image as a performance leader was damaged in 1990 when Motorola, its sole source for microprocessors, was delayed in shipping its newest products. Suddenly Apple's computers looked overpriced and underpowered. And those were not the only problems, according to John Sculley:

We were increasingly viewed as the "BMW" of the computer industry. Our portfolio of Macintoshes were almost exclusively high-end, premium-priced computers that our market research suggested would continue to have limited success in penetrating the corporate marketplace. Without lower prices, we would be stuck selling to our installed base. We were also so insular that we could not manufacture a product to sell for under $3000. We constantly fell into the trap of "creeping elegance" with our NIH—not invented here—mentality. We spent more than two years, for instance, designing a portable computer that had to be "perfect." But in the end, it was a disaster—it was 18 months late and 10 pounds too heavy. Our distribution was also an issue. Five large dealers were selling 80 percent of our products. Given the evolution of the computer industry, we concluded that drastic action was necessary; there could be no sacred cows. The result was a dramatic shift in Apple's strategy and culture. We still want to change the world, but we have to transform the company and industry for it to work. We cannot permit the commoditization of this industry to continue.

THE NEW APPLE

In October of 1990, Apple began a process of repositioning its entire business. This repositioning included new financial and manufacturing policies, a new marketing mix (new products, pricing, and distribution), and new relationships with other companies, including its own subsidiaries, IBM, and a variety of Japanese firms.

New Marketing Mix The key to Apple's ongoing business, noted John Sculley, was that "Apple could no longer be a niche player. We were going to enter the mainstream with products and prices designed to regain market share." With that philosophy, Apple embarked on an ambitious strategy of expanding its product portfolio to include low-cost, low-priced computers for the larger business and individual market. With the introduction of the Mac Classic with a street price of $999 in October of 1990, Apple would be competing head-on with the clones and go for volume (see Exhibit 4). Sales of Macs rose from 9.8 percent of U.S. computer stores' unit sales in Q2 1990 to 17 percent market share one year later.

But Sculley did not believe that volume was enough. In 1990, he also appointed himself the chief technology officer, and made it a priority to get products out faster and extend the hardware and software product lines. "To build on our core differentiation," commented Sculley, "we will bring out a series of 'hit products' through the first half of the 1990s." "Hit products" were defined as new products and derivations of older products that could be produced with very rapid cycle times. Sculley believed that product turns would have to be every 6 to 12 months. By the end of 1991 he noted with pride that 80 percent of Apple volume was coming from products introduced in October of 1990. In the previous year, only 35 percent of revenue came from new products. Two more hit products were introduced in late 1991 and early 1992. The first were aggressively priced notebook computers, called Powerbooks. Notebook computers were the fastest-growing segment of the computer market since 1989, but it was a segment where Apple had previously failed. When the Powerbook shipped in October 1991, it got rave reviews. Analysts predicted the Powerbook might generate a billion dollars in revenue in its first year. Sculley's second effort was unveiled shortly thereafter. In January 1992, Apple introduced a new software product, called Quicktime, which put Apple at the forefront of multimedia technology. One month later, Apple announced software that would allow Macs to respond to commands from the human voice, without special hardware or training. In both areas, Apple was probably 12–18 months ahead of the competition.

To complement the hit products strategy, Sculley also proclaimed that Apple would restructure its distribution strategy. Apple maintained a direct sales force of approximately 300, one-third covering large corporate accounts, two-thirds focused on education and other markets. Most products, however, were still sold through computer stores. Bob Puette, president of Apple USA, described the problem succinctly: "How do we move to the Dell model without killing our existing business?" In late 1991, Apple decided that it would sell its products through superstores and started to offer limited direct end-user telephone support.

Finance and Manufacturing Apple's historical financial model was based on one simple principle, Sculley's "50-50-50" rule: If Apple could sell 50,000 Macs a month, with a gross margin of 50 percent, Apple would have a stock price of $50. In 1987, Sculley wrote in his autobiography, "It was critical to have high gross margins to pay for the huge research and development expenses to support a proprietary technology." And until 1990, Apple followed these policies religiously, achieving all of Sculley's objectives.

New, low-end products designed to gain market share as well as "hit products" with short product life cycles could not operate on the same principle. Joe Graziano, Apple's CFO remarked, "We have no choice. We must bring down our expense structure, raise our productivity, and fundamentally alter the way we do business." If Apple wanted to match the computer hardware industry's average (see Exhibit 7), it would have to cut costs drastically. Yet Apple was also a software company, which meant that Apple had less flexibility than other PC companies in cutting certain expenditures, especially R&D. Sculley nonetheless decided to trim Apple's entire cost structure before a crisis emerged. In May of 1991, Apple reduced its workforce by 10 percent or 1,560 people. But as Kevin Sullivan, S.V.P. Human Resources, explained, the cuts went much deeper:

> This was not a drive to lower expense rates in response to temporary market conditions, but rather to get cost out of the system permanently. We had to change the way we did our work . . . we attacked how we spent our money rather than reducing our expenses. Actions ranged from consolidating buildings, cutting away cafeteria subsidies, charging for the use of the Fitness Center, subcontracting the management of the Child Care Center, etc. . . . In addition, we cut some projects and activities that some people felt were important to us, especially in sales and marketing. We let people go who were very talented and doing great work, but we chose not to do that work any more. We also stated that we were going to be moving jobs out of California . . . The Campus was no longer the Center of the Universe . . . Finally, we changed many of our relationships with the channel, large accounts and developers. We got much tougher on selecting who they were and what kind of service or response they would get from us. We were building a new Apple

that had to be leaner and swifter. Finally, we had to do layoffs, and layoffs are layoffs, any way you cut it.

Part of Apple's greatest challenge was in manufacturing, which historically was a centerpiece of Apple's sole-source strategy. In the past, virtually *everything* was done in-house. But now manufacturing had new instructions: Anything that could be bought on the outside should be subcontracted rather than developed. NIH was no longer acceptable. At the same time, manufacturing facilities were expanded to build a greater variety of products that could be ramped faster to global volumes.

Relationships with Other Companies

To get a better understanding of the competitive environment, Sculley and his COO, Michael Spindler, spent nine months in 1990 visiting with the senior executives of major computer companies, including Sun, Hewlett-Packard, IBM, DEC, and the large Japanese and European companies. Sculley said, "We discovered that we were out of touch. We did not really understand open systems, how to penetrate big corporations, and we did not realize that firms like IBM had big leads in semiconductor technology." Sculley's conclusion was that Apple should build a "federation" of alliances with partners that could help leverage Apple's strengths in software, especially user-friendliness, multimedia, and networking. He said, "We have to have partners; we have to become more open; we have to penetrate a broader market or our application developers will abandon us; we have to license technologies in and be willing to license technologies out." A key to the federation concept was that the core Macintosh business would be largely separate from the new ventures and prod-

uct groups. Spindler would run the Mac business, while Sculley could operate the alliances and federation like Silicon Valley start-ups. (See Exhibit 8.) However, Apple shocked the world when it chose its first significant alliance partner—its longtime nemesis, IBM.

The Apple–IBM Joint Ventures During the summer of 1991, IBM and Apple formed two joint ventures—Taligent and Kaleida. Sculley listed four major objectives in working with IBM:

> First, we had to overcome the resistance of MIS managers in large corporations to buying Apple computers. We called this our Enterprise Systems effort. The alliance attacked this problem in three ways: (1) We got IBM's stamp of approval; (2) IBM's sales force would offer Mac communication products; and (3) we both committed to achieve "interoperability" (seamless connections between the varying IBM and Apple computers). Second, our current microprocessor technology from Motorola would not carry us through the 1990s. We saw IBM's RS6000 RISC microprocessor as the best technology in the industry. Since IBM also agreed to work with Motorola as a second source for the technology, we reduced our vulnerability from being dependent on a sole source. We would call this new generation of computers the "PowerPC." Third, we formed Taligent to develop our next generation OS, which we internally called Pink. Pink will be a major breakthrough in software technology.[7] However, to pay for Pink, we

---

[7] This new technology, known as "object-based systems," was so complicated that it would take several hundred million dollars and at least three years to complete the project. Pink promised to increase significantly a computer user's productivity

needed money and a broader market. IBM and Apple together would have the resources and large installed base. In addition, Pink would be written to run on Apple's installed base of Motorola chips, the new IBM chip, as well as the Intel X86 chips. Lastly, we formed Kaleida to create standards in multimedia technologies, like putting full motion video on the personal computer.[8]

The underlying concept of the IBM–Apple relationship was that both companies could share the costs and risks of developing new technologies, but ultimately, the parents would compete in the market place for computers. The JVs would operate independently, shipping their software products to both parents at agreed-upon transfer prices. IBM would provide the semiconductor technology while Apple would provide most of the software technology and personnel. Six months after the JV was formed, the parents appointed a CEO from IBM and COO from Apple.

Claris To help create a supply of applications for the Mac in the mid-1980s, Apple created a software subsidiary called Claris. Claris was responsible for many of the important programs for the Mac, like MacDraw and MacWrite. However, in an effort to reduce potential conflicts of in-

terest with Apple's ISVs, Sculley decided to spin off a portion of Claris to the public. Although Apple ultimately decided to keep 100 percent of Claris in 1990, it kept Claris operationally independent (see Exhibit 8). By 1992, Claris was the second leading supplier of applications to the Mac with 15 percent of the market (compared to Microsoft's 30 percent share of Mac applications) and was in the top 15 application software companies in the world. Analysts estimated that Claris had broken even on roughly $100 million in sales in 1991. As part of Sculley's strategy to be a more open computer company, Claris would not have to dedicate itself in the future to Mac applications. It could write applications for DOS, Windows, and OS/2, as well as the Mac. Although Claris was behind other companies, like WordPerfect, Lotus, and Microsoft, its goal was to be in the top five software companies by the mid-1990s.

Alliances with Japanese Firms Beyond reinvigorating its core business with the IBM alliance and expanding its application software sales, Sculley believed that Apple had to break out of the mold set by other computer companies and look for major innovations that would change the way people used computers. In the near future, Sculley argued, computers would be pervasively networked. His vision of the year 2001 saw computers, telecommunications, consumer electronics, publishing, and a variety of other technologies merging together (see Exhibit 9). Apple, he believed, had unique software technology that could exploit these linkages. Rather than everyone using general-purpose PCs in the future, computing would be increasingly specialized.

---

by making the writing of customized software applications very easy. If on schedule, Pink would probably give IBM and Apple at least a two-year lead on Microsoft. In a parallel, independent effort, Apple was developing the follow-on OS to System 7. This follow-on OS could be designed to run on multiple microprocessors, such as the RS6000.

[8]A fifth objective was highly technical—creating a joint Apple–IBM version of UNIX, which was another OS that both companies wanted to use for certain large corporate applications.

Sculley announced to the world at the Consumer Electronics Show in January of 1992 Apple's intention of creating a new era of "personal electronics" with "personal digital assistants (PDAs)." In describing the product concept, Sculley recalled the words of Dr. Edwin Land of Polaroid, who said, "We really don't invent new products, but the best ones are there already, only invisible, just waiting to be discovered." In this vein, Apple would introduce an executive organizer that would fit in the palm of your hand and keep track of telephone numbers, calendars, and so on. It would have built-in wireless communications and would have the capability of displaying best selling book titles. Other products would include portable MultiMedia Players that used computer and CD technology, and a portable pen-based computing product. Sculley even suggested at the public gathering that Apple would license its GUI and operating systems for other companies' consumer electronic products, possibly including digital television.

These types of computing and consumer electronics products, however, required expertise that exceeded Apple's core skills and competencies. While Apple could pioneer the computing hardware and software technologies, it lacked distribution and marketing expertise for consumer electronics, LCD display technology needed for hand-held computers, and very low-cost manufacturing for miniaturized products. For these new technologies to be successful, analysts speculated that they would have to be priced under $500. Given the ambitious nature of these projects, Sculley also believed that no one company could pursue all of these avenues by itself. Sony had already manufactured one of Apple's new portable computers, and a number of other Japanese companies might be candidate partners to work with Apple in this new realm.

GOING FORWARD IN 1992

Sculley told his sales force in late 1991, "The industry must once again become innovation driven, move away from commodity status, and provide value-added products and services. I believe Apple has a chance to make the difference. In fact, Apple may be one of the few great hopes for turning things around." The questions Sculley posed in March 1992 were: Can our actions to date achieve the objective of changing the industry structure? Would other steps be necessary? Was it even required that Apple change the industry structure to be successful in the future? And were there other alternatives that Apple might consider?

EXHIBIT 1
DETAILED FINANCIALS OF APPLE OVER TIME

	1991	1990	1989	1988	1987	1986	1985	1984	1983	1982	1981
Total revenues ($ millions)	$ 6,309	$ 5,558	$ 5,284	$4,071	$2,661	$1,902	$1,918	$1,516	$ 983	$ 583	$ 334
Cost of sales	3,314	2,606	2,695	1,991	1,296	891	1,118	879	506	288	170
Research and development	583	478	421	273	192	128	72.5	71	60	38	21
Marketing and distribution	1,740	1,556	1,340	908	655	477	478	399	230	120	55
General and administrative	224	207	195	180	146	133	110	82	57	35	22
Operating income	447	712	634	620	371	274	103	86	130	102	66
Net income	310	475	454	400	218	154	61.3	64.1	77	61	39
Property, plant, equipment, and other	275	321	284	186	121	67	66	53	64	30	NA
Depreciation and amortization	204	202	124	77	70	51	41	37	22	16	NA
Cash dividends paid	56	53	50	39	15	—	—	—	—	—	NA
Cash and temporary cash investment	893	997	809	546	565	576	337	115	143	153	73
Accounts receivable	907	762	793	639	406	263	220	258	136	72	42
Inventories	672	356	475	461	226	109	167	265	142	81	104
Property, plant, and equipment	448	398	334	207	130	222	176	150	110	57	31
Total assets	3,494	2,976	2,744	2,082	1,478	1,160	936	789	557	358	255
Total current liabilities	1,217	1,027	895	827	479	138	90	255	129	86	70
Total shareholders' equity	1,767	1,447	1,486	1,003	837	694	550	465	378	257	177
Permanent employees	12,386	12,307	12,068	9,536	6,236	4,950	4,326	5,382	4,645	3,391	2,456
International sales/sales (%)	45	42	36	32	27	26	22	22	22	24	27
Gross margin/sales (%)	47	53	49	51	51	53	42	42	49	51	49
R&D/sales (%)	9	9	8	7	7	7	4	5	6	7	6
ROS* (%)	4.91	8.55	8.59	9.83	8.19	8.10	3.20	4.23	7.83	10.46	11.68
ROA† (%)	8.87	15.96	16.55	19.21	14.75	13.28	6.55	8.12	13.82	17.04	15.29
Return on equity (%)	19	32	36	44	28	28	12	15	24	28	44
Stock price range	40.5–73.3	24.3–47.8	32.5–50.4	35.5–47.75	20.3–59.8	10.8–22	7.3–15.6	10.8–17.25	8.6–31.6	5.5–7.5	6.8–7.3
PE/ratio	12.9	10.5	12.9	13.6	20.3	11.6	22.1	26.7	30.6	16.1	24.3
Market value‡	6,751	4,150	5,166	5,033	4,914	2,004	1,360	1,694	2,368	742	1,320

Sources: Apple annual reports and Value Line.
*ROS = net income/total revenues.
†ROA = net income/total assets.
‡Year-end stock price times the number of shares outstanding.

EXHIBIT 2
PC CONSUMER PREFERENCES—MAJOR BRANDS (TIER I) VERSUS OTHER SECONDARY
COMPANIES—BASELINE STUDY (MARCH 1991–MAY 1991)

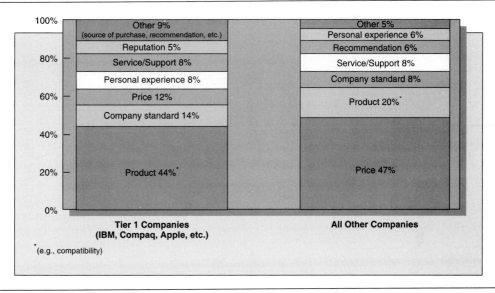

Source: Compiled from Intellitrack data, 1991.

EXHIBIT 3
PC DISTRIBUTION CHANNEL BREAKDOWN*

	Direct	Dealer	Superstore	VAR	Mass Merchant	Consumer Electronics	Mail Order
(%) of Total Unit Shipments							
1987	17.4	58.9	0	11.3	3.4	4.1	4.3
1988	12.3	61.7	0	12.4	3.9	4.3	4.8
1989	8.6	63.2	0	13.9	4.1	4.7	4.8
1990	8.0	58.3	1.1	14.7	5.2	5.2	6.1
1991	7.9	55.7	2.0	15.2	6.4	6.4	6.2
1992[†]	8.3	51.6	2.9	15.7	7.5	7.5	6.2
(%) of Total Value Shipments							
1987	31.0	49.0	0	13.2	1.4	1.8	2.3
1988	25.3	52.9	0	14.3	1.7	1.9	3.2
1989	17.3	56.9	0	17.1	1.9	2.1	3.7
1990	18.4	52.7	0.7	18.0	2.9	2.5	5.1
1991	14.7	51.7	1.6	18.7	3.9	3.7	4.6
1992[†]	14.4	50.0	2.5	19.0	4.1	4.0	4.9

Source: Compiled from International Data Corporation data, 1991.

*Estimated sales do not equal 100% because of rounding.

[†]Projected figures.

EXHIBIT 4
ESTIMATED PC WORLDWIDE MARKET SHARE RANKED BY MANUFACTURER REVENUE*

Rank	Company	1981	1982	1983	1984	1985	1986	1987	1988	1989	1990	1991
1	IBM	6.04%	11.47%	21.34%	29.96%	29.04%	25.28%	25.27%	21.54%	18.65%	17.94%	16.05%
2	Apple	8.82	7.34	7.10	10.10	8.78	7.98	7.99	8.83	9.98	10.22	10.49
3	NEC	3.92	4.30	4.79	4.64	6.33	6.70	7.11	6.04	5.65	5.81	5.79
4	Compaq	0.00	0.00	0.73	1.52	2.25	2.48	3.47	4.93	5.36	4.77	4.44
5	Olivetti	2.27	2.08	1.76	1.28	2.63	3.37	3.14	3.12	2.79	2.92	3.10
6	Toshiba	0.60	1.68	0.94	0.46	0.24	0.74	1.32	1.58	1.68	2.44	2.72
7	Epson	0.00	0.01	0.41	0.62	0.66	0.96	1.26	1.81	2.11	2.39	2.67
8	Tandy	10.57	10.42	7.22	3.92	4.32	3.66	3.14	2.81	3.28	2.38	2.57
9	AT&T	0.63	0.35	0.39	0.98	3.18	3.24	2.95	2.70	2.13	1.92	2.09
10	Zenith	2.03	1.65	1.30	1.24	1.71	2.31	2.78	3.05	2.60	1.70	1.79
11	Philips	0.73	0.59	0.97	0.98	1.33	1.70	1.45	1.25	1.60	1.83	1.75
12	Siemens	0.00	0.00	0.01	0.05	0.26	0.62	1.14	1.45	1.51	1.58	1.62
13	HP	2.66	2.25	2.26	2.66	2.70	2.20	1.44	1.74	1.81	1.67	1.58
14	Acer	0.27	0.63	0.25	0.21	0.28	0.53	0.92	1.28	1.29	1.34	1.30
15	Packard Bell	0.00	0.00	0.00	0.00	0.00	0.01	0.04	0.13	0.72	1.05	1.20
16	Unisys	0.64	2.57	2.27	2.74	2.87	2.27	2.01	1.81	1.58	1.36	1.11
17	Dell	0.00	0.00	0.00	0.02	0.11	0.23	0.46	0.63	0.74	0.99	1.10
18	Other	60.83%	54.66%	48.26%	38.62%	33.30%	35.71%	34.13%	35.29%	36.54%	37.68%	38.18%

ESTIMATED PC WORLDWIDE MARKET SHARE BY INSTALLED UNITS*

Company	1981	1982	1983	1984	1985	1986	1987	1988	1989	1990	1991
IBM	1.35%	2.73%	4.60%	8.64%	11.09%	12.07%	13.12%	13.68%	13.68%	13.36%	12.81%
Apple	8.85	6.65	6.09	7.80	8.27	8.22	8.23	8.21	7.98	7.63	7.90
NEC	4.28	3.55	3.77	4.53	5.23	5.53	5.63	5.51	5.35	4.97	4.79
Compaq	0.00	0.00	0.27	0.70	1.08	1.37	1.66	2.04	2.38	2.57	2.74
Olivetti	1.78	1.03	0.78	0.68	0.99	1.25	1.50	1.69	1.79	1.72	1.66
Toshiba	0.29	0.86	0.84	0.74	0.68	0.77	0.83	0.98	1.18	1.59	1.98
Epson	0.00	0.01	0.18	0.38	0.50	0.70	0.95	1.36	1.85	2.18	2.40
Tandy	0.00	0.00	0.00	0.00	0.00	0.12	0.33	0.48	0.64	0.80	0.89
AT&T	0.26	0.10	0.09	0.25	0.79	1.08	1.24	1.34	1.33	1.24	1.20
Zenith	0.98	0.66	0.53	0.56	0.80	1.14	1.60	2.02	2.18	2.05	1.96
Philips	0.20	0.19	0.22	0.25	0.38	0.53	0.62	0.76	0.91	1.03	1.08
Siemens	0.00	0.00	0.00	0.02	0.06	0.14	0.27	0.41	0.53	0.61	0.68
HP	1.29	1.00	0.96	1.08	1.19	1.20	1.07	1.04	0.92	0.84	0.84
Acer	0.21	0.20	0.13	0.16	0.25	0.44	0.76	1.12	1.37	1.55	1.68
Packard Bell	0.00	0.00	0.00	0.00	0.00	0.00	0.02	0.07	0.34	0.58	0.80
Unisys	0.18	0.33	0.36	0.46	0.51	0.60	0.71	0.75	0.76	0.70	0.65
Dell	0.00	0.00	0.00	0.01	0.05	0.11	0.23	0.30	0.38	0.47	0.59
Other	80.32%	82.69%	81.18%	73.73%	68.14%	64.73%	61.23%	58.24%	56.43%	56.12%	55.34%

Source: Adapted from InfoCorp data.

*Market share includes all computer sales under $12,000. Commodore and Sharp have been included in the "other" category even though their share exceeds 1 percent. However, both companies derive a large percentage of their revenues from nontraditional computer products (e.g., palmtop computers, organizers, and computers designed primarily for entertainment), which are not directly comparable to IBM PCs and Macs.

EXHIBIT 5
SELECTED COMPETITOR/SUPPLIER FINANCIAL STATISTICS—1982–1992 ($ MILLIONS)

IBM	**1991**	**1990**	**1988**	**1986**	**1984**	**1980**
Revenues	$64,792	$69,018	$59,681	$51,250	$45,937	$26,213
Cost of goods sold	32,474	30,723	25,648	22,706	18,919	10,149
R&D expense	6,644	6,554	5,925	5,221	4,200	1,520
Selling, general, and administrative	24,732	20,709	19,362	15,464	11,587	8,804
Net income	−2,827	6,020	5,491	4,789	6,582	3,563
Total assets	92,473	87,568	73,037	63,020	42,808	26,703
Long-term debt	13,231	11,943	8,518	6,923	3,269	2,099
Stockholders' equity	37,006	42,832	39,509	34,374	26,489	16,453
ROS %*	−4.4	8.7	9.2	9.3	14.3	13.6
ROA %[†]	−3.1	6.8	7.5	7.6	15.4	13.3
ROE %[‡]	−7.6	14.8	14.9	14.4	26.5	22.7
Stock prices ($/share)						
High	139.8	123.1	130	162	128.5	72.8
Low	92	94.5	104.5	119	99	50.4
P/E ratio	21.2	10.4	11.9	18	10.6	10.4
Market valuation[§]	50,285	64,523	70,210	72,720	75,399	39,115

Compaq	**1991**	**1990**	**1988**	**1986**	**1984**	
Revenues	$ 3,271	$ 3,598	$ 2,066	$ 625	$ 329	
Cost of goods sold	2,054	2,058	1,233	361	232	
R&D expense	197	185	75	27	11	
Selling, general, and administrative	721	706	397	152	66	
Net income	131	455	255	43	13	
Total assets	2,826	2,717	1,589	378	231	
Long-term debt	73	74	275	73	0	
Stockholders' equity	NA	1,859	815	183	109	
ROS %*	4	12.6	12.3	6.9	3.9	
ROA %[†]	4.6	16.7	16	11.3	5.6	
ROE %[‡]	6.9	30	42	26.8	12.9	
Stock prices ($/share)						
High	74.3	68	33	10.8	7.3	
Low	29.9	35.5	21	5.8	1.8	
P/E ratio	28.2	10.3	8.9	11.7	14.5	
Market valuation[§]	2,244	4,859	4,312	1,026	325	

Dell Computer[‖]	**1992**	**1991**	**1990**	**1989**	**1988**	**1987**
Revenues	$ 890	$ 546	$ 389	$ 258	$ 159	$ 70
Cost of goods sold	608	364	279	176	109	54
R&D expense	33	22	17	7	6	2
Selling, general, and administrative	180	114	80	50	27	10
Net income	51	27	5	14	9	2
Total assets	560	264	172	167	56	24
Long-term debt	42	0	0	0	0	0
Stockholders' equity	274	112	80	75	9	3
ROS (%)*	5.7	4.9	1.3	5.4	5.7	28.6
ROA (%)[†]	11.9	10.2	2.9	8.4	16.1	8.3
ROE (%)[‡]	18.6	24.1	6.3	18.7	100	66.7
Stock prices ($/share)						
High	NA	36.3	18.8	10.6	12.6	NA
Low	NA	15.8	4.6	5	7.7	NA
P/E ratio	NA	13.2	8.3	26	12.5	NA
Market valuation[#]	900	614	339	108	187	NA

EXHIBIT 5 (continued)

Intel	1991	1990	1988	1986	1984	1982
Revenues	$4,778	$3,921	$2,875	$1,265	$1,629	$ 900
Cost of goods sold	1,898	1,638	1,295	687	774	467
R&D expense	618	517	318	228	180	131
Selling, general, and administrative	765	616	456	311	316	NA
Net income	818	650	453	−173	198	30
Total assets	6,292	5,276	3,550	2,080	2,029	1,056
Long-term debt	363	345	479	287	146	197
Stockholders' equity	4,558	3,592	2,080	1,275	1,360	552
ROS %*	17.0	17.0	16.0	−14.0	12.0	3.0
ROA %[†]	13	12.3	12.8	−10.3	9.8	2.8
ROE %[‡]	20.4	18.1	21.8	−16.3	14.6	5.4
Stock prices ($/share)						
High	59.3	52	37.3	21.5	29	13.8
Low	37.8	28	19.3	10.9	16.5	6.9
P/E ratio	11	12.3	11.4	NA	21.2	48.7
Market valuation[§]	10,045	7,600	4,344	3,717	4,788	5,032

Microsoft	1991	1990	1988	1986	1984	1982
Revenues	$ 1,843	$ 1,183	$ 591	$ 197	$ 98	$ 25
Cost of goods sold	363	253	148	41	23	NA
R&D expense	235	181	70	21	11	NA
Selling, general, and administrative	596	357	185	76	35	NA
Net income	463	279	124	39	16	4
Total assets	1,644	1,105	493	170	48	15
Long-term debt	0	0	0	2	1	0
Stockholders' equity	1,350	1,105	493	171	31	8
ROS* (%)	25.1	23.6	20.9	19.7	16.3	16.0
ROA[†] (%)	28.2	25.2	25	22.9	33.3	23.3
ROE[‡] (%)	40.8	37.7	40.3	40.5	70	62.1
Stock prices ($/share)						
High	115	53.9	23.5	8.5	NA	NA
Low	49	28	5.2	6.5	NA	NA
P/E ratio	22.6	19.9	25.2	19.5	NA	NA
Market valuation[§]	19,380	12,788	8,533	NA	NA	NA

Sources: *Value Line* and companies' annual reports.

*ROS = net income/total revenues.

[†]ROA = net income/total assets.

[‡]ROE = net income/total stockholders' equity.

[§]Number of shares outstanding (*Value Line* 1992) times the year-end stock price (NYSE and OTC daily stock price reports).

[||]Fiscal year ends in February.

[#]Market capitalization as of March 17th.

EXHIBIT 6
SHIPMENTS AND INSTALLED BASE OF VARIOUS MICROPROCESSORS, 1981–1991 (MILLION UNITS)

	1981	*1982*	*1983*	*1984*	*1985*	*1986*	*1987*	*1988*	*1989*	*1990*	*1991*
Intel X86 microprocessors											
Shipments											
Units shipped	0	0.2	1	2.6	3.7	5.5	10.2	14	16.1	18.3	20.2
Installed base	0	0.2	1.2	3.7	7.4	12.9	23.1	37	53.1	71.4	91.6
Motorola microprocessors											
Shipments											
Units shipped	0	0	0	0.5	0.7	0.9	1.2	1.6	1.8	2.9	3.3
Installed base	0	0	0.1	0.5	1.3	2.2	3.4	5	6.4	9.3	12.6
RISC											
Units shipped	0	0	0	0	0	0	0	0	0	0.2	0.4
Installed base	0	0	0	0	0	0	0	0	0.1	0.3	0.7

Source: Adapted from InfoCorp, 1992.

EXHIBIT 7
AVERAGE OPERATING RATIOS IN 1990*

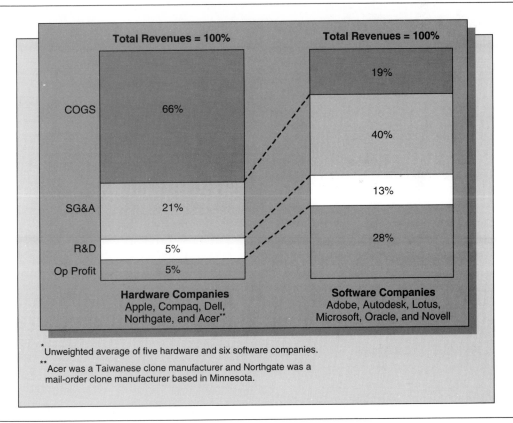

*Unweighted average of five hardware and six software companies.

**Acer was a Taiwanese clone manufacturer and Northgate was a mail-order clone manufacturer based in Minnesota.

Sources: Morgan Stanley; DLJ; annual reports.

EXHIBIT 8
APPLE'S FEDERATION CONCEPT

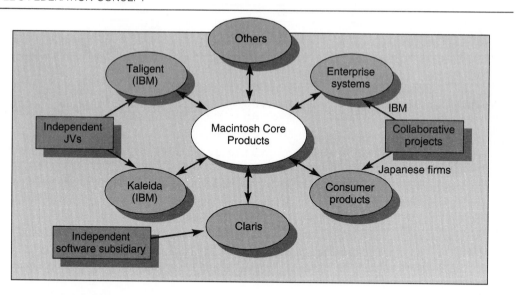

Source: Casewriter's representaiton.

EXHIBIT 9
INFO INDUSTRY, 2001: FUSION POWERED

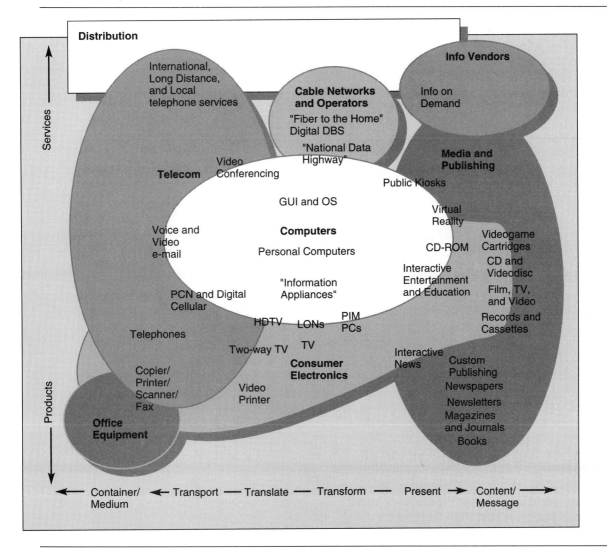

Source; Presentation by John Sculley at Harvard University—program on Information Resources Policy, 1992.

Bill Gates and the Management of Microsoft

*Despite the fact that we've been success-
ful financially, there's an ongoing need
to anticipate where this industry is going, and to be at the forefront of changing
the products. And this is every bit as
challenging as it's ever been—and perhaps more so.*

—Bill Gates, Microsoft Chairman
and CEO, 1991

On June 30, 1991, Microsoft Corporation closed the books on another year of
dazzling growth. Revenues for the Redmond, Washington, software developer
surpassed $1.8 billion, up 56 percent from
the previous year, and 10 times the level
of 1986 (see Exhibit 1). Profitability remained exceptionally high, with net income reaching $463 million, 25 percent of
revenues (see Exhibit 2).

The founder and chief executive of this
company was 35-year old William H. (Bill)
Gates III, arguably the most influential
person in the computer industry. He was
also one of the wealthiest Americans, owning 30 percent of Microsoft stock with a
market value of $4 billion. Under Gates's
leadership, Microsoft had successfully
navigated the transition from a start-up
firm to a major corporation. The dominant
supplier of personal computer (PC) operating system software during the 1980s,
Microsoft had by the end of the decade
surpassed such competitors as Lotus Development Corporation in sales of applications software. The release in 1990 of
Windows 3.0, which enabled applications
programs to work together in a user-
friendly graphics environment, had been
a spectacular success, selling over three
million copies in its first year. Microsoft's
success was reflected in a stock price of 30
times earnings, well above the industry
average. Adjusting for splits, the stock
price had increased by a factor of 20 since
the company went public in 1986 (see
Exhibit 3).

Looking ahead, however, Microsoft confronted a fresh set of challenges. It had
expanded into new areas, including networking and consulting, and faced in-

creasingly strong competition from a growing number of firms. Product development was becoming more complex and demanded an integrated approach that was not part of the company's tradition. In addition, Microsoft's sheer growth imposed a number of organizational and managerial challenges. As Gates and his top management team developed their strategy for the 1990s, they recognized that further transitions would be necessary to ensure continuing success.

MICROSOFT: THE EARLY DAYS

Bill Gates was the middle child of a prominent Seattle family. As a boy he attended the Lakeside School, where he was introduced to computers. Along with several other classmates, including Paul Allen, Gates spent many free hours and evenings learning about computing and programming. By the time Gates was 14, he and Allen had developed an expertise as programmers and had formed their own company.

In 1973, Gates began his college studies at Harvard. The next year, Paul Allen moved to the Boston area and took a job with Honeywell. Both were convinced that huge opportunities lay ahead in the computer industry, and they looked for an opportunity to which they could apply their programming talents. The right opportunity soon materialized. Stopping at a newsstand in Harvard Square in the autumn of 1974, Allen spotted the current issue of *Popular Electronics* with a headline trumpeting the "World's First Microcomputer Kit." The machine was the Altair 8080, marketed by a small company called MITS, with a price tag of $397. Built around an Intel 8080 microprocessor, the Altair was little more than a set of boards and switches. It came with neither a screen

nor a keyboard and contained only 256 bytes of memory, expandable to 4K. A further limitation was that the Altair could be programmed only in the complex 8080 machine-level language. A first step toward making the Altair usable was to provide it with a programming language.

Excited by the opportunity, Gates and Allen threw their energies into the development of a BASIC language for the Altair, no small challenge given the 4K memory constraint. After long days and nights of programming, they accomplished their goal, and licensed the resulting program to MITS. A few months later, Allen moved to New Mexico to work more closely with MITS, and Gates followed the next year, abandoning his studies at Harvard.

Gates and Allen recognized that the Altair was only the beginning in a computing revolution. Intel's 8080 was a considerable improvement over its predecessor, the 8008, but was only one of many steps in the ongoing improvement of semiconductor technology. Integrated circuits were growing exponentially in power and were simultaneously dropping in price. If that trend continued, Gates and Allen reasoned, at some point in the future computers would be infinitely powerful and would cost nothing. And if computer hardware were available to everyone, then computer software would become the scarce resource. Rather than focus on building hardware, as their peers at Apple were doing, Gates and Allen decided to devote themselves to developing software. In 1975, Microsoft was created as a partnership, with Gates owning 60 percent to Allen's 40 percent, reflecting Gates's greater share of the development of BASIC.

For the next three years, Gates and Allen lived in Albuquerque and developed other languages for the 8080, including FORTRAN and COBOL. Along the way, they hired a few additional programmers. In 1977 Microsoft developed BASIC for Tandy's TRS-80 computer and also licensed a version of BASIC for a new personal computer called the Apple II. Two years later, with sales continuing to grow and the company expanding in size, Microsoft moved its operations from New Mexico and set up shop in an office building in Bellevue, Washington, near Seattle. By 1980 the firm had 38 employees and revenues of $8 million. In addition to his duties as a programmer, Gates took responsibility for marketing and negotiations. Sensing a need to bolster the company's management, he contacted a friend from Harvard days, Steve Ballmer, and for a 6 percent stake in the company brought him aboard as assistant to the president. In time, Ballmer became indispensable to Gates as a sounding board, marketing expert, and coleader.

In 1980, IBM began to develop its own personal computer and needed an operating system. It contacted a number of software firms and, not wanting to rely on a single operating system, chose three. Among them was Microsoft's entry, called MS-DOS (Microsoft Disk Operating System). Because the success of an operating system depended on the popularity of applications programs that used it, Gates worked feverishly over the next several months with independent software firms, urging, prodding, and cajoling them to develop a family of products that would run on MS-DOS. The effort paid off—MS-DOS became the most popular operating system and eventually the de facto industry standard. "Believe me, it was not IBM who made MS-DOS the standard," Gates asserted. "It was up to us to get people to focus their development on it, and to get

other PC manufacturers to license it." Soon every IBM PC and IBM-compatible PC was sold with MS-DOS, bringing a steady flow of royalties to Microsoft. By 1990, there were more than 70 million users of MS-DOS PCs worldwide.

During the early 1980s Microsoft consisted of a small band of bright young software developers. The prevailing credo, according to one long-time employee, was "reverence for the developer." The tone at Microsoft reflected the qualities of its leader: self-assured, energetic, creative, and intense. The atmosphere was informal but hard-driving, passionate about software development, and highly competitive. Employees worked long hours, often staying overnight developing key products. Their drive was based on a love of the product, not on projections that Microsoft would one day make them wealthy. Salaries were modest, and as revenues grew, there was a need to let employees earn shares of the company. As a partnership, Microsoft could not easily distribute shares, so in 1981 Microsoft incorporated, with Bill Gates the chairman and CEO. Paul Allen held the largest number of shares after Gates, and continued to work actively in programming until 1983, when he was diagnosed with Hodgkin's disease and took a leave of absence from the company.

Looking back on those early days, one veteran employee remembered, "When I joined Microsoft in 1981, we used to argue about whether there could ever be a $100 million PC software company. It didn't seem possible at the time." But Gates never doubted the potential market for PC software. He predicted publicly in 1981 that Microsoft would surpass $100 million in revenues by 1985. In fact, 1985 revenues reached $140 million.

Building Management Systems

By 1982, Microsoft had 220 employees and revenues of $24 million. Expanding beyond operating systems software, which controlled the inner working of the computer, the firm introduced its first applications software product: Microsoft Multiplan electronic worksheet. But the firm was reaching the limits of its administrative capacity. Microsoft needed more than brilliant software developers—it also needed management processes to handle the growing administrative, financial, and logistical duties. "When Bill realized we had crossed a certain point," one employee recalled, "he knew he needed professional managers."

In July of 1982, Gates hired James F. Towne, an experienced manager at Tektronix, Inc., as Microsoft's president and chief operating officer (COO). The relationship between Gates and Towne did not work well, in part because Gates was very product-oriented and found it difficult to communicate with an executive from a different industry. Within a year Gates decided that a change had to be made, and Towne resigned. As a replacement, Gates chose Jon Shirley, a 25-year veteran of Tandy and at the time its vice president of Computer Merchandising. Gates had known Shirley for years, as Tandy had been a retail outlet for Microsoft products. Among his peers, Shirley was regarded as "the ultimate businessman": professional in manner and experienced in running a business.

Jeff Raikes, a veteran software developer, recalled:

> Bill always had a high degree of respect for Jon. Jon was someone who loved computer products, but he also had knowledge of marketing, of finance, and

of the computer industry. Plus, Jon was a known quantity, and it was extremely important for Bill to hire a known quantity at that time. What if Bill had made a mistake with a second COO? Would he ever have had the confidence to get a third COO?

Hiring Jon Shirley turned out to be an excellent choice. Industry watcher Stewart Alsop noted, "As you watch how Microsoft has developed, what you see is Gates realizing well in advance what he's not good at and finding exactly the right person to do the job. [When Towne left] Gates went out and hired Jon Shirley. And he was absolutely the right guy ... The process of identifying the mistake, figuring out the problem, and fixing it is what makes Bill Gates different. I've seen him do it over and over again."

When Shirley joined Microsoft in 1983, he found little of the infrastructure needed to run a $50 million business. Corporate accounting was handled on an outdated Radio Shack PC. Orders were entered on a time-share system based in San Francisco that was frequently inaccessible. The manufacturing operation was little more than a parts warehouse from which work was subcontracted.

"I was hired to give Bill more time, to take things he worried about off his back," Shirley recalled. Leaving Gates to focus on the technical side of Microsoft, Shirley set about building the financial, manufacturing, and human resources systems. One of his first moves was to hire Frank Gaudette as Microsoft's first chief financial officer (CFO). Gaudette put in place a managerial accounting system that tracked revenues and expenses by each product and each sales channel, providing exceptional visibility for decision making. It also extended profit and loss responsibility to as many managers as possible and was flexible enough to accommodate a rapidly growing company. "One of the smartest things Bill ever did was bring in business people and let them do their thing," Gaudette remarked.

Microsoft's compensation policy continued to emphasize employee participation in the company's fortunes. In addition to salaries, which were somewhat below industry levels, new employees received a sizable stock grant that vested fully over four and a half years. After three years, employees were considered for an additional stock grant. While some prospective employees were reluctant to accept a lower salary than available elsewhere, others found the principle of participating in the firm's growth to their liking.

By 1985, Microsoft employees numbered over 1,000. Gaudette remembered:

> Shortly after I got here, Bill said to me, "Frank, I don't know everybody's name anymore." He acted like that was bad. I said, "Bill, we can make it small again if that's what you really want."

Despite its surging growth, Microsoft tried to retain the feel of a small firm. Once a year, all Microsoft employees came together for a presentation from top management. At Christmas time, employees gathered for a holiday party; in the summer, they held picnics. Many employees cited the extensive use of electronic (e-) mail as an important element of direct and open communication: Employees used e-mail to communicate directly to Gates and Shirley on a variety of issues, and typically received answers quickly and personally.

But Microsoft's informal manner belied its intense atmosphere. "The Microsoft style is pretty aggressive," remarked one manager. "People jump on each other all the time—but it's not personal. It's a challenging, aggressive style." Stories abounded of combative meetings and "yelling matches" between groups of software developers, each advocating features for coming products. Critical e-mail messages, often sarcastic or sharp in tone, were known around the company as "flame mail."

Young Developers, Experienced Managers

"We're in the intellectual property business," Gates remarked. "It's the effectiveness of developers that determines our success." Because of the constant need to develop new and better products, hiring top talent and quickly bringing their contributions on-line was a top priority. Gates described Microsoft's approach:

> We've always had the most aggressive approach of any software company in finding people with high IQs and bringing them in. We wanted to be known as *the* software company that knew how to take people right out of college and turn talent and energy into a good development engineer. That was very explicit. We also pushed to the absolute limit the number of smart people that we brought in from overseas. It was also explicit that we design a development methodology that was not dependent on a few prima donnas but that could make use of many people's talent.

Steve Ballmer took a leadership role in college recruiting, seeking out bright graduates with high aptitude for problem solving under pressure. In contrast to its practice of hiring software developers out of college, Microsoft often sought for key managerial positions people with significant industry experience. In addition to

Shirley and Gaudette, key managers in marketing and international positions had substantial experience. "Although the software industry was new, and we were creating the rules," Gates recalled, "we found that the business experience these people had was very valuable."

Software Development

As the company grew, Gates remained in charge of product development, overseeing directly the development of systems software and applications software. He was a demanding manager with strong ideas about the future of personal computing and about specific features of new products. Product review meetings with Gates, known as "Bill meetings," were legendary, characterized by sharp and relentless questioning, stinging criticism, and ambitious deadlines. But along with a reputation for being abrupt and hard-driving, Gates was also described by a long-time software developer as attentive to individual needs:

> Bill is not a nerd like some people think. He can be very attuned to personal issues. He can go in and pump you up and make you feel that you're handling a really great mission for the company. There's great attention to keeping people happy.

Unlike its early language products, such as BASIC, and its operating system, MS-DOS, several of Microsoft's products were not immediately successful. Its first applications program, Multiplan, was intended to overtake the popular spreadsheet, Visi-Calc, but was soon overtaken by an even stronger program, Lotus Development Corporation's popular 1-2-3, and registered disappointing sales. In 1983, Microsoft began to focus on a graphics user interface, a system by which users could interact easily with computers. In 1985, after lengthy delays in development, Microsoft introduced Windows, a graphics-based operating environment that ran on MS-DOS and allowed users to run several programs at the same time. Windows used drop-down menus and icons that gave users visually oriented tools for easy interaction with their computers. The first version of Windows, however, was slow, had poor graphics, and met with only limited success. In subsequent years, new versions of operating systems and applications products were released with improved features and greater efficiency.

During the mid-1980s, Microsoft released updated versions of MS-DOS, along with applications software products including Excel (spreadsheet), Word (word processing), and Works (multi-purpose software). Microsoft products were sold through two channels: original equipment manufacturers (OEMs) and retailers. The OEM channel comprised computer manufacturers who bundled Microsoft operating systems with their products. OEM sales provided Microsoft with a steady flow of royalty income. The retail channel consisted of stores that stocked their shelves with applications programs such as spreadsheets and word processing programs. The mix of revenues among these channels reflected an increasing reliance on applications (see Exhibits 4 and 5), which reached 48 percent in 1990. In addition, Microsoft had aggressively established subsidiaries abroad in the early 1980s, and by 1989 foreign sales exceeded U.S. sales.

By 1988, Microsoft had overtaken major competitors such as Lotus Development Corp., VisiCorp, MicroPro, and Ashton-Tate to become the market leader in PC applications software as well as operating systems software (see Exhibit 6). While its spreadsheet program, Excel, remained second to Lotus 1-2-3, and its word processing program, Word, ranked second to WordPerfect, Microsoft was in first place overall. Gates credited Microsoft's success to its commitment to graphics user interface and to its efficient development process.

Management Accounting

Microsoft's philosophy of personal responsibility was reinforced by a management accounting system in which, as CFO Frank Gaudette stressed, "Everyone has a profit and loss statement." Under this system, all revenues and costs, identified by product and by sales channel, were fed into a single, consolidated ledger. This database was then exploded into many P/L statements, each focusing on a particular business unit, marketing channel, or geographic area. Every business unit manager, channel manager, and foreign subsidiary manager had a profit and loss statement which revealed his or her contribution to Microsoft's bottom line. For example, the sale of an Excel spreadsheet through the retail channel would appear as revenue in two places: the analysis business unit and the retail channel. The same held for the OEM sales of MS-DOS in Germany: Both the systems business unit and the German subsidiary recorded the sale as revenue, from which each deducted its controllable and allocated costs to determine its contribution to Microsoft profits.

Microsoft's largest discretionary cost was for marketing, and was controlled according to a strict formula: 12 percent of targeted revenues were budgeted for marketing expenses, with occasional exceptions made for major product introduc-

tions, variations across countries, or for opportunities to gain market share. The marketing budget was divided between product marketing (roughly 60 percent) and channel marketing (roughly 40 percent). Expenses were monitored closely, with managers responsible not only for meeting profitability targets but also for meeting each line item of expense. Actual sales and expense figures could be reviewed via an on-line system, which displayed results according to product, channel, and geographic region. Frank Gaudette provided a monthly review of financial results for the board, which also met quarterly to review Microsoft's financial performance. Although Gates left the analysis of week-to-week financial results to others, he examined monthly and quarterly results in detail. "At the quarterly meetings," said Gaudette, "Bill zeroes in on everything."

GENERAL MANAGEMENT IN 1991

In 1990, Jon Shirley retired after seven years as Microsoft president and COO. At 52 years of age, and with more than one million shares of Microsoft stock, Shirley decided to trade in the long hours at Microsoft for a less consuming schedule. He expressed his desire to retire in 1989, giving the Microsoft board one year to find a replacement. Following an extensive search, the Microsoft board selected Michael R. Hallman, a 20-year veteran of IBM and president of Boeing Computer at the time. Hallman's experience with Boeing made him especially well qualified as Microsoft increasingly relied on sales to corporate customers.

Hallman inherited a much different company from the one Shirley had encountered seven years earlier. Whereas Shirley had imposed management controls on the growing business, Hallman found that he had to scale back certain controls:

> When I got here, I found the president had to sign all employment requisitions, even for temporary employees. I was the fourth signature needed to approve a resignation! Once I asked, What would happen if I didn't sign? Would we really hold the fellow hostage?
>
> The degree of centralized approval just wasn't sustainable as we got larger. Delegation was needed for two reasons: not only because it was too cumbersome to continue to centralize, but also to make sure that others were trained to take responsibility.

Gates and Hallman divided the responsibilities of general management. "If you look at the organization chart," said Gates, "you see that only the COO reports to me. But if there's a product strategy question, I'll be involved. I work more closely with Steve Ballmer and Mike Maples than Mike Hallman does." Hallman agreed: "Chief Operating Officer is the right title for my job. Bill Gates manages product development directly. I deal with technical projects only on an administrative basis." Hallman described his priorities as sales and marketing, including calling on major customers, and managing the operations. Gates and Hallman divided foreign reviews equally: Each visited half the subsidiaries around the world one year, switching the following year to visit the other half.

By the summer of 1991, Microsoft employed more than 8,000 people, almost all of whom were located at the Microsoft "campus" on a large tract of wooded land in Redmond, 10 miles east of Seattle. Software development was concentrated in a series of contiguous buildings on the campus. Manufacturing plants were situated in nearby Bothell, WA, as well as in Puerto Rico and in Dublin, Ireland. Customer service and support were handled from three centers, two in the Seattle area and one, established in 1990, in North Carolina. Microsoft's 21 foreign subsidiaries were spread from Italy to India, from Argentina to Korea.

Microsoft's organization structure was split into two major divisions: product development and product sales (see Exhibit 7). Product development, in turn, was divided into systems software, run by Steve Ballmer, and applications software, headed by Mike Maples, a 23-year veteran of IBM who joined Microsoft in 1988. Manufacturing, logistics, finance, and human resources all reported to Frank Gaudette, senior vice president of administration and CFO. At the next level, product development was composed of nine business units, each responsible for a family of products and run by a business unit manager (BUM). The business units were organized functionally, with managers for Product Development, Testing, User Education, Program Management, and Product Marketing. Domestic sales and channel marketing were handled by the U.S. Sales and Marketing Division (USSMD), while foreign sales were the responsibility of the 21 foreign subsidiaries.

Managing Innovation and Product Development

Bill Gates worked out of a modern but unimposing office in Microsoft's executive suite. Five personal computers—usually switched on and running various programs—occupied desks and tabletops, making Gates's office look more like a software lab than the chairman's office of a $1.8 billion corporation. One large bookshelf was crammed end-to-end with software documentation. Another held biographies of scientists and businesspeople, novels, and a half-dozen atlases. Over Gates's desk was the framed photo and autograph of another American industrial pioneer—Henry Ford.

Gates estimated that he spent half of his time on direct contact with major customers, industry relations, visits to subsidiaries, review meetings, and acting as ambassador for the company. He was known for having a "broad bandwidth"—company terminology for expertise in a wide variety of issues, including legal, financial, administrative, and industry matters. "I'm very much the CEO," he noted. The other half of his time continued to be devoted to managing new product development.

As Gates described it, "My role is to set the product direction for the company." Starting with an idea for a new product—what it should do and when it should be released—Gates and his top managers worked backward to determine the level of staffing and other resources required. Several top managers marveled that major allocations did not require 100-person task forces or lengthy written reports. The key, according to one, was Gates's judgment: "Bill will not study an issue to death. Once Bill is convinced, he'll get his best brains together and say, 'Let's do it.' " For example, the development of Multimedia, which enabled personal computers to integrate information from a variety of forms —including text, sound, graphics, and video—was based on a simple conviction, according to one executive: "We decided four years ago that we would invest whatever it takes, irrespective of revenues." Similarly, perseverance in the development of Windows was due to Gates's unwavering confidence in the project.

Once the product direction had been set, Gates remained directly involved in many product development efforts, work-

ing with the top technical architects to make sure they shared a common vision. Six top software architects, possessing the highest ranking of "Level 15," reported directly to Gates. "I also make sure I spend time with the developers one notch down from that, the 14s," Gates added. Mike Maples concurred: "Bill knows the developers and he reviews all of their products. He likes to take part in arguments about product features. He challenges developers; he stretches them." Gates estimated that he knew more than 150 developers personally.

As the complexity of Microsoft programs grew, the demands for product development shifted. Mike Maples observed:

> Our applications products used to work on a stand-alone basis. They were like tools: you could make an electric drill, you could make a hammer, and you could make a saw, and put them on the same rack, but they were integrated by the user. What we're headed for is where the products have to work together.

The need for software products to work together required a change in Microsoft's approach toward product development. As one manager noted, "Our culture has been: 'I'm going to get a small band of guys and against all odds I'm going to build this great product.' " But as Microsoft products increasingly had to work together, product development required the simultaneous efforts of multiple teams. Most important was not excellence in individual design, but excellence in overall systems architecture. As a consequence, Gates assumed a central role in coordinating the efforts of development teams. At times, he determined the composition of development teams: "If I see that a group is having unexpected difficulties or is moving slowly, I might assign a 14 to join the group, determine the problem, and help out." At other times, Gates interceded directly in discussions among various development teams whose efforts were interdependent. One development team might point out that their program depended on a certain feature that a second team was developing, and that second team might, in turn, be dependent on a third team. Gates's approach was to say to each, "Don't worry about the others; I'll guarantee that they deliver their product with the right specifications at the right time. You just develop your piece and don't worry about the rest." This way, the various teams could work simultaneously rather than sequentially, speeding up the development process and avoiding friction of having to negotiate with each other.

GOING FORWARD: MICROSOFT IN THE 1990S

As Microsoft moved into the 1990s, several forces were changing the way it did business. Most notable were improvements in microprocessor technology and the increasing sophistication of computer users. These trends were described in Microsoft's 1989 annual report:

> The role of the personal computer is changing.
> "One person, one computer" was miracle enough just a few years ago. But as hardware evolves and the market grows, customers are beginning to realize that no computer is an island and that interconnections of business require that the tools of business be interconnected, too.
> Microsoft's vision was always ambitious—the idea of "a computer on every desk" suggests that people will want to share information and ideas from one desktop machine to another. So it's no

surprise that local area networks (LANs) are among the fastest-growing segments in the computer business.

Advances in the power of microprocessors meant that companies no longer linked "dumb" terminals to mainframe computers or minicomputers, but could place powerful PCs on every desktop. Increasingly they sought to link these PCs into corporatewide networks. At the same time, improvement in computer power was matched by the growing sophistication of computer users. Corporations relied more and more on their information systems, of which Microsoft products were an increasingly vital part. Microsoft products no longer performed isolated functions for individual users, but were frequently essential to the customer's operations. In industry parlance, Microsoft products were often "mission critical." In response to these trends, Microsoft moved beyond PC operating systems and PC application software and began to address the integrated computing needs of customers.

The 1990s: Strategic Challenges

In a memo to senior managers in May 1991, Gates reviewed the company's competitive position and outlined its strategic challenges. Some ongoing challenges included an FTC investigation and a pending lawsuit by Apple Computer, which alleged that Microsoft had improperly used the "look and feel" of the Macintosh. More significantly, the company faced growing competition on several fronts. In operating systems software, Microsoft's collaboration with IBM had ended, and IBM was seeking to develop its own successor to MS-DOS. Novell, the leader in networking software, enjoyed a substantial head start over Microsoft. Software firms like Borland, which acquired Ashton-Tate in July 1991, offered high-quality applications programs at prices that undercut Microsoft. The combined effect of these competitive threats constituted a serious challenge. If Microsoft could not maintain strength in these three areas, it risked losing its position of prominence.

Microsoft's response to these challenges rested on Windows. "Our strategy for the 1990s is Windows," Gates declared in his memo to managers. "Everything we do should focus on making Windows more successful." Despite Microsoft's record of growth, Gates recognized that continued success could not be taken for granted. He reflected:

> Growth isn't a given at all. I don't wake up in the morning and think, "Of course we're going to continue to grow, now let's think about how many employee picnics we should have this summer." I wake up and think, "What are we going to do to have better products to sell more software?" Growth isn't a given, it's a variable. And we're not going to continue growing unless we come up with some incredibly good products.

Developing "incredibly good products" depended, as always, on having top software talent. In addition to its ongoing college recruiting of entry-level software developers, Microsoft began to hire several senior software developers from other companies. "We've done real well at bringing strong technical people in," Gates allowed. "If you ask me what I'm most excited about today, it's the two senior developers we hired just recently."

Product Usability and Support

Another emerging challenge was posed by exploding product support costs, stimulated by the combination of hugely increasing numbers of Microsoft users and by the growing complexity of product features. Microsoft's Product Service and Support (PSS) group, which fielded phone calls from users, was finding it increasingly difficult to handle the volume of calls. By 1991, service and support costs had surpassed 5 percent of total revenues. These costs were allocated to the products according to their share of total revenue.

The size and rate of growth in support costs prompted much discussion in Microsoft's executive suite. Mike Hallman noted:

> Microsoft has been known for its products. We're not well known for our customer support. By 1995, I want Microsoft to be as well known for its customer service and support as for its products. I want Microsoft to be the "Maytag repairman" of software.

The emphasis on reducing product support costs was one aspect of a larger emphasis on improved quality. As Microsoft dealt directly with customers, built mission-critical applications, and grew in size, greater attention to quality in all phases of the operation—from product development to product support—was vital. Bill Gates agreed that software usability and support had received insufficient attention and urged that it become a top priority. Mike Halliman remarked:

> This whole issue of total quality and continuous improvement is critical. But we can't impose a campaign of Total Quality, with banners and everything, like they do at some other companies. Having a "Vice President of Total Quality" wouldn't work here.

Corporate Sales and Consulting

By 1991, Microsoft recognized that it had undergone a fundamental change in its relationship to customers. Hallman explained:

> Five years ago, we built operating systems that we sold through OEMs, and we never talked to end users. Then we developed applications which we sold through retail channels, and still we never talked to end users. It's only in the last two years that we've come to grips with the fact that, at least for large corporations, we are a strategic technology provider. We're on all of their PCs and operating systems, we're a key part of their applications strategy, and they often use our networking products.
>
> More than one company has come to us and said, "We're trying to identify our strategic technology partners and we list AT&T and IBM and Digital, yet we find we may have most dependency on you. How do we deal with you?"

Microsoft's emergence as a "strategic technology provider" made direct contact between Microsoft and its corporate customers very important and led to the creation, in 1990, of Microsoft Consulting Services. It was led by vice president Bob McDowell, who explained, "The customer says, 'If I'm going to bet part of the farm on this product, I'll need dedicated technical assistance. I get that kind of help from IBM—and I'll need it from Microsoft.' "

The growing importance of selling and consulting to corporations was indicative of a broader shift in Microsoft's activities. Many senior managers believed that future success depended on the ability to understand customer needs and to present Microsoft products as an integrated information systems solution. In McDowell's words, the traditional credo of "reverence for the developer" had to be matched by "reverence for the customer." Other managers, however, were concerned by Microsoft's shift away from the traditional

emphasis on technical skills. As one software development manager observed:

> We have always been a technically driven company. What if our sales and support staffs keep growing at their present rates? Will we still be a technical company, with a small and elite technical corps, or will the technical people get overwhelmed?

Managing Growth: Organizational Issues

As it grappled with the new challenges of networking, consulting, and usability, Microsoft also faced the challenge of executing its traditional operations on a bigger scale. Top executives estimated that if Microsoft's Windows strategy continued to be successful, the company could reach $5 billion in sales and employ between 14,000 and 16,000 people by 1995. Such growth posed a set of internal challenges, quite apart from strategic and product development issues.

As Microsoft grew, its organizational subunits had become larger. The Office Business Unit, for example, had grown in revenues from $100 million in 1988 to $400 million in 1990. In an effort to retain the benefits of smaller organizations, Jeff Raikes, manager of the Office Business Unit, divided his unit into three subunits, each of which would be responsible for program management, project management, and so forth. Further subdivisions were anticipated, as well. Yet the desire to retain small working units ran headlong into the need to coordinate product development across organizational units. Mike Maples noted the conflict:

> I'm going to keep subdividing business units. I think that communication and development work are so much more efficient—maybe by orders of magni-

tude—in small teams than in big teams. The question is, How do you make sure that these small teams share technology and experiences so that everything works together?

One solution was to establish linking mechanisms across subunits. Committees were established to agree on consistency in key issues, such as the use of direct marketing, approaches to the educational market, and the use of computer-based training. Furthermore, one employee in each functional area was designated a "director" and coordinated that function across the various business units, producing a kind of matrix. Thus, there was a director of Marketing, a director of Development, and a director of Program Management. Employees began serving as directors on a part-time basis, in addition to their regular jobs; in a few instances, however, where these responsibilities demanded full-time attention, the directorship became a full-time assignment which rotated among employees.

In addition, Gates noted the importance of focusing each business unit on the competitive task at hand. He observed:

> It's important to set the image of what competition means to us. It doesn't mean pricing our software very low, and it doesn't mean undermining our competitors. We have to make sure that's well understood. Competition to us means coming out with very innovative products.
>
> Each business unit is focused on its competition. We have a Spreadsheet Business Unit; they wake up every morning thinking about Lotus. We have a Word Processing Business Unit 1; they wake up thinking about WordPerfect. We have a Networking Business Unit 1; and they wake up thinking about Novell. Those are very entrenched competitors, and we're going to have to develop far

better products in order to dislodge them. We're not going to back off competing with them. There are other competitors that can write software well, like Borland, that would come along if we weren't pushing ourselves to the max.

Managing Growth: Hiring, Training, and Compensation

The prospect of doubling the number of employees in four years posed severe challenges in management development. By 1991, Microsoft's rapid growth meant that management slots were opening faster than employees could fill them. Existing employees were not gaining experience on the job quickly enough, and in sufficiently large numbers, to fill management openings internally. One executive commented, "We can't wait for the demographics to catch up with demand."

Microsoft responded by hiring more experienced people with specific skills. It also began to place concerted attention on employee development and training programs. Frank Gaudette asserted:

> We've got to keep training employees if they're going to grow. That's the only thing you can do when each person is doing the biggest job they've ever done.
>
> We have to create a part of our corporate culture that wasn't here in the early days. We need to agree that training, too, is part of our culture. When people talk about Microsoft, we want them to say, "Boy, they can train!"

At the same time, the company was considering a change in its compensation policy, moving to a more traditional reliance on salary, with stock grants somewhat less important in the future. Although managers remained optimistic about the growth potential of Microsoft stock, they recognized that it was not likely to continue growing 20-fold in five years. Gaudette explained:

> The law of diminishing returns applies to us, too. There will have to be a shift in compensation—we'll have to get more traditional in the methodology. But the underlying philosophy in wage and salary administration will remain: We are a meritocracy. Compensation is always related to contribution.

Growth in the company workforce also forced managers to think about physical expansion. Many questioned whether a single site was practical if Microsoft grew to more than 14,000 employees. Some managers argued that a second site would allow Microsoft to tap a new labor market, but others countered that it would inevitably make coordination and integrated product development more difficult and could further erode Microsoft's traditional small-company feel.

Continuing growth also spelled changes for the work environment. E-mail threatened to smother top management; in 1991, Gates and Hallman were receiving up to 100 e-mail messages per day. Change was also evident in growing measures to ensure security. Top managers had been concerned about lax security for a number of years but had been reluctant to impose stricter measures unilaterally. Frank Gaudette recalled:

> When I got here in the mid-1980s, asking employees to wear a badge would have been considered "Big Brother"-ism. But over time, it was the software developers, who had always been against rules, who said, "We've got all this valuable software lying around where anyone can walk in and see it—we better get this stuff locked up!"

After much discussion, a security system was installed, and employees were given picture-badges with magnetic strips that allowed them entry to specific buildings. Wearing a badge remained optional during working hours but was mandatory after-hours and on weekends. "Where we have become more bureaucratic," Gaudette explained, "it's because employees determined it was the right thing to do, and not because some executive decided it was the right thing to do."

The combined effect of these changes engendered concern among several managers. A human resources manager noted, "Some companies are concerned about cultural change. My biggest mission here is 'culture keep'—how to keep what's good about the company alive and well." A vice president commented:

> In a small company you can lead by example. But as the newer hires become further and further removed from the old-timers, how do they pick up the company's values? How do they see that the extra weekend they work, or the good idea they have, really makes a difference in a $5 billion company? How do they develop that commitment to be successful?

Looking Ahead

In the summer of 1991, Microsoft could look back on a 16-year history of remarkable technical and financial achievement. Its growth and consistently high profits bore witness to a successful transition from start-up company to major corporation. Going forward, Gates had enunciated a clear strategic vision for the company in the 1990s based on Windows. Yet he realized that the company faced many challenges, and that questions remained as to how Microsoft should be managed as it pursued that strategy.

Reflecting on these challenges, Gates remarked:

This is a business where if you don't stay ahead, you can lose market share very quickly. We have to figure out what the opportunities for innovation will be, based on changes in hardware and changes in what users want, and then we have to implement those things very rapidly. For us, that means setting systems standards and shipping innovative applications.

This business is getting more and more complex, yet it has to be fun for people, so that they feel empowered and feel they can do things. At the same time, the products have to fit together. It's a very tough problem.

EXHIBIT 1
EMPLOYEE AND REVENUE GROWTH AT MICROSOFT
CORPORATION, 1975–1991

Year	Employees	Revenues ($000)	Net Income ($000)
1975	3	16	N/A
1976	7	22	N/A
1977	9	382	N/A
1978	13	1,356	N/A
1979	28	2,390	N/A
1980	38	8,000*	N/A
1981	130	16,000*	N/A
1982	220	24,486	3,507
1983	476	50,065	6,487
1984	778	97,479	15,880
1985	1,001	140,417	24,101
1986	1,442	197,514	39,254
1987	2,258	345,890	71,878
1988	2,793	590,827	123,908
1989	4,037	803,530	170,538
1990	5,635	1,183,446	279,186
1991	8,226	1,843,432	462,743

Source: Microsoft Corporation.

*Approximate figure.

EXHIBIT 2A
MICROSOFT CORPORATION INCOME STATEMENT, 1986–1991 ($ MILLIONS)

	1991		1990		1989		1988		1987		1986	
Net revenues	$1,843	100%	$1,183	100%	$803	100%	$591	100%	$346	100%	$197	100%
Cost of revenues	363	20	253	21	204	25	148	25	74	21	41	21
Research & development	235	13	181	15	110	14	70	12	38	11	21	11
Sales & marketing	534	29	318	27	219	27	161	27	85	25	58	29
General & administrative	62	3	39	3	28	3	24	4	22	6	18	9
Operating income	$ 650	35	$ 393	33	$242	30	$187	32	$127	37	$ 61	31
Nonoperating income	21		23		17		11		9		5	
Stock option program expense			(6)		(8)		(14)		(14)		—	
Income before taxes	671	36	411	35	251	31	184	31	121	35	66	34
Provision for taxes	208	11	131	11	80	10	60	10	49	14	27	14
Net income	$ 463	25%	$ 279	24%	$171	21%	$124	21%	$ 72	21%	$ 39	20%

Source: Microsoft Corporation annual report.

EXHIBIT 2B
MICROSOFT CORPORATION BALANCE SHEET, 1986–1991 ($ MILLIONS)

	1991	1990	1989	1988	1987	1986
Assets						
Current assets						
Cash & short-term investments	$ 686.3	$ 449.2	$300.8	$183.2	$132.5	$102.7
Accounts receivable	243.3	181.0	111.2	93.6	55.1	34.5
Inventory	47.1	55.6	37.8	53.5	16.6	8.0
Other	51.8	34.1	19.2	15.0	8.8	2.8
Total current assets	$1,028.5	$ 719.9	$468.9	$345.3	$213.0	$148.0
Property, plant, & equipment	530.2	325.4	198.8	130.1	70.0	19.5
Other assets	85.5	60.0	52.8	17.6	4.7	3.2
Total assets	$1,644.2	$1,105.3	$720.6	$493.0	$287.8	$170.7
Liabilities & shareholders' equity						
Current liabilities						
Accounts payable	85.9	51.0	42.0	43.1	20.5	9.7
Customer deposits	25.7	17.2	10.0	6.0	6.3	7.0
Accrued compensation	41.6	28.8	25.7	15.1	5.1	1.3
Notes payable	19.5	6.5	25.4	20.3	5.2	—
Income tax payable	44.4	42.6	30.3	16.1	2.2	7.5
Other	76.2	40.8	25.4	17.0	9.3	5.9
Total current liabilities	$ 293.4	$ 186.8	$158.8	$117.5	$ 48.6	$ 31.4
Stockholders' equity	394.5	219.5	110.5	90.0	76.8	50.8
Retained earnings	956.3	688.9	455.6	285.0	161.1	89.2
Translation adjustment	0.0	10.2	(4.3)	0.3	1.1	(0.7)
Total stockholders' equity	$1,350.8	$ 918.6	$561.8	$375.5	$239.1	$139.3
Total liabilities & stockholders' equity	$1,644.2	$1,105.3	$720.6	$493.0	$287.8	$170.7

Source: Microsoft Corporation annual report.

EXHIBIT 3
GROWTH OF MICROSOFT CORPORATION SHARE PRICE, 1986–1991

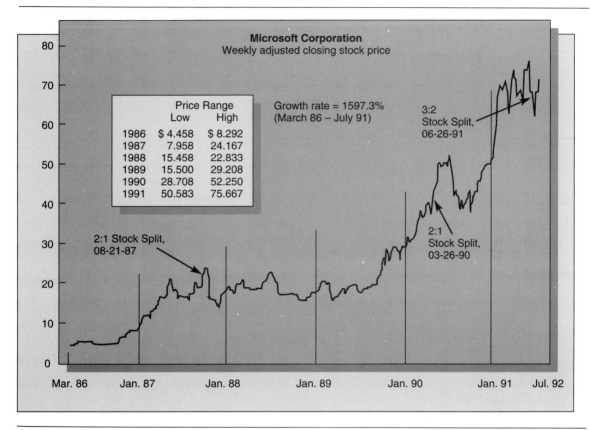

Microsoft Corporation
Weekly adjusted closing stock price

	Price Range	
	Low	High
1986	$ 4.458	$ 8.292
1987	7.958	24.167
1988	15.458	22.833
1989	15.500	29.208
1990	28.708	52.250
1991	50.583	75.667

Growth rate = 1597.3%
(March 86 – July 91)

3:2
Stock Split,
06-26-91

2:1 Stock Split,
08-21-87

2:1
Stock Split,
03-26-90

Source: Interactive Data Corporation.

EXHIBIT 4
MICROSOFT CORPORATION SOFTWARE AND HARDWARE PRODUCTS, 1989 (PARTIAL LISTING)

	Operating System	
	MS-DOS	Apple Macintosh
Business application software		
Microsoft Chart	X	X
Microsoft Excel	X	X
Microsoft File		X
Microsoft Learning DOS	X	
Microsoft Mail	X	X
Microsoft Multiplan®	X	X
Microsoft PowerPoint®		X
Microsoft Project	X	
Microsoft Word	X	X
Microsoft Works	X	X
Microsoft Write		X
The Microsoft Office		X
Systems/languages software		
Microsoft BASIC	X	
Microsoft C	X	
Microsoft COBOL	X	
Microsoft FORTRAN	X	
Microsoft Macro Assembler	X	
Microsoft Pascal	X	
Microsoft QuickBASIC	X	X
Microsoft QuickC Compiler	X	
Microsoft QuickC Compiler with Quick Assembler	X	
Microsoft QuickPascal	X	
Microsoft Windows/286	X	
Microsoft Windows/386	X	
Hardware, recreation, and CD-ROM products		
Microsoft Mouse	X	
Microsoft Flight Simulator®	X	X
Microsoft Bookshelf (CD-ROM)	X	
Microsoft Programmer's Library (CD-ROM)	X	
Microsoft Small Business Consultant (CD-ROM)	X	
Microsoft Stat Pack (CD-ROM)	X	

Source: Microsoft Corporation 1989 annual report.

EXHIBIT 5
DISTRIBUTION OF REVENUES BY PRODUCT, CHANNEL, AND REGION, 1986–1990

	1990	1989	1988	1987	1986
Revenue by product group					
Systems/languages	39%	44%	47%	49%	53%
Applications	48	42	40	38	37
Hardware, books, other	13	14	13	13	10
Total	100%	100%	100%	100%	100%
Revenue by channel					
Domestic OEM	13%	14%	17%	21%	25%
Domestic retail	30	29	32	35	32
	43%	43%	49%	56%	57%
International OEM	13	18	14	14	21
International finished goods	42	37	34	28	19
	55%	55%	48%	42%	40%
Microsoft Press & other	2	2	2	2	3
Total	100%	100%	100%	100%	100%

EXHIBIT 6
MICROSOFT CORPORATION SHARE OF THE PC SOFTWARE MARKET

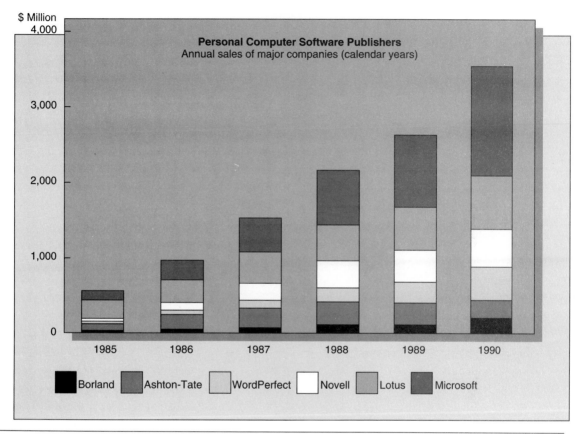

Source: Softletter, Watertown, MA.

EXHIBIT 7
MICROSOFT CORPORATION, PARTIAL ORGANIZATION CHART, 1991

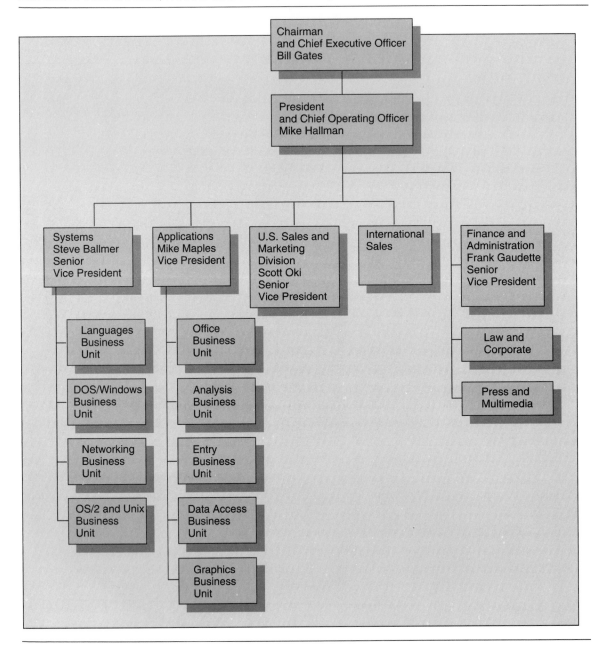

■

Chapter 3

Personal Values and Corporate Strategy

INTRODUCTION

At this point in our exploration of general management we shift emphasis from the fundamentals of economic strategy, which permit us to test the sustainability of corporate purpose, to consider how and why strategy is made. When we do, we find that the general manager's own preferences and values play a central role in the process.

This should be no surprise. We see the same phenomena at work in every other sphere of endeavor, and much writing about business in the news media emphasizes the role played by leaders' values in shaping the direction of their companies.

- Kenneth Olsen wanted to build a computer company that served the needs of engineers. He believed strongly that it was possible to provide computing capability by a means that was independent of the large and increasingly bureaucratic corporate computer rooms where mainframe IBM equipment sat in air-conditioned splendor. His solution was the PDP—a personal data processor that could be located close to the engineers that used it. This vision was the basis for the first minicomputer company—Digital Equipment. Olsen's high ethical standards were reflected in every aspect of the company from its advanced human relations policy to its salaried sales force.

- Many Japanese companies were built by men who felt strongly the importance of freeing Japan from dependence on foreigners. The founders of Hitachi, Canon, and Matsushita were all driven by nationalistic spirit. They persevered through years of travail and profitless growth before they achieved the technological competence to free themselves from dependence on foreign licenses. Even today, the commitment of Japanese managers to the well-being of their country is evident as they try to devise strategies that will enable them to respond to the very strong yen without causing undue hardship to their employees.

■ Southwest Airlines has been the only consistently profitable U.S. air carrier for the last decade. Ed Kelleher, its founder and chief executive, has infused the organization with his commitment to delivering good low-cost service to the public. To achieve that goal, every member of the organization pitches in to get planes loaded and unloaded to meet tight schedules. Even pilots move luggage, and ticket personnel come out to help clean the planes when necessary. The high-spirited and performance-oriented work environment of Southwest reflects the dedication of its leader, who spends hours delivering his message personally.

The importance of a general manager's personal values to the purpose and functioning of a firm is an odd paradox. On the one hand, it certainly is natural that the boss puts his or her imprint on the direction of the company. After all, isn't that what bosses do? But in this day and age, such a dominant role played by one individual smacks of dictatorial powers incongruent with contemporary attitudes. And given the scale of large organizations, it would seem to be an impossible feat. How could it be?

The question comes close to the heart of the contribution that general managers make to their businesses. To understand it, we must recognize that firms are social and political as well as economic institutions. Firms are where we spend most of the day when we are not eating or sleeping. We not only earn our living there but also have much of our identity defined and our nonmonetary needs satisfied.

WE ALL HAVE VALUES

It is an apparently obvious thing to say, but each of us brings to the workplace a set of beliefs about people, about relationships among people, about companies and how they should operate, and about the role of companies in society. It is not uncommon for young people to take these beliefs for granted. They think that all others share the same ideas.

For example, it is not unusual for people who grew up and were educated in the middle of a family involved in business and management to believe that private enterprise has a clearly defined role in the society and that management has clearly defined rights. They know that managers "think" and workers "do" so that the rights of managers are clear. They know that unions are at best an administrative cost and at worst a real obstruction to the proper functioning of a firm.

Others believe that money is a remarkably good measure of value. Large profits justify large salaries. Indeed, paying for performance is the only appropriate way of providing incentives. It is a wonderful thing that the functioning of free markets permits talented individuals working within the law to earn millions of dollars in a year.

It is sometimes a shock for people to learn that other apparently sensible, talented, and managerially capable people do not share their values. Some believe that the role of firms is to provide great products and services as well as good jobs in healthy working conditions. They think adequate rewards to investors come naturally over time when firms fulfill their proper function. The credo of Johnson & Johnson, reflecting the values of the company's founder General Robert Johnson and reinforced by his successor James Burke, is a good example of this approach. (See page 366).

Scientists who enter business often bring with them a commitment to the advancement of knowledge that shapes the way they think about their company. Seymour Cray is a good example of a business leader dedicated to the excellence of his product above and beyond the economic success of his company. Cray left Control Data Corporation, where he had helped to build their largest computers, in order to found a company that would simply build the fastest, most powerful computers in the world. While he was aware of the importance of customers, he was sure that there would always be organizations that needed bigger and faster computers, and he would serve them. When the professional management brought in to help manage the growth of the company he founded allocated scarce research resources away from the fastest and most powerful to the larger markets just behind the edge of speed and power, Cray left to found a new firm committed to his goals.

Conflicts of values can be devastating to a company, especially when they involve the division of rewards. *The Year They Sold Wall Street* tells the story of what happened at the New York investment bank Lehman Brothers as the culture of the firm's traders, led by Lou Glucksman, clashed with that of the "white shoe" investment bankers led by Lehman's CEO, Pete Peterson.[1] In the world of the traders there was only one issue—how current profits were shared among those who earned them. The idea that Lehman was a great merchant bank with a reputation in corporate finance dating back to the turn of the century that provided the basis for long-term profitable banking business was irrelevant. It was intolerable that current power and rewards did not reflect the way income

---

[1] Tim Carrington, *The Year They Sold Wall Street* (Boston: Houghton Mifflin, 1985).

Our Credo

We believe our first responsibility is to the doctors, nurses, and patients,
to mothers and all others who use our products and services.
In meeting their needs everything we do must be of high quality.
We must constantly strive to reduce our costs
in order to maintain reasonable prices.
Customers' orders must be serviced promptly and accurately.
Our suppliers and distributors must have an opportunity
to make a fair profit.

We are responsible to our employees,
the men and women who work with us throughout the world.
Everyone must be considered as an individual.
We must respect their dignity and recognize their merit.
They must have a sense of security in their jobs.
Compensation must be fair and adequate,
and working conditions clean, orderly, and safe.
Employees must feel free to make suggestions and complaints.
There must be equal opportunity for employment, development,
and advancement for those qualified.
We must provide competent management,
and their actions must be just and ethical.

We are responsible to the communities in which we live and work
and to the world community as well.
We must be good citizens—support good works and charities
and bear our fair share of taxes.
We must encourage civic improvements and better health and education.
We must maintain in good order
the property we are privileged to use,
protecting the environment and natural resources.

Our final responsibility is to our stockholders.
Business must make a sound profit.
We must experiment with new ideas.
Research must be carried on, innovative programs developed,
and mistakes paid for.
New equipment must be purchased, new facilities provided,
and new products launched.
Reserves must be created to provide for adverse times.
When we operate according to these principles,
the stockholders should realize a fair return.

Johnson & Johnson

was being generated. The struggles for control of the firm were so
tumultuous that sale seemed the sensible way out.

The battle at Lehman Brothers was extreme, but the issues were typical
of what happens when different groups in a company have substantially
different objectives. The distribution of rewards and power is fundamental because it is a direct reflection of the strategy of the firm. In this case,
the warring parties had dramatically different views of how Lehman
should have deployed its assets to deal with the conditions in the
financial markets of the 1980s. What looked like a squabble over money
was also a civil war about the corporate strategy of Lehman Brothers.

VALUES ARE KEY TO LEGITIMATE ACTION

At roughly the same time that Lehman was in trouble, the venerable Morgan Guarantee bank began a metamorphosis that transformed it from a traditional commercial bank focused on large corporate and country customers to an investment bank with a very aggressive trading operation. But because there was a shared understanding of what the organization was trying to accomplish, and because the values of the institution were preserved, there was none of the uproar that tore Lehman apart. The leadership of Morgan was able to recognize oncoming changes in the financial markets and plan changes that were quite dramatic involving new kinds of people, modifications of compensation, and a new culture. The values and needs of investment bankers and traders were integrated into the firm. Yet for the members of the old organization the core of Morgan remained.

This is a difficult feat to manage. In many companies, the decade of the 1980s seemed to involve abandoning all but economic values, defined as who would pay the most for the common shares this week. During the 1960s and 1970s several countries in East Asia led by Japan developed highly competitive export-oriented economies. The large open markets of the U.S. were their primary target. The power of this attack was compounded by a highly overvalued dollar. American manufacturers discovered that their cost structures were totally inappropriate to the trading conditions in which they found themselves. Wages were too high, and tiers of middle management and staff were not only costly but also interfered in the design of an effective competitive response.

The restructuring of our major corporations has involved massive layoffs. For managers and workers who lost jobs, the experience has been one of a broken contract. Somehow, the world in which they were promised income for a lifetime if they showed up and worked hard was shattered. It seemed that the managers who remained were paid large bonuses for destroying the lives of the losers who were paying the price for the sins of past company and macroeconomic mismanagement. These sentiments were captured in the sobriquet given to Jack Welch, the chief executive of General Electric. In the first four years of his leadership, the firm laid off 70,000 workers. Welch was called "Neutron Jack" because "he killed the people and left all the buildings." He felt the name was distinctly unfair because the alternative for GE if it did not become a nimble, lean, innovative giant was even more damaging. The losses would have been far greater, Welch believed, had he not driven GE to become a high-productivity company.

But notice that the legitimacy of these painful actions taken for economic reasons is not just shareholder return. The principal justification is competitive conditions. Welch did not use the language of shareholder value to explain his actions. Instead his entire thrust was to do whatever was necessary to make GE a strong global competitor.

The cases in this book describe managers in the rich countries of Europe and the United States competing against wonderfully educated, hardworking, low-salaried Asians. Devising an effective response involves difficult ethical dilemmas. The managers know that they must deliver to their customers goods and services of equivalent quality and price despite very different employment costs. In many countries in Europe, management's ability to respond is substantially constrained by legislation. A social safety net going back to Bismarck institutionalizes a contract that promises reasonable income and medical care in return for willingness to participate in the industrial system. How is a manager to make a company competitive if this seems to involve a set of working conditions that violate the social contract?

Research that has examined the challenges faced by managers in the midst of restructuring industries reveals that establishing legitimacy is a key task for those involved in shutting down capacity or merging companies.[2] The manager who leads this work must believe—like a surgeon—that the destruction associated with the cutting is vital to the survival and future health of the patient.

Executives with the required fortitude are rare. In one industry that we studied, steel in the United States, a substantial portion of the restructuring of the long products sector (about half the capacity of the integrated manufacturers) was accomplished by one man, Tom Graham, as he moved from LTV to USX to Armco. Mr. David Roderick, his superior while at USX, commented on the problem.

> Most executives tied to steel probably won't make hard decisions. People that spent their whole lives in steel plants, that came up through the plants, have too many friends, too many neighbors, too many ties. They are too close to these people to make rational decisions.

Our values give us the courage to make hard choices that will influence the lives of those we are responsible for managing.

AWARENESS OF VALUES

In considering how awareness of our values can play a role in shaping of corporate purpose, we cannot do better than quote Kenneth Andrews from the seventh edition of this book.

---

[2] Joseph L Bower, *When Markets Quake* (Boston: Harvard Business School Press, 1986), chapter 9.

Our interest in the role of personal values in strategic formulations should not be confined to assessing the influence of other people's values. Despite the well-known problems of introspection, we can probably do more to understand the relation of our own values to our choice of purpose than we can to change the values of others. Awareness that our own preference for an alternative opposed by another stems from values as much as from rational estimates of economic opportunity may have important consequences. First, it may make us more tolerant and less indignant when we perceive this relationship between recommendations and values in the formulations of others. Second, it will force us to consider how important it really is to us to maintain a particular value in making a particular decision. Third, it may give us insight with which to identify our biases and thus pave the way for a more objective assessment of all the strategic alternatives that are available. These consequences of self-examination will not end conflict, but they will at least prevent its unnecessary prolongation.

The object of this self-examination is not necessarily to endow us with the ability to persuade others to accept the strategic recommendations we consider best; it is to acquire insight into the problems of determining purpose and skill in the process of resolving them. Individuals inquiring into their own values for the purpose of understanding their own positions in policy debates can continue to assess their own personal opportunities, strengths and weaknesses, and basic values by means of the procedures outlined here. For a personal strategy, analytically considered and consciously developed, may be as useful to an individual as a corporate strategy is to a business institution. The effort, conducted by each individual, to formulate personal purpose might well accompany his or her contributions to organizational purpose. If the encounter leads to a clarification of the purposes one seeks, the values one holds, and the alternatives available, the attempt to make personal use of the concept of strategy will prove extremely worthwhile.

Introducing personal preference forces us to deal with the possibility that the strategic decision we prefer (identified after the most nearly objective analysis of opportunity and resources we are capable of) is not acceptable to other executives with different values. Their acceptance of the strategy is necessary to its successful implementation. In diagnosing this conflict, we try to identify the values implicit in our own choice. As we look at the gap between the strategy that follows from our own values and that which would be appropriate to the values of our associates, we look to see whether the difference is fundamental or superficial. Then we look to see how the strategy we believe best matches opportunity and resources can be adapted to accommodate the values of those who will implement it. Reconciliation of the three principal determinants of strategy that we have so far considered is often made possible by adjustment of any or all of the determinants.

The role of self-examination in coming to terms with a conflict in values over an important strategic determination is not to turn all strategic decisions into outcomes of consensus. Some organizations—you can see them in this book—are run by persons who are leaders in the sense that they have power and are not afraid to use it. It is true that business leaders, in

Zaleznik's words, "commit themselves to a career in which they have to work on themselves as a condition for effective working with other people."[3] At the same time a leader must recognize that "the essence of leadership is choice, a singularly individualistic act in which a (person) assumes responsibility for a commitment to direct an organization along a particular path . . . As much as a leader wishes to trust others, he has to judge the soundness and validity of his subordinates' positions. Otherwise, the leader may become a prisoner of the emotional commitments of his subordinates, frequently at the expense of making correct judgments about policies and strategies."[4]

When a management group is locked in disagreement, the presence of power and the need for its exercise condition the dialogue. There are circumstances when leadership must transcend disagreement that cannot be resolved by discussion. Subordinates, making the best of the inevitable, must accept a follower role. When leadership becomes irresponsible and dominates subordinate participation without reason, it is usually ineffective or is deposed. Participants in strategic disagreements must know not only their own needs and power but those of the chief executive. Strategic planning, in the sense that power attached to values plays a role in it, is a political process.

You should not warp your recommended strategy to the detriment of the company's future in order to adjust it to the personal values you hold or observe. On the other hand you should not expect to be able to impose without risk and without expectation of eventual vindication and agreement an unwelcome pattern of purposes and policies on the people in charge of a corporation or responsible for achieving results. Strategy is a human construction; it must in the long run be responsive to human needs. It must ultimately inspire commitment. It must stir an organization to successful striving against competition. People have to have their hearts in it.

---

[3] Abraham Zaleznik and Manfred F R Kets de Vries, *Power and the Corporate Mind* (Boston: Houghton Mifflin, 1975), p. 207.
[4] *Ibid.*, p. 209.

Salvatore Ferragamo, SpA

Wanda Ferragamo looked around the room. A lively discussion was taking place among the members of Ferragamo's board of directors, composed mainly of her six children, a son-in-law, and Wanda herself. All had been active in helping her, as president, build on the legacy of her husband, Salvatore. Since his death in 1960, Wanda had expanded the company from a small base to a significant international presence that in 1990 included luxury shoes, clothing, and accessories for women and men.

Earlier that morning, while walking down the streets of Florence on her way to the meeting, Wanda had noticed many of her competitors' shops. Their offerings were more varied and modern, designed to appeal to a younger, more fashion-driven market; their product lines had expanded to include watches, perfumes, and a variety of sportswear. These competitors were, she knew, opening new stores throughout the world. Yet, Wanda felt that with rapid expansion many had reduced the quality of both their designs and their workmanship.

Wanda was dedicated to maintaining Salvatore's lifelong commitment to quality, value, and fairness with employees, suppliers, and customers. But now, in late 1990, the board had gathered to hear a presentation from Geraldo Mazzalovo, an Italo-French MBA from Columbia University who had recently been brought into the company by her son Ferruccio, Ferragamo's chief administrative officer.

As a backdrop for Mazzalovo's presentation, Wanda stressed that he had been asked—by Ferruccio and herself—to recommend the steps needed to double Ferragamo's sales over the next five years (from $200 million to roughly $400 million). "The market is growing and changing," she said, "we must grow with it. I'm convinced this kind of growth is possible, but Mr. Mazzalovo is here to tell us what changes he thinks we need to make in order to reach such an ambitious growth target."

Despite her 68 years, Wanda believed she could still make major contributions to the business; she had no desire to retire.

Change itself was not frightening, and she wanted to continue pursuing her husband's dream of a House of Ferragamo. At the same time, she did not want to erode the family spirit that had been so important in her company's success thus far.

SALVATORE FERRAGAMO: THE BUSINESS IN 1990

Salvatore Ferragamo, SpA, was a Florence-based maker of high-quality Italian clothing and leather goods, which began as the small, handmade shoe business of Salvatore Ferragamo (see Appendix A). Since his death 30 years earlier, Wanda had presided over the company's growth, managing the business with her six children. Unlike the Gucci or Benetton families, the Ferragamos placed a premium on consensus decision making and had developed the company gradually in order to preserve product quality.

Salvatore's distinctive italic signature adorned a complete line of luxury products, all manufactured in Italy according to strict specifications. The Ferragamo business grew steadily from $20 million to $200 million in 1990, with profits hovering around 5 percent of sales. (See Exhibit 1-A and 1-B for financial information and Exhibit 2 for Ferragamo's sales and production by division for 1990.) Much of that growth was internally instigated rather than market-driven: A family member would recommend a new product line or a new store location and, upon agreement from the other Ferragamos, investment in the opportunity would follow. While the company continued to introduce new products, such as men's ties in 1988, its major product lines had existed for 15 years. Women's shoes continued to account for over half of the company's business, although Ferragamo also sold a range of other items. (See Exhibits 3-A and 3-B for information on product volumes and trends.) Thirty-three Ferragamo boutiques sold the full product line throughout North America, Asia, and Europe, with dozens of other independent retail outlets carrying selected merchandise in Ferragamo "corners."

The company was roughly divided into six organizational units, each run by one of the Ferragamo children. As president, Wanda was actively involved in both design and administration for the entire business. The three daughters managed design and merchandising for their respective product lines. Fiamma, the eldest, was in charge of women's shoes and handbags; Giovanna, women's ready-to-wear (RTW) clothing; Fulvia, the youngest, scarves and other accessories. The three brothers focused more on management and administration. Eldest son Ferruccio served as managing director and chief administrator of the company. Middle son Leonardo was responsible for expanding the Ferragamo brand across Europe and Asia, while youngest son Massimo led the U.S. operations as general manager of the Moda Imports subsidiary.

Located some 300 kilometers from the Italian fashion capital of Milan, company headquarters was the Florentine palazzo where Salvatore had set up his first assembly line. Elaborately frescoed rooms served as impressive product showrooms, with the company's flagship boutique on the ground floor. Administrative offices and product inventory were based in Osmannoro, a suburb 30 kilometers from Florence. The company directly employed 457 people worldwide and supported thousands more through controlled contract manufacturing. Ferragamo also retained showrooms and offices in Milan, New York, and Hong Kong, with the New York and Hong Kong offices managed as distribution subsidiaries.

Products

Ferragamo's product line was divided into four categories: Women's Shoes, Women's RTW, Women's Accessories, and Men's Shoes/RTW.

Women's Shoes Women's shoes, for which Ferragamo was best known, consisted of two lines. The more expensive Salvatore Ferragamo "originals" historically provided the largest volume, while the unlined "Salvatore Ferragamo Boutique" collection, by 1989, had grown to be nearly as large as the "originals." Two full shoe collections were introduced annually. Styles were manufactured in 14 sizes with 6 widths per size (roughly 100 sizes for each style).

Providing a broad range of sizes was deemed critical. "No matter how beautiful the shoe looks, it must support the foot properly or we won't manufacture it," Fiamma Ferragamo continually exhorted her staff. Fiamma, who was awarded the Neiman Marcus Fashion Award in 1967 (20 years after Salvatore received it in 1947), supervised an international staff of seven designers who developed the shoe through the prototype stage. She also determined the final choice of styles for each collection. While Salvatore's shoe designs had been fantastic, using outrageous shapes and colors to create a new effect (see Appendix B), Fiamma's designs typically were conservative and consistent over seasons. "The women of today demand a practical shoe," Wanda affirmed, "so why shouldn't we give them one?"

Stringent manufacturing standards assured such uniform sizing that some women bought the shoes without trying them on. Some customers even knew the manufacturing code—the last number written inside the shoe—of their favorite styles. "We frequently have women come in with a Ferragamo shoe they've worn daily for five years, asking for the same style again," a Saks Fifth Avenue buyer had told Massimo. Customer satisfaction kept orders exceeding manufacturing capacity. However, the family opposed a rapid step-up of its shoe production, as it was not willing to sacrifice product quality. Said Ferruccio, "The ideal manufacturing volume is one pair less than the customer wants.

Women's Ready-to-Wear (RTW) Twice each year in Milan, Ferragamo introduced its women's RTW collection, which included suits, separates, dressy and casual clothes, and a full line of knitwear. The basic RTW collection featured 90 different styles, varying by color or fabric to provide 250 versions, while the knitwear collection generally comprised 60 styles with 180 variations.

Women's RTW Director Giovanna worked with a head designer and four assistants to fashion styles attractive to an international customer. From the palazzo—a site which provided "daily inspiration"—the design team worked directly with fabric manufacturers to create special material, often woven exclusively for Ferragamo. Design was determined by "inspiration" and the continuity of the Ferragamo look. Prototypes were then developed and refined according to price and aesthetics. Ferragamo's RTW prices were somewhat lower than the name designers', but the company felt its products offered higher-quality materials and better workmanship.

As each season's collection emerged, a French freelance fashion coordinator, Yolaine Borghini, coordinated the shoe, accessory, and RTW components. Working with the three sisters, she developed a complementary palette and encouraged design synergies wherever possible—for instance, using similar buttons on a belt, dress, and handbag. Together with the sisters, she also selected the items to be featured in firmwide advertising and fashion shows.

Despite solid sales growth, Giovanna sought increased consumer recognition for her division, particularly in the United States: "People are always saying, 'Great—Ferragamo now has dresses to go with the shoes,' but of course we've had them for 25 years!" RTW sales were strongest in Asia, Ferragamo's newest market. Suspecting that the traditionally conservative design limited her collection's appeal, Giovanna had, in recent years, greatly expanded the line to include more dramatic colors, with younger-looking separates (such as miniskirts) to be worn with her basic styles.

Accessories   These comprised two types: leather purses and "soft" lines. Purses were a historic Ferragamo strength. The soft (nonleather) accessories division designed silk scarves, ties, pareus, blankets, pillows, umbrellas, and towels. Division Director Fulvia Ferragamo kept strict control over all Ferragamo accessories, including the silk ties and scarves that were traditionally manufactured under license for other prominent fashion houses. She supervised two designers and ran the important Milan office, situated near the famed silk printers of Lake Como. The team developed 24 new scarf and 24 new tie designs twice each year, frequently using Ferragamo's highly recognizable animal motifs.

Like Giovanna, Fulvia wanted to attract a younger, broader customer base to her products. Her jungle animal scarves, introduced 20 years earlier, continued to be her most successful pieces, fast becoming collector's items. After learning that sofa cushions were being made from her scarves, she introduced decorative pillows. Endeavoring to keep a "Ferragamo personality," Fulvia was pursuing more innovative designs as a way to strengthen her division's relatively weak position. She was frustrated, however, by the division's limited understanding of its market and customers.

Men's Shoes and Ready-to-Wear   Ferragamo's men's lines were a small but growing part of the company's business. Unlike the women's lines, however, they did not have the benefit of a full-time family member in charge. Usually, the men's lines drew heavily from the women's designs, and received part-time attention from the sisters.

Men's products were showcased in five free-standing "Salvatore Ferragamo Uomo" boutiques, each featuring a full line of men's shoes and clothing items. Sales outside the boutiques were largely limited to shoes, although a new men's tie line—using Ferragamo's scarf designs—had been a huge success in 1989. The family agreed that its men's lines needed more management attention, and they were committed to hiring at least two experienced outsiders to run that part of the business in 1991.

Manufacturing

Ferragamo manufactured its products through strictly controlled relationships with highly skilled suppliers; existing contracts had been originated by Salvatore himself. A Ferragamo production expert supervised each of the three major types of manufacturing—leather, clothing, and silk printing. Ferragamo's system of external manufacture was common among Italian luxury goods companies; as *The Economist* chronicled, "Giorgio Armani has no factory; Gucci is little more than an office ... Benetton employs fewer than 2,000 workers and puts out four-fifths of its business to a network of small firms."[1] Ferragamo, however, stood apart in the closeness and duration of relationships with its 18 approved manufacturers.

A cousin, Jerry Ferragamo, had been carefully trained by Salvatore to oversee this aspect of the business. It took 12 months (or more) for a new factory to be qualified to produce Ferragamo shoes, after which Ferragamo agreed to absorb 100 percent of the factory's output. The company often helped finance the expansion of its approved suppliers, and worked closely with them when operating problems cropped up.

Unwilling to compromise control of the product, the family refused to license the Ferragamo name to other manufacturers. As Fulvia affirmed, "If the label says Ferragamo, then there is a Ferragamo behind it, from design to sale." Wanda and her six children believed the customer bought Ferragamo because she or he could trust the quality of the product carrying their name.

The company's purchasing activities were supervised by Giuseppe Anichini, an accountant who had served in the company for 32 years and was also an important advisor to Ferruccio. Raw materials were obtained in Italy[2] through an established network of weavers, tanners, and silk printers who supplied materials to Ferragamo's exact specifications. Products were sourced by division through Osmannoro, although Anichini was modi-

fying the process to achieve synergies of purchasing wherever possible.

Ferragamo was widely respected in the industry for its vigilant policing of the brand. A full-time staff person was employed to guard against copies, simulations, and cheaper-priced interpretations to which luxury goods were especially vulnerable. For example, the company ensured that Ferragamo's scarf dies were not "borrowed" to print bootleg designs on cheaper silk, and that its gold-toned signature hardware was doled out to manufacturers by the piece.

Marketing and Distribution

Ferragamo's operations on three continents differed in sales and opportunities (see Exhibit 4-A and 4-B). The U.S. market, reflecting Salvatore's early success in Hollywood, was historically Ferragamo's largest and most important, accounting at one time for as much as 70 percent of the company's total sales. Products were sold mainly through department stores and franchised outlets, but by the end of 1990, company-owned boutiques were also significant. Until 1982, the U.S. market had been run largely from Florence. At that point, Wanda had decided to place a family member on site, and Massimo (then 25 years old) agreed to run Moda Imports, the U.S. operating company.

Under Massimo, the U.S. business grew rapidly and exerted increasing influence over the company's direction. Recognizing this, Massimo built a staff of experienced outsiders to help him run the operations, which by 1990 consisted of a staff of 53, three company-owned boutiques (with a fourth, in Beverly Hills, to open in 1991), and an extensive retail network in the United States and Canada. They, in turn, had put increased pressure

---

[1] *The Economist*, May 26, 1990.
[2] Ferragamo utilized Chinese silk on occasion.

on Florence to move faster and to broaden the company's product offerings.

Massimo felt the American market offered significant additional growth through opening more company-owned outlets and building sales in key department stores such as Saks Fifth Avenue, Nieman Marcus, and Nordstrom. In particular, the Saks relationship, which dated to Salvatore's days, had helped the company gain representation in other prestige retailers over the years. Ferragamo was one of the top three suppliers to these retailers in 1990.

Ferragamo's European business was relatively underdeveloped; outside of Italy, Spain, and the U.K., the brand was relatively unknown. Since the mid-1980s, Leonardo Ferragamo had been responsible for correcting this oversight. He recently hired a department store expert from England to help him pursue opportunities in France, Germany, and Eastern Europe, and also set up a Hong Kong office to develop his Asian business. Aiming to expand distribution, Leonardo's market development group launched an ambitious Asian growth campaign in 1988. Within two years, they had opened 13 new boutiques and 10 "corners" in Hong Kong, Thailand, Korea, Malaysia, and Taiwan. And they had developed a substantial Japanese business through an exclusive distributor in that country.

Overall, compared with many other fashion houses, Ferragamo was considered quite fussy about store sites, designs, and merchandising. Each of its 17 company-owned and 16 franchised boutiques was expected to carry a full line of Ferragamo products—particularly shoes—and each boutique manager came to Florence twice a year to select merchandise from the Ferragamo collections. Ellen Bygrave, an experienced retailer from Singapore, was in charge of all company-owned boutiques.

Despite a strong presence in tourist areas, stores were designed to attract the local population first, and secondarily any transient customers. Boutiques were situated in the most desirable shopping area of a major city, and featured significant street frontage for display windows. Ferragamo was quick to remove stores from shopping areas that had declined in status. Like the company-owned stores, the franchised stores were subject to rigid standards of store design, merchandising, product pricing, and selling. (See Exhibit 5 for a list of retail stores.)

With department store distribution, the company had far less control over what was stocked and where and how it was sold. It focused almost exclusively on the top one or two high-end department stores in each market, where competition for representation was fierce. The strength of Ferragamo's local consumer franchise essentially determined what those retailers would stock. In the United States, for instance, this was mainly shoes, although the other lines were gradually gaining distribution. In Europe, the major goal was to gain a market foothold through shoe distribution. In Asia, stocking the whole line was important. According to Massimo, getting high-end department stores in the United States to handle Ferragamo's nonshoe lines would require a major step-up in the company's design and merchandising skills. However, he was concerned that recent RTW upgrading efforts—while they had helped build sales—might have confused customers about what Ferragamo stood for.

While each division had a rough customer profile, Ferragamo lacked detailed information about buyer habits or demographics. The company surmised that the contemporary female customer began buying in her forties, and was loyal primarily to one division: She was, for example, a shoe customer who occasionally bought a scarf or dress. Financially secure, she was interested in value, but spurned clothing emblazoned with designer insignia. The company knew much less about its male customers.

Ferragamo's marketing efforts up through 1990 were successful but relatively undermanaged. Since no one was responsible for corporate marketing, there was no formalized corporate marketing strategy or plan. Wanda had a special interest in advertising, on which the firm spent about $9 million annually, and supervised relationships with the agency. The three sisters exerted considerable influence on how their products were marketed, and Massimo and Leonardo played a role in their respective geographic markets. Although Wanda and the family had recently decided to bring in a top marketing executive, they were as yet undecided about how that function would be organized and staffed.

THE LUXURY GOODS INDUSTRY

The luxury goods industry flourished during the booming world economy of the late 1980s, reaching $52 billion by 1990; a rapidly growing class of newly rich consumers seemed willing to pay high prices for prestigious labels. Well-known purveyors of high-fashion clothing, perfume, and other expensive wares increased production of "exclusive" products and concocted new items to sell, typically under the same upmarket brands. Many firms made a fortune: The members of Comité Colbert, an association of 70 of France's biggest luxury companies, increased its sales by 25 percent in 1989 to $5.4 billion.[3]

In a market where even poorly managed luxury firms made a profit, "creativity" and "style," rather than hardheaded business strategies, were typically viewed as the keys to success. Once-staid luxury houses like Gucci, Chanel, and Hermès updated product and marketing strategies during the late 1980s to capture the younger, trendier customer who accounted for the fast-growing clientele of most luxury firms by 1990.[4] Gucci downplayed its familiar, old-fashioned G symbol and revamped its product line, offering loafers in red and mustard-yellow suede along with the traditional black and brown leather, and a new line of RTW, featuring pumpkin-orange wool coats and leggings. Chanel hired two renowned designers—Lagerfeld and Stein—to style and run its RTW and accessories lines; by 1990 they had built a powerful and growing international high-fashion business. Hermès also assembled a new design team which, while keeping the classics, gradually introduced a few fresh new styles, including brightly colored silk-print body stockings. Where Hermès had traditionally considered it vulgar to use models in advertisements and had featured its colorful silk scarves in black and white line drawings, that policy changed in 1984.

As a full-line retailer of luxury goods, Ferragamo's boutiques competed with the Hermès, Valentino, and Chanel boutiques, often located along the same street. In this environment, Ferragamo's prices were somewhat lower than the others, reflect-

---

[3] "The Lapse of Luxury," *The Economist*, January 5, 1991, p. 49.
[4] The typical luxury customer, once over 40, was 30 to 40 years old in 1990. [Nina Carnton, "New Life in Old Houses," *Newsweek*, August 26, 1990.]

ing a customer-perceived difference in chic and styling.

In department stores, Ferragamo's products faced a broader range of competitors. In women's shoes, the Ferragamo customer compared shoes by Joan & David, Jourdan, and Bruno Magli. Men's shoes were measured against Cole-Haan and Bally. The price tag carried greater weight in the department store than in the boutique, although fashionability remained important. Ferragamo shoes were competitively priced in the upper part of the market, where its breadth of sizes and styles made Ferragamo the leading brand.

In women's RTW, Ferragamo's collection hung in department stores beside the most exclusive designer sportswear names: Genny, Escada, Ms. V, and, to a lesser extent, Valentino, Armani, and Ungaro. Ferragamo competed most effectively when shown in an in-store boutique environment, where its RTW collection could be featured in interchangeable pieces. Some of Ferragamo's classic women's ensembles were less striking than those of its high-fashion competitors, although recent collections had made progress in this area.

With the exception of neckties, which competed directly with Hermès as "status" silks in better department stores, men's RTW was primarily featured in Ferragamo Uomo boutiques. This pitted the company against other European-style men's designers, such as Armani and Versace, whose boutiques often faced those of Ferragamo.

MANAGING THE COMPANY

Ferragamo's organization was highly personal and drawn largely around comfortable family relations, not by a formal hierarchical structure (see Exhibit 6).

Wanda sat at the top of a flat pyramid. Eldest son Ferruccio functioned as the company's chief operating officer. Informally, the other family members and all outsiders reported directly to him.

The board of directors consisted of Wanda as chairman plus her six children, son-in-law Giovanni Gentile, and two outsiders. Normally, the board dealt mainly with routine legal and tax matters rather than key policy decisions.

The recent addition of Geraldo Mazzalovo was largely motivated by Ferruccio's concerns that Ferragamo had begun to outgrow its very informal organizational setup. During his brief tenure, Mazzalovo had already begun to update, strengthen, and formalize the company's financial statements, control reports, and reporting relationships. He had also been inserted into the store site selection process and he had begun to recruit experienced outsiders to increase the company's technical capabilities.

Wanda's Role

By the end of 1990, Wanda's role had evolved to something like a U.S.-style board chairman, primarily focusing on the work environment, strategy/resource allocation, and fashion aspects of the company. As one of her children put it:

> Wanda has three remarkable skills that have helped us become a successful company:
> She has a clear vision of how the fashion world is evolving. She is the one who has pushed us into new markets like the Far East. She has also helped us decide to deemphasize franchises in favor of department stores and company boutiques.

Despite being untrained in finance and accounting, she has a great feeling for how to make money. For instance, she saw the leverage we get from owning prime retail locations in key cities around the world. Today those store sites are an extremely valuable hard asset to Ferragamo.

And she understands better than anyone what will sell and how to deal with our retailers. She serves as a sounding board for our new collections. When someone has a wild idea, they'll show it to Mother and she'll know if it's right.

When she was not meeting with customers or officials or visiting new markets and stores, Wanda worked in the palazzo from 8:30 AM to 7 PM, and frequently spent evenings devoted to business. "We can never rest on our laurels—for 30 years there has been so much to do," she would often proclaim. She was always accessible to family members, and other managers were also very comfortable asking for her opinions. Even family gatherings weren't exempt from business discussions. Said Leonardo, "When we get together, we often talk about family matters—until Mother shows up. Then it's back to business!"

Family Involvement

Nonfamily employees marveled at the Ferragamos' ability to work together and respect each other's opinions. Wanda insisted that the family "work as a team," encouraging the children to iron out any differences among themselves. She believed the family should form a cohesive decision-making body, "like seven arteries to the heart." However, if eventually they could not arrive at a consensus, she was quite comfortable stepping in as a "facilitator." She rarely made controversial decisions herself but had become quite adept at guiding the discussions to a satisfactory decision. One major U.S. retailer who knew the family well commented, "They are a remarkable group. Each one is an able manager and a significant contributor. They all share their mother's dedication to quality and integrity. For example, Massimo, the one I know best, would be a big success in most any business."

Anticipating conflicts, Wanda had forbidden spouses from joining the company long before any of the children married. Even Giovanna's husband, Giovanni Gentile, who consulted nearly full time to the Data division, was not an employee of Ferragamo.

Although none of Wanda's 17 grandchildren was yet old enough to join the firm, the Ferragamos insisted that they must earn a position through education and experience. Wanda asserted that "they must prove their skill in some other business and then dedicate their lives to the business." Although the company's ownership would eventually pass to the next generation, the family expected only a few grandchildren to become company managers.

Some nonfamily members admitted their frustrations with the family's slow decision making, and cited the occasional decision which was more conducive to maintaining family harmony than to furthering the business. One recently hired manager commented on the stress inherent in a system in which company position paralleled birth order and, to some extent, professional success. He pointed out that, "Everyone knows the Ferragamos make the key decisions and hold the top jobs." However, another senior outsider commented that the family was open-minded to advice from its key employees.

Work Environment

Wanda stressed that the family's serious work ethic provided an important example for employees: "Our people see us working hard alongside them when they know we could be at home, or on a boat, or on holiday." She credited the emphasis on "family values" with inspiring a cordial atmosphere, "not like a cutthroat business empire."

Ferragamo approached hiring with caution as, like other Italian companies, it hired "for life" (employees could not be fired except for major shortcomings). Thus, employees felt "taken care of" by the company, which offered help with pensions, medical needs, tuition, and even house purchases. Employees were also well paid: The company offered salaries and benefits comparable to other Florentine businesses and would match fashion industry salary levels where appropriate. Top managers also received incentive compensation and bonuses tied to their division and the company performance as a whole. Ferruccio determined the bonuses and viewed them as an important motivator.

Ferragamo's atmosphere was much less formal than many European businesses, although the grandeur of the palazzo inspired a degree of decorousness. In a country where titles were important indicators of power, Wanda preferred to be called "Signora Ferragamo" rather than the proper "Presidentessa." According to Giovanna, "Mama has the mind of a businesswoman, but the heart of a Neapolitan mother!" The six children were addressed officially as "Signor Ferruccio," "Signora

Giovanna," and more frequently by their first name alone. The rest of the professional staff were addressed by their first names.

The company conducted most of its work in Italian, although professionals were comfortable speaking English and other European and Asian languages. While the support and manufacturing staff were mostly Italian, the management staff was multinational. Wanda considered the diversity of managerial perspective beneficial to the company's international clientele and important for future operations.

MAZZALOVO'S PRESENTATION

Mazzalovo's presentation to Ferragamo's board outlined the opportunity the company faced and then focused on the management changes needed to capitalize upon it.

Mazzalovo began by agreeing with Wanda's conclusions:

> The global leisure market offers Ferragamo a huge opportunity. It is a large, growing, and profitable market. And, aside from shoes, we really haven't scratched the surface. As a company, we have some enormous strengths on which to build: tremendous product quality, fine brand awareness, a positive corporate culture, and the willingness to invest in the long term. And we have a strong, experienced management team at the top.
>
> However, if we are going to expand into higher fashion lines, we must make some adjustments to become more aggressive in several areas.
>
> ■ We need to make faster decisions. For example, our site selection criteria often puts us in the position of losing good sites while we debate on small details.

- We must improve our interdepartmental communications and coordination. Ferragamo must stand for a consistent image, and individual product lines must reinforce one another, not go off in different directions.

- We must also become more market-focused, and less product-focused. For example, we know very little about our customers and why they buy our products. We also know very little about the pricing elasticity on our kinds of products.

- We must strengthen our distribution base; we are too dependent upon a few major department stores.

The company will have to change significantly to grow in this highly competitive, volatile luxury goods marketplace. Specifically, we must first develop and adhere to a focused brand strategy, and second, create an organizational structure which is more responsive to the market and possibly less dictated by current management's concerns.

Mazzalovo stressed the need for the company to launch a full-scale strategy study to examine its products, markets, and competition. Pausing to distribute handouts (see Exhibits 7 and 8), he then offered his recommendations for Ferragamo's future position:

> I envision a full-line luxury house strategy. We could build Ferragamo by featuring a full line of products, similar to what Chanel and Hermès have done. New items such as cosmetics, perfume, watches, or evening clothes could be added to our existing product lines. This would enable Ferragamo to command higher prices, particularly in RTW, but would subject us to the volatility of the high-fashion business. It would require a significant investment in advertising and market expansion.

To assist Ferragamo's geographic expansion, Mazzalovo proposed that the company retain a management consulting firm to help develop a strategic plan for each of its three key markets—America, Europe, and Asia. He recommended McKinsey & Company because of their worldwide office network. Concurrent with the market and strategy study, Mazzalovo emphasized the need for continued adjustment of the company's organizational structure, with special attention to how it supported or inhibited a product's path from design to market. He then challenged:

> Now that you know what's involved, my questions to you are, Do you still want to go for it, and are you prepared to make the changes necessary to achieve that goal?

THE FAMILY MEETING AT FIESOLE

On the Sunday following Mazzalovo's presentation, the Ferragamos met for their bimonthly family gathering at Wanda's 15th-century villa in Fiesole. Wanda and her children wanted to be sure that "the grandchildren" were informed about the program that was being considered, since it affected the future of the company. While all 17 grandchildren were present, the discussion—led by Ferruccio—was aimed chiefly at those who were 14 and older.

Once the grandchildren's meeting had been completed, the family enjoyed dinner together, after which, while the grandchildren were being settled, Wanda moved into the living room for a more comprehensive yet informal discussion of Mazzalovo's plan. At dinner, Giovanna had urged the family to forge ahead, arguing that, "We've been doing the same thing for 30 years—it will do us good to stand back and learn." Seeing that her children had reassembled, Wanda reminded them, first of all, that the decisions they made in the next few days could determine the company's direction over the next decades. She also said:

> The Salvatore years were characterized by product innovation and creative design. The family years have been characterized by building product dedication and brand integrity. You have created demand and trust for the Ferragamo brand. We have established a strong base on which to build. Now, our challenge is to combine the strengths of these two eras. Yet we must do this carefully to avoid destroying the things that have made us so successful as a family business. After all, our major goal is to build the right kind of a business, not just make ourselves wealthier.
>
> Whether that can be accomplished by Mazzalovo's plan is for us to discuss this evening.

EXHIBIT 1-A
SALVATORE FERRAGAMO SPA CONSOLIDATED
INCOME STATEMENT ($000)

	1988	1989	1990
Net sales	158,983	193,510	202,742
Cost of sales	94,699	111,040	114,450
Gross profit	64,284	82,470	88,292
Operating expenses	51,106	57,801	57,900
Operating profit	13,178	24,669	30,392
Financial (costs) revenues	(1,636)	409	(7,758)
Real estate (costs) revenues	2,149	4,179	3,668
Nonoperating costs	1,787	4,417	4,044
Extraordinary items	(2,864)	(9,881)	(12,563)
Profit before taxes	12,614	23,793	17,783

Note: Some yearly fluctuations are the result of translating liras into
       dollars at prevailing rates, and some numbers have been altered
       to preserve confidentiality.

EXHIBIT 1-B
SALVATORE FERRAGAMO SPA CONSOLIDATED BALANCE SHEET ($000)

	1988	1989	1990
Assets			
Cash	8,730	13,989	21,504
Accounts trade receivable	23,599	24,436	18,940
Other receivables	16,419	22,484	17,401
Short-term investments	35,706	32,119	12,687
Net inventories	23,535	27,543	41,589
Total current assets	107,989	120,571	112,121
Long-term investments	35,668	33,616	26,124
Tangible assets	70,187	56,264	57,952
Intangible assets	31,531	31,872	23,764
Total fixed assets	137,386	121,752	107,840
Total assets	245,375	242,323	219,961
Liabilities & stockholders' equity			
Banks & loans	53,425	36,084	15,145
Accounts trade payable	12,170	14,621	20,219
Taxes	12,727	9,839	4,922
Other payables	67,863	17,852	9,433
Total current liabilities	146,185	78,396	49,719
Banks & loans	26,445	72,689	71,045
Provision	5,220	8,571	7,299
Total long-term liabilities	31,665	81,260	78,344
Equity	61,955	70,020	79,727
Net result current year	5,570	12,647	12,171
Total equity	67,525	82,667	91,898
Total liabilities & equity	245,375	242,323	219,961

Note: Numbers have been altered somewhat to preserve confidentiality.

EXHIBIT 2
FERRAGAMO SALES AND PRODUCTION FOR 1990 BY DIVISION

Division	Sales (millions $)	No. Items Sold/Year (thousands, units)	Retail Price
Women' s shoes			
Boutique	60	300	$110–$160
Originals	70	500	$175–$275
Women's RTW collections			
Standard	8	60	$400–$700
Sweaters & knitwear	4	60	$200–$400
Accessories			
Bags & leather	12	200	$175–$250
Leather accessories	3	40	$110–$225
Ties	4	400	$ 85
Scarves	2	16	$140
Men's shoes and RTW	40	250	$180–$320
Total	$ 203		

EXHIBIT 3-A
FERRAGAMO BUSINESS VOLUME BY PRODUCT CATEGORY AND MARKET IN 1989*

Product Item	U.S.	Asia	Europe	Italy	TOTAL
Shoes, women	65.8%	32.1%	49.7%	25.6%	57.3%
Shoes, men	14.0	5.4	2.7	3.3	10.6
Sweaters, women	2.8	14.1	11.5	15.2	5.9
Sweaters, men	0.8	1.8	0.0	2.0	0.6
Clothes, women	4.4	21.9	17.4	7.4	8.9
Clothes, men	1.8	2.7	0.0	1.6	1.3
Bags/leather	6.0	11.1	9.4	14.8	7.8
Leather accessories[†]	0.8	2.9	1.5	4.4	1.1
Ties	1.8	3.5	2.7	10.0	2.8
Other accessories[‡]	1.5	4.4	5.1	15.7	3.7
Total	100.0%	100.0%	100.0%	100.0%	100.0%

*Most recent categorical data available for all countries outside of the United States.

[†]Includes small leather goods such as datebooks, keychains, and wallets.

[‡]Includes women's scarves, pillows, towels, and the like.

EXHIBIT 3-B
FERRAGAMO PRODUCT SALES TRENDS IN THE UNITED STATES

Product Item	1990	1985
Shoes, women	68.2%	78.5%
Shoes, men	14.1	10.7
Sweaters, women	2.6	2.0
Sweaters, men	0.3	0.5
Clothes, women	3.9	3.2
Clothes, men	0.6	1.2
Bags/leather	6.7	3.0
Leather accessories	0.4	0.1
Ties	1.9	0.2
Other accessories	1.3	0.6
Total	100.0%	100.0%

EXHIBIT 4-A
FERRAGAMO BUSINESS BY AREA

Market	1990	1985
U.S.	53%	65%
Asia	13	5
Europe (excluding Italy)		
Boutiques	3	2
Duty-free	1	0
Wholesale	7	3
Italy		
Boutiques	19	20
Wholesale	4	5
Total	100%	100%

EXHIBIT 4-B
FERRAGAMO BUSINESS VOLUME BY OUTLET

	1990	1985
Company-owned boutiques	18.0%	15.0%
Department stores and specialty stores	82.0	85.0
Total	100.0%	100.0%

EXHIBIT 5
FERRAGAMO BOUTIQUE RETAIL STORES

Location		Number	Relationship
Italy			
Florence	Via dei Tornabuoni	(1)	Company-owned
Milan	Via Montenapoleone (Uomo)	(2)	Company-owned
Rome	Via Condotti (Uomo)	(2)	Company-owned
Naples	Piazza dei Martiri (Uomo)	(2)	Company-owned
Genova	Via Roma	(1)	Company-owned
Torino	Via Roma	(1)	Company-owned
Bari	Via Sparano	(1)	Company-owned
Capri	Via Vittorio Emanuele (Uomo)	(2)	Company-owned
England			
London	Old Bond Street	(1)	Company-owned
Switzerland			
Zurich	Bleicherweg	(1)	Company-owned
Spain			
Barcelona	Avenida Diagonal	(1)	Franchised
United States			
New York	Fifth Avenue (Uomo)	(2)	Company-owned
Palm Beach	Worth Avenue	(1)	Company-owned
Honolulu	Royal Hawaiian Shopping Center	(1)	Franchised
Canada			
Vancouver	Robson Street	(1)	Franchised
Japan			
Tokyo	Imperial Hotel	(1)	Franchised
Osaka	Hotel New Otani	(1)	Franchised
Hong Kong	The Mandarin Oriental	(1)	Franchised
	Queen's Road Central	(1)	Franchised
	The Regent Hotel	(1)	Franchised
	The Peninsula Hotel	(1)	Franchised
	Causeway Bay	(1)	Franchised
	Pacific Place	(1)	Franchised
	Matsuzakaya	(1)	Franchised
Singapore	The Paragon Orchard Road	(1)	Franchised
Malaysia			
Kuala Lumpur	Hilton Hotel	(1)	Franchised
South Korea			
Seoul	Samkyung Building	(1)	Franchised
Taiwan			
Taipei	Tung Hwa South Road	(1)	Franchised

EXHIBIT 6
FERRAGAMO ORGANIZATIONAL CHART, 1990

EXHIBIT 6
FERRAGAMO ORGANIZATIONAL CHART, 1990

Board

President Wanda

Managing Director Ferruccio

Moda Imports Massimo

Price Committee

Asia/Europe Leonardo

Image Committee

Retail Director

Marketing Director

Strategy and Finance Mazzalovo

Personnel

Data

General Affairs Anichini

Sourcing

Organization and Strategy

Finance

Control

Production Leather

Production RTW

Production Accessories

Shoes Fiamma

RTW Giovanna

Accessories Fulvia

Fashion Coordinators

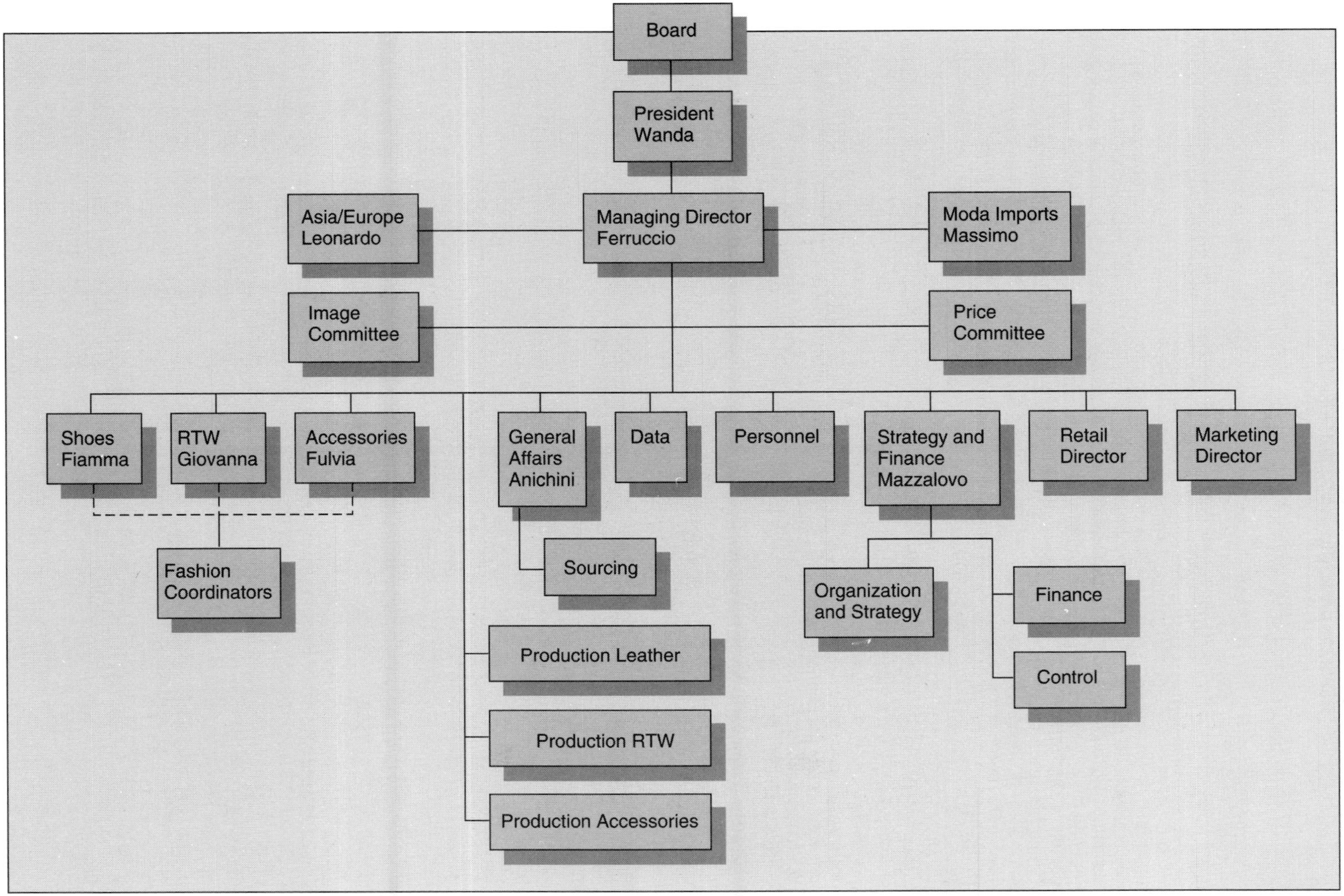

Exhibit 7
Mazzalovo's Report
Summary of Observed Problems

Strategic	Organizational	Operational

Product orientation
 • Inattentive to the market
    • Insufficient knowledge of customers & competitors
    • Poor coordination between Marketing, Design, and Production
    • No analysis of specific markets (geographic and cultural aspects, income levels . . .)
 • Slow market penetration
 • Risky client portfolio:
    • 51 percent sales to 6 clients
    • 70 percent sales to 16 clients
 	
 Crisis of identity
 • Timid, immobilized
 • Inconsistent image (incongruous ad campaigns, prices, designers)
 • No strategic plan
 	
 Organizational structure not ready to expand
 	
 Minimal use of new technologies
 	
 Rigid productioin processes
 	
 Strong influence of U.S. market
 	
 Lack of orientation to objectives and results
	Structure
	 • Not clear
	 • Not formalized
	 • Certain functions missing, others undeveloped
	
	 Poor coordination
	 • Functions segmented: Marketing/Design/P.R./Publicity Competitive position/Finance/CED
	
	 Minimal interdepartmental communication between:
	 • Production/Shipping
	 • Design/Production
	 • Production/Sales
	 • Publicity/Florence/United States
	 • Sales/Finance and Administration
	 • Florence/foreign stores
	 • Florence finances/foreign offices
	
	 Management style
	 • Slow decision making
	 • Centralized; "presidential"
	 • Reactive (little planning)
	 • Minimal delegation
	 • Senior managers involved with operating details
	 • 18 employees report to one manager
	
	 Human resources
	    Poorly managed
	
	 Culture—conservative
		Functions missing
		 • Strategic planning
		 • Organization
		 • Monitoring of competitors/customers
		 • Internal auditing
		 • Investment evaluations
		 • Business development
		 • Marketing
		
		 Functions to implement
		 • Development of products
		 • Control
		
		 Functions needing improved coordination
		 • Design/production/sales
		 • Public relations/publicity
		 • Management of stores and boutiques
		 • Logistics
		 • Personnel
		 • Finance and administration

These hypotheses must now be verified by a strategic study.

EXHIBIT 8
MAZZALOVO'S RECOMMENDATIONS FOR CHANGE

Revamp organization to bring it in line with chosen strategy.	• Hire management consultants.
	• Perform organizational study to:
	  • Formalize distribution of responsibilities.
	  • Improve productivity.
	  • Align organizational structure with the general orientation of the company.
	  • Recommend specific organizational changes and alternatives.
	  • Perform strategic studies (control and information systems, etc.).

Create a formal structure for the Market Development Division.	• Division should perform small-scale research studies on issues including the company's Japanese distribution process and American pricing procedure.
Establish Finance and Administrative Dept.	• Internal audits. • Coordinate and systematize billing and payment procedures. • Establish internal control models for international stores (review operations, bank accounts . . .).
Reorganize Men's Divisions as a prototype for other divisions.	• Hire two professionals as division directors for Men's Shoes and RTW. • Give Men's directors broad charters to supervise the entire process, including product sales and marketing.
Develop a more aggressive marketing concept.	• Hire a senior executive with experience in the international luxury goods and fashion industries as marketing director. • Marketing director should sit on Image Committee.

APPENDIX A

THE SHOEMAKER OF DREAMS: EARLY FERRAGAMO HISTORY

Salvatore Ferragamo made his first pair of shoes when he was nine years old to save his sister the shame of going barefoot to her First Communion. By age 12 he was the shoemaker of choice in his Neapolitan village of Bonito, Italy. Handmaking shoes was slow work and provided a meager living: While Salvatore could produce five pairs on a good day, the week's tiny margins could be eroded by one wrong cut of the leather or slip of the hammer. At the age of 16 in 1914, Salvatore left for America to investigate the emerging mechanized shoemaking industry and to find ways to improve the process.

Dissatisfied with the low-quality machined shoes produced by the shoe factories of Massachusetts, Salvatore sought customers willing to pay more for handmade shoes. In 1915 he set up a small shoemaking business near the burgeoning motion picture industry in California. Commissions from film stars and costume designers established his business, and his original styles were showcased in dozens of films. In a short time, Ferragamo earned renown for his creative, unusual, and comfortable shoe designs. Customers often paid Ferragamo more than he asked, claiming that such exquisite shoes "should cost more." By 1927 he had a booming business, an international clientele, and a desire to expand his empire.

Returning to Florence, Salvatore established a shop with 60 shoemakers in the Palazzo Feroni Spini on the Arno River. In 1940 he married Wanda Miletti, the daughter of the mayor in his hometown of Bonito. Despite the bankruptcy of an early partnership, his business thrived. Production leapt to 350 pairs of shoes a day by 1950, handcrafted by 700 Italian artisan employees, mostly for the American market.[5] Retaining personal control over shoe design, Salvatore experimented with shoemaking technology and devised a method for the consistent measurement and manufacture of shoes. Throughout his 57-year career, he strove to make shoes that would fit the foot properly. Taking medical school courses in anatomy, Salvatore created a "legacy of comfort" which revolutionized the industry. His creative fervor was such that he produced over 20,000 shoe styles in his lifetime, including the famous steel-frame stiletto heel worn by Marilyn Monroe, the wedge-heeled cork sandal, the platform heel, and a series of shoes made of raffia, cellophane, bark, and seaweed during the war when the leather supply was restricted. By the time he died in 1960, the self-styled "shoemaker of dreams" had achieved a worldwide reputation for exquisitely designed shoes of the finest quality.

Wanda Takes Over

Salvatore's death left his widow with six children to raise and a company to run. Receiving several offers to sell, Wanda was loath to abandon the company's 100 employees and business her husband had spent a lifetime to build. Within three weeks after his death, she assumed his role as president of Salvatore Ferragamo, SpA. Lack of business experience did not deter the 38-year-old signora, whose youngest child, Massimo, was only two years old. Over the course of their close marriage—"he would tell me everything"—she had taken to heart the

---

[5] Salvatore Ferragamo, *Shoemaker of Dreams* (George G. Harrap & Co. Ltd, 1957).

three tenets of Salvatore's business philosophy:

1. to be honest and fair with employees, suppliers, and customers,
2. to build a product of the finest quality, and
3. to provide excellent value for the money.

As president, Wanda had two major goals: to continue her husband's work, and to encourage her children to join her in the family enterprise. She also wished to fulfill Salvatore's dream: to build a fashion house that would "clothe a woman elegantly with Ferragamo products, from top to toe." At the time she took over, the business had shoe sales of about $20 million, evenly divided between the Italian and American markets, with profits around 5 percent.

APPENDIX B

SALVATORE FERRAGAMO'S "LEGACY OF CREATIVITY"

APPENDIX C

THE FERRAGAMO FAMILY

Front row, left to right: Giovanna Gentile Ferragamo, Fiamma di San Giuliano Ferragamo, Mrs. Wanda Ferragamo, Fulvia Visconti Ferragamo. Back row, left to right: Leonardo Ferragamo, Ferrucio Ferragamo, Massimo Ferragamo.

Schlumberger, Ltd.: Jean Riboud
Excerpts from "A Certain Poetry"
by Ken Auletta

Jean Riboud

From the windows of Jean Riboud's New York office, on the 44th floor at 277 Park Avenue, one can see the buildings that house the headquarters of such corporate giants as Warner Communications, Gulf & Western, Citicorp, International Telephone and Telegraph, Colgate-Palmolive, United Brands, Bankers Trust, CBS, RCA, and International Paper. All of them are better known than Schlumberger, Ltd., the company that Riboud is chairman and chief executive officer of, but none of them can match Schlumberger's profits. In stock-market value—the number of outstanding shares multiplied by the price per share—only three companies were worth more than Schlumberger at the end of 1981. They were AT&T ($48 billion), IBM ($34 billion), and Exxon ($27 bil-

lion). Schlumberger was then worth $16 billion.

Riboud has offices in New York and Paris, and both are rather ordinary except for the art on the walls—works by Picasso, Klee, Max Ernst, Magritte, Jasper Johns, Victor Brauner, and Janez Bernik. His New York office is a snug corner—16 feet by 20 feet—with beige walls. An adjoining conference room, 17 feet by 18 feet, has one couch and a round wooden table with six chairs. Riboud's office has a single telephone with just two lines, and no private bathroom; there are white blinds on the windows and a simple beige sisal carpet on the floor. His desk is a long, rectangular teak table with chrome legs; on it are a few memorandums but no "in" or "out" box and no books. His personal New York staff consists of one secretary, Lucille Northrup, to whom he rarely dictates; memorandums and paperwork are frowned upon at Schlumberger, and when Riboud wants to send out a memorandum, he first writes in longhand. His Paris office is equally uncluttered.

Riboud is 63 years old. He is 5 feet 10 inches tall and slight of build, with wavy gray hair combed straight back. His nose is long and thin; his lips are narrow. His suits come in conservative shades, and his shirts are usually quiet solid colors. He speaks softly, sometimes almost inaudibly, in accented English, rarely gesticulates, and is an intense listener, usually inspecting his long fingers while others speak. Everything about Riboud conveys an impression of delicacy except his eyes, which are deep brown and cryptic. He arrives at work around 10 AM and he takes at least six weeks' vacation annually. Yet he is no figurehead; rather, he believes in delegating authority—a principle that no doubt accounts for the calm of Schlumberger's offices in New York and Paris. Schlumberger employs 75,000 people, and of that number only 197 work at the two headquarters.

As the chief executive of a multinational corporation—Schlumberger does business in 92 countries—Riboud has a somewhat surprising talent for avoiding publicity. He is a stranger to most other corporate executives, deliberately keeping his distance from them. He sits on no other company's board of directors.

Riboud has been the chief executive of Schlumberger for the past 18 years. Because the corporation does no mass advertising, of either the consumer or the institutional sort, because it retains no lobbyist in Washington and no public-relations agency in New York or Paris, and because it has never been involved in a public controversy, Schlumberger (pronounced "shlum-bare-zhay") remains one of the world's lesser-known major corporations. It is a high-technology company that generates the bulk of its income from the oil-field-service business—making tools that enable oil companies to find and drill for oil with great precision. The information gained and the techniques learned in oil-field services have helped the company to expand into such fields as electric, gas, and water meters; flight-test systems; transformers and semiconductors; automatic test equipment for integrated-circuit chips; electronic telephone circuits; computer-aided design and manufacturing processes; and robotics. Schlumberger is recognized on Wall Street as one of the world's best-managed multinational companies, and financial analysts can point to a number of facts to document its success. Its net income has grown by about 30 percent in each of the past 10 years up to 1981. Its earnings per share rose by more than 30 percent annually between 1971 and 1981, even though the price of oil remained stable or declined in several of those years. Its profit in 1982 totaled $1,350,000,000 on revenues of $6,284,000,000, for a profit as a percentage of revenue of 21 percent —higher than that of any of the thousand other leading industrial companies in the world. Its return on equity in 1981 was 34 percent, while the median for the *Fortune* 500 companies was 13⁸⁄₁₀ percent. Schlumberger has relatively little long-term debt: it amounted to just $462,000,000 at the end of 1982, or 3 percent of the company's total capitalization. And while the profits of most oil and oil-field-service companies fell sharply in 1982, Schlumberger's net income rose by 6 percent.

Science is the foundation of Schlumberger. Science is the link between the various corporate subsidiaries, for the task of most of them is collecting, measuring, and transmitting data. Science, and particularly geophysics, was at the core of the careers of Conrad and Marcel Schlumberger, the company's founders. Ever since the first oil well was drilled in 1859, oil companies had longed for a technology that would help them find oil. Initially, prospectors had to painstakingly extract core samples and drill cuttings from rock formations, haul them slowly to the surface, ship them to a laboratory, and await a chemical analysis. This tedious, expensive process enabled the oil companies to determine whether there was oil in a given area and even to determine its quality, but not its precise quantity or the exact shape of the well; and it did not enable them to pinpoint where to drill. Conrad, having discovered a new geophysical principle, assigned the job of fashioning a tool and testing it to Henri Doll, who was a brilliant young engineer and also the husband of Conrad's daughter Anne. Doll's task was to chart the electric current as it encountered various kinds of rock, water, and oil. By comparing the actual current coursing through the earth with records showing the electrical resistivity of each substance, the brothers and Doll hoped to produce what amounted to the world's first X-ray of an oil well.

Today, the tools are more refined, but the basic process—wireline logging, as it came to be known—is a measurement taken on just about every oil or gas well drilled in the world. And today, without benefit of a patent on its basic logging process, Schlumberger—as the original partnership was renamed in 1934—has a near-monopoly on this business, logging some 70 percent of the world's wells. In the United States alone, in 1981 the company hired 1 percent of all the engineers graduating from American colleges.

Over the years, Schlumberger's oil-field business has expanded beyond logging measurements to include a broad range of other services: drilling, testing, and completing wells; pumping; and cementing.

The company's Forex Neptune subsidiary, formed in the 1950s, is now the world's largest oil-drilling company. The Johnston-Macco and Flopetrol subsidiaries provide an assortment of testing and completion services after drilling has started. A subsidiary called The Analysts provides continuous detailed logs of oil wells from the moment drilling begins, in contrast to most logs, which are prepared only before drilling begins or after it ceases. The Dowell Schlumberger company, which is jointly owned by Schlumberger and Dow Chemical, offers pumping and cementing services. Together with the Wireline division, these companies make up the Oilfield Services—one of two major parts of the Schlumberger empire. The other major part is known as Measurement, Control, and Components. Its subsidiaries include the world's largest manufacturer of electric, gas, and water meters; a leading manufacturer of transformers; a producer of valves and safety controls for nuclear power systems; and a manufacturer of flight-control and signal-processing systems for aerospace and military use. The Fairchild Camera & Instrument Corporation, a California-based semiconductor company that Schlumberger acquired in 1979, manufactures, among other products, integrated circuits such as microprocessors and memories; advanced bipolar microprocessors for the F-16 fighter plane; and electronic telephone circuits. Applicon, another subsidiary, is among the pioneers in computer-aided design and other efforts to automate factories.

Schlumberger has a total of 43 major subsidiaries, most of which rely on science and technology. The jewel in Schlumberger's crown is the Wireline, which in 1981 generated 45 percent of the company's $6 billion in revenues and about 70 percent of its $1,200,000,000 in profits. Many of Schlumberger's subsidiaries rank at or near the top of their various industries. The investment banker Felix Rohatyn, who serves on the boards of eight major corporations, including Schlumberger, and is a close friend of Riboud's, says, "By the standard of profit margins, return on investment, compound growth rate, of remaining ahead of the state of the art technically and having an efficient management structure, over the last 20 years —until the recent drastic change in the energy environment—Schlumberger might well have been the single best business in the world." Rohatyn's enthusiasm is shared by independent analysts at the major Wall Street brokerage firms, and their judgment has been reflected in research reports issued by, among others, Morgan Stanley, Merrill Lynch, Paine Webber, Wertheim, L. F. Rothschild, Unterberg , and Towbin. An analysis issued by Barton M. Biggs, managing director of Morgan Stanley, in January of 1982, reads, "Here is this immense, superbly—almost artistically—managed company booming along with a 35 percent compound annual growth rate in earnings and 37 percent in dividends between 1975 and 1980 . . . Our analysis of earnings variability from growth trend shows Schlumberger as having the most consistent, high-growth track of any company in the 1,400-stock universe of our dividend discount model."

Even though Schlumberger is a competitive company devoted to ever-higher profits, over the years its executives have shown a predilection for the politics of the left. Paul Schlumberger urged his sons to share the profits of their company with employees. He financed his sons only on the condition that "the interest of scientific research take precedence over financial ones." Conrad was a pacifist and a socialist until Stalin's Russia disillusioned him.

Rene Seydoux, the husband of Marcel's daughter Genevieve, who ran Schlumberger's European wireline operations, and to whom Riboud reported after Marcel's death in 1953, was an ardent and active supporter of the French Socialist Party. Jean de Menil, who supervised all South American operations in the period after the Second World War, supported various liberal causes in the United States. Along with his wife, Dominique, a daughter of Conrad Schlumberger, de Menil became a major financial contributor to Martin Luther King, Jr., and the American civil-rights movement. And in 1981 Jean Riboud, as an intimate of President Mitterrand, supported the Socialist government's proposed nationalization of 46 enterprises.

Riboud is a man of contrast. He is a hugely successful capitalist, with an annual salary of $700,000 and Schlumberger stock worth about $33 million, yet he calls himself a socialist. He loves business, yet most of his friends are from the worlds of art and politics. He was born into a French banking family in Lyons, the historical birthplace of the French ruling class, yet he says that one of his principal goals in life is to battle this class. He has deep roots in France, yet he considers himself an unofficial citizen of India and of the United States. He places a premium on loyalty and sentiment, yet he is a tough businessman who has unhesitatingly fired loyal executives and has had a hand in easing out four members of the Schlumberger family. He is charming yet distant. He is a strong and independent man, yet he has a history of "more or less falling in love"—in the words of his friend the writer Francoise Giroud—with leading French politicians of the left.

Even to many of his friends, Riboud is an enigma. They do not understand his success as a capitalist—in part because he does not speak of Schlumberger to them. "Jean Riboud impersonates a businessman who is trying to hide a certain poetry," Saul Steinberg says. "He is in some sort of Sydney Greenstreet business, as far as we see it—oil, Arabia. I say, 'What's this pussycat doing as director of this company? I can see the pussycat. But where is the crocodile?' Now, no pussycat becomes officer in charge of such a company, and I tell myself that in order to be good on the highest level of anything you need mysterious sources."

Few cities dominate nations the way Lyons once dominated France. A city of over half a million people in the center of France, Lyons was synonymous with the French business establishment. The Ribouds were Roman Catholic—the right religion—and comfortable. The family lived in an apartment in Lyons until 1929, when they moved to a spacious house in the suburb of Ecully. Summers were spent 55 miles north of Lyons, at La Carelle, an estate of 1,300 acres of farmland and wooded hills, which has been in the family since 1850. Like many members of the French establishment, Camille Riboud, Jean's father, attended L'Ecole des Sciences Politiques, in Paris, where his circle of friends included Georges Boris, who became a close associate of Pierre Mendes-France; Andre Istel, a future banker; Maurice Schlumberger, who became a banking partner of Istel's; and Jean Schlumberger, who became a writer of some distinction. Maurice and Jean Schlumberger were brothers of Conrad and Marcel. Jean Riboud says, "My father was an enlightened conservative. He was really part of the establishment and wanted to be part of the establishment, and yet he wanted to be entirely independent-minded—independent of the establishment." His days were

devoted to commerce. At night, he read to his children: Homer, Euripides, Baudelaire, Verlaine, Rimbaud.

Camille's wife, Helene, grew up in Lyons and spent her summers in the nearby town of Givors, where her father's family owned a bottling factory. Helene Riboud was taught to be a devout, unquestioning Catholic, to obey her husband, to control her emotions, and to organize a good home. She "was not a silly woman," Antoine Riboud says, but she was "ordinary" —without "the sparkle of my father." Jean Riboud offers a different memory of Helene. "She was a lively, attractive, gay woman, without the culture of my father," he says. "But she was not an ordinary person." The qualities that Jean remembers most vividly are "an extraordinary dignity and an extraordinary sense of duty." Krishna Riboud remembers her mother-in-law, who died in 1957, as a woman of "great determination and great character," but she also says that Jean has a romanticized view of his father. "He feels that all his cultural background comes from his father," she says. "All the authority he has comes from the mother. I see more of the mother in him than the father."

In 1939, at the age of 53, Camille Riboud died of a heart attack, and Jean, who was then 19, became the de facto head of the family. "Jean is exactly the portrait, the figure of my father," Antoine Riboud says. "He has the same intellectual way of thinking as my father. To all the children, he was the second father."

In 1939, after graduating from L'Ecole des Sciences Politiques, he volunteered for the army but was rejected because, at 19, he was too young. The next year, though, he joined the army as a tank officer, and when Germany invaded France he was sent into battle in the Loire Valley. He was captured in June of 1940, but he escaped. In the spring of 1941, he went to the Sorbonne to study law and economics and prepare for the Civil Service. He studied and lived for two years in occupied Paris, and during this time he kept in touch with the budding Resistance movement in Lyons, attending organizational meetings and slipping back and forth between occupied France and Vichy France.

In the summer of 1943, he and a fellow student, Yves Le Portz, were urged by others in the Resistance to join the Free French Army in North Africa. To get there, they decided to take a route that had been used by, among others, Georges Schlumberger, a son of Maurice: to Perpignan, in the south, by bicycle, and from there the 25 miles or so to Spain by kayak. On a moonless August night, Riboud and Le Portz hid their bicycles at the top of a cliff, put their kayak into the water, and paddled furiously, hoping to parallel the coastline just out of sight. But a storm came up, sending water crashing into their tiny craft and shoving them out into rough seas. Frantically, they struggled back toward the shore, where the water was calmer, and then they made their way south, to a point where the Pyrenees plunged straight down into the Mediterranean. They spotted a cave and, leaving their kayak outside, crawled in to sleep. They were awakened a short while later by officers from a German patrol boat, who, after one look at the detailed maps of the coast of Spain the two were carrying, arrested them. The Germans took them to be interrogated by a colonel, who first saluted their bravery and then turned them over to the Gestapo in Perpignan. After two weeks of questioning, they were taken to the city of Compiegne, north of Paris, and in September they were among 1,200 prisoners shipped by train to Buchenwald.

When Riboud and Le Portz arrived at Buchenwald, experienced prisoners gave them some advice: The Gestapo will ask if you are able to do mechanical work. Say yes. "We had no idea of mechanics at all," recalls Le Portz, who is today chairman of the European Investment Bank. But they followed the advice and were sent to an aircraft-construction plant near Buchenwald. Prisoners who said they were ignorant of mechanics were sent on to Dachau, the extermination camp. Buchenwald was brutal—particularly the long hours working outdoors in winter without a coat. In addition to the cold, the hard labor, and the Gestapo, prisoners of war had to contend with common criminals whom the Germans had rounded up and sent to the camps. "To divide us, they mixed ordinary criminals with members of the Resistance," Le Portz says. "There were as many conflicts among inmates as between inmates and guards. Unity among the prisoners was essential."

Riboud recalls that in many of the camps "some of the Christians and the Communists became forces of order." They helped their fellow prisoners not to lose faith, and to accept discipline and solidarity. Riboud himself soon emerged as a leader at Buchenwald. "We didn't speak German," Le Portz says. "Yet a few months after entering the camp Jean was the official German interpreter for the prisoners—and he'd read German newspapers to them. Moreover, he was a man of extraordinary humor. He tried to make life as easy as possible for other prisoners. Jean managed to establish contact with the outside world and get information to the camp. He was not a passive man."

Of his years at Buchenwald, Riboud says, "I've seen the worst and the best of human beings, to an extent that I never thought could be as bad and as good, as ominous and as perfect." The experience contributed to a lifelong conviction that, in Riboud's words, "in the presence of death there are the ones who fight and the ones who give up, the ones who survive and the ones who do not." Antoine Riboud says that Buchenwald made his brother "more liberal" and also made him "very strong, very capable of resisting anything."

With the war behind him, Jean assumed that a job in his father's bank awaited him. A career in banking had been Camille Riboud's wish for him, and though Jean had no ambitions along those lines he decided to fall in with his father's plan. He recalls, "I went to see the man who was the head of the bank"—his father's partner—"and he said to me, 'There is no room in the bank.'" The partner also told Riboud that he had "no gift for banking." Unsure of what he wanted to do, he went to Paris to have an interview for a job in industry, and while he was there he also went to see Andre Istel, who had been a banking partner of Maurice Schlumberger. Istel, a French Jew, had fled to the United States during the war, and now he planned to open a New York banking office, to be called Andre Istel & Company. Among Istel's clients was the oil-field-service company Schlumberger.

Two months later, in September of 1946, Riboud opened Istel's New York office, working at a salary of $200 a month. "It was another planet," he says. "Europeans had absolutely nothing. I took all my belongings to America, and I remember that they were one pair of shoes and two shirts. That's all I had—that was everything." For a year, Riboud rented a furnished room on the East Side, and then, his salary having risen, he moved into a $125-a-month apartment on Sixty-third Street between Madison and Fifth Avenues. A number of art galleries were nearby, as was the Museum of Modern Art, which he particularly enjoyed. Again, as at Buchenwald, Riboud quickly learned the language being spoken around him.

As a young man, Riboud had become accustomed to meeting his father's literary friends, and he had read the classics; he had always cared about art and about politics; and now he shared the passions and interests of his new friends in the New York literary and artistic community.

Riboud did well at the bank. He came to know some conservative businessmen and formed friendships with several—notably Garrard Winston, an attorney whose bloodline stretched back to the early days of the American republic. But investment banking did not inspire Riboud the way politics did. His was a generation that had been dominated from its early years by political questions: by Fascism, the Spanish Civil War, Hitler, the Second World War, the Holocaust, the United Nations, and colonialism; and now by Senator Joseph McCarthy. "We had to choose," Riboud says. He wanted the left to remain united, to remain focused on traditional enemies, to help prevent the Cold War. When Riboud thought of Communists, he thought not of a Stalin Gulag but of Buchenwald, populated in part by Communists "who had convictions and integrity," and who had saved his life.

The Schlumberger family had been keeping an eye on Jean Riboud. Glowing reports arrived from Andre Istel and Maurice Schlumberger. The Schlumbergers had come to know Riboud directly because a third of the investment bank's financial-advisory business was with their company or with the family itself. Riboud was invited to family dinners and impressed other guests with his knowledge of politics, art, and literature. One day, Marcel Schlumberger arrived at the house of his niece Anne, in Ridgefield, Connecticut. She recalls that he seemed depressed. Schlumberger had always been a family company, and Mr. Marcel, as he was called, usually hired its engineers himself. But the company was growing rapidly—it now had offices not only in Paris but also in New York, Ridgefield, and Houston—and Marcel worried that it was becoming too successful, too bureaucratized, and would lose its sense of intimacy and fall into the hands of men without character. Anne listened to Marcel's lament, and after a while the talk turned to Jean Riboud. "You see him now and then," he said. "What do you think of this lad?"

In "The Schlumberger Adventure," a family memoir published in the United States in January of 1983, Anne (who, divorced from Henri Doll, had become Anne Gruner Schlumberger) writes that she replied, "I think he has a heart—a feeling for humanity, I guess I want to say. That's rare enough in someone committed to high finance. If you're thinking of taking him on, I'll be surprised if he disappoints you."

"Oh, I find him *sympathique*," Marcel said. "We'll see." He paused, then added, "I wouldn't know how to use him. Finance is not our business, and I don't believe in it."

Marcel arranged to have lunch with Riboud in Paris in July of 1950. Jean and Krishna had had a son, Christophe, that year, and had talked often of starting a new life in France. Riboud felt unfulfilled as an investment banker. He was restless in America and was concerned that he was losing touch with France. Moreover, he had never been to India; he wanted to go there, and then settle in Paris and maybe open a bookstore. Earlier that year,

he had notified Andre Istel that he planned to leave the banking business and go to India for six months. Now, when Marcel learned of these plans, he offered Riboud an undefined position with Schlumberger. "I haven't the foggiest idea what you'll do," he said at lunch. He offered to pay Riboud $500 a month —$2,500 a month less than he was then making. He proposed to send him to Houston as an assistant to his son, Pierre, but Riboud, because of his Indian-born wife, preferred not to live in the South. Still, he was intrigued by Schlumberger and by the sense of adventure that the oil business promised. He agreed to go to work for the company, but on two conditions: he must first visit India, and he must work at Schlumberger's Paris office. Marcel accepted his terms.

Upon returning to France, in May of 1951, Riboud went to work at Schlumberger. He worked on finances, on merging what had become four independent Schlumberger companies into one, but mostly he listened. "For the first year, I really did nothing except listen to Marcel," he says. "Marcel used him as a gadfly," says Paul Lepercq, who is also from Lyons and was recruited by Riboud as his replacement at the New York bank; today Lepercq is the second-longest-serving member of the Schlumberger board of directors. Riboud watched Marcel—the "adapter," as Paul Schlumberger called him—spend hours asking penetrating questions, or sit through meetings without saying a word, his eyes unreadable under thick eyebrows, his expression blank. Marcel focused on personnel decisions, which, he told Riboud, were the most important decisions an executive had to make. Even though Marcel was approaching 70, he would cross the ocean to attend meetings of engineers and managers. William Gillingham, a British-born engineer who had been hired by Marcel in 1934 and had become the head of Schlumberger's oil-field-service operations, recalls saying, "Mr. Marcel, you must enjoy coming over here and hearing these technical papers," and that Marcel glared at him and said, "Mr. Gillingham, I don't come here to hear these papers. I can read them in my office. I come here to see what kind of people are running *my* company."

Despite his flaws, Marcel communicated to Riboud his almost religious devotion to Schlumberger. As with other corporate pioneers—Thomas J. Watson of IBM, A. P. Giannini of the Bank of America, Henry Ford—this devotion became a legend. Riboud speaks of an incident that took place in 1940, when the Germans had invaded Belgium and were poised to overwhelm France. Erle P. Halliburton, the head of the Halliburton Oil Well Cementing Company, which was Schlumberger's chief oil-field-service rival, paid a visit to Marcel. "Everybody knew that France was going to be defeated, that Paris would be totally cut off from Houston, and that Houston wouldn't survive by itself, without Paris," Riboud says. Halliburton offered to buy Schlumberger for $10 million. Marcel made no reply but slowly rose from his chair and beckoned Halliburton to follow him. They walked silently to the elevator, where Marcel thanked his visitor and said goodbye. Another executive might have hesitated, Riboud says. Why didn't Marcel? "Because there are some questions you never discuss," he says. "If somebody were to come and ask you to sell your wife, you wouldn't hesitate, would you?" Riboud draws a lesson from this tale: Marcel Schlumberger was never swayed by passing storms because he remained anchored to a set of beliefs. "The first was, think for yourself," Riboud says. "What-

ever is happening at the moment, try to think for yourself." In the summer of 1953, at the age of 69, Marcel died of heart failure.

Although Marcel's corporate heirs shared his sense of the company's special mission, his death robbed Schlumberger of its central authority. Feuds surfaced among the branches of the Schlumberger family. No one emerged as chief operating officer to replace Marcel. Instead, the company was divided into four fiefdoms, each ruled by a family member. The technical side of the business was the domain of Henri Doll. But Doll was a scientist, not a corporate manager; although he ranked first in seniority when Marcel died, he chose not to assume the leadership of the company.

Pierre Schlumberger, the only son of Marcel—and the only son of either founder—ruled the most profitable division: Schlumberger's North American wireline operations. Schlumberger came out of the war a weakened company, with its executives scattered. In 1946, Pierre set up an organization in Houston that would keep pace with the growing American oil market. Like his father, Pierre was a man of simple convictions. With his father gone, he came to believe that if Schlumberger was to grow it had to become a public company rather than remaining a family one, and that it had to make its financial operations more professional—to codify a set of rules rather than follow the whims of one man. Pierre had ambitious plans, but the other family members resisted them.

A third sector—Schlumberger's wireline operations in South America and the Middle East—was run from Houston by Jean de Menil, the husband of Conrad's daughter Dominique. For eight years after his marriage, de Menil, a Paris banker, resisted Marcel's importunings to join the company, but in 1939 he did, and became responsible for Schlumberger's financial structure. During the war de Menil successfully schemed with Marcel to free the company from potential Nazi control by shifting its base of operations from France to Trinidad. And after the war de Menil played a large part in making Schlumberger a truly international corporation by requiring that all business be conducted in English and that the dollar be the common currency, as is now customary in the oil business. Like Conrad Schlumberger, de Menil was an idealist and lent his financial support to political and artistic movements that challenged the status quo. And, also like Conrad, he believed that Schlumberger's ability to help others find oil was a natural extension of his political beliefs. "You were bringing to human frontiers technology that helped people," says his son George de Menil, who is a professor of economics. "During the war, it contributed something crucial to the war effort. After the war, it contributed something crucial to the growth of the world economy."

Schlumberger's European operations—the fourth fiefdom—were run by Marcel's son-in-law Rene Seydoux. Like de Menil, he had intense political convictions, and he became a supporter of the French Socialist Party. During the war, he was captured by the Germans and sent to a prisoner-of-war camp. After the war, he returned to Schlumberger and was made head of its Paris office. Among those who worked for him following Marcel's death was Jean Riboud, who admired his gentle nature. Through Seydoux, Riboud came to know many Socialist Party leaders. Of the four family members, a person who knew them well says, "The others were stronger

personalities in a sense, but Rene Seydoux was always the cement, trying to hold things together."

The cement did not adhere. For three years after Marcel Schlumberger's death, the company remained divided into four parts. Relations among the family members were amicable, professional, often affectionate. The four parts were united in their devotion to Schlumberger and its mission, but there was no central planning and coordination. Riboud and other executives disliked this arrangement and campaigned to restructure the corporation. Finally, in 1956, a new parent company, Schlumberger, Ltd., was created to unify operations. Pierre Schlumberger became president; Henri Doll was elected chairman of the board. The company was incorporated on the island of Curaçao, in the Netherlands Antilles, which was then becoming one of the world's major tax havens.

In 1959, however, Pierre's wife died, and over the next 18 months Pierre stayed at home most days. When he did come to the office, he was irritable and autocratic. "Pierre was very fragile and lost his balance," observes his cousin.

The branches of the Schlumberger family disagreed about many things, but not about the value of Riboud. Everyone saw in him familiar qualities. In early May of 1965, the family asked Riboud to replace Pierre Schlumberger. Riboud says that he immediately resigned, declaring, "I will not replace Pierre, because I owe too much friendship to him. The only decent thing for me to do is to resign." The family prevailed on Pierre to resign first, and then asked Riboud to become president and chief executive officer of Schlumberger. He did so on May 13, 1965.

For 18 years, Riboud has ruled Schlumberger, in the words of one company executive, "like an absolute constitutional monarch." Felix Rohatyn says, "He is the absolute, unquestioned boss in the company. His authority is as absolute as that of any chief executive I've seen." When Riboud speaks of Schlumberger, he often does so in the first person singular. Explaining, for example, Schlumberger's 1979 acquisition of the Fairchild Camera & Instrument Corporation, he says, "It seemed to *me* . . ." Although he is not a Schlumberger, his authority within the family is comparable to that of Conrad or Marcel. "He has the unanimity of the family behind him," according to Dominique de Menil, who is now 75 and is a close friend of Riboud. Since the Schlumberger family owns about a fourth of the company's stock, the support of the family is significant. Still, because Schlumberger has generated consistently higher profits under his reign, because he has succeeded in completing the transformation of a family enterprise into a public company, because he is acclaimed on Wall Street, and because he has at times ruthlessly asserted his authority, Riboud has assured his independence.

The only overt challenge to Riboud's reign has come from Jerome Seydoux. From the time Jerome was a little boy, Marcel Schlumberger had urged his grandson to become an engineer. By the end of the sixties, he had caught the attention of Riboud. In 1969, Jerome's father, Rene, retired from the board of directors, and Riboud invited Jerome to join it. He hailed the younger Seydoux as one of the brightest men of his generation, valued his advice, and took him into his counsel, as Marcel Schlumberger had done with Riboud.

In 1969, while Seydoux was vacationing in the South of France, Riboud phoned and asked to meet him on a matter of urgency. Seydoux still remembers the date of the meeting—the first day of May. Riboud offered Seydoux a job with Schlumberger. Some months later, Schlumberger acquired the Compagnie des Compteurs, a French manufacturer of electric meters and other instruments, and Riboud offered Seydoux the job of president. The company had been losing money, but Riboud believed that it could become profitable. Riboud remembers telling Seydoux that if he succeeded with the new acquisition, he would have "a big future." Seydoux remembers Riboud's saying that he would become president of Schlumberger. In any case, Seydoux did succeed, transforming the company into a profitable operation that is now known as Measurement & Control—Europe. Five years later, in September of 1975, Riboud appointed Seydoux president of Schlumberger, retaining the positions of chief executive officer and chairman of the board. Seydoux remained president for just 18 weeks. His memory of his tenure remains vivid. Now president of Cargeurs S.A., a Paris transportation company, Seydoux recently told a visitor to his office, "I always worked very well with Riboud. We talked easily and communicated well. Yet a few days after I became president he wasn't happy. It lasted four and one-half months, but I really think it lasted only a week. Very soon after I became president, we stopped communicating."

In the opinion of people who knew him then, Seydoux began acting as if he were the chief executive—as if the family dynasty had been restored. When he moved into his new office, one of his first acts was to hang on the wall over his desk a picture of his grandfather, Marcel Schlumberger. Riboud thought that Seydoux was acting like someone who believed that his station was inherited, not earned. Riboud's unease was intensified by complaints from executives who had been instructed to report to Seydoux. Jerome was too officious, too brusque, they protested. William Gillingham says that Jerome lacked "the human touch." Some executives were doubtless unhappy that they no longer reported directly to Riboud, and Riboud himself was unhappy because he had discovered that at the age of 55 he did not want to step aside.

Riboud, having decided to dismiss Seydoux, carefully met with or telephoned every other member of the board—there were 16 members—and said that there was not room for two corporate heads at Schlumberger and that he planned to dismiss Seydoux. With the board's approval, he visited and won the concurrence of five of the six branches of the Schlumberger family. And then, one winter morning, he summoned Seydoux to his New York apartment, at the Carlton House, on Madison Avenue. In his soft, polite way, Riboud said that he was unhappy with the current arrangement and asked Seydoux to leave.

Riboud, as he demonstrated with Seydoux, is not timid about firing people. "Jean has less difficulty facing up to tough personnel decisions than any other executive I know. Most executives dread it," Felix Rohatyn says. Carl Bucholz, an American who started as an engineer, was once vice president of personnel, and is now president of The Analysts, says, "One of my predecessors sat outside Riboud's office all day, and Riboud wouldn't talk to him. If someone was blowing hot air in my office, I'd say, 'Get the hell out of here!' If you're blowing hot air around Riboud, he'll smile and put his arm around you and walk you to the door and make you feel good—and you'll never get in there again."

A man who sulks after losing at golf or at gin rummy—something that Riboud does—is capable of holding grudges. "When something goes wrong, it's finished," says Jeanine Bourhis, Riboud's secretary in Paris for the past 13 years. "Jerome Seydoux was family. He liked Jerome very much, too. And all of a sudden—*phiff!*"

"Riboud handles personnel matters as if no personalities were involved," says Benno Schmidt, who is a managing partner of J. H. Whitney & Company and was a member of Schlumberger's board from 1973 to 1982. "If he considers you the wrong man, he'll remove you in five seconds. He's invariably generous as far as the personal welfare of the person is concerned, but he feels no obligation to keep people in jobs they're not doing. It's matter-of-fact." Several months after making those remarks, Schmidt himself felt the cold side of Riboud. Riboud visited Schmidt in his office, on Fifth Avenue, and told him that after prolonged deliberation he had decided that Schmidt and three other board members should retire. (Board members who were not also employees of the company received $24,000 annually for their services, and $9,000 more if they served on the executive committee, the audit committee, or the finance committee.) Riboud did not ask whether Schmidt, a sometime golfing partner and a member of the Schlumberger executive committee, wanted to step aside. He simply told Schmidt politely that he must go.

Whatever personal pain Riboud feels is soothed by the conviction that loyalty to the company outweighs personal loyalties. He believes that he is simply doing his duty. "If you want to be St. Francis of

Assisi, you should not head a public company," he says.

At the beginning of 1982, 70 percent of the world's active oil-drilling rigs outside the Soviet bloc were in the United States and Canada. Because of the current oil glut, the number of active drilling rigs in North America fell from 4,700 in January of 1982 to 1,990 in March of 1983, but that was still more than the 1,200 active rigs operating in the rest of the non-Communist world. The United States produces more barrels of oil daily (about 8,600,000) than Saudi Arabia (about 4,600,000). And Schlumberger's Wireline division generates 45 percent of the corporation's revenues and an estimated 70 percent of its net profits. It is therefore not surprising that this division occupies much of Riboud's time.

On a recent Friday afternoon, Riboud, accompanied by Andre Misk, a former field engineer who is a vice president and the director of communications, went to Teterboro Airport, in New Jersey, and boarded one of six jet airplanes belonging to the company for a flight to Houston.

On Monday morning at nine, Riboud went to the office of Ian Strecker, who has been in charge of Schlumberger's wireline, engineering, and manufacturing operations in North America since the beginning of 1982. Strecker is a burly, gregarious man of 43 whose normal work outfit consists of cowboy boots, an open-necked sports shirt, and slacks. He joined Schlumberger 21 years ago in England, where he was born, and has since held 20 jobs in 18 different locations. Part of Riboud's purpose in meeting with Strecker was to get a feel for him and other employees in order to gauge, in Marcel Schlumberger's words, "what kind of people are running *my* company." One of Riboud's preoccupations is that Schlumberger will lose its drive as a company and grow complacent—a concern he had discussed on the plane to Houston. "Any business, any society has a built-in force to be conservative," he said. "The whole nature of human society is to be conservative. If you want to innovate, to change an enterprise or a society, it takes people willing to do what's not expected. The basic vision I have, and what I'm trying to do at Schlumberger, is no different from what I think should be done in French or American society." In other words, sow doubt. Rotate people. Don't measure just the profits in a given division—measure the man in charge, too, and his enthusiasm for change. Strecker's predecessor, Roy Shourd, learned at first hand just what Riboud means. Shourd headed the North American Wireline division from 1977 through 1981, and in those years its profits rose an average of 30 percent annually. But Riboud worried that Shourd was growing complacent with success, that he was surrounding himself with an inbred group of executives and becoming too clubby with the Houston oil establishment, so late in 1981 he suddenly shifted Shourd to New York and a staff job. (Typically, one year later, in another surprising move, Riboud elevated Shourd to the position of executive vice president for drilling and production services. Riboud was satisfied that Shourd's year in exile had reignited his competitive spirit.)

This visit to Houston allowed Riboud to take the measure of Strecker, whom he did not know well. Strecker's office is in a three-story red brick building overlooking Houston's Gulf Freeway. Strecker and Riboud sat down at an oval cherrywood conference table, and then Riboud, who had arrived with no reports or notes, silently inspected his fingernails, formed his long fingers into a steeple, on which he rested his chin, and began the meeting. He asked how Strecker's wife, Elaine, had adjusted to Houston, how their two sons, who had remained in school in England, were getting on, how the Streckers had enjoyed a recent visit to England. Before long, the meeting got around to specific employees. Riboud made detailed comments on them, giving not only his impression of their abilities but also his impression of how well their abilities were matched to their jobs. He emphasized that final judgments on all employees were Strecker's to make. After Riboud had finished with the personnel matters, he asked Strecker if he had been spending much time in the field—among 1,800 field engineers whom Schlumberger employed in North America.

"I feel that my biggest challenge here in the next couple of years is engineering," Strecker replied, referring to engineering research. "So I'm spending most of my time there now." He said that the next day he would join all the engineering department heads for a three-day retreat in California, at which they would evaluate priorities and challenges. Riboud suggested that the engineers might want to consider pushing the manufacturing section of Schlumberger Well Services, in Houston, which produces 60 percent of the equipment used by the Schlumberger field engineers. Even though this is more than the company's other manufacturing plant, in Clamart, France, produces, Riboud is not satisfied. He wants Schlumberger to become totally self-sufficient—to farm out less work to such companies as Grumman and International Harvester, which makes the frames for Schlumberger's trucks.

There was a long silence. Riboud sat inspecting the fingers of one hand, and finally Strecker asked if Riboud had any further questions.

"I've got a major concern about what happens to your business in the next few years," Riboud said. He then noted that Strecker's monthly report for January, which he had received in New York, revealed that North American logging operations were 11 percent below plan and that operations in completed wells—so-called cased-hole explorations—were 5 percent below plan. "The January report blames the weather," he said. "But then I read and see that the biggest decline was in log interpretation, and you can't blame the weather for that." Riboud said he was confident that the world would remain dependent on oil for at least 50 years longer, but he added that two unknowns threatened oil exploration—and thus Schlumberger revenues—in the immediate future. One was the faltering American economy. The other was a decline in the price of oil.

Even in a recession, Strecker said, independent oil drillers can earn enough to continue searching for oil as long as the price is at least $30 a barrel. He observed that after President Carter began to decontrol the price of oil in 1979, the number of oil rigs in North America climbed from 2,500 to 4,750 between 1979 and 1981. "Decontrol caused that rapid growth," Strecker said. But now, with the real price of oil declining, with the economy in recession, and with abundant, if perhaps temporary, oil surpluses, the number of rigs was back down to just under 2,500. Strecker said the natural-gas picture was totally different, with supplies plentiful but the price "probably too high."

"It's funny—the gas manufacturers are lobbying in Washington today against decontrol of all gas prices," Riboud said.

If gas should be fully decontrolled, Strecker said, gas producers would not be able to sell all their supplies in this sluggish economy, and the price should drop. (It has not yet done so.) With lower prices, gas producers would concentrate on shallow-well drilling, which was less expensive. Deep-well drilling would become prohibitively expensive, just as it was for independent oil prospectors whenever the price dipped below about $30 a barrel.

Riboud and Strecker, their session over, walked to the office of Robert Peebler, the North American Wireline's vice president of finance, to review the division's business projections for February. Surveying the expected rig counts of Schlumberger and of its competitors, Riboud seized on the figure of 90 rigs credited to competitors off the Gulf Coast. "I'm always surprised by how many offshore rigs our competitors have," he said. Peebler replied that competitors had only 10 percent of the offshore market, but this did not seem to appease Riboud; he asked Peebler to forward an analysis of the situation to his New York office. Riboud's message was clear: Only total victory counts. Schlumberger could lose its edge; competitors with more to prove could be hungrier and more aggressive. Already, Wall Street analysts who examined oilfield-service companies had reported that Dresser Industries' Atlas Oilfield Services Group, a worldwide competitor, was leading in the development of the Carbon/Oxygen log and the Spectralog—two advanced logging tools. Gearhart Industries, which was bidding for a larger share of the American market, claimed to have hired 300 graduate engineers in 1981—an increase of 100 percent over 1980. (Because of the drop-off in drilling and the recession, the number fell to 140 in 1982.) Schlumberger remains far ahead of its competitors, but to stay there, Riboud feels, it must continue to challenge its employees.

After Riboud's meeting with Peebler came a slide presentation by engineers and scientists, who talked about such things as a "neutron porosity tool," a "Gamma Spectroscopy Tool," the "radial geometric factor," and the "finite element code." The advanced technology that such arcane terminology represents is perhaps the major reason that Schlumberger stays ahead of its competitors—who concede that Schlumberger's tools are generally more advanced than theirs. And since Schlumberger spends $125 million annually on wireline research—a sum greater than the profits of any wireline competitor—its lead will be difficult to overcome. Much of the research is designed to perfect drilling and logging tools that help identify hard-to-reach oil in already drilled wells and help extract it. This residual oil is expensive to recover, and oil companies claim that as long as the price per barrel stays below $30 pursuing it is not profitable. But if the price rises above $30, and if supplies become scarce (they are now abundant), new opportunities await the oil companies and Schlumberger. An analysis made by Philip K. Meyer, a vice president with the Wall Street firm F. Eberstadt & Company, in April of 1981 explains why: "We have found in the United States roughly 450 billion barrels of original-oil-in-place, of which only some 100 billion barrels have been produced to date. This means we know the location of 350 billion barrels of remaining (residual)-oil-in-place . . . If only a third of this residual-oil-in-place were to economically respond to tertiary recovery, over 100 billion barrels would be added to U.S. reserves."

Riboud listened intently to the engineers and scientists, and when the presentation was over, he said, politely, "I have read all this. You are just preaching motherhood. Where are the problems?"

Not long after the engineering presentation, Riboud had lunch in the executive dining room with three dozen section heads, most of them in their late twenties or early thirties. A number of them said that at Schlumberger they didn't feel isolated in their offices or laboratories, as they had at other places they had worked, and that they weren't dependent on memorandums or rumors to gauge the reactions of their superiors.

"I was at Bell Labs for four years, and I don't think I ever met the vice president of research," said Dennis O'Neill, who was head of the informatics section and had been with Schlumberger for five years. "Here within six months I was making presentations to the executive vice president of the Wireline." James Hall, who had been employed by Schlumberger for 10 years, said he had had the same experience. "It's a lot more personal at Schlumberger," he said. With a Ph.D. in nuclear physics from Iowa State University and two years of advanced doctoral work at the Swiss Federal Institute of Technology in Zurich, Hall was the head of the engineering–physics section. While he was completing his studies, he worked for Mobil Oil. "You felt more isolated there, because contact with management was much less," he said of that experience. "You had contact just with your bosses. You didn't feel the direct contact with your managers you have here. It tends to build more of a team spirit when not only your boss comes to talk to you about a project but several levels of command above as well. To me, in engineering that's what the Schlumberger spirit is. The individual design engineer feels that the responsibility of the company is placed on him."

In Riboud's field visits, time is often set aside for questions from employees like Hall. During the lunch in Houston, the first question was from a young engineer–researcher, who asked for Riboud's "view of the nonwireline" part of the Schlumberger's empire.

"You are an engineer," Riboud said. "Be a little more precise in your question." Riboud did not wait for the young man to rephrase the question. He apparently sensed that, like many wireline employees, the young man was concerned about Schlumberger's purchase, for $425 million, of the Fairchild Camera & Instrument Corporation—a giant semiconductor company, which lost $30 million the second year after the purchase. Now Riboud went on, "The question is really: When we have this little jewel of a wireline business, why do we bother à la Fairchild and so forth? It's really a philosophical problem. Why does the company have to grow, and in which direction? I'm not saying I'm right, but I feel two things—two dangers. One danger is of becoming a conglomerate and trying to do everything. The other danger is of just staying a wireline company. I don't think we could have maintained the profit margin we had and the motivation of our people if we'd done that. The real problem in any organization is to have new challenges, new motivations."

Lunch was followed by a session with department heads from the manufacturing division, which employed 950 people and produced $400 million worth of field equipment annually. The heads of the materials-management and purchasing sections presented Riboud with flow charts and graphs showing a steady rise in their productivity, and spoke in the self-assured language of American business schools. Riboud's eyes narrowed. He listened politely but impatiently; finally he leaned forward with his elbows on the conference table and explained why the company could not measure productivity by price or sales alone. "Since we are selling equipment to ourselves, it is hard to measure," he said. There was no competition over price or product or speed of production, he said, and the charts were therefore relatively worthless.

Later that afternoon, Riboud met with the 27 executives and department heads who supervise the North American Wireline division. Many of them also inquired about the acquisition of Fairchild and about Schlumberger's stock. And they asked why Schlumberger had organized a division in the Far East much like the one in Houston. Japan and the rest of the Far East, Riboud repeated, are the frontier of the eighties, as Houston was in the late forties and fifties. There are vast reserves of oil in China. The Japanese have moved ahead of the West in consumer electronics and office automation; they are threatening to move ahead in the development of computers, semiconductors, and genetic engineering. Singapore, Hong Kong, South Korea, Taiwan, and Japan manufacture goods more cheaply and more efficiently than the West does. If Schlumberger does not feel the threat of competition in North America or the Middle East, then it will feel it from the Far East. Schlumberger has been so successful for so long, he said, that it risks losing its "intellectual humility." He added, "We have the King Kong attitude."

Riboud toured the center and then went to the company cafeteria, where he had coffee with several dozen employees. Gene Pohoriles, the general manager of this unit, was a veteran Schlumberger engineer and, like many old-timers, wore in his lapel a gold Schlumberger pin, with stars that symbolize the number of years he had served the company. Pohoriles introduced Riboud to the employees and then asked the first question: Why did Schlumberger dilute the value of its stock by buying Fairchild?

"Let me be blunt about it," Riboud answered. "What people in the Wireline are asking is: Why did Riboud screw up the Schlumberger stock by purchasing Fairchild?"

"Close," Pohoriles said.

Fairchild was a necessary acquisition, Riboud told him. "I felt strongly that 20 years down the road we had to have a semiconductor capacity." Schlumberger's basic business, he went on, is information, not oil, and what the Wireline does is provide information to oil companies to help them make accurate decisions. The next generation of wireline and meter equipment, he said, will be more dependent on tiny microprocessors and semiconductors.

Riboud's reaction to Pohoriles—admiring his courage while excusing what Riboud thought was an ignorant question—hinted at Riboud's style of management at Schlumberger. On several occasions, he has said that the company's goals should be "to strive for perfection." To this end, he searches for fighters, for independentminded people who don't, in his words, "float like a cork." In 1974, when he appointed Carl Buchholz his vice president of personnel, it was largely because Buchholz was not afraid to speak out. Riboud recalled first seeing Buchholz at a Schlumberger management conference near Geneva. "All the people were reciting the Mass, and suddenly Buchholz said, 'You're full of it!' I said, 'This is a fellow who speaks his mind.'" The subject under discussion at the conference,

Buchholz later recalled, was the development of managers. The executives in attendance rose, one after another, to congratulate themselves on their success, and finally Buchholz stood up and said that in fact the executives were not successfully developing managers at all. A debate ensued, and Riboud sided with Buchholz. Afterward, Riboud made a point of getting to know him, and not long after the conference Buchholz, who had been assistant vice president of operations for Schlumberger Well Services in Houston, was promoted to vice president of personnel and transferred from Houston to New York, where he quickly developed a reputation as an in-house critic.

Of all the people who have surrounded Riboud at Schlumberger over the years, probably none has been closer than Claude Baks, who was hired by Marcel Schlumberger as an engineer in 1946 and left the company only in the fall of 1982. An enigmatic man with a blunt manner, Baks had no official duties, but he could enter any meeting uninvited and he reported only to Riboud. He was born in 1917, in Latvia. His parents were Jewish, and with the outbreak of the Second World War he joined the Free French Army, fighting in North Africa and Europe. On assignment for the company in Venezuela some years after he was hired, Baks met Krishna and Jean Riboud, who were traveling there. When he returned to Paris on holiday, he looked up the Ribouds, and became close to them and their son, Christophe. Riboud, who was then general manager of Schlumberger's European operations, had a hand in getting Baks transferred from Venezuela to Paris, where he was given a staff job. Admiring Baks's independence, Riboud asked him to become his adviser.

At this time, Riboud, with Henri Langlois, was raising money to finance a 12-hour film, directed by Roberto Rossellini, about the history of the world. (They raised $500,000, including $100,000 from Schlumberger.) Baks shared Riboud's interest in film and worked closely with both Langlois and Rossellini on Riboud's behalf. Baks had no family of his own, and the Ribouds in effect became his family.

Riboud and Baks were an unlikely pair. Riboud is a man of delicate appearance and subdued manner. Baks has bushy black eyebrows, a stubbly black beard, and a bulbous nose; he is missing a few front teeth. He has a deep, raspy voice, which some find intimidating, and he is usually wearing a dirty raincoat, a baggy sports jacket, and baggy pants. His office, a cubicle on the fourth floor of Schlumberger's Paris headquarters, was just two doors from Riboud's. He kept the blinds closed and would not open the windows, and visitors seldom stayed long. The walls were bare, the desktop was clear, and besides the desk the only furniture was two chairs and three metal file cabinets. Yet fellow employees went to Baks's office to try out ideas, to get clues to Riboud's thinking, to learn something of the company's history, and to ingratiate themselves with Baks.

In trying to explain the role that Baks played, Riboud has said, "His main contribution at Schlumberger has been to prevent Schlumberger from becoming an establishment." He went on, "He has never had a title in 35 years. He has never had a secretary. He has never written a letter. He has no responsibilities. Schlumberger is not a bank where everyone has to have a niche. Over the years, he's had more purpose than 90 percent of the people I know. He forces people to think." What Baks helped do was keep alive, under chairman Riboud, a sort of permanent "cultural revolution" at Schlumberger.

"Generally, after a while people repeat themselves," observes Michel Vaillaud, who until December of 1982 was one of two Schlumberger executive vice presidents for operations, his sphere being all oil-field services. "You know what they will ask you. With him, you never feel safe. Never." Vaillaud, who is 51 years old, is a lean, regal-looking man. When he met Riboud, in 1973, he was a career civil servant. He had graduated first in his class from L'Ecole Polytechnique, which Conrad Schlumberger attended, and which is acknowledged to be the best scientific school in France. He then received an advanced degree from mining and petroleum schools and, entering the Civil Service, rose rapidly in the French Ministry of Industry. When Riboud and Vaillaud met, Vaillaud was the Ministry's director for oil and gas. Some weeks later, Vaillaud recalls, Riboud offered him a position at Schlumberger. Although Vaillaud's training and experience were in petroleum, Riboud asked him to move to New York and become vice president of Schlumberger's electronics division. Vaillaud spoke little English, and he felt unsure of himself in electronics, but he accepted the offer.

Two months after Vaillaud took the job, Riboud called and asked to spend the day with him in New York. Vaillaud remembers feeling that he gave inadequate answers to persistent questions from Riboud. "I came back and told my wife, 'We should pack—I'm going to be fired.' Then I heard nothing the next day, or the next." At the time, Vaillaud did not understand that his uncertain technical answers to Riboud's questions were secondary. Riboud was taking his measure as a man, not as a technocrat. Computers could give out data; Riboud was searching for character. Two years later, Vaillaud returned to France as president of the Compagnie des Compteurs. Then in 1981, when Riboud decided to divide Schlumberger into two basic parts—the Oilfield Services and Measurement, Control, & Components—Vaillaud and most Schlumberger executives expected him to make Vaillaud the head of the electronics division and Roland Genin, who had been an executive vice president and manager of Drilling and Production Services, the head of the oil-field division. These appointments would have had a certain logic to them, for Vaillaud had mastered electronics and Genin had spent his career in the oil-field division, beginning in 1950, when he joined Schlumberger as a field engineer. Riboud did just the opposite: Vaillaud became the head of the oil-field division, Genin the head of the electronics division. Riboud picked the less experienced man for each job because, he says, each would bring a "totally different view," a "fresh imagination" to his new task. Riboud had taken a similar unexpected step a year earlier when he chose Thomas Roberts, a West Point graduate who had become the vice president of finance, to be the new president of Fairchild. Roberts had asked him why, and Riboud had answered, "I like to shake the tree."

If an eagerness to shake the tree is one of Riboud's most prominent management traits, another one—allied to it—is, obviously, his preoccupation with personnel matters. As his meetings in Houston showed, he is familiar with people at many levels of the organization. Instead of closeting himself with a few top executives, he meets with large groups of employees. The vice president of personnel at Schlumberger—the job is now held by Arthur W. Alexander—reports to the president, not to an executive vice president, as is often the case at other companies. "Riboud spends more time on people and people problems, in contrast to business and business problems, than any other chief executive I've ever seen," says Benno Schmidt. "I think the thing he's most concerned with in running this vast business is coming as near as possible to having exactly the right man in the right place all the time. Most people who run a company are much more interested in business, new products, research—all that."

When it comes to evaluating individuals, Riboud can be quite blunt. Once a year, he meets with each of his top executives to offer an evaluation of their performance. Carl Buchholz remembers one of his evaluations: "He said, 'Let's talk about the Buchholz problem.' He talked about my relations with other people and how I ought to improve them. He talked about what he wanted done that wasn't being done. He was quite specific."

Like his predecessors, Riboud wants people at Schlumberger to have a feeling of independence. Day-to-day decisions are left to those in the field. Riboud's job, as he sees it, is primarily to think 5, 10, 20 years ahead and to set the basic direction of the company. On September 30, 1977, at a celebration of the 50th anniversary of the Schlumbergers' first log, he remarked, "I should say that the most important thing I learned from Marcel Schlumberger was to have an independent mind—to think for oneself, to analyze by oneself, not to follow fashions, not to think like everyone else, not to seek honor or decorations, not to become part of the establishment." On another occasion, he said,

"When you fly through turbulence, you fasten your seat belt. The only seat belt I know in business turbulence is to determine for oneself a few convictions, a few guidelines, and stick by them."

Riboud the businessman puzzles many of his nonbusiness friends. For years, Henri Cartier-Bresson has wondered why Riboud worked in a corporation instead of plunging full-time into art or politics. Cartier-Bresson—a shy man with pale blue eyes, gold-framed eyeglasses, and close-cropped white hair—recalls asking Riboud, "What are you doing there? You're not a scientist. You have no passion for making money," and that he replied, "I'm a corkscrew."

"It means he knows how a bottle must be opened—delicately and firmly," Cartier-Bresson says.

Riboud sees his work at Schlumberger as an extension of his political views. "Running a company is like politics," he says. "You are always balancing interests and personalities and trying to keep people motivated." On being asked how he would like to be characterized as an executive, he replied, "I would like it to be said that I'm bringing about in my professional life what I'm trying to bring about with myself—it's one and the same thing." Like Marcel and Conrad Schlumberger, the two brothers who founded the company in 1926, Riboud thinks of the company as an extension of personal values—humility, loyalty, preserving faith in an idea, serving people, being trusting, being open-minded to different cultures, being ambitious and competitive and yet mindful of tradition. The key in a corporation or in government, Riboud says, is "motivating people" and forging a consensus. "We are no longer in a society where the head of a corporation can just give orders," he says. People need to believe in something larger than themselves. To be successful, he thinks, a corporation must learn from the Japanese that "we have the responsibility that religion used to have." A good company must not be just a slave to profits; it must strive to perform a service and to beat its competitors. But more, he feels, it must measure itself against a higher standard, seeking perfection.

There is another way in which Schlumberger is an extension of Riboud's political philosophy—in its international character. Riboud says that with the possible exception of the oil company Royal Dutch/ Shell, Schlumberger is "the only truly multinational company that I know of." Schlumberger has long since ceased to have a single national identity. "If I have one purpose today," Riboud says, "it is to expand the concept of merging together into one enterprise Europeans, Americans, and citizens of the Third World; to bring in Asians, Africans, and Latin Americans so they feel at home with their own culture, their own religion, and yet feel that Schlumberger is their family."

"I think politics is a contradiction in Riboud," says Bernard Alpaerts, who began his career with Schlumberger 30 years ago as an engineer and retired this year as executive vice president of the company's Measurement & Control operations worldwide. "Politics is far removed from the management of this company. Schlumberger is almost a company without a nation. Riboud knows very well that most of his managers don't have the same political opinions he has. And, honestly, he doesn't mind. Sometimes you don't recognize in his business decisions the political opinions he has." The investment banker Felix Rohatyn says, "Riboud is compli-

cated. There is this mixture in the man of being the hardheaded manager of a huge company that is as intensely capitalistic as any organization I know, and at the same time being clearly involved with the Socialist government of France."

This is one of several contradictions in Riboud. He is, for example, a loyal family man—devoted to his wife, to his son and daughter-in-law and their three children, yet he has had sometimes stormy relationships with his brothers and sisters. He takes pride in being open-minded and a foe of bigotry, yet Christophe Riboud says that his father is "one of the most determined and prejudiced men I know."

Why is it that a company like Schlumberger succeeds? In order to answer this, one should probably first inquire into the degree of success of the company's various components. Schlumberger, according to Wall Street analysts, had a near-monopoly on the wireline business—about 70 percent of the world market. (Its nearest wireline competitor, Dresser Industries' Atlas Oilfield Services Group, has just over 10 percent.) And Schlumberger retains its near-monopoly even though it charges higher prices than its competitors. "We believe we are entitled to a certain return on investment, which we intend to maintain, and we price accordingly," says D. Euan Baird, who is 45, Scottish-born, and, like most of the company's top executives, started as a Schlumberger field engineer. A policy first established by Marcel Schlumberger remains in force today: Schlumberger charges its wireline customers twice the amount of its costs. Because Schlumberger does not sell, or even lease, its equipment, and because its equipment is the most technologically advanced, so that the company provides the best technical service, it remains the most highly regarded company in the oil-field-service industry. Of course, oil companies can afford to pay its prices. Since the cost of logging a well—the wireline process—is only 2 to 5 percent of the oil company's cost, wrote John C. Wellemeyer, managing director of the investment-banking firm of Morgan Stanley, in 1973, "Schlumberger should be able to increase prices as much as required to maintain its margins." Until the current oil shock, that is what it has done.

To isolate the specific reasons for Schlumberger's success, one needs to start where Conrad and Marcel Schlumberger did—with technology. Competition in the oil-field-service business hinges on technology. Marvin Gearhart, president of Gearhart Industries, an aggressive domestic competitor of Schlumberger, says, in reference to the industry and Schlumberger, "It's a high-technology business, and they've been the leader in high technology."

Helped by the Fairchild subsidiary and by a heavy investment in what is called artificial intelligence, Schlumberger may be nicely positioned for the future. In recent years, advanced technology has brought about an explosion of the well-log data that are generated at every well site. Concurrent advances in data processing have helped cope with this explosion, but an isolated field engineer cannot quickly interpret so much data, and none of Schlumberger's 44 data processing centers—which may be hundreds, or perhaps even thousands, of miles away from an oil well—can entirely replicate the skills of a trained field engineer. Consequently, a bottleneck has formed in the oil-field-service industry, with clients desperate for all possible information before they make their expensive decisions, and logging companies unable to provide a

complete on-the-spot analysis of their complex logs. Enter the new world of artificial intelligence. Fairchild is at the center of a strategy to forge ahead in artificial intelligence.

Schlumberger's reliance on research and technology suggests a second reason for the company's success: Schlumberger executives are trained to think in 10-year and 20-year cycles. "The time horizon there is longer than that of any other company I know in being willing to wait for a return on their investment," says Felix Rohatyn. Riboud points out that after the Compagnie des Compteurs was acquired in 1970, it took Schlumberger seven years to transform it into a success. "We could afford to take the seven years, because we had our basic business," he says. "If it had been 10 or 12 years, though, people would have lost faith in what we were doing." The Compagnie des Compteurs is actually one of relatively few that Schlumberger has acquired: 15 or so over the past 20 years—a tiny number for a company of such size and cash reserves. This is in marked contrast to the current trend among American corporations. Between 1978 and 1982, American corporations spent an estimated $258 billion to acquire other companies, many of them in unrelated fields.

Schlumberger, on the other hand, has not assumed that because it was successful in one field it could succeed in unrelated fields. This refusal to shed its basic identity is a third reason for its success. Schlumberger, Riboud says, will not engage in an unfriendly takeover of another company, believing that the hostility generated poisons the corporate atmosphere required for success.

Schlumberger's determination to stick with what it knows best contributes to a fourth reason for its success: it is relatively unburdened by debt. Unlike, say, the Du Pont company, which had long-term corporate debts of $5,700,000,000 in 1982, Schlumberger's long-term debt as of December 1982 was a mere $462 million; moreover, it had a readily available cash pool of $2,300,000,000 in short-term investments. Such a balance sheet, says Elizabeth Taylor Peek of Wertheim & Company, is "incredible for a company of that size." Interest income alone brought Schlumberger $254 million in 1982.

Schlumberger is exceptional in a fifth way: it is in good standing in the Third World. There are several reasons for Schlumberger's standing in the Third World. "You can't nationalize a spirit or brains," Riboud has said. "They could nationalize a few trucks, but what would they have? The concept from the beginning was to do everything ourselves—to manufacture the equipment and deliver the services. We never sold equipment. So how do you nationalize a service?" Schlumberger has escaped troubles of the sort that befell many oil companies in the Middle East and the United Fruit Company in Latin America, partly because it has striven to remain inconspicuous. It does not own natural resources (oil) in any nation but services those who do. It does not engage in consumer advertising, and it does not lobby governments, so it is less of a target than the well-known big corporations.

The key executives of most multinational companies tend to be of a single nationality. For example, IBM has 23 members on its board of directors, all but one of whom are Americans. Exxon has three non-Americans on its 19-member board. General Electric has only Americans on its 18-member board. This has not been the case at Schlumberger. Its board was evenly divided in 1982 between French and American nationals.

What Riboud has called "the will to win" hints at a final reason for Schlumberger's success—what employees refer to as "the Schlumberger spirit." Riboud likens the Schlumberger spirit to a religion. "It is our greatest asset, our unique strength," he says. The reason the Japanese have done so well, he told the New York Society of Security Analysts in March of 1980, is so simple and so obvious that it has been overlooked. It has less to do with their technological prowess, their productivity growth, the assistance they receive from their national government than with spirit. "They had the same faith that the great religions had in past centuries," he said. Riboud then tried to define what makes up the Schlumberger spirit:

> (1) We are an exceptional crucible of many nations, of many cultures, of many visions. (2) We are a totally decentralized organization ... (3) We are a service company, at the service of our customers, having a faster response than anybody else. (4) We believe in the profit process as a challenge, as a game, as a sport. (5) We believe in a certain arrogance; the certainty that we are going to win because we are the best—arrogance only tolerable because it is coupled with a great sense of intellectual humility, the fear of being wrong, the fear of not working hard enough.

Where does this spirit come from? Surely—in part, at least—from the personalities at the top: from the Schlumberger brothers and from Jean Riboud. "Conrad and Marcel created this spirit of friendship and honesty, and Riboud kept it," says Anne Gruner Schlumberger, a daughter of Conrad Schlumberger. "Riboud is loved because he is very friendly. It is the love of people, and the interest in their life. When people left for America and Russia, Conrad escorted the engineers to the railroad station to give them advice. He knew their families, their children." The brothers communicated shared democratic values within the Schlumberger hierarchy, as Riboud does today.

The company's spirit also comes in part from the special nature of Schlumberger's business. From the start, Schlumberger has been the only wireline company to refuse to turn over raw data to clients, insisting that it alone must process these data, for it is producing a service, not a commodity. Anne Gruner Schlumberger has written that "the high quality of human relations" at the company "took its start from a 'noble' activity, in the sense that nothing produced there was mere merchandise." She goes on, "The object conceived and made there was not such as fall into an anonymous market and in their turn become anonymous. This sonde, the galvanometer, were not for sale. The tie between the man who makes and the thing made was not cut." The Schlumberger brothers stipulated at the outset that the company would not own oil wells or permit employees to buy shares in oil companies. Schlumberger was to be trusted to keep oil-company secrets, it had to be "pure." Dominique de Menil, another daughter of Conrad, who was trained as an engineer and worked closely with her father, has recalled, "You had to be totally honest and independent of any interest." Engineers at Schlumberger sensed that they were embarking not just on a career but a calling. They were not just merchants but missionaries.

Summing up, Riboud said, "If we lose the drive, and fear searching for new technologies, or fear taking incredible gambles on new managers," or fear to heed the voices of "other countries and cultures, then we will become an establishment." If that happens, Schlumberger may remain powerful and profitable for the moment, but ultimately it will decline. "It's easy to be the best," Riboud has said many times. "That's not enough. The goal is to strive for perfection."

In sum, Riboud remains a mystery even to his friends. "He is a man who cannot be classified in any way," says Charles Gombault, the former editor of *France-Soir*, who came to know Riboud through Pierre Mendes-France. "Is he an intellectual? I don't think so. Is he a merchant? I don't think so. Is he an industrialist? It doesn't show. He is one of the few men with a strong influence over the President of France, but he will never talk about it. He never shows off. If you see La Carelle, you will understand. It's a beautiful old house with lots of antiques everywhere, extremely comfortable. But if you want to have the feeling of fortune you do not have it looking at the house. You have it looking at the ground as far as you can see. He is a man of the earth."

The Body Shop International

Business people have got to be the instigators of change. They have the money and the power to make a difference. A company that makes a profit from society has a responsibility to return something to that society.

—Anita Roddick, founder and managing director of The Body Shop

"Let's face it, I can't take a moisture cream too seriously," Anita Roddick was fond of saying. "What really interests me is the revolutionary way in which trade can be used as an instrument for change for the better." This heretical statement by the head of the fastest-growing company in the cosmetics industry reflected her habit of going against the tide of the industry's established practices.

The Body Shop did not advertise, avoided traditional distribution channels, spent as little as possible on packaging, and used product labels to describe ingredients rather than to make miraculous claims. Its products were based on all-natural ingredients and were sold in refillable, recyclable containers. But the most unconventional of all was The Body Shop's strong social message. As Roddick explained, "There hasn't been an ethical or philosophical code of behavior for any business body ever, and I think it's going to have to change."

From a single storefront in 1976, The Body Shop had grown to 576 shops by 1991, trading in 38 countries and 18 languages. Worldwide retail sales from company stores and licensees were estimated at $391 million. Along the way, The Body Shop was voted U.K Company of the Year in 1985 and U.K Retailer of the Year in 1989. In addition, Roddick had been the Veuve Cliquot Businesswoman of the Year in 1985 and Communicator of the Year in 1987. In 1988, she was awarded the prestigious Order of the British Empire by Queen Elizabeth (who herself was rumored to use The Body Shop's Peppermint Foot Lotion).

But in the early 1990s, some began wondering if The Body Shop's phenomenal run of success was fading. Could its unconventional retailing approach succeed in the highly competitive U.S. market? Would its quirky organization and values be effective as it grew in size and scope? And could it survive the eventual departure of its founder?

ANITA RODDICK: THE ENTREPRENEUR

> The world of business has taught me nothing . . . I honestly believe I would not have succeeded if I had been *taught* about business.
>
> —*Anita Roddick*

Born to Italian-immigrant parents, Roddick (née Perella) grew up working in the family-owned café in Littlehampton, West Sussex. Trained in education, she taught briefly in a local elementary school before accepting a position as a library researcher for the *International Herald Tribune* in Paris. Next, she moved to Geneva, where she joined the United Nations International Labor Organization to work with issues of Third World women's rights. With money saved, she traveled throughout the South Pacific and Africa, developing a fascination along the way for the simplicity and effectiveness of the beauty practices of the women she encountered.

Returning to England, she met Gordon Roddick, a Scots poet and adventurer who shared her love of travel. The birth of two daughters forced the Roddicks to settle down, and the couple decided to convert a Victorian house in Brighton into a hotel. In 1976, however, they sold their business so Gordon could fulfill a lifelong dream of riding on horseback from Buenos Aires to New York City—a journey that would take up to two years. Anita agreed to the plan ("Gordon never was a boring man") and, at 33, undertook to support the family. She had an idea for a shop.

With a £4,000 bank loan (approximately $6,000), Roddick developed a line of 25 skin and hair care products based on natural ingredients. Sourcing exotic ingredients like jojoba oil and rhassoul mud from a local herbalist, she prepared the first product batches on her kitchen stove and packaged them in the cheapest containers she could find—urine-sample bottles. Handwritten labels provided detailed information about the ingredients and their properties. A local art student designed her logo for £25. The Body Shop name—a tongue-in-cheek inspiration Anita took from auto repair shops she had seen in the United States—turned out to be a potential liability when she located her first shop in a small storefront near a funeral parlor. When her new neighbor's lawyer threatened to sue unless she changed her shop's name, Roddick took the story to the local newspaper. The curiosity inspired by the subsequent article assured that her first day of business, March 27, 1976, was an unqualified success.

Roddick gradually developed a loyal clientele. Some found the natural products less irritating to sensitive skin; others liked their novel aromas and textures; and many just enjoyed the relaxed, honest shop environment. As the sole employee, Anita formulated new products, ran the store, purchased supplies, kept the books, and constantly tried to draw attention to her business. (In one successful ruse, she sprinkled strawberry essence along the street leading to her door in an attempt to lure customers by the pleasing aroma.)

After a successful summer, Roddick exchanged a half share in her fledgling business for a £4,000 investment by a local businessman, funding the opening of a second store. In April 1977, when Gordon returned (his horse had died in the Andes), he hit upon the idea of franchising as a way to continue expansion despite limited capital. When the first two

franchises in nearby towns both succeeded, the Roddicks began receiving calls
from other interested parties. The business began to take off.

Founding Concepts and Practices

From the beginning, the company was
an extension of Anita Roddick's personal
philosophy and convictions. Although
these were not formalized early on, her
intense involvement in the growing organization shaped its operations. Yet she
freely acknowledged she "didn't have a
clue about business matters," and from
the early days, Gordon managed the financial and administrative aspects.

Roddick's first goal for the company
was simple: survival. To make her original selection look larger, for example, she
offered each product in five sizes—
creating a choice much appreciated by her
customers. Due to a cash flow that prevented her buying more bottles, she created a refill service at a 15 percent discount. This service subsequently appealed
to a new generation of environmentally
conscious consumers. Detailed labeling
information had originally been necessary
because of the products' unfamiliar ingredients but later seemed totally in tune
with a consumer awareness movement.
Even the trademark Body Shop green
color—now so politically correct—was
chosen originally because it was most
effective in concealing the damp that
showed through the walls of the first
store. Roddick recalled:

> There was a grace we had when we
> started—the grace that you didn't have to
> bullshit and tell lies. We didn't know
> you could. We thought we had to be
> accountable. How do you establish ac-
> countability in a cosmetics business? We
> looked at the big companies. They put

labels on the products. We thought what
was printed on the label had to be truth-
ful. I mean, we were really that naïve.

In addition to the products, Roddick
also strove to create a unique environment
in her stores—one of honesty, excitement,
and fun. Rather than become overly sophisticated, she focused on the elements
of what she called trading: "It's just buying and selling, with an added bit for me,
which is the magical arena where people
come together—that is, the shop," she
said. "It's all just trading."

Building on the Foundation

The Body Shop experienced phenomenal growth through the 1980s, expanding
sales at a rate of 50 percent yearly (see
Exhibit 1). In April 1984, when the stock
was floated on London's Unlisted Securities market, it opened at 95 pence and
closed that afternoon at 165 pence. In
January 1986, when it obtained a full
listing on the London Stock Exchange, the
stock was selling at 820 pence and had
become known as "the shares that defy
gravity." [1] By February 1991, the company's market value stood at £350 million
($591 million).

The products and the stores had also
evolved but had remained true to the original concepts. Entering a Body Shop anywhere in the world, the customer experienced brightly lit open spaces, trimmed in
dark green, with a black-and-white tiled
floor. Neat stacks of black-capped, green-
labeled plastic bottles lined wall shelves,
their monotony broken by pyramids of

---

[1] The Roddicks retained 30 percent of the equity;
Ian McGlinn, the source of the original £4,000 investment, held another 30 percent, and an additional
7 percent had been distributed to franchisees.

brightly colored soap bars or displays of natural loofah back scrubbers, potpourri, and T-shirts. Cards in front of each display offered information about products with simple and descriptive names like Orchid Oil Cleansing Milk, Carrot Moisture Cream, and Seaweed and Birch Shampoo. A self-service perfume bar featured natural oils that could be either used as perfume or added as scents to a selection of nonperfumed lotions. The whole experience, in Roddick's vision, was designed to be "theater, pure and simple."

Products were priced more expensively than mass-merchandised cosmetics but well under exclusive department store lines. Sales staff were trained to be friendly and knowledgeable but never overbearing. Stacks of pamphlets provided information on a range of topics, from "Hair, Who Needs It?," to "The Body Shop Approach to Packaging," or "Against Animal Testing." In one corner, a giant product information manual described each product in detail. Noticeably lacking, for a cosmetics retail company, were any photographs of models with beautiful hair and perfect skin. Roddick was fond of saying that her concept of beauty was Mother Theresa, not some bimbo: "There are no magic potions, no miracle cures, no rejuvenating creams. Skin care products can do nothing more than cleanse, polish, and protect. That's it. End of story."

THE BODY SHOP APPROACH

> It turned out that my instinctive trading values were dramatically opposed to the standard practices in the cosmetics industry. I look at what they are doing and walk in the opposite direction.
>
> —Anita Roddick

As she built her business, Roddick developed most of the Body Shop's unique operating practices and management policies to respond to opportunities she perceived. From product development to human resource management, The Body Shop had been described as "innovative," "daring," and even "radical." But there was no question it was successful. (See Exhibit 2.)

Franchising

The company's explosive international growth was driven by its franchising program, and by early 1991 there were 586 shops worldwide (see Exhibit 3). Of these, only about 10 percent were company-owned, but these served the important role of testing new products and marketing concepts and sensing customer interests and trends. By appointing a head franchisee in each major national market, Roddick was able to concentrate on the development of new product lines and the company's global vision rather than worry about the complexities of administration or personnel management The franchise contract was for 5–10 years and involved an investment of £150,000 to £250,000 ($270,000–$450,000). The start-up cost included shop fittings, opening day stock, a percentage of the location's rent (The Body Shop chose the sites and maintained the lease), and a licensing fee of between £5,000 and £25,000 ($9,000 to $45,000) for The Body Shop name. Typically, it took a franchise two to three years to become profitable (see Exhibit 4).

Roddick felt that one reason why the cosmetics industry had become exploitative was that it was dominated by men who traded on women's fears. She felt business practices could be improved substantially "if they were guided by 'feminine principles'—like love and care and intuition," and openly acknowledged a preference for women as franchisees:

> What is wonderful about the company is that 90 percent of the people running the shops are female, have no formal business training, and yet are brilliant retailers and brilliant business people . . . This business is run by women. Policy decisions are made by women, all the words are written by women, product development is controlled by women. So our customer, our female customer, believes that we have a covert understanding of women. It gives us an extraordinary edge. It's The Body Shop's secret ingredient.

Anita Roddick kept strict control over the franchising process—no small task with over 5,000 applicants at any one time. The process, which involved a personality test, a home visit, and an assessment of the candidate's business acumen and attitude toward people and the environment, took as long as three years. Roddick liked to conduct the final interview, and was known for asking unexpected questions. ("How would you like to die?" "Who is your favorite heroine in literature?") Her objective was to ensure that The Body Shop image and the principles it was based on were not diluted through franchising. "We choose as franchisees only people who are passionate about our product and our ideas," she explained. Once selected, the candidate was required to undergo extensive training on product knowledge, merchandising, and store operations.

Cathy Stephensen was, in many ways, a typical franchisee. Selected from over 2,000 unsolicited inquiries from would-be franchisees in her large urban center, she had given up a secure, twenty-year career in financial and investment management in order to run a Body Shop. She reflected on her decision:

> I was interested in issues of motivation, social responsibility, and particularly in the concept of a corporation that could do good as well as do it profitably . . . I didn't have a list of franchise or business opportunities. It was The Body Shop or nothing. I think that was the case with a lot of franchisees.
>
> I sense that the store does make a difference in people's lives, and I feel really good about that . . . I don't think you become a Body Shop franchisee for the money. You do it because you believe in the principles. Somehow you think it will all work out all right in the end. That's very much the common profile [of Body Shop franchisees].

Product Development and Production

Believing that the cosmetics industry had a lot to learn from the skin and hair care practices of women all over the world, Roddick spent two to four months of every year traveling to remote corners of the world with an anthropologist. In Sri Lanka, she saw women rubbing their faces with the skins of freshly cut pineapple, producing a fresh, clean look. Later, she learned that pineapple had an enzyme which acted to remove dead cells from the surface of the skin. This was translated into The Body Shop's Pineapple Face Wash. In the Polynesian islands, she saw women rubbing an untreated extract from the seeds of the cocoa plant into their hair to make it shine. Cocoa butter was then incorporated into a number of products, making The Body Shop one of the world's largest importers of this raw material. In Ghana, she discovered Shea-butter oil, a product extracted from an African tree nut; in Hawaii, she learned of anfeltia conccina, a seaweed extract incorporated into her Seaweed and Birch Shampoo; in Japan, she picked up tsubaki oil, extracted from camellias.

Even back in England, Roddick would approach anyone, "from taxi drivers, to shop assistants, to your mother-in-law," to inquire about personal care habits. She wrote the chairman of Quaker Oats, in Chicago, to ask about the cosmetic properties of oatmeal. He sent her a formula for a protein extract which she discovered could be used in a range of products such as eye shadow and soap. After reading about huge stockpiles of powdered milk in U.K. warehouses, she telephoned the Milk Marketing Board for information, a conversation which resulted in The Body Shop's Milk Bath. Instead of market research, The Body Shop relied on direct customer ideas and feedback obtained through the widely used suggestion boxes located in each outlet; six staff members cataloged and replied to ideas submitted.

Initially, product development had been driven by samples brought back in Anita's backpack and the creativity of the herbalist she had worked with since the start-up. Testing had been done on staff volunteers, and because ingredients had been used for centuries, risks were minimal. Eventually, the company employed an outside academic to test for toxicity and effectiveness, and finally, by 1990 established a formal research department. There was some debate about the extent to which The Body Shop's products were "natural," and the company acknowledged using some synthetic preservatives, ingredients derived from petrochemicals, and artificial colors.

Although over 70 percent of Body Shop products were supplied by outside contractors, the company hoped to increase its in-house manufacturing from 30 percent to 50 percent by the early 1990s. Most of its production occurred in Wick, West Sussex, where the company had 320,000 square feet of production and warehouse space.

Marketing

As a cosmetic retailer, The Body Shop defied most accepted marketing practices. In an industry where 30 cents on every dollar of sales was typically devoted to advertising, the company had no marketing or advertising department. It made no elaborate claims or promotions. And the products, still packaged in plain plastic bottles, were never "sale" priced. Said Roddick:

> (The cosmetics industry) makes its money through packaging and advertising, which together are 85 percent of its costs. Charles Revlon, the founder of Revlon, said, 'In the factory we make cosmetics, in the store we sell hope." And he's right The cosmetics industry is a dream machine.

Roddick recognized the value of publicity, however, and by 1980 had hired a PR consultant. She openly courted the press, and by her own estimate, generated £2 million worth of free publicity in a year. She was a natural for the role: "The press like us. I'm always available. I'm loud-mouthed and quotable."

Because the stores represented the company's primary marketing tool, Roddick used regular visits by regional managers to keep tight control over layout, literature, window displays, and operating style. The company's Write Stuff Department—five writers and six graphic designers—created The Body Shop's constantly changing brochures and displays. In 1990, when The Body Shop was nominated to the U.K- Marketing Hall of Fame,

Roddick insisted her approach was only common sense:

> The trouble with marketing is that consumers are hyped out. The din of advertising and promotion has become so loud, they are becoming cynical about the whole process. What we have tried to do is establish credibility by educating our customers ... It humanizes the company, and makes customers feel they are buying from people they know and trust.

Organization and Human Resources

As The Body Shop grew, so too did Roddick's recognition of the need to maintain the enthusiasm and commitment of her employees, 75 percent of whom were women under 30:

> Most businesses focus all the time on profits, profits, profits ... I have to say I think that is deeply boring. I want to create an electricity and passion that bonds people to the company. You can educate people by their passions, especially young people. You have to find ways to grab their imagination. You want them to feel that they are doing something important. . . I'd never get that kind of motivation if we were just selling shampoo and body lotion.

Roddick constantly worked at communications within the company. Every shop had a bulletin board, a fax machine, and a video player through which she bombarded staff with information on topics ranging from new products, or causes she supported, to reports on her latest trip or discussions of "dirty tricks in the cosmetics industry." The in-house video production company produced a monthly multilingual video magazine, *Talking Shop*, as well as training tapes and documentaries on social campaigns.

Roddick also encouraged upward communication through a suggestion scheme to DODGI (the Department of Damned Good Ideas), through regular meetings of a cross section of staff, often at her home, and through a "Red letter" system which allowed any employee to bypass management and communicate directly with a director. But she was equally aware of the power of informal communication, and unabashedly tapped into the grapevine by planting rumors with the office gossips. She explained the motivation behind her intensive communications:

> What's imperative is the creation of a style that becomes a culture. It may be forced, it may be designed. But that real sense of change, that anarchy—I tell Gordon we need a Department of Surprises —we do whatever we must to preserve that sense of being different Otherwise, the time will come when everyone who works for us will say The Body Shop is just like every other company.

Roddick took advantage of her travel to visit stores regularly. Appearing in jeans and carring a knapsack, she typically told stories, joked about embarrassing moments in her travels, described new products or projects she was working on, and listened to employees' concerns. She encouraged employees to "think frivolously" and "break the rules," and tied bonuses to innovative suggestions. She also introduced a system of two-way assessment, asking staff to evaluate their managers' effectiveness. She detested bureaucracy and kept meetings short by requiring participants to stand through them. Roddick explained:

> I tend to encourage separateness and eccentricity ... For me, the bottom line is keeping my company alive in the most imaginative, breathless, honest way I can.

I don't think in all the years I've been running this business there has been one meeting, except for the end-of-year results, where profit has been mentioned.

Extending the family feeling, the company built a £1 million day care facility at its Littlehampton headquarters. The charge for this service was staggered by salary level, and free day care slots were offered to social service organizations. In 1986, a training center opened in London and began offering courses on the company's products and philosophy, problem hair and skin care, and customer service. Soon, however, there were sessions on topics as diverse as sociology, urban survival, aging, and AIDS. Any employee of the company or its franchisees could sign up, and all courses were free. "You can train dogs," explained Roddick. "We wanted to *educate* and help people realize their own potential."

THE BODY SHOP PHILOSOPHY

All the Body Shops around the world form part of a whole that is held together by a common bond. It is underwritten by a common philosophy. This is the strong foundation on which a thriving and successful international company has been built.

—Anita Roddick

As The Body Shop became increasingly successful in a period often characterized as "The Decade of Greed," Roddick kept pushing herself and others to define the appropriate role for their growing corporation. Going public did not seem to reduce the company's quirkiness as some had predicted. Indeed, Roddick seemed little concerned about the investment community's view of The Body Shop and routinely referred to investors in the stock as "speculators":

Most are only interested in the short-term and quick profit; they don't come to our annual meetings and they don't respond to our communications. As far as I am concerned, I have no responsibility to these people at all.

Indeed, in her view, The Body Shop's stock flotation marked a very different historic watershed:

Since 1984, the year The Body Shop went public, as far as I am concerned, the business has existed for one reason only—to allow us to use our success to act as a force of social change, to continue the education of our staff, to assist development in the Third World, and above all, to help protect the environment.

Environmental Consciousness

Long a critic of the environmental insensitivity of the cosmetics industry ("Its main products are packaging, garbage, and waste," she claimed), Roddick found in this area a natural focus for her redoubled commitment to a social agenda. Within months of the public stock issue, she entered into an alliance with Greenpeace and began campaigning through the shops to "save the whales." The link was natural since several Body Shop products were based on jojoba oil, a plant-based product that she argued could be substituted for the oil from sperm whales widely used in the cosmetics industry. When several franchisees expressed concern that the campaign was becoming "too political," she dismissed their protests.

Within a couple of years, disagreements with Greenpeace led Roddick to switch her primary allegiance to Friends of the Earth, jointly promoting awareness campaigns on acid rain, recycling, and ozone layer depletion. Again, she turned over display windows to posters, and distributed literature through the shops. Simultaneously, she set up a four-person Environmental Projects Department not only to coordinate the campaigning but also to ensure that the company's own products and practices were environmentally sound. In addition to using biodegradable packaging and refilling 2 million containers annually, the company expanded its use of recycled paper, substituted reusable cases for cardboard shipping boxes, and offered refunds on returned packaging. It also banned smoking in all its offices and shops and provided bicycles at low prices to over 350 headquarters employees.

Feeling frustrated with the bureaucracy of Friends of the Earth, in 1987 Roddick decided that The Body Shop should define and implement its own environmental and social campaigns. She enjoyed the freedom of being able to pick her own issues and respond rapidly to crises.

Community Activity

About the same time, Roddick was looking for ways to become more active at the local level. As she put it, "We had to neutralize the corrupting effect of our wealth by taking positive steps to ensure we remained a humane and caring company. She set up a Community Care Department and began talking to franchisees about having every shop commit to a local need and supporting it by allowing staff time off to work on the project. Most responded positively, and soon shops worldwide were working with disabled centers, AIDS support groups, and homeless programs. But Roddick still fretted that some were not imaginative enough, and some "malingerers" remained uninvolved:

If a shop didn't have a project and said, in effect, it didn't give a damn about the community, it was usually the franchisee speaking, not the staff . . . If they absolutely refused to become involved, there was not much I could do—other than to make quite sure they did not get another shop.

As she launched into the social and environmental projects, Roddick became sensitive to some associated risks. First, she didn't want to make potential customers feel guilty or overwhelmed by the campaigning. Second, she saw a risk that staff could become so enamored with the causes that they neglected their "trading" role. But the biggest risk was that the company's motivations would be questioned. An article in *Marketing* noted, "There are times when Roddick's thirst for publicity seems almost insatiable. She has associated herself with every conscience-raising exercise from Third World development to a cheap condom campaign to curb the spread of AIDS." Her response to such criticism varied from defensive to dismissive:

A poster to stop the burning of the rain forest creates a banner of values, it links us to the community, but it will not increase sales.

To cynics, altruism in business is disarming. But the bottom line is, you keep your staff—and good staff are hard to keep, especially in retail.

The absolute truth is that nothing of what we do is undertaken with an eye to our "image". . . If there is a single motivation for what we do, it is, in the words of Ralph Waldo Emerson, "to put love where our labor is."

Trade Not Aid

Her regular travels made Roddick acutely aware of the huge development needs that existed in the Third World; but her experience with the ILO in Geneva convinced her that aid programs were not the answer. In 1987, she launched a "Trade Not Aid" policy with the objective of "creating trade to help people in the Third World utilize their resources to meet their own needs." Eventually, she hoped to trade directly with those who grew or harvested all the raw ingredients The Body Shop used. By 1991 two major projects had been initiated.

During a visit to southern India in 1987, Roddick visited a group of farm communities set up by a British expatriate to train poor and homeless boys. Impressed, Roddick agreed to make Boys Town the primary supplier of Footsie Rollers—serrated pieces of acacia wood sold by The Body Shop as foot massagers. A price was calculated using first world wage rates—four times the local norm. The boys were paid local wages, with the balance being deposited in a trust account for each worker to receive as he left to start an independent life at the age of 16. Retail profits from the Footsie Rollers funded the boys' health care and education.

Returning home, she raised the money required to open a new village, and in 1989 returned to India to set up The Body Shop Boys' Town, with facilities to house and employ 85 boys. This led to other contracts to produce soap bags, woven baskets, Christmas cards, and silk-screened T-shirts. Over the next three years, The Body Shop proudly reported that 3,000 jobs were created as the impact of the programs spread into surrounding communities. By 1990, Roddick had plans to establish Boys Town Trusts in Mexico, Africa, and Thailand.

On a trip to Nepal, Roddick found entire villages unemployed as a result of a government limit on the harvest of the lokta shrub—the traditional source of material for their handmade paper. Seeing the possibility of setting up another Trade Not Aid project, she brought in an expert who found alternative sources of paper fiber—water hyacinth, banana tree fiber, and sugar cane. Roddick then committed The Body Shop to an order for bags, notebooks, and scented drawer liners that allowed a large family paper factory to convert to the new production. In June 1989, this company bought the land needed for another papermaking factory that employed 37 people. A portion of The Body Shop's profits were used to replant the area, and another 10 percent went to the Nepal Women's Association.

Some ventures, however, resulted in frustration, failure, and even occasional disillusionment. The Boys Town project, for example, ended in what Roddick described as "a cruel deception," with work being subcontracted to local sweatshops at a fraction of the price The Body Shop was paying. The contract was canceled and relationships severed. A textile project in Bangladesh and a sponge sourcing venture in Turkey were also aborted due to various supply problems. Yet Roddick remained committed to Trade Not Aid and was pursuing projects in Somalia, Malaysia, the Philippines, and Kenya.

The Soapworks Project

In 1989, Roddick turned the principles of her Trade Not Aid campaign to what she termed "Britain's own third world." A visit to the depressed Glasgow suburb of Easterhouse, a 55,000-person slum with 37 percent unemployment, resulted in the decision to locate a new 33,000-square-foot soap factory in the town, almost 400 miles from the company's other facilities. She explained:

It certainly would have been more conventional to set up the Soapworks factory near Littlehampton. But it's more fun, more motivating, and better for morale to do it here. It's not economic in terms of transport, but it's easier to inculcate our ideas here.

Eight months and £1 million later, Soapworks opened, staffed by 16 of the community's chronically unemployed. After two weeks' training, they returned to Easterhouse on Littlehampton wages—a third higher than local rates. By 1991, the payroll had reached 100, and eventually Soapworks was expected to provide a third of The Body Shop's worldwide soap needs. Once the factory became profitable (expected in 1991), 25 percent of after-tax profits were to be placed in a charitable trust for the purpose of benefiting the community.

Although the project was highly praised by public officials and was widely reported by the press, a few Easterhouse residents felt that The Body Shop had a patronizing and even exploitative attitude about Soapworks. When Roddick referred to the community as a location "where angels fear to tread," for example, one observer remarked, "To hear her speak . . . you might think The Body Shop was the only industrial employer in Easterhouse. But as you can see, her plant is on a small industrial estate surrounded by several busy factories." In typical fashion, Roddick's response was, "Cynics—up yours!" She hoped that she would inspire other firms worldwide to establish similar projects. In her view, "The Body Shop will have failed by 50 percent if we don't provide a role model for other companies."

Political Involvement

In the late 1980s, The Body Shop's social and environmental activities became increasingly political. Although the company had long required suppliers to vouch that their ingredients had not been tested on animals in the past five years, in 1989 it escalated its activities in this area. In response to a 1989 EC draft directive proposing that all cosmetics be tested on animals, Roddick mounted a massive media blitz and began a petition in her shops. With 5 million supporting signatures, the petition was influential in the bill's eventual withdrawal.

Critics within the industry claimed that her cruelty-free platform was a marketing ploy. Indeed, they claimed that most base cosmetics ingredients—including many used by The Body Shop—had originally been tested on animals. Roddick responded:

> Although we recognize that, realistically, most existing ingredients used in the cosmetics industry have been tested on animals by someone, somewhere, at some time, we make sure that no animal testing is carried out by us or in our name.

Roddick's environmental concerns also became more political in nature as she became committed to the protection of the rain forests. After a visit to Brazil to attend a rally protesting the construction of a dam which would flood 15 million acres of rain forest, Roddick returned to England to take action. She held a franchisee meeting where she raised £200,000, initiated a "Stop the Burning" poster campaign, and organized a petition which collected 1 million signatures in four weeks. Followed by a small media army, Roddick and 250 of her staff marched on the Brazilian Embassy in London and tried to deliver the sacks of protest letters to the ambassador. Several franchisees expressed concern about such high-profile political activity, and one wondered if The Body

Shop was going into the "rent-a-mob" business.

The Body Shop also began associating itself with several other organizations such as Amnesty International and FREEZE, the antinuclear weapons group. It was this latter campaign that finally brought a strong reaction from several franchisees who felt that Roddick should not be speaking for them on such issues.

> My first reaction was "if you support nuclear weapons, what the hell are you doing in one of my shops?" ... But then I realized I did not necessarily have the right to speak for The Body Shop on every issue ... I accepted that principle—and completely ignored it. I have never been able to separate Body Shop values from my own personal values.

Profit with Principle

Roddick acknowledged that she was on a mission to create "a new business paradigm"—one in which companies accepted the responsibility that came with their economic power and became engines of social change. To implement her vision, however, she recognized she had to overcome two major impediments. Externally, she rejected the pressures of shareholders and the financial community to focus companies on profits to the exclusion of other objectives:

> The responsibility of business is not to create profits but to create live, vibrant, honorable organizations with real commitment to the community ... I certainly believe that companies should not be evaluated solely on their annual report and accounts.

Equally threatening to Roddick was the growing complacency among employees as The Body Shop became larger, more widespread, and more successful:

> What worries me now is that within the company there is an umbrella of corporate goodness which some people are hiding under, saying, "I work for The Body Shop, therefore I am sincere, good, caring, humane, and so on." It really depresses me ... We talk about being lean and green, but I can see a fat cat mentality creeping in: paper being wasted, lights left on after meetings. What it comes down to is arrogance.

THE U.S. MARKET CHALLENGE

> *It was Gordon's view that while the United States offered The Body Shop the greatest potential for growth, it also represented the greatest potential for disaster.*
>
> —Anita Roddick

In early 1991, observers wondered whether The Body Shop could maintain its phenomenal growth. They pointed to the fact that sales in the United Kingdom, which represented 67 percent of the company's total, had grown by only 1 percent after inflation and new store openings had been removed from the 1990 figures. Although the $12 billion U.S. cosmetics market clearly represented the company's greatest growth opportunity, Gordon was particularly nervous about entering what had been described as "a graveyard for British retailers."

Entry into the U.S. Market

In 1988, with over 200 stores in 33 countries, The Body Shop finally committed to a 50,000-square-foot production and warehouse facility in Morristown, New Jersey. Under the direction of a British expatriate, who was previously the president of Unilever's fragrance subsidiary, 12 company-owned shops were opened on the East Coast. Total investment exceeded £10 million. In mid-1990, the company began franchising, and by year's end, 37 shops had been opened. Anita Roddick explained the delay: "We wanted to wait for two years to see how we would do . . . We don't advertise. We've never gone into shopping malls, and we were terrified of those. The question was, 'Were we good enough?' " By 1990, U.S. sales were £5.8 million, or 7 percent of total revenues. Due to the high cost of the initial infrastructure, however, the U.S. operations were still running at a loss.

Challenges of the U.S. Market

Whether these initial losses would continue or, indeed, whether stores remained open depended on how the company dealt with a different set of challenges. First, environmental concern had been less of a public issue in the United States during the 1980s, and it was not certain that The Body Shop's strong image and unfamiliar practices would appeal to them. A 1990 Price Waterhouse report commented:

> The link between common ideals and store loyalty is not yet proven . . . Some customers may be willing to pay $3.00 for a bar of soap, knowing that some of the money is going to a worthy cause. Others will be turned off to a company that uses its profits to support such a bold political agenda. The diversity of the U.S. market, in terms of consumer values and demand, and the vocal nature of dissident groups may make it difficult for The Body Shop to find a solid platform on which to build a business.

Roddick learned how difficult it was to transfer her values even within her organization. It was hard to recruit staff who embraced Body Shop values and could fit into what she called "our quirky, zany organization." "I thought our values were global," she said, "and that our image and style were so strong that they would be easily transferable across the Atlantic. I was wrong."

She was also amazed by how constrained business was in a country that epitomized the free enterprise system. The Food and Drug registrations, the various state and city regulations, and the lawyers' horror stories all made Roddick nervous about her decision. Under warnings about product liability and the likelihood of litigation, for example, she was advised not to offer a refill service in the United States. Lawyers also convinced her to drop her "Against Animal Testing" logo on products for fear of retribution by the cosmetics industry. "They really put the frighteners on us," she said. "We felt we had to modify our trading practices drastically."

Furthermore, some experts questioned whether The Body Shop's resistance to advertising would limit growth in the communications-intensive U.S. market. Price Waterhouse calculated that The Body Shop's target of 1,500 shop openings by 1995 implied sales of $685 million, equivalent to a 17 percent share of the top third of the cosmetics industry where it competed. Analysts predicted that this would be a difficult challenge without advertising. David Altschiller, chief executive of the New York advertising agency handling the $10 million Liz Claiborne fragrance account, commented, "It's very hard to cultivate awareness and familiarity among consumers here without media advertising. Many highly successful European concepts have fizzled . . . when they're plunked down unadulterated in the American market." Roddick acknowledged, "There's no example of anyone doing what we're doing in America and making it work . . . I think I have to become slightly more eccentric and slightly more theatrical to get my point across."

Finally, The Body Shop's global success had not gone unnoticed in the cosmetics industry. Betting that the "green consumer" population would continue to grow, many leading firms were introducing "natural" lines and revamping the look and the marketing pitch of their products. Revlon was marketing "New Age Naturals"—a line of cosmetic products with names like Peppermint Skin Toner and Almond and Walnut Scrub. In 1990, Estée Lauder created Origins, a product line based on plant oils and extracts. It sold them in recycled (and recyclable) containers and emphasized that no animal testing had been carried out on its ingredients within six years. Lauder planned to market this line in stand-alone stores, the first of which was scheduled to open in Cambridge, Massachusetts, in mid-1991. And Leslie Wexner, founder of the hugely successful retailer, The Limited, had opened 42 Bath and Body Works shops. *Business Week* reported that Roddick was so concerned about the shops which looked "astonishingly like Body Shops" that her lawyers were discussing the concern with The Limited. "People think we're a flaky New Age company," Roddick declared. "But my God, we defend ourselves like lions."

As The Body Shop entered the 1990s, the price of "the shares that defy gravity"

seemed to reflect some of the uncertainty the company faced in its markets (see Exhibit 5). Some analysts felt that the company had outgrown its historical strategy, organization, and even its leadership. Could the company adequately defend itself against the wave of new competition without resorting to advertising, they wondered? Should it—indeed, could it—adjust its quirky and sometimes radical organizational and cultural values in response to the rising chorus of skeptics and cynics? And how would it survive the eventual change of leadership?

At least the last question seemed to be one that concerned the Roddicks. Commented Anita:

> Leadership of a company should encourage the next generation not just to follow, but to overtake . . . The complaint Gordon and I have is that we are not being overtaken by our staff.

Announcing the 1990 results, Gordon added:

> The thing we now have to do is reduce the dependence of the business on Anita and Gordon. You can either create a structure where the business is unable to do without you because you hang on to all the bits, or you can create a structure where they are pleased to see you, but they can do without you. That is our aim.

EXHIBIT 1
KEY FINANCIAL DATA FOR THE BODY SHOP, 1984–1990 (IN £'000)

(Year ended)	1984 9/30	1985 9/30	1986 9/30	1987 9/30	1989* 2/28	1990 2/28
Turnover	4,910	9,362	17,394	28,476	55,409	84,480
of which:						
Overseas	20%	21%	22%	25%	25%	33%
United States					874	5,839
Profit before taxes	1,044	1,929	3,451	5,998	11,232	14,508
Dividends	75	150	300	605	1,439	1,558
Transferred to reserves	414	871	1,762	3,129	7,114	6,977
Tangible fixed assets	608	676	1,744	4,093	15,606	31,442
Net current assets	524	1,265	1,948	2,772	8,630	1,515
Long-term liabilities	(320)	(258)	(230)	(120)	(239)	(5,991)
Minority interests	—	—	(17)	(158)	(520)	(974)
Shareholders' funds	812	1,683	3,445	6,587	23,477	25,992
Weighted average number of shares ('000)	na	80,000	80,000	80,397	84,908	85,306
Number of outlets						
United Kingdom	45	66	77	89	112	139
Overseas	83	102	155	186	255	318
Total	128	168	232	275	367	457

Source: Body Shop annual reports.

*Financial year changed. 1989 data reflects results from March 1, 1988, to February 1, 1989.

EXHIBIT 2
THE BODY SHOP PERFORMANCE VERSUS U.K. INDUSTRY SEGMENT STANDARDS
(DECEMBER 31, 1990)

	The Body Shop	Industry* Lower Quartile	Industry Median	Industry Upper Quartile
Return on capital	43.6%	3.1%	16.5%	41.2%
Return on total assets	20.2%	−.9%	6.8%	14.2%
Pretax profit margin	17.2%	0.0%	4.8%	10.5%
Sales/total assets	117.9%	111.8%	159.7%	192.9%
Average remuneration	£10,424.5	£6,740.7	£9,000.0	£12,269.2
Sales/employee	£66,782.6	£32,927.6	£50,483.9	£99,252.1

Source: ICC Online. Ltd., *Financial Datasheets,* November 5, 1990.

*Industry comparison against U.K. Chemical Industries Manufacturing: Perfumes, Cosmetics, and Toilet Preparations. Category includes perfumes. hair preparations. bath salts, shampoos, toothpastes, and other toilet preparations.

EXHIBIT 3
WORLDWIDE SHOP LIST (MARCH 1991)

No. of Shops		Overseas History — First Shops Opening In:	
Antigua	1	1978	Belgium (Brussels)
Australia	31		
Austria	5	1979	Sweden (Stockholm)
Bahamas	4		Greece (Athens)
Bahrain	1		
Belgium	4	1980	Canada (Toronto)
Bermuda	1		Iceland (Reykjavik)
Canada	87		
Cyprus	1	1981	Denmark (Copenhagen)
Denmark	5		Finland (Tampere)
Eire	5		Eire (Dublin)
Finland	11		
France	3	1982	The Netherlands (Leiden)
Germany	28		France (Paris)
Gibraltar	1		
Grand Cayman	1	1983	Australia (Melbourne)
Greece	14		Cyprus (Limassol)
Holland	23		Germany (Cologne)
Hong Kong	7		Singapore
Indonesia	1		Switzerland (Zurich)
Italy	22		UAE (Dubai)
Japan	1		
Malta	1	1984	Hong Kong (Tsjmshatsui/Kc)
Malaysia (E)	3		Italy (Catania/Sicily)
Malaysia (W)	7		Malaysia (Kuala Lumpur)
New Zealand	3		
Norway	13	1985	Bahamas (Nassau)
Oman	2		Bahrain (Manama)
Portugal	5		Norway (Oslo)
Qatar	1		
Saudi Arabia	6	1986	Austria (Vienna)
Singapore	6		Kuwait (Safat)
Spain	17		Oman (Muscat)
Sweden	30		Portugal (Lisbon)
Switzerland	18		Spain (Madrid)
Taiwan	3		
UAE	1	1987	Antigua (St. John's)
USA	39*		Saudi Arabia
			Malta (Sliema)
			Bermuda (Hamilton)
		1988	USA (New York)
			Gibraltar
			Taiwan (Taipei)
		1989	New Zealand (Wellington)
		1990	Indonesia
			Japan (Tokyo)
Overseas	412	Number of countries we trade in: 38	
UK & Channel Isles	174†	Number of languages we trade in: 18	
Grand total	586		

Source: The Body Shop press office.
*Franchise 23, Company 14
†Franchise 133, Company 41

EXHIBIT 4
FRANCHISE FINANCIAL PROJECTIONS, YEAR 1

Store sales	100.0%
Total cost of goods sold	55.8
Gross profit	44.2
Employee costs	23.6
General administration, marketing	16.4
Interest expense	2.7
Total expenses	42.7
Net income	1.5%

EXHIBIT 5
THE BODY SHOP'S STOCK PRICE MOVEMENT, 1984–1990 (IN POUNDS)

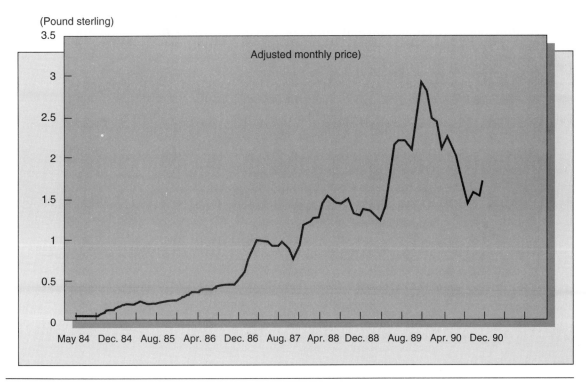

Source: Interactive Data Corp.

Adjusted Six-Monthly Closing Price*		
June 84 £0.058	June 87 £0.971	June 90 £2.11
Dec. 84 £0.143	Dec. 87 £0.865	Dec. 90 £1.80
June 85 £0.189	June 88 £1.526	
Dec. 85 £0.258	Dec. 88 £1.297	
June 86 £0.349	June 89 £1.780	
Dec. 86 £0.476	Dec. 89 £2.923	

*Adjusted for five 2-for-1 splits.

APPENDIX

THE BODY SHOP: A TIMELINE OF KEY EVENTS AND MILESTONES

1976 First shop opens in Brighton (March). Second shop opens in Chichester (November).

1977 First franchises granted.

1978 First franchisee outside the United Kingdom—in Belgium.

1984 The Body Shop goes public on the U.K. unlisted securities market in April.

1985 Anita Roddick selected as the Veuve Cliquot Business Woman of the Year.

1986 SAVE THE WHALE campaign launched with Greenpeace.
New £4 million headquarters and 320,000 square foot warehouse and production facility opened. Environmental Projects department and Body Shop training school established.

1987 FRIENDS OF THE EARTH campaign launched.
Jacaranda, the company's own independent video company, is established.
Named Company of the Year by the Confederation of British Industry (CBI).

1988 Queen awards Anita Roddick the Order of the British Empire (OBE).
The first U.S. branch of The Body Shop opens in New York.
Soapworks, a 33,000-square-foot soap factory, opens in Easterhouse, Scotland.

1989 The Body Shop is voted Retailer of the Year.
"STOP THE BURNING" rainforest campaign launched.

1990 AGAINST ANIMAL TESTING campaign is launched.
The first Body Shop opens in Tokyo.
Among many 1990 awards are the Queen's Award for Export, U.K. Hall of Fame Marketing Award, the Animalia Award for animal protection, the U.K. Environmental Management Award, the International Women's Forum Award, and the U.S. Environmental Protection Agency's Environmental Achievement Award.

Chapter 4

■

Relating Strategy to Social Responsibility

INTRODUCTION

For a general manager, little is quite so perplexing and often so disturbing as the challenges of responding to changes in the social responsibilities of the corporation. The challenge is particularly vexing for managers who believe, as the economist Milton Friedman has put it, that "the social responsibility of a businessman is to improve his profits."

For many managers, Friedman summarizes precisely the view to which they subscribe. For them, their social responsibility is to run a profitable corporation as long as their efforts are within the law. Serving customers and coping with suppliers while fending off competitors is their idea of dealing with the world outside their firm. And free markets are the best mechanism for governing those transactions. These managers have what might be called a "pre-Copernican" view of their role, in which their firm is at the center of the universe and other forces revolve around it in subordinate roles.

That others might have a broader view of their responsibility was captured at a conference at Harvard some years back by a U.K. executive listening to U.S. executives explain how they were circumventing certain manifestations of anti-inflationary policy of the federal government that they found obnoxious. "If I understand what you are saying," he said, "you think it perfectly acceptable to act in opposition to declared government policy as long as it is legal. I find that extraordinary!" He was an outsider in that discussion, but his views were by no means unusual. U.S. businessmen might be astonished to learn that imprisonment is a potential consequence for violating government regulation of prices in places such as Singapore.

At the same time, it is also true that others take a far narrower view than the U.S. executives. The comment in that discussion of an executive from a developing country is illustrative. He remarked that U.S. executives were making little progress in his country because they seemed to think that in a market characterized by great scarcity, product quality was important and bribing key government officials was inappropriate. He found the Foreign Corrupt Practices Act an example of cultural imperialism.

In fact, the managers of multinational companies come quickly to understand that their responsibilities extend well beyond the basic economic tasks of the firm, and that standards and expectations vary widely by country. It is sometimes hard, however, for executives to accept the same breadth of responsibilities in the United States. Yet the range of company activity that has significant societal impact, and the range of social and political concerns that has tangible and even strategic implication for their company are very wide. Those crafting corporate strategy must necessarily consider how the social responsibilities of their firm should and will be interpreted.

Responsibility for Economic Action

Decisions that company managers take for granted to be their private preserve, such as plant location, innovation plans, make vs. buy in sourcing, choice of technology, and pricing, have major impact on the pattern of employment, the trade balance, the condition of the environment, and the relative fortunes of local communities. For many governments that we think of as Western, capitalistic democracies, there is no question but that government will intervene in various ways to influence the consequence and often the substance of these decisions. At the same time, public interest in education, health, housing, transportation, and even justice leads to legislated and administrative action by government bodies that has far-reaching effects on companies.

In the last decade, it has been common to see Japanese industrial and trade policies discussed in some detail, so that many understand how differences in patent policy, for example, have influenced the relative ability of companies in Japan and elsewhere to compete. French subsidies to Air France, and to French steel and chemical companies also receive attention. But apparently minor matters, such as the accounting treatment of goodwill in mergers, have major influence on the ability of companies domiciled in the United States to compete with foreign companies when seeking acquisitions.

On the European side of the Atlantic, a different problem exists. During the 1970s and 1980s, a substantial welfare state was built up in all European states. The result was a considerable rigidity built into the economies. Not only did the cost of labor rise dramatically, but also a web of rules was constructed that made organized European labor highly inflexible. For European company management, the result was a competitive weakness in the global battle against Asian and also the rapidly improving U.S. corporations. (The cases on Opel in Chapter 5 and General Electric in Chapter 7, deal directly with these problems.)

A different version of virtually the same problem has come home to roost in Japan. Managers of Japanese companies, accustomed to three decades of steady growth, now face the challenge of how to maintain their commitment to a costly and aging workforce in the face of a stagnant domestic economy, a still-strengthening yen that raises export prices, and vigorous competition from increasingly successful challengers based in Korea, Taiwan, and other parts of East Asia. It is hard to capture the depth of confusion among managers whose concept of the Japanese management system includes permanent employment as a cornerstone. They see providing secure lives for their employees and steady business for suppliers and customers as a central aspect of their responsibility as business managers. The first line of the Mitsui mission statement, more than three hundred years old, is "Serve the nation." How can the nation be served by exporting jobs? Nonetheless, outsourcing and direct foreign investment have increased and layoffs have begun.

What these brief descriptions highlight is the broader consequences —what economists call the public consequences—of private action. In a world where a rising standard of living is a nearly universal political objective, business managers everywhere find that their actions are considered to have important public consequences and therefore receive a good deal of attention. And within limits that vary by country and by individual it would be a fair generalization to say that managers understand this concern by government officials.

To the extent that the concern is reflected in broad economic policies that make trading conditions orderly and stable, managers usually support government. Businesses like cheap money and cheap supplies, as well as protection from predatory competitors, especially if they are foreign. Where managers have problems is where they perceive politically motivated bodies intervening in ways that constrain their ability to operate. Tight money, price controls, and labor and safety laws all seem to reflect a short-sighted view that government can usefully intervene in the specific decisions of firms. In the United States, this aversion is often expressed in some version of the phrase "The government is lousy at picking winners." Research suggests that the truth is much more complicated, that there have been notable successes (e.g., agricultural fertilizer) as well as failures (mass-produced housing) and that neither affects attitudes toward massive intervention that is politically popular, such as the interest deduction on home mortgages. And when one distinguishes among firms, there are often as many supportive of a particular piece of intervention as opposed. Finally, in many parts of the world it is taken for granted that the government will intervene to support a healthier economy. In such countries the only argument is about the effectiveness of particular policies.

**Responsibility for
Social Action**

When we consider the *social* consequences of economic action, the picture is somewhat different. Over the course of history, the attitudes of society toward particular arrangements have changed. In democracies, when business management has not responded to perceived social needs, political pressure has built up to the point where legislation followed. The right to collective bargaining was a response to labor conditions in the early part of the industrial revolution, as were child labor laws. Food and drug and later product safety laws were a response to a perceived need to control anonymous suppliers to the new mass consumer markets. Environmental legislation followed the growth of popular concern for clearly perceivable deterioration in the physical environment.

In almost all these instances, business managers—as opposed to individual businesspeople in their role as private citizens—opposed the legislation as an illegitimate interference in their ability to manage their enterprise in a responsible way. They believed that their right to manage so that they could fulfill their duty to those who owned the enterprise would be compromised. They saw the costs involved in meeting a particular legislatively mandated social objective, such as clean air or a racially integrated society, as inappropriately having been made a cost of doing business.

Of course, in the narrowest sense they were correct that a cost had been imposed. There are many ways of achieving social objectives. That we have defense contractors rather than government-owned arsenals is simply a decision about how to spend money for defense equipment. In the same way, mandating that the effluent from a factory be clean is simply an alternative to taxing that company and having the government build a water treatment plant with the proceeds, or taxing those who drink the water and having them build the plant. Insisting that companies doing business with the government hire in proportion to the racial balance of a community is a way of imposing on companies the achievement of a goal that the community undermines through segregation in housing. While in the long run the laws may improve the economic efficiency of the society, in the short run they impose the costs of social goods on private enterprise.

How should general managers think about problems such as these? To begin, it helps to be aware of the issues and recognize that they have the potential for being strategic. Certainly if the ways they are resolved change the relative position of the firm vis-à-vis competitors, suppliers, customers, or substitutes, they deserve the same kind of attention that would be given to forces perceived to be strictly economic. Second, some problems that appear first to involve only costs turn out after careful examination and imaginative investment to be opportunities for gaining competitive advantage. Just as "the cost of quality" has frequently turned out to be negative, so that improving quality pays, the costs of "environmentally friendly" manufacturing processes have been found to yield even greater economic benefits.[1]

Third, in some situations individual firms can band together to share costs, thereby reducing their strategic impact. For example, a large number of U.S. chemical manufacturers joined together to form the Chemical Industry Institute of Toxicology in order to share the cost of research necessary to deal with the toxicological aspects of their products.[2] The CIIT also provides an independent forum that can deal with the government on a firmer basis of trust than would be possible for profit-making firms. Other examples of such joint ventures are the Electric Power Research Institute, the Institute of Nuclear Power Operators, and so familiar an organization as the Underwriters Laboratory.[3] Organizations of this sort spread the cost of dealing with a problem across many firms. This has the effect of lowering costs, reducing duplicative effort, and eliminating the possibly disruptive strategic advantages that might be gained by free riders who ignore the problem and pay no cost.[4]

A fourth approach is political action. Companies often decide that the issue they are facing is so significant that it is worth entering the political fray as an individual company, as part of an industry group, or as part of an even larger multi-industry effort. How to approach each issue depends a great deal on the nature of the question and the state of play in the political process. Generally speaking (there are always exceptions), companies can be effective on their own when an issue is being dealt with primarily on technical grounds by low-level, technically competent administrative employees. In contrast, when an issue has developed into a full-blown political cause, it is almost always vital to cloak oneself in the membership of a large and presumably broadly interested group. The National Association of Manufacturers and the Business Roundtable are two of the most prominent broadly based groups of this sort.

Outside the United States, there is much clearer recognition of the usefulness and legitimacy of this function. Each country usually has a confederation of employers, which itself may be organized by industry and subindustry. Examples are the Confederation of British Industry, the Confindustria (Italy), and the Keidanren (Japan).

For the individual company management, knowing how to pick up issues early, diagnose their social and political context, and devise an

---

[1] Christopher D Ittner, *The Economics and Measurement of Quality Costs: An Empirical Investigation* (DBA Thesis, Harvard University, Graduate School of Business Administration, 1992); and Sue Hall, June 1992, unpublished working paper.

[2] "The Chemical Industry Institute of Toxicology," Harvard Business School Case #9-382-167; and Joseph L Bower, *Two Faces of Management* (Boston: Houghton Mifflin, 1983), p. 236.

[3] Joseph L Bower, "The Organization of Markets," Harvard Business School Working Paper # 92-032, 1991.

[4] The pros and cons of this approach are discussed in Bower (1983), chapter 9.

action plan is a vital part of the general management task. Involved are an understanding of issue, legislative, and bureaucratic politics in the context of different governments—local, state, and national. These three types of politics are quite separate but interacting. *Issue politics* involve broad public groups and the media. *Legislative politics* have to do with the detailed procedures by which a legislature is organized and the rules by which it operates. *Bureaucratic politics* involve the organizational arrangements of legislative staffs and administrative agencies. Many issues also require knowledge of the different branches of the judicial system.

Because few firms have the talent among their executives to deal with such questions, it is common to draw upon the services of law firms and lobbyists. Managing their efforts is at least as demanding as managing those of the kinds of consultants normally hired to help with building economic strategy.

Equally important, however, are all the problems with building strategy and organization that we discuss in the subsequent chapters. It is not enough for the leader of a large organization to come to some intellectual realization that a particular course of action makes sense. The challenge is to develop that idea as an actionable program to which his or her organization is committed. Where the objective is not broadly considered to be in the economic interest of the firm and its managers, it may be especially difficult to devise and implement a successful strategy.

THE MORAL DIMENSIONS OF STRATEGIC ACTION

It is useful to think about the range of problems and responses just discussed above as defining a kind of action space in which issues can be arrayed. As one tries to sort out where responsibility lies and what an ethical course of action would look like, it is important to understand whether (a) one is acting as a principal bearing the costs and benefits of the consequences or (b) one is an agent of a publicly owned firm whose employees and owners bear the costs. Whereas the use of resources of a privately owned firm to pursue management's political or social objectives is usually thought to be legitimate, the same behavior by leaders of publicly owned firms is widely debated. It is also important to understand whether the problem is primarily economic and within the purview of the firm's expertise, or whether primarily social or even political questions are being confronted.

The appropriate course of action is likely to differ depending upon where in the space the decision is located. Bribery of a local customs official in a country where this practice is pervasive, by the owner of an exporting firm domiciled in a country that is equally complacent, is very different from bribery associated with the export of contraband for political purposes by a large publicly owned corporation. The decision to

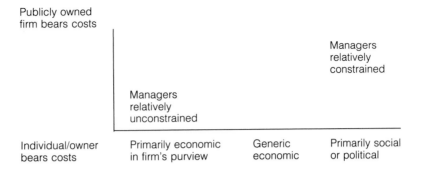

abandon operations in a foreign market because of legislation or a consumer boycott is made more difficult if, for example, in the case of South Africa, the management of a public firm believes that its presence as an employer is of significant positive benefit to the black population and its withdrawal causes serious harm. A private firm might believe it correct to make choices that the public firm could not.

Appropriate action also depends on the administrative feasibility of the response. The corporation top management that pledges a response opposed by its members has taken on a potentially costly obligation because the likelihood of appearing hypocritical is very high. There is a real possibility of such an awkward discrepancy developing when the arena of action is social and the firm is public.

This is no small matter. The evaluation and incentive systems of contemporary firms—especially those making a point of "paying for performance"—communicate a powerful message about the importance of growth and economic return in the minds of corporate leaders. Unless those incentive systems are modified so that rewards are congruent with the stated noneconomic objectives, it is hopeless to expect large numbers of subordinates to comply with what appear to be pious paper mandates.[5] The problem exists even around simple issues of honesty. When the perpetrator is a top producer, corporations can find it difficult to fire even those who steal or otherwise violate the law. First-line supervisors may prefer to keep a "great guy" who didn't hurt anyone rather than be embarrassed by the knowledge that the "great guy" was the only one to be caught or by the thought that firing the individual will make public a lapse the company would rather keep private.

It helps enormously if company leadership has made clear that illegal behavior will not be tolerated. Some chief executives find pronounce-

---

[5] See, for example, Robert Ackerman's study of racial integration at Xerox in the 1970s, *The Social Challenge to Business* (Cambridge: Harvard University Press, 1975), chapters 8 and 9, pp. 163–286.

ments of this sort to be uncomfortable "speechifying," but clear statements reinforced by rapid enforcement provide a powerful message for those tempted to be weak.

Again, Kenneth Andrews provides a succinct summary:

> Policy for ethical and moral behavior, once the level of integrity has been decided, is not complicated by a wide range of choice. The nature of the company's operations defines the areas of vulnerability—purchasing rebates, price fixing, fee splitting, customs facilitation, bribery, dubious agents' fees, conflict of interest, theft, or falsification of records. Where problems appear or danger is sensed specific rules can be issued. . . . These should not be over detailed or mechanical, for there is no hope in anticipating the ingenuity of the willful evader. Uncompromising penalties for violation of policy intent or the rarely specified rule will do more to clarify strategy in this area than a thousand words beforehand.[6]

Strong, clear words can also help set a tone for an industry. One of the most remarkable aspects of the business world is the extent to which standards are enforced by private sanctions that govern behavior in entire industries. Even more remarkable is the variation in these standards. In some industries, firms go bankrupt before they break oral agreements. (Hardwoods has this reputation.) In others, thick contracts are regularly abrogated and lawsuits provide a constant background to business. It is remarkable what can be achieved when the leaders of an industry cooperate to set standards of behavior.[7]

STRATEGY FOR SOCIAL ACTION

How managers should view the social responsibilities of their firm can be considered with the same framework of strategic analysis as we have developed for economic questions. The choice of where and how to respond should be guided by the nature of the business—the products and markets as well as the resources of the firm and the opportunities for positive change. Much of the groundwork that permitted peaceful acceptance of the necessity to end apartheid in South Africa was laid by giant corporations—Shell and Anglo-American—whose resources and domicile outside the United States permitted them to take a very broad and long view of what had to be done. For a small, entrepreneurial venture such an approach would be foolhardy.

In Chapter 3, however, we saw in The Body Shop a relatively small corporation that has made the support of social causes a central part of their corporate system. In Chapter 9, Ben & Jerry's, a still smaller company, provides another example. The two cases included in this

---

[6] This text, 7th edition, p. 428.

[7] See, for example, Lisa Bernstein, "Opting Out of the Legal System: Extralegal Contractual Relations in the Diamond Industry," *Journal of Legal Studies* 20 (January 1992), pp. 115-157.

chapter illustrate the range of the problems we are considering. The BayBank case involves the pattern of lending to minorities and the subtle organizational considerations that influence how a bank ought to respond to government regulators, while RU 486 deals with explosive concerns of some consumers with the use to which a product may be put. Most of the questions raised in this chapter's discussion can be asked explicitly in the context of these cases. In making such decisions, personal values play an important role, but so also does careful understanding of the strategic situation of the firm.

BayBank Boston

As Richard Pollard, chairman of BayBank Boston, got off the phone with Richard Syron, president of the Boston Federal Reserve Bank (the Fed), he could not help but feel a mixture of concern and satisfaction about the results of the Fed's new study of mortgage lending. A bomb was dropped on the Boston banking industry in 1989 when a Fed study of neighborhood lending patterns provided evidence of discrimination. A 1990 analysis of home mortgage lending data seemed to confirm the earlier study. Local bankers had been quick to point out that neither of these studies reflected all the variables that go into a lending decision. The bankers argued that the patterns discovered by the Fed could simply reflect differences in the quality of loan applications rather than racial discrimination.

The 1992 study was designed to meet this objection, thanks in large part to the participation of Boston bankers, who voluntarily opened up their mortgage files to the Fed researchers. As Syron explained it, the researchers confirmed Pollard's belief that the banks were not turning down qualified black applicants. Rather, the study detected a more subtle source of bias in the mortgage lending process. (See Exhibit 1 for BayBank's mortgage loan process.) According to the new study, applicants who met the credit criteria on the first cut were given loans without regard to race. However, a large number of applicants (80 percent) initially failed to meet standard credit criteria. In most of these cases, the problems were eventually overcome and a mortgage was approved. It was in this discretionary process of working the application that racial differences were found, even after all credit factors were considered. Black and Hispanic applicants were more likely to be denied a mortgage. The racial disparity found in this study was much lower than that implied by the previous studies, but it was significant nonetheless. (See Exhibit 2 for excerpts from the 1992 study.)

During the last three years, Pollard had spent a tremendous amount of time and energy as the chairman both of BayBank Boston and of the Massachusetts Bankers

This case was written by Christine C. Remey under the direction of professor Gregory J. Dees of the Harvard Business School. Copyright © 1993 by the President and Fellows of Harvard College. Harvard Business School case 393-095 (revised June 21, 1993).

Association (MBA) dealing with the issues raised by the earlier studies. The new study forced Pollard to ask himself, Would existing programs adequately address the problem? If not, what else needed to be done to provide equal access to banking services and resources? Was BayBank Boston doing enough?

THE EVOLUTION OF BAYBANKS, INC.[1]

Once called Baystate Corporation, Bay-Banks had always had a strong regional presence in the suburbs around Boston. Until the mid-1970s, Baystate was made up of 11 banks, each with its own name, identity, and customer base. Baystate was a substantial player in the state, holding 11 percent of Massachusetts's deposit base throughout the late 1970s. By 1976, its eight banks in the Boston suburbs had 144 branches. Its hallmark was a commitment to customer service and an appeal to local bank loyalty.

William Crozier's Plan In the mid-1970s, Baystate began to reevaluate its decentralized structure and local marketing strategy. William Crozier, then newly appointed chief executive officer and chairman, proposed a common corporate identity to improve marketing and advertising impact and to increase operating efficiency by centralizing data processing. With the approval of the Baystate shareholders in the spring of 1976, Crozier's proposal became a reality and BayBanks, Inc., was born. The local banks took on the new BayBank name and retained their

regional identity as a surname. For instance, Harvard Trust in Cambridge became BayBank/Harvard Trust.

Crozier also made a decision to strengthen the corporate side of the business. A presence in Boston's financial district was essential to corporate banking in Massachusetts. Richard Pollard, a commercial banker from the Chase Manhattan Bank, was hired and a new bank, BayBank Boston, was created to house the corporate banking function. The bank eventually became a base for retail expansion in Boston with subsequent expansion into the so-called streetcar suburbs of Boston.

Electronic Banking In a preemptive strike, Crozier bet early and heavily on technology, particularly automatic teller machines (ATMs) and electronic funds transfer capabilities. Crozier's bet turned out to be a good one.

> As the growth of the 1980s erupted on all fronts, BayBanks met market needs by launching an expansion program unparalleled in the company's history. The stars of that expansion were the BayBank Card and the X-Press 24[SM] network, one of the most successful electronic banking programs ever executed in the United States.[2]

By the middle of 1989, BayBank ATMs had 39 percent of Suffolk county's ATM market share. BayBanks, Inc., profited financially due to a boost in individual accounts and service charges. By the end of the 1980s, BayBanks, Inc., was approaching $10 billion in total assets.

Adjusting to Life in the City Over the course of a decade, BayBanks, Inc., had created an organization that incorporated the strengths of the suburban community

---

[1] Unless otherwise noted, facts and figures from this section were drawn from Professor Walter J. Salmon's "Baystate Corporation" cases [HBS cases (A) No. 579-117, (B) No. 579-118, and (C) No. 579-119].

[2] BayBanks, Inc., annual report, April 1990, p. 6.

banks, aggressive corporate marketing, an extended ATM network, and a growing corporate business. As the rapid growth of the 1980s subsided, BayBanks management decided to expand the Boston branch network beyond the downtown business district and the airport into some of the residential neighborhoods.

> The prospect of slower economic growth requires a modification of the rapid expansion strategies that worked to our great advantage during the 1980s . . . To be sure, growth opportunities continue to present themselves. For example, we are now engaged in a major program of service to residential communities of the City of Boston where we have not had a presence.[3]

BayBank Boston planned to capitalize on the retail banking skills developed by its parent. However, just as this expansion strategy was being developed in 1988, events began to unfold that made it all too clear that doing business in the city was quite different from serving the suburbs. Not only were the economics and competitive dynamics of city banking different, but city banks had to deal with a much more complex set of social and political issues.

THE CHALLENGES OF INNER-CITY BANKING

Over several decades, the living conditions in U.S. urban centers had steadily deteriorated. "Crime rates were soaring, riots were erupting in black neighborhoods, city treasuries were empty, city streets were clogged with traffic, and signs of continued decline were pervasive."[4]

According to many community activists, banks had facilitated the decline through "redlining" and "disinvestment." Redlining referred to "a practice by which local lenders draw a red line around sections of a city, literally or figuratively, to delineate areas within which they will not lend."[5] Disinvestment was defined as taking deposits from an inner-city community and using them to make loans elsewhere. Critics argued that restricted access to bank credit had several negative effects on inner-city neighborhoods: constraining opportunities for home ownership, discouraging rehabilitation and maintenance of residential and commercial property, and undermining local business development efforts. The credit gap had been filled in part by higher-priced less carefully regulated sources: rent-to-own programs, consumer credit companies, second-mortgage companies, even loan sharking.

The bankers' response stated simply was, If fewer loans have been made in inner cities, it has largely been because inner cities present fewer prudent and profitable loan opportunities. Banks had an obligation to their depositors (including inner-city depositors) and to their shareholders to allocate loan funds to their most profitable use within the constraints of prudent lending practices. Because banks operated on rather thin margins, it took only a small increase in loan default rates to eliminate the profit on a large loan portfolio. Concerns about prudence were enforced by banking regulators and by secondary markets. By the 1980s, it had become common practice for banks to sell the mortgages they originate to organiza-

---

[3] *Ibid.,* p. 7.

[4] Jon C. Teaford, *The Rough Road to Renaissance: Urban Revitalization in America, 1940–1985* (Baltimore, MD: The Johns Hopkins University Press, 1990), p. 168.

[5] Katharine L. Bradbury, Karl E. Case, and Constance R. Dunham, "Geographic Patterns of Mortgage Lending in Boston, 1982–1987," *New England Economic Review* (September/October 1989), p. 3.

tions (such as Federal National Mortgage Association) that package them as mortgage-backed securities. These organizations have criteria for the kinds of mortgage loans they will purchase. Banks that did not comply limited their capacity to originate new loans. Accordingly, bankers argued that the lack of bank credit should be seen more as a syinptom, rather than a cause, of urban decline.

Trying to Be Part of the Solution In the early 1960s, in response to public criticism, a number of Boston savings banks formed the Boston Banks Urban Renewal Group (B-BURG).[6] Working with Mayor Collins, the group committed $2.5 million to rehabilitate affordable housing and to provide home ownership loans insured by the Federal Housing Administration (FHA). By 1968, with inner-city tensions at new heights, newly elected Mayor Kevin White attempted to reinvigorate and to expand B-BURG by arranging a $29 million low-income, minority loan pool funded by large financial institutions and insured by the FHA. The results of this expanded effort were tragic.

> In the early 1970s, more than 70 percent of B-BURG-assisted homeowners were unable to keep up their mortgage payments . . . The banks foreclosed on more than a thousand single-family homes and multiunit dwellings in the area. The local HUD [Housing and Urban Development] office took over these houses.[7]

Shoddy underwriting practices and drive-by inspections contributed to the extraordinary default rate. "It was simple human nature. With the government assuming the risk, screening standards always seemed to diminish."[8] Because the target area for B-BURG loans was limited to the Jewish communities of Dorchester and Mattapan, B-BURG has also been criticized for indirectly destroying those communities. With B-BURG money readily available to black applicants, "opportunistic real estate brokers fueled white flight by engaging in unscrupulous blockbusting practices, resorting to threats and even break-ins and arson to encourage Jews to sell their homes at below-market prices."[9]

Increasing Federal Regulatons Lobbying by community groups generated enough political awareness that inner-city residents were starting to demand legal recourse for lending injustices. In response to the public outcry, the Home Mortgage Disclosure Act of 1974 (HMDA) required that banks submit information on mortgage application denial and acceptance percentages to the federal regulators. The idea was that this data could identify patterns of discrimination.

Three years later, Senator William Proxmire (D, Wisconsin) introduced the Community Reinvestment Act (CRA) to reinforce the idea that "a bank charter carries with it an obligation to serve the credit needs of the area the bank is chartered to service, consistent with prudent lending practices."[10] A supporter of the CRA, Ralph Nader, urged that the CRA "would, in effect, interject the community service factor into the market calculations of depository institutions."[11] Bankers rejected the need for regulation and claimed that if good business were present, the bankers

---

[6] See *The Death of an American Jewish Community* (The Free Press, 1990), for details about B-BURG.
[7] *Ibid.*, p. 332.

[8] *Ibid.*, p. 175.
[9] *Ibid.*
[10] Congressional Record S. 406, January 24, 1977, p. 1.
[11] *Ibid.*, p. 20.

would find it, as A.A. Milligan of the American Bankers Association articulated:

> We do not deny that there is a problem . . . we believe that competitive pressures will in the future, as they have in the past, force [any offending] banks to change their policies. Their competitors within their communities will take advantage of these local loan opportunities and will advertise the fact that they are concerned about community development, whereas the other institutions are not.[12]

Nader pushed the Senate Committee to put some "teeth" in the CRA, while others like Senator Jake Garn (R, Utah) objected:

> The answer isn't more rules and regulations. Piecemeal, we are heading for credit allocation and government bureaucrats back here interfering with the private sector. I'm sick and tired of the antibusiness attitude of this committee . . . the Ralph Naders have their asses kissed every day and are told how wonderful their testimony is over and over again, while we are building up a regulatory burden that is going to destroy the housing industry in this country.[13]

Despite Garn's objections, the CRA was passed in 1977. (See Exhibit 3.) It would be enforced by the banking regulators, such as the Federal Reserve Board and the Comptroller of the Currency. Banks reported on their community activities and were given a rating by their federal supervisory agency. Furthermore, bank regulators considered CRA compliance in approving or denying bank requests for branch expansion, merger, or acquisition. It was in this process that community groups had their leverage.

THE BOSTON BANKING CONTROVERSIES, 1989–92

For a decade, the passage of the CRA appeared to many community groups as merely a symbolic victory. As Nader feared, the CRA seemed to lack "teeth." Bank credit was still perceived as a major problem in inner-city communities. CRA reports seemed superficial, and few banks got unsatisfactory ratings. By 1988, "of more than 50,000 applications for merger or expansion by banks made since the act took effect, only eight have been denied on grounds that banks were not complying."[14]

Leak of the Fed Study

In 1988, a group of researchers at the Boston Federal Reserve Bank began working with 1982–87 real estate transaction data to explore "how the Community Reinvestment Act (CRA) could be used more effectively to promote the creation of affordable housing."[15] Just as BayBank Boston began to establish a presence in city neighborhoods, news began to leak about the Boston Fed's research. January 11, 1989, was a day that would change the next three years for Pollard, BayBanks, and the Boston banking industry because of the following headline:

> **Inequities Are Cited in Hub Mortgages Preliminary Fed Finding Is "Racial Bias"**[16]

---

[12] *Ibid.*, p. 315.

[13] *Ibid.*, p. 324.

[14] Teresa M. Hanafin, "Lending Law Is Faulted as Largely Ineffective," *The Boston Globe*, January 11, 1989, p. 13.

[15] James T. Campen, "The Struggle for Community Investment in Boston, 1989–1991" in Gregory D. Squires (ed.), *From Redtining to Reinvestment: Community Responses to Urban Disinvestment* (Philadelphia: Temple University Press, 1992), p. 38.

[16] Steven Marantz, "Inequities Are Cited in Hub

The Boston newspapers had received a copy of a preliminary draft of the study. The article stated that the study

> concludes from statistical analysis that if banks and thrifts competed with equal aggressiveness in white and minority neighborhoods, they would have made "far fewer loans in predominantly white neighborhoods . . . and would have more than doubled their actual number of mortgage loans in the predominantly black areas of Mattapan/Franklin Park and Roxbury." . . . "Long after the passage of the CRA, banks and thrifts continue to compete more aggressively in white neighborhoods and leave minority neighborhoods to mortgage companies," the study says. "Boston has become a city with significant unmet credit needs for affordable housing and continues as a city with significant racial lending bias."[17]

This story started an avalanche of media attention. One banking expert claimed that in the 90 days after January 11, the Boston media did not miss a single day of coverage. Racial bias, redlining, disinvestment—none of these charges was new; so how could this headline capture the attention of journalists, readers, viewers, and bankers? James Campen, a professor at the University of Massachusetts, suggested that

> What mattered even more than the study's findings . . . was its sponsorship. This was the first study ever by any of the four federal bank regulatory agencies that had contained such conclusions. The fact that the study was done at the Fed gave it and its findings a respectability and credibility that no study sponsored

by community advocates or the media could hope to achieve.[18]

Richard Syron, the week-old president of the Boston Fed, called the conclusions of the study "premature" and stated that his staff "had a responsibility to pursue them and make some determination whether the Boston-area banks were discriminating."[19] More research into lending practices was planned.

The Banking Industry Response Bankers were convinced that they were being falsely accused. Pollard remembered his own reaction:

> Banks wanted to make mortgages. In the late 1980s, the competition was fierce. The banks were booming and mortgage companies were stealing our business. We wanted all the mortgages we could get—black or white—it did not matter. If anything, we were willing to stretch to make a mortgage to a minority applicant just because we needed the volume. It was inconceivable to us that we could be discriminating.

Other industry executives echoed this response. The Massachusetts Bankers Association's (MBA) president, Robert Sheridan, encouraged further study, stating, "I think the record of the industry is impeccable, and we would welcome any intensive scrutiny . . . A thorough, complete analysis will show no bias."[20]

Falsely accused or not, Pollard suspected that this issue would dominate his

---

Mortgages," *The Boston Globe*, January 11, 1989, p. 1.
[17] *Ibid.*

[18] James T. Campen, "The Struggle for Community Investment in Boston," in Gregory D. Squires (ed.), *From Redlining to Reinvestment: Community Responses to Urban Disinvestment* (Philadelphia: Temple University Press, 1992), p. 41.
[19] Peter G. Gosselin, "Boston Fed Chief Promises Further Study," *The Boston Globe*, January 11, 1989, p. 13.
[20] Steven Marantz and Teresa Hanafin, "Report of Lending Bias Draws Mix of Reactions," *The Boston Globe*, January 12, 1989, p. 1.

professional life for a while. Not only was he chairman of a Boston bank, but he was to become chairman of the MBA in June. The MBA represented more than 200 financial institutions. Edward P. Shea,[21] vice president of the MBA, recalled, "Our pitch was that we, as the trade association, could represent their combined interests, or they [the banks] could take a chance on their own." As the media, the politicians, and the community groups probed into the allegations of the leaked study, the banks opted for a collaborative effort. Though it put pressure on Pollard as incoming MBA chairman, collaboration was welcomed by BayBank Boston. As the newcomer to city banking, BayBank Boston did not have much experience to draw on, and its record of lending in inner-city neighborhoods was nearly nonexistent. There was strength in numbers.

Given its expansion plans, BayBanks, Inc., was vulnerable to attentive CRA scrutiny. BayBank Harvard Trust had made a formal request to open a new branch in Allston, a working-class neighborhood on the west end of Boston. Community groups were aware of BayBank's request and used the opportunity to express their concerns. They picketed an existing branch to fuel opposition to the Allston request. Community activists felt that Bay-Bank should not be allowed to expand until it addressed CRA issues. Pollard remembered that day well "because once they finished picketing at the branch, the community activists walked a few blocks to my house, where they demonstrated and left messages in my mailbox."

Fortunately, Crozier, chairman of Bay-Banks, Inc., had anticipated the need for expertise in community relations. After a lengthy "courtship," Crozier hired Thomas Kennedy. Kennedy was well versed in the issues of inner-city life. While studying at the Episcopal Theological School, Kennedy had volunteered for an internship program in New York City, working as a retail salesman and living in East Harlem. Kennedy reflected on his experience as "formative and pivotal, exposing me to urban living and poverty." Upon returning to Boston and being ordained as an Episcopal priest, Kennedy spent a number of years in church-sponsored outreach activities that he referred to as "street ministry," including a period as dean of the Cathedral Church of St. Paul. He first met Crozier serving on a private school board in 1971. Kennedy remembered a conversation they had in 1987:

> Crozier was talking stream of consciousness, saying that his bank needed to reach out to the community and understand its needs. As he described the role of an individual helping the bank in that capacity, I looked at him and said, "Are you talking about having a clergyman come to your bank?" This was the craziest idea I had ever heard. However, he was persistent. By May of 1989, I was community affairs officer at BayBanks, reporting directly to Pollard and indirectly to Crozier.

Kennedy worked with Pollard, tackling the sensitive issues of discrimination and inner-city lending.

As BayBanks dealt with the Allston branch challenge, members of the MBA met weekly for breakfast to discuss the scope of the problem, possible explanations, and an industry response. Pollard analyzed the discussions:

---

[21] The author would like to thank Ed Shea for his time and counsel in preparing this case. Special thanks also go to the staff of the MBA for sharing information on this subject.

The key was to break the issue into its elements. We decided that the mortgage lending issue was the tail wagging the dog. It was the symptom of the disease —not the disease. The inability of a minority applicant to get a mortgage is caused by disinvestment in that community, lack of economic growth, poor income level—all of which needed to be dealt with differently.

This realization led to the identification of four problem areas: mortgage lending, affordable housing, access to bank services, and small-business loans. Each problem was addressed by the MBA by setting up task forces chaired by bankers. Clark Miller, executive vice president of the Bank of Boston, offered to lead the effort on mortgage lending. Richard Driscoll, chairman of The Bank of New England, who had been active in the housing issues, volunteered to work on affordable housing. Pollard assumed responsibility for banking services. Finally, Shawmut Bank's president, John P. Hamill, took the lead on small-business lending.

Further Government Pressure On several fronts, regulatory pressures concerning community banking practices were mounting. While the Boston Fed continued its research, Boston Mayor Ray Flynn, working through the Boston Redevelopment Agency (BRA), decided to hire Charles B. Finn of the Hubert H. Humphrey Institute of Public Affairs at the University of Minnesota. Finn's 1988 studies of home mortgage lending in Detroit[22] and Atlanta[23] heightened public awareness of discrimination in lending. Ulti-

mately, Detroit and Atlanta financial institutions donated funds for a below-market-rate mortgage loan pool similar to B-BURG.

1989 saw significant activity on a national level as well. In a highly visible case, the Federal Reserve Bank of Chicago employed the CRA to halt an acquisition by Continential Bank.[24] By March, the federal financial supervisory agencies completed a review of the CRA and its enforcement. The agencies stated that

> the CRA and the implementing regulations place upon all financial institutions an affirmative responsibility to treat the credit needs of low- and moderate-income members of their community as they would any other market for services that the institution has decided to serve. As with any other targeted market, financial institutions are expected to ascertain needs and demonstrate their responses to those needs.[25]

Specific suggestions for effective programs included more flexible lending criteria, participation in government-insured lending programs, improved advertising and marketing efforts, involvement at all levels of management, improved customer assistance, adoption of a branch closing policy (specifically appropriate notice), assistance in community development programs, establishment of a community development corporation, the funding of a small-business investment corporation, and investments in state or municipal bonds. Finally, amendments to the Financial Institutions Reform, Recovery, and

---

[22] "The Race for Money," a newspaper series printed in *The Detroit Free Press*, July 24–27, 1988.

[23] The series, "The Color of Money," was written by Bill Dedman of *The Atlanta Journal & Constitution*, May 1 through November 3, 1988.

[24] Bill Barnhart, "Fed Hits Continental's Civic Investment," *The Chicago Tribune*, February 16, 1989, Sec. 3, p. 1.

[25] Joint Statement of the Federal Financial Supervisory Agencies Regarding the Community Reinvestment Act, March 21, 1989.

Enforcement Act of 1989 clarified and strengthened the CRA reporting and evaluation process. CRA evaluations would be more detailed and publicly available. (See Exhibit 4.) Lenders would be required to provide information on the sex, race, and income of mortgage applicants, as part of their HMDA reporting. These additions permitted more thorough analysis of mortgage lending practices.

Community Groups' Response The news of the Fed study energized a number of community groups. It was just the sort of credible evidence that they needed to press their case for more community banking. There were many local community groups interested in the CRA and its interpretation. The Massachusetts Urban Reinvestment Advisory Group (MURAG) had been formed nearly 20 years earlier to focus attention on the disinvestment problem. The Dudley Street Neighborhood Initiative, a Roxbury community group, was involved in "a grassroots effort to preserve and redevelop our neighborhood for the people who live and work in it."[26] The Greater Roxbury Neighborhood Authority, Nuestra Communidad Community Development Corporation, and Urban Edge Community Development Corporation were also active. Another participant was the statewide affordable housing coalition, the Massachusetts Affordable Housing Alliance. A Boston union of hotel workers, Local 26, through their subsidiary, Union Neighborhood Assistance Corporation (UNAC), was involved because of a housing trust fund benefit that had recently been granted. These community groups threatened class action suits, organized demonstrations, and submitted informa-

tion to the media. Also active nationally but sited in Boston, the Reverend Charles Stith and his group, the Organization of a New Equality (O.N.E.), encouraged the efforts. No one organization or individual emerged as the leader. In addition, representing the business interests of the minority community, the Minority Developers Association took an active interest. The groups shared a common concern about the problem while representing a diversity of interests and political perspectives.

Working toward a Solution

During the spring of 1989, industry, community groups, and government agencies worked separately. The MBA needed time to analyze the problem from the perspective of the industry as a whole and individually within each financial institution. Several of the community groups united as the Community Investment Coalition (CIC) and insisted on representation in the bankers' meetings. By early June, three forums were scheduled by the MBA, each one dealing with a facet of the problem. The Boston Fed agreed to host the forums so that all parties would feel comfortable. The MBA made an effort to be inclusive and thereby opened the forums to everyone. Of course, not all of the participants agreed with this collaborative approach. Bruce Marks of UNAC refused to attend the forums. Instead his group organized a sit-in at the Bank of Boston.

The Forums As Pollard entered the first forum on small-business lending, a reporter inquired, "Do you think that the banks have caused these problems?" He responded, "I do not know if the banks are part of the problem, but we are certainly part of the solution." This was the tone the MBA tried to set. The bankers and the community representatives were addressing the issues and designing solutions

---

[26] Dudley Street Neighborhood Initiative, *A Neighborhood Building Its Future*, 1991.

together. Shea of the MBA explained that the emphasis of this first forum was to explore ways "to develop jobs, incomes, stability, and savings, so that residents will be able to afford housing on truly market standards."

The second forum addressed affordable housing. Richard D. Driscoll's comments reinforced the emphasis on problem solving:

> The problem of affordable housing in our community is critical and needs more involvement by everybody, certainly by banks . . . Everybody has to abandon old ideas about how this problem will be solved. Certainly banks have to stop saying "we've never done it this way before" or "our current policies prevent us from doing that" or "it's not my problem, let's give it to the government.[27]

In July, the third session, addressing bank services, was held. The concerns raised ranged from branch openings and closings to cashing welfare checks.

With over 90 bankers and over 100 community representatives at each of the forums, recognition of the needs of the community as well as the limitations on private organizations were acknowledged by participants. After the forums, the bankers' task forces continued to work on solutions. Yet, there were some skeptics. Peter Dreir of the Boston Redevelopment Authority (BRA) commented, "This could be a window of opportunity or it could simply be a window dressing."[28] Another doubter, Representative

Joseph P. Kennedy (D, Massachusetts) stated, "While it's encouraging to see the formation of task forces, and forums . . . I still am unclear at what specific measures came out of them."[29] The MBA promised to reveal their plan and the banks' commitments to the reinvestment efforts in late September.

Negotiating a Settlement

While the bankers were drafting a plan, pressure continued to mount from the media, community groups, and politicians. The Greater Roxbury Neighborhood Authority printed and circulated their study on patterns of mortgage discrimination. Peter Dreir of the BRA continually made reference to the Finn study, but failed to state when the study would be released to the public. On August 24, the Community Investment Coalition (CIC) took a stand "calling for the infusion of $2.1 billion in private bank loans and the reopening of closed bank branches to redress years of lending bias and neglect."[30] As reported, the CIC groups "want the city's largest banks to finance the construction and rehabilitation of 12,000 housing units. They want a program of discounted mortgage rates at 5 percent and 15 more bank branches and ATMs for the minority communities."[31] The CIC sent their 29-page analysis and plan to all of the banks in Boston. Pollard reported that in the enclosed letter the CIC stated, "While the

---

[27] Steven Marantz, "Bank of N.E. Official Urges More Community Lending," *The Boston Globe*, June 23, 1989, p. 21.

[28] James T. Campen, "The Struggle for Community Investment in Boston," in Gregory D. Squires (ed.), *From Redlining to Reinvestment: Community Responses to Urban Disinvestment* (Philadelphia:

Temple University Press, 1992), p. 48.

[29] Steve Marantz, "Banks Eye Kennedy-Amended Bailout Bill," *The Boston Globe*, August 2, 1989, p. 25.

[30] "Roxbury Leaders Ask $2.1-B in 'Bias Loan,'" *The Milford Daily News*, August 25, 1989, p. 20.

[31] MaryAnne Kane, *Channel 7 WNEV TV*, August 24, 1989, transcript published by New England Newswatch (Framingham, MA).

details of the plan are open for discussion, its scope is nonnegotiable." The CIC insisted on a response by September 11 and urged that the bankers open their discussions up to CIC representatives.

Official Release of the Federal Reserve Study   On August 31, 1989, the final version of the Fed study was released. The study had compared mortgage origination patterns in predominantly black and predominantly white neighborhoods. The researchers found significantly lower mortgage activity in predominantly black neighborhoods, even controlling for income and wealth levels. The central findings were:

> Controlling for all the economic and other nonracial factors, the results suggest that neighborhoods with over 80 percent black residents would still have 24 percent fewer mortgage loans relative to the housing stock than neighborhoods with less than 5 percent black residents.[32]
>
> ... While realtors, developers, lenders, and others probably all share some responsibility for the racial pattern of mortgage activity, one group stands out as having a special role to play in correcting this situation. Not only are banks and thrift institutions central to the home ownership process, but unlike other lenders they have an affirmative obligation under the Community Reinvestment Act to help meet the credit needs of their entire community.[33]

In response to the official release of the study, Pollard maintained his early position that "if people think that somehow banks don't want to make mort-

gages in black areas, that couldn't be further from the truth."[34] Many bankers concurred. Some privately expressed skepticism regarding whether there was even enough good business in the urban centers for all the banks to fulfill their CRA obligations.

The conclusions of the Fed study further verified the allegations the CIC had been making over the summer. The local newspaper and television coverage continued to push the discrimination theme, as is evident in this cartoon (see page 455).[35]

In lieu of a specific counteroffer to the CIC proposal, the MBA scheduled an open meeting on September 8. Following the meeting, the community groups hosted a meeting of their own to discuss their proposal and to negotiate the specifics of a plan. At this meeting in Roxbury, Pollard commented, "It is clear at this point that there is no single answer ... The possible solutions we have identified all depend on cooperation among bankers, government officials, and community leaders. We think we have already gone a long way and we expect more progress in the months to come."[36] Pollard went on to commit $150,000 of the MBA funds to establish a community banking council. Throughout the fall, the MBA task force meetings were open to all interested parties.

Struggling to Reach an Agreement   As the MBA worked on a four-pronged plan for community investment, BayBank Boston announced its intention to locate

---

[32] Katherine L. Bradbury, Karl E. Case, and Constance R. Dunham, "Geographic Patterns of Mortgage Lending in Boston, 1982–1987," *New England Economic Review* (September/October 1989): 21.

[33] *Ibid.*, p. 26.

[34] Allan R. Gold, "Racial Pattern Is Found in Boston Mortgages," *The New York Times*, September 1, 1989, p. A20.

[35] Dan Wasserman, *The Boston Globe*, September 5, 1989, p. 14. Copyright, 1989, Boston Globe. Distributed by the Los Angeles Times Syndicate. Reprinted with permission.

[36] Media Advisory, "Massachusetts Bankers Association Testifies on Community Reinvestment Issues," September 29, 1989.

branches and install new ATM machines in minority neighborhoods. Thomas Kennedy of BayBank Boston explained,

> We were already committed to doing something in the neighborhoods of Boston. In fact we applied to open a branch in Allston and already had approval for a branch in Jamaica Plain, which are both low- to moderate-income neighborhoods. The preliminary work had already been done. In response to the pressure, we analyzed our customers by residential zip codes. It turned out we had over 16,000 BayBank customers in the neighborhoods of Roxbury, Mattapan, and Dorchester—and they had no place to bank in their community.

Other Boston banks were developing plans to commit their personnel, funds, and branches to the MBA plan. The atmosphere was generally positive.

However, the negotiations stalled due to disagreement on the mortgage lending issue. The community groups and the bankers could not reach resolution over the mortgage rates. The CIC, with political support in the mayor's office, demanded rates 2 percent below standard rates with no up-front point charges, but the bankers criticized the proposal as unsustainable in the long term. The bankers offered standard rates with two points. John Hamill of Shawmut vowed that "[w]e're 90 percent there . . . We're going to keep working until we have something everybody is happy with."[37] Ultimately, the bankers were able to sell the community groups on market-rate mortgages. They did this by addressing inequities in the loan underwriting criteria and by arranging a program to assist with down payments. For instance, in the past, rent payments did not have the same weight as prior mortgage payments in demonstrating creditworthiness. This would be changed in the new program.

In December of 1989, just as the final details of an agreement between the banks and the community groups was being worked out, the BRA finally released the study by Charles Finn. It again hit hard at the theme of discrimination and the special role of banks in exacerbating the problems of inner-city neighborhoods. The Finn study went beyond the Federal Reserve study in its evaluation of individual banks, and BayBank stood out because of its history as a suburban bank.

The mayor and BRA officials wanted to use the Finn study to pressure the banks into a below-market-rate mortgage program. However, many observers of the summer forums and participants in the fall meetings felt that the release of the Finn study by the BRA did more harm than good, a sentiment that was captured in this cartoon (see page 458).[38]

Pollard, speaking on behalf of the MBA, admitted, "We have to pause a minute to see what's happening here ... the BRA study has thrown everything into confusion ... You do not want to look reactive, you want to look positive. If we don't come out with something this week it's not because we don't have it."[39] A local editorial writer wondered,

> Who figures to be hurt most by this? Who else but the people whom the program would benefit the most? As one activist put it, "The bottom line is that if this process goes by the wayside it's the black community—not some of those people who are part of the negotiations—that will suffer." Neither Mayor Flynn nor the BRA want this, we're sure—but what are they going to do to prevent it?[40]

Breaking the Stalemate It was in this atmosphere of urgency and confusion that racial tensions were dramatically heightened in the city of Boston. In October, the police reported that Carol Stuart, a pregnant white female, had been shot and killed while driving through Mission Hill with her husband, Charles. Since the horror of that day, an investigation had begun to find the assailant, as described by Charles Stuart, "a black, with a raspy voice, high strung, wearing a black jogging suit."[41] Police were very aggressive in their tactics and incurred the anger and frustration of the black community. By early January 1990, the investigation began to focus on Charles Stuart as the murderer of his wife as a result of his leap to death off the Mystic River Bridge. Members of the city's black community demanded a public apology from Flynn for the aggressive police tactics. Flynn refused to apologize.

---

[37]Steve Marantz, "No Agreement on Neighborhood Lending," *The Boston Globe*, December 15, 1989, p. 80.

[38] Reprinted with permission from *The Boston Herald*, December 26, 1989.

[39]Steve Marantz, "Aftermath of the BRA'S Mortgage Lending Report: Hub Bankers Postpone Unveiling of $1 Billion Reinvestment Plan," *The Boston Globe*, December 21, 1989, p. 41.

[40] "The Timing Was Terrible," *The Boston Herald*, December 22, 1989, p. 34.

[41] Peggy Hernandez, "Minority Leaders in City Demand an Apology," *The Boston Globe*, January 5, 1990, p. 21.

BOSTON'S LARGEST BANKS (1981–1987)

Bank	Total Deposits ($000)	Mortgage Loans White/Minority
The First National Bank of Boston	$7,482,003	2.1:1
Bank of New England	6,029,462	1.9:1
State Street Bank	3,983,204	*
Shawmut Bank	3,131,746	2.3:1
Boston Five	1,466,343	0.9:1
The Provident	1,146,728	4.2:1
Home Owners	1,105,742	2.6:1
United States Trust Company	886,691	1.8:1
South Boston Savings Bank	766,185	7.4:1
Neworld Bank for Savings	754,818	1.9:1
First Mutual of Boston	563,696	2.5:1
BayBank Boston, Harvard Trust, Norfolk	433,230	11.7:1
First American Bank	386,451	0.6:1
Capital Bank and Trust	328,718	10.2:1
Haymarket Co-Operative Bank	325,606	No mortgage loans to minority neighborhoods

Source: Adapted from Charles Finn, "Mortgage Lending in Boston's Neighborhoods 1981–1987," December 1989.

*Too few mortgages to calculate ratio.

Revived racial tensions made it hard for Flynn's administration to take further steps to threaten the carefully negotiated MBA reinvestment plan, a plan in which many community leaders had invested a great deal of time and energy. The reinvestment plan was announced, in January 1990, at the annual Martin Luther King Day Breakfast, cosponsored by Union United Methodist Church and St. Cyprian's Episcopal Church. The MBA plan called for concerted activity on all four fronts of mortgage lending, affordable housing, economic development, and access to banking services. (See Exhibit 5 for an overview of The Massachusetts Bankers Association Community Investment Program.) Many of the programs were innovative. General Electric Credit and Fannie Mae had agreed to insure and purchase loans made with underwriting criteria more appropriate for low- to moderate-income home buyers. The Minority Enterprise Investment Corporation (MEIC) planned to work closely with mi-

nority loan applicants to help make their businesses viable candidates for financing, blending business consultation with traditional, hard-nosed underwriting. Nearly all Massachusetts banks agreed to cash government checks even for individuals who did not have accounts at the bank. And the Massachusetts Community and Banking Council (MCBC) planned to keep alive an ongoing dialogue between the community groups and the bankers.

Reactions to the MBA Plan

The community representatives were pleased with the MBA plan. Willie Jones of the CIC commented that the MBA program "should provide for the level of affordability we've been striving for."[42] At the announcement of the program, the Reverend Charles Stith, pastor of the United

---

[42] Stteve Marantz, "$400m Investment Plan for Hub," *The Boston Globe*, January 11, 1990, p. 51.

Methodist Church and head of Organization for a New Equality (O.N.E.), was ecstatic, exclaiming, "I have never been more proud to be a citizen of this city than I am today."[43] The new year was devoted to establishing the new corporations, getting the products to the public, locating affordable housing projects, and finding sites for branch openings. Many of these activities were followed up on by the task forces, while others were up to individual banks.

BayBank Boston was satisfied with the MBA plan and its opportunity for participation. Pollard viewed it as "a permanent thing in which the funds will be replenished over and over. In the long run, it will have a more significant impact."[44] The BayBanks board had been following the progress throughout 1989; therefore, the board quickly approved multiple commitments. BayBanks' contributions were:

- $5 million for mortgage lending at a discounted rate
- $10 million in equity participation for the development of affordable housing (for which the bank received tax credits)

---

[43] Ibid.

[44] Steve Marantz, "Banks' $1 Billion Reinvestment Plan Called National Model," *The Boston Globe*, January 15, 1990, p. 22.

- $2 million to Massachusetts Minority Enterprise Investment Corporation ($.5 million in equity investments and $1.5 million in loans)
- five branches and 25 ATMs in low- and moderate-income areas
- Pollard would chair the Massachusetts Community and Banking Council.

As the new player in the city and in keeping with its ATM strategy, BayBank Boston had decided to take the lion's share of the MBA's promised total of nine new branches and 30 ATMs.

Members of the MBA were particularly delighted that they had avoided the temporary and potentially disastrous remedy of a below-market minority loan pool. They believed that they would avoid another B-BURG and they had not repeated what they perceived to be the mistakes made in Atlanta and Detroit. As Sheridan of the MBA commented,

> Without question, the "big bang" approach of a one-shot loan pool would have put money out on the street sooner. However, the Association is convinced that if the mandate of the Community Reinvestment Act is to be taken seriously, it must be seen as a coherent, financially sound enterprise that will live on after media and even advocate attention has moved on to other things.[45]

The financial soundness of the MBA plan was crucial to the Massachusetts banks and to banking regulators. The turn of the decade brought with it a recession that hit the northeastern states particularly hard. After several years of boom, Massachusetts experienced high unemployment and a major decline in real estate values. These economic strains took their tolls on the banks. The most dramatic evidence of this was the failure of the Bank of New England, as well as many smaller banks. The Bank of New England's chairman, Richard Driscoll, who had headed the MBA task force on affordable housing, resigned from the bank while the MBA process was unfolding. Many banks were reporting losses and cutting dividends. In this environment, BayBanks, Inc., reported its first loss ever. It lost nearly $70 million in 1990. Following a rash of failures in the savings and loan industry, both banks and their regulators had a special interest in assuring that a community investment program be consistent with the safety and soundness of the financial institutions.

Second Mortgage and Home Improvement Loans

Media and advocacy attention did subside for close to a year—until the Bank of New England was to be purchased by Fleet/Norstar Financial Group. Bruce Marks of UNAC assembled documents showing that Fleet as well as other banks had financed private mortgage companies which in turn charged customers interest rates well above the typical bank market rate. He alleged that Fleet was indirectly "lending at loan-shark rates."[46] Not only was this usurious, according to Marks, but it led to an unfortunately high number of foreclosures.

After a 90-day moratorium on foreclosures in Suffolk and Hampden counties, the allegations had been reviewed by the federal regulators. Fleet's purchase of the Bank of New England was approved. However, this issue did not end there. Community groups demanded a more thor-

---

[45] Statement issued by Robert K. Sheridan, President of the Massachusetts Bankers Association, August 1990.

[46] Peter Canellos and Gary Chafetz, "Mortgage Companies Got Credit from Fleet," *The Boston Globe,* May 8, 1991, p. 18.

ough investigation. Despite an aggressive advertising program, called "Setting the Record Straight,"[47] Fleet continued to be featured in the Boston press as the financier of "loanshark" loans to elderly and minority communities. Once again the Boston Fed was called upon—this time to study second mortgage and home improvement lending. Their August 1991 study concluded that

> Certain individuals have suffered great hardship, including the loss of their homes, because of burdensome second mortgages. High rates are only one dimension of the second-mortgage problem, but it is one that permits quantification. We estimate that loans with interest rates of 18 percent or more account for 1.4 percent of the nonaquisition[48] mortgages made in Suffolk county from 1987 to 1990. In the [predominantly black] neighborhoods of Roxbury and Mattapan, 5.1 percent of nonacquisition mortgages carried rates of 18 percent or more. These mortgages are supplied by a relatively small number of specialized lenders. Banks are not providers of high-rate second mortgages, although they are important suppliers of nonacquisition mortgages throughout Suffolk county. The major Boston banks have at times provided financing to some of the high-rate lenders or purchased loans from these lenders; but most of the larger high-rate lenders have many other funding sources. Finally, our survey revealed that many different lenders—banks, mortgage companies, finance companies,

contractors, and individuals—operate throughout Suffolk county, offering borrowers a spectrum of rates.[49]

ESTIMATES OF NONACQUISITION LOANS IN SUFFOLK COUNTRY

Interest Rate	Total Suffolk County	Roxbury and Mattapan
18% or greater	698	207
15% to 18%	1,630	298
Less than 15%	39,581	2,147
Unidentified	9,314	1,370
Total	51,223	4,022

Source: Adapted from Table 1 of Alicia Munnell and Lynne Browne, "Second Mortgages in Suffolk County," The Federal Reserve Bank of Boston, August 14, 1991, p. 12.

Media coverage expanded to cover loans made by home improvement companies as well. Several of the major Boston banks, including BayBanks, were named as financiers of questionable lenders. One television station ran a hard-hitting investigative report on the tragedies that sometimes resulted from questionable lending practices. The Massachusetts attorney general initiated a probe of the banks and their relationships with private mortgage and home improvement companies.

In October 1991, an analysis of 1990 HMDA data was released. 1990 was the first year that race, sex, and income data were reported. The data once again showed racial differences, even when income level was held constant. The release of this data made national news with lead stories in major newspapers. Though it was unrelated to Boston's second-mortgage problem, this information simply fueled the fire.

Accused of forcing as many as 1,000 people out of their homes by "strip-mining

---

[47] Doug Bailey, "Ad Campaign Responds to Critics," *The Boston Globe*, June 18, 1991, p. 1.

[48] The Boston Fed defined nonacquisition mortgages as "second mortgage loans, refinancings of first mortgages, and first mortgages on properties with no existing mortgage." (Alicia Munnell and Lynn Browne, "Second Mortgages in Suffolk County: 1987–1990," The Federal Reserve Bank of Boston, August 14, 1991, p. 1.)

[49] Alicia Munnell and Lynn Browne, "Second Mortgages in Suffolk County: 1987–1990," The Federal Reserve Bank of Boston, August 14, 1991, pp. 10–11.

the equity from minority communities,"[50] Fleet terminated business with 38 private mortgage companies. In defending Fleet Finance, the subsidiary involved, a spokesperson explained, "The higher the risk, the higher the rate. It's not illegal to make a profit."[51] Nonetheless, working with Mayor Flynn, Fleet agreed to establish an $11 million fund to refinance 550 cases on more favorable terms.

Employing the concept of lender liability, the attorney general threatened to investigate the banks individually. BayBanks was the major provider of financing to home improvement companies in Massachusetts. BayBanks managers felt that they had been careful in selecting the home improvement companies with which they dealt. As Pollard explained,

> The only way to control this business is on a complaint basis. BayBanks was legally bound to repair anything that broke down, to replace poor workmanship, or to complete an incomplete project. When a home improvement salesman carried BayBanks's paper, the consumer was protected. In general, there were no complaints. When we did receive two or three complaints from the same company, we dropped them. We policed that part of our business.

He felt that the media and community activists had overestimated the problem, at least as it related to companies funded by the banks. He also wondered why banks were being held responsible for their customers' behavior. Nonetheless, Pollard wanted to resolve this issue quickly. BayBanks entered into discussions with the community and the attorney general.

On February 19, 1992, the attorney general announced an agreement with BayBanks. The agreement drew on the organizations created by the MBA reinvestment plan. BayBanks created a Victim Resolution Program to be run through the recently created MCBC, improved procedures for indirect home improvement lending by offering a product directly to the consumer, committed at least $5 million to a home improvement loan program, and committed $6 million in loans to another MBA-created entity, MHIC. In addition to the commitments made to the attorney general, BayBanks got out of the business of funding home improvement companies. The results were immediate: "[e]ven before hearing a word of the settlement, activists said BayBanks's combination of financial aid and corporate responsibility set a new standard for other banks in Massachusetts and across the country."[52] Shortly after BayBanks announced their agreement, Shawmut Bank agreed to a similar resolution plan, facilitated by the MBA corporations and council. Fleet's earlier plan was characterized by community activists as "totally inadequate . . . purely political and it flies in the face of justice and fair play."[53] In response to these comments and upon further investigation, Fleet also settled with the attorney general two months later.

Continuing National Attention

In May 1992, the nation focused on urban poverty as South Central Los Angeles erupted in riots after the Rodney King

[50] John R. Wilke, "Back Door Loans: Some Banks' Money Flows into Poor Areas—And Causes Anguish," *The Wall Street Journal*, October 21, 1991, p. A1.
[51] *Ibid.*
[52] Mitchell Zuckoff, "Shawmut Is Said to Settle Over Loan Scams," *The Boston Globe*, February 22, 1992, p. 1.
[53] *Ibid.*

verdict was announced. Despite a video-tape depicting several white police offic-ers severely beating Rodney King, a black male motorist whom they had stopped, the officers were found not guilty of crimi-nal wrongdoing. The verdict fueled a sense of injustice. After the riots, the federal government began to talk more seriously about improving urban conditions. And racial discrimination became an even more prominent topic of discussion.

At the same time, the Office of the Comptroller of the Currency began an investigation of 266 banks, all of which had shown a disparity in their lending patterns, according to the HMDA data. Bankers and industry experts hoped that the result would not be further regula-tions. Banks, it was felt, cannot bail out the nation's inner cities. In a *New York Times* editorial, Lawrence White, finance professor at New York University, argued that enough was enough in terms of regu-lations:

> The Community Reinvestment Act is at best obsolete . . . [I]n today's competitive environment, banks need no assistance in discovering good customers. If serving the local community is profitable, the law is unnecessary. If it is not profitable, a bank must earn extra profits from other activities to subsidize those losses. But banks and nonbank rivals have com-peted so fiercely in other financial ser-vices that extra profits are scarce—leaving banks with a choice of shirking their community reinvestment require-ments or suffering losses . . . If supplying unprofitable financial services to local companies and households serves a pub-lic purpose, that case should be made explicitly, and *public* resources should support those services.[54]

These concerns were raised at a time when banking regulators were described as "schizophrenic" because "[t]he Bush administration, fretting that tight-fisted bankers are hobbling economic recovery, wants more aggressive lending. Congress, worried that another savings and loan mess is about to land on it, has ordered tighter regulation to cut risk."[55]

When Racial Disparity Persisted

Pollard was concerned about the regu-latory issues, but for the moment he had to focus specifically on Boston. The Federal Reserve Bank of Boston had just com-pleted the "end all–be all" study of mort-gage lending patterns. The researchers at the Fed had worked with the bankers to understand the practical criteria for evalu-ating a loan, and they had complete access to loan files. The methodology was thor-ough. Because of their cooperation in the study, it would be hard for the banks to ignore the results.

Richard Syron, president of the Fed, had called to tell Pollard that even with all this information, evidence of racial disparity remained. The results reflected aggregate patterns; individual bank perfor-mance was not studied. But there was no reason to think that BayBank would be an exception. What held in the aggregate probably held for BayBank Boston. The question was, What, if anything, should he do about it?

---

[54] Lawrence J. White, "Don't Handcuff the Healthy Banks," *The New York Times*, May 17, 1992, p. F13.

[55] Mike McNamee and Tim Smart, "The Head-Spinning Split Over Banking," *Business Week*, June 8, 1992, p. 43.

EXHIBIT 1
BAYBANK MORTGAGE LOAN APPROVAL PROCESS

STEP 1: Preliminaries

  a) A potential applicant identified a property to purchase and negotiated a price.

  b) The applicant decided to approach BayBank for a mortgage.

STEP 2: The applicant inquired at branch office

  a) A mortgage specialist conducted the preliminary interview focusing on the applicant's ability to service the debt, based on gross income.

  b) If the applicant was interested in applying for one of the mortgage products offered, he/she was given a BayBank Mortgage Application Package.

STEP 3: Branch review of completed application

  a) After the mortgage specialist received the application, an appointment was made to review the application process with the applicant.

  b) At the appointment, the application was reviewed for completeness and for any obvious obstacles to making the loan. If there were any missing forms or problems, the applicant may be asked to supply additional information.

  c) The applicant paid an application fee and one point (1% of the loan).

STEP 4: Bank underwriting process at BayBank Mortgage Corporation

  a) An underwriter and loan processor reviewed the application using secondary market criteria. Credit reports were ordered, income and bank accounts were verified, and the property was assessed.

  b) A senior underwriter reviewed the work of the underwriter and loan processor. The file was passed through a quality control process. The senior underwriter finalized the decision and sometimes recommended an alternative method for making the loan.

  c) If the underwriter recommended the loan be denied, the senior underwriter must review the loan to assure that all possibilities for approving the loan have been exhausted. If the senior underwriter agreed with the recommendation, the loan was given to the CRA manager for review. If the CRA manager did not find an alternative program to grant the loan, the loan was reviewed by senior staff at BayBank Mortgage Corporation. If senior staff agreed with the decision, a denial letter was written that explained the reasons for denial.

  d) The bank's closing department prepared instructions and closing documents for the bank's attorney. The attorney made an appointment with the applicant for the closing.

EXHIBIT 2
EXCERPTS FROM "MORTGAGE LENDING IN BOSTON: INTERPRETING HMDA DATA" (1992)

The Home Mortgage Disclosure Act (HMDA) data for 1990, which were released in October 1991, showed substantially higher denial rates for black and Hispanic applicants. These minorities were two to three times as likely to be denied mortgage loans as white applicants were. In fact, high-income minorities in Boston were more likely to be turned down than low-income whites. The 1991 HMDA data, which are being released currently, show a similar pattern.

This pattern has triggered a resurgence of the debate on whether discrimination exists in home mortgage lending. Some people believe that the disparities in denial rates are evidence of discrimination on the part of banks and other lending institutions. Others, including lenders, argue that such conclusions are unwarranted, because the HMDA data do not include information on credit histories, loan-to-value ratios, and other factors considered in making mortgage decisions. These missing peices of information, they argue, explain the high denial rates for minorities.

The results of this study indicate that minority applicants, on average, do have greater debt burdens, higher loan-to-value ratios, and weaker credit histories and are less likely to buy single-family homes than white applicants, and that those disadvantages do account for a large portion of the difference in denial rates. Including additional information on applicant and property characteristics reduces the disparity between minority and white denials from the originally reported ratio of 2.7 to 1 to roughly 1.6 to 1. But these factors do not wholly eliminate the disparity, since the adjusted ratio implies that even after controlling for financial, employment, and neighborhood characteristics, black and Hispanic mortgage applicants in the Boston metropolitan area are roughly 60 percent more likely to be turned down than whites. This discrepancy means that minority applicants with the same economic and property characteristics as white applicants would experience a denial rate of 17 percent rather than the actual white denial rate of 11 percent. Thus, in the end, a statistically significant gap remains, which is associated with race.

Estimating an equation that includes an explicit measure for race is not the only way to test whether race is an important factor in the mortgage lending decision. An equally good alternative is to estimate an equation for white applicants and then plug in the obligation ratios, loan-to-value ratio, credit history, and other values for each black/Hispanic applicant to calculate that applicant's probability of denial. The resulting discrepancy between the actual minority denial rate and the estimated minority denial rate based on the white equation can be interpreted as the effect of race on the mortgage lending decision.

PROBABILITY OF BLACK/HISPANIC DENIALS BASED ON WHITE EXPERIENCE

Chacteristics and Experience	Denial Rates (%)
Actual denial rate for blacks/Hispanics in sample	28.1%
Denial rate for blacks/Hispanics with black/ Hispanic characteristics but white experience	20.2
Denial rate for blacks/Hispanics with white characteristics but black/Hispanic experience	18.2
Actual denial rate for whites in sample	10.3

If blacks/Hispanics had their own characteristics, that is, high obligation ratios, weaker credit histories, higher loan-to-value ratios, and being less likely to buy a single-family home, but were treated by lenders like whites, their average denial rate would be 20.2 percent rather than the actual 28.1 percent experienced by minority applicants. In other words, economic, property, and neighborhood characteristics explain much of the higher minority denial rate, but 7.9 percentage points remain unexplained.

If the 7.9-percentage-point discrepancy is attributed to the effect of race on the lending decision, this amount can be added to the white denial rate to estimate the racial impact starting from the white base. That is, the third line [in the table] shows what the denial rate would have been for black and Hispanic applicants if they had white obligation ratios, loan-to-value ratios, credit histories, and other characteristics but were treated by lenders like minorities. Thus, even if minorities had all the economic and property characteristics of whites, they would have experienced a denial rate of 18.2 percent, 7.9 percentage points more than the actual white denial rate of 10.3 percent.

EXHIBIT 2 (continued)

This study has examined one avenue through which differential treatment could affect minorities' access to credit and opportunities for home ownership. It found that black and Hispanic mortgage applicants in the Boston area were more likely to be turned down than white applicants with similar characteristics.

It is important to clarify the limited focus of this analysis; it abstracts from discrimination that may occur elsewhere in the economy. For example, if minorities are subject to discrimination in education or labor markets, they will have lower incomes and their applications may reflect higher obligation ratios, greater loan-to-value ratios, or poorer credit histories. Similarly, if blacks and Hispanics are discouraged from moving into predominantly white areas, they will limit their search to neighborhoods sanctioned for minorities. They tend to be older central cities with high-density housing, such as two- to four-family homes. Denial of a mortgage loan application on the basis of either these economic or property characteristics would not be considered discriminatory for the purpose of this study.

Even within the specific focus of conventional lenders, the reported measure of the hurdles faced by minorities should be placed in perspective; differential treatment can occur at many stages in the lending process. For example, minorities may be discouraged from even applying for a mortgage loan as a result of a prescreening process. Similarly, if white applicants are more likely than minority applicants to be "coached" when filling out the application, they will have stronger applications than similarly situated minorities. In this case, the ratios and other financial information in the *final* applications, which were the focus of this analysis, may themselves be the product of differential treatment. This study does not explore the extent to which coaching occurs, but rather focuses on the impact of race on lenders' decisions regarding the final applications received from potential borrowers.

Source: Alicia H. Munnell, Lynn E. Browne, James McEneaney, and Geoffrey M.B. Tootell, "Mortgage Lending in Boston," Federal Reserve Bank of Boston, Working Paper No. 92-7, October 1992.

EXHIBIT 3
EXCERPTS FROM THE COMMUNITY REINVESTMENT ACT OF 1977

Findings and Purpose

Section 2. (a) The Congress finds that—

    (1) regulated financial institutions are required by law to demonstrate that their deposit facilities serve the convenience and needs of the communities in which they are chartered to do business;

    (2) the convenience and needs of the communities include the need for credit services as well as deposit services; and

    (3) regulated financial institutions have continuing and affirmative obligation to help meet the credit needs of the local communities in which they are chartered.

(b) It is the purpose of this Act to require each appropriate Federal financial supervisory agency to use its authority when chartering, examining, supervising, and regulating financial institutions, to encourage such institutions to help meet the credit needs of the local communities in which they are chartered consistent with the safe and sound operation of such institutions.

Community Reinvestment Programs and Procedures

Section 4. Each appropriate Federal financial supervisory agency shall develop programs and procedures for carrying out the purposes of this Act. Such programs and procedures shall include—

(1) requiring that in connection with an application for a deposit facility, the applicant

    (A) delineate the primary savings service area for the deposit facility;

    (B) analyze the deposit and credit needs of such area and how the applicant proposes to meet those needs;

    (C) indicate the proportion of consumer deposits obtained from individuals residing in the primary savings service area by the deposit facility that will be reinvested in that area; and

    (D) demonstrate how that applicant is meeting the credit needs of the primary savings service areas in which it or its subsidiaries have already been chartered to do business;

(2) using, as factors to be considered in approving applications for deposit facilities, the applicant's record in meeting the credit needs of the primary savings service areas in which it or its subsidiaries have already been chartered to do business, and its proposal for meeting the credit needs of the primary savings service area associated with the pending application;

(3) permitting and encouraging community, consumer, or similar organizations to present testimony at hearings on applications for deposit facilities on how the applicant has met or is proposing to meet the credit needs of the communities served by or to be served by the applicant or its subsidiaries; and

(4) requiring periodic reports from regulated financial institutions concerning the amount of credit extended in the institutions' primary savings service areas and making such reports available to the public.

Annual Report

Section 5. Each appropriate Federal financial supervisory agency shall include in its annual report to the Congress a section outlining the actions it has taken to carry out its responsibilities under this Act.

EXHIBIT 4
AMENDMENTS TO THE FINANCIAL INSTITUTIONS REFORM, RECOVERY, AND ENFORCEMENT
ACT OF 1989

As of July 1, 1990, CRA ratings are no longer on a numerical basis; rather they are written evaluations using a four-tier descriptive system:

Outstanding record of meeting community credit needs;
Satisfactory record of meeting community credit needs;
Needs to improve record of meeting community credit needs;
Substantial noncompliance in meeting community credit needs.

Each institution will have its performance reviewed in five major categories:

1. Ascertainment of community credit needs;
2. Marketing and types of credit extended;
3. Geographical distribution and record of opening and closing offices;
4. Discrimination and other illegal credit practices; and
5. Community development.

An "outstanding" rating will be achieved only by financial institutions that demonstrate certain qualities, including leadership in ascertaining community needs, participation in community revitalization, and affirmative involvement in planning, implementing, and monitoring their CRA-related performance. Most CRA observers agree that "outstanding" ratings will be difficult to achieve.

CRA evaluations can be found at an institution's main office and designated branch in each of its local communities. They are not, however, required to provide free copies.

Source: Virginia M. Mayer, Marina Sampanes, and James Carras, *Local Officials Guide to the Community Reinvestment Act*, Washington, D.C.: National League of Cities, 1991, p. 15.

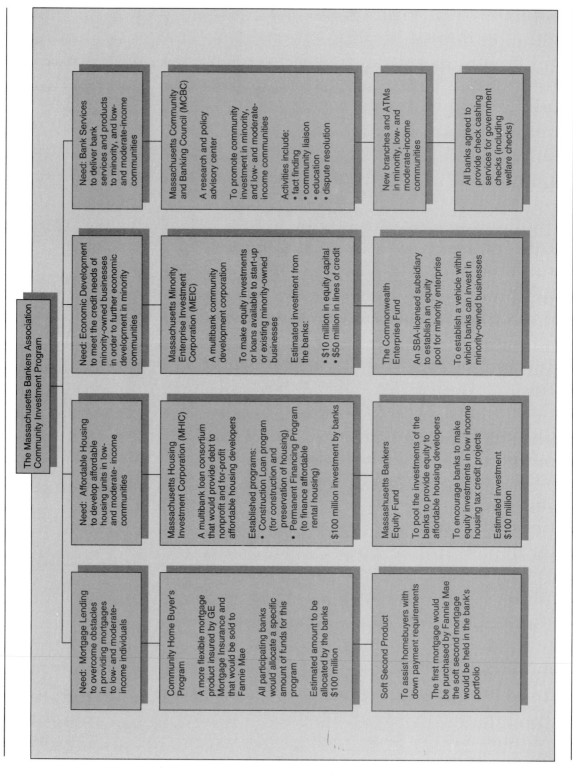

The Massachusetts Bankers Association Community Investment Program

Need: Mortgage Lending to overcome obstacles in providing mortgages to low- and moderate-income individuals

Community Home Buyer's Program

A more flexible mortgage product insured by GE Mortgage Insurance and that would be sold to Fannie Mae

All participating banks would allocate a specific amount of funds for this program

Estimated amount to be allocated by the banks $100 million

Soft Second Product

To assist homebuyers with down payment requirements

The first mortgage would be purchased by Fannie Mae the soft second mortgage would be held in the bank's portfolio

---

Need: Affordable Housing to develop affordable housing units in low- and moderate-income communities

Massachusetts Housing Investment Corporation (MHIC)

A multibank loan consortium that would provide debt to nonprofit and for-profit affordable housing developers

Established programs:
• Construction Loan program (for construction and preservation of housing)
• Permanent Financing Program (to finance affordable rental housing)

$100 million investment by banks

Massachusetts Bankers Equity Fund

To pool the investments of the banks to provide equity to affordable housing developers

To encourage banks to make equity investments in low income housing tax credit projects

Estimated investment $100 million

Need: Economic Development to meet the credit needs of minority-owned businesses in order to further economic development in minority communities

Massachusetts Minority Enterprise Investment Corporation (MEIC)

A multibank community development corporation

To make equity investments or loans available to start-up or existing minority-owned businesses

Estimated investment from the banks:
• $10 million in equity capital
• $50 million in lines of credit

The Commonwealth Enterprise Fund

An SBA-licensed subsidiary to establish an equity pool for minority enterprise

To establish a vehicle within which banks can invest in minority-owned businesses

---

Need: Bank Services to deliver bank services and products to minority, and low- and moderate-income communities

Massachusetts Community and Banking Council (MCBC)

A research and policy advisory center

To promote community investment in minority, and low- and moderate-income communities

Activities include:
• fact finding
• community liaison
• education
• dispute resolution

New branches and ATMs in minority, low- and moderate-income communities

All banks agreed to provide check cashing services for government checks (including welfare checks)

RU 486 (A)

In late October 1988, Edouard Sakiz, chairman of the French pharmaceutical company, Groupe Roussel UCLAF, faced several decisions about RU 486, a new drug the company had developed. When used in conjunction with another drug, RU 486 was 90 to 95 percent effective in causing a miscarriage in the first five weeks of a pregnancy. The drug also had properties that could make it effective for treating several serious illnesses.

Sakiz had to decide whether to market the drug in France and in China and how to do so. Both countries had already given Roussel UCLAF approval to sell RU 486. Sakiz also had to decide whether to seek approval from the Food and Drug Administration to sell the drug in the United States.

THE DEVELOPMENT OF RU 486

RU 486 was developed as a result of a joint effort of private industry and members of the medical and scientific communities. In addition, the personal efforts of one man, Etienne-Emile Baulieu, were critical. Baulieu, a medical doctor by training, was a highly successful research biochemist and a specialist in the study of steroid hormones. He had long been affiliated with INSERM (the National Institute of Health and Medical Research), a laboratory run by the French government, and he also taught biochemistry at the university level and consulted for pharmaceutical companies.

Baulieu made his mark early with the discovery in 1959 of soluble steroids secreted by the adrenal glands, a breakthrough that led to advances in the treatment of adrenal cancer. Later, Baulieu worked with Gregory Pincus, a biochemist at Boston University who played a major role in the development of the contraceptive pill. Baulieu was involved in the testing of the pill and later served on a World Health Organization committee on contraception.[1] Pincus helped Baulieu se-

[1] Steven Greenhouse, "A New Pill, A Fierce Battle," *New York Times Magazine*, February 12,

cure funding from the Ford Foundation for research at INSERM.[2] This work led ultimately to the development of RU 486.

Methods of birth control such as the rhythm method, oral contraceptives, and IUDs depend upon knowledge about physiological events during a woman's menstrual cycle and the ways hormones trigger these events. The rhythm method is preferred by women who oppose the use of other contraceptive methods for religious or other reasons. It makes no use of scientific innovations per se, but rather seeks to take advantage of the temporary incapacity of the uterus to receive fertilized eggs early in a menstrual cycle.[3]

Oral contraceptives—commonly called "the pill"—usually work by suppressing the hormones that trigger the production and release of an egg. (Some forms of the pill permit a sperm to fertilize an egg but then prevent the fertilized egg from implanting on the wall of the uterus where it would continue development.) The contraceptive pill is almost 100 percent effective when used as directed. However, many side effects have been attributed to the increased levels of estrogen the pill induces. Minor side effects include nausea, weight gain, bleeding, and migraine headaches. Major side effects include blood clots, heart attack, benign liver tumors, elevation of blood sugar levels, and increased susceptibility to some kinds of cancer.

Another method of fertility control, the intrauterine device or IUD, functions mechanically rather than chemically. An IUD is a semipermanent implant in the wall of the uterus. This foreign object changes the uterus in several ways that prevent a fertilized egg from being implanted on the wall of the uterus. IUDs can have serious side effects, including infections that can lead to infertility. Because of these risks, IUDs are illegal in many countries, and pharmaceutical companies that produced the IUDs that led to infection have faced costly lawsuits.

Baulieu's research focused on the way a woman's body receives messages from reproductive hormones, particularly the hormone progesterone. In 1970, Baulieu successfully isolated the receptors in the cells of the uterus that receive messages from progesterone. His research team then began searching for a chemical that would keep these receptors from getting the hormone's signals to prepare the uterus to receive and nurture an embryo.[4]

Soon, Baulieu's efforts were joined by chemists at Roussel UCLAF, which was a leader among pharmaceutical companies working in steroid biochemistry. Roussel UCLAF chemists tested a variety of molecules and in 1978 created a synthetic steroid whose chemical structure closely resembled progesterone. This molecule, it seemed, might "trick" the progesterone receptors in the uterus and halt further production of progesterone. This would cause the lining of the uterus to break down and be expelled, as in normal menstruation. If a fertilized egg were attached to the lining, it, too, would be expelled. Roussel UCLAF registered the synthetic steroid as RU 38486.

Since the full role of progesterone in reproduction remained unclear, testing of

---

1989, p. 23.

[2] Jeremy Cherfas and Joseph Palca, "The Pill of Choice?" *Science*, September 22, 1989, p. 1324.

[3] *Contraception at UHS* (Harvard University Health Services, September 1989), p. 37.

[4] Jeremy Cherfas, "Etienne-Emile Baulieu: In the Eye of the Storm," *Science*, September 22,1989, pp. 1323–4.

RU 486 was necessary to confirm Baulieu's suspicion that blocking progesterone would terminate a pregnancy. Initial tests on monkeys confirmed that progesterone was necessary for the maintenance of an embryo.[5] The first test of RU 486 on human subjects was done in collaboration with a professor of medicine at the University Hospital of Geneva. Eleven women who were in the first trimester of pregnancy and wanted abortions were administered doses of RU 486 over four days. Nine of the women aborted successfully; the other two had successful surgical abortions.[6] A subsequent study involved one hundred women desiring abortions who were referred to researchers within 10 days of an expected missed period. The women took various doses of RU 486 over various time periods, ranging from 400 mg. over four days to 800 mg. over two days. RU 486 caused abortions for 85 of the women, though a minority of them experienced complications, including heavy uterine bleeding, nausea, fatigue, and uterine contractions more painful than those in normal menstruation.[7]

The success rate of 85 percent was considered too low, so the researchers decided to give women RU 486 along with a small dose of synthetic prostaglandin, a reproductive hormone that induces contractions of the uterus. Subsequent studies showed that this combined treatment would raise the success rate of both drugs and diminish side effects of each. RU 486 blocks the normal effect of progesterone on the uterus and prevents it from accepting or sustaining an embryo; prostaglandin encourages the uterus to contract and expel its contents. This method, a combined dose of RU 486 and synthetic prostaglandin, was ultimately adopted for the use of RU 486.[8]

The testing of RU 486 revealed that the drug had other properties. It also blocked the receptors for the glutocorticoid hormone. This suggested the drug could be used to treat Cushing's syndrome (a life-threatening disease), certain kinds of breast cancer, and certain benign brain tumors.[9]

The early tests also suggested that RU 486 might be used as a form of birth control with similarities to the contraceptive pill. The earliest tests on monkeys showed it to be 100 percent effective in preventing pregnancy if taken once a month. This suggested that if a woman were not pregnant, taking RU 486 could induce menstruation. If a woman were pregnant, RU 486 would end the pregnancy. Baulieu and others had expressed the hope that RU 486 might someday be commonly used as a "once-a-month pill."[10] In commenting on the possible uses of RU 486, an article in the *New England Journal of Medicine* stated:

> Demographic surveys estimate that there are approximately 90 million births worldwide each year and 40 to 50 million abortions . . . Thus, unfortunately,

---

[5] Beatrice Couzinet, Nelly Le Strat, André Ullmann, Etienne-Emile Baulieu, and Gilbert Schaison, "Termination of Early Pregnancy by the Progesterone Antagonist RU 486 (Mifepristone)," *New England Journal of Medicine* 315:25 (December 18, 1986): 1565–70.

[6] W. Hermann, R. Wyss, A. Riondel, D. Philibert, G. Teusch, E. Sakiz, and E.-E. Baulieu, "Effet d'un stéroide antiprogestérone chez la femme: interruption du cycle menstruel et de la grossesse au début," *Comptes Rendues des Scances de l'Academie des Sciences* [iii] 294 (1982), pp. 933–938.

[7] *Ibid.*

[8] *Ibid.*

[9] Cherfas et al., p. 1322.

[10] *Ibid.*

in the last quarter of the 20th century, abortion, with its risks and sequelae, is the most widely used method of fertility regulation. The need for a safe, convenient, and effective method of preventing or terminating pregnancy is obvious.[11]

Some doctors predicted that within a decade RU 486 or a pill like it could be used for a third of France's abortions.

Baulieu held similar beliefs, saying:

> I want to help women. I have not dedicated my life to abortion. I am not anti-children. I have three children and seven grandchildren. But women die in botched abortions. Two hundred thousand every year. RU 486 can save them.[12]

Baulieu viewed RU 486, not primarily as a new abortion technology, but as an advance in fertility control. RU 486 resembled other methods of fertility control that manipulated hormones. Like some of these methods, RU 486 functioned *after* a fertilized egg had implanted in a woman's uterus and had begun to develop. Baulieu preferred to call the pill a "contragestive," a way of halting gestation, not an "abortificant." He said, "I resent it when people present the very early interruption of pregnancy as killing a baby, morally or physically."

ROUSSEL UCLAF

Roussel UCLAF was partially owned by Hoechst, the German pharmaceutical and chemical conglomerate. Hoechst owned 54.5 percent of Roussel UCLAF; the French government owned another 36.25 percent. Hoechst had made its first investment in Roussel UCLAF in 1968 because it was attracted by Roussel UCLAF's creative R&D in biochemistry. In 1987, Hoechst was the fourth largest chemical company in the world, as measured by sales, and the seventh largest pharmaceutical company. (See Exhibit 1.)

Roussel UCLAF was the third largest chemical–pharmaceutical company in France and the 42nd largest in Europe. It specialized in steroids and related drugs so the research and marketing of RU 486 fell within its company's area of expertise. Health care products were Roussel UCLAF's main business, but roughly a third of its sales came from chemicals, pesticides and insecticides, veterinary products, and nutrition products. Roussel UCLAF's profits had been weak in recent years, in part because of French price controls and competition from generic drugs. In early 1988 Banque Paribas Capital Markets had advised its clients to reduce their holdings of Roussel UCLAF shares. (See Exhibit 2.)

Two-thirds of Roussel UCLAF's sales were made outside France. Roussel UCLAF's U.S. sales amounted to approximately $120 million, or roughly 7 percent of Roussel UCLAF's total sales of $1.7 billion, and they had been growing rapidly. The company's health care sales in the United States were made through Hoechst Roussel UCLAF Pharmaceuticals, which was majority-owned by Hoechst.

Roussel UCLAF's involvement with RU 486 was due largely to the company's chairman, Edouard Sakiz. At the age of 20, Sakiz left his native Turkey to study medicine in Paris, and he soon became involved in research on hormones. A journalist described Sakiz as "a sensitive,

---

[11] Couzinet et al., p. 1565.

[12] Jeremy Cherfas, "Etienne-Emile Baulieu: In the Eye of the Storm," *Science*, September 22, 1989, p. 1323.

courteous man" who had "flourished in the rarefied environment of academia."[13] As a skilled endocrinologist, Sakiz was involved in the discovery of the steroid molecule which constitutes RU 486 and in its earliest testing. Though he was chairman of Roussel UCLAF at the time, Sakiz joined Baulieu in signing the article that announced to the medical and scientific communities the results of the first tests of RU 486.

During his mid-20s, Sakiz became a research assistant to a leading French biochemist at an elite research institute. He had published many scientific papers and served as Roussel UCLAF's research director before he became its chairman. Sakiz was also a personal friend and former classmate of Etienne-Emile Baulieu. During the 1960s, after Sakiz had returned to France from an academic appointment in the United States, Baulieu recommended him for his first post at Roussel UCLAF, as director of biological research. Sakiz in turn played a role in Baulieu's appointment as a consultant to Roussel UCLAF in the late 1960s, and he later encouraged the transfer of Baulieu's research on progesterone receptors to Roussel UCLAF's labs. Since the mid-1960s, Baulieu had been an "independent and exclusive" consultant to Roussel UCLAF.

Sakiz and Baulieu shared a long-standing interest in reproductive technology. In Sakiz's case, this interest had a corporate side: He remembered Roussel UCLAF's decision in the 1960s not to produce the contraceptive pill, even though it fell clearly within the company's capabilities. The decision was the result of resistance to the pill in France. Sakiz later commented, "We lost the market for contraceptives even though we were the most important steroid company in the world. And now contraceptives are considered natural; they aren't at all controversial."[14]

EARLY OPPOSITION TO RU 486

Pressure against Roussel UCLAF for involvement with RU 486 began long before the French government approved the sale of the drug. In February of 1988, more than seven months earlier, the *New York Times* reported that U.S. companies had been threatened with boycotts if they sold or conducted research on abortion-inducing drugs like RU 486. The paper also reported that representatives of Hoechst-Roussel UCLAF, the American subsidiary of Roussel UCLAF's parent company, had stated that their company would not seek approval for RU 486 from the Food and Drug Administration.[15] A company official had said, "We're not in that business—we don't want to get into it."

Protests soon reached Roussel UCLAF. By June 1988, Sakiz was receiving threatening letters every day. Some said, "Assassins, stop your work of death," or, "Your pill kills babies and you will suffer the consequences." Opponents of abortion had also begun to picket the company's headquarters on the Boulevard des Invalides in Paris, sometimes marching just below the window of Sakiz's office. The company also received bomb threats;

---

[13] Steven Greenhouse, "A Fierce Battle," *New York Times Magazine*, February 12, 1969, p. 24.

[14] *Ibid.*

[15] Gina Kolata, "Boycott Threat Blocking Sale of Abortion-Inducing Drug," *New York Times*, February 22, 1988, p. A1.

antiabortion groups and Catholic hospitals in France said they would stop buying Roussel UCLAF and Hoechst products if the company marketed RU 486: protestors handed out leaflets calling RU 486 a "chemical weapon" that would "poison the still-tiny children of a billion Third World mothers." Some opponents of RU 486 emphasized that before and during World War II Hoechst was a leading member of German chemical industry conglomerates that manufactured cyanide gas for the Nazi gas chambers. (Other evidence suggests that the gas was manufactured with concentration camp labor.) Protesters compared RU 486 to the Holocaust: "You are changing the uterus into a death oven," some charged. Sakiz believed these personal challenges and indictments were taking a toll on the morale of Roussel UCLAF's employees.[16]

The chairman of the Hoechst Group, Wolfgang Hilger, had stated that an abortion pill would violate the support for life expressed in Hoechst's corporate credo. Hilger was personally opposed to abortion. Nevertheless, he had stated in 1988 that "Hoechst subsidiaries are active worldwide under their own responsibilities and at their own initiative within the framework of shared goals."[17] In 1988 West German law permitted abortions only when a pregnant woman's life was threatened, when the pregnancy resulted from rape or incest, or if birth could create severe social and economic hardship. Violators of the law faced heavy fines.

There was also opposition to RU 486 within Roussel UCLAF. On June 23, 1988,

a rally of hundreds of antiabortion protesters took place in front of Roussel UCLAF's headquarters during the company's annual meeting. The highlight of the meeting was to have been Sakiz's announcement of a significant improvement in profits, but the protests and discussions of RU 486 eclipsed the announcement. Xavier Dor, a member of the Roussel UCLAF's board of directors who opposed abortion, made the new drug the focus of the meeting.

Other foes of RU 486 inside the company said they opposed selling the pill because of the boycott threat. (Hoechst sales in North America, principally the United States, exceeded $5 billion in 1988 and represented a quarter of the company's world sales and profits. Forty percent of U.S. sales were fibers; the rest were chemicals, pharmaceuticals, and plastics.) Three of the RU 486 opponents were members of Roussel UCLAF's five-person Executive Committee. Two were about to retire, but the other, Alain Madec, was 43 years old and the third-ranking executive at Roussel UCLAF.[18]

The situation grew more complex on September 18, 1988, when the government of China gave Roussel UCLAF approval to market RU 486. This was the first step in an arrangement Roussel UCLAF had made with the World Health Organization for distribution of RU 486 at cost to Third World countries. China wanted RU 486 as part of its population control program. The country's population was already 1.1 billion, and Chinese demographers described the early 1990s as "the Himalayas of population growth"

[16] Greenhouse, p. 24.
[17] Roussel UCLAF annual report, 1988, p. 6.

[18] *Ibid.*

because 150 million women, born in a baby boom during the 1960s, would reach their prime child-bearing age. (China's leader at the time, Mao Zedong, had opposed birth control, calling it "bloodless genocide encouraged by China's enemies.") The country's decade-old "one couple, one child" policy seemed to be failing, even though contraceptives, abortions, and sterilization were available at no cost and living, housing, and education policies favored couples who followed the one-child rule. China seemed unlikely to meet its national goal of a population no greater than 1.2 billion in the year 2000.

On September 23, Claude Evin, the French Minister of Health, approved a trial period of sale for RU 486. The French government would fully fund the distribution of the pill to certain approved clinics throughout France, where women seeking abortions could obtain free treatment with RU 486.

French law permitted abortions during the first three months of pregnancy in cases of "distress." In practice, this was a policy of abortion on request since a woman decided whether she met the "distress" condition and did not need legal or medical permission for an abortion. After three months, abortion was allowed only if a woman's life or physical health was at stake or if there was a risk of fetal handicap. Approximately 160,000 abortions were carried out in France during 1987. Abortions cost roughly $200 and were available at nearly 800 authorized clinics. The government reimbursed 80 percent of the cost. Roussel UCLAF expected the government to pay it $52 for the three RU 486 pills each woman would take.

The Ministry of Health had approved the distribution and marketing of RU 486 with prostaglandin under strict procedures comparable to those of narcotics distribution. Each package would be numbered, distribution was to be limited to authorized hospitals and clinics, and a special register would record the name of physicians and patients. Women would make four medical visits to use RU 486. The first was simply to request an abortion since French law required a woman to wait one week between a request and an abortion. On the second visit, a woman would take three tablets of RU 486. On the third, 36 to 48 hours later, she would receive prostaglandin by injection or suppository and then rest for two to three hours before returning home. Eighty percent of the women would expel the embryo—roughly the size of a pea—during the next 24 hours. Two-thirds of the women would have bleeding heavier than in their normal periods.

About a week later, the abortion would be confirmed during a final visit. If RU 486 had not worked, a surgical abortion would be performed because of the possibility of birth defects. RU 486 could be used only during the first five weeks of pregnancy, or up to about three weeks after a woman has missed a period. (After this point, natural progesterone in the uterus seemed likely to keep the pill from working.)

Sakiz had hoped that the protests against the pill were aimed mostly at preventing this approval. Instead, during the month after the French government's decision, the protests from opponents of abortion increased. The Catholic Church publicly opposed RU 486. Jean-Marie

Lustiger, then the Archbishop of Paris, said the pill was "extremely dangerous." In making his decisions, Sakiz also had to consider factors outside France. In particular, Roussel UCLAF's decision would influence and be developed in the United States.

ABORTION IN THE UNITED STATES

Until the late 1960s, when many states rewrote their abortion laws, abortion was illegal in the United States. In 1973, the Supreme Court ruled in its landmark *Roe v. Wade* decision that state governments could not prohibit abortions during the first three months of pregnancy and could regulate it in the following months. After the decision, there emerged a "pro-life" political movement of people opposed to abortion, and it came to wield considerable political lorce. President Reagan opposed abortion, but his administration, which produced three new Supreme Court justices, did not overturn *Roe v. Wade*. Only one Supreme Court decision, *Webster v. Reproductive Health Services* in 1989, was thought to have weakened the rights granted by *Roe v. Wade* because it gave states broader rights to limit abortion.

The strategy of the right-to-life movement involved political lobbying against proabortion legislation, as well as direct confrontational action aimed at preventing abortions or ostracizing women who have them and doctors who perform them. The antiabortion movement gained exposure in the media through the picketing of abortion clinics and offices of doctors who perform abortions, civil disobedience, and, on occasion, the bombing of abortion clinics. Pro-life activists also produced and distributed films like *The Silent Scream* which graphically depict

what happens to an embryo or fetus during an abortion.

Supporters of abortion rights responded with vigorous political efforts, including lobbying for proabortion legislation, marches for abortion rights that had drawn hundreds of thousands of people, and counterdemonstrations at sites where right-to-life protesters were picketing. The Supreme Court's *Webster* decision, and the possibility of a reversal of *Roe*, posed a new challenge for the pro-choice movement and seemed to have reinvigorated it.

The United States had one of the highest abortion rates of all developed countries. Each year, approximately 28 of every 1,000 women of child-bearing age had abortions. Since the late 1960s, more than 24 million legal abortions had been performed in the United States. approximately one-quarter of all pregnancies.[19] The number of abortion providers had been declining since 1985,[20] and doctors who provided abortions were distributed unevenly. In 1985, 82 percent of counties in the United States had no doctors who performed abortions, even though these counties accounted for 30 percent of women of child-bearing age. Only 2 percent of abortions in the mid-1980s took place outside of metropolitan areas.

A *New York Times* article describing the obstetricians and gynecologists opposed to abortions quoted Dr. Curtis E. Harris, the head of the American Academy of Medical Ethics, an organization that favored restrictions on abortion, who called abortion "a real contradiction since most gynecologists work to bring a child

---

[25] Food and Drug Administration, "RU 486" (FDA Import Bulletin 66-B13), September 26, 1988.

[19] Alan Guttmacher Institute, "Facts in Brief: Abortion in the United States" (two-page pamphlet), 1990.

[20] *Ibid.*

into the world in a healthy state."[21] Other doctors had been intimidated by vocal public opposition to abortion. Facing picketing, harassment, and occasional acts of violence, some doctors who did not oppose abortions in principle declined to perform them. Several doctors quoted in the article stated that the medical community ostracized doctors who perform abortions. The article said one doctor feared that her two-year-old son would be taunted and thought she would lose patients who now come to her for gynecological care if she performed abortions. Some doctors who believed that abortions should be available feel an ambivalence about performing them themselves because of the strong emotions aroused.

Dr. Louise Tyrer of Planned Parenthood offered another explanation for the decreasing interest in performing abortions: "The older doctors like myself who used to see women by the hundreds in hospitals suffering complications of illegal abortions and even dying were highly motivated to change that." Younger doctors, she said, "have not seen any of that—they're not aware of the horrors."[22]

One gynecologist who believed that abortions should be legal and available said that "as long as there is someone else to provide abortions, I'd rather not do it."

REGULATION AND LITIGATION IN THE UNITED STATES

Some observers underlined other factors that contributed to the unavailability of drugs like RU 486. The pharmaceutical firm Upjohn, for example, denied that it had stopped its fertility research because of the boycott. Rather, a spokesperson said the company halted this research for two reasons: "an adverse regulatory climate in the United States . . . and a litigious climate. Litigation is terribly expensive, even if you win."[23]

A drug can be marketed in the United States only if the Food and Drug Administration (FDA) approves it. Both RU 486 and its accompanying synthetic prostaglandin required FDA approval. (The prostaglandins already approved by the FDA were natural prostaglandins and were not strong enough for use with RU 486.) According to the provisions of the Food and Drug Act of 1964, the FDA was required to approve only drugs that were demonstrated, through extensive and documented testing, to be "safe and effective" for their intended purpose. The drug-approval process, from research to approval, took six to ten years. Furthermore, only a fifth of drugs for which Investigational New Drug Applications were submitted were eventually approved.

Groups concerned with AIDS had recently succeeded in getting the FDA to allow drugs that were available abroad but not approved by the FDA to be imported through the mail for personal use by people with "life-threatening conditions like AIDS and cancer."[24] On September 26, 1988, wary of the potential applicability of this directive to RU 486, Burtin I. Love of the FDA clarified the new rule with this statement:

---

[21] Gina Kolata, "Under Pressures and Stigma, More Doctors Shun Abortion," New York Times, January 18, 1990, p. A1.

[22] Ibid.

[23] Ibid., and Gina Kolata, "After Large Study of Abortion Pill, French Maker Considers Wider Sale," New York Times, March 8, 1990, p. 1.

[24] Food and Drug Administration, "Pilot Guidance for Release of Mail Importations" (FDA policy directive), July 20, 1988.

"RU 486" or "Mifepristone" manufactured by Roussel UCLAF Laboratories, Paris, France, has been approved in France and in China. The drug is used to induce abortion and can be used up to 49 days after a woman's last menstrual period.

This drug will not be allowed entry under the "Pilot Guidance for Release of Mail Importations" issued on July 20, 1988, because it does not meet the criteria in the policy statement.[25]

The federal government had been strongly influenced by the politics of abortion. This was especially true during the Reagan administration, which staunchly opposed abortion. From the beginning of Reagan's first term, the government had prohibited federal funding of research relating to abortion. Antiabortion members of Congress had already focused on RU 486. Representative Robert Dornan of California wrote a "Dear Colleague" letter to members of the House entitled "Death Pill." In the letter, Dornan wrote, "The proponents of abortion want to replace the guilt suffered by women who undergo abortion with the moral uncertainty of self-deception. Imagine, with the 'death pill,' the taking of a pre-born life will be as easy and as trivial as taking aspirin."[26] Dornan also offered an amendment to a Health and Human Services Appropriations Bill which would have prohibited FDA funding for testing of what he called RU 486—The "Death Pill." The amendment did not pass.

The antiabortion movement in the United States had also influenced international organizations. In 1985, the Agency for International Development withheld $10 million from a United Nation's agency that had funded birth control programs in China, where many abortions occurred during the last three months of pregnancy, sometimes against a woman's wishes. The United States did not contribute to the World Health Organization's special program on human reproduction and the director of the WHO feared the United States would stop supporting other WHO programs if the organization conducted research on RU 486.

Many observers believed that the antiabortion movement had discouraged pharmaceutical companies from producing abortion-inducing drugs. The *New York Times* reported in early 1988 that "National Right-to-Life and other groups opposed to abortion have served notice to drug companies that if any company sold an abortion-inducing drug the millions of Americans who oppose abortion will boycott all the company's products."[27]

ABORTION-RELATED RESEARCH IN THE UNITED STATES

Several pharmaceutical companies had already faced boycotts because of research on or marketing of abortion-related drugs. The National Right-to-Life group had called on its members to boycott the Upjohn Company of Kalamazoo, Michigan, because it sold three such drugs.[28] In 1985, after a two-year boycott by members

---

[26] Robert K. Dornan, "Death Pill" ("Dear Colleague" letter to members of Congress), July 29, 1986.

[27] Gina Kolata, "Boycott Threat Blocking Sale of Abortion-Inducing Drug," *New York Times*, February 22, 1988, p. A1.

[28] John C. Wilke, "Abortion Drugs—What's the Situation Now?" *National Right-to-Life News*, January 22, 1989, p. 3.

of National Right-to-Life, fertility research in Upjohn's labs ceased altogether.

Winthrop Sterling USA of New York had developed a drug called "Epostane" which has abortive properties similar to those of RU 486. A spokesman for Sterling said the company had no plans to market Epostane because it would not be "consistent with Sterling's strategic goals." John Wilke, president of the National Right-to-Life Committee, had said that Sterling was in communication with the NRL and

> ... has given us written assurances that they are removing this drug from the scene completely. They will not do any more research on it. They will not give or sell the license for it to any other company. They will not allow any other research to be done on the drug. In effect, it has been put in a deep freeze. For this, we are deeply grateful to the Winthrop Sterling Drug Company and to its owner, Eastman Kodak.[29]

The caution these companies showed was, in a sense, industrywide. The Pharmaceutical Manufacturers Association, which develops positions on public policy issues affecting the industry, had no policies on abortion-inducing drugs and said they were not an industrywide matter.[30]

While abortion remained a diverse political issue in the United States, there were indications that antiabortion sentiment was waning. Many political candidates, including a number of Republicans, had shifted their views in a pro-choice direction. A Harris poll had found that 59 percent of those polled said they would favor "a new birth control method ... to terminate unintended pregnancy in its first few weeks by taking a pill." Thirty-three percent opposed the "new method," and 8 percent were unsure.

The "adverse regulatory climate" and the "litigious climate" cited by Upjohn also described the U.S. context for the development and marketing of reproduction-related drugs. Of 17 major companies doing research on contraceptives before the 1980s, only one, Ortho Pharmaceutical Corp., was continuing the research in the late 1980s. No new contraceptive methods had been introduced in the United States in the 30 years since the introduction of the oral contraceptive pill and intrauterine devices. Only two pharmaceutical companies still sold IUDs, and many doctors refused to prescribe them.[31]

In November 1989, the World Bank and the International Planned Parenthood Federation issued a joint statement criticizing the lack of leadership the United States had shown in developing contraceptives. Barber Conable, president of the World Bank, cited an "ideological hangup" in the federal government as the reason the government had not funded international family planning programs.[32]

Similarly, a panel formed by the National Academy of Sciences concluded that:

- the slowing pace of research in the development of contraceptives has left the United States far behind Europe;
- the number and kind of contraceptives available to people in the United States has not changed substantially in 30 years (since the

---

[29] *Ibid.*

[30] Ellen Benoit, "Why Nobody Wants $1 Billion: How a Small Band of Activists Has Intimidated Some of the World's Biggest Companies," *Financial World*, June 27, 1989, p. 35.

[31] "Birth Control Group Urges More Research," *Boston Globe*, January 30, 1980, p. 8.

[32] *Ibid.*

introduction of the oral contraceptive and the IUD);

- the abortion rate, and the number of people who are choosing sterilization early in their reproductive lives, are increasing;
- there are "shortcomings of existing products, including characteristics related to health risks, effectiveness, and convenience as well as to other user preferences."[33]

According to the report, the groups particularly ill-served by these methods were teenagers and people in their early 20s. Available methods did not take account of behavioral difficulties that made even slightly inconvenient methods ineffective for this age group. Also, women who could not use a particular effective method for health reasons—many women cannot safely take the pill—had few alternatives left. The report's "wish list" included RU 486, as well as contraceptive vaccines, long-acting implantable steroids, reversible male and female sterilization, new spermicidal agents with antiviral properties, a once-a-month pill acting as a menses inducer, new methods for ovulation prediction and self-detection, and methods interfering with spermatogenesis.[34]

Opponents of abortion criticized the report. The legal director of the NRL said his group believed the report was part of a national campaign by abortion rights activists and family planning organizations to get abortion drugs on the market in the United States, particularly RU 486.[35]

Moreover, another NRL report expressed concern for the safety of RU 486 for "anemic, malnourished women" in developing countries who might be given the drug under Roussel UCLAF's agreement with the WHO. The report said, "the company is promoting this drug as safe, but we don't have any idea of what the long-term effects will be."[36]

Safety concerns were shared by some supporters of abortion rights. A discussion paper for the board of directors of the National Women's Health Network, a women's advocacy group, asked whether current studies actually showed that RU 486 was safe and whether in the long run it would be proven safer than currently accepted techniques.[37] The paper also noted that the pill and the IUD turned out to have serious, unanticipated side effects.

In September 1988, when Sakiz had to make several critical decisions about RU 486, the drug had not been tested under any of the FDA's procedures. Drugs submitted to this process typically had to be introduced by a pharmaceutical company, by the National Institutes of Health or some other federal institution, or by private institutions. Since federal funds could not be used for abortion-related research, Roussel UCLAF would have to reverse its policy and seek approval itself or permit other groups to submit RU 486 pill for approval.

---

[33] Luigi Mastroianni et al., "Development of Contraceptives—Obstacles and Opportunities," *New England Journal of Medicine*, vol. 322, no. 7 (February 15, 1990): 482–4.

[34] *Ibid.*

---

[35] *Ibid.*

[36] Kolata, March 9, 1990.

[37] Cindy Pearson, "RU 486: What Will It Mean for the Women's Health Movement?" (three-page discussion paper for the Board of Directors of the National Women's Health Network), November 12, 1988.

EXHIBIT 1
HOECHST AG: BASIC FINANCIAL DATA ($ MILLIONS)

	1986	1987
Sales	$17,518	$20,531
Net income	645	849
Profit margin (%)	3.7	4.1
Capital spending	1,235	1,330
R&D	986	1,232
Employees	181,000	168,000

Source: *Chemical and Engineering News*, June 18, 1990, p. 75.

EXHIBIT 2
ROUSSEL UCLAF: BASIC FINANCIAL DATA ($ MILLIONS)

	1983	1984	1985	1986	1987
Sales	$ 1,217	$ 1,243	$ 1,314	$ 1,480	$ 1,611
Net income*	43	52	56	47	31
Funds from operations	87	100	128	104	98
R&D	99	108	129	171	203
New fixed assets and investments	66	82	75	110	93
Stockholders' equity	448	338	477	517	658
Employees at year-end	$17,003	$17,266	$17,830	$16,322	$14,786

Source: Roussel UCLAF annual reports.

Roussel UCLAF financial data is reported in French francs and was converted into dollars using the average exchange rate for each year. The ratio of FF to $ was 7.62 in 1983, 8.74 in 1984, 3.99 in 1985, 6.93 in 1986, and 6.01 in 1989.

*Excluding capital gains.

Chapter 5

■

Building Strategy

INTRODUCTION

As the concept of corporate strategy has become appreciated by an increasingly wide audience, chief executives have typically approached the academics and consultants familiar with the ideas in order to get help in developing strategy for their companies. What they soon find is that it is much easier to get a thoughtful analysis of a company's position in an industry and what might be done about it than it is to develop a useful approach to changing the policies and capabilities of the firm.

The reasons are many. Some were laid out in Chapter 1. Action in a company turns on concrete phenomena, not on abstractions or labels. Consequently in assessing opportunities and capabilities, accurate understanding of the company and its competitors is fundamental. Knowing that a new technological approach to a problem is more efficient does not mean that a particular company might not have driven old technology to unappreciated levels through incremental improvement. Showing that increases in cumulative volume have permitted some firms to lower their costs in proportion to their learning and experience does not mean that some firms will not learn to bypass or accelerate the learning process. As a consequence of these complex realities, technical experts in the companies and their consultants often have differing views that general managers cannot easily reconcile.

Another problem is also inherent in what is implied by a strategy. Almost inevitably, a careful examination of where opportunity may lie in the future means that a shift in the firm's center of gravity will be necessary. Resources ought to be transferred in the direction implied by movement in the markets. That in turn means a shift in the relative power of executives who manage different areas of the business, for executives are obviously not homogeneous in experience, knowledge, and skill.[1] Delicate balances of influence among key players in a company can be challenged by what might seem to be mere words on paper about hypothetical futures.

Shifts in the allocation of resources have broader implications for the careers of all of those in the organization. Engineers, marketers, operations managers, and related staff all need resources to build the businesses for which they are responsible. They are evaluated on their performance, not on whether they might have done better if resources were not shifted toward the company's "new strategic thrust."[2] Their views color the way studies develop.

Managers also find that when they ask their executives to take part in strategic studies, they often are unable to contribute useful views. In a sense, if they understood what was happening in the market or with new technology, there would not have been the need for the strategic study. The managers are part of the problem.[3] Even where managers have truly useful understanding of markets and technology, they often lack any strategic sense. They understand how to make progress as long as everything else around them is relatively static. They lack an understanding of how to perceive a competitor's strategy and respond to the implications of that analysis with a revised strategy of their own. An extreme example of this approach, probably apocryphal, was supplied in the 1980s by a foreman in a deserted Glasgow shipyard. "Everything would be fine if they would let us do what we always did well," he said, "build wooden ships."

A final kind of problem can be found in the best-managed companies. There the careful work of building systems and processes to link those responsible for innovation with their counterparts at leading customers creates a peculiar blindness to new technological ideas that the customers find uninteresting.[4] For example, the reluctance of General Motors to put radial tires on its new cars delayed by years their development at Goodyear. It is at least partly for the same sort of reason that IBM was so late in entering the mini- and microcomputer market and why disk drive specialist Seagate missed the 3.25-inch drive.

---

[1] Building on Michel Crozier's discussion of relative power in *The Bureaucratic Phenomenon* (Chicago: University of Chicago Press, 1967), C K Prahalad studied the way relative power shifted as strategy was reoriented. See *The Strategic Process in a Multinational Corporation* (DBA Thesis, Harvard Business School, 1975).

[2] Joseph L Bower, *Managing the Resource Allocation Process* (Boston: Harvard Business School, Division of Research, 1973), chapter 2.

[3] Joseph L Bower, *When Markets Quake* (Boston: Harvard Business School Press, 1986), p. 71 and chapter 10.

[4] Clayton M Christensen and Joseph L Bower, "Customer Power, Strategic Investment, and the Failure of Leading Firms," *Strategic Management Journal*, forthcoming.

Improving the strategic direction of a company, in other words, is not a question of doing some analysis for top management, disseminating the message in a speech, and starting up the new system. It is a time-consuming process that is difficult to manage.

THE PROCESS OF STRATEGIC DEVELOPMENT

For the chief executive seeking to drive change in his or her company's corporate strategy, the process often feels like Mao's long march with many steps. At the start there is often no consensus that anything needs to change. Results are good, the stock market is happy, and the business press flattering. In a healthy enterprise, the signals that a modification in strategy may be appropriate accumulate slowly. And as we have seen, they are easy to miss.

Studies of the strategy-making process reveal that it is hard to see when the premises of a business are being undermined.[5] Sometimes the first people to see the problems are at low levels of the organization. Other times, it is only the chief executive that has the perspective that permits picking up the problem. In the Cleveland Twist Drill case, it is the sales force that picks up the emergence of low-cost, high-quality foreign product in the market. In Schlumberger, it is the chief executive, Jean Riboud, who sees early the necessity of acquiring capability in electronics.

How this information and an awareness of the need for change are created and shared varies widely. A variety of activities might be involved ranging from very direct action when an owner entrepreneur has active control and makes a decision to change things, to a decade of work when the leader of a large corporation embarks on significant change. Two examples make the contrast clear.

- In 1992, the Chairman of Knoll International, the parent company of Color Tile—a chain of tile and carpet stores—paid his first visit to a Home Depot store. He returned "frightened to death," and ordered that Color Tile be sold.[6]

- In the late 1970s Philip Caldwell was running the Philco division of Ford Motor Company. On a trip to Taiwan he was able to compare the productivity of Toshiba and Philco plants. The only difference that could account for the inferior performance of the Philco plant was their management. Possessed of this fundamental insight, Caldwell and his

---

[5] Aguilar, Francis J. and Arvind Bhambri, "The Johnson & Johnson (A), Harvard Business School Case No. 384-053 and Johnson & Johnson (B): Hospital Services, Harvard Business School Case No. 384-054; and Burgelman, Robert A., "Intel Corporation (A): The DRAM Decision," Stanford University Graduate School of business Case No. PS-BP-256, Rev. 1990.

[6] "Tiffany's Sparkle May Have Blinded Investcorp," *Business Week*, Aug. 29, 1994, p. 86.

successor "Pete" Peterson would take until the late 1980s to transform the organization and practices of Ford so that product design, costs, and the innovation cycle were competitive with Japanese manufacturers. In the process, literally thousands of managers had to learn the nature of the competitive threat and come to acknowledge that the way they managed Ford was not efficient or effective, and then accomplish the Herculean task of changing almost all policies and practices.

The differences are instructive. In one case, one man had to reach a strategic conclusion that could be implemented by outside lawyers and investment bankers. In the second, an organization of hundreds of thousands had to be transformed. When Phil Caldwell recognized that management practices at Ford had to be fundamentally changed, he had no idea that "Team Taurus" would be created to develop the most successful car of the decade. He just knew that he had to lower Ford's costs and improve quality or Ford would succumb to its Japanese competitors. For Ford, creating awareness involved countless studies of competitors' products and manufacturing processes. Hundreds of managers had to be brought on board before plans for concrete change could be developed.[7]

Three other examples illustrate how daunting the first steps can be.

- In 1959, T. Vincent Learson of IBM reached the conclusion that IBM's computer business was vulnerable to what today we would call "being niched to death" by competitors with superior products at different points in IBM's product line. Somehow technological obstacles would have to be overcome so that product proliferation was replaced by a new product line with full compatibility. The path-breaking scientific work required to resolve the problem would eventually be recognized by a separate issue of the journal *Annals of Computing*, but getting the organization to accept the challenge was a harder management task. Eventually key managers would be removed, the company reorganized several times.

- In 1975, the top leadership of Hitachi, the great Japanese electrical machinery and electronics firm, had concluded that future progress required the company "to be more international." The Dutch multinational Philips looked like an attractive example of the capability and strategic position they wished Hitachi to possess. Beyond that, it was difficult to provide a more concrete specification of strategic objective. The president captured his dilemma using a baseball analogy as he surveyed his head office organization in Tokyo. "Overseas, we have some very good pitchers, but in Tokyo we have only very bad catchers."

---

[7] "The Transformation at Ford Motor Company," HBS Case #9-390-083, 1990.

Domestically oriented managers could think of foreign markets solely in terms of exports.[8]

- In 1982, Colin Hampton, the leader of Union Mutual Life Insurance company, saw that the deregulation of financial service industries could threaten the survival of his company as presently constituted. It seemed clear to him that in order to devise a strategic response appropriate for a large specialist in a world of many giant players, he had to transform the fundamental character of his company. What did that mean? He was shocked when the consultant he employed suggested that it would probably mean that half his top management team would leave, but even more surprised when some of his top management team could not or would not work on the problem with him.

In general laying an effective foundation for making new strategic arrangements involves the following steps:

- Awareness of the need for change must be shared with a critical mass of top executives. It is not enough that a leader have a powerful vision of what may be. It needs to be shared.

- The exisiting corporate strategy must be carefully identified and critiqued given studies of the trends in markets and competition. (It is precisely for such purposes that a "five forces" analysis may be appropriate.) The result of such work may be what some have called a mission or a strategic vision, and others call strategic intent.[9] Top management workshops that share the concept of corporate strategy and apply it to the company have proved useful in accomplishing this step.

- Operating managers must be involved so that the technical estimates involved in the studies can be checked against the best knowledge of those inside and outside the company. It took Learson three years to get proper cooperation from powerful IBM division heads.

- Out of this process will come plans for change. Almost always these turn out to be hypotheses about what the company ought to do rather than useful schedules of action, but that is seldom clear at the time. IBM's triumphal 360 series of computers did not emerge until 1966, by which time IBM had to deal with major unforeseen questions concerning time-sharing and integrated circuits. At Union Mutual, the company had to learn what would be involved in overcoming severe legal hurdles including taxing lawsuits from life insurance agents as management "demutualized" the company.

---

[8] Author interviews with Hitachi management, 1975.

[9] See Fred Gluck, "Vision and Leadership in Corporate Strategy," *McKinsey Quarterly,* Winter 1981; and C K Prahalad and Gary Hamel, "Strategic Intent," *Harvard Business Review,* May–June 1990.

> **Because the desired change almost always fits poorly with the way the company is configured, functions and products may have to be regrouped, and acquisition or disposition of pieces of businesses or even whole businesses may be appropriate.**

Although research suggests that it is useful for this learning activity to precede major commitments, it is certainly common for companies to move with far less preparation. Sometimes it is sloppy management, but other times it reflects a willingness to move opportunistically to gain the advantages of being first or a conscious willingness to learn about a new arena through trial and error.

Again research shows that early moves in the direction of strategic change usually lead to a phase in which new structure is required.[10] The problem is straight-forward. As far back as Henri Fayol, we have known that the logical sequence of administrative action was plan, organize, implement, control. In the context of large corporations, Alfred D. Chandler Jr. showed that the logic implied that structure needed to be revised when strategy changed. What Chandler did not point out was that structure also shapes strategy.[11] The way the members of an organization think about a problem is substantially determined by how they are organized. A group of successful country managers with important local positions based on their local facilities has a very hard time devising a concept for rationalizing the company's assets on an international basis. It is not just turf. From the perspective of managers responsible for the on-going progress of businesses, it is difficult to rethink the fundamental premises that provide the foundation for the jobs at which they are successful. So in order merely to get useful analysis of the concrete strategic situation, it is often necessary to change the organization or withdraw the managers involved in planning change from their operating structural context.

- At a minimum some crude regrouping of activities into new groups or divisions is required. At IBM, the power of the World Trade group that handled international activity had to be reduced. More important, the management of two hugely successful product groups that accounted for the bulk of the domestic computer business had to be smashed into submission so that they would cooperate with the "New Product Line" project.

- Alternatively or as a prior step, working groups of key managers are assembled, sometimes with outside consultants, in order to design a

---

[10] Alfred D Chandler, Jr., *Strategy and Structure* (Boston: MIT Press, 1962).

[11] This point was first developed in Bower (1973), *Managing the Resource Allocation Process*, and later developed by Robert Burgelman and Leonard Sayles in *Inside Corporate Innovation* (New York: Free Press, 1986).

road map for change. At Union Mutual, a task force spent nearly a year trying to understand what the product line would be for an appropriately focused company.

- The new subunits identified may then engage in studies that actually provide the basis for new strategy. At IBM, groups of this sort saw the need to add time-sharing to the list of capabilities in the 360 series of computers.

The result of these rearrangements and building of new structure and systems is often a new awareness of the capabilities necessary for continued development along the lines that have been emerging. Additional technical talent was needed at IBM, while Union Mutual found that new executives were required to pursue product development.

What happens is that as managements begin to implement their plans, whether opportunistically, or boldly in a quantum move following extensive study, or in a step-by-step fashion, they learn of new capabilities required—sometimes merely to survive, but normally to be competitive or to exploit unexpected opportunity. As the operating organization begins its work, it gathers experience that permits managers to learn what will have to be done to implement the strategy. As we observed in Kawai's Komatsu, this often involves a sequence of steps by which capability is accumulated: At Komatsu this meant high quality first, then low cost, then international distribution, and then product diversification. The process is iterative, and at any one stage in the process, it is entirely possible that subsequent stages are not anticipated.

The experience of the Italian appliance manufacturer Merloni is illustrative.[12] In the mid-1970s, preparatory analysis revealed the importance of improving the quality of their Ariston brand products, as well as the usefulness of developing foreign sales. The company introduced a radically advanced line of highly styled appliances called "Open Space Ariston" and opened sales agencies in Paris, London, and Düsseldorf. The OSA line failed, but the quality improvements developed for that line enabled a substantial upgrading of Merloni's core products. Over a decade, the international operations put in place in the 1970s were steadily improved so that by the 1990s, volumes and profits in France and the United Kingdom were attractive. Germany remained an unresolved problem.

At Merloni, building their foreign operations turned out to require a special breed of executives who could live well in a company based in North Central Italy, while conducting business in London or Paris. New

---

[12] Joseph L Bower, "Merloni Elettrodomestica," Harvard Business School Case #9-690-003.

information and logistics systems were required as well. It took time and patience to assemble these capabilities. By the late 1980s, however, Merloni management had learned a great deal about how to manage the addition of layers of strategic capability. Their cost postition was perhaps the best in Europe, their market share was number four behind the North Atlantic giants (Electrolux, Whirlpool, and GE) and the company was the only major independent player.

The Merloni experience and the other examples cited are important because they reveal the length of time involved in building strategy. The examples also suggest that what strategists do is exactly what Schon has in mind when he describes "reflection in action."[13] Great general managers in their role as strategists possess the skill to see the need to change and the courage to take steps forward knowing that partial failure is the likely cost of a chance to learn. Building strategy consists of taking selected steps— most of which involve building organization and undertaking trial operations in order to learn and acquire capability.

SUMMARY

If we now step back, we can understand why the word *strategy* can be used in so many different ways. For a chief executive, strategy is always a project—the evolving purpose and programs of the organization that change in response to intended extensions of capability, to moves of competitors, to the social and political environment, and to unanticipated developments in his or her own organization. At any point in time one can look back and identify what strategy has emerged; and formally identifying and assessing the economic strategy of component businesses can be extremely useful. One can also look forward to explore and try to determine the future directions in which the strategic postition of the organization should be pushed. That effort, in turn, must reflect the limitations of resources and environment, but also will reflect the values of the leader.

The discussion also makes clear that the management work of building strategy is not independent of what must be involved in building the organization that can translate the intentions of management into improved strategic position. The two are closely interdependent, because the information required to build a strategy is usually acquired on the job while building the capability to implement the strategy. The examples we have discussed suggest that building organizational capability is a time-consuming process involving careful work with individual managers as well as groups. It is to those processes that we now turn.

---

[13] Donald A Schon, *The Reflective Practitioner* op cit.

Adam Opel AG (A)

My first time in East Germany was in July of '89. Words cannot describe this experience. Imagine driving from Hamburg to Berlin along the transit corridor, an autobahn financed by the West German government, and going through a no-man's land, going past bunker after bunker, watchtowers, guard dogs, barbed wire, soldiers. You felt you were going into a high-security penitentiary, only it was a penitentiary with 17 million people. It was scary the first time. To see that system all of a sudden unravel, disintegrate over a matter of months, was really an extraordinary experience.

Speaking was Louis R. Hughes, head of Adam Opel AG. He continued:

At that time I could not have imagined that less than half a year later, on January 8, 1990, I would be traveling to *Automobilwerke Eisenach*, East Germany's second largest car factory, to begin discussions on a possible joint venture. I will never forget that day as long as I live. It was a really gray and dreary kind of day. Most of the border points were still closed. They had in the countryside a couple of provisional crossing points that had just been put up, and so we drove over this lonely country road through a sea of barbed wire and bunkers and watchtowers to this little trailer, and there was a sign: *Willkommen*. As we drove to Eisenach (it was a 40-minute drive), house after house had West German flags flying from them. Now, this was only two months after the wall had come down, and the Communist government was still firmly in power. When we got to the factory, someone had, clearly without the consent of the factory management, put up a couple of West German flags within the factory and on one of the water towers. It gave you a feeling that political change was in the air, was in the wind.

We met the management. They were an old group and looked like they had served the Communist party faithfully for many years. Only the managing director was a fairly young guy in his mid-40s. He seemed very tense. They took us through the factory. The factory was a disaster. Employment was about six times larger than you would find in the West for its output. And the factory was filthy; you couldn't begin to produce quality there. The air was also dirty because the East Germans used for their heating a very soft, high-sulphur-content coal called *braunkohle*. It permeates the air with a sort of sweet, heavy smell that really chokes you. That was the environment, a sort of brown haze of smoke and dirt everywhere. I couldn't believe it was actually Germany. It was like stepping into a time machine.

OPEL IN 1989

Adam Opel AG in 1989 was one of Europe's major automobile producers. Wholly owned by General Motors since 1930, it produced 1.2 million cars in 1989 with an employment of close to 55,000 and sales of almost DM 21 billion.[1] According to Hughes, "our profit margins are larger than those of Daimler-Benz and Volkswagen, and we are the fastest-growing manufacturer." Success had not always been an Opel trademark. Its cars had been unexciting, with a lower-middle-class image. During the early 1980s, the product line was completely redesigned, with a strong focus on both technological and environmental leadership. Opel was a pioneer in introducing catalytic converters in Europe, with which, by 1989, all of its cars sold in Germany were equipped. In 1989 Opel could not keep up with demand, and

waiting lists for its various models were common. A true renaissance had occurred.

Adam Opel and the German market played a pivotal role in GM's European operations. Close to half of Opel's sales were made in Germany, with most of the remainder going to other European countries. Germany accounted for 36 percent of GM's European sales, followed by the United Kingdom with 20.6 percent (supplied by its wholly owned Vauxhall subsidiary). In 1989, Volkswagen was market leader in Germany with 21.9 percent of new car registrations. Opel was in second place with 16.1 percent, followed by Ford (10.1 percent), Mercedes (9.2 percent), BMW (6.8 percent), and VW-owned Audi (5.6 percent). Japanese imports had a 14.9 percent share. (See Exhibit 1 for European market shares.) In 1986 Opel had a 14.9 percent share, compared with 23.3 percent for Volkswagen, and had thus narrowed the gap.

A regional headquarters office called General Motors Europe (GME) had been established in 1986 near Zurich to plan and coordinate GM's European activities. Five years later *The Economist*[2] commented on this move:

> GM's success has been founded on a restructuring of its European operations. These used to be run by Opel, the company's German subsidiary, which is based at Rüsselsheim. GM uses the Opel name in continental Europe, but the name of its British subsidiary, Vauxhall, is used in Britain. Ford, which uses the same name across Europe, has adopted a pan-European approach to car making ever since Henry Ford II foresaw that one

---

[1] The exchange rate for the dollar was 1.77 Deutschmarks in December 1989 and 1.68 Deutschmarks in February 1990.

[2] *The Economist*, March 9, 1991, p. 63.

day most of Europe would be a single market. He established Ford of Europe to coordinate sales and manufacturing back in 1968. Unlike GM's European operations, Ford's were consistently profitable throughout the 1980s.

An executive who has worked for both companies recalls that GM's top European managers used to be swamped by German issues and the day-to-day problems of running Rüsselsheim, the company's biggest manufacturing complex. A further difficulty was that Rüsselsheim employs generations of workers from the same family. That meant there was stiff resistance to change—and to investment in manufacturing facilities outside Germany.

GM decided to set up a pan-European headquarters in 1986, but it wanted to better Ford's example. Ford's European headquarters is in Britain, at Brentwood. This is also the base of Ford's British operations. GM decided it needed somewhere completely neutral, away from all its manufacturing fiefs. It eventually chose Zurich, in the German-speaking part of Switzerland, for its GM Europe head office and its 200 staff.

An equally important decision meant that GM's bosses back in Detroit were persuaded to invest more in Europe and to broaden the company's product line. The most significant new factory is its plant in Zaragoza in Spain, which produces the Opel Corsa (also sold as the Vauxhall Nova). This is the smallest car ever made by GM and is now responsible for more than 20 percent of its total European sales.

On April 1, 1989, shortly after celebrating his 40th birthday, Lou Hughes became chairman of the Adam Opel *Vorstand* (Executive Board). He had grown up in Cleveland in a working class environ-

ment, had graduated in 1971 as a Bachelor of Mechanical Engineering from General Motors Institute, and had obtained his MBA at the Harvard Business School two years later. He subsequently joined the financial staff of General Motors in New York and became assistant treasurer in 1982. In this capacity he played a major role in negotiating the NUMMI joint venture between GM and Toyota in Fremont, California. In 1985 he moved to Canada as vice president of finance when his former mentor on the financial staff in New York, Jack Smith, became head of Canadian operations. In early 1987, when Jack Smith became president of General Motors Europe, Hughes followed him to Switzerland as chief financial officer.

When Hughes received the Opel assignment, it was suggested that he try to change the bureaucratic and hierarchical organizational structure. When Hughes came to Opel's Rüsselsheim headquarters close to the Frankfurt airport, he was the only American in the Vorstand, which, in typical German fashion, operated on a collegial basis. Also, by German law, management had to consult on a number of important decisions with the *Betriebsrat* (works council), which consisted of members elected by the employees. Hughes found that relations had been quite adversarial, and his goal was to try to change this climate. Also, like his other GME colleagues, he was eager to introduce "lean" manufacturing techniques, being concerned that the European automobile industry was far less efficient than the Japanese. After arriving at Opel, Hughes began working hard on his rudimentary German, refusing to speak English with his colleagues, but by early 1990, in his own words, "my German proficiency equaled that of a six-year-old."

As he began to carry out his initial game plan, Hughes was suddenly confronted with the totally unexpected developments in East Germany.

POLITICAL DEVELOPMENTS IN EAST GERMANY DURING 1989

In January of 1989, Erich Honecker, 77, who had ruled the DDR (*Deutsche Demokratische Republik* = German Democratic Republic) for 18 years, predicted that the Berlin wall could stand for 100 years. *Time* in September 1989 described Honecker as "a stern holdout against Gorbachev-style reform. With such Communist neighbors as Poland and Hungary experiencing a bracing splash of economic and political change, East Germany remains shackled by a regime that refuses to look beyond a Stalinist status quo." The DDR had been separated from its sister state by barbed wire and minefields as well as the famous Berlin wall. Its citizens were not allowed to travel to the West; the only tourism permitted was to the other Eastern European countries.

In May, Hungary had begun to dismantle the barbed wire along the Austrian border. On June 4, Solidarity scored an overwhelming victory in Poland's first free parliamentary elections. Frustrated by the lack of political and economic progress at home, thousands of East Germans decided to flee to West Germany, where, upon arrival, they would receive a passport, the equivalent of $125 in cash, unemployment, and health benefits, as well as free meals, temporary lodging, and low-interest loans. Their first route was via an officially allowed vacation to Hun-

gary and from there to Austria and West Germany, after the Hungarian government suspended a bilateral treaty forbidding unauthorized travel into third countries. When the DDR government subsequently disallowed travel to Hungary, East Germans went to Czechoslovakia. Since Prague's hard-line regime did not follow Hungary's example, the refugees camped on the grounds of the West German embassy. When they numbered 5,000, the situation became untenable, and on September 30 the West German Foreign Minister arrived in Prague with a diplomatic agreement for passage to the West. As the trains traveled through East Germany, 15,000 people had to be kept away from Dresden's railway station, while others boarded the trains en route. With Gorbachev as his guest of honor, Honecker celebrated the DDR's 40th anniversary on October 7. Soon thereafter the famous Leipzig demonstration of some 70,000 people took place. A crackdown appeared imminent. However, on October 18 Honecker stepped down. Demonstrations all over East Germany continued, one time numbering 300,000 in Leipzig. Then, on November 9, the world was stirred by the epoch-making event of the 28-year-old Berlin wall coming down.

Freedom of movement across the hitherto closed border became possible. East Germans now had access to what they considered West Germany's shopping paradise. They exchanged their Ostmarks on the black market at rates far below the official one. This gave West Germans the opportunity to travel east to buy already low-priced subsidized goods with their cheaply acquired black market Ostmarks.

As political and economic chaos spread in the DDR, West Germany's chancellor,

Helmut Kohl, took the initiative on November 28, just days before the Malta summit between Bush and Gorbachev, by proposing, without prior consultation of his allies, his personal plan for German reunification. He suggested a first stage requiring free elections in East Germany in exchange for economic aid from the West. This step was deemed essential to stem the flow of emigrants. As a second stage after the elections, "confederal structures" would be set up for various forms of cooperation between the two sovereign states. The third stage would be a "federal state system in Germany." However, German reunification still seemed far away. The allies, which had paid lip service to the reunification desires of the German people when that realization was totally out of the question, were suddenly confronted with a political dilemma because of strong domestic resistance to the idea. Also, Russian acquiescence seemed highly unlikely. In its February 12, 1990, issue *Time* commented: "Although unification may be an idea whose time has come, it is still an idea; German officials and their respective allies have months, perhaps years, of negotiation ahead."

THE EAST GERMAN AUTOMOBILE INDUSTRY[3]

The entire East German automobile industry was managed through a single state enterprise, the *VEB IFA Kombinat PKW*,[4] located in Karl Marx Stadt (Chemnitz).

---

[3] Portions of the following description have been excerpted from *Die Automobilindustrie in der DDR*, dated February 26, 1990, and prepared by the Verband der Automobilindustrie E.V.

[4] VEB = Volkseigener Betrieb, factory belonging to the people; IFA = Industrieverband Fahrzeuge, industrial association for vehicles; PKW = Personenkraftwagen, automobiles.

Trucks and buses were produced by a different Kombinat, as were two-wheel vehicles. These three Kombinate reported to the *Ministerium für Maschinenbau* (ministry for production of machines) in Berlin, which in turn received its instructions from the *Staatliche Plankommission* (State Planning Committee) in Berlin. This group, in turn, received its signals from the Politburo. The economic czar of the Politburo was Günter Mittag, a powerful party official with firm ideas who had consistently opposed modernization of both the industry's product and facilities. Contradicting him, it was felt, meant almost certain career suicide. Also, insiders said that when the Kombinat general directors met with the Politburo, the latter were seated while the former were left standing during the entire meeting. Mittag, regarded as a potential Honecker successor, was removed from the Politburo concurrently and subsequently jailed on corruption charges.

The Kombinat PKW had some 66,000 employees. A DDR Kombinat engaged in both economic and social pursuits, such as hospitals, restaurants, or day care centers. Thus, the payroll was huge, the decision processes were multifaceted, and the factory directors were powerful figures in their local communities. Thirty factories in the automotive Kombinat supplied parts to two assembly plants. The biggest factory in Zwickau, near Chemnitz in the southeastern part of the DDR, assembled the Trabant, which accounted for about half of the 3.7 million cars on the road in the DDR and for 146,000 of the 217,000 units produced in 1989. The remaining 71,000 units were assembled under the Wartburg name and represented the Kombinat's mid-priced entry. East Germany exported 69,000 units to other East European countries, usually under long-term trade agreements involving transfer rubles rather than hard currency. Almost all of the 20,000 units imported also came from Eastern Europe. Vehicle imports from the West were minimal, allowed only under special circumstances and if the car model had been approved. Regulations for the importation of used cars were expected to be liberalized in early 1990, but the enormous import duty remained a formidable hurdle. Since no hard currency was made available, trade with East Germany involved barter arrangements. Even under these circumstances, automotive exports from West to East Germany amounted to DM 137 million in 1988, largely consisting of parts and equipment, while West German imports from the East stood at DM 76 million.

Antiquated factories and equipment, resulting from the industry's low-priority status with the Politburo, made for low productivity. Thus, the Trabant required some 3,300 man-hours versus only 925 for the Fiat Uno. There was a labor shortage, and the industry employed workers from Poland, Vietnam, Cuba, Angola, and Mozambique. Wages, which were similar for workers and engineers, were one-fourth of those in the West. The work week amounted to 43.75 hours, and monthly take-home pay was about 1,100 Ostmarks.

Backward integration was the norm, with some 80 percent of components and much of the equipment manufactured within the Kombinat. A so-called Monokultur existed whereby assemblers were forced to rely on a sole supplier for a given component. The only significant category sourced from outside was electrical components. In spite of this extensive in-house production, parts shortages were most common. This problem was aggravated by the long transport times due to the poor condition of both the railroads and the road network. Thus, the plants tried to keep unusually large inventories to protect against a common problem of assembly line stoppages.

Antiquated design and severe shortages also applied to the finished product. The Trabant and Wartburg models dated from the mid-1960s. Thus, East Germany's auto industry not only suffered from a productivity gap but also from a technology gap, in terms of both performance and environmental protection (see Exhibits 2 and 3). In order to remedy this problem, the Kombinat had entered into two supply arrangements, one with Citroen for drive shafts and one with Volkswagen for engines. For example, in 1984 VW had granted a license for two of its engines to the Kombinat. The DM 500 million facility would produce 300,000 units per year, of which 100,000 would be exported to VW over a four-year period to pay for it. This investment was essential because the two-stroke East German cars began to lose their export capability in East European countries, thus forcing the Politburo to reverse its long-standing policy of concentrating solely on two-stroke engines. The Kombinat developed a long-term modernization strategy. In 1988 the Wartburg had been equipped with the four-stroke engine, to be followed by the Trabant in 1990. A new Trabant body would be developed with Volkswagen's help for introduction in 1992, and VW would also assist in creating a new body for the Wartburg by 1996.

Demand by far outstripped supply. Thus, the waiting period for a Trabant was 13 years and for the Wartburg 17 years. The order book of the Kombinat by the end of 1989 stood at 6.2 million units. Placing an order committed only the Kombinat and not the purchaser, thus likely inflating this figure. Nevertheless, experts in the Kombinat saw a pent-up demand in East Germany of at least 3 million cars. This estimate was based on East Germany's 1988 ratios of 4.67 inhabitants per car and 54.7 cars per 100 households as well as a saturation target of 75–80 cars. This demand, according to a 1989 Kombinat statement, would require doubling East Germany's car production to a 425,000-unit output. At the time, the Kombinat planned to continue manufacturing the two-stroke Trabant through 1993 and increase its output to 175,000 units per year. Given the lack of available goods and services, and given the low cost of their subsidized basic needs, East Germans had been prodigious savers and thus possessed the purchasing power to pay for much of this pent-up demand.

The Kombinat had its own sales outlets all over Germany. With the long waiting period they were strictly order-taking and distribution outlets, and they did not engage in car repairs. Car prices ranged from about 11,000 Ostmarks for the two-stroke Trabant to 30,000 Ostmarks for the four-stroke Wartburg. A new four-stroke Trabant was to be introduced at 20,000 Ostmarks. Car prices were subsidized at the assembly level. Thus, parts suppliers passed on their continuously rising costs to the assemblers, who were compensated by the government for the shortfall between their costs and revenues.

A separate Kombinat, reporting to the transport ministry, handled repairs, with 600 exclusive Wartburg repair shops. Cars were also repaired by cooperatives or private mom-and-pop repair shops. With the average age of the East German car amounting to over 13 years in 1989, repairs were in great demand, especially for the older vehicles. Old or damaged cars were almost always rebuilt, given the long waiting periods for new cars. Also, car registration papers were hard to obtain and sold for as much as 5,000 Ostmarks. Even though replacement parts amounted to 30 percent of the automobile Kombinat's output, shortages were rampant, leading to long waiting periods. The Kombinat was able to produce only 70 percent of demand. Sometimes an individual wishing to have a car repaired went to the repair shop and first opened the trunk. Depending on the nature of the gift inside the trunk, the customer was given either an early or a late repair appointment. A separate Kombinat, *Minoel*, ran the few available gas stations.

THE EAST GERMAN MARKET OPPORTUNITY

Among the Eastern European states, East Germany was considered to be the most prosperous (see Exhibit 4). The economic outlook for the DDR was seen as very good, given the likely support from West Germany and its de facto European Community membership through its trading arrangements with its Western neighbor. In addition, its population was well educated.

The DDR was seen as a growth market for automobiles (see Exhibit 5). Its car density was at southern European levels, such as Spain, and only one-half that of West Germany. Density in the DDR paralleled that of West Germany in the 1970s. Said Hughes, "There was no reason why the East German market should not follow a very similar pattern. We expected the market to more than double by the year 2000."

Market research had indicated that East Germans by far preferred Western automobiles over their local outmoded models. The main problems for the Western automobile companies were their ignorance of the DDR market, their lack of sales and service outlets, and the unavailability of hard currencies. Companies had to devise strategies through which they could offset imports into the DDR with exports from there. Thus, car manufacturers began to analyze their purchasing requirements to determine sourcing possibilities in the DDR. As of December 1989 the economics of manufacturing in the DDR appeared tempting. On December 5, 1989, *Die Welt* quoted a VW executive: "Why go to Korea when next door wage costs are only one-fourth of ours."

With the opening of the Berlin wall a large number of automotive manufacturers and suppliers began to explore the DDR market. BMW was reported to be visiting frequently the Kombinat factory in Eisenach; Mercedes-Benz was said to be negotiating with the Kombinat that produced heavy vehicles; while Peugeot/Citroen, having been supplied with drive shafts from the Zwickau plant for a number of years, apparently had offered the Kombinat a joint venture. Ford approached East Germany through its regional headquarters in the United Kingdom and was supposed to be negotiating for a sales/service location in East Berlin. Some Japanese manufacturers, such as Nissan and Mitsubishi, were also rumored to be exploring the East German scene. Opinions were voiced that the DDR automotive industry should concentrate on becoming a parts supplier and import finished cars exclusively from the West. The Kombinat spoke out strongly against such an approach, supported by the workers in its assembly plants in Zwickau and Eisenach.

As of December 1989 the prevailing opinion was that the Communists would remain in power and that the DDR would remain a separate state with its own non-convertible currency, its own legal system, and its own social and economic institutions as well as its protected borders. The DDR government began paving the way for joint ventures, hitherto illegal, and was anxious to obtain technical and monetary assistance from the West. However, COMECON rules continued to apply, making it impossible to export advanced equipment to the DDR. Given the prevailing unrest, the East German government moved the automobile industry into the third slot on its priority list of industries, thus making additional investments highly likely. The centrally planned economy, although somewhat loosened, continued to persist.

VOLKSWAGEN'S PREEMPTIVE STRATEGY

On December 4, 1989, Carl H. Hahn, Volkswagen's CEO, proposed in his birthplace Chemnitz to the automobile Kombinat the creation of a joint venture to develop, produce, and market cars. Hahn made this proposal upon receiving the first engine as part of the barter deal concluded with the Kombinat in 1984. Subsequently, he met with Hans Modrow, head of the DDR government. Of the Western car makers, VW had the most extensive contacts with the DDR. In the past, it had supplied 27,000 Golf units and had purchased annually DM 50 million in parts and equipment from the Kombinat. On December 22, 1989, a joint venture arrangement to study possible cooperation was signed. Together, VW and the Kombinat would work on replacing the Trabant in 1993 with an internationally competitive car. VW spoke of making investments on the order of some DM 5 billion to DM 6 billion. Said Dieter Voigt, the 51-year-old general director of the

Kombinat, "We wanted to develop with VW both in Zwickau and also in Eisenach a complete car manufacturing setup. VW and we operated on the assumption that the DDR would remain a closed market for quite a while longer in which we could sell 400,000 to 450,000 cars" (interview in *Der Spiegel*, March 19, 1990).

OPEL'S RESPONSE TO THE EAST GERMAN OPPORTUNITY

In late November 1989, a few days after the wall came down, Lou Hughes received a phone call from Jack Smith, who had become GM's vice chairman responsible for its overseas activities, inquiring what Opel was planning to do in terms of East Germany. Later, Jack Smith commented, "There was never any question at GM that the DDR was Opel's responsibility. They spoke the language, were of the same nationality, and also they were our largest and strongest European unit. GME had been assigned the rest of Eastern Europe, and they had their hands full in exploring opportunities there." Said R. J. Eaton, GME's president, "Germans always saw West and East Germany as a single country. Thus, it was perfectly logical to assign the DDR to Opel. Opel has been part of the German landscape for decades and is viewed as a German company."

Since Opel had done no business with the DDR and was completely ignorant about the East German consumer, Mr. Georg Hehner, Vorstand member in charge of sales, approved in November a request by his staff to conduct a market survey by interviewing East Germans who had only recently arrived in the West. He said, "For us, the DDR is a no-man's land." In spite of their physical separation, East Germans were not totally ignorant of the West German car market because they were able to receive the West German television stations and hence their commercials. In mid-December the results became available (see Exhibits 6, 7, and 8). Opel was regarded as a German brand in contrast to Ford, which was viewed as a U.S. brand. Distressing to Opel management, however, were the much lower ratings of Opel compared to VW along a number of dimensions (Exhibit 9).

As movement across the East–West border became possible after the wall came down, and given the expectation that visa requirements for West Germans traveling to the DDR would be dropped by Christmas, Opel as well as its competitors quickly began to explore the possibilities of establishing service and repair outlets in East Germany to serve the emerging tourism. Immediately after November 9, Opel had received dozens of unsolicited applications from former East German dealers. Hehner and his marketing team decided that there was no time to prepare extensive strategy papers. Planning had to be based on existing East German census data, leading to the conclusion that 350 to 400 dealers were needed to cover the country adequately. The decision was also made to ignore the existing Kombinat repair shops and sales offices and to concentrate on private independent dealers. In January, six three-person teams were dispatched to the DDR to acquire dealerships. In addition, liaison responsibilities were assigned to Opel dealers located near the border, with the expectation that they would not only provide repair service but also sell used cars to East German customers. On the manufacturing side, by late November an analysis had been made to determine to what extent parts and equipment could be sourced from the DDR.

Lou Hughes also began to explore market and manufacturing opportunities at the highest levels. In early December, he visited the U.S. ambassadors to both West and East Germany, two think tanks in Berlin, as well as high-ranking economic officials in both the West and East German governments. Simultaneously, the VW proposal and the subsequent signing of the joint venture agreement hit the news. Commented an industry observer:

> Volkswagen had put together a strategy to take over the entire industry, build a brand new small car tailored to the East German market by 1994, spend 5 billion marks, and employ about 30,000. As almost everybody else, they must have thought at that time that the wall was down but the Communist government was still firmly in power. There were no agreements whatsoever with the Soviets, who had some 400,000 soldiers in the DDR. So it was a situation where there was a separate economy, with a German-speaking population and some historical ties, and where Volkswagen had done some business. Volkswagen must have hoped it could take the whole thing on a silver platter and, as that economy grew, maybe eventually it would become more liberalized and VW could get a lock on that new market with its relatively high disposable income compared to the other Eastern European countries.

Hughes reflected on the Volkswagen move in retrospect:

> We were deeply concerned. First of all, we saw this brand-new market, 17 million people, about 25 percent of the total German population. We wanted to par-

ticipate in that growth. We knew from looking at the overall demographic data that we were going to have to expand our capacity in any event. The complication in all this was that we always had a moving target. Here we were going through a decision process involving the investment of roughly a billion Deutschmarks in a constantly changing economic and political climate. I negotiated with four separate economic ministers. It was the most unstable situation one could imagine.

> In looking at Volkswagen's strategy in the DDR we felt that they would focus on Zwickau, near Hahn's birthplace, where the Trabant was built. Their whole strategy seemed based on replacing the Trabant, and they still had to devise a strategy for what they were going to do with the other assembly plant in Eisenach. So we wanted to take advantage of this window of opportunity before Volkswagen could figure out what they wanted to do with Eisenach. Even though an East German government official had advised us not to contact Eisenach directly, we did so anyway through the intermediary of a member of our Betriebsrat who had relatives in Eisenach. The contact was made between Christmas and the New Year, and a meeting was arranged for the first day everyone would be back from the holidays.

AUTOMOBILWERKE EISENACH (AWE)

Eisenach was located in the southwestern part of the DDR close to the West German border (see Exhibit 10). It had a rich history, often involving the Wartburg, a castle overlooking the city from a high hilltop. While hiding in the Wartburg castle, Martin Luther translated the Bible. The first automobile had been produced in Eisenach in 1898 with Wartburg as its trademark. When BMW decided to commence the manufacture of automobiles in 1929, it did so by acquiring the Eisenach company. After the Second World War the factory was "owned by the people" and was subsequently incorporated into the automotive Kombinat.

In 1953, AWE was instructed to concentrate on manufacturing a small two-door, two-stroke car based on a 1940 Audi design. However, under the dynamic leadership of the factory director, without knowledge or approval from above, an in-house version of a four-door, much larger car was developed. When presented with this model, the top brass approved and it was launched in 1955. The Eisenach engineers also developed a four-stroke engine by 1959. This development, however, was stopped in 1961 by party and ministry officials, and it was not until 1988 that the first four-stroke Wartburg was built, using the engine produced under VW license. A new Wartburg with front-wheel drive was launched in 1966 and was still being produced in 1990. Prior to the launching of this new model, substantial factory modernization investments were made with the assistance of Renault and a West German company. The years following 1966 were frustrating for the Eisenach engineers. Through in-house developments they attempted to prevent their models from falling too far behind Western developments. In 1969 they resumed work on a four-stroke engine, and in 1974 and again in 1978 they produced a prototype version of a new Wartburg. AWE was ordered by the highest government levels to abandon both projects. Even ministry approvals were sometimes overturned by the Politburo, especially when significant investments were involved. When the Kombinat developed its new long-term strategy, it was

clear that the new 1996 Wartburg could not be manufactured in the old inefficient factory, and management received funds to gradually develop a greenfield facility outside Eisenach. It was still only partially completed by 1990.

In 1987, the factory director was dismissed because of health problems. However, it was also alleged that he was forced to leave because of his independent stance, which was in contradiction to party instructions, and that, since the other members of management were felt to be loyal to their dismissed boss, an outsider was brought in, Dr. Wolfram Liedtke. Liedtke, 42 years old at the time, had previously managed a unit of the public transportation Kombinat in the small town of Nordhausen. A mechanical engineer by training, he had worked in the Zwickau factory early in his career.

Lou Hughes described his first encounter with Eisenach management as follows:

> We were surprised. We thought they would be very proud of their car, try to cling to the past. But they didn't; they were very realistic. They said, "We know our car is uncompetitive, we know we can't survive, we know we can't continue building cars with 9,000 people." They were ready to talk, and that was the biggest surprise. Also, there was an historical rivalry between the Sachsen region, where Zwickau is located, and the Thüringen area where Eisenach is. So there were a lot of things playing there, historical, rational, everything. But not to be underestimated.

Following the January 8 visit to Eisenach, AWE management was invited to visit Opel at Rüsselsheim. The return visit took place from February 1 through 3. It included not only the usual meetings and factory visit but also an afternoon at the test track and a two-day visit on two chartered jets to Spain to visit GM's factory in Zaragoza and also to visit the city of Toledo. Throughout, Opel management treated the AWE executives as equals and rolled out the red carpet.

After this visit, contacts intensified between technical and manufacturing people to explore possible joint activities. Opel made cars available to the Eisenach management so they could familiarize themselves with the Opel product line. Where all this would lead, however, was still unclear. Eisenach was not a legally separate company but part of the Kombinat. And the Kombinat was tied to Volkswagen through its 50–50 joint venture. In early 1990 there were thoughts expressed in East Berlin that single factories could possibly leave a Kombinat and become separate entities. Nothing of this kind, however, had occurred to date.

MAKING THE CASE FOR EISENACH

A few days after his return from the January 8 visit to Eisenach, Lou Hughes had dispatched a memo to Bob Eaton and to Jack Smith. The memo stated, after describing the visit, the Kombinat, the market, and the Eisenach factory:

> The management showed a great deal of realism about the plant's competitive position in a liberalized economy and the need to cooperate with a Western partner. The Opel team was impressed by their technical competence and apparent absence of ideological bias. What was also impressive was the evident grassroots support throughout the community for change (even reunification). The team saw West German flags hanging from many homes throughout the countryside and even in the Eisenach factory.
>
> We are planning to immediately form a joint study team with the Eisenach man-

agement. The study would have three areas of focus: (a) source tooling, jigs, fixtures, and transport racks from DDR suppliers (could be implemented relatively soon); (b) develop DDR component suppliers; (c) produce passenger cars.

> VW reportedly plans to close its deal before the May 6 elections, which puts a great deal of pressure on us to quickly develop a proposal. We are forming a GM/Opel team to develop an approach consistent with our corporate strategy for Eastern Europe. As a footnote, Eisenach management have already been approached by Peugeot, Nissan, and BMW. However, the chemistry between the Opel and Eisenach management was very good—open, honest, and constructive. As a result, we intend to move ahead aggressively.

Two days later, Joachim Beickler, comptroller, went to regional headquarters to present to the new business development steering committee the economic rationale for studying a potential linkup with Eisenach (see Exhibit 11). Beickler, a German 1982 Harvard MBA graduate, had been recruited by Hughes and had subsequently worked with him in his various assignments. On February 7, Hughes went to Zurich to present his case to the GME strategy board, of which he also was a member and at which key policy decisions for GME were made. Hughes put forth a two-step manufacturing proposal for Eisenach. A modest effort to assemble some 10,000 completely knocked-down Opels would be started in 1991–1992 (advanced to June 1990 later in February) with a second step involving body building, painting, and final assembly of some 150,000 vehicles a year starting in 1994. The plant could also include a facility for transmission production and potentially sheet metal manufacture. The investment of the first step would involve only DM 15 million, while the financial requirements for the second step were estimated at DM 1.4 billion.

The Eisenach proposal had been developed by Dr. Friedrich Lohr, who was not only a member of the Opel Vorstand but also the head of GME's technical design center (TDC) as well as a member of GME's strategy board. Having been in charge of the technical design function for some 15 years, he was a veteran in formulating and assessing plant proposals. He also had accumulated extensive experience in Eastern Europe. He commented:

> What really made a difference to us at Opel was the phone call from Jack Smith. We felt that somebody in the States really cared. By coincidence, I had been in Berlin on business on November 9. We heard, in disbelief and with tears in our eyes, the news of the wall opening. We went to the Brandenburg Gate where a huge crowd had assembled. I will never forget that night of celebration. It was only in the early morning that I returned to my hotel room. When we went to Eisenach on January 8, I feared that the AWE people might have a hostile reaction to a visit by an American company. I knew we had to build mutual confidence. Our visit to Spain helped a great deal, including our bumpy return on the chartered planes during one of Europe's worst storms.
>
> Having spent my career with General Motors, I know that, even though we feel patriotic about an Eisenach factory, we will have to justify it to the parent company on the basis of dollars and cents. Such considerations often favor the less developed southern part of Europe, where governments grant significant incentives which, under European Community rules, are permitted there but not in the north. Thus, GM has built a large factory in Spain specializing in the two lower-end-of-the-line models. This move

reflected two aspects of GM's European strategy. First, our European manufacturing facilities concentrate on specific models. This division of labor allows GME to maximize scale economies. Second, GM management wishes to reduce its dependence on high-labor-cost countries where, for historic reasons, many of our factories are located and where most of our cars are sold.

> We all agree at Opel and at GME that Eisenach cannot be viewed as strictly a German project within Opel. Building automobiles in Eisenach will be part of a European-wide decision by GM as to how and where to add much-needed capacity. As my visits to Eisenach have escalated, I have become concerned about the size of the investment. The planned factory is getting larger and larger. On my last trip, sitting around the table drinking beer, I took my beer coaster and sketched out a factory layout. I told my East German friends that, if we were not able to reduce our project to this size, we would have no chance to obtain parent company approval. Also, we need to run the plant on a three-shift basis for the economics to come out right. The AWE people are simply not used to thinking in these terms.
>
> I am having just as much trouble convincing my colleagues that we should plan to manufacture the Kadett, our second smallest model, and not the Corsa, our lowest-priced car. Many people feel that the Corsa is the ideal car for East Germany, given their low purchasing power. A number of us, based on our market research, feel that the Kadett will have a much better chance. Anyway, not everybody feels that Eisenach is the way to go. I can't blame them. Everything is moving so fast and changing so quickly, and there are lots of uncertainties and question marks.

One of those question marks was the labor situation. Regional headquarters was reluctant to expand manufacturing capacity in high-cost Western Germany. Even though in January of 1990 East Germany was viewed by many as a low-labor-cost paradise, some executives felt that other Eastern European countries were even lower-cost locations. Concerns were also expressed about East Germany's low productivity and about the danger that the low DDR wages might rapidly approximate those in West Germany. Workers in other Eastern European countries could not easily leave their jobs as could East Germans, who always had the option of moving to the western part of their country. Also, West German unions were believed to be pushing for a reduction of the wage differential. Absenteeism and a poor work ethic were also important fears. It was learned that the average absenteeism for the DDR was between 10 percent and 11 percent. At Eisenach it amounted to 6 percent to 8 percent. Also, the poor infrastructure in the DDR was seen as a liability. Finally, the exchange rate between the Deutschmark and the Ostmark was a source of concern: Would it be determined by economic realities or political desires? In early 1990, the official rate was one to one, but in the black market several Ostmarks were needed to buy one Deutschmark. Bob Eaton commented, "The unofficial rate would fluctuate between five and ten Ostmarks for a Deutschmark. This black market rate was probably more representative of the productivity and technology gap between the two Germanies. But at the time it was also doubtful whether such a drastic reduction in East German purchasing power was politically feasible."

The Opel Vorstand was also unsure whether it would get much support from the United States, where GM was closing several plants. As the parent company was curtailing operations and experiencing difficult times, would GM's top executives support a new plant in a country under Communist control with all the attendant political and economic risks? The East German political and economic situation continued to be most volatile, with assumptions and estimates changing by the day. At the same time, the Vorstand felt that for competitive reasons speed was essential. How would the financial staff at headquarters respond when asked to analyze a capital appropriation request based on so many uncertain assumptions? Also, large proposals had to be approved by the overseas policy group (OPG) before being submitted to the board of directors. The OPG, at which concurrence was obtained on important issues, consisted of both domestic and overseas top management.

In Rüsselsheim, some members of the Vorstand were enthusiastic while others were lukewarm about a possible Eisenach venture or felt that the chances of pulling Eisenach away from the Kombinat were extremely remote. They wished to concentrate on the West German market, in which they were gaining on Volkswagen and for which they did not have enough cars. Also, they felt that Opel was totally ignorant about the DDR market and relatively unknown to the East German consumer, thus best leaving that slowly emerging market to the dealers near the border or to other entrepreneurs trying to sell used Opels in the East. Some members of the Betriebsrat were concerned about moving production to a low-wage area, even if it were part of Germany. They were concerned about employment in the West, reflecting a general union concern about unfair competition from the DDR and about the pressure refugees were creating in the West German labor market.

One argument which Hughes kept stressing was the importance of a manufacturing presence as a prerequisite for a significant market share. GM's market shares were much higher in the United Kingdom, Spain, and Germany, where it was producing cars, than in France and Italy where GM had no manufacturing presence. Within Germany there were also substantial differences between those Länder (states) where Opel produced cars and those where it did not (see Exhibit 12). Thus, a manufacturing presence was considered to be of strategic importance.

Finally, there was the question of a market share target. In his discussions with his marketing people, Hughes had been given their East German forecasts in which market shares paralleled those existing in West Germany. Thus, he found Opel again positioned as an eternal second behind the leader Volkswagen. He decided to send the forecasts back with the target to become number one in the DDR. Hughes commented:

> I was convinced that our product had reached a level of acceptance in the Western market where everyone was telling us we were every bit as good. Here was going to be a unique window of opportunity. If, somehow, someway, we could become number one in this brand-new market. Two competitors entering this market for the first time, and the underdog suddenly becoming number one. People throughout the media and the industry will notice something is fundamentally different. Here is a group of customers who have no preordained notions.

EXHIBIT 1
WESTERN EUROPEAN MARKET SHARES — 1989 (percentages)

Country	[# cars]*	VW Group†	Fiat‡	PSA§	Ford‖	GME	[# cars]#	Renault	Japanese**	Others††
Total	[13,402]	15	14.5	12.7	11.8	11.6	[1,554]	10.4	11	12.1
Germany	[2,832]	28.3	4.9	3.6	10.2	16.6	[470]	3.4	14.9	17.2
Italy	[2,306]	12.5	56.4	7.7	4.9	4.2	[96]	7.0	1.8	4.6
United Kingdom	[2,301]	6.0	3.4	8.9	27.1	15.7	[362]	3.8	11.3	22.3
France	[2,274]	9.2	7.3	32.8	7.1	5.2	[119]	29.1	3.0	5.7
Spain	[1,126]	20.0	7.6	17.9	14.2	14.5	[163]	19.2	1.3	4.8
Netherlands	[496]	11.3	6.4	11.9	10.4	14.4	[72]	5.9	26.2	12.1
Belgium/ Luxembourg	[476]	16.6	5.0	15.1	10.5	11.3	[54]	10.2	19.2	11.3
Switzerland	[341]	15.6	9.5	7.5	7.4	14.7	[50]	5.4	29.0	9.3
Sweden	[307]	12.2	2.3	5.1	9.4	16.9	[52]	1.7	24.8	27.3
Austria	[276]	20.4	6.3	6.8	9.3	12.2	[34]	4.9	30.6	8.9
Portugal	[193]	12.6	17.8	16.1	8.0	11.8	[23]	19.9	6.7	7.0
Finland	[178]	8.4	4.1	8.4	7.2	14.5	[26]	1.2	38.9	16.9
Greece	[86]	14.2	14.2	6.2	3.2	6.6	[6]	4.9	28.5	15.9
Denmark	[78]	8.6	5.6	14.6	10.9	15.0	[12]	1.5	31.7	11.7
Ireland	[78]	7.8	4.5	6.3	15.4	11.9	[9]	4.5	40.0	7.5
Norway	[55]	11.9	1.5	9.1	1.4	4.7	[8]	2.1	57.9	11.1

Source: Company records.

*Number of cars sold in thousands of units.

†Includes VW (10.1%), Audi (2.7%), Seat (2.2%).

‡Includes Fiat (10.7%), Alfa Romeo (1.66%), and Lancia/Ferrari (2.2%).

§Includes Peugeot (7.9%) and Citroen (4.8%).

‖Includes 0.2% for Jaguar.

#Includes 0.5% for Saab.

**The Japanese market share of 11% includes Nissan (3%), Toyota (2.6%), Mazda (1.8%), Mitsubishi (1.2%), Honda (1%), Suzuki (0.7%), Subaru (0.4%), and Daihatsu (0.3%).

††Includes Rover (3.1%), BMW (2.8%), Mercedes (3.2%), Volvo (2.0%), Lada (0.8%), and Skoda (0.2%).

EXHIBIT 2
WEST GERMAN AND EAST GERMAN CAR MODELS

1989 Opel Kadett · 1989 Opel Corsa · 1989 Wartburg · 1989 Trabant · 1989 VW Golf · 1989 VW Polo

Source: Company records.

EXHIBIT 3
SPECIFICATIONS FOR THE GOLF, KADETT, TRABANT, AND WARTBURG

	Acceleration (0–62 mph)	Top Speed (mph)	Fuel Economy (mpg)
VW Golf 1.3 l	16.7	94	39.8
Opel Kadett l .3 l	15.5	100	39.8
Trabant 0.6 l	60.0	62	35.3*
Wartburg 1.0 l	20.0	81	26.4*

Source: Company records.

*Using 2-stroke fuel.

EXHIBIT 4
DATA ON EASTERN EUROPEAN ECONOMIES

Country	Population (in millions)	GDP/person	Economic Outlook
East Germany	16	$9,000	Very good
Hungary	10.6	6,500	Fairly good
Czechoslovakia	15.6	8,000	Fairly good
Yugoslavia	24	7,000	Moderate
Poland	37.8	5,500	Moderate
Romania	23.1	5,500	Poor/moderate
Bulgaria	9	5,000	Poor/moderate
Soviet Union	288	7,000*	Poor/moderate

Source: Company records.

*Average of range of estimates.

EXHIBIT 5
EAST GERMANY NEW PASSENGER CAR MARKET DEVELOPMENT

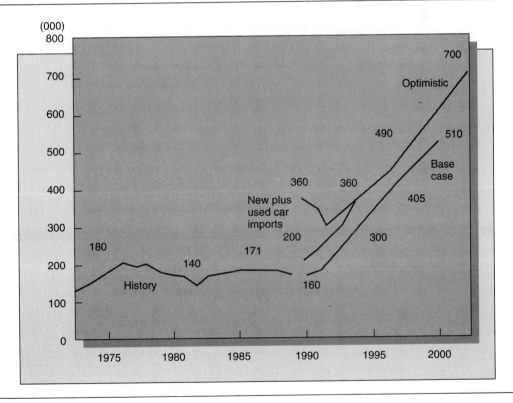

Source: Company records.

EXHIBIT 6
GDR MARKET RESEARCH: LIST OF BUYING PRIORITIES

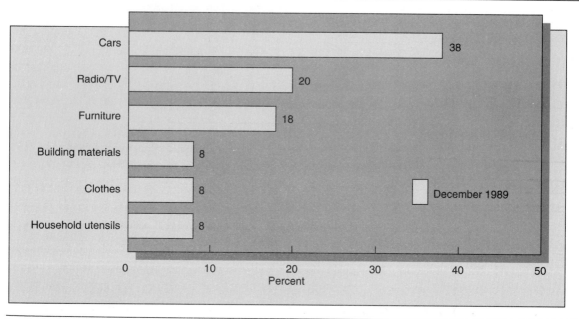

Source: Company records.

EXHIBIT 7
GDR MARKET RESEARCH: BRAND AWARENESS UNPROMPTED

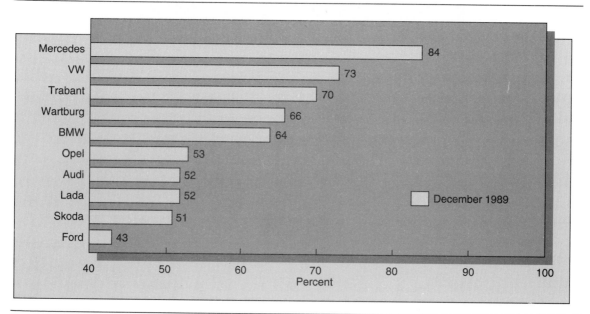

Source: Company records.

EXHIBIT 8
GDR MARKET RESEARCH: MODEL AWARENESS UNPROMPTED

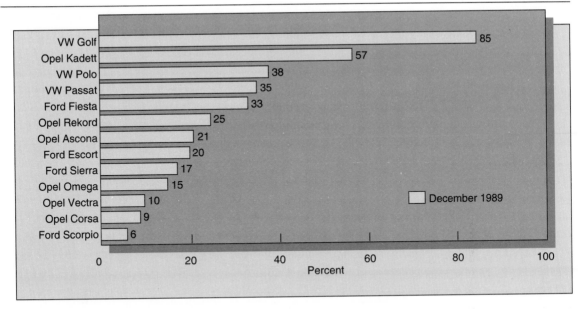

Source: Company records.

EXHIBIT 9
GDR MARKET RESEARCH: BRAND IMAGE 12/89

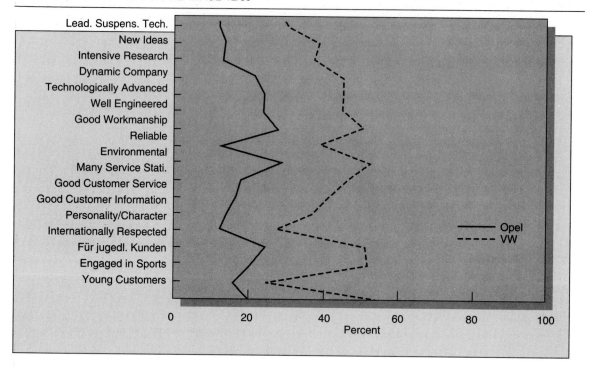

Source: Company records.

EXHIBIT 10
WEST GERMAN PLANT LOCATIONS

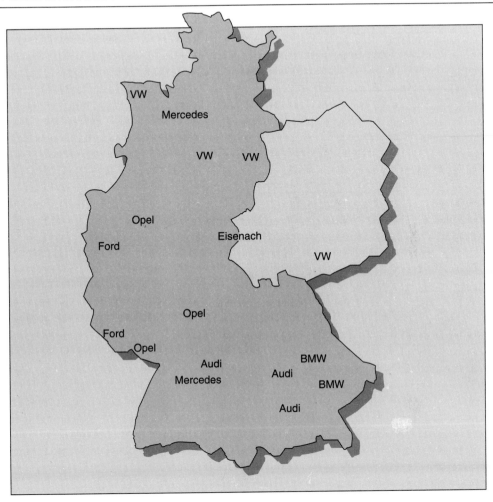

Source: Company records.

EXHIBIT 11
STUDY OF POTENTIAL LINKUP WITH IFA-EISENACH

Economic rationale:
- Market potential
- Economic reforms imminent
- Hard currency shortage likely to persist
- Potential to use GDR as export base for COMECON

In view of strong competitive interest in GDR as a market and as an industrial base, imperative to reach go/no-go decision quickly.

Source: Company records.

EXHIBIT 12
OPEL'S MANUFACTURING PRESENCE AND MARKET SHARES

Manufacturing Presence		No Manufacturing Presence	
United Kingdom	15.2%	France	5.1%
Spain	14.3%	Italy	4.0%
Germany	16.1%		
		Germany	
Hessia	18.7%	Bavaria	13.3%
North Rhine		Lower Saxony	14.2%
Westphalia	19.5%		

Source: Company records.

Intel Corporation—Leveraging Capabilities for Strategic Renewal

1990, a glorious year for Intel, was drawing to a close, and Andy Grove, Intel's CEO, was reflecting on what the future portended:

> We are currently a leader in semiconductors, and my hope and vision is that our technology is going to be the heart and spine of the entire computer industry. But crucial resource allocation decisions among our three divisions— microcomputers, memory products, and systems— and strategic choices within each division will determine Intel's trajectory well into the next decade.

Once again, Intel was poised at strategic crossroads, as it so often had been over the previous 30 years. Grove believed the company's experience in transforming itself from a memory producer to a microprocessor supplier would prove invaluable in surmounting the challenge of constant strategic renewal and revitalization. However, skeptics were predicting that Intel's glory days were coming to a close, and the company faced the threat "of turning into just another big company, helplessly swatting at its smaller and swifter rivals."[1]

THE EARLY YEARS (1968–1980)

Birth of the Company

Intel was founded in 1968 by Robert Noyce and Gordon Moore, pioneers in the emerging semiconductors industry, and a team of scientists, prominent among whom was Andy Grove. (See Exhibit 1 for biographical profiles of senior Intel executives.) An Intel manager remarked:

> The whole was greater than the sum of the parts, so nicely did they fit together,

[1] Kathleen Wiegner, "The Empire Strikes Back," *Upside*, June 1992, pp. 30–52.

and play off each other's strengths. Noyce looked after external relations, Andy was responsible for internal operations, and Gordon Moore was the resident genius responsible for technology strategy.

They first set their sights on replacing magnetic-core computer memories, which accounted for as much as 60 percent of the cost of a computer, with semiconductor memories. "It's very tempting for a little company to run in all directions," remarked Moore, "but we went the other way—it was our objective to dominate any market in which we participated."[2] Yet this commitment to focus was balanced by an equally strong belief in "buying options"—systematically exploring alternatives—an approach that not only provided flexibility but also generated internal competition. For example, even in their earliest resource-constrained days, they established two teams to work simultaneously on different semiconductor technologies—bipolar and MOS. (See Appendix I for a description of technical terms.)

In mid-1969, barely nine months after start-up, the bipolar team introduced Intel's first product, a bipolar static random access memory (SRAM). (See Exhibit 2 for a chronology of product introductions.) Several months later, the MOS design team, led by Les Vadasz, used a relatively new manufacturing process to introduce the first commercial 256-bit MOS SRAM, the 1101. Moore, Noyce, and Grove then decided to drive for a dynamic random access (DRAM) chip of the same size with four times the memory capacity. The re-

sult was the 1K chip, which Intel called the 1103 DRAM. Grove recalled:

> The general feeling was that if the 1103 failed, Intel might not get another chance. As it turned out, the 1103 was universally preferred to magnetic-core memories and soon became an industry standard. Within one year, we had transformed ourselves into a high-volume, low-cost manufacturer of standardized products. By 1971, the 1103 was [the] world's largest-selling semiconductor memory.

Expanding the Industry's Frontiers

Soon after Intel's early success, competitors entered the DRAM market, and a dynamic game developed in the industry that forced companies to balance the benefits of driving production down a steep experience curve[3] against technological leapfrogging to the next generation. Moore explained:

> This business lived on the brink of disaster As soon as you learned enough to make a device with high yield, you calculated that you could decrease costs by trying to make something four times as complex, which brought your yield down again. The technology-development process became rather predictable: every three years or so, a new generation of chips was developed with four times the capacity of its predecesor. Because I preached it so often, people around here began to refer to this phenomenon as Moore's law!

---

[2] J.B. Quinn, "Intel Corporation," in H. Mintzberg and J.B. Quinn, *Cases and Text in Management,* 1985, p. 166.

[3] The semiconductor industry had a 70% experience curve—costs fell by 30% as cumulative volume produced doubled (G.W. Cogan and R.A. Burgelman, "Intel Corporation (A): The DRAM Decision," Graduate School of Business, Stanford University, case no. PS-BP-256, rev. 1990, p. 3).

1971 became a landmark year when Intel introduced two more path-breaking products which shaped the development of the industry and Intel's position in it. The first was the erasable programmable memory device, EPROM 1702, to which Moore committed the company even though its applications were not immediately obvious. The second product was even more significant since it led Intel to diversify from memory devices into microprocessors. Convinced that a chip that Intel engineers had developed for a Japanese calculator manufacturer had potential beyond its immediate use, Intel bought back the rights to market it for noncalculator applications. In 1971, the company offered its first microprocessor, the 4-bit 4004.

In April 1974, Intel introduced the 8-bit 8080, the first general-purpose microprocessor. Although sales of the device recovered its R&D costs in the first five months of shipments, further development became a matter of heated debate between the sales and engineering groups. Initially, management committed to a program under Vadasz's guidance to develop the 432, a microprocessor with a revolutionary new architecture favored by Intel's development engineers. But because it was technologically aggressive, the 432 program ran into delays. At the same time, competitive offerings from Motorola and Zilog began challenging Intel's dominance in the 8-bit microprocessors business. Intel's sales staff, under Ed Gelbach, contended that a completely new technology would take too long and would be too risky, and wanted Intel to take a more evolutionary approach, building on the existing 8080. The executive committee resolved the internal conflict of views between Vadasz, the 432 sponsor, and Gelbach, the sponsor of the evolutionary

approach, by deciding to explore both options and, in 1976, authorized a second 16-bit project, the 8086.

Developed along more conventional lines, the 8086 microprocessor was introduced in 1978. But sales started slowly and didn't meet forecasts for the first two years. When Motorola's competitive 16-bit microprocessor began gaining momentum, Intel responded by initiating Operation Crush—an "all-out combat" plan, complete with war rooms and SWAT teams, to make the 8086 architecture the industry standard. Enormously successful, Operation Crush also led to perhaps the most significant design win of the industry when IBM chose in 1980 to put the 8088 (an 8-bit version of the 8086) in its Personal Computer (PC). Placed at the heart of the first IBM PC, Intel's microprocessors rode the rising demand for PCs in the following years.

Meanwhile, development on the revolutionary 432 continued, and the product was finally introduced as a 32-bit microprocessor in 1981, seven years after it was conceived. It soon became clear, however, that the 432 would not achieve wide commercial acceptance. To some in Intel it was a huge failure, to others it was a courageous attempt to tap the technology of the future. "The technology and concepts learned from the 432 project," Noyce remarked later, "have had enormous applicability to some other things we are doing and doing well. It may be that the nature of such high-technology research is that you may not find what you were looking for, but you find something else equally important."

By the early 1980s, Intel had come a long way. Although memory products were still its dominant business (EPROM 2716, introduced in 1977, was becoming an industry standard), the microprocessor business was also growing rapidly. Intel had also introduced its first EPROM microcontroller in 1976, and its microcontrollers soon became the industry's leading architectures. Intel also began selling system-level products in the mid-1970s. According to Vadasz, the principal motivation was "to educate new users and create 'friendliness' for Intel products." By 1980, this business represented about a quarter of the company's revenues.

INTEL'S CULTURE AND ORGANIZATION

The 2-in-a-Box Management Philosophy

As the combination guiding Intel operations over the years, Moore and Grove had become a complementary team. Moore was quiet, long-term oriented, and philosophical, while Grove was vocal, aggressive, and demanding. Functionally, Moore emerged as the technology futurist, and Grove as the details-oriented pragmatist. Moore remarked, "Looking back, we split the job. I worried about what to do, Andy about how to do it." Grove reflected:

> Since my combination with Gordon turned out to be serendipitous, we were inspired to introduce an unusual management concept: the 2-in-a-box. It became normal in Intel for two executives with complementary skills to share the responsibilities of one role.

The 2-in-a-box form was used at all management levels to stabilize a transition, start-up, or a reorganization, or to broaden the bandwidth of a job, such as getting a marketing-oriented person and a production-oriented person together. Pairing was also done sometimes to groom successors or to act as a buffer from burn-out. However, some viewed the 2-in-a-box as an inefficient and countercultural form. One executive remarked:

> Whereas Intel encourages healthy egos and fierce independence, the 2-in-a-box role-models collaboration. It resembles an arranged marriage. It takes quite a while to develop, if at all, and even then, remains personality-driven to a considerable extent. It can limit the responsibility and accountability of both partners, the subordinates may end up "playing Mom against Dad," and if egos enter the picture, it can be a spectacular failure.

Organizing Flexibly

This unconventional approach typified management's attitude toward the organization. Moore and Grove wanted permeable membranes, not barriers, in Intel's organization. All employees' offices were in cubicles located off one big hall. Only low partitions separated executives from the rest of the workforce, and executive offices were dispersed rather than clustered. Rooms were set aside for meetings, available, like the parking spaces, on a first-come, first-served basis. Ties and suits were dispensed with.

Although Intel had started as purely a functional organization, in 1976 the first divisions were established in order to focus the managers' attention on emerging business segments. Through all such structures, Intel maintained a fluid organization, and over time, matrix-relations had begun to develop across business and functional lines. (Exhibit 3 represents the 1990 Intel structure.) "Organizational forms developed not because they were good, but because they were necessary," remarked Vadasz. "Our strength has been to recognize that all such forms are ultimately transitory, and their purpose is to respond to the needs of the time."

To facilitate the matrix relationships, a whole range of cross-boundary devices were set up—task forces focusing on specific projects, councils addressing long-term issues, and ongoing cross-departmental programs. Administration staff reported principally to corporate office and on dotted lines to functional general managers; divisional marketing staff reported principally to their divisional heads and on dotted lines to corporate marketing. Engineering was matrixed into manufacturing. Informal relationships crisscrossed functional boundaries.

New ideas usually originated from small, highly motivated, and innovative teams, and they rode on the backs of "product champions"—middle managers within Intel who became fanatically wedded to these ideas. The design teams and "product champions" then had to overcome a series of potential rejections from their superiors up the Intel hierarchy. The company had a very sharp and well-defined sense of its history and identity. Stories of how product champions had transformed their dreams into amazingly successful products were recounted over the years and became part of the company's mythology. With each revolutionary new product, the names of its developers and champions came to be inseparably linked within Intel: Hoff and Fagin with the microprocessor, Frohman with the EPROM, and others.

As Intel's structure grew more complex, Moore became concerned that Intel could no longer rely on informal processes to shape and communicate its strategy. With the objective of building on the company's early traditions of strategic initiative emerging from the front lines, he asked Vadasz in 1979 to head up a formal Strategic Long-Range Planning (SLRP) process. The new system required middle-level managers to prepare strategies for their business segments, which were then evaluated by senior executives at annual meetings. Crosscutting these business segment strategies were planning systems called strategic capability segments for developing functional capabilities.

Moore also firmly believed in performance-based incentives. "One of our unspoken rules at Intel," he remarked, "is that if you can't measure something, you don't understand it." He administered employee bonuses, determined annually according to company profitability and achievement of previously negotiated individual targets.

Grove focused more on individuals and took great pride in putting people where they were needed. He said:

> In our business, there are the quick, and there are the dead. So we have to be very flexible in moving our human resources as needs change, and our open culture helps us take such decisions pragmatically. Any time we reorganize, people end up moving in every direction—upward, sideways, downward. That is because careers advance at Intel not by moving up or down the organization but by individuals filling corporate needs.

However, another executive felt that the process had become too mechanical:

> In our horror of getting too bureaucratized, we have too many reorganizations, and this leads to unnecessary attrition in our knowledge base. We just design an organization chart that seems to meet current requirements, move people into it, and then walk away. But that's only the beginning. Things are vastly more

complicated from then on since the human relations side has yet to be handled.

Management Style and Culture

Intel's operating style evolved very much in Grove's mold of what one executive described as "aggressive brilliance." He elaborated:

> Andy's so incredibly articulate and so powerful that he can tear anybody apart. He's going to push you till he's sure you know what you are doing, and in the scuffling, he gauges you. Irritating though this can be, you've got to respect his keen mind and tremendous knowledge of business and management. His direct approach has encouraged everybody to open his mouth and be contentious, even if the CEO is in the room. Unfortunately, as a result, our interpersonal communication skills have become rather primitive. We have people who model Andy's confrontational style, but end up being just loud, nickel-and-dime imitations.

Intel employees thought of themselves as a special breed of people, a Marine Corps of the industry. Grove remarked:[4]

> Being a manufacturer of high-technology jelly beans, Intel needed a special blend of two types of people. The wild-eyed, bushy-haired boy geniuses that dominate laboratories could never have taken the technology to the mass-produced jelly-beans stage. But the straight-laced, crew-cut manufacturing operators of conventional industry would never generate the technology in the first place.

An executive reflected on the profile of a typical Intel employee:

> We're bright, opinionated, macho, rude some would say, rather arrogant, impatient, and very informal. The negative side of our personality is that in going for results, sometimes we ignore the niceties about how we get them. Besides, we lose out on the quiet, shy, good type of people. People who are looking for stable environments do not last very long at Intel.

This action orientation carried into the frequently held internal meetings, which had to have agendas, and had to close with action plans and deadlines. During a meeting, participants were encouraged to debate the pros and cons of a subject aggressively through "constructive confrontation," as Grove labeled it. But once something had been decided on, Intel had the philosophy "Agree or disagree, but commit."

MANAGING RAPID TRANSITIONS (1980–1990)

Riding Out the Recession

The 1980s dawned with economy-wide recession. (See Exhibit 4 for Intel's financial data.) About the same time, the U.S. semiconductor industry was also facing intense competition from the vertically integrated Japanese electronic giants, "companies with deep pockets and big appetites," as Grove characterized them. By 1979, Japanese semiconductor manufacturers had 40 percent of the worldwide 16K DRAMs market and a lead in the introduction of the next-generation 64K DRAMs. When the U.S. companies introduced comparable 64K chips in 1981, the Japanese companies, already well down their experience curves, resorted to severe price cuts. In the EPROM market also, prices dropped by 75 percent as Intel's competitors brought out new products.

---

[4] The quote is a combination of Grove's comments to the case writers and his remarks, quoted in J.B. Quinn, *op. cit.*, p. 167.

While some companies implemented major cutbacks and layoffs, Intel's top management decided to minimize layoffs and accelerate product introductions. To boost efficiency, Grove instituted the "125 percent solution," in which all salaried employees worked an additional 10 hours per week without additional compensation. In this period, Intel developed the next generations of microprocessors and EPROMs and advanced its process technology. Circuit design and fabrication operations were increasingly automated. Moore also consciously delayed a plant start-up, forgoing six months of production of 4-inch wafers in order to jump to making 6-inch wafers, which were much more difficult to manufacture but offered greater production economy. When the recession continued into 1982, Grove negotiated financial support from IBM through their acquisition of a $250 million (slightly under 20 percent) interest in the company.

The $2 Billion Memory Products "Bloodbath"

As the economy pulled out of the recession and the semiconductor industry rebounded by the end of 1982, healthy revenues and profits returned to Intel, spurred on by the market success of its new-generation microprocessors, the 16-bit 80286, and the recently introduced EPROM 2764.

Encouraged by rising demand, semiconductor manufacturers began to ramp up memory products production capacity in their quest for market share and consequent learning economies. But by 1985, the industry was in another downturn, triggered by soft demand and overcapacity. The Japanese firms were growing increasingly skilled in process improve-

ments and manufacturing efficiency. By 1983, production yields of Japanese semiconductor companies exceeded those of U.S. companies by up to 40 percent. When the market shrank by over 50 percent in 1985, the Japanese firms again chose to protect market share through deep price cuts. In the ensuing price war during 1985–86—DRAM prices fell as much as 40 percent in three months—the U.S. semiconductor producers collectively lost about $2 billion. (See Exhibit 9.)

Intel suffered operating losses totaling $255 million over 1985–86. Describing the 1985–86 price war as "a bare-knuckle fight with the Japanese," Grove decided to exit the DRAM business. He recalled that the decision to exit the business was an emotional and difficult one:[5]

> Although Intel had created the business, we had become a nonfactor in DRAMs with 2–3 percent market share. Yet, many people were still holding on to the "self-evident truth" that we were a memory company. I went to see Gordon and asked him what a new management would do if we were replaced. The answer was clear: Get out of DRAMs. So, I suggested to him that we go through the revolving door, come back in, and just do it ourselves.

Because DRAMs had always been the first high-volume product line to employ new technology, they were recognized within the industry as technology drivers. "We used to drive our learning from the DRAM volume runs," Barrett, Intel's executive vice president, remarked, "but

---

[5] The quote is taken from B. Graham and R.A. Burgelman, "Intel Corporation (B): Implementing the DRAM Decision," Graduate School of Business, Stanford University, case no. PS-BP-256B, 1991, p. 1.

now we have to depend more on intelligent engineering."

In the same period, Grove decided to take other draconian measures that essentially transformed Intel's business. (See Exhibit 5.) "We tore the company down and put it back together," he recalled later. By the end of 1986, Intel exited both DRAM and SRAM businesses, stopped development of E^{2}PROMs (a more flexible version of EPROMs), and got out of other low-margin product lines such as memory systems and bubble memory. Eight plants were shut down, one of the three development sites was closed, and the Intel workforce was reduced by 30 percent.

In making these changes, however, Grove again tried to protect the engineering knowledge and production expertise that Intel had so carefully developed. In order to minimize separations, he proposed the "90 percent solution"—the workforce took a 10 percent pay cut rather than suffer further separations. He tried to selectively minimize the separations of development engineers by initiating retraining of memory product engineers in microprocessors engineering. "Our culture has always been to work hard and learn," recalled Albert Yu, the co-general manager of the microcomputer components group, "and constant relearning, as the company changes its focus, has become the norm."

Microprocessors Business to the Rescue

Within a month of making the DRAM-exit announcement in 1985, Intel announced shipment of the 32-bit 386 as the successor to the very successful 80286. In introducing the 386, Grove departed from Intel's traditional practice of licensing other suppliers in response to customers' pressure to provide second sources for its microprocessors. There were 12 second sources for 8086, Intel's 16-bit microprocessor, and four for 80286, its follow-on microprocessor. (See Exhibit 11.) For the 32-bit microprocessor 386, Grove granted only one license—to IBM, to manufacture up to 50 percent of its own captive demand. This strategy freed Intel from competitive pressures from close substitutes but put enormous customer pressure on the company to build capacity and establish itself as a dependable supplier. In response, AMD, a traditional Intel licensee, took Intel to arbitration complaining that Intel was reneging on a licensing agreement.

Noyce's observation that "brainpower is the entire franchise in this industry" was never more true. Whereas its memory products had been repeatedly copied earlier by competitors who had then aggressively gained market share through process development, Intel was trying to protect its intellectual rights in microprocessors by limiting second sourcing and legally challenging unauthorized cloning. In 1984, Intel aggressively sued NEC, the largest semiconductor manufacturer in the world, for infringing on its microprocessor design copyright. While the 1989 judgment was hailed as a victory by both sides, NEC had effectively been held off in the interim.

The 386 garnered over 200 design wins within a year of introduction. By 1987, Intel had shipped about 800,000 units and was back on the path of rapid growth and high profitability. (See Exhibit 5 for sales breakdown of Intel by product lines.) Convinced of Intel's future well-being, IBM had sold the last of its shares in the company in that year.

Intel's systems business, begun with the objective of accelerating customer acceptance of Intel components, also began growing rapidly by opening new technology-intensive, high-margin business opportunities. One of the rising stars was the supercomputers business group. Intel was poised as the industry leader with one-third of the market for massively parallel computers, regarded by experts as the next wave in supercomputing.

Partnership and Alliances

In eliminating second sources for the 386, Intel signaled its cautiousness toward the wave of strategic partnerships sweeping the semiconductor industry. Barrett remarked on Intel's attitude:

> In this world, being fellow travelers works easily, not marriages; alliances work easily, not joint ventures. Meaningful technological partnerships are possible only if the partners bring equal technical contributions, and that is very difficult. We are strategically allied with IBM, Compaq, and Microsoft in that we have common hardware and software standards. Our actions aren't coordinated, but we do have an amoebic relationship since subtle signals do get exchanged.

Intel's perspective on partnerships was influenced by its experience with SEMATECH. In 1986, 14 U.S. chipmakers, including Intel, IBM, and AT&T, had formed this consortium with government blessing and financial support to develop advanced chipmaking process techniques in response to the Japanese challenge. But the consortium was bedeviled from the beginning by bickering over how to accomplish its objectives and by charges of pork-barrel politics. Despite the fact that Intel's Noyce agreed in 1988 to become its CEO, Grove opined that there was "a 50–50 chance of SEMATECH being successful, since the people joining SEMATECH have been more effective competitors rather than collaborators."[6]

In 1988, despite his skepticism about the value of partnerships, Grove announced the establishment of BiiN, a 50–50 percent joint venture with Siemens to develop fault-tolerant computer systems. However, the venture was dissolved in October 1989 since "the investment needed to make BiiN a success was too high." Most of the Intel staff in BiiN was reassigned to developing the P6, a futuristic microprocessor, where the expertise gained in BiiN could hopefully be utilized. Intel also joined U.S. Memories, an IBM-led joint venture among U.S. manufacturers set up in 1989 to design 4M DRAM chips, but the venture folded within a year due to lack of cooperation.

Strengthening Internal Operations

Intel's focus on self-reliance forced it to continuously sharpen its capabilities, and in the late 1980s, the company made several adjustments in order to upgrade its design, manufacturing, and sales processes. To speed the design process, computerized "libraries" of circuit layouts were established in the hope of future use, and computer verification and simulation techniques were enhanced. In order to reduce the "time-to-money" cycle, Intel designers began to involve manufacturing and customers early during chip design. "We broadened the scope of development work to include manufacturability," Moore remarked, "and put development people in charge of these facilities." Overall, the company projected spending $600 million on R&D in 1991.

---

[6] "What the Chip Wars Taught Intel's Andy Grove," *Chief Executive*, Nov.–Dec. 1987.

Changes were also introduced into manufacturing. "Perhaps we have been forced by a heritage of manufacturing inefficiency to be creative in product development," remarked Barrett, "but now we have to be closer to the low-cost production of the Japanese companies than they are to our innovative ability." Intel closed inefficient plants, experimented with work weeks, enhanced clean-room discipline, and moved toward dedicated plants and more automation. Manufacturing and assembly facilities were established all over the world, and with Europe 1992 approaching and outside suppliers facing stiff duties, Intel had just begun to set up a $500 million production facility in Ireland. (See Exhibit 6 for a description of Intel's geographical expansion.) Overall, the company was budgeting $1 billion for new capital expenditure in 1991.

To deal with a rapidly globalizing market, the sales department was divided along geographical lines into Europe, Japan, Asia–Pacific, and North America operations. By 1990, more than half of Intel's sales would come from out of the United States, with huge opportunity for further penetration of overseas markets. In particular, the company was working to capitalize on the 1986 U.S.–Japan trade agreement in which the Japanese government undertook to open its domestic semiconductor market to U.S. suppliers.

Organizational Evolution

Managing the roller coaster of rapidly changing fortunes led Grove to make organizational changes as well. Grove was becoming increasingly aware of the problems associated with formally letting middle managers drive strategy. He remarked:[7]

> The SLRP process was turning into an embarrassment. Top managers were trying to get middle managers, who had neither positional nor informational power, to come up with strategies and then taking pot shots at them. The middle managers were gaming the system, regularly coming up with unrealistically high projections.

Eventually, Grove changed the SLRP in 1987. Vadasz described the new system:

> The new, more informal SLRP system is a mix of top-down and bottom-up approaches. The top-management group sets the parameters of corporate strategy, and business units operate within that locus. Besides, strategic planning is tightly intermeshed with operational planning and control, which involve short-term forecasting and business planning with clear objectives, detailed reviews, and close attention to financial figures.

In 1988, an organizationwide survey was conducted on the employees' understanding of Intel's culture. An emerging concern was that the officers increasingly felt the need to focus on human relations. An executive described the changing attitudes:

> Our intensity is wrapped around an entrepreneurial 30 percent per annum growth culture. We like home runs. But

---

[7] The quote is a combination of Grove's comments to the case writers and his remark in R.A. Burgelman, 1991, "Intraorganizational Ecology of Strategy Making and Organizational Adaptation: Theory and Field Research," *Organizational Science*, 2:3, August, p. 244.

that does not work out to a very stable work environment. After the mid-80s cataclysm, folks have become more sensitive to the people side of things. Increasingly, you feel that things can get done without leaving human devastation along the way. And, maybe we're getting older as an organization, but long-term career growth issues have begun to surface. We have to tell an average performer that he or she is not the bottom of the pile but is OK. We have to change our career focus from moving up an increasingly narrow corporate ladder to enjoying a rich work atmosphere. But it has been tough for old-timers to change, including some of our top managers. They feel that when we've done very well so far, why worry about changing our culture now.

In response to the survey, a document was framed to clarify Intel's organizational values. (See Exhibit 7.) Grove, a great believer in discipline and keeping work and leisure activities separate, began supplementing the task focus of the organization with concern for a friendly work environment. For example, to counter burnout, all employees became eligible after a certain length of service for an eight-week paid sabbatical to do whatever they wanted. He also agreed to build recreation facilities, and an executive recalled the inauguration ceremony:

Andy had long resisted the idea of having recreation facilities in the company. "This is not a country club, guys. You come here to work," he'd say. But when he gave in on this issue, he made a celebration of being beaten down. At the dedication of the facilities, he appeared in his bathing suit and took a shower under a big banner which read, " 'There

will never be any showers at Intel'— Andy Grove.''

Passing on the Baton

There was a growing concern within Intel that people were so focused on the internal environment that they lacked a broad perspective. "The company has become too dependent on in-house management," complained an executive, "On the other hand, several senior executives have left because they didn't see any room at the top." Partly in response to such concerns, Grove announced in 1988 that he would retire from the CEO position at age 55 in 1991. He decentralized operations by delegating budget approval power and strategic planning to Intel's three operating groups. "We're deregulating the company a bit," Grove remarked. "We'll be less synergistic, but we'll move faster and more decisively."

In January 1990, Grove named Barrett executive vice president. Barrett joined Moore and Grove in Intel's executive committee.[8] He described the distribution of responsibilities:

I am going to be responsible for the internal wheels and gears of the company, even as Andy Grove shifts his attention more to external relations, product-line strategies, and major alliances, and Gordon Moore does the long-

---

[8] Noyce, who had distanced himself from day-to-day management in Intel since becoming chairman of SEMATECH, died in June 1990. Several newspapers featured his death with the headline, "The Father of Silicon Valley Passes Away." Intel management decided to dedicate Intel's new corporate office to Noyce's memory.

run technology planning for the company.

Barrett was perceived within Intel as Grove's heir apparent. But a senior executive remarked that the transition from Grove to Barrett was not proceding entirely smoothly:

> The whole of Intel is intensely molded in Andy's personality, and he's running the company with a stronger hand than ever before: Even Craig isn't sure who reports to Andy and who to him. It is very difficult for Andy to let go, especially to a person who is not like him. Andy epitomizes the constructive confrontation approach through his emotional intensity, but Craig is cerebral and operates more at an intellectual level. He's not as extroverted as Andy, although he is very bright and analytical.

Barrett was a champion of quality orientation, customer focus, and employee empowerment. An executive remarked on the change he was bringing about:

> Craig is convinced that people closest to the work know how best to work. He is very much the facilitator, a believer in the moderating, rather than the confronting, role of senior management. While the old culture was macho, confrontative, and tough, Craig is bringing in a management style focusing on processes of consensus.

EMERGING CHALLENGES

As the 1990s dawned, semiconductor companies had to make increasingly greater up-front capital investments, even though new products were rapidly emerging and industry standards had not yet stabilized. Through the 1990s, micropro-

cessor performance was expected to evolve at 5 percent per month. R&D cost of developing a new family of memory chips had risen from $100,000 in 1970, to $2 million in 1980, to $100 million in 1985, and was expected to rise further to $350 million in 1991 and $1 billion in 1999. In 1978, it cost $10 million to build a fabrication facility; by the mid 80s, the figure was about $35 million; by 1990 it was estimated to climb to above $100 million.[9] (See Exhibit 8.) An industry analyst commented on the effect of having to make escalating investments in the face of increasing uncertainty:[10]

> It is a lot like Russian roulette now, except that you pull the trigger, put the gun to your head, and then wait two years to find out whether or not you've blown your brains out. You've got to make numerous choices, with expectations of how they're going to turn out, and what your competition is going to do over the next two years, and you just have to charge ahead. At the end of two years you find out whether the trade-offs you made really worked out or not.

The press and the investment community were proclaiming Intel as one of the premier U.S. manufacturers of "electronic building blocks," but new and intricate challenges were emerging. As Grove looked to the future, he observed:

---

[9] Estimates derived from F.M. Scherer's 1991 *Industry Analysis and Government Policy* lecture at the Kennedy School of Government, *Business Week* article "Talk About Your Dream Team," 07/27/1992, pp. 59–60, and *Upside* interview with Michael Slater, June 1992, pp. 64–77.

[10] Michael Slater, quoting John Moussouris, in *Upside*, June 1992, pp. 64–77.

Once again, we are standing at a fork in the road, and have to decide soon the direction we're going to take, or else we risk hitting the divider. Investment in our industry is so astronomical that we will end up betting our company on whatever choices we eventually make. So, I am really paranoid that we should be able to identify which opportunities to exploit, and how to exploit them.

Grove had to allocate resources among the three Intel divisions, and within each division also, strategic choices needed to be made. David House, who was in charge of the microcomputer components group, characterized the debate on resource allocation:

Essentially, the microcomputers division is the goose laying the golden egg for Intel today. Some of us, including me, are suggesting that we feed this goose and invest intensively in microprocessors. But others, including Les Vadasz, worry what if the x-86 microprocessor success is a flash in the pan and the present demand bubble will burst one day. They feel that we need to develop the systems business as insurance against downswings in the components business—to mix metaphors, they want us to spread our eggs in several baskets.

The Continuing Battle in Memory Products

Grove faced a wrenching decision in EPROMs, the only memory segment in which Intel was still active. Intel had lost money and market share in EPROMs since 1986. (See Exhibit 9.) Since 1986, Hitachi, NE C, and Toshiba had begun to challenge Intel for leadership by aggressively introducing new EPROM generations. (See Ex-

hibit 2.) Many felt that the DRAM story was about to repeat itself in EPROMs.

Meanwhile, 256K DRAM prices, which had been about $2 per chip in 1985, firmed up to $6 per chip by 1988, but by then, Japanese firms accounted for 75 percent of the world's supply of the next generation 1M DRAMs. The forbidding DRAM forward economics still favored the Japanese low-cost manufacturing powerhouses. "Japanese and Korean companies play by different rules," Moore commented, even as Intel's executive committee decided that, rather than reenter the business, the company would market in the United States DRAMs sourced from NMB Japan.

On the other hand, Intel engineers were exploring a revolutionary new technology which could potentially replace floppy disks and mechanical disk drives with thin, credit-card-sized multichip packages called Flash memory modules. The product had enormous potential, especially in the portable PC market. Two and a half million Flash chips had been sold worldwide in 1990, and Dataquest was predicting a $1.5 billion market by 1995. (See Exhibit 9.) Intel was well positioned since it had by far the largest market share in the emerging market. But several Japanese companies—Toshiba, Mitsubishi, Oki, and Fujitsu—were also jockeying for technology leadership in the field. While Intel and other U.S. companies were on the leading edge of design, Japanese companies had available capacity and the edge in manufacturing expertise.

Grove was wondering how far to support memory products business. Maintaining a presence in EPROMs would require redoubled R&D efforts so that Intel could continue to lead in future EPROM generations. On the other hand, exit would be more or less irreversible, as the DRAM exit had been. If Intel were to pursue the Flash business aggressively, it would need to commit significantly greater resources than before in R&D and production.

Competitive Challenges in Microprocessors Business

Grove felt that Intel's microprocessor division had several layers of capabilities which would help it meet the emerging needs of the PC market in the 1990s. (See Exhibit 10.) However, competition was looming from RISC processors at the upper end and from imitator manufacturers at the lower end. Engineering workstations, which are more complex than PCs, had experienced dramatic sales increases during the 1980s. (See Exhibit 11.) Workstations were powered by microprocessors supplied by several Intel competitors including Motorola, NEC, and Fujitsu using the RISC design approach, which competed against Intel's CISC design. As workstations became more user-friendly and moved to attract mass markets, and as PCs became more powerful, the two computer classes were becoming increasingly competitive as alternate desktop offerings. In 1989, Intel had introduced the 486, its next-generation microprocessor, initially targeted at the workstations market.

Intel engineers first dismissed the RISC approach as "the hope of the have-nots." But RISC processors offered technical advantages such as enhanced computer performance, which led Dataquest to predict that RISC's share of the worldwide 32-bit microprocessor market would grow from 9 percent in 1988 to 39 percent by 1992. Vadasz described Intel's response to the RISC approach:

Intel design engineers proposed several times that we also develop RISC-based products, so that if the market split between RISC and CISC architectures, we would have a position in both. We were concerned that a RISC-based product should not cut into our existing CISC-based businesses. But our organization works with decision proposals starting at the bottom and bubbling their way up the chain, drawing support and opposition from middle managers, and over time, management's decision emerges. Sometimes, the decision could be to take both options in the short term and allow the market to decide. We did it earlier with the 432 and the 8086, and we've done it again to some extent, in the RISC–CISC debate. Aggressive product champions within Intel and changing market conditions have led to our announcing our first two RISC chips in 1989.

The i860 RISC chip was aimed at the emerging parallel supercomputers market, which placed great premium on computational speed. The i960 was targeted to the microcontrollers market, in which Intel's market share has dwindled over the years. However, Grove had to decide what position Intel needed to take in the long run in the RISC vs. CISC decision. While RISC architecture offered performance benefits, CISC architecture provided software compatibility with past microprocessor generations.

Not only did Intel have to focus on RISC at the upper end of performance, but it also had to fortify its lower end against imitator manufacturers. Intel had profited greatly from the 386 by virtue of its position as a sole supplied. By 1988, 386 was generating over 30 percent of Intel's revenue, and was projected to contribute as much as $2 billion of profits through 1991. But Intel's monopoly position was about to be breached. While the arbitration on AMD's claim to the 386 license was continuing in 1990, several companies, including AMD, were very close to reverse-engineering the 386. Besides, while the Japanese companies had concentrated thus far on memory products, analysts believed that they were waiting in the wings for the legal battles on intellectual property to end before entering the microprocessors market as well. House commented on the increasing concern within Intel about the company's future market position:

> We don't have enough supply ability to prevent shortages till well into 1991. I am worried that we may be hurting our own long-term prospects by limiting the spread of our chip architecture through licensing, by creating too attractive a target for Intel-clones, and by antagonizing customers and pushing them to our competitors in the future.

Increasingly faced with the possibility of competition from imitators, Grove began planning a multipronged response. "We will guard our intellectual property like a hawk," he said, "but ultimately, speed is the only weapon we have. Rapid introduction of new generations should motivate computer makers who want to keep moving up the performance curve to stay with Intel." In 1988, 386SX, a cheaper, low-end version of the 386, was introduced. The 486 was introduced in 1989. Grove accelerated the development of P5, Intel's next-generation microprocessor, so that it could be introduced by 1992. A P6 was being planned, and the company was trying to halve the time between chip generations from four years in the 1980s to two years through most of the 1990s, mainly by concurrent development of multiple generations.

To combat imitators, Intel management also took a risky approach of directly appealing to the end users. Intel marketing executives began chalking an ambitious two-year $250 million advertising campaign—"Intel Inside"—in order to develop brand loyalty among computer customers for its microprocessors. "Like Nutrasweet and Dolby have done before," observed Yu, "we would like to be able to win brand recognition for an ingredient of the final consumer product." Intel salespersons would attempt to get their systems customers to put an "Intel Inside" sticker on their point-of-sale materials and to use the logo as part of their advertising.

Looking Downstream

Intel had largely maintained a commitment to the upstream R&D and manufacturing activities.[11] Because of this focus, the company had missed seemingly attractive opportunities for expanding into downstream markets, as Moore recalled:

> We were coming up with too many opportunities for a company our size to manage, which is what every good engineering company should do. But the end markets fell a little out of our range of intuition. I personally turned down the idea of our entering the PC business. Then, we absolutely missed the workstations revolution, even though we were pioneers in the business.

---

[11] Early in Intel's history, management had made a few limited, and not always successful, advances downstream. In 1972, Intel initiated a brief but disastrous foray into consumer marketing when it acquired Microma Watches. It exited the business in 1978. Moore continued wearing an old Microma watch "to remind me, if I ever find myself thinking of getting into other consumer products, of the trouble we'd be getting into." (D.B. Yoffie and A.G. Wint, "Intel Corpration 1987," HBS case N9-388-051, p. 5)

In 1989, Grove decided to expand the systems business by offering platform computer systems, essentially entire computers minus monitors, keyboards, and application software, to OEM assemblers, who would box and sell the systems under their own brand names. Several of Intel's component customers expressed dismay that Intel was coming out with competitive offerings.

"Partly in deference to their sensitivities," remarked Vadasz, who had moved back from the systems division to corporate business development in 1990, "we have drawn a clear line—we will restrict our systems-level sales to OEM customers only." Over the long term, Grove had to decide how far down the vertical channel Intel should venture, and importantly, what new capabilities Intel needed to develop in venturing downstream. An industry observer conjectured that Intel's moves to come closer to the final customer could be part of a long-range strategy:

> It is possible that Intel's tactics are only precursors to some more grandiose future plans. Currently, it is mainly a chip manufacturer. By going into systems and launching the "Intel Inside" campaign, it may be creating an option by establishing the capability of later entering the computer business on its own. In the last few years, components technology has been growing much more critical for computer assemblers than the other way round. Therefore, Intel can perhaps push computer assemblers with announcements such as overdrives and systems sales without serious retaliatory threats.

Conclusion

As Moore surveyed the options facing Intel, he mused:

> We have been extremely successful these last few years, and even that is somewhat of a concern, since the biggest curse in our business is having too much money: You become sloppy and dabble in too many things. But nobody is getting crazy here, offering harebrained or diversification projects, simply for the sake of utilizing available cash. We recognize that one sunny day doesn't a summer make. Most of us have lived through the semiconductor bloodbath, and know that if demand falls, the cash drain is also very fast. Available reserves help us sleep easier. But we are in a very expensive business, and have had a relatively short period of prosperity. We have to be very careful which options to choose, since we shall again end up betting the company on these options.

EXHIBIT 1
BIOGRAPHICAL PROFILES OF INTEL'S PAST AND PRESENT EXECUTIVE
COMMITTEE MEMBERS

Robert Noyce and Gordon Moore

Noyce was a physics PhD from MIT and Moore was a chemistry PhD from CalTech. Moore and Noyce were among the first engineers to work in 1955 with William Shockley, who shared the 1956 Nobel Prize as coinventor of the transistor. By 1957, differences had emerged in Shockley's team, and Noyce, Moore, and six others left to join Fairchild Camera and form Fairchild Semiconductors.

Noyce coinvented the integrated circuit in 1959, for which he was awarded the national medal of science in 1979. In 1968, Noyce, then general manager of Fairchild, and Moore, director of research and development, left to found Intel. Noyce and Moore were recognized as fellows of the Institute of Electrical and Electronics Engineers (IEEE) in 1966 and 1968 respectively. Noyce was awarded the National Medal of Technology in 1987, and Moore was also awarded the medal in 1990. At the time of Noyce's death on June 2, 1990, at age 62, Noyce was vice-chairman of Intel, and Moore was chairman.

Andy Grove

A Hungarian refugee at age 20, András Gróf had worked his way as waiter through City College of New York. Changing his name to Andrew S. Grove, he then got a doctorate from the University of California at Berkeley in chemical engineering.

He started working in 1963 at Fairchild as assistant to Moore, and was assistant director of research and development in 1968, when he accompanied Moore and Noyce to Intel. Grove was recognized as an IEEE fellow in 1972.

He oversaw Intel's internal operations from the beginning, and was appointed to Intel's executive committee in 1976. He was named president and COO in 1979, and CEO in 1987. Besides working at Intel, Grove had found time to write a weekly syndicated business column and publish two books on management.

Craig Barrett

Barrett had taught engineering at Stanford University for 10 years before joining Intel in 1974. At Intel, he ran a major part of the components group in 1985, was co-general manager of the microprocessors group for about a year in 1989, and was appointed executive vice president in January 1990.

EXHIBIT 2
TIME LINE OF MAJOR INTEL AND COMPETITOR PRODUCT INTRODUCTIONS

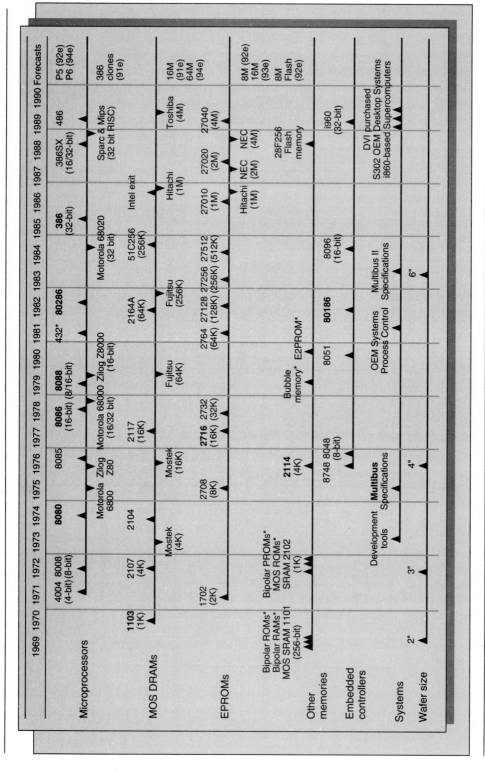

Intel product introductions are marked by ▲ on the time line, and competitive product introductions are marked by ▼ on the time line.
The table charts only major product introductions. Besides, Intel product introductions in peripherals and coprocessors, software, and microcommunications are not charted.
Competitive product innovations are charted partially, and only in microprocessors, DRAMs, and EPROMs.
Intel products which became industry standards are marked in bold. Product lines marked by asterisks (*) were discontinued or sold at a later date. e = estimate.
Sources: Intel 1988 annual report, Dataquest, & G.C. Cogan and R.A. Burgelman, op cit.

EXHIBIT 3
INTEL CORPORATE STRUCTURE—PARTIAL ORGANIZATIONAL CHART, MID-1990

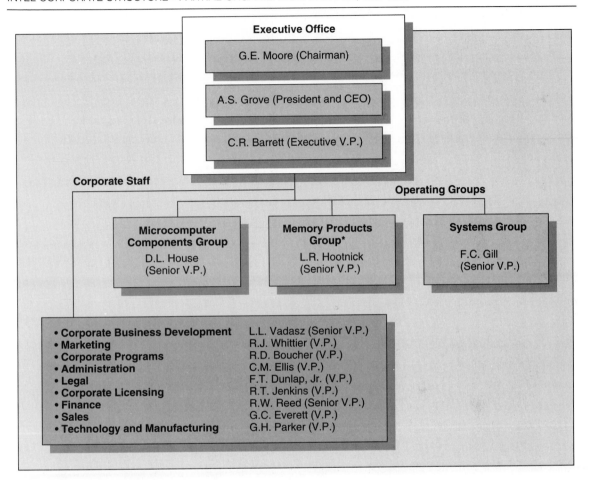

Each operating group was evaluated on ROI basis, and had sales, engineering, and manufacturing reporting to it. Several corporate functions were matrixed into operating group responsibilities through dotted-line relationships. Intergroup product transfers were priced on cost-plus basis, except 80×86 processors, which were "sold" to the systems group at most favored customer prices.

*The full name of the Memory Products Group was Embedded Controllers and Memory Products Group.

EXHIBIT 4
INTEL'S FINANCIAL PERFORMANCE 1969–1990

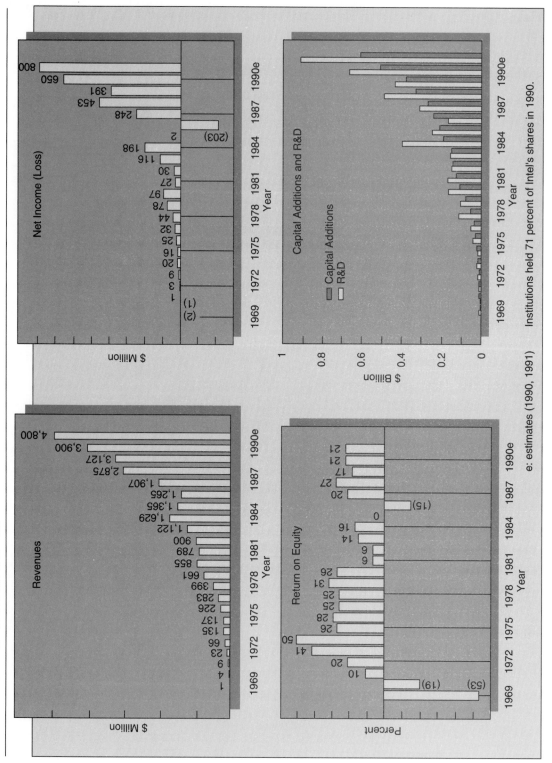

Source: Intel annual reports.

EXHIBIT 5
ESTIMATED PRODUCT-LINE BREAKDOWN OF INTEL REVENUES AND PROFITS

Product Line	1983	1984	1985	1986	1987	1988	CAGR(%)
Revenues ($ million)							
Microprocessor							
8-bit	316	419	95	24	12	5	(56)
80186/80286	28	282	444	411	476	450	74
386			2	43	349	1,100	N.A.
Subtotal	344	701	542	478	836	1,555	35
MDS memory							
EPROM	237	211	180	186	203	311	6
DRAM	66	61	25				N.A.
SRAM	13	55	49	48	41		N.A.
Other	19	66	58	25	23	24	5
Subtotal	335	392	312	259	267	335	0
Other semiconductor	123	209	206	208	250	276	18
Total semiconductor	802	1,302	1,060	946	1,353	2,165	22
Systems	321	327	305	319	554	710	17
Total	**1,122**	**1,629**	**1,365**	**1,265**	**1,907**	**2,875**	**21**
Operating Profits ($ million)							
Microprocessor							
8-bit			(4)	(1)	0	0	
80186/80286			14	6	92	80	
386			(12)	(9)	97	431	
Subtotal			(1)	(4)	189	511	
MOS memory			(66)	(124)	3	0	
Other semiconductor			4	(5)	15	15	
Total semiconductor			(63)	(132)	207	526	
Systems			3	(1)	39	68	
Total			**(60)**	**(133)**	**246**	**594**	
Profitability (%)							
Microprocessor							
8-bit			(4)	0	0	0	
80186/80286			3	1	19	18	
386			(600)	(20)	28	39	
Subtotal			0	(1)	23	33	
MOS memory			(20)	(48)	1	0	
Other semiconductor			2	(2)	6	5	
Total semiconductor			(6)	(14)	15	24	
Systems			1	0	3	10	
Total			**(4)**	**(11)**	**13**	**21**	

Source: R. Lurie, B. Huston, and D.B. Yoffie, "Intel Corporation 1988," HBS case no. 389-063, 1989.

Figures in parentheses are negative. N.A. : not applicable.

1986 operating losses do not include one-time $60 million charge toward "restructuring of operations."

EXHIBIT 6
DOMESTIC AND INTERNATIONAL EXPANSION

Year	Site	Facility
1968	Mountain View, CA	Intel founded
1969	Geneva, Switzerland	Sales and marketing started from
	Japan	Intel Europe and Intel Japan
1972	Penang, Malaysia	Components assembly and testing
1973	Livermore, CA	Wafer fabrication
1974	Manila, Phillipines	Components assembly and testing
	Haifa, Israel	Logic products design center
1976	Aloha, Oregon	Wafer fabrication
1977	Santa Clara, CA	Wafer fabrication
	Barbados, W. Indies	Components assembly
1979	Deer Valley, Arizona	Domestic production sites
	Hillsboro, Oregon	Systems manufacturing
1980	Chandler, Arizona	Wafer fabrication, components assembly, and testing
	Rio Rancho, New Mexico	Logic, EPROM, and microcontrollers
1981	Tsukuba, Japan	Logic products design center
	Las Piedras, Puerto Rico	Systems manufacturing
1983	Albuquerque, New Mexico	Wafer fabrication
1984	Folsom, CA	Microcomputers and memory products divisions
	Singapore	Systems manufacturing
1988	Jerusalem, Israel	Wafer fabrication
1989	Leixlip, Ireland	Components fabrication and systems manufacturing facility costing $500 million

Geographical Breakdown of Sales by Intel

Market	1990e	% share 1989	1988
Americas	49	57	57
Europe	22	22	24
Japan	10	11	11
Asia–Pacific	19	10	8

Source : Intel annual reports.

EXHIBIT 7
INTEL VALUES DOCUMENT

Our Mission is to do a great job for our shareholders, customers, and employees by being the preeminent building block supplier to the computing industry.

Our Values:

Risk Taking
To maintain our innovative environment, we strive to:

- Embrace change.
- Challenge the status quo.
- Listen to all ideas and viewpoints.
- Encourage and reward informed risk taking.
- Learn from our successes and mistakes.

Quality
Our business requires continuous performance improvement. We strive to:

- Set challenging and competitive goals.
- Do the right things right.
- Continuously learn, develop, and improve.
- Take pride in our work.

Discipline
The complexity of our work and our tough business environment demand a high degree of discipline. We strive to:

- Properly plan, fund, and staff projects.
- Pay attention to detail.
- Clearly communicate intentions and expectations.
- Make and meet commitments.
- Conduct business with uncompromising integrity and professionalism.

Customer Orientation
Partnerships with our customers and suppliers are essential to our mutual success. We strive to:

- Listen to our customers.
- Communicate mutual intentions and expectations.
- Deliver innovative and competitive products and services.
- Make it easy to work with us.
- Serve our customers through partnerships with our suppliers.

Results Orientation
Output is the measure of success. We strive to:

- Set challenging goals.
- Execute flawlessly.
- Focus on output.
- Assume responsibility.
- Confront and solve problems

Great Place to Work
A productive and challenging work environment is key to our success. We strive to:

- Respect and trust each other.
- Be open and direct.
- Work as a team.
- Recognize and reward accomplishments.
- Be an asset to the community.
- Have fun!

Source: Company documents.

EXHIBIT 8
GLOBAL SEMICONDUCTOR DEMAND TREND ($ M)

Product Class	1985	1986	1987	1988	1989	1990e	1991e	1992e	1993e	1994e	1995e
Total semiconductor	27,116	33,729	41,478	54,521	61,454	62,772	69,232	78,767	91,055	102,193	110,352
N. American captive	2,773	2,895	3,227	3,662	4,241	4,547	5,584	6,556	7,518	8,407	8,691
Merchant semiconductor	24,343	30,834	38,251	50,859	57,213	58,225	63,648	72,211	83,537	93,786	101,661
MOS digital	10,103	12,815	17,473	26,988	33,024	32,292	35,926	42,496	50,980	58,661	64,546
Microcomponents	2,745	3,489	5,108	7,144	8,202	10,068	12,063	14,494	17,465	19,982	22,216
Microprocessors						2,413	2,939	3,518	4,243	4,896	5,209
Microcontrollers						4,472	5,138	6,032	7,027	8,024	8,955
Microperipherals						3,183	4,041	5,357	6,647	7,156	7,440
Memory	3,817	4,511	6,056	11,692	16,361	13,091	13,418	15,958	19,378	22,583	24,447
Logic	3,541	4,815	6,309	8,152	8,461	9,133	10,445	12,044	14,137	16,096	17,883
Other semiconductors	14,240	18,019	20,778	23,871	24,189	25,933	27,722	29,715	32,557	35,125	37,115

Refer to Appendix I for classification of semiconductors into product categories.

Top 10 Merchant Semiconductor Suppliers

Company	Worldwide Revenues ($ billion)		
	1990e	1989	1988
NEC	5.0	5.0	4.5
Toshiba	4.9	4.9	4.4
Hitachi	3.9	3.9	3.5
Motorola	3.7	3.3	3.0
Intel	3.1	2.4	2.4
Fujitsu	3.0	3.0	2.6
Texas Instruments	2.6	2.8	2.7
Mitsubishi	2.5	2.6	2.3
Matsushita	1.9	1.9	1.9
Philips	1.9	1.7	1.7

Top 10 MOS Digital Semiconductor Suppliers

1976	$ million	1981	$ million	Top 10 Market-Share Rankings	
				1989	$ million
TI	135	Intel	491	NEC	3,604
Intel	132	NEC	438	Toshiba	3,100
NEC	74	Motorola	372	Intel	2,420
GI	68	TI	350	Hitachi	2,407
National	67	Hitachi	288	Fujitsu	1,958
Hitachi	63	National	255	Motorola	1,705
AMI	59	Toshiba	250	Mitsubishi	1,676
Mostek	56	Fujitsu	218	TI	1,603
Motorola	55	Mostek	210	Samsung	1,066
Rockwell	50	GI	141	Oki	1,028

Source: Dataquest.

EXHIBIT 8 (continued)
GLOBAL TRENDS IN THE SEMICONDUCTOR INDUSTRY

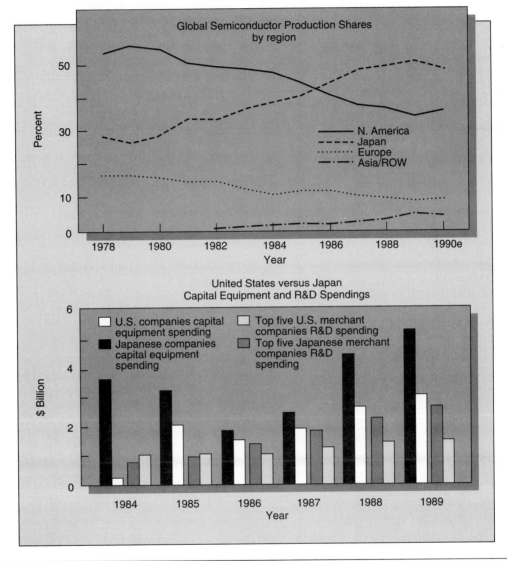

Source: Dataquest.

Source: *Financial Times*, March 21, 1991.

EXHIBIT 8 (continued)

Selected Competitor Data for 1988 and 1984

FY	Item	Intel	NS	TI	AMD	Motorola	Hitachi	Toshiba	NEC	Fujitsu
1988	Sales	2,875	1,648	6,294	1,125	8,250	39,800	28,579	21,893	16,374
	COGS	1,505	1,280	5,778	661	5,040	29,535	20,583	15,120	10,713
	PBT	631	(187)	516	14	611	2,649	1,003	566	849
	PAT	453	(23)	366	19	445	1,094	485	204	337
	Assets	3,550	1,416	4,427	1,081	6,710	44,969	27,673	23,426	18,532
	Long-term debt	479	52	623	130	343	3,462	4,423	3,576	2,413
	Owners' equity	2,080	848	2,243	645	3,375	16,148	5,743	4,784	6,616
1,984	Sales	1,629	1,655	5,741	583	5,534	18,528	11,003	7,476	5,401
	COGS	883	1,146	4,190	276	3,206	13,632	8,182	5,117	3,346
	R&D	180	158	367	101	411	898	597	391	n.a.
	PBT	299	103	525	98	466	631	572	367	523
	PAT	198	64	316	71	387	709	250	189	297
	Assets	2,029	1,156	3,423	512	4,194	7,997	N.A.	N.A.	5,699
	Long-term debt	146	24	380	27	531	1,379	1,830	1,524	915
	Owners' equity	1,360	619	1,540	278	2,278	6,118	2,191	1,728	1,935

All figures are in $ million. Figures in parentheses are negative. NS : National Semiconductors. N.A. : not available.

Source: Cogan & Burgelman, *op cit.*

EXHIBIT 9
WORLDWIDE MEMORY FORECAST

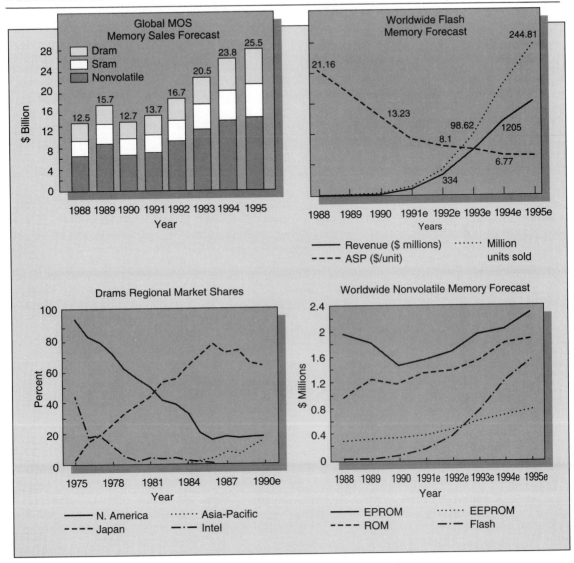

Source: Dataquest.

EXHIBIT 9 (continued)
GLOBAL MARKET SHARES IN EPROMS

Year	Market Share (%)											Total Market ($ million)
	Intel	Hitachi	Mitsu-bishi	NEC	Fujitsu	AMD	National	TI	Toshiba	SGS-Thomson*	Others	
1976	74							4	22			11
1977	59				2		4	10	19		8	79
1978	44	1	4		2	3	8	28			10	124
1979	27	6	2		5	4	7	30	2		17	380
1980	23	9	4	2	9	3	5	24	3		18	514
1981	29	12	6	4	8	4	4	20	1	3	9	326
1982	28	12	10	10	12	7	4	8	3		6	543
1983	24	15	9	8	11	9	5	11	2	1	5	879
1984	16	17	13	6	11	10	4	11	4	2	6	1,320
1985	18	16	11	9	12	11	3	6	6	3	5	866
1986	23	16	14	9	9	8	2	4	7	3	5	910
1987	19	11	10	5	12	8	5	6	10	6	8	1,350
1988	17	5	9	5	10	8	7	8	8	10	13	1,947
1989	17	4	7	6	10	11	7	11	6	9	12	1,808
1990e	16	7	5	5	7	16	7	12	5	11	9	1,446

*Figures until 1986 give sales of SGS, which merged in 1986 with Thomson to form SGS-Thomson.

Top Five MOS Memory Suppliers—1990

Company	Revenue ($ billion)
Toshiba	1.6
NEC	1.4
Hitachi	1.4
Fujitsu	1.0
Samsung	1.0
Top Five Market Share	49%

Flash Market Shares (%)

Company	1990	1989	1988
Intel	85	68	68
SEEQ	1	5	10
Toshiba	10	26	22
Atmel	3	1	0
TI	1	0	0

e: estimate.

Source: Dataquest.

EXHIBIT 10
INTEL'S CORPORATE STRATEGY FOR THE 1990S

Business Thrusts

Connectivity   Processor power   Mobility   Natural data

To provide computer-supported collaboration
in the conduct of "just-in-time" business

Capabilities

Silicon technology & manufacturing (circuit linewidth reduction)

Architecture/Platform (Intel x86 as industry standard)

Design technology (increasing transistor count per chip)

Information/Service/Support

Brand recognition ('Intel Inside' campaign)

Source: Company documents.

EXHIBIT 11
GLOBAL MICROPROCESSORS MARKET

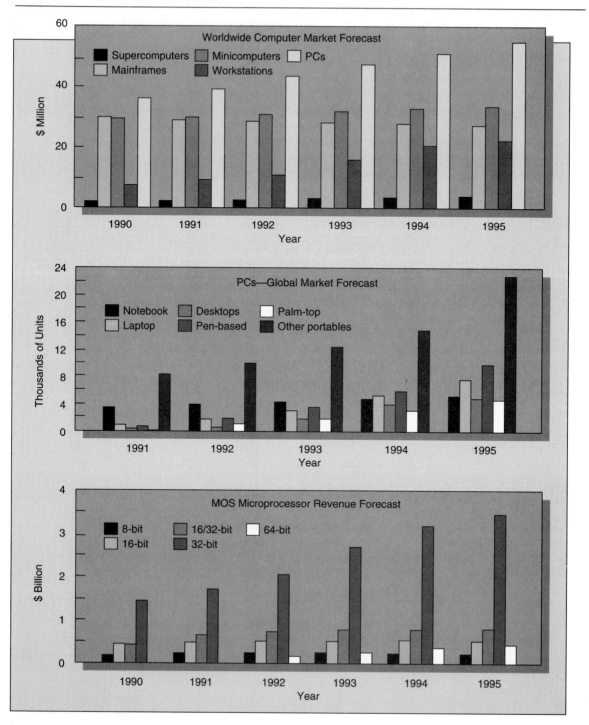

Source: Dataquest.

EXHIBIT 11 (continued)

Market Shares of Top 10 Microcomponent Suppliers

Company	Revenues ($ million)	
	1989	1990e
Intel	1,929	2,726
NEC	841	981
Motorola	767	970
Hitachi	505	546
Mitsubishi	431	441
Toshiba	361	386
TI	252	320
Matsushita	218	250
Chips & Technologies	216	240
Fujitsu	197	213

Microcomponents include microprocessors, microcontrollers, and peripherals (refer to Appendix 1).

Source: Dataquest.

Market Shares of Top 10 Microprocessor Suppliers

Company	Revenues ($ million)	
	1989	1990e
Intel	1,204	1,826
Motorola	275	291
AMD	105	110
NEC	69	72
Hitachi	68	72
National Semiconductor	55	66
SGS-Thomson	53	53
Harris	48	45
Toshiba	41	42
Zilog	25	25

Source: Dataquest.

Increasing Complexity of Microprocessor Chips

Intel Micro	Intro. Year	Transistor Count	MIPS*	Circuit Line Size (μ)	Wafer size
4004	1971	2,300	0.06	6.5	2"
8080	1974	6,000	0.29	4.5	3"
8085	1976	6,500	0.37	3	4"
8086/88	1978–79	29,000	0.75	3	4",6"
80286	1982	134,000	1.50	2.5	6"
386	1985	275,000	5	1.5	6"
486	1989	1,200,000	27	1	6"
i860	1989	2,500,000	100	0.8	6"

*MIPS (millions of instructions/sec) is a measure of chip performance.
$1\mu = 10^{-6}$ meter.

Source: Company records.

EXHIBIT 11 (continued)
The Evolving Global Market for Microprocessors (by Word Length)

	1975	1976	1977	1978	1979	1980	1981	1982	1983	1984	1985
4-bits											
Units sold (000s)	251	464	352	369	274	128	72				
8-bits											
80x86 class M/S (%)				37	40	27	20	19	22	34	36
Intel M/S (%)	76	47	22	17	15	12	12	10	11	12	9
Zilog M/S (%)	0	1	3	8	10	12	12	9	11	10	8
Units sold (000s)	341	817	3090	6763	12494	22391	33840	47991	67797	75128	51933
16-bits											
80x86 class M/S (%)							33	28	37	76	84
Intel M/S (%)							30	20	23	48	56
AMD M/S (%)							1	2	4	8	9
Units sold (000s)	7	84	196	355	515	784	1703	3871	6256	7823	5910
16/32-bits											
80x86 class M/S (%)											
Intel M/S (%)											
Motorola M/S (%)						100	78	64	53	57	61
Units sold (000s)						21	69	250	882	2238	2450
32-bits											
x86 class M/S (%)											2
Intel M/S (%)											2
Motorola M/S (%)											55
Units sold (000s)							2	4	4	1	100
64-bits (000s)											

The Evolving Global Market for Microprocessors (by Word Length)

	1986	1987	1988	1989	1990e	1991e	1992e	1993e	1994e	1995e
4-bits										
Units sold (000s)										
8-bits										
80x86 class M/S (%)	30	30	29	23						
Intel M/S (%)	8	7	8	7						
Zilog M/S (%)	10	17	18	21						
Units sold (000s)	55094	54310	63560	64790	74900	73500	75000	73000	73000	71000
16-bits										
80x86 class M/S (%)	81	87	83	79						
Intel M/S (%)	46	49	49	39						
AMD M/S (%)	15	19	21	23						
Units sold (000s)	8480	14701	19500	23962	26300	29700	33500	36500	38000	39000
16/32-bits										
80x86 class M/S (%)			5	16						
Intel M/S (%)			5	16						
Motorola M/S (%)	69	65	66	61						
Units sold (000s)	3022	5730	10349	13934	17700	24400	28900	32500	35000	37000
32-bits										
x86 class M/S (%)	18	40	54	45						
Intel M/S (%)	18	39	54	45						
Motorola M/S (%)	49	42	35	39						
Units sold (000s)	459	1799	4702	6345	8500	11700	16700	26000	37000	46000
64-bits (000s)							100	200	400	700

e: estimate; M/S: market share. The x86 class includes all manufacturers supplying x86-type microprocessors. Motorola and Zilog microprocessors don't belong to this class, while AMD microprocessors do.

Source: Dataquest.

APPENDIX I

TECHNICAL APPENDIX

The electronics industry permeates daily life through several applications —data processing, consumer goods, industrial products, communications, and so on. The **semiconductor devices,** which are assembled by electronic equipment suppliers in various configurations, can be classified as **discrete devices,** which perform a single function, and **integrated circuits (ICs),** single devices comprising several active components.

An IC can incorporate anything between a few and millions of transistors —the more transistors per IC, the more "large scale" the integration on the IC. A **transistor** is the basic semiconductor unit—it is a solid-state device which works as an electronic switch. ICs are fabricated on a round slice of silicon, called a **wafer.** When the ICs on a wafer are cut and individually packaged, they are called **chips.** IC fabrication may be done by **bipolar** or **MOS** processes. A bipolar transistor is faster than a MOS transistor but consumes more power.

ICs may be principally classified into memory, microcomponent, and other devices. A **memory IC** stores and retrieves information in the form of bits. A **bit** constitutes the vocabulary of a device. 1K bits $= 2^{10}$ ($= 1,024$) bits; 1M $= 2^{20}$ ($= 1,048,576$) bits. The more bits of information a memory chip can save, the greater is its capacity.

A memory device may be volatile or nonvolatile. A **volatile memory device** can retain information only so long as it is supplied with power. A **nonvolatile memory** product doesn't lose information when power is removed. Most nonvolatile memory devices are **Read Only Memory (ROM)** chips whose information can be accessed but not altered. **EPROMs** are a variety of ROMs whose information can be erased (by ultraviolet light), and which can then be reprogrammed. Most volatile memory devices allow both storage and retrieval of information and are referred to as **Random Access Memory (RAM)** chips. **Static RAM (SRAM)** devices retain data so long as they are supplied with power. **Dynamic RAM (DRAM)** chips minimize power consumption, but the information written on them has to be rewritten periodically, else it gets erased. **Flash memories** can be considered to be like electrically erasable EPROMs or like nonvolatile DRAMs.

Microcomponents[a] can be categorized into microprocessors, microcontrollers, and peripherals. A **microprocessor** comprises the central processing unit (CPU) of a general-purpose system. A **microcontroller** is often dedicated to a particular application and contains a CPU, memory, and input/output capability. A **peripheral** device supports a microprocessor or a microcontroller.

CISC (Complex Instruction Set Computing), the traditional microprossor architecture, uses a large set of instructions to perform its tasks. **RISC** (Reduced Instruction Set Computing) offers faster computational speed at the cost of a smaller set of instructions. Within each architectural class, a microprocessor operates on a group of bits simultaneously—the number of bits in one group is called the microprocessor's **word length.**

---

[a] Microcomponents categorization follows Dataquest classification.

The Harvard Business School
Strategies from Inception through World War II

In 1908, Henry Ford introduced his Model T at $845. On the first of October of that same year, the Harvard Graduate School of Business Administration, with a faculty of 15 including its dean, opened its doors to 24 regular MBA students and 35 "special" students taking one or more courses. This event occurred during the final year of Charles W. Eliot's 40-year-long Harvard presidency. Just before becoming president in 1869, at the age of 34, Eliot, an MIT chemistry professor, had published two articles on education in the *Atlantic Monthly*, starting with the question:

> What can I do with my boy? I want to give him a practical education that will prepare him better than I was prepared to follow my business or any other active calling. The classical schools and the colleges do not offer what I want. Where can I put him? Here is a real need and a very serious problem.

Upon assuming the Harvard presidency, Eliot found a moribund undergraduate curriculum and graduate schools of uncertain quality. At the Medical School, there were no entrance examinations; as a result, large numbers of underqualified students were admitted, some of whom could barely read or write. Final examinations were oral, as in the college; at the Medical School, moreover, they were only five minutes long, and a student needed to pass exams in only five out of nine subjects to graduate. In short order, Eliot raised the school's standards for admission, instruction, and examination, which gradually elevated it to preeminence in its field. The Law School experienced a similar upheaval. In 1869, half of its students had no college training, and after being enrolled for 18 months, students were eligible to receive a degree. Again, Eliot pushed for higher standards, and also forced a skeptical faculty to accept a new "case method" of teaching.

Although this experiment became the focus of an international debate, its eventual success brought worldwide acclaim to the Law School.

Eliot himself considered the reestablishment of the elective system in the college a key accomplishment of his presidency. Against strong opposition, Eliot gave increasing numbers of undergraduates the opportunity to design their own educations. In these and other policies, the president emphasized the practical and the relevant in education. At a 1905 alumni dinner, he summed up his feeling on the subject: "We seek at Harvard to put all the various sciences and arts into practice so that public advantage may result. We seek to train doers, achievers—men whose successful personal careers are made subservient to the public good. We are not interested here in producing languid observers of the world, mere spectators in the game of life, or fastidious critics of other men's labors. We want to produce by hundreds and thousands strenuous workers in the world of today—a more interesting world, I venture to say, than has yet offered a field for splendid intellectual and moral achievement . . ."

ELIOT'S CONTROVERSIAL CREATION

Within this context, Eliot was sympathetic to a proposal for training business leaders: A considerable number of executives "have told me with a great deal of urgency that the universities were not supplying the great business corporations with well-trained young men who would make responsible managers." However, others in the business community doubted whether universities could contribute anything useful, as expressed by one skeptic:

College authorities, instead of laying the facts before the young men who are preparing to enter college . . . will go right on deceiving as many as they can and taking the money of those to whom they can give nothing in return but useless knowledge. Practically they stand on the same level as the merchant who sells goods which he knows to be shoddy.

Academics raised similar doubts:

The professional knowledge and skill of physicians, surgeons, dentists, pharmacists, agriculturalists, engineers of all kinds, perhaps even of journalists, is of some use to the community at large, at the same time that it may be profitable to the bearers of it . . . But such is not the case with the training designed to give proficiency in business . . . The work of the College of Commerce is a peculiarly futile line of endeavor for any public institution, in that it serves neither the intellectual advancement nor the material welfare of the community.

Yet, in 1881, Wharton, an imaginative Philadelphia ironmaster, had donated $100,000 to the University of Pennsylvania for the creation of the "Wharton School," intended to offer courses of instruction in finance and commerce. By 1889, the school's success within the university's college of liberal arts had led to the creation of a wide-ranging undergraduate curriculum of a full four years.

The department head in economics, a strong supporter of a business school at Harvard, wrote in 1906, "the more I think of it, the more I am convinced that we must have, not a department of the Graduate School [of Arts and Sciences] or the college, but a separate professional school, with a separate faculty, whose object would be purely to train men for their career, as the Law and Medical Schools do. We must take men without regard to what they have studied in college, and we must teach them business, not political economy." Thus, a *Graduate* School of Business *Administration* was established the following year. There had not previously been a graduate school of business—indeed, it seems that no institution had yet called itself a "school of business." The addition of the word "administration" was a further distinction, which would take on unanticipated significance in years to come. Three small rooms in University Hall, then Harvard's central administration building, were set aside for the dean of the Business School. Located one floor below the president's office, this suite of offices would for the next two decades give the struggling school a great advantage: access to Harvard's president. Edwin F. Gay, a Harvard professor in economic history, was appointed as the school's first dean.

GAY'S INITIAL CHALLENGE

In his eleven years as dean of the Harvard Business School, Edwin Gay faced a formidable array of challenges. Foremost among these was a question of invention: What *was* a graduate school of business administration? What sort of intellectual capital should it attempt to generate? What sort of graduate should it hope to produce?

Gay and his small faculty solicited opinions on these basic questions from both industry and academia. The contradictory answers they heard, early in the course of their decade of experimentation, led them to several important conclusions. The "profession" of business that they intended to serve, they realized, was far from a final definition. Furthermore, with the increasingly rapid pace of change

and diversification that then characterized business, it appeared that the profession might never be clearly defined. What the Harvard Business School needed to invent, it seemed, was a wholly new educational structure, able to respond to changing realities and to redefine itself over time.

Manufacturing and Marketing

The theory underlying the school's "scientific endeavor" in 1910 was indeed simple. Gay hypothesized that the art of business consisted of two major functions: production and distribution. In part to distinguish his new school from existing schools of economics, he called those basic functions "manufacturing" and "marketing." For Gay, the school's role was to discover and teach the principles that underlay the fields of manufacturing and marketing. In the process, the school would help to define the profession of business, both by providing it with scientifically derived information and by training qualified managers for its ranks. But how much intellectual territory could a faculty of 15, with no precedents to build upon and an operating budget of $29,000 a year, expect to cover, and cover well enough to justify the school's continued existence?

As Gay looked ahead from 1908, he saw that two processes had to occur simultaneously. A curriculum had to be devised, which could be relied upon to produce the business leaders of the 1920s and beyond; and at the same time, the school needed to define territories in which it could make a clear and significant contribution to business theory—and practice—in the short run. The two processes were closely linked: Because no texts or lectures existed for a graduate school of business, business theory had to be developed in a way that would inform the curriculum. Where were those territories which would provide new materials for teaching —territories significant enough to warrant the attention of business, yet manageable enough to be comprehended by the scarce resources of the Harvard Business School?

They were not, Gay concluded, in the manufacturing field. For one thing, manufacturing was too large, complex, and changeable. Furthermore, there was already an impressive body of knowledge on this topic. It had been developed, for the most part, by a small but growing group of mechanical engineers; they called their field "scientific management," and they were the disciples of the founder of scientific management, Frederick W. Taylor. Taylor had proposed that manufacturers should determine scientifically what workers ought to be able to accomplish, given the available equipment and materials. (This involved using time-and-motion studies to break down each task into its component parts.) With this information in hand, the manufacturer should then prescribe productivity levels. Taylorism represented concrete evidence that there might indeed be a science underlying the practice of business, at least on the manufacturing side. Gay decided, in effect, to cede that territory to Taylor: He would incorporate scientific management in the Business School curriculum, and meanwhile invest the school's limited resources for research elsewhere. He initiated a correspondence with Taylor, and won a grudging agreement from the engineer to lecture at the school in the spring of 1909.

The marketing side of Gay's scientific endeavor was influenced by Arch W. Shaw, a Chicago-based publisher whose flagship publication was *System*—"the

magazine for management" (later purchased by McGraw-Hill and renamed *Business Week*). Shaw began to visit the school regularly in 1910, attending classes and talking with the faculty. In early 1911, he sent Gay a formal note: "I wish to give for use in this school a fund which shall be applied for the purpose of investigation of business problems, primarily for the problem of distribution of products."

The fund, gratefully accepted by Gay, amounted to $2,200. It was an ample sum of money to investigate *some* aspect of distribution; now the question became, where to start? Gay and Shaw shared a conviction that the work they were about to begin would ultimately be taken over by some government agency. It therefore seemed logical to focus on a subject that hitherto had been ignored by government. They settled on the small retailer, convinced that the federal government—then preoccupied with "big" business—might eventually do for "little" business what the Agriculture Department was doing for farmers. By gathering information on agricultural techniques and crop yields from large numbers of farmers, the department had been able to provide individual farmers with standards of productivity. Could Harvard do the same for the small retailer—and simultaneously develop much-needed material for its curriculum?

The Bureau of Business Research

In the summer of 1911, two representatives of the school's newly created "Bureau of Business Research" set off for the Midwest. Their mission seemed modest: to establish definitively the costs of operating a retail shoe business. The initial results were discouraging. They soon discovered that no two retailers kept exactly comparable records. The Bureau of Business Research—which at that point consisted of nothing more than its two investigators—decided to organize a committee of manufacturers and retailers, public accountants, and Harvard faculty members to establish a standard classification of accounts for retailers in the shoe industry.

The committee met intermittently during the academic year of 1911–1912, and by the summer of 1912, the standard classification system was available for use. As soon as it was ready, a young faculty member used it to obtain information on the operating expenses of shoe stores in the East and Midwest. Over 130 stores were included in the survey, most of them visited in person to explain the purposes of the study and to overcome through dogged persistence the merchants' reluctance to divulge what they considered proprietary information. Some retailers refused to cooperate. "Why, damn it, man, you're asking for the guts of this business," complained one president of a New York department store. "That's exactly what I'm asking for," was the reply. In this case, as in others, it later emerged that the executive actually was more embarrassed by the inadequacy of his accounting system than he was concerned about revealing trade secrets.

The fruits of these efforts appeared in May of 1913—exactly coincident with the end of the school's five-year trial period—when the Bureau of Business Research issued its first bulletin: *Object and History of the Bureau with Some Preliminary Figures on the Retailing of Shoes.* The "object and history" section of the report said that the bureau represented "an approach to the scientific study of business, which up to the present time has developed in the main in an empirical, rule-of-thumb fashion. There is in

general a feeling that the time is now at hand for the businessman to have more scientific information to aid him in meeting and solving his problems."

There were two reasons for publishing "preliminary figures": Dean Gay was anxious to have a research product in hand as soon as possible, and the director of the bureau wanted something tangible to show to the next round of shoe retailers. Immediately after the publication of the bulletin, five "field agents" left Cambridge once again, soliciting data from additional shoe retailers. This time out they reported a perceptible difference: The first bulletin had been well received in trade publications, and retailers were now much more willing to cooperate.

In all, some 10,000 shoe retailers were surveyed: the first organized research in the field of business administration. In 1914, the bureau undertook a study of operating expenses in the retail grocery trade and eventually secured the cooperation of some 14,000 grocers. Wholesale shoe firms, wholesale grocers, retail general stores, retail hardware dealers, retail jewelers, and department and specialty stores were subsequently studied. Within four months of the publication of the first bulletin concerning the retail grocery trade, for example, some 15,000 individual orders for the findings had been received, thus proving the existence of a need for this kind of research.

Most important, the bureau established effective working relationships with thousands of retail and wholesale businesses. In the process, it earned for the Harvard Business School a reputation for integrity and competence. Business managers learned that operating-expense information—hitherto a jealously guarded secret—could be divulged with confidence, with the knowledge that the figures would be employed for the general good. In 1920, at the beginning of the bureau's second decade of operation, this record of accomplishment allowed, as will be discussed later, the bureau's researchers to take on a significant new role: case collection.

Business Policy

Early in 1911, *System* publisher Arch Shaw complained to Dean Gay that the school's courses were too general and descriptive, and that its students "wouldn't recognize a problem if they saw one." "If you know so much about it," Gay replied, "why don't you tackle it yourself?" Shaw and Gay agreed upon the concept of a required second-year course, to be called Business Policy. Shaw would be the course head; his experiment would attempt to integrate the lessons of the first year by adopting the vantage point of the upper-level manager. Shaw decided to take a new approach to getting students to "recognize a problem." He secured the cooperation of 15 senior managers, each of whom agreed to present a real problem to the class over the course of a week. In the first of three sessions, the businessman would explain his problem and answer students' questions regarding it. In the second class meeting, two days later, students would hand in a written "problem analysis" with a recommended solution. In the third session, at the end of the week, the businessman would discuss the reports.

Curriculum Design

In its early years, the Business School conducted a number of experiments in industry-specific courses. A Technique of Printing course, first offered in 1911, had been preceded by a course in fire insurance, as well as courses in railroading and banking. In 1914, a new array of specialized offerings appeared: in chamber of commerce and trade association work, in lumbering and forestry, and in public utilities operation. In 1916, water transportation was added to the curriculum. A definite enrollment pattern soon emerged—students consistently favored the functional courses (and the "tool" courses, including accounting practice and business statistics) over both the theoretical and the industry-specific courses.

In a school with limited resources and an uncertain curriculum, student preferences had an immediate impact. "Voting with their feet," as the faculty later came to refer to it, was immediately established as a Business School tradition. Arch Shaw's Business Policy course was elected by some 70 percent of the eligible students the first time it was offered; the specialized courses, on the other hand, were generally underattended, particularly as better functional courses became available. By 1918, the faculty agreed that the "Harvard Business School sought to train *generalists*—and although a student might desire training in a specialized field, he would nevertheless be required to become familiar with 'the general aspects of business.' The purpose of the school is not to teach rules and methods and specific facts about business, but to train men who have initiative and intellectual capacity in such fashion that they can analyze business problems and make decisions on the strength of knowledge and experience."

Few Graduates

Since the school's founding, the faculty had required every second-year student to "submit a thesis dealing with some concrete problem in the business which he plans to enter and embodying the results and conclusions derived from his original investigation of actual business conditions." But only 207 of the 1,442 students who enrolled at the school in its first 11 years ever satisfied that requirement—because, for the most part, students stayed for only one year of Harvard's new experiment in business education, and then left to take jobs. In the school's first half-dozen years, many students left because of dissatisfaction with their first-year studies and because of the unimpressive reputation of the second-year curriculum. It was a period of experimentation, and many of the curricular innovations of the day—such as the thesis requirement, which was abandoned in 1922—proved unsatisfactory.

DONHAM SHAPES THE SCHOOL

At the October 7, 1919, Business School faculty meeting, President Lowell introduced the school to its second dean: Wallace Brett Donham, a Boston banker, and Lowell's protegé during Donham's college and law school years.

A School Without a Home

Donham, who would hold the deanship for 23 years through the boom of the 1920s, the depression of the 1930s, and the early war years, immediately was confronted with a deluge of students. While four students had graduated in June of 1919, four months later, total enrollment stood at 412, almost double the previous 1916 high. By 1926, enrollment again had doubled. As a result, Donham's early tenure was characterized by inadequate physical facilities. He wrote, "The school is scattered all over the Cambridge buildings of the university without proper ad-

ministrative quarters, professors' studies, classrooms, laboratory facilities, library and reading room quarters, or dormitories." The problem gave rise to discontent that manifested itself in some unusual ways: Disaffected Business School students had established a tradition of cheering noisily for the visiting teams at Harvard's football games—a practice which President Lowell found irritating.

Donham was increasingly preoccupied by the dormitory question: "Without [our own dormitories] . . . particularly with our lack of centralized administration and teaching space, the faculty feel the great difficulty of developing the professional spirit without which we are hardly justified in having such a school. [It is much harder] to build up a professional attitude toward business than it is to build up a knowledge of the ethics and practices of law or medicine. Dormitories would help us immensely in accomplishing this result."

A month into his tenure, Donham began soliciting comments from the faculty, and soon established a "Building Committee of the Faculty." He submitted his own recommendations to the building committee on January 13, 1920—three months after assuming the deanship. Intensive architectural planning, lobbying within the university, and almost full-time fundraising efforts followed, leading to the famous April 21, 1924, offer by George F. Baker, in response to a $1 million solicitation, that "if by giving $5 million I could have the privilege of building the whole school, I should like to do it." Donham and his architectural adviser spent the ensuing summer on the Cape to prepare a very specific plan for the ensuing architectural competition. McKim, Mead, and White emerged as the winners, Frederick Law Olmsted's firm was hired to landscape the campus, and on June 4, 1927, the new Harvard Business School campus was dedicated in the presence of 87-year-old George F. Baker.

The Case Method

Early in his first week as dean of the Harvard Business School, Donham asked marketing professor Copeland to join him in his University Hall office for a conference. Donham quickly got to the point: He understood that Copeland planned to produce a textbook for the first-year marketing course. The dean argued against that plan and proposed instead that Copeland produce a "problem book." Donham had ample reason for experimenting with a new teaching technique. Business School students—already annoyed by their cramped physical circumstances—were beginning to voice complaints about the curriculum's seeming lack of relevance and the inadequate teaching skills of certain professors. Students had taken to stamping their feet during lectures they considered boring or irrelevant. Perhaps a variation on the "case method" that had informed and enlivened his own law school education could be devised to solve the problem. Without a doubt, students encountering a modified case method would be forced to become "more active mentally," as he later put it—more actively engaged in the learning process.

With Copeland at work on his compilation of problems, Donham began engaging the rest of the faculty in a broad discussion of the school's course content and methods. He prepared a lengthy memorandum, circulated to the faculty in early 1920, which effectively defined the new dean's conception of the school. By favoring a *functional* course orientation, Donham was going against a powerful

external trend toward industry specialization. When the Wharton School established its MBA program in 1921, for example, it did so in the interest of specialization: Its new MBA candidates were to acquire superior "technical equipment" by taking 10 of their 28 courses, as well as writing a thesis, in a specialized field of study.

Donham proposed that instruction be "based in large part on specific facts or problems stated in varied forms as they present themselves to the businessman. The student should be required in each course to investigate facts, to sort undigested material, to state problems, to analyze problems, to reach conclusions, and to present the subject matter and his decision orally and in writing as he will be required to do in business." Donham constantly emphasized facts for methodological reasons. Every case, he noted, must have "the atmosphere and detail of reality." It was facts, meticulously recorded by firsthand observation, that would recreate the reality of business for the student and enable him to enhance his "executive judgement." Reality, therefore, was to be brought to the classroom, and Donham was searching in particular for the reality of *decision making*. Later he wrote, "I distrust intensely principles divorced from facts. To me, method is so much more important than content that there is no comparison."

The subject of teaching *method* was never brought to a formal vote by the faculty. "Some members of the faculty," recalled Copeland, "welcomed enthusiastically the innovation which the dean was sponsoring. The attitudes of other members ran all the way from lukewarmness to covert hostility." However, Donham was, by all accounts, persuasive. Throughout the early 1920s, he sponsored a series of faculty lunches which focused on the problems of collecting and using cases. Also, the faculty was expanding rapidly—from 15 in 1919 to 24 in 1923—and Donham was careful to appoint new members who would be sympathetic to his goals. By 1923, two-thirds of the school's courses were taught by the case system. Once again, student enrollment patterns were helping to determine the direction of the school. A few polished lecturers continued to enjoy large and attentive audiences, but students were drifting away from the faculty's less stimulating lecturers and toward case-oriented courses.

By October of 1921, some $25,000 had been spent on case writing. Donham likened these costs to capital expenditures in industry, which could not be fairly charged to current students in the form of tuition fees. He therefore took personal responsibility for raising the needed funds among supporters in the business community. And while fund-raising for case research proved a difficult task, it was facilitated by evidence of solid progress. The research effort had produced immediate results: There were now in print four additional "case books"—as they were beginning to be called—with another expected shortly. Some 90,000 mimeographed pages of case material had been prepared for distribution to students between November 1920 and July of the following year. By the summer of 1925, 5,000 cases had been produced.

From Applied Economics to the Human Factor

The gradual acceptance of the case method by other educators, as well as the school's own growing reputation, validated Wallace Donham's innovative approach to business education. But the school's conception of itself—as a school of applied economics, devoted to the practical illustration of known economic principles—was dissolving with equal rapidity. Later, Copeland wrote, "Most of the economic theory concerning the business firm was restricted to hypothetical states of equilibrium under restrictive sets of static assumptions which completely ignored many of the most significant elements of business strategy and behavior, as well as many of the most important issues involved in the decisions facing an active business executive." "The facts of concrete situations," Donham later recalled, "refused to stay within the concepts of our economists, who were thinking in terms of applied economics. In spite of the fact that our reporters were trying to ignore noneconomic factors, noneconomic facts persisted in coming into situations. By so doing, they forced us to recognize that problems faced by men of affairs—either public or private—can almost never be treated as problems in applied economics."

In the summer of 1925, Donham sought out George Elton Mayo, an Australian scholar and philosopher who had combined a variety of clinical and practical experiences to forge a new discipline: industrial sociology. His studies had focused on the psychological and physiological aspects of factory work, and his research on the textile business had revealed the link between high turnover and low productivity and the monotony and fatigue associated with textile mill work. His suggestions to incorporate a regular schedule of breaks during the workday led to increases in productivity, and he won the respect of both workers and management.

After joining the Harvard Business School faculty in 1925, Mayo responded to an invitation in 1928 to assist in interpreting the conflicting data then emerging from a company-sponsored research project at Western Electric's Hawthorne Works. This manufacturing facility employed over 40,000 workers, who manufactured most of the telephones made in America, as well as products for its parent company, American Telephone and Telegraph. Western Electric researchers had set up a special facility, later known as the "Relay Assembly Test Room," in April of 1927. Five workers had agreed to assemble telephone relays under conditions of close scientific observation, but without formal company supervision. Their output was first determined under normal working conditions; it was then measured again when the workers were transferred to the test room. At staged intervals, changes were introduced into the working environment: pay incentives, various rest schedules, shorter work weeks, and so on. Taken as a whole, the productivity of the workers rose consistently. A return to the original working conditions reduced productivity somewhat, but not to the levels originally recorded.

The correlation that *did* seem promising to Mayo and his assistants was the one which apparently existed between supervision and productivity. Throughout the studies, the test room workers' comments had suggested the importance of their relative autonomy and of the sympathetic attention they were receiving from their observers. In subsequent interviews, Mayo proposed an indirect approach. Rather than interrogation, he argued for sympathetic listening—much like the attention enjoyed by the test room workers. The interviewer was to pay close attention to the interviewee, to refrain from arguing or offering advice, to listen for and test the validity of patterns in the interviewee's responses, and to treat all responses as confidential. Interviews conducted along

these lines would begin to answer the question that Mayo had defined as critical: How does the worker's psychological state relate to his or her productivity?

This observation, which seemed to contradict prevailing stereotypes of the industrial workplace and its effect on the worker, convinced Mayo that he was involved in a "major revolution in industrial method," comparable in its impact to the Industrial Revolution. "If all fear of bullyragging can be taken out of supervision, and if a majority of supervisors are trained interviewers," he wrote in October 1929, "industry will enter upon a new and undreamed era of active collaboration that will make possible an almost incredible human advance."

Mayo subsequently decided to write a full account of the Hawthorne studies. Glaucoma prevented him from doing so, however, and the task of chronicling the Hawthorne studies eventually fell to Harvard's Roethlisberger and Western Electric's Harold Wright and William Dickson. *Management and the Worker*, published in 1939, indisputably defined a new field of social research. In the process, it shaped the research agenda and methodology of the Harvard Business School and validated Wallace Donham's concept of field-based empirical research, aimed at addressing key social and industrial issues.

By the mid-1930s, the Mayo research was becoming integrated into the school's curriculum. Mayo had suggested a conceptual model to replace the discredited model of applied economics. The approach of the medical clinician, defined most broadly, seemed a much more workable basis for business research and teaching than did economics. The physician, in a sense, replaced the economist; the "clinical method" supplanted the illustration, through case research, of established economic theory.

It was a conceptual scheme largely out of step with prevailing trends in business education and in the broader society. The Wharton School, for example, embarked upon a deliberate effort to reconstruct itself as a school of applied economics. In the same period, the federal government turned increasingly to economists, such as Harvard's influential Alvin Hansen and Seymour Harris, for social prescriptions. Donham deplored this trend in particular, for it failed to consider "the most important variables in practically every problem, and because it ignores them, it leads to action which would not have been taken if the problem had been conceived more broadly and more premises had been taken into account."

Educational Impact

Under Donham's tenure, a rare degree of consensus regarding method and values developed, which Professor Malcolm McNair captured when he wrote, "We have forced [the student] to acquire knowledge by the hard route of the case method instead of the easy route of the textbook and lecture." Rather than providing a specific body of knowledge, the school offered a means of analyzing a situation, working out a program of action, and carrying out that program.

Sumner Slichter stipulated:

> Something should happen to men who come to the Business School which could not happen to them anywhere else in the world, and which will leave its mark on them for the rest of their lives—even though the distinctive qualities that they get from two years at the Business School may not manifest themselves (and probably should not) for 10 or 20 years after their graduation.

On one occasion, an alumnus, more than 10 years out of school, responded to Donham's question, "What did the school do for you?" as follows: "That is simple. It gave me a sense of assurance that I could tackle any problem, either because I had the experience to justify handling it myself, or because I knew in what direction to turn in situations where my experience was inadequate."

THE SECOND WORLD WAR

Adjusting Strategy

By March of 1939, as Donham and other faculty members at the Harvard Business School had already concluded that American intervention in the widening war was inevitable, the school set out to build upon its long history of collaboration with the armed forces. In the early 1920s, the War Department had established a school (which became the Army Industrial College) for the training of selected Army officers in business affairs. A similar program was established by the Navy. Donham had been particularly involved in the creation of the Army school and had recommended that Army officers be sent to the Business School in preparation for teaching at the Army Industrial College—a practice already observed by the Navy. By the end of the 1930s, half of the faculty of the Army Industrial College were Business School graduates.

In the fall of 1940, Donham announced two new courses related to defense production and procurement. He then confronted the threat of a precipitous drop in enrollment, as more and more men left to fight in the war. He presented to the faculty Committee on Instruction his proposal that the school should admit 750 first-year students, rather than the 600 students accepted under normal circumstances. At the end of the first year, qualified students—up to two-thirds of the class—would go on to the second year. The remaining third of the students, however, would receive three months of specialized training and be awarded a "Bachelor of Commerce" degree in their field of specialization.

As the dean had anticipated, his plan for a bachelor's degree aroused bitter opposition within the faculty, who were reluctant to compromise the quality of instruction. Nonetheless, the result, after a protracted and sometimes acrimonious debate, was the authorization of an "Industrial Administrator" (IA) program, a three-term program to be offered in twelve months of continuous training. It was designed for students "going into government service or into industries connected with national defense." Drawing most of its elements from the MBA program, the IA curriculum emphasized production at the expense of marketing and policy issues. The IA program successfully addressed the need to link the school's curriculum with war-preparedness training, while also making up the enrollment deficit.

The Stat School

In June 1941 Army Chief of Staff General George C. Marshall created the "Army Air Forces" (AAF). In order to keep track of personnel, training, and planes—over 230,000 by war's end—a "Statistical Control Division" at AAF Headquarters was created in 1942, and a decision was soon made to "subcontract" the training of the statistical officers. Harvard was selected for this purpose in May 1942. AAF officials stressed that the Statistical School (or "Stat School," as it was soon known)

had the highest military priority, and they planned to send the first class to Soldiers Field in June—only three weeks from that date. When over 100 statistical officers-in-training gathered at Soldiers Field in June for the school's first five-week session, teaching material was in hand for only three weeks' worth of classes. While that material was being presented, other researchers were still scrambling in the field, developing cases and related materials for the final two weeks of the program.

The Stat School was able to build upon an innovative course developed for the IA program on Management Controls which combined accounting with business statistics as well as human relations concepts to focus on the pragmatic objective of securing and subsequently *using* information most effectively. The accounting portion had its origin in a second-year course first offered in 1936, which pioneered the use of accounting for internal as well as external purposes. Its focus on managerial planning and control helped, in the words of a contemporary faculty member, bring accounting "out of the green-eyeshade era to become a tool of general management." Subsequently, in 1939, the hitherto unpopular but required Business Statistics course had been revamped at Donham's directive to emphasize the use of figures in management decision-making, and judgment in the use of figures. Donham also had wanted the human relations concepts taught by Mayo and Roethlisberger to have a prominent place in the new Management Controls course.

Early in 1943, on behalf of the Stat School, George Lombard began six weeks of daily visits to a small AAF base outside Boston—actually only a pair of fighter strips set at right angles in a cornfield—to research the human and structural challenges associated with the rapid expansion of the organization. He tried to ob-serve as much as possible about the human interactions at the base without disrupting normal routines. He recorded not only what various individuals said, but also what they did; and how what they did affected the work of others around them. This research drew upon the lessons of the Western Electric experi-ments of the 1930s to assess and depict the inherent complexities of a human or-ganization.

Lombard quickly perceived a collision of values and a pronounced incompatibil-ity between old and new types of warfare. The "old guard" in the Army, for ex-ample, placed great emphasis on the morning report, a daily personnel sum-mary which dated back to Revolutionary War days. More recently commissioned officers, however, tended to dismiss the morning report as time-consuming and irrelevant. For one thing, it failed to link the availability of people and the avail-ability of machines. Furthermore, the sheer scope of the AAF, and the nature of its new assignments, made "counting noses" a nearly hopeless task. In 1943 alone, for example, the AAF produced 65,000 pilots, 14,000 navigators, 14,000 bombardiers, 82,000 aerial gunners, and 530,000 technicians, many of whom re-ported for duty without official assign-ments. The result, in many cases, was chaos.

Small as it was, the air base being studied by Harvard's researchers offered homely examples of these same growing pains. One morning, for example, Lom-bard accompanied the adjutant—the staff officer responsible for personnel and ad-ministration, and a career officer—on a tour of the base. Crossing the cornfield, they came upon a private who was tend-

ing a small fire. The young man was evidently boiling some water. "What are you doing, soldier?" asked the adjutant. "Just making some hot water to wash my socks, sir," replied the private sheepishly. "Why aren't you on duty?" the adjutant demanded. "What's your assignment? What are you supposed to be doing?" The questions were critical ones, given the severe manpower shortages faced by this and similar units across the country. "I don't *have* an assignment, sir," came the response. "I don't know."

Starting with the summer of 1943, the first case that the incoming students were asked to consider, on their first day at Soldiers Field, was "The Umpteenth Fighter Squadron"—a rich, complicated, and jarringly realistic summary of George Lombard's study of the fighter squadron in the cornfield. The case raised numer-ous human and organization issues, in-cluding impetuousness, failure to del-egate authority, lack of persuasiveness, violation of the chain of command, and a general lack of coordination—in short, the reality that most of the statistical officers would soon encounter firsthand. The Umpteenth Fighter Squadron case became celebrated for the heated classroom ses-sions it provoked. Typically, the consen-sus of the first hour of discussion was simple: "Court-martial everybody!" But eventually, other voices would begin to be heard in the classroom: "But that doesn't make sense. It's obviously not that simple."

The subject matter at hand at the Stat School was not, in fact, statistics, but rather *administration* in the broadest sense. The statistical officers were being trained to assist their superiors in making informed decisions; therefore, they had to understand the problems and responsibilities faced by those superiors. After members of the school's first class had already demonstrated their utility, other AAF commands began putting in their requests for statistical assistance.

The AAF statistical control system had a major impact for two reasons. First, through a system of new and modified reports, new types of information were generated, including daily reports on aircraft status. Second, the information developed was used much more objectively, since it flowed up to Air Force headquarters through a parallel and largely independent command structure. This model of statistical control, furthermore, was adopted after the war by numerous companies. Perhaps the best-known example is the Ford Motor Company, which employed former Stat School researcher and faculty member Robert S. McNamara in precisely this capacity. By the end of the European war, the Statistical School had trained more than 3,000 officers.

A "Retread" Program

At the May 20, 1942, meeting of the Harvard Business School faculty, Dean Donham reported on the school's ever-changing relationship with the federal government. Donham, six weeks from retirement, proposed the last major initiative of his deanship. Envisioning a way to assist the war effort on a new level, he suggested the creation of a retraining program aimed at facilitating the conversion from peacetime to wartime employment. "War Production Training" was established to train up to 150 accomplished executives between the ages of 35 and 60. The course would be long—fifteen weeks—intensive, and residential.

Throughout the fall of 1942, the school had assumed that Harvard's name, combined with the widespread desire to contribute to the war effort, would be sufficient to populate the course. In fact, despite an approving New York Times editorial, only a few dozen inquiries had been received by early December. Donham's successor, Dean Donald David, promptly sent his administrative aide for the proposed program, Eugene M. Zuckert, on a cross-country quest to solicit participants. Zuckert's charge was to convince Harvard's friends in industry to identify "stranded" executives in their own cities and pay their expenses while they attended Harvard's retraining course. The sponsoring companies might (or might not) hire the retooled executives when they returned home. Officials at General Electric and Kodak—Zuckert's first two stops—were not persuaded. The program, they told him, was too broad-gauged. Furthermore, anyone who was valuable enough to warrant four months of intensive training was probably not stranded. Such an executive, they pointed out, would have already found war-related work.

At his next stop, headquarters of the Curtiss-Wright Corporation, Zuckert found the answer. With new facilities and thousands of workers in a setting of intense activity and seeming chaos, Peter Jansen, director of the airplane division, listened in silence to Zuckert's proposal. "Let me get this straight," he finally responded in a pronounced Dutch accent. "I should go downtown, and get dumbkopfs, send them to your school, and hire them when they get back?" "Mr. Jansen, that is exactly right," Zuckert replied. "Tell me," Jansen continued wryly, "why I should go downtown to get dumbkopfs, when I have so many right here?" The idea, although obvious in hindsight, simply hadn't before been considered: that companies could send their *own* employees to be retrained.

In reviewing the value of retraining, the program's principal architect, Professor Franklin E. Folts, concluded that it resulted from the broadening of executives who had narrow business experience: "They are shaken out of grooves." Housed together, without spouses or children, the retreads had a concentrated learning experience in and out of the classroom. The curriculum was demanding, in part because the program was under the close scrutiny of Washington, and in part because the chief executives with whom Folts had discussed the program liked the idea of "hard training for their promising men." Significantly, Folts saw personal growth not only in the students taking the course, but also in the faculty members who taught it. This suggested that responsibility for teaching in the program should be rotated among a larger faculty group—perhaps the whole Business School faculty.

How were the retreads "shaken out of grooves"? Folts mentioned several key factors: the four-month course was long, by executives' standards; it was intensive; and it was residential. But the retraining program had two additional strengths. First, it was an *integration* of various related subjects, achieved through careful faculty coordination. Second, the course rapidly evolved away from its original production-apprenticeship approach to a new general management model. The retraining program gradually began to emphasize the "administrative point of view." "This intensive course allows participants to handle greater responsibilities and to recognize and deal sympathetically with the problems of other departments and phases of production other than strictly their own. Their broad understanding would tend to eliminate factionalism." In an article on the retraining course in the magazine *Modern Industry*, published in the summer of 1943, the author wrote approvingly of Harvard's efforts to instill "the airplane view"—in other words, the general management perspective. "This advanced training course attempts to give the trainee an overall picture that might otherwise take him years to acquire."

As early as 1943, after only one run of the retraining course, the school was considering whether or not to continue it in some form after the war. Dean David felt the course *should* continue, and a faculty Subcommittee on Adult Education shared his conviction. The school could not be content with educating only MBAs—the business leaders of 10 and 20 years hence. "If the Harvard Business School wishes to make its greatest possible contribution to greater efficiency in American business," a faculty report stated, "the teaching and research facilities of the school must be made available to business executives who are *now* in positions of authority and responsibility." Not to be ignored were the potential benefits to be gained at Soldiers Field: "It may well be that one of the greatest benefits to the school of a program of this type will be the continued rounding out of the experience and background of the faculty itself."

Chapter 6

■

Building Organizational Capabilities

INTRODUCTION

The general manager's work of building and applying organizational capabilities is usually discussed as if it were independent from the formulation of strategy. It is clear from the preceding discussion of building strategy that this doesn't make a lot of sense. The activities involved are seldom separate and distinct. Crafting a strategy is an iterative process. Feedback from operations gives notice of changing environmental factors and changing resources to which strategy must be adjusted. To stay competitive, a business strategy must change in response to factors such as evolving knowledge and skills of its members, changes in the markets it services, and as fundamental a matter as the success or failure of the basic ideas in which the strategy is grounded.

Nonetheless, having acknowledged this close relationship, in this chapter we shift our focus from the general manager as strategist to the critical role of organization builder. As organization builder, the general manager's immediate challenge is to ensure that existing capabilities are tailored and applied to the strategic tasks at hand. With a longer time perspective, the challenge is cumulatively to build the capability of the organization so that its increasing breadth and depth give strategic flexibility to the corporation by increasing its range of response to emerging opportunities and threats.

TAILORING THE ORGANIZATION TO STRATEGY

For people to contribute creatively and effectively to the performance of the enterprise, the structure of the organization—its formal organizational design and the information, measurement, planning, resource allocation, compensation, and incentive systems that support it—must be tailored to the relevant aspects of corporate strategy and current conditions. This sounds like a fairly didactic statement and to some extent it is. There is a certain amount of straightforward architecture in the design of organization, which is reflected in the following discussion. There is also a top-down quality to the presentation because the design—which implicitly means the delegation of responsibility—is inherently the task of a business leader. Even if a general manager chooses some version of self-managed teams as an organizational form, he or she has to assign responsibility to the team and be sure that the information, measurement, resource allocation, and inventive systems are congruent.

Nonetheless, the way in which the task of design is accomplished—especially whether organization members are involved in the process—has a dramatic impact on the usefulness of the result. A more dynamic view of the design process is developed in the subsequent sections of the chapter. Finally, the cases make clear that what is presented neatly here with the aim of clarity can become quite messy in the conditions of an operating company.

Many steps are involved in the process of design, and the sequencing can be quite important. Though they are described here in a linear fashion, it is often necessary to approach steps in parallel or even reverse order.

1. Once a strategy is tentatively or finally set, the key tasks to be performed and the kinds of decisions required for its implementation must be identified. This analysis is hard work. It is the sort of project currently associated with reengineering.

2. Responsibility for key tasks and decisions must be assigned to individuals or groups in a manner that permits their efficient performance. For this purpose, understanding the capability of the people and subunits of the company relative to competition is vital. Many attempts at strategic change fail because the reorganization designed to facilitate implementation assigns new tasks without reference to the knowledge, experience, or skill of the people involved. This is especially true when individuals with narrow functional backgrounds are assigned to general management roles—for example, when profit centers are first introduced.

3. Formal provision for the coordination of activities thus separated must be made in various ways. (Profit centers are one popular example.) In addition to new layers of organization, supervisory project and committee organizations, task forces, and other ad hoc units are often economical. Unfortunately, the prescribed activities of these formally constituted bodies turn out never to be adequate by themselves; people have to want to make them work, and that usually means that they are supplemented by spontaneous voluntary coordination.[1] As we shall see, new incentives may be necessary to induce separate and potentially competitive constituencies to cooperate.

4. Information systems adequate for coordinating divided functions must be designed and installed. These systems tell those performing part of the task what they may need to know about the rest and let supervisors know what is happening within the scope of their responsibility. This task has ordinarily been considered routine, but research by Robert Kaplan and others has suggested that as fundamental a category of information as the cost of operations has often been distorted by outdated accounting systems.[2]

5. The tasks to be performed need to be arranged in a sequence comprising a program of action or a schedule of targets to be achieved at specified times. While long-range plans may be couched in general terms, operating plans must be relatively detailed. They help coordinate and pace the efforts of multiple units and establish standards against which short-term performance can be judged. Recently, managers have found it useful to examine these plans by mapping processes in detail. The result of such work often highlights the administrative infeasibility of some objectives given resources allocated or configured. Alternatively, it may be possible to reengineer the processes so that they require far fewer resources or less time for their accomplishment. This sort of work then necessitates a rethinking of strategy and organization.

6. Once the basic structure is settled, individuals and teams must be recruited and assigned to essential tasks in accordance with the skills that they possess or can develop. Training programs and pilot efforts may turn out to be critical aspects of a successful transition. Learning is seldom accomplished efficiently through random efforts at new tasks.

7. Actual performance, as described by formal reports and assessed by managers and customers, must be compared with plans and standards in order to measure organizational achievement, individual and subunit competence, and the adequacy of internal standards. Performance measures are fundamental to the process; if they don't change, it is rare that the behavior of the organization in question changes at all.

8. The compensation and incentive schemes of the company need to be examined to ensure that the way individual performance is measured in both quantitative and qualitative terms is aligned with the corpora-

---

[1] Chester Barnard called this the "informal organization." See Chester Barnard, *The Functions of the Executive* (Cambridge: Harvard University Press, 1939), chapter 9.

[2] See Robert S Kaplan and H Thomas Johnson's discussion of the need for activity-based costing in *Relevance Lost* (Boston: Harvard Business School Press, 1991).

tion's goals. Since individual motives are complex and multiple, incentives should range from those that are universally appealing—such as adequate compensation and a supportive organizational climate—to specialized financial rewards and other forms of recognition designed to fit individual needs and unusual accomplishments.

9.   In addition to financial and nonfinancial incentives and rewards for performance, what Robert Simon calls "boundary systems" of constraints and controls must be devised to contain inappropriate activity and enforce standards, especially ethical standards.[3] These boundary controls, like incentives, are both formal and informal. In an era where it is often deemed highly desirable to pay significant incentives for unusual levels of current performance, general managers often find that much time and attention need to be devoted to ensuring that managers avoid the temptation to cross the boundaries of corporate and legal standards in order to earn more for themselves.

10.   Provision for the continuing development of required technical and managerial skills is a high priority, beyond the kinds of special training and development needed for the implementation of reorganization. The development of individual capabilities must take place in the context of their assigned responsibilities. General managers often find it useful to supplement this kind of on-the-job development with intermittent formal instruction and study. The process of building general management careers is discussed in Chapter 9.

11.   Finally, energetic personal leadership is necessary for growth and achievement in any organization. Organizations, particularly successful ones, have a tendency to run down, in the process of which individual contributors at all levels become complacent. A key task of general managers is to fight complacency. The style with which this is accomplished may vary. Some managers use fear, others uncertainty, and others intracompany competition; examples of each are evident in this book's cases. But leadership must be expressed in a clearly perceived fashion that is natural for the manager and consistent with the requirements imposed upon the organization by its strategy and membership.

The cases in this chapter provide the opportunity to assess the appropriateness of the current structure and systems to the chosen strategy and competitive environment. In Colgate Palmolive, for example, you are asked to consider the structures and human resource policies that will best enable the company to take advantage of its corporatewide assets and its presence in dozens of countries.

The general manager must be concerned not only with the intellectual logic of aligning the organization and strategy as just outlined but also with the psychodynamics of aligning management processes and the

---

[3] Robert Simons, *Levers of Control* (Harvard Business School Press, 1995), chapters 6 and 7.

people who effect implementation. Increasingly managers recognize that superior organizational performance requires high member commitment to both corporate ends and means.

For commitment to develop, the structural elements and systems must be congruent with the company's strategic tasks and with the needs and aspirations of its middle managers and other employees. For example, the division of labor and definition of jobs must both efficiently address strategic tasks *and* meet the needs of those who occupy the jobs. In addition, a common theme in especially effective organizations in the 1990s is involvement designed to unleash the ideas and commitment of members.

BEYOND ORGANIZATION AS AN ARCHITECTURAL TASK

The effective general manager leads strategy and implementation but provides others with opportunities to influence them. Indeed, the interdependence of strategy formulation and implementation makes middle management and employee involvement essential in both. To achieve planned results, goals must be known; to achieve superior results, goals and means must be so wholly accepted that they stimulate extraordinary effort and ingenuity. Consider a most common example. Sales or service persons often encounter in the field early clues to the need for change. Textbooks have always urged companies to tap this early warning system, and most try. But if sales and service people doubt the interest of top management in their response, they may shrug their shoulders and shift their attention to other immediately rewarding tasks. In contrast, if they believe that top management is open to influence, they will go out of their way to report the opportunity and seek whatever communication channels are open to them.

Effective general managers express by their actions, if not in so many words, that their intention is as much to maintain and develop a cooperative and creative organization and to foster effective execution as it is to lay plans and measure performance against plan. Another example helps illustrate the point. To involve committed team members in building strategy, some leaders invite their comments on the feasibility of strategic alternatives. The natural resistance to change that can be expected to generate negative response to new ideas can be turned to constructive use if managers involve the operating organization in consideration of such objections before plans are frozen. By attempting to achieve amendment, acceptance, and understanding beforehand, management can use the process of change as an experience that reinforces the leadership's commitment to the members.

The implication of these examples is that the process of modifying company organization, structure, and administrative policies and practices can permit and sustain involvement and increase commitment to company purposes. Having a clearly defined job with lateral and upper limits has become less and less attractive to present generations of educated employees and middle managers. The values they bring to a company include independence, aversion to arbitrary or unreasoned authority, and ambition to do something important enough to deserve recognition. They expect to be treated as persons capable of responsibility and judgment. They will wish to have room to experiment and explore as they carry out their assignments and reach beyond them.

For a company to tap the latent energy and creativity its employees bring to the job, they must be involved in the processes that shape the strategic aspects of their work. Some of the companies we study go beyond mere exposure of strategic possibilities for comment. Little Johnsonville Sausage involves factory workers in capital budgeting decisions, while General Electric uses a system called "work out" to form problem-solving teams that involve knowledgeable and affected workers from across all organizational lines. It is clear in these cases that when general managers take these steps that break down conventional hierarchical relationships, they have to be careful to deal sympathetically with the virtues and shortcomings of the results.

The cases in this chapter provide many examples of the potential for such involvement and describe a variety of approaches toward member involvement by the respective general managers, including at one end of the spectrum, in Johnsonville Sausage, delegation and empowerment as the major organizing principle. In this and other cases you can (a) consider whether top management provides for the appropriate involvement by the people who must implement strategy and (b) assess the effect of this involvement on company performance.

BUILDING ORGANIZATION CAPABILITY

Thus far, we have argued that ensuring the fit of the organization structure and systems with present strategic tasks is a vital responsibility of the general manager. Without that fit, the existing capabilities of the company are likely to be diffused or even misused. People and groups work at cross purposes, costs are too high, and morale suffers.

Building new organization capabilities is even more important for long-term performance of the corporation. Although an organization can hire new talent relatively quickly and consultants can bring new knowledge, the more complex repertoire that enables an organization to use people and knowledge effectively can be built only by coordinated actions on many fronts over a long time. A pervasive example of this idea is provided by the relative failure of most efforts at total quality management (TQM). It is easy enough to hire experts or bring in consultants, but the comprehensive and consistent effort required to make total quality a part of company culture has eluded most of those corporations that have tried.

Equally challenging to general managers is the fact that as they build new capabilities, they must attend to maintaining and renewing old ones from time to time. If maintenance activities are neglected, core organizational capabilities erode; if renewal activities are absent, the capability may become obsolete—out of sync with the competitive strategy. The challenge is analogous to that of a football coach. The basic skills of the team must be maintained and even improved at the same time that new systems of offense and defense are developed and deployed. Without sound blocking and tackling, a team cannot win, but in a truly competitive league, they must be innovative as well.

What do we mean by capabilities? In the management literature today, it is common to hear the concepts "organizational resources," "organizational competences," and "organizational capabilities" used more or less interchangeably.[4] Some authors try to make careful distinctions among them, but general usage is sloppy, with the same consequences noted in the discussion of strategy in Chapter 1. In this book we will distinguish between tradable assets such as machines, information, and experts—all of which can be bought or hired—and the ability of the organization to use technology, its reputation in the markets, and its knowledge about markets to serve customers. That ability is not tradable in the sense that you cannot buy it or sell it. It is what the organization knows how to do. And perhaps more important, capabilities include assumptions about people and how they should relate, the contribution made by the company's products and services, and ideas about how the company will compete—all of which give meaning to the working lives within the organization.

How do general managers think about organizational capabilities? They tend to regard the capabilities as embedded in the "organizational culture" or "work environment," the latter of which is the term we will use here. The work environment is the composite of particular values, beliefs, attitudes, practices, behavior patterns, and skills that are the manifestation of how the organization does business. Effective general managers place high priority on formulating the ideal work environment for their organization and on shaping the organization to this ideal.

We have already seen in many of the cases the potential power of unique work environments shaped by the general managers. Consider the

---

[4] B Barney, "Firm Resources and Sustained Competitive Advantage," *Journal of Management* 17 (March 1991), pp. 99–120; K R Conner, "A Historical Comparison of Resource-Based Theory and Five Schools of Thought within IO Economics," *Journal of Management*, March 1991; C K Prahalad and Gary Hamel, "The Core Competence of the Corporation," *Harvard Business Review*, May–June 1990; Hiroyuki Itami, "Over Extension and Invisible Assets," *Managing Invisible Assets* (Cambridge: Harvard University Press, 1987), chapter 8; Birger Wernerfelt, "A Resource-Based View of the Firm," *Strategic Management Journal*, 1984, pp. 171–180; J Pfeffer and G Salancik, *The External Control of Organizations* (New York: Harper & Row Publishers, 1978).

Schlumberger organization. It was characterized by humility despite the company's dominating position in the wire line business and its sustained record of high performance; this humility kept members on their toes, constantly striving for excellence. Schlumberger also promoted a "missionary" mentality among its engineers out in the field. The sense of a calling rather than a mere commercial occupation helped ensure that engineers far from headquarters would perform their mission in the best interests of both the customer and Schlumberger. At the same time the company maintained its dominance with heavy R&D investments. Over two decades, CEO Jean Riboud carefully and consistently built these and other qualities into the Schlumberger work environment. For example, he promoted humility and continual renewal by challenging the organization to strive for "total victory" and by "shaking the tree."

The cases that follow will permit you to analyze the nature of the work environment, how it contributes to capabilities and performance, and the levers the general manager is using to shape it. Each company's work environment is unique in the configuration of specific elements that comprise it as well as the particular competitive and administrative setting. Nonetheless, most work environments address certain common issues. Among the most important of these are the following:

- The necessity of maintaining an *outward* orientation toward customers, competitors, suppliers, and other potentially important groups at the same time that enormous effort is exerted inwardly to achieve efficiency and cooperation
- The necessity of *avoiding complacency*, of maintaining a sense of urgency in the face of the organization's desire for the peace of routine relationships and activity
- The importance of establishing the appropriate balance between *teamwork* and *star* contributors
- The necessity of *shared purpose* that makes pursuit of corporate objectives a unifying and exciting enterprise

Most enterprises start out with a keen sense of their markets and awareness of their competitors; some organizations nurture this outward orientation, and others become preoccupied with internal matters and lose their sense of the marketplace. Some companies preserve a sense of urgency and commitment to continuous improvement, while others become complacent with success.

These ideas are well illustrated in our cases. The two biggest players in the earth-moving equipment industry—Caterpillar and Komatsu—had come to differ sharply on these aspects of their work environments in the early 1980s, with important consequences for their competitiveness. Komatsu, the challenger with a growing share of the world market, was keenly aware of industry leader Cat's strengths and weaknesses, copying the former and exploiting the latter. Komatsu's CEO Kawai promoted this aspect of the work environment with the rallying cry "Maru C" (beat Cat) cited earlier and by insisting upon careful monitoring of Cat's products and practices. Meanwhile the relatively inward-oriented Caterpillar organization—smug about its impressive historical leadership position gained in the aftermath of World War II and confident of the traditional strategic and organizational formula that produced its past success—failed to take Komatsu seriously and to respond effectively to the challenge it posed. The "yellow paint in the blood" of Cat managers bound them together but blinded them to new threats.

It is hard to exaggerate the range of differences that can be observed in the weight that general managers place on teamwork (Nike and Microsoft) and individual stars (Apple's Steve Jobs and Jean-Louis Gassé). The contrast between the highly individualistic styles of the Apple project leaders and the apparently faceless contributions of Microsoft's "#15's" is dramatic. The contrast between the pair of earth-moving equipment competitors is also illustrative. Komatsu was strongly characterized by teams operating at many organizational levels, while Caterpillar was marked by jealously guarded silos of functional specialties that bucked issues up to the top of the company for resolution.

The cases also illustrate the power of shared purpose. We could see how the early work environment of Nike was energized by the shared objective of a bunch of Oregon amateurs to set back the world and beat Adidas. In the same way, the young talent of Microsoft was excited by the unbelievable prospect of building a $100 million company. But the giant Schlumberger and Marks & Spencer were also galvanized by powerful commitment to a strategy of providing unusual value for their respective consumers. This is the aspect of corporate strategy discussed in Chapter 1 that goes so far beyond mere economic positioning.

It is interesting that this strategic aspect of a company's work environment often uniquely reflects the metaphors its leaders and then its members employ. Several of our cases illustrate the idea. Nike was like a sports team—cooperating internally to win against the competition. The Apple organization aspired to be like the products it made. "Here's the most interesting thing about our culture—we are what we make!"[5] And Serengeti was characterized internally by the same type of partner relationships that underpinned its competitive strategy.

The way work environments are shaped to motivate, unify, employ teams and stars, and direct attention outward are only some of their important aspects. As you study the cases in this section, you will discover other aspects of work environments with important implications for the organizations' capabilities.

---

[5] "Reshaping Apple Computers' Destiny," Harvard Business School case 9-393-011, p. 3.

How Work Environments Contribute to Capability

A company's work environment can contribute to its capability and performance in many different ways. For example, shared commitment to corporate purpose focuses behavior on strategic tasks. We will see in Chapter 7 how important is Marks & Spencer's commitment to unique value. The work environment in Nordstrom, another retail chain, focuses everyone on serving the customer. A work environment can enable people to identify with the company, as did Apple's ideal of "empowering people through technology," or can be a source of meaning and motivation as in The Body Shop, where the "electricity and passion" bonded people to the company and energized them. It can provide shared criteria for decision making as illustrated by Schlumberger.

Work environments that are sufficiently distinctive to be known to job applicants can help recruit and select those who will probably prosper most in the environment. Lincoln Electric illustrates this advantage. Finally, work environments help shape the values and skills of future leaders and promote continuity over time. This source of continuity is an advantage in an organization like Hewlett-Packard, where the work environment has continued to be largely an asset, but was a disadvantage in the 1980s in IBM, General Motors, and Caterpillar, where the once powerfully effective work environments were not renewed and became barriers to the development of new capabilities.[6]

The Forces That Shape Work Environments

How are work environments shaped? General managers use many levers to form the unique set of elements that comprise the work environment. Their definition of goals and strategic imperatives can play a key role. Over two decades beginning in the mid-1960s, Komatsu's Kawai set a succession of very ambitious goals for quality, cost, and product performance features, each goal challenging the organization to new heights and together combining to create an extraordinary "can do" attitude on the part of Komatsu employees.

General managers' own styles can play a major role in setting the tone. Recall Anita Roddick's proposition, "What's imperative is the creation of a style that becomes a culture," and consider whether she in fact practiced what she proposed.

The structures and systems tailored to focus effort on strategic tasks have a powerful, longer-term effect on the work environment. They are the structural context for organizational activity. We can see at Marks & Spencer, for example, that structures and systems designed to achieve unusual lateral coordination along the value chain from suppliers and through the organization to customers not only channel present behavior

---

[6] Dorothy A Leonard-Barton, "Core Capabilities and Core Rigidities: A Paradox in Managing New Product Development," *Strategic Management Journal* 13, (1992), pp. 111–125.

but also shape mindsets, skills, and habits that become part of the work environment. Flatter structures, such as those Greenbury introduced, shorten vertical communication and also promote an egalitarian culture, while profit centers designed to coordinate effort around differentiated products, like those at Adams, can break down a cooperative culture. You will find many examples in the cases to come that powerfully illustrate the role of systems and structures in shaping work environments.

General managers also use the recruitment and promotion processes to shape and reinforce the desired work environment. Recall how Bill Gates recruited for raw intelligence, Jean Riboud recruited for character, and Anita Roddick recruited for social values. One could argue that each of these selection patterns not only aligned individuals with the strategy and organization but also helped create and reinforce the work environment.

SUMMARY

A critical role of the general manager is aligning the organization with the key tasks implicit in the chosen strategy, relying upon the design of structures, integrative mechanisms, information systems, work schedules, controls, rewards, selection criteria, and development programs. These elements of organization building are the basic blocking and tackling of strategy implementation. Each structural dimension must be aligned with others and with the strategy. In the cases that follow, it will be important to assess the quality of these alignments and identify elements, if any, that are weak links.

The effective general manager also takes a longer perspective and seeks to build powerful organization capability for the future; with this perspective he or she is likely to focus on the work environment. The work environment is distinct; it is the personality of the company, the derivative of many forces including many components of structural context as well the style of the manager. The work environment's effects are powerful and long term precisely because they are what gives meaning to work and what provides a basis for individuals to identify with the company. They provide shared but implicit decision criteria and shape the skills and mindsets of the future membership and leadership of the organizations.

The Adams Corporation (A)

In January 1987, the board of directors of the Adams Corporation simultaneously announced the highest sales in the company's history, the lowest aftertax profits (as a percentage of sales) in many decades, and the retirement (for personal reasons) of its long-tenured president and chief executive officer, Jerome Adams.

Founded in St. Louis in 1948, the Adams Brothers Company had long been identified as a family firm in both name and operating philosophy. Writing in a business history journal, a former family senior manager commented:

> My grandfather wanted to lead a business organization with ethical standards. He wanted to produce a quality product and a quality working climate for both employees and managers. He thought the Holy Bible and the concept of family stewardship provided him with all the guidelines needed to lead his company. A belief in the fundamental goodness of

mankind, in the power of fair play, and in the importance of personal and corporate integrity were his trademarks. Those traditions exist today.

In the early 1960s, two significant corporate events occurred. First, the name of the firm was changed to the Adams Corporation. Second, somewhat over 50 percent of the corporation's shares were sold by various family groups to the wider public. In 1980, all branches of the family owned or influenced less than one-fifth of the outstanding shares of Adams.

The Adams Corporation was widely known and respected as a manufacturer and distributor of quality, brand-name consumer products for the American, Canadian, and European (export) markets. Adams products were processed in four regional plants located near raw material sources. (No single plant processed the full line of Adams products, but each plant processed the main items in the line.) The products were stored and distributed in a series of recently constructed or renovated distribution centers located in key cities throughout North America, and they were sold by a company sales force in thousands of retail outlets—primarily supermarkets.

In explaining the original, long-term financial success of the company, a former officer commented:

> Adams led the industry in the development of unique production processes that produced a quality product at a very low cost. The company has always been production-oriented and volume-oriented, and it paid off for a long time. During those decades the Adams brand was all that was needed to sell our product; we didn't do anything but a little advertising. Competition was limited, and our production efficiency and raw material sources enabled us to outpace the industry in sales and profit. Our strategy was to make a quality product, distribute it, and sell it cheap.

> But that has all changed in the past 20 years. Our three major competitors have outdistanced us in net profits and market aggressiveness. One of them—a first-class marketing group—has doubled sales and profits within the past five years. Our gross sales have increased to over $1 billion, but our net profits have dropped continuously during that same period. While a consumer action group just designated us as "best value," we have fallen behind in marketing techniques; for example, our packaging is just out of date.

Structurally, Adams was organized into eight major divisions. Seven of these were regional sales divisions with responsibility for distribution and sales of the company's consumer products to retail stores in their areas. Each regional sales division was further divided into organizational units at the state, county, and/or trading-area level. Each sales division was governed by a corporate price list in the selling of company products, but each had some leeway to meet the local competitive price developments. Each sales division was also assigned (by the home office) a quota of salespeople it could hire and was given the salary ranges within which these people could be employed. All salespeople were on straight salary with an expense reimbursement salary plan, which resulted in compensation under industry averages.

A small central accounting office accumulated sales and expense information for each of the several sales divisions on a quarterly basis, and it prepared the overall company financial statements. Each sales division received, without commentary, a quarterly statement showing the following information for the overall division: number of cases processed and sold, sales revenue per case, and local expenses per case.

Somewhat similar information was obtained from the manufacturing division. Manufacturing division accounting was complicated by variations in the cost of obtaining and processing the basic materials used in Adams's products. These variations—particularly in procurement—were largely beyond the control of the division. The accounting office, however, did have one rough external check on manufacturing division effectiveness: A crude market price existed for case lot goods, sold by smaller firms to some large national chains.

Once every quarter, the seven senior sales vice presidents met with general management in St. Louis. Typically, management discussion focused on divisional sales results and expense control. The company's objective of being number one—the largest selling line in its field—directed group attention to sales as compared to budget. All knew that last year's sales targets had to be exceeded, no matter what. The manufacturing division vice president sat in on these meetings to explain the product availability situation. Because of his St. Louis office location, he frequently talked with Jerome Adams about overall manufacturing operations and specifically about large procurement decisions.

The Adams Corporation had a trade reputation for being very conservative with its compensation program. All officers were on a straight salary program. An officer might expect a modest salary increase every two or three years; these increases tended to be in the thousand-dollar range, regardless of divisional performance or company profit position. Salaries among the seven sales divisional vice presidents ranged from $125,000 to $170,000, with the higher amounts going to more senior officers. Jerome Adams's salary of $200,000 was the highest in the company. There was no corporate bonus plan. A very limited stock option program was in operation, but the depressed price of Adams stock meant that few officers exercised their options.

The corporate climate at Adams had been of considerable pride to Jerome Adams. "We take care of our family" was his oft-repeated phrase at company banquets honoring long-service employees. "We are a team, and it is a team spirit that has built Adams into its leading position in this industry." No member of first-line, middle, or senior management could be discharged (except in cases of moral crime or dishonesty) without a personal review of his case by Mr. Adams; as a matter of fact, executive turnover at Adams was very low. Executives at all levels viewed their jobs as lifetime careers. There was no compulsory retirement plan, and some managers were still active in their mid-70s.

The operational extension of this organizational philosophy was quite evident to employees and managers. For over 75 years, a private family trust provided emergency assistance to all members of the Adams organization. Adams led its industry in the granting of educational scholarships, in medical insurance for employees and managers, and in encouragement of its members to give corporate and personal time and effort to community problems and organizations.

Jerome noted two positive aspects of this organizational philosophy:

> We have a high percentage of long-term employees—Joe Girly, a guard at East St. Louis, completes 55 years with us this year, and every one of his brothers and sisters has worked here. And it is not uncommon for a vice president to retire with a blue pin—that means 40 years of service. We have led this industry in manufacturing process innovation, quality control, and value for low price for decades. I am proud of our accomplishments, and this pride is shown by everyone from janitors to directors.

Industry sources noted that there was no question that Adams was number one in terms of manufacturing and logistic efficiency.

In December 1986, the annual Adams management conference gathered over 80 members of Adams's senior management in St. Louis. Most expected the usual formal routines—the announcement of 1986 results and 1987 budgets, the award of the "Gold Flag" to the top processing plant and sales division for exceeding targets, and the award of service pins to executives. All expected the usual social good times. It was an opportunity to meet and drink with "old buddies."

After a series of task force meetings, the managers gathered in a banquet room—

good-naturedly referred to as the "Rib Room" since a local singer, Eve, was to provide entertainment. In the usual fashion, a dais with a long, elaborately decorated head table was at the front of the room. Sitting at the center of that table was Jerome Adams. Following tradition, Adams's vice presidents, in order of seniority with the company, sat on his right. On his left sat major family shareholders, corporate staff, and a newcomer soon to be introduced.

After awarding service pins and the Gold Flags of achievement, Adams formally announced what had been corporate secrets for several months. First, a new investing group had assumed a control position on the board of Adams. Second, Price Millman would take over as president and CEO of Adams.

Introducing Millman, Adams pointed out the outstanding record of the firm's new president: "Price got his MBA in 1978, spent four years in control and marketing, and then was named as the youngest divisional president in the history of the Tenny Corporation. In the past years, he has made his division the most profitable in Tenny and the industry leader in its field. We are fortunate to have him with us. Please give him your complete support."

In a later informal meeting with the divisional vice presidents, Millman spoke about his respect for Adams's past accomplishments and the pressing need to infuse Adams with "fighting spirit" and "competitiveness." He said, "My personal and organizational philosophy are the same—the name of the game is to fight and win. I almost drowned, but I won my first swimining race at 11 years of age! That philosophy of always winning is what enabled me to build the Ajax Division into Tenny's most profitable operation. We are going to do this at Adams."

In conclusion, Miliman commented:

> The new owner group wants results. They have advised me to take some time to think through a new format for Adams's operations—to get a corporate design that will improve our effectiveness. Once we get that new format, gentlemen, I have but one goal—each month must be better than the past.

Colgate-Palmolive: Company in Transition (A)

As Reuben Mark, currently president of the Colgate-Palmolive Company, and about-to-be-elected chief executive officer, prepared for a presentation to the members of CP's board of directors on May 3, 1984, he picked up a newly circulated investment analyst's report downgrading the company from a "buy" to a "hold" recommendation with the comment:

> Because of another quarter of lackluster profits, we suggest this stock only for those investors seeking a defensive posture in the event of a repeat of our recent recession.

As he read, Mark reflected on the words "lackluster" and "defensive" and the real challenge that these identified for him as the company's new CEO. He thought too of the five years of rebuilding and reestablishment of old values upon which his predecessor, Keith Crane, and he had worked so hard. He felt the success of

these efforts had positioned the company once again with the strengths it had enjoyed for much of its 178-year history. Now was the time to capitalize on the strengths. The question was how.

BACKGROUND

The Colgate-Palmolive Company (CP) was one of the oldest manufacturers of consumer products in the United States, tracing its roots back to Colgate and Co., which was founded in 1806. Upon the merger in 1928 of Colgate and the Palmolive-Peet Company, a major soap producer, the foundations for the modern Colgate-Palmolive Company were laid. At the time of the acquisition, oil and perfume processing companies owned by the two firms were sold to allow them to concentrate on the production and marketing of such products as Palmolive soap, Fab washing powder, and Colgate Ribbon dental creme. In 1938, the last of the Colgate family to hold the position of president relinquished it to E.H. Little, a director and senior marketing manager.

The Little–Lesch Era

Mr. Little was to lead the company for 23 years. During this time, primary emphasis was placed on the development of CP's international business. In 1938, the company realized 28 percent of its $99.4 million in sales and 41 percent of its $4.9 million in profits from international operations. By 1961, international sales represented 53 percent of the company's total of $604.9 million, with profits from international business making up 78 percent of the total for that year of $22.2 million. By 1961, CP was conducting business in one form or another in 85 countries. It was during this time that a global organization philosophy was developed as well, with every senior executive expected to have extensive foreign experience.

Little's successor, George Lesch, had worked in Mexico for 15 years prior to taking responsibility for European operations. During his years as CEO (1960–1971), he adopted much the same philosophy and policies of his predecessors. He was followed by David Foster, who set out to recast the company in a different mold.

The Foster Era—A Change in Emphasis

Foster had spent his business career at Colgate, having started in the export department of the U.K. company. After becoming U.K. general manager, he had the responsibility for Europe, prior to moving to the U.S. company and then to corporate. He concluded that Colgate was a company with all of its investment in consumer businesses that he felt had limited growth potential. For that reason, in the early 1970s, he set out to diversify the company's operations. Colgate entered the health care products business in 1972 with the acquisition of the Kendall Company, a manufacturer and marketer of disposable health care products. The following year, CP acquired Helena Rubenstein, a marketer of women's cosmetics. A golf and tennis sporting goods division was begun with the acquisition in 1974 of the Ram Golf Corp. and the Bancroft Racket Co., followed by other small sport equipment companies in the United States and overseas. To promote these businesses, major sponsorship activity was initiated with women's golf and tennis tournaments.

Soon thereafter, the company acquired Riviana Foods, the largest U.S. producer and marketer of rice sold under several brand names. Also included in the company was Hill's Pet Products, a manufacturer and marketer of specialty (dietary) pet foods sold through veterinarians, breeders, and pet stores. As part of an effort to explore alternative marketing methods, in 1978 CP acquired Princess House, Inc., a U.S. company in the business of offering crystal glassware and other "top of the table" items through a party plan (in-home) sales method.

Foster's concept was that these diverse business groups would provide greater growth than Colgate could achieve in its traditional markets. A complete list of CP's acquisitions during this era is presented in Exbibit 1. Unfortunately, the anticipated growth did not occur and profitability was less than planned, putting excessive demands for profitability on the traditional businesses.

The Crane Era—Back to Basics

By 1979, when Keith Crane (who had worked across the globe for Colgate, as well as run Kendall) succeeded Foster as CEO, Colgate could claim to be a significantly diversified consumer goods company, with 30 percent of its revenues realized from products other than those in the traditional household and personal care markets. But Crane realized that the broad diversification was not working as forecast. What he inherited was a loose confederation of companies, associated with a company whose main-line general managers had seen much of the cash generated from their household and personal care products siphoned off to finance acquisitions and the operations of other businesses. And the anticipated return was nowhere in sight.

As Crane analyzed the overall business, he concluded that Colgate had become a company that was losing momentum in its traditional business. In particular, he was concerned about the quality of the company's soaps and dentifrices, the lack of aggressive research and development activity, and the reactive nature of much of CP's marketing efforts, particularly in the United States, where it ranked poorly in many product categories behind Procter & Gamble and Lever Brothers. He also did not like the fact that managers of the company's traditional businesses thought that they were being measured on the various ways that they were able to reduce the costs of ongoing business activity, rather than on their talent to manage their individual subsidiaries. This situation had been compounded as the size of the staff at the company's headquarters in New York had increased to track their progress, and other staff had been added to try to improve the performance of the newly acquired firms.

Crane, described by his associates as a quiet, thoughtful professional with an excellent grasp of the global business and brilliant recall, set out to get CP's management "back to basics" and put a dispirited organization back on track. Among other

things, he established a pattern of visiting every one of the company's global subsidiaries at least every other year. According to one of Crane's contemporaries, "He went around the world. The people in the field couldn't wait to have him back. They knew he didn't forget, and they knew that he basically was on their side. He was the first CEO to recognize that all areas of the business were important to the whole, not just marketing. He preached the need for the total manager."

As one country manager at the time put it,

> During the Foster era, the company lived off the fat built up during the heyday of international expansion under E.H. Little and George Lesch. However, in 1979, the company was centralized and operated by putting increasing profit demands on its base businesses, especially outside the United States. I nearly quit that year. Why? Because I couldn't build the business by just delivering profits without a longer view which included investment funds. Without that outlook, the company would continue to be a mediocre performer. It was only the prospect that Crane would redirect the company against its core strength that made me decide to stay on. And that is what Crane did.

Product Health

The major rallying cry of the Crane era became "product health." One of the operating vice presidents remembered a typical meeting with a country GM at that time:

> The GMs had been rewarded for saving product costs an inch a year. Keith would ask why the formula was inferior to competition, and why it hadn't been fixed. The GM would say, "I can't fix it; it'll

reduce profits." Keith would reply, "Put that aside. Fix it. Without a competitive product, there soon won't be any profits."

The 1982 annual report focused on this effort, emphasizing significant increases in investment in research and development, capital expenditures for new plant and equipment, product quality, advertising effectiveness, and sales "firepower," which meant improving and increasing the size of the corporation's many sales departments around the world. Nearly all of this investment was centered on household and personal care (especially dental) products. Exhibit 2 contains information showing trends in investments in product health between 1979 and 1983. These investments had produced a negative cash flow position for the company in recent years.

Global product and market information posed another problem. According to Reuben Mark, whom Crane named president and chief operating officer in 1982, "We couldn't make any sense out of the data we had. For a given product line, it was collected and analyzed in countries all around the world under different assumptions and with different methods."

In spite of the staff organization in New York, there was limited communication or coordination among country managers. In part, this was a legacy from an era where each country manager operated very independently. Managers of CP's most successful businesses in countries such as France, Mexico, Australia, Colombia, and the Philippines had been left to manage their businesses as they saw fit, linked only by financial reporting requirements. While this resulted in an organization able to respond to local competitive pressures, it impeded the exchange of

important information about new formulas, products, advertising, manufacturing, or sales techniques that were suitable for more than one country. Further, corporate support efforts tended to be splintered by too many individual country requests, with the larger countries dominating the available resources. The result was that the company was not making use of its global strengths and knowledge to advance its business.

Business Development Groups

In 1981, Colgate decided to create Business Development Groups (BDGs) responsible for coordinating product development, manufacturing, and marketing for core product categories (oral, detergents, soaps, liquid cleaners) on a worldwide basis. Described by one manager as "the best thing as a company we ever did," the groups were officed in New York and staffed with experienced, strong general managers from CP's operating subsidiaries. Although the BDGs were organized as staff versus line, the experience level of each group, plus the corporate commitment to support them, gained them respect in the field, where their suggestions received very serious attention. As one senior executive put it, "Since no one had any experience with the BDG concept, there was skepticism in the field as well as among N.Y. staff. In retrospect, I can't imagine how we operated without the BDGs."

The first BDG to be created was for oral products. According to the vice president selected to head it:

> I was managing Spain at the time, having come previously from the U.K. operation. The basic goal was to fix and strengthen the oral business on a global

basis, primarily through coordinated research and development and marketing. We began comparing product quality across countries. We asked whether we were getting proper share of market and "share of voice" in our advertising. It required a lot of traveling, up to 100 days per year. I divided my time between the general manager and marketing manager in each country. On a cross-boundary product introduction, for example, the hardest person to persuade was the first guy. We didn't ever say you had to do it; but we could make cooperation sound awfully attractive. What we did insist on is that country GMs have strategies for every brand. We encouraged them to tap into us for new ideas. And if the idea was especially good, we occasionally said, "You are going with it unless you can make a good argument for not doing it."

The BDG concept was well entrenched by the end of 1983. As a result, the company experienced an increase in situations where a product developed internally in one country could be introduced rapidly across the globe. In their report to shareholders for 1983, Crane and Mark pointed out that:

> Worldwide, the company's market share advanced in several key categories, following the aggressive introduction of 162 new and revitalized products in 44 countries coupled with programs to increase the consumer franchise of existing brands. The development of our business was global in nature with a substantial portion of the direction and guidance being centrally driven by the Business Development Group, which manages our global category activities.

A summary of market share data for all countries in which Colgate-Palmolive sold its products is shown in Exhibit 3.

Research and Development

With the BDGs' increasing emphasis on global strategies and product development, research and development for household and personal products were given clear direction on development needs. Over 200 additional professionals were hired to support the global activity and to develop the new products needed for the future. Most of these were added to the staff of the company's primary research and development facility at Piscataway, N.J.

Advertising Effectiveness

To facilitate more effective investment in advertising, and particularly to increase the creative excellence required around the world, the number of advertising agencies worldwide to which CP entrusted its advertising efforts was reduced from 13 to 3. As pointed out in the 1983 annual report, "The alignment of our major core brands with three international agencies will provide greater coordination and marketing thrust."

The Operating Committee

Keith Crane also formed an operating committee, composed of seven senior executives chaired by Reuben Mark, to coordinate worldwide business activities. According to one senior executive, "Keith and Reuben set about to expand these people's understanding of the business. Global business reviews were held, with all senior executives expected to attend. Over time all members of management benefited, because each gained an overall knowledge of the worldwide business and thus was more effective in their own responsibilities."

Divestiture

To refocus its efforts and free up the capital to invest in its core businesses, CP's management also began divesting some of the businesses acquired in the previous era. The first to go was Maui Divers of Hawaii Ltd. It was followed by many others, as indicated in Exhibit 1.

Control Systems

A budget was negotiated between corporate and the field. Once agreed, each subsidiary company and operating unit supplied a series of financial reports, including a breakdown of the budget by month and a substantial amount of detailed analysis, to the corporate controller's office at headquarters. After consolidation of each set of divisional data by the corporate controller's office, the resultant reports and supporting detail were then reviewed (respectively) with the three executive vice presidents, each of whom controlled about one-third of the world. Debates between the controller's office and divisional management often ensued, resulting in detailed and protracted discussions over the accuracy of the information and its significance for identifying the strengths and weaknesses of the respective areas.

Performance Measurement

Although everyone had agreed upon a budget, its use as a measurement of subsequent performance was of minimal significance, since typically it was immediately superseded each year by the "latest estimate" system, a monthly submission of performance data and updated estimates from each operating unit. As a result, a general manager's remuneration and bonus, far from being related directly to performance versus his agreed budget, was often equally based on a division manager's view of how a particular GM was doing. At the time a GM's bonus amounted to only a small proportion of his salary (salaries typically ranged from $75,000 to $125,000). Stock options existed, although distribution of this benefit was also believed to be based more upon arbitrary judgment than on performance.

Strategic Planning

Prior to 1982, no real strategic plan existed, nor did the function exist.

One of Colgate's major strategic issues centered around the wide range of success the company experiences from market to market. In Europe, for example, their indices of per capita sales vary dramatically from a high of 22.70 in France, to a low of 3.73 in Holland (Exhibit 3A). Moreover, in weaker markets, such as the United Kingdom, Colgate frequently has one or two strong product lines, plus a larger number of weaker product entries (Exhibit 3B).

As Colgate's top management pondered the issue of supplying strategic direction, they were unclear about which product categories and markets to emphasize, as well as how to think about low-share brands and marginal product categories within each market.

Besides the issue of whether to emphasize strong markets or bolster weaker ones, Reuben Mark faced the added complication of how to coordinate global brand plans with local market plans. Should strategic control and resource allocation decisions be vested at headquarters, with the Europe GM (Exhibit 3C), or with the local market GM? And how much local initiative and flexibility would be possible, given Colgate's limited resources and the many demands on them? For example, would Mark and his colleagues at corporate headquarters have to first develop a corporate strategy for Colgate and its major product lines, or could he let the countries (or regions) operate largely on their own?

Competition

Colgate's two principal competitors were Unilever and Procter & Gamble. While Colgate faced several sizeable local competitors in a few countries, their chief competitor was nearly always one of these two giants.

Within the United States, P&G was the dominant soap and toilet goods producer. They were regarded as aggressive, technologically strong, and a "world class" marketer. They had a long history of successful new products and product improvements aimed at giving them a performance edge with consumers. As a result, they were the category leader in most of their key categories. P&G was a strong company financially and they consistently spent roughly 3 percent of sales on R&D and 8.5 percent on advertising.[1]

Outside the United States, Colgate's primary competitor was nearly always Unilever. In the United States, their Lever Brothers' subsidiary had historically been the second or third entry in the category behind P&G and, sometimes, Colgate. But internationally, Unilever's market position was often number one or a strong number two. Like P&G, Unilever was strong technically and an aggressive marketeer. For example, they typically spent 2 percent of sales on R&D and 7.5 percent on advertising. They were also regarded as a truly global company, capable of adapting successfully to a wide variety of local competitive challenges. Thus, on a worldwide basis, Colgate management regarded Unilever as its chief competitive threat.

Thus, in developing its local strategies, Colgate could usually focus its efforts mainly against Unilever or P&G.

In the marketplace, however, Colgate had to take into account its key distributor customers, if they were to be successful. For they often faced a serious problem in competing for shelf space and promotional support from their retailers and wholesalers. Moreover, in most major countries, the distributive trade was growing more concentrated and, consequently, more difficult to deal with. This was a particular problem for smaller manufacturers and lower-volume brands, but also for the second or third competitor in the major categories.

THE COMPANY IN 1984

In early 1984, Reuben Mark could look back on a number of accomplishments that he and Crane had achieved. In his words:

> The BDGs were humming. Our investment in manufacturing to catch up was largely completed; we were now going further to invest in several large, new facilities. The product quality battle was being won. Our managers had their eyes once again on the core categories. Our

---

[1] In comparison, Colgate spends 2 percent on R&D and 6.7 percent on advertising, but on a much narrower product range.

shares were coming back from the brink of having them fall away from us.

Colgate's worldwide market shares in selected product categories for 1979 and 1984 were:

	1979	1984
Colgate toothpaste	29.8%	33.9%
Detergents	9.8	11.1
Hard surface cleaners	15.1	18.0

Mark believed, however, that several strategic challenges still remained. Although volume and market share growth had occurred among some products and in some markets, holes existed in the product lines themselves. In addition, product category growth between 1983 and 1988 was expected to slow to a level below that achieved between 1977 and 1983.

A chart of the organization Mark inherited in 1984 is shown in Exhibit 4. He wondered whether any major changes would be required in order to manage the company more aggressively and competitively.

One thing the company had not done in the eyes of a number of observers was convert strengths to profits. The latter had been relatively flat, as shown in Exhibits 5, 6, and 7.

CONVERSATIONS WITH MANAGEMENT

When Keith Crane told him confidentially in late 1983 that he was thinking about retirement, Reuben Mark initiated a series of informal conversations with his senior managers in an attempt to elicit their views about where the company should be going and how it might get there.

One country GM had offered the following:

Somewhat to my surprise, the BDGs have worked in bringing new ideas to us. But unless you rekindle the long-held attitude among each of us that "I'm the fastest gun in my territory," we won't move fast enough to take advantage of the opportunities and stay profitably ahead of competition.

Also, what we really need to do is increase our ability to make acquisitions at the country level in order to fill in gaps in our product offerings. For example, the U.K. has no presence in the household detergent market.

Another had commented:

It was hard to get through to New York for awhile. Keith changed that by coming out here a lot. But you've still got too many people in the New York office who can shut down lines of communication. What are we going to do about that? You want results, not reports.

The manager of a BDG stated:

When this function was created, we pulled some of our best people from out of our subsidiaries. I think that seriously depleted the management in several of those countries. We're going to have to think about how to fix that.

One country GM complained:

We used to be able to count on being in a country long enough, sometimes 8 to 10 years, to really understand the issues and make a significant impact. That has changed in the past few years as new positions had to be filled. How do you expect us to move every several years and do much more than learn where to shop for groceries before we're moved again? It may be great for my exposure but it isn't doing much for the management of my subsidiary.

A senior manager who previously had had responsibility for a major European subsidiary with significant manufacturing capability remarked:

> We keep our eye on marketing strategy and product quality, but have not devoted enough attention to manufacturing costs. As a result, they have edged up steadily. Surely, there is a place for new techniques such as just-in-time procedures in our business. It may cost money, but it should be seen as part of our effort to build product health. Given the volume of certain products that we produce, we should be the low-cost producer. We're not.

The GM for the United States, in discussing the performance of his organization, suggested:

> You know, it's difficult operating under the nose of corporate management. As a result, it's not the preferred assignment among country GMs. The U.S. company has never been run as a free-standing subsidiary. That has to change. We need to be given the tools to be the masters of our destiny, like other CP subsidiaries. And of course this is Procter & Gamble's stronghold. You can develop an inferiority complex in the United States if you don't watch out.

One senior manager in the New York office commented:

> We've regained some lost ground in research and development. But that's just a beginning. We've rebuilt the core products. Now we need new products.

Another field manager said:

> In the process of emphasizing cost-cutting to supply money for the late

1970s' acquisitions, and to cover profit forecast shortfalls, we beat what entrepreneurial spirit there was out of our managers. They contributed but never benefited. That doesn't develop superior managers, only defensive ones.

Importantly, though, Mark also heard managers express the opinion that politics had never played a significant role in company management. As one put it, "Tirecutters don't stay around here long." They hoped it could be kept that way.

One senior manager, whose experience, like most of those in the New York headquarters, had been solely with the core CP businesses, said:

> We have divested a number of the businesses that were acquired in the 70s. But those we have left still constitute a major distraction. Why don't we get rid of the lot? There is plenty of opportunity in our core businesses.

One vice president in New York commented:

> We've been able to make progress without a major change in organization. Whether this can continue or not, I'm not sure. While we've sold off companies, the closest we've come to letting anyone go in our remaining firms was an early retirement program last year. This is almost a Japanese company, in which people rarely have been terminated for reasons of poor performance. We don't even take the job of appraising performance seriously, nothing like what I experienced in the company I worked with before coming here. My experience has been that people want to be tougher appraisers but don't know how to do it. And given the geography of this company of 40,000 employees, we're going to have to supplement the "world tour" as a means of communicating. We've just started bringing in managers to our lower

ranks from outside; we'll have to decide whether to accelerate the program and begin to fill more senior positions that way, too, if the company significantly changes its goals for growth.

Yet another vice president in the New York office expressed the opinion that:

> During the recent programs to rebuild the product lines, the GMs in the countries have started to develop bad habits. They're beginning to forget that the purpose of rebuilding is to strengthen our businesses in order to increase our profitability, not just stay even.

One of Mark's greatest concerns was how to reintroduce a spirit of independence and entrepreneurship that had once characterized the company's management. He envisioned the need as ranging from the contribution of new ideas of all kinds to the internal development of new products and even new businesses.

REUBEN MARK BECOMES CEO

When Keith Crane approached him to become the new CEO of Colgate, Mark echoed his thoughts:

> I was surprised by the suddenness. Keith was only 60 and I thought that he wanted to stay until at least 62. Nevertheless, it was a dream I had been holding inside for years—running my own company. Being given the opportunity to direct and lead a company like Colgate, especially since it was already on the road to recovery, and making it succeed, was something I had waited for all my life. I was a little apprehensive about taking on the many essential duties that required immediate attention, yet at the same time was very excited by the challenge.

Mark was viewed as a very open, people-oriented leader and a strong moti-

vator.[2] Outgoing by nature, Mark took delight in knowing many of the company's employees on a first-name basis. He connected with people on the plant floor as easily as he did in the boardroom.

On his plant visits he not only would address many employees individually, but would also listen and learn about their jobs, their problems, and their frustrations. More important, he acknowledged each person's advice and responded personally afterwards—by letter, phone call, or card—whenever possible.

Knowing how to motivate also meant knowing when to recognize and reward good performance. Mark's "You Can Make a Difference" award was one example of his recognition of a job well done. By the same token, he did not pass out compliments for the sake of "winning" people over to his way of thinking. Instead, he opted for open discussions, inviting criticism and suggestions from his executives when disagreements arose.

Mark realized that one man could not do it all. He firmly believed that the success of Colgate was dependent not only upon his leadership ability, but also on the people who worked for and reported to him. "Mark has allowed people to take risks," stated one senior general manager. Mark knew that he needed support from people at every level who understood his goals, believed in them, and then committed themselves to making them happen. He was energetic and sensitive in his dealings with people, but direct and decisive when the circumstances warranted. Colleagues commented that "he doesn't have an outsized ego," and he is very much a down-to-earth individual.

---

[2] "The Man Brushing Up Colgate's Image," *Fortune,* May 11, 1987, p. 107.

Those who knew him well, both inside and outside the corporation, recognized him most for his excellent marketing mind and for an instinct that was unbeatable in the marketplace—adding to his intellectual capability and incredible memory. He had a solid financial background and an amazing talent for handling numbers.

As Reuben Mark considered his new responsibilities, he drew three important conclusions. First, he would have to be very careful to set the right priorities in order to avoid spreading himself, his organization, and the company's resources too thinly. Despite the company's recent progress, there were still many problems to be addressed in all aspects of the business. Mark also knew that catching his two major competitors—P&G and Unilever—was not a realistic short-term goal for Colgate. Both companies had clearly superior resources, so he hoped to avoid a head-on battle with either one. But he did attach a high priority to becoming a more aggressive competitor globally.

Second, he felt Colgate's major strength was the quality of its managers around the world. While many industry observers felt that Colgate needed a major input of management talent to change itself into a more effective worldwide competitor, Mark disagreed. "If we can free our key managers to operate, they know what to do. They are a tremendous resource, and it's my job to marshal them into action."

Third, he was concerned that Colgate's survival as a major global player would require a significant change in the company's work environment. This meant reestablishing the winner's attitude that once prevailed in Colgate's International Division. He felt this would be the key to unleashing the management talent as well as providing a backdrop for strategy initiatives in his far-flung global company.

EXHIBIT 1
COMPANIES BOUGHT AND SOLD BY THE COLGATE-PALMOLIVE COMPANY
BETWEEN 1970 AND EARLY 1984

Company	Products	Year Bought	Year Sold
Kendall Co.	Disposable health care products for consumer and hospital use	1972	—
Helena Rubenstein	Cosmetics	1973	1980
Ram Golf Corp.	Golf equipment	1974	1979
Bancroft Racket Co.	Tennis equipment	1974	1980
Charles A. Eaton Co.	Golf and tennis footwear	1976	—
Riviana Foods	Food products (rice, caviar, kosher meats, pet foods)	1976	1980 (portions)
Marisa Christina Inc.	Sport sweaters	1976	1981
Joseph Terry & Sons (U.K.)	Boxed chocolate candy	1977	1982
Respiratory Care Inc.	Health care equipment	1977	—
Maui Divers of Hawaii Ltd.	Inexpensive cosmetic jewelry	1977	1979
Leach Industries	Sport equipment for racquet ball	1977	1980
MedaSonics, Inc.	Health care equipment	1977	—
Princess House, Inc.	Glass and tableware sold via party plan sales technique	1978	—
AJD Cap Corp.	Sport caps	1978	1981
NDM Corp.	Cardiac electrode equipment	1978	—

EXHIBIT 2
TRENDS IN COMPANY INVESTMENTS IN "PRODUCT HEALTH" BETWEEN 1979 AND 1983

	1979	1980	1981	1982	1983
Sales (in millions)	$4,494	$5,130	$5,261	$4,888	$4,865
Media advertising (as % of sales)	6.1%	5.6%	5.8%	6.5%	6.8%
R&D expenditures (as % of sales)	0.9	0.9	1.0	1.3	1.5
Capital expenditures (as % of sales)	3.1	2.3	2.0	2.8	3.8

EXHIBIT 3
WORLDWIDE HOUSEHOLD AND PERSONAL CARE MARKET SHARES—
CATEGORY SUMMARY

Set out below is a summary of the company's international market share summary data for its main categories of business. This analysis covers all those markets where the corporation has a *subsidiary* presence and an active marketing effort. It does not therefore include export territories or markets assigned to licensees.

| | | Number of Countries | | |
| | | Brand | | |
Category	Sold in	Leader	No. 2	50% Share or More of Category
Dentifrices	48	18	4	7
Toilet soaps	46	3	6	—
Fabric softeners	24	9	2	4
Detergents	35	3	3	1
Light-duty liquids	39	9	3	3
Fine fabric detergents	16	2	—	1
All-purpose cleaners	40	3	8	2
Shampoos	36	10*	10*	1*
Total	284	57	36	19

*Category data only.

EXHIBIT 3A
PER CAPITA SALES BREAKDOWN

Country	Indexed per Capita Sales
France	22.70
Germany/Austria	10.53
Italy	7.91
U.K.	5.68
Nordic Group	9.99
Spain	3.34
Greece	11.37
Belgium	9.31
Switzerland	11.39
Portugal	6.35
Holland	3.73

EXHIBIT 3B
MARKET BREAKDOWN—U.K. MARKET

	Total Retail Market (thousands)	Colgagte's Share of Market
Dental cream	207,000	32.8
Toothbrush	54,800	1.6
Body cleaning	162,500	8.2
Shampoo	216,000	3.9
Deodorants	207,500	10.8
Shave preps	39,800	29.3
Fabric softeners	145,400	6.1
Hand dishwashing	188,000	7.0
Scouring powders	5,500	44.5
Cream cleaners	57,200	22.3

Note: 1. Colgate has no entry in the heavy-duty detergent segment in the U.K., while P&G and Unilever both have strong positions in that large category.

2. Data have been disguised to protect Colgate's competitive positions.

EXHIBIT 3C
EUROPEAN ORGANIZATION, 1985

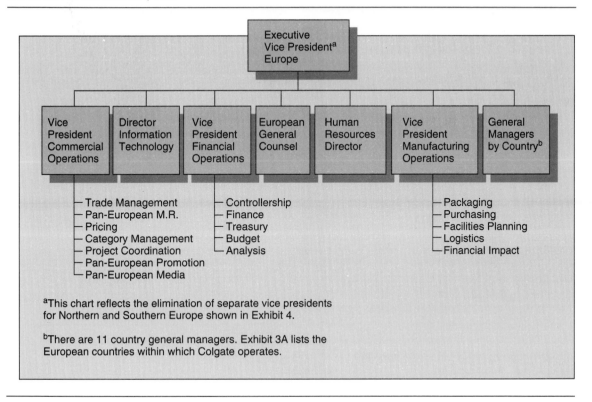

[a]This chart reflects the elimination of separate vice presidents for Northern and Southern Europe shown in Exhibit 4.

[b]There are 11 country general managers. Exhibit 3A lists the European countries within which Colgate operates.

EXHIBIT 4
ORGANIZATION CHART (1984)

Board of Directors

Chief Executive Officer and President

Special Projects

Executive Assistant to Chairman and Chief Executive Officer

Chief Financial Officer Legal–Executive Vice President

Legal Department

Financial–Controller
Treasurer
Tax and Real Estate
Investor Rel
Auditing

Human Resources Vice President

Chief Development Officer Senior-Executive Vice President

Manufacturing/ Engineering Vice President

R&D– Vice President

Packaging

Purchasing/ Travel

Consumer Relations

Communications

International Business Development Vice President

Export

Special Countries

Chief Strategic and Business Development Officer Senior-Executive Vice President

Strategic Planning

Business Development

HDD

Oral
Toilet Soap
HS Cleaners
Liquids

Toiletries

Acquisitions

MIS

New Products
New Categories
Traditional and nontraditional
New ventures
Princess House

Market Research

Chief of Operations Worldwide Colgate and Related Companies Senior-Executive Vice President

Operations Executive Vice President

Americas/ Southern Hemisphere Vice President

Central America Northern

Southern

Americas Vice President

Riviana

Etonic

Bike

Far East Vice President

A.P. Division

Operations Executive Vice President

European North Vice President

Europe South/ Africa Vice President

Chief of Operations Kendall and Related Hospital, Industrial, and Fiber Businesses Senior-Executive Vice President

U.S. Company

France

Kendall

Hospital

Industrial

EXHIBIT 5
INDUSTRY SEGMENT DATA FROM CONTINUING OPERATIONS ($000s)

	1980	1981	1982	1983	1984*
Net sales:					
Household and personal care	$3,569,610	$3,639,200	$3,458,222	$3,321,340	$3,368,959
Health care and industrial	719,766	772,378	748,180	800,239	803,103
Food	653,872	658,680	492,726‡	512,209	482,114
Specialty marketing	187,216	191,106	188,867	231,010	255,781
	$5,130,464	**$5,261,364**	**$4,887,995**	**$4,864,798**	**$4,909,957**
Operating profit:					
Household and personal care	$ 290,151	$ 289,242	$ 218,560	$ 184,994	$ 190,156
Health care and industrial	83,655	86,780	81,782	96,215	63,885
Food	51,324	50,911	52,866‡	48,041	46,452
Specialty marketing	21,387	30,301	41,035	52,095	48,620
	$ 446,517	**$ 457,234**	**$ 394,243**	**$ 381,345**	**$ 349,113**
Net unallocated expenses†	(82,689)	(62,328)	(16,516)	(30,857)	(233,719)
PBT	**$ 363,828**	**$ 394,906**	**$ 377,727**	**$ 350,488**	**$ 115,394**
Identifiable assets:					
Household and personal care	$1,409,697	$1,409,672	$1,265,346	$1,312,300	$1,344,758
Health care and industrial	360,896	388,345	391,605	466,541	545,592
Food	390,542	329,961	260,993‡	257,149	220,854
Specialty marketing	117,020	96,082	100,481	114,677	128,575
	$2,278,155	**$2,224,060**	**$2,018,425**	**$2,150,667**	**$2,239,779**
Corporate assets	309,636	406,767	555,988	513,298	328,564
Total assets	**$2,587,791**	**$2,630,827**	**$2,574,413**	**$2,663,965**	**$2,568,343**
Capital expenditures:					
Household and personal care	$ 76,465	$ 66,343	$ 89,154	$ 101,859	$ 146,501
Health care and industrial	29,027	26,220	36,659	66,961	83,863
Food	9,359	9,216	8,542	8,958	7,713
Specialty marketing	2,230	5,470	4,795	4,763	5,711
	$ 117,081	**$ 107,249**	**$ 139,150**	**$ 182,541**	**$ 243,788**

*Projected.

†Net unallocated expenses include general corporate expense and income, net interest, and the 1984 provision for restructured operations.

‡Due to the divestment of certain subsidiaries, including Joseph Terry & Sons Limited in early 1982, net sales, operating profit, and identifiable assets were reduced by $83,336, $2,546, and $55,614, respectively, in the Food segment.

EXHIBIT 6
GEOGRAPHIC AREA DATA FROM CONTINUING OPERATIONS ($000s)

	1980	1981	1982	1983	1984
Net sales:					
United States	$1,982,665	$2,170,467	$2,029,189	$2,208,713	$2,342,678
Western Hemisphere	932,567	1,049,983	1,004,304	854,471	873,086*
Europe	1,586,537	1,378,953	1,231,568	1,156,416	1,086,286*
Africa and Far East	628,695	661,961	622,934	645,198	607,907*
	$5,130,464	**$5,261,364**	**$4,887,995**	**$4,864,798**	**$4,909,957**
Operating profit:					
United States	$ 154,907	$ 168,124	$ 171,474	$ 198,899	$ 181,116
Western Hemisphere	106,760	124,349	89,806	78,780	95,308*
Europe	94,301	81,816	71,752	46,369	25,682*
Africa and Far East	90,549	82,945	61,211	57,297	47,007*
	$ 445,517	**$ 457,234**	**$ 394,243**	**$ 381,345**	**$ 349,113**
Identifiable assets:					
United States	$ 920,436	$ 989,386	$ 963,595	$1,090,890	$1,252,867
Western Hemisphere	423,502	413,207	344,584	335,881	346,122*
Europe	659,295	573,364	467,485	474,766	409,171*
Africa and Far East	274,922	248,103	242,761	249,130	231,619*
	$2,278,155	**$2,224,060**	**$2,018,425**	**$2,150,667**	**$2,239,779**

*When the financial statements of non-U.S. operations are translated into U.S. dollars, they are, of course, affected by exchange rate changes between the dollar and local currencies. In particular, European results were negatively affected by the strengthening of the dollar between 1980 and 1984 (e.g., the French franc moved from 5.8 to the dollar in 1980 to 9.4 in 1984).

EXHIBIT 7
FINANCIAL PERFORMANCE: COLGATE VERSUS P&G AND UNILEVER

	1982	1983	1984
Colgate			
Sales	$ 4,888	$ 4,865	$ 4,910
Operating income	394	381	349
Operating income (%)	8.1%	7.8%	7.1%
Net income	197	198	72
Net income (%)	4.0%	4.1%	1.5%
ROE	15.0%	14.0%	11.7%
ROC	11.7%	11.2%	10.0%
Stock price			
Low	16	19	21
High	23	25	27
EPS	$ 2.41	$ 2.42	$ 0.64
*P&G**			
Sales	$11,994	$12,452	$12,946
Operating income	1,365	1,529	1,287
Operating income (%)	11.4%	12.3%	10.7%
Net income	777	866	890
Net income (%)	6.5%	7.0%	6.9%
ROE	19.4%	19.8%	18.4%
ROC	15.5%	16.1%	14.1%
Stock price			
Low	39	51	46
High	61	63	60
EPS	$ 4.69	$ 5.22	$ 5.35
Unilever			
Sales	$21,277	$19,410	$18,760
Operating income	1,141	1,085	1,078
Operating income (%)	5.4%	5.6%	5.8%
Net income	607	559	583
Net income (%)	2.9	2.9	3.1
ROE	12.9	12.3	13.6
ROC	9.3	8.8	8.6
Stock price			
Low	10	13	15
High	15	17	18
EPS	$ 2.16	$ 1.99	$ 2.08

Source: Colgate, P&G, and Unilever finance departments.

*P&G financial statistics reflect a fiscal year-end of June 30.

The Lincoln Electric Company

We're not a marketing company, we're not an R&D company, and we're not a service company. We're a manufacturing company, and I believe that we are the best manufacturing company in the world.

With these words, George E. Willis, president of The Lincoln Electric Company, described what he saw as his company's distinctive competence. For more than 30 years, Lincoln had been the world's largest manufacturer of arc welding products (Exhibit 1). In 1974, the company was believed to have manufactured more than 40 percent of the arc welding equipment and supplies sold in the United States. In addition to its welding products, Lincoln produced a line of three-phase alternating-current industrial electric motors, but these accounted for less than 10 percent of sales and profits.

Lincoln's 1974 domestic net income was $17.5 million on sales of $237 million (Exhibit 2). Perhaps more significant than a single year's results was Lincoln's record

of steady growth over the preceding four decades, as shown in Figure A.

During this period, after-tax return on equity had ranged between 10 and 15 percent. Lincoln's growth had been achieved without benefit of acquisition and had been financed with internally generated funds. The company's historical dividend payout policy had been to pay to the suppliers of capital a fair return each year for its use.

COMPANY HISTORY

Lincoln Electric was founded by John C. Lincoln in 1895 to manufacture electric motors and generators. James F. Lincoln, John's younger brother, joined the company in 1907. The brothers' skills and interests were complementary. John was a technical genius. During his lifetime he was awarded more than 50 patents for inventions as diverse as an apparatus for curing meat, an electric drill, a mine-door-activating mechanism, and an electric arc lamp. James's skills were in management and administration. He began as a salesman but soon took over as general manager. The Lincoln Electric Company was undeniably built in his image.

FIGURE A

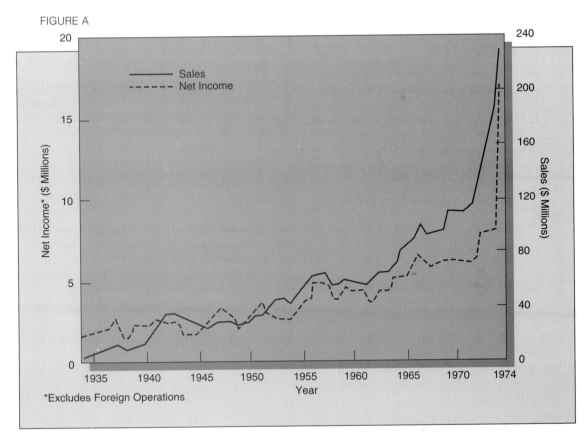

In 1911, the company introduced its first arc welding machine. Both brothers were fascinated by welding, which was then in its infancy. They recognized it as an alternative use for the motor-generator sets they were already producing to recharge the batteries for electric automobiles. The success of Ford, Buick, and others indicated that the days of the electric auto might be numbered, and the brothers were anxious to find other markets for their skills and products.

John's mechanical talents gave the company a head start in welding machines which it never relinquished. He developed a portable welding machine (a significant improvement over existing stationary models) and incorporated a transformer to allow regulation of the cur-

rent. As his biographer noted, "This functional industrial development gave Lincoln Electric a lead in the field that it has always maintained, although the two giants—Westinghouse and General Electric—soon entered the market."[1]

By World War II, Lincoln Electric was the leading American manufacturer of arc welding equipment. Because of the importance of welding to the war effort, the company stopped producing electric motors and devoted its full capacity to welding products. Demand continued to outpace production, and the government

---

[1] Raymond Moley, *The American Century of John C. Lincoln* (New York: Duell, Sloan & Pearce, 1962), p. 71.

asked the welding equipment manufacturers to add capacity. As described by Lincoln's president, George Willis:

> Mr. Lincoln responded to the government's call by going to Washington and telling them that there was enough manufacturing capacity but it was being used inefficiently by everyone. He offered to share proprietary manufacturing methods and equipment designs with the rest of the industry. Washington took him up on it and that solved the problem. As a result of Mr. Lincoln's patriotic decision, our competitors had costs which were close to ours for a short period after the war, but we soon were outperforming them like before.

In 1955, Lincoln once again began manufacturing electric motors, and since then its position in the market had expanded steadily.

Through the years, Lincoln stock had been sold to employees and associates of the Lincoln brothers. In 1975, approximately 48 percent of employees were shareholders. About 80 percent of the outstanding stock was held by employees, the Lincoln family, and their foundations.

In its 80-year history, Lincoln had had only three board chairmen: John C. Lincoln, James F. Lincoln, and William Irrgang, who became chairman in 1972.

STRATEGY

Lincoln Electric's strategy was simple and unwavering. The company's strength was in manufacturing. Management believed that Lincoln could build quality products at a lower cost than their competitors. Their strategy was to concentrate on reducing costs and passing the savings through to the customer by continuously lowering prices. Management had adhered to this policy even when products were on allocation because of shortages in pro-

ductive capacity. The result had been an expansion of both market share and primary demand for arc welding equipment and supplies over the past half century. Lincoln's strategy had also encouraged the exit of several major companies (including General Electric) from the industry and had caused others to seek more specialized market niches.

Management believed its incentive system and the climate it fostered were responsible in large part for the continual increase in productivity upon which this strategy depended. Under the Lincoln incentive system, employees were handsomely rewarded for their productivity, high quality, cost reduction ideas, and individual contributions to the company. Year-end bonuses averaged close to 100 percent of regular compensation, and some workers on the factory floor had earned more than $45,000 in a single year.[2]

Lincoln's strategy had remained virtually unchanged for decades. In a 1947 Harvard Business School case study on the company, James F. Lincoln described the firm's strategy as follows:

> It is the job of The Lincoln Electric Company to give its customers more and more of a better product at a lower and lower price. This will also make it possible for the company to give to the worker and the stockholder a higher and higher return.

In 1975, Chairman William Irrgang's description was remarkably similar:

> The success of The Lincoln Electric Company has been built on two basic ideas. One is producing more and more of a

---

[2] By contrast, the median income for U.S. manufacturing employees in 1974 was less than $9,200, according to Bureau of Labor Statistics data.

progressively better product at a lower and lower price for a larger and larger group of customers. The other is that an employee's earnings and promotion are in direct proportion to his individual contribution toward the company's success.[3]

Management felt it had achieved an enviable record in following this strategy faithfully and saw no need to modify it in the future. Lincoln Electric's record of increasing productivity and declining costs and prices is shown in Exhibit 3.

COMPANY PHILOSOPHY

Lincoln Electric's corporate strategy was rooted in the management philosophy of James F. Lincoln, a rugged individualist who believed that through competition and adequate incentives every person could develop to his or her fullest potential. In one of his numerous books and articles he wrote:

Competition is the foundation of man's development. It has made the human race what it is. It is the spur that makes progress. Every nation that has eliminated it as the controlling force in its economy has disappeared, or will. We will do the same if we eliminate it by trying to give security, and for the same reason. Competition means that there will be losers as well as winners in the game. Competition will mean the disappearance of the lazy and incompetent, be they workers, industrialists, or distributors. Competition promotes progress. Competition determines who will be the leader. It is the only known way that leadership and progress can be developed if history means anything. It is a hard taskmaster. It is

completely necessary for anyone, be he worker, user, distributor, or boss, if he is to grow.

If some way could be found so that competition could be eliminated from life, the result would be disastrous. Any nation and any people disappear if life becomes too easy. There is no danger from a hard life as all history shows. Danger is from a life that is made soft by lack of competition.[4]

Lincoln's faith in the individual was almost unbounded. His personal experience with the success of Lincoln Electric reinforced his faith in what could be accomplished under the proper conditions. In 1951 he wrote:

Development in many directions is latent in every person. The difficulty has been that few recognize that fact. Fewer still will put themselves under the pressure or by chance are put under the pressure that will develop them greatly. Their latent abilities remain latent, hence useless . . .

It is of course obvious that the development of man, on which the success of incentive management depends, is a progressive process. Any results, no matter how good, that come from the application of incentive management cannot be considered final. There will always be greater growth of man under continued proper incentive . . .

Such increase of efficiency poses a very real problem to management. The profit that will result from such efficiency obviously will be enormous. The output per dollar of investment will be many times that of the usual shop which practices output limitation. The labor cost per piece will be relatively small and the overhead will be still less.

---

[3] *Employee's Handbook* (Cleveland: The Lincoln Electric Company, 1974).

[4] James F. Lincoln, *Incentive Management* (Cleveland: The Lincoln Electric Company, 1951), p. 33.

The profits at competitive selling prices resulting from such efficiency will be far beyond any possible need for proper return and growth of an industry . . .

How, then, should the enormous extra profit resulting from incentive management be split? The problems that are inherent in incentive dictate the answer. If the worker does not get a proper share, he does not desire to develop himself or his skill. Incentive, therefore, would not succeed. The worker must have a reward that he feels is commensurate with his contribution.

If the customer does not have a part of the saving in lower prices, he will not buy the increased output. The size of the market is a decisive factor in costs of products. Therefore, the consumer must get a proper share of the saving.

Management and ownership are usually considered as a unit. This is far from a fact, but in the problem here, they can be considered together. They must get a part of the saving in larger salaries and perhaps larger dividends.

There is no hard and fast rule to cover this division, other than the following. The worker (which includes management), the customer, the owner, and all those involved must be satisfied that they are properly recognized or they will not cooperate, and cooperation is essential to any and all successful applications of incentives.[5]

Additional comments by James F. Lincoln are presented in Exhibit 4.

COMPENSATION POLICIES

Compensation policies were the key element of James F. Lincoln's philosophy of "incentive management." Lincoln Electric's compensation system had three components:

- wages based solely on piecework output for most factory jobs,
- a year-end bonus which could equal or exceed an individual's full annual regular pay, and
- guaranteed employment for all workers.

Almost all production workers at Lincoln were paid on a straight piecework plan. They had no base salary or hourly wage but were paid a set "price" for each item they produced. William Irrgang explained:

Wherever practical, we use the piecework system. This system can be effective, and it can be destructive. The important part of the system is that it is completely fair to the worker. When we set a piecework price, that price cannot be changed just because, in management's opinion, the worker is making too much money. Whether he earns two times or three times his normal amount makes no difference. Piecework prices can only be changed when management has made a change in the method of doing that particular job and under no other conditions. If this is not carried out 100 percent, piecework cannot work.

Today piecework is confined to production operations, although at one time we also used it for work done in our stenographic pool. Each typewriter was equipped with a counter that registered the number of times the typewriter keys were operated. This seemed to work all right for a time until it was noticed that one girl was earning much more than any of the others. This was looked into, and it was found that this young lady ate her lunch at her desk, using one hand for eating purposes and the other for punching the most convenient key on the typewriter as fast as she could; which simply goes to show that no matter how good a

---

[5] *Ibid.*, pp. 7–11.

program you may have, it still needs careful supervision.[6]

A Time Study Department established piecework prices, which were guaranteed by the company until methods were changed or a new process introduced. Employees could challenge the price if they felt it was unfair. The Time Study Department would then retime the job and set a new rate. This could be higher or lower but was still open to challenge if an employee remained dissatisfied. Employees were expected to guarantee their own quality. They were not paid for defective work until it had been repaired on their own time.

Each job in the company was rated according to skill, required effort, responsibility, and so on, and a base wage rate for the job was assigned. Wage rates were comparable to those for similar jobs in the Cleveland area and were adjusted annually on the basis of Department of Labor statistics and quarterly to reflect changes in the cost of living. In this way, salaries or hourly wages were determined. For piecework jobs, the Time Study Department set piece prices so that an employee producing at a standard rate would earn the base rate for his or her job.

The second element of the compensation system was a year-end bonus, which had been paid each year since 1934. As explained in the *Employee's Handbook*, "The bonus, paid at the discretion of the company, is not a gift, but rather it is the sharing of the results of efficient operation on the basis of the contribution of each person to the success of the company for that year." In 1974, the bonus pool totaled

$26 million, an average of approximately $10,700 per employee, or 90 percent of prebonus wages.

The total amount to be paid out in bonuses each year was determined by the board of directors. Lincoln's concentration on cost reduction kept costs low enough that prices could generally be set (and not upset by competition) on the basis of costs at the beginning of the year to produce a target return for stockholders and to give employees a bonus of approximately 100 percent of wages. The variance from the planned profits was usually added to (or subtracted from) the bonus pool to be distributed at year-end. Since 1945, the average bonus had varied from 78 percent to 129 percent of wages. In the past few years, it had been between 40 percent and 55 percent of pretax, prebonus profit, or as high as twice the net income after taxes.

An individual's share of the bonus pool was determined by a semiannual "merit rating," which measured individual performance compared to that of other members of the department or work group. Ratings for all employees had to average out to 100 on this relative scale. If, because of some unusual contribution, an individual deserved a rating above 110, he or she could be rewarded from a special corporate pool of bonus points without any penalty to coworkers. Ratings above 110 were thus reviewed by a corporate committee or vice president, who evaluated the individual's contribution. Merit ratings varied widely, from as low as 45 to as high as 160.

In determining an employee's merit rating, four factors were evaluated separately:

- dependability
- quality

---

[6] William Irrgang, "The Lincoln Incentive Management Program," Lincoln Lecture Series, Arizona State University, 1972, p. 13.

- output
- ideas and cooperation

Foremen were responsible for the rating of all factory workers. They could request help from assistant foremen (dependability), the Production Control Department (output), the Inspection Department (quality), and the Methods Department (ideas and cooperation). In the office, supervisors rated their people on the same items. At least one executive reviewed all ratings. All employees were urged to discuss their ratings with their department heads if they were dissatisfied or unclear about them.

Lincoln complemented its rating and pay system with a Guaranteed Continuous Employment Plan. This plan provided security against layoffs and assured continuity of employment. Every full-time employee who had been with the company at least two years was guaranteed employment for at least 75 percent of the standard 40-hour week. In fact, the company had not had any layoffs since 1951 when initial trials for the plan were put into effect. It was formally established in 1958.

The guarantee of employment was seen by the company as an essential element in the incentive plan. Without such a guarantee, it was believed that employees would be more likely to resist improved production and efficiency for fear of losing their jobs. In accepting the guaranteed continuous employment plan, employees agreed to perform any job that was assigned as conditions required, and to work overtime during periods of high activity.

The philosophy and procedures regarding the incentive plan were the same for management and workers, except that William Irrgang and George Willis did not share in the bonus.

EMPLOYEE VIEWS

To the researchers, it appeared that employees generally liked working at Lincoln. The employee turnover rate was far below that of most other companies, and once a new employee made it through the first month or so, he rarely left for another firm (see Exhibit 5). One employee explained, "It's like trying out for a high school football team. If you make it through the first few practices, you're usually going to stay the whole season, especially after the games start."

One long-time employee who liked working at Lincoln was John "Tiny" Carrillo, an armature bander on the welding machine line, who had been with the company for 24 years. Tiny explained why:

> The thing I like here is that you're pretty much your own boss as long as you do your job. You're responsible for your own work and you even put your stencil on every machine you work on. That way if it breaks down in the field and they have to take it back, they know who's responsible.
>
> Before I came here, I worked at Cadillac as a welder. After two months there I had the top hourly rate. I wasn't allowed to tell anyone because there were guys who still had the starting rate after a year. But, I couldn't go any higher after two months.
>
> I've done well. My rating is usually around 110, but I work hard, right through the smoke breaks. The only time I stop is a half hour for lunch. I make good money. I have two houses, one which I rent out, and four cars. They're all paid for. When I get my bills, I pay them the next day. That's the main thing; I don't owe anyone.
>
> Sure, there are problems. There's sometimes a bind between the guys with low

grades and the guys with high ones, like in school. And there are guys who sway everything their way so they'll get the points, but they [management] have good tabs on what's going on . . .

A lot of new guys come in and leave right away. Most of them are just mamma's boys and don't want to do the work. We had a new guy who was a produce manager at a supermarket. He worked a couple of weeks, then quit and went back to his old job.

At the end of the interview, the researcher thanked Tiny for his time. He responded by pointing out that it had cost him $7.00 in lost time, but that he was glad to be of assistance.

Another piece worker, Jorge Espinoza, a fine-wire operator in the Electrode Division, had been with the company for six years. He explained his feelings:

I believe in being my own man. I want to use my drive for my own gain. It's worked. I built my family a house and have an acre of land, with a low mortgage. I have a car and an old truck I play around with. The money I get is because I earn it. I don't want anything given to me.

The thing I don't like is having to depend on other people on the line and suppliers. We're getting bad steel occasionally. Our output is down as a result and my rating will suffer.

There are men who have great drive here and can push for a job. They are not leaders and never will be, but they move up. That's a problem . . .

The first few times around, the ratings were painful for me. But now I stick near 100. You really make what you want. We just had a methods change and our base rate went from 83 to 89 coils a day. This job is tougher now and more complex. But, it's all what you want. If you want 110 coils you can get it. You just take less

breaks. Today, I gambled and won. I didn't change my dies and made over a hundred coils. If I had lost, and the die plugged up, it would have cost me at least half an hour. But, today I made it.

MANAGEMENT STYLE

Lincoln's incentive scheme was reinforced by top management's attitude toward the men on the factory floor. In 1951, James Lincoln wrote:

It becomes perfectly true to anyone who will think this thing through that there is no such thing in an industrial activity as Management and Men having different functions or being two different kinds of people. Why can't we think and why don't we think that all people are Management? Can you imagine any president of any factory or machine shop who can go down and manage a turret lathe as well as the machinist can? Can you imagine any manager of any organization who can go down and manage a broom—let us get down to that—who can manage a broom as well as a sweeper can? Can you imagine any secretary of any company who can go down and fire a furnace and manage that boiler as well as the man who does the job? Obviously, all are Management.[7]

Lincoln's president, George Willis, stressed the equality in the company:

We try to avoid barriers between management and workers. We're treated equally as much as possible. When I got to work this morning at 7:30, the parking lot was three-quarters full. I parked way out there like anyone else would. I don't have a

---

[7] James F. Lincoln, *What Makes Workers Work?* (Cleveland: The Lincoln Electric Company, 1951), pp. 3–4.

special reserved spot. The same principle holds true in our cafeteria. There's no executive dining room. We eat with everyone else.[8]

Willis felt that open and frank communication between management and workers had been a critical factor in Lincoln's success, and he believed that the company's Advisory Board, consisting of elected employee representatives, had played a very important role in achieving this. Established by James F. Lincoln in 1914, the board met twice a month, providing a forum in which employees could bring issues of concern to top management's attention, question company policies, and make suggestions for their improvement. As described in the *Employee's Handbook*:

> Board service is a privilege and responsibility of importance to the entire organization. In discussions or in reaching decisions Board members must be guided by the best interests of the Company. These also serve the best interests of its workers. They should seek at all times to improve the cooperative attitude of all workers and see that all realize they have an important part in our final results.

All Advisory Board meetings were chaired by either the chairman or the president of Lincoln. Usually both were present. Issues brought up at board meetings were either resolved on the spot or assigned to an executive. After each meeting, William Irrgang or George Willis

would send a memo to the executive responsible for each unanswered question, no matter how trivial, and he was expected to respond by the next meeting if possible.

Minutes of all board meetings were posted on bulletin boards in each department, and members explained the board's actions to the other workers in their department. The questions raised in the minutes of a given meeting were usually answered in the next set of minutes. This procedure had not changed significantly since the first meeting in 1914, and the types of issues raised had remained much the same (see Exhibit 6).

Workers felt that the Advisory Board provided a way of getting immediate attention for their problems. It was clear, however, that management still made the final decisions.[9] A former member of the Advisory Board commented:

> There are certain areas which are brought up in the meetings which Mr. Irrgang doesn't want to get into. He's adept at steering the conversation away from these. It's definitely not a negotiating meeting. But, generally, you really get action or an answer on why action isn't being taken.

In addition to the Advisory Board, there was a 12-member board of middle managers which met with Irrgang and Willis once a month. The topics discussed here were broader than those of the Advisory Board. The primary function of these meetings was to allow top management to get better acquainted with these individu-

---

[8] The cafeteria had large rectangular and round tables. In general, factory workers gravitated toward the rectangular tables. There were no strict rules, however, and management personnel often sat with factory workers. Toward the center was a square table that seated only four. This was reserved for William Irrgang, George Willis, and their guests when they were having a working lunch.

[9] In some cases, management allowed issues to be decided by a vote of employees. Recently, for example, employees had voted down a proposal that the company give them dental benefits, recognizing that the cost of the program would come directly out of their bonuses.

als and to encourage cooperation between departments.

Lincoln's two top executives, Irrgang and Willis, continued the practice of James F. Lincoln in maintaining an open door to all employees. George Willis estimated that at least twice a week factory employees took advantage of this opportunity to talk with him.

Middle managers also felt that communication with Willis and Irrgang was open and direct. Often it bypassed intermediate levels of the organization. Most saw this as an advantage, but one commented:

> This company is run strictly by the two men at the top. Mr. Lincoln trained Mr. Irrgang in his image. It's very authoritarian and decisions flow top-down. It never became a big company. There is very little delegated and top people are making too many small decisions. Mr. Irrgang and Mr. Willis work 80 hours a week, and no one I know in this company can say that his boss doesn't work harder than he does.

Willis saw management's concern for the worker as an essential ingredient in his company's formula for success. He knew at least 500 employees personally. In leading the researcher through the plant, he greeted workers by name and paused several times to tell anecdotes about them.

At one point, an older man yelled to Willis good-naturedly, "Where's my raise?" Willis explained that this man had worked for 40 years in a job requiring him to lift up to 20 tons of material a day. His earnings had been quite high because of his rapid work pace, but Willis had been afraid that as he was advancing in age he could injure himself working in that job. After months of Willis's urging, the worker switched to an easier but lower-paying

job. He was disappointed in taking the earnings cut and even after several years let the president know whenever he saw him.

Willis pointed out another employee, whose wife had recently died, and noted that for several weeks he had been drinking heavily and reporting to work late. Willis had earlier spent about half an hour discussing the situation with him to console him and see if the company could help in any way. He explained:

> I made a definite point of talking to him on the floor of the plant, near his work station. I wanted to make sure that other employees who knew the situation could see me with him. Speaking to him had symbolic value. It is important for employees to know that the president is interested in their welfare.

Management's philosophy was also reflected in the company's physical facilities. A no-nonsense atmosphere was firmly established at the gate to the parking lot where the only mention of the company name was in a sign reading:

> $1,000 REWARD for information leading to the arrest and conviction of persons stealing from the Lincoln Electric parking lot.

There was a single entrance to the offices and plant for workers, management, and visitors. Entering, one could not avoid being struck by the company motto, in large stainless steel letters extending 30 feet across the wall:

THE ACTUAL IS LIMITED
THE POSSIBLE IS IMMENSE

A flight of stairs led down to a tunnel system for pedestrian traffic which ran under the single-story plant. At the base of the stairs was a large bronze plaque on which were inscribed the names of the eight employees who had served more than 50 years, and the more than 350 active employees with 25 or more years of service (the Quarter Century Club).

The long tunnel leading to the offices was clean and well lit. The executive offices were located in a windowless, two-story cement-block office building which sat like a box in the center of the plant. At the base of the staircase leading up to the offices, a Lincoln automatic welding machine and portraits of J. C. Lincoln and J. F. Lincoln welcomed visitors. The handrail on the staircase was welded into place, as were the ashtrays in the tunnel.

In the center of the office building was a simple, undecorated reception room. A switchboard operator/receptionist greeted visitors between filing and phone calls. Throughout the building, decor was spartan. The reception room was furnished with a metal coat rack, a wooden bookcase, and several plain wooden tables and chairs. All of the available reading material dealt with Lincoln Electric Company or welding.

From the reception room, seven doors each led almost directly to the various offices and departments. Most of the departments were large open rooms with closely spaced desks. One manager explained that "Mr. Lincoln didn't believe in walls. He felt they interrupted the flow of communications and paperwork." Most of the desks and files were plain, old, and well worn, and there was little modern office equipment. Expenditures on equipment had to meet the same criteria in the office as in the plant: The Maintenance Department had to certify that the equipment replaced could not be repaired, and any equipment acquired for cost reduc-

tion had to have a one-year payback.[10] Even Xerox machines were nowhere to be found. Copying costs were tightly controlled and only certain individuals could use the Xerox copiers. Customer order forms which required eight copies were run on a duplicating machine, for example.

The private offices were small, uncarpeted, and separated by green metal partitions. The president's office was slightly larger than the others, but still retained a spartan appearance. There was only one carpeted office. Willis explained, "That office was occupied by Mr. Lincoln until he died in 1965. For the next five years it was left vacant, and now it is Mr. Irrgang's office and also the Board of Directors' and Advisory Board meeting room."

PERSONNEL

Lincoln Electric had a strict policy of filling all but entry-level positions by promoting from within the company. Whenever an opening occurred, a notice was posted on the 25 bulletin boards in the plant and offices. Any interested employee could apply for an open position. Because of the company's sustained growth and policy of promoting from within, employees had substantial opportunity for advancement.

An outsider generally could join the company in one of two ways: either taking a factory job at an hourly or piece rate, or entering Lincoln's training programs in

---

[10] Willis explained that capital projects with paybacks of up to two years were sometimes funded when they involved a product for which demand was growing.

sales or engineering.[11] The company re-cruited its trainees at colleges and graduate schools, including Harvard Business School. Starting salary in 1975 for a trainee with a bachelor's degree was $5.50 an hour plus a year-end bonus at an average of 40 percent of the normal rate. Wages for trainees with either a master's degree or several years of relevant experience were 5 percent higher.

Although Lincoln's president, vice president of sales, and personnel director were all Harvard Business School graduates, the company had not hired many recent graduates. Clyde Loughridge, the personnel director, explained:

> We don't offer them fancy staff positions and we don't pretend to. Our starting pay is less than average, probably $17,000–$18,000[12] including bonus, and the work is harder than average. We start our trainees off by putting them in overalls and they spend up to seven weeks in the welding school. In a lot of ways it's like boot camp. Rather than leading them along by the hand, we like to let the self-starters show themselves.

The policy of promoting from within had rarely been violated, and then only in cases where a specialized skill was required. Loughridge commented:

> In most cases we've been able to stick to it, even where the required skills are

entirely new to the company. Our employees have a lot of varied skills, and usually someone can fit the job. For example, when we recently got our first computer, we needed a programmer and systems analyst. We had 20 employees apply who had experience or training in computers. We chose two, and it really helps that they know the company and understand our business.

The company did not send its employees to outside management development programs and did not provide tuition grants for educational purposes.

Lincoln Electric had no formal organization chart, and management did not feel that one was necessary. (The chart in Exhibit 8 was drawn for the purposes of this case.) As explained by one executive:

> People retire and their jobs are parceled out. We are very successful in overloading our overhead departments. We make sure this way that no unnecessary work is done and jobs which are not absolutely essential are eliminated. A disadvantage is that planning may suffer, as may outside development to keep up with your field.

Lincoln's organizational hierarchy was flat, with few levels between the bottom and the top. For example, Don Hastings, the vice president of sales, had 37 regional sales managers reporting to him. He commented:

> I have to work hard, there's no question about that. There are only four of us in the home office plus two secretaries. I could easily use three more people. I work every Saturday, at least half a day. Most of our regional men do too, and they like me to know it. You should see the switchboard light up when 37 re-

---

[11] Lincoln's chairman and president both advanced through the ranks in Manufacturing. Irrgang began as a pieceworker in the Armature Winding Department, and Willis began in Plant Engineering. (See Exhibit 7 for employment history of Lincoln's top management.)

[12] In 1975, the median starting salary for Harvard Business School graduates who took positions in industrial manufacturing was $19,800.

gional managers call in at five minutes to twelve on Saturday.

The president and chairman kept a tight rein over personnel matters. All changes in status of employees, even at the lowest levels, had to be approved by Willis. Irrgang also had to give his approval if salaried employees were involved. Raises or promotions had to be approved in advance. An employee could be fired by his supervisor on the spot for cause, but if the grounds were questionable, the decision had to be approved afterward by either Willis or Irrgang. Usually the supervisor was supported, but there had been cases where a firing decision was reversed.

MARKETING

Welding machines and electrodes were like razors and razor blades. A Lincoln welding machine often had a useful life of 30 years or more, while electrodes (and fluxes) were consumed immediately in the welding process. The ratio of machine cost to annual consumables cost varied widely, from perhaps 7:1 for a hand welder used in a small shop to 1:5 or more for an automatic welder used in a shipyard.

Although certain competitors might meet Lincoin's costs and quality in selected products, management believed that no company could match the line overall. Another important competitive edge for Lincoln was its sales force. Al Patnik, vice president of sales development, explained:

> Most competitors operate through distributors. We have our own top field sales force.[13] We start out with engineer-

ing graduates and put them through our seven-month training program. They learn how to weld, and we teach them everything we can about equipment, metallurgy, and design. Then they spend time on the rebuild line [where machines brought in from the field are rebuilt] and even spend time in the office seeing how orders are processed. Finally, before the trainees go out into the field, they have to go into our plant and find a better way of making something. Then they make a presentation to Mr. Irrgang, just as if he were one of our customers.

> Our approach to the customer is to go in and learn what he is doing and show him how to do it better. For many companies our people become their experts in welding. They go in and talk to a foreman. They might say, "Let me put on a headshield and show you what I'm talking about." That's how we sell them.

George Ward, a salesman in the San Francisco office, commented:

> The competition hires graduates with business degrees (without engineering backgrounds) and that's how they get hurt. This job is getting more technical every day ... A customer in California who is using our equipment to weld offshore oil rigs had a problem with one of our products. I couldn't get the solution for them over the phone, so I flew in to the plant Monday morning and showed it to our engineers. Mr. Willis said to me, "Don't go back to California until this problem is solved ..." We use a "working together to solve your problem" approach. This, plus sticking to published prices, shows you're not interested in taking advantage of them.

> I had a boss who used to say, "Once we're in, Lincoln never loses a customer

---

[13] The sales force was supplemented in some areas by distributors. Sales abroad were handled by wholly owned subsidiaries or Armco's International Division.

except on delivery." It's basically true. The orders I lost last year were because we couldn't deliver fast enough. Lincoln gets hurt when there are shortages because of our guaranteed employment. We don't hire short-term factory workers when sales take off, and other companies beat us on delivery.

The sales force was paid a salary plus bonus. Ward believed that Lincoln's sales force was the best paid and hardest working in the industry. He said, "We're aggressive, and want to work and get paid for it. The sales force prides itself on working more hours than anyone else . . . My wife wonders sometimes if you can work for Lincoln and have a family too."

MANUFACTURING

Lincoln's plant was unusual in several respects. It seemed crowded with materials and equipment, with surprisingly few workers. It was obvious that employees worked very fast and efficiently with few breaks. Even during the 10-minute smoke breaks in the morning and afternoon, employees often continued to work.

An innovative plant layout was partly responsible for the crowded appearance. Raw materials entered one side of the plant and finished goods came out the other side. There was no central stockroom for materials or work-in-process. Instead, everything that entered the plant was transported directly to the work station where it would be used. At a work station, a single worker or group operated in effect as a subcontractor. All required materials were piled around the station, allowing visual inventory control, and workers were paid a piece price for their production. Wherever possible, the work flow followed a straight line through the plant from the side where raw materials

entered to the side where finished goods exited. Because there was no union, the company had great flexibility in deciding what could be performed at a work station. For example, foundry work and metal stamping could be carried out together by the same workers when necessary. Thus, work could flow almost directly along a line through the plant. Intermediate material handling was avoided to a great extent. The major exception arose when multiple production lines shared a large or expensive piece of machinery, and the work had to be brought to the machines.

Many of the operations in the plant were automated. Much of the manufacturing equipment was proprietary,[14] designed and built by Lincoln. In some cases, the company had modified machines built by others to run two or three times as fast as when originally delivered.

From the time a product was first conceived, close coordination was maintained between product design engineers and the Methods Department; this was seen as a key factor in reducing costs and rationalizing manufacturing. William Irrgang explained:

> After we have [an] idea . . . we start thinking about manufacturing costs, before anything leaves the Design Engineering Department. At that point, there is a complete "getting together" of manufacturing and design engineers—and plant engineers, too, if new equipment is involved.
>
> Our tooling, for instance, is going to be looked at carefully while the design of a product is still in process. Obviously, we can increase or decrease the tooling very materially by certain considerations in

---

[14] Visitors were barred from the Electrode Division unless they had a pass signed by Willis or Irrgang.

the design of a product, and we can go on the basis of total costs at all times. In fact, as far as total cost is concerned, we even think about such matters as shipping, warehousing, etc. All of these factors are taken into consideration when we're still at the design stage. It's very essential that this be done: otherwise, you can lock yourself out from a lot of potential economies.[15]

In 1974, Lincoln's plant had reached full capacity, operating nearly around the clock. Land bordering its present location was unavailable, and management was moving ahead with plans to build a second plant 15 miles away on the same freeway as the present plant.

Over the years, Lincoln had come to make rather than buy an increasing proportion of its components. For example, even though its unit volume of gasoline engines was only a fraction of its suppliers', Lincoln purchased engine blocks and components and assembled them rather than buying completed engines. Management was continually evaluating opportunities for backward integration and had not arbitrarily ruled out manufacturing any of Lincoln's components or raw materials.

ADMINISTRATIVE PRODUCTIVITY

Lincoln's high productivity was not limited to manufacturing. Clyde Loughridge pointed to the Personnel Department as an example: "Normally, for 2,300 employees you would need a personnel department of about 20, but we have only 6, and that includes the nurse, and our

responsibilities go beyond those of the typical personnel department."

Once a year, Loughridge had to outline his objectives for the upcoming year to the president of the company, but as he explained, "I don't get a budget. There would be no point to it. I just spend as little as possible. l operate this just like my home. l don't spend on anything I don't need."

In the Traffic Department, workers also seemed very busy. There, a staff of 12 controlled the shipment of 2.5 million pounds of material a day. Their task was complex. Delivery was included in the price of their products. They thus could reduce the overall cost to the customer by mixing products in most loads and shipping the most efficient way possible to the company's 39 warehouses. Jim Biek, general traffic manager, explained how they accomplished this:

> For every order, we decide whether it would be cheaper by rail or truck. Then we consolidate orders so that over 90 percent of what goes out of here is full carload or full truckload, as compared to perhaps 50 percent for most companies. We also mix products so that we come in at the top of the weight brackets. For example, if a rate is for 20,000 to 40,000 pounds, we will mix orders to bring the weight right up to that 40,000 limit. All this is computed manually. In fact, my old boss used to say, "We run Traffic like a ma and pa grocery store."

As in the rest of Lincoln, the employees in the Traffic Department worked their way up from entry-level positions. Jim Biek had become general traffic manager after nine years as a purchasing engineer. He had received an MBA degree from Northwestern after a BS in mechanical engineering from Purdue, started in the engineering training program, and then spent five years in Product Development and Methods before going to Purchasing and finally to Traffic. Lack of experience in Traffic was a disadvantage, but the policy of promoting from within also had its advantages. Biek explained:

> One of my first tasks was to go to Washington and fight to get welders reclassified as motors to qualify for a lower freight rate. With my engineering experience and knowledge of welders, I was in a better position to argue this than a straight traffic man . . .
>
> Just about everybody in here was new to Traffic. One of my assistant traffic managers had worked on the loading platform here for 10 years before he came into the department. He had to go to night school to learn about rates, but his experience is invaluable. He knows how to load trucks and rail cars backward and forward. Who could do a better job of consolidating orders than he does? He can look at an order and think of it as rows of pallets.
>
> Some day we'll outgrow this way of operating, but right now I can't imagine a computer juggling loads like some of our employees do.

Lincoln's Order Department had recently begun computerizing its operations. It was the first time a computer had been used anywhere in the company (except in engineering and research), and according to Russell Stauffer, head of the Order Department, "It was a three-year job for me to sell this to top management." The computer was expected to replace 12 or 13 employees who would gradually be moved into new jobs. There had been some resistance to the computer, Stauffer noted:

> It's like anything new. People get scared. Not all the people affected have been here for the two years required to be eligible for guaranteed employment. And even though the others are assured a job, they don't know what it will be and will have to take what's offered.

The computer was expected to produce savings of $100,000 a year and to allow a greater degree of control. Stauffer explained:

> We're getting information out of this that we never knew before. The job here is very complex. We're sending out more than 2 million pounds of consumables a day. Each order might have 30 or 40 items, and each item has a bracket price arrangement based on total order size. A clerk has to remember or determine quickly whether we are out of stock on any items and calculate whether the stock-out brings the order down into another bracket. This means they have to remember the prices and items out of stock. This way of operating was okay up to about $200 million in sales, but now we've outgrown the human capability to handle the problem.

Although he had no previous experience in computers, Stauffer had full responsibility for the conversion.

> I've been here for 35 years. The first day I started, I unloaded coal cars and painted fences. Then I went to the assembly line, first on small parts, then large ones. I've been running the Order Department for 12 years. Since I've been here, we've had studies on computers every year or two and it always came out that we couldn't save money. Finally, when it looked like we'd make the switch, I took some courses at IBM. Over the last year and a half, they've totaled eight and a half weeks, which is supposed to equal a full semester of college.

To date, the conversion had gone well, but much slower than anticipated. Order pressure had been so high that many mistakes would have been catastrophic. Management thus had emphasized assuring 100 percent quality operations rather than faster conversion.

LINCOLN'S FUTURE

The 1947 Harvard Business School case study of Lincoln Electric ended with a prediction by a union leader from the Cleveland area:

> The real test of Lincoln will come when the going gets tough. The thing Lincoln holds out to the men is high earnings. They work like dogs at Lincoln, but it pays off . . .
>
> I think [Mr. Lincoln] puts too much store by monetary incentives—but then, there's no denying he has attracted people who respond to that type of incentive. But I think that very thing is a danger Lincoln faces. If the day comes when they can't offer those big bonuses, or his people decide there's more to life than killing yourself making money, I predict the Lincoln Electric Company is in for trouble.

Lincoln's president, George Willis, joined the company the year that this comment was made. Reflecting on his 28 years with the company, Willis observed:

> The company hasn't changed very much since I've been here. It's still run pretty much like Mr. Lincoln ran it. But today's workers are different. They're more outspoken and interested in why things are being done, not just how. We have nothing to hide and never did, so we can give them the answers to their questions.

Looking forward, Willis saw no need to alter Lincoln's strategy or its policies:

> My job will continue to be to have everyone in the organization recognize that a common goal all of us can and must support is to give the customer the quality he needs, when he needs it, at the lowest cost. To do this, we have to have everyone's understanding of this goal and their effort to accomplish it. In one way or another, I have to motivate the organization to meet this goal. The basic forms of the motivation have evolved over the last 40 years. However, keeping the system honed so that everyone understands it, agrees with it, and brings out disagreements so improvements can be made or thinking changed becomes my major responsibility.
>
> If our employees did not believe that management was trustworthy, honest, and impartial, the system could not operate. We've worked out the mechanics. They are not secret. A good part of my responsibility is to make sure the mechanics are followed. This ties back to a trust and understanding between individuals at all levels of the organization.
>
> I don't see any real limits to our size. Look at a world with a present population of just under 4 billion now and 6.25 billion by the year 2000. Those people aren't going to tolerate a low standard of living. So there will be a lot of construction, cars, bridges, oil, and all those things that have got to be to support a population that large.
>
> My job will still be just the traditional things of assuring that we keep up with the technology and have sufficient profit to pay the suppliers of capital. Then, I have to make sure communication can be maintained adequately. That last task may be the biggest and most important part of my job in the years ahead as we grow larger and still more complex.

EXHIBIT 1
ARC WELDING

Arc welding is a group of joining processes that utilize an electric current produced by a transformer or motor generator (electric or engine powered) to fuse various metals. The temperature of the arc is approximately 10,000 Fahrenheit.

The welding circuit consists of a welding machine, ground clamp, and electrode holder. The electrode carries electricity to the metal being welded, and the heat from the arc causes the base metals to join together. The electrode may or may not act as a filler metal during the process; however, nearly 60 percent of all arc welding that is done in the United States utilizes a covered electrode that acts as a very high-quality filler metal.

The Lincoln Electric Company manufactured a wide variety of covered electrodes, submerged arc welding wires and fluxes, and a unique self-shielded, flux-cored electrode called Innershield. The company also manufactured welding machines, wire feeders, and other supplies that were needed for arc welding.

Lincoln Arc Welding Machines

EXHIBIT 2
LINCOLN'S STATUS IN 1974

Statement of Financial Condition
(Foreign Subsidiaries Not Included)

December 31	1974
Assets	
Current assets	
Cash and certificates of deposit	$ 5,691,120
Government securities	6,073,919
Notes and accounts receivable	29,451,161
Inventories (LIFO basis)	29,995,694
Deferred taxes and prepaid expenses	2,266,409
Total	73,478,303
Other assets	
Trustee—notes and interest receivable	1,906,871
Miscellaneous	384,572
Total	2,291,443
Intercompany	
Investment in foreign subsidiaries	4,695,610
Notes receivable	0
Total	4,695,610
Property, plant, and equipment	
Land	825,376
Buildings*	9,555,562
Machinery, tools, and equipment*	11,273,155
Total	21,654,093
Total assets	$102,119,449
Liabilities and shareholders' equity	
Current liabilities	
Accounts payable	$ 13,658,063
Accrued wages	1,554,225
Taxes, including income taxes	13,262,178
Dividends payable	3,373,524
Total	31,847,990
Shareholders' equity	
Common capital stock, stated value	281,127
Additional paid-in capital	3,374,570
Retained earnings	66,615,762
Total	70,271,459
Total liabilities and shareholders' equity	$102,119,449

*After depreciation.

Exhibit 2 (continued)

Income and Retained Earnings Year Ended December 31	1974
Income	
Net sales	$232,771,475
Interest	1,048,561
Overhead and development charges to subsidiaries	1,452,877
Dividend income	843,533
Other income	515,034
Total	236,631,480
Costs and expenses	
Cost of products sold	154,752,735
Selling, administrative, and general expenses and freight out	20,791,301
Year-end incentive bonus	24,707,297
Pension expense	2,186,932
Total	202,438,265
Income before income taxes	34,193,215
Provision for income taxes	
Federal	14,800,000
State and local	1,866,000
	16,666,000
Net income	$ 17,527,215

EXHIBIT 3
LINCOLN ELECTRIC'S RECORD OF PRICING AND PRODUCTIVITY

A. Lincoln Prices* Relative to Commodity Prices,[†] 1934–1971

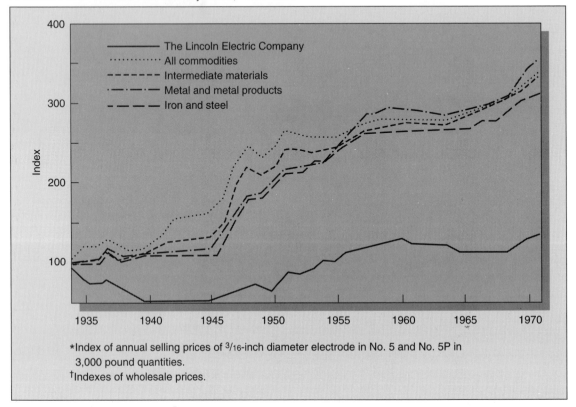

*Index of annual selling prices of $3/16$-inch diameter electrode in No. 5 and No. 5P in 3,000 pound quantities.
[†]Indexes of wholesale prices.

Source: Company records.

EXHIBIT 3 (continued)

B. Lincoln Prices‡ Relative to Wholesale Machinery and Equipment Prices, 1939–1971

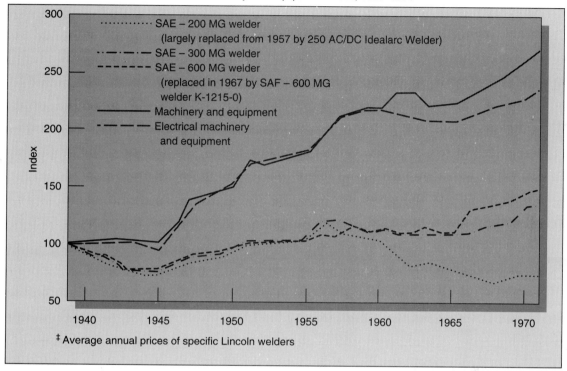

‡ Average annual prices of specific Lincoln welders

Source: Company records.

EXHIBIT 3 (continued)

C. Productivity of Lincoln Production Workers Relative to Workers in Manufacturing and Durable Goods Industries, 1934–1971

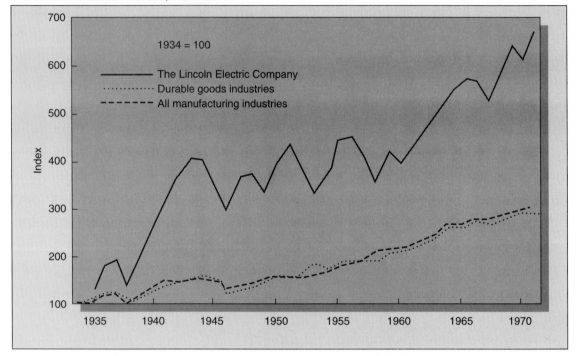

Source: Company records.

EXHIBIT 3 (continued)

D. Lincoln Productivity Relative to Three Other Companies: Sales Value§ of
Products per Employee, 1934–1971

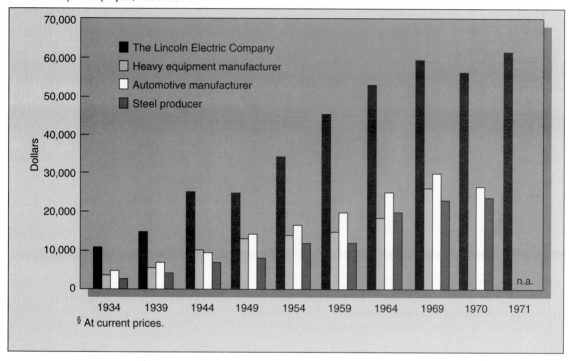

§ At current prices.

Source: Company records.

EXHIBIT 4
JAMES F. LINCOLN'S OBSERVATIONS ON MANAGEMENT

- Some think paying a man more money will produce cooperation. Not true. Many incentives are far more effective than money. Robert MacNamara gave up millions to become Secretary of Defense. Status is a much greater incentive.
- If those crying loudest about the inefficiencies of labor were put in the position of the wage earner, they would react as he does. The worker is not a man apart. He has the same needs, aspirations, and reactions as the industrialist. A worker will not cooperate on any program that will penalize him. Does any manager?
- The industrial manager is very conscious of his company's need of uninterrupted income. He is completely oblivious, though, to the worker's same need. Management fails—i.e., profits fall off—and gets no punishment. The wage earner does not fail but is fired. Such injustice!
- Higher efficiency means fewer manhours to do a job. If the worker loses his job more quickly, he will oppose higher efficiency.
- There never will be enthusiasm for greater efficiency if the resulting profits are not properly distributed. If we continue to give it to the average stockholder, the worker will not cooperate.
- Most companies are run by hired managers, under the control of stockholders. As a result, the goal of the company has shifted from service to the customer to making larger dividends for stockholders.
- The public will not yet believe that our standard of living could be doubled immediately if labor and management would cooperate.
- The manager is dealing with expert workers far more skillful. While you can boss these experts around in the usual lofty way, their eager cooperation will not be won.
- A wage earner is no more interested than a manager in making money for other people. The worker's job doesn't depend on pleasing stockholders, so he has no interest in dividends. Neither is he interested in increasing efficiency if he may lose his job because management has failed to get more orders.
- If a manager received the same treatment in matters of income, security, advancement, and dignity as the hourly worker, he would soon understand the real problem of management.
- The first question management should ask is: What is the company trying to do? In the minds of the average worker the answer is: "The company is trying to make the largest possible profits by any method. Profits go to absentee stockholders and top management."
- There is all the difference imaginable between the grudging, distrustful, half-forced cooperation and the eager, whole-hearted, vigorous, happy cooperation of men working together for a common purpose.
- Continuous employment of workers is essential to industrial efficiency. This is a management responsibility. Laying off workers during slack times is death to efficiency. The worker thrown out is a trained man. To replace him when business picks up will cost much more than the savings of wages during the layoff. Solution? The worker must have a guarantee that if he works properly his income will be continuous.
- Continuous employment is the first step to efficiency. But how? First, during slack periods, manufacture to build up inventory; costs will usually be less because of lower material costs. Second, develop new machines and methods of manufacturing; plans should be waiting on the shelf. Third, reduce prices by getting lower costs. When slack times come, workers are eager to help cut costs. Fourth, explore markets passed over when times are good. Fifth, hours of work can be reduced if the worker is agreeable. Sixth, develop new products. In sum, management should plan for slumps. They are useful.
- The incentives that are most potent when properly offered are:
    Money in proportion to production.
    Status as a reward for achievement.
    Publicity of the worker's contributions and skill.
- The calling of the minister, the doctor, the lawyer, as well as the manager, contains incentive to excel. Excellence brings rewards, self-esteem, respect. Only the hourly worker has no reason to excel.
- Resistance to efficiency is not normal. It is present only when we are hired workers.
- Do unto others as you would have them do unto you. This is not just a Sunday school ideal, but a proper labor-management policy.
- An incentive plan should reward a man not only for the number of pieces turned out, but also for the accuracy of his work, his cooperation in improving methods of production, and his attendance.
- The progress in industry so far stems from the developed potentialities of managers. Wage earners, who because of their greater numbers have far greater potential, are overlooked. Here is where the manager must look for his greatest progress.
- There should be an overall bonus based on the contribution each person makes to efficiency. If each person is properly rated and paid, there will not only be a fair reward to each worker but friendly and exciting competition.

EXHIBIT 4 (continued)

- The present policy of operating industry for stockholders is unreasonable. The rewards now given to him are far too much. He gets income that should really go to the worker and the management. The usual absentee stockholder contributes nothing to efficiency. He buys a stock today and sells it tomorrow. He often doesn't even know what the company makes. Why should he be rewarded by large dividends?

- There are many forms and degrees of cooperation between the worker and the management. The worker's attitude can vary all the way from passivity to highly imaginative contributions to efficiency and progress.

Source: *Civil Engineering*, January 1973, p. 78. Reprinted by permission.

EXHIBIT 5
STABILITY OF EMPLOYMENT

A. Lincoln and Industry Labor Turnover Rates, 1958–1970

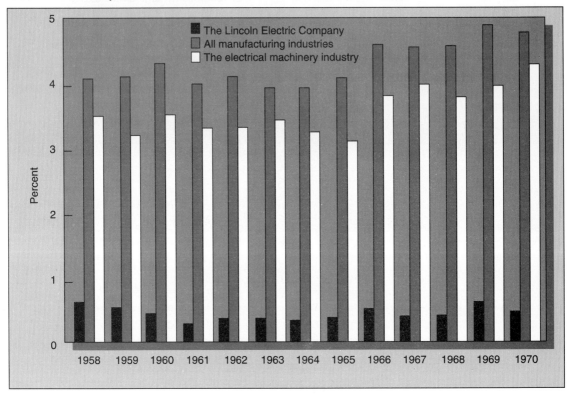

B. Employee Distribution by Years of Service, 1975

Emloyee's Years of Service	Number of Employees
Less than 1	153
1	311
2	201
3	93
4	34
5	90
6–10	545
11–20	439
21–30	274
31–40	197
41–50	27
51 or more	1
Total	2,365

EXHIBIT 6
MANAGEMENT ADVISORY BOARD MINUTES

September 26, 1944
Absent: William Dillmuth

A discussion on piecework was again taken up. There was enough detail so it was thought best to appoint a committee to study it and bring a report into the meeting when that study is complete. That committee is composed of Messrs. Gilletly, Semko, Kneen, and Steingass. Messrs. Erickson and White will be called in consultation, and the group will meet next Wednesday, October 4th.

The request was made that the members be permitted to bring guests to the meetings. The request was granted. Let's make sure we don't get too many at one time.

The point was made that materials are not being brought to the operation properly and promptly. There is no doubt of this difficulty. The matter was referred to Mr. Kneen for action. It is to be noted that conditions of deliveries from our suppliers have introduced a tremendous problem which has helped to increase this difficulty.

The request was made that overtime penalty be paid with the straight time. This will be done. There are some administrative difficulties which we will discuss at the next meeting but the overtime payment will start with the first pay in October.

Beginning October 1st employees' badges will be discontinued. Please turn them in to the watchmen.

It was requested that piecework prices be put on repair work in Dept. J. This matter was referred to Mr. Kneen for action.

A request was made that a plaque showing the names of those who died in action, separate from the present plaques, be put in the lobby. This was referred to Mr. Davis for action.

The question was asked as to what method for upgrading men is used. The ability of the individual is the sole reason for his progress. It was felt this is proper.

J. F. Lincoln
President

September 23, 1974 (Excerpts)
Members absent: Tom Borkowski, Albert Sinn

Mr. Kupetz had asked about the Christmas and Thankgiving schedules. These are being reviewed and we will have them available at the next meeting.

Mr. Howell had reported that the time clocks and the bells do not coincide. This is still being checked.

Mr. Sharpe had asked what the possibility would be to have a time clock installed in or near the Clean Room. This is being checked.

Mr. Joosten had raised the question of the pliability of the wrapping material used in the Chemical Department for wrapping slugs. The material we use at the present time is the best we can obtain at this time . . .

Mr. Kostelac asked the question again whether the vacation arrangements could be changed, reducing the fifteen-year period to some shorter period. It was pointed out that at the present time, where we have radically changing conditions every day, it is not the time to go into this. We will review this matter at some later date. . .

Mr. Martucci brought out the fact that there was considerable objection by the people involved to having to work on Saturday night to make up for holiday shutdowns. This was referred to Mr. Willis to be taken into consideration in schedule planning . . .

Mr. Joosten reported that in the Chemical Department on the Saturday midnight shift they have a setup where individuals do not have sufficient work so that it is an uneconomical situation. This has been referred to Mr. Willis to be reviewed.

Mr. Joosten asked whether there would be some way to get chest X-rays for people who work in dusty areas. Mr. Loughridge was asked to check a schedule of where chest X-rays are available at various times . . .

Mr. Robinson asked what the procedure is for merit raises. The procedure is that the foreman recommends the individual for a merit raise if by his performance he has shown that he merits the increase . . .

Chairman
William Irrgang: MW
September 25, 1974

EXHIBIT 7
EMPLOYMENT HISTORY OF TOP EXECUTIVES

William Irrgang, Board Chairman
1929 Hired, Repair Department.
1930 Final Inspection
1934 Inspection, Wire Department
1946 Director of factory engineering
1951 Executive vice president for manufacturing and engineering
1954 President and general manager
1972 Chairman of the board of directors

George E. Willis, President
1947 Hired, Factory Engineering
1951 Superintendent, Electrode Division
1959 Vice president
1969 Executive vice president of manufacturing and associated functions
1972 President

William Miskoe, Vice President, International
1932 Hired, Chicago sales office
1941 President of Australian plant
1969 To Cleveland as vice president, international

Edwin M. Miller, Vice President and Assistant to the President
1923 Hired, factory worker
1925 Assistant foreman
1929 Production Department
1940 Assistant department head, Production Department
1952 Superintendent, Machine Division
1959 Vice president
1973 Vice president and assistant to the president

D. Neal Manross, Vice President, Machine and Motor Divisions
1941 Hired, factory worker
1942 Welding inspector
1952 General foreman, Extruding Department, and assistant plant superintendent
1953 Foreman, Special Products Department, Machine Division
1956 Superintendent, Special Products Division
1959 Superintendent, Motor Manufacturing
1966 Vice president, Motor Division
1973 Vice president in charge of Motor and Machine Divisions

Albert S. Patnik, Vice President of Sales Development
1940 Hired, sales student
1940 Welder, New London, Conn.
1941 Junior salesman, Los Angeles office
1942 Salesman, Seattle office
1945 Military service
1945 Reinstated to Seattle
1951 Rural Dealer Manager, Cleveland sales office
1964 Assistant to the vice president of sales
1972 Vice president

Donald F. Hastings, Vice President and General Sales Manager
1953 Hired, sales trainee
1954 Welding engineer, Emeryville, Cal.
1959 District manager, Moline office
1970 General sales manager, Cleveland
1972 Vice president and general sales manager

EXHIBIT 8

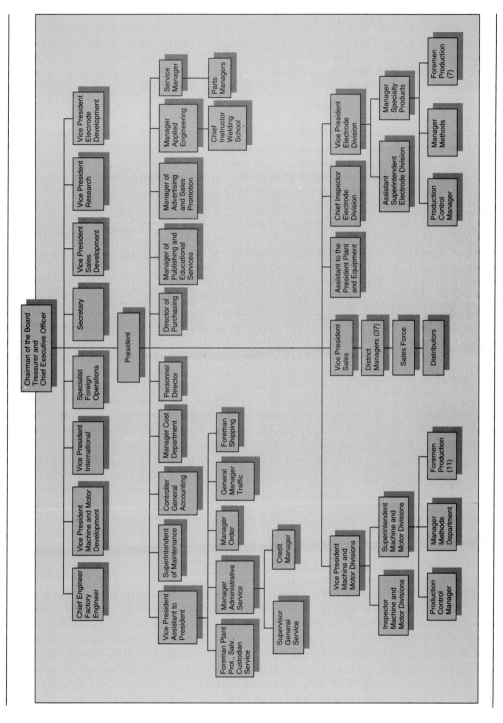

EXHIBIT 9
LINCOLN COMMENT ON THE CASE

After reading the 1975 Harvard case study, Richard S. Sabo, manager of publicity & educational services, sent the following letter to the casewriter:

July 31, 1975
To: Mr. Norman Fast
Dear Mr. Fast:

I believe that you have summarized the Incentive Management System of The Lincoln Electric Company very well; however, readers may feel that the success of the Company is due only to the psychological principles included in your presentation.

Please consider adding the efforts of our executives who devote a great deal of time to the following items that are so important to the consistent profit and long-range growth of the Company.

I. Management has limited research, development, and manufacturing to a standard product line designed to meet the major needs of the welding industry.
II. New products must be reviewed by manufacturing and all production costs verified before being approved by management.
III. Purchasing is challenged to not only procure materials at the lowest cost, but also to work closely with engineering and manufacturing to assure that the latest innovations are implemented.
IV. Manufacturing supervision and all personnel are held accountable for reduction of scrap, energy conservation, and maintenance of product quality.
V. Production control, material handling, and methods engineering are closely supervised by top management.
VI. Material and finished goods inventory control, accurate cost accounting, and attention to sales costs, credit, and other financial areas have constantly reduced overhead and led to excellent profitability.
VII. Management has made cost reduction a way of life at Lincoln, and definite programs are established in many areas, including traffic and shipping, where tremendous savings can result.
VIII. Management has established a sales department that is technically trained to reduce customer welding cost. This sales technique and other real customer services have eliminated nonessential frills and resulted in long-term benefits to all concerned.
IX. Management has encouraged education, technical publishing, and long-range programs that have resulted in industry growth, thereby assuring market potential for The Lincoln Electric Company.

Richard S. Sabo

bjs

The Johnsonville Sausage Co. (A)

Ralph Stayer hung up the phone and leaned back in his chair, deep in thought. One of Johnsonville Sausage's private label customers—Palmer Sausage—was considering a huge increase in its Johnsonville purchases. In fact, the company was talking about placing an order that, if accepted, would account for 25 percent of Johnsonville's annual sales volume. Ralph wondered how he should react.

THE BUSINESS

The Johnsonville Sausage Co. was based in Johnsonville, Wisconsin, a small town about 60 miles north of Milwaukee. In 1945, when Ralph's parents purchased it, the company was a rural meat market—a family home with a storefront, a sausage kitchen, and a slaughter shed and smokehouse out back. The Stayers opened retail food stores between 1946 and 1952. Mr.

Copyright © 1986 by the President and Fellows of Harvard College. Harvard Business School case 387-103 (revised December 20, 1993).

Stayer bought livestock from local suppliers, slaughtered the animals, and sold meat in the three retail stores. He also made fresh sausage, which had acquired an excellent reputation in the area. He managed these stores, and Mrs. Stayer kept the books for the business.

When Ralph graduated from Notre Dame in 1965 with a bachelor's degree in business, he and his father took a hard look at Johnsonville's wholesale and retail operations. The wholesale business looked more promising, and the Stayers decided to focus their efforts on building this segment of the business. Ralph built the company's wholesale business to $4 million in sales in 1975, $15 million in 1980, and $50 million in 1985. Between 1980 and 1985, return on equity climbed from 18 to 27 percent, and the debt-to-equity ratio hovered between 55 percent and 65 percent. The company had become a business of well over 500 employees. Ralph assumed most of the day-to-day decision-making authority for the wholesale business in the early 1970s, and was officially named president in 1978.

Products

Johnsonville Sausage's product line consisted of three types of sausage, which in total accounted for approximately 120 different items:

> **Fresh sausage**—Made from freshly butchered pork and beef cuts. Popular fresh sausage products included bratwurst, Italian sausage, breakfast links and patties, and kielbasa. Fresh products had a shelf life of approximately three weeks.

> **Smoked sausage**—A sausage made in the same manner as a fresh sausage, but to which nitrates and nitrites were added as a "cure." The sausage was then cooked for two to four hours in a hot oven with smoldering wood chips to impart a smoked flavor. Smoked sausage had a shelf life of approximately two months.

> **Semidry sausage**—Semidry sausage, also called summer or slicing sausage, was made like a smoked sausage but was cooked for three or four days. It was typically much larger than an average sausage and could be sliced like a salami. Semidry sausage had a shelf life of at least four months.

Product varieties within each of these three categories were created by varying the spices, the link length, and the casing.

Production

All sausage began as a combination of beef and pork cuts. Live hogs were purchased weekly, and they were slaughtered daily at the company's slaughterhouse in Watertown, Wisconsin. The butchered pork was shipped daily in 2,000-pound bins to the Johnsonville plants.

The processing plants ran on a two-shift basis. Fresh meat was delivered to the plant by 10:00 PM, when the first shift began to turn this meat into sausage filler: meat was ground and spices and flavorings added. At 6:00 AM, the second shift arrived and began making sausages by stuffing casings with this mixture.

- The sausage meat was emptied into a large hopper and was extruded by machine into the casing.
- For fresh sausage, the links were then placed by hand on styrofoam trays, flash frozen, wrapped in cellophane packages, and packed in boxes to be shipped.
- For smoked or semidry sausage, the links were placed in the smokehouse and cooked or smoked for a time with a seasoned wood.

Virtually all of this process was carried out in a refrigerated environment. The process was somewhat capital-intensive since large, mechanized equipment was used to grind the meat, stuff the sausage, and freeze the links. The average industry cost breakdown of a pound of sausage was as follows:

Raw materials	58%
Direct labor	4
Manufacturing overhead	20
Sales and marketing	9
Warehouse/distribution	3
Contribution to corporate overhead and profit	6
Total	100%

Workers tested samples of each product for fat, protein, and moisture content and reported the results to the USDA. Sausage production was typically finished by 3:00 or 4:00 PM, a scant 24 hours after the hog had been butchered.

Inventory was kept at a minimum—two days or so—and all products were made in response to customer orders. During the summer months, fresh sausage was extremely popular, particularly the bratwurst for which the company was famous in Wisconsin.

There were significant fluctuations in demand, due to both seasonal variations and the impact of the company's own promotion and marketing efforts. To deal with these fluctuations, Johnsonville's workforce was flexible and could work more or less than a 40-hour standard week, as needed. In addition, part-time or seasonal workers were hired during the busy summer months. From this pool, employees could select workers to fill full-time openings.

Johnsonville built a new plant in 1978, adjacent to its older facility. The new plant was used only for fresh products; the old factory was used strictly for smoked and semidry products.

Sales and Distribution

Johnsonville relied on a combination of brokers and its own direct sales force to sell its product. The firm employed 25 salespeople in 1985 and used food brokers outside Wisconsin. It used part-time "demonstrators" to cook and distribute free samples of product in retail stores. It began print advertising in 1975. Johnsonville also worked with stores to develop promotions, which typically included discounts on the prices of certain products as well as co-op advertising.

Fresh bratwurst was the product most responsible for Johnsonville's growth; "brats" were sold at the Milwaukee Brewers' stadium and were extremely popular. In fact, several annual polls of sportswriters and broadcasters revealed that John-

sonville's bratwurst was the favorite "stadium food" available anywhere:

> Bratwurst is one of the passions that consumes, and is consumed by, Bob Costas [NBC sportscaster]. Name a ballpark, and Costas will tell you the best item on the menu ... And when it comes to ballpark food, no other stadium occupies a more hallowed spot in Costas's heart, on his palate, or in his stomach than Milwaukee's County Stadium. "The single best ballpark item anywhere, at any ballpark, hands down, is the bratwurst with the sauerkraut and red sauce, at County Stadium," he said, "It's not even close."[1]

Markets

In its early years, Johnsonville served the local area through its retail outlets. It started wholesaling when Ralph began selling to other stores in 1965 and added some other jobbers between 1968 and 1972. Once Ralph signed an outlet as an account, jobbers took weekly orders for the products. In 1978, the company opened its new production facility and began serving the state of Indiana; Ralph's sister Launa was the sales representative for that state.

As time went on, the company continued to expand its distribution both within and outside the state. Under Ralph's direction, Johnsonville expanded to Iowa, Indiana, Illinois, Minnesota, and several other neighboring states. Meanwhile, the firm's market position in Wisconsin continued to strengthen. Its share of the bratwurst market in the greater Milwaukee market rose from 7 percent in 1978 to 46 percent in 1985. The company's Italian

---

[1] *Milwaukee Journal*, July 21, 1985, p. 6.

sausage was number two in this market, and its breakfast sausage ranked number four.

MANAGEMENT

As the company grew; it underwent a series of changes. Ralph described his early approach to managing the business:

> I ran the business from the sausage stuffer. I lived right on the shop floor, making sausage at the same time I was making all the decisions about purchasing, production scheduling, pricing, and advertising. I called on our major accounts.
>
> We had some office help to handle the payroll and receivables and payables. But I made all the decisions. As the company grew, I did hire a financial person and a sales manager. I still made all the decisions and let them handle the implementation details.

In 1980, however, Ralph began to feel uncomfortable with the business and the way in which he was managing it:

> I was fed up with the business. The quality of our product was slipping and no one seemed to care. I had always been proud of the fact that people seemed to enjoy their jobs and took pride in their work. But that seemed to change. People were careless—equipment was being poorly cared for, and bad product was making its way into the market. We did an attitude survey, and general morale was just even with the national average.
>
> One incident particularly sticks in my mind. I'd hired someone early on who was very competent. Then one day it struck me that he was just a soldier, carrying out my orders. I tried to get him to take more responsibility, but he couldn't; I'd ruined him. A few years of my style had beaten the independence

out of him. I vowed I'd never do that again to a man.

During the time that Ralph was attempting to work through his thoughts and feelings about the business, he happened to hear a lecture by a professor from the University of Wisconsin. Dr. Lee Thayer was addressing how managers could change their philosophy and style of management. Thayer, who began working with Ralph, described the process:

> It was a long, slow process. The new philosophy had several dimensions.
>
> ■ First, performance is key. And in a well-developed system, there is no conflict between what is best for the company and what's best for the individual.
>
> ■ The second element is the idea that people do need help to accomplish their objectives, and that *this* is the job of management. We can help them by defining very carefully what their job is, defining explicitly what the performance standards are, and giving them the resources they need.

Thayer described the change process at Johnsonville:

> The first task was to develop a new model of managerial performance in Ralph Stayer's mind. There were several elements to the process. First, he participated in several seminars where we reviewed the new philosophy. Next, he would call me frequently with questions regarding particular decisions that had to be made. We discussed how these issues should be handled if we wanted to be true to the philosophy we were trying to implement. It was very difficult work. As much as Ralph wanted to change, it was still difficult to do.

Ralph described Thayer's role as vital in this organizational transition. He helped him understand his own role as a leader and the importance of that role to the organization. Even more important, he was a sounding board for working through specific issues and problems. Said Ralph: "He was an objective voice that could help us see when we were slipping back toward our old ways. We wouldn't be where we are today without him."

Ralph spoke about how he had come to view his job:

> My first task is a developer of people: our organization's "members." I spend a lot of time with people in the organization just talking things through. I don't tell them what to do anymore; I send them out to make their own decisions. If two people come to me—say manufacturing and marketing—to resolve a dispute, I send them back out; I'm not paying them to push tough decisions up to me; I'm paying them to think.
>
> My job is as a coach, a supporter, a resource. I'm here to help them do their jobs better. I've figured out the few key things I need to know and don't bother with the rest. I'm proud of the fact that there are a lot of details about the business that I just don't know—advertising and promotion plans, for example.
>
> We have a motto here that "Your job is to eliminate your job!" By that, we mean that a manager should delegate his responsibility and develop the capability of his people to work together to such an extent that his existing job virtually disappears—it has been delegated to those who work with him or her. Of course, that person's job continues to evolve as the people they work with delegate new responsibilities to them.
>
> Whenever I see a problem, I look at myself, not "them." First, I assume that if people aren't achieving the performance results we've decided upon, that some of the problem is my fault—I'm not creating the right environment or giving them the

kind of support they need. I need to figure out what part of the problem I am, and how I can change to eliminate it.

> It's my job to ask questions, to surface and describe issues, and to create an environment where all of the relevant parties can discuss these issues.

THE TRANSITION

The Johnsonville Philosophy

Ralph regarded the change in philosophy as the most important change at Johnsonville. The new philosophy included a deep moral commitment to the individual. The primary objective was to make *people* better, not to make the business better. Ralph spoke about this:

> We have gone from a company where I made all of the decisions to one in which responsibility for decisions is distributed to the area best suited to make them. Rather than one entrepreneur on top, we want an organization where everyone is an entrepreneur, where each person is the instrument of his or her own destiny.
>
> We are on the leading edge of developing a far better way to live and work together. The system builds on itself. As people grow, opportunities for sales and profits grow, which in turn provides more opportunities for people to grow.
>
> The key is that *people see Johnsonville as a means to their ends, not vice versa.* We are not the means to the end of profit. It's the other way around: profit is the means to our ends. Profit is not unimportant. It is the seed corn that makes everything else work. Our increase in profits has allowed us to increase our investments in the business and increase the compensation for our people at the same time. This has all occurred in a mature, consolidating industry where both profit margins and compensation have been declining overall.

The first step, then, is getting together and deciding what our ends are.

We begin at a fairly high level of abstraction: clearly, we all want job security, increasing compensation, and a rewarding job. We have attacked each of these objectives, thinking about each one in more detail.

Job security comes from customer demand for our product. It is everyone's responsibility to make a quality product, to innovate and to think about the future. The key here is to be clear about what our performance objectives are and how we are meeting them.

Compensation is the bottom line in this company, not profit. We will work to make this as big as we can. The smarter we work, the more we satisfy customers, and the bigger the payoff. Job security and compensation will both increase.

Finally, the job should be rewarding. Work is a very large part of our lives—all of our lives. It provides the things we want for ourselves and our families. But if we cannot make our work lives more fulfilling, more challenging, more rewarding—more fun—then we're all losers in the game of life. We spend more of our waking hours in our jobs than in any other single thing in life. If all we had to show for it was a paycheck, we would be poor indeed.

The beauty of this philosophy and our objectives is that they all fit together—there is no conflict in achieving these goals. That is because they all revolve around performance.

Structure

As the organization's structure evolved, Ralph emphasized allocating responsibility properly: "deciding who owns the problem." As an example, customer letters of complaint or praise were typically directed to line workers. Complaints about too much salt or a "flavor pocket" (i.e., all the spices in one bite of sausage) were routed to the employees in the meat-grinding room who added the spices. Complaints about tough or split casings went to the sausage stuffers. Workers wrote customers letters explaining the cause of the problem, outlining the steps that were being taken to avoid it, and apologizing for the inconvenience. Employees could send coupons for free product to such customers.

During the early stages of the organization's transition, Ralph found that some individuals at Johnsonville were unable to accept the kind of responsibility that was required. Ralph brought in new people to the three key positions that reported to him. These individuals had considerable experience in their respective functions. Moreover, Ralph had screened them carefully to ensure that they would enthusiastically embrace the firm's philosophy.

Ralph hired Bob Salzwedel from a CPA firm in 1981 to manage the finance function. His responsibilities included acquisitions, cost and financial accounting, accounts credit and collections, and data processing. Bob felt that the job of the finance area was to provide people with the information that they needed to run the operation themselves. Thus, billing and credit were placed under the sales function, and cost accounting under manufacturing. In Ralph Stayer's words, "We do two things here—make sausage and sell it. They are the two line functions, and as close as possible to 100 percent of what we do should fall under one of these two areas. All support functions—including me—are here to serve these two functions. We work for them."

Dissatisfied with the way his 1980 hire was managing the manufacturing organization, Ralph let him go and hired Russ

Wiverstad in May of 1982. Russ had been with Oscar Mayer for 30 years, rising to a plant manager position in which he was responsible for 700 employees. Russ talked about why he had left Oscar Mayer and joined Johnsonville:

> My job at Oscar Mayer was essentially the enforcement of company policy—policy doesn't exist unless it's enforced. They had standards based on time and motion studies, and if a group wasn't up to par, it was my job to yell at the supervisor. I got sick of it.

Russ commented on the changes that had transpired since he joined Johnsonville:

> When I joined the company, Ralph was making all of the day-to-day operating decisions in the manufacturing area: ordering, scheduling, and the like. It took a little while for Ralph to develop trust and confidence in my abilities, but once he did, he delegated a lot of responsibility to me. Over the years, he's become even less involved in the day-to-day operations. Our relationship works on the principle that it's my job to keep him informed, not his job to ask me the right questions. One factor that allowed our working relationship to evolve so well was that Ralph didn't *have* to delegate. He was doing it out of choice, not necessity.
>
> So, it could happen slowly, at a pace he was comfortable with, and that let him develop confidence in me. As Ralph delegated to me, I delegated to my subordinates. Where all the budgeting and planning used to be done by the vice president of manufacturing, those numbers now come from the shop floor.

Originally Russ was responsible for Plant 1 (old), Plant 2 (new), and the slaughtering operation. Over the years, as new functions in the organization were articulated, Russ also assumed responsibility for engineering (developing plans for new plant and equipment); research and development (USDA testing, packaging, product and process development); purchasing (buying meat, spices, and packaging); and personnel development (education and training).

Ralph hired Mike Roller in mid-1984 to replace a 1981 hire, who, after an unsuccessful shift in marketing strategy, had resigned in late 1983. It fell upon Mike to reorganize sales and marketing operations in order to set the stage for further growth and development. The company's first formal marketing plan was developed, including volume and expense budgets that the line managers had developed. Information systems were established to monitor actual results against this plan. Mike added a sales coordinator to eliminate coordination problems between sales and manufacturing; a food service director to direct the company's expansion into food service institutions; a marketing coordinator to implement the company's promotional activity (coupons, demonstrations, and so on); and a national account manager to begin developing Johnsonville's business with major national accounts.

Manufacturing

The supervisor position in the manufacturing area was eliminated. Each function—grinding, packing, stuffing, and so on—had a designated "lead person." Within a given function, workers worked as a team. They alternated specific jobs —e.g., a worker who picked sausages off a conveyor belt and placed them on a styrofoam tray switched jobs with a person who wrapped the sausage or who packed the wrapped trays in boxes. This system was one that the workers had proposed to help eliminate the routine of some of the jobs. It fit with the company's philosophy in a number of ways. If the workers had true responsibility for performance, then it was up to them to organize the line as they saw fit. Doing so increased their own enjoyment of their jobs and improved performance. Job switching had broadened the scope of workers' knowledge and skills. As a result, workers had come up with new ideas for organizing the work and for new equipment that would make them more productive.

Each Monday, production schedules for the coming week were developed by the plant coordinator. These schedules set daily production volumes. Required production targets then cascaded back to create production goals for each area (grinding, mixing, stuffing, packing, and so on).

Area leaders made a commitment to provide the next area in the production flow with the inputs they required to complete their tasks. Materials were weighed and their movement charted throughout the day. Thus, if there was a problem meeting the production target on a given day, the source of that problem was identified.

Daily production scheduling involved delicate tradeoffs. For instance, it might be easiest for the grinding area to produce all the brat mixture in the morning and all the slicing sausage mixture in the afternoon. But this approach might leave other steps in the production cycle—stuffing or packing, for instance—without the inputs they needed to work efficiently. To achieve efficiency overall, therefore, some areas had to work at less than peak efficiency in order to permit other areas to work more efficiently. One worker in the grinding area described how the system worked:

Some days we do stuffing or packing a favor, some days they help us out. If we spent our time fighting with one another, we'd never get any work done.

The lead person's responsibilities were not to supervise the other workers, but to collect data, help train new workers, and give workers the information and help they needed to improve their own performance.

A group of workers met each morning to taste a sample of the previous day's production and discuss any ideas on how the product could be improved. Manufacturing performance was evaluated against budget. On an annual basis, beginning each fall, two or three line workers from each area within manufacturing became part of a budget team, together with people from sales and accounting. Working with the sales force, the line workers developed a sales forecast for the coming 12 months, by product line. They then developed budgets and set goals for certain key measures, including:

- Labor efficiency (pounds of sausage per man-hour)
- Yield (pounds of meat used per pound of sausage produced)
- Labor cost (dollars of labor per pound of sausage)

Workers collected the data required to measure their progress toward these goals, and analyzed and posted results versus budget on a monthly basis. Daily figures for yield, efficiency, and costs were produced.

The capital budgeting process was part of this cycle as well. Line workers developed proposals for new capital equipment. They justified qualitatively why the purchase of the equipment was warranted and then performed a more complex financial analysis, estimating return on assets. Income-producing projects were judged against a 25 percent ROA (pretax) hurdle rate, whereas safety and quality-oriented investments were evaluated according to a less quantitative measure. During this process, the finance area was viewed as a resource to be used; it did not manage the budgeting process but provided service as needed to the line workers.

Personnel

As the organization placed more emphasis on individual responsibility, the personnel function changed dramatically. In 1980, Donna Schwefel, a secretary, had started the personnel department. It hired most of the direct labor, kept pay records, administered the benefit programs, and maintained other personnel records required by law. But Ralph felt that the personnel function should be a line responsibility: "The only difference between Johnsonville and its competitors is our people."

In practice, many of the typical personnel functions became the responsibility of "the line."

- Lori Lehmann, who packed on the bratwurst line, observed the frustration of new workers thrown onto the production line with no training or orientation. Lori suggested a training/orientation program for new hires. She was encouraged to develop a training/orientation guide for all the manufacturing workers in the new plant. Lori presented this program to all new employees.

- Lori also suggested that workers interview prospective hires. When this procedure proved successful, in early 1986, management eliminated personnel's role in hiring.

The performance review process was also removed from the personnel area. It worked as follows:

- Each individual worker developed his or her own job description, listing responsibilities, the performance objectives for each responsibility, and the standard measures along which performance would be judged.

- The individual and his or her supervisor had to agree on the job description and performance standards.

- Individuals updated their job descriptions whenever their responsibilities changed and, again, agreed on the changes with their supervisor.

- Individuals also measured their own performance, analyzed their deficiencies, and suggested ways in which they would improve.

- Individual workers met twice annually with their leader to review these results and agree on the performance evaluation. These meetings were supplemented with almost daily discussion about objectives and performance.

- Based on the semiannual reviews, leaders assigned workers points, from 1 to 100, for their performance. The points were then totaled on a companywide basis, and the bonus pool ("company performance share") was allocated in proportion to points earned.

The company did not have an employment security policy. Ralph explained:

> The best people—people who are really good at what they do—always have job security. To rely on the company to provide this, rather than one's self, is foolish. We provide an opportunity and environment where people can learn and become great; this is what the company can do.

The personnel fuction shifted its focus to the human development area. Terri Case, a local high school teacher, was hired in mid-1985 in response to a

Johnsonville ad seeking an individual "committed to lifelong learning." Ralph Stayer, as part of his emphasis on "people development," wanted Johnsonville to be a vehicle through which individuals could accomplish their own personal goals, whatever they might be. Every individual in the company was given an $80 educational allowance, to be spent in whatever manner they wished. Some took cooking or sewing classes, others flying lessons. Magazine subscriptions were another popular use for these funds. The company also had arranged for all workers to receive a free economics course, taught on plant premises by a local professor.

The hiring process also was unusual. In addition to the typical questions about prior experience, potential hires were asked:

- Why do you want to work for Johnsonville?
- How do you spend your leisure time?
- What would you like to be doing in five years?
- How do you define cooperation?
- How do your friends describe you?
- What do you have to offer a group?

In Terri's words, "If someone isn't sharp enough to write a well-thought-out paragraph on why they want to work here, they are probably not qualified to handle the type of responsibility we give people."

Compensation

Before the transition, workers were paid strictly on an hourly basis, at a rate that was about equal to the local average. Hourly increases typically were granted once a year. In 1979, the company introduced a profit-sharing plan that contributed toward a worker's pension fund.

Management viewed it as unsuccessful because it did not tie compensation to individual performance; it did not seem to influence worker motivation, perhaps because its effect was not immediate.

In 1982, the company instituted a policy of no across-the-board wage increases. Increases would be given only for an increase in responsibilities. Workers' responsibilities were traced via job descriptions, which were reviewed formally twice a year.

In addition to wages, workers received a company performance share, which was a function of both the firm's and the individual's performance. There were three "pools" to which a share of the company's profits was added semiannually:

- hourly workers
- salaried workers
- the three senior-level managers (not including Ralph Stayer)

Ralph described the philosophy behind the compensation system:

> To get great performance, it is necessary to build a system where only great performers can survive. Our compensation system is a good example. In the executive group, Russ, Bob, and Mike split their bonus completely upon the basis of what they did to build people during the year. This same percentage was used to compute their share of a net worth incentive—they can each get an additional bonus of up to 5 percent of the company's annual increase in net worth.

Employees received bonus payments based on individual performance as part of Johnsonville's company performance share (CPS). Since this plan was introduced, average payments to production workers had been as follows (individual payments had varied plus or minus 35 percent, depending on performance):

1982—$200

1983—$700

1984—$350

1985—$800

The 1985 payment represented 4 to 5 percent of the average worker's annual wage. Management hoped to increase this percentage to 25 percent over the next several years. Ralph gave his views on the compensation levels at Johnsonville:

> Our "average" wage has improved over the last five years, with respect to both our local area and the industry. Because we've grown so quickly, a relatively high proportion of our work force is new and hasn't had the chance to work their way up through responsibility and pay levels.
>
> But if you compare someone who has been here for two years with the average local employee, we've moved from about average to the 80th percentile or so. Only workers in heavy industry represented by the big, national unions do much better.
>
> With respect to the industry, we are below the national master union contract that binds Oscar Mayer and Hormel. Still, we've moved from about 50 percent of the national master contract level to 85 to 90 percent of that level. During a time that competitive pressures have forced them to decrease their wages, we've been able to *increase* ours.

Some workers were very enthusiastic about CPS. Typically, they had increased their responsibilities over the years and had received hourly increases as well, so they viewed the CPS as a true "bonus." Other workers, however, complained that they had not received any wage increase over the past three to four years. Most of these workers had failed to assume new responsibilities at Johnsonville. They felt that the CPS was a poor substitute for the annual wage increase that they had formerly enjoyed. In addition, workers seemed to think that there was little variation between the best and worst performers. The compensation system did seem to have broadened individuals' perspective on the company, however. People began to question Ralph Stayer about the impact of acquisitions and capital investments on the company's performance and the CPS.

Research and Development

Before Johnsonville's transition, the research and development area was not formally delineated in the organization; Ralph worked on his own ideas. Now R&D was viewed as everyone's responsibility. One of the company's recent, and successful, new products, "Beer 'n Bratwurst," was developed by a team within the company. The bratwurst was made with beer, instead of water, to replicate the flavor that many brat fans achieved by soaking the product in beer. The idea came out of a brainstorming session held during summer 1984. Together with individuals from the sales and research areas, this team tested and refined the product, which was introduced six months later.

A similar process resulted in the company's ham and cheese sausage, a mild bratwurst containing bits of ham and cheese. Ralph Stayer was not even aware that the product was under development until he was presented with samples.

Systems and Controls

Johnsonville emphasized "self-control." In Ralph Stayer's words, "The notion of control systems is an illusion; the only real control is when people control themselves." In line with the company's philosophy, individual performance was key to the achievement of both the individual's and the firm's goals. Thus, the control system began with great emphasis on describing responsibilities and performance targets at an individual level. Individual salespeople developed the budgets and forecasts to which they were willing to be held accountable. Manufacturing employees used these forecasts to develop budgets and production targets to which they agreed to be held accountable.

Out of these individual commitments, firmwide projections and budgets were developed. These budgets were used as a yardstick against actual performance and as a control on spending. Nonbudgeted items over $500 had to be approved at the vice president level.

Subordinates were responsible for demonstrating their performance to their superiors, not vice versa. There was great emphasis on monitoring one's own performance. Manufacturing workers collected the data to evaluate their own performance daily. Salesmen received weekly and monthly reports on their performance versus budget. It was viewed as the individual employee's job to analyze these data and understand them. If there was a shortfall compared with expectations, what was the cause? If plans were being exceeded, what lessons could be learned?

Workers did punch a time clock but did not punch out for lunch, and their hours were no longer tallied by accounting. It was each individual employee's responsibility to total his or her hours weekly.

Ralph described the issues the firm faced in developing its information and control systems:

> Traditional flows of information are totally inappropriate for what we are trying to accomplish. Traditional information systems transfer the problems away from those individuals that are best suited to deal with them effectively. The key is to develop systems to push problems back to where they belong. We divide information into two types—history and control. Control data are developed to help each person or group control their own operations. They are generated and kept at the operational level. Historical information shows trends and overall performance and flows to whoever is interested.

One example of the manner in which Johnsonville worked was a specific problem the firm had experienced with "leakers"—vacuum-packed plastic packages of sausages that "leaked" air back into the package, thereby shortening shelf life. One worker described how the problem would have been handled before the transition:

> Someone from Quality Assurance would have been measuring the total quantity of leakers, and when it reached a certain point, they would yell at the foreman and tell him to reduce the number of leakers and the guy wouldn't have a clue what to do about it, so he'd just yell at the people who worked for him. That's the whole reason you need a foreman, so you have someone to yell at when there's a problem.

The leaker problem, however, was handled very differently. A "Pride Team" of volunteers was formed to address the problem. This team of first-line workers, with the help of a manufacturing specialist, investigated the leakers and discovered four possible sources:

- The die, which punched out the plastic package;
- The plastic film, which was used for the plastic packages;

- The packaging machine, which actually shrink-wrapped the sausage; or
- The placement of the sausage in the wrapper.

Only this last cause was a human source of leakers; the rest were machine- or materials-related. The workers developed a set of priorities for attacking these problems, based on their analysis of the frequency with which each of these causes contributed to the leaker problem.

The workers attacked each problem, working with material suppliers, making adjustments to equipment or the manner in which it was used. Within two months, the machine/materials problems, which accounted for over 80 percent of the leakers, were completely eliminated. The team developed new practices for line workers, solving the worker-related leaker problems as well. As a final step in the program, representatives from the Pride Team visited retail outlets to educate them on how to handle and store the product once it had left the plant in order to decrease problems caused at the store level. During this process, the workers collected, analyzed, and posted the data every day to determine how they were progressing on the leaker problem.

Results to Date

Ralph Stayer was encouraged by the improvements in performance recorded in the past several years. Sales revenue per dollar of compensation doubled between 1983 and 1986. The ratio of complaints to compliments received from customers declined from 10:1 to 1:1 in the same three-year period. Ralph also observed impressive strides in other areas, such as the percentage of trucks on time and correct invoices.

Employee commitment to the new organizational philosophy was growing. When Ralph first began explaining the philosophy, many people were opposed to it, some charging that he was playing "mind games" with them. Even though in 1986 some people still opposed the philosophy, the large majority was committed, and the trend continued for other employees to buy in.

Although much responsibility at Johnsonville was now delegated to the functional units, some decisions still cut across these functions. Ralph described how he viewed such decisions:

> When we have an issue that involves several different areas, I try to get together the key functional managers and let them work on it. I'd rather not make a decision, but expose it to them, and let them decide and learn from it. I believe I have a certain responsibility to the shareholders—including myself—and if I thought a decision was endangering the economic health of the organization, I would veto it. But—so far at least—that hasn't happeneed.
>
> Basically, I don't want to rob the organization of the opportunity to learn.
>
> The greatest joy for me has been watching people take the program and run with it. Seeing people's expectations of themselves and of what they might become being lifted to levels that would not have been possible any other way.

THE PALMER SAUSAGE DECISION

The employees of Palmer Sausage had gone out on strike in mid-1985, and the company had farmed out its production of sausage items to a number of subcontractors. Johnsonville had produced ring bologna and wieners for Palmer, and the products had sold so well that Palmer asked Johnsonville to continue making the product even after the strike was settled. Palmer sold these products outside the geographic regions in which Johnsonville competed.

In mid-1986, Ralph Stayer received a phone call from Palmer's vice president of manufacturing, informing him that Palmer was thinking of closing one of its midwestern plants and would consider giving the lion's share of the business to Johnsonville. As was standard practice in the industry, any contract for private label production would permit cancellation of the business with 30 days' notice.

Ralph described the thoughts that raced through his mind:

> On one hand, we would love to have the business. We make a 25 percent return on assets on this private-label business—it is profitable for us. But in our last business plan, we decided that we did not want to push private label business over 15 percent; after that point, it

would begin to compete for capital with the rest of our business. This order alone is for a dollar volume that will represent 25 percent of our sales.

> We are runing at a very high capacity utilization now. In order to process this business, we will have to run two long shifts, six or seven days a week. [Johnsonville could not operate more than 18 hours per day because it was necessary to break down the equipment and clean it on a daily basis.] This will really push us to our limits. It could have a demoralizing impact on our own people and cause the quality of our own products to suffer.

> Longer term, it will force us to build another plant much sooner than we had anticipated. Suppose we build for this business and then they cancel our contract? Our return on that investment will drop dramatically, and we will have to lay off the workers we hired for this business.

Ralph wondered what he should do.

Banc One—1993

Banc One is different than its peers—different in a good way . . . this company knows how to motivate people to act as if they were entrepreneurs.
—Morgan Stanley Research Report,
June 1992

In December 1992, Goldman Sachs analyst Robert Albertson labeled Banc One "a premier bank acquirer. . . (with) the most experience and the most impressive repeat performance success rate in accretive acquisitioning."[1] Six months later, UBS Securities reported that Banc One had acquired 137 banks in 74 different transactions in the 25 years since its first acquisition, seeking "average banks," not troubled institutions, and making them better by "generating an average 40–70 percent return on assets improvement." UBS Securities considered Banc One's long-term performance as "great and sus-

Copyright © 1993 by the President and Fellows of Harvard College. Harvard Business School case 394-043 (revised June 21, 1994).

[1] Robert B. Albertson, "Banc One Corporation, the Right Bank at the Right Time and the Right New Product," *Goldman Sachs, Investment Research* (December 7, 1992).

tainable," continuing, "It averaged 17 percent ROE over the past decade with below-average financial leverage. Its success stems from mastering the basics. While accretive acquisitions have contributed significantly to its 13 percent historical earnings growth rate, internally generated growth has resulted in about 70 percent of the growth."

By mid-1993, Banc One, headquartered in Columbus, Ohio, ranked eighth among U.S. banks in total assets and second in market value. Its nearly $15 billion market capitalization exceeded that of American Express, Time Warner, Boeing, or J.P. Morgan. In 1980, Banc One's market value had been $222 million, when its stock price stood at 82 percent of book value. By the end of 1992, Banc One's share price was 249 percent of book value. From 1982 to 1992, the number of employees increased from 4,939 to 32,700, while assets skyrocketed from $5 billion to $61.4 billion. For nine years, Banc One's net interest margin had consistently ranked number one among the top 25 U.S. banks, exceeding their median by 42 percent in 1992. Its price–earnings ratio of 16.2 topped their median by 37 percent in 1992. (See Exhibit 1, Performance Averages, 1983–1992.)

AN OUTSIDER LOOKING IN

Dennis F. Shea, author of the Morgan Stanley report, participated in a two-day planning session attended by 300 Banc One executives in early 1992. Afterward, he described "a banking culture that is unique in the industry." He observed:[2]

> Bank One's culture is pervasive and infectious. Management goes to great lengths to motivate the employees of newly acquired companies to do things the Banc One way. Most important, the culture is not imposed on the acquired company by sending in waves of Banc One people. In fact, the opposite is true: waves of people from the acquired company come to Columbus and other locations. Overwhelmingly, local autonomy—the so-called uncommon partnership between the company and the subsidiary banks—was most often cited as a strength.
>
> Innovation is encouraged at Banc One. Obviously, some innovations don't produce the desired results and others produce unintended consequences. In these cases, the fallout is contained. However, if an experiment works and makes sense, then it is duplicated throughout the system by bank managers who want to mimic that success.
>
> Share and compare were some of the watchwords used at the conference, and those words are the key to Banc One's success. Banks within the system compare and contrast successes and failures. The folks that manage the banks pounding out returns on assets up around 2

> percent seem to be sought after by employees at banks with lower ROAs. Share and compare is possible because all the banking subsidiaries use the same financial reporting and control systems, and everyone has access to the performance of each bank within the system.
>
> Over half the people I polled mentioned the management information and control system as one of the bank's great assets. Managers at individual banks believe they have an edge over the competition because they have better information. Every month a comprehensive analysis of each bank's results is produced and then pored over by the bank's management as well as by internal bank analysts who work for the holding company . . . Banc One refuses to rest on its laurels. I find this relentless introspection refreshing, especially in an industry that all too often has seemed content with mediocrity.
>
> The big challenge at Banc One is maintaining the strong culture which binds all the affiliates together, at least according to the employees I polled. They are concerned about how the company can motivate all the new employees from the recently or soon-to-be-acquired affiliates to adapt to the Banc One culture.

THE INSIDE VIEW

Banc One's 1991 annual report cover featured a picture of several shiny nuts and bolts and the slogan, "Building shareholder value by sticking to the nuts and bolts." The report stated in its preface,[3] "Bank analysts who have heard the Banc One story over the years often comment that it does not change much. It is constantly refined, but the message is always the same. More than one analyst has com-

---

[2] Dennis F. Shea, "Banc One (ONE): Cultural Immersion," *Morgan Stanley, U.S. Investment Research* (June 1, 1992).

[3] Banc One Corporation: 1991 annual report.

mented that we seem to have a good understanding of the 'nuts and bolts' of the business. We are proud of their assessments. Over the years, we have worked hard to develop a straightforward and simple strategy for the continued success of this company."

The 1992 annual report, virtually identical to the one delivered a year earlier,[4] cited the following as basic strategies:

- Serving retail and middle-market customers through community banks, which operate with significant local autonomy, coupled with strong central financial and credit controls;
- Investing in and implementing technologies which enhance retail products, create competitive advantages, provide operating efficiencies, and generate nontraditional bank revenue sources; and
- Treating bank acquisitions as an ongoing line of business, requiring rigorous pricing and management disciplines.

Management believed that banks would succeed or fail in the 1990s primarily on how well they did four things: manage opportunities, make affiliations work, create value, and develop human and financial capital. The first challenge was managing the opportunities created by structural changes in the banking industry, including deregulation, intensified competition, automation, and an increasingly global banking environment. Banc One's chairman, John B. McCoy, reported to shareholders that "with overabundance of opportunity also comes an overabundance of risk . . . If a company lacks the capacity and capability to take advantage of opportunity, trying to manage it is meaningless." McCoy felt that Banc One

was especially good at evaluating new opportunities. He commented, "We are very good at due diligence. We really have very few surprises because we've been at it so long. We know where to look underneath the covers to see what's good and what's bad."

Making affiliations work was the second major task. Banc One's president, Don McWhorter, reflected on the organization's success on this front: "One of the things we do better than anybody else is to acquire a bank and then significantly improve its earnings in a relatively short period of time." "Affiliated," rather than "acquired," was the term used at Banc One. The 1992 report stated, "The very basis of our culture is steeped in what we call an Uncommon Partnership philosophy. This philosophy is one of the cornerstones of our success, based on three principles: decentralizing the people side of the business; centralizing the paper and electronic transaction sides of the business; and operating under a superb financial management system which continuously measures and reports the successes of our efforts." McCoy explained, "If it involves people, we do it at the local level; if it involves paper, we centralize it." (See Exhibit 2 for a description of organizational responsibilities at Banc One.)

Focusing on the third major difference among banks in the 1990s, McCoy asserted, "The ability to create and to maintain a perception of value will be crucial in an increasingly concentrated and competitive banking environment. One critical element in perceived value and pricing will be customer service, still considered scarce in our industry. Since it is scarce, we have found that customers are willing to pay for superior service. Our goal is to continue to refine the capability

---

[4] Banc One Corporation: 1992 annual report.

through 'total quality management,' which begins with determining customer needs and ends with exceeding those needs. Like return on assets and return on equity, return on our quality effort is just as important."

Banc One's management recognized that the fourth critical measure of bank competitiveness was human and financial capital. Banc One was committed to developing its own "human capital." McCoy stated, "At Banc One we try to be very open, exciting, opportunistic. We run a very decentralized organization and I think that a decentralized organization allows and encourages innovation. I think it attracts stronger people. The real key to attracting people is that you have to provide them opportunity and you have to give them authority and responsibility. One of the things that's been very good for our company is that we are growing so fast, there is plenty of opportunity. People would rather be president than be manager, so we create those opportunities where each one has his own market. We now have 100 presidents in this company. We try to treat people the right way, and I've always described it as 'I want to treat people the way I'd like to be treated.' For instance, when I look at myself, I don't remember my successes. It's the mistakes that I made that I learned from, and so I try to reward mistakes as a rule of thumb." McWhorter amplified, "Decisions are made at a very low level. People really do run their own show and have the discretion to make major decisions. That turns them on like lightning. They have an opportunity early on to try their wings with the full understanding that we have a great tolerance for mistakes. We certainly permit experimentation and expect that some of those experiments will fail, and

we have our share of skinned knees. However, if you look back through the history of our successes you will find that almost all the good ideas germinated at rather low levels of our organization. That fact excites and stimulates people throughout our organization."

As to "financial capital," McCoy stated, "Equity is a prime determinant of growth, even survival, in the new banking environment. Banking organizations with the strongest capital positions have the most options as the industry continues to consolidate. . . they will be the survivors."

A SECOND OPINION

In June of 1993, a UBS Securities report confirmed Banc One's self-assessment. The report enumerated Banc One's strengths:[5]

- A strong service orientation will continue.
- A retail/middle-market focus provides high margins.
- Subsidiary banks have significant local autonomy.
- Central support is strong but not obtrusive.
- Nontraditional banking activities have been consolidated within Banc One Diversified Services Corporation.
- Fee-income sources are expanding.
- Customer loyalty should aid growth of fee-based products.
- Growth plans are backed by good research.

The report offered evidence to support its findings. For example, it noted the customer service orientation expressed by Banc One's corporate slogan, "Whatever it

---

[5] Michael L. Mayo and Brent Erensel, "Banc One, The Largest U.S. Community Bank," *UBS Securities Report, draft* (June 23, 1993).

takes," was exemplified by its more than 1,000 conveniently located branches staying open 8:00 AM to 6:00 PM rather than the more typical 9:00–5:00 banking hours and 80 percent of the branches opening for business on Saturday. Banc One broke the mold of traditional banking by setting up shop in supermarkets and, where appropriate to the business, by opening on Sunday as well (20 percent of the branches had Sunday hours).

UBS noted that, in spite of Banc One's rapid climb into the ranks of the largest U.S. banks, it had never wavered from its commitment to the retail market. Consumer and small-company loans continued to provide the bulk of Banc One's business. In fact, at the time of the report, Banc One had no loans over $65 million and only five were greater than $50 million.

UBS credited much of Banc One's success to its decentralized management, noting that decisions were made by employees who best knew customers' needs. Centralized services, including market research, a strategic banking system (combining product profitability and household demographic data), and data management, were other important Banc One strengths cited by UBS.

When assessing Banc One's future, UBS analyst Michael Mayo considered the consolidated Diversified Services Corporation an important factor. DSC was formed to provide a focused strategy for boosting income from nontraditional banking sources. Its goal was to build strategic partnerships with each subsidiary bank to sell mortgages, brokerage services, insurance, mutual funds, and other fee-related products. Noting that DSC had the capability to generate significant fee income from Banc One's loyal customer base,

Mayo was optimistic about the organization's ability to build new business with existing Banc One clients.

THE McCOY FACTOR[6]

Though Banc One could trace its roots back to 1868,[7] its signature policies and practices had been molded by three generations of McCoys. John Hall McCoy took the helm in 1935 and was soon dubbed "5 percent McCoy" because he stubbornly charged 5 percent though prevailing interest rates following the depression were much lower. He believed that customers would pay for good service, and he concentrated on retail banking for two reasons. While serving as a Hoover appointee to the Reconstruction Finance Corporation, John H. noticed that installment loan companies continued to prosper. Furthermore, when he took over leadership of the ailing bank, it was clear that two larger Columbus banks were dominating trust and commercial lending.

His son, John Gardner McCoy, became president and CEO in 1958 only after the board of directors agreed to his three conditions. "First," he recalled, "I wanted a Tiffany bank—not a Woolworth operation with linoleum floors."[8] Second, he wanted

---

[6] Portions of the following two sections, "The McCoy Factor" and "The Banc One Glue," contain material taken from an earlier Banc One case, No. 9-390-208, prepared by Paul S. Myers under the supervision of Professor Rosabeth Moss Kanter, with additional contributions by Professor Paul W. Marshall.

[7] Banc One's predecessor organizations include First Banc, Ohio (1967–1979), City National Bank, Columbus (1929–1967), and Sessions and Company (1868–1929).

[8] Robert Teitelman, "The Magnificent McCoys: Running America's Best Bank," *Institutional Investor* (July 1991).

the board to give him the power to hire and set salaries. Third, he insisted that 3 percent of profits be reserved for research, though he was not then entirely sure what the research would encompass. Once satisfied that he could run the bank his way, John G. took the reins of the organization confidently. One of his first acts was to hire John Fisher, a former disc jockey, to develop ad campaigns for new retail products. In 1962, Fisher hired Phyllis Diller, a local comedienne whom he had seen in Columbus clubs, to make Banc One commercials. Her irreverent style caused some board members to complain that the ads lacked dignity. McCoy responded, "It is very simple: You can have either dignity or dividends. I vote for dividends."

The research investment John G. had insisted on making resulted in the development of state-of-the-art data processing capabilities. In 1966, Banc One (then City National Bank) took a bold step by introducing the first BankAmericard (now VISA) outside of California, a move that marked the beginning of the national charge card revolution. In 1970, Banc One was again the first to introduce plastic-card automated teller machines. In 1976, Merrill Lynch selected Banc One for its new Cash Management Account venture because of its superior data processing capabilities. Though Banc One established its reputation as an industry innovator, it also had some unsuccessful new ventures in the 1970s, including a point-of-sale credit card network in 1977 and an attempt to launch at-home banking in 1979.

In 1967, John G. created a bank holding company, First Banc Group of Ohio. (The spelling Banc resulted from the Ohio law prohibiting holding companies from being called banks. Only local bank affiliates used the regular spelling, i.e., Bank One of Columbus.) In 1979, anticipating structural changes in the banking industry, he registered the holding company to do business in every state. When he found that the First Banc name was already taken in several states, he commissioned a study for a powerful alternative. Banc One was the result. John G. believed that when the laws against intra- and interstate banking were relaxed, Banc One would be well positioned to expand by building "uncommon partnerships." Fisher had coined the phrase in 1968, when the first small rural banks were acquired, to describe the company's unique acquisition and operating strategy. In 1980, when banks were permitted to expand across county borders, Banc One immediately began the affiliation process with larger, urban Ohio banks.

In 1970, John B. joined the organization, starting in the company computer room and moving on to the credit card business. He recalled his return to Columbus, fresh out of Stanford Business School and three years in the military as an administrator at an Air Force hospital. "In my mind the toughest year was the first year because everybody knew who I was. My father ran the company, and it seemed like everybody expected failure. I started in operations, so I was at least 15 miles from wherever his office was. I was in the bowels of the company. In the first year, I had some real successes. And people started saying, 'Hey, I'd like him to work for me because I think he can do a good job,' as opposed to, 'Oh God, I've got the chairman's son coming over.' And so in my mind, the toughest year I had in the company was the first year. Once I'd demonstrated that I could perform, then I was on the same level playing field that everybody was." Still early in his career, John

B. returned from an international banking conference in New York City where he had

> learned how some smart bankers were making a killing by loaning money to the Swedish government. He hurried to his father's office to explain how Banc One was missing the great Swedish opportunity. John G. barked to his only son, "You sit at my desk, and you write down everything you know about Sweden." Time went by, and the white sheet of paper in front of the young McCoy remained blank. Young McCoy walked away from this experience with two lessons. The first was in banking: Don't rush into unfamiliar territory. The second was in McCoy family dynamics: Taking over the bank from his father was not going to be easy or a dead certainty. As he began to rise in the corporate ranks, John B. always knew that his relationship to his father cut both ways. "I could always lose my father and my job. On the other hand, I could always call him at home after all was said and done and ask him why the hell he did what he did."[9]

Later, "there were the usual whispers and jokes when John B. edged closer to the executive suite: John G. was "John God," and John B. was "John Boy."[10] In 1984, John Bonnet McCoy became CEO at the age of 40. Two years later, as restrictions on interstate banking were eased, banks in Indiana and Kentucky became the first non-Ohio affilliates. Michigan and Wisconsin followed in quick succession. In 1989, at the invitation of the FDIC, Banc One participated in the bidding to acquire a large, defunct Texas bank, MCorp. To the surprise of some of the contenders, the Banc One bid was successful. The acquisition marked Banc One's first move outside the Midwest and portended other large-scale acquisitions to follow in the 1990s, including Colorado, Arizona, Illinois, and West Virginia affiliations. (See Exhibit 3, Banc One Locations and Market Share.) With several of its new affiliates, Banc One got more than an extended retail banking network. Many of the new banks had already developed financial services and products that went beyond the traditional banking categories.

After taking over as president and CEO, and particularly after 1987, when John G. retired as chairman, John B. became not only the undisputed leader at Banc One, but also one of the nation's most profiled bankers. In less than a decade (1984–1993), John B. McCoy took Banc One assets from 37th to 8th place among U.S banks. At the same time, the staff grew by more than 25,000, while the stock price increased 500 percent. The July 1991 *Institutional Investor* cover featured "The Magnificent McCoys: Running America's Best Bank." In 1993, *American Banker* selected John B. as "Banker of the Year."

Banc One's leader was praised as both a strategist and an operator, but John B. put the greatest emphasis on the management of people. He noted, "Banking is people. I would guess about 70 percent of my time is on personnel. My belief in people is that everyone wants to learn. My belief in people is that everyone wants to do a better job. And my whole point is, if you get the right people in the right job, you won't have anything to do. At Banc One, we are constantly fiddling, constantly patting them on the back, motivating them, then letting them run. This company is too big for me to say, 'Okay, here's the new

---

[9] *Ibid.*
[10] *Institutional Investor, op. cit.*

product that I thought of.' We have a lot of people working on that, so I'm the chief personnel officer, the drum major, and the symphony conductor."

Though "headhunters" frequently combed the company's ranks, Banc One held on to its best managers, and few managers had been stolen away by other companies. And because Banc One's high standards applied to individuals as well as banks, jobs were not sinecures. McCoy remembered an affiliate bank president with 20 years' service whose job grew too big for him to handle:

> I told him I was convinced he couldn't do [the job], that I'd given him a chance for the past year, and that I had to make a change. I said he had two choices: We could get him an outplacement counselor to help him get an outside job or he could become the president of a smaller bank. He chose to take the outside job. It was announced in the company that he simply wanted that job. There was no embarrassment, no cutting him off at the knees. That's the style I want. If everyone feels the hammer is coming right at him, it's harder to get good performance. Of course, if someone breaks the law, they're out the next minute; that's happened.

The acquisition of new affiliates absorbed some 20 percent of McCoy's time. Working with Executive Vice President Bill Boardman and a small staff, he was often on the road, inspecting potential affiliates and working on deals. Acquisitions of banks with less than $1 billion in assets were initiated and managed by the state holding companies and supported by a corporate review process; larger deals were handled by Boardman and McCoy. From initial meetings to the closing, McCoy enjoyed being involved in the "deal-making." He commented that he often found his responsibilities for people and acquisitions intertwined:

> Besides being chief personnel officer, my other job is that of Goodwill Ambassador. There are times I feel I'm running for office. On the first day in Texas, I tried to walk around as many floors as I could, let people see who we are. We had dinners for all the officers; I talked about our philosophy.

Before McCoy's father completed his first deal, in 1968, he had determined that new acquisitions would work only if they became part of the "uncommon partnership." A longtime Banc One employee explained: "The interpretation may have changed over the years, but it really means local autonomy and keeping the existing management team in place." New affiliates had "sister" or "mentor" banks, and cooperative learning was fostered throughout the organization, but John B. was also a strong believer in what he called "creative conflict." Every bank received a monthly "peer report," and there was as much competition to stay out of last place as there was to be in first. McCoy saw the competition as very healthy and depended on it to inspire innovation. When senior managers proposed a program to consolidate a number of credit card operations Banc One had acquired through its affiliates (a total of eight companywide by early 1993), McCoy insisted that they be consolidated into several operations rather than one. He noted that internal competition among the separate card companies would result in honing a competitive edge and should lead to greater innovation.

At the corporate level, McCoy and McWhorter managed in an informal style, convening weekly staff meetings almost interchangeably, depending on who was available and what issues needed attention. People from throughout the organization were invited to join the meetings to discuss particular agenda items. Monthly policy committee meetings brought the holding company presidents to Columbus to meet with the officers and to review pending business issues and operating results on a companywide basis. In addition to chairing board meetings, McCoy attended the state Presidents' Council meetings. He commented, "When things are running well, I don't have to go to a lot of meetings. Because of the strengths of our forecasts and financial systems, we don't do a lot of reviews—only if there is a problem. In fact, no one wants to take my phone calls, because they know that I call only when there's trouble." In a crisis, McCoy acted decisively. "His reaction is 'Get the people we need in this room, right now,' " said a Banc One officer. "He shuns memos. His frequent response to suggestions: 'Why would we want to do that?' Turf battles and parochial interests are squelched with a sometimes thundering, 'We've got to do what's best for Banc One Corporation.' "

THE BANC ONE GLUE

In the early 1980s, though Banc One was still very much a Columbus bank, it had completed several acquisitions. With additional acquisitions on the horizon, John Fisher felt the need to develop unifying devices. He recalled his early discussions with both McCoys:

> If this continues, every time we do a merger we'll begin to look a lot more like the new affiliates and less like ourselves. You can just see how if we replicate the mergers, down the road there would be no surviving Banc One operating philosophy or culture. We needed to develop

things we could transfer to new affiliates to glue us together as a single organization.

The following year, John B. McCoy became president and CEO. Fisher, sensing that he was searching for a platform to call his own, a way to make his own mark on the company, proposed a plan that included establishing a corporate positioning theme, a training program for executives, and an enhanced internal communications network. Early in 1985, Banc One selected the theme "Nine Thousand People Who Care" as the statement of its common goal.

While attending an IBM function with Fisher and hearing its company song, McCoy commented, "We'd never sing a song in our company." Fisher replied, "We will, and you'll have tears in your eyes." In 1986, Banc One introduced its own song, which its broadcast advertising included and which employees sang at various celebrations and company events. McCoy encouraged employees to get together and record their performances of the company song. The winners would star in a music video produced for companywide broadcast.

The Bank One College, founded in 1985, provided an internal training program for senior managers, especially new affiliate presidents and new corporate executives. Designed to bring new managers together and to be a catalyst for collaboration and exchange, its motto was, "We create our own future." The college took participants from geographically dispersed locations and immersed them in two weeks of intense day and evening experiences ranging from physical workouts to intensive case studies. Top executives, including McCoy, presented the corporate operating philosophy, plans, and issues. Outward Bound–style exercises were used to develop teamwork and trust. Though the semiannual program had a long waiting list of participants, some were skeptical about the college. John B. McCoy was often involved in the final selection of candidates, and when, occasionally, a candidate resisted participating, he would urge the individual to attend and to follow up with an evaluation. The training helped managers both to clarify the company's philosophy and operating style and to adapt them to their own. Though the intensive orientation and training were praised by most managers, some decided they could not accept the basic Banc One philosophy and actually resigned after their college experience. Besides providing needed information and training, Bank One College helped build a network of relationships among affiliates. Annual reunions of all the graduates reinforced these ties.

The Banc One Code of Ethics represented one of the most controversial aspects of the corporate philosophy. Deeply embedded in the culture since the days of John Hall McCoy, the Banc One ethics were defined by accountability and responsibility to depositors and shareholders. When a new bank affiliated with Banc One, each of its employees received a copy of the Code of Ethics and was asked to sign a statement attesting to knowledge of and agreement with its content. The code specifically addressed conflict of interest, personal conduct, and financial affairs. A recently hired Banc One manager described the code as "very conservative."

Though signing the Code of Ethics and attending the college were one-time experiences, other communications within Banc One were frequent and detailed. The monthly company newsletter, The Wire, reported the latest events, internal organizational changes, promotions, employment anniversaries, and other items of employee interest. As Banc One grew, both local and corporatewide editions were published. In 1986, Banc One initiated a systemwide, 30-minute network news–style broadcast, The Quarterly Report. Standard features were the Chairman's Report and financial highlights for the previous quarter. Local affiliates taped professional-quality reports, and senior managers regularly appeared to answer questions about company issues. As affiliates from new regions of the country joined Banc One, the videos included geography and economics lessons about the areas. Outstanding affiliate performance was often recognized on the videos, and banks cited for innovative programs were frequently besieged by calls from other affiliates wanting more information.

Awards were abundant. The Chairman's Award was given annually at the Corporate Quality Awards banquet. "We Care" awards were presented regularly to employees to recognize individual or group contributions to superior customer service; in 1992, 560 employees earned this recognition. The most coveted was the Blue One award, given to the bank scoring highest on profitability, credit quality, reserves and liquidity, and productivity. Other banks scoring highest in each of these individual categories received awards called the Best of the Best. Names and photos of award recipients appeared regularly in The Wire and were sometimes featured in the annual report.

Though building and maintaining the culture was important, the process was also dynamic. When John Fisher retired in 1989, the company song was no longer in popular use, and the slogan was in the process of being updated from "People

Who Care" to "Whatever it takes." Some of the old-timers noted the changes with a certain sense of loss.

SHARE AND COMPARE

Information sharing and idea exchange were basic components of Banc One's operating success. Management stressed face-to-face meetings, preferring personal interaction. State holding company presidents had monthly policy committee meetings in Columbus. The annual Presidents' Council meetings brought together all bank presidents to discuss current issues with corporatewide relevance.

Banc One relied on its powerful financial control system, Management Information Control System (MICS), to provide key operating information, using it at every level of the company to help the banks set and meet performance targets. One way affiliates could keep score on performance was through the monthly peer comparison report, which included results both for the current period and for the full year. The May 1993 two-page peer comparison sorted affiliates alphabetically within one of three peer groups determined by asset size: 19 large banks, comprising some 75 percent of Banc One assets and income; 29 midsize banks, accounting for some 16 percent of total assets and earnings; and 50 small banks. The only dollar figures reported were end-of-period assets and net income, and the remaining data were percentages: equity/ assets, ROA, ROE, net interest margin (NIM), and noninterest expense (NIE)/ revenue (see Exhibit 4, peer comparison report, large banks).

Another more detailed scorecard was available within a few days of the period's closing. The monthly comparative analysis report contained in-depth financial information (see Exhibit 5, comparative analysis for a Colorado bank, with explanatory note). The report included an earnings analysis and ratio analyses of income, loan quality, balance sheet items, liquidity measures, productivity, and noninterest expense control. At the highest level of aggregation, the comparative analysis was provided for the nine state holding companies. At the next level, the total figures for the individual state holding company were detailed for each constituent bank (e.g., Banc One Colorado and each of its six member banks). The same information was available for each member bank (e.g., Denver) in a one-page report labeled "Major Highlights." However, at the individual bank level, the comparison was made not with peers, but with the bank's own prior forecast and monthly budget commitments. Sixty additional pages of information allowed an examination into the finest details (see explanatory note of Exhibit 5).

Managers placed strong emphasis on the MICS numbers. Though the original budgets stood as the commitment to achieving a stated earnings level, actual results led to revisions in monthly targets. One affiliate manager explained:

> The MICS printout doesn't go into a black binder and get hidden away in some drawer. It's the Banc One Bible. The monthly printout is required reading for all officers and supervisors—those people who make the business forecasts—and it is an operating tool for all managers.

One of the most popular stories at Banc One concerned McCoy's attention to MICS. He was said to have placed a call to a new affiliate president a few days after the close of that bank's first month of business with Banc One. He inquired about performance numbers, and the president replied that the information would not be available for weeks. McCoy impressed his new colleague with the Banc One way when he responded, "I'm looking at them now." Another Banc One officer commented, "You can ask new affiliates what they found the worst part of Banc One and they'll say, 'MICS.' Ask them what they found to be the best and they'll say, 'MICS.' " McCoy amplified, "We've bought banks where we go in and say, 'How much are you going to make next year?' and the guy says, 'I'll tell you at the end of the year.' He'd tell you that he's bottom line oriented, he just never put a budget together. At Banc One we are *really* bottom line oriented. Every division, every individual, has a target that he is aiming at and knows what he has to do to get this done. We have a monthly policy committee meeting where we spend three hours on what the earnings are going to be and we go through each bank. Our management information system teaches the culture."

McCoy considered MICS to be one of his most powerful general management tools, noting, "Everyone has access to everyone else's numbers. They can see who is the best, who is the worst. If you see you're the worst, you pick a better bank and see what's happening there. It's friendly peer competition, but not deadly competition. You're in the same company but not competing in the same market. So there's a willingness to share. If I run the Columbus Bank and I've got a great idea, I'm sort of proud of that idea but I will share it with the guy in Dayton because he may have a great idea as opposed to me competing against Dayton and deciding I'm not going to show him anything because I want to take his customers."

While affiliates learned from their peers, they judged their performance against Banc One standards. To qualify for bonus participation, a minimum ROA of 1.15 percent *and* a minimum increase in earnings of 5 percent over the previous year had to be met. Target bonuses ranged from 10 percent to 50 percent of salary. To earn 100 percent of the target bonus, a 1.35 percent ROA coupled with earnings growth of 10 percent had to be met. Several senior managers acknowledged that though the monetary bonus played a significant motivating role, it was no more important than pride, loyalty, and competition.

THE UNCOMMON PARTNERSHIP

Banc One's acquisition strategy remained virtually unchanged throughout the years. As regulatory changes allowed John B. to look across county and, later, state lines, Banc One continued to pursue only successful banks run by managers with proven track records. Other guidelines included do not overpay (make only nondilutive acquisitions); make no hostile takeovers; and make no single acquisition with assets greater than one-third Banc One's size. McCoy explained, "We are always concerned that every time we buy somebody else we could become a little bit more like them and less like us. If we buy a bank less than a third of our size, two things will happen: Our culture will be the surviving culture and secondly, we ran some numbers that show that if we bought something a third of our size and it didn't work, our company would still survive. We will not take dilution so we have a very strict pricing discipline. We've found that we can pay only so much for a bank and once we go past that line, we don't earn the return that we have to earn. We want to buy banks in markets where we can be number one, two, or three in market share. We don't have to start one, two, or three in market share, but over time we have to be able to build up to that."

McCoy commented in 1986 that "the success [of our acquisitions] will be achieved through basically two things: a local management team that knows the market and a similarity between the two organizations' products and services." Of the deals that were not completed, 80 percent failed because of Banc One's lack of confidence in the potential acquisition's management. With few exceptions, incumbent officers remained in place after the affiliation occurred. McCoy recounted a story that became a part of the company folklore:

> When my dad was running the bank, the head of the largest bank in Cleveland called and said, "Why don't we take you and us and form one bank—we'd be really strong." My dad thought that was a great idea, so he invited the guy to his house for breakfast to discuss putting the three banks together. As breakfast was about to be served, Dad asked, "So, what will I do in the new bank?" He was told, "Oh, there wouldn't be any need for you!" That was that. The Cleveland guest was gone before the strawberries were on the table. Our issue [when we make acquisitions] is how to use current management, not how to get rid of it.

With such a strategy, the assessment of people became central to all acquisition decisions. In the spring of 1989, during the due diligence period in Texas, a team of 20 Banc One analysts and executives from affiliate banks studied MCorp's operations. Senior management had already

been removed by the FDIC, but the officers and staff immediately below that level remained in place. McCoy recalled:

> Our accounting guy said, "The controls aren't good, but I'm impressed by the people." Then the next guy said something similar. So we went back to focus on the people: why they're here, who the boss is, why they haven't left. When we got comfortable with the people, we went ahead.

McCoy always expected the existing bank managers to operate the new affiliates profitably and soundly, applying pressure on them to attain higher earnings. Banc One advisers provided what they described as a waterfall of opportunities to increase profitability, with specific examples of earnings improvements on both the revenue and the cost sides. The recommended changes often totaled 2–3 percent ROA. A new affiliate had to implement some, but not all, of the suggested changes to reach the targeted 1.4 percent. The average acquisition increased its ROA by 62 percent, with most of the improvement coming in its first year of affiliation.

The autonomy Banc One allowed affiliates in choosing how to reach the goals was "uncommon" in the banking world, where most holding companies imposed uniform rules and practices on every member bank. At Banc One, each affiliate had its own bank charter, board of directors, and chief executive officer; formulated its own business plan; controlled all personnel and lending functions; and determined all product pricing and marketing, based on local market conditions. However, Banc One provided a uniform product line with standardized features and marketing approaches. Though certain of the products were mandatory, each affiliate was free to select from an additional menu of products those that best served its local market.

In addition to providing corporate support for new affiliates, Banc One assigned a mentor, or sister, bank of comparable asset size and demographic features to each one to demonstrate just how improvements could be made. The sister bank shared information and expertise with the newcomer and helped build competence in the use of Banc One's products, systems, and operating procedures. Typically, the mentor bank president and several staff members would spend two or three days visiting the new affiliate, though more of the learning and sharing was done at the mentor bank when affiliates came to observe Banc One operations in process. One affiliate president remarked:

> The operating culture gets transmitted in part by sharing information between the one with the Banc One culture and the one without. It's easy to see when you have an ROA of .6 percent and the other bank has 1.5 percent that there are [better] ways of doing things that you can learn.

The corporate office in Columbus provided (for a fee) central services, including legal, new product development, and marketing. Banc One's centralized procurement program, originally developed by Banc One, Wisconsin, and implemented companywide on a voluntary basis, saved the company more than $36 million from 1990 to 1992. One subscribing affiliate noted that the group must serve him at least as well as, if not better than, his in-house operations had. "I have the authority to find my own suppliers if I'm not happy with the job Columbus is doing." Affiliation allowed banks to draw

from a broad range of system-supported products not usually provided by small independent banks, such as leasing and commercial lending. An Ohio affiliate president concluded:

> The uncommon partnership offers our customers the best of both worlds: those local [lending] decisions as well as services not generally offered by a $100 million bank. Because of that partnership, we're allowed to spend more time with our customers. For example, I don't have my staff bogged down with tracking the changes in regulations. The corporate legal staff does that. We can instead focus on serving the customers.

Responding to the question whether more services would have to be centralized, McCoy responded, "Never use the word 'centralized.' We use the word 'standardized.' And there is a big difference and we talk a lot about it."

INDUSTRY PRESSURES

Banc One was consistent in meeting its goal of increasing shareholder value. In 1992, the company reported its 24th consecutive year of increased earnings per share, 22nd of increased cash dividends to shareholders, 24th of return on assets greater than 1 percent, and 17th of return on equity in excess of 15 percent. For Banc One employees, the company's growth and success had provided unique career opportunities and engendered a sense of excitement and innovation throughout the organization. President Don McWhorter characterized Banc One as "a company that doesn't stand still. While many other companies are downsizing we are expanding at breakneck speed. Everyone likes to be part of a winning team. Our growth stimulates exceptional personal performance because there is opportunity for each and every employee to succeed."

Though Banc One's focused growth strategy and "nuts and bolts" execution had yielded the desired results for more than a decade, company leaders saw several significant challenges in the future. The first was the redefinition of the industry in which Banc One would compete. They saw increasing pressures on both the loan and the deposit sides of the business. External changes—in demographics, competition, interest rates, product demand, the regulatory environment—all compelled Banc One to look beyond the conventional boundaries of banking and commit itself to becoming a "provider of financial services." Banc One experts estimated that traditional banking products accounted for no more than 25 percent of the financial activities of its customers. In mid-1993, McWhorter recalled, "With all the new competition for financial services, you could make a strong case for the fact that traditional banking is dead."

While loan demand was growing soft, new competitors were vying for the business that existed, and most were playing by a different set of rules. The entry of nonregulated competitors such as GE Credit, General Motors, Ford, Sears, and Merrill Lynch into the credit business added to the growing price and volume pressures. "When we look at our regulatory environment, we think it probably costs us 50 basis points. . . and these people have none," reported a senior bank official. On the deposit side, plummeting interest rates were driving banking customers to look for alternative investments. Core deposits were migrating into mutual funds, and even relatively unsophisticated consumers were learning about a whole new array of financial products. As

to margins, McWhorter anticipated a compression in the difference between the cost of funds and the rates at which they could be lent, noting, "If the spread moves from the current 300 basis points back to the traditional 175, it will mean $100 million loss in income."

McCoy commented that perhaps the most significant development in the early 1990s was the renewed activity in bank mergers and consolidations, citing the megamergers of BankAmerica and Security Pacific, NCNB and C&S/Sovran, and Fleet/Norstar's acquisition of Bank of New England as examples. While Banc One viewed the consolidations as positive steps toward building a stronger industry, it cautioned that overestimates of potential performance were driving up prices and sometimes resulting in unrecoverable dilution. Other superregional banks were also aggressively pursuing acquisitions in many of the same markets Banc One was considering. Though Banc One's uncommon partnership often made it the acquirer of choice for potential affiliates, it had to reckon with increasingly strong contenders in the marketplace.

A BROADER STRATEGY

McCoy planned to stick to the basics in acquisition and core business growth, continuing to rely on the uncommon partnership. But he also looked to the addition of a line of nonbanking businesses offered by Diversified Services Corporation, formed in 1990 to provide new sources of revenue. McCoy explained, "We came to the conclusion that we had a number of nonbanking businesses out there that had a lot of potential, but we weren't managing them very well. So that's when we went out and hired Paul Walsh and set up this thing called DSC." (Walsh's banking experience included three years at another superregional bank holding company, the Minneapolis-based Norwest, where he had been Senior Vice President of Capital Management and Trust, and 13 years with Citicorp prior to that.) "We said, 'Paul, we are going to give you all these businesses and what you have to do is to come back and tell us what makes sense.' And I took great care to explain to him that if he had all these businesses reporting to him in two years from now, I would not think he had done a good job. There's this ego thing, 'the more things I have reporting to me, the better,' but I've always had a philosophy that the fewer things you have reporting to you, the better you can do with them."

"The first thing I wanted to do was get a buy-in. I said, 'Listen, Paul, you've got to go out and talk to the individuals and convince them that you are right.' I told him about a guy in the car leasing business who came here and said, 'Gee, I've got a great idea. Here's what I want to do. You just tell the banks at the next meeting that this is what we're going to do.' I said, 'What I'll do is call three banks. I'll call four banks. I'll tell them that you are the best thing since sliced bread and I've gone through this program. It's nifty and I'd like you to go visit each one of them. You'll be there and then we'll go from there.' He said, 'That's only four banks.' I said, 'That's only two banks, because only two of them will do it. Two of them won't even do it, but we will get the two that will and you focus on them and then we'll start publishing the numbers. You may think it is going to take longer, but you are only going to be working with the people that really want to do it, instead of going out and saying, 'Okay, we are going to do this,' and find out you spend all your time with people who aren't interested.' "

Walsh first evaluated each of the existing 12 nonbank businesses on the basis of product profitability, market share, and customer service potential. One was sold, another shut down, several similar services merged, and one was returned to a state holding company. The remaining products were grouped into two categories, asset-based services (mortgage, commercial and consumer finance, and leasing products) and investment services (brokerage, insurance, investment advisory, and trust businesses). Walsh recalled that his intellectual choice to draw on the Banc One customer base to build each of these businesses into one of the top 10 performers in its relevant industry was the easy part. The implementation proved to be a far greater challenge. He initially considered Diversified Services as a separate line of business that would grow quickly by piggybacking on Banc One's customers. When he introduced DSC to affiliates as a centrally managed business that would "leverage the [banking] franchise," he was, at first, received coolly. By the time he got to Indiana, the audience was downright "hot."

Walsh went back to the drawing board and found ways to make the programs mutually beneficial in order to gain cooperation in an organization where each bank had a strong voice. His new proposal for a strategic partnership allowed individual banks to participate in the program's financial rewards and gave bank presidents some input on local staffing decisions. Commenting on Banc One's way of doing things, McWhorter remarked, "An outsider would say, 'Boy, you guys talk things to death,' because we are great consensus builders. We agonize over things that tend to invade somebody's local territory. We believe so strongly in the creative entrepreneurial spirit that we recognize that we have to change some things, but we do it with great, great caution . . . Maybe it's slow, but when we're finished, everybody says, 'Yeah, that's the thing we ought to do' . . . So it's the buy-in. There's nothing these people can't do. You get them pointed in the same direction, and I wouldn't want to be on the other side."

Though the repositioning of the services was important, Walsh noted that "the watershed event" in building support and even enthusiasm for the Diversified Services Corporation among the Banc One affiliates was the appointment of Don McWhorter as president in 1992. He recalled that, though there was no model in the industry for the integrative approach he proposed, McWhorter was willing to support the program and cooperate in getting DSC off the ground. McWhorter commented on the DSC–local bank partnership: "There are products, such as trust and credit cards and mortgages, that clearly need to be run on a consolidated basis just because the expertise is such that they will have a better chance of success. However, we are not comfortable going straight from where we've been to a functional line of business operation. We think that it's too important that the relationship with the local bank be maintained. It is kind of an in-between spot that we're pretty comfortable with. We want to make sure we avoid separating these centralized products from the local bank distribution system and marketplace. We think they are very closely linked and we want to maintain that link."

Banc One planned to distribute the new financial services through Personal Investment Centers (PICs) that would be located within the branch offices. In 1992, six test locations yielded encouraging product and market information. Based on early suc-

cesses, Banc One and participating affiliates had committed to opening more than 400 such centers in 1993. Each PIC was expected to offer a full range of nontraditional financial services, including insurance, brokerage, consumer finance, sophisticated mortgage processing and servicing, and a range of mutual funds as well as some of the existing products available through the branches.

McWhorter outlined plans for making the strategic partnership work: "Even though several of the DSC products will be offered and managed on a centralized basis, local bank presidents will be responsible for the penetration of those products in their marketplace. In this organization, it's the bottom line that gets everybody's attention. If we leave the profits in the local bank, they're going to work pretty hard to see that these products are sold . . . For example, each state will have a trust head (who) will report to the head of the trust company but will also have a very strong dotted-line (responsibility) to the state CEO. So this person will literally become part of the management team of the state because he's going to be a major contributor to the overall profit of that state. On the other hand, he'll work with the trust company to develop products, to develop marketing. It may not work—this is something new."

Goldman Sachs praised the initiative as "a better mousetrap," saying, "We believe their PIC could be the leading bank breakthrough in providing investment services to the individual." The report praised Banc One for resisting any temptation to pursue the "infamous, but limited high-net-worth individual customer" and targeting instead individuals defined as "the mezzanine investors" with up to approximately $75,000 in investable, discretionary assets, and in the late 40s to early 50s age bracket. Roughly one-third of Banc One's 4.5 million customers fitted the description.

ORGANIZATIONAL CHALLENGES

Looking to the future, McCoy commented, "We've got to become more sales-oriented. If we are going to hold the president or the branch manager accountable as the market manager, then he's accountable for everything that happens to that market, and that doesn't mean that everybody reports to him in that market. But when we add up the scores at the end of the year and look at Columbus and Indianapolis and, say they are the same, if we sold a billion dollars of mutual funds at Indianapolis and $500 million in Columbus, we are going to say that that guy in Columbus didn't do the job as the market manager. And then he'll come back and say, 'Well, we didn't do as well because we didn't have good people.' And we'll say, 'Well that's your responsibility. If you don't like the people, you have to get out there and talk to Paul and change that.' "

Banc One confronted several additional challenges in mid-1993. Customer service received intense study. McCoy commented, "We have struggled with how to measure customer service. It is sort of interesting: I can sit down and pick up the financial statement of this company or any bank and in about three minutes I can give you a good opinion of how that company is doing. So what I've always struggled for is, 'What are the three numbers, or four numbers or the five numbers that I can look at to tell me about customer service?' And on the other hand, it's probably more important, not for me to know about customer service, but for the front line people to know." To demonstrate its

importance, management decided to make service a line on the MICS report, to be measured by customer retention, depth of service (number of Banc One products used by each customer), and customer feedback as determined by surveys. Managers were to be evaluated not only on financial results, but also on service performance, and bonuses would be tied to both. However, in early 1993, McWhorter was still struggling with how best to measure service. "How do you define and measure quality? We are deeply committed to the concept and our people have worked on developing and implementing a total quality management system over the years. However, we are still not comfortable with the results. We needed a program that was simple to implement, simple to monitor, and very effective in terms of measures. That is why we believe that customer satisfaction and customer retention represent at least two key elements that are absolutely going to be measured throughout our company."

Banc One was also confronted with difficult technological challenges. It had already made heavy investments in the development of its new Strategic Banking Systems with EDS and was updating its MICS reporting system. The acquisition pace had put severe strains on the Service Corporation that provided Banc One's operating and applications systems. A vice president of Banc One's data processing division noted that every new affiliate had to be converted to Banc One's systems. The process usually took several months to a year, and making the transition work smoothly had taken top priority over the development of new products. As Banc One was acquiring larger holding companies, it was finding that some had state-of-the-art systems and were balking at accepting what they considered inferior Banc One systems. The 1993 conversion of Colorado's six banks had not gone smoothly. When the systems were changed statewide just two months after completion of acquisition, bank customers found themselves standing in long lines as tellers struggled with system delays of several minutes for each entry.

McWhorter commented that the company had always lived on the revenue side, but that Wall Street would value operating efficiencies more highly in the future. Feeling it was important to establish Banc One as a low-cost provider, he was asking for cuts in operating budgets of $150 million in 1993.

A 1992 McKinsey presentation to management on "How to win in an upside-down world" graded Banc One's performance in five areas: (1) "fail-safe" approach to risk management, (2) continu-ous improvement approach to cost management, (3) superior value delivered to customers, (4) ongoing M & A success, and (5) management system that sets new standards of excellence. The report concluded that "Banc One and several others have turned the tables on the once mighty." (The others included Nations-Bank, PNCF, First Union, Norwest, and First Wachovia.)

The McKinsey study, however, also stated that "several uncertainties lie before the new front-runners." It saw a third round of bank consolidation emerging after round one, during which banks "filled in the map" within states, and round two, a consolidation involving state winners leaping across state lines to drive regional mergers. Round three would see the emergence of superregional contenders and a possible endgame resulting in a few dominant institutions per region.

EXHIBIT 1
BANC ONE 10-YEAR AVERAGE PERFORMANCE, 1983–1992

Average 1983–1992	Banc One (originally reported)	Median 25 Largest U.S. Banks	Banc One Rank
Return on average assets	1.38%	.67%	1st
Return on common equity	16.92	11.97	1st
Average equity to assets	7.97	5.62	1st
Nonperforming assets	1.63	NA	NA
Net charge-offs	1.10	NA	NA
Efficiency ratio*	56.00%	NA	NA

*Noninterest expense/total income (interest and noninterest income, but without securities gain).

EXHIBIT 2
RESPONSIBILITIES AT BANC ONE IN 1992

Banc One Corporation provides
- Systems and operations development, direction, and support
- Treasury menagement
- Financial monitoring and control
- Mergers and acquisitions
- Corporate marketing
- Legal and compliance administration
- Cross-fertilization of ideas across afflliates

State holding companies provide
- State financial analysis
- Goal setting, measurement, and compensation

Affiliate chief executive officers
- Function as independent CEOs of banks
- Choose to use optional central resources

Systemwide committees
- Develop standardized products
- Share best practices
- Establish human resources policies

EXHIBIT 3
BANC ONE LOCATIONS, CURRENT AND PENDING, WITH MARKET SHARE

State	Assets ($billion)	State Rank
Ohio	19.3	2
Texas	18.8	3
Arizona	9.8	2
Indiana	7.5	2
Wisconsin	6.7	3
Illinois	3.9	8
Nebraska (pending)	3.0	2
West Virginia (pending)	3.0	1
Colorado	2.8	3
Kentucky	1.7	4
Utah	0.9	4
Michigan	0.6	11
Oklahoma (pending)	0.5	6

Source: UBS Securities Report, June 1993, and Banc One Corporation annual report, 1992.

EXHIBIT 4
BANC ONE MICS FULL-YEAR PEER COMPARISON REPORT FOR LARGE BANKS, MAY 1993

Assets	Equity/ Assets	Net Income	ROA	ROE	NIM	NIE/REV
11,228,011	11.17	139,388	2.22	25.01	10.18	48.01
6,539,556	10.98	134,236	2.12	24.18	8.65	49.03
5,834,680	10.02	121,580	1.97	22.22	7.08	49.47
4,626,288	9.74	90,128	1.93	22.14	7.05	49.61
4,429,304	9.42	56,010	1.89	21.54	6.95	49.97
3,523,315	9.22	54,304	1.68	21.28	6.75	51.23
2,919,340	9.00	47,204	1.68	21.15	6.36	55.79
2,306,245	8.93	43,112	1.65	21.00	6.34	57.69
2,271,216	8.74	34,701	1.53	20.30	6.26	58.73
1,852,069	8.71	31,319	1.41	19.95	6.08	58.81
1,846,283	8.46	23,722	1.41	18.26	5.76	60.83
1,487,213	8.40	18,894	1.39	17.76	5.73	61.57
1,136,174	8.21	18,073	1.36	16.99	5.69	62.31
1,117,913	8.17	14,805	1.30	16.92	5.66	63.76
1,047,775	7.68	14,411	1.29	15.85	5.33	63.96
906,849	7.51	11,896	1.26	15.39	5.27	67.58
887,306	6.95	11,375	1.17	13.10	5.14	68.30
823,893	6.65	10,300	1.05	11.72	5.10	68.51
764,101	6.54	7,305	0.88	8.56	5.08	68.97
Total 55,546,531	8.49	882,763	1.62	19.79	6.46	56.65

Each column has been sorted to show the range of performance from best to worst in the category. Therefore, the rows do not correlate to the performance of a single affiliate.

Large bank affiliates included Akron, Austin, Arizona, Chicago, Cincinnati, Cleveland, Columbus, Dallas, Dayton, Denver, Fort Worth, Houston, Indianapolis, Lexington, Lima, Midcities, Milwaukee, Rockford, and Youngstown in June 1993.

Assets are forecast for the end of the full (calendar) year. Net income includes year-to-date actuals and projections for the remaining periods. Ratios are computed on the basis of full-year forecasts. Forecasts are revised every month.

The following data show the performance for three of the above affiliates.

City X	4,626,288	11.17	90,128	1.97	18.26	6.26	49.61
City Y	2,306,245	7.51	34,701	1.53	21.00	6.95	58.73
City Z	905,849	7.68	11,896	1.29	17.76	5.76	61.57

EXHIBIT 5
BANC ONE MICS COMPARATIVE ANALYSIS REPORT, JUNE 1993

Banc One, Denver
Major Highlights
For the month of June, 1993

Earnings Analysis

	Jun Actual	B/(W) Pr Fcst	B/(W) Budget	Full Year Forecast	B/(W) Pr Fcst	B/(W) Budget	Pr Year 4th Qtr	First Quarter	Second Quarter	Third Quarter	Fourth Quarter
Loan int	4,988	20	(216)	62,647	179	(1,569)	15,261	15,098	14,893	16,028	16,628
Loan fees	6	(69)	(141)	606	(165)	(1,166)	376	168	80	179	179
Inv inc	1,388	(1)	(264)	16,818	(61)	(3,008)	5,533	4,894	4,414	3,898	3,613
Other int inc	—	—	—	—	—	—	—	—	—	—	—
Int exp	(1,638)	(101)	321	(20,114)	(11)	4,017	(5,714)	(5,387)	(5,069)	(4,849)	(4,809)
NIM	4,843	(167)	(299)	61,190	(88)	(1,728)	15,727	15,033	14,575	15,601	15,981
Provision	1,000	1,200	1,280	(1,480)	1,450	2,420	(1,100)	(680)	600	(500)	(900)
Net fnds fnct	5,843	1,033	981	59,710	1,362	692	14,627	14,353	15,175	15,101	15,081
Service chgs	655	(124)	(150)	9,042	(147)	(364)	2,319	2,245	2,269	2,264	2,264
Non-int inc	405	(75)	76	7,111	(320)	1,541	2,610	1,961	1,698	1,618	1,834
Non-int exp	(3,935)	655	438	(53,015)	190	(1,189)	(15,624)	(13,460)	(12,922)	(13,440)	(13,194)
Pretax net	2,868	1,506	1,343	21,616	1,115	682	3,661	4,839	5,961	5,199	5,616
Net tax	892	(502)	(436)	6,461	(377)	(129)	1,086	1,432	1,806	1,548	1,674
NOE	1,976	1,003	907	15,156	737	553	2,575	3,407	4,155	3,651	3,943
Net sec	—	—	—	(7)	—	(7)	—	(12)	5	—	—
Net income	1,976	1,003	907	15,149	737	546	2,575	3,394	4,160	3,651	3,943

Ratio Analysis

Income

	Jun Actual	B/(W) Pr Fcst	B/(W) Budget	Full Year Forecast	B/(W) Pr Fcst	B/(W) Budget	Pr Year 4th Qtr	First Quarter	Second Quarter	Third Quarter	Fourth Quarter
Loan yield %	8.46	.12	(.21)	8.42	.05	(.20)	8.79	8.64	8.42	8.46	8.46
Inv yield %	7.52	(.28)	.36	7.18	(.06)	.17	7.57	7.34	7.40	7.49	7.39
E/A yield %	8.35	.02	(.01)	8.23	.02	(.06)	8.54	8.39	8.27	8.35	8.36
Overall rate	2.10	.04	.31	2.16	.04	.27	2.29	2.25	2.16	2.09	2.10
NIM %	6.27	(.23)	.06	6.34	(.00)	.13	6.36	6.25	6.17	6.44	6.49
Funds fnct %	7.57	1.33	1.69	6.18	.15	.37	5.92	5.97	6.42	6.23	6.12
ROA %	2.10	1.00	.95	1.35	.05	.07	.92	1.23	1.49	1.30	1.39
ROE %	26.92	13.75	12.33	17.06	1.20	.85	11.81	15.46	18.59	16.60	17.54
KMIC ROA %	2.10	1.00	.95	1.35	.05	.07	.92	1.23	1.49	1.30	1.39
Loan quality											
Res ratio EOM%	1.69	(.17)	(.11)	1.70	(.05)	(.10)	1.78	1.81	1.69	1.68	1.70
Chg-offs/Ins %	.24	(.14)	(.33)	.08	.13	.24	.50	.13	.08	(.09)	.21
NPL/loans %	1.76	(.12)	(.17)	1.08	—	—	2.49	2.28	1.76	1.33	1.08

Banc One, Denver
Major Highlights
For the month of June, 1993

Ratio Analysis (continued)

	Jun Actual	B/(W) Pr Fcst	B/(W) Budget	Full Year Forecast	B/(W) Pr Fcst	B/(W) Budget	Pr Year 4th Qtr	First Quarter	Second Quarter	Third Quarter	Fourth Quarter
Balance sheet											
T. assets ADB	1,143,876	66,629	12,273	1,120,890	12,234	(18,066)	1,112,827	1,120,707	1,118,986	1,115,182	1,128,660
Whlsle growth %	13.67	2.70	(5.40)	11.04	.23	2.28	7.59	2.81	18.78	14.12	6.85
Retail growth %	46.50	(9.27)	(2.86)	12.35	(1.09)	(2.64)	16.73	10.99	(6.05)	30.66	12.28
Loan growth %	32.91	(4.32)	(4.65)	11.83	(.56)	(.68)	13.04	7.74	3.70	23.92	10.12
Core growth %	24.43	65.31	19.52	(6.06)	2.26	(1.73)	29.21	(37.89)	23.56	(12.64)	4.35
Dep. growth %	24.23	65.90	19.86	(7.19)	2.23	(3.36)	23.79	(39.65)	21.87	(13.38)	3.77
Loan/deposit %	74.06	(4.42)	(2.41)	82.55	(2.46)	2.40	68.51	77.38	74.06	81.27	82.55
Lg liab dep %	9.72	(.71)	1.61	10.08	.13	1.84	4.64	11.60	9.72	11.10	10.08
Equity/assets %	7.56	(.72)	(.29)	7.99	(.47)	.02	7.45	7.99	7.56	7.83	7.99
Productivity											
FTE/MM assets	.52	(.06)	(.08)	.49	(.03)	(.06)	.52	.49	.53	.50	.49
Dep's/office	109,851	5,834	1,149	107,155	2,576	(3,881)	115,459	104,171	109,851	106,146	107,155
Salary/FTE	27.4	4.0	2.6	27.9	.6	.9	26.3	27.9	26.5	27.6	28.0
Headcount	590	(96)	(96)	553	(39)	(56)	579	553	590	555	548
NIE TO											
Revenue %	66.7	6.6	3.0	68.5	(.2)	(2.0)	75.6	70.0	69.7	69.0	65.7
Assets %	4.19	1.00	.52	4.73	.07	(.18)	5.59	4.87	4.63	4.78	4.64
Risk adj rev %	68.3	5.6	.8	69.1	.6	(.5)	79.0	70.8	70.2	68.4	67.1

(continued)

EXHIBIT 5 (concluded)
HOW TO READ BANC ONE MICS COMPARATIVE ANALYSIS REPORT*

Explanation of the Report

The first section provides an analysis of earnings data. Revenue entries include loan interest, loan fees, investment income, and other interest income. Deducting interest expense from these revenues yields net interest margin (NIM). A provision for loan losses is deducted from NIM (or added when reserves are reduced) to determine the next line entry, net funds function. Other income items (service charges and noninterest income) are added and noninterest expenses are deducted to compute pretax net earnings, which, minus net tax, give the net operating earnings. Net security transactions are then added (or subtracted) to determine net income.

The second section provides ratio analyses of key income indicators. Yield rates are provided for loans, investments, and earnings/assets. Overall rate indicates the cost of funds rate. Other income ratios include net interest margin and net funds function percentages, ROA, ROE, and KMIC ROA (the adjusted ROA used for key management incentive compensation).

In the third section, loan quality is measured by several key ratios, including end-of-month reserves/assets, charge-offs/loans, and nonperforming loans/total loans.

Balance sheet indicators include total assets (average daily balance) and growth percentages for wholesale, retail, loan, and core deposits. (Core deposits include interest checking, savings, money market, and IRA accounts as well as retail CDs.) Deposit growth includes core deposits plus jumbo CDs and public funds.

Liquidity measures include loans/deposits and large liabilities dependence (net earnings from potentially volatile funding sources/assets) and equity/assets percentages.

Productivity measures include the full-time employees per milllion dollars of assets and deposits per office (average deposits per branch in the state holding company). Head count is also tallied monthly for each group.

Controllable cost performance indicators include noninterest expenses as a percentage of revenues, of assets, and of risk-adjusted revenues (risk-adjusted revenues are NIM − charge-offs + other income).

The "Major Highlights" report for each individual bank compared (better or worse) both the curent month and the full-year projections with the forecast revised the previous month and budget (numbers agreed to and locked in by October of the prior year). It also included the prior year's fourth quarter and all current-year quarters. The highlights were followed by a two-page income statement that disaggregated items such as interest or fees on loans into specific loan categories. Noninterest expense was similarly broken down to individual entries such as salaries, occupancy, and so on. Similar backup information was available to provide detail for the average-daily-balance and end-of-month balance sheets. Any item on the highlights report could be examined in finest detail with the information provided in six pages of financial information and 18 pages of statistical support. The 30-page report was followed by another 30 pages of comparisons and variances. The differences between the current month's results and the previous forecast, budget, and prior month's performance were included, as was information about whether the year-to-date performance was under or over budget. The forecast for the next month was compared with the budget and with the current month. Finally, the forecast for the full year was included with a comparison with budget and the previous forecast.

Explanation of Abbreviations

B/W	= Better or worse	KMIC	= Key management incentive coopensation
Pr fcst	= Forecast revised the previous month	Res ratio EOM	= Reserve ratio end-of-period
Pr year	= Prior year		
Int	= Interest	Chg-offs/lns	= Charge-offs/loans
Inv inc	= Investment income	NPL/loans	= Nonperforming loans/loans
Int exp	= Interest expense	T. assets ADB	= Total assets (average daily balance)
Nim	= Net interest margin		
Net fnds fnct	= Net funds function	Dep. growth	= Deposit growth
NOE	= Net operating earnings	Lg liab dep	= Large liabilities dependence
Net sec	= Net security transactions	FTE/MM assets	= Full-time employees per million of assets
E/A	= Earnings/assets		
		Dep's/office	= Deposits per office

---

*The Comparative Analysis Report is a Banc One internal management tool. It does not follow the format as the more formal corporate reports prepared in accordacce with GAAP for external use.

ABB Deutschland

For 1991 I am aiming for a profit before taxes of DM 500 million. This is a five-fold increase of our 1988 budgeted figure. Thus, we have to close a profit gap of about DM 400 million. As a result, a big challenge lies ahead of us. However, increased profitability is essential to meet our target of a 17 percent return on equity.

The challenge of a fivefold profit increase in four years was Eberhard von Koerber's message to his colleagues on the Vorstand (executive committee) of ABB's German subsidiary as he chaired his first meeting on January 8, 1988.

ASEA BROWN BOVERI

Asea Brown Boveri (ABB) was four days old at the time of von Koerber's pronouncement. ABB (see Exhibits 1 and 2) had been created through the merger of Sweden's Asea and Switzerland's Brown Boveri (BBC), leading electrotechnical companies, which had been fierce competitors all over the world. The merger decision, voted on by both boards on August 10, 1987, was preceded by only six weeks of negotiations, conducted without investment bankers by both companies' top management and their major shareholders, namely, Peter Wallenberg for Asea and Stephan Schmidheiny for Brown Boveri. It had been possible to maintain complete secrecy, and the announcement, which called the merger "an important contribution to strengthening European industry," came as a complete surprise. Said Schmidheiny in retrospect, "Nobody really expected this merger, because it was unthinkable. But this is precisely it: to think the unthinkable and then act. It took courage to merge without analysis."[1] Percy Barnevik later commented, "There were no lawyers, no auditors, no environmental investigations, and no due diligence. Sure, we tried to value assets as best we could. But then we had to make the move, with an extremely

---

[1] Werner Catrina, *BBC: Glanz, Krise, Fusion* (Zurich 1991), p. 244 (translated from the German).

thin legal document, because we were absolutely convinced of the strategic merits."[2]

The strategic logic was driven by the recognition that "the ongoing transformation of the electrotechnical industry into an electronics industry has raised the critical minimum sales threshold required to sustain successful research and development." ABB would become number one in the electrotechnical field. Synergies from merging Asea and BBC, which differed in terms of both product segments and geographic markets, were significant. Not only could the development of the next generation of electronic and software components be more easily supported, but product and manufacturing specialization, as well as better utilization and rationalization of marketing and distribution organizations, would reduce costs. Access to export credit institutions in several countries would allow ABB to handle larger projects. Finally and importantly, there would be one fewer competitor in what had become a stagnating and fiercely competitive electrotechnical market with abundant excess capacity.

Reactions in financial circles were overwhelmingly positive. Yet, some commentators wondered whether this merger would suffer the same fate as previously announced transnational European mergers which had failed, such as Dunlop and Pirelli or Citroen and Fiat. Would ABB, which adopted the U.S. dollar as its reporting currency and English as the corporate language, be able to follow in the footsteps of the two successful transnational mergers of the early part of the century which had created Royal Dutch Shell and Unilever? Asea and BBC's corporate cultures and organizational traditions were on opposite ends of the spectrum. Also, the Scandinavian and Germanic mentalities of the executive cadres were very dissimilar. Against the background of failures of most far-reaching international mergers, and confronted with major hurdles in terms of corporate and national cultures, what were the chances that the ABB merger would succeed? Barnevik was confident, however. In January of 1988, at ABB's first press conference, he said, "The ABB merger will become a success. The combination is a marriage without a divorce possibility. We are condemned to succeed."

Asea

Asea, founded in 1883 and headquartered in Västerås, Sweden, had been a success story during the 1980s in spite of stagnation and competition in its traditional markets. This was quite a change from the late 1970s when Asea was viewed as a company in trouble. As a technically dominated firm, it was seen as unresponsive to its markets, often selling at a loss, and having to support a huge bureaucracy at headquarters. Thus, in 1980, a concerned Marcus Wallenberg brought in 39-year-old Percy Barnevik as Asea's first CEO without an engineering degree. Barnevik had studied economics at G2teborg and Stanford and, after a three-year stint at Axel Johnson, had joined the Swedish steel company Sandvik. After six years as controller, he became president of Sandvik's troubled U.S. subsidiary in 1975. By accomplishing a successful turn-

---

[2] This and the following Barnevik quotes are from William Taylor, "The Logic of Global Business: An Interview with ABB's Percy Barnevik," *Harvard Business Review* (March–April 1991).

around, he caught Wallenberg's eye and joined Asea.

According to *Manager Magazin*, after a few months of studying the Asea situation in 1980, Barnevik set four goals. First, losses would be eliminated by either divesting or closing units which were in the red or by drastically reducing their excess capacities. Second, internationalization would be pursued through either acquisitions or more exports. A first priority was to strengthen Asea's hold on the Nordic countries. Third, financial goals and controls, aimed at demanding profitability targets, would be instituted. Fourth, decentralization would be the name of the game. The head office bureaucracy would be cut back and function only as a holding company. Operational responsibility would be delegated to over 30 divisions which, in turn, would be broken down into separate profit centers.

The results were dramatic. During Barnevik's first five years sales increased fourfold and profits tenfold (followed by two years of stagnating profits). The headquarters staff had been reduced from 2,500 to 300 people. Early during his tenure, Barnevik replaced about half of Asea's top 79 people. Manufacturing capacity for power plants was cut in half, particularly after Sweden's ambitious nuclear energy program ground to a halt, and both capacity and product range for transformers were also cut back. In both instances the red ink turned black. Some 20 units were either divested or closed. Even though 4,000 jobs had been eliminated, 6,000 new ones had been created. Many small and some large acquisitions accelerated Asea's growth, both in its traditional fields and in unrelated activities, such as air handling and pollution control, industrial robots, and financial services. These unre-

lated activities accounted for about one-third of Asea's 1986 sales.

Brown Boveri

Brown Boveri, after Nestlé and Ciba-Geigy the third largest company in Switzerland, had been founded in 1891 by an Englishman, Charles Brown, and a German, Walter Boveri, with money borrowed from Boveri's future Swiss father-in-law. The brilliance of the founders led to rapid growth and international expansion. Except for difficult years during the Great Depression, BBC, until the 1980s, knew mostly success and prosperity, which reached a peak during the post–World War II period. With its home base in one of the few countries undamaged by the war, BBC could quickly and significantly participate in the postwar reconstruction. Power generation and distribution benefited from mega-orders from mostly state-owned utilities and overshadowed BBC's other activities such as the electrical equipment for locomotives and other traction vehicles, the electrical and control equipment for a broad range of industries, electronics (information technology and broadcasting transmitters), turbochargers for la·ge diesel engines, and standard electrical products for residential, commercial, and industrial buildings. With demand booming, BBC focused on its core businesses and continuously added capacity (as late as 1976) to meet customer demands. The 1973 oil crisis reduced demand in the industrial world, but it was replaced by large orders from the oil-producing states. Thus, BBC continued to thrive.

With the collapse of the world economy after the second oil crisis, BBC was suddenly confronted with declining demand

and increasing competition. BBC's heavy dependence on its core businesses made it particularly vulnerable when the market collapsed. Its highly focused strategy of the 1960s and 1970s backfired in the 1980s. It was compounded by the fact that most of its capacity was located in Switzerland and Germany, two countries with some of the world's highest wages and strongest currencies, and by BBC's deliberate policy of maintaining its highly skilled workforce so that their know-how would not be lost. The only way to keep these workers employed was to accept loss orders. Management justified this policy by pointing out that the power generation business was bound to revive, at which point BBC would be ideally placed to take advantage of the next boom. A Swiss journalist in October 1985 labeled this strategy "management by hope." Also, in 1985, *Manager Magazin* chose BBC Germany for its monthly rubric on "mismanagement" and labeled the article "Mit voller Kraft in müde Märkte" (with full force into tired markets).

BBC's corporate organization from the outset had stressed local autonomy. It was felt that local management was best placed to negotiate with the public utilities and railroads, which were mostly state-owned. Almost always, local nationals managed the foreign subsidiaries. The local autonomy was also a consequence of the minority holdings in many of BBC's subsidiaries. The local autonomy policy was especially appropriate during the long periods both before and after the second world war when trade and foreign exchange restrictions made local manufacture essential. Another reason for local autonomy was the strictly local competition. For example, in Germany BBC competed with German-based Siemens and AEG. Duplication of manufacturing facili-

ties was common so that local products could be offered in each market. Duplication of R&D also occurred in the larger affiliates. The subsidiaries paid license fees to the parent and sometimes dividends. The executive committee reflected BBC's geographic focus with each member responsible for a major country or geographic area. Only beginning in 1987 did BBC shift to a new divisional organization based on 24 business units. This new organization was viewed as a prerequisite to reduce the bulky organization and to eliminate duplication.

At that time, however, there were doubts as to whether the power of the geographic units could really be broken, and whether management at all levels would show the necessary strength and determination to take the drastic measures required. While lip service was paid to cooperation, independence still prevailed when tough capacity or personnel reduction decisions had to be made. In spite of the divisional organization, business unit heads felt that operational decision-making remained in the geographic units and left them with the task of writing strategy papers which were not implemented in the countries.

A prime example was the medium-voltage field. The new business unit head had plainly identified the situation: BBC had by far the largest market share in Europe, yet it was losing money because of excessive fragmentation. Each local unit not only manufactured a broad line, but also had developed different solutions for the same customer need. The remedy for this duplication and proliferation was simple: rationalize and specialize the many local manufacturing facilities and standardize and reduce the extensive product line. However, when it came to implementation, the local princes dug in to defend their product solutions and manufacturing facilities. Cost comparisons were difficult, compounded by a high proportion of allocated costs. Thorough analyses and lengthy negotiations, trademarks of the past, did not disappear. Thus, action remained slow while the red ink was flowing.

THE MESSAGE FROM CANNES

After the January 8th meeting, at which von Koerber enunciated his fivefold profit improvement target, the Mannheim Vorstand and other German top managers traveled to Cannes to attend ABB's first top-management meeting. The message from Cannes, in essence, dealt with four topics: strategy, organization, behavior, and financial targets. The strategy message came as a surprise to the BBC contingent. BBC's crisis had been attributed to its highly focused strategy. Asea, in contrast, had successfully diversified into environmental controls, robotics, and even financial services. Thus, everyone expected a message of continued diversification away from the core businesses.

Instead, power was portrayed as a winner, providing ABB with a unique opportunity to achieve both world leadership and profitability. ABB's focus would be on the electrotechnical and related areas, and no major unrelated diversification was contemplated. To some of the BBC attendees, it almost sounded like a vindication of BBC's former, much maligned focused strategy. Barnevik put forth a set of powerful, clear, and simple messages. He said, "Remember: (1) You do not have to be in high-growth business to make big money (sometimes a reverse correlation); (2) you can achieve good/high growth in worldwide mature business (product and country niches, competitors disappearing,

etc.); (3) to go against the mainstream is often profitable; and (4) with the right strategy and properly implemented—a lot of money is to be made in the electrotechnical industry." He put 10 questions (see Exhibit 3) to the audience and concluded, "Yes on 6–7 out of 10 questions: Power is a winner. Yes on 8–10 out of 10: Power is a sure winner and will propel ABB into high profitability."

The Cannes message also put forth ABB's organizational philosophy. At its core was the principle of decentralizing responsibility and authority as far down into the organization as possible. The fundamental guiding principle was enunciated to organize the group "in clear profit centers with individual accountability as the only way to lift profitability and keep it there. The many profit centers reflect a *far-reaching decentralization of responsibility and authority* into, as much as possible, 'self-contained and manageable' units with overview." The 180,000 employees, grouped in between 3,000 and 4,000 profit centers, would be acting in, and controlled by, ABB's "international matrix" (see Exhibit 4). According to Barnevik, "The only way to structure a complex, global organization is to make it as simple and local as possible. ABB is complicated from where I sit. But on the ground, where the real work gets done, all of our operations must function as closely as possible to stand-alone operations. Our managers need well-defined sets of responsibilities, clear accountability, and maximum degrees of freedom to execute."

The responsibilities of business area (BA) management were defined (see Exhibit 5). Barnevik subsequently described the role of the BA leader as "a business strategist and global optimizer. He decides which factories are going to make what products, what export markets each factory will serve, how the factories should pool their expertise and research funds for the benefit of the business worldwide. He also tracks talent—the 60 or 70 real standouts around the world.''

Country management's responsibilities were also defined (see Exhibit 6). Barnevik later amplified, "So we have a Norwegian company, ABB Norway, with a Norwegian CEO and a headquarters in Oslo. The CEO has the same responsibilities as the CEO of a local Norwegian company for labor negotiations, bank relationships, and high-level contacts with customers. This is no label or gimmick. We *must* be a Norwegian company to work effectively in many businesses.''

The international matrix resulted in two bosses for managers running a business area in a country, namely, his local superior and the BA head. These managers, according to Barnevik,

> need a different set of skills. They must be excellent profit center managers. But they must also be able to answer to two bosses effectively. After all, they have two sets of responsibilities. They have a global boss, the BA manager, who creates the rules of the game by which they run their businesses. They also have their country boss, to whom they report in the local setting. These managers have to handle that ambiguity. They must have the self-confidence not to become paralyzed if they receive conflicting signals, and the integrity not to play one boss off or against the other.

ABB's executive committee would be located in Zurich with a small staff. BA heads, however, would have their offices in many different places. Thus, ABB would not have a single large head office. In fact, a large headquarters bureaucracy became taboo. Barnevik showed a slide on how to minimize overhead and allocated costs:

Central Staff Functions Financed by Allocations Eliminated Solutions:

- Elimination of function (30 percent)
- Decentralize to profit centers (as needed) (30 percent)
- Create service centers, charging market rates (30 percent)
- Remaining central staff (10 percent)

Subsequently, he described ABB's headquarters philosophy as follows:

> We operate as lean as humanly possible. It's no accident that there are only 100 people at ABB headquarters in Zurich. The closer we get to top management, the tougher we have to be with head count . . .
>
> Being simultaneously big and small, decentralized and centralized . . . [requires] a structure at the top that facilitates quick decision making and carefully monitors developments around the world. That's the role of our executive committee. The 13 members of the executive committee are collectively responsible for ABB. But each of us also has responsibility for a business segment, a region, some administrative functions, or more than one of these. Eberhard von Koerber, who is a member of the executive committee, is responsible for Germany, [some adjoining countries], and Eastern Europe. He is also responsible for a worldwide business area and some corporate staff functions.

Barnevik summarized ABB's organizational philosophy as follows:

> ABB is an organization with three internal contradictions. We want to be global and local, big and small, radically decentralized with centralized reporting and

control. If we resolve those contradictions, we create real organizational advantage.

That's where the matrix comes in. The matrix is the framework through which we organize our activities. It allows us to optimize our businesses globally *and* maximize performance in every country in which we operate. Some people resist it. They say the matrix is too rigid, too simplistic. But what choice do you have? ... It's a fact of life. If you deny the formal matrix, you wind up with an informal one—and that's much harder to reckon with. As we learn to master the matrix, we get a truly multidomestic organization.

Barnevik also used the Cannes meeting to put forth a set of behavioral priorities. He stressed the importance of being close to the customer and close to the market. A slide on general principles of management behavior was shown:

1. To take action (and stick out one's neck) and do the right things is obviously the best,
2. To take action and do the wrong things is second best (within reason and a limited number of times),
3. Not to take action (and lose opportunities) is the only unacceptable behavior.

Barnevik later explained:

> To make real change in cross-border mergers, you have to be factual, quick, and neutral. And you have to move boldly. You must avoid the "investigation trap"—you can't postpone tough decisions by studying them to death. You can't permit a "honeymoon" of small changes over a year or two. A long series of small changes just prolongs the pain. Finally, you have to accept a fair share of mistakes. I tell my people that if we make 100 decisions and 70 turn out to be right, that's good enough. I'd rather be roughly right and fast than exactly right and slow. We apply these principles everywhere we go ... Why emphasize speed at the expense of precision? Because the costs of delay are vastly greater than the costs of an occasional mistake.

Not only speed was deemed essential. It was also stressed that volume increases were no solution to cost problems. A two-stage rocket approach, with profit coming before growth, was advocated: Get competitive and profitable first and only subsequently expand from a profitable position. Another element was called the fixed cost of change: "The merger creates a reconstruction program anyway: Speed up the planned activities and take deeper cuts if necessary." The importance of spending time with customers in the midst of merging was also stressed. The attendees were told to keep up pressure in the marketplace and not to lose market share. Barnevik called for a determined selling effort, labeling it the "battle of 1988." Finally, acceptance of loss orders became taboo. Policies for change were summarized in a series of overheads shown in Exhibit 7.

Cannes not only stressed strategic, organizational, and behavioral elements but also addressed ABB's financial goals. Targets were set for return on equity (net income as a percentage of stockholders' equity), return on capital employed (earnings after financial income and expense —adding back interest expense—as a percentage of stockholders' equity plus interest-bearing liabilities), result margin (operating earnings after depreciation as a percentage of sales), capital turnover (sales divided by average total assets), as well as receivables and inventory turnover as a percentage of sales. These targets required substantial improvements. For example, return on capital employed was to be raised from 12.5 percent to 20 percent (see Exhibit 8). Also, volume growth (in real terms) was targeted at 5 percent per year, 3 percent through internal growth and 2 percent through acquisitions.

THE BBC HERITAGE

BBC's Corporate Culture

To comprehend the magnitude of the merger implementation task and von Koerber's challenge to implement the message from Cannes, it is important to take a closer look at the Brown Boveri corporate culture and at the Germanic traditions prevailing in both Switzerland and Germany. BBC's corporate culture reflected both European and Germanic organizational traditions in the characteristics of its business and environment as well as in the training and motivations of its executives.

First and foremost, Brown Boveri was a fraternity of engineers. The focus at BBC was on technology. The proof of success was the many licensing agreements through which BBC became the leading supplier outside the United States of technology to others. These successes bred a certain arrogance and a not-invented-here syndrome. This applied to outside customers and inside affiliates alike. Thus, it was not uncommon to have Switzerland and Germany work toward different technical solutions to the same customer problem. Lacking in the BBC culture was a focus on the market and the customer. Through pioneering inventions they had created their markets. Their task was to deliver the very best product to the customer. Quality would sell itself. Hence an external sales orientation was lacking.

BBC was a company of technicians and not a company of salesmen.

Perfectionism became a trademark resulting from the engineering domination. Problems would be thoroughly analyzed and extensively discussed. Slow, deliberate decision making attempted to come up with the perfect solution. Unfortunately, when the perfect solution was arrived at, it was often too late. Lacking were quick decision making, acting on the basis of imperfect information, and seeking entrepreneurial results.

Specialization and compartmentalization also resulted from the technical orientation. It was at that time a European tradition to have a tight compartmentalization of the different functional activities. Thus, Chinese walls separated engineering from manufacturing, and they existed between other functions as well. During the 1980s, BBC used its technological skills as a differentiating competitive weapon. However, the development engineers did not coordinate sufficiently with manufacturing. Their sophisticated advanced designs resulted in higher costs which could not be converted into higher prices or, worse, they resulted in quality problems as designs exceeded manufacturing capabilities. Lack of coordination and one-dimensional thinking were significant weaknesses of the BBC organization.

Centralized decision making was another trademark of BBC's culture. It resulted not only from prevailing European tradition, but also from the characteristics of BBC's core businesses. Big-ticket sales were made infrequently to a few large, important customers. Not surprisingly, in such a delicate and high-stakes game, top management was intimately involved. Centralized decision making brought with it a large head office bureaucracy, referred to as *Stammhaus* in Baden and *Zentrale* in Mannheim. This, in turn, often resulted in a *Papierkrieg* (paper war). Many trivial decisions were pushed upstairs, often all the way to the top. Orders or decisions from above educated middle management to become dependent and not take initiatives or make decisions. There was not much delegation. Prior to the merger, a director observed:

> We have far too much faith in paper and too little faith in people. I wish we had fewer minutes, fewer questionnaires, fewer specifications and all of those things that just fill up the filing cabinets, and I wish we would talk more with each other. Think more about human contacts among ourselves, rather than trying to get everything on paper so we'll be able to prove three years from now that we said the right thing back then. We concentrate far too much on the organization itself, and for that reason, on internal politics. We have little principalities, we have walls, we delineate very exactly where the line is rather than concentrating on profit, on costs, on goals, and especially on results.

Within this context, internal politics took on great importance, as did internal competition, often resulting in trench warfare. Said the director, "We are far too internally oriented, always thinking about internal competition rather than tackling the outside competition. I often get the feeling that we compete with each other more than we do with our real competitors." A Danish executive reflected, "Four-fifths of my time is spent on internal discussions." Spending time with customers and seeking customer satisfaction took the back seat in this organization. Also, the collegial leadership body at the top produced mostly compromise decisions, if any at all. Decisive, quick, and tough leadership was lacking.

Identification of executives was strongest with their national unit rather than the parent. Duplication was considered not only a fact of life but a competitive necessity in the local market. Taking a global approach in this context with rationalization as its goal seemed doomed from the outset.

Finally, a financial and strong performance orientation was lacking. BBC executives were not hard-nosed taskmasters working around the clock. To the contrary, they were an extremely cultured, cosmopolitan, and socially responsive group. They put the human dimension first. Employees felt they were treated as human beings and were extremely loyal to the company. In host countries, BBC executives adapted smoothly to local habits and conditions, and at home its social security provisions for its workers were ahead of their time. Executives found time to play the piano and collect art and were extremely well read. At the time of the merger, in contrast to Asea's predominantly Swedish management, many nationalities were represented. The BBC executive committee showed an even Swiss–German distribution, and business units were not only led by nationals from these two countries, but also included nationals from Norway, Denmark, Netherlands, Austria, the United Kingdom, and the United States, as well as Italy.

The Baden–Mannheim Relationship

BBC as a multinational company headquartered in Baden, Switzerland, had its largest subsidiary in Mannheim, Germany. This subsidiary was twice as large as the parent's Swiss operation and, until 1986, was only 56 percent owned. BBC cannot be understood without understanding the Baden–Mannheim relationship. From its founding, BBC Germany had conducted its affairs independently in accordance with BBC's local autonomy philosophy. This quickly led to a duplication of activities, which was consistent with the strategy to supply important markets from local factories. Baden and Mannheim, however, found themselves on a collision course when the German operation, confronted with a saturating local market in the 1960s, also wanted to export. The two organizations found themselves face-to-face in third countries. This rivalry was compounded by the Swiss resentment that the Germans were able to benefit from more generous export insurance and financing help from their government and also from more advantageous bilateral tax treaties. The Germans, on the other hand, resented that they had to get Baden's approval and had to pay the traditional license fee, which they felt put them at a disadvantage vis-à-vis their German competitors. Even though Germany was the largest unit in BBC, it was only a distant second in its home market behind Siemens. Mannheim management felt that Baden interference added an unnecessary handicap in their competitive battles with Siemens.

These conflicts involving export sales were aggravated by a number of other factors. First of all, Mannheim had established an impenetrable Siegfried line by hiding behind German corporate, fiscal, and codetermination law. Corporate law made it impossible for Baden to issue orders given the substantial minority hold-

ings in BBC Deutschland. Tax law made transfers of profits prohibitively expensive. Codetermination law required agreement with the Betriebsrat (works council), which defended the local interests tooth and nail. German executives became experts in the use of these defenses. If they did not use them, they were locally treated as traitors. The Swiss, on the other hand, felt that Mannheim was using these devices shamelessly to thumb their noses at Baden.

There were also many personality conflicts. To paraphrase George Bernard Shaw, Baden and Mannheim were two organizations separated by the same language. The Germans would view the Swiss as provincial, while the Swiss saw the Germans as arrogant. At a meeting involving the KL and the Vorstand, each Vorstand member drove up with chauffeur in a company Mercedes, while the Swiss KL members drove their own personal cars, which were mostly modest. The Germans were more aggressive and resented when the prudent Swiss slowed them down. The Swiss, in turn, were reluctant to have an already big German subsidiary get even bigger. The Germans, being bigger, felt more important and resented being dependent on their much smaller Swiss parent. This antagonism led to a long war of attrition as both organizations competed for the same business in third countries, often with different designs. According to many executives, Baden and Mannheim would sometimes compete more fiercely with each other than with their outside competitors. Enormous energy and time went into the solution of internal conflicts. The constant tug-of-war took a severe toll.

The New Boss

When von Koerber enunciated his five-fold profit improvement target on January 8, 1988, his words fell on an icy silence and were met with visible disbelief by the four old-timers on the Vorstand. Sales and profits had stagnated during the previous five years. Markets were saturated as well as fiercely competitive. Previous profit-improvement programs had failed to produce significant results. Tension and uncertainty in the organization were rampant. The popular head of the Vorstand had been replaced by von Koerber, and two Swedish Asea executives were also appointed to the Vorstand. Even though ABB was a 50–50 merger between equals, Asea's 46-year-old Percy Barnevik had become CEO, and many feared that the Swedes were taking control. Two months earlier, Barnevik had publicly commented that "it is not too bold or undiplomatic to state that BBC has a large inherent potential to improve its earnings. BBC is today in the situation where Asea was at the beginning of the 1980s."

Also a member of the ABB executive committee, von Koerber, 49, divided his time between Zurich and Mannheim. He had joined the BBC executive committee in September of 1986. Born in Germany and having studied law and economics in his home country and in Switzerland, he had previously worked mostly for BMW, where he joined the Vorstand in 1984 in charge of sales and marketing. He had spent nine years overseas, both in finance and administration and as country head. He was reluctant to take on the Mannheim assignment since his wife was terminally ill with cancer and there was a nine-year-old daughter at home.

One of his few lucky breaks in inheriting the ABB German operation was the minor overlap between BBC and Asea, given the fact that Asea's beachhead in Germany and the rest of the European Community was very modest indeed. As a result, ABB Deutschland consisted largely of the previously BBC-owned operations. However, the ABB international matrix immediately went into effect. As a result, Vorstand members, who were responsible for business segments (involving a half-dozen related business areas) would report geographically to von Koerber as well as to another member of the ABB executive committee with respect to their business segments. Likewise, the business area heads in Germany would report both to a Vorstand member and to the worldwide ABB business area head.

EXHIBIT 1
ASEA BROWN BOVERI ORGANIZATION CHART

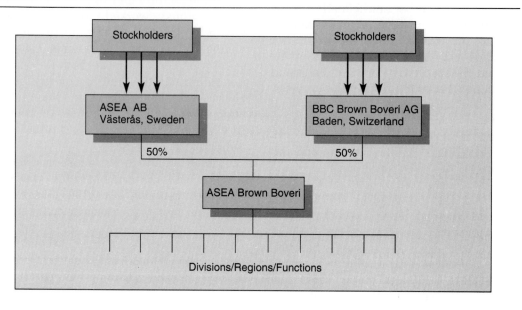

Source: Company records.

EXHIBIT 2
THE WORLD'S LEADING ELECTRICAL COMPANIES

Sales (billions of U.S. dollars)	Electro-technical Area	Total Sales	Number of Employees
ABB	18	18	180,000
Siemens	11	28	363,000
Hitachi	11	36	164,000
General Electric	11	36	304,000
Westinghouse	10	12	125,000
CGE	8	14	150,000
Mitsubishi	7	15	71,000
Toshiba	6	24	120,000
AEG	4	7	78,000
GEC	3	10	165,000

Source: Report from Asea's Extraordinary Shareholders' Meeting on
November 11, 1987. Sales figures converted from Swedish krona into
U.S. dollars.

EXHIBIT 3
GOOD OR BAD TO BE STRONG IN POWER?

1. Have or are we developing technologies for the future?
2. Are we able to use merger opportunities, cut capacity and costs to be low-cost producer?
3. Can we exploit opportunities in niches and service?
4. Do we keep up quality, reliability, and services?
5. Do we have domestic markets with entrenched positions?
6. Can we exploit export financing opportunities?
7. Can we use competitors' decline and exit ambitions?
8. Do we have staying power for the 1990s?
9. Can we project ourselves worldwide as the company in power, someone for utilities to rely on long term?
10. Do we have the flexibility and strategic ability to position ourselves in this turbulent and mixed scenario?

Source: Company records.

EXHIBIT 4
THE INTERNATIONAL MATRIX

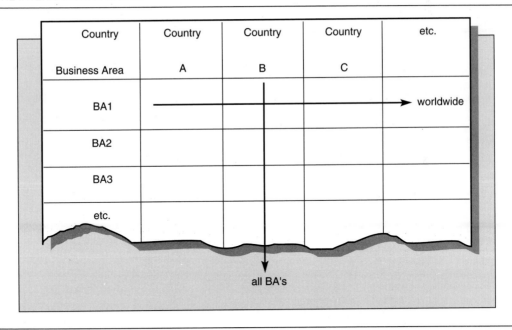

Source: Company records.

EXHIBIT 5
GROUP ORGANIZATION

BA Management Responsibilities

- Worldwide result and profitability
- Establishing a management team—preferably consisting of members from different countries
- Developing a worldwide strategy
- Basic development (typically CAD)
- Coordinating delegated development
- Market allocation scheme and/or tender coordination

- Transfer price schemes
- Price strategy—price coordination
- Product and production allocations
- Coordination of purchasing power
- Coordination and transfer of experience and know-how in design, production, and quality
- External transfer of technology
- Acquisitions

Source: Company records.

EXHIBIT 6
GROUP ORGANIZATION: COUNTRY MANAGEMENT

- Size and complexity of local structure in line with ABB's business presence
- In smaller countries: single company with departments
- In larger countries: holding structure with many subsidiaries and operating units
- Local entities serve their respective markets in line with BA objectives, strategies, and guidelines—they have responsibility for operational results

Source: Company records.

EXHIBIT 7
POLICIES FOR CHANGE

- Identified necessary changes implemented as fast as possible. Small risk that negative changes not considered enough.
  - Concentrate on the ones with biggest profit improvements (80–20 rule)
  - 10 times more common to delay than the opposite
- Get over with "negative" changes in a lump sum; avoid prolonging the process, and cut it up in pieces. Packages with "positive" and "negative" changes desirable. Important to quickly focus on new opportunities. Means earlier focus on positive changes.
- No "fair" reductions in terms of equality between locations—
  Improvements of group profitability count as main criteria in a broad sense.
- Most major changes must be started first year.
  - "Honeymoon" of small changes would be detrimental.
  - What is not started the first year will be a lot more difficult later.
- The merger creates unique possibilities ("excuses") to undertake long-overdue actions which should have been undertaken anyway.
- Upcoming merger problems must be resolved fast and on lowest possible level.
- Example:
  - First cutting capacity, merging, and streamlining costs
  - Then with increased competitiveness—growth and new opportunities
  Volume increase is no solution to cost problems.

Source: Company records.

EXHIBIT 8
LONG-TERM PROFITABILITY REQUIREMENTS

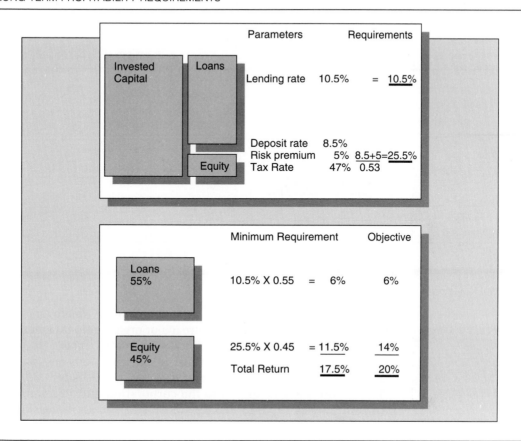

Chapter 7

■

Transforming an Organization

INTRODUCTION

Effective organizations are not forever. General managers often find themselves in situations that require major organizational surgery or other forms of transformation. Indeed, the ability to effect major transformation became more critical to the survival of organizations in the 1980s and 1990s than it had been for the preceding several decades.

Trends and forces external to the corporation and internal conditions have both played a role in making transformation an increasingly important aspect of management. Several broad external forces have contributed:

- The sharpening of global competition among countries and companies including the rapid industrialization of many developing nations
- The development of technologies that make existing strategies obsolete and even change industry structures
- The development of progressively higher standards for winning and keeping customers
- The impact of larger and more fluid financial markets that facilitated major transfers—voluntary and otherwise—of corporate control
- The growing utilization of different organizational forms, including strategic alliances

In addition to these external dynamics that can make competitive strategies and core capabilities obsolete or dramatically raise performance standards, internal developments can cause deterioration in a company's organizational capability. Because these are directly subject to a general manager's influence, it is important to explore the common types of organizational maladies that erode capability. These maladies were increasingly identified as problematic for companies in the 1980s and 1990s, especially in conglomerate corporations such as Allied Chemical and ITT and other giant companies such as IBM, General Motors, AT&T, and the nearly profitless Japanese trading companies. These maladies were also found in other companies such as Caterpillar, Ford, Kodak, and Xerox and the non-American cousins such as FIAT, Renault, Volvo, Daimler Benz, and Nissan.

What are the maladies often associated with growth, size, and diversification that have afflicted corporations, including many of those just cited? The two main causes are strategic and organizational. Understanding them, we can both see how general managers can build the case for change and define the types of reforms the transformation must include for remedies to be adequate.

One set of corporate ills has the effect of confusing the sense of direction. Especially in diversified firms, corporate strategy often lacks clarity and power and is confusing to managers as well as to the financial community. Partially as a consequence, financial resources tend to be spread around to keep all parts of the organization satisfied rather than concentrated on strategic opportunities and diverted from lost causes. This tendency of corporate-level management to respond fairly to the demands of divisions blunts the potential disciplinary effects of the marketplace on individual businesses or product groups. A different strategic problem develops in even the best-run companies when knowledge of the marketplace is confined to what very good customers teach. If the early phases of new technological development take place in new markets, great companies can miss important innovation.[1]

Another set of maladies tends to erode organizational capability and depress performance. These ills include growth in bureaucracy, layering of organizational levels, staff groups that dominate line management, and a tendency for form to drive out substance. The effects are low risk taking, lax standards, low cost effectiveness, and managers who think and act more like hired hands than owners. A further consequence is that the corporation becomes a weak magnet for new talent and a poor developer of existing talent.

You may have observed some of these maladies in several of the companies studied earlier. In a few cases the maladies may have been in an advanced state; in others, management may have detected them at an

---

[1] Clayton M Christensen and Joseph L Bower, "Customer Power, Strategic Investment, and the Failure of Leading Firms," *Strategic Management Journal*, forthcoming.

early stage and taken steps to head them off. In the cases that follow, you can assess whether these corporate illnesses are present, calibrate their consequences, and consider alternative remedial steps.

The question to which we now turn is, How can general managers transform their organization in response to the fundamental but inevitable strategic and organizational inertia that characterizes large, diversified, or merely well-established companies?

INGREDIENTS OF SUCCESSFUL PLANNED CHANGE

Transformation involves managing three ingredients of planned change[2]—the *motivation* to change, the *vision* of new strategy and organization to guide change efforts, and the transition *processes* themselves. Each ingredient is essential—the absence or weakness of any one of the three can doom a planned change. Without a significant level of motivation to depart from the status quo, a vision of the future remains a dream, and transition steps will be implemented pro forma, if at all. Without a vision or model of the future to guide change initiatives, high motivation to change and effective transition processes will produce random change initiatives potentially inconsistent in their direction. Similarly, without competent and effective management of transition processes, a strong motivation to change and a clear sense of direction for the change will produce nothing but frustration.

Thus, the level of motivation, the clarity and attractiveness of the vision, and the effectiveness of the transition processes have more than an additive impact on the overall effectiveness and result of a transformation effort. All three ingredients must be present to some threshold level. Beyond this level, the stronger each ingredient is, the greater the likelihood of pulling off a major transformation. Effective general managers understand these ideas, whether they use the terms adopted here or others.

Let us examine, in turn, what is involved in managing motivation to change, visions of the future, and transition processes.

Building Motivation

General managers must ensure that an adequate level of motivation to change exists throughout the organization. The greater the magnitude of change contemplated, the higher the level of motivation required.

---

[2] John R Kimberly, Robert H Miles, and Richard E Walton, *The Organizational Life Cycle* (San Francisco: Jossey-Bass Publishers, 1980).

Leaders can generate and sharpen two types of motivation for change —dissatisfaction with the status quo and positive interest in an alternative future. Dissatisfaction can push an organization toward change, and interest in an attractive alternative future can pull it.

It is not sufficient for the leader and his or her immediate associates to be dissatisfied; they must create a shared dissatisfaction among the groups whose cooperation is required in planning and implementing the transformation. Obvious examples are a shared dissatisfaction with recent performance in the marketplace—loss of market share or profit shortfalls. It is possible to generate widely shared dissatisfaction by involving members of the organization in benchmarking strong competitors (their products, processes, and services) and by bringing members into contact with customers—to learn firsthand their needs and expectations.

Honda management required managers and engineers to disassemble and examine their best competitors' auto parts and to spend time in the field learning about customers' habits and needs (e.g., spending a day in a Disneyland parking lot to discover how people use their car trunks). Champion Paper International enabled workers who loaded rolls of paper into rail cars to visit customers to observe how the paper was unloaded and how different loading techniques would create less damage and more convenience for customers.

These outside forces can be enlisted even more actively as a force for change. Customers can be given a forum for telling the company that it has become arrogant—a distinct possibility for a successful, dominating company whether it makes earth-moving equipment, performance shoes, computers, or copiers. Financial analysts' views can be made known inside the organization. For example, when analysts lambasted IBM in the 1980s and early 1990s for the perceived slow pace of their workforce reduction, top management had the choice of either discounting these reports or using them internally to create greater readiness for change.

General managers can harness social as well as economic sources of dissatisfaction. In organizations needing major change, inevitably there exist not only market failures and economic shortfalls, but also human disappointment and frustration. People may feel underutilized in their narrow jobs; they may recognize the amount of energy wasted in internal conflict; they may understand the stultifying effect of the inherent bureaucracy; and they may feel badly about compromises they feel forced to live with concerning the products they make or the services they deliver. By conveying an understanding of these social issues and an intention to address them in the change process, the general manager can mobilize both economic and social dissatisfaction in creating a readiness for change.

In addition to using these steps to create dissatisfaction and a motivation to change, an effective general manager will anticipate and deal with resistance to change. As noted in Chapter 5, the resistance is often rational, based on real threats to the status, power, and economic welfare of groups and real prospects for obsolescence of the well-developed competencies of individuals. The resistance is sometimes also based on an almost romantic attachment to the current organization, especially its work environment (an attachment that we could observe in both Nike and Apple.)

These rational and emotional sources of resistance to change, together with ingrained habits of behavior and mindsets, create what can be called "organizational inertia." During the 1980s, the business media commented frequently on the challenge for chief executives in major corporations to overcome organizational inertia. The CEOs of IBM, General Motors, Caterpillar, and AT&T were among those facing major organizational inertia at a time when they were feeling mounting external pressures to change. These and other corporations with similar internal problems were likened to battleships or aircraft carriers: They could only be turned around very slowly because their momentum would continue to take them in the initially plotted direction for some time, until finally the new actions designed to change course could take effect. But in the same period managers of far smaller companies faced similar challenges. Many general managers have experienced great frustration and sometimes career disappointments when they discovered that they could not turn the ship around in time, even when it was a PT boat.

In the cases on transformation that follow, it is useful to assess the adequacy of strength of motivation for change and the steps general managers have taken and could have taken to mobilize organizationwide energy to create change. Considering alternative approaches not taken can be illuminating, especially when there is no apparent crisis to drive change.

We referred earlier to positive interest in an alternative future as well as dissatisfaction with the status quo, noting that they are different forms of motivation for change. Positive motivation to pull the change depends ultimately upon the nature of the vision of the future toward which change will be directed and whether or not it is attractive and reasonable.

Formulating a Vision

However you label it— vision, model, desired future state, goals, and so on—some preference about the future must provide a foundation for planned change in strategy and organization. Even though the picture evolves in direction and concreteness, coherent transformation is impossible without some target.

In the decades before the 1980s, general managers seldom referred to their change objectives in terms of a "vision of the future enterprise." Today, however, this term is used more frequently, in part because the changes that today's general managers have in mind represent a radical departure from the organization of yesterday, and in part because they want the outline of the future organization to be compelling and inspiring to members of the organization. The word *vision* suggests both these attributes or effects.

Usually the vision is not a complete picture; it specifies some features of the ideal future, such as an "empowered workforce" or a "customer-focused organization" or "a world-class competitor". Nor is it a strategy embodying means as well as ends. It is intended to provide directional guidance rather than define the end state or specify how to get there. And—like strategy—it can evolve over time as a manager works out important elements of the vision.

We have seen in many cases how conceptual models or visions of company founders were instrumental to the development and maintenance of organizations over time; the management philosophies of Anita Roddick and James Lincoln come to mind. We could also observe general managers employing models to guide change in Serengeti Eyewear and Johnsonville Sausages. In this chapter, we develop the concept of transformation further by taking a closer look at the role of such visions in the change process in a single company—one not included as one of our case studies.

Champion International Corporation, a large pulp and paper company, launched a major transformation effort in the mid-1980s that is still going on nearly a decade later. The project—really many projects—has produced dramatic improvements in operating capabilities throughout the organization, reflected in the yield of expensive raw materials, reduction in downtime of capital-intensive processes, and increases in the productivity of highly paid employees. Changes have occurred in all parts of the company, including its pulp and paper mills, forest products units, technology center, other professional units, office staff, and the executive suite.

The idea that guided Champion's initial change efforts in a pilot mill was to create a high-commitment, high-performance organization. Once this effort proved to yield results, the goal of transforming the entire organization was labeled top priority by the CEO, and the vision was summarized by an overriding goal of providing "customer-driven quality." The means chosen to achieve this goal included "workforce empowerment", "customer focus," and "process improvement." A bull's-eye diagram (shown in Figure 7-1) was used to show the interrelationship among these three guiding tasks and the final objective of customer- driven quality.

The bull's-eye vision called for a type of attention to the customers' needs that required internal changes in virtually every department. Identifying the three means made clear that profound changes were required in the management of employees, the engineering of businesses, the administrative and operating processes, and the entire organization's mindset toward the customer.

FIGURE 7–1

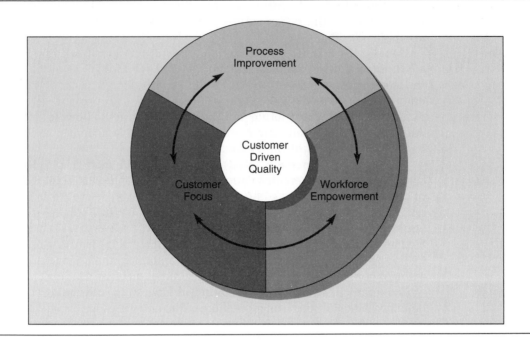

The vision was then translated into more specific terms as it was applied to particular operating units. Here is how it was detailed for the Champion Paper mills at one time. The following are just four of seven paragraphs:[3]

    1. Imagine a mill where each employee knows what he needs to do in his job to contribute to the whole organization running smoothly. He and his team manage by facts and know how to analyze problems using simple tools for understanding process variability. Everyone on the team knows the most important variables to control in order to satisfy customers and to guarantee effectiveness and efficiency. To accomplish all of this, the team meets regularly, using a disciplined meeting process, but employees also have the information, skill, and freedom to make process improvements on-the-run in the daily flow of the manufacturing process.

---

[3] From company documents drafted by Richard Ault and Mark Childers.

2. Imagine a mill where employee/management teams meet to interview and select new members as well as to certify skill levels of existing members. All members are encouraged and rewarded for increasing their skill and knowledge in technical, social, and business terms. To prepare themselves, managers and workers are both trainers and trainees. Training is systematic, ongoing, and based on clear definition of the competencies needed for outstanding performance.

3. Imagine a mill where the leadership team, consisting of both top mill managers and local union presidents, develops clear targets around a few key indicators, and every employee at every level knows these targets and indicators and what they can do to help achieve them. Each area has measurable milestones that are at all levels. All employees, including managers, are compensated in part by their organization's performance against these targets.

4. Imagine a mill where all problems and challenges are met by a group of appropriate people regardless of their levels, functions, or jobs within the organization. These cross-functional teams even include individuals from groups outside the mill when appropriate, such as suppliers, sales, and other corporate staff and even customers. Midlevel mill managers and support staff work together in teams to optimize total system performance rather than maximize departmental objectives.

Champion's use of visions in its sustained change process is illustrative of the transformation process in a number of respects. It shows how visions evolve with experience—in this case from one focused almost exclusively on worker participation to one with relevance for all parts of the organization and the enterprise's infrastructure. And it illustrates the wide but concrete dimensionality of the desired future state reflected in the evolution from the bull's-eye diagram to the detailed image of the daily behavior of mill personnel.

Using this example, we can identify a number of lessons associated with effective use of visions to guide transformation.

- The vision needs to be clear, compelling, and credible. (If the Champion vision had been complex or detailed earlier, it would not have been credible. At the outset, even the single simple idea of "empowerment" had to be demonstrated before it became credible.)
- The vision was effective because it eventually was widely shared and embraced. This required not only that it was presented repeatedly by many leaders, but also that as many groups in the organization as possible must actively engage the vision by translating its implications for their own units and by using it to redesign their work and the structures for which they are responsible.

Above all, we learn that the vision must be ambitious or it will not be compelling or provide the basis for a process of major transformation. The ideals embraced in a vision often are ends toward which the organization will strive, but not end states that can ever be fully achieved. This is especially true when, as we see in many of our cases, the vision of the future organization calls for achievement of both of two qualities commonly thought to be opposing. In effect, the vision may call for achieving "the best of both worlds":

- Take advantage of market power of bigness *and* have the agility of smallness.
- Think globally *and* act locally.
- Innovate *and* control.
- Tough-mindedness *and* soft-heartedness.
- Internal competition among peer units *and* cooperation.
- Self-assurance of being the best *and* "running scared" of potential competition.

Note that in discussing the use of "vision," we emphasized that its effectiveness depended on the process by which it was communicated and the degree to which it was embraced by the members of the organization. This highlights the importance of processes of transformation, to which we now turn.

Managing the Process of Change

Books have been written on the topic of managing change.[4] They discuss the same challenge of developing and sharing awareness in order to provide motivation for those affected and the critical role that a powerful vision plays in that process. But the lengthy chapters tend to revolve around orchestrating the many processes that must be managed as the entire context and culture of the firm are modified. For purposes of dicussion here, all that space allows is identifying some of the most significant processes and major choices that must be made in managing a transformation.

The process of changing goals and redesigning the organization as well as developing the broad outlines of an implementation plan is always the early and central concern of the company's leadership. Depending on the approach taken relatively few people may be involved or a large segment of the

---

[4] Some stimulating examples are Rosabeth Moss Kanter's *Change Masters* (1983) and *When Giants Learn to Dance* (1989); Andrew Pettigrew's *Managing Change for Competitive Success* (1991); and Peter Senge's *The Learning Organization* (1993).

organization may be engaged. That choice is fundamental for the leaders. The general manager must make a judgment as to how important it is to involve members and layers of the organization in order to enlist greater cooperation and commitment. The decision involves myriad factors:

- What is the minimal group that has to be involved for the knowledge basis of the choices to be adequate?
- Is it important to involve younger members of the organization so that the next generation of leadership is committed to the decisions made?
- To avoid creating problems, who has to be involved among those who have power but will not be affected by the likely consequences of the choices?
- How much time and distraction from other organizational work can the company stand?
- Since the costs are high, can the benefits of more extensive involvement be gained through means other than a process with wide participation?

The planners of change also need to consider the steps they will follow:

- Will a pilot site such as a plant or division be appropriate for testing the new concepts and flushing out problems of implementation, or is it better to plunge ahead and roll out the changes across the entire organization? Eisenach was attractive to Opel's Lou Hughes because of follow-on effects.
- As we noted in the discussion of motivation and vision, a critical practical aspect of planning is communication. An effective transformation requires that an enormous amount of attention be given to how the rationale for change, the nature of the change, and the planned steps will be communicated to all members of the organization. Because they are perceived as inevitable and powerful, external crises—such as East Asian competition—make for powerful communication. In addition to cascading this information down the hierarchy by encouraging each level to engage the next level in dialogue about the changes coming, leaders often travel the circuit giving stirring speeches about the need for change and the vision of the future. When spreading bad news, leaders often use disinterested outside experts to add credibility.
- A critical step to be worked out is how to deal with inertia and even active resistance to change. The individuals and organizations that will provide the biggest problem can often be anticipated. The mix of "fostering"and "forcing" techniques needs to be thought through. Should reliance be placed exclusively on fostering achieved by persistent selling of the change, involvement of members in the planning process, and use of incentives to induce support? Or should change be

forced on reluctant managers, staff groups, workers, and labor leaders? The decisions were central to von Koerber in Battle of Mannheim (Chapter 7).

- Other processes are needed to ensure that the necessary knowledge and competence are brought to bear. Consultants may be used to help in the design and implementation of the changes, such as total quality management, empowerment, and reengineering. Even more important is the training and education of members of the organization to perform effectively in the "new" organization. In a transformation, most employees need to know much more about the business than before and need to develop and employ increased analytical, technical, and organizational skill sets. Building these skills often requires a significant new mandate for training.

- Still another dimension requiring attention is the process of business and management performance measurement including measuring the process of change. New systems may be necessary to capture performance, especially where responsibility for profit is being driven to lower levels of the organization. Viewed from the perspective of managing the change, there need to be milestones and metrics for assessing progress and creating forms of recognition to reinforce it.

- This is turn relates to the processes by which incentives are designed and managed. Changes in the systems that affect career progress and employee incomes have awesome power. Whether the way in which change is made is perceived as legitimate or not can have critical influence on the success or failure of a transformation. It is especially important that changes in compensation be introduced in ways that are congruent with the espoused values underlying the new vision.

This list may seem long and inclusive, but it merely shows the range of processes that need modification as part of a major transformation. The number and variety of implementing activities that often must be coordinated to produce desired change can be illustrated by returning to the example of Champion. Figure 7-2 shows the list of activities and redesigned systems that were added to the bull's-eye vision in Figure 7-1 in order to display all the tools that were used to promote each of the three major elements of the vision of empowerment, process improvement, and customer focus.

CONTINUAL RENEWAL

The situation in a company that brings a general manager to plan the kind of fundamental change that we have called transformation is not inevitable—although the long list of great companies that fell from the heavens in the 1980s and 1990s is a caution. These situations can be avoided if managers regularly track the changing environment, frequently

FIGURE 7–2
CHAMPION CHANGE PROCESS

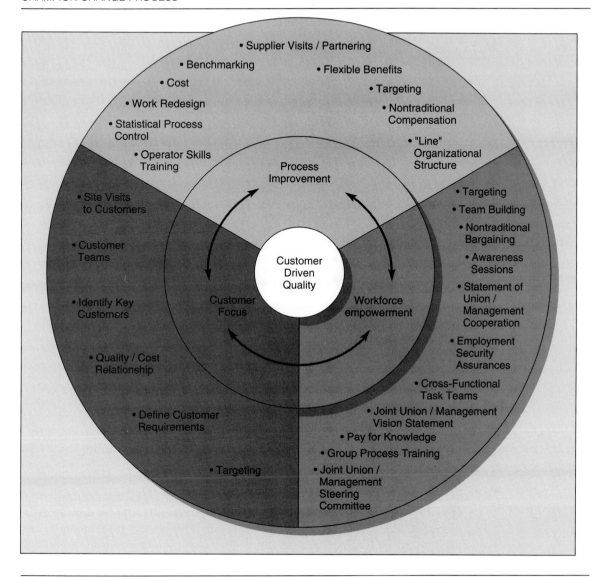

test the premises and logic of their business strategies, and continually review the liveliness of their organization.

Drawing on our discussion of building strategy and organizational capability in Chapters 5 and 6 and the preceding discussion of transformation, we can identify in the actions of general managers we have studied the steps that they have taken to deter the inward focus and complacency that come with success and instead encourage renewal.

Managers like Zaki Mustafa, Jack Welch, and Sir Richard Greenbury espouse continual renewal as a central theme in the growth of their enterprises. Some version of renewal is included in all statements concerning the company vision and management philosophy. Jack Welch uses a powerful image of growth. "I want to start the day the dumbest that I'll ever be." That notion of learning becomes a part of the social contract between the organization and its members.

With phrases like "customer oriented" and "boundaryless" or systems like "best practice," general managers focus the organization outward on customers' evolving needs, on industry leaders' best practices, and on competitors' changing products and market tactics and strategies.

With arrangements like Banc One's uncommon partnership and comparative reports like MICSs, general managers like John McCoy keep raising the performance bar, setting both organizational and individual goals higher. "Restless dissatisfaction" (Marks & Spencer) and obsession with winning market share (Schlumberger) are ways that general managers push their organizations to ever-higher levels of performance.

Repeatedly we see that the structures and systems of great companies are designed to promote lateral processes of communication and coordination between those in direct contact with customers (such as Lincoln's welding-trained sales force) and those involved with internal functions of the organization. The linkage of suppliers with technology in selector–merchandiser teams at Marks & Spencer is so powerful that the suppliers are called "retailers without stores" and Marks & Spencer "a manufacturer without factories." These companies develop processes for sharing and comparing among peer groups that identify and rapidly diffuse better ways of managing. In addition we see extensive incentives and awards offered to encourage experimentation and continuous performance improvement. Still other general managers use systems or their personal intervention to control recruitment and job assignment so that talent is moved in, out, and around the organization (such as Riboud at Schlumberger, Barnevik at ABB, and Welch at GE). With this movement of talent comes the sharing of knowledge and experience.

Last, but hardly least, we can see in case after case that general managers "walk the talk" on this issue. Their own style poses a challenge to complacency. With the outgoing and even outrageous cheerfulness of Anita Roddick, the intense passion of Bill Gates, the social commitment of Ben Cohen, the mystery of Riboud, or the in-your-face toughness of Jack Welch, general managers drive renewal in the way they live their lives.

SUMMARY

We have been considering the situation confronting a general manager in which a major transformation is required. These situations can often be avoided by regularly monitoring the external environment, frequently revisiting the competitive strategy, and continually reviewing the state of the organization.

Drawing upon our earlier discussion in Chapter 6 of building the organizational capability and the discussion here of organizational transformation, we can summarize actions general managers can take to ensure continual renewal of the organization.

First, it is important to espouse continual renewal as a central theme in the growth of the enterprise. It should be included in all statements concerning the company vision and/or the management philosophy, and it must become a part of the social contract between the organization and its members.

Second, the general manager should emphatically focus the organization outward—on customers' evolving needs, on competitors' changing products and market tactics and strategies, and on the industry leaders' best practices.

Third, the general manager must repeatedly raise the performance bar, both in terms of organizational goals and challenges and in individual expectations.

Fourth, the structures and systems should be designed to promote lateral processes, including communication and coordination, between those in direct contact with customers, competitors, and suppliers and those involved in the internal functions of the organization. Processes should be developed to encourage sharing and comparing among peer groups and, hence, improve the internal diffusion of best-practice processes. In addition, incentives and awards should be offered to encourage experimentation and other initiatives to continuously improve performance. Still other systems that control recruitment and job assignment can be employed to move talent in, out, and around the organization—and with this movement of talent also comes the movement of knowledge and experience.

Finally, as we emphasized in our discussion of how work environments are shaped, the general manager's leadership style can often play a crucial role in challenging complacency, confronting opponents of change, and otherwise promoting a continued sense of urgency in the organization.

Richardson Sheffield

As Bryan Upton, chairman of Richardson Sheffield, proudly showed a visitor around a display room bulging with a glittering array of knives in countless designs and presentations, he suddenly turned reflective. "I've been 30 years with this company and I've seen my share of ups and downs. But I can't think of a time when we've had more opportunities or challenges facing us."

This was quite a statement coming from a person who had steered Richardson Sheffield through one of the severest shakeouts experienced by an industry anywhere. In the decade from 1975 to 1985, while U.K. cutlery production plummeted by 60 percent, Richardson's sales had grown fourfold and profits eightfold in real terms. Upton had taken a mature industrial operation in a 19th-century industry and turned it into a growth company.

Yet his mixture of optimism and concern was understandable. In 1989, Richardson was poised on the threshold of a major international expansion that could continue the growth trajectory through the 1990s. But would the ongoing transformation in the organization and the nature of the business facilitate or impede that future growth?

INDUSTRY AND COMPANY BACKGROUND

Although the industry environment and business situations that Upton encountered over his 33 years with Richardson had been extraordinarily challenging, he had somehow negotiated himself and his company through the turbulence remarkably successfully.

The U.K. Cutlery Industry

The cutlery industry in Sheffield, England, which predated the Industrial Revolution, grew with the worldwide reputation of its quality silverware until it employed 30,000 people in the 1950s. Soon thereafter, however, increasingly in-

It draws on "The Richardson Sheffield Story" by R. M. Grant and C. Baden Fuller (London Business School Case Series No. 2, 1987). Copyright © 1992 by the President and Fellows of Harvard College. Harvard Business School case 392-089 (revised April 15, 1993).

formal lifestyles shrank the demand for silverware. In addition, mass production of stainless steel cutlery helped manufacturers in the Far East build an increasingly dominant position in the world market. Even within the U.K. market, by the mid-1980s imports had captured over 50 percent of the market by value and a much larger share in units. As a result, by 1989 industry employment had plunged to 2,500 in Sheffield (see Exhibit 1). Within this devastated industry, only a few segments, such as silverplated tableware and kitchen knits, had survived by focusing on quality.

The kitchen knife segment was highly fragmented, with two dominant suppliers—Richardson Sheffield and Kitchen Devils. Kitchen Devils had become the largest manufacturer of kitchen knives in Britain during the 1970s. It was acquired by Wilkinson Sword in 1984; Wilkinson Sword was in turn acquired by British Match, which was then bought out by Swedish Match. Later, Fiskar of Finland bought the knives and scissors division from Swedish Match. Kitchen Devils had lost its momentum as a consequence of all these moves and, by the mid-1980s, its business had stagnated.

Richardson's Rebirth: The Scalpel and The Hammer

Founded in 1839, Richardson Sheffield remained a family company until 1956, when Jerome Hahn, an American, acquired a 51 percent share. Hahn wanted a captive blade supplier to supply his U.S.-based cutlery company, Regent Sheffield.

When Hahn visited Richardson Sheffield in 1959, he asked a young employee named Bryan Upton if he had any suggestions on improving productivity. Upton had left school in 1945 at the age of 13.

After 14 years as a die sinker in the cutlery industry, he joined Richardson as a "progress chaser," a job requiring him to coordinate with nine chargehands to match production with order requirements. As Upton later recalled, "I told Jerry Hahn that the chargehands were not productive and were obstructing smooth factory operations. Senior executives told him I was crazy, but he still made me works manager and told me to try out my ideas." Upton immediately replaced the chargehands with three others. "They worked better than the nine ever had," he recalled, "and they went on to have lifetime careers with our company."

By 1960, Hahn owned 100 percent of the company. Committed to building it, he drew no salary and took no dividends, reinvesting all profits in the business. However, problems at Richardson persisted, and in 1966, Hahn appointed Upton as managing director. He immediately stopped uncontrolled spending and instead concentrated on increasing productivity. To keep management lean, Upton recruited an active board of three nonexecutive directors in finance, sales, and external relations. Their expertise supplemented his manufacturing experience.

Gordon Bridge, the finance director, felt that Hahn and Upton ideally complemented each other:

> Jerry was a brilliant systems man. He introduced labor and steel utilization control systems and imposed the discipline of part numbers and standard costs for every item in the plant. The systems let him review an entire business, spot the mistakes, identity solutions, and come up with great ideas. Eighty percent of his ideas were unworkable, but 20 percent were phenomenal! But Jerry couldn't run the business. Bryan, on the other hand, went deep into the operating

details of the business. While Jerry was like a scalpel with his keen mind and sarcasm, Bryan was like a hammer with his dogged determination and direct forcefulness. Hahn was the ideas man and Upton was the action man—a great team!

THE DEVELOPING BUSINESS CAPABILITIES

Richardson's evolution from a commodity blade supplier to a manufacturer and marketer of a distinctive line of kitchen knives was driven by Upton's belief in continuous upgrading in production and engineering, aggressive product development, and focusing on the customers.

Productivity-Driven Engineering

When Upton took over in 1966, operators sitting astride their grindstones pulled blades across the wheels. Motivated by piecework pay, they would produce about 700 blades a day. To bring about change, Upton got rid of the piecework ("a constant source of tension and dispute that reduced our flexibility and willingness to change") and closed down the knife assembly operations ("We had to concentrate on making blades right before we could pay attention to handles and assembly"). Upton then focused on improving the blade production process, reinvesting most of the earnings in modifying and upgrading equipment. "I didn't want to risk having a machine supplier take ideas he developed with us and sell them to our competitors, so we developed our own equipment," he said.

Existing operations were semiautomated, largely through the use of electromechanical systems. Central to this effort was Bob Russell, a young engineer whom

Upton tapped to head up the development process. Russell recalled:

> Our blade-grinding machines cut the operation from a 35-second manual job to a five-second automatic cycle. Better still, one operator could supervise five or six machines. These were pretty simple, straightforward machines, but by the time we'd built 100, making marginal improvements on each one we built, we had the design very refined. That's how most improvements have happened here—gradually and continuously.

When this technology appeared to be reaching its limit, Upton recruited David Williams, a young engineer who had been experimenting with the possibility of applying electronics and computer-based systems to cutlery manufacturing. When Williams joined as manufacturing systems manager in 1985, Upton focused Russell's responsibilities more on machine installation and the civil engineering tasks of plant expansion. Gordon Bridge commented:

> We were a mechanical and pneumatic manufacturer, but Bryan foresaw the increasing need for electronics and robotics. So far, David and his small team have developed and installed electronic sensors that tell the operator when to change grinding wheels, computer controls that monitor the output and quality by machine, and automated grinding and polishing techniques that reduce labor input in these key operations.

By 1989, the company had 50 computer-controlled, edge-grinding machines monitored by eight operators, with each machine producing 6,000 blades a day. Williams was proud of the progress he and his team had been able to achieve. "There are probably only 30 other production monitoring systems like this in the country," he said, scanning a monitor screen that showed what each machine on the shop floor was doing at that moment. "Most of the others are in high-tech or high-capital process industries. We have the only one in the cutlery industry." Williams and his team had won a British Machinery award in 1988 for an electronically controlled scalloping machine that improved the grinding unit's productivity by 100 percent.

Bryan Upton reflected on the central importance of this process development effort: "What distinguishes us from the rest of the industry is that we are engineers, not cutlers. As a result, we have been able to continuously improve our operating efficiencies—sometimes very dramatically" (see Exhibit 2).

Innovation-Driven Product Development

In 1979, Jerry Hahn presented a challenge to Bryan Upton that triggered a major change in Richardson's strategy. Hahn knew that Sears was looking for a supplier that could produce a unique kitchen knife—one that never needed sharpening. On his next visit to England, he asked Upton if he could develop and manufacture such a product. "If you can," he said, "I have a great name for it—the Laser knife."

Working with a variety of blade angles, edges, and tiny serrations, Upton and his development team finally came up with a product they felt was truly a breakthrough. In typical fashion, they developed a new model of grinding machine to produce the special blade. To show their confidence, they backed the product with a 25-year guarantee; the reaction of British store buyers, however, was one of complete lack of interest. They already had strong brands, they told Richardson. Upton was

fighting mad and took his crusade to the national press:

> I told them that here was a major technical innovation—the sharpest knife in the world—developed and manufactured in Britain, and the stores were turning us away. That did the trick. Without spending a penny on advertising, we got massive coverage and the stores were forced to stock Laser. The knife sold extremely well from the start, and by 1989, Richardson had secured 45 percent of the domestic knives market.

It did not take foreign competitors long to see the product's success and copy it. Richardson responded by improving the Laser's design and performance. In 1982, it introduced Laser 5 and, four years later, Laser 7. The company was planning to introduce Laser 10 in 1990.

With the success of Lasser, the company accelerated its shift from blade producer to knife manufacturer. In the early 1980s, Richardson was buying 25 percent of the plastic knife handles produced by Elford Plastics, a nearby manufacturer, and Upton and Bridge decided they should buy the company. A quick review convinced Jerry Hahn of the merits of the idea and, in April 1984, the deal was consummated.

This spurred another round of innovation focused on the handle. "We realized that there was a fashion element to our business also," said Upton, "so we began experimenting with different handle colors and shapes. They were a great success."

To cope with the surge in its knife business, the company had purchased a 140,000-square-foot factory site in 1986, which it used exclusively for knife assembly. About half of the blades it was making were now being turned into knives.

That same year, Richardson overtook Kitchen Devils as the U.K. market leader and became the largest supplier of kitchen knives in Western Europe. The success of the Laser knife encouraged the company to think about extending the product line, and by 1989, designs had been finalized for a line of Laser scissors.

Customer-Driven Marketing

The development of the Laser knife thrust Richardson into the mainstream of consumer marketing in the 1980s. But, even when the company was basically a blade producer supplying other knife manufacturers, it had developed a strong market consciousness. The concern for customer responsiveness was ingrained into every member of the company in what were known as "Upton's four golden rules." Upton explained:

> A letter received today must be answered today, a sample requested today must be ready today, telexes and faxes must be responded to in minutes, and if the customer needs delivery tomorrow, he'll get it tomorrow. This quick response is appreciated by our customers and often means the difference in getting an order.
>
> For example, seven days before our Christmas shutdown, Shell asked us to supply 80,000 knives to Ireland on four days' notice. We were just coming out of the rush period, and some thought we could never make it. But we accepted the order and delivered. No competitor can match that performance. As a result, we got a repeat order.

However, it had taken many years to convert Richardson from a blade supplier to a customer-sensitive knife marketer. Not surprisingly, the effort started at the shop floor level, as Production Manager Denise Ogden explained:

> Since my earliest days, Mr. Upton constantly stressed that our edge is our customer orientation, and for those of us in the factory that means quick reaction and attention to quality. Everybody understands and there is a strong belief here that we have to keep improving if we are to remain the leaders.

As part of his ongoing effort to expand the company's knife business, in 1975 Upton hired Kathy Sanchez as customer liaison and asked her to start exploring the international market. Sanchez recalled:

> I began doing some simple, basic things, like corresponding in German with German agents. After a visit to the Cologne trade fair in 1976, I became convinced we could do very well internationally, and Bryan supported my initiatives. I looked up the business directory and wrote personal letters to 300 traders all over the world, enclosing our prices and catalogs. Our export sales rose dramatically, and we won the Queen's award for export achievement in 1986. Today, 60 percent of our sales are overseas.

But Upton was wary of sophisticated marketing practices. When Laser was introduced, he relied heavily on the product's superior performance and Richardson's basic customer orientation to sell it. He remarked:

> We didn't need a marketing staff or an advertising campaign. We had a great product, and Laser was a terrific brand name. Then we got excellent free publicity to bring it to public attention and get it in the stores, and we had the drive of Kathy Sanchez, whom I had promoted to sales director.

THE DISTINCTIVE WORK ENVIRONMENT

"Central to our success," said Bryan Upton, "are our continual attention to engineering and production, our hands-on management style, and the quality of our people." The following pages describe a few of Richardson's unique organizational characteristics.

Upton's Management Style

A newspaper article once described Bryan Upton as a man "who never says no to an order, and never takes no for an answer." In his straightforward Yorkshire manner he confessed, "I am not an easy person to get along with. But I am not difficult. I'm just demanding!" He looked at himself as a hands-on manager. "Even as the chief executive of the company," he said, "I will unload lorries on the dock, if need be. I'm often the first in and the last out. I believe in leadership by example."

Within the company, he was viewed as a mix of coach, controller, and company conscience. For example, on one of his frequent shop floor rounds, he saw knife blades that had been dropped near a machine. He took some 10 pence coins from his pocket, threw them on the floor and, in full hearing of the workers, asked the supevisor, "Would you leave these coins lying on the floor? Well these blades are worth much more!"

Upton's attention to detail was legendary. "When Bryan visits the shop floor," remarked a production executive, "he doesn't just pass through—he pokes around, and he sees things you have missed. He knows a lot more about the business than I do, and he has answers for every problem. More often than not, he's

right, but sometimes it gets frustrating. His style is direct, and he'll beat you over the head every day with an awful lot of common sense. You sometimes may not like him, but in the end you respect him."

Organization Culture and Values

Many of Richardson's organizational norms and management practices had been deeply influenced by the leader's management style—his bias for action, attention to detail, commitment to customer service, and dedication to the company had all been absorbed into the company culture. Said one executive:

> Bryan personalizes the culture of our company. In order to survive here, you have got to be very open and have a sunny personality, yet be able to work under pressure and give and take with Bryan and others. Those who are quiet or sensitive are so unhappy that they have to leave. And yet, we have built a great team here. Many in the company would walk through fire for Bryan. He is very enthusiastic and his enjoyment of what he is doing is very infectious. You see Kathy Sanchez, Bob Russell, Tony Seagrave, Denise Ogden, and others who have molded themselves very much in Bryan's image.

Sanchez had risen rapidly within the company based on her hard work, skills, dedication, and toughness—all attributes Upton admired. These skills also brought results, and in 1987 she won an award as Salesperson of the Year from the British Sales and Marketing Association. Sanchez acknowledged:

> I have consciously copied Bryan's style. It works, although for a long time I found it difficult to delegate responsibility. But, as work has increased, I have had to form

priorities, I have had to identify key people and put my faith in them.

A sales executive confirmed her view:

> Kathy strives for the best, and she expects 110 percent from you. Like Bryan Upton, she is a very hardworking person, and the company is a big part of her life—perhaps too big. Both of them are approachable, they teach you, they back you up on crazy schemes, they are always motivating people, bringing people into their projects. But they will also give you a "rocket" if you have made a mistake.

As a result, Richardson's work environment was most often referred to as "demanding" and usually involved very high time commitment of its executives. "I work more than 60 hours a week," said one manager, "because the expectation is that everything has to be done immediately. Sometimes it is tiring, and I find myself wondering if it is worth it." Bryan Upton himself warned prospective employees, "It is not only you, but your spouses and your families may have to sacrifice, too."

The work pressure was felt in all parts of the company. David Williams, the manufacturing systems manager, felt that Bryan Upton subjected him to time pressures and deadlines inappropriate for a development laboratory. "I have learned to take the flak from these people and do what I can at my pace," he said. "But, it can be hard when long-term development projects are turned on and off depending on the latest crisis."

Another term often used by managers to describe their work environment was "unstructured." Said one:

> We have an active, even unsociable culture, and people who revel in unstructured situations, and are self-motivated

and pressure-driven, will do well here. When I joined the company, I was depressed that people didn't have time to meet with me. I later realized that they hold off to see if the new person is going to stay. However, once you're on board, this company works like a family. But you are not mollycoddled—you have to be self-directed. It's fun if you like living on your adrenaline.

Human Resources Management

Cutlery was a low-paid seasonal industry, traditionally dominated by relatively low-skilled female employees. Richardson employed between 250 and 450 workers, many on short-term contracts. Average earnings for such workers was about £100 ($155) a week. Richardson had de-skilled operations to simplify recruiting and training in an environment of fairly high labor turnover. Absenteeism ran at about 15 percent.

Upton was philosophically opposed to the idea of a personnel department, believing that matters relating to people should be managed by those who had responsibility for them. Consequently, all personnel functions were handled by line managers who were responsible for the recruitment, development, and deployment of people in their respective departments. Management was developed from within where possible and recruited from outside when inside capabilities were lacking. Upton described how he selected people who would fit into this unique environment:

> I interview all candidates for management positions, and my criteria are straightforward. First, the person should be ready to work 24 hours a day for the company. Second, the person should be very flexible since there are no sharp

lines between jobs here. Third, he or she should be able to react quickly. Finally, the person should really believe from within that the business exists to serve the customer. Given all this, I tell prospective employees to join us only if they feel that they need to come here more than we need them to come.

I can tell a lot about a candidate very quickly. If you walk slow and talk slow, you will not get in my office. If you are overweight, chances are you will not be employed. I may give you a page with dots on it and ask you to draw circles around them. If you are not fast, you are out. We don't need capable people as much as we need those who are quick and responsive.

One prominent aspect of Upton's management approach was his deep interest in the development of those working with him. He explained:

I feel I have a natural ability to spot and develop talent that is right for this company. For example, when Kathy Sanchez joined us in the customer liaison role 13 years ago, I noticed that she was unbelievably bright. I kept giving her increasing responsibilities, and today she is our director of sales and marketing. Denise Ogden is another good example. She joined this company as a worker when she was 15 years old, and today she is a production manager. These are people we have been able to develop in the company, knowing our business and the way we manage. It's a huge asset.

Denise Ogden had risen rapidly on the basis of her deep commitment to the company, unswerving sense of purpose, and strict discipline. She looked on Bryan Upton as a teacher and a role model:

I came here 16 years ago straight from school, and Mr. Upton has taught me everything I know. He made me aware

that the most important task is to ensure that orders and samples go out on time, so that the customers are served well. If he asked me for a sample, I knew he wanted it not the same day, but within 15 minutes. He taught me how to manage people. I learned to keep watch on my workers, be aware of where they were and what was happening at any moment.

One manager described a recent incident when a young worker had left footprints on a wall when he climbed up to get supplies from a high shelf. Ogden made him walk through the plant to get a bucket of water and clean off the footprints while all his co-workers watched. "It was a great lesson in production floor cleanliness," he observed, "but it was a lesson in discipline Denise had learned painfully some 15 years earlier. As a young line worker, she had taken rivets from the plant and tossed them at a friend on her way home. Bryan had called in the police to talk to her, and that public humiliation shook her up and sent a lesson to the others."

Although the company had been very successful in developing talent internally, there were no formal training programs or career development schemes. It was all done through capable people being given new—often additional—responsibility. Gordon Bridge gave an example:

Our marketing manager left us recently. We have not replaced him. Instead, we had the marketing assistant report directly to Kathy. He is under tremendous pressure to take over much of the work of his previous boss, but he also has a great opportunity. We have succeeded in the past in management development by the "pressure cooker" method.

The company also had no hesitation in redeploying those it felt could do better in another position or firing those who were not contributing. Bryan Upton gave an example of how he tried to fit people and jobs:

> Tony Seagrave was in charge of our production for many years, but with all the changes, the pressure was getting too much for him, so I moved him to special projects. He's now in a niche where he can contribute much more and where he will eventually be much happier because of that.

"I used to come in at 6:00 in the morning and leave at 10:00 in the night," recalled Seagrave, "and I'd come in on Sundays to do the production planning. I had my finger in everythmg. Then, three years ago, Bryan shifted me to special projects."

Richardson's worker turnover was quite low. Most management turnover occurred within the first few months of employment as people decided whether they liked the Richardson environment, and the company decided whether they could contribute. Bryan Upton commented:

> Turnover in the sales department has been high. Kathy Sanchez is a very demanding person. One U.K. sales manager who came to us with a good record at Kellogg and Duracell was with us only four weeks. He and Kathy had gone with a salesman to a meeting with an important customer. After the meeting, Kathy let him have it in front of the salesman. She asked why he had forgotten whom he had met at the previous meeting, why he had not brought along a notebook, why he had let her control the meeting, and why he had no price list readily available. When she finished, he told her he was quitting.

Sanchez gave her perspective on the turnover issue:

> One reason for our high turnover may be recruitment of people who are poorly matched to our requirements. Our standards are quite different and our jobs are much less structured than in most companies. It is very difficult to find the kind of committed people we demand, and some people just cannot take our pace physically. What seems a high turnover is really an initial weeding out of misfits.

RECENT CHANGES, NEW CHALLENGES

In the late 1980s, several internal and external developments were converging to challenge some of the basic strategic directions and organizational foundations Bryan Upton had laid over the previous two decades.

International Expansion

The first major change was occurring in Richardson's markets. As European market harmonization approached, management began looking toward continental Europe. "After 1992, German and French manufacturers will try to enter the U.K.," said Bryan Upton, "and the competitive game will become much tougher."

In 1988 and 1989, Richardson established small sales branches in Germany, France, and Scandinavia. Although these branches were growing steadily, it was a difficult task penetrating further into new markets, slower than the rapid expansion direct exports had brought earlier. Established supplier relationships, local differences in product preferences, and parochial national attitudes all represented important entry barriers. Upton and Bridge acknowledged it would be difficult to continue on their current growth trajectory without taking bold new steps. But there were skeptics who questioned whether this strongly Sheffield-rooted company with its unique culture and style had the management capability to grow into a much larger or much more diverse organization.

The McPherson's Takeover

In 1986, Jerry Hahn sold his U.S. and U.K. cutlery companies to McPherson's Ltd., an Australia-based company that was diversifying out of its core industrial metals business into consumer products, mainly housewares. After the acquisition, the consumer products division was split into regional offices with McPherson's consumer group taking responsibility for Asia–Pacific, the Regent Sheffield unit covering North America, and Richardson Sheffield handling Europe.

McPherson's had developed the Wiltshire Staysharp line of knives, which came in scabbards with tungsten carbide insets that sharpened the knife edge each time the blade was withdrawn or replaced. Because of its design and its higher price, Staysharp required more sophisticated marketing than the impulse-buy Laser with its "never-needs-sharpening" concept. In order to launch the Staysharp line in the United Kingdom, Richardson established its first-ever, five-person marketing department and went in for heavy TV advertising. (Exhibit 3 describes Richardson's principal products; Exhibit 4 provides financial information.)

After the McPherson's takeover, Richardson augmented its top management group. In particular, they felt it was important to fill the top production manager's job, to build a stronger marketing organization, and to reinforce the financial control staff. Richardson implemented these changes over the next few years. By

1989, a new production director had been hired and integrated into the management, and a McPherson's financial manager had been added to the staff. However, the new marketing manager had lasted only two years, running into a conflict of management styles with Upton and Sanchez. Sanchez was made directly responsible for marketing also in her new position as director of sales and marketing.

When Richardson's nonexecutive board was dissolved after its acquisition, Upton persuaded Gordon Bridge to become a full-time deputy managing director. Then, in 1988 when Upton was appointed chairman, Bridge succeeded him as managing director. (See Exhibit 5.)

With the change in ownership and leadership, many wondered if Richardson Sheffield could, or indeed should, continue to remain the same company. Some newer executives had started pushing to formalize systems and tighten policies. The financial analyst was working to upgrade what be termed "rather primitive" management information and costing systems. And the production director was asking the sales department for periodic forecasts by product so he could better plan production. On the other hand, some older employees were concerned by what they saw as a dilution of company values. Bob Russell, chief engineer, reflected:

> As we've grown, personal commitment has diffused. We are split into tiny domains, and there are little managers sitting in little offices instead of managing the work. We're not knit together like we were, and as a result, there's not the same loyalty to the company. Just as bad is the red tape and paperwork that is creeping in. I hate the cost systems and analyses that delay us without improving produc-

tivity. Yet, despite the fancy systems, the floodgates have been opened on overhead costs.

Yet, Kathy Sanchez was optimistic about the future:

> The key is retaining our team's overriding commitment to the company. It has given us freedom, opportunities, and enthusiasm. There is an energy—a fire—which used to come from Jerry Hahn, which comes from Bryan, and which now is within me and others in the next generation. That's the vital element that will keep pushing us to think of new and better ways to build this company.

LOOKING TO THE FUTURE

There was a widespread feeling that Richardson Sheffield faced a momentous point in its history. One executive suggested:

> We will either burst through this phase or fall back. If we can adapt by becoming

truly professional and multinational, our horizons are fantastic. But our management must decouple from the operational details so they can guide us strategically. The alternative is that Richardson remains the size management is comfortable with.

Gordon Bridge described the challenge:

> We can't continue to run an operation of this size and complexity through personal intervention. We have to develop more managers who think and act like Bryan—managers with a hands-on instinct. To do that, I have got to stop Bryan from taking unnecessary responsibility.

Bryan Upton saw the situation simply:

> Like a Liverpool football club, we've learned that it's very hard getting to the top of the first division. But we also understand it's even harder staying there. We're at the top of the league in this knife business, and we are determined to stay there.

EXHIBIT 1
THE CUTLERY INDUSTRY IN THE UNITED KINGDOM

The cutlery industry can be divided into table cutlery, kitchen knives, and scissors and razors. The scissors and razors market is excluded from these tables.

1A
U.K. Manufacturers' Production of Table Cutlery and Kitchen Knives

	1975	1983	1984	1985	1986	1987
Gross index of production (1980 = 100)	160	73.8	75.0	74.5	66.6	65.5
Production (£ million at manufacturer sale price)						
Table cutlery		19.9	20.0	21.7	20.5	21.3
Kitchen knives		6.4	9.7	10.6	12.4	17.8

1B
Export and Import of Cutlery (£ million at manufacturers' sale price)

	1983	1984	1985	1986	1987
Kitchen knives					
Export	3.5	4.4	4.7	6.0	5.7
Import	2.4	2.3	2.4	3.6	3.2
Table cutlery					
Export	10.0	9.0	8.9	9.2	8.7
Import	14.7	18.8	21.3	19.7	25.8

EXHIBIT 2
RICHARDSON'S COST AND PRODUCTIVITY DATA

2A
Summary of Productivity Data, 1975–1988*

Year	Revenue	Profit (£'000s)	Stocks	Capital	Labor Cost/ Revenue (%)	Employees
1975	752	44	91	280	17.1	103
1976	1,113	42	196	324	15.6	112
1977	1,595	107	327	408	12.6	120
1978	2,422	254	503	662	11.9	134
1979	2,222	199	703	843	12.2	155
1980	2,446	210	703	1,074	12.2	160
1981	2,698	227	787	1,292	11.0	159
1982	3,458	263	823	1,537	11.0	176
1983	5,059	410	1,130	1,955	11.4	221
1984	7,000	554	1,417	2,302	9.5	339
1985	8,683	856	2,147	2,626	8.5	338
1986[†]	4,826	942	2,428	3,531	9.5	367
1987	11,751	2,124	3,303	10,879	8.9	410
1988	17,268	1,693	4,287	11,809	8.9	442

Note: Profit figure is before interest and tax.

*Data have been disguised.

[†]Data for six months.

2B
Costs and Expenses as Percentage of Revenue, 1989 Data[‡]

Revenue	100
Less:	
Materials	37
Labor	9
Production expenses	10
Total direct expenses	56
Gross profit	44
Selling expenses	19
Distribution	5
General administration	11
Net profit (before interest and tax)	9

[‡]Data have been disguised.

EXHIBIT 3
RICHARDSON SHEFFIELD'S PRODUCT RANGE

Range	Product	Features
Laser knives		25-year guarantee
	Laser	Original knives with hardwood handles, brass compression rivets, and stainless steel blades; also available in wooden blocks and gift sets
	Laser 5	Made of permanently bonded, contoured polypropylene handles. The knife had a dishwasher-resistant ink marking. Also available in polystyrene wall racks, wooden wall racks, steak sets, dishwasher-safe polystyrene blocks, and wooden blocks.
	Laser 7	Laser 7 knives had three rivets, instead of the two in Laser knives. Their blades were made of thicker-gauge steel, and their handles were of pakkawood.
	Laser 2000	Satin finish and PTFE nonstick coating
Wiltshire Staysharp	Knives-900	Tailor-made sharpening scabbards; dishwasher-safe polypropylene handles
	Knives-1200	Tailor-made sharpening scabbards; rosewood handles with brass reinforcing rivets
	Scissors	Scissors in sharpening scabbards
Sabatier knives	Sabatier 1	High-quality professional knives with steel bolsters and hand-crafted blades
	Sabatier 2	Professional knives at a lower price, with aluminum bolsters
Others		10-year guarantee
	Kitchen King	Range of precision-ground knives
	Prestwood	Hollow ground blades and hardwood handles.
	Cuisine	Satin finish stainless steel blades with hardwood handles and brass compression rivets
	Supersharp	Dishwasher-safe, stainless steel blades and polypropylene handles with decorative studs
	Carlton	Unbreakable polypropylene handles
	Thrifty	Lowest-priced, but dishwasher-safe
	Snac-Pac	Knife, fork, and spoon set, complete with salt and pepper shakers

EXHIBIT 3 (continued)

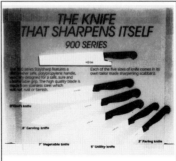

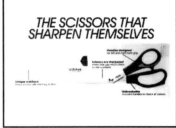

EXHIBIT 4
FINANCIAL PERFORMANCE OF RICHARDSON SHEFFIELD

	6/87	6/88
Profit and loss statment (£ '000s)		
Sales	11,751	17,268
Gross profit	5,372	6,997
Less overheads	3,248	5,304
Net profit (loss) before interest and tax	2,124	1,693
Balance sheet (£'000s)		
Capital, reserve, and liabilities:		
Capital and reserves	469	1,428
Creditors	3,071	3,539
Taxation	1,309	1,016
Loan—bank	5,000	5,000
—McPherson's	—	1,100
McPherson's Ltd.	1,209	(79)
Total	11,058	12,004
Short-term debt	(179)	(195)
Total	10,879	11,809
Assets:		
Debtors	2,202	2,059
Stock	3,301	4,287
Plant and machinery—net	1,691	1,852
Land and buildings—net	1,682	1,784
Investments	2	2
Intangibles	185	175
Goodwill	1,816	1,650
Total	10,879	11,809

Note: £1 = $1.55 in June 1989.

EXHIBIT 5
ORGANIZATION CHART OF RICHARDSON SHEFFIELD, 1989

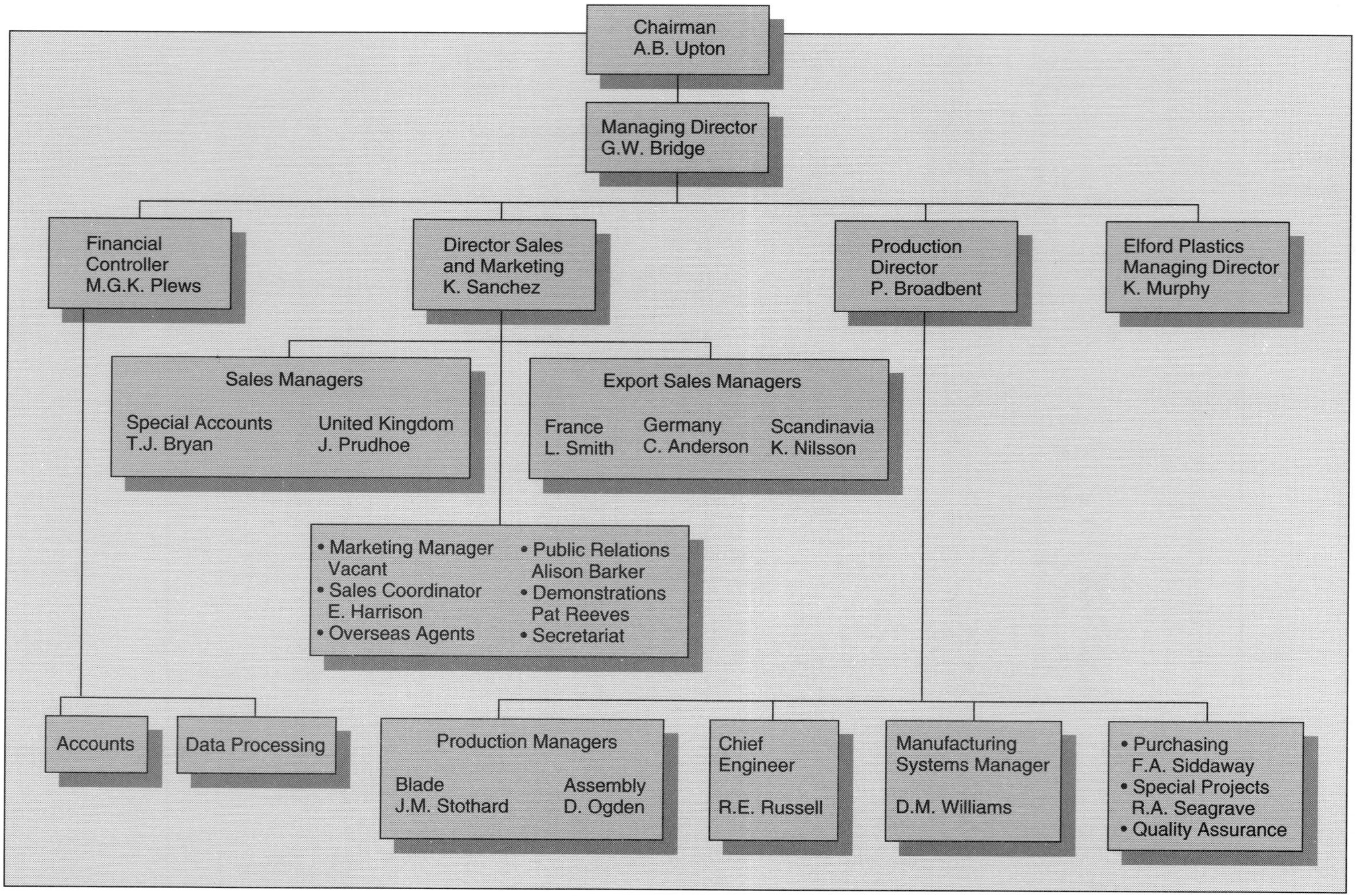

Chairman
A.B. Upton

Managing Director
G.W. Bridge

Elford Plastics
Managing Director
K. Murphy

Production
Director
P. Broadbent

Director Sales
and Marketing
K. Sanchez

Financial
Controller
M.G.K. Plews

Manufacturing
Systems Manager
D.M. Williams

Chief
Engineer
R.E. Russell

Production Managers

Blade   Assembly
J.M. Stothard D. Ogden

Purchasing
• F.A. Siddaway
• Special Projects
  R.A. Seagrave
• Quality Assurance

Export Sales Managers

France   Germany   Scandinavia
L. Smith   C. Anderson K. Nilsson

Sales Managers

Special Accounts   United Kingdom
T.J. Bryan   J. Prudhoe

Marketing Manager   • Public Relations
Vacant   Alison Barker
• Sales Coordinator   • Demonstrations
  E. Harrison   Pat Reeves
• Overseas Agents   • Secretariat

Accounts

Data Processing

Jack Welch: General Electric's Revolutionary

In 1993, Jack Welch might be satisfied that the ultimate arbiter of value, the stock market, seemed to appreciate GE's achievements under his leadership. From a multiple of 7 in 1982, the price/earnings ratio had climbed to 16—a clear signal that the stock market was enamored with the changes Welch was making at GE. Over a period when the S&P 500 had risen 326 percent, GE market value had grown 498 percent. (See Exhibit 1.) If GE was not yet as "lean and agile" as Welch might want, it was surely a far more nimble giant than the company he had inherited from the "management legend" Reg Jones.

In fact, as GE entered its 12th year with Welch at the helm, the company was once again being studied widely as a model of how a giant corporation ought to be managed. Fundamentally, Welch appeared to be pulling off the impossible. He was making one of the largest, most complex companies in the world perform like a growth company. At first, the accomplishment was merely discounted. By 1993, however, Welch was being credited with a world-class achievement in management. Having concluded that Jack Welch had done the impossible and transformed giant GE, everyone interested in management wanted to know whether it was fluke of personality or whether generalizable principles, useful for all, underlay Welch's achievement. Had Jack Welch presided over the invention of a new approach to managing a complex organization?

GE AS AN INVENTOR

Founded to exploit Thomas Edison's patents, the company that later became GE soon assembled a range of businesses, wide for the time, dedicated to the generation, distribution, and use of electric power. Later, businesses such as aircraft engines, engineering plastics, nuclear power, and computers were added to the basic businesses of generators, transformers, wire and cable, lighting, and home appliances.

GE's size and complexity had always proved a challenge for its leaders. In the 1930s to help control its diversity, GE had developed a powerful financial staff. Later, in the 1950s in order to develop a more entrepreneurial culture suited to diversification, profit centers and group staff were introduced by CEO Ralph Cordiner. As the post-war trendsetter of divisionalization, GE was broken up into more than 100 businesses. When these grew large, they were again broken up. Cordiner's organizational arrangements for managing diversity became a role model and were widely copied. In the 1960s, to provide substantive analysis to deal with the stagnant profits that resulted from the consequent dispersion of resources, Fred Borch used his planning staff and leading consulting firms to develop PIMS and portfolio strategic planning. Once again GE's innovations were widely imitated by companies around the world.

Borch's consultants argued that allocating resources on the basis of projected ROI led to waste because incremental investments almost always looked attractive even when the business was poor. But there was no system for looking at businesses. The consultants recommended that GE should reorganize completely into what they called Strategic Business Units (SBUs). The special characteristics of an SBU were a unique set of integrated strategic plans and the ability for the unit manager to "call the shots" on all the factors crucial to the success of the business. Thus, where there had been profit centers for ranges, refrigerators, and dishwashers, there would now be only a home appliance SBU.

THE JONES LEGACY

When he was named GE's new chairman and CEO in 1972, Reg Jones took over a company consisting of 10 groups, 46 divisions, and 190 departments. These were organized into 43 SBUs that were intended to provide a basis for better planning and investment. Jones asked each to hire a strategic planner.

By the mid-1970s, some GE managers believed that SBU planning, while helping to strengthen GE's competitive positions and to improve profits, was also leading to a balkanization of the company. GE appeared to be moving in the direction of becoming a holding company.

In Jones's mind, another problem was that corporate review of SBU plans also suffered from overload. He explained:

> Right from the start of SBU planning in 1972, the vice chairmen and I tried to review each plan in great detail. This effort took untold hours and placed a tremendous burden on the corporate executive office. After a while, I began to realize that no matter how hard we would work, we could not achieve the necessary in-depth understanding of the 40-odd SBU plans. Somehow, the review burden had to be carried on more shoulders.[1]

In 1977, Jones announced a "sector" organization structure as a new level of management that represented a macrobusiness or industry area. Jones's objective was to spread the review load and also to add more value at the corporate level. After allowing time for the six-

---

[1] "General Electric: Strategic Position, 1981" (HBS Case No. 381-174), by Professors Francis J. Aguilar and Richard G. Hamermesh. © 1981 by the President and Fellows of Harvard College.

sector structure to take root, Jones concluded, "The sector approach . . . exceeded my expectations. Now I can look at six planning books and understand them well enough to ask the right questions."[2] *Fortune* anointed Jones a "management legend" for his accomplishments.

Jones also had a private reason for this organizational change. He thought it time to consider succession, and the sector executive position would provide visibility for the candidates in a horse race for CEO. The position also enabled him to broaden the managers by assigning them responsibilities for businesses new to them. Jack Welch, for example, was reassigned from engineering plastics, where he had succeeded in building up a magnificent high-tech business, to sector executive for home appliances. From that position he was elected CEO.

A Harvard Business School professor who had invited Welch to his class on a number of occasions during the 1970s later wrote:

> Welch's youth, extremely high energy level, candor in responding to tough questions, and obvious leadership qualities combined to captivate my students. Welch was engaged in a horse race, and I told my students that. In the class following each of Welch's appearances, I asked the students whether they thought he would be the next chairman of GE, winning out over six other candidates. Knowing nothing about the other six candidates, my students, each time, concluded that Welch did not fit their stereotype of GE's CEO, and the job would probably go to someone more conventional. Welch was a maverick, he let the students know

it, and they loved him for it, but that's what happens to mavericks. I didn't know the other candidates either, but I shared my students' view, and was astonished at the announcement in December 1980 that Welch had won the race. The outcome that I admire is that somehow the officers and directors of GE were able to select a new CEO who was more likely to make difficult changes than some of the other contenders for the job. The core issue in CEO selection is the tension between continuity and change. In this case, GE was able to select an "outsider" from inside.[3]

Welch's Background[4]

According to Welch, most of his values and beliefs had been shaped during his childhood years:

> I was an only child. My parents were about 40 when they had me, and they had been trying for 16 years. My father was a railroad conductor, a good man, hard-working, passive . . . [My mother] always felt I could do anything. It was my mother who trained me, taught me the facts of life. She wanted me to be independent. Control your own destiny —she always had that idea. Saw reality. No mincing words. Whenever I got out of line, she would whack me one, but always positive, always constructive, always uplifting. And I was just nuts about her.[5]

---

[2] *Ibid.*

[3] Richard F. Vancil, *Passing the Baton* (Boston, MA: Harvard Business School Press), 1987.

[4] This section has been taken from "General Electric: Jack Welch's Second Wave (A)" (HBS Case No. 391-248), by Research Associate Kenton W. Elderkin and Professor Christopher A. Bartlett. © 1981 by the President and Fellows of Harvard College.

[5] Stratford Sherman, "The Mind of Jack Welch," *Fortune*, March 27, 1989.

One of Welch's high school classmates described him as "a nice, regular guy, but always very competitive, relentless, and argumentative." A college classmate said, "The desire to win was in his eyes. He was always looking one step ahead." Another classmate said, "He hated losing—even in touch football," and another said, "Jack wasn't blessed with a lot of grace or athletic ability. He trounced people by trying harder." One of Welch's most remembered comments was, "We're still friends?"[6]

Years later, a colleague would claim that Welch's management style was built on his hockey-playing years. "Hockey is the kind of game where people bang you up against the boards and then go out and have a drink with you after," he said. Using "constructive conflict" Welch often forced managers to defend their views, even if that meant getting into shouting-match arguments. "Jack will chase you around the room, throwing arguments and objections at you," said one executive. "Then you fight back until he lets you do what you want, and it's clear you'll do everything you can to make it work." According to another manager, "If you win, you never know if you've convinced him or if he agreed with you all along and was just making you strut your stuff."

Welch was the first engineer to earn a PhD from the University of Illinois in only three years. Graduating in 1960, he joined GE's plastics division in Pittsfield, Massachusetts. In 1968, at age 32, he became the youngest division manager in GE. Because people neither really knew what the unit was doing nor had high expectations for it, Welch got a considerable degree of freedom and responsibility. Starting with the Detroit automakers, he rapidly expanded his sales to OEMs worldwide. Overseas operations reinforced his autonomy, allowing him to transform the small plastics operation into a $400 million business. Always open, he distrusted anyone who hoarded information or surrounded themselves with staffs.

Transferred to corporate headquarters in Fairfield, Connecticut, in 1977, Welch was astonished at the byzantine nature of GE's bureaucracy. In his view, corporate staff was interfering too much in line activities—requiring presentations, demanding reports—but doing little to create or sell more products. He felt that this led line people to waste their time playing political games with corporate staff in the hope that they would receive some benefit. He cringed as he recalled the $30,000 the light bulb business had spent to produce a film in order to make its case with corporate for a new piece of production equipment.

JACK WELCH TAKES CHARGE

Jack Welch took office in April 1981 shortly after his 45th birthday. As the new chairman and chief executive officer of General Electric, he described his vision for GE:

> A decade from now I would like General Electric to be perceived as a unique, high-spirited, entrepreneurial enterprise . . . a company known around the world for its unmatched level of excellence. I want General Electric to be the most profitable, highly diversified company

---

[6] Marilyn Harris et al, "Can Jack Welch Reinvent GE?" *Business Week*, June 30, 1986.

on earth, with world-quality leadership in every one of its product lines.[7]

Welch, in his 1989 *Harvard Business Review* interview, noted, "In 1981, when we first defined our business strategy, the real focus was Japan. The entire organization had to understand that GE was in a tougher, more competitive world, with Japan as the cutting edge of the new competition. Nine years later, that competitive toughness has increased by a factor of 5 or 10."[8] Also, when Welch took office, the U.S. economy was in serious decline aggravated by soaring interest rates and a strong dollar.

In terms of GE's strategic response, Welch told an HBS audience that "you can't set an overall theme or a single strategy for a corporation so diverse as GE." Instead, Welch determined that the goal was to be number one or number two in every business the company was in. Achieving this required a common concern for quality and excellence. "To me, quality and excellence mean being better than the best . . . If we aren't, we should ask ourselves, 'What will it take?' then quantify the energy and resources to get there. If the economics, the environment, or our abilities determine that we can't get there, we must take the same spirited action to disengage ourselves from that which we can't make better than the best."

As GE built and exited businesses, Welch found that he needed a concise way to give strategic meaning to his actions. In 1983, he developed the "three circle concept" as it came to be called (after a drawing he made for a reporter). All businesses were divided into (1) core, (2) high technology, or (3) service areas. Only the 15 businesses that dominated their markets would be placed in a circle. (See Exhibits 2 and 3.) The others either had to come up with a strategy for achieving dominance or be divested. Welch decreed that core businesses were to focus on "reinvestment in productivity and quality," and the high-tech businesses were to "stay on the leading edge" through acquisitions and large R&D investments; the services were to grow by "adding outstanding people who create new ventures and by making contiguous acquisitions." Welch noted that "we have our hands on a simple, understandable strategy for where we are, where we are not, where we can't find a solution, and where we have to disengage. We have to get used to the idea that disengaging does not mean bad people or bad management; it's a bad situation, and we can't tie up good dollars chasing it." The major moves Welch made into and out of businesses in order to be number one or number two are shown in Exhibit 4. Profits from divestitures were used to fund acquisitions and growth of remaining businesses.

To deal with a corporate bureaucracy that seemed out of place in the new GE, he emphasized what became known as "destaffing." From 1980 to 1984, the total workforce was reduced from 402,000 to 330,000. While the press nicknamed him "Neutron Jack," after the neutron bomb, which wipes out people but leaves build-

---

[7] "General Electric: 1984" (HBS Case No. 385-315), by Professors Francis J. Aguilar and Richard G. Hamermesh and Research Assistant Caroline Brainard. © 1985 by the President and Fellows of Harvard College.

[8] Noel Tichy and Ram Charan, "Speed, Simplicity, Self-Confidence: An Interview with Jack Welch," *Harvard Business Review*, September–October 1989, p. 114.

ings intact, Welch believed the label to be exaggerated. He was convinced that a company the size of GE needed to stay "lean and agile" to be competitive. He acknowledged that becoming lean required destaffing, but he stated that the company had no intention of becoming "mean" in the process.

Welch also believed that the planning system had evolved from being fresh, idea-oriented, and effective to becoming bureaucratic and inhibiting. To increase candor and constructive discussions, planning reviews were restructured so Welch and the two vice chairmen talked with individual SBU managers privately and informally. Rather than focusing on comprehensive strategic documentation or planning concepts, Welch directed the review around the key issues for each business. Welch cut the 200-person corporate planning staff in half by 1984. His objective was to get "general managers talking to general managers about strategy, rather than planners talking to planners."[9]

GE'S CULTURAL CHANGE

Going for the Leap

By 1984, in spite of substantial accomplishments, Welch claimed that he was only at the 15 percent mark of what he intended to do. Said Welch, "A company can boost productivity by restructuring, removing bureaucracy, and downsizing, but it cannot sustain high productivity without cultural change." Addressing GE employees in 1985, he suggested:

For me, the idea is: shun the incremental and go for the leap. Most bureaucracies —and ours is no exception—unfortunately still think in incremental terms rather than in terms of fundamental change. They think incrementally primarily because they think internally. Changing the culture—opening it up to the quantum change—means constantly asking not how fast am I going, how well am I doing versus how well I did a year or two before, but rather, how fast and how well am I doing versus the world outside. Are we moving faster, are we doing better against that external standard?

Changing the culture starts with an attitude. And I would suggest it starts at the top—with the CEOs and the boards of directors that are charged with leading our institutions. More boards have to be thinking, How much can this organization take, how much can it absorb, is it being stressed too little or too much—constantly challenging the pace. How does an institution know when the pace is about right? I hope you won't think I'm being melodramatic if I say that the institution ought to stretch itself, ought to reach, to the point where it almost comes unglued."[10]

Welch's People

In his *Harvard Business Review* interview, Welch stated:

Good business leaders create a vision, articulate the vision, passionately own the vision, and relentlessly drive it to completion. Above all else, though, good leaders are open. They go up, down, and around their organization to reach people. They don't stick to the established channels. They're informal. They're straight with people. They make

---

[9] Information in the preceding three paragraphs is drawn from "General Electric: 1984," *op. cit.*

[10] Tichy and Charan, *op. cit.*, p. 112.

a religion out of being accessible. They never get bored telling their story.

Real communication takes countless hours of eyeball to eyeball, back and forth. It means more listening than talking. It's not pronouncements on a videotape; it's not announcements in a newspaper. It is human beings coming to see and accept things through a constant interactive process aimed at consensus. And it must be absolutely relentless. That's a real challenge for us. There's still not enough candor in this company.[11]

I mean facing reality, seeing the world as it is rather than as you wish it were. We've seen over and over again that businesses facing market downturns, tougher competition, and more demanding customers inevitably make forecasts that are much too optimistic. This means they don't take advantage of the opportunities change usually offers. Change in the marketplace isn't something to fear; it's an enormous opportunity to shuffle the deck, to replay the game. Candid managers—leaders—don't get paralyzed about the "fragility" of the organization. They tell people the truth. That doesn't scare them because they realize their people know the truth anyway.

We've had managers at GE who couldn't change, who kept telling us to leave them alone. They wanted to sit back, to keep things the way they were. And that's just what they did—until they and most of their staffs had to go. That's the lousy part of this job. . . . The point is, what determines your destiny is not the hand you're dealt; it's how you play the hand. And the best way to play your hand is to face reality—see the world the way it is—and act accordingly.

For a large organization to be effective, it must be simple. For a large organiza-

tion to be simple, its people must have self-confidence and intellectual self-assurance. Insecure managers create complexity. Frightened, nervous managers use thick, convoluted planning books and busy slides filled with everything they've known since childhood. Real leaders don't need clutter. People must have the self-confidence to be clear, precise, to be sure that every person in their organization—highest to lowest—understands what the business is trying to achieve. But it's not easy. You can't believe how hard it is for people to be simple, how much they fear being simple. They worry that if they're simple, people will think they're simple-minded. In reality, of course, it's just the reverse. Clear, tough-minded people are the most simple.[12]

Simple *doesn't* mean easy, especially as you try to move this approach down through the organization. When you take out layers, you change the exposure of the managers who remain. They sit right in the sun. Some of them blotch immediately; they can't stand the exposure of leadership.[13]

Welch made similar statements at the 1989 GE shareholders' meeting:

We found in the 1980s that becoming faster is tied to becoming simpler. Our businesses, with tens of thousands of employees, will not respond to visions that have subparagraphs and footnotes. If we're not simple, we can't be fast . . . and if we're not fast, we can't win.

Simplicity, to an engineer, means clean, functional winning designs, no bells or whistles. In marketing, it might manifest itself as clear, unencumbered proposals. For manufacturing people, it would produce a logical process that

---

[11] *Ibid.*, p. 113.

[12] *Ibid.*, pp.113–114.
[13] *Ibid.*, p. 116.

makes sense to every individual on the line. And on an individual, interpersonal level, it would take the form of plain speaking, directness, honesty.

But just as surely as speed flows from simplicity, simplicity is grounded in self-confidence. Self-confidence does not grow in someone who is just another appendage on the bureaucracy, whose authority rests on little more than a title. People who are freed from the confines of their box n the organization chart, whose status rests on real-world achievement—those are the people who develop the self-confidence to be simple, to share every bit of information available to them, to listen to those above, below, and around them and then move boldly.

But a company can't distribute self-confidence. What it can do—what we must do—is to give each of our people an opportunity to win, to contribute, and hence earn self-confidence themselves. They don't get that opportunity, they can't taste winning if they spend their days wandering in the muck of a self-absorbed bureaucracy.

Speed ... simplicity ... self-confidence. We have it in increasing measure. We know where it comes from ... and we have plans to increase it in the 1990s.

Welch wanted to keep directly in touch with the rich resource that he believed existed in GE's employees. For this reason, he retained the sophisticated management development process (known as CI and CII reviews) that had long been part of the company's tradition. For three hours each spring and again in the fall he met with each business to review their human resource potential and how it was being developed. He was a big supporter of Crotonville, GE's education center, but focused it more on specific company-related development activities.

Welch's Organization

In addressing the 1989 GE shareholders' meeting, Welch also commented:

> We had constructed over the years a management apparatus that was right for its time, the toast of the business schools. Divisions, strategic business units, groups, sectors, all were designed to make meticulous, calculated decisions and move them smoothly forward and upward. This system produced highly polished work. It was right for the 1970s, a growing handicap in the 1980s, and it would have been a ticket to the boneyard in the 1990s.
>
> So we got rid of it, along with a lot of reports, meetings, and the endless paper that flowed like lava from the upper levels of the company. When we did this, we began to see people—who for years had spent half their time serving the system and the other half fighting it—suddenly come to life, making decisions in minutes, face-to-face, on matters that would have once produced months of staff gyrations and forests of paper. But this transformation, this rebirth, was largely confined to upper management. In the 1990s we want to see it engulf and galvanize the entire company.

One year later the 1990 annual report stated:

> The walls within a big century-old company don't come down like Jericho's when management makes some organizational changes—or gives a speech. There are too many persistent habits propping them up. Parochialism, turf battles, status, "functionalitis," and, most important, the biggest sin of a bureaucracy, the focus on itself and its inner workings, are always in the background.

Surveying organizational changes, Welch commented, "We're now down in some businesses [from nine] to four [layers] from the top to the bottom. That's the ultimate objective. We used to have things like department managers, section managers, subsection managers, unit managers, supervisors. We're driving those titles out ... We used to go from the CEO ... to sectors, to groups, to businesses. We now go from the CEO ... to businesses. Nothing else. There is nothing else there. Zero."[14]

In the *Harvard Business Review*, Welch elaborated:

> Layers hide weaknesses. Layers mask mediocrity. I firmly believe that an overburdened, overstretched executive is the best executive because he or she doesn't have the time to meddle, to deal in trivia, to bother people. Remember the theory that a manager should have no more than six or seven direct reports? I say the right number is closer to 10 or 15. This way you have no choice but to let people flex their muscles, let them grow and mature. With 10 or 15 reports, a leader can focus only on the big important issues, not on minutiae.
>
> We also reduced the corporate staff. Headquarters can be the bane of corporate America. It can strangle, choke, delay, and create insecurity. If you're going to have simplicity in the field, you can't have a big staff at home. We don't need the questioners and the checkers, the nitpickers who bog down the process, people whose only role is to second-guess people who clog communication inside the company. Today people at headquarters are experts in taxes, finance, or some other key area that can help people in the field. Our corporate staff no longer just challenges and questions; it assists. This is a mind-set change: staff essentially reports to the field rather

than the other way around ... Each staff person has to ask, "How do I add value? How do I help make people on the line more effective and more competitive?" In the past, many staff functions were driven by control rather than adding value. Staffs with that focus have to be eliminated. They sap emotional energy in the organization.[15]

> Cutting the groups and sectors eliminated communications filters. Today there is direct communication between the CEO and the leaders of the 14 businesses. We have very short cycle times for decisions and little interference by corporate staff. A major investment decision that used to take a year can now be made in a matter of days.[16]
>
> I operate on a very simple belief about business. If there are six of us in a room and we all get the same facts, in most cases, the six of us will reach roughly the same conclusion. And once we all accept that conclusion, we can force our energy into it and put it into action. The problem is we don't get the same information. We each get different pieces. Business isn't complicated. The complications arise when people are cut off from information they need. That's what we're trying to change.[17]
>
> We also run a Corporate Executive Council, the CEC. For two days every quarter, we meet with the leaders of the 14 businesses and our top staff people. These aren't stuffy, formal strategic reviews. We share ideas and information candidly and openly, including programs that have failed. The important thing is that at the end of those two days everyone in the CEC has seen and discussed the same information. The CEC creates a sense of trust, a sense of personal familiarity and mutual obligation at the top of

---

[14] Anonymous, "GE Chief Hopes to Shape Agile Giant," *Los Angeles Times*, June 1, 1988.

[15] Tichy and Charan, *op. cit.*, p. 114.
[16] *Ibid.*, p. 115.
[17] *Ibid.*, p. 116.

the company. We consider the CEC a piece of organizational technology that is very important for our future success.

People always overestimate how complex business is. This isn't rocket science; we've chosen one of the world's more simple professions. Most global businesses have three or four critical competitors, and you know who they are. And there aren't that many things you can do with a business. It's not as if you're choosing among 2,000 options.

At our 1986 officers' meeting, which involves the top 100 or so executives at GE, we asked the 14 business leaders to present reports on the competitive dynamics in their businesses. How did we do it? We had them each prepare one-page answers to five questions: What are your market dynamics globally today, and where are they going over the next several years? What actions have your competitors taken in the last three years to upset those global dynamics? What have you done in the last three years to affect those dynamics? What are the most dangerous things your competitor could do in the next three years to upset those dynamics? What are the most effective things you could do to bring your desired impact on those dynamics?

Five simple charts. After those initial reviews, which we update regularly, we could assume that everyone at the top knew the plays and had the same playbook. It doesn't take a genius. Fourteen businesses each with a playbook of five charts. So when [vice chairman] Larry Bossidy is with a potential partner in Europe, or I'm with a company in the Far East, we're always there with a competitive understanding based on our playbooks. We know exactly what makes sense; we don't need a big staff to do endless analysis. That means we should be able to act with speed.

Probably the most important thing we promise our business leaders is fast action. Their job is to create and grow new global businesses. Our job in the executive office is to facilitate, to go out and negotiate a deal, to make the acquisition, or to get our businesses the partners they need. When our business leaders call, they don't expect studies—they expect answers.

Take the deal with Thomson, where we swapped our consumer electronics business for their medical equipment business. We were presented with an opportunity, a great solution to a serious strategic problem, and we were able to act quickly. We didn't need to go back to headquarters for a strategic analysis and a bunch of reports. Conceptually, it took us about 30 minutes to decide that the deal made sense and then a meeting of maybe two hours with the Thomson people to work out the basic terms. We signed a letter of intent in five days. We had to close it with the usual legal details, of course, so from beginning to end it took five months. Thomson had the same clear view of where it wanted to go—so it worked perfectly for both sides.[18]

Welch also made some important changes to GE's traditional personnel practices. To accelerate the change process, Welch believed that he had to overhaul the way the company compensated its managers and other employees. He wanted to give more recognition to individual contributors and higher rewards to those who produced superior results. He said:

A flat reward system is a big anchor to incrementalism. We want to give big

---

[18] *Ibid.*, pp. 115–116.

rewards to those who do things but without going after the scalps of those who reach for the big win but fail. Punishing failure assures that no one dares.[19]

Breaking with tradition, Welch's redesigned bonus system reached deep into middle management but was much more discriminating. Widespread 10 to 15 percent bonuses at the top levels were replaced by 30 and 40 percent bonuses to fewer managers—and more who were awarded no bonus. Similarly, routine 4 to 5 percent pay increases were replaced by 10 to 15 percent raises for superstars and only routine rewards for routine performance. Finally, he gave stock options as rewards to thousands of employees rather than reserving them for only the top echelon as had been the practice historically.

Many GE managers and workers had negative reactions to the changes. Some felt overworked, and some felt that the bonds of loyalty that made GE a great corporation were shattered by Welch's performance orientation. Trading the consumer electronics business for Thomson's medical systems struck many as the ultimate signal that anything was for sale. Welch was well aware of the existence of discontent but spoke passionately of the need for change. In his *Harvard Business Review* interview, he commented:

> Like many other large companies in the United States, Europe, and Japan, GE has had an implicit psychological contract based on perceived lifetime employment. People were rarely dismissed except for cause or severe business downturns, like in aerospace after Vietnam. This produced a paternal, feudal, fuzzy kind of

loyalty. You put in your time, worked hard, and the company took care of you for life.

> That kind of loyalty tends to focus people inward. But given today's environment, people's emotional energy must be focused outward on a competitive world where no business is a safe haven for employment unless it is winning in the marketplace. The psychological contract has to change. People at all levels have to feel the risk–reward tension.

> My concept of loyalty is not "giving time" to some corporate entity and, in turn, being shielded and protected from the outside world. Loyalty is an affinity among people who want to grapple with the outside world and win. Their personal values, dreams, and ambitions cause them to gravitate toward each other and toward a company like GE that gives them the resources and opportunities to flourish.

> The new psychological contract, if there is such a thing, is that jobs at GE are the best in the world for people who are willing to compete. We have the best training and development resources and an environment committed to providing opportunities for personal and professional growth.[20]

Work-Out

One dramatic step in bringing about cultural change at GE was Work-Out, a major effort to spread across the company the sort of rough-and-tumble approach to discussing and solving problems that Welch thought he experienced when he worked with groups of GE managers attending the general management course at

---

[19] *Ibid.*

[20] Tichy and Charan, *op. cit.*, p. 120.

the company's Crotonville management development center.

According to *Fortune*,[21] Work-Out is, essentially, a forum where three things can happen: Participants can get a mental workout; they can take unnecessary work out of their jobs; they can work out problems together. Work-Outs started in March 1989.

> Initially, all followed the same format, which Welch likens to a New England town meeting. A group of 40 to 100 people, picked by management from all ranks and several functions, goes to a conference center or hotel. [Dress is informal.] The three-day sessions begin with a talk by the boss, who roughs out an agenda—typically to eliminate unnecessary meetings, forms, approvals, and other scut work. Then the boss leaves. Aided by the outside facilitator, the group breaks into five or six teams, each to tackle part of the agenda. For a day and a half they go at it, listing complaints, debating solutions, and preparing presentations for the final day.
>
> It's the third day that gives Work-Out its special power. The boss, ignorant of what has been going on, comes back and takes a place at the front of the room. Often senior executives come to watch. One by one, team spokesmen rise to make their proposals. By the rules of the game, the boss can make only three responses: he can agree on the spot; he can say no; or he can ask for more information—in which case he must charter a team to get it by an agreed-upon date.
>
> "I was wringing wet within half an hour," says Armand Lauzon, the burly, blunt-spoken head of plant services at the GE Aircraft Engines factory in Lynn,

Massachusetts. His employees had set up the room so that Lauzon had his back to his boss. "They had 108 proposals; I had about a minute to say yes or no to each one, and I couldn't make eye contact with my boss without turning around, which would show everyone in the room that I was chickenshit." Ideas ranged from designing a plant-services insignia as a morale booster to building a new tinsmith shop, and Lauzon said yes to all but eight.

> Electrician Vic Slepoy makes no apology for the ordeal Lauzon suffered: "When you've been told to shut up for 20 years, and someone tells you to speak up—you're going to let them have it." Lauzon is not complaining. Work-Out proposals will save plant services more than $200,000 in 1991. The biggest hit: a yes to letting Lynn's tin knockers bid against an outside vendor to build new protective shields for grinding machines, based on a design an hourly worker sketched on a brown paper bag. They brought in the job for $16,000 versus the vendor's quoted $96,000.
>
> These first sessions are really about building trust. Says Welch, "You have to go through the administrative part of it. If you jump right into complicated issues, no one speaks up, because those ideas are more dangerous." That's because they cross functional boundaries where people feel their turf is being encroached upon. To make that step, the Work-Out process changes. Later Work-Outs are still "unnatural acts," but now they're "in natural places," in [one of the Work-Out facilitator's] words—meaning that teams are made up of people who work together day to day or who are involved in different steps of the same process, like packers and shippers or purchasing agents and parts managers. Often they are commissioned at town meetings to gather data on a knotty problem.
>
> Technician Al Thomas led one such team at GE Plastics' Burkville, Alabama,

---

[21] Thomas A. Stewart, "GE Keeps Those Ideas Coming," *Fortune* © 1991 Time Inc. All Rights Reserved.

plant, which makes Lexan, a polycarbonate used in auto bumpers and milk bottles. Its mission: to increase the "first-pass yield"—the percentage of resin that ends up as salable pellets without having to be melted and run again through the factory's extruders. "There were no home runs," Thomas says, but the team hit 26 singles. They installed a computer terminal on the extrusion floor to give workers early warning of problems upstream where resins are made. They realigned pipes that pour pellets into cartons to reduce spillage. They vetted the procedures manual; a Post-it note on one page reads, "This procedure is totally unnecessary and useless." Hourly workers, not engineers, are writing a new version. The team met daily for three months and spent about $10,000. When they were done, 37 percent of the waste was gone. And, says Thomas, it was fun: "We learned a lot without bosses looking over our shoulders."

Now Work-Outs are enrolling customers and suppliers as well as colleagues. A team in the locomotive paint shop in Erie, Pennsylvania, found that a major cause of delays and rework was inconsistency in the paint because GE was buying it from two suppliers. Team members persuaded their boss, Ralph Schumacher, to use just one, Glyptal Corp., and asked its chemist to join up. Together they wrote standards for color and consistency, eliminating the need for dual inspections, and hooked up a direct phone line between the two shops. A paint job now takes 10 shifts, down from 11 or 12 before. GE's Monogram Retailer Credit Services, which manages Montgomery Ward's charge card business, teamed with Ward to tie its cash registers directly to GE's mainframes, cutting the time for opening a new customer account from 30 minutes to 90 seconds.

In his *Harvard Business Review* interview, Welch elaborated:

Work-Out has a practical and an intellectual goal. The practical objective is to get rid of thousands of bad habits accumulated since the creation of General Electric. How would you like to move from a house after 112 years? Think of what would be in the closets and the attic—those shoes that you'll wear to paint next spring, even though you know you'll never paint again. We've got 112 years of closets and attics in this company. We want to flush them out, to start with a brand new house with empty closets, to begin the whole game again.

The second thing we want to achieve, the intellectual part, begins by putting the leaders of each business in front of 100 or so of their people, 8 to 10 times a year, to let them hear what people think about the company, what they like and don't like about their work, about how they're evaluated, about how they spend their time. Work-Out will expose the leaders to the vibrations of their business—opinions, feelings, emotions, resentments, not abstract theories of organization and management.

Ultimately, we're talking about redefining the relationship between boss and subordinate. I want to get to a point where people challenge their bosses every day: "Why do you require me to do these wasteful things? Why don't you let me do the things you shouldn't be doing so you can move on and create? That's the job of a leader—to create, not to control. Trust me to do my job, and don't make me waste all my time trying to deal with you on the control issue."

Now, how do you get people communicating with each other with that much candor? You put them together in a room and make them thrash it out.[22]

We have to apply the same relentless passion to Work-Out that we did in sell-

---

22 Tichy and Charan, *op. cit.*, p. 118.

ing the vision of number one and number two globally. That's why we're pushing it so hard, getting so involved.[23]

Best Practices

Best Practices was, according to *Fortune*,[24] another assault on business-as-usual. Again, the impetus was Welch's pursuit of ideas to increase productivity. It was Welch himself who first voiced what later seemed obvious. Other companies get higher productivity growth than GE. Why not kick their tires?

The assignment went to the business development staff in Fairfield, which scrutinizes acquisition candidates and thus has wide knowledge of other companies. In the summer of 1988, the group began scouring the business press and canvasing GE executives, looking for companies worth emulating. From an initial list of about 200, they found two dozen that had achieved faster productivity growth than GE and sustained it for at least 10 years. Half of the survivors agreed to the proposition GE made: Let us send some people to your shop to learn about your best management ideas; in return, we'll share the study with you and let you ask about our methods. Participants included electronic components maker AMP, Chaparral Steel, Ford, Hewlett-Packard, Xerox, and three Japanese companies. The Project, which GE called Best Practices, took more than a year.

Basically, GE's question was, "What's the secret of your success?" Surprise: The answers were remarkably similar. Almost every company emphasized managing processes, not functions; that is, they focused less on the performance of

individual departments than on how they work together as products move from one to another. They also outhustled their competitors in introducing new products and treated their suppliers as partners. And they managed inventory so well that they tied up less working capital per dollar of sales than GE.

The implications of the Best Practices study were earthshaking. GE realized it was managing and measuring the wrong things. The company was setting goals and keeping score; instead, says business development manager George Zippel, "We should have focused more on *how* things got done than on *what* got done."

Best Practices provided an empirical basis for changing what GE manages. The corporate audit staff—[since the 1930s] GE's fearsome cadre of traveling checkers—altered its methods. Auditors, youngsters picked for their high potential, used to come from finance backgrounds; now half are operations or information systems experts. Says audit staff head Teresa LeGrand: "When I started 10 years ago, the first thing I did was count the $5,000 in the petty cash box. Today we look at the $5 million in inventory on the floor, searching for process improvements that will bring it down."

Crotonville turned the Best Practices findings into a course, which it gives to a dozen people a month from each of GE's 10 manufacturing businesses. The service businesses, which need to pay special attention to issues like managing information technology, have their own course, based on research at nonmanufacturing companies like American Express.

Nowhere have GE's new management techniques come together more impressively than in the appliance business. A year ago senior vice president Gary Rogers toured the Montreal plant of GE Appliances' Canadian subsidiary, Camco, to see how it had adapted the ideas of a

[23] *Ibid.*, p. 118.
[24] Stewart, *op. cit.*

small New Zealand appliance maker, Fisher & Paykel. Camco's manufacturing head, Serge Huot, had found a way to transfer Fisher & Paykel's job-shop techniques to the high-volume Canadian factory, automatically speeding operations. The change hadn't been trouble-free— Camco had problems making all models available at all times—but the normally taciturn Rogers was excited.

What happened next shows how GE's new management techniques work. Rogers called a town meeting Work-Out to introduce the ideas and the vision —which amounts to a build-to-order manufacturing style. For example, building a dishwasher takes just hours, but it takes about 16 weeks for a change in the pattern of consumer demand to affect the product mix at the end of the assembly line in Louisville. The goal: Reduce that cycle by 90 percent while actually increasing availability—the odds that a given model is on hand when a customer orders it. Finance manager David Cote assembled a cross-functional team to install Camco's system, now called Quick Response. Work-Out teams began sticking process maps on the walls—more than 500 in all. One result among many: Workers in the distribution center now get production schedules in a new way that allows them to tell truckers well in advance when their loads will be ready —a simple change that will save almost a day's time and will cut $3 million in inventory.

More than 200 Louisville managers and employees toured the Montreal operation. Others took a GE jet to Crotonville to take the Best Practices course, including a group with two shop stewards from the refrigerator plant. The trip was meant to show union and management leaders the potential payoff from process-oriented, nonhierarchical cooperation and to help soften a relationship that had become a rigid that's-not-my-job-description face-off. Another purpose was to study companies—one of them a textile manufacturer—that had mastered high-volume, build-to-order manufacturing.

Since implementing Quick Response in January, GE Appliances has cut its 16-week cycle by more than half while increasing product availability 6 percent. Inventory costs have plunged more than 20 percent—a major reason the group has weathered the recession with steady profits despite a 5 percent decrease in volume. The program has cost less than $3 million, Roger says, and has already returned a hundred times that.

That's not counting the benefits to other GE businesses. Quick Response, the result of a Best Practice from an outside company, has made Appliance Park the hottest destination on GE's internal Best Practices circuit. Two years ago the business's combination of low margins, tough unions, and brutal competition made Louisville the last place an ambitious GE manager wanted to be—"an isolation ward," says one. Now groups from every other GE business have taken up residence there to learn how to adapt the process to their needs.

The revolution at General Electric is still fragile, and middle management is one of the weaker points. David Genever-Watling, senior vice president of industrial and power systems, says, "You need unselfish, open-minded executives to run the process," and they are still a rare breed at GE or anywhere else . . . The same goes for workers. In Schenectady, New York, union business agent Lou Valenti says, "I'm behind the process 200 percent," and was reelected without opposition last year; in Lynn, workers who went through Work-Out were told by colleagues that it's a ploy to win votes for the new contract—but in July the Lynn local approved a three-year national pact for the first time since 1982.

Welch can point to results where they will always matter most at GE, in the numbers. Productivity—which GE measures by dividing real revenues (with price increases factored out) by real costs (after discounting for inflation)—will rise 5 percent in 1991, according to Welch, "with almost no layoffs and, due to the recession, no increase in volume." GE expects to get five dollars in sales for every dollar of working capital invested—16.3 percent more than in 1988, the year before Work-Out and Best Practices began.

Welch admits that it will take a decade before GE's new culture becomes as hard to change as the one it is supplanting. By then, he says, GE's hierarchies could actually wither away.

Boundary-less Integrated Diversity

In the 1990 GE annual report, Welch put forth yet another challenge for his organization, intending to make GE into a truly "boundary-less" company.

> In a boundary-less company, suppliers aren't outsiders. They are drawn closer and become trusted partners in the total business process. Customers' vision of their needs and the company's view become identical, and every effort of every man and woman in the company is focused on satisfying those needs.
>
> The boundary-less company blurs the divisions between internal functions; it recognizes no distinctions between "domestic" and "foreign" operations; and it ignores or erases group labels such as "management," "salaried," and "hourly," which get in the way of people working together.

An additional challenge was to link GE's 13 businesses through what Welch termed "integrated diversity," the ability to transfer the best ideas, most developed knowledge, and most valuable people freely and easily across businesses in a boundary-less company. For Welch, the learning associated with the Quick Response project—from the New Zealand supplier, to Canadian subsidiary, to Louisville, to the rest of GE—was an apt illustration of the concept.

Both insiders and outsiders had reservations about how much change these initiatives could achieve and how quickly. Said one senior manager, "Of course, Jack has to make it seem achievable—even easy. But it's not. It's one thing to study another company's best practices—it's quite another to transplant that change into a company like GE."[25]

In his *Harvard Business Review* interview, Welch was asked, "When will we know when these changes have worked?" Welch responded:

> A business magazine recently printed an article about GE that listed our businesses and the fact that we were number one or number two in virtually all of them. That magazine didn't get one complaint from our competitors. Those are the facts. That's what we said we wanted to do, and we've done it.
>
> Ten years from now, we want magazines to write about GE as a place where people have the freedom to be creative, a place that brings out the best in everybody. An open, fair place where people have a sense that what they do matters, and where that sense of accomplishment is rewarded in both the pocketbook and the soul. That will be our report card.[26]

---

[25] Elderkin and Bartlett, *op. cit.*
[26] Tichy and Charan, *op. cit.*, p. 120.

EXHIBIT 1
GENERAL ELECTRIC'S PERFORMANCE IN THREE ERAS (millions of dollars)

	Borch			Jones			Welch		
	1961	1970	CAGR	1971	1980	CAGR	1981	1992	CAGR
Sales	$ 4,666.6	$ 8,726.7	7.2%	$ 9,557.0	$ 24,959.0	11.2%	$ 27,240.0	$ 57,073.0	7.0%
Operating profit	$ 431.8	$ 548.9	2.7%	$ 737.0	$ 2,243.0	13.1%	$ 2,447.0	$ 6,273.0	9.9%
Net earnings	$ 238.4	$ 328.5	3.6%	$ 510.0	$ 1,514.0	12.8%	$ 1,652.0	$ 4,725.0	10.0%
ROS	5.1%	3.8%		5.3%	6.1%		6.1%	8.4%	
ROE	14.8%	12.6%		17.2%	19.5%		18.1%	20.1%	
Stock market capitalization	$ 6,283.7	$ 7,026.7	1.2%	$ 10,870.5	$ 12,173.4	1.3%	$ 13,765.4	$ 68,594.7	15.7%
S&P 500 Stock Price Index—Composite	65.7	83.0	2.6%	97.9	119.4	2.2%	126.4	413.0	11.4%
Employees	279,547	396,583		402,000	366,000		404,000	231,000	
U.S. GNP ($ billion)	$ 523.0	$ 982.0	7.2%	$ 1,063.0	$ 2,626.0	10.6%	$ 2,708.0	$ 5,951.0	7.4%

Source: GE Annual Reports, *Moody's Industrial Yearbook*, Survey of Current Business.

EXHIBIT 2
GENERAL ELECTRIC COMPANY WORLDWIDE BUSINESS PROFILE*

GE is committed to enhancing the global competitiveness of its 13 key businesses through internal growth, acquisitions, and joint ventures and by eliminating the boundaries that exist among its businesses, customers, suppliers, and employees.

Aerospace   A leading U.S. provider of satellites, radar systems, integrated software systems, and other advanced technologies for use in defense, space, and aviation.

Aircraft Engines   The world's leading manufacturer of large jet engines for commercial and military aircraft, and the supplier of both large and small engines powering nearly 18,000 aircraft in service today.

Appliances   A world leader in major appliances for the home, providing high-quality products under the GE, Monogram, RCA, and Hotpoint brand names.

Capital Services   One of the largest and most diversified finance companies in the United States, providing financial products and services tailored to customer needs through GE Capital, Employers Reinsurance, and Kidder Peabody.

Industrial and Power Systems   A global leader in providing utilities and other customers with products that generate and deliver electricity as well as systems that improve air quality.

Lighting   Not only the originator of the incandescent lamp but also now the world's biggest supplier of lightbulbs and a global leader in lighting technology.

Medical Systems   The global leader in diagnostic imaging systems used by hospitals, clinics, and health care professionals to provide the best health care possible for their patients.

NBC   The top-ranked television network in the United States in 1990 in terms of viewer ratings and advertising revenues.

Plastics   A world leader in high-performance engineering plastics that can be used in innovative ways to replace metal, glass, and other traditional materials.

Information Services   Helping customers worldwide to be more productive through the use of computers, teleprocessing networks, satellites, cellular phones, and other information technologies.

Electrical Distribution and Control   An industry leader in products that distribute, control, and protect electrical power and a supplier of factory automation equipment.

Motors   The U.S. market leader in energy-efficient motors and one of the largest suppliers of AC and DC electric motors in the world.

Transportation Systems   One of the world's largest manufacturers of diesel electric locomotives and a leading supplier of propulsion systems for rapid-transit cars and electric wheels for off-highway vehicles.

*Description of business position and GE's strategic position as described in GE's 1991 annual report.

EXHIBIT 3
GENERAL ELECTRIC—INDUSTRY SEGMENT INFORMATION

	1992	1991	1990	1989	1988	1987	1986	1985	1984	1983	1982	1981
Revenues												
Aerospace	NA	NA	12.5%	12.4%	13.3%	13.0%	11.8%	10.5%	9.1%	7.5%	NA	NA
Aircraft engine	18.3%	19.6%	16.7	16.1	16.1	16.7	16.3	15.8	12.9	12.4	11.5%	10.8%
Appliances	13.2	13.2	12.5	13.2	13.1	11.7	11.8	12.4	12.6	11.1	10.1	11.5
Broadcasting	8.4	7.9	7.2	8.0	9.0	8.0	4.9	NA	NA	NA	NA	NA
Industrial	17.2	17.1	14.8	16.6	17.5	16.4	12.8	13.7	13.6	14.0	17.3	19.7
Materials	12.1	12.0	11.5	11.6	8.8	6.8	6.3	8.0	7.3	7.1	6.6	7.5
Power systems	15.8	15.6	12.5	12.0	11.9	12.3	14.3	18.4	20.0	20.5	22.4	22.1
Technical products and services	11.6	11.8	9.5	10.7	11.0	9.1	8.2	17.1	15.8	13.6	13.0	11.0
Corporate items and eliminations	-0.9	-1.2	-0.6	-3.3	-3.7	-3.2	-2.9	-3.1	-3.5	-2.8	-2.3	-3.0
Total GE	40,254	39,594	44,879	42,650	40,292	40,516	36,728	29,272	28,936	27,681	27,192	27,240
GEFS												
Financing	57.2%	61.4%	60.9%	56.6%	54.7%	42.6%	100.0%	100.0%	100.0%	100.0%	100.0%	100.0%
Insurance	20.9	18.2	19.3	20.9	23.3	27.0	NA	NA	NA	NA	NA	NA
Securities broker–dealer	21.8	20.4	19.8	22.4	21.7	30.3	NA	NA	NA	NA	NA	NA
Total GEFS	18,440	16,399	14,774	12,945	10,655	8,225	5,814	499	448	397	286	239
Consolidated revenues	57,073	54,629	52,619	55,595	50,947	48,741	42,542	29,772	29,384	28,078	27,478	27,479
Operating Profit												
Aerospace	NA	NA	8.9%	9.5%	11.2%	13.6%	14.1%	10.7%	8.8%	NA	NA	NA
Aircraft engines	23.4%	26.3%	17.1	15.4	17.5	21.2	20.2	16.5	12.2	13.4%	NA	12.1%
Appliances	7.1	8.1	6.3	5.9	1.1	11.0	10.7	0.5	0.4	12.7	NA	0.0
Broadcasting	3.7	3.9	6.5	8.9	9.4	11.3	5.6	16.2	12.6	NA	NA	NA
Industrial	16.3	15.6	11.4	12.5	14.0	6.8	13.3	9.8	10.1	6.3	NA	18.6
Materials	13.6	14.9	13.8	15.5	12.8	11.4	9.8	8.1	11.8	10.9	NA	0.0
Power systems	19.1	17.3	10.0	7.5	8.8	4.5	8.2	18.2	14.5	23.6	NA	16.8
Technical products and services	16.8	13.9	8.1	8.7	8.5	6.2	2.6	0.5	-0.2	12.8	NA	9.4%
Total GE	5,441	5,377	7,385	6,801	5,715	4,440	4,310	4,068	3,779	3,009		2,600

continued

EXHIBIT 3 (continued)

	1992	1991	1990	1989	1988	1987	1986	1985	1984	1983	1982	1981
GEFS												
Financing	59.2%	70.0%	90.8%	101.2%	87.5%	111.2%	162.3%	118.2%	125.4%	100.0%	NA	100.0%
Insurance	40.8	30.0	32.8	31.7	32.5	32.0	−216.4	10.6	0.8	NA	NA	NA
Securities broker–dealer	CF	CF	−3.9	−4.7	6.2	−4.0	−136.1	0.0	0.0	NA	NA	NA
Total GEFS	2,307	1,895	1,395	1,138	1,027	572	−62	424	354	290	NA	129
Consolidated operating profit	7,748	7,272	8,780	7,939	6,742	5,012	4,249	4,492	4,133	3,299	NA	2,789
Depreciation												
Aerospace	NA	NA	11.2%	10.0%	11.2%	9.8%	7.6%	NA	NA	NA	NA	NA
Aircraft engines	19.8%	20.6%	19.0	17.9	16.5	15.7	13.3	13.1%	12.4%	11.9%	9.6%	9.8%
Appliances	7.1	7.4	6.5	7.3	6.9	6.0	6.5	6.4	6.8	6.3	7.6	0.0
Broadcasting	5.5	5.9	5.5	5.2	4.6	4.1	1.9	NA	NA	NA	NA	NA
Industrial	19.0	18.3	16.9	16.3	16.4	20.4	13.4	13.3	13.7	14.6	14.4	10.5
Materials	26.5	25.8	21.2	20.9	16.6	13.1	17.9	19.9	18.8	18.7	12.4	0.0
Power systems	10.7	10.1	9.1	8.9	9.1	10.5	11.8	13.5	16.3	16.0	19.2	20.5
Technical products and services	5.0	6.9	6.6	10.1	11.0	11.0	12.7	19.2	15.1	11.4	11.0	11.8
Corporate items and eliminations	6.0	6.2	4.3	3.3	6.7	5.4	3.6	4.0	3.1	4.0	3.1	2.2
Total GE	1,483	1,429	1,534	1,524	1,522	1,544	1,460	1,226	1,100	1,084	964	882
GEFS												
Financing	94.3%	94.8%	93.9%	92.8%	93.4%	88.1%	92.3%	NA	NA	NA	NA	NA
Insurance	1.0	0.7	1.1	1.1	0.8	1.1	1.1	NA	NA	NA	NA	NA
Securities broker–dealer	2.5	3.1	3.2	4.4	4.3	7.6	3.6	NA	NA	NA	NA	NA
Total GEFS	1,335	1,225	976	732	744	369	365	NA	NA	NA	NA	NA
Consolidated depreciation	2,818	2,654	2,333	2,256	2,266	1,913	1,460	1,226	1,100	1,084	964	882

Source: General Electric annual reports.

EXHIBIT 4
RESTRUCTURING AT GE, 1981–1993

ACQUISITIONS

1981
- Calma Company, CAD/CAM supplier
- Intersil, semiconductor manufacturer
- Structural Dynamics Research Co. (48%)
- 4 niche software companies
- Air pollution control business from Envirotech

1984
- Employers Reinsurance Corp.

1988
- Montgomery Ward Credit Corp.
- Roper Corp., appliances
- Borg-Warner chemical business
- Baltica-Nordisk Insurance of Denmark

1991
- Financial News Network
- EMI Thorn, U.K., light source business
- British Airways engine overhaul facility
- Chase Manhattan leasing operation
- Bank of New York
- Itel Corp.
- CMV Leasing

1982
- 16% share of GEISCO (GE Information Service Co.) owned by Honeywell
- GEVENCO (GE Venture Capital Co.) invested in 7 new businesses
- 17.5% of Gearhart Industries

1986
- RCA
- Kidder Peabody (80%)

1989
- Tungsram Co. of Hungary, lighting (50% +)
- FGIC Corp. (remaining 62%)

1983
- AMIC Corp., mortgage insurer
- Reuter-Stokes, high-tech niche instruments
- Rail car management company
- GEVENCO invested in 10 new companies
- GEVENCO increased investments in 15 companies

1987
- CGR, medical diagnostic imaging swapped with Thomson of France
- Navistar Financial Canada
- Gelco Corp., auto fleet leasing
- D&K Financial, auto leasing

1990
- Kidder Peabody (remaining 20%)
- MNC Financial leasing operation
- Burton Group of U.K.
- Travelers Mortgage Services
- ELLCO Leasing Corp.
- Repurchased 38 million GE shares

Jack Welch takes office as CEO in April, 1981

1981   1982   1983   1984   1985   1986   1987   1988   1989   1990   1991   1992   1993

DIVESTITURES

SUMMARY

1981–85 GE acquired over 300 businesses.
1985–90 GE acquired over 70 businesses.
          GE divested over 200 businesses.
1981–90 GE invested over $17 billion in acquisitions.
          GE received over $9 billion from divestitures.
          GE sold businesses making up 25% of 1980 sales.

1982
- Pathfinder Mines Corp.
- Central air conditioning business
- Mining products business

1985
- Australian Coal Properties
- Remainder of GE Cablevision operations

1983
- Utah International
- Housewares business sold to Black & Decker
- 8 radio and 2 TV broadcasting stations
- Family Financial Services
- Data Communications Products
- Trapper Mines
- 17.5% interest in Gearhart Industries

1987
- Consumer electronics business swapped to Thomson of France
- NBC radio networks
- NiCad battery, ballast lighting, nuclear waste, and HVDC power transmission businesses
- Donated David Sarnoff Research Center to SRI

1990
- Ladd Petroleum

1984
- GE Cablevision Corp. merged with United Artists Cablesystem

1988
- RCA Global Communications
- GE Solid State, semiconductor business
- Sadelmi-Cogepi, foreign construction firm

1991
- Columbia Home Video JV

1992
- GE Aerospace, GE Government Services, Knolls Atomic Power Labs combined with Martin Marietta

The Battle of Mannheim

A HOT WINTER IN MANNHEIM

"Koerber raus, Koerber raus" (Koerber get out) shouted a crowd of about 4,500 ABB employees outside the Käfertal head office building in Mannheim. This March 24, 1988, demonstration was part of a two-hour strike to protest a newspaper interview in the local paper by Eberhard von Koerber, head of the Vorstand of ABB's German subsidiary. The interview was viewed as a provocation by the union leadership. They blamed von Koerber for going public with the results of a confidential meeting which management and the Betriebsrat (works council) had attended two days earlier at the invitation of Lothar Späth, prime minister of the federal state of Baden-Würtenberg, in which Mannheim was located. A member of the Betriebsrat shouted through the megaphone that von Koerber had broken an agreed-upon silence. By doing so, he had poisoned the atmosphere for further talks and had been trying to marshal public opinion against the Betriebsrat and the employees. In several passages of the interview he had "lied," according to the Betriebsrat spokesman. During the joint meeting with Späth, union members had understood that the concept of the Vorstand was still open for modifications. In the interview, however, von Koerber repeated the need to reduce the ABB German workforce of 36,000 by some 3,500–4,000 people. IG Metall,[1] the union representing the blue-collar workers, feared that employment might be reduced by as much as 6,000 people. DAG,[2] the union representing the white-collar employees, blamed von Koerber for not being interested in maintaining Mannheim as ABB's German base. Peter Toussaint, the IG Metall representative in Mannheim and an employee representative on the ABB Deutschland supervisory board, stated, "It is no concept, when von Koerber claims that where we make losses, we have to eliminate the losses. BBC today as in the past is still a healthy company."

[1] IG stands for Industriegewerkschaft or industrial union.

[2] DAG stands for Deutsche Angestellten Gewerkschaft.

The March 24 demonstration was yet one more event in the hot Mannheim winter of 1988. ABB had been founded on January 4, 1988. On January 8, von Koerber enunciated his target of a fivefold profit increase and, subsequently, ABB Deutschland top managers attended the Cannes meeting. Thereafter, on January 14, Percy Barnevik presided over ABB's first press conference at which a Mannheim reporter was present. A few days later, a lengthy lead article appeared in the local paper describing how Barnevik had initiated a powerful tempo in order to take advantage of the early merger honeymoon to break the prevailing crusty and immobile structures, especially at BBC. The reporter indicated that to date it had been impossible to overcome the "narrow-mindedness and jealousy in the tense German–Swiss corporate relationship." The article concluded:

> "Restructure first, grow afterward" is the current ABB formula. But in times of codetermination, this is easier said than done. Restructuring is a euphemism for job reduction. Barnevik knows full well that only with drastic cuts in employment can he succeed in his ambitious goal to make ABB through cost reductions into one of the world's most profitable electrotechnical companies. How skillful the Swedes will turn out to be will be determined by how successfully they deal with the "social forces," particularly in Germany, Switzerland, and Scandinavia.

The author finally suggested that Barnevik's goals were probably too ambitious given the likely organizational and social resistance.

The first shot in the impending battle was fired by Toussaint. In an early February interview he indicated that several hundred jobs were in jeopardy in the Mannheim area. He said, "The catastrophe will be twice as big as we had feared in our wildest dreams. IG Metall recognizes that restructuring measures are necessary, but we did not expect such massive targets." He severely criticized the Swedish managers in ABB and particularly Percy Barnevik. Later, Toussaint commented:

> We were very concerned when we learned about the merger between Asea and BBC. We felt that Asea got the better part of the deal. Admittedly, they were more profitable, but with their restructuring in Scandinavia they had essentially reached the end of the line. Their technology was weaker than that of BBC and they virtually had no beachhead in the European Economic Community. Barnevik, furthermore, with his American-style management approach, was a known quantity. BBC had a lot of unrealized substance, and Barnevik was obviously going to squeeze everything out until the last drop. We had to get ready to resist this approach. We had to protect jobs, particularly in Mannheim, which already had the highest unemployment rate in the state and where BBC was the largest industrial employer. We were not going to surrender without a long hard fight.

The predicted war broke out on February 23. In the early hours of the morning both the mayor of Mannheim and the economics minister of Baden-Würtenberg in Stuttgart were informed that a "reduction of employment of about 10 percent will have to be accomplished during the next three years." At 8:00 AM the Betriebsrat received the news, subsequently IG Metall was informed, and at 11:30 AM a press conference was held Two units in the Käfertal factory complex would be heavily impacted. The Betriebsrat was told that the transformer plant, employing over 500, would have to be closed, and 700 out of the 4,000 workers in the power plant unit would lose their jobs. The company also indicated that a complete overhead analysis would be made by McKinsey to prune the administrative apparatus. According to the Betriebsrat, some 20 percent of the administrative jobs were at risk. With BBC employment standing at 36,000, the local newspaper carried as a headline the next day that 4,000 jobs would be eliminated. The television newscast that evening stated that Mannheim was footing the bill for the elephant marriage between Asea and BBC. Toussaint later commented, "When this announcement came, we decided to engage in a deliberate confrontation with management."

The initial reaction in the local newspaper showed understanding for the Vorstand's position:

> BBC Germany and particularly its Mannheim location have been chronically ill for years. With or without merger, major surgery would have been inevitable sooner or later. A reproach clearly is in order. Management should have attempted much earlier, and in smaller steps, to bring about the slow recovery of the sick company units. This applies not just to the German but to the entire BBC organization. If inaction would have continued a few more years, maybe BBC would have turned into a second AEG.

(AEG, Germany's third largest electrotechnical concern, had been previously near bankruptcy and had to be rescued by Daimler Benz.) The Käfertal employees felt differently. Spontaneously, about 4,000 people met outside the head office building to be "informed" by the Betriebsrat. This was the prevailing approach in Germany to stop work while still getting paid. Even though works assemblies, involving management, the Betriebsrat, and the employees, were scheduled at regular intervals five times a year, workers could always request to be informed when

events triggering the codetermination law were occurring.

The waves resulting from the February 23 announcement remained not limited to the Käfertal complex. Mannheim's socialist mayor immediately called on the Christian democratic state government for help to alleviate Mannheim's 10 percent unemployment rate. With state elections scheduled for March 20, he knew that his call would almost certainly yield a response. Observers had been surprised that von Koerber dropped his bomb before the election. He had visited Helmut Kohl in Bonn in early February and had initially announced that it would take time to work out the restructuring measures and that definite plans would not be submitted until March. The rumor mill and the resulting uncertainty in Käfertal had made it impossible to stick to this initial timetable.

The union response to the February 23 announcement was prompt and strong with the statement that these "plans had nothing to do anymore with restructuring but would lead to the destruction of the German BBC." Several aspects of the Mannheim situation gave the opposition some tactical advantages. They could count on a great amount of sympathy given Mannheim's high unemployment rate and its social-democratic political landscape. In addition, BBC was heavily concentrated in its Käfertal complex, which housed not only several important product groups but also all administrative activities.[3] A single Betriebsrat, comprising 31 elected members, represented all of Käfertal's 7,700

---

[3] Every German factory above a minimal size had an elected Betriebsrat. Its size varied, depending on the number of workers represented. When several factories and/or offices were involved, the single, large works council was referred to as Gesamtbetriebsrat.

employees. Four members of the Betriebsrat, while small in number but strong in political influence, belonged to the extreme left of the political spectrum. Finally, under German law, the announced measures, with their personnel and social consequences, required information, consultation, and decision sharing by the Betriebsrat. Compounding the situation was the traditional rivalry between the German and Swiss organizations. Each side traditionally feared that it was taken advantage of at the expense of the other.

Thus, union members were constantly able to exploit numerous occasions to call for work stoppages. One occurred on February 29 with another one following on March 4, each time involving several thousand people. On Tuesday, March 8, almost 6,000 people showed up for the works assembly at 9:30 AM. Von Koerber, flanked by two Vorstand colleagues in charge of power plants and human relations, had to listen to a day of speeches and insults. At the beginning of the meeting some 500 workers from the transformer factory, which was to be closed, walked by the Vorstand's table, each of them depositing a wooden cross on it. The union raised another topic: It alleged that certain activities, which were being transferred to Switzerland, had been financed with German government research grants. Thus, the Swedes and Swiss were portrayed as carrying away technology financed by the German taxpayer. The union also announced counterproposals: for example, the suggestion that Asea robots also be manufactured in Mannheim. The meeting continued for a total of three days (after the first day without von Koerber), thus becoming the longest in German codetermination history.

Outside support continued to grow. Union leaders had established contacts with unions in other countries. Sympathy

meetings of other BBC Betriebsrat in Germany were held. Church leaders expressed their sympathy and support. Protesters were able to corner Späth at an election campaign meeting, which was also attended by Kohl. Workers refused to work overtime. Two political parties, the SPD and FDP, were planning moves in the Bundestag. Späth promised he would write letters to the two major shareholders in ABB, Peter Wallenberg in Sweden and Stephan Schmidheiny in Switzerland. Finally, on March 22 a three-hour meeting took place involving Späth, the Betriebsrat, and the BBC Vorstand. On the heels of this meeting came the von Koerber interview which led to the "Koerber heraus" demonstration. Interestingly, the title of the interview was "Construction Rather Than Destruction at BBC," and in it von Koerber promised a real 5 percent annual growth rate for BBC in the next few years resulting from its changed focus on growth segments. This was in line with a Barnevik comment to a local reporter in January in which he emphasized that the German operation of the new ABB would benefit the most from the merger in the midterm. ABB wanted to exploit the large German market more fully. However, the union leadership was clearly on a confrontation course and seemed to be unwilling to listen and compromise.

RESTRUCTURING IN POWER PLANTS

Power plants were the lions of the BBC product line. They also were one of the main battlegrounds of the Swiss–German rivalry. The worldwide recession of the early 1980s, the high real interest rates, and the debt crisis of many developing nations resulted in a severe drop in demand for power plants, creating enormous excess capacities and making export markets fiercely competitive. Not surprisingly, under these conditions, the rivalry between Switzerland and Germany became fiercer as well. At that time, the BBC head office was unable to give binding instructions to BBC Mannheim with its large block of minority shareholders. Only in 1986, after acquiring over 75 percent of the shares of its German subsidiary, did it become possible. Just before the ABB merger, BBC ended five years of unsuccessful efforts to jointly rationalize the Swiss and German power plant operations. It adopted a plan, labeled manufacturing alliance, under which Switzerland would make all the rotating pieces while Mannheim would limit itself to the stationary pieces and the final assembly. As part of the plan, one of the two Swiss factories would be closed.

The alliance itself was not subject to the German codetermination law, but its impact in terms of personnel reductions required involvement of the Betriebsrat. The purpose of the plan was not only to bring about specialization of the two hitherto full-line Swiss and German operations but also to reduce capacity in both countries. Thus, 700 out of the 4,000 workers would lose their jobs in Käfertal. One of the power plant executives commented:

> Up to now both Germany and Switzerland have been making the full product line. In the past, our large home market allowed us to subsidize our exports. But since several years now, the home market has virtually disappeared. We have been accepting export orders at prices which clearly do not cover our costs, simply to keep the factory going. But the factory still is too big even though we are fully integrated by making almost everything in house. In 1987, we incurred DM 130 million[4] in costs which we could

have avoided if our capacity had been adjusted to our production volume. Also, we are having difficulty in allocating our indirect costs to specific projects. As a result, we incurred DM 240 million in unallocated costs in 1987.

Another executive talked about the poor pricing of the export orders. He said:

> Here at BBC we are outstanding engineers but poor businessmen. We have been signing orders just to keep the factory going. For some time now I have been concerned about this policy, not only because of the red ink but also because we have been exposing ourselves to substantial technical risks in accepting highly sophisticated, hitherto unproven projects. Keep in mind that these units have to be installed in developing countries. Fine-tuning this equipment at its destination is no easy task.
>
> I have the Cannes statement on my desk, which states, "In a highly fixed-cost, mature, and highly competitive industry we often deal with crazy pricing from competition. It is then necessary to get our own managers away from routine contribution and cash-flow thinking if we ever shall reach satisfactory profitability. *All costs must be covered.* A loss order is a serious matter and can only be accepted on high management level. We need *more courage to say no* to further worsening of sales conditions or price concessions. That may mean loss of some orders, but it will raise average margin." Time will tell whether this new policy will bring about a change in our behavior. Our previous BBC management for sure was deeply concerned about keeping the factory filled.

In charge of the Mannheim power generation restructuring program was Udo Werlé, who had only recently been transferred from a smaller BBC subsidiary, where he had been engaged in an earlier restructuring effort He said:

---

[4] In the first quarter of 1988, DM 1.68 = $1.

Reducing capacity is nothing new to our power plant operation. By the late 70s the factory operated on the basis of 1.4 million manhours. This figure has already been reduced to 0.9 million manhours. However, in spite of these previous manpower reductions, we never reduced capacity enough. We had unused capacity year in, year out. This led to poor motivation of the workforce. We simply cannot continue operating this way. Unless we are competitive, particularly in terms of price, we are placing the entire Käfertal location in jeopardy. Thus, we will be taking measures on three fronts: First, McKinsey will start with us in terms of its overhead analysis. Second, we have the manufacturing alliance with Switzerland. Third, we are planning to drastically reduce capacity not just in terms of manpower but also in terms of machines and factory space. Of course, the Betriebsrat has the right of codetermination. Unfortunately, at Käfertal we do not have a Betriebsrat just for the power plant factory but one for the entire area. This makes life more difficult, particularly since we have granted too many concessions to them in the past. It is about time that they learn that the good old days of the power plant business have been gone for several years. With Germany having some of the highest wages in the world, we cannot run our factory like a country club if we are going to survive in world competition. The Betriebsrat will have to face these facts of life whether they like it or not.

RESTRUCTURING IN TRANSFORMERS

Transformers had been a perennial poor performer at BBC Mannheim. From 1981 through 1987 sales averaged DM 100 million per year, while losses stood on average at DM 20 million per year. The lowest loss year was 1984 with DM 12.5 million,

while losses peaked in 1987 at the DM 31.9 million level. The high 1987 loss was in part caused by two very large orders from abroad, accounting for 60 percent of sales, which were technically unusually demanding. These orders resulted in both penalties and expensive reworkings. To meet these demands, the Käfertal operation borrowed workers from the power plant sector as well as from BBC's Geneva transformer operation.

Transformers were a mature product subject to intensive competition from the industrial and developing world as well as from the Eastern Bloc. In this market BBC pursued a strategy of technological differentiation. However, the traditional organizational separation of R&D and manufacturing led to poor coordination among these functions. As a result, manufacturing was unable to deliver the products on time and with the promised quality and specifications.

BBC was one of five companies producing transformers in Germany. Siemens was the largest producer. BBC and Lepper, which had been acquired by Asea in 1965, were of about equal size. Two other producers were somewhat smaller, with one being controlled by Siemens and the other by a large German utility. The domestic market was small and could have been supplied entirely by one of the five producers. Thus, all producers were forced to compete in the extremely price-sensitive export markets.

Transformers were one of the two German Asea operations which, prior to the merger, overlapped with BBC's activities. During the mid-1980s, the Asea affiliate had been restructured, and, at the time of the merger, the Asea mentality was already deeply embedded in this formerly family-owned company. Thus, Lepper, which was located in Bad Honnef near Cologne, produced almost the same volume as BBC with half the people, and its production throughput times took only one-third of the time required at Käfertal. Most importantly, Lepper made a profit.

During the fall of 1987, a working team was appointed to investigate the two parallel German transformer operations and to submit recommendations. Concurrently, the BBC general manager for transformers was relieved of his job and was replaced by Horst Stange, who continued as head of the Bad Honnef operation. Karl-Heinz Barz, who had been transferred in 1986 from the standard products division as controller, was also made responsible for plant management. In early 1988, the technical and marketing directors in Käfertal also left. The responsibility for marketing was transferred to the Bad Honnef organization. Thus, the Mannheim transformer operation was virtually without a top-management team. Käfertal's three-story factory was viewed as out of date and inefficient. Thus, it came as no surprise that the study team recommended that the Käfertal facility be closed. Moreover, in the words of one of the former Asea executives,

> The situation in Käfertal was beyond belief. The technical problems were enormous, deliveries were delayed, and the factory looked like a gigantic traffic jam with stuff standing around everywhere. Also, wages were high since the work force was covered by the same agreement as the more highly skilled power plant workers. Yet, because of heavy turnover, a good part of the people were new and inexperienced.

The project team indicated that Käfertal had too high a proportion of exports. Thus, the combined capacity of Bad Honnef and Käfertal should be reduced from DM 200 million to about DM 130 million.

The alternative to the closing of Käfertal would be a split of the volume with 55 percent Bad Honnef, 45 percent Käfertal, and some product specialization, much like the power plant arrangement between Mannheim and Switzerland This approach, however, would be DM 8 million/year more costly even after reducing manpower in Käfertal by 70 percent from over 500 to about 150 people and cutting invested capital by one-half. Such drastic cuts, and forgoing loss orders, would be required for Käfertal to reach a break-even level in bad years and profitability in good ones. The project team felt that this second alternative would be difficult to achieve and strongly recommended the first alternative, namely, to close the Käfertal transformer factory and to concentrate all production at the Bad Honnef site. This recommendation, which was communicated to the Betriebsrat, resulted in the 500 wooden crosses ending up on the Vorstand table at the outset of the three-day works assembly.

BACK TO BASICS

The Cannes financial targets were translated by von Koerber into a demanding set of performance requirements for ABB's German operations. BBC Mannheim's 1987 performance was not only way below the Cannes targets but also below the current ABB averages. For example, its ROCE stood at 9.9 percent, and no real growth had occurred during the last several years. Von Koerber saw opportunities for improvements on all fronts. One major effort was to focus on asset reduction, encompassing three elements. The first element involved working capital management. Receivables by 1990 were to be reduced from 17 percent to 16 percent and inventory from 44 percent to 34 percent of sales. The second element related to a reduction in fixed assets. By reducing excess capacity, floor space could be freed and rented out or sold. The third element consisted of the sale of unneeded property. This was seen as a significant contributor, with gains helping to offset the nonrecurring expenses which the restructuring effort would entail.

A second major effort focused on costs. A hiring stop was ordered; only von Koerber's office was able to grant exemptions. Productivity improvements should be accomplished along several dimensions: reduction of personnel, of floor space, and of throughput times. More subcontracting should be pursued vigorously to replace expensive in-house manufactured parts. A particularly significant opportunity was seen in purchasing. Mannheim's annual purchases amounted to DM 2.4 billion, and it was felt that this large volume would allow it to squeeze at least DM 100 million out of suppliers. Finally, it was felt that the overhead analysis, for which McKinsey had been engaged, would yield substantial cost savings. Von Koerber felt that the added cost of the consultants would be more than offset by the speedy and earlier implementation of the many cost saving actions. He said: "There is no doubt that, in a turnaround, consultants have a very short payback period if they are able to identify quick cost reductions. Of course, this is pure cost cutting and has nothing to do with strategy."

A third major effort involved the sales front. More aggressive pricing was suggested, and loss orders became taboo. In addition, McKinsey would be engaged to help Mannheim management search for additional sales opportunities in their existing markets. Von Koerber was convinced that, given the previous lack of market and customer orientation, many such opportu-

nities existed. Thus, after several years of stagnation, Mannheim management was faced with demanding and increasing targets for both orders and sales.

DECENTRALIZING THE SALESFORCE

In February 1988, Georg Demling, a newly elected member of the Mannheim Vorstand responsible for the standard products group as well as for sales, and Josef F. Becker, head of centralized sales in Germany, had recommended to decentralize the pooled BBC sales force. At the Cannes conference a month earlier two principles had been stressed which both executives fully shared, namely, a strong customer orientation and a need to decentralize as much as possible. Traditionally, BBC's sales organization had been centralized as a single profit center consisting of 43 offices and employing 1,500 people. Each customer should have a single contact with the company, a Mr. BBC so to speak. This person would try to sell BBC's entire broad product line, allowing synergies to be reached among the different product lines.

Demling and Becker, however, felt that the advantages of a single salesperson were more than outweighed by its disadvantages. Said Demling:

> First, we had a Chinese wall between central sales and the business units. These units did not interface directly with the customer, and, as a result, their operating and strategic understanding of the market was either underdeveloped or nonexistent. Second, we had long and conflict-rich decision-making processes. Pricing for large orders and product adaptations in response to customer requests gave rise to many battles. The business units did not respect central sales as a customer. Instead they treated

us like colleagues and engaged in lengthy intramural battles. When we finally reached a consensus, it was often too late for the marketplace. Third, central sales sold a very broad range of products. Thus, the salesmen had a very broad but also only a somewhat superficial knowledge of our product offerings. Many of them simply did not have the technical competence expected by our customers. Thus, they often could not handle complex customer requests and had to ask for help from the business units.

The merger was seen as an excellent opportunity to eliminate these disadvantages. Demling stressed three advantages of decentralization: First, business units would be in closer touch, both operatively and strategically, with the market. In the past, they did not always have the right products and these problems would likely disappear. Second, integration would be easier by shortening the decision process and by eliminating the joint responsibilities, especially in terms of pricing. Third, it would be possible to specialize the sales force, which would be better for the customer. As a result of these advantages, an increase in market share was targeted. Some of the Vorstand members felt that the potential of the decentralization was exaggerated. It certainly applied to the standard products, but for the power generation and distribution segments as well as the industry segment and the transportation business area ABB would continue to have to deal at a top-management level with its few large customers, such as utilities, industrial giants, or the Bundesbahn. Thus, sales to these customers were already de facto decentralized, given the different responsibilities of the Vorstand members involved. Some Vorstand members saw the improvement opportunity primarily in pruning the large empires which several sales office heads had cre-

ated. Thus, the Vorstand had already approved an overhead reduction analysis by McKinsey in the hope that the administrative sales apparatus could be trimmed by some 25 percent.

VON KOERBER'S REMAINING DILEMMAS

In spite of being immersed in restructuring activities, von Koerber was also talking about growth opportunities in the ABB portfolio. He commented:

> Right now everybody seems to ask me about our growth strategy: Prime Minister Späth, journalists, church leaders, and employee representatives. All I can do at this point is make headlines without substance. We are at present in a battle for survival and have neither time nor the energy to develop a growth strategy. Yet, everybody wants a description of a bright future although we have no idea what the future holds. When I talk about our growth strategy, I feel as though I am dancing on a tightrope.

Von Koerber was also wondering how he could take advantage of Mannheim's unique position in the ABB group. He saw ABB Deutschland as ABB's platform in the European Community. His unit was the largest in ABB. Mannheim accounted for the bulk of ABB's sales in the EC. ABB's position in France was virtually nil given BBC's earlier withdrawal; it was modestly represented in the United Kingdom, and only in Italy, by virtue of BBC's earlier involvement, did it have a position of some significance. Germany had many advantages, such as its export financing and insurance facilities. Also, research support came from both Bonn and Brussels. Human resources for R&D were available in Germany, well trained and highly committed. Cooperative ventures with universities and other research institutes were possible. In sum, German R&D was seen as fully competitive with Japan and the United States.

Others were less sanguine. They pointed out that ABB Deutschland was a relatively small number two in its home market. German wages were among the highest in the world, and productivity improvements needed worker approval under the code-termination law. Also, wouldn't ABB's multidomestic concept with factories all over the world decrease German exports, and wouldn't increased subcontracting from low-wage countries result in further reductions in employment? What would be Mannheim's future if ABB carried through its intentions to specialize and optimize on a worldwide basis?

One of von Koerber's major headaches was his concern about management depth in Mannheim. Management development, he felt, had been ignored. How many Mannheim managers would be able to rise to the challenges resulting from ABB's international matrix? Also, he was not only fighting with the Betriebsrat but also encountering open and underground management resistance to his restructuring plans, even at the highest levels. Barnevik later commented: "The silent resistance from managers was more formidable. In fact, much of the union resistance was fed by management." On how much talent, motivation, and cooperation could von Koerber count? He said:

> Our hard-nosed confrontation strategy is subject to lots of criticism not only on the outside but also inside ABB, both in Mannheim and Zurich. Many of my colleagues from the BBC side are urging me to move more gently and slowly. Keep in mind that I am a newcomer here. How do I know what is really going on? Sometimes I feel that I am sitting on top of a huge pudding without knowing what's inside. Middle management normally resists change and rightly so because they are usually the losers, not top management or the workers. This problem is compounded by the fact that these people, given the previous Baden–Mannheim relationship, are trained to resist. Resistance in Mannheim is fine-tuned, invisible, and very well organized. As a newcomer, it is difficult for me to know where to act first.

> To bring about change, you usually rely on the young people in an organization. But there are very few of them here. Because BBC did not grow and had to cut costs, no people have been hired in recent years. I am now starting to bring in some fresh blood, but the degree and speed at which they can be digested, absorbed, and integrated by the organization is limited. Thus, in addition, I am relying on a few trustworthy colleagues and associates whom I am sure were frustrated in the past and are determined to contribute to a better future. I am using a number of task forces consisting of loyal lieutenants. Also, a dozen McKinsey people are of great help to me. To silence resistance, I am moving some people around and have made a few top-management changes. I know I need to rock the boat, but I don't want to rock it so hard that it capsizes and sinks. I have to watch the point beyond which the boat would capsize. My nightmare is that I will exceed the limit and that we will all sink together.

Marks & Spencer: Sir Richard Greenbury's Quiet Revolution

THE CHAIRMAN

In 1994, Marks & Spencer was the United Kingdom's most profitable retailer with profits of £851 million on sales of £6.5 billion. Immediately following the publication of its annual results in his third year as chairman, Sir Richard Greenbury talked about the problems he faced as he guided perhaps the world's greatest clothing and food retailer toward the challenges of the next century.

The second chairman from outside Marks & Spencer's founding families, Greenbury had joined the company from grammar school[1] as a junior management trainee in 1953. Following nine years in the stores, he joined the Baker Street head office, where he served in management and executive positions in the buying areas. He was appointed to director in 1970. In 1986, he was made chief executive officer under the then chairman, Lord Rayner, and then was appointed to chairman in April 1991.[2] The challenges he faced both at home and abroad were considerable.

> As I became chairman, this country was in the worst recession for 60 years. That was my priority. I had no illusion. The U.S. economy, on which we also depend, was also in trouble. But the United Kingdom was the worst.

Coupled with the recession was the issue of the perceived maturity of the business in the United Kingdom. Greenbury and his colleagues were convinced that the potential for continued growth in the United Kingdom was still there, but that this potential was being undervalued.

The chairman felt costs had become "too fat and comfortable" and requested a review at all levels.

[1] Until they were largely abolished in the 1970s by the Labour government, grammar schools were the higher academic grade of state secondary schools in the United Kingdom.

[2] In 1992, he was knighted in the New Years Honours list.

We had put our margins up to cover the cost of new IT systems and overheads. I wanted to see if we could bring costs down, so that we could then bring our margins down and pass the benefits on to our customers, thus generating higher sales and profits.

Following the chairman's initiatives, processes and procedures were reviewed, paperwork at all levels reduced, unnecessary tasks eliminated, and costs questioned in a more creative way than ever before. In addition, there was a complete structural review in the stores and head office which led to some reduction in numbers and resulted in "faster, more efficient communication" and people with "greater responsibility and job satisfaction throughout the business."

On the product side, more accurate buying was greatly helped by the introduction of new systems. This allowed significant savings to the end-of-season cost of reductions—a major benefit.

With the attack on costs and inefficiency under way, Greenbury focused his attention on a third priority, the issue of driving up the sales. The "high street"[3] was under attack from mass discounting, which had destroyed the price credibility of many retailers. In response, Greenbury launched an "Outstanding Value" campaign. On many key major lines, customers were offered permanent lower prices. Key to these "outstanding values" were volume deals with suppliers and the ability of the business with the reduction in its cost base to accept lower gross margins. At the same time, capital expenditure remained high, at around £300m per year, allowing for continued footage expansion with particular emphasis on the development of the new out-of-town/edge-of-town stores and the enlargement of major high street stores to provide a departmental store concept in the major regional centers.

Another approach to value was product development. Despite the fact that many markets were mature, gains were to be made from new departments and increases in market share in established ones. Home furnishings and childrenswear, both with low market share, were given new impetus. In core areas such as ladies outerwear and lingerie new techniques, innovative product development, and better values provided impetus for growth.

In the spring of 1994, it appeared that these moves had proved themselves. Sales and profit were strong in the United Kingdom and the competition weak. (See Exhibits 1 and 2.) The company seemed to have weathered recession in the United Kingdom well, and following the chairman's policies, was well placed for the future. The supply base had never been stronger or closer, and the U.K. store operation had been extended and modernized.

At home, financial services were also growing fast and the product offer expanding away from the core Chargecard business. Loans, unit trusts, and PEPs[4] were already established and the company had announced the entry into the life insurance market in 1995. The very high levels of customer trust and brand image enjoyed by Marks & Spencer provided significant opportunities for further development of financial service products.

Still another challenge inherited by Sir Richard was that Marks & Spencer's diffi-

---

[3] English for "main street."

[4] *P*ersonal *E*quity *P*lans (a tax-benefited way of buying common stock).

culties in North America had created a credibility problem affecting their thrust overseas.

> Canada had taken 30 minutes of criticism at the AGM for 20 years . . . the problem posed . . .was that they cast a cloud in shareholders' eyes on our ability to develop overseas.[5]

He was convinced that

> Internationally . . . there is a pot of gold at the end of the rainbow, but trading overseas as a retailer is not easy. Except for shops with very focused ranges, nobody that I know has cracked this internationally . . . I am wary of the situation, but I am not frightened of it. I do know that I do not believe in acquisition retailing. We will put a store down in a local market and grow from that presence organically.

In Western Europe, the business was now over £200m a year primarily in France, Spain, and also in Belgium and Holland. Profit performance was strong and the focus on considered growth in targeted countries. The chairman's view was that it would take five years to "get where we want to be in Western Europe."

The chairman also wondered how fast to grow in the Far East. The impetus for this was in the success of the Hong Kong operation with annual sales of £60m off 80,000 square feet of selling space. In addition, the franchise operation was doing very well in Southeast Asia.

> The two big plums are China and Japan. I have put two groups into place to study the question—should we, and how to go about it?

They are both timing issues. In China, how long will it be before 10 percent of the population can afford to shop at M&S? Shanghai No. 1 Department Store has three times the traffic of Marble Arch, but they are buying junk.[6] To what extent can we get good suppliers for the local market? If we move too soon, we might struggle. But the people who come in early when there are still problems are the ones who will make friends and relationships.

In Japan, the market was also large and the country moving out of recession. However, for the chairman there were two major concerns—too-high property prices and employment practices and wages out of line with poor labor productivity.

The third area of overseas business was the fast-developing franchise network, already in 22 countries throughout the world. The concept provided for a low-cost, low-risk way of entering an unknown country without direct ownership, linked in with a local partner who had good market knowledge. Franchises were seen as a beachhead into new markets, but clearly as the pace of international development grew, close consideration had to be given as to whether this was the right approach for entry into each new country. Europe, Asia, and franchises were each promising, but how to allocate resources was not obvious.

While those responsible for development pushed hard to move aggressively, the chairman was concerned to avoid major mistakes. As well, he knew adjustments would have to be made in an orga-

---

[5] The Annual General Meeting of shareholders.

[6] Marble Arch was the M&S flagship. With sales of $250 million on 150,000 square feet, it was considered one of the best stores in the world.

nization traditionally designed for the geographically compact United Kingdom in order to deal with the exploding matrix of product and country.

Finally, Sir Richard was concerned with the people of the business, especially what he believed was the excessively autocratic style of the business and the challenge of planning a line of succession.

> I followed a series of outstanding chairmen. But they were quite autocratic. If Teddy Sieff disagreed with you, he'd say, "Nonsense laddie!" This aspect of the culture had to change.
>
> Past succession issues had been clear; Israel Sieff's becoming chairman was automatic when Simon died. Teddy (Israel's brother) being chairman was automatic because Marcus (Israel's son) was too young. Then, Marcus was the clear successor and so was Derek (later the Lord Rayner, a brilliant protégé of the Sieffs). I was more or less in line because of age. Derek, Brian Howard, and Henry Lewis were all the same age, Clinton was close, and I was 10 years younger.
>
> Now, eight members of the board are of similar age—mid-50s, which is a problem. It is why we have a board that's too big. We have to have some continuity.

Keith Oates, who had joined Marks & Spencer in 1984 with a distinguished background in international business and finance, had ably complemented Silver as managing director. But developing a cadre of managers who could take over at the end of Greenbury's tenure occupied a good deal of his personal agenda.

Following three years as his deputy chairman, Clinton Silver was to retire in July 1994 after 42 years, service in the business. He had provided the chairman with enormous support and expertise in this period, with particular responsibility for all merchandise procurement.

MARKS & SPENCER ORIGINS

In 1882, Michael Marks, a Polish Jew who had escaped from the pogroms, arrived in the north of England and began "hawking" merchandise. In 1884, he met Isaac Dewhirst, a wholesaler of small goods who gave Marks a £5 credit to obtain stock, and began trading from a stall outside Leeds. Due to language difficulties, Marks sold under a small sign: "don't ask the price, it's a penny," a wonderful marketing slogan. It also meant that a wide variety of goods that could be sold for a penny had to be sourced and that he had to concentrate on volume, given the low profit margin of such goods.

In 1894, Marks formed a partnership with Thomas Spencer, a cashier at Dewhirst, and the business began to grow. In 1917 Spencer retired and a new board was formed, which included Simon Marks, Michael's son, and Israel Sieff. Their close partnership on the board was to last almost 50 years until the death of Simon in 1964, their friendship going back even further to when the two were at school in Manchester, and reinforced when they each married one another's sister.

During World War I, Chaim Weizmann had a remarkable influence on both Simon Marks and Israel Sieff as well as on the future policies of the firm. Weizmann was a great scientist and statesman—a key figure in the development of Zionism. He drew both Marks and Sieff into the movement and encouraged their commitment to the benefits and applications of technology. Weizmann also stimulated in them a sense of social responsibility so that they came to see, through their business, a means of creating a service for both the customer and their employees. These ideas were to become cornerstone tenets of the modern Marks & Spencer.

During the 1920s, after visiting America and seeing the growth of major retail chains such as Woolworth, Simon Marks returned, determined to transform the company into a national chain store group using principles learned at Sears Roebuck. This would involve control of merchandise generated by a central organization with systems that could be acutely sensitive to consumer demand, adjusting the production and flow of goods from factory to shops as required. Marks became very aware of the need for accurate, speedy sales information, and, in addition, "I learned the value of counter footage—that is, each counter foot of space had to pay my wages and rent and earn a profit."

Tied in with these concepts, Marks & Spencer also began its then-revolutionary policy of buying directly from manufacturers. Although it met with enormous resistance from wholesalers, this philosophy, new to the United Kingdom, allowed Marks & Spencer to specify its own standards of manufacture and simplify its range of products.

In 1926, Marks & Spencer became a public company, and in 1928 the St. Michael trademark was registered, Simon Marks wishing to commemorate his father's name. In 1931, when the turnover was £5.3m and profit £0.5m, a new food department was opened, selling fruit, vegetables, and canned goods. By 1960, Marks & Spencer was 100 percent St. Michael and was becoming a national institution.

As the business grew (by 1956 turnover was over £100m), the complexity and rigidity of the business became apparent as

costs rose disproportionately. This prompted Lord Marks and Sieff to institute a "simplification" program followed by a good housekeeping campaign. Its hallmark was a vast reduction in the number of administrative procedures, reporting "by exception," and "sensible approximation" for the sake of simplicity. All staff were involved in the process, and the immediate effects of the change were dramatic: a drastic cut in the volume of paper, a cut in the number of store office staff, a sharp reduction in head office costs, and a passing on of cost reductions to customers in the form of better values. But beyond cost, simplification freed managers from their desks to become more involved with the flow from supplier to customer.

During the 1970s, worried by the impact on the United Kingdom of Labour governments, the chairman, Lord Sieff,[7] began to take the company abroad. In 1972, a company was formed jointly with People's Department Stores Ltd. of Canada under the name of St. Michael's shops of Canada Ltd. In 1975, the first European store was opened in France. After Lord Rayner assumed the chairmanship in 1983, this trend toward internationalization accelerated with the purchase of Brooks Brothers, a world-famous U.S. group of high-quality mens' clothing shops, and the New Jersey–based Kings Super Market chain. Also in the 1980s, Marks & Spencer changed dramatically at home. Out-of-town/edge-of-town stores were developed. Major regional centers were expanded. Marks & Spencer moved to expand its product range, for example, the expansion of home furnishings and

---

[7] Marcus Sieff, son of Israel Sieff, succeeded his uncle J. Edward Sieff.

footwear. The Chargecard was launched in 1985 and following its success came a range of consumer financial services.

By 1994 Marks & Spencer's business overseas had grown to £940m with a profit of over £60m, up from £269m and £30m in 1990, respectively. The success of the U.K. business, coupled with methodical expansion of international operations and the shunning of acquisitions, had allowed Marks & Spencer cash reserves to balloon. Marks & Spencer required no source of capital other than their ongoing operations, and even if dividends were increased significantly, the company would still have a large positive cash flow. "What do we do," asked Robert Colvill, director of finance, "with all this money?"

THE MARKS & SPENCER TOP MANAGEMENT STRUCTURE AND RESPONSIBILITIES

Reporting to Sir Richard were two joint managing directors, Clinton Silver—deputy chairman—and Keith Oates. The remaining board was composed of thirteen executive directors with various functional responsibilities, the majority of whom had a hallmark of longevity of service in the company and senior management experience across a broad range of disciplines. (See Exhibit 3 for the board's composition and profiles of board members as of late spring 1994.) Silver called Greenbury's accession to the chairmanship in 1991 a "watershed" in the board's structure and style. Greenbury strengthened the subcommittee structure (handling issues such as capital expenditure reviews and information technology plans) and expanded the board membership as a way of developing younger executives. Another significant change was

in instituting a board style where open debate could take place. Said Greenbury:

> Board meetings now take up to four hours. There is debate—and if there is not, I force debate. Today, after a board meeting we are all with the decision. When everybody is expected to contribute and has the chance to contribute, I expect them to work to make the decision a success with every ounce of their energy.
>
> I think that this attitude is going down right through the business—a more open style. We are much better than we used to be; things are not foisted upon the staff. So through the board, I indirectly devolved a lot back to the stores, whose management is closest to the customers. I suppose it is not surprising; I spent nine years in the shops.

In addition to regular Monday morning meetings of the executive directors with their management teams and monthly meetings of the board, the board also met for a major strategic conference every two years. Extensive analysis was performed and detailed study papers were prepared by members prior to these conferences. The June 1994 conference was to focus on international issues.

The board also had a considerable committee structure. Two of the most active and visible committees were the Information Technology Review Committee (ITRC) and the Capital Expenditure Committee (CEC) (Exhibit 4 shows the membership of these committees). Both were chaired by Keith Oates. "When I became chairman, I asked whether we were getting the necessary benefits out of our huge investment in IT," said Greenbury. "I did not think that we were."

To monitor IT investment and set IT strategy, Oates had assumed leadership of the ITRC in 1987. Composed of over one-half of the executive board, it met four to five times annually. The committee's purpose was to ensure that IT investment was consistent with the company's primary business objectives, such as applying IT for even faster flow of merchandise from suppliers to the customer. Another important aim of the committee was to ensure that consistent IT systems were being implemented worldwide to ease the process of international expansion.

The profit and return on capital performance information, developed under Keith Oates, subsequently served as one of the main bases for capital allocation decisions both in the United Kingdom and overseas. The CEC was formed to analyze requests for capital and to allocate Marks & Spencer's annual £380m capital budget—all of which was funded by cash generated from ongoing operations. (Exhibit 5 shows the 1993–1994 budget.) Any individual capital project over £15m went through the CEC first before approval by the executive board. The CEC had sole decision-making authority for projects in the £4m to £15m range. Past implementation reviews of all capital projects ensured desired corporate returns were being met and modifications to policies made quickly. Group return on capital had risen consistently.

Since his arrival, Oates had instituted a dynamic revenue and capital operating plan process for the whole business, which rolled up through the divisional directors and ultimately up to the executive directors. A new management accounting system showed product profitability and return on capital by product group. Previous to this, business planning was managed through central estimates for sales and stock and production requirements without formal plans covering profit.

Under the new process, the operating plan preparation each spring resulted in a financial plan for the new financial year covering all revenue and cost areas of the business owned by each board member responsible. In the various merchandise areas, the operating plan objectives drove the buying department's plans. During the year, the plan was formally reviewed on a quarterly basis by the board and careful scrutiny made of sales or cost revisions in order to project the overall profit targets. For the financial planning staff in Baker Street, these planning cycles became an ongoing, year-round process. This attention to financial detail had proved invaluable to M&S as it progressed through the early 1990s. "We could not have managed our way through the last recession," said Oates, "without these financial control systems."

THE MARKS & SPENCER CULTURE

The heart of the United Kingdom business organization lay in its Baker Street offices with over 3,000 employees. There, the buying offices and supporting testing rooms and laboratories were located next to group managers of store operations, personnel, finance, public relations, customer services, and the executive directors and chairman. The emphasis was on efficiency and teamwork. When the researcher first studied the company in 1975, great deference was given to senior management. In 1994, it was clear that while the respect and politeness remained, junior managers spoke far more confidently of their own initiatives and views.

Outsiders were impressed with the effectiveness of communication at Marks & Spencer. Both formal and informal communication was aimed at ensuring a wide understanding of current issues. Standard practice, when one wanted a word, was to knock on an office door, enter, politely interrupt for a conversation unless clearly inappropriate, and leave.

Informal practices were complemented by a series of cascading meetings every Monday. The board met at 10:30 AM after the executive directors had had time to meet with their people so that they were prepared to present their issues and debate others. The executive directors then contributed to the preparation of a minute sent out by Wednesday of that week to all managers in head office and stores.

In turn, the management from Baker Street was very regularly in the stores, "probing" to see what was working and where the sales/flow of goods had changed so that correction was needed. Many directors and executives were again in the stores on Saturday, shopping for their own needs and to see what was going on for themselves.

The mood of Marks & Spencer was "restless dissatisfaction." Executives were constantly pushing to see if they could find a way to improve the goods through better quality, value, and service.

Marks & Spencer management were also very concerned to protect the company's public image. They knew that the British public believed in the high standards that Marks & Spencer brought into their approach to customers, staff, product quality, and safety. To maintain that reputation, Marks & Spencer management was obsessive about response to customers' comments, about staff needs, and about hygiene and reliability. In a typical instance, the researcher's interview with a director of technology was interrupted by a subordinate who wanted a review of a briefing paper he had prepared for the press and BBC concerning sandwich hygiene. Newspapers had reported high bacteria count in the sandwiches sold by "retailers," and noted Marks & Spencer's impeccable quality only by leaving it out of the story. Called for comment by the media, these managers saw an opportunity to stress again to the public the quality of their products and the seriousness in which quality standards were upheld.

PERSONNEL AND WELFARE

To work at Marks & Spencer was to work for Europe's most admired company.[8] For university graduates, an entry-level position at Marks & Spencer represented the quintessential "good" job. Long before governments or companies focused on welfare, the firm had a tradition of dedication by and to its workforce. In 1994, Marks & Spencer still had some of the best benefits of any company in the United Kingdom, and their attention to the welfare of their employees had not waned. Marks & Spencer human relations policies had, however, been modernized.

In response to his concern with inefficiency caused by excess numbers and bureaucracy that had been allowed to creep in, Greenbury delayered and then led a downsizing. Staff levels at Baker Street had been reduced from over 4,000 in 1986 to about 3,100 by 1994. "The structure was shaped like a diamond," said Greenbury, "big in the middle." Across the entire corporation, there had been staff reductions as well. It was a

---

[8] In June 1994, the *Financial Times* reported that M&S had been awarded this distinction by 697 peer companies. Though not always first in Europe, M&S was a regular leader in their poll.

difficult time for the organization, which Marks & Spencer management buffered as well as they could through a generous redundancy package and an active placement program. In fact, the 300 compulsory redundancies in head office and 300 in stores were followed by 350 volunteers, highlighting the package's attractiveness.

There had been changes in the stores as well. According to Clara Freeman, the divisional director of personnel:

> This is not necessarily a job for life. But there is a security level—a social contract with our staff to be fair—that still exists. It used to be that the personnel manager protected the staff from the realities of life; now the whole management team is required to manage properly the human resources of the store.

The classic early progression was to spend three to eight years "in the shops," after which time the high performers were pulled out into the buying departments—often in the merchandising function. Freeman explained:

> We encourage the building of a career profile. One of our goals, as we move through the 1990s, is to have staff at every level with a broader range of skills to provide us with more flexibility. We have fewer people now, so they have to be more flexible. The result is less emphasis on straight-line career development.

THE PRODUCT RANGE

Marks & Spencer's retail product range consisted of two broad categories: food (representing 40 percent of the total group turnover) and general merchandise, the latter including womenswear, menswear, childrenswear, toiletries and cosmetics, and home furnishings. There was also a growing line of financial service products. Compared to traditional department stores, the Marks & Spencer range was narrow and deep and focused 100 percent on the single brand, St. Michael.

Clothing In 1994, Marks & Spencer was a clothing powerhouse with an 18 percent share of the United Kingdom market. On any given day, one out of every three British women was wearing Marks & Spencer undergarments; one in every 10 pairs of ladies' shoes was bought from Marks & Spencer. Women's outerwear and lingerie were the largest areas of the general merchandise business. Market share was massive in a number of core areas, up to 40 percent in bras and underwear and in the high teens in many fashion departments. Menswear was also a major product area. The company enjoyed 35 percent of the men's underwear and 20 percent of the U.K. men's suit markets.

Although having smaller market share, childrenswear and home furnishings were viewed as growth areas with a focus on providing for the family. Following a policy of creating destination shops in major sites, the home furnishings range had expanded to the extent that a special catalogue and the United Kingdom's first national computerized wedding list service were introduced.

Food Marks & Spencer staff liked to say that they "sell food that eats well —Rolls Royce food at Ford prices." The company had differentiated itself from its large supermarket competitors in the United Kingdom. Marks & Spencer did not aim to be a one-stop commoditybased shop such as Tesco and Sainsbury, with up to 18,000 lines on display, covering a mass of brands. Rather Marks & Spencer had created a niche market driven by high quality, chilled specialty, and convenience items. The key to this was a focus on food freshness, flavor, quality, innovation, and direct involvement with the suppliers, particularly in the sourcing of raw materials. With only 2,500 items in the range, all own-brand, 800 were changed annually, highlighting the emphasis on newness and innovation. In 1979, they had started a now extensive range of "ready-prepared" recipe dishes—fresh foods (as opposed to frozen), ready for the oven or dinner table. Examples included Indian specialties such as tandoori chicken and tikka marsala, Chinese crispy duck, Italian fine pasta meals, and other delicately prepared fish and meat dishes. In 1980, they introduced high-quality prepared sandwiches, which in 1994 represented as much as 6 percent of the total food business in some stores. In general, convenience was often the key to the success of the product, whether it was for a special occasion or family eating.

BUYING

The focal point for the procurement of both foods and general merchandise was the Baker Street buying team, whose departmental heads were typically located three organizational levels from the executive board (shown in Exhibit 6). The traditional category of "buyer" did not exist in Marks & Spencer—rather the function was split between the role of the merchandiser and that of the selector. Because Marks & Spencer developed its St. Michael brand ranges, the product development role of the selector was a key. The logistical and financial role was covered by the merchandiser. The third role of technologist was responsible for setting the product specification with the suppliers and the development of new raw materials and manufacturing methods.

By removing layers of supervisory managers, Greenbury placed greater responsibility on the buying teams. Teamwork across the three disciplines was essential to a successful end result.

Merchandiser Merchandisers had day-to-day financial planning and operational responsibilities for the buying departments. This included management of the selling price structure, margin, and costs of reduction. Also involved were the management of their supply base, planning production and commitment, and negotiating cost prices. On the selling side, they managed store stocks, the catalogue, and the communication of layout and display priorities. The buying departments had worldwide responsibility for Marks & Spencer including all emerging international businesses.

The increasingly sophisticated use of information technology to track demand at the store level had improved the buying tools available to the merchandiser and enhanced the roles of managing the supplier base and merchandise distribution. In spite of these new tools providing immediate and accurate information, visiting stores and suppliers to see for oneself what was happening was still an essential part of the job. The "why" could only be answered in this way.

Selector With the guidance of the merchandiser, the selector's key responsibility was product development and the creation of each season's range. Selectors were responsible for the "look" of the product itself, including the monitoring of fashion trends, in conjunction with the design department that pursued a common group policy.

Technology Marks & Spencer was unique among retailers in their emphasis on the importance of technical personnel in direct liaison with their suppliers, including their procurement of raw materials and audit of supplier systems and quality. In their work they tracked the leading edge of textile and agribusiness technology around the world. Many commercial breakthroughs had come from technical developments either originated by or exploited by Marks & Spencer technologists. The researchers were intrigued by one instance where fabric-printing technology had been adapted to buttering bread for sandwiches.

Design   The general merchandise buying departments were also supported by a 30-member specialized central design staff. This group of design experts researched and forecast major fashion trends and, most importantly, developed Marks & Spencer's biannual overall design directions and themes that ensured a consistency of look across all departments in line for the season one year ahead. By melding an understanding of the design forecasts with an extensive internal database that revealed patterns in how customers' tastes evolved, the buying department developed a range that they believed was abreast of fashion.

Based on its fashion forecasts, Marks & Spencer made substantial commitments to its suppliers. However, departments were constantly looking at ways of increasing flexibility for certain buying decisions until the season had begun. In some areas, by making the garment "in the griege," using IT to track color preferences, and dyeing made-up garments during the selling season, Marks & Spencer could customize the flow of high-volume manufacturing to the subtle shifts in consumer taste.

Relationship with the Supplier Base

Marks & Spencer saw its future growth linked with the need for a dynamic dedicated core group of United Kingdom–

based suppliers, whose size allowed them to invest in people and machinery as required. To this end, it had actively encouraged the move toward supplier consolidation. As shown in the table, concentration was considerable.

SHARE OF MARKS & SPENCER BUSINESS BY GENERAL MERCHANDISE SUPPLIERS

	1990	1992	1993
Top 5	38%	43%	45%
Top 20	73%	80%	80%

In total, 260 suppliers served the general merchandise departments and 400–450 the food group. This supplier network was in many ways an extension of Marks & Spencer's own buying department organization—so much so that many senior people in the supply base were ex–Marks & Spencer employees and functions and responsibilities between the organizations were closely linked. Suppliers were required to have their own product test laboratories, but these had to be accredited and were periodically audited for that purpose in order to maintain consistent standards.

This close relationship was also reflected in supplier organizational structures that paralleled the Marks & Spencer buying department structure. Relationships with large suppliers spanned every level of the two organizations' structures. Executive board members of Marks & Spencer and its large suppliers met in regularly scheduled joint strategy meetings, where close personal relationships formed and coordination issues were discussed candidly. In addition, suppliers were required to have a dedicated team to interact with individual Marks & Spencer buying departments. Colin Dyer, director of Mark & Spencer operations for Courtaulds Textiles—a £870m firm—explained:

Along with our own fabric suppliers and the Marks & Spencer buying departments, we move in like a vortex on product solutions. It is like a spiderweb of communication between their merchandisers and selectors and our designers and sales staff. Their technologists work closely with our factory production staff, designers, and material suppliers.

We cannot do without them, but they cannot replace us quickly either. Other new suppliers cannot bring the Marks & Spencer culture on board rapidly enough to survive the first few crises. Our relationship is one of trust. It is robust. There are important nods and winks between us. It takes three-quarters of an hour for a message to move through the Marks & Spencer hierarchy, and because of our connections at every level of the organization, we hear the exact same information in an hour and a half.

The electronic integration of Marks & Spencer and its suppliers was increasing. Two-way electronic equipment had been developed to allow, for example, intercommunication of stock availability. On-screen interactive computer-aided design links were being "trialed," which would allow for both faster new product development and existing designs to be changed—thereby allowing the buying team to respond even more rapidly to demand shifts during the selling seasons.

Marks & Spencer typically retained six weeks of stock in their distribution system and stores. The suppliers financed the balance of finished stock, which was kept strictly under control. In addition, of enormous benefit was the fact that suppliers were paid within 21 days of receipt of goods.

Overall, doing business as a Marks & Spencer supplier was demanding. Nonetheless, becoming part of the Marks & Spencer supplier base was viewed as a prize to be treasured. Smaller, innovative firms were constantly approaching Marks & Spencer with their products, hoping that they could grow their companies through the giant retailer. Executives from large, established suppliers, such as Coats Viyella, admitted that "we jealously guard our relationship with Marks & Spencer." Through targeted acquisitions and conscious internal expansion, Courtaulds Textiles had increased its business with Marks & Spencer to over 40 percent of its total revenue. Working closely with Marks & Spencer allowed the manufacturer to focus on production issues while reducing longer-term uncertainty surrounding end-consumer demand.

Marks & Spencer, in turn, viewed their supplier arrangements as long-term partnerships. The merchandiser in charge of boyswear explained Marks & Spencer's commitment to suppliers this way:

> When we start a relationship with a supplier, we do it one way—we will share the rewards and mistakes with them. But we do not start something without the intention that it will be there in 100 years. To start a new supplier relationship requires a disproportionate amount of time and patience. As hard as it is to increase the supply base, it is harder still to decrease it. It is a major decision to drop a supplier.

In 1994, 80 percent of M&S supplies were sourced in the United Kingdom.

Merchandise Flow

Sir Richard Greenbury noted that:

> In the 1950s and 1960s, we were a production-led business, where the product was pushed and manufacturing was king. In the 1970s and early 1980s it was a product business, where the retailer was the king. In the 1980s, it became a pull business that was customer led. Now we always say, "Buy what we sell, not sell

what we buy," because, as we move through the 1990s, the customer is no longer king—the customer is the dictator.

The company's merchandise flow, allocation, and distribution operated increasingly as a pure customer-pull system. Sales assistants used small handheld terminals to check on the availability of stock allocated to them in a central warehouse facility. Allocation of product was done under the guidance of the merchandiser. However, so important was it to Marks & Spencer to fulfill the customers' needs that a computer-based customer ordering system was being implemented in the stores where, if the customer could not find the product, size, or color that he or she wanted, it could be ordered directly from the store and subsequently transferred from anywhere else in Marks & Spencer's U.K. merchandise stock system, often within 24 hours.

The company was beginning to roll out a more advanced pull-oriented stock replenishment system based on real-time bar code data generated from the till. The sales assistants could augment the automatic reorder amounts on their handheld terminals in anticipation of certain events, sales conditions, and holidays.

Inventory had decreased in recent years from 8–10 weeks down to 6–6.5 weeks in general merchandise. Approximately half the stock was in the stores, while the other half was in the regional warehouses. Faster flow had improved space efficiency in the stores and the warehouses. "We have moved from the concept of warehouses to hold stock," related the Marks & Spencer executive for buying group systems, "to a concept of warehouses to manage stock throughput efficiently." The redundant stockroom space available in many stores was a vital benefit to the

business. Particularly in city centers, where many stores were landlocked, it allowed for the release of space much needed for further development.

STORE OPERATIONS

The tradition at the old Marks & Spencer had been to have a dual authority structure in the stores, consisting of the store manager, who was primarily responsible for sales, and the staff manager who was responsible for the welfare of the staff. The store manager's primary role had been to focus on achieving maximum sales and ensuring his customers received the highest level of service. He affected his stock where he could but had no knowledge of the cost base of the store.

By the 1980s, it became apparent that many costs, such as personnel expenses and theft and loss, could be best controlled at the store level. The first step in this direction had been a cultural and structural change in the management of each store, initiated in the mid-1980s by the previous chairman, Lord Rayner. Store management structure was changed to provide a commercial manager, personnel manager, and financial manager, who worked as a team reporting to the store manager. Store managers were given much more financial information regarding the profitability of their unit. While stores had no control over buying margins and still operated within well-laid-down central guidelines, for Marks & Spencer, this was significant.

Soon after, store management received profit data, and a decision was made by the executive board to reorganize and delayer the 280 U.K. stores. In addition, the principle of store regionalization was introduced to raise the standards of smaller units by putting them under the management of major store teams. For example, in Oxford, the store manager not only supervised the commercial manager, the personnel manager, and the financial manager in that recently expanded 75,000-square-foot facility, but was also responsible for a smaller 30,000-square-foot operation 30 miles away in Banbury. Many jobs were made bigger and more interesting, e.g., a young woman, formerly financial manager from the Oxford facility, was promoted to unit manager in the Banbury store. With the substantial reduction in management overhead, a number of small unprofitable units returned to profitability. In the process, total store management personnel were cut from 1,960 in 1990 to 1,510 in 1994.

Where regionalization helped to improve the store performance within given regions, the institution of "best achiever" store rankings helped to diffuse operating excellence across stores and regions. The annual rankings provided a ready operating benchmark for similar stores (by geography and size) in such categories as staff costs as a percentage of revenue, theft and loss, food waste as a percentage of food sales, returns to warehouse, till throughput, and overall profitability. Although not directly tied to store manager compensation, receiving "best achiever" status was high praise within Marks & Spencer. (Exhibit 7 provides for a sample Marks & Spencer "best achiever" report sent to store managers.)

Many of the best achiever stores also operated as idea generators and new product or process innovation test beds. For example, the edge-of-town Camberley store was often visited by buying department personnel and suppliers alike to get direct customer feedback via the floor supervisors and sales assistants. Innovative product displays were often devel-

oped there. Schemes to increase till throughput and productivity were initiated by the Camberley till operators themselves, perfected, and rolled out to other Marks & Spencer stores across the United Kingdom.[9] They provided the basis for eliminating a layer of supervisors.

ESTATES AND STORE DEVELOPMENT

During the previous decade, Marks & Spencer had followed a three-pronged strategy for store development that Greenbury sought to consolidate. (See Exhibit 8 for store numbers and footage.) In 23 major regional locations, M&S sought to create superstores that had the square footage and the full M&S range of goods so as to define the Marks & Spencer image. In addition, the flagship Marble Arch store was expanded to 150,000 square feet and refurbished.

As their competition moved away from the city center, Marks & Spencer continued to develop with new high street locations. Roger Aldridge, the director of estates and store development, stated, "We have to treat the town center as our mall." Many local Marks & Spencer store managers were active in their high street communities to develop easier store access, pedestrian walkways, and outdoor security systems, working with both city officials and other local businesses.

The other major change was the development of 16 large out-of-town/edge-of-town stores, the majority of which were approximately 70,000 square feet. These highly profitable stores were the largest growth area of the business with 12 per-

---

[9] The fact that Camberley was close to the chairman's weekend home undoubtedly influenced its role as a laboratory in the Marks & Spencer system.

cent of the footage. They appealed to the carborn shopper, in particular the family. Their catchment area was far greater than with high street stores.

Marks & Spencer's intention was to continue to focus investment on their network of complementary regional center and out-of-town stores, which now accounted for 60 percent of total sales. Below this level of store operated a further 200 stores in high street locations of varying size. Their offer varied from a good range of clothing and food for the family down to focused food-only locations.

FINANCIAL SERVICES

Up until 1985, all transactions in the stores were either through cash or check. No financial service products existed.

By 1994, financial activities were generating a profit of £41.7m. The Marks & Spencer cardholder base comprised 2.7m accounts and 3.5m cardholders, accounting for 20 percent of retail sales in the United Kingdom. (See Exhibit 9 for the growth of financial services.) However, the company still retained the policy of not accepting outside credit cards.

The introduction of the Chargecard in 1985 was Marks & Spencer's entry into financial services. It was viewed as being strongly anchored to their core retail business. As Robert Colvill, the finance director, related, "We realized the future was going to be transaction-related. There will be ongoing innovation at the till; we will not be able to avoid it."

By employing their own Chargecard instead of accepting bank credit cards, they were able to avoid the major cards' 2–4 percent transaction charges. Moreover, the controller of the card service owned Marks & Spencer customer purchase behavior data. Keith Oates, the managing director responsible, said:

If you accept other cards, then they have the data and you do not. Part of the reason that we introduced the card is that we realized we needed the customer database. Our marketing programs can be more focused with this data. It is used for store building and development plans. The data can be used to market other financial services products.

After the Chargecard was up and running, it allowed Marks & Spencer to consider other financial products, such as personal loans, PEPs (Personal Equity Plans), and Unit Trusts. Entry into life insurance was planned in 1995. (The cartoon captures some of the public reaction to Marks & Spencer's diversification.)

The concept underlying the expansion in the financial services product offer was to provide a product coupled with reliable service, just as with any other product sold in the stores. It was thought that success would be helped by the company's strong brand and reputation for product quality and value. But this also implied a responsibility by the company. Explained Colvill:

It is not so much the Marks & Spencer label as it is the Marks & Spencer culture. The public trusts Marks & Spencer people and co-owns the culture. They believe that we are straight and fair dealers. They know that they only have to raise a point with us and we will address it. We wanted to carry this relationship into financial services.

In fact, soon after the introduction of the Chargecard, Marks & Spencer moved quickly to integrate backward, replacing their chosen "supplier," a bank retained to run the operation, due to perceived customer service quality problems. The aim was to protect the Marks & Spencer name. Similarly, Marks & Spencer consciously chose not to enter the home mortgage market, although it would be

Source: *The Guardian*, February 2, 1994.

"a natural" for them. "It is not in the Marks & Spencer culture to repossess a house," said Oates. "There is a good possibility that we would damage our reputation."

As the financial services product line was expanded, the strategy of MSFS was to extend the virtuous circle to this new area. So as Colvill related:

> We have two things going for us: the Marks & Spencer name and our deliberately low-cost base. We will move into products where we can compete in a

low-cost way—in volume—and that will also strengthen the Marks & Spencer brand.

THE CHALLENGE OF INTERNATIONAL OPERATIONS AND EXPANSION

Greenbury's goal was for Marks & Spencer's international operation to grow "organically."

> We are a mature business in the United Kingdom and a great business, but we have to be able to operate across a range of countries. No business will fire on all cylinders at all times. We have dominant shares in the United Kingdom, so we have to grow abroad. But we also had a credibility problem among financial experts with our performance in Canada and our perceived mistake in paying too much for Brooks and Kings.

The importance placed on the development of the overseas base by the chairman was highlighted by the board restructure in April 1994, which made a director responsible for each of the major trading blocks—Europe, North America and Asia. (Exhibit 10 provides a geographic breakdown of sales, and Exhibit 3 shows board responsibilities before April 1994's changes.)

Europe Despite the impact of slower growth during the European recession, Europe's profit performance remained comparable with the United Kingdom. Since the first store opened in Paris in 1975, a further 23 stores had been developed with a total of 680,000 square feet—14 in France, three in Belgium, four in Spain, and two in Holland.

Within these chosen countries, a policy was being pursued of developing clusters of stores in key major city centers for maximum impact and benefits of econo-

mies of scale. Already three cities, Paris, Madrid, and Barcelona, had been selected and European managers parleyed for rapid expansion, perhaps by acquisition.

Although local European managers were pushing to expand faster, Greenbury expounded the conservative growth policy:

> We intend to grow the chain of continental stores in prime locations as quickly as sites become available at the right price. I know that I can double or treble that business. So the current £250 million can get to £750 million. The problem is that if I press them to expand, then we will make mistakes. We need to be patient. My guess is that it will take us five years to get to where we want to be in Western Europe.

Expansion was favored in Europe because of its proximity to the United Kingdom and the greater consistency with the United Kingdom in seasonality and dressing styles. However, Marks & Spencer learned that while store catalogues could be set centrally to reflect the core purchases, even Europe required adjustment for profile, fit, size, and climate. (See Exhibit 12.) The challenge for the buying departments was to recognize the national differences as well as the similarities.

With the scale of growth in Europe making it an ever more important proportion of the business, improvements were made to the efficiency of the flow and handling of goods, and the ITRC decided to standardize and enhance the flow of information.

Far East Whereas Marks & Spencer had a chosen strategy for European expansion, managers were less certain how to approach the large Asian market. Marks & Spencer management was buoyed by Hong Kong's "enormous success," even though most of the merchandise was sourced from the United Kingdom and then airfreighted. Greenbury was emphatic that

> Before I retire, we shall have to decide how we will deal with the opportunities posed by China and Japan. They are the two great areas of growth in the next decade. So the critical decision facing us is how far and how fast we will expand in the Far East.

In 1994, Marks & Spencer was concentrating on building a suitable distribution infrastructure to supply merchandise accurately, timely, and cost-effectively. A growing supply base in Asia could make products locally, thus avoiding all the logistical issues of freighting from Europe, while making use of abundant high-quality local fabrics (already sourced by Marks & Spencer's manufacturers) and avoiding tariffs on imported goods.

The development of this business was providing key lessons in operating in that part of the world. The product profile had identified the need to provide appropriately sized merchandise for the Asian population. One of the earlier successes was the development of the Asian fit bra. Since the climate was hot all year round, light-weight fabrics were particularly needed.

By virtue of being in Hong Kong, Marks & Spencer was going to be in China. Both the China and Japan markets were being reviewed by study teams that were to look at the issues of entry timing and potential partners. The early opinion of Marks & Spencer management was that China and Japan were contrasting situations. For China, the issue was the development of the national infrastructure to support a major retailer and the current restrictions on imports through tariffs. For Japan, the issue was whether that £8b clothing market was too mature—whether Marks & Spencer was too late. Here, as well as in Europe, Marks & Spencer was determined to move carefully. Explained Greenbury, "I do not want people to say that China and Japan were for me what Canada was for Marcus. I do not want that."

North America When Greenbury took over, he saw it as a priority to resolve the situation in Canada once and for all. A major review of the Canadian business was undertaken, and as a result a large segment was sold off and the remainder downsized in order to relate to the retail and economic situation in Canada. Two small businesses remained; in total Canada had been reduced in size from a turnover of over £200m in 1990 to only £83m in 1994. Profitability had also been reestablished to a break-even level.

Greenbury regarded Brooks Brothers as "a good business," although he was concerned that the general perception in the financial community was that Marks & Spencer had overpaid to acquire the company. In 1994, following several years of work involving senior U.K. management relocated to the United States, the business was showing its third year of increasing sales and profits.

Greenbury also believed that Kings Super Markets was making "good progress." Its product range was being revamped to include much more fresh food than its local "commodity-based" competition. Compared to other U.S. retail operations of its type and size, it was highly profitable. Limited expansion was planned into adjacent counties to broaden its customer base.

Franchising Management in Baker Street viewed franchising as a low-capital beachhead into new national markets. Growth was strong and profitable. Inherent in franchising was the recruitment of and contracting with a local partner, often a necessity to navigate successfully through the specific regulations and customs in a new country. These arrangements were made purposely flexible to allow the company to assume control of the franchise if that became desirable. By 1994, franchise operations existed in 22 countries—a total of 76 shops. (Exhibit 11 shows stores and performance.)

Franchise operation management in Baker Street believed that the group had the potential to achieve retail sales approaching £400m and profits of over £30m by growing their existing accounts. In addition, they were studying expansion into Italy and also beginning to consider broadening their focus beyond Western Europe and Asia to Central and Eastern Europe and India. As Nigel Colne, executive director responsible for international franchising, said, "Our pace of expansion is driven by three factors—Marks & Spencer human resources, the choice of the right country and partner, and effective supply chain systems."

Managers in the franchise group believed that the typical Marks & Spencer attention to detail in managing their supplier partnerships was being extended into developing franchise partnerships as well. One called the choice of partner "absolutely critical." The group had an "R&D" function which assessed and prioritized new market opportunities and carried out the search and final selection of a local partner. The process from research to final partner selection took a year.

Many of the franchise group's development programs concentrated on involving their chosen partners in Marks & Spencer's operations. They were invited to Baker Street twice a year. In addition, the group called upon store managers and assistant managers to carry out one- to two-year attachments based in franchise accounts around the world. This was part of the high level of attention that was paid to ensure that franchise operations were consistent with Marks & Spencer's image. By 1994, there were five such attachments, and a proposal sought three more. Staffing, theft and loss, and other Marks & Spencer cost control practices were the areas where these Marks & Spencer people "on the ground" were intended to show their worth.

As Marks & Spencer grew internationally, staff rotation through international assignments became an important management development device, not only in franchise arrangements, but also in the company's directly owned operations. Clara Freeman commented on the challenge in exporting the Marks & Spencer way of doing business through the international attachments:

> We really have not dealt fully with the issue yet. I would say that we are a bit schizophrenic about it. We still manage Europe—at the top anyway—as an extension of the United Kingdom with expatriates. We have not melded the local management with the expatriates as well as we would have liked. We have wanted to export the way we do things. So we deal with this through trials. Some international managers will do 6 to 18 months in some of our larger U.K. stores. We are trying to get a more even exchange both ways. The deputy manager in our Manchester store is a Frenchman on attachment. He will manage the new rue de Rivoli store in Paris.

At its soul, Marks & Spencer had a strong predisposition to "buy British." With 80 percent of all goods made in the United Kingdom, a majority of their internationally sold product was sourced from the United Kingdom. However, Marks & Spencer suppliers such as Courtaulds Textiles and Coats Viyella had moved, on a selective basis, some production abroad. This trend afforded Marks & Spencer the opportunity to extend their existing supplier relationship to promising international markets more easily in locales such as the Far East and India. In food, local sourcing was necessary, and Marks & Spencer management believed that developing new food supplier relationships in Europe and Hong Kong was presenting a constraint on the growth of the food business abroad. Most food products still came out of the United Kingdom to supply Europe.

Because of the inherently decentralized nature of international operations, some Baker Street managers were concerned that the international operations were beginning to "reinvent the wheel." In a related area, although they had worldwide product responsibility nominally, the buying groups were just beginning to view their responsibilities as being global. Greenbury was concerned about this tension:

With international markets, you have conflict at the U.K. buying level. The buying departments have purchase responsibility—credit for the right decisions and kicks for the bad one. Hong Kong, though, has its own operating plan, but they do not have authority over buying. They have an attitude: "I am not going to be asking this guy in Baker Street what I want." The guy in Baker Street, however, is going to be judged against the U.K. operating plan alone. Right now, I try to appeal to their sense of being a single business—Marks & Spencer—but it is a problem.

The top management of M&S together with its nonexecutive directors was taking two days in July after the AGM for a retreat to discuss the many questions raised by success and expansion. Several managers wondered aloud what readers of this case would suggest that they do.

EXHIBIT 1
GROUP SUMMARY FINANCIAL INFORMATION—FIVE YEARS, 1990–1994
(FISCAL YEAR ENDING MARCH 31) (£ millions)

	1994	1993	1992	1991	1990
Income statement					
Sales					
General	3,785.7	3,432.7	3,371.6	3,376.0	3,221.5
Food	2,632.7	2,408.2	2,357.7	2,307.3	3,306.0
Financial activities	122.8	109.9	98.2	91.5	80.6
Total	6,541.2	5,950.8	5,827.5	5,774.8	5,608.1
Sales:					
U.K. and Ireland	5,601.7	5,115.0	5,014.7	5,037.7	4,884.8
Continental Europe	243.3	235.6	195.0	149.9	121.1
Rest of world	609.0	526.9	555.1	528.2	458.4
Export	87.2	73.3	62.7	59.0	49.3
Total	6,541.2	5,950.8	5,827.5	5,774.8	5,608.1
Operating profit:					
U.K. and Ireland	809.9	683.9	640.1	606.2	605.1
Other	63.5	56.0	39.1	32.0	30.0
Total	873.4	739.9	679.2	638.2	635.1
Net profit (before dividends)	578.2	495.5	368.0	397.3	389.0
Dividends	255.5	223.6	195.5	182.0	172.5
Balance sheet					
Fixed assets	3,110.9	2,928.6	2,781.4	2,612.6	2,468.5
Current assets					
Cash and securities	814.7	688.0	538.3	321.8	294.7
Inventory	354.6	344.2	338.3	351.1	374.3
Receivables	884.4	729.5	648.2	617.7	537.6
Current liabilities	1,181.0	1,230.7	1,168.8	896.7	925.0
Net current assets	872.7	531.0	356.0	393.9	281.6
Long-term debt	640.2	492.1	477.3	568.7	569.5
Shareholders' equity	3,343.4	2,966.9	2,660.1	2,437.8	2,180.6

Source: Marks & Spencer annual reports.

EXHIBIT 2
PERFORMANCE VS. PRIMARY U.K. COMPETITION (£ millions)

	1993	1992	1991	1990	1989
Marks & Spencer:					
Turnover	5,950.8	5,827.5	5,774.8	5,608.1	5,121.5
Operating profit	739.9	679.2	638.2	635.1	658.3
Turnover growth	2.1%	0.9%	3.0 %	9.5%	
% Operating profit	12.4	11.7	11.1	11.3	11.1
Burton (general merchandise competitor)					
Turnover	1,893.1	1,764.6	1,661.1	1,788.7	1,808.0
Operating profit	60.9	35.3	46.2	194.8	255.3
Turnover growth	7.3%	6.2%	−7.1 %	−1.1%	−
% Operating profit	3.2	2.0	2.8	10.9	14.5
Sainsbury (food competitor):					
Turnover	10,269.7	9,202.3	8,200.5	7,257.0	5,915.1
Operating profit	785.0	666.0	585.0	470.7	372.9
Turnover growth	11.6%	12.2%	13.0 %	22.7%	−
% Operating profit	7.6	7.2	7.1	6.5	6.3
Tesco (food competitor):					
Turnover	7,582.0	7,097.0	6,346.0	5,402.0	4,718.0
Operating profit	583.0	545.0	417.0	327.0	265.0
Turnover growth	6.8%	11.8%	1.75%	14.5%	−
% Operating profit	7.7	7.7	6.6	6.0	5.6

EXHIBIT 3
EXECUTIVE BOARD PROFILE—MARCH 1994

Name	Age	Joined M&S	Buying	Service
Sir Richard Greenbury Chairman	57	1953 (Stores nine years)	Merchandising various clothing groups Management to Joint M.D. all clothing Joint M.D. Foods & Homeware	All U.K. departments as Joint M.D.
Clinton Silver C.B.E Deputy Chairperson Joint M.D.	64	1952 (Stores three years)	Merchandising and management in various clothing groups Director of Foods Director of Clothing	
Keith Oates Joint M.D.	51	1984	(Finance with IBM, Black & Decker Brussels, Thyssen-Bornemisza N.V., Monaco)	Director of finance and financial activities. Added all overseas operations as Joint M.D.
Roger Aldrige Director Estates & Store Development	47	1973	(Estates with J. Hepworth)	Company estates manager then divisional director including International. Added Store Development as director.
Jim Benfield Director of Childrenswear and Home Furnishings	44	1970 (Stores three years)	Merchandising various food groups Divisional director Ladieswear then Foods	Divisional director Store Development Construction and H.O. Premises
Nigel Colne C.B.E. Director of International Franchise Group	54	1960 (Stores six years)	Merchandising and management in various clothing groups Senior executive Ladieswear	Director Store Operations, Estates; I.T. and Physical Distribution; North America, Far East, and Europe PA to Michael Sieff
Robert Colvill Director M&S FS	53	1985	(Morgan Grenfell, Samuel Montague, Chemical Bank)	Managing director of Marks & Spencer Financial Services, Treasury
Chris Littmoden Director Financial Control and Management Accounting	50	1974 (British Oxygen)	Executive, Foods	Financial Control; various buying groups P.A. to Lord Sieff Divisional director Group Financial Control and Management Accounting

EXHIBIT 3 (continued)

Name	Age	Joined M&S	Buying	Service
Guy McCracken Director Food	45	1975 (3 years in Food Processing)	Technologist and management in various food groups Divisional Director Clothing and Homeware Technology Merchandise director in Clothing, Home Furnishings, and Direct Selling	P.A. to Lord Rayner
Joe Rowe Director Food	46	1968	Merchandising in Foods, management in Foods and Clothing Divisional director Ladieswear	P.A. to Lord Sieff
John Sacher C.B.E. Director I.T., Physical Distribution and Retail Systems	53	1968 (Great-grandson of Michael Marks) (three years in Merchant Banking)	Management and director in Clothing and Homeware	Director Europe Personnel Europe
Peter Salsbury Director Personnel and Store Operations	44	1970 (Stores three years)	Merchandising and management in various clothing and homeware groups Divisional director Womenswear	Director Personnel
David Sieff Director Corporate and Government Affairs	54	1957 (Stores three years) (Son of Lord Sieff)	Management and director Foods, Homeware, Technology	Director Export Personnel Construction and H.O. Premises
Paul Smith Director North American Operations	53	1965 (Stores three years)		Management in Personnel and Office Services. Divisional Director Personnel then Store Development and Construction Services, then Far East
Andrew Stone Director Womenswear	51	1966 (Family fabric business) (Store three years)	Merchandising and management of various clothing groups. Divisional director Menswear and Childrenswear	P.A. to Lord Sieff
Don Trangmar Director Menswear	55	1965 (Stores two years)	Merchandising and management in various clothing groups. Director of Homeware	P.A. to Lord Sieff

EXHIBIT 4
MEMBERSHIP OF THE INFORMATION TECHNOLOGY REVIEW AND
CAPITAL EXPENDITURE COMMITTEES OF THE BOARD

CEC	ITRC
Mr. J. K. Oates, Chairman	Mr. J. K. Oates, Chairman
Mr. R. Aldridge	Mr. N. L. Colne
Mr. J. R. Benfield	Mr. J. R. Benfield
Mr. N. L. Colne	Mr. R. W. C. Colvill
Mr. R. W. C. Colvill	Mr. P. G. McCracken
Mr. P. G. McCracken	Mr. S. J. Sacher
Mr. P. L. Salsbury	Mr. P. L. Salsbury
Mr. A. Z. Stone	Mr. D. G. Trangmar

EXHIBIT 5
GROUP INVESTMENT PROGRAM 1993–1994—
SEPTEMBER 1993 ESTIMATES

	Full Year 1993–1994 £ (millions)
U.K. and Republic of Ireland	
Construction	
Edge of town	49.8
Regional centers	44.5
High street	20.2
Neighborhood stores	2.1
Subtotal construction	116.6
Estates	52.3
Store development	86.6
Total development	255.5
Information technology	25.0
Other (including head office premises)	17.5
Marks & Spencer Financial Services	2.1
Total U.K. and Republic of Ireland	300.1
Overseas	
Europe	54.1
North America	26.4
Far East	4.3
Total overseas	84.8
Total group	384.9

EXHIBIT 6
BUYING DEPARTMENT STRUCTURE, EXAMPLE: LADIES' UNDERGARMENTS

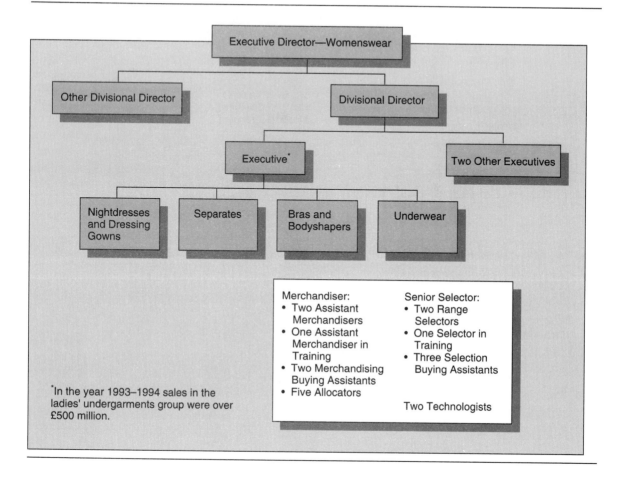

Executive Director—Womenswear

Other Divisional Director

Divisional Director

Executive*

Two Other Executives

Nightdresses and Dressing Gowns

Separates

Bras and Bodyshapers

Underwear

Merchandiser:
- Two Assistant Merchandisers
- One Assistant Merchandiser in Training
- Two Merchandising Buying Assistants
- Five Allocators

Senior Selector:
- Two Range Selectors
- One Selector in Training
- Three Selection Buying Assistants

Two Technologists

*In the year 1993–1994 sales in the ladies' undergarments group were over £500 million.

EXHIBIT 7
BEST ACHIEVERS

Group	Total Staff Cost	Theft & Loss	Food Waste % to Food Sales	Energy, Wrap Materials, Other Controllables
Marble Arch	6.61	0.61	1.77	0.35
Central London	Leadenhall 5.72 (10.61)	Bayswater 0.64 (0.83)	Brent Cross 1.37 (1.74)	Leadenhall 0.49 (1.24)
Edge of town	Camberley 5.25 (8.49)	Fosse Park 0.39 (0.98)	Metro Centre 0.91 (4.19)	Camberley 0.48 (1.29)
Major regional	Aberdeen 6.17 (7.47)	Nottingham 0.41 (8.87)	Newcastle 1.03 (1.87)	Edinburgh 0.52 (0.76)
Regional centers	Inverness 6.08 (9.07)	York 0.42 (0.88)	Canterbury 1.05 (1.76)	York 0.63 (0.99)
High street	Carlisle 6.87 (10.86)	Chesterfield 0.32 (1.06)	—Derby —Doncaster —Llandudno 1.17 (3.17)	Derby 0.66 (1.43)
Small stores	Hamilton 7.31 (12.81)	Mansfield 0.28 (1.24)	Darlington 1.23 (4.36)	Hamilton 0.75 (1.67)
Neighborhood	Leeds Moor 6.25 (11.67)	Chiswick 0.15 (1.00)	St. Helen 1.29 (5.33)	Bury 0.79 (2.82)
Potential savings 1993–1994 £ (millions)	65	12	9	11

(Figures in brackets indicate the worst store.)

In total, if all stores by shape of chain were to achieve the best achiever percentages, net profit would increase by £97 million.

EXHIBIT 8
GROUP STORE NUMBERS AND FOOTAGE

	March 1993		March 1994	
	Numbers	Gross Sq. Ft.	Numbers	Gross St. Ft.
U.K. and Republic of Ireland				
Edge of town	13	997	16	1,191
Town center	238	8,437	228	8,567
Neighborhood	3	117	3	118
Total	302	10,387	306	10,759
Continental Europe				
France	12	381	14	428
Belgium	3	83	3	83
Spain	2	68	4	108
Holland	2	71	2	71
Total	19	603	23	689
Canada				
Marks & Spencer	41	412	40	412
D'Allaird's	113	376	105	351
Total	154	788	145	750
United States				
Brooks Brothers	66	587	84	653
Kings	18	312	19	330
Total	84	899	103	983
Far East				
Hong Kong	5	57	6	70
Japan—Brooks Brothers	44	60	50	66
Total	49	117	56	136
Group total	608	12,694	633	13,317

EXHIBIT 9
FINANCIAL SERVICES PERFORMANCE

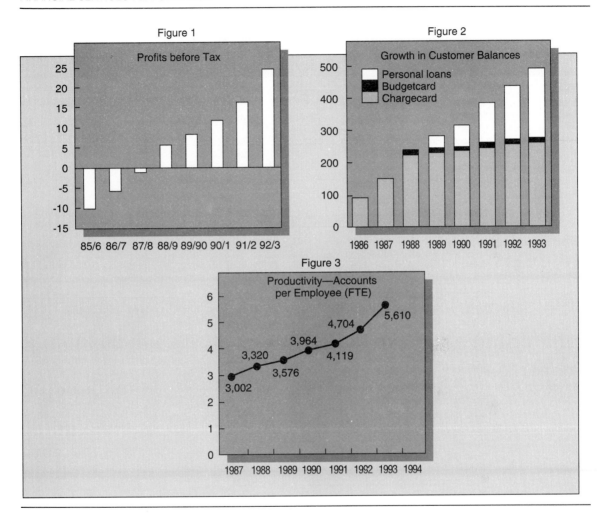

Figure 1
Profits before Tax

Figure 2
Growth in Customer Balances
- Personal loans
- Budgetcard
- Chargecard

Figure 3
Productivity—Accounts
per Employee (FTE)

3,002 3,320 3,576 3,964 4,119 4,704 5,610

EXHIBIT 10
NONFRANCHISE OVERSEAS SALES AS A PERCENTAGE
OF TOTAL OVERSEAS SALES
(26 WEEKS ENDING SEPTEMBER 25 FOR
1992 AND 1993)

	1993 (%)	1992 (%)
Continental Europe		
France	19.7	21.0
Belgium	3.1	3.5
Spain	3.3	4.9
Holland	1.7	1.9
Total	27.8	31.3
United States		
Brooks Brothers	22.9	21.2
Kings	26.9	24.6
Total	49.8	45.8
Canada		
Marks & Spencer	5.6	6.7
D'Allaird's	4.2	5.6
Total	9.8	12.3
Far East		
Hong Kong—M&S	6.1	4.7
Japan—Brooks Brothers	6.5	5.9
Total	12.6	10.6
Total overseas	100.0	100.0

EXHIBIT 11
INTERNATIONAL FRANCHISE GROUP (RETAIL SALES)

	Actual 1987–1988 £ (million)	Actual 1993–1994 £ (million)
Jersey	18.0	22.5
Guernsey	6.0	11.0
Singapore	4.0	24.0
Greece	2.0	15.0
Portugal	—	17.0
Israel	6.0	12.5
Top six accounts—total	**36.0**	**102.0**
Austria	—	3.0
Hungary	—	1.5
Turkey	—	—
Malaysia	—	1.0
Indonesia	—	4.0
Thailand	—	2.0
Czech Republic	—	—
New Accounts	**—**	**11.5**
Philippines	1.0	5.0
Cyprus	3.0	8.0
Malta	2.0	4.0
Gibraltar	3.0	5.0
Caribbean	6.0	4.0
Others	25.0	20.5
Total	**76.0**	**160.0**

EXHIBIT 12
INTERNATIONAL PROFILES

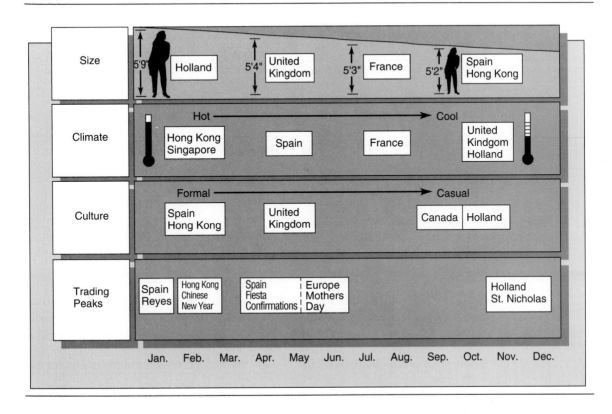

Chapter 8

■

Building Relationships

INTRODUCTION

In this chapter we continue our exploration of the work involved in building strategy and organization. Previously we have considered how general managers design structure and systems and build layers of organizational capability tailored to corporate and business unit strategy. And we have examined how they affect major transformations of established organizations by either revolution as in the GE case or evolution as illustrated in Marks & Spencer.

In order to accomplish these tasks, general managers need the active support of a wide range of constituencies. Like Lou Hughes at Opel, they must seek resources and allies inside and outside the organization. They need to structure and maintain relationships with these individuals and groups to help them communicate, facilitate, and implement their objectives.

To illuminate the general manager's challenges in building relationships, the cases that follow focus on general managers like Lou Hughes and Zaki Mustafa at the middle level of large organizations. We refer to these managers as "unit managers" or "division managers." While each division general manager has a major profit and loss responsibility, he or she must manage this responsibility within the context of a larger corporate hierarchy. As a result, these general managers must not only manage "down" like Phil Knight, building and rearranging relationships with subordinates, but also manage "up," structuring relationships with bosses and corporate staff. Each of these general managers also has a distinct set of customers and suppliers and therefore must manage "out," as well as a set of organizational peers that may call on them to manage "across" the organization, for example borrowing or lending key talent or resources. Thus general managers in the middle must be prepared to build relationships in four directions—up, down, out, and across.

BUILDING RELATIONS WITH DIRECT REPORTS

In most of our cases, we have observed general managers vitally concerned with managing down—to ensure that the troops are all moving smartly in the right direction. We have emphasized how general managers rely upon developing the work environment to help them manage down; in large companies this occurs through several layers of organization. But they also must build relationships with their immediate staff.

Ideally, the relationships a general manager builds with the people who work with him or her directly are characterized by common purpose, mutual trust, two-way communication, and loyalty. For example, you may recall how Zaki Mustafa, who headed Corning's Serengeti division, placed high priority on developing intimate relationships with the key managers who opted to stay in his division. At the CEO level Phil Knight had to build similar relationships to manage Nike's successful growth to a billion-dollar company.

What does it take to build effective relationships with key subordinates? First, it helps if the general manager and a direct report can make a mutual choice when entering into their formal relationship. If the general manager hires or selects his or her subordinate, the two parties not only are likely to be on the same wavelength about organizational purpose and assigned responsibilities but also are likely to feel mutually committed to each other. It is hard to develop such committed, transparent relationships when one inherits "the other." Several of the managers we have studied, like Eberhard von Koerber or John Sculley, "parachuted" into their jobs, and this certainly complicated the challenge they faced.

Next, the general manager must provide challenging tasks, set high standards, and enforce accountability while at the same time providing his or her direct reports with the freedom, resources, and support necessary to get the job done. Situations such as the one in this chapter facing Cleveland Twist Drill's Jim Bartlett can pose a formidable test.

Third, a general manager needs to show an interest in the personal and professional development of subordinates. Although it is common today to emphasize pay for performance, most of us respond very positively to efforts by others that help us to grow. When individuals believe that they are being given the best chance imaginable to use and further develop their talents, they are likely to be both excited and loyal.

General managers can build constructive relationships with their team by managing their interactions with individual subordinates so as to take account of this broad agenda of objectives. Common purpose, trust, and loyalty may be even more important in a particular interaction than substance. The same objectives may also be pursued indirectly by building team relations among the group of direct reports. For this purpose, work and social meetings need to be shaped so that norms develop covering the sharing of resources, mutual accountability, joint problem solving, and professional development. A good example of this sort of activity is provided by James Houghton's work with Corning's "6 pack."

BUILDING RELATIONSHIPS UPWARD

The need to manage upward is a key distinction between middle level managers and CEOs. Chief executives do have their board of directors and major shareholders, as well as regulators, and these present them with complex challenges. Division managers, in contrast, must *always* be concerned with line superiors, sometimes several levels of them, and with corporate staff groups. Division managers have a lot at stake in these relations because typically they are not only in the middle of the organization, they are in the middle of their careers. How they are *perceived* as performing will have a great deal to do with the resources and support they are given and whether they are promoted to more responsible positions.

The ideal relationship between a division manager and his or her superiors is not easy to define because circumstances vary so widely, affecting, for example, how much autonomy for the division could reasonably be expected. Personal styles and preferences vary greatly. Still, when managed well, certain aspects of how division general managers relate to their various superiors are almost always important assets. Especially important are

- an ability to persuade higher-level managers to endorse division proposals for resources to support research, new products, capital programs, shifts in strategy or organization, or requests for personnel.
- an ability to secure from superiors rewards and other signs of recognition for the division's achievements.
- a protégé–mentor relationship that provides coaching and other support.

The fact is that in the terms just specified poor relationships with individuals and groups up the line are just as common as good relationships. It is not uncommon for unit managers to be so jealous of their autonomy or resentful of "heavy-handed intervention from on high" that they ignore, manipulate, or challenge higher-level staff groups or line managers. Their behavior heightens distrust and reinforces "we–they" attitudes and game playing. We can observe problems of this sort in the Kentucky Fried Chicken case.

How can middle managers build relationships up the line that are responsive and supportive, allow latitude for action, provide recognition, and allow mentor–protégé relations to develop? We have observed several types of actions that help general managers build such relationships with superiors and offer four of them as general guidelines.[1]

First, division managers need to thoroughly understand the position of the corporate office on issues that impinge on the division. While this may involve interpreting or translating general objectives into more specific implications, the general manager should think through how corporate strategy might impose requirements on the unit's product market strategy; how corporate requirements for information and control and coordination might impose legitimate burdens on the unit; and how corporate resource constraints might affect the plans put forward by the unit. Only with a sympathetic understanding of the corporate perspective can a division manager sort out which corporate initiatives, if any, to resist and also help his or her own staff make appropriate interpretations of these corporate initiatives. Additionally, the more clearly the divisional general manager conveys to corporate officials an understanding of the division's perspectives, the more likely are the latter to take seriously and address on their merits any response by the division that takes exception to their initiatives.

An especially valuable way of building understanding is to make sure that the division takes advantage of whatever expertise corporate staff can offer. There is no better way to communicate respect for staff than to put their ideas to work in ways that improve performance.

Division managers also need to engage in sufficient "face work" with key corporate managers to build a level of interpersonal rapport that permits trust and fast communication when the situation calls for it. If headquarters is at a distance, this can involve travel, but it is vital work. There simply is no substitute for friendly face-to-face interaction so that the folks at the other end of the fax line or reading a memorandum know how to calibrate what they are reading.

Third, division general managers should invest in keeping superiors well informed with timely information. It is especially important to avoid surprises such as significant news—usually bad—that reveals far later in the day than necessary that results are different from plans. Managing the expectations of superiors sounds manipulative, but a division manager that gives his or her superiors early warning of changes in the offing can make allies. Managers who surprise their bosses make enemies. This aspect of the middle management job resembles the CEO's relationship with the board of directors. Surprises are anathema.

The reason is straightforward. To begin, surprises suggest that plans were made on the basis of poor information and understanding. But surprises have two other more important implications. They suggest that

---

[1] The interested reader can find a full discussion of this relationship in Joseph L Bower, *Managing the Resource Allocation Process* (Boston: Harvard Business School, 1970), chapters 3, 9, and *passim*; as well as Jay W Lorsch and Steven A Allen III, *Managing Diversity and Interdependence* (Boston: Harvard Business School, 1973), chapter 4.

the manager involved has not kept careful track of what is going on and does not understand that early warning of a shift in circumstances—the date of project completion or the profitability of operations—is valuable because other adjustments can be made.

Finally, at the same time that division managers are opening up the lines of communication, they need to be careful to avoid "bucking issues up." It is important to resist the temptation to involve superiors in making decisions delegated to the division. Even though it may seem natural to clarify the intention of corporate superiors when facing a difficult choice, it is easy to convey the impression that one is attempting to blur responsibility for difficult or risky decisions.

BUILDING RELATIONS WITH CUSTOMERS AND SUPPLIERS

Building relationships with customers and suppliers is an important dimension of all general management jobs. Just how important depends upon the business, but as we noted in Chapter 6, it has been given increasing priority in the past decade as companies face intensified competition.

A general manager's close relationship with customers not only may help make a sale (the traditional rationale for such contacts) and get the division's story told, but also helps keep the general manager and the organization focused on the changing needs of customers. Close relationships between a division manager and key suppliers may permit coordinated management of inventories, product development and process development, all to the mutual advantage of the division and its suppliers. As described in the case study, Marks & Spencer has raised such relationships to an art form.

Finally, partnership relations with labor unions, not always readily achievable, often spell the difference between satisfactory and superior operating performance. Of course, in all of these and similar relationships with other external entities, a division manager's personal investment in these relationships signals their importance to other members of the division.

What is required to achieve constructive and sometimes close relations with other entities? The general manager needs to understand the interests and priorities of the other entity, for example, a supplier or union official; to assess the other entity's options and how its actions can help or hurt the division; and to formulate possible arrangements that would best integrate the interests of the two parties. Then the general manager must formulate a plan and possess the skill to negotiate a win–win solution. When it appears impossible to negotiate an integrative solution, a general manager must have the stomach and nerve for confrontation and conflict as well as a plan to mobilize the power to prevail. And because confrontation and conflict may alter the expectations of the other party, general managers need to be alert to the possibility that as a consequence of conflict, a more cooperative search for solutions may become feasible.

BUILDING RELATIONSHIPS ACROSS THE ORGANIZATION WITH PEERS

The interdependence among general managers as peers takes many different forms. In the extreme, one division may be the supplier or customer of another. A division may depend on others for assistance such as information or services. It will compete with all other units for corporate resources. It may have joint or overlapping responsibilities with some units for developing technology or going to market. And the managers of other units may be important sources of counsel and suggestions.

These interdependencies have long characterized organizational life. Traditionally, they have been managed with corporate plans, procedures, transfer pricing schemes, or ad hoc decisions by common superiors, but experience has revealed the usefulness of relying less on formal organizational hardware and more on informal software, in other words, relationships.[2] Today their management is increasingly assumed to be the responsibility of the participants themselves. With a desire to rely less on bureaucracy, less on hierarchical controls, and more on lateral processes to coordinate and control business processes has come a need for middle level managers to pay more attention to building these peer relationships and resolving issues within them.

The characteristics of constructive peer relations and the means for building and managing them are in many ways similar to those associated with the previous three types of relationships. It is important to convey understanding of the others' needs; to search for integrative solutions with corporate goals clearly in mind; to spend time and energy in "face work"; to develop norms of reciprocity; and to plan to cooperate if possible but be prepared to confront if necessary.

In the cases that follow we can see middle managers in action. They are confronted with a variety of challenges, including getting approval of a major proposal, preserving the character and autonomy of a subsidiary, and turning around a faltering business. We can pay particular attention to how in the context of addressing these challenges the division managers draw upon existing relationships and build new ones, and we can notice which of their actions are effective and which are ineffective. In addition, each reader can reflect on whether he or she would have the insight and skill to manage these relationships as well as or better than our middle manager protagonists.

---

[2] See, for example, Robert G Eccles, *The Transfer Pricing Problem: A Theory for Practice* (Boston: Lexington Books, 1985).

Basic Industries

In May 1966 Pete Adams, plant manager of Basic Industries' Chicago plant, was worried about the new facilities proposal for Toranium. His division, Metal Products, was asking for $1 million to build facilities that would be at full capacity in less than a year and a half, if forecast sales were realized. Yet the divisional vice president for production seemed more interested in where the new facility was to go than in how big it should be. Adams wondered how his salary and performance review would look in 1968 with the new facility short of capacity.

METAL PRODUCTS DIVISION

Basic Industries engaged in a number of activities ranging from shipbuilding to the manufacture of electronic components. The corporation was organized into five autonomous divisions (see Figure A), which in 1965 had sales totaling $500

million. Of the five, the Metal Products Division was the most profitable. In 1965, this division realized an after-tax income of $16 million on sales of $110 million and an investment of $63.7 million.

Metal Products had not always held this position of profit leadership within the company. In fact, in the early 1950s Basic's top management had considered dropping the division. At that time, the division's market share was declining owing to high costs, depressed prices, and a lack of manufacturing facilities.

A change in divisional management resulted in a marked improvement. Between 1960 and 1965, for example, the division's sales grew at 8 percent a year and profits grew at 20 percent a year. The division's ROI rose from 12 percent to 25 percent over the same period.

Ronald Brewer, president of Metal Products Division since 1955, explained how this growth had been achieved:

> Planning goes on in many places in the Metal Products Division, but we do go through a formal planning process to establish goals. We establish very specific goals for products and departments

FIGURE A
ORGANIZATION CHART

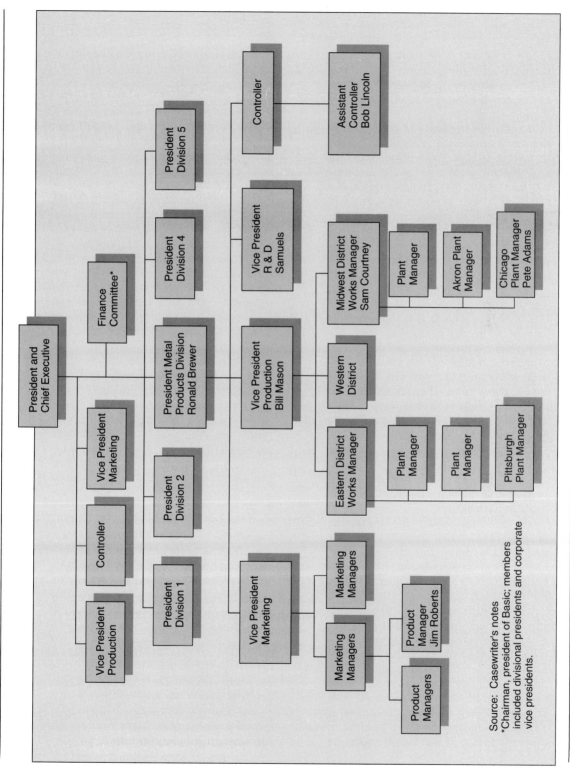

Source: Casewriter's notes
*Chairman, president of Basic; members included divisional presidents and corporate vice presidents.

Source: Casewriter's notes.

in every phase of the business. This formal and detailed planning is worked out on a yearly basis. We start at the end of the second quarter to begin to plan for the following year.

We plan on the basis of our expectations as to the market. If it's not there, we live a little harder. We cut back to assure ourselves of a good cash flow. Our record has been good, but it might not always be. Some of our products are 30 years old. We've just invested $5 million, which is a lot of money for our division, in expanding capacity for a 25-year-old product. But we're making money out of it and it's growing.

Along with detailed planning for the year to come, we ask for plans for years three and four. Our goal is to make sure that we can satisfy demand.

Any time we approach 85 percent of capacity at one of our plants, our engineers get busy. They will give the plant manager the information as to what he needs in the way of new equipment. The plant manager will then fit the engineer's recommendation into his expansion plans. The plant manager's plan then goes to our control manager. The marketing people then add their forecasts, and by that time we have built up the new facilities proposal.

On the other hand, the marketing people may have spearheaded the project. Sometimes they alert the plant manager to a rapid growth in his product, and he goes to the engineers. In this division, everyone is marketing-minded ... We measure plants, and they measure their departments against plan. For example, we have a rule of thumb that a plant must meet its cost reduction goals. So if one idea doesn't work out, a plant must find another one to get costs to the planned level. We make damned sure that we make our goals as a division. Our objective is to have the best product in the market at the lowest cost. It's a simple concept, but the simpler the concept, the better it's understood.

Well, on the basis of his performance against plan, a man is looked at by his superior at least once a year, maybe more. We take a pretty hard-nosed position with a guy. We tell him what we think his potential is, where he is going to go, what he is going to be able to do. We have run guys up *and* down the ladder. In this division, it's performance and fact that count. We have no formal incentive plan, but we do recognize performance with salary increases and with promotions.

You know, we have divisions in this company which are volume happy. We here are profit conscious—we had to be to survive. What I'd like to see is interest allocated on a pro rata basis according to total investment. I grant you that this would hurt some of the other divisions more than us, but I think that treating interest as a corporate expense, as we do, changes your marketing philosophy and your pricing philosophy.

For example, most new facilities proposals are wrong with respect to their estimates of market size—volume attainable at a given price—and timing. You can second-guess a forecast, though, in several ways and hedge to protect yourself. There is a feeling at Basic Industries that there is a stigma attached to coming back for more money. That means that if you propose a project at the bare minimum requirement and then come back for more, some people feel that you've done something wrong. Generally, this leads to an overestimate of the amount of capital required. It turns out that if you have the money you do spend it, so that this stigma leads to overspending on capital projects. We at Metal Products are trying to correct this. First, we screen projects closely. We go over them with a fine-toothed comb. Second, internally, we set a goal to spend less than we ask for where there is a contingency.

Also, when a project comes in at an estimated 50 percent return, we cut the estimate down. Everyone does. The figure might go out at 30 percent. But this practice works the other way too. For example, in 1958 Bill Mason [Metal Products' vice president of production] and I worked like hell to get a project through; although it looked like 8 percent on paper, we knew that we could get the costs way down once it got going, so we put it through at 12 percent. We're making double that on it today. We haven't had a capital request rejected by the finance committee in eight years [see Figure A].

Of course, every once in a while we shoot some craps, but not too often. We are committed to a specific growth rate in net income and ROI. Therefore, we are selective in what we do and how we spend our money. It's seldom that we spend $500,000 to develop something until we know it's got real market potential. You just don't send 100 samples out and then forecast a flood of orders. New products grow slowly. It takes six or seven years. And, given that it takes this long, it doesn't take a lot of capital to develop and test out new ideas. Before you really invest, you've done your homework. Over the years we've done a good job in our new products, getting away from the aircraft industry. In 1945, 70 percent of our business was based on aircraft. Today it's 40 percent. The way we do things protects us. We have to have a very strong sense of the technical idea and the scope of the market before we invest heavily.

Metal Products Division's main business was producing a variety of basic and rare nonferrous metals and alloys such as nickel, nickel-beryllium, and titanium in a myriad of sizes and shapes for electrical, mechanical, and structural uses in industry. One of the division's major strengths was its leadership in high-performance material technology, thanks to patents and a great deal of proprietary experience. Metal Products had a substantial technological lead on the competition.

Toranium

In the late 1950s, Metal Products decided to follow its technological knowledge and proprietary production skills into the high-performance materials market. One of Metal Products' most promising new materials was Toranium, for which Jim Roberts was product manager.

Roberts was 33 years old and had a PhD in chemical engineering. Prior to becoming a product manager, he had worked in one of Metal Products' research labs. Roberts explained some of Toranium's history:

> Developing Toranium was a trial-and-error process. The lab knew that the properties of the class of high-performance materials to which Toranium belonged were unusually flexible and therefore felt such materials had to be useful. So it was an act of faith that led R&D to experiment with different combinations of these materials. They had no particular application in mind.
>
> In 1957 we developed the first usable Toranium. Our next problem was finding applications for it. It cost $50 a pound. However, since a chemist in the lab thought we could make it for less, we began to look for applications.
>
> In 1962 I entered the picture. I discovered it was an aerospace business. When the characteristics of our material were announced to the aerospace people, they committed themselves to it. Our competitors were asleep. They weren't going to the customer. I went out and called on the customers and developed sales.

In 1963 we decided to shift the pilot plant from the lab and give it to the production people at Akron. We decided that we simply were not getting a good production-oriented consideration of the process problems. The people at Akron cut the costs by two-thirds, and the price stayed the same.

In 1963 I also chose to shut off R&D on Toranium because it couldn't help in the marketplace. We had to learn more in the marketplace before we could use and direct R&D.

I ought to mention that, under the management system used by Mr. Samuels [vice president of R&D], the product manager—along with R&D and production—shares in the responsibility for monitoring and directing an R&D program. This arrangement is part of an attempt to keep everyone market oriented.

From 1962 to 1965, sales of Toranium increased from $250,000 a year to $1 million a year just by seeking them, and in 1965 we put R&D back in.

This material can't miss. It has a great combination of properties: excellent machinability, thermal shock resistance, and heat insulation. Moreover, it is an excellent electrical conductor. We can sell all that we can produce. Customers are coming to us with their needs. They have found that Toranium's properties and our technical capabilities are superior to anything or anyone in the market.

Moreover, pricing has not been a factor in the development of markets to date. In fact, sales have been generated by the introduction of improved grades of Toranium at premium prices. Presently, General Electric represents our only competition, but we expect that Union Carbide will be in the marketplace with competitive materials during the next few years. However, I don't expect anyone to be

significantly competitive before 1968. Anyway, competition might actually help a little bit in expanding the market and stimulating the customers as well as in educating our own R&D [people].

Now, if one assumes that no other corporation will offer significant competition to Toranium until 1968, the only real uncertainty in our forecasts for Toranium is related to Metal Products' technical and marketing abilities. R&D must develop the applications it is currently working on, and production will have to make them efficiently.

This production area can be a real headache. For example, R&D developed a Toranium part for one of our fighter bombers. However, two out of three castings cracked. On the other hand, we've got the best skills in the industry with respect to high-pressure casting. If we can't do it, no one can.

The final uncertainty is new demand. I've got to bring in new applications, but that shouldn't be a problem. You know, I've placed Toranium samples with over 17 major customers. Can you imagine what will happen if even two or three of them pay off? As far as I'm concerned, if the forecasts for Toranium are inaccurate, they're underestimates of future sales.

NEW FACILITIES PROPOSAL

Sam Courtney, district works manager (to whom the plant managers of the Chicago, Akron, and Indianapolis plants reported), explained the origin of the new Toranium facilities proposal:

The product manager makes a forecast once a year, and when it comes time to make major decisions, he makes long-range forecasts. In January 1965 we were at 35 percent of the Toranium pilot-plant capacity. At that time we said, "We have to know beyond 1966; we need a long-range forecast. Volume is beginning to move up."

The production control manager usually collects the forecasts. Each year it is his responsibility to see where we are approaching 85 percent or 90 percent of capacity. When that is the case in some product line, he warns the production vice president. However, in this instance, Toranium was a transition product, and Akron [where the pilot plant was located] picked up the problem and told the manager of product forecasting that we were in trouble.

The long-range forecast that Courtney requested arrived at his office early in March 1965 and clearly indicated a need for new capacity. Moreover, Roberts's 1966 regular forecast, which was sent to production in October 1965, was 28 percent higher than the March long-range projection. It called for additional capacity by October 1966.

Courtney's first response was to request a new long-range forecast. He also authorized the Akron plant to order certain equipment on which there would be a long lead time. The district works manager explained. "It is obvious we are going to need additional capacity in a hurry, and the unique properties of Toranium require special, made-to-order equipment. We can't lose sales. Producing Toranium is like coining money."

At the same time, Courtney began discussions on the problem with Bill Mason, vice president of production for Metal Products. They decided that the Akron plant was probably the wrong location in which to expand the Toranium business. Courtney commented, "There are 20 prod-

ucts being produced at Akron, and that plant cannot possibly give Toranium the kind of attention it deserves. The business is a new one, and it needs to be cared for like a young child. They won't do that in a plant with many important, large-volume products. We have decided over a period of years that Akron is too complex, and this seems like a good time to do something about it."

The two locations proposed as new sites for the Toranium facilities were Pittsburgh and Chicago. Each was a one-product plant that "could use product diversification." While Pittsburgh seemed to be favored initially, Mason and Courtney were concerned that the Toranium would be contaminated if it came in contact with the rather dirty products produced at Pittsburgh. Therefore, Courtney asked engineering to make studies of both locations.

The results of these initial studies were inconclusive. The Pittsburgh plant felt that the problem of contamination was not severe, and the economic differential between the locations was not substantial.

After the initial studies were completed, Roberts's new long-range forecast arrived. Table A compares this forecast with Roberts's previous ones.

In response to this accelerating market situation, Courtney and Mason asked Adams, plant manager at Chicago, to make a "full-fledged study of the three locations" (Akron, Pittsburgh, and Chicago). At the same time, Mason told Brewer, president of Metal Products:

> We're now about 90 percent certain that Chicago will be the choice. Associated with the newness of the material is a rapidly changing technology. The Metal

TABLE A
ACTUAL AND PROJECTED SALES ($ MILLIONS)

Date of Forecast	1965	1966	1967	1968	1969	1970	1971
Projected Sales							
March 1964	1.08	1.3	—	—	2.2	—	—
March 1965	1.17	1.4	1.6	—	—	2.8	—
March 1966	—	1.8	2.5	3.4	—	—	5.6
Actual Sales	1.0	—	—	—	—	—	—

Products R&D center at Evanston is only 10 minutes away. Another important factor is Adams. Titanium honeycomb at Chicago was in real trouble. We couldn't even cover our direct costs. Adams turned it around by giving it careful attention. That's the kind of job Toranium needs.

Peter Adams was 35 years old. He had worked for Basic since he graduated from college with a BS in engineering. After spending a year in the corporate college training program, Adams was assigned to the Metal Products Division. There he worked as an assistant to the midwestern district manager for production. Before becoming Chicago plant manager in 1963, Adams had been the assistant manager at the same plant for two years.

In working through the financial data on the Toranium project, Adams chose to compare the three sites with respect to internal rates of return (see Table B). He made this comparison for the case where capacity was expanded to meet forecast sales for 1967 ($2.5 million), the case where capacity was expanded to meet forecast sales for 1971 ($5.6 million), and the case where capacity was expanded from $2.5 to $5.6 million.

While the economics favored Akron, Adams was aware that Mason favored Chicago. This feeling resulted from conversations with Courtney about the Toranium project. Courtney pointed out the importance of quality, service to customers, liaison with R&D, and production flexibility to a new product like Toranium. Furthermore, Courtney expressed the view that Chicago looked good in these respects, despite its cost disadvantage. He also suggested that a proposal asking for enough capacity to meet 1967 forecast demand would have the best prospects for divisional acceptance.

By the end of April 1966, Adams's work had progressed far enough to permit preparation of a draft of a new facilities proposal recommending a Chicago facility. Except for the marketing story he obtained from Roberts, he had written the entire text. On May 3, Adams brought the completed draft to New York for a discussion with Mason and Courtney. The meeting, which was quite informal, began with Adams reading his draft proposal aloud to the group. Mason and Courtney commented on the draft as he went along. Some of the more substantial comments are included in the following excerpts from the meeting.

MEETING ON THE DRAFT PROPOSAL

Adams: We expect that production inefficiencies and quality problems will be encountered upon start-up of the new facility in Chicago. In order to prevent these problems from interfering with

TABLE B
COMPARISON OF SITES AND INTERNAL RATES OF RETURN
($ IN THOUSANDS)

	Chicago	Pittsburgh	Akron
1. Incremental capital investment for capacity through 1967	$980	$1,092	$675
Internal rate of return	34%	37%	45%
2. Incremental capital investment for capacity through 1971	$1,342	$1,412	$1,272
Internal rate of return	52%	54%	55%
3. Incremental capital investment to raise capacity from $2.5 to $5.6 millon	$710	$735	$740
Internal rate of return	45%	47%	46%

the growth of Toranium, the new facilities for producing Toranium powder, pressing ingots, and casting finished products will be installed in Chicago and operated until normal production efficiency is attained. At that time, existing Akron equipment will be transferred to the Chicago location. Assuming early approval of the project, Chicago will be in production in the first quarter of 1967, and joint Akron and Chicago operations will continue through September 1967. The Akron equipment will be transferred in October and November 1967, and Chicago will be in full operation in December 1967.

Mason: Wait a minute! You're not in production until the first quarter of 1967, and the forecasts say we are going to be short in 1966!

Adams: There is a problem in machinery order lag.

Mason: Have you ordered a press?

Adams: Yes, and we'll be moving by October.

Mason: Well, then, say you'll be in business in the last quarter of 1966. Look, Pete, this document has to be approved by Brewer and then the finance committee. If Chicago's our choice, we've

got to *sell* Chicago. Let's put our best foot forward!

The problem is to make it clear that, on economics alone, we would go to Akron . . . but you have to bring out the flaw in the economics: that managing 20 product lines, especially when you've got fancy products, just isn't possible.

Courtney: And you have a better building.

Mason: All of this should be in a table in the text. It ought to cover incremental cost, incremental investment, incremental expense, incremental ROI, and the building space.

And Sam's right. Akron is a poor building; it's a warehouse. Pittsburgh is better for something like high-pressure materials. But out in Chicago you've got a multistory building with more than enough space that is perfect for this sort of project.

Courtney: Pete, are we getting this compact enough for you?

Mason: Hey, why don't we put some sexy-looking graphs in the thing? I don't know, but maybe we could plot incremental investment vs. incremental return for each location. See what you can do, Pete.

Courtney: Yes, that's a good idea.

Mason: Now, Pete, one other thing. You'll have to include discounted cash flow on the other two locations. Some of those guys [division and corporate top management] are going to look at just the numbers. You'll show them they're not too different.

Mason: [*A bit later in the discussion*] The biggest discussion will be, "Why the hell move to Chicago?"

Courtney: You know, Pete, you should discuss the labor content in the product.

Mason: Good. We have to weave in the idea that it's a product with a low labor content and explain that this means the high Chicago labor cost will not hurt us.

Adams: One last item: Shouldn't we be asking for more capacity? Two and one-half million dollars only carries us through 1967.

Mason: Pete, we certainly wouldn't do this for one of our established products. Where our main business is involved, we build capacity in five- and ten-year chunks. But we have to treat Toranium a little differently. The problem here is to take a position in the market. Competition isn't going to clobber us if we don't have the capacity to satisfy everyone. If the market develops, we can move quickly.

After the meeting, Courtney explained that he and Mason had been disappointed with Adams's draft and were trying to help him improve it without really "clobbering" him. "Adams's draft was weak. His numbers were incomplete and his argument sloppy. I've asked him to meet with Bob Lincoln [assistant controller for Metal Products] to discuss the proposal." The result of Adams's five meetings with Lincoln was three more drafts of the Toranium proposal. The numerical exhibits were revised for greater clarity and the text was revised to lessen the number of technical terms.

Adams, however, was still very much concerned with the appropriate size of the new facility. "Mason is only interested in justifying the location of the new facility!" Adams exclaimed. "We plan to sell $5.6 million worth of Toranium in 1971, yet we're asking for only $2.5 million worth of capacity. It's crazy! But, you know, I think Mason doesn't really care what capacity we propose. He just wants 'sexy-looking graphs.' That's OK for him, because I'm the one who's going to get it in the neck in 1968. So far as I can see, Brewer has built his reputation by bringing this division from chronic undercapacity to a full-capacity, high-ROI position."

The next step in the Toranium facilities proposal was a formal presentation to the top management of Metal Products on June 2, 1966. There were two capital projects on the agenda. Brewer began the meeting by announcing that its purpose was to "discuss the proposals and decide if they were any good." He turned the meeting over to Mason, who in turn asked Adams to "take over and direct the meeting."

Adams began reading the draft proposal, after first asking for comments. He had gotten halfway down the first page when Brewer interrupted.

Brewer: Let me stop you right here. You have told them [*the proposal was aimed at Basic Industries' financial committee*] the name, and you have told them how much money you want, but you haven't told them what the name means, and you haven't told them what the products are.

At this point a discussion began as to what the name of the project was going to be. The meeting then continued with Adams reading and people occasionally making comments on his English and on the text.

Brewer: Look, let's get this straight. What we are doing in this proposal is trying to tell them what it is we are spending their money on. That's what they want to know. Tell me about the electronic applications in that table you have there. I have to be able to explain them to the finance committee. I understand "steel" and "aerospace" but I don't understand "electronic applications" and l don't understand "electronic industry." I need some more specific words.

Samuels: [VP of R&D] Let me ask you a question which someone in the finance committee might ask. It's a nasty one. You forecast here that the industry sales in 1971 are going to be about $7 million, or maybe a little less. You think we are going to have 75 percent or 85 percent of this business. You also think we are going to get competition from G.E. and others. Do you think companies of that stature are going to be satisfied with sharing $1.5 million of the business? Don't you think that we may lose some of our market share?

This question was answered by Roberts and pursued by a few others. Essentially Roberts argued that the proprietary technology of the Metal Products Division was going to be strong enough to defend its market share.

Brewer: Let me tell you about an item which is much discussed in the finance committee. They are concerned—and basically this involved other divisions —with underestimating the cost of investment projects. I think, in fact, that there was a request for additional funds

on a project recently which was as large as our entire annual capital budget [$7.9 million in 1965]. Second of all, as a result of the capital expenditure cutback, there was a tendency—and again it has been in other divisions—to cut back on or delay facilities. Now, it's not really just the capital expenditure cutback that is the reason for their behavior. If they had been doing their planning, they should have been thinking about these expenditures five or six years ago, not two years ago. But they didn't do the estimates, or their estimates weren't correct, and now they are sold out on a lot of items and are buying products from other people and reselling them and not making any money. It's affecting the corporate earnings, so the environment in the finance committee today is very much (1) "Tell us how much you want, and tell us *all* that you want," and (2) "Give us a goddamned good return." Now I don't want us to get *sloppy*, but, Bill, if you need something, ask for it. And then make Pete meet his numbers.

Adams: Well, on this one, as I think you know, the machinery is already on order, and we are sure that our market estimates are correct.

Brewer: Yes, I know that. I just mean that if you want something, then plan it right and tell them what you are going to need so you don't come back asking for more money six months later.

———

Brewer: I am going to need some words on competition. I am also going to need some words on why we are ready so soon on this project. We are asking for money now, and we say we are going to be in operation in the fourth quarter.

Samuels: Foresight [*Followed by general laughter*].

Mason: Well, it's really quite understandable. This began last October, when we thought we were going to expand at Akron. At that time, it was obvious that we needed capacity, so we ordered some machines. Then, as the thing developed, it was clear that there would be some other things we needed, and because of the timing lag we had to order them.

Brewer: OK, now another thing. Numerical control is hot as a firecracker in the finance committee. I am not saying that we should have it on this project, but you should be aware that the corporation is thinking a lot about it.

Brewer: [*Much later in the discussion*] There are really three reasons for moving. Why not state them? (1) You want to free up some space at Akron, which you need. (2) There are 20 products at Akron, and Toranium can't get the attention it needs. (3) You can get operating efficiencies if you move.

If you set it out, you can cut out all of this "crap." You know, it would do you people some good if you read a facilities proposal on something you didn't know beforehand. [The finance committee reviewed about 190 capital requests in 1965.] You really have to think about the guy who doesn't know what you're talking about. I read a proposal yesterday that was absolutely ridiculous. It had pounds per hour and tons per year and tons per month and tons per day and—except for the simplest numbers, which were in a table —all the rest were spread out through the story.

The meeting continued for several hours, taking up other agenda items.

Adams indicated that he was disappointed with the meeting. Brewer seemed to him to be preoccupied with "words,"

and the topic of additional capacity never really came up. The only encouraging sign was Brewer's statement, "Tell us all that you want." But it seemed that all Mason "wanted" was $2.5 million worth of capacity.

Adams saw three possibilities open to him. First, he could ask for additional capacity. This alternative meant that Adams would have to speak with Courtney and Mason, and, as Chicago plant manager, he viewed the prospect of such a conversation with mixed feelings. In the past his relations with Courtney and Mason had been excellent. He had been able to deal with these men on an informal and relaxed level. However, the experience of drafting the Toranium proposal left Adams a little uneasy. Courtney and Mason had been quite critical of his draft and had made him meet with Bob Lincoln to revise it. What would be their reaction if he were to request a reconsideration of the proposal at this late date? Moreover, what new data or arguments could he offer in support of a request for additional capacity?

On the other hand, Adams saw a formal request for additional capacity as a way of getting his feelings formally on record. Even if his superiors refused his request, he would be in a better position with respect to the 1968 performance review. However, Adams wondered how his performance review would go if he formally requested and received additional capacity and then the market did not develop as forecast.

As his second alternative, Adams believed he could ask that the new facilities proposal specify that Metal Products would be needing more money for Toranium facilities in the future. This alternative did not pose the same problems as the first with respect to Courtney and Mason. Adams felt that saying more funds might be needed would be acceptable to Courtney and Mason, whereas asking for more might not be. However, the alternative introduced a new problem. Brewer had been quite explicit on insisting that the division ask for all that was needed, so that it would not have to come back and ask for more in six months. To admit a possible need for additional funds, therefore, might jeopardize the entire project.

In spite of this drawback. Adams felt that this alternative was the best one avail-able. It was a compromise between his point of view and Mason's. And, if top management felt that the future of Toranium was too uncertain, then why not ask for contingent funds? This would get Adams off the hook and still not actually increase Metal Products' real investment.

As his third alternative, Adams decided he could drop the issue and hope to be transferred or promoted before 1968.

Kentucky Fried Chicken (Japan) Limited

In January 1983, Dick Mayer leaned back in his chair and gazed absent-mindedly at the Norman Rockwell portrait of Colonel Sanders on his office wall. Mayer, a veteran Kentucky Fried Chicken (KFC) executive, had recently been promoted from vice chairman and head of the company's U.S. operations to chairman and chief executive officer, and for the past few weeks had been focusing his attention on the challenges facing him in Kentucky Fried Chicken-International (KFC-I). As he talked to KFC-I managers about their problems, opportunities, and challenges, he was exposed to a wide range of opinion on what was needed to continue KFC's growth and profitability overseas.

At one end of the spectrum was Loy Weston, president of KFC's highly successful joint venture in Japan. Weston's view was that in recent years headquarters staff interference in local national operations was increasingly compromising the spirit of entrepreneurship that had built the overseas business. In Louisville, however, Mayer heard a different story. For example, Gary Burhow, vice president of strategic planning, felt that the lack of effective planning and control in the early years of KFC-I had led to suboptimal financial performance, inconsistent strategies, and stalled expansion into new markets. He emphasized that the recent efforts by headquarters staff were aimed at supporting the overseas subsidiaries and bringing to them the very considerable resources and experience of the parent company.

THE BEGINNINGS

Harland Sanders was born in Henryville, Indiana, in 1890, the son of a farmhand. A sixth-grade dropout, he occasionally worked as a cook. In his late 40s, he developed a recipe for chicken based on a pressure cooking method and a secret seasoning mix of eleven herbs and spices. When Sanders's gas station, restaurant, and motel were bypassed by the new interstate highway system in 1956, he decided to try to franchise his chicken recipe. With his white suit, goatee, string tie, and benign charm, he sold some 700 franchises in less than nine years. In allocating franchising rights for KFC, Sanders was generous to his friends and relatives. His management style was to rely on the basic goodness of the people around him and trust his franchisees to play fair. There were no management systems or strategic controls.

Industry Growth and Development

Colonel Sanders became a pioneer in one of the fastest-growing industries of the postwar era. Many of the practices he initiated were quickly imitated by others, and within a few years several "rules of the game" came to be accepted in the U.S. fast food industry.

One of the first norms to be established was expansion through franchising. The high capital cost of opening new stores, together with the need to expand rapidly to stake out the territory, quickly forced companies toward this option. Franchising also allowed companies to capture operating economies, particularly in advertising and raw materials purchasing. As franchises matured, chain managements often became interested in buying them back or opening their own stores. This not only gave them better understanding and control of operations, it also allowed franchising fees to be supplemented by profits.

At the store level, the importance of scale economies was also quickly recognized. Because each restaurant outlet had high fixed costs and small returns on unit sales, traffic volume was crucial. This made location a key success factor, and

decisions on which region, town, neighborhood, or even side of the street could mean the difference between success and failure.

Within the industry, companies soon learned that effective store management was also a key factor in profitability. Because margins were small and the opportunities for waste, shrinkage and inefficiency were many, it took a special kind of individual to keep a fast food outlet operating smoothly and profitably. In addition to ensuring short-term profits, store managers were also responsible for building local public relations, maintaining employee morale, developing customer goodwill, keeping tab on competing chains, and so on. And yet the salaries paid to these entrepreneurial individuals were relatively low for the 60–80 hours a week they devoted to their work. Most were attracted to the company-owned outlets by the prospects for promotion into regional and divisional positions.

As the industry developed, the importance of the chain's overall market image also became increasingly clear. The need for a focused theme or product line was acknowledged to be critical, as was the importance of the consistency and reliability of the product throughout the chain. Successful new product innovations were difficult, and management was always conscious of the risk of confusing the chain's image if it deviated too far from its basic menu and core theme.

Acquisition and Growth: The Late 1960s

By 1964 the 700 KFC outlets were grossing over $37 million a year and the colonel, now in his mid-70s, had begun to mutter that the "damned business is beginning to run right over me." The time seemed ripe for a change of ownership.

When a 29-year-old Kentucky lawyer, John Y. Brown, and a 60-year-old financier, Jack Massey, offered Sanders $2 million, a lifetime salary, and a position in charge of quality control in the business, the colonel accepted.

Under Brown and Massey, growth exploded. During the next five years, KFC's revenue grew 96 percent a year (from $7 million to $200 million). In 1970, the company was building 1,000 stores a year in the United States. Brown recognized that the key to continued growth was to find, motivate, and retain hard-working and entrepreneurial managers and franchisees. His philosophy was that everyone involved with a KFC operation had a right to expect to become wealthy.

But with the rapid growth, problems soon cropped up. KFC headquarters experienced high turnover in its management ranks, with a number of senior executives leaving in quick succession to become franchisees for KFC's new ventures. If he was to keep these key people, Brown had to find new challenges and promotion opportunities within the company.

About this time, Brown became fascinated with the apparently boundless opportunities for KFC to expand overseas. The rapid economic growth and trend toward two-income families that had fueled the growth of the fast food industry in the 1950s and 1960s were appearing in the late 1960s in other countries. Despite warnings from some who felt that food tastes differed widely from one country to the next, and that the whole concept of fast food was a cultural phenomenon that could not be transported outside the United States, Brown was convinced there was an opportunity. Besides, he felt he would be able to keep some of his entrepreneurial executives challenged by sending them to start new KFC ventures

abroad. One executive later described Brown's international expansion strategy in these terms: "He just threw some mud against the map on the wall and hoped some of it would stick."

The country managers were like Roman governors sent to govern distant provinces with nothing more than an exhortation to maintain Rome's imperial power and reputation. Few had any operating expertise, they were offered little staff support, and the only attention paid to operations was Colonel Sanders's personal efforts to maintain the quality of his original product. Each country manager was on his own to make a success of his venture, and most had to learn the business from scratch.

CHANGES IN THE EARLY 1970s

KFC (Japan): Getting Started

It was against this background that Mitsubishi approached KFC with a proposal to start a joint venture in Japan. The giant Japanese trading company had a large poultry operation and wanted to develop the demand for chicken in its home country. Finding a perfect fit with his priorities, Brown was quick to seize the opportunity. The only problem was, he had nobody in the company equal to such a challenging assignment. But he thought he knew a good candidate—an IBM salesman named Loy Weston.

During the Korean War, Weston had been stationed in Japan and became intrigued with Japanese culture. After the war, he joined IBM's sales department and studied law at night. While at IBM, he started a dozen entrepreneurial ventures in his spare time, including airplane leasing, coffee machine sales, and sandpaper wholesaling. In the 60s he was based in

Lexington, Kentucky, as a member of IBM's new-product sales group. It was then he met John Y. Brown.

After the Mitsubishi contact in 1969, Brown called Weston and asked if he would go to Japan and start a new company. Weston agreed, and soon the two men were discussing how to make the venture work. Brown's directions to Weston were simple. He asked him not to franchise until he had proven the fast food concept with company-owned stores. Brown's dictum was "Build a store and make it work; then build another and another." Weston was to receive $200,000 as start-up capital and an annual salary of $40,000. He was promised an expense account after the company had been successfully established. His training consisted of two weeks cooking chicken at a KFC restaurant in Detroit.

Heading east to Japan, Weston decided to stop over in Greece. In Athens, he met the president of Dai Nippon, an Osaka-based printing firm. When the Japanese manager learned that Weston was going to start a new company that would require a lot of printing, he offered to telex to his office and have someone meet Loy. That individual was Shin Ohkawara, a Dai Nippon sales representative.

Weston thought he recognized some real potential in this young salesman and decided to cultivate a friendship with a view to persuading him to join KFC. He asked Ohkawara to take him to different restaurants so he could learn more about the Japanese food industry. This gave Loy an opportunity to scout the market and at the same time to get to know the young Japanese man better. Weston used these occasions to impress Ohkawara with the grand plans he had for the new company, playing up the Mitsubishi connection to emphasize KFC's strength and commit-

ment. After about six months, Shin Ohkawara agreed to join KFC.

Despite the fact that no formal joint venture agreement had been signed between Mitsubishi and KFC in the six months following his arrival in Japan, Weston had gone ahead with the test marketing of KFC products in a local department store, although without a Japanese partner such an operation was strictly illegal. He found that Japanese disliked the mashed potatoes in the KFC standard menu and that the coleslaw was too sweet for local palates. On the spot Weston decided to substitute french fries for the prescribed mashed potatoes and reduced the coleslaw sugar content from the company-set standard. "These were no-brainers. The idea of getting clearance from the United States didn't even occur to me." The first real KFC store was in the American Park in the EXPO-70 in Osaka. KFC Corp. sent the equipment from Louisville, and the store was erected in just two weeks.

The joint venture agreement was finally signed on July 4, 1970. To build on the exposure gained at EXPO-70, two more stores were opened in Osaka. Sites were chosen where land was relatively cheap and where new shopping centers were opening up. In keeping with U.S. practice, stores were large, free-standing structures with 4,400 square feet of floor space. Shin Ohkawara, who managed one of the stores, recalled the early days:

> The stores were exact replicas of the U.S. take-out stores. Although the distinctive architecture was a big plus in the United States, nobody in Japan recognized what we were selling, and sales were very poor. The U.S. manual said that we could not keep the food more than two hours after cooking. So we threw out more chicken than we sold.

The new venture was soon in trouble. Losses mounted, and the company had exhausted the $400,000 put up by the joint venture partners. Weston needed to borrow more. Meanwhile he also had to recruit people to run the existing stores. Both he and Ohkawara were putting in 15-hour days, and they knew they could not do that indefinitely. The latest threat was the appearance of McDonald's in Tokyo. With all its problems, it appeared KFC-J was heading for an early demise, and Weston wondered how he could turn the operation around.

U.S. Operations: Emerging Problems

By late 1970, KFC faced a changed environment in the United States. The economy went into a recession and the company's revenues and profits began to plateau. Meanwhile, its new diversification ventures, like fish and chips and roast beef, were failing to meet expectations. KFC's stock price fell from a peak of $58 to $18, leading many of those who had hoped to get rich to quit the company. As the management exodus continued, Brown saw an opportunity to install a more professional team to build the systems necessary to gain control.

Competition in fast food in the United States was becoming more intense, and an industry shakeout began. KFC managers started hearing field reports about poor product quality and customer service in their stores. So concerned were they about the emerging economic, competitive, and operating problems in the United States that they tended to leave the foreign operations to fend for themselves. Amid all this came a rift in the echelons of top management, and in mid-1971, Brown and Massey sold KFC in an exchange of stock valued at more than $275 million to

Heublein, Inc., a packaged goods company that had developed strong brand franchises such as Smirnoff Vodka in the United States and many other countries.

To fit into the Heublein organization, which was structured along domestic and international lines, KFC's small international staff was merged with Heublein's international group in Farmington, Connecticut, and a manager from Heublein's international operations was brought in to serve as the vice president of KFC-International. A small staff was assigned exclusively to KFC-I to serve as a link between the overseas subsidiaries and Heublein headquarters. (See Exhibit 1A.)

Despite efforts to establish more control over the subsidiaries, headquarters management found KFC-I's independent-minded subsidiary managers uncooperative. Reports often came too late or with too little information. Sometimes they were not sent at all. Although visits from corporate headquarters to the subsidiaries became more frequent, they were usually limited to general exchanges of views about the way the subsidiaries were functioning. In the end, each country manager was left with responsibility for expanding within his territory, using funds generated from his existing operations.

LURCHING TOWARD THE MID-1970s

KFC (Japan): Shaky Beginnings

In the early 1970s, KFC-J was struggling to get on its feet. After heavy losses in Osaka and a not-so-propitious start in Kobe, the company was operating on a shoestring. In early 1972 Weston went to the United States to make a pitch to the new parent company for additional financing. To his surprise, Heublein agreed to increase their share of KFC-J's equity by

$400,000. With matching funds from Mitsubishi and bank guarantees from both parents, he now received a warmer welcome when he applied for additional debt. Now all he had to do was to make the stores work.

As he continued to wrestle with the start-up challenges, Weston was struck by what he described as a "simple but profound insight." He began thinking of KFC-Japan not as a fast food company but as a firm in the fashion industry.

> Recognizing that we were selling to young, trendy Japanese who wanted to emulate American habits helped us develop a totally new strategic vision. It also led to lots of changes. First, it meant we had to focus on Tokyo since this was the center of fashion and the source of new trends in Japan. Then we began to focus all marketing efforts on our target group—upscale young couples and children.

These decisions resulted in further changes in product and market strategy. To build volume, stores were located not in suburban shopping centers but near key stations on the commuter lines. High rents and limited space forced them to reduce the standard store size to less than half the area specified in the KFC operations manual. This meant kitchens and equipment had to be totally redesigned. To build volume Loy and his team also decided to add fried fish and smoked chicken products—two favorite foods of the Japanese—to the menu. They also adjusted prices to compete with a typical take-out Japanese pork dish called *katsudon*. Advertising increasingly deviated from KFC themes, and to accommodate smaller Japanese appetites, "mini-barrels" with 12 rather than the U.S. standard of 21 chicken pieces were introduced. All these

decisions, Loy Weston proudly acclaimed, were made locally, without consulting corporate headquarters.

By the end of 1972, the company had opened 14 new stores, most of them in Tokyo. In 1973, 50 more were added. Weston was optimistic that 1974 would be the year KFC-J would turn its first profit. Then the oil crisis hit the Japanese economy, and continuing losses forced a refinancing and a slowdown in store expansion. Loy felt he was starting all over again.

U.S. Operations: Facing Difficulties

Meanwhile KFC's domestic operations were in turmoil. Many former franchisees who had become corporate executives under Brown either left on their own or were fired. KFC's sales stagnated. There was widespread discontent among the franchisees, some of whom felt the new owners did not understand the chicken business and were not providing the leadership expected from a franchisor. There was even talk of a class action suit against Heublein among the more disgruntled franchisees. Company stores floundered and began underperforming the franchised operations, further convincing franchisees that the company did not know its own business. Even founder Colonel Sanders was reported to be unhappy, telling a group of journalists that the "chain's gravy was beginning to acquire the look and taste of wallpaper paste." Such disarray was a boon for competitors. The emerging Church's franchise and a number of regional chains began to cut deeply into KFC's dominance of the market.

Not only had growth stopped, but by 1976 KFC's sales actually showed a four-year decline of 8 percent. Store-level profits were declining 26 percent annually. As

Dick Mayer was to recount later, "Quality, service, and cleanliness [in the company-owned stores] were just terrible . . . Product ratings were inconsistent, standards were almost nonexistent, service time was highly variable, employees were often surly, and the buildings were dirty and run-down." In this period, Heublein was not keen on committing funds to what appeared to be a lost cause. Except for sending a few cost-cutting experts to help ease the cash flow problems, management did little to deal with the developing crisis. The prevailing attitude seemed to be that they were in a competitive segment of a saturated industry, and better opportunities lay in diversification.

THE LATE 1970s: NEW DIRECTION

KFC-I: Changes in Management

In late 1975, Michael Miles was appointed vice president of international operations for Heublein. At the time, he had had no international experience. Miles had a journalism degree from Northwestern and, before joining KFC in 1971, had spent 10 years with the Leo Burnett Advertising Agency, where he had been responsible for the Colonel Sanders account. In 1972, he was named a Heublein vice president and became the head of the Grocery Products Division, which marketed the Grey Poupon, Ortega, and A1 Steak Sauce brands. In that capacity, he initiated and completed the first strategic plan for the company. Strategic planning was to become his credo.

As vice president of the international group, Miles was responsible for all of Heublein's international operations, which were primarily its offshore KFC stores and its non-U.S. liquor business. He quickly decided that the collection of largely autonomous KFC subsidiaries would require most of his attention. The performance of many of them left much to be desired. The few operating standards that had been communicated were poorly controlled. Even the basic menu varied widely—South Africa offering hamburgers, Australia serving roast chicken, Japan with its fish, and Brazil with a full-scale wide-choice menu. Some, like KFC-J, had yet to achieve break-even, and other more established operations had begun to show declining profits. Many cited market saturation and more competitive environments as the reason for these poor results. Miles approached the international operations with a firm conviction that overseas subsidiaries needed more support and control from corporate headquarters, and that a good strategic planning system was the basic starting point. (See Exhibit 1B for organizational impact of changes.)

Recognizing that he was in unfamiliar territory, however, Miles moved with deliberation. He saw planning essentially as an approach to foster a thought process among the country managers. He wanted those individuals who knew how to run the business to make the plans and implement them. Despite immense resistance from the subsidiaries, he persisted in his efforts, and the subsidiaries gradually began adopting his strategic planning approach.

Miles also offered to help the subsidiaries develop new marketing skills. Through periodic seminars he introduced them to market research and new techniques in television advertising that would enhance brand awareness. After about two years, most of the subsidiaries had learned to use these tools and were beginning to apply them routinely.

KFC (Japan): Maturing Operations

In recalling Miles's efforts to introduce planning systems, Loy Weston was blunt:

> One fine morning, he rolled out this nine-page planning document. Headquarters wanted all kinds of data—environment conditions, strengths and weaknesses of our operation, objectives for the next five years, projections, action plans, and so on. It was useless for our needs. It was the same thing with marketing. They said we should be more professional. They asked us to hire a market research company to do a consumer survey. We paid a lot of money for that, and what did it show? That people bought our chicken because it tasted good. Fascinating!

Shin Ohkawara was a little less blunt, but also appeared somewhat skeptical:

> It was ironic. Here we had built our business from scratch with no assistance from the United States and were finally approaching break-even. In contrast to the situation in the States, our stores were known for their quality, service, and cleanliness, and we had a highly motivated team. Yet the people from the United States were trying to teach us how to manage. They even sent over an American controller so their monthly reports would be filled in correctly.
>
> But we learned to live with it. The strategic planning exercises actually helped us by forcing us to project and to quantify uncertainty for the first time. Of course, we adapted it to Japanese practices. Our Presidents Review is a handwritten document that comes up from all sections and is collated into two 3-inch-thick books. We go through this process the first month of the year—not six months ahead as required by the U.S. planning cycle, and obviously not in their prescribed format.

> We also learned how to manage our relationships with headquarters better. We learned the rules of the game, like "never show a big jump" and "manage sales and profit to show consistent growth."

In 1976, KFC-J reported its first profit, a modest 14 million yen. Miles offered warm congratulations all around.

THE EARLY 1980s: REORGANIZATION

Headquarters Changes: U.S. Turnaround

During the latter half of the 1970s, KFC's domestic operations continued to slide to the point that the problems could no longer be ignored. In early 1977, Mike Miles was given the company's most challenging assignment: to find out what was wrong with the U.S. business, which accounted for two-thirds of KFC's worldwide sales, and fix it. Miles asked Dick Mayer, who was Heublein's vice president for marketing and planning in the Grocery Products Group, to come to KFC's Louisville headquarters to help with this Herculean task. Mayer worked with Miles and played a major role in developing a turnaround strategy for KFC.

Just as he had done in international, Miles's first act as president of Kentucky Fried Chicken was to introduce a strategic planning process. His analysis identified that the company had lost touch with its customers and was being outflanked by aggressive new competitors such as Church's. The centerpiece of Miles's turnaround program was what he called a "back-to-basics" program. It stressed quality, service, and cleanliness (QSC) inspections by headquarters-directed mystery shoppers, training programs, strict management control systems, five-year rolling plans, a revamped advertising approach, investments to improve the visual image of stores, and effective franchise relationships.

By 1979, these various programs were beginning to show results. Average sales per store turned around and began increasing at a better than 10 percent per annum rate. Store-level profits rebounded even more dramatically, bringing them close to the levels of industry leader McDonald's.

In July 1981, with his reputation greatly enhanced, Mike Miles was named senior vice president responsible for all Heublein's food products in the United States and internationally. Immediately, his attention returned to KFC's foreign subsidiaries, where he saw great opportunity to benefit from the techniques just applied so successfully in turning around the U.S. operations.

Soon after taking charge of KFC-I, Miles made three important organizational changes. First, he decided that the international operations could learn more from the U.S. experience if the KFC-I headquarters were moved back to Louisville with the rest of KFC. Second, he hired as the new president of KFC-I a professional manager with extensive experience in consumer products marketing (with Procter & Gamble) and general management (with the Swift Group of Esmark Corporation). Third, he expanded the staff expertise at KFC-I headquarters to reinforce the planning, service, and control functions he felt were required (Exhibit 2).

Bob Hiatt, the new president of KFC-I, outlined his broad objectives:

> When I came here in September 1981, the strategic planning mode was well on its way, but the subsidiaries' independent heritage was still clearly evident. Our objective was to convince them that

better strategic plans meant better bottom-line results. In operating terms, you could say our aim was and is to achieve consistency and control worldwide. We want consistency of products and facilities, and we need to control the production and marketing approaches if we are to maintain that consistency.

Gary Buhrow, vice president of strategic planning for KFC-I, discussed the changes in his area of responsibility:

> Up to 1981 planning in international had really been a perfunctory exercise. Miles wanted me to make it a more integrated, ongoing activity. To ensure consistency, we developed a standard format to be used by all subsidiaries, we adopted a five-year rolling plan process, and we implemented a more formal staged review procedure (Exhibit 3). As might be expected, the country managers were not overjoyed.

Donald Lee was the financial vice president at KFC-I. Earlier he had been the international controller and had also served at Heublein headquarters in the finance area. He said:

> The number of reports we require has multiplied over the years (Exhibit 4). But we don't apply our requirements rigidly. KFC-Japan is a good example. They balked when we introduced the new capital expenditure approval procedure for new store openings, and argued that they had traditionally been making such investment decisions without headquarters approval. They also said that Mitsubishi did not require prior approval. So we agreed to give them a blanket approval for capital expenditures in the beginning of the year. The problem is that by making such exceptions you weaken the whole system, leaving yourself open for other subsidiaries to demand similar treatment.

In general, we tend to treat the folks in Japan with kid gloves. Loy claims that staff interference will only stifle him. But Loy and Shin cannot take this autonomy business too far. They must realize they are part of a company with lots of opportunities and needs. We need procedures like the capital expenditure approval so we can make sensible choices among competing demands. In Tokyo, they think that we should take a long-term view and ignore short-term losses. But the reality is we are an American public company and Wall Street will start screaming if the quarterly earnings dip.

In addition to the strategic and financial systems, a new set of controls was introduced at this time. The international operations group was established to transfer to KFC's overseas companies some of the database management systems that had been so helpful in turning around its U.S. business. Gary Masterton, a key manager in the international operations group, explained:

Our objectives are simple—to increase efficiency and ensure standards on a worldwide basis. The product is sacred, and we must do all we can to ensure its quality and consistency. The sooner we get back to basics—eliminating the ribs in England and the fish in Japan—the sooner we can get control and squeeze out cost savings. And if the U.S. operations were able to use our database system to help drive up per store sales by 60 percent and to double store-level margins in less than six years, we'd be crazy not to try to learn from them in our overseas units.

The new operations control systems asked for store-level information on numbers of chickens, customer traffic, ticket average, menu mix, and speed of service. The availability of comparable data on a worldwide basis, as well as some expert input such as time and motion studies to establish labor efficiencies, allowed management to set standards, measure performance, and reward store managers. Efficiency targets, QSC ratings, and performance bonus levels were introduced, and reports on trends at the store level were produced.

The subsidiaries' reactions to the new database operations system varied. For example, New Zealand adopted it with enthusiasm, but in Australia there was a lot of resistance. But there had been a disturbing deterioration in quality, service, and cleanliness in the Australian outlets in recent years, and the Louisville operations group used the resulting decline in sales and profits as the opportunity to step in and implement the back-to-basics program and the supporting database system. Japan also questioned its need to adopt the new systems and programs and challenged headquarters' ideas. Louisville management emphasized it was trying not to be too dogmatic and was willing to adapt the system to their special needs. "We don't ram it down their throats, but we do want the system operating universally," said Masterton. "Those that accept it find it can be a very useful system they can apply locally, and not just data sent back to headquarters for control. We want this to be one of *their* management tools."

KFC (Japan) Reaction

The new management direction and systems of 1981 did not sit well with Loy Weston:

We are slowly being reduced to the role of order-takers. In the first year after Miles came back, we had 22 man-weeks of visitors from the corporate headquarters. Quality control audits, computer people, planners, operations guys, and so on. They questioned everything from our store designs to the smoked chicken, yogurt, and fish on our menu. They gave us hurdle rates for real estate and operating instructions straight from the American manuals.

They acted as if they had all the answers and we knew nothing. Just because they had introduced crispy chicken in the United States, they thought we should too. I knew it wouldn't work. But I agreed to a test market. It bombed. They didn't like our TV commercials so they made one for us that was so inappropriate we never aired it. Finally, I had to remind them they couldn't do this. We are a joint venture, not a wholly owned subsidiary.

Shin Ohkawara sounded philosophical:

I guess it is all inevitable as we change from a venture-oriented to a professionally managed company. They want us to follow their ideas. OK, we will give them a try. But we kept thinking there were lots of ways they could also learn from us. For instance, we felt that our 12-piece "mini-barrel" could be a big success elsewhere. And our small store layouts, with their flexible kitchen design, might be very suitable for U.S. shopping malls. We were even experimenting with chicken nuggets in 1981 until we were told to stop.

What worries me, though, is this constant pressure from the United States for improved margins. (Incidentally, Mitsubishi has never asked us for more profit.) People at headquarters want to know why we have not raised prices for four years now, and only twice in the last 12 years. By pricing our products just 20 percent above supermarket fresh chicken prices, we have expanded demand tremendously. If we use the U.S. pricing formula we will just invite competition.

New Challenges

Just as its new international programs were shaping up, KFC entered an important new chapter in its history. Attracted by Heublein's solid sales growth and strong profit performance, R.J. Reynolds (RJR) acquired the company in October 1982 as part of its continuing strategy of diversifying away from tobacco products (Exhibit 5 shows overall Heublein performance by business). Soon thereafter, Mike Miles was offered the opportunity to become president of Dart and Kraft and was succeeded as chairman and chief executive of KFC by Richard Mayer.

Mayer, an MBA from Rutgers, had begun his career at General Foods. He joined Heublein in 1973 as director of business development and subsequently became vice president of strategic planning and marketing at the time Miles was trying to get the company to take a more sophisticated approach to such matters. As the driving force behind KFC's more professional management approach, Mayer held strong convictions about the value of strategic planning:

Strategic planning pervades everything we do at KFC. It has brought great and effective change to our business and the way we market. (But) it clearly reduced marketing's ability to "do its own thing." As more people knew precisely what was going on, there was less tap dancing and more accountability in the marketing function. For example, all menu and pricing proposals required exhaustive marketing analysis. Proposals were reviewed by top management and evaluated by how they would help meet long-term strategic goals, not quarter-to-quarter earnings spikes . . .

Our best marketing people have become even better after exposure to the planning process. They quickly saw the logic and applied this tool to improve the business ... and their careers. Our weaker performers—the "tap dancers" who never saw the light—are now tap dancing on someone else's stage.

As he reviewed the international operations, Dick Mayer focused a good deal of time on KFC-Japan. Not only was it one of KFC-I's largest, fastest-growing, and highest-potential units, but in many ways it reflected the challenges that faced the company's entire international operations. Four issues seemed of particular importance in Japan, and indeed for KFC-I.

The most fundamental issue concerned the appropriate level of performance expectations for the overseas units (Exhibit 6 shows KFC-J's growth record). For example, although KFC-Japan expected to open its 400th store by the end of 1983, on a per-capita basis this represented less than one-quarter the level of penetration in the United States. And penetration levels in other countries were even lower. Mayer felt it was important for management to resist the temptation to regard the more established overseas units as mature. KFC-I had to maintain its drive for aggressive growth. But what did he need to do to ensure that such growth would continue?

The second challenge related to the overall issue of headquarters control of international operations. Mayer was aware of resistance to the administrative operational controls and systems and considered how hard he should push for their implementation. For example, how could headquarters turn a blind eye to the fact that some overseas units were force-fitting their numbers to meet hurdle rates, submitting approval forms after decisions had been implemented, and writing management reports to appease headquarters

rather than provide proper analysis? Should they be willing to accept operational variations like the Japanese company's continued resistance to suggestions that it give up its obsession with menu expansion and devote more attention to improving the basics of its operations? At headquarters, managers claimed there was proven evidence that menu diversity affected the bottom line and hurt quality, but Japan rejected both notions.

A third important issue Mayer identified was the continuing problem of how to expand into new countries. Six countries (Japan, Australia, South Africa, New Zealand, the United Kingdom, and Germany) accounted for over 95 percent of overseas earnings, and over the past decade numerous attempts to expand into a variety of new countries had met with very limited success (see Exhibit 7). A diversity of opinion existed on how the company should proceed. Gary Buhrow, vice president–strategic planning, felt the company had to move away from the highly opportunistic and people-dependent approach of the past:

> The world is more complicated than it was 15 years ago. We have to pay more attention to political risks, currency risks, and legal issues. And we need more sophisticated measures of market potential. We have begun to develop a capability at headquarters, a systematic analysis and comparison of new market risks and opportunities. This has helped us prepare a list of priority international market opportunities for KFC. In addition, when managers make market entry proposals and present details of their entry strategy, we have much more data against which to evaluate it and to set financial and operational expectations.

Loy Weston, on the other hand, felt that the string of failures and below-expectation performances in new markets could be tied directly to the deviation from John Y. Brown's mud-on-the-map approach of selecting entrepreneurs, giving them the challenge, and leaving them alone. He explained:

> Expansion into new markets requires a combination of sensitivity and entrepreneurial spark that is found in a different kind of person from your normal breed of corporate officer. When you find the right person—someone with energy, vision, imagination, and, above all, willingness to make quick and unorthodox decisions —you have to leave him alone. You can't succeed if there are constant audits, visits, and forms to fill in for headquarters.
>
> Hong Kong is a perfect example of what not to do. They sent an insensitive and patronizing Australian who saw himself as a high-powered corporate executive. He breezed in, hired a secretary, bought a Mercedes, and immediately began driving around to inspect potential sites. There was no effort to understand local tastes or customs. He paid exorbitant prices for the sites, entered a joint venture with, of all parties, a U.K.-based conglomerate, and set up standard stores with standard menus. When stores opened, he was not close to the operations and wasn't even aware that the fish meal–fed chicken he was buying had a strong unpleasant taste. It was a total disaster.

Dick Mayer had an open mind on the issue. But he was concerned that KFC had such limited positions in Korea, Taiwan, Thailand, and Hong Kong—four of the highest-priority countries identified by the new market potential analysis. He learned that these countries were the responsibility of Loy Weston who, four years earlier, had been named vice president for the

North Pacific. Shin Ohkawara had succeeded Weston as president and chief executive in Japan, leaving Loy free to concentrate entirely on new market entries, but progress was slow. Mayer wondered if he should leave Weston alone, or whether he should authorize more headquarters involvement at this stage.

The question raised the whole issue of the appropriate management skills required to manage the company's overseas operations, and this topic represented the fourth item on Mayer's list of challenges. In considering the matter, he theorized that there were three stages in country management evolution:

> In the entrepreneurial stage there is not much room for managerial orientation. Loy Weston is a real go-getter. But he is an organizational nightmare who gets great joy in pricking the balloons of bureaucracy. At the second stage, we see the development of local baronies as managers use their local knowledge and developing operating skills to build their autonomy. The third stage is marked by the appearance of professional management who respond to planning, measurement, and business development ideas. Only this group can build for the long term.
>
> Unfortunately, there is a widespread belief that professional managers cannot be venturesome or entrepreneurial. But a fast food operation is inherently an entrepreneurial venture, and the country manager has to deal with the franchisees, who are generally entrepreneurs themselves. If you want to succeed in this business, you can't be a pinstripe type. So by a kind of natural selection, the right types of managers rise to the top. I believe our professional managers can be the source of the entrepreneurial expansion we are looking for.

EXHIBIT 1
KFC-INTERNATIONAL: ORGANIZATIONAL STRUCTURE

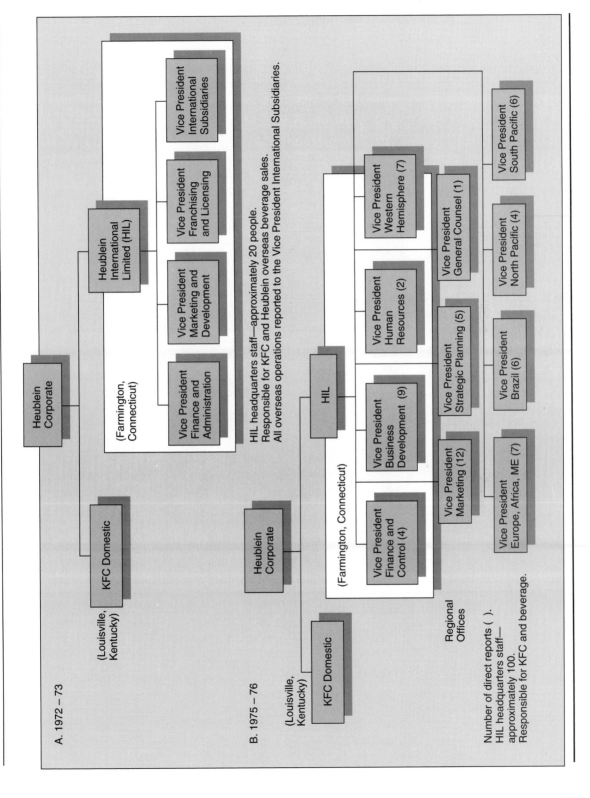

A. 1972 – 73

Heublein Corporate

KFC Domestic
(Louisville, Kentucky)

Heublein International Limited (HIL)
(Farmington, Connecticut)

Vice President Finance and Administration

Vice President Marketing and Development

Vice President Franchising and Licensing

Vice President International Subsidiaries

HIL headquarters staff—approximately 20 people.
Responsible for KFC and Heublein overseas beverage sales.
All overseas operations reported to the Vice President International Subsidiaries.

B. 1975 – 76

Heublein Corporate

KFC Domestic
(Louisville, Kentucky)

HIL
(Farmington, Connecticut)

Vice President Finance and Control (4)

Vice President Business Development (9)

Vice President Human Resources (2)

Vice President Western Hemisphere (7)

Vice President Marketing (12)

Vice President Strategic Planning (5)

Vice President General Counsel (1)

Regional Offices

Vice President Europe, Africa, ME (7)

Vice President Brazil (6)

Vice President North Pacific (4)

Vice President South Pacific (6)

Number of direct reports ( ).
HIL headquarters staff—approximately 100.
Responsible for KFC and beverage.

801

EXHIBIT 2
KFC-INTERNATIONAL ORGANIZATION: 1981

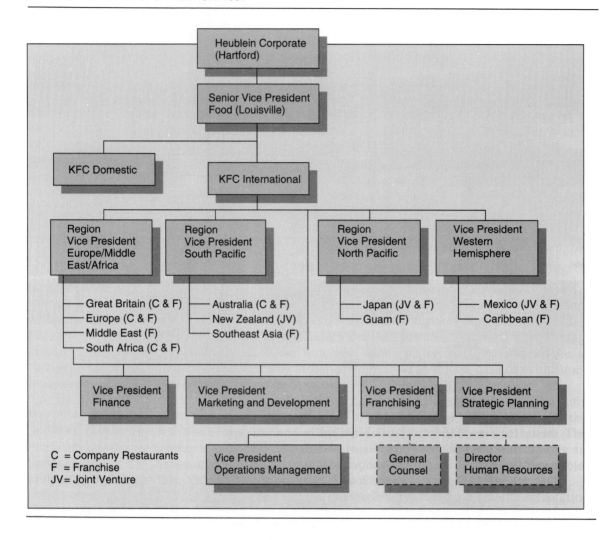

EXHIBIT 3
KFC-I PLANNING CYCLE OF CALENDAR

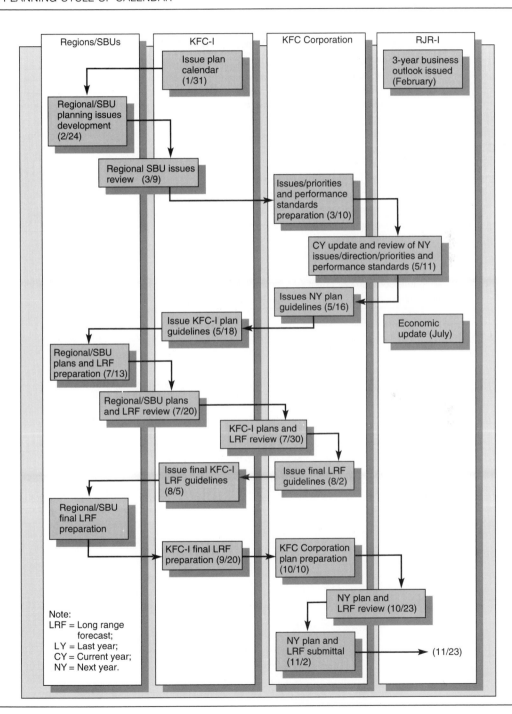

Regions/SBUs | KFC-I | KFC Corporation | RJR-I

Issue plan calendar (1/31)

3-year business outlook issued (February)

Regional/SBU planning issues development (2/24)

Regional SBU issues review (3/9)

Issues/priorities and performance standards preparation (3/10)

CY update and review of NY issues/direction/priorities and performance standards (5/11)

Issues NY plan guidelines (5/16)

Issue KFC-I plan guidelines (5/18)

Economic update (July)

Regional/SBU plans and LRF preparation (7/13)

Regional/SBU plans and LRF review (7/20)

KFC-I plans and LRF review (7/30)

Issue final KFC-I LRF guidelines (8/5)

Issue final LRF guidelines (8/2)

Regional/SBU final LRF preparation

KFC-I final LRF preparation (9/20)

KFC Corporation plan preparation (10/10)

NY plan and LRF review (10/23)

NY plan and LRF submittal (11/2)

(11/23)

Note:
LRF = Long range forecast;
LY = Last year;
CY = Current year;
NY = Next year.

EXHIBIT 4
LIST OF REPORTING SCHEDULES IN THE MONTHLY
FINANCIAL PACKAGE

1.	Statement of Earnings—Local Currency: Current Month
1A.	Statement of Earnings—Local Currency: Year-to-Date
2.	Statement of Earnings—U.S. $
3.	Full Year Forecast—Local Currency
4.	Current Forecast—U.S. $: Full Year
4A.	Current Forecast—U.S. $: Quarter by Month
5.	Balance Sheet
6.	Balance Sheet Variance Analysis
7.	Other Earnings Data
8.	Personnel Status Report
8A.	Equivalent Employee Analysis
9.	Capital Expenditure Status Report
10.	Intercompany Transactions—Statement of Earnings
11.	Store Closing Report—Reserve Reconciliation
11A.	Store Closing Report—Explanation
12.	Risks and Opportunities
13.	Receivables Management Report
14.	Intercompany Account Reconciliation
14A.	Intercompany Charges/Payments

Source: KFC-International.

EXHIBIT 5
SUMMARY FINANCIAL DATA OF HEUBLEIN, INC.

The company operated worldwide principally in four business segments: production and marketing of distilled spirits and prepared cocktails (Spirits); production and/or marketing of wines and brandies (Wines); production and sale of specialty food products (Grocery); and operating and franchising principally Kentucky Fried Chicken restaurants (Restaurants). The business segment information for each of the five years ended June 30 is presented below:

(in thousands)	1982	1981	1980	1979	1978
Revenues:					
Spirits	$ 877,041	$ 876,546	$ 883,419	$ 819,563	$ 742,575
Wines	387,130	378,497	386,938	368,972	324,794
Grocery	173,545	153,552	131,511	114,193	118,160
Restaurants	699,687	641,526	520,011	466,346	434,583
Consolidated	$2,137,403	$2,050,121	$1,921,879	$1,769,074	$1,620,112
Operating profit:					
Spirits	$ 114,696	$ 107,078	$ 93,341	$ 87,599	$ 73,105
Wines	25,965	26,551	32,655	29,422	28,895
Grocery	26,447	21,545	17,904	17,989	17,949
Restaurants	84,087	69,126	51,302	34,966	26,711
Consolidated	251,195	224,300	195,202	169,976	146,660
Interest expense	33,214	28,581	25,361	23,106	25,041
Corporate and miscellaneous—net	20,251	27,683	22,933	15,851	12,319
Income before income taxes	$ 197,730	$ 168,036	$ 146,908	$ 131,019	$ 109,300
Identifiable assets:					
Spirits	$ 312,322	$ 318,695	$ 320,379	$ 300,605	$ 272,257
Wines	310,984	318,137	308,445	281,969	221,748
Grocery	58,389	61,601	63,219	66,696	61,170
Restaurants	353,882	316,519	276,682	242,266	227,659
Corporate	140,531	107,900	80,067	80,382	100,412
Consolidated	$1,176,108	$1,122,852	$1,048,792	$ 971,918	$ 883,246

Source: Form 10-K reports.

EXHIBIT 6
KFC-JAPAN PERFORMANCE CHARTS, 1978–1982

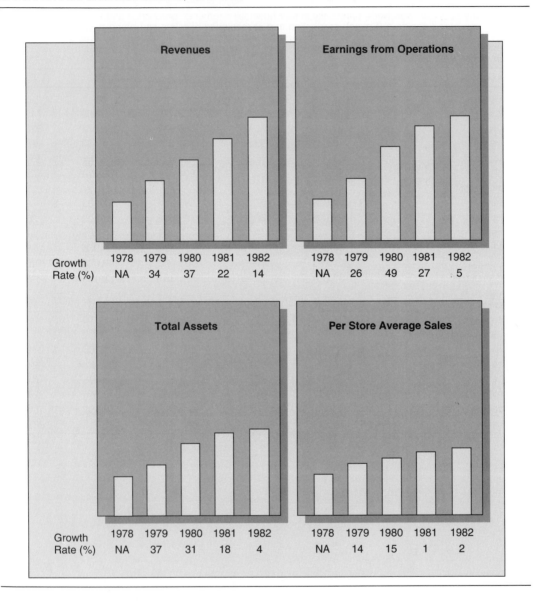

EXHIBIT 7
KFC SUBSIDIARIES ABROAD IN 1983

Country	Number of Stores Company	Number of Stores Franchise	Number of Stores Total	Country	Number of Stores Company	Number of Stores Franchise	Number of Stores Total
Europe, Middle East, and Africa				**North Pacific**			
South Africa	48	95	143	Japan	149	270	419
Great Britain	61	308	369	Guam	—	3	3
Germany	3	11	14	Saipan	—	1	1
Holland	5	2	7				
Spain	4	6	10		149	274	423
Denmark	—	3	3	**Western Hemisphere**			
Iceland	—	1	1				
Sweden	—	1	1	Argentina	—	1	1
Switzerland	—	1	1	Aruba	—	1	1
Kuwait	—	15	15	Bahamas	—	11	11
U.A.E.	—	10	10	Barbados	—	3	3
Saudi Arabia	—	7	7	Bermuda	—	1	1
Bahrain	—	2	2	Curaçao	—	3	3
Qatar	—	1	1	Grand Cayman	—	1	1
Lebanon	—	2	2	Haiti	—	3	3
Yemen	—	2	2	Jamaica	—	10	10
Egypt	—	6	6	Martinique	—	1	1
				St. Maarten	—	1	1
	121	473	594	St. Croix	—	3	3
South Pacific				St. Thomas	—	3	3
				Trinidad	—	8	8
Australia	157	69	226	Costa Rica	—	4	4
Fiji	—	1	1	Panama	—	7	7
Indonesia	—	20	20	Ecuador	—	5	5
Malaysia	—	27	27	Paraguay	—	1	1
New Zealand	42	—	42	Peru	—	4	4
Philippines	—	15	15	Venezuela	—	1	1
Singapore	—	23	23	Puerto Rico	26	—	26
				Mexico	38	18	56
	199	155	354		64	90	154
				Grand Total	533	992	1,525

Source: KFC-International.

Cleveland Twist Drill (A)

"Run a tight ship and manage for cash."

This was the seemingly uncomplicated mandate given by Acme-Cleveland's CEO Chuck Ames to Jim Bartlett when Bartlett assumed the presidency of Cleveland Twist Drill (CTD)—a subsidiary of Acme-Cleveland Corporation—in August 1981.

The economy, however, had been souring; sales and profitability were declining considerably. Rather than fine-tuning a sound business, Jim Bartlett soon found himself overhauling CTD's entire organization and strategy. He realized that his immediate priorities were to make CTD competitive in labor costs and to rationalize a product line that had proliferated to over 16,000 products.

His approach to these goals, however, had somewhat disoriented the old-line management, who found it difficult to accept the dramatic change in the character and direction of this 107-year-old company. Conse-

quently, Bartlett brought in a new team and replaced virtually all of the inherited department heads, many of whom had devoted their entire careers to the company.

Although Bartlett felt he had been able to formulate the main elements of a turnaround, he knew some major unresolved problems still stood in the way of achieving his objectives. To address the issue of labor costs, Bartlett had to decide whether he should (1) request from the Acme-Cleveland board $17 million to build new manufacturing facilities in lower-cost locations or (2) attempt to win concessions from the existing workforce in Cleveland. Even if Bartlett got the relocation funds, he was unsure how he should handle the prospect of major workforce reductions in Cleveland. In addition, Bartlett faced a host of other problems in consolidating CTD's operations and changing its strategy: How could the unwieldy product line be rationalized? How could he maintain morale and a sense of purpose during a period of retrenchment? How could he turn a manufacturing-driven company into a marketing-driven one?

INDUSTRY BACKGROUND

In 1981 Cleveland Twist Drill was the second largest U.S. manufacturer of cutting tools. The high-speed drills, reamers, taps, dies, gauges, end mills, saws, cutters, and other products of this approximately $1 billion industry were used primarily in metalworking, where they were expendable "razor blades" in machining and metal removal (see Exhibit 1).

The cutting tool industry was mature, with little prospect of long-term real growth. In fact, unit demand had declined approximately 1 percent to 2 percent per year during the 1970s. Three major trends were evident:

1. conglomerate acquisition of privately owned firms,
2. a change in product demand, and
3. increasing foreign competition.

Industry Undergoes Changes in Ownership

Until the late 1960s, all of the firms in the expendable cutting tool industry were privately owned. Between 1965 and 1970, however, most were acquired by conglomerates such as Litton, TRW, and Bendix. During this period, Cleveland Twist Drill merged with National Acme, a machine tool manufacturer, to form Acme-Cleveland and reduce the probability of being acquired by a much larger company. Since more than half of Acme-Cleveland's top management came from Cleveland Twist Drill, the latter was able to remain relatively unchanged. But CTD's competitors changed rapidly from family-owned and family-managed concerns to publicly owned and professionally managed firms.

In the early 1970s United Greenfield, a TRW subsidiary and CTD's largest competitor, built a major new facility in Augusta, Georgia. CTD did not build its first southern plant until almost nine years later, and even then the new plant's output was an insignificant percentage of the company's total production.

Change in Product Demand

New materials, technologies, and methods were steadily reducing demand for the industry's bread-and-butter product, high-speed steel drills. Titanium nitride coatings and carbide solid and tipped tools, while priced higher than steel, had a significantly longer wear life. Lasers were being used increasingly as a cutting medium, and a shift from fastening to bonding of metal parts eliminated the need for drills.

Also affecting demand was a trend from specialty to commodity products in much of the market. Traditionally, cutting tool manufacturers had established close working relationships with the manufacturing and engineering departments of their customers. This enabled them to demonstrate the technical superiority of their products and qualified them to bid on high-quality jobs that commanded a price premium. The entry of new competitors and the centralization of purchasing in many large companies increased the importance of price in the buying decision. This, together with a shrinkage of perceived quality differentiation between top-line manufacturers like CTD and the new entrants, had divided the marketplace into a large commodity-like segment and a small high-quality segment. In the commodity segment, service was less valued, and many manufacturers sold directly to the end users through their sales force.[1]

Increased Competition

In the mid-1970s CTD's major end-user customers, such as Boeing, began informing CTD of the availability of high-quality tools at a lower price from Canada, Japan, and Yugoslavia. CTD management felt that this competition was in the lower price and quality end of the market and hence not a significant threat. Competition continued to increase, however, as Japanese and Western European manufacturers increased their shares of the American market. In addition, automated equipment for producing cutting tools eliminated many key skills normally required in manufacturing a quality product, thus opening the door for competition from Third World and Eastern bloc countries. Also, small, "short-line" specialists based in the United States were gaining ground against major competitors like CTD.

COMPANY BACKGROUND

Cleveland Twist Drill was founded in 1876 by Jacob Dolson Cox in partnership with C. C. Newton. Although neither of Cox's two sons followed in his father's footsteps, the business continued to grow under family ownership. CTD's growth paralleled the growth of industrial distributors, and it was through its distributor network that CTD became the dominant force in the industry. Bert Finlay, vice president for sales and marketing

who had joined the company in 1956, recalled:

> From 1930 to 1950 CTD concentrated on building market share and distribution channels. When I came aboard in 1956, CTD had control of the marketplace and maintained that position right up to the Vietnam War. The distributors having the CTD line had virtual entrée to any other line [of complementary industrial products].

In 1968 Arthur Armstrong, Cox's son-in-law and CTD's chief executive, engineered a merger with the slightly larger National Acme. As stated in their first combined annual report:

> The result is a major resource for production systems, know-how, tools, and automated machines which increase efficiency and reduce costs. Virtually every product manufactured by industry, from surgical needles to automobiles to spacecraft, requires products such as we design, produce, and market throughout the free world.

The new company grew rapidly, from combined sales of $109 million in 1968 to $405 million by 1980. Profits increased more slowly, from $9 million to $16 million. (See Exhibit 2 for financial highlights.) Some old-timers saw this merger as a turning point for CTD. According to one:

> This was the beginning of the decline. There really was no synergy in the two businesses getting together. National Acme was the sick company which never got well. The top management of the merged company tried to bail out National Acme's business by using CTD's resources. As a result they did not pay enough attention, or allocate enough resources, to keep CTD in the forefront. As business boomed, we could not make our

---

[1] In 1981 approximately 60 percent of cutting tools were sold through industrial distributors and 40 percent by company sales forces.

delivery commitments. Though the product quality was good, Manufacturing was not responsive to the needs of the customer; Product and Applications Engineering and Sales would want to respond to the customers' needs, and Manufacturing would not, and therein lay the conflict.

Enter Jim Bartlett

After graduating from the Harvard Business School in 1961, Jim Bartlett joined McKinsey & Co. in New York City. Two years later he was selected to move to Cleveland, where McKinsey was opening a new office. The partner in charge was Chuck Ames.

After five years with McKinsey, Jim went into the venture capital business, first with Laird & Co. and then with a group of partners. Their business was essentially one of acquiring privately held companies ranging from $2 million to $30 million in revenues. Jim's group increased the companies' profitability, installed professional management, and then sold them at a gain. In his 15-year involvement in venture capital, Jim and his partners actively invested in and managed roughly 20 privately held manufacturing businesses. Not only did they achieve a solid return on their investment, but Jim found this work challenging and satisfying. A minority investor and participant in some of Jim's ventures was Chuck Ames, his old boss and mentor from McKinsey.

In 1972 Ames left McKinsey to become president and chief operating officer of Reliance Electric Company. In 1976 he was made chief executive officer. During his tenure, Reliance's sales rose from $339 million in 1972 to $1.34 billion in 1979, net earnings rose from $13.6 million to $67.9 million, and ROE went from 11 percent to 22 percent. In 1979 Reliance was acquired by Exxon for $1.2 billion. Chuck Ames resigned a year after the acquisition was completed.

For over 10 years Arthur Armstrong, the chief executive officer of Acme-Cleveland, had been a member of the board of directors at Reliance. By 1980 Armstrong and his key associate and successor, Paul Cooper, decided to reach out to Chuck Ames to lead Acme-Cleveland through the coming difficult period. Ames, having served on the board of Acme-Cleveland, was familiar with the situation facing the firm.

Shortly after he became president in January 1981, Ames called Jim Bartlett and offered him the presidency of his Cleveland Twist Drill division. "I need management," Chuck said to Jim, but Jim Bartlett was not interested. His venture capital firm had just bought another company, which he was in the process of guiding through the transition to professional management. Despite Jim's initial lack of interest, Chuck continued to pursue him. Finally, in March 1981, Jim agreed to join Acme-Cleveland as president of Cleveland Twist Drill. But he could not start until August because he had to wind up his affairs and help find some professional management for the company he was running.

Between March and August, Bartlett had several discussions with Chuck Ames about CTD's history, present status, and mission. According to Jim, Ames's perception was that CTD was a very solid business that merely needed a good general manager who could set an explicit long-term strategy. Ames and the rest of Acme's board considered CTD as "solid as the Bank of England . . . number one in the industry . . . a flagship company . . . with unassailable strength."

JIM BARTLETT'S FIRST NINE MONTHS

Strategic Planning at CTD

When Bartlett arrived, CTD was in the midst of preparing its 1982 budget and sales forecasts. He decided to involve himself in the process right away and asked to see management's strategic plans. Bartlett described what he found:

> For at least three years prior to my arrival, the strategic planning process had consisted primarily of the top management of the division getting together at a hotel and committing to some broad goals which did not change much from year to year, except for increased sales and profit projections. Their strategy could best be captured by the opening statement of the five-year, long-range plan developed in 1978: "In 1983 CTD will be the same as it is today, but different. The essential difference will be REAL GROWTH in sales and profits, as compared with 1978." The opening sentence of the 1980 five-year, long-range plan was exactly the same: "In 1985 CTD will be the same as it is today, but different. The essential difference will be REAL GROWTH in sales and profits, as compared with 1980 results."

This real growth in sales was projected as shown in Table A.

TABLE A
CTD'S PROJECTED REAL GROWTH IN SALES AND PROFITS ($ MILLIONS)

	1978	1979	1980	1981	1982	1983
1978 Plan	$92	$103	$114	$126	$146	$160
1980 Plan	—	—	$126	$133	$156	$183

Profit growth was projected at 6 percent of sales in the 1978 plan and was raised to 6.5 percent in the 1980 plan. As for the actual strategies to achieve these projections, Bartlett said:

> This was merely an exercise where the outside consultant who had been brought in would ask the managers everything they would like to do during the next five years. As a result, the major strategies for the last three years were generalizations that did not amount to much. Their key strategy statements were (1) to achieve increased productivity in manufacturing and throughout all division operations; (2) to achieve conversion from purchased to manufactured for major items now resold; (3) to provide management depth and skilled employees required to achieve the division's long-range growth goals; (4) to be more responsive to the physical, emotional, and social needs of employees and to the needs of our communities; and (5) to expand international market participation.
>
> Upon learning this, I immediately came to the conclusion that planning would have to change because we needed to develop much more relevant strategies. Besides, Chuck Ames had already suspended these kinds of long-range planning efforts and asked the divisions to focus on their short-term results. In a memo to the division heads, Chuck had written, "I would suggest that the operating division heads begin to think through the strategy they will employ to raise the return on sales of their division to 7 percent on a continuing basis. And that all of us think in terms of the strategy required to achieve, on a continuing basis, returns of 7 percent on sales, 22 percent on equity, and 14 percent growth rate in earnings per share."

Bartlett indicated how the 1982 plans were completed:

When I arrived, CTD was about to complete fiscal 1981. At that time we expected the sales volume for the year to come in at about $120 million, and the people there had viewed the results for the year as being pretty good. Like most others at that time, the people in the division had assumed that the economy would rebound in 1982, and so the forecast of $140 million for 1982 seemed pretty reasonable to me.

Within six months into the fiscal year Bartlett realized that not only would he not achieve his forecast but he would be hard-pressed to even do as well as the last year. He felt the plan relied too heavily on assumptions about economic recovery, which did not happen. Bartlett believed, however, that this downturn was a double-edged sword. He explained:

> The bad edge of the sword was that the decline in sales had caused considerable profit pressures on the business. The good or opportunity edge of the sword was that these results produced a climate that made it easier to institute strategic changes, which otherwise would have been much more difficult to get people to accept.

Manufacturing

Because CTD was basically a manufacturing company, the next task Bartlett set for himself was to learn about its manufacturing capabilities and vulnerabilities. CTD's facilities comprised 10 acres of manufacturing floor space, including 19 buildings. The main plant, a 5-story, 500,000-square-foot building on top of which sat CTD's headquarters, was located on East 49th Street, just one block from Lake Erie, in a heavily industrialized section of Cleveland. The Cleveland plant complex accounted for 75 percent of domestic production. Another 15 percent was produced in Mansfield, Massachusetts; the remaining 10 percent was produced in Cranston, Rhode Island, and Cynthiana, Kentucky.[2] There were also three foreign plants, but they were of only minor importance.

CTD had traditionally organized its manufacturing operations by process. Grinding was done in one area, testing in another, milling in another, and finishing in yet another. Many of the processes were not even in the same building. One department did nothing but move goods in process from one floor to another, from one building to another, and even between plants in Cleveland, Cynthiana, and Cranston. One result of this practice and the plant layout was that CTD had more indirect than direct labor costs.

When Jim Bartlett arrived, he got involved in the manufacturing budget right away and targeted a $5 million reduction in manufacturing wages. He asked the manager of industrial relations, Gordon Streit, for ideas on how to achieve this. Streit, who was 57 years old and had spent his entire career at CTD, seemed to be confused by this approach and was at a loss for suggestions. According to Bartlett, Streit made some suggestions like "maybe we should cut salaries by 10 percent across the board." Bartlett, finding such responses totally inadequate, fired Streit during his first week at CTD. Needless to

---

[2] In total, CTD had 524,000 square feet of manufacturing space in Cleveland; 65,000 square feet in Mansfield; 49,000 square feet in Cranston; and 145,000 square feet in Cynthiana. The number of hourly employees at these locations was approximately 530, 100, 50, and 90, respectively.

say, Streit was shocked and asked Bartlett, "How can you do this to me? No one has ever told me I was not doing my job well."

Streit was the first among Bartlett's inherited, nine-member top management team to be dismissed. Bartlett commented, "Firing Gordon was an unpleasant and difficult thing to do, and I sensed that most of the employees felt I was shooting from the hip. But I couldn't tolerate a key executive who could not give me any good ideas on the major problems we faced. Of course, we made a generous severance arrangement with Gordon."[3]

Streit was replaced by Jack Sims from the corporate industrial relations staff at Acme-Cleveland. Bartlett asked Sims to investigate how CTD's wages compared with those of competitors. By contacting the Metal Cutting Tool Institute (the industry trade association), Sims was able to develop a comparison between CTD's wages (excluding benefits) and the industry averages (see Table B). When benefits were included, the gap between CTD and its competitors widened to $4.50 per hour in the Cleveland area.

In addition, CTD's productivity and quality were compared with competitors' levels. These studies showed that productivity varied little throughout the industry and that CTD's quality ran somewhat higher. From these studies, Bartlett concluded that CTD was at a competitive disadvantage and that significant changes in manufacturing strategy would be required:

> When I started at CTD, I thought the company was in reasonably good shape

and that I would be addressing the longer-term issue of substitute products. Instead, within the first month or two, I realized that the company faced a very serious and dangerous cost situation that had to be corrected. And with our industry actually decreasing in size and with very tough competition, I concluded that our survival was at stake.

Bartlett then met with the head of manufacturing, Sam Colt—42 years old and described as articulate, soft-spoken, well liked by the rank and file, and a hard worker. Colt had started as a trainee at CTD, had worked his way up, and was considered the number one candidate to succeed to the top position (so Bartlett had been informed upon joining the company). All the manufacturing plants reported to Colt. As a hands-on manager, he knew the production output for every plant on a shift-by-shift and product-by-product basis.

According to Bartlett, when he and Colt started discussing manufacturing strategy, Colt wanted to talk only about operating data. Bartlett had to steer the conversation around to CTD's comparative cost position in order to impress on Colt that CTD was not cost competitive in its present facilities and would always have trouble catching up with competitors that had more efficient facilities.

In October 1981 Bartlett asked Colt to begin work on a change in CTD's manufacturing strategy. In a four-page memo a month later, Bartlett spelled out specifically what he was looking for. The memo began this way:

> The presentation for preliminary five-year plans by each product group is now scheduled for February 25, 1982. These plans will have a major influence on the direction CTD will take in the location and very nature of its manufacturing

---

[3] Streit was given one year's salary as severance pay, was allowed to begin to collect retirement benefits as if he were 65, and was offered the services of an outplacement company at CTD's expense.

TABLE B
COMPARATIVE WAGE ANALYSIS: INDUSTRY VERSUS CTD

Industry Average		CTD Average	
United States (excluding CTD)	$7.51	Mansfield, Mass.	$ 9.89
New York, New England, Mid-Atlantic	7.15	Cranston, R.I.	7.32
Chicago and West	7.55	Cynthiana, Ky.	7.65
Cleveland and Detroit (excluding CTD)	$8.30	Cleveland	$10.67

base. However, as we discussed earlier, there are a number of questions that must be addressed, the answers to which will have a major impact on how we should reposition our manufacturing base. Your responsibility in preparing for the late February meeting is to develop the clearest possible answers to these questions.

There followed a series of questions (see Exhibit 3) listed under four headings: (1) East 49th Street Dispersion; (2) Plant Network Design; (3) Organization and Staffing; and (4) Capital Investment. This memo was never answered to Bartlett's satisfaction, and in February 1982 Sam Colt was fired. Bartlett commented:

> This was a very difficult decision because Sam was so well liked and because he really was just a product of the corporate culture he had grown up in. When I called my first staff meeting, for example, Sam and his people got up to leave when the marketing people arrived. Cross-functional discussion just wasn't part of the culture. Despite all my sympathy and efforts, I realized that it would be impossible to achieve what we had to without someone else in Sam's position.

Sam Colt was replaced by Pete Manzoni, former vice president of manufacturing for Bailey Controls, a division of Babcock & Wilcox. Manzoni explained how he came to join CTD:

> I have always played the stock market, and my investment philosophy is to buy shares in companies where there is some major change or chance for change going on. In about half of the situations, I am able to win big, and in the other half I hope to break even by getting out in time. Thus, when Chuck Ames joined Acme-Cleveland, knowing of his track record at Reliance, I bought a large block of shares in Acme-Cleveland. A year later, when Acme's stock had gone down, and having read in the local papers about management changes at Acme and CTD, I wrote a letter to Ames stating that all he had done was fire a lot of people and changed around positions, but the business meanwhile had continued to go downhill. As a result of this letter, Ames contacted me, and soon I was talking to Jim Bartlett about joining CTD, which I did on March 1, 1982.

After about a month on the job, Manzoni, with Bartlett, began formulating a manufacturing strategy for CTD.

Labor Relations

Only the Cleveland and Mansfield plants were unionized, though with different unions and separate labor agreements. Management's relationship with the workers in Cleveland was not only conflict-free but benevolent and harmonious. While the Mansfield workers were represented by the United Steel Workers union, the Cleveland plant had its own house union.[4] The company's relationship with this union was quite good and rather informal. Until 1969 there was not even a written labor contract. Instead, verbal agreements and clarifying memos were used. All through the 1960s and 1970s, as CTD prospered, it shared its gains generously with its workers. The company was one of the first to provide dental insurance and unlimited medical coverage. A provision in its contract for a cost of living allowance (COLA) was without a cap to enable the workers to recover fully increases in the consumer price index (CPI); moreover, the company had agreed in 1972 to an 8 percent minimum annual COLA, which in 1980 turned out to be slightly higher than the increase in the CPI. CTD also had a long tradition of providing piece-rate incentives for increased productivity, ranging from 25 percent to 40 percent of base salary.

There had never been a layoff in the company's history. During the 1974–1975 recession the salaried employees took a 10 percent cut, but the hourly workers kept working full time and built up inventory that was used later when business picked up. Morale was high, and management and the workers were close; not only the plant manager, but also the president, spent considerable time on the shop floor and knew people by their first names.

Management's benevolence toward its workers included not only financial rewards, but also psychological and social benefits. In the 1970s, CTD had a bowling league with about 40 teams, 2 golf leagues, and a softball league. There were also an annual sports awards banquet, a big Christmas dinner, and a Christmas party for the children—the personnel department kept track of all the employees' children's ages and sexes to ensure that they received the appropriate presents. A club for retirees offered medical check-ups, social events, and other benefits.

Other employee-assistance programs listed in the company's 1978 and 1980 long-range plans were alcohol- and drug-abuse counseling, physical fitness courses, CPR and first aid classes, preretirement counseling, financial planning and tax return preparation at company expense, legal referrals, and marital, family, and personal counseling. Social activities included photography and radio classes, picnics, open houses, and family activities. To serve the community there were plans for trial job interviews for high school students, summer jobs at CTD for local teachers, economics courses for employees and students, and encouragement for employees to serve on local community agencies and educational boards.

But all was not a bed of roses. Roy Martin, 38, newly promoted Cleveland plant manager and a 20-year veteran, provided a perspective on CTD's culture and the changes Jim Bartlett had made:

> Even before Jim came, things had started to change. In the recession of 1975, they cut out the Christmas party for the kids. Also for the banquet, instead of the shrimp cocktail and steaks, we had a spaghetti dinner in the basement. There were also some management layoffs and a 10 percent salary cut. Basically these were the easy things. The tough things had not been done and the tough questions were, do we really need all these

---

[4] A house union is an independent union organized solely within a specific company and has no affiliation with international unions.

levels of management, and do we even need all these managers?

I was one of the last of the manufacturing guys left, and I suddenly went from a Young Turk to the last of the good old boys. This put me in a peculiar position. I was Sam Colt's lieutenant, and when Sam was fired by Bartlett this was a real blow culturally to the organization because Sam was well liked. Conceptually I did not have a problem with what Jim wanted to get done and so in a way I had one foot in either camp; one camp wanted to continue as before and not make too many changes, while the other camp wanted to do things differently and change the business practices. So the new team basically wanted to make all the changes, and the old people were in a way divided.

What hurts us the most is the COLA provision, which was negotiated in 1972, that went out of control. The incentive program was out of control too. Previously it was about 25 percent of the base; now 10 years later it is 42 percent of the base, and the problem is that everyone expects to get it, so it is no longer a real incentive. When people don't get the incentives that they have come to expect, we get grievances that our standards are too tight.

Having collected comparative wage data, management was in a quandary on how to proceed because contract negotiations were not due until November 1983. Some of the senior management wanted to seek immediate wage and work rule concessions from the union bargaining committee (the most important work rule change would be a reduction in the over 500 job classifications, which seriously reduced plant flexibility). There was, however, legitimate concern that the rank and file would resist even if the union leadership went along because they had never

been told there were any real problems. The workers' perception of the company and their part in it was that they produced the best-quality goods and as a result CTD was the leader in the industry. Other members of senior management felt CTD should communicate the grim realities directly to the workers.

Against this backdrop Pete Manzoni, with Bartlett's concurrence, began informal discussions with the union bargaining committee in the middle of March. The committee was headed by Greg Thompson, who had recently been reelected president of the house union. Thompson was a decent, understanding sort of person who was sympathetic to CTD's problems. So far not much had been accomplished by these talks. According to Manzoni:

> Thompson's reaction to our proposals has been one of absolute shock, followed by disbelief and anger. His reaction has been something like this: "You guys are new here, and you don't know what's going on. We have been here for 25 years and we have never been treated like this by past management. They never told us there was any big wage- or benefit-differential problem. I don't know where you got your numbers from, but they can't be right. Besides, our productivity and quality are much higher than our competition's, so the numbers are not even comparable."

Bartlett soon realized that they had placed Thompson in a terrible bind:

> Thompson is a very intelligent, sensitive man who is well respected by his union members. He is a real statesman. He has calmed many management–labor problems and relationships in the past. Now we're telling him to convince his rank and file that a major concession has to be made before the contract expires.

Marketing and Sales

CTD's traditional market objectives were to serve as broad a market as possible and to maintain the highest product quality. To achieve these goals, CTD supplied a very large distributor network with a product line that included about 16,000 standard products and many specials. It also had on its own payroll 70 highly trained service representatives who worked directly with end users to solve problems with the existing products and to design new ones for special applications.

Largely because of the sales reps' work, CTD had established a reputation for superior quality. In recent years, however, other manufacturers had improved the quality of their products considerably, and CTD had not sufficiently kept abreast of technological advances to maintain its position. It became increasingly difficult for CTD to obtain a price premium for its products, and top management began questioning the wisdom of an annual outlay of approximately $5 million to maintain a specialized service force.

Drills accounted for 40 percent of CTD's product. Four other important product groups each accounted for between 10 percent and 13 percent of the total: (1) reamers; (2) taps, dies, and gauges; (3) end mills and aircraft specials; and (4) assembled threading tools (ATT).

Three other categories—Nobur, saws and cutters, and miscellaneous tools—accounted for the remaining 10 percent. (See Exhibit 4 for market segment analysis and six-year market share trends.)

Before Jim Bartlett arrived, P&L responsibility at Acme-Cleveland rested primarily with the president of each division or subsidiary. Both Chuck Ames and Bartlett believed, however, that product managers should also have profit responsibility (see Exhibit 5). Accordingly, Bartlett, shortly after his arrival, appointed three product managers who would have P&L responsibility for major segments of the business: one for drills and reamers; one for end mills, taps, dies, gauges, and Nobur; and one for ATT, saws, and cutters. Before, the product manager position had reported to the vice president for sales and was basically a staff position (Exhibit 6); now the product managers would report directly to the president (Exhibit 7).

Although the product managers had P&L responsibility, they had no product-line P&Ls with which to manage. As Jack Massey, the vice president of finance, put it:

> There are big problems in getting product-line profitability data. When I got here I started looking at the financial systems and there was no way to do a good analytical job. The people in the financial department were just bookkeepers. There were no proper information systems. All we had was a P&L and balance sheet—one for the United States, one for Canada, one for Mexico, one for Germany, and one total consolidated. There were no other operating reports to identify profitability, inventory turnover, variance analysis, or efficiency. All they were used to doing was looking at inventory cycles. Also, there was no way to identify opportunities or problems. We thought we would have product-line performance in place within six months. Now it seems it's going to take us two years. The problem is that people don't report against the routings; they just produce pieces and get paid, and there are no cost standards. Also, with business going down, we can't afford to allocate the resources to develop the information we need.

Besides the problem of establishing profitability figures, the product managers also found themselves spending more time responding to short-term pressures. One said:

> As demand began to fall, more and more of our time is being spent in forecasting sales figures and renegotiating production targets with manufacturing. Also, pricing issues have become quite important in the face of declining demand. There was, for example, pressure to lower prices so as to keep up demand. However, analysis showed that each 10 percent cut in prices would require 20 percent more sales to make up the lower level of profit. In light of declining overall demand, such a sales increase would have been most unlikely.

The product managers did not have an easy time dealing with the sales organization, either. The vice president for sales, Bert Finlay, had been with CTD for over 20 years and was described as "a very bright, energetic guy, though he was not on board with the new concept." Over time, the product managers hired product specialists to help them with their jobs. When they tried to fill these positions from the field sales and service organization, they encountered considerable opposition from Finlay, who resisted the development of the product-manager organization at the expense of field sales.

The product managers also faced a difficult task in developing strategies for growth markets. In addition to finding a very broad product line that was almost unmanageable, they found their competitors firmly entrenched in the commodity segment of the drill market (see Table C). At the high-quality end of the market, in spite of a strong engineering and R&D department, CTD found itself far behind in seeking growth opportunities outside

high-speed steel tools. As one of the product managers summed it up:

> The market perception of CTD is one of a high-cost producer resting on past successes, with little growth or technological drive. Though our premier product line—Cleforge—is still well respected in the industry, it is too high-priced for the price-conscious buyers.
>
> Our lower-priced line—Cleline—with which we can be price competitive, is not broad enough. We consistently have trouble putting together complete packages in this line. We really have no choice here. The commodity segment is now more than half the market and growing. We must have a complete, price-competitive line.

BARTLETT'S OPTIONS

In the past nine months, Jim Bartlett had dramatically changed the organizational structure of CTD and put new people in most of the key management positions. The administrative staff had also been cut back, and there had been significant volume-related layoffs in manufacturing. Even before Bartlett took over, Chuck Ames had begun restructuring and cutting back the entire Acme-Cleveland organization, and CTD had received a taste of the new management style when 75 management positions had been pared away.

Jack Sims, vice president of personnel, described how there had been opportunities to do away with entire departments:

> Since June 1981, 341 salaried people have been let go, for an annual savings of $10.6 million. For example, there was the wage standards department with 15 people who spent all their time administering the incentive system and writing job descriptions. This department was

TABLE C
1982 ESTIMATED SALES OF HIGH-SPEED STEEL DRILL COMMODITY SEGMENT
($ IN MILLIONS)

CTD	Company A	Company B	Company C	Company D	Company E	Others
$4	$40	$20	$15	$15	$10	$25.5

cut to one person. There was a customer service department with 70 people; these people did nothing but order processing and order entry. That responsibility has now been put into the hands of the sales offices, and the customer service department has been cut to 10 or 12 people. They also had 17 people in the personnel department administering all sorts of programs. That has now been cut to 5 people. And the company also employed its own cafeteria workers, paying them a wage rate of $10 per hour and $5 per hour in benefits; in addition, the cafeteria operation was being subsidized by $300,000 a year. All of these workers were let go, and a food service company was hired to run the cafeteria.

Sims continued:

I am thoroughly convinced that we are doing the right thing here. We should have addressed these issues many years ago. Of our salaried people, about one-half of them were in shock when we started to make the changes, but the other half felt that it was about time. I think that the greatest risk of what we are doing is that we may be doing too much too soon. There is just a lot of change all at once.

While Bartlett was pondering the pros and cons of the various options, he knew he had to act fast because of CTD's poor performance. For the first six months of fiscal 1982, sales were already 10 percent below the previous year and 15 percent below budget. While earnings were slightly above the previous year, they were considerably below budget. More disturbing was that the trend in both sales and earnings had been deteriorating.

Jim Bartlett realized that many of CTD's problems were rooted in the sharp decline in demand caused by the recession, but he also felt that the recession only highlighted CTD's underlying weaknesses. As Bartlett looked back, he realized he had got into more than he had bargained for. The industry had matured. CTD's sales were on the decline, and he had a major problem with the union on wages and benefits.

By early April 1982, Bartlett felt he knew what had to be done. First, he had to improve CTD's competitive cost position dramatically in its core markets while maintaining service and delivery. Achieving a competitive cost position was essential for CTD to compete effectively in the large and growing commodity segment and maintain its position in the high-quality segment. As he wondered how he could pull this off, three possibilities kept churning in his mind:

1. He could step up the pace and pressure of negotiations with the union bargaining committee and hope for an early breakthrough.

2. He could bypass the bargaining committee and appeal directly to union employees.

3. He could immediately seek board approval for the necessary funds to proceed with plans to transfer work to other locations without involving the union leadership or its members.

None of these alternatives was particularly attractive. Whether Greg Thompson could persuade his union members to accept something as traumatic as wage concessions was an open question. For Thompson to endorse or recommend pay and benefit givebacks might seem tantamount to selling out to the new management.

Going directly to the rank and file might have been feasible a couple of years earlier, when there was still a very strong family feeling. But recently, because of the firings and forced retirements of many of the managers who had spent their entire careers with the company, and because many of the company's beneficences, like Christmas dinner and other social activities, had already been cut out, the production employees were already wary.

Requesting board approval for funds to transfer work at this stage also concerned Bartlett. He had a mandate to "manage for cash." To request $15 million to $20 million—when Acme-Cleveland was considering several acquisitions—might be viewed as contradicting that mandate. Because Acme-Cleveland was having a bad year, all capital requests were given very close scrutiny. And because most of the board had strong ties to Cleveland, a major move out of Cleveland might not be looked on favorably. Finally, although CTD had begun limited production at its Cynthiana, Kentucky, plant in early 1979, Bartlett wondered how responsible it would be to his employees and the community in Cleveland to launch a full-scale "southern strategy" before at least exploring all possible alternatives to gain wage and benefit concessions.

Complicating these alternatives were the facts that the current contract wasn't due to expire for 18 months and that it would take one to two years to bring any new facilities to competitive levels of productivity. Bartlett feared a three-year delay in achieving a competitive cost position if he waited to negotiate a new contract and then was unable to gain the necessary concessions.

Bartlett's second major objective was to maintain CTD's position in the marketplace because its sales and customer order backlog were dropping precipitously. What the company needed here were sound product-line strategies. But this component still perplexed him because CTD had no financial analysis or history on the profitability of its product lines.

The third major element of Bartlett's program was to move CTD into established growth markets. To accomplish this, CTD needed to develop a capability in new technologies, such as titanium nitride coatings, powdered metallurgy, and ceramics, rather than continue its investments in high-speed steel.

Thus, as shown in Exhibit 8, Bartlett felt he had conceived the main aspects of his strategy. What he needed to establish now was how the key elements of each aspect would be realized.

EXHIBIT 1
PRODUCTS MANUFACTURED BY THE CLEVELAND TWIST DRILL CO.

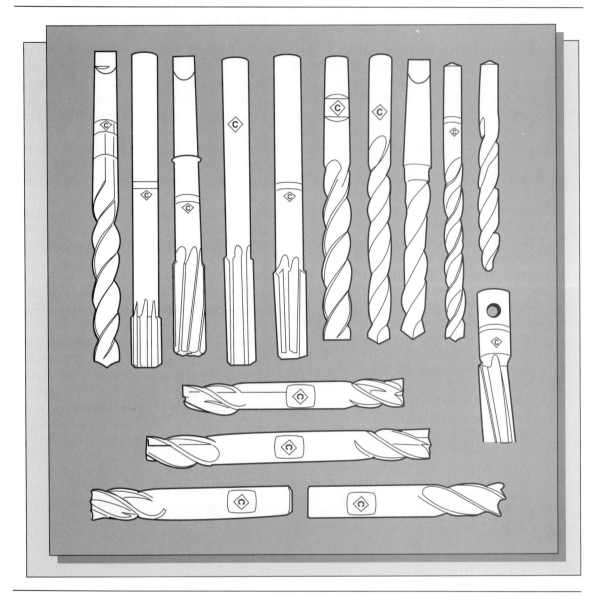

EXHIBIT 2
ACME-CLEVELAND'S FINANCIAL PERFORMANCE, 1973–1981

	1981	1980	1979	1978	1977	1976	1975	1974	1973
I. Financial Highlights									
Summary of operations									
Net sales	$400,743,537	$405,235,999	$344,460,395	$289,509,329	$218,191,699	$194,088,642	$231,489,665	$169,442,363	$127,850,966
Cost of products sold	318,721,315	301,847,698	246,286,255	210,201,261	160,159,308	143,008,384	170,670,207	126,022,710	90,417,166
Interest expense less interest income	6,942,653	6,651,559	3,592,141	4,328,008	4,756,829	4,756,829	6,569,948	3,102,128	672,111
Earnings before taxes	18,145,346	27,931,887	35,832,636	24,971,294	8,753,201	5,389,716	12,771,499	10,493,880	12,563,828
Income taxes	7,214,000	10,949,000	16,357,000	11,813,000	3,915,000	2,478,000	5,816,000	4,785,000	5,876,000
Net earnings	10,931,346	16,982,887	19,475,636	13,158,294	4,838,201	2,911,716	6,955,499	5,708,880	6,687,828
Net earnings to net sales	2.7%	4.2%	5.7%	4.5%	2.2%	1.5%	3.0%	3.4%	5.2%
Earnings per common share	2.41	3.96	4.34	2.96	1.08	.65	1.56	1.43	1.74
Dividends per common share	1.40	1.35	1.15	.80	5.25	.50	6.25	1.00	.82
Other financial information									
Current assets	168,751,234	182,884,833	156,791,868	132,945,224	123,794,140	100,570,415	129,570,415	133,731,029	72,362,351
Current liabilities	70,964,020	71,953,727	59,461,457	39,394,887	41,166,527	26,264,216	46,884,880	47,980,021	27,206,073
Working capital	97,787,214	110,931,106	97,330,411	93,550,337	82,627,613	74,306,199	82,685,535	85,751,008	45,156,278
Property, plant, and equipment—net	75,596,288	75,120,585	56,196,074	47,716,898	44,352,655	44,259,575	47,054,224	43,890,446	31,169,157
Capital expenditures	16,299,044	26,097,516	14,732,829	9,005,924	4,608,876	8,528,286	8,235,977	5,968,552	5,023,718
Depreciation	8,042,833	6,370,516	5,340,020	5,032,188	4,817,117	4,925,867	4,757,590	3,706,216	3,234,652
Long-term obligations	53,082,173	70,534,284	49,737,582	47,017,089	42,195,043	38,849,752	45,153,231	51,075,644	9,679,581
Total assets	252,437,417	263,712,017	219,574,767	184,463,445	171,071,286	150,001,052	178,141,229	179,894,704	105,258,535
Redeemable preferred shares	162,874	162,874	—0—	62,215	62,215	62,125	62,215	62,215	—0—
Shareholders' equity	121,668,098	116,330,248	107,079,591	93,964,096	84,255,799	81,800,056	81,160,550	77,028,520	66,855,616
Shareholders' equity per common share	$27.15	$26.37	$23.81	$21.10	$18.92	$18.37	$18.22	$17.28	$17.42
II. Expendable Products Segment* ($000)									
Total sales	$148,360	$148,045	$144,521	$115,207	$97,277	$89,854	$91,416	$94,620	$80,653
Operating profit	14,188	10,795	21,665	17,092	11,895	10,516	7,155	10,901	11,325
Identifiable assets	86,444	95,071	72,741	69,135					
Depreciation	3,845	3,347	2,940	2,799					
Capital expenditures	$7,321	$13,338	$8,113	$3,947					

Note: Fiscal years ended September 30.

*This includes products other than those manufactured by Cleveland Twist Drill.

EXHIBIT 3
EXCERPTS FROM JIM BARTLETT'S MEMO (11/13/81) TO SAM COLT ON MANUFACTURING STRATEGY

I. East 49th Street Dispersion

- What are the common manufacturing operations at East 49th Street to *all* the products manufactured there? How many hourly persons function in relevant departments and what are the costs associated today?
- What skills are required by hourly operators in these departments? What is the age and seniority profile of these persons performing these operations today? Which of these skills will disappear via attrition over the next five years that are not being replaced through training?
- Through matrix analysis, where does each major product group produced at East 49th Street depart from a list of operations common to all? Which of these product groups, by virtue of their separate (or separable) manufacturing process, lend themselves to relatively easy exit?
- Of those products that are readily separable from a process viewpoint, which represent the highest content of critical manual skills? Which represent a high "automation cost" if duplicated elsewhere?

II. Plant Network Design

- How many plants should we have? What is the optimum size of a plant?
- How many different product lines should be produced in each plant? To what extent can we continue to do early-stage operations on a tool class in one plant to support the production of other plants?

III. Organization and Staffing

- What should the organization be for each of our plants presently on line, including East 49th Street?
- What management resources are available to us in developing the necessary details to execute a major series of manufacturing moves (plant start-ups, line relocations, etc.)? What must be done to shore up these resources in time to have knowledgeable people making decisions and carrying out the required actions?
- What services, support, or direction will manufacturing require from outside its own organization?

IV. Capital investment

- What are the major elements of our existing in-place capital structure for manufacturing? Which of these elements (heat treating, centerless grinding, NC equipment, broaching, etc.) will require major overhaul or substantial capacity upgrading during the next five years?
- Again using matrix analysis, where do we have duplication of facilities or equipment today? What additional duplication (or capacity) is already programmed through our present Cranston and Cynthiana moves?
- Are there major segments of capital equipment capability missing in our present plants that impair our competitive ability? What investments might we make to add to our productivity today?

EXHIBIT 4
MARKET SEGMENT AND MARKET SHARE TRENDS

A. Market Segment Analysis

Segment	Mix	Market Share	Competitive Market Share	
Drills and reamers	52%	14%	Company A	15%
			Company B	13%
Taps and dies	13%	9%	Company B	15%
			Company C	
End mills and aircraft specials	11%	10%	Company D	20%
			Company B	20%
			Company E	10%
			Company F	10%
ATT (assembled threading tools)	10%	33%	Company B	35%
			Company G	20%
Saws and cutters	4%		(Over 100 domestic manufacturers)	
Other/miscellaneous	10%			
	100%			

B. 6-Year Market Share

	1981	1980	1979	1978	1977	1976
Drills	21.4	21.2	22.3	22.9	21.3	21.6
Reamers	21.5	21.5	22.2	23.0	21.8	22.8
End mills	10.9	11.6	10.3	10.7	10.5	10.8
Taps and dies	10.7	11.7	10.7	10.0	10.0	9.9

Note: Some figures have been disguised. Key relationships have been preserved.

EXHIBIT 5
BARTLETT'S MEMO ON PRODUCT MANAGEMENT CONCEPT

Date: March 31, 1982

To: Field Selling Organization   Office:

From: J. T. Bartlett   Office:

Subject: Role of the Product Manager in Our Business

Even though we have done considerable communicating about the role of the Product Manager in our business, I think we have a way to go in making this concept work to produce solid benefits. I am therefore writing to underscore some fundamental points about the product management function and how it should work in CTD's business.

The first and most important point you should understand is our Product Managers' function as general managers. They have Profit and Loss responsibility for major segments of our business. Whenever there is a problem in the Field, whenever a customer is not being served, whenever we are missing a promised delivery date, whenever a competitor is introducing a product or launching a new initiative in pricing or promotion, the Product Managers should know. When you are not receiving the kind of support you need from the Managers of manufacturing, engineering, or customer service, you should immediately contact your Area Manager who in turn will call the appropriate Product Manager. If your Area Manager is not available and the situation is urgent, you should reach Bert Finlay or one of the Product Managers directly. Let me stress that this does not mean that the Product Managers are a "dumping ground" for minor complaints and petty gripes. On the contrary, we expect you to handle that level of customer dissatisfaction.

However, if we are about to miss a major opportunity because of our inability to respond in a timely manner, the Product Manager should know. Only by communication at this level will it be possible for the Product Managers to be effective.

Secondly, it is impossible for our Product Managers to function unless they are aware of our competitors' moves and your thoughts on how we should serve our customers or markets better. I never cease to be impressed when I'm with you to hear your ideas and market intelligence. These ideas, particularly those coming from your knowledge of competitors, are invaluable input for our tactical planning as well as our long-term strategic thinking. We need to hear as much as we can from the Field about these activities. Without a keen sense of competition, we are surely going to hit endless foul balls in our marketing direction. Hence, everything you know relating to our competition must be communicated to the Product Managers. A written format for this information will be forthcoming.

EXHIBIT 6
ORGANIZATION CHART AS OF JANUARY 1981

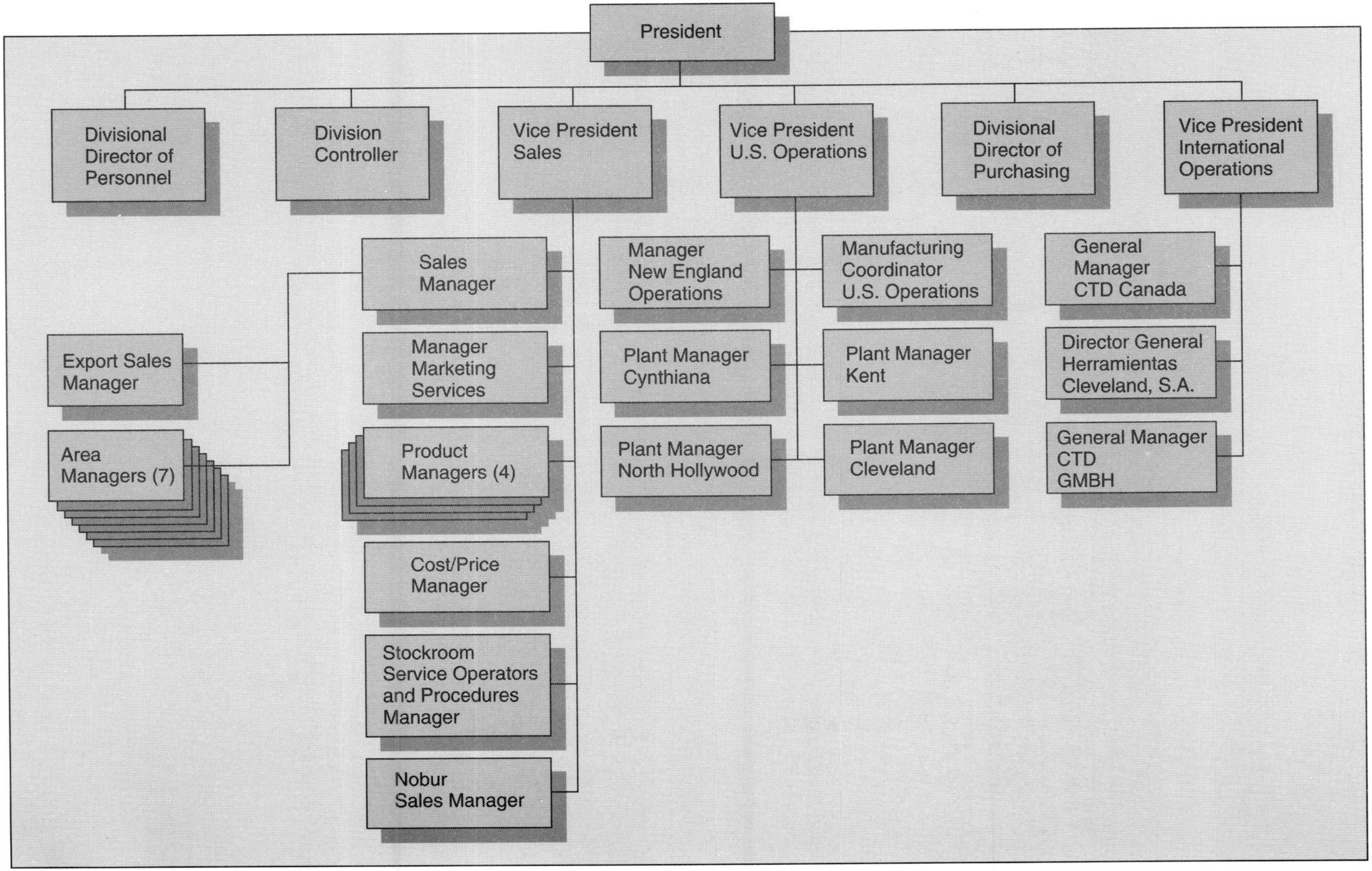

EXHIBIT 7
ORGANIZATION CHART AS OF APRIL 1982

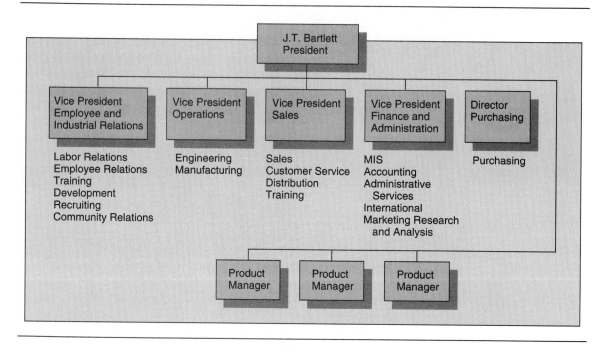

EXHIBIT 8
CTD FIVE-YEAR STRATEGIC PLAN SUMMARY

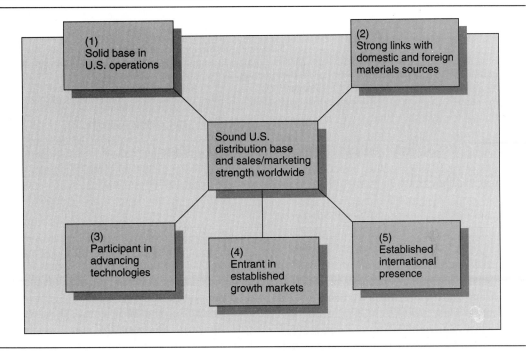

Richardson Hindustan Limited (Abridged)

Two projects of major potential interest to the Richardson-Vicks Inc. (RVI) Indian subsidiary were very much on the mind of Gurcharan Das, president of Richardson Hindustan Limited (RHL), as he reviewed his company's strategic plan in early 1984. The first would take the Indian firm into products not included among the parent company's worldwide offerings. The second would set up RHL as a supplier of a key raw material for RVI's global operations. Both propositions went counter to existing corporate policies and practices which stressed products capable of being transferred to markets around the world and which favored investments in marketing over manufacturing. A recent forced reduction of RVI's ownership from 55 percent to 40 percent was sure to affect corporate management's thinking about these two ventures as well as about a host

of other activities and expectations which defined the relationship between parent and its distant subsidiary.

"Balancing the requirements of headquarters and those of the local organization in a way which serves the long-term interests of both is clearly one of the most critical parts of my job," noted Das.

> RHL is a loyal subsidiary, yet it has a kindred spirit of its own. As a result, I have to promote RHL's interests at headquarters and then turn around to promote RVI's interest in Bombay. Luckily, I am dealing with excellent people at both ends, or the job would not be much fun.

RVI and RHL

Richardson-Vicks, Inc., was a leading worldwide marketer of branded consumer products for health care, home care, and nutritional care. The company's product line could be traced to 1905, when Lunsford Richardson, a North Carolina pharmacist, formed a company to sell Vicks VapoRub, which he had developed "especially for children's croup or colds." The company experienced rapid growth following World War II with the addition of new products and the expansion of overseas operations.

In management's view, marketing had been the key to RVI's success. The 1982 annual report described RVI's corporate strategy as follows:

> The company seeks leadership positions for each of its brands by developing products that meet distinct consumer needs. It then produces them under high manufacturing standards to ensure high performance and consumer acceptance. Finally it supports them with outstanding advertising, promotion, and distribution.

In 1983, RVI had revenues of $1.1 billion based on the sales of such products as Vicks VapoRub (cold product), Oil of Olay (skin care), Clearasil (acne medication), Vidal Sassoon (hair care), Vicks Throat Drops (cough drops), Sinex (nasal spray), NyQuil (nighttime cold medication), and Homer Formby (home care products). According to company records, one out of every four dollars spent in the United States on cold remedies went to purchase a Vicks product. Overseas sales had grown even faster than domestic and in 1983 accounted for more than half the company's total sales and profits. Exhibit 1 shows financial information for RVI.

RHL was one of more than 30 subsidiaries in the Richardson-Vicks worldwide network. The Indian company was founded in 1964 to oversee the construction of a pharmaceutical plant and to take over the marketing efforts then being handled by a small RVI branch operation. Upon completion of the plant in 1966, 45 percent of RHL's equity was sold to the Indian populace through a public stock offering. RVI retained 55 percent ownership.

Starting from annual sales of $2.5 million in its first year of operation (1966–67 fiscal year), RHL posted a record sales volume of $23 million in 1983 and had become an important unit to the parent company. Its facilities in 1984 included headquarters office space in Bombay, a modern 160,000-square-foot factory located on a 16-acre site at Kalwa (20 miles north of Bombay), and a menthol distillation center located at Bilaspur (150 miles north of Delhi).

Gurcharan Das

Born in 1943, Das, the eldest of three children, left India at the age of 12, when his father, a government official, was transferred to Washington, D.C. After completing high school at the age of 16, he studied philosophy and politics at Harvard, graduating magna cum laude.

At the age of 20, Das joined Richardson-Merrell (subsequently Richardson-Vicks) as a way to spend a few years in India before going on to graduate studies. His first boss believed the best training to be selling Vicks products, and Das spent 15 out of the next 24 months on the road. This experience was to have a profound effect on Das, as he later recalled:

> When I was traveling, getting to know my country and getting to know the trade and consumers made for very exciting days. But the evenings were pretty lonely and dull. So I started reading a lot of history about the areas in which I was traveling. I also observed the people and their way of life. I started writing a diary about my observations and impressions.
>
> In Chandigarh, looking through some records of the Punjab government, I came

across the history of Sir Henry Lawrence and his contemporaries. This account had all the ingredients of a novel—passion, intrigue, jealousy, fighting, and love. I became excited by this story about India of 120 years ago, when the British first conquered the Punjab. Since I was not confident of my ability to handle a novel, I decided to write a play.

As a result, Das won his first public acclamation in India as the 25-year-old author of the award-winning play "Larins Sahib." He had already begun work on his second play about Mira Bai—a 16th-century poetess, priestess, and saint—when in December 1968 he was reassigned to Richardson-Merrell's headquarters in New York en route to a position in Mexico.

After two years in the United States and a year in Mexico, Das returned in 1971 to Richardson Hindustan as marketing manager. Four years later, he went to Mexico as general manager, Nutrition Division, of the Richardson-Merrell subsidiary. In January 1980, feeling frustrated with an apparent lack of opportunity for advancement, Das left the company to join General Foods as assistant general manager of its Spanish operations. A year later, his supporters in Richardson lured him back with an offer to lead Richardson-Hindustan.

Gurcharan Das at Richardson Hindustan Limited

When Das returned to his native India in January 1981 to head RHL, he found a company in trouble. He recounted his initial impressions:

> I was very excited to go back home as head of the company where I had started as a trainee 18 years earlier. But what I found when I got there was a real mess.

The company was cash-poor, morale was low, labor was hostile, labor–management relations were adversarial, and turnover in the management ranks was very high. Because of governmental price controls, management for years had stressed volume, selling at any price and producing at any cost. I can tell you, it was a difficult homecoming for me.

Das, together with RVI management, quickly mapped out a strategy to turn the situation around. He explained the resulting priorities and actions:

> The top priority was to increase profitability. We raised prices wherever we could, reduced inventories and accounts receivable, cut low-yielding sales and distribution activities, and got the sales force to push the more profitable lines. RHL suffered some decline in volume, but not as much as the marketing people had predicted in resisting these moves. The cash flow improved dramatically.
>
> Next, I dealt with the labor situation. Labor relations could be characterized as bitterly adversarial. Management advocated the approach of "stick it to the workers," and the workers, I am sure, would have happily done the same back.
>
> I set out to convince the workforce that we had a problem which could only be worked out together. To help change the prevailing hostile attitudes, we mounted an attitude-change program—first for managers, then for supervisors, and finally for workers. In October 1981, the old personnel manager was replaced by someone who shared my views on how to work with labor instead of against it. A year later we succeeded in signing a three-year contract which made sense to both sides.
>
> The final step was to identify and commit to new opportunities for future growth. I tend to favor participative management and have found the strategic planning process to be a splendid vehicle

for involving and motivating the young managers throughout the organization.

As a result of the turnaround, profits had almost doubled, return on equity had increased from 20.3 percent to 27.1 percent, accounts receivable had reduced from 70 days outstanding to 30, and head-count had decreased from 750 to 675. In tune with these results, RHL stock prices had more than doubled from Rs.20 to Rs.45. (See Exhibit 2 for the RHL financial results.)

Das summed up his assessment of RHL's situation as of mid-1984:

> Given the results for 1983 and the situation today, the company has more than met the objectives I had set in 1981. Profits are good, relations with the government have improved greatly, labor is happy, and management is enthusiastic —not one key manager has left the company in the past 18 months. The central challenge for us now is profitable growth.

RHL'S STRATEGIC PLAN

RHL's five-year growth objectives were to double sales revenues and to triple profits by 1988. (See Exhibit 3 for the company's key financial projections.) An expansion and extension of RHL's core product lines was to serve as the basis for this growth. The company planned to launch 12 new products and relaunch one other product during this period. Entry into two new businesses had also been proposed to serve as a base for future growth as well as a hedge against the possible underachievement of the projected sales growth for core products.

RHL's strategic plan predicted a climate of steady business growth. Over the next five years, population was expected to grow at 2.2 percent (adding the equivalent of one Australia to India's population

every year); the economy and consumer spending were projected to grow at 3–4 percent p.a.; per capita income of the top 20 percent of the population would continue to grow modestly; and the rupee would gently weaken (5 percent to 8 percent p.a.) against the U.S. dollar.

The strategic plan predicted political stability: Democracy would continue; the ruling party was expected to return to power in 1985; regional problems would be contained, with devolution of power from the center to the states; "pragmatic socialism" would continue to be the government's ideology; and the high degree of bureaucratic control would continue. The report predicted continuing decontrol of prices and the unlikelihood of dramatic changes in taxes except for discontinuation of advertising disallowance in 1985.

Core Products

RHL prided itself as a marketing company; its advertising programs and extensive distribution system were the primary engines for sales growth. Arun Bewoor, general sales manager, explained the company's approach:

> About 75 percent of the Indian population lives in some 526,000 rural communities. That's a potential market of almost one-half billion people. And RHL has built the largest rural distribution structure in our field. We do grassroots marketing and draw upon Indian culture for unique campaign ideas. India is a country with many people outside the monied economy, so we sell small tins of Vicks for 15 cents. Television is still in its infancy so we advertise through the movie halls. Our market research showed that people had colds in the rainy season as well as winter, so we started to do

intensive market promotion during the monsoons. The land and people are heterogeneous, so we segment our advertising based on language, economic development, and market development.

Cold care and casual therapeutics products accounted for about 80 percent of RHL's 1983 total sales. The strategic plan aimed to continue the company's dominance in these market segments in order to generate funds for new product expansion. Vicks VapoRub was the single largest product in its category and its dominance was expected to continue. However, competition was intensifying from lower-priced regional "look-alike" brands. According to Arun Bewoor,

> We have a lot of problems with mushroom competitors. These are small, fly-by-night manufacturers who make copies of VapoRub, sell them for a month or two, and then disappear, only to reappear somewhere else later. When RHL raised its price on the popular five-gram tin from one rupee to two rupees, we brought these hit-and-run outfits out in droves.

Dominant in the casual therapeutic line of products was Vicks Cough Drops, which accounted for about 20 percent of RHL's total sales. It held a 40 percent national market share, followed by Boots' Strepsils (23 percent) and Halls (17 percent). Arun Bewoor noted,

> Cough drops have big growth potential, and Halls is a big threat as it moves more aggressively in the north and south of India from its strong base in Bombay. It was Hall's successful growth which prompted us to launch a single-portion twist-wrapped candy throat drop to combat their successful offering of this product type.

Clearasil was synonymous with pimple care in India and overwhelmingly dominated the acne remedy market. According to market studies, while only about 24 percent of young urban pimple sufferers used acne medication, increasing urbanization, literacy, social interaction, and spending power would make young people more and more conscious of their facial skin problems. For this reason, management considered the young people's skin care market segment as ready for a major takeoff. The strength of the Clearasil franchise was reflected in its ability to hold sales volume while its price tripled to almost $1 per tube. To capitalize on this potential, the company planned to introduce related Clearasil products (soap, medicated cleanser, and super-strength lotion).

Ayurvedics

Das and Dr. Victor Moreno, vice president of research and development for Vick Americas/Far East division, had been intrigued for some time with the possible opportunity to commercialize the supply of herbal medicines which had been widely popular in India for some 2,000 years. Das characterized ayurvedic, or natural (herbal), medicines as safe, slow, and long-term-acting, and therefore ideally suited for chronic diseases. Herbal formulas were even thought capable of curing some chronic diseases over time as compared to the Western approach of alleviating symptoms. As a result of this thinking, Dr. Moreno and Das hired Dr. T. G. Rajagopalan in 1982 to develop an ayurvedic line of products. Rajagopalan had received a master's degree in biochemistry from the University of Madras and a PhD in the same field from Duke University. He had worked in Ciba Geigy's laboratories as a biochemist for 15 years before joining RHL.

Rajagopalan described his approach to this challenge:

> To decide on the best initial target areas, we began with a broad study of 12 areas of medicine, such as skin, liver, hair/ teeth, respiratory, etc. With the help of a consultant and several university students, we collected over 7,000 ayurvedic recipes, which had to be translated from Sanskrit. These recipes included anywhere from one to 90 plants. Since the plant names were only in Sanskrit, it was a task to find the equivalent botanical names.
>
> We next developed a computer program to categorize the pharmacological properties of the plants as well as the vehicles for administering the medication. Since we wanted to meet Western pharmacological and toxicity standards, we screened the products to show toxicity based on reports in Western literature published from 1905 to 1982. The data bank we have on herbal plants is unique. Nobody has done this before.

Opinions about RHL's entry into ayurvedic products differed widely. Das saw great commercial possibilities in India and eventually abroad from ayurvedic medications and personal care products. Bharat V. Patel, vice president of marketing for RHL, was much less enthusiastic about its market potential, viewing the effort as more of a move to gain favor with the Indian government by promoting indigenous medicinal practices. He questioned RHL's ability to devise an ayurvedic product which could compete with the efficacy of a Western drug:

> I am opposed to the idea of our introducing a serious drug for several reasons. First, such a drug would take us into a domain where doctors hold sway. RHL does not have expertise in this arena; our strength is in over-the-counter products. Second, ayurvedics will never be able to provide the quick relief that people want in this day and age. Finally, such a product does not fit in our specialty of casual therapeutics for minor ailments.
>
> If we do come out with such a product, the company should not project it as an ayurvedic drug. It should be offered with modern packaging emphasizing its attributes rather than its natural herbal content.

Somewhat in line with Patel's thinking, RHL management's objective was to offer proprietary medicinal products which could be advertised and sold over the counter rather than ethical drugs. Furthermore, introducing ayurvedic toiletries was seen as easier than herbal medicinal products because of the latter's more stringent requirements for quality consistency (difficult to achieve with natural plants).

Lou Mattis, who had line responsibility for RHL as general manager for Vick Americas/Far East, was undecided as to the project's profit potential, but willing to give it a try. In 1984, RHL was committed to constructing an R&D facility for developing ayurvedic products. Construction was estimated at $275,000 and initial equipment orders would run about $330,000. Das estimated these investments would increase to a total of $1 million in two years and to $2 million in five years.[1]

Dextromethorphan-Hydrobromide

As a way of increasing exports and of making a high-technology basic drug to comply with government pressures, RHL management began looking into the pos-

---

[1] All figures on the new businesses have been disguised.

sibility of producing dextromethorphan-hydrobromide, an antitussive ingredient used in products to counter cough symptoms. RVI was reportedly the world's largest consumer of dextro with annual purchases of almost $9 million (at the 1983 price of $285 per kilogram) from two established suppliers. RHL proposed to become a global source of dextro for RVI, producing the same quality product at a lower price with the aim of making a profit and of gaining important goodwill with the government.

The person pushing the dextro manufacturing venture was B. K. Patney, RHL's vice president of manufacturing. He planned to import the intermediate materials and produce the dextromethorphan at a cost 20 percent below RVI's current price. While he preferred to license the process in Italy or even to develop his own version, Patney proposed to license from one of the current suppliers, despite the higher cost, so as to more readily gain headquarters' approval.

Tax savings were also an important element in the dextro proposal. If the manufacturing facility were to be located in a duty-free and free-trade site and the manufacturing process added more than 30 percent value to the imported intermediate chemicals, then the company would qualify for a duty drawback on imported chemicals, cash incentives on exports, and no income tax for seven years on profits arising from the facility. Investment in the dextro facilities would total about $2.2 million. RHL executives estimated that the payback for this investment would be less than two years.

Notwithstanding RHL's enthusiasm for the dextro project, Das perceived RVI's response as unenthusiastic. He recognized several reasons for headquarter's reluctance. Perhaps most important was RVI's policy of focusing its resources on marketing investments and keeping down its investments in manufacturing plant. Moreover, dextromethorphan-hydrobromide was a complicated chemical compound requiring special processes with which RVI had no direct experience.

RHL's failure to deliver on an earlier promise to produce low-cost menthol exports possibly provided some people with further grounds for opposing the project. In the 1960s, RHL management had proposed to grow the mentha arvensis plant in India both as a means of import substitution and as a source of low-cost menthol for the parent company. For a variety of agricultural reasons, the costs for producing menthol in India turned out to be much higher than had been anticipated when compared to production in Brazil.

On the positive side, Das felt that RHL's strong financial performance over the past two years had done much to improve its credibility at headquarters. Patney's successful track record in manufacturing also went a long way toward headquarters' taking the dextro project seriously. He had developed a reputation as a person who submitted carefully prepared capital investment proposals and who had successfully implemented each approved project within a typically tight budget limit.

Despite these strong pluses for the dextro project, Das recognized their limits: "RHL is 10,000 miles from the home office in Wilton, Connecticut. And so there is still a healthy dose of skepticism there as to what RHL can do."

BUILDING AND BALANCING CONSTITUENCY RELATIONSHIPS

Notwithstanding his deep interest and involvement in products and markets, Das saw that a special part of his job was serving several important RHL constituencies: the parent company, the RHL employees, the Indian government, and the Indian shareholders. The requirements and expectations of these parties were different and often in direct conflict. Not only was it important for Das to figure out what balance to strike with respect to specific decisions, but it was also vital to convince each party to accept the concessions it might perceive itself making. His ability to argue each case on its own merits was limited where RHL was viewed as only a small element in a total picture, such as might be the case for an RVI headquarters executive or even more so for an Indian government official.

RVI Headquarters

As a worldwide marketer of branded consumer products, RVI followed a strategy of developing or acquiring a brand leader in one market and then transferring its experience to other markets around the world. Each of the operating divisions was relatively autonomous and had complete responsibility for its product line.

Louis Mattis, president and general manager of the Vick Americas/Far East division since 1982, was responsible for 13 country managers and 26 countries with sales of $232 miilion in 1983. He had joined the company in 1979 from Warner-Lambert Co. At the age of 42, he had established a reputation as a hard-driving, successful consumer product manager who encouraged and expected high-level performance from his people. Lou Mattis was to become an executive vice president of RVI and a member of a newly formed corporate strategic planning committee, along with the company's other two executive vice presidents, as of January 1, 1985. With this promotion, he would also gain responsibility for RVI's nutritional care products in the United States.

Mattis described the evolution of corporate/divisional relations as follows:

> We've gone through several stages of evolution in dealing with our multicountry operation. In the 1960s we said, "Young man, go do your thing." We had a very small home office staff and exercised loose control. In the 1970s, the pendulum swung to the other end and the division was centralized very tightly in terms of home office control. Staff was set up in every function—manufacturing, personnel, finance, policy. The staff became decision makers and the field were implementers.
>
> My predecessor made some really good decisions and business did very well in the 1970s . . . But the control system had an impact on the country managers. They became upward looking, bureaucratic, and procedural-oriented.
>
> In the last four years, we have given country managers independence with financial controls. We still use a continuous planning and review system but staff executives don't have to concur on the line manager's decisions before they can be implemented, as was true earlier.

To achieve decentralization, four areas had been created (namely, Mexico, Japan, Canada and South America, and Australia and the Far East) with an area director in charge of each. As Mattis described it:

> We've put line responsibility and authority with the area directors. The staff is a resource to the countries and to me. The way our process works, the country managers first discuss their ideas and then budget with their area director and then with the home office staff. Only then do the country managers come with their area director to me for approval. My

review is for each country, not for an areawide budget.

Capital expenditures require corporate approval and so I get involved. I also get into plans for products that are new to the entire division. If a product is new to a country but is already in the division, it is the area director's concern.

Area Director Don Glover was area director for Australia and the Far East, an area that covered 11 countries and some South Pacific islands. Eight of these countries had independent companies. The area director's staff consisted of a marketing research director, a personnel director, and a finance director. He described his role as follows: "The work of the area director is not to be a policeman. It's a link between the country manager and the home office and between countries. We look for similarities and common problems so that we can avoid reinventing the wheel."

Country Manager Under Mattis, the country manager played a pivotal role with full responsibility for the bottom line of the subsidiary company. RVI's manager's guide defined the main role of the country manager as follows: "To ensure that the market strategic and operational objective and standards set and implemented are the most advantageous for the market environment and are consistent with area and division plans and policies."

With this purpose in mind, the manager's guide defined a set of nine key result areas by which country managers were to be evaluated:

- Market strategic plans
- Profitability
- Today's products and markets
- Tomorrow's products and markets
- Organizational effectiveness
- Corporate responsibilities
- Social responsibilities
- Supply of product
- Asset protection and utilization

A typical career path for a country manager was to start in marketing, move on to marketing director, next to general manager in a small country with no manufacturing operations, then to a small country with integrated operations (marketing and manufacturing), and finally to head up a major national organization.

RHL Organization

Gurcharan Das's philosophy and style of management set the tone for the RHL organization. His stress on people was clearly signaled in a letter accompanying the first annual report after he became president, "Our success over the years is a result of the development of our people . . . We seek the best-qualified individuals we can find for every job. Employment, training, advancement, and compensation are on the basis of merit."

The following year, the introductory letter was devoted exclusively to the subject of "people excellence." In it, Das stated:

My main job today is to create an environment where new ideas thrive and people develop their full potential. Otherwise good people do not stay. At RHL, we are working hard to create a climate which fosters innovativeness and encourages risk taking.

Our philosophy of growth through people excellence is based on the following tenets:

1. A basic belief that people can grow.
2. To help people grow, we need to invest in them.

3. We believe that a consultative and participative management style is more effective than an authoritarian or paternalistic one.

4. We believe the best form of motivation is through achievement.

In practice, Das spoke softly, listened well, smiled often, and had an air of enjoying his work. He interacted frequently with his managers individually and in groups, encouraging debate and seeking new ideas. He was respected and well liked by his subordinates.

Ginil Shirodkar, vice president-personnel, saw RHL as being in transition from a task-oriented organization to one concerned with task *and* people. In an organizational development plan, the earlier managerial atmosphere was described as one characterized by "jockeying for power, functional empires, interfunctional conflicts, low morale, legalistic management style, low mutual trust, and high management turnover." Faced with this company culture, he set out to replace it with one reflecting the philosophy Das had articulated.

To help change attitudes, Shirodkar developed a training and development program for people at all levels of the organization. One of the most important elements in this program, in his view, was a series of top-management workshops in team building and sensitivity training held in March 1982, September 1982, and February 1983. The objectives for these sessions were to build management teamwork, to set new goals, and to instill the new RHL values. Other elements in the overall program included a 10-day residential workshop for field sales supervisors and managers which focused on people-management and selling skills; a

one-week residential program for senior middle managers with emphasis on developing general management skills; a personal growth laboratory for union leaders, workers, supervisory staff, and executives; and a team-building workshop for manufacturing managers.

The training program was connected with a formal appraisal system. Shirodkar described the procedure:

> At the start of each year, every manager and his immediate superior agree on several major objectives for the junior manager. At the end of the year, both of them rate the assessee's performance. It is mandatory for the appraisal interview to last for at least two hours. It may go on for six hours. The discussion of the junior manager's strengths and weaknesses forms the basis on which the senior manager prepares a report identifying the training needs of the assessee.

Subsequently, the assessee and the appraiser–senior manager individually charted out a career path for the assessee. These were compared and the objectives for the next year were set by agreement. To ensure objectivity, a second appraiser then made an independent assessment of the appraisee's performance potential and charted a career path. For the "high fliers" in each division, Shirodkar would meet with Das and the relevant functional director to chart out a separate five-year career path.

Shirodkar was increasingly concerned that nonmarketing managers perceived themselves as having a second-class status within RHL. In an in-house management seminar held in January 1984, several middle-level managers in manufacturing and finance voiced unhappiness with the limitations their careers faced because of the importance Das attached to the marketing function. This strong focus on marketing was evident in a remark made on another occasion by Patney:

> This is a consumer marketing–oriented company. Everything else must fall in line. It's very difficult to talk to top management about manufacturing or the need to invest there. They will spend $5 million on advertising at the drop of a hat but will study to death a $50,000 capital investment for plant.

Das acknowledged this bias and was puzzled as to how he could deal with it:

> This company will live or die on its marketing. I would like all of our managers to gain firsthand experience in marketing, but so far I have not had much success in getting my managers in finance or manufacturing to transfer to a marketing position.

Indian Government

Taxes, price controls, and licenses made the government a significant factor in the business planning for any company operating in India. As a low-technology, high-return, foreign-owned consumer product company, RHL was particularly vulnerable to governmental restrictions and penalties. Patel summed up the company's situation, saying, "Selling our kind of products in India is not difficult. The real problem is to get the government's permission to sell it and to do so profitably, given the complex and tough tax structure."

Most of the company's decisions with respect to products, markets, and investments attempted to reduce this vulnerability and to build goodwill by being "a good citizen." This approach reflected the parent company's deep-seated commitment to conducting a sound business in an ethical manner. In management's think-

ing, everyone involved—the consumer, the host country, and RVI—had to benefit for the business to be sound.

Faced with an effective income tax rate of 76 percent (basic corporate income tax of 55 percent, a surcharge of 15 percent, and disallowance for income tax purposes of 20 percent of advertising expenditure), management viewed the reduction of taxes as the most important element in its plan to improve RHL's profitability. Besides the income tax, the company paid federal excise tax of 105 percent of the sale price for toiletries, and various state and city taxes (e.g., 4 percent for Bombay and 15 percent state sales tax for Maharashtra, in which Bombay was located).

RHL's management aimed to reduce the effective income tax rate to 48 percent by 1987–88 by using tax incentives offered by the Indian government as a means of directing business investments for social and economic improvement. Management planned to construct a satellite plant in an industrially backward area. The tax incentive for a new manufacturing unit was an 8- to 10-year tax holiday on 25 percent of profits; locating in a backward area qualified an additional 20 percent of profits for the tax holiday. The company planned to introduce toiletries based on natural herbs, in line with Indian government policy of favoring the sale of such products by excusing them from excise tax. In addition, Das was also actively engaged in working with industry associations to convince the government to eliminate the advertising disallowance.

At times, tax consequences played an important role in RHL's efforts to obtain headquarters' approval for new investments. Sumit Bhattacharya, vice president-finance, noted, "Last year the government imposed a heavy tax on advertising [the 20 percent disallowance]. Investments in

R&D, however, could serve as a tax set-off. This certainly helped RHL to get approval for additional R&D expenditures."

Along these lines, Patney remarked:

> Over the years, I've learned the need to justify my requisitions for plant and equipment investments for other than manufacturing reasons. Let me give you an example. With the introduction of the new herbal drops, the plant needed additional capacity. Any request for added capacity based on a straightforward manufacturing rationale would have been hard to sell. Headquarters would probably have urged me to squeeze more production out of my existing plant. My approach, therefore, was to emphasize the tax advantages we could obtain from setting up new equipment The tax savings alone would pay for the equipment in eight to nine months. Since the equipment has to be installed within a year from the time the product is introduced, I received approval in record time.

Das noted in connection with this new capacity investment, "Here's a good case in point where a tax incentive benefited everyone involved. RHL got needed additional capacity, RVI got an attractive investment, and India got new, efficient facilities for a new product."

Taking into account business–government relations in India as a whole, Das noted:

> The environment in India is generally not supportive of business and certainly not of multinational corporations operating in India. The private sector and the market mechanism are constantly questioned. The government evaluates business with respect to the extent to which it can help the country to achieve national social objectives. As a result of this situation, RHL's credentials are constantly challenged, making it important for us to prove that we are contributing to

Indian society. The proposals to increase exports and to develop products with a social benefit, such as an ayurvedic remedy for chronic pain, are good examples of how RHL is attempting to strengthen its national franchise by helping to solve Indian problems.

Shareholders

The Indian government's regulations also led to a change in RHL's shareholders structure in 1983. RHL came under the Foreign Exchange Regulation Act (FERA) because it had greater than 40 percent foreign equity. Manufacture and sale by all industrial companies in India had to be carried out in accordance with industrial licenses issued by the Indian government. Since many companies, including RHL, were outgrowing their industrial license, the Indian government had been obliged from time to time to grant both general increases in production in excess of licensed capacity as well as specific requests for such increases. As had been the case with all FERA companies, however, RHL's request for grants of specific production increases had been rejected. For Das, this situation presented serious limits to growth.

Then in the late 1970s, the Indian government began to push for reducing foreign ownership to no more than 40 percent in all companies except those involved in high technology or those primarily in export. Several FERA companies complied. Some companies, notably IBM and Coca Cola, preferred to withdraw from India rather than dilute their shareholding. Das described his experience in dealing with this challenge to RVI, with its 55 percent equity share of RHL:

> A number of the corporate executives were strongly opposed to any dilution of

RVI's holdings in RHL. For one thing, RVI has 100 percent ownership of most of its subsidiaries and does not hold a minority position in any. For another, the sale of shares would incur a book loss. Major devaluations in the rupee resulted in RVI's investment being overvalued on the balance sheet.

Whatever the merits of individual cases, the Indian government was committed to the electorate for reducing foreign ownership in Indian companies. RHL's management tried to get an exception on the grounds that its pioneering work in developing a strain of mentha arvensis which was sufficiently drought and disease resistant to be grown in India qualified the company as involved in high technology. The Indian government rejected this claim on the basis of the low manufacturing technology involved in producing RHL's products.

While battling the Indian government for an exception to the new requirement for foreign ownership, Das was at the same time trying to convince headquarters of the advantages attached to reducing its ownership to 40 percent. This reduction in foreign ownership would remove the company from the severe FERA restrictions to growth. Das explained:

> I tried to make clear that RVI would do better owning a smaller share of a larger operation than a larger share of a smaller one. In any event, the company might have been able to delay the equity restructuring for another year or two by dragging out the dispute in the courts, but eventually it would have been compelled to reduce its ownership.

A senior executive at RVI headquarters provided further perspective to management's thinking:

> To start with, there was a major split in headquarters on whether or not to reduce RVI's ownership to a minority position. It was not a matter of being unwilling to share the profits or to open our affairs to scrutiny. After all, Indian investors already owned 45 percent of RHL. Rather it was a reluctance to lose positive control of a business with our good name on it. RVI holds its managers to high standards of behavior as well as of performance. And there were those of us who opposed any possible impairment of our ability to ensure that these standards be met. After all, our name and reputation mean a lot to us.

Following RVI's decision to reduce its ownership to 40 percent, Das made every effort to reassure headquarters of his intentions to continue his dedication to RVI. The strategic plan stated:

> Our objective will be to continue to get full and continuing access to RVI products, technology, and ways of working. In turn we will manage the Indian business in order to maximize RVI's interest and continue to add value to RVI through transfer of management people to RVI subsidiaries ... After deconsolidation, our focus should shift from operating profit to profit after tax.

As of late 1984, 60 percent of RHL equity was owned by approxtmately 8,750 Indian shareholders, with an average holding of approximately 100 shares. The largest Indian shareholders were government-owned financial institutions and Mr. S. C. Banta, RHL chairman, with respectively 10.7 percent and 6 percent shares in RHL. The 1984 shareholders' annual meeting, held in a theater, was attended by some 1,200 shareowners.

EXHIBIT 1
RICHARDSON-VICKS INC. FINANCIAL SUMMARY, 1979–1983 ($ MILLIONS)

	Year ended June 30				
	1983	1982	1981	1980	1979
Summary of operations					
Sales	$ 1,116	$ 1,116	$ 1,088	$ 929	$ 829
Investment, royalty, and other income	9	17	16	14	8
Total income	$ 1,125	$ 1,133	$ 1,104	$ 943	$ 837
Cost of products	444	433	428	360	329
Selling, advertising, and administrative	517	502	485	408	362
Research	35	32	29	22	19
Interest	21	23	14	11	9
Other	10	29	13	11	20
Total costs and expenses	$ 1,027	$ 1,019	$ 969	$ 812	$ 739
Earnings before taxes	$ 98	$ 114	$ 135	$ 131	$ 98
Income taxes	46	47	52	56	50
	$ 52	$ 67	$ 83	$ 75	$ 48
Discontinued operations	-	-	(4)	9	15
Earnings for the year	$ 52	$ 67	$ 79	$ 84	$ 63
Earnings per common and common equivalent share	$ 2.10	$ 2.74	$ 3.31	$ 3.56	$ 2.66
Key statistical data					
Cash	$ 119	$ 91	$ 106	$ 109	$ 142
Tangible net assets	265	395	361	461	373
Working capital	245	225	198	290	268
Current ratio	2.0	2.1	1.8	2.0	2.2
Long-term debt	168	41	13	18	19
Stockholders' equity	471	486	452	550	498
Property, plant, and equipment (net)	242	247	209	184	209
Expenditures for property, plant, and equipment	34	58	49	53	48
Depreciation	21	19	16	13	12
Advertising and promotional expenditures	278	276	268	230	206
Average common and common equivalent shares (in thousands)	24,511	24,448	23,982	23,678	23,706
Cash dividends paid per-share common	$ 1.48	$ 1.48	$ 1.32	$ 1.20	$ 1.06
Number of employees	10,700	11,000	10,800	15,000	15,000
Stock price					
High	32.5	30.9	42.5	27.0	31.0
Low	22.4	20.5	22.3	17.5	19.8

Source: Annual reports.

EXHIBIT 2
RHL FINANCIAL HIGHLIGHTS (table in lakhs: units of 100,000 rupees)
(1983 financial details in $ millions)

| Summary of Operations | Years Ending June 30 | | | | | | | | | |
	1983	1982	1981	1980	1979	1978	1977	1976	1975	1974
Sales	2,330	2,000	1,919	1,656	1,335	1,389	1,247	1,086	889	738
Earnings before taxes	390	229	159	174	96	201	185	125	124	57
Income taxes	297	155	103	123	71	156	132	85	92	36
Earnings after taxes	92	74	56	51	25	45	53	40	32	21
Dividends	54	36	36	30	18	36	26	26	26	11
Retained profits	39	38	20	21	7	9	27	14	6	10

Profit and loss account for year ended June 30, 1983			**Balance sheet as of June 30, 1983**	
Sales	$23.3		Current assets	$7.2
Expenses	19.7		Inventories	5.3
Raw and packaging materials		8.0	Fixed assets	3.0
Wages		2.7	Total assets	$10.2
Operations		5.5	Current liabilities	5.6
Sales and excise taxes		3.3	Long-term debt	1.0
Other		0.2	Deferred payment credits	0.2
Profit before taxes	3.9		Equity	3.4
Profit after taxes	0.9		Total liabilities	$10.2

Source: Richardson Hindustan Limited annual report.

Note: The exchange rate as of late 1983 was approximately 10 rupees to one U.S. dollar.

EXHIBIT 3
KEY FINANCIAL OBJECTIVES (COMPARISON TO INDUSTRY AVERAGE)

Our financial performance for 1982–1983 compares favorably with industry average on all financial indicators. Our financial ratios are expected to further improve by 1987–1988.The most dramatic improvement is expected in the PAT ratio, which will rise as a result of our plan to invest in tax-designated areas. Our tax rate would come down to 48 percent as a result and PAT ratio go up to 11.6 percent. In the interest of producing a conservative plan we have not projected the full benefit of tax incentives and have shown tax rate at 66.4 percent (versus 76 percent today).

	Industry Average* (1982)	Our Company	
		Actual 1982–1983	Objective 1987–1988
Sales growth (five-year compound)	15.2	10.7	20.0
Earnings before tax (% sales)	9.8[†]	19.1[†]	22.3
Earnings growth (five-year compound)	9.2	14.2	23.9
Earnings after tax (% sales)	3.9[†]	4.6[†]	7.5
Debt/equity	0.43	0.33	0.30
Return on shareholders' equity (%)	21.8	27.1	36.0
Price earnings multiple	8.1	9.6	10.0

Source: RHL strategic plan, August 1983.

*Industry average is based on performance of following companies:

1. Warner Hindustan
2. Pfizer
3. Abbott Laboratories
4. Parke-Davis
5. Colgate-Palmolive
6. Beechams (HMM)
7. Cadbury
8. Ponds
9. Nicholas
10. Nestle (FS)
11. Brooke Bond
12. German Remedies
13. May & Baker
14. Cyanamid

†Industry sales figures include excise tax (10%–15%), thus increasing the denominator, while RHL figures exclude excise taxes from sales. If excise taxes had been included in RHL fiscal 1983 sales (as in Exhibit 2), earnings would have been 16.7% before tax and 4.0% after tax.

Chapter 9

■

Building a General Management Career

GENERAL MANAGEMENT SKILLS

In this book we have discussed at some length the skills required by those who fill general management roles. More important, your discussion of the cases in class should have given you a strong sense for the extent to which different leaders approach the tasks of general management in varying ways depending upon their personality, their values, and most of all the skills that they bring to the job or are able to develop.

Because the role of general manager seems unbounded in its demands, virtually everything about a person appears relevant to the job. Personality, education, and experiences all contribute to the repertoire of responses that are available to deal with constantly changing environmental settings. Jean Riboud is perhaps a most extreme example because his preparation for the general management of Schlumberger involved harsh wartime experiences, banking, and an apprenticeship mostly observing Marcel Schlumberger. But each manager we have studied developed a way of motivating people and unleashing their capabilities; keeping their focus external, on the customer and away from bureaucratic issues; integrating their efforts even when objectives such as globally strong but locally responsive seemed contradictory; and most of all driving the organization so that it could build and sustain strategic direction.

Building a general management career involves acquiring a wide set of skills. Because we are in a learning environment, the skill that often gets the most emphasis is *analytic ability*. In some ways, it is the easiest to see and admire whether employed in shaping the strategy of the firm, designing structure or systems, or devising a rapid response to a competitor's thrust. But because analytic skills are visible, they are often given more emphasis than they may deserve. For example, it was important that Bill Gates saw the central role that software would play, but it was his skill in building an organization in which towering programming talents could work effectively without their egos destroying the team spirit of Microsoft that underlay the spectacular profitable growth. All the general managers we studied seemed to have considerable analytic skill, but it wasn't analysis primarily that made them successful.

Perhaps more rare and certainly more central was their *creativity*. Where did Anita Roddick get the idea of The Body Shop? While certainly serendipity played its role, where did she develop the range of skills that enabled her to turn necessity into the remarkable theater stage that we know today as a Body Shop store?

The general managers we have studied often displayed good *judgment*, especially in their assessment of people. They seemed able to observe what was happening and draw useful conclusions for their company. Bill Gates could see that Towne was not the right person and hired Jon Shirley in Towne's place. Lou Hughes could see in the communist aparatchnik Liedke a man who had the skill to lead the workers of Eisenach out from under the tutelage of the Kombinat.

As well, the general managers we have studied were often skilled at *risk taking*. It was not so much that they bet their companies as it was that they bet their careers. They took positions that were not obvious to others and by doing so drove their organizations forward at difficult times. Hirotaro Higuchi committed Asahi's fortunes to dry beer. Ralph Stayer risked transforming himself as a manager in order to build a more effective organization. Eberhard von Korber announced a profit improvement goal of 500%.

And in their roles of building the work environment and as performers, we have seen remarkable skills in *human relations—persuading, communicating, charming, integrating* and even *wheeling and dealing* in order to motivate, coordinate, and direct the efforts of normally fractious employees, peers, superiors, and interested parties in the government and community. Zaki Mustafa and Lou Hughes demonstrated how entrepreneurs can function in large organizations, in Hughes's case, right through the turmoil of political upheaval. John McCoy was able to articulate a vision and manage the detail of his organization's life so that highly decentralized bank managers functioned as a closely cooperative and mutually supportive team.

The obvious question any student must ask is, "How can I acquire the skills I need that my parents didn't give me?"

STEPS IN A GENERAL MANAGEMENT CAREER

For most students, the first skills to be acquired are analytic. We go to school before we start to manage, and unless we have unusual experience in our extracurricular life, most of what we learn consists of substance and the tools of analysis. Much professional school education involves acquiring mastery of a relevant set of tools, relevant substantive knowledge, and—at least as important—the perspective and values of the field. A general manager's perspective is necessarily rich and complex. It must encompass the views from the orbiting satellite, the helicopter, and the trenches, and its territory includes the functions, the markets, and the people and practices of the company. Both short and long term are important. And as we have seen, the professional manager *serves* his or her organization, so an ethical perspective on the activities of the organization is vital. Concepts and tools for understanding these problems should be the core of a business management curriculum.

Following school, the first job for many graduates is a kind of postgraduate education in analysis working in a staff capacity or as a consultant. While consulting may also develop skills in communication and persuasion, the work is intensely analytical, especially in the early years. Some managers argue that consulting also develops a person's awareness of the centrality of a client's needs as opposed to his or her own. But the lack of responsibility for outcomes, so vital to development as a manager, is what many believe to be the key drawback of consulting as a training ground for general management.

General management skills are usually acquired on the ground in trench warfare—inch by inch. The work of a consultant often involves viewing problems from helicopter or even satellite level. One works with data and recommendations rather than individuals whose daily patterns of behavior have to change.

For those who actually become general managers, it is typical to begin working in an operating function developing the skills of supervision and the knowledge of a field of activity necessary to produce results. It is as a performer that one gets evaluated and promoted in the early years of a career.

The shift from doing to managing is the next big transition. For many, it is extremely difficult. To put the matter in as extreme a fashion as possible, doers promoted to managers discover that their first instinct is to substitute their effort for that of those they are supposed to help and direct, or even to compete with them. It takes time to realize that they must "get ahead of the curve" by setting the agenda and marshaling resources so that their organization can move effectively. Budgets emerge as a tool for planning and resource allocation rather than a nuisance, and the world of peers and superiors becomes a network of potential allies and counselors rather than competitors and evaluators.[1]

---

[1] Linda Hill's *Becoming a Manager: Mastery of a New Identity* (Boston: Harvard Business School Press, 1992) provides a graphic description of this transition.

The next to last major step comes when a manager is asked to move from a functional role to take on responsibility for an entire business unit. As we have seen in Chapter 8, even for middle managers, managing a business unit requires new skills—those we associate with the leader of an entire enterprise. Integrating the work of the functions and providing strategic direction are the critical new components of the task. Inevitably this means working on problems where many of those contributing know more about their particular areas than does the manager, and where many of the key parameters are unknown because they turn on the future behavior of competitors, regulators, and the broader economic environment.

The final step comes when a general manager takes on the responsibility for the total enterprise. This means caring for the balance sheet and working with the sources of finance. The media and politicians may pose demands that are far more difficult to sort out than those of customers and suppliers. Balancing the requirements of financial and product markets with the desires and needs of the internal organization while inventing a future that is strategically sound is the ultimate task of top management.

Learning comes from reflecting on experience. Involved are improved recognition of problems, or the potential for problems, and an improved repertoire of responses. A sensitivity to the importance of sequence and forum for action is acquired, as well as skill in carrying out different sorts of tasks. For example, very few people start working life able to give negative feedback effectively. As a consequence many do the job poorly if they even attempt it. Yet an effective general manager must find a way to accomplish that critical activity even if it means teaming with a colleague who is good at the task.

Accelerated learning comes when managers are able to get others to help them in self-reflection or in developing their repertoire. This is what mentors do for their protégés. By pointing out patterns in behavior that are strengths or weaknesses, by offering tips on tactics at key moments, and by pointing out role models or offering useful rules of thumb, friends and supervisors can speed up the growth process. In effect, these are what musicians call "master classes" where top performers watch younger players go through their paces and give them hands-on coaching.[2]

In some business societies, this activity is routine. In Japan, for example, it is common for superiors to take individuals or small groups out for dinner and drinking. These informal occasions provide a comfortable venue for the very delicate discussion that coaching represents. In the United States, it is less common to see this work carried out routinely by

---

[2] Donald A Schon's *The Reflective Practitioner: How Professionals Think in Action* (New York: Basic Books, 1983) is perhaps the first academic treatment to call attention to this phenomenon. Chapter 8 discusses the work of managers in a "learning organization."

senior managers. Instead, one of the more important skills for the aspiring general manager to develop is the identification and nurturing of mentors.

As individuals develop as managers, they typically begin to build a rudimentary theory of what it is they are doing. These theories provide answers to questions such as "What motivates people?" "How is their capability best unleashed?" "How are individual efforts best integrated?" "How can I best learn what my customers want?" "How can I avoid being blindsided by change?" There is a surprising degree of variation in the answers given, some emphasizing money, others insecurity or fear, others empowerment and the intrinsic rewards of accomplishment. Some managers work heavily with outsiders, consultants, or members of their board of directors. Others spend extensive time going around lines of authority to meet with low level people who are actively engaged in the field. But an adequate theory must be consistent in all respects. It takes time before a manager can expound a theory like James Lincoln's. But the experience of Ralph Stayer at Johnsonville Sausage suggests that with effort and help, radical improvement is possible.

Many young managers hope that they can move quickly to general management by starting with a small or a family organization. They quickly learn that if these more entrepreneurial businesses are largely free of bureaucratic constraints, they are full of the human and political problems associated with dominant personalities—the sort of people who build new companies. The contrast between the career choices facing Gurcharan Das at Procter & Gamble, Geraldo Mazzalovo at Ferragamo, or Chuck Lacey at Ben & Jerry's illustrates the opportunities and problems in large multinational corporations and small family organizations.

Our hope in preparing this book is that you can accelerate your learning by studying the work of the 36 general managers who are presented in the cases. Examining their progress as strategists, organization builders, and performers, you can develop your skills of analysis and problem solving, so important to the work of general management. You can also examine the other dimensions of your toolkit to see where on-the-job training is badly needed and then plan your job search and career to build on your strengths and correct your weaknesses. General management is a fascinating and rewarding career.

Gurcharan Das's Career Choices

In November 1985, Procter & Gamble (P&G) unexpectedly acquired Richardson-Vicks (RVI) and greatly changed Gurcharan Das's professional situation as president of Richardson-Hindustan (RHL). RVI's strong international presence offered P&G an opportunity to accelerate its mounting overseas thrust. The opportunity to enter India held a special appeal, not only because of its enormous population, but also because it had long been the almost private preserve of archrival Unilever. Under Das, RHL, with its direct coverage of 220,000 outlets, would lead the attack.

The union with P&G had other profound implications for RHL and Das. Under Richardson-Vicks, marketing was king, queen, and jack. P&G's emphasis on product technology elevated the importance of research and product development. According to Das, "For the first time, we are talking about technology-led products, as against marketing-led products. For us,

the immediate challenge is to learn how to manage properly the research and development functions."

Das's response was to overhaul RHL's management structure and process by delegating operating responsibilities to product teams, comprising middle-level managers from marketing, manufacturing, R&D, finance, and purchasing. Senior executives were to be looked upon as resources only. This new approach was entirely in line with Das's personal preference for participative management. And along with the resulting increase in emphasis on manufacturing and research, the product team was also consistent with another P&G basic policy—promoting from within. The product team provided a ready vehicle to train and develop people for increased responsibility.

In 1987, as Das looked forward into the future, he could see the possibility of many opportunities opening up to him. P&G management had come to regard him highly, and the company certainly had a growing need for people with his talents. This need pertained to its future corporate global strategy. At the same time, he had been contacted by some of Rajiv Gandhi's close advisers to explore the possibility of taking on an important government post. Finally, Das continued to be tugged by his broad intellectual interests and by the pleasure he derived from writing about Indian history and politics.

INTERVIEW WITH GURCHARAN DAS NOVEMBER 6, 1986

Even before the merger, I was at a crossroads with Richardson-Vicks. I had turned around the business in India, and they wanted me to take on additional responsibility. But India was one of the few countries that was really growing explosively, and so they did not want to take me out of India. And so about a year ago they added Thailand and Indonesia to my Indian responsibility. Now, with the merger with P&G, the opportunities have become even more exciting, because P&G does not exist in India. They are keen to enter the Indian market, recognizing, of course, that Lever has a fortress here. So, there is a desire on their part to keep me in India to build that business. I think that they would also like me to play a larger role on a larger canvas. The Indian opportunity itself could be a very huge opportunity that could make the Indian company grow by leaps and bounds. And given my responsibility during 1985 and 1986 for Thailand and Indonesia, some of the same principles would apply, to introduce the broad stream of P&G products, competing against Lever in these three countries.

From a personal standpoint, I am happy to stay on in India, but equally comfortable abroad. I have a deep sense of Indian identity—a sense of responsibility to the country in which I was born and where I was initially educated. I have the desire to give back to the Indian society what I have taken from it.

In the 40 years since independence, India has been governed under well-motivated socialist policies. These policies had tremendous flaws and have kept India back. I have strong convictions about what needs to be done and would like to be able to influence government in that direction. My advice has been sought, off and on, in various forums. It is something that I like doing, something which I feel I should be doing.

I had a liberal education at Harvard. A sense of responsibility and obligation is built into you as a Harvard undergraduate. At least this was true when I was there in the early 60s. We were challenged to contribute to society. I think that this has always been with me, a need to justify that what I am doing is somehow for the greater good.

We have a relatively small business today with sales about $35 million. But it is a highly profitable business, one of the most profitable subsidiaries in the company. With the broad stream of P&G products, I think within five years we can increase sales manyfold. We can finance this growth largely through our own reserves and local borrowing. Let me remind you that P&G only owns 40 percent of RHL's equity. The other 60 percent is divided amongst 10,000 Indian shareholders.

I think the connection with P&G will make us more product-driven. P&G puts tremendous emphasis on the superiority of its products, on technology. Frankly, we would not be entering the Indian market unless we have products which can win in blind product tests against the leading competitive product in the category. So it will force us to innovate, because you cannot really bring a ready-made product which is being sold in the U.S. or other parts of the world into India. The market needs are often distinctive, and one also encounters supply constraints in India. You have to formulate the product using Indian materials. Take soaps for example. India does not allow tallow-made soaps. Soaps have to be made with vegetable oil. This would be a special challenge for us because P&G's soap technology is largely tallow-based.

One department in our company that would really become strong, and happily so, would be R&D. As you know, we have already set up a center for herbal medicine. But where P&G will make its biggest impact will be in connection with its household products, building our consumer-oriented technical skills in India. One of the things that has struck me about P&G is how consumer-oriented their product development people are, much more so than our own research people. I think this is one of the keys to P&G's success. They will make us a lot more product-quality-driven, and this will be good for the Indian consumer.

The merger with P&G has been viewed positively by our people. It has thrown a range of new products right into our laps. This has happened at a time when the government is decontrolling great parts of the economy. We are in a good takeoff position because we have a strong organization which is highly regarded in India for marketing and even more so for sales and distribution. Our capabilities in the distribution area are probably second only to those of Lever.

We are now assessing which P&G product categories make the most sense for India, which are the most attractive. In the last three months we have been working fairly intensely with the help of some P&G people to study consumer habits in India. We are trying to find out their unfulfilled needs, their level of satisfaction and dissatisfaction with the products that are available to them in the various categories in which P&G participates. P&G has around a hundred products, and it is important that the first one we choose for India should be a hit, a winner.

In terms of human resources, we will have the possibility of bringing some people from P&G into India. Parenthetically, P&G has a large number of Indians working for them all over the world. We are hoping that some of these Indians would want to come back and work in India. Whether they are willing to come back and work as local managers rather than expatriates is yet questionable. We would not be able to justify to our own people bringing in other Indians and putting them on expatriate salaries. Yet, we are optimistic that we will be able to attract some of them. Also, we have a number of good people in all functional areas who could be sent out to P&G for training and brought back to manage these new products.

P&G has recently created a brand-new division to be responsible for business operations in Asia and the Pacific. This is significant because they do not create a new division every day. They have selected a person from Richardson-Vicks to head the division. This person, Todd Garrett, who had been in charge of Richardson-Vicks's operations in the Far East and Latin America, in fact, was my former boss. He reports directly to the president of P&G International.

Soon after the merger, we had a meeting in Hawaii with the senior people from RVI and P&G to review the activities of the two companies in the various countries. I met one day with Ed Artzt [vice chairman of the board and president, Procter & Gamble International] and the next day with John Smale [president and chief executive, Procter & Gamble]. Both of these meetings were very positive. We basically agreed that P&G would enter India using Richardson-Hindustan as the vehicle.

Since then, we have had quite a few P&G people visit and work with us. For example, a product development expert, who happened to be Indian, spent a month doing habits studies. He was, of course, helped by our own market research people. Manufacturing people have also been working with us to determine our capabilities for proceeding with expansion. So we have had a fair amount of contact with people from there, but basically, the contacts have been initiated by us, as should be the case.

An international career would be very rewarding, and it would be a lot of fun pioneering businesses in different parts of the world. There is another concern my wife and I have. We have two sons who are now 13 and 14. What brought us back to India was in fact our desire that our boys, who were seven and eight at the time, ought to get rooted in their own culture. I believe it is very important in this world to have a sense of identity. A sense of identity to me meant that wherever I was abroad, I knew who I was. I found that expatriate children were often confused and did not know who they were.

When the time comes, I would like the boys to experience the kind of undergraduate education that I did in a good university in America or England. While they are in a good school in Bombay, by Indian standards, the method of education is the very old-fashioned rote system. I would like them to learn to question more, to think independently. Against those benefits of a better education abroad, one has to balance the cost of again removing them from India.

Cervantes makes a wise comment in this connection. When Don Quixote returns to his village in the Mancha, after traveling around fighting windmills and helping maidens in distress, he observes that the universal is really in your backyard. In effect, cosmopolitan life is at odds with the universal. We have certainly found that there is a value in being in one's own country.

The basic values we grew up with were not very different from middle-class values elsewhere. My mother instilled in us the value of hard work and integrity. I remember as children, at night

before going to bed, she would read to us excerpts from the Hindu epics Mahabharata and Ramayana. These are illustrative of the models of behavior. My father was spiritually inclined. All his vacations and spare time would be spent visiting the ashram [refuge] of his guru. Ever since I can remember, he meditated for an hour each morning and evening.

What has been most rewarding to me has been to witness the development of RHL and of its people over the past five years. I have gained a great satisfaction from seeing my people grow in their capabilities, from creating a sense of teamwork amongst them, and from having given them a vision of leadership.

From the very first day that I came back from India, I constantly talked about values. The values I talked about were the obvious ones, respecting the individual both inside the organization and outside, building strong relationships with suppliers, being close to the customer, and innovativeness. Over the years we have evolved a philosophy of what RHL is all about. This year's company annual report is focused precisely on these values [Exhibit 1 contains a copy of the president's letter].

As to the difficult side of the work, two or three things come to mind. Dealing with the government bureaucracy is one of the more frustrating parts of the job. I have to go to Delhi to obtain licenses or price increases when our products are price-controlled. You might have to wait in corridors, sometimes for hours, until some junior functionary deigns to see you. That is a frustrating, unrewarding part of the job.[1]

---

[1] In this connection, a *Wall Street Journal* article on Indian bureaucracy, published November 7, 1986, contained the following quoted comment by a government functionary: "I don't have money, I don't have intellectual power, but what I can do [in reference to one of India's leading industrialists] is

Another negative side to my job has been the need to fire people. I have not had to fire too many people, but certainly my share of them. Some people who had worked for the company for many years had to be fired for incompetence. One person had to be fired for lack of integrity. It was shocking to discover a person who had worked for the company for 20-odd years involved in a fraud. Finally, I had to fire one person who was almost too brilliant for the organization, but who just could not fit in. Another frustrating experience in my career was when I had to report to a boss whom I viewed as incompetent.

For the last five to six years I have been working slowly, over weekends and vacations, on a novel. Having a very demanding job and a fairly time-consuming avocation has meant less time for the family. This is one of the problems. I like to feel that when I am with them, I am there with them all the way. But I know that a particularly trying day often does have a way of filtering into the evening and night.

As far as the children are concerned, my wife has given them warmth and love. She is constantly available for them. I, in my own way, have tried to instill in them a sense of liberal values, of the ambiguities of life, and of a tolerance for different points of view. I find it curious that my adolescent boys are a lot more oriented to getting on and making money than I was. I never really particularly thought about making a lot of money. Financial rewards have obviously come, but they have always come sort of on their own without my really thinking much about them.

As I look back on a career of 22 years in business and look forward to probably another 20 years that remain, it strikes me that one of the reasons why I have

done well is that I have had a degree of detachment. Because of the type of education I had, I never really saw the business world as the be-all and end-all of life. I was not the typical gung ho MBA. I think a strong humanistic background, a broad liberal background with a continuing interest in literature and humanities has provided me with a counterpoint. I think this detachment has been useful and allowed me to cut off at the end of the day easier than might otherwise have been true.

Even today, I still see business with all its limitations. My friends in Bombay and around the world are from many professions. I like to keep in touch with literary people, people who are in the university, people who are in government. These diverse relationships help me to find meaning in something beyond the business world.

In a sense, this detachment is similar to my father's. His first priority was his search for God. But my upbringing has been such that I am agnostic. It is very hard with the kind of background that I went through to be anything else. But this agnosticism is coupled with an intense search for meaning in life. That is why I studied philosophy. I changed over from the sciences because I thought maybe in philosophy there might be answers. It turned out, in fact, there were just more questions. Philosophy taught you to ask the right questions.

EXCERPTS FROM INTERVIEWS WITH FAMILY, FRIENDS, AND COLLEAGUES DECEMBER 13, 1986, AND MARCH 20, 1987

Bunu Das

(Born and raised in Kathmandu, Nepal, Bunu met Gurcharan Das in New York. They were married in 1971 and had two sons.)

---

keep J. R. D. Tata waiting outside my office for 20 minutes.''

I have always enjoyed traveling and meeting people. But now that we are in India, I am reluctant to leave again. I suppose, as one grows older, one wants to return to one's own support system. Gurcharan's brother lived for 18 years in the United States. Over time, his wife increasingly missed India, and they finally returned. The dilemma for most expatriate Indians is that they dream to go home but are reluctant to give up the economic advantages connected with living abroad.

As I see it, if we had to leave India for P&G, there is little likelihood of ever returning while on that career track. Government service, on the other hand, frightens me. Gurcharan is naive about government work . . . he thinks he will be able to achieve something, but politics cannot be changed in two or three years.

Would he be happy writing full-time? Not yet. He *likes* what he does as a manager. Then there is the matter of living standard. Neither one of us has family wealth. We own a house in the country which could be sold, and we have a small pension in the United States. These funds would permit us to live modestly, but we could not afford to send the children abroad to top universities. Perhaps after another five or six years, when the boys have completed college, we could consider it.

The only thing I resent with our present life is that Gurcharan is always in a rush. There are only 24 hours in a day. Gurcharan works long hours, he is fond of sports, he needs to write. As a result, we greatly limit our social engagements. Even then, he does not have enough time for the children. As adolescents, they need a father's attention.

My family heritage has been with the civil service. I have had to learn what business life is all about. The more I learn about private business, the more I dislike it. There always seem to be people who are trying to advance at someone else's expense. This happens in government too, but there is a big difference. One might

not reach the top, but one is never shipped out as can happen in business.

Despite his success to date, Gurcharan will face problems whichever direction he takes. On the one hand, his U.S. education and his long association with American multinational firms would make him vulnerable in government. Indian officials are paranoid about CIA spies and U.S. financing of Pakistan. On the other hand, being brown-skinned could hurt his chances of moving into a high executive rank in an American corporation.

At some point, one has to come to terms with what life is all about. What is success? What is doing well? Is it increasing sales and making more profits? Is that good for mankind? At what point do you say enough is enough? Now I am happy to drive a small car. When will I want a big car? Now I have 15 saris. When will I want 300 saris?

There is another issue which concerns me. The P&G executives' wives I have met were more involved with the company than were RVI wives. Since I value my private life, I am not sure just how I will react to a more closely knit corporate culture. I see many benefits to this way of life and quite liked the wives I met. But I fear that the increased involvement could lead to problems, since a wife's standing in the corporate family surely depends on her husband's standing.

Were Gurcharan offered an opportunity requiring our departure from India, my initial reaction will be that I do not want to go. Then I will begin to reconsider, rationalizing the benefits associated with the opportunity and will go along with Gurcharan's desire. I come from an Eastern tradition. What will happen will happen. It is predestined.

Udain Patel

(A psychoanalyst by profession, Dr. Patel, age early 40s, was a longtime friend of Gurcharan Das.)

There are two aspects of Gurcharan's personality. He has ambitions to succeed in the corporate world. He also has a deep emotional tie to India. In my view, while Gurcharan would gain some satisfaction from the power, the trappings, and the accomplishments in corporate life, business success would not satisfy the passionate side of his personality.

A government job would most suit his emotional needs. Contributing to India would be in tune with Gurcharan's idealism. But this route would be risky. He would need a clear-cut job and responsibility. Otherwise, he will experience great frustration getting enmeshed in politics and bureaucracy. He is too straightforward an individual to deal with political machinations.

He likes to delegate. But that style probably would not work in government. The Indian bureaucracy fosters an attitude of distrusting people. Of course, if Gurcharan were able to change this attitude to one of trust by demonstrating its organizational power, he would derive great satisfaction from such an accomplishment.

His choice then comes to this. A career in government offers Gurcharan the greatest potential psychic rewards but carries an enormous risk of frustration and failure. A career in multinational corporate life offers much satisfaction and is less risky in that the outcome depends so much more on his performance. But it fails to correspond to an important emotional need.

What are Gurcharan's strengths and weaknesses? One of his strengths is his ability to pick out patterns from information. He has a good sense of what matters in a situation. Second, he has high ethical standards in dealing with his people. For example, he has literally agonized about how to help a key subordinate develop as a manager without intruding inappropriately in his personal life. Most other corporate presidents would take the position that such a person has to make it or fail on his own. Gurcharan has great concern for his colleagues as people. Third, Gurcharan is able to delegate and not interfere in his subordinates' work.

On the weakness side, he seems to have a growing problem with his span of attention. He frequently interrupts his train of thought and seems distracted, making it difficult for others to interact with him with any comfort. Perhaps this just reflects the life of a corporate executive, where one must constantly jump from one issue to another.

Allocating his time between career, family, and his other interests is already a problem for Gurcharan, and it will become more severe as he climbs up the ladder. The artistic man in Gurcharan needs unstructured time. He is not getting time for reflection these days. One can sense the pressure on him.

Camelia Panjabi

(Ms. Panjabi, vice president of marketing for the Taj luxury hotel chain, was a longtime friend of Gurcharan Das.)

Gurcharan was never your typical corporate man. In the early years he was always talking about whether to go off to an apple orchard and write. It is surprising to see him return to writing after so many years. Most of us give up on our youthful ideals.

What is remarkable about Gurcharan is how he solves problems. He is a great example of a lateral thinker, coming up with solutions most others would never conceive.

If the government gave Gurcharan a good offer, he would jump at it. Most of us in our 40s are inclined that way. Just children when independence came, we are the first generation who can consider themselves pure nationals, not former British subjects.

I do not think that he will leave India. If he did, he would soon regret it and would probably come back if opportunity beckoned. It would depend on what he does, of course. Just taking on responsibility for a broader geographical scope would probably not offer him the intellectual challenge he needs. Expanding the ayurvedic business might. It would be breaking new ground and would in some ways retain his connection with India.

He suffers the schizophrenia common to Indians with a Western mind and an Indian soul. The synthesis of the two is difficult; contradictions question every line of action. I often wonder how he succeeds in the competitive business world being as gentle as he is. It is an enigma to me.

Bansi Mehta

(Mr. Mehta, a distinguished chartered accountant and a member of the Richardson Hindustan board for 10 years, was friend and adviser to Gurcharan Das. They also shared an interest in theater and classical Indian music.)

Gurcharan has brought a sea-change to the company. His sensitivity to management style and his responsiveness to issues stand out. In India, he would be called a "radical humanist"—someone who is different and who relates well to people. As a director, I would hate to see him leave RHL. He has shown that a person can be different and a humanist and still succeed in business. It is most unusual for someone at his level in India.

His strengths include a razor-sharp mind incisive in grasping issues, his ability and inclination to delegate, and his ability to communicate. This last characteristic is probably his greatest strength. He can deal with people at their level. My only possible reservation about his management abilities is that I am not sure that he can handle a crisis situation.

So far he has faced circumstances which allowed time for persuasion. But there are times when decisive, even militant actions are called for, and he might not be able to act accordingly.

In RHL he has a good situation. He has a track record which gives him license to experiment. And he has built up a management team that appreciates him and what he stands for. He would be giving up a lot were he to leave. It would take him a long time to achieve the same favorable circumstances.

On the other hand, I do not think that we can retain Gurcharan for very long as full-time president—perhaps five to seven years. He might move into politics in such a way—becoming a member of Parliament, for example—so as to allow him a continued affiliation with the company in a reduced capacity. He could become a part-time executive director or chairman of the board.

A full-time high government position is another possibility, but this is probably not the right time for him to go. For one thing, it is very difficult to be a professional manager in today's government. Gurcharan is apolitical and would be frustrated by the political maneuverings. For another, any job with the present government could be short-lived. The political situation is somewhat unsettled at present. Then too, a top government job pays about 8,000 rps per month. Gurcharan would have to downgrade his standard of living by 75 percent were he to switch.

He will not go to another company; he is too committed to RHL for that. If he dilutes his involvement in RHL or leaves it, it will be because of political activities.

Gurcharan is an Indian in the full sense—in his thoughts, his expressions, and his philosophy. He yearns to maintain his ties to India. Even if he goes elsewhere, he will come back. He could not get what he wants outside India.

EXCERPTS FROM INTERVIEWS
WITH P&G EXECUTIVES
JULY 6, 1987

Todd A. Garrett, General Manager, Asia/Pacific Division, P&G International

(Garrett had started his career with P&G, serving as brand manager during his five years' employment. Leaving because of his desire to live in the Northeast, he spent the next 17 years in marketing and general management with Richardson-Vicks. He returned to Cincinnati as a result of the 1985 merger. In January 1987 he was selected to head the newly created Asia/Pacific Division, with responsibility for all operations in Australia, Hong Kong, India, Indonesia, Malaysia, New Zealand, the Philippines, Singapore, Taiwan, and Thailand, and the Richardson-Vicks business in Japan.)

(When asked about P&G's objectives for Richardson-Hindustan Limited (RHL), Garrett noted two. First, RHL was to maintain its strong market share in its core businesses. Second, it was to serve as the conduit for P&G to introduce new categories of products into India. He continued, "In a more general sense, RHL has several things to offer P&G. First, it is a source of earnings in its own right. This past year alone, RHL grew 28 percent in volume and more than doubled its profits. Second, it has an ayurvedics laboratory which has the potential to develop products for India and beyond. Third, with its strong distribution and marketing, RHL can help P&G to learn about consumers' needs in India and the relevance of its products to the Asian market. In effect, India can serve as a greenhouse for P&G's ideas in the Far East.")

Das has a very strong track record. He is a mature and proven person. He has always shown strong market direction and leadership, and he is now showing strong general management leadership abilities. He seems to be adapting to the P&G purpose and way of doing things. He is intelligent, creative, knows how to guide organizations and work, and his business is booming. In terms of recent accomplishments, Das has completed a major restructuring of the Indonesian sales organization and, very important in P&G, has developed a successor. He has met all financial goals. His career possibilities are good. He is a multicultural person with many languages, and he is sensitive to different cultures.

His big move will be to show that he can manage outside of his home country. He did demonstrate this to a certain extent in Mexico, in the United States, in Spain with General Foods, and in his last two years with regional responsibility for Thailand and Indonesia. This latter task is particularly difficult for an Indian, since they are often disliked as merchants of the Far East.

He is favorable about P&G. He is lured by the government and in fact received a proposal about a month ago. He spoke to me and to Ed Artzt during a meeting in June. I know Ed spent quite some time talking to him. Others in the company would be staying and continuing to establish their track records of business accomplishment, which is one of the main criteria for career advancement at P&G. I told him that he would have to be the one to decide what he wanted to do over the next 15 years.

The company is going to celebrate this year its 150th anniversary. In preparation for this event, a statement of purpose was written last year. It is to be a living and breathing document. For example, every manager will have responsibility for recruiting at colleges. The whole thing starts with recruiting, and then in challenging individuals.

Results are the great equalizer in P&G. People are promoted on merit and only from within. This policy forces managers to take people development seriously. When you know that you will be working with the same people the rest of your life, you have to be honest with each other. In this company, people care about each other. There is a real loyalty to the firm, and that will be a major competitive advantage over the next 15 years. There is a feeling that *we* are P&G; it's the glue that holds the place together.

Don't get me wrong. No place is perfect. Actions will happen here that don't conform to all our ideals. But by and large, the heart is in the right place, and the people try to do the right thing.

Stanley D. Hanson, Personnel Manager, Asia/Pacific Division

(Hanson was from Richardson-Vicks and had worked for Todd Garrett before the merger.)

There was a good fit between P&G's and RVI's Far Eastern operations. It was total immersion for us right away. We were "Procterized." One big difference was P&G's 100-percent-promotion-from-within policy and the resulting importance of college recruiting. At RVI, we might have had 75 percent promotions from within, and that can make a big difference in people-development practices. Another difference is that people jump from function to function more in P&G than they did at RVI. They also move faster from job to job, averaging perhaps two and a half years.

The personnel staff is now quite lean compared to what it was in RVI. With a larger personnel staff and a smaller size company, there was much more direct involvement by headquarters people in the career planning at RVI than is true at P&G. In P&G, everyone knows everyone else, and the selection of people is based on personal knowledge. There is a gut feel about fit and ability based on years of association. At RVI, we depended on a more explicit measurement system. I have had a close association with Das

and his people for some years and have worked directly with them on career planning.

For Gurcharan, there is now much more competition, but there is also much more opportunity. In RVI he had a chance to become one of four division presidents. In P&G, there are many more divisions. Das's job for the next three or four years will be to build India. His job after that could take him anywhere.

Ed Artzt, Vice Chairman of P&G and President of P&G International

Career planning—keeping good people here—is the lifeblood for P&G. We have a strict policy of promotion from within. Each generation of future management is already in the company. It has to be identified and developed. We have an understanding right away with our new people that they are going to be here for a long time.

We look for individuals with intelligence and promise. We put them in work situations where their development will be greatest. We believe in a diversity of experience and responsibilities for our people. People need to get exposed to different organizational environments to give them a diverse experience. We ask our good people to make moves that would not necessarily be ones they themselves would select. We often toss good guys into snake pits. What is key is to let the managers know that the moves are in their best interest. In my view, good career paths often contain more obstacles than people would select on their own. People have to be challenged and grow up the hard way. Accepting tough assignments requires that the people have faith and trust in the company. People have to believe in the policies and that their performance will form the basis for advancement in the company.

Das is a capable guy at a crossroads in his career. He is strongly motivated to achieve and is comfortable in facing up to challenges. What Das needs to know is that we really mean it when we say that he will get the same opportunities as anyone else in the company and that he is not just a good Indian manager doing a job that no one else can or wants to do.

His problem is in feeling that he is not a "Procter guy." As one RVI person said to me recently, "I know two years ago I was acquired, like furniture, but I was never hired. Now that you have given me a new assignment I feel for the first time that I have been hired. I now think differently about the company and about myself." You have to give new people a reason to believe that they are now part of the team and make them feel that they are hired. You have to demonstrate that you have career plans for them and that these career plans are no different than for your other people. People need to have a sense of being on a level playing field in competing for higher positions. We have good role models to show that foreigners can do well in P&G. Three group vice presidents in international are foreigners, and the head of R&D is an Egyptian who has worked in Europe most of his life.

We used to have a problem in that you were favored if you were associated with soaps and detergents and to some extent if you were in the marketing function. This is largely breaking down.

The main problem in "Procterizing" the RVI people is to get them to understand what that means. Many of them think that the P&G culture means that you promote from within, that you write one-page memos, that the basis of accounting is statistical cases, that everything is in writing, and that you have a hardy, disciplined management. "Procterizing," as we see it, includes the following three things: (1) that the business is product-driven (in RVI it was advertising-driven); (2) that data-based marketing analysis underlies strategy planning; and (3) that organizational development rests on recruiting and training. In RVI, they had a great deal of detail on how a person performed, but never did anything about it. In effect, they had a good report card to evaluate a person, but did little to improve that person. In contrast, in P&G, the trainer is evaluated by his performance in bringing up his people. In effect, each manager has to be very concerned on how he develops his people.

I told Das that we thought a great deal of him and that we were prepared to risk commitments that we would not do without him there. I told him that we had confidence in him and that the investments in India would be based on this confidence. Once he was able to get a new framework in place in India and launch some new products, his career would blossom. This is a tall order for Das. RHL is good, but small. It has never really bellied-up with a tough competitor.

What complicated the situation is that we had decided to take Thailand away from him in mid-1987 since it was a small operation and distracted him excessively. We would rather have him spend the 25 percent of time that he spent on Thailand dealing with the challenges in India. We had to somehow convince him that this was not a diminution of his power and authority. That little wrinkle complicated the discussions.

We figure that it will take about three to five years for him to get P&G off to a good start in India. I told him that this was the most important thing that he could do anywhere in the company.

I also told him to trust us. We are reluctant to make promises. We don't want to make promises we can't keep. Also, we like to keep our options open. We might have to put a person in a lesser position than we had originally intended. For a person to accept this, there has to be faith in the company and in the superior. There also has to be a payoff eventually.

J. Allan Campbell, Personnel Manager, P&G International

P&G and RVI were alike in basic values but very different in the way they did things. For example, RVI had a policy of 75 percent promotion from within but in some parts of International did not achieve that goal. As a result, there was not sufficient pressure in the system to develop its own people. RVI's paperwork was better than P&G's, but our knowledge of the people is greater since we grew up together. What has helped the acculturation is that the RVI managers have welcomed the additional training and the investment in research. As of today, this combination is working well.

P&G International has about 5,000 to 7,000 management employees out of 23,000 total. Of the 35 general managers abroad, only three are American. More and more countries are being run by local or third-country nationals.

The company does not really use organizational charts or sophisticated long-term replacement tables like other companies. That's just our culture. But it does maintain a formal inventory of top development people. On the international side, there is an inventory of everyone with potential for general management ranks.

Smale (P&G chairman and CEO), Pepper (P&G president), Artzt, the group vice presidents, and the senior vice president meet one time a year to review the top people. They spend two to four full days doing this. In addition, the administrative committee, including 30 or so top managers in the company, meet every Tuesday at 10:00 AM to discuss business and people-change proposals. It is an informational affair, ensuring that important moves are first reported to this group of people.

There are any number of practices that help to unify this company. For example, the company holds meetings every November with every general manager in the world attending, and one-half of the managers at the next level. These sessions involve reporting business results, training, communications, and "taking communion," if you will, to our direction and to our principles. Then there is our policy of moving people around in their job assignments. Also important, the top people constantly travel around and are highly visible and accessible. Artzt travels a lot. He is on the ground in each International Division at least once and sometimes several times each year. And Smale joins him two or three times each year. There is a great deal of face-to-face contact in P&G. We spend an enormous amount of money getting people around the world and in training. This creates a commonness of purpose.

It is not necessary for Das to have experience in Cincinnati. There are several top people who have spent little or no time in Cincinnati. The company is so homogeneous in values, even though each business has its own personality, that a person can be anywhere and get a comparable exposure.

If a person is really talented, P&G has an ability to be loose/tight. Tight in carrying out its principles, but free to accommodate various styles. There is lots of discussion, a river of information, in this company on how people feel about their jobs and about possible opportunities. We try to accommodate our people. People can say no to assignment proposals and survive at P&G.

EXHIBIT 1
PRESIDENT'S LETTER, RICHARDSON HINDUSTAN ANNUAL REPORT, 1985–1986

Shaping Our Future Through Commitment to Core Values

We at RHL, have come to realize that our future depends on our being able to define for ourselves a set of core values. Well-defined values help people in knowing the boundaries of freedom and provide a practical guide to day-to-day decision-making, managing people and setting high standards of performance. They also enable individuals to work in harmony and eventually give the business an unassailable competitive edge.

A Journey of Discovery

It is not enough that a few people in the organization believe in these values. Each and every person has to be committed to them. The development of this credo has been a journey of discovery for all of us at RHL. Over a period of time, through a number of ways, we have identified three common basic beliefs:

1 *Existing for the Customer* - All our actions within and outside the company have an impact on our customers. This probable impact should be the keystone of decision-making at RHL. Every activity in the company should be tested to see whether it gets us new customers or satisfies existing ones. Once this belief in the importance of the customer becomes widespread in the company, it will be translated each day into hundreds of small activities, all with a customer focus.

2 *Respect for the Individual* - It is a company's people who make it prosper–the "average" person (not the "star"), who once he becomes committed, makes the big difference. For individuals at every level make countless small decisions daily that make for success or failure of the whole enterprise. And people behave according to how they are treated. If we repect them and create an atmosphere of openness, trust and where people feel confident and motivated, then we will succeed.

3 *Continuing Innovation* - I believe that much of our success can be attributed to our desire to do things in a better way. Experimentation is the proven route to innovation. That is why we value people who are restless, who experiment, and who show initiative. We must also remind ourselves that innovation is quickly stifled unless failure is tolerated.

This is the set of beliefs each member of the RHL family is committed to, but only after discovering a personal meaning in it. We are constantly reviewing our policies and practices so that they reflect this commitment. Recently, we introduced the concept of Product Teams at RHL. Each team has the responsibility for a product and consists of young executives from marketing, manufacturing, R&D, purchase, etc. Through these teams, we find our people performing with greater autonomy, demonstrating far more concern for the customer, and removed from the hierarchical structure, showing much more initiative and innovation. Some of the teams are already behaving like minicompanies within RHL, producing and marketing their products.

The ultimate test of beliefs is in their practice (for only when they are practiced do they become values). In this report you will observe people at RHL talking about how these beliefs affect their work lives.

President

Ben & Jerry's Homemade Ice Cream Inc.: Keeping the Mission(s) Alive

As Chuck Lacy composed his thoughts before the September 1990 Ben & Jerry's board meeting, he knew that the central decision of the day would set the tone of the company for years to come. And because he was to assume the presidency in January, Chuck felt a special need to put his imprint on that decision.

From the beginning, Ben & Jerry's was determined to be a company with a strong and unique set of values. It wanted to be a force for social change. It wanted to stand for something better than the typical corporation. A key policy exemplifying that intention was the 5-to-1 salary ratio, which dictated a maximum spread between the lowest- and highest-paid employees of five times—a dramatically narrower differential than the 90 to 1 norm in American business. (See Exhibit 1 for a description of the policy.) The policy aimed to recognize the contribution of lower-level employees and to link top-management rewards to companywide compensation. It also made a philosophical statement that corporate America tended to overpay top management and underpay entry-level employees, and that corporations should strive to reduce discrepancies in wealth distribution. A source of great company pride, this policy had drawn more attention, internally and externally, than any other at Ben & Jerry's.

In recent years, however, the board and various company members had begun to question its fairness and effectiveness. Ben & Jerry's had grown much larger and more complicated. New positions that required a higher level of management skill and professionalism were being created, and the 5-to-1 rule was a major barrier to offering competitive compensation packages to prospective candidates. Midlevel employees saw limited incentive for promotion, as salary compression began to equalize middle- and upper-level compensation. Top management was paid substantially below market rates for their work.

Moreover, growth had brought people to the company who questioned the underlying assumptions of justice and equity behind the rule. To many, arbitrarily tying compensation levels to a specific ratio was not necessarily more fair than using market rates for the jobs performed.

Ben Cohen was unimpressed by these arguments. As a founder of the company and a driving spirit behind its development, he was completely committed to the philosophy behind the 5-to-1 policy. He was not willing to sacrifice the principle behind the policy for any reason. Many in the company and on the board agreed with Ben. They believed that the 5-to-1 rule symbolized values which were central to the company's identity and success, and that morale would be devastated by a change in the policy. Accordingly, they sought managers who supported the social mission and who were willing to make the financial sacrifices it entailed.

The debate about the policy had gone on for almost two years and was beginning to erode board morale. Chico Lager, the outgoing chief executive officer, strongly believed that the policy had to change. The board would soon decide the fate of the 5-to-1 rule.

BEN & JERRY'S

In 1963, Ben Cohen and Jerry Greenfield became friends at their Long Island, New York, high school. Fourteen years later, dissatisfied with their respective careers, they decided to start a food company together. Resolving to live in a rural area more consistent with their 1960s counterculture perspective, they moved to Vermont. After an initial attempt at starting a bagel delivery service, they enrolled in a $5 correspondence course on ice cream making from Penn State. They incorporated their company on December 16, 1977, and opened the first Ben & Jerry's homemade ice cream shop in Burlington four months later with an investment of $12,000.

The shop was an immediate success. By 1980, relatively low wintertime demand at the shop drove the pair to package their ice cream in pints and to start selling them to small retail outlets in the area. In 1981, sales had increased enough to require expansion of manufacturing into a second building.

The company was able to sell as much ice cream as it could make; growth consistently averaged over 60 percent annually (see Exhibit 2), and came mainly from entering new geographic markets with pint-sized containers. By 1990 the company was selling its products in all major markets and had a fairly high penetration of the relevant supermarkets and "mom-and-pop" stores that represented the bulk of ice cream sales (see Exhibit 3).

In 1988, Ben and Jerry were named U.S. Small Business Persons of the Year at a White House ceremony. The company had become a phenomenon.

THE ICE CREAM INDUSTRY

The total retail value of ice cream and all related products sold in the United States was roughly $9.3 billion in 1990, or almost 1.5 billion gallons. The frozen dessert market was large, slow-growing, and fragmented into a host of mainly local and regional companies. It was segmented into categories based on butterfat and air content according to the proportions shown in Table A.

Virtually all superpremium ice cream was marketed in round containers by the pint. Other categories were typically sold in rectangular containers, primarily by the

TABLE A
SEGMENT SHARE OF U.S. PACKAGED FROZEN DESSERT MARKET, 1990 (RETAIL VALUE)

	(%)	Total Sales ($ millions)
Packaged ice cream		$2,100
Superpremium*	9.5%	
Premium	38.1	
Regular	38.1	
Economy	14.3	
Ice milk		$ 500
Superpremium	0.4%	
Premium	54.4	
Regular	36.4	
Economy	8.7	
Frozen yogurt		$ 350
Superpremium	15.7%	
Premium	67.4	
Regular	16.4	
Economy	0.5	
Frozen novelties		$3,200

Source: International Ice Cream Association, June 1992
*Containing more than 14% butterfat and 20% or less air.

half gallon (see Exhibit 4). Distribution cost was an important factor, particularly in the lower-priced, bulkier segments.

Although the mix of products changed significantly over time (see Exhibit 5), per capita consumption of ice cream barely rose from roughly 15 quarts per year in 1970 to almost 17 quarts in 1990. Ninety-four percent of all households ate ice cream, and consumption was highest among families with young children and persons over 55 years old. This demographic fact indicated that per capita ice cream consumption could exceed in the 1990s the 19.5 quart per year peak hit during the early 1960s. (Exhibit 6 indicates per capita consumption in the United States by region.)

Ice cream consumption was not as seasonal as one might suspect: the three months of summer accounted for about 30 percent of the annual consumption of ice cream. Supermarket ice cream inventories turned 35 times per year, and the product

generated five times more profits per square foot than the average product sold in the supermarket. Producing ice cream, from mix creation to packaging and freezing, required almost six hours. The highest-quality products cost the most to produce. Ben & Jerry's products, for example, were known for having numerous and large chunks of added ingredients, a process that was much more difficult and costly to achieve than using smaller pieces. Consumers considered taste and creaminess the key qualities of an ice cream.

The Superpremium Ice Cream Market

Superpremium ice cream was distinguished from other ice creams by its higher fat content and its lower level of "overrun," the amount of air contained in the ice cream. As a result superpremiums tended to taste richer and creamier than traditional ice creams. Competition in the superpremium category was focused on product quality, flavor differentiation, and marketing. Once a consumer had made the choice to "invest" in a superpremium ice cream at twice the price per ounce of premium ice creams and three or four times the price of regular ice creams, a 5- or 10-cent-per-pint price differential was not a critical factor in the ultimate purchase decision.

It was only in the 1980s that several companies began to capitalize on market research that showed that ice cream consumers valued quality over price. Major packaged food companies such as Kraft (Frusen Gladje) and Pillsbury (Häagen-Dazs) flooded the market with new varieties of ice cream and other frozen novelties. Several small companies briefly flourished and then stumbled (Steve's

Homemade Ice Cream) or perished (Shamitoff Foods). During the 1980s, product quality and price points trended upward as consumers came to view ice cream as an affordable luxury. This attitude allowed premium and superpremium ice cream volumes to grow at a 14 percent annual rate during the 1980s, about seven times as fast as the average consumer product.

As aging baby boomers began to see their waistlines expand, processors responded with "reduced guilt" products with lower fat and cholesterol, enabling light and fat-free ice cream categories to develop. At the same time, demand for superpremium ice creams continued to grow.[1] As ice cream manufacturers addressed smaller market niches in order to stimulate growth, the market fragmented into hundreds of flavors and a half dozen gradations of fat, from superpremium with 20 percent butterfat to fat-free frozen desserts with no sugar. During the 1980s, virtually all of the gains generated by the superpremium and premium categories came at the expense of the middle brands. This trend was projected to continue into the 1990s.

Following this initial period of rapid growth, the superpremium ice cream market experienced a "shake-out" in the late 1980s that, according to industry analysts, continued into 1990. Initially, some of the smaller players that had not established a strong retail foothold were eliminated. Since then, the shake-out was expedited by a shelf space crunch in the freezer cabinet as retailers made room for the increasingly popular frozen yogurts, ice milks, and nonfat ice creams. (Exhibit 7 shows the leading superpremium producers in 1990.)

The superpremium ice cream market in 1990 separated into two relatively distinct subsegments: producers oriented toward traditional flavors such as vanilla, chocolate, coffee, and chocolate chip; and "mix-in" flavors. Mix-in flavors generally consisted of a base ice cream of vanilla or chocolate to which chunks of candy bars, cookies, nuts, and/or fruits were added. Mix-in costs ranged from zero for vanilla to as much as a third of cost of goods sold for some flavors. Selling prices, however, were the same for all flavors. Thus, a product mix skewed toward traditional flavors would produce significantly higher gross margins than those of a mix-in specialist. Häagen-Dazs and Frusen Gladje primarily targeted the traditional flavor subsegment, while Ben & Jerry's and Steve's focused on the mix-in category. During the 1980s, Häagen-Dazs and Ben & Jerry's emerged as the dominant forces in their respective categories. (See Exhibit 8 for Ben & Jerry's market share figures.) Häagen-Dazs had attempted to introduce flavors more toward the mix-in side of the spectrum in order to abate the rapid market share growth of Ben & Jerry's. This effort was only modestly successful, as it appeared that the new flavors had cannibalized Häagen-Dazs's existing line while Ben & Jerry's continued to flourish.

Ice cream was a flavor-loyal business. Consumers typically perused a variety of familiar ice cream brands and selected an appealing flavor or arrived at the store with a particular flavor in mind. Producers could alleviate the risk of losing a potential sale by having a broad selection of flavors in stock as often as possible. The

---

[1] The ice cream market reflected a 1980s trend—that consumers were interested in only the very best or the very best value.

"hit ratio" could be raised by having a higher percentage of the company's flavors on the shelves and/or by increasing the number of flavors the consumer would buy through constant flavor innovation.

By 1990, the competitive environment had become more intense and difficult. Penetration of the leading brands had been achieved in all significant markets. Market growth was projected to slow dramatically to rates of roughly 4 to 5 percent. These factors were creating strong pressure for competitors to fight each other for market share in order to achieve acceptable growth rates. At the same time, local competitors had sprung up—some mimicking Ben & Jerry's iconoclastic style. Potential competition from traditional ice cream makers became a greater threat as these producers became increasingly aware of the segment's attractions.

Future competition in the industry would require a more sophisticated approach to product innovation and product line management. Consumer tastes were changing, requiring products with lower cholesterol and calories than the traditional superpremium ice cream without sacrificing taste. Light ice milk, frozen yogurt, and frozen novelties were being introduced by the superpremium competitors in order to respond to these requirements. Indeed, at least eight competitors had introduced superpremium[2] frozen yogurt by late 1990, and sales in this segment were expected to double in 1991. These new products vied with existing products for shelf space. Broader product lines, more complicated manufacturing and distribution systems, and more so-

phisticated marketing and promotion programs would increasingly be required in the 1990s.

Distribution

Due to the importance of product quality, flavor selection, and shelf space in gaining share of the superpremium ice cream market, product distribution became a major focus for market participants. The distribution method of choice was "direct store delivery" whereby the ice cream was delivered directly to the store and placed on the shelf by a distributor representative. Häagen-Dazs created such a system at great cost and distributed roughly 50 percent of its products through company-operated distributors versus outside distributors. Ben & Jerry's, alternatively, had two primary distributors, Dreyer's Grand Ice Cream, Inc., and Sut's Premium Ice Cream, as well as several other local distributors that serviced limited market areas. In 1990, sales to Dreyer's accounted for 43 percent of total company sales,[3] and sales to Sut's represented 10 percent. Dreyer's distributed Ben & Jerry's in all of the company's markets except New England, Florida, and Texas, and Sut's distributed Ben & Jerry's ice cream in parts of New England.

Both Frusen Gladje and Steve's were losing distribution at a rapid pace in 1990. Since 1989, Frusen Gladje's grocery store distribution dropped roughly 15 percent in Ben & Jerry's core markets, and its

---

[2] Superpremium loosely defined as being those products sold in pints and in the same price range as superpremium ice creams.

[3] Ben & Jerry's represented a significant component of Dreyer's business, accounting for roughly 12 percent of that company's sales in 1990. At the same time, Dreyer's had been instrumental in Ben & Jerry's success at penetrating markets, specifically in the West Coast where Dreyer's has a dominant market share.

market share fell about five share points. At the same time, Steve's share had declined two to three percentage points. Industry analysts believed that virtually all of the market share losses of Frusen Gladje and Steve's had been picked up by Ben & Jerry's, while Häagen-Dazs' share had increased only slightly. Combined, Frusen Gladje and Steve's had almost 10 percent of the market, but this was down from 25 percent roughly two years earlier and was still shrinking.

Ben & Jerry's Position

By 1990, Ben & Jerry's had established itself as a strong number two in the super-premium ice cream market nationwide and was the fifth largest ice cream maker of any type. Ben & Jerry's products were sold in bulk to its own retail scoop shops and to the food service industry, but the vast majority of its sales were through grocery stores in pint containers. Since most outlets carried only one or two brands of superpremium ice cream, being number one or number two was crucial in the business.

Ben & Jerry's distributed its products through a variety of channels. The largest distributor, Dreyer's Grand Ice Cream, Inc., was also the producer and marketer of Edy's brand ice cream. Dreyer's also produced approximately 25 percent of Ben & Jerry's ice cream in a plant in Indiana. This arrangement had been struck when Ben & Jerry's capacity had not increased rapidly enough to meet demand. Interested in penetrating new markets quickly, Ben & Jerry's management saw the Dreyers arrangement as a temporary stopgap. In order to maintain the made-in-Vermont character of Ben & Jerry's ice cream, Vermont dairy products were shipped to Indiana for processing in the Dreyer's plant.

The arrangement caused some controversy for the company, and the press had run several stories speculating about how the relationship between the two companies might evolve.

Ben & Jerry's ice cream came in a wide range of innovative flavors, including Cherry Garcia and Chunky Monkey. Except for the temporary arrangement with Dreyer's, it was made in Vermont with only Vermont dairy products. The higher costs of using Vermont dairy products depressed margins but were thought to be outweighed by the image of quality and purity which the policy conveyed. The ice cream contained no artificial ingredients or preservatives, although some of the candy and cookies used in various flavors did. The company claimed to add one and a half to two and a half times more flavorings to its products than any other competitor. The rumor inside the company was that Ben had a sinus problem and thus had difficulty tasting any flavor until it was quite potent.

In 1988 the company began to make Peace Pops and Brownie Bars to supplement its product line and to gain shelf space. In 1989 it added Ben & Jerry's Light, with one-third less fat and 40 percent less cholesterol than its regular superpremiums. A frozen yogurt line was planned for 1991.

By 1990, two plants were operating at full capacity and a third was planned. Approximately 330 people worked at the company, with over 220 in the manufacturing operations at these facilities; fewer than 20 people were employed outside of Vermont. A strong commitment to quality and an emphasis on manufacturing skills pervaded the organization.

Although Ben was by far the largest shareholder, stock in the company was publicly traded (see Exhibit 9).

Continued Growth at Ben & Jerry's

Until 1990, much of Ben & Jerry's rapid sales growth had been a function of the company's expansion into new geographic markets. In the future, industry analysts believed that the company would be increasingly dependent on further penetrating existing markets, given that it had developed a strong distribution network. Ben & Jerry's had identified 12 core markets, representing roughly two-thirds of total U.S. superpremium sales, and had achieved distribution in every major chain in those markets by late 1990.

Flavor differentiation also played an essential role in the growth of Ben & Jerry's product line. The company steadily added new flavors to the line and eliminated slower-moving flavors in order to have a constantly improving flavor selection available. Ben & Jerry's aggressively introduced new flavors in 1990, including Chocolate Fudge Brownie, Rainforest Crunch, Wild Maine Blueberry, and Fresh Georgia Peach Light, which contributed to the company's 24 percent volume increase by late 1990. Ben & Jerry's product mix in 1990 was heavily weighted toward lower-margin products. Looking ahead, industry observers saw opportunity to promote some of the higher-margin products and/or introduce new products that incorporated lower mix-in costs, such as Ben & Jerry's Frozen Yogurt, being introduced in 1991. Clearly, these developments in the marketplace posed some new challenges for Ben & Jerry's management, including the need to develop innovative marketing strategies and programs and fast-response management information systems.

THE SOCIAL MISSION

The growth and success of the firm had not been the original intention or expectation of the two founders; they each had serious misgivings about the idea of building a substantial profit-making corporation. They both held strong antibusiness biases growing out of their 1960s radical backgrounds. The fact that their scoop shop in rural Vermont had become a significant and well-known company was a somewhat uncomfortable surprise to them. In fact, Jerry left the company in 1982 to be with his companion in Arizona while she attended graduate school. Part of his reasoning (reversed by his return in 1985) was that, with 20 rather overworked employees, the company was becoming too impersonal for him. Although sharing these concerns, Ben was convinced by a friend that, with the right approach, a large and growing company could become a large and growing force for social change. With that expectation, Ben stayed on and became the dominant personality and driving spirit behind the development of the company's unique culture of social activism.

The company developed in a manner referred to internally as "caring capitalism" and which some observers have called zany, adventurous, and antiestablishment. These beliefs showed up in practices and policies throughout the company.

The company's approach to marketing and promotion reflected these attitudes. Ben had always taken a personal interest in this area. Traditional approaches to marketing were rejected. No market research, media spending, or test marketing was employed. Ben decided that the marketing and promotional approach of the company should be educational events focused on social issues. They should be fun as well. With this basic philosophy, a variety of creative and effective promotional activities were developed. The company's pint containers were used to promote campaigns for such issues as support for the family farm and to ban Bovine Growth Hormone. The company sponsored summer music festivals across the country. Its factory tour in the Waterbury plant became the second most popular tourist attraction in Vermont, with one-half of the tour admissions going to local charities. Its annual meetings became highly publicized "events"—activities that lasted several days and included promotions for world peace, environmental, and other social causes. A converted bus with solar-powered systems carried a traveling vaudeville act around the country. The publicity surrounding these types of promotional activities was extensive. The company developed a distinctive image as a result.

Ingredient sourcing was pursued with a social purpose. For example, a Native American farming group supplied all the blueberries for the Wild Maine Blueberry flavor; a New York bakery run by homeless people supplied all the brownies for a flavor called Chocolate Fudge Brownie; and a flavor called Rainforest Crunch, using ingredients native to the Brazilian rainforest, was developed to encourage its preservation.

In 1985, the Ben & Jerry's Foundation was established to fund community projects. It was financed by a 7½ percent pretax profit contribution, the highest level of charitable contribution of any U.S. public company.

The company planned to open a plant and adjacent scoop shop in Karelia in the Soviet Union to promote peace.

Ben organized 400 companies into a group called 1 Percent for Peace, which worked toward efforts to encourage peace through understanding.

Environmental issues were taken seriously and included investment in state-of-the-art greenhouse technology for waste-

water treatment at the plants and the appointment of an environmental affairs director.

Internally, the company attempted to be progressive and caring. Free employee assistance programs helped with any type of personal problem. On-site day care facilities were started. Employee benefits were comprehensive. The company tried to create an atmosphere where employees could be "real." Dress was casual, even in the offices, and company meetings were celebratory bashes. The tone and style of the organization were friendly, informal, and direct, and the management philosophy was participatory. Hierarchy was viewed with suspicion and distaste. No organization chart existed, although jobs and responsibilities were generally understood. Jerry was head of the Joy Gang, whose purpose was to "spread joy" across the company.

The overwhelming majority of employees believed that the company did a good job as a socially conscious company contributing to its various communities. In the 1989 annual report, William Norris, founder and chairman emeritus of Control Data Corporation, signed the social audit, which the company conducted each year, with a statement that his "conclusion is that Ben & Jerry's has the most thoughtful, comprehensive social concerns program of which I am aware."

The firm's socially conscious approach was not part of a carefully crafted commercial strategy but resulted from the personal orientation and interests of the founders. Ben commented in the March/April 1988 issue of *New Age Journal:*

> Jerry and I never planned on going into business, so we don't have your normal business head. We didn't go to business school. I didn't graduate from college. Jerry was going to premed when we

opened up this homemade ice cream parlor pretty much on a lark. We were looking to make a livable wage, but we were not looking to get rich, and I think that's what's really different about us and our motivation to go into business . . . It's really interesting what you can do with business when you don't care about making a lot of money.

As the company grew, gained recognition, and succeeded financially, the need to be more explicit about the role of social activism in the company increased. A series of discussions to develop a mission statement resulted (see Exhibit 10). Arriving at the three elements of the mission—product, economic, and social—was fairly easy. Deciding the relative importance of each proved much more difficult. Some people advocated a focus on the economic mission of profit, shareholder value, and employee rewards. This, they argued, was the heart and foundation of any company. Others, led by Ben, argued for an emphasis on the social mission. This, they argued, was the spirit that drove the firm and the main reason for their support for it. Eventually, the board agreed to assign equal importance to each element of the mission and to highlight their interdependence. This theme was reinforced by Ben in a statement in the 1989 annual report:

> It's our objective to run Ben & Jerry's for long-term financial and social gain. We are becoming more comfortable and adept at functioning with a two-part bottom line, where our company's success is measured by both our financial and our social performance.
>
> We are convinced that the two are intertwined. And, we are convinced that attention to excellence, quality, and the social needs of our communities will lead to solid, stable growth of both our bottom lines.

Observers of the company who agreed with Ben's statement pointed to a number of factors. The unusual strength of the social mission caused a promotional boost, as interested reporters covered the company extensively. Many employees were motivated at least partly by it, and morale was high (see Exhibit 11). A Roper poll indicated that 52 percent of the population would pay 10 percent more for a brand made by a socially responsible company. The idea that doing well and doing good are consistent had gradually gained converts as the company continued to progress in both dimensions.

The orientation to the social mission had some questionable repercussions at the firm, however. Much less attention to cost and profit was demonstrated than in most businesses. For example, the company's three-year business plan contained no numbers and only 3 of 70 points in the plan referred to economic characteristics of the firm. Some traditional business methods that might have strengthened the company were either rejected in the zeal for an antiestablishment ethic or not discovered in the first place. The self-conscious rejection of hierarchy at the company made decision making and communication laborious and complicated. Everyone felt comfortable going to see Chico with problems or suggestions. This put an enormous burden on Chico, who was not necessarily the right person to deal with the issue in the first place.

As the number of people in the company grew, not everyone necessarily subscribed to the company philosophy. Practical pay and promotion issues predominated with many of them. As the potential for chaos increased with size and complexity, a smoothly functioning, well-organized system became more important.

The company didn't rate as well on these issues as on others (see Exhibit 12).

Ben, Chico, and Chuck

Proud of being a Vermont company, the management team and workforce were made up of people who lived in or were willing to move to a rural environment. The management group was young, with most of its members in their 20s and 30s. (Exhibit 13 describes the backgrounds of the management team.)

Ben was the clear leader of the company; he approved products, directed marketing and promotion, and was the driving force behind the social mission. A 40-year-old, bearded man who was forced to borrow a waiter's uniform for his 1988 White House award because he had no suits of his own, Ben personified the spirit of the company. Ben was not, however, interested in managing the details involved in building the organization. He was unequivocal about the values that he believed the company should represent, but the process of managing the company was unappealing to him.

As a result, in 1982 he brought Fred "Chico" Lager into the company as general manager. Armed with an MBA, a professional approach to his job, and a basic appreciation of the social mission of the company, Chico became the de facto head of the "economic mission" and the builder of the organization. As time went on, Ben's presence diminished. He even hired a marketing director in 1986—the job for which he had always taken personal responsibility. Chico was running the company.

As Ben observed the development of the company, he became increasingly concerned that the social mission was being lost. He expressed his concerns repeatedly. Ben's pressure did result in the

mission statement and a more sophisticated understanding of the value of the company, but it contributed to wearing Chico out. He was leaving for a six-month trip around the world in January, when Chuck Lacy would take over.

The 5-to-1 Debate

The discussions about the 5-to-1 compensation rule had become a symbol of the philosophical tension between the more "businesslike" faction headed by Chico and the "socially minded" faction headed by Ben. Feelings about the issue represented by the 5-to-1 rule were strong on both sides. As one director stated:

> The dissolution of the company is at stake. It is a battle for the heart and soul of the company.

Ben's side of the argument was clear and unequivocal. Whatever the apparent effects on the functioning of the company as a profit-making enterprise, the policy was simply morally correct. If it was impossible to do the right thing and to be involved in a commercially successful venture, then Ben and his compatriots would quit. Moreover, they believed that in fact the policy was part of the animating spirit at the company and that it was a key source of pride, cohesion, loyalty, and motivation, which were central to the long-term success of the company.

On the other hand, many others thought that this perspective was naive and dangerous. With a tougher market and competitive environment looming, and with a larger and more complicated company to manage, hiring and retaining the best possible managers would be crucial for the company's future. The 5-to-1 policy resulted in above-market compensation for the lower pay levels and a substantial penalty at the top levels (see Exhibit 14).

Pay constraints had already caused problems in attempts to hire some competent professionals into key spots. Morale of existing managers was also affected by the rule. Wall Street analysts had been making comments about high management turnover.

Chico Lager described his own attitude toward the policy:

> My problem with the ratio was that it didn't allow me, as the CEO of the organization, to recruit and put in place the management staff I needed to run the company. Trying to recruit senior-level positions became a nightmare. Most job searches lasted over a year. By offering compensation packages which were sometimes 25–50 percent below market rates, we limited the pool of applicants we considered. It was, in my opinion, one of the reasons why we often hired senior managers who didn't work out. Keep in mind that not only were we asking people to take large pay cuts from their existing salary to join the company, but we were also telling them that even if they did great work, their future compensation would be limited to minimal raises that were going to be based on whether or not we could afford to increase the pay scale for the entire company.
>
> The vacancies in senior management created a tremendous stress on the organization. We came very close to a financial meltdown during the period of time we were recruiting a CFO. Our existing finance staff was overwhelmed by the growth of the company. Our ability to manage the company intelligently, based on budgets, forecasts, what-if scenarios, etc. was nonexistent
>
> I also had feelings regarding the 5-to-1 from a personal standpoint, although these were definitely secondary to my concerns for the company. Still, in 1990, I was making the same amount of money (approximately $81,000) that I had made in 1988. During that time the company had grown from $47 million to $77 million. Every other employee had received annual salary adjustments during that time. My salary was tied to the employee who was about to be hired. Unless I increased the starting wage for full-time scoopers in our company-owned ice cream shops, I couldn't give myself a raise. Any increase to the entry-level wage for scoopers would have repercussions throughout the company's salary structure and major bottom-line impact. I was happier to make $5,000 less and have the company make $200,000 more. It wasn't worth the added stress that the added expenses would bring to my job.

For Chuck Lacy, the debate had special significance. He had been recruited to Ben & Jerry's in 1988. A tall 33-year-old with a trademark Ben & Jerry's beard, Chuck had observed the disagreement between Ben and Chico. He had grown concerned about Ben's disenchantment with the direction of the company. He believed that Ben's creativity and visionary leadership was a huge asset for the company. He also supported the principles behind the social mission.

He recognized the need for discipline, order, professionalism, and profit orientation. Everyone at Ben & Jerry's knew that the company was changing. The family spirit of the company was tested by the arrival of more and more newcomers. Controls, departments, memos, and procedures had inevitably made the company seem more traditional, corporate, and businesslike. This was a fact that everyone, including Ben, had to accept.

Chuck knew that he would bear a big share of the burden of seeing Ben & Jerry's grow from adolescence to adulthood. A few key decisions early in his tenure would set the tone for the future. The 5-to-1 ratio was probably the most important one.

EXHIBIT 1

TO: All Employees
FROM: Chico
RE: The 5-to-1 Salary Ratio

Employee compensation at Ben & Jerry's is based on several components. These include profit sharing, a stock purchase plan, and a benefit package. In addition, the company has a corporate salary policy that we believe is unique: a compressed salary structure in the ratio of 5 to 1. Basically, this policy means that the highest-paid employee of Ben & Jerry's (this includes corporate officers) will be paid at the rate no more than five times what the lowest-paid employee could earn for an equivalent workweek. The policy is implemented as follows:

1. The policy applies only to all full-time employees who have completed their probationary period. A full-time employee is defined in the employee handbook as ". . . one assigned to an established position with a regular workweek of at least (30) hours."
2. After six months of employment, all full-time employees receive the same basic benefit package, regardless of their salary or wage level. Some special benefits, such as stock options or stock grants, may be based upon salary. For example, stock options may be granted in proportion to an employee's annual wage.
3. The maximum annual salary payable under the 5-to-1 ratio is five times the lowest straight-time hourly rate paid any full-time, permanent, nonprobationary employee, multiplied by 48 (hours) and 52 (weeks). For example, if the lowest straight-time hourly rate were $6.50 per hour, the maxmium annual salary payable under this policy would be $81,120 ($6.50 × 48 × 52 × 5). The ratio is based on a 48-hour week to take into consideration that high-level salaried employees customarily work more than 40 hours per week.
4. The compensation of corporate officers may be a combination of salary and performance bonus. Combined, these two forms of cash compensation must be within the limitations of the 5-to-1 ratio as calculated above.
5. Employee salaries are determined by the company and its board of directors. Other than prescribing the maximum salary that *may* be paid to an employee, the 5-to-1 ratio has no effect on the amount of individual employee salaries.
6. The board of directors reserves the right to modify the compressed salary ratio.
7. The board of directors may at any time change or eliminate the 5-to-1 salary ratio.

The board of directors of Ben & Jerry's implemented the 5-to-1 salary ratio because of a belief that:

1. Everyone who works at Ben & Jerry's is a major contributor to the success of the company;
2. Corporate America overpays top management and underpays entry-level employees;
3. Corporations should attempt to reduce wealth distribution discrepancies; and
4. This board of directors of Ben & Jerry's recognizes that their compensation is linked to others in the company and that they benefit as others benefit.

Policy Goal

The corporate goal is to maintain excellent compensation packages for entry-level employees and thereby enable top management to achieve market rates.

EXHIBIT 2
BEN & JERRY'S—FINANCIAL HIGHLIGHTS ($000)

	1990 Forecast	1989	1988	1987	1986	1985	1984	1983	1982	1981
Net sales	$75,000	$58,464	$47,561	$31,838	$19,954	$ 9,858	$4,115	$1,815	$968	$615
Cost of sales		41,660	33,935	22,673	14,144	7,321	2,949	1,239	586	309
Gross profit		$16,804	$13,626	$ 9,165	$ 5,810	$ 2,537	$1,166	$ 576	$382	$306
Selling, general, & admInistrative		13,009	10,655	6,774	4,101	1,812	822	479	366	273
Operating income		$ 3,795	$ 2,971	$ 2,391	$ 1,709	$ 725	$ 344	$ 97	$ 16	$ 33
Other income		(362)	(274)	305	208	(31)	(13)	(26)	(11)	(4)
Income before tax		3,433	2,697	2,696	1,917	694	331	71	5	29
Income taxes		1,380	1,079	1,251	901	143	118	14	0	0
Net income	$ 2,400	$ 2,053	$ 1,618	$ 1,445	$ 1,016	$ 551	$ 213	$ 57	$ 5	$ 29
Balance sheet data										
Working capital		5,829	5,614	3,902	3,678	4,955	676	57	43	24
Total assets		28,139	26,307	20,160	12,805	11,076	3,894	509	295	193
Long-term debt		9,328	9,670	8,330	2,442	2,582	2,102	157	80	69
Stockholders' equity		13,405	11,245	9,231	7,758	6,683	1,068	154	21	77

EXHIBIT 3
MARKET SHARES AND PENETRATION IN MAJOR MARKETS, AUTUMN 1990

Market	Ben & Jerry's Share (Penetration)		Häagen-Dazs Share (Penetration)	
Baltimore/ Washington	34%	(84%)	48%	(79%)
Boston	53	(100)	39	(99)
Chicago	28	(88)	64	(93)
Denver	34	(88)	47	(98)
Houston	41	(74)	57	(64)
Los Angeles	20	(84)	70	(89)
Miami	26	(95)	68	(96)
New York	28	(93)	55	(100)
Philadelphia	31	(80)	52	(89)
San Francisco	38	(99)	60	(100)

EXHIBIT 4
PERCENT OF VOLUME OF PACKAGED ICE CREAM

Package Size	Economy	Regular	Premium	Superpremium	Total
Cup	1%	3%	1%	*%	1.8%
Pint	*	3	7	30	4.4
Quart	*	1	4	13	2.0
Half gallon	75	63	58	24	62.7
Gallon	5	7	1	2	4.6
Bulk	20	23	30	33	24.9
	100%	100%	100%	100%	100 %

Source: International Ice Cream Association, 1990.

*Less than 1%; Note: Totals may not add due to rounding.

EXHIBIT 5
SEGMENT SHARE TRENDS IN THE U.S. FROZEN
DESSERT MARKET

	1985	1990	1995E
Economy	13%	13%	12%
Regular	46	34	24
Premium	26	34	39
Superpremium	6	8	10
Ice milk	6	5	5
Frozen yogurt	3	6	10

Sources: International Ice Cream Association, National
Ice Cream Retailers Association, and Wessels, Arnold,
and Henderson.

EXHIBIT 6
PER CAPITA ICE CREAM PRODUCTION BY REGIONS,* 1989

	New England	Mid Atlantic	E.N. Central	W.N. Central	South Atlantic	South Central	Mountain	Pacific	United States
1987	23.42	16.96	15.31	23.44	11.69	12.51	12.01	15.44	15.26
1988	22.11	16.14	14.08	21.30	11.02	11.67	12.31	14.77	14.35
1989	19.44	14.67	12.15	21.18	10.89	11.03	9.72	13.841	3.39

Source: International Ice Cream Association, 1990.

*Per capita production is often used as a proxy for per capita consumption.

EXHIBIT 7
MARKET SHARES IN MAJOR U.S. MARKETS, SUPERPREMIUM ICE CREAM, 1990

Company	National	Boston	New York	Florida	Midwest	San Francisco	Los Angeles
Häagen-Dazs	49%	39%	55%	70%	70%	60%	70%
Ben & Jerry's	27	53	28	25	25	38	20
Frusen Gladje	8	3	4	3	4	1	2
Steve's	2	2	8	0	0	0	0
All others*	14	3	5	2	1	1	8

Source: A.C. Nielson; Wessels, Arnold, and Henderson.

*Includes a half-dozen very small regional companies such as Double Rainbow in San Francisco.

EXHIBIT 8
BEN & JERRY'S SHARE OF THE U.S. FROZEN DESSERT MARKET (wholesale, $ millions)

	1990 Market Size	1990 B&J Market Share	1990 B&J Sales	1994 Est. Market Size
Superpremium ice cream	$ 200	27%	$54	$ 241
Superpremium ice milk	10	60	6	0
Superpremium frozen yogurt	55	0	0	100
Novelties	1,000	NM	6	1,000
Bulk (foodservice)	NA	NA	9	NA
Retail	NA	NA	3	NA
Total			$78	

Source: William Blair & Company, April 1991.

EXHIBIT 9
BEN & JERRY'S STOCK PRICE AND STOCK OWNERSHIP

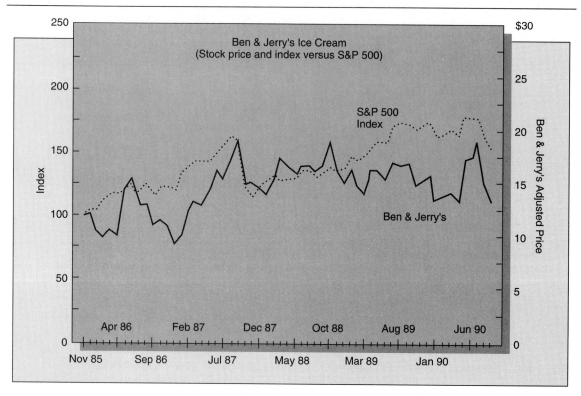

Source: Interactive Data Corp.

EXHIBIT 9 (continued)
BEN & JERRY'S STOCK PRICE AND STOCK OWNERSHIP

BEN & JERRY'S STOCK OWNERSHIP AS OF MAY 1990

Owner	Ownership of Class A Stock		Ownership of Class B Stock		Ownership of Preferred Stock	
	No. of Shares	% Shares[a] Outstanding	No. of Shares	% Shares[a] Outstanding	No. of Shares	% Shares Outstanding
Ben Cohen[b]	441,987	21.8	243,938	42.6	—	—
Mr. & Mrs. Fred Lager	41,600	2.1	26,800	4.7	—	—
Jeffrey Furman[c,d]	22,200	1.1	15,150	2.6	—	—
Merritt C. Chandler	36	*	15,150	2.6	—	—
All executive officers & directors as a group (7 persons)	506,062	24.9	285,906	49.9	—	—
Jerry Greenfield[c]	72,500	3.6	45,000	7.9	—	—
Elizabeth Bankowski	—	—	—	—	—	—
The Ben & Jerry's Foundation, Inc.[e]	—	—	—	—	900	100

*Less than 1%.

(a) As of 5/11/90. Each share of Class A common stock entitles holder to one vote; each share of Class B common stock entitles holder to 10 votes.

(b) Under the regulations of the Securities & Exchange Commission, Mr. Cohen may be deemed to be a parent of the company.

(c) As two of the three current directors of the foundation, which has the power to vote or dispose of the preferred stock, both Mr. Greenfield and Mr. Furman may be deemed, under the regulations of the Securities & Exchange Commission, to own beneficially the preferred stock.

(d) Does not include 210 shares of Class A common stock and 105 shares of Class B common stock owned by Mr. Furman's wife.

(e) While the foundation is an entity legally separate from the company, it may be deemed to be an affiliate of the company under the securities laws.

EXHIBIT 10
BEN & JERRY'S STATEMENT OF MISSION

Ben & Jerry's is dedicated to the creation and demonstration of a new corporate concept of linked prosperity. Our mission consists of three interrelated parts:

Product Mission:

To make, distribute, and sell the finest quality all-natural ice cream and related products in a wide variety of innovative flavors made from Vermont dairy products.

Social Mission:

To operate the company in a way that actively recognizes the central role that business plays in the structure of society by innovative ways to improve the quality of life of a broad community: local, national, and international.

Economic Mission:

To operate the company on a sound financial basis of profitable growth, increasing value for our shareholders and creating career opportunities and financial rewards for our employees.

Underlying the mission of Ben & Jerry's is the determination to seek new and creative ways of addressing all three parts, while holding a deep respect for individuals, inside and outside the company, and for the communities of which they are a part.

EXHIBIT 11
BEN & JERRY'S EMPLOYEE ATTITUDE SURVEY—1990

	% Satisfied		
	Low	Middle	High
Pay	26%	11%	63%
Benefits	16	3	81
Job security	15	9	76
Coworkers	3	4	93
Chances for accomplishment	15	8	76
Chances for development	24	8	69
Chances for advancement	31	12	57
Overall job satisfaction	5	5	90

EXHIBIT 12
BEN & JERRY'S EMPLOYEE ATTITUDE SURVEY—VALUES VERSUS PRACTICES

Two-thirds of Ben & Jerry's people say that the company "really practices what it preaches." The great majority understand and support the company's social mission. Sixty-one percent say it is "in tune" with their own values (12 percent say too conservative and 27 percent say too radical). See the chart below:

To What Extent Does B&J's:	To Some Extent	A Great Extent
Produce the highest-quality products?	5%	95%
Give customers high-quality service?	6	93
Set a positive example for other business?	7	92
Effectively meet its social responsibilities?	10	89
Make work as joyful and pleasant as possible?	27	67
Treat people with dignity and respect?	31	63
Recognize and reward good performance?	39	49
Respect people's home and family responsibilities?	42	42

EXHIBIT 13
COMPANY OFFICERS

Ben Cohen, a founder of the company, was president and chief executive officer from January 1983 until February 1989. Currently, Mr. Cohen spends the principal portion of his time on marketing and promotion. Mr. Cohen first became involved with ice cream in 1968 as an independent mobile ice cream retailer with Pied Piper Distributors, Inc., Hempstead, New York, during three summers. He was promoted within the Pied Piper organization, and his responsibilities were broadened to include warehousing, inventory control, and driver training. He spent three years, from 1974 to 1977, as a crafts teacher at Highland Community, Paradox, New York, a residential school for disturbed adolescents, before moving to Vermont to form the company with Jerry Greenfield. Mr. Cohen has been a director of the company since 1977. Mr. Cohen is a director of Community Products, Inc., manufacturer of Rainforest Crunch candy, a member of the Council of Economic Advisers to the Governor of Vermont, a director of Oxfam America, and a trustee of Hampshire College.

Fred ("Chico") Lager joined the company as treasurer and general manager in November 1982 and has served as a director since 1982. In February 1989 he was named president and chief executive officer of the company. Mr. Lager shares responsibility for day-to-day operations of the company with Chuck Lacy and is responsible for long-term strategic planning. From 1977 until 1982, Mr. Lager was the owner/operator of Hunt's, a Burlington, Vermont, nightclub and restaurant. After five years of successful operation, Mr. Lager sold Hunt's and joined the company.

Charles Lacy joined the company in 1988 as director of special projects and became general manager in February 1989, succeeding Mr. Lager when he was named president. Mr. Lacy shares with Mr. Lager responsibility for the day-to-day operation of the company. From 1984 until joining Ben & Jerry's, Mr. Lacy was a finance and business development executive with United Health Services, a chain of nonprofit hospitals and clinics in upstate New York.

Jeffrey Furman has been an officer, legal consultant, and director of the company since 1985. His office is in Ithaca, New York. Mr. Furman has been a member of the New York Bar since 1969. From 1976 until 1984 he worked for Raven Management Associates as a senior consultant to small business throughout New York State. Since March 1984, Mr. Furman has devoted all of his professional time to the company. Effective January 1, 1988, Mr. Furman became a full-time employee of the company. Effective March 31, 1990, Mr. Furman has resigned as vice president of the company and continues as a consultant and director. Mr. Furman is a director of Community Products, Inc., manufacturer of Rainforest Crunch candy.

Merritt C. Chandler became a director of the company in 1987. He has been business manager of the Addison, Vermont, Central Supervisory Union, a group of school districts, since 1985. Until 1982, Mr. Chandler was an executive of Xerox Corporation. From 1982 until 1985 he was an independent business consultant. Mr. Chandler acted as project manager in connection with the construction of the company's Waterbury, Vermont, plant.

Henry Morgan became a director of the company in 1988. He is Dean Emeritus of the Boston University School of Management, having served as dean from 1979 to 1986. He is a director of Cambridge Bancorporation, MedCem Products, Inc., and Symbolics, Inc.

Other Key Personnel

Jerry Greenfield, age 38, a founder of the company, was president from 1977 until January 1983. After graduating from Oberlin College in 1973 with a BA in Biology, Mr. Greenfield engaged in biochemical research at the Public Health Research Institute in New York City and then at the University of North Carolina, Chapel Hill. Mr. Greenfield moved to Vermont to establish the company with Mr. Cohen in 1977. Effective in January 1983, Mr. Greenfield elected to withdraw from the daily operations of the company and moved to Arizona. Mr. Greenfield moved back to Vermont in 1985 and through 1986 was a consultant to the company, participating in promotional activities, special projects, and certain major policy decisions. Effective January 1, 1987, Mr. Greenfield became a full-time employee of the company and serves as director of promotions.

James Miller, age 38, joined the company as production manager in September 1985, became plant manager in May 1986, and was named director of manufacturing in February 1989. From 1976 to 1981, he was a production supervisor and assistant plant manager for Land O'Lakes Incorporated, in Mora, Wisconsin (a manufacturer of dairy products). From 1982 to 1983, Mr. Miller was a shift supervisor at Schepps dairy in Terrell, Texas. From March 1983 until he joined the company, Mr. Miller was an assistant plant superintendent and plant superintendent for the Specialty Foods Division of Southland Corporation in McKinney, Texas.

EXHIBIT 13 (continued)

Richard Brown, age 33, joined the company as director of sales in January 1986. From 1981 to 1984, Mr. Brown was a food service sales manager and western regional sales manager for Chipwich, Inc., Ft. Lee, New Jersey (an ice cream novelty manufacturer). From May 1984 until he joined the company, Mr. Brown was national sales manager for Schamitoff Foods (a frozen novelty manufacturer).

France Rathke, age 29, joined the company in April 1989 as its controller and was promoted to chief financial officer in April 1990. From September 1982 to March 1989, Ms. Rathke was a manager at Coopers & Lybrand, independent public accountants, in Boston, Massachusetts. Ms. Rathke is a certified public accountant.

David Barash, age 34, joined the company as director of community relations in August 1985 and became director of human resources in April 1988. From 1979 to 1985, he developed and directed public programs for Shelburne Farms, Inc., an agricultural organization in the Burlington, Vermont, area, and operated his own consulting business.

Steven Ramlal, age 42, joined the company as director of quality assurance in April 1989. From June 1981 to April 1989 he was corporate quality assurance manager for Schwan's Sales Enterprises, a manufacturer of ice cream and other frozen dairy and entree foods. He held progressively more responsible microbiology positions with Schwan's from April 1978 to June 1981. Prior to this, he was a senior bacteriologist with Kraft and a chemist with Coca-Cola USA.

EXHIBIT 14
BEN & JERRY'S COMPENSATION VERSUS MARKET RATES

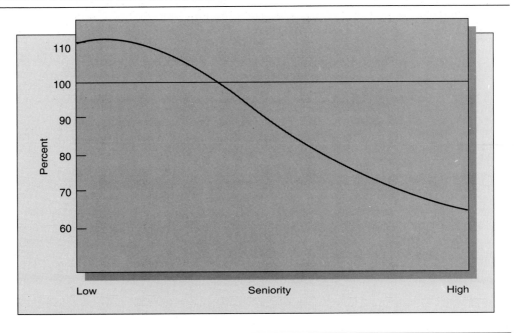

INDEX OF CASES